HOLT
LITERATURE AND LANGUAGE ARTS

Second Course

Kylene Beers
Carol Jago
Deborah Appleman
Leila Christenbury
Sara Kajder
Linda Rief

Senior Program Consultants for English Language Development

Robin Scarcella
Mabel Rivera
Héctor Rivera

Mastering the California Standards
Reading, Writing, Listening, Speaking

HOLT, RINEHART AND WINSTON

ISBN 978-0-03-099290-2
ISBN 0-03-099290-7

2 3 4 5 048 11 10 09

Program Authors

Kylene Beers is the senior program author for *Holt Literature and Language Arts*. A former middle school teacher, she is now Senior Reading Advisor to Secondary Schools for Teachers College Reading and Writing Project at Columbia University. She is the author of *When Kids Can't Read: What Teachers Can Do* and co-editor (with Linda Rief and Robert E. Probst) of *Adolescent Literacy: Turning Promise into Practice*. The former editor of the National Council of Teachers of English (NCTE) literacy journal *Voices from the Middle*, Dr. Beers assumed the NCTE presidency in 2008. With articles in *English Journal, Journal of Adolescent and Adult Literacy, School Library Journal, Middle Matters,* and *Voices from the Middle,* she speaks both nationally and internationally as a recognized authority on struggling readers. Dr. Beers has served on the review boards of *English Journal, The ALAN Review,* the Special Interest Group on Adolescent Literature of the International Reading Association, and the Assembly on Literature for Adolescents of the NCTE. She is the 2001 recipient of the Richard W. Halley Award given by NCTE for outstanding contributions to middle school literacy.

Carol Jago is a teacher with thirty-two years of experience at Santa Monica High School in California. The author of nine books on education, she continues to share her experiences as a writer and as a speaker at conferences and seminars across the country. Her wide and varied experience in standards assessment and secondary education in general has made her a sought-after speaker. As an author, Ms. Jago also works closely with Heinemann Publishers and with the National Council of Teachers of English. Her long-time association with NCTE led to her June 2007 election to a four-year term on the council's board. During that term she will serve for one year as president of the council. She is also active with the California Association of Teachers of English (CATE) and has edited CATE's scholarly journal *California English* since 1996. Ms. Jago served on the planning committees for the 2009 NAEP Reading Framework and the 2011 NAEP Writing Framework.

Deborah Appleman is professor and chair of educational studies and director of the Summer Writing Program at Carleton College in Northfield, Minnesota. Dr. Appleman's primary research interests include adolescent response to literature, multicultural literature, and the teaching of literary theory in high school. With a team of classroom teachers, she co-edited *Braided Lives,* a multicultural literature anthology. In addition to many articles and book chapters, she is the author of *Critical Encounters in High School English: Teaching Literary Theory to Adolescents* and co-author of *Teaching Literature to Adolescents.* Her most recent book, *Reading for Themselves,* explores the use of extracurricular book clubs to encourage adolescents to read for pleasure. Dr. Appleman was a high school English teacher, working in both urban and suburban schools. She is a frequent national speaker and consultant and continues to work weekly in high schools with students and teachers.

Leila Christenbury is a former high school English teacher and currently professor of English education at Virginia Commonwealth University, Richmond. The former editor of *English Journal,* she is the author of ten books, including *Writing on Demand, Making the Journey,* and *Retracing the Journey: Teaching and Learning in an American High School.* Past president of the National Council of Teachers of English, Dr. Christenbury is also a former member of the steering committee of the National Assessment

PROGRAM AUTHORS continued

of Educational Progress (NAEP). A recipient of the Rewey Belle Inglis Award for Outstanding Woman in English Teaching, Dr. Christenbury is a frequent speaker on issues of English teaching and learning and has been interviewed and quoted on CNN and in the *New York Times, USA Today, Washington Post, Chicago Tribune,* and *US News & World Report.*

 **Sara Kajder,** author of *Bringing the Outside In: Visual Ways to Engage Reluctant Readers* and *The Tech-Savvy English Classroom,* is an assistant professor at Virginia Polytechnic Institute and State University (Virginia Tech). She has served as co-chair of NCTE's Conference on English Education (CEE) Technology Commission and of the Society for Information Technology and Teacher Education (SITE) English Education Committee. Dr. Kajder is the recipient of the first SITE National Technology Leadership Fellowship in English Education; she is a former English and language arts teacher for high school and middle school.

 **Linda Rief** has been a classroom teacher for twenty-five years. She is author of *The Writer's-Reader's Notebook, Inside the Writer's-Reader's Notebook, Seeking Diversity, 100 Quickwrites,* and *Vision and Voice* as well as the co-editor (with Kylene Beers and Robert E. Probst) of *Adolescent Literacy: Turning Promise into Practice.* Ms. Rief has written numerous chapters and journal articles, and she co-edited the first five years of *Voices from the Middle.* During the summer she teaches graduate courses at the University of New Hampshire and Northeastern University. She is a national and international consultant on adolescent literacy issues.

Program Consultants

 **Robin Scarcella** is a professor at the University of California at Irvine, where she also directs the Program in Academic English/English as a Second Language. She has a Ph.D. in linguistics from the University of Southern California and an M.A. in education/second language acquisition from Stanford University. She has taught all grade levels. She has been active in shaping policies affecting language assessment, instruction, and teacher professional development. In the last four years, she has spoken to over ten thousand teachers and administrators. She has written over thirty scholarly articles that appear in such journals as the *TESOL Quarterly* and *Brain and Language.* Her most recent publication is *Accelerating Academic English: A Focus on the English Learner.*

 Mabel Rivera is a research assistant professor at the Texas Institute for Measurement, Evaluation, and Statistics at the University of Houston. Her current research interests include the education of and prevention of reading difficulties in English-language learners. In addition, Dr. Rivera is involved in local and national service activities for preparing school personnel to teach students with special needs.

 Héctor H. Rivera is an assistant professor at Southern Methodist University, School of Education and Human Development. Dr. Rivera is also the director of the SMU Professional Development/ESL Supplemental Certification Program for Math and Science Teachers of At-Risk Middle and High School LEP Newcomer Adolescents. This federally funded program develops, delivers, and evaluates professional development for educators who work with at-risk newcomer adolescent students. Dr. Rivera is also collaborating on school reform projects in Guatemala and with the Institute of Arctic Education in Greenland.

Marilyn Astore is a former teacher, principal, and county office assistant superintendent with over 20 years of classroom experience and over 40 years in the field of education. In her role as chair of both the California Curriculum Commission and its Reading/Language Arts/English Language Development Subject Matter Committees, she worked with other commissioners to advise the California State Board of Education on the adoption of curricular and instructional materials. She has taught teacher education classes at California State University, Sacramento; the University of San Diego; and the University of California, Davis, University Extension. Ms. Astore presents and consults on K–12 reading issues and intervention for older struggling readers.

Isabel L. Beck is professor of education and senior scientist at the University of Pittsburgh. Dr. Beck has conducted extensive research on vocabulary and comprehension and has published well over one hundred articles and several books, including *Improving Comprehension with Questioning the Author* (with Margaret McKeown) and *Bringing Words to Life: Robust Vocabulary Instruction* (with Margaret McKeown and Linda Kucan). Dr. Beck's numerous national awards include the Oscar S. Causey Award for outstanding research from the National Reading Conference and the William S.

Gray Award from the International Reading Association for lifetime contributions to the field of reading research and practice.

Margaret G. McKeown is a senior scientist at the University of Pittsburgh's Learning Research and Development Center. Her research in reading comprehension and vocabulary has been published extensively in outlets for both research and practitioner audiences. Recognition of her work includes the International Reading Association's (IRA) Dissertation of the Year Award and a National Academy of Education Spencer Fellowship. Before her career in research, Dr. McKeown taught elementary school.

Amy Benjamin is a veteran teacher, literacy coach, consultant, and researcher in secondary-level literacy instruction. She has been recognized for excellence in teaching from the New York State English Council, Union College, and Tufts University. Ms. Benjamin is the author of several books about reading comprehension, writing instruction, grammar, and differentiation. Her most recent book (with Tom Oliva) is *Engaging Grammar: Practical Advice for Real Classrooms,* published by the National Council of Teachers of English. Ms. Benjamin has had a long association and leadership role with the NCTE's Assembly for the Teaching of English Grammar (ATEG).

Sandra Carsten has over thirty-seven years of experience as a teacher and administrator in the Fresno Unified School District. She has been a leader in curriculum, instruction, and professional development and has supervised national grants. As an assistant superintendent for curriculum and instruction, she implemented standards-based programs, benchmark assessments, and protocols for monitoring student achievement. In addition, Ms. Carsten served for five years as the director of the Association of California School Administrators.

Eric Cooper is the president of the National Urban Alliance for Effective Education (NUA) and co-founder of the Urban Partnership for Literacy with the IRA. He currently works with the NCTE to support improvements in urban education and collaborates with the Council of the Great City Schools. In line with his educational mission to support the improvement of education for urban and minority students, Dr. Cooper writes, lectures, and produces educational documentaries and talk shows to provide advocacy for children who live in disadvantaged circumstances.

Harvey Daniels is a former college professor and classroom teacher, working in urban and suburban Chicago schools. Known for his pioneering work on student book clubs, Dr. Daniels is author and co-author of many books, including *Literature Circles: Voice and Choice in Book Clubs and Reading Groups* and *Best Practice: Today's Standards for Teaching and Learning in America's Schools.*

Judith L. Irvin taught middle school for several years before entering her career as a university professor. She now teaches courses in curriculum and instructional leadership and literacy at Florida State University. Dr. Irvin's many publications include *Reading and the High School Student: Strategies to Enhance Literacy* and *Integrating Literacy and Learning in the Content Area Classroom.* Her latest book, *Taking Action: A Leadership Model for Improving Adolescent Literacy,* is the result of a Carnegie-funded project and is published by the Association for Supervision and Curriculum Development.

Patrick Schwarz is professor of special education and chair of the Diversity in Learning and Development department for National-Louis University, Chicago, Illinois. He is author of *From Disability to Possibility* and *You're Welcome* (co-written with Paula Kluth), texts that have inspired teachers worldwide to reconceptualize inclusion to help all children. Other books co-written with Paula Kluth include *Just Give Him the Whale* and *Inclusion Bootcamp.* Dr. Schwarz also presents and consults worldwide through Creative Culture Consulting.

Marianne Steverson is currently president and COO of the educational services company known as Smar²tel Learning Links. She has forty-two years of diversified experience in the public school sector and private educational therapy practice. She coordinates the company's in-school professional development for teachers of reading. She also manages the development of new products and methodologies. Her areas of specialization include teaching struggling readers and teaching students who use African American Vernacular English.

Critical Reviewers

Program Advisors

Mastering the Standards Reading • Writing • Listening • Speaking

Contents in Brief

 Chapter Standards Focus

Chapter Standards Focus

CHAPTER 1

Plot and Setting

"Be careful what you set your heart upon—for it will surely be yours." —**quoted by James Baldwin**

What Do You Think? What kinds of wishes might cause more heartache than joy?

 California Standards

Word Analysis, Fluency, and Systematic Vocabulary Development
1.2 Understand the most important points in the history of the English language and use common word origins to determine the historical influences on English word meanings.

Reading Comprehension (Focus on Informational Materials)
2.3 Find similarities and differences between texts in the treatment, scope, or organization of ideas.

Literary Response and Analysis
3.2 Evaluate the structural elements of the plot (e.g., subplots, parallel episodes, climax), the plot's development, and the way in which conflicts are (or are not) addressed and resolved.

3.4 Analyze the relevance of the setting (e.g., place, time, customs) to the mood, tone, and meaning of the text.

Writing Applications (Genres and Their Characteristics)
2.1 Write biographies, autobiographies, short stories, or narratives:
   a. Relate a clear, coherent incident, event, or situation by using well-chosen details.
   b. Reveal the significance of, or the writer's attitude about, the subject.
   c. Employ narrative and descriptive strategies (e.g., relevant dialogue, specific action, physical description, background description, comparison or contrast of characters).

Character

"It is the ability to choose which makes us human."
—**Madeleine L'Engle**

What Do You Think? When do people stand up
for what they believe in?

 California Standards

Word Analysis, Fluency, and Systematic Vocabulary Development
1.2 Understand the most important points in the history of English language and use common word origins to determine the historical influences on English word meanings.

Reading Comprehension (Focus on Informational Materials)
2.2 Analyze text that uses proposition and support patterns.

Literary Response and Analysis
3.3 Compare and contrast motivations and reactions of literary characters from different historical eras confronting similar situations or conflicts.

Writing Applications (Genres and Their Characteristics)
2.1 Write biographies, autobiographies, short stories, or narratives:
  a. Relate a clear, coherent incident, event, or situation by using well-chosen details.
  b. Reveal the significance of, or the writer's attitude about, the subject.
  c. Employ narrative and descriptive strategies (e.g., relevant dialogue, specific action, physical description, background description, comparison or contrast of characters).

Theme

"In spite of everything, I still believe that people are really good at heart." —**Anne Frank**

What Do You Think? How can we do the best with what we're given?

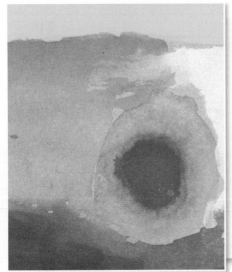

 California Standards

Word Analysis, Fluency, and Systematic Vocabulary Development
1.3 Use word meanings within the appropriate context and show ability to verify those meanings by definition, restatement, example, comparison, or contrast.

Reading Comprehension (Focus on Informational Materials)
2.3 Find similarities and differences between texts in the treatment, scope, or organization of ideas.

Literary Response and Analysis
3.5 Identify and analyze recurring themes (e.g., good versus evil) across traditional and contemporary works.

Writing Applications (Genres and Their Characteristics)
2.4 Write persuasive compositions:
  a. Include a well-defined thesis (i.e., one that makes a clear and knowledgeable judgment).
  b. Present detailed evidence, examples, and reasoning to support arguments, differentiating between facts and opinions.
  c. Provide details, reasons, and examples, arranging them effectively by anticipating and answering reader concerns and counterarguments.

Comparing Texts

Informational Text Focus

CHAPTER 4

Style

"Could it think, the heart would stop beating." —**Fernando Pessoa**

What Do You Think? Which is better—acting from the mind or from the heart?

California Standards

Word Analysis, Fluency, and Systematic Vocabulary Development
1.1 Analyze idioms, analogies, metaphors, and similes to infer the literal and figurative meanings of phrases.

Reading Comprehension (Focus on Informational Materials)
2.4 Compare the original text to a summary to determine whether the summary accurately captures the main ideas, includes critical details, and conveys the underlying meaning.

Literary Response and Analysis
3.6 Identify significant literary devices (e.g., metaphor, symbolism, dialect, irony) that define a writer's style and use those elements to interpret the work.

Writing Applications (Genres and Their Characteristics)
2.2 Write responses to literature:
   a. Exhibit careful reading and insight in their interpretations.
   b. Connect the student's own responses to the writer's techniques and to specific textual references.
   c. Draw supported inferences about the effects of a literary work on its audience.
   d. Support judgments through references to the text, other works, other authors, or to personal knowledge.

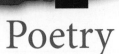

CHAPTER 5

Poetry

"The poetry and the songs that you are supposed to write, I believe are in your heart. You just have to open up your heart and not be afraid to get them out." —Judy Collins

What Do You Think? How important is it that we express our feelings?

California Standards

Word Analysis, Fluency, and Systematic Vocabulary Development
1.1 Analyze idioms, analogies, metaphors, and similes to infer the literal and figurative meanings of phrases.
Literary Response and Analysis
3.1 Determine and articulate the relationship between the purposes and characteristics of different forms of poetry (e.g., ballad, lyric, couplet, epic, elegy, ode, sonnet).
Writing Applications (Genres and Their Characteristics)
2.6 Write technical documents:
  a. Identify the sequence of activities needed to design a system, operate a tool, or explain the bylaws of an organization.
  b. Include all the factors and variables that need to be considered.
  c. Use formatting techniques (e.g., headings, differing fonts) to aid comprehension.

CHAPTER 6

Reading for Life

"Problems can become opportunities when the right people come together" —Robert Redford

What Do You Think? How can we solve the problems we face in daily life?

 California Standards

Reading Comprehension (Focus on Informational Materials)

2.1 Compare and contrast the features and elements of consumer materials to gain meaning from documents (e.g., warranties, contracts, product information, instruction manuals).

2.5 Understand and explain the use of a complex mechanical device by following technical directions.

2.6 Use information from a variety of consumer, workplace, and public documents to explain a situation or decision and to solve a problem.

Writing Applications (Genres and Their Characteristics)

2.5 Write documents related to career development, including simple business letters and job applications:

   a. Present information purposefully and succinctly and meet the needs of the intended audience.

   b. Follow the conventional format for the type of document (e.g., letter of inquiry, memorandum).

World Almanac

Expository Critique

"Get the facts, or the facts will get you. When you get them, get them right, or they will get you wrong." —Dr. Thomas Fuller

What Do You Think? How do you judge the ideas you encounter in text?

California Standards

Reading Comprehension (Focus on Informational Materials)
2.7 Evaluate the unity, coherence, logic, internal consistency, and structural patterns of text.

Writing Applications (Genres and Their Characteristics)
2.3 Write research reports:
  a. Define a thesis.
  b. Record important ideas, concepts, and direct quotations from significant information sources and paraphrase and summarize all perspectives on the topic, as appropriate.
  c. Use a variety of primary and secondary sources and distinguish the nature and value of each.
  d. Organize and display information on charts, maps, and graphs.

Informational Selections

CHAPTER 8

Literary Criticism: A Biographical Approach

"Nothing which has entered into our experience is ever lost."
—William Ellery Channing

What Do You Think? How do the things we have experienced in our lives continue to affect us?

 California Standards

Word Analysis, Fluency, and Systematic Vocabulary Development
1.2 Understand the most important points in the history of English language and use common word origins to determine the historical influences on English word meanings.

Literary Response and Analysis
3.7 Analyze a work of literature, showing how it reflects the heritage, traditions, attitudes, and beliefs of its author. (Biographical approach)

Writing Applications (Genres and Their Characteristics)
2.1 Write biographies, autobiographies, short stories, or narratives:
  a. Relate a clear, coherent incident, event, or situation by using well-chosen details.
  b. Reveal the significance of, or the writer's attitude about, the subject.
  c. Employ narrative and descriptive strategies (e.g., relevant dialogue, specific action, physical description, background description, comparison or contrast of characters).

Barbara Diamond Goldin

Skills, Standards, and Features

READING SKILLS FOR LITERARY TEXTS

SKILLS, STANDARDS, AND FEATURES continued

WORKSHOPS
WRITING WORKSHOPS

PREPARING FOR TIMED WRITING

LISTENING AND SPEAKING WORKSHOPS

MEDIA WORKSHOP

FEATURES
LITERARY PERSPECTIVES

SKILLS, STANDARDS, AND FEATURES continued

Selections by Genre

SELECTIONS BY GENRE continued

NONFICTION
AUTOBIOGRAPHIES

BIOGRAPHIES

DIARY

INTERVIEW

NOTE

SPEECHES

SELECTIONS BY GENRE continued

English–Language Arts Content Standards
Grade 8

READING

 1.0 Word Analysis, Fluency, and Systematic Vocabulary Development

Students use their knowledge of word origins and word relationships, as well as historical and literary context clues, to determine the meaning of specialized vocabulary and to understand the precise meaning of grade-level-appropriate words.

VOCABULARY AND CONCEPT DEVELOPMENT

1.1 Analyze idioms, analogies, metaphors, and similes to infer the literal and figurative meanings of phrases. **Chapters 4, 5**

1.2 Understand the most important points in the history of English language and use common word origins to determine the historical influences on English word meanings. **Chapters 1, 2, 8**

1.3 Use word meanings within the appropriate context and show ability to verify those meanings by definition, restatement, example, comparison, or contrast. **Chapter 3**

 2.0 Reading Comprehension (Focus on Informational Materials)

Students read and understand grade-level-appropriate material. They describe and connect the essential ideas, arguments, and perspectives of the text by using their knowledge of text structure, organization, and purpose. The selections in *Recommended*

Literature, Kindergarten Through Grade Twelve illustrate the quality and complexity of the materials to be read by students. In addition, students read one million words annually on their own, including a good representation of narrative and expository text (e.g., classic and contemporary literature, magazines, newspapers, online information).

STRUCTURAL FEATURES OF INFORMATIONAL MATERIALS

2.1 Compare and contrast the features and elements of consumer materials to gain meaning from documents (e.g., warranties, contracts, product information, instruction manuals). **Chapter 6**

2.2 Analyze text that uses proposition and support patterns. **Chapter 2**

COMPREHENSION AND ANALYSIS OF GRADE-LEVEL-APPROPRIATE TEXT

2.3 Find similarities and differences between texts in the treatment, scope, or organization of ideas. **Chapters 1, 3**

2.4 Compare the original text to a summary to determine whether the summary accurately captures the main ideas, includes critical details, and conveys the underlying meaning. **Chapter 4**

2.5 Understand and explain the use of a complex mechanical device by following technical directions. **Chapter 6**

2.6 Use information from a variety of consumer, workplace, and public documents to explain a situation or decision and to solve a problem. **Chapter 6**

EXPOSITORY CRITIQUE

2.7 Evaluate the unity, coherence, logic, internal consistency, and structural patterns of text. **Chapter 7**

 3.0 Literary Response and Analysis

Students read and respond to historically or culturally significant works of literature that reflect and enhance their studies of history and social science. They clarify the ideas and connect them to other literary works. The selections in *Recommended Literature, Kindergarten Through Grade Twelve* illustrate the quality and complexity of the materials to be read by students.

STRUCTURAL FEATURES OF LITERATURE

3.1 Determine and articulate the relationship between the purposes and characteristics of different forms of poetry (e.g., ballad, lyric, couplet, epic, elegy, ode, sonnet). **Chapter 5**

NARRATIVE ANALYSIS OF GRADE-LEVEL-APPROPRIATE TEXT

3.2 Evaluate the structural elements of the plot (e.g., subplots, parallel episodes, climax), the plot's development, and the way in which conflicts are (or are not) addressed and resolved. **Chapter 1**

3.3 Compare and contrast motivations and reactions of literary characters from different historical eras confronting similar situations or conflicts. **Chapters 2, 3**

3.4 Analyze the relevance of the setting (e.g., place, time, customs) to the mood, tone, and meaning of the text. **Chapter 1**

3.5 Identify and analyze recurring themes (e.g., good versus evil) across traditional and contemporary works. **Chapter 3**

3.6 Identify significant literary devices (e.g., metaphor, symbolism, dialect, irony) that define a writer's style and use those elements to interpret the work. **Chapter 4**

LITERARY CRITICISM

3.7 Analyze a work of literature, showing how it reflects the heritage, traditions, attitudes, and beliefs of its author. (Biographical approach) **Chapter 8**

WRITING

 1.0 Writing Strategies

Students write clear, coherent, and focused essays. The writing exhibits students' awareness of audience and purpose. Essays contain formal introductions, supporting evidence, and conclusions. Students progress through the stages of the writing process as needed.

ORGANIZATION AND FOCUS

1.1 Create compositions that establish a controlling impression, have a coherent thesis, and end with a clear and well-supported conclusion. **Chapters 3, 4, 7**

1.2 Establish coherence within and among paragraphs through effective transitions, parallel structures, and similar writing techniques. **Chapters 1, 5, 8**

1.3 Support theses or conclusions with analogies, paraphrases, quotations, opinions from authorities, comparisons, and similar devices. **Chapter 3**

ENGLISH–LANGUAGE ARTS CONTENT STANDARDS continued

RESEARCH AND TECHNOLOGY

1.4 Plan and conduct multiple-step information searches by using computer networks and modems. **Chapter 7**

1.5 Achieve an effective balance between researched information and original ideas. **Chapters 3, 7**

EVALUATION AND REVISION

1.6 Revise writing for word choice; appropriate organization; consistent point of view; and transitions between paragraphs, passages, and ideas. **Chapters 2, 6, 8**

 ## 2.0 Writing Applications (Genres and Their Characteristics)

Students write narrative, expository, persuasive, and descriptive essays of at least 500 to 700 words in each genre. Student writing demonstrates a command of standard American English and the research, organizational, and drafting strategies outlined in Writing Standard 1.0.

Using the writing strategies of grade eight outlined in Writing Standard 1.0, students:

2.1 Write biographies, autobiographies, short stories, or narratives:

a. Relate a clear, coherent incident, event, or situation by using well-chosen details.

b. Reveal the significance of, or the writer's attitude about, the subject.

c. Employ narrative and descriptive strategies (e.g., relevant dialogue, specific action, physical description, background description, comparison or contrast of characters). **Chapters 1, 2, 8**

2.2 Write responses to literature:

a. Exhibit careful reading and insight in their interpretations.

b. Connect the student's own responses to the writer's techniques and to specific textual references.

c. Draw supported inferences about the effects of a literary work on its audience.

d. Support judgments through references to the text, other works, other authors, or to personal knowledge. **Chapter 4**

2.3 Write research reports:

a. Define a thesis.

b. Record important ideas, concepts, and direct quotations from significant information sources and paraphrase and summarize all perspectives on the topic, as appropriate.

c. Use a variety of primary and secondary sources and distinguish the nature and value of each.

d. Organize and display information on charts, maps, and graphs. **Chapter 7**

2.4 Write persuasive compositions:

a. Include a well-defined thesis (i.e., one that makes a clear and knowledgeable judgment).

b. Present detailed evidence, examples, and reasoning to support arguments, differentiating between facts and opinions.

c. Provide details, reasons, and examples, arranging them effectively by anticipating and answering reader concerns and counterarguments. **Chapter 3**

2.5 Write documents related to career development, including simple business letters and job applications:

a. Present information purposefully and succinctly and meet the needs of the intended audience.

b. Follow the conventional format for the type of document (e.g., letter of inquiry, memorandum).

Chapter 6

2.6 Write technical documents:

a. Identify the sequence of activities needed to design a system, operate a tool, or explain the bylaws of an organization.

b. Include all the factors and variables that need to be considered.

c. Use formatting techniques (e.g., headings, differing fonts) to aid comprehension.

Chapter 5

WRITTEN AND ORAL ENGLISH LANGUAGE CONVENTIONS

The standards for written and oral English language conventions have been placed between those for writing and for listening and speaking because these conventions are essential to both sets of skills.

 1.0 Written and Oral English Language Conventions

Students write and speak with a command of standard English conventions appropriate to this grade level.

SENTENCE STRUCTURE

1.1 Use correct and varied sentence types and sentence openings to present a lively and effective personal style. *Warriner's Handbook Second Course* **Chapters 1, 7, 18**

1.2 Identify and use parallelism, including similar grammatical forms, in all written discourse to present items in a series and items juxtaposed for emphasis. *Warriner's Handbook Second Course* **Chapter 18**

1.3 Use subordination, coordination, apposition, and other devices to indicate clearly the relationship between ideas. *Warriner's Handbook Second Course* **Chapters 5, 6**

GRAMMAR

1.4 Edit written manuscripts to ensure that correct grammar is used. *Warriner's Handbook Second Course* **Chapter 17**

PUNCTUATION AND CAPITALIZATION

1.5 Use correct punctuation and capitalization. *Warriner's Handbook Second Course* **Chapters 13, 14, 16**

SPELLING

1.6 Use correct spelling conventions. *Warriner's Handbook Second Course* **Chapter 16**

ENGLISH–LANGUAGE ARTS CONTENT STANDARDS continued

LISTENING AND SPEAKING

 1.0 Listening and Speaking Strategies

Students deliver focused, coherent presentations that convey ideas clearly and relate to the background and interests of the audience. They evaluate the content of oral communication.

COMPREHENSION

1.1 Analyze oral interpretations of literature, including language choice and delivery, and the effect of the interpretations on the listener. **Chapters 1, 4**

1.2 Paraphrase a speaker's purpose and point of view and ask relevant questions concerning the speaker's content, delivery, and purpose. **Chapters 5, 7**

ORGANIZATION AND DELIVERY OF ORAL COMMUNICATION

1.3 Organize information to achieve particular purposes by matching the message, vocabulary, voice modulation, expression, and tone to the audience and purpose. **Chapters 1, 2, 3**

1.4 Prepare a speech outline based upon a chosen pattern of organization, which generally includes an introduction; transitions, previews, and summaries; a logically developed body; and an effective conclusion. **Chapters 3, 7**

1.5 Use precise language, action verbs, sensory details, appropriate and colorful modifiers, and the active rather than the passive voice in ways that enliven oral presentations. **Chapters 3, 8**

1.6 Use appropriate grammar, word choice, enunciation, and pace during formal presentations. **Chapters 1, 4, 7, 8**

1.7 Use audience feedback (e.g., verbal and nonverbal cues):

  a. Reconsider and modify the organizational structure or plan.

  b. Rearrange words and sentences to clarify the meaning.

Chapters 4, 7

ANALYSIS AND EVALUATION OF ORAL AND MEDIA COMMUNICATIONS

1.8 Evaluate the credibility of a speaker (e.g., hidden agendas, slanted or biased material). **Chapters 5, 7**

1.9 Interpret and evaluate the various ways in which visual image makers (e.g., graphic artists, illustrators, news photographers) communicate information and affect impressions and opinions. **Chapter 6**

 2.0 Speaking Applications (Genres and Their Characteristics)

Students deliver well-organized formal presentations employing traditional rhetorical strategies (e.g., narration, exposition, persuasion, description). Student speaking demonstrates a command of standard American English and the organizational and delivery strategies outlined in Listening and Speaking Standard 1.0.

Using the speaking strategies of grade eight outlined in Listening and Speaking Standard 1.0, students:

2.1 Deliver narrative presentations (e.g., biographical, autobiographical):
  a. Relate a clear, coherent incident, event, or situation by using well-chosen details.
  b. Reveal the significance of, and the subject's attitude about, the incident, event, or situation.
  c. Employ narrative and descriptive strategies (e.g., relevant dialogue, specific action, physical description, background description, comparison or contrast of characters).
Chapters 2, 8

2.2 Deliver oral responses to literature:
  a. Interpret a reading and provide insight.
  b. Connect the students' own responses to the writer's techniques and to specific textual references.
  c. Draw supported inferences about the effects of a literary work on its audience.
  d. Support judgments through references to the text, other works, other authors, or personal knowledge.
Chapter 4

2.3 Deliver research presentations:
  a. Define a thesis.
  b. Record important ideas, concepts, and direct quotations from significant information sources and paraphrase and summarize all relevant perspectives on the topic, as appropriate.
  c. Use a variety of primary and secondary sources and distinguish the nature and value of each.
  d. Organize and record information on charts, maps, and graphs.
Chapter 7

2.4 Deliver persuasive presentations:
  a. Include a well-defined thesis (i.e., one that makes a clear and knowledgeable judgment).
  b. Differentiate fact from opinion and support arguments with detailed evidence, examples, and reasoning.
  c. Anticipate and answer listener concerns and counterarguments effectively through the inclusion and arrangement of details, reasons, examples, and other elements.
  d. Maintain a reasonable tone.
Chapter 3

2.5 Recite poems (of four to six stanzas), sections of speeches, or dramatic soliloquies, using voice modulation, tone, and gestures expressively to enhance the meaning. **Chapter 1**

Why Be a Reader/Writer?

by **Kylene Beers**

You've heard this story before, haven't you?

Once upon a time there were three bears—Mama Bear, Papa Bear, and Baby Bear.

Goldilocks "visits" the Bear home while the family is out. She destroys their place while searching for the food, chair, and bed that are *just right* for her. When the Bear family returns, Goldie runs off without even an "I'm-so-sorry" apology.

The Bears are left to clean up everything—end of story.

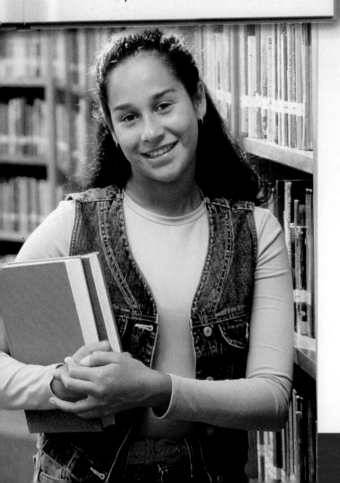

What Is the Message?

Isn't this an odd story to tell young children? Is it trying to teach them that

- children can be more trouble than bears?
- we must lock the door when we leave the house?
- sometimes people might do things they know are wrong?

The message I like most is that we are all searching for the things that are *just right* for us. While I don't like the way Goldilocks went about getting what she wanted, I do understand her need to find the food, the chair, and the bed that were *just right*.

Goldilocks wanted things that fit her needs. Interestingly, as she grows and changes, those needs will change. She'll outgrow the *just right* chair, and the *too big* chair will fit *just right*.

The *Just Right* Reading / Writing Experience

When you read and write, you're often looking for the *just right* experience that fits your needs. *Holt Literature and Language Arts* gives you many opportunities to find out how a book is *just right* for you.

Using the Standards to Set the Standard

Sometimes we need lessons to help us accomplish all the things a skilled reader can do. This book is designed to help you master the skills you need to be a strong reader *and* writer. The California standards are your tour guide. They will lead you through this book, helping you learn the literacy skills you'll need for this year, for your remaining years in school, and for all your life as a member of society.

Everyone who worked on this book—the people who chose the reading selections, the people who wrote the activities, the people who chose the artwork—continually asked themselves, "How do we create a book that not only meets the California standards but also *sets* the standard when it comes to helping students become readers and writers?" We think that, as you read through this book, you'll find that we answered that question by providing you with

- interesting selections to read
- powerful models to help you learn to write
- many opportunities to practice new skills
- specific information about each standard—so that you will always know what is expected of you
- the kinds of topics and art that middle-schoolers have told us interest them

In this book, then, you'll get practice in all kinds of language skills.

- You will read a variety of material, from ads to odes, from stories to Web pages.
- You will learn better ways to speak, listen, and write.
- You will understand more, sound better, and be more confident about what you know and understand.

There are many reasons to be a skillful reader and an effective writer—good grades, passing tests, getting into college. The best reason—the *just right* reason—has to do with reading and writing to discover more about yourself and the world you live in.

So, let what you read and write this year act as a *mirror* that shows you more about yourself or a *window* that shows you worlds beyond where you live.

Whichever you do, you'll be discovering the reason that is *just right* for you.

Kylene Beers

Senior Author
Holt Literature and Language Arts

How to Use Your Textbook

Getting to know a new textbook is like getting to know a new video game. In each case, you have to figure out how the game or book is structured, as well as understand its rules. If you understand the structure of your book, you can be successful from the start.

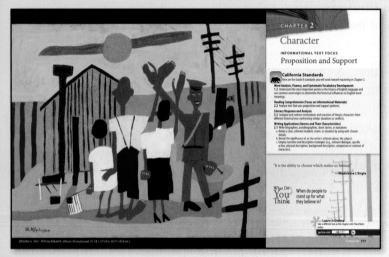

Chapter Opener

What is the focus of each chapter, or section of the book? What does the image suggest about what the chapter will cover? On the right, you'll see a bold heading that says "Plot and Setting" or "Character." These are the **literary skills** you will study in the chapter. Also in bold type is the **Informational Text Focus** for the chapter. These are the skills you use to read informational texts such as a newspaper or Web site. Keep the **What Do You Think?** question in mind as you go through the chapter. Your answers may even surprise you.

Literary Skills Focus

Like a set of rules or a map, the **Literary Skills Focus** shows you how literary elements work in stories and poems, helping you navigate through selections more easily. The Literary Skills Focus will help you get to your destination— understanding and enjoying the selections.

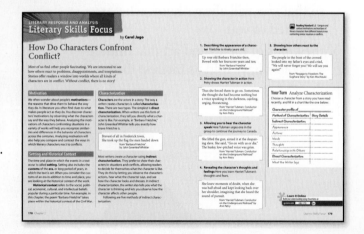

Reading Skills Focus

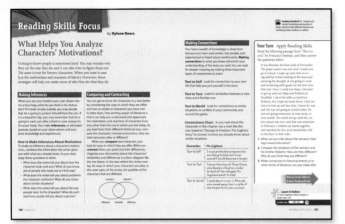

Your mind is working all the time as you read, even if you're not aware of it. Still, all readers, even very good ones, sometimes don't understand what they've read. **Reading Skills Focus** gives you the skills to help you improve your reading.

Reading Model

You tend to do things more quickly and easily if you have a model to follow. The **Reading Model** enhances your learning by demonstrating the literary and reading skills that you will practice in the chapter.

Wrap Up

Think of **Wrap Up** as a bridge that gives you a chance to practice the skills on which the chapter will focus. It also introduces you to the **Academic Vocabulary** you will study in the chapter: the language of school, business, and standardized tests. To be successful in school, you'll need to understand and use academic language.

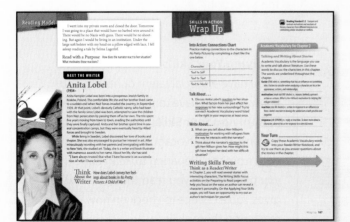

How to Use Your Textbook

Literary Selection Pages

Preparing to Read

If you have ever done something complicated, you know that things go more smoothly with some preparation. It is the same with reading. The **Preparing to Read** page gives you a boost by presenting the literary, reading, and writing skills you will learn about and use as you read the selection. The list of **Vocabulary** words gives the words you need to know for reading both the selection and beyond the selection. **Language Coach** explains the inner workings of English—like looking at the inside of a clock.

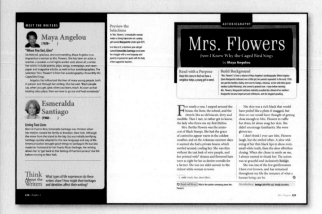

Selection

Meet the Writer gives you all kinds of interesting facts about the authors who wrote the selections in this book. **Build Background** provides information you sometimes need when a selection deals with unfamiliar times, places, and situations. **Preview the Selection** presents the selection's main character and hints at what is to come. **Read with a Purpose** helps you set a goal for your reading. It helps you answer the question, "What is the point of this selection?"

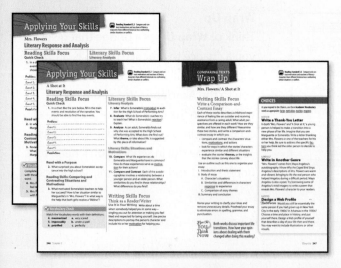

Applying Your Skills

If you have a special talent or hobby, you know that you have to practice to master it. In **Applying Your Skills,** you will apply the reading, literary, vocabulary, and language skills from the Preparing to Read page that you practiced as you read the selection. This gives you a chance to check on how you are mastering these skills.

Comparing Texts

You probably compare people, places, and things all the time, such as a favorite singer's new songs with her previous album. In **Comparing Texts,** you will compare different works—sometimes by the same author, sometimes by different authors—that have something in common.

Informational Text Focus

When you read a Web site or follow a technical manual, you are reading informational text. The skills you use in this type of reading are different from the ones you use for literary text. **Informational Text Focus** helps you gain the skills that will enable you to be a more successful reader in daily life and on standardized tests.

Standards Review

Do you dread test-taking time? Do you struggle over reading the passage and then choosing the correct answer? **Standards Review** can reduce your "guesses" and give you the practice you need to feel more confident during testing.

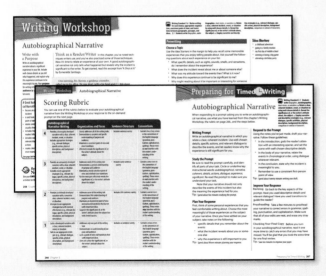

Writing Workshop

Does a blank piece of paper send shivers up your spine? **The Writing Workshop** will help you tackle the page. It takes you step-by-step through developing an effective piece of writing. Models, annotations, graphic organizers, and charts take the "What now?" out of writing for different purposes and audiences.

Preparing for Timed Writing

What is your idea of a nightmare? Maybe it is trying to respond to a writing prompt. **Preparing for Timed Writing** helps you practice for on-demand, or timed, writing so that you can realize your dreams of success.

Plot and Setting

INFORMATIONAL TEXT FOCUS

Treatment, Scope, and Organization of Ideas

 California Standards

Here are the grade 8 standards you will work toward mastering in Chapter 1.

Word Analysis, Fluency, and Systematic Vocabulary Development
1.2 Understand the most important points in the history of the English language and use common word origins to determine the historical influences on English word meanings.

Reading Comprehension (Focus on Informational Materials)
2.3 Find similarities and differences between texts in the treatment, scope, or organization of ideas.

Literary Response and Analysis
3.2 Evaluate the structural elements of the plot (e.g., subplots, parallel episodes, climax), the plot's development, and the way in which conflicts are (or are not) addressed and resolved.

3.4 Analyze the relevance of the setting (e.g., place, time, customs) to the mood, tone, and meaning of the text.

Writing Applications (Genres and Their Characteristics)
2.1 Write biographies, autobiographies, short stories, or narratives:
 a. Relate a clear, coherent incident, event, or situation by using well-chosen details.
 b. Reveal the significance of, or the writer's attitude about, the subject.
 c. Employ narrative and descriptive strategies (e.g., relevant dialogue, specific action, physical description, background description, comparison or contrast of characters).

" Be careful what you set your heart upon—for it will surely be yours."

—**quoted by James Baldwin**

 What Do **You** Think? What kinds of wishes might cause more heartache than joy?

Literary Skills Focus

by **Carol Jago**

What Are the Structural Elements of Plot?

When you describe your favorite movie to friends, you probably explain to them the structural elements of plot. You describe the conflict, or problem, the character faces. You discuss the way the character addresses the problem. You probably mention the climax, the most exciting moment when the outcome is determined. These are structural elements that are essential to all stories.

Plot

Plot The chain of related, or connected, events that tells you what happens in a story is called **plot.** When a plot is well developed, or explained, you can't stop reading the story. The element of the plot that keeps you reading is usually a **conflict,** or problem faced by a character. You become curious and want to see the way the conflict is addressed, or handled. Finally, you want to learn how the conflict is **resolved,** in other words, how the story turns out.

Most plots are built on these structural elements:

- **Basic situation** The part of the story in which you meet the characters and find out what they want.
- **Conflict** In this part of the story, the main character faces a conflict. The conflict may be with another character, with a force of nature such as a tornado, or within the main character's own heart and mind.

- **Complications** Now the plot develops, and more problems arise that prevent the main character from getting what he or she wants.
- **Climax** is the point at which you see the characters address the story's main conflict. Very often, the climax is also the emotional high point of the story.
- **Resolution** is the closing part of the story in which you learn how the characters have dealt with the outcome of the conflict.

Here is how the **structural elements of plot** are traditionally diagrammed. Note that the climax is the high point of the story.

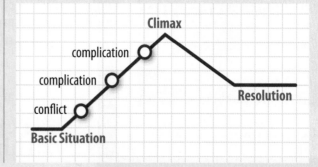

Subplots If you consider movies you've seen and novels you've read, you know that stories often contain subplots. A **subplot** is a minor plot that is related to the main story. (The prefix *sub–* means "under" or "less important than.") In "Flowers for Algernon" by Daniel Keyes, the main plot is centered on Charlie's surge in intelligence following surgery. The development of Charlie's relationship with his doctors is one of the story's ongoing subplots. As Charlie becomes more intelligent, his perception of the doctors changes:

> When I left afterwards, I found myself trembling. I don't know why for sure, but it was as if I'd seen both men clearly for the first time.
>
> from "Flowers for Algernon"
> by Daniel Keyes

Parallel Episodes You might be familiar with the story of the Three Little Pigs. You might recall that the Big Bad Wolf goes to each pig's house and says, "Little pig, little pig, let me in." Each pig addresses the wolf's challenge. The events are similar each time, with only minor differences. These events are examples of **parallel episodes,** in which a writer addresses a similar event several times throughout a plot's development.

Your Turn Analyze Plot

Map out the structural elements of the plot of a story from a book, a TV show, or a movie you are familiar with. Use a story map like this:

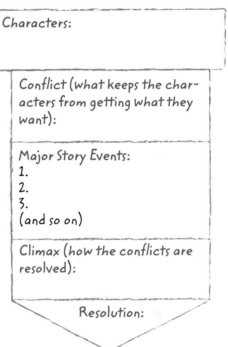

Characters:

Conflict (what keeps the characters from getting what they want):

Major Story Events:
1.
2.
3.
(and so on)

Climax (how the conflicts are resolved):

Resolution:

Make note of any **parallel episodes.** If you can find **subplots** in your story, complete another chart just like this one.

Peanuts
©United Feature Syndicate, Inc.

Learn It Online
To understand the role of literary elements in novels, visit *NovelWise* at:

go.hrw.com   H8-5   Go

Literary Skills Focus

by **Carol Jago**

How Is Setting Relevant to the Meaning of a Text?

The plot of a story may take place in a crazy world, as in Lewis Carroll's *Alice's Adventures in Wonderland,* or in a mysterious farmhouse, as in the story "The Inn of Lost Time." The setting—where and when a story takes place—is at the center of what happens in all works of literature.

Setting

The **setting** of a story is the time and place in which the events occur. Writers create believable settings by appealing to your senses.

> The dark sky, filled with angry, swirling clouds, reflected Greg Ridley's mood as he sat on the stoop of his building.
>
> from "The Treasure of Lemon Brown" by Walter Dean Myers

As you read, you see darkness in the sky and the movement of the clouds. You touch the stoop that Greg is sitting on. These details make you feel as if you are sitting with him, ready to share the adventures that come his way.

The Relevance of Setting Setting is not simply the place where the plot develops. Writers create settings that are **relevant,** or important, to the meaning of a text. Sometimes the setting can create a conflict for the story's characters. In the passage that follows, notice that the time and place creates problems that a character must address.

> Around nine o'clock the temperature had risen to almost one hundred degrees. I was completely soaked in sweat and my mouth felt as if I had been chewing on a handkerchief. I walked over to the end of the row, picked up the jug of water we had brought, and began drinking.
>
> from "The Circuit" by Francisco Jiménez

The **customs,** or way of life, that the characters follow are also relevant to the meaning of a story. The passage below is from a story set in sixteenth-century Japan. Notice how the customs from this time period affect the way characters react to one another.

> While the girl served the wine, the host looked with interest at my swords. From the few remarks he made, I gathered that he was a former samurai, forced by circumstances to turn his house into an inn.
>
> from "The Inn of Lost Time" by Lensey Namioka

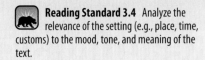
Mood

The overall atmosphere in a work of literature is called its **mood.** Setting affects the mood of a story. A murder will always be solved in a murder mystery—but compare the coziness of a solution arrived at in the cozy library of an English country house with the gritty feel of a clue found in the basement of a dark, abandoned warehouse.

Mood is often created by precise descriptions and by adjectives, such as *scary, tense,* or *uplifting.* Writers create mood by using specific details that appeal to your senses. How would you describe the mood the writer conveys in this passage?

> Outside, the wind had picked up, sending the rain against the window with a force that shook the glass in its frame. A car passed, its tires hissing over the wet street and its red taillights glowing in the darkness.
>
> from "The Treasure of Lemon Brown" by Walter Dean Myers

Tone

The writer's attitude about a place or a character is called **tone.** Writers reveal their tone by carefully choosing words that convey how they feel about a setting. In this passage the words *tired* and *sunk* convey a tone of weariness and exhaustion.

> When the sun had tired and sunk behind the mountains, Ito signaled us that it was time to go home.
>
> from "The Circuit" by Francisco Jiménez

When you speak, your tone of voice gives added meaning to what you say. Writers are skillful at using written language to achieve effects similar to those that people achieve with their voices.

Language is what creates that setting. When you read a story with a vivid setting, look for words that help you use your senses. Find words that let you *see* the purple towers or the littered streets, *smell* the arsenic poison or the musty closets, *hear* the sounds of creaky doors and droning bees, *taste* the hot chilies or the pancake syrup, *feel* the tropical breezes or the Arctic blasts.

Your Turn Analyze Setting

Analyze the relevance of the setting in a story you have read recently. Describe the setting in a sentence or two. Imagine if the story took place in a different setting—your own neighborhood, for example, or another planet. Record three significant ways in which the story would be affected by the change in setting.

Title: _____

Setting: _____

Alternate Setting: _____

Changes to Story: _____

1. _____

2. _____

3. _____

Learn It Online

Do pictures help you learn? Try the *PowerNotes* version of this lesson at:

go.hrw.com   H8-7   **Go**

Reading Skills Focus

by **Kylene Beers**

How Do You Analyze Plot and Setting?

Great stories are sometimes complicated. Writers don't set out to make their stories difficult to read, but the complexity of the tale they tell often requires you to work hard to understand the significance of a subplot or the relevance of a setting. Such stories challenge you to build your reading muscles. One way to exercise these muscles is to practice retelling a complex story.

Retelling

Keeping up with the development of plot and the way conflicts are addressed and resolved can be challenging. **Retelling,** or restating, a story's events will help you analyze the structural elements of plot. You can retell the basic structural elements of plot by using a strategy called Somebody Wanted But So.

First, write the four words on a piece of paper, as shown in the chart below. Write the main character's name under the heading "Somebody." Under the heading "Wanted," write down what the character wants. In the "But" column, record how the character is prevented from getting what he wants (the cause of the story's conflict). The way the conflict is addressed and resolved is placed in the "So" column. When you complete the chart, you will have one sentence. It might require more than one Somebody Wanted But So statement to identify all of the structural elements of a plot.

You'll have the opportunity to practice using Somebody Wanted But So later in this chapter.

Somebody	Wanted	But	So

Analyzing Details

When you read a short story, paying close attention to important details will help you evaluate the plot, analyze the characters, and **visualize,** or picture, the setting.

Look especially for details related to plot and setting as you read the stories in this chapter.

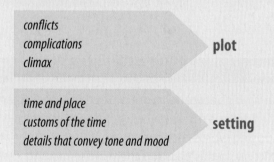

conflicts
complications
climax
→ **plot**

time and place
customs of the time
details that convey tone and mood
→ **setting**

In the example that follows, specific details reveal the main character's hopes and fears. The reference to nurses shows that the setting is a hospital or doctor's office.

> Im skared. Lots of people who work here and the nurses and the people who gave me the tests came to bring me candy and wish me luck. I hope I have luck.
>
> from "Flowers for Algernon"
> by Daniel Keyes

Sequence in Stories

Many stories are told in **chronological order,** or the sequence in which events happen. Record the sequence of a story's events by making a chart like this:

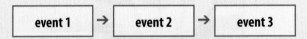

The chart above will work for the main structural elements of a simple story, but you'll find that most stories are more complicated.

"The Inn of Lost Time," for example, is actually three stories in one. Two guests trade stories with a farmer and his wife. To follow all story events, you may want to make three separate sequence charts.

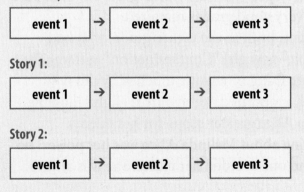

Main Story:

event 1 → event 2 → event 3

Story 1:

event 1 → event 2 → event 3

Story 2:

event 1 → event 2 → event 3

When you read long stories like "Flowers for Algernon," charts like the ones shown above can help you keep track of the sequence of subplots and parallel episodes.

Your Turn Apply Reading Skills

Read the passage below. Then, read it a second time and identify the details that reveal the conflict the characters face. List and analyze details that help you visualize the setting.

> The second day of our journey was a particularly grueling one, with several steep hills to climb. As the day was drawing to its close, we began to consider where we should spend the night. I knew that within an hour's walking was a hot-spring resort known to have several attractive inns.
>
> But Tokubei, my employer, said he was already very tired and wanted to stop. He had heard of the resort and knew the inns there were expensive. Wealthy as he was, he did not want to spend more money than he had to.
>
> While we stood talking, a smell reached our noses, a wonderful smell of freshly cooked rice. Suddenly I felt ravenous. From the way Tokubei swallowed, I knew he was feeling just as hungry.
>
> from "The Inn of Lost Time"
> by Lensey Namioka

Now go to the Skills in
Action: Reading Model

Learn It Online
To become an expert on tracking story events, visit the interactive Reading Workshops on:

go.hrw.com   H8-9   **Go**

Girl (1963) by Roy Lichtenstein. © Estate of Roy Lichtenstein.

Read with a Purpose
Read this story to discover what Melinda Alice does with the wishes she is granted.

Those Three Wishes

Analyzing Visuals   **Connecting to the Text** In what ways does the girl in this painting remind you of Melinda Alice?

by **Judith Gorog**

No one ever said that Melinda Alice was nice. That wasn't the word used. No, she was clever, even witty. She was called—never to her face, however—Melinda Malice.[1] Melinda Alice was clever and cruel. Her mother, when she thought about it at all, hoped Melinda would grow out of it. To her father, Melinda's very good grades mattered.

It was Melinda Alice, back in the eighth grade, who had labeled the shy, myopic[2] new girl "Contamination" and was the first to pretend that anything or anyone touched by the new girl had to be cleaned, inoculated,[3] or avoided. High school had merely given Melinda Alice greater scope for her talents.

The surprising thing about Melinda Alice was her power; no one trusted her, but no one avoided her either. She was always

---

1. **malice** (MAL ihs): a wish to hurt others; ill will.
2. **myopic** (my AHP ihk): nearsighted.
3. **inoculated** (ih NAHK yuh layt ihd): vaccinated.

included, always in the middle. If you had seen her, pretty and witty, in the center of a group of students walking past your house, you'd have thought, "There goes a natural leader."

Melinda Alice had left for school early. She wanted to study alone in a quiet spot she had because there was going to be a big math test, and Melinda Alice was not prepared. That A mattered; so Melinda Alice walked to school alone, planning her studies. She didn't usually notice nature much, so she nearly stepped on a beautiful snail that was making its way across the sidewalk.

"Ugh. Yucky thing," thought Melinda Alice, then stopped. Not wanting to step on the snail accidentally was one thing, but now she lifted her shoe to crush it.

"Please don't," said the snail.

"Why not?" retorted Melinda Alice.

"I'll give you three wishes," replied the snail evenly.

"Agreed," said Melinda Alice. "My first wish is that my next," she paused a split second, "my next thousand wishes come true." She smiled triumphantly and opened her bag to take out a small notebook and pencil to keep track.

Melinda Alice was sure she heard the snail say, "What a clever girl," as it made it to the safety of an ivy bed beside the sidewalk.

During the rest of the walk to school, Melinda was occupied with wonderful ideas. She would have beautiful clothes. "Wish number two, that I will always be perfectly dressed," and she was just that. True, her new outfit was not a lot different from the one she had worn leaving the house, but that only meant that Melinda Alice liked her own taste.

After thinking awhile, she wrote, "Wish number three. I wish for pierced ears and small gold earrings." Her father had not allowed Melinda to have pierced ears, but now she had them anyway. She felt her new earrings and shook her beautiful hair in delight. "I can have anything: stereo, tapes, TV videodisc, moped, car, anything! All my life!" She hugged her books to herself in delight.

By the time she reached school, Melinda was almost an altruist;[4] she could wish for peace. Then she wondered, "Is the snail that

---

4. **altruist** (AL troo ihst): person who helps others without expecting anything in return.

Literary Focus

Plot and Setting The writer explains Melinda Alice's **conflict**—she is not prepared for her math test—and describes the **setting**—a sidewalk on the way to school.

Reading Focus

Retelling Here's one way to retell what has happened: "Melinda Alice almost steps on a snail, who offers her three wishes. Her first wish is to be granted her next thousand wishes."

Reading Focus

Sequence in Stories Melinda Alice has now made three wishes: to have a thousand wishes, to be perfectly dressed, and to have pierced ears and earrings.

powerful?" She felt her ears, looked at her perfect blouse, skirt, jacket, shoes. "I could make ugly people beautiful, cure cripples . . ." She stopped. The wave of altruism had washed past. "I could pay people back who deserve it!" Melinda Alice looked at the school, at all the kids. She had an enormous sense of power. "They all have to do what I want now." She walked down the crowded halls to her locker. Melinda Alice could be sweet; she could be witty. She could—The bell rang for homeroom. Melinda Alice stashed her books, slammed the locker shut, and just made it to her seat.

"Hey, Melinda Alice," whispered Fred. "You know that big math test next period?"

"Oh, no," grimaced Melinda Alice. Her thoughts raced; "That stupid snail made me late, and I forgot to study."

"I'll blow it," she groaned aloud. "I wish I were dead."

Read with a Purpose What do you think about the way Melinda Alice handles her wishes?

Literary Focus

Plot Melinda Alice makes her final wish here at the **climax** of the story—the point when you know what will happen. The **resolution,** or final part of the story, is left to your imagination.

MEET THE WRITER

Judith Gorog
(1938–   )

World Traveler

Judith Gorog has been traveling all her life. Born in Wisconsin, she has lived in many parts of the United States and also in Germany and Italy. She has traveled far and wide—to Peru, Japan, Europe, and Indonesia.

All along the way, Judith writes stories. She says, "I have always written, and began to write stories for children when I was a child, making up stories and plays and rewriting the Greek myths with myself taming Pegasus."

Think About the Writer Based on the information above, choose two adjectives that describe the author.

Reading Standard 3.2 Evaluate the structural elements of the plot (e.g., subplots, parallel episodes, climax), the plot's development, and the way in which conflicts are (or are not) addressed and resolved. **3.4** Analyze the relevance of the setting (e.g., place, time, customs) to the mood, tone, and meaning of the text.

Into Action: Story Map

"Those Three Wishes" is a very short story with a dramatic climax. Fill in a story map like the one below and then retell the story.

> Characters:
> Melinda Alice & snail
>
> Conflict:
>
> Complications:
> 1.
> 2.
> 3.
>
> Climax:
>
> Resolution:

Talk About . . .

1. With a partner, discuss the parallel episodes and setting of "Those Three Wishes." Try to use each Academic Vocabulary word listed at the right at least once in your discussion.

Write About . . .

Answer the following questions about "Those Three Wishes."

2. Evaluate whether the plot would have been better developed if it had included a resolution.

3. Analyze the relevance of the setting to the plot's development. How do the story's time and place create a conflict for the main character?

Writing Skills Focus
Think as a Reader/Writer

In Chapter 1 the Writing Skills Focus activities on the Preparing to Read pages will guide you in understanding how writers develop their plots and settings. On the Applying Your Skills pages, you'll have a chance to practice using those writers' techniques.

Academic Vocabulary for Chapter 1

Talking and Writing About Plot and Setting

Academic Vocabulary is the language you use to write and talk about literature. Use these words to discuss the stories you read in this chapter. The words are underlined throughout the chapter.

analyze (AN uh lyz) *v.:* examine in detail. *Analyze the way the writer creates mood through her word choice.*

aspect (AS pehkt) *n.:* one part of a situation, plan, or subject. *The class debated several difficult aspects of the plot's development.*

evaluate (ih VAL yoo ayt) *v.:* judge. *Evaluate whether the way the plot was resolved is satisfying.*

relevance (REHL uh vuhns) *n.:* quality of being important or meaningful. *People's customs have relevance to the setting of a story.*

structural (STRUHK chuhr uhl) *adj.:* relating to the way the parts of something connect to form a whole. *A plot diagram reveals the structural elements that make up a plot.*

Your Turn

Copy these Academic Vocabulary words into your *Reader/Writer Notebook,* and try to use them as you answer questions about the stories in Chapter 1.

THE TREASURE OF LEMON BROWN

by **Walter Dean Myers**

Music Lesson #2 (2000) by Colin Bootman. Oil on board

What aspects of life
are really important?

 QuickWrite

Think about something important you would like to teach or te
younger than you. What would it be? How would you do it?

 **Reader/Writer Notebook**

Use your **RWN** to complete the activities for this selection.

Reading Standard 3.2 Evaluate the structural elements of the plot (e.g., subplots, parallel episodes, climax), the plot's development, and the way in which conflicts are (or are not) addressed and resolved.

Literary Skills Focus

Conflict and Resolution The plot of a story almost always involves **conflict.** Usually a conflict arises when a character wants something very badly but is prevented from getting it. A story can have **external conflicts**—struggles with outside forces, such as a hurricane—or **internal conflicts**—struggles within a character's heart or mind, such as fighting shyness. In "The Treasure of Lemon Brown," the main character faces many conflicts, both external and internal. These conflicts are introduced throughout the story. Most are addressed and settled during the course of the story. As you read, look for one conflict that remains unresolved at the end of the story.

TechFocus As you read the story, pay attention to how one character describes music called the "blues." Make a list of details to research for a short presentation.

Reading Skills Focus

Retelling You can use the strategy called retelling to help you recognize the <u>structural</u> elements of plot as you read.

Into Action As you read the story, questions at the bottom of the pages will ask you about the characters' conflicts and will prompt you to stop and retell main events. Record conflicts and complications on a chart like the one below.

Characters	Conflicts	Complications (Main Events)
Greg		
Lemon Brown		

Writing Skills Focus

Think as a Reader/Writer

Find It in Your Reading Walter Dean Myers uses precise details to portray the setting, New York City's Harlem. As you read, record in your *Reader/Writer Notebook* some of the details that help you imagine this urban neighborhood.

Vocabulary

impromptu (ihm PRAHMP too) *adj.:* unplanned. *Greg's friends had an impromptu checkers tournament.*

tentatively (TEHN tuh tihv lee) *adv.:* in an uncertain or hesitant way. *Greg pushed tentatively on the apartment door.*

intently (ihn TEHNT lee) *adv.:* with close attention. *Greg listened intently to the sounds in the room.*

probing (PROHB ihng) *v.* used as *adj.:* searching or investigating. *Greg, probing his leg, did not find any injuries.*

ominous (AHM uh nuhs) *adj.:* threatening. *After the crash, Greg heard only an ominous silence.*

Language Coach

Related Words An *omen* is an event that hints at a future event. Although an omen could indicate a happy event to come, omens are usually associated with upcoming danger. Which word on the list above is related to the word *omen*?

Learn It Online
Listen to a professional actor read this story at:
go.hrw.com   H8-15   Go

Walter Dean Myers
(1937–)

Fostering a Talent

Walter Dean Myers was born in Martinsburg, West Virginia; he was one of eight children. Myers's mother died when he was two, and when he was three, his father sent him and two of his sisters to New York City to be raised by foster parents. The Deans guided him through the rough times of his youth and taught him to appreciate both storytelling and education. When he became a published writer, Myers added their name to his to show how important they were to him.

> "My foster father was a wonderful man. He gave me the most precious gift any father could give to a son: He loved me. . . . My foster mother understood the value of education. . . . She also understood the value of a story, how it could serve as a refuge for people like us."

Michael L. Printz AWARD

Think About the Writer What do you think inspired Myers to become a writer?

Build Background

This story is set in Harlem, a neighborhood in New York City. After World War I, Harlem was the center of an African American literary explosion called the Harlem Renaissance. Important writers, such as Langston Hughes and Zora Neale Hurston, lived in Harlem during this time. Though Harlem has always been a vibrant place, full of life, many of its buildings were not maintained for many years and were abandoned. Recently, however, Harlem has enjoyed a new wave of development and restoration.

Preview the Selection

In this story, you'll meet a boy named **Greg,** who learns some life lessons from a person he meets in an unlikely place.

THE TREASURE OF LEMON BROWN

by **Walter Dean Myers**

The dark sky, filled with angry, swirling clouds, reflected Greg Ridley's mood as he sat on the stoop of his building. His father's voice came to him again, first reading the letter the principal had sent to the house, then lecturing endlessly about his poor efforts in math.

"I had to leave school when I was thirteen," his father had said; "that's a year younger than you are now. If I'd had half the chances that you have, I'd . . ."

Greg had sat in the small, pale-green kitchen listening, knowing the lecture would end with his father saying he couldn't play ball with the Scorpions. He had asked his father the week before, and his father had said it depended on his next report card. It wasn't often the Scorpions took on new players, especially fourteen-year-olds, and this was a chance of a lifetime for Greg. He hadn't been allowed to play high school ball, which he had really wanted to do, but playing for the Community Center team was the next best thing. Report cards were due in a week, and Greg had been hoping for the best. But the principal had ended the suspense early when she sent that letter saying Greg would probably fail math if he didn't spend more time studying.

"And you want to play *basketball*?" His father's brows knitted over deep-brown eyes. "That must be some kind of a joke. Now you just get into your room and hit those books." Ⓐ

That had been two nights before. His father's words, like the distant thunder that now echoed through the streets of Harlem, still rumbled softly in his ears.

Ⓐ **Reading Focus** **Retelling** Explain Greg's conflict. What does he want? What stands in his way?

It was beginning to cool. Gusts of wind made bits of paper dance between the parked cars. There was a flash of nearby lightning, and soon large drops of rain splashed onto his jeans. He stood to go upstairs, thought of the lecture that probably awaited him if he did anything except shut himself in his room with his math book, and started walking down the street instead. Down the block there was an old tenement that had been abandoned for some months. Some of the guys had held an impromptu checkers tournament there the week before, and Greg had noticed that the door, once boarded over, had been slightly ajar. **Ⓑ**

Pulling his collar up as high as he could, he checked for traffic and made a dash across the street. He reached the house just as another flash of lightning changed the night to day for an instant, then returned the graffiti-scarred building to the grim shadows. He vaulted over the outer stairs and pushed tentatively on the door. It was open, and he let himself in. **Ⓒ**

The inside of the building was dark except for the dim light that filtered through the dirty windows from the street lamps. There was a room a few feet from the door, and from where he stood at the entrance, Greg could see a squarish patch of light on the floor. He entered the room, frowning at the musty smell. It was a large room that might have been someone's

parlor at one time. Squinting, Greg could see an old table on its side against one wall, what looked like a pile of rags or a torn mattress in the corner, and a couch, with one side broken, in front of the window.

He went to the couch. The side that wasn't broken was comfortable enough, though a little creaky. From this spot he could see the blinking neon sign over the bodega[1] on the corner. He sat awhile, watching the sign blink first green, then red, allowing his mind to drift to the Scorpions, then to his father. His father had been a postal worker for all Greg's life and was proud of it, often telling Greg how hard he had worked to pass the test. Greg had heard the story too many times to be interested now.

For a moment Greg thought he heard something that sounded like a scraping against the wall. He listened carefully, but it was gone.

Outside, the wind had picked up, sending the rain against the window with a force that shook the glass in its frame. A car passed, its tires hissing over the wet street and its red taillights glowing in the darkness.

Greg thought he heard the noise again. His stomach tightened as he held himself still and listened intently. There weren't any more scraping noises, but he was sure

---

1. bodega (boh DAY guh): small grocery store.

Ⓑ **Literary Focus** Conflict What internal conflict is Greg thinking about when it starts to rain?

Ⓒ **Read and Discuss** What is Greg doing?

Vocabulary **impromptu** (ihm PRAHMP too) *adj.*: unplanned.
tentatively (TEHN tuh tihv lee) *adv.*: in an uncertain or hesitant way.
intently (ihn TEHNT lee) *adv.*: with close attention.

Connecting to the Text In what ways is the boy in this picture similar to and different from Greg?

Jim (1930) by William H. Johnson.
Oil on canvas (21 5/8" x 18 1/4").

he had heard something in the darkness—something breathing!

He tried to figure out just where the breathing was coming from; he knew it was in the room with him. Slowly he stood, tensing. As he turned, a flash of lightning lit up the room, frightening him with its sudden brilliance. He saw nothing, just the overturned table, the pile of rags, and an old newspaper on the floor. Could he have been imagining the sounds? He continued listening, but heard nothing and thought that it might have just been rats. Still, he thought, as soon as the rain let up he would leave. He went to the window and was about to look out when he heard a voice behind him.

"Don't try nothin', 'cause I got a razor here sharp enough to cut a week into nine days!"

Greg, except for an involuntary tremor in his knees, stood stock-still. The voice was high and brittle, like dry twigs being broken, surely not one he had ever heard before. There was a shuffling sound as the person who had been speaking moved a step closer. Greg turned, holding his breath, his eyes straining to see in the dark room. **D**

The upper part of the figure before him was still in darkness. The lower half was in the dim rectangle of light that fell unevenly from the window. There were two feet, in cracked, dirty shoes from which rose legs that were wrapped in rags.

"Who are you?" Greg hardly recognized his own voice.

"I'm Lemon Brown," came the answer. "Who're you?"

"Greg Ridley."

"What you doing here?" The figure shuffled forward again, and Greg took a small step backward.

"It's raining," Greg said.

"I can see that," the figure said.

The person who called himself Lemon Brown peered forward, and Greg could see him clearly. He was an old man. His black, heavily wrinkled face was surrounded by a halo of crinkly white hair and whiskers that seemed to separate his head from the layers of dirty coats piled on his smallish frame. His pants were bagged to the knee, where they were met with rags that went down to the old shoes. The rags were held on with strings, and there was a rope around his middle. Greg relaxed. He had seen the man before, picking through the trash on the corner and pulling clothes out of a Salvation Army box. There was no sign of the razor that could "cut a week into nine days." **E**

"What are you doing here?" Greg asked.

"This is where I'm staying," Lemon Brown said. "What you here for?"

"Told you it was raining out," Greg said, leaning against the back of the couch until he felt it give slightly.

"Ain't you got no home?"

"I got a home," Greg answered.

"You ain't one of them bad boys looking for my treasure, is you?" Lemon Brown cocked his head to one side and squinted one eye. "Because I told you I got me a razor."

"I'm not looking for your treasure," Greg answered, smiling. "*If* you have one."

"What you mean, *if* I have one," Lemon Brown said. "Every man got a treasure. You

---

D **Literary Focus** Conflict What new conflict is Greg facing?

E **Read and Discuss** What does this information suggest about Lemon Brown?

don't know that, you must be a fool!"

"Sure," Greg said as he sat on the sofa and put one leg over the back. "What do you have, gold coins?"

"Don't worry none about what I got," Lemon Brown said. "You know who I am?"

"You told me your name was orange or lemon or something like that."

"Lemon Brown," the old man said, pulling back his shoulders as he did so, "they used to call me Sweet Lemon Brown."

"Sweet Lemon?" Greg asked.

"Yessir. Sweet Lemon Brown. They used to say I sung the blues so sweet that if I sang at a funeral, the dead would commence to rocking with the beat. Used to travel all over Mississippi and as far as Monroe, Louisiana, and east on over to Macon, Georgia. You mean you ain't never heard of Sweet Lemon Brown?"

"Afraid not," Greg said. "What . . . what happened to you?"

"Hard times, boy. Hard times always after a poor man. One day I got tired, sat down to rest a spell and felt a tap on my shoulder. Hard times caught up with me." **F**

"Sorry about that."

"What you doing here? How come you didn't go on home when the rain come? Rain don't bother you young folks none."

> GREG TURNED, HOLDING HIS BREATH, HIS EYES STRAINING TO SEE IN THE DARK ROOM.

"Just didn't." Greg looked away.

"I used to have a knotty-headed boy just like you." Lemon Brown had half walked, half shuffled back to the corner and sat down against the wall. "Had them big eyes like you got. I used to call them moon eyes. Look into them moon eyes and see anything you want."

"How come you gave up singing the blues?" Greg asked.

"Didn't give it up," Lemon Brown said. "You don't give up the blues; they give you up. After a while you do good for yourself, and it ain't nothing but foolishness singing about how hard you got it. Ain't that right?"

"I guess so." **G**

"What's that noise?" Lemon Brown asked, suddenly sitting upright.

Greg listened, and he heard a noise outside. He looked at Lemon Brown and saw the old man was pointing toward the window.

Greg went to the window and saw three men, neighborhood thugs, on the stoop. One was carrying a length of pipe. Greg looked back toward Lemon Brown, who moved quietly across the room to the window. The old man looked out, then beckoned frantically for Greg to follow

---

F **Literary Focus** Conflict What do you think Lemon Brown means by "hard times"? What kinds of conflict might he have faced? Explain your answer.

G **Read and Discuss** What is Lemon Brown saying?

Analyzing Visuals **Connecting to the Text** How is the view of
Harlem seen in this photograph similar to Walter Dean Myers's description? How is
it different?

him. For a moment Greg couldn't move. Then he found himself following Lemon Brown into the hallway and up darkened stairs. Greg followed as closely as he could. They reached the top of the stairs, and Greg felt Lemon Brown's hand first lying on his shoulder, then probing down his arm until he finally took Greg's hand into his own as they crouched in the darkness.

"They's bad men," Lemon Brown whispered. His breath was warm against Greg's skin.

"Hey! Ragman!" a voice called. "We know you in here. What you got up under them rags? You got any money?"

Silence.

"We don't want to have to come in and hurt you, old man, but we don't mind if we have to."

Lemon Brown squeezed Greg's hand in his own hard, gnarled fist.

There was a banging downstairs and a light as the men entered. They banged around noisily, calling for the ragman.

"We heard you talking about your treasure." The voice was slurred. "We just want to see it, that's all."

"You sure he's here?" One voice seemed to come from the room with the sofa.

"Yeah, he stays here every night."

"There's another room over there; I'm going to take a look. You got that flashlight?"

"Yeah, here, take the pipe too."

Greg opened his mouth to quiet the sound of his breath as he sucked it in uneasily. A beam of light hit the wall a few feet opposite him, then went out.

"Ain't nobody in that room," a voice said. "You think he gone or something?"

"I don't know," came the answer. "All I know is that I heard him talking about some kind of treasure. You know they found that shopping-bag lady with that money in her bags."

"Yeah. You think he's upstairs?"

"HEY, OLD MAN, ARE YOU UP THERE?"

Silence.

"Watch my back, I'm going up." **Ⓗ**

There was a footstep on the stairs, and the beam from the flashlight danced crazily along the peeling wallpaper. Greg held his breath. There was another step and a loud crashing noise as the man banged the pipe against the wooden banister. Greg could feel his temples throb as the man slowly neared them. Greg thought about the pipe, wondering what he would do when the man reached them—what he *could* do.

Then Lemon Brown released his hand and moved toward the top of the stairs. Greg looked around and saw stairs going up to the next floor. He tried waving to Lemon Brown, hoping the old man would see him in the dim light and follow him to the next floor. Maybe, Greg thought, the man wouldn't follow them up there. Suddenly, though, Lemon Brown stood at the top of the stairs, both arms raised high above his head.

"There he is!" a voice cried from below.

"Throw down your money, old man, so I won't have to bash your head in!"

Vocabulary **probing** (PROHB ihng) *v.* used as *adj.*: searching or investigating.

Ⓗ **Reading Focus** Retelling What has happened to put Greg and Lemon Brown in danger?

Lemon Brown didn't move. Greg felt himself near panic. The steps came closer, and still Lemon Brown didn't move. He was an eerie sight, a bundle of rags standing at the top of the stairs, his shadow on the wall looming over him. Maybe, the thought came to Greg, the scene could be even eerier.

Greg wet his lips, put his hands to his mouth, and tried to make a sound. Nothing came out. He swallowed hard, wet his lips once more, and howled as evenly as he could.

"What's that?"

As Greg howled, the light moved away from Lemon Brown, but not before Greg saw him hurl his body down the stairs at the men who had come to take his treasure. There was a crashing noise, and then footsteps. A rush of warm air came in as the downstairs door opened; then there was only an ominous silence.

Greg stood on the landing. He listened, and after a while there was another sound on the staircase.

"Mr. Brown?" he called.

"Yeah, it's me," came the answer. "I got their flashlight."   ❶

Greg exhaled in relief as Lemon Brown made his way slowly back up the stairs.

"You OK?"

"Few bumps and bruises," Lemon Brown said.

"I think I'd better be going," Greg said, his breath returning to normal. "You'd better leave, too, before they come back."

"They may hang around outside for a while," Lemon Brown said, "but they ain't getting their nerve up to come in here again. Not with crazy old ragmen and howling spooks. Best you stay awhile till the coast is clear. I'm heading out west tomorrow, out to East St. Louis."

"They were talking about treasures," Greg said. "You *really* have a treasure?"

"What I tell you? Didn't I tell you every man got a treasure?" Lemon Brown said. "You want to see mine?"

"If you want to show it to me," Greg shrugged.

"Let's look out the window first, see what them scoundrels be doing," Lemon Brown said.

They followed the oval beam of the flashlight into one of the rooms and looked out the window. They saw the men who had tried to take the treasure sitting on the curb near the corner. One of them had his pants leg up, looking at his knee.

"You sure you're not hurt?" Greg asked Lemon Brown.

"Nothing that ain't been hurt before," Lemon Brown said. "When you get as old as me, all you say when something hurts is, 'Howdy, Mr. Pain, sees you back again.' Then when Mr. Pain see he can't worry you none, he go on mess with somebody else."

Greg smiled.

"Here, you hold this." Lemon Brown gave Greg the flashlight.

He sat on the floor near Greg and carefully untied the strings that held the rags on his right leg. When he took the rags away, Greg saw a piece of plastic. The old man

Vocabulary ominous (AHM uh nuhs) *adj.*: threatening.

❶ **Reading Focus** Retelling How do Lemon Brown and Greg scare off the thugs?

carefully took off the plastic and unfolded it. He revealed some yellowed newspaper clippings and a battered harmonica.

"There it be," he said, nodding his head. "There it be."

Greg looked at the old man, saw the distant look in his eye, then turned to the clippings. They told of Sweet Lemon Brown, a blues singer and harmonica player who was appearing at different theaters in the South. One of the clippings said he had been the hit of the show, although not the headliner. All of the clippings were reviews of shows Lemon Brown had been in more than fifty years ago. Greg looked at the harmonica. It was dented badly on one side, with the reed holes on one end nearly closed.

"I used to travel around and make money for to feed my wife and Jesse—that's my boy's name. Used to feed them good, too. Then his mama died, and he stayed with his mama's sister. He growed up to be a man, and when the war come, he saw fit to go off and fight in it. I didn't have nothing to give him except these things that told him who I was, and what he come from. If you know your pappy did something, you know you can do something too.

"Anyway, he went off to war, and I went off still playing and singing. 'Course by then I wasn't as much as I used to be, not without

> "WHAT I TELL YOU? DIDN'T I TELL YOU EVERY MAN GOT A TREASURE?" LEMON BROWN SAID.

somebody to make it worth the while. You know what I mean?"

"Yeah," Greg nodded, not quite really knowing.

"I traveled around, and one time I come home, and there was this letter saying Jesse got killed in the war. Broke my heart, it truly did. **ⓙ**

"They sent back what he had with him over there, and what it was is this old mouth fiddle and these clippings. Him carrying it around with him like that told me it meant something to him. That was my treasure, and when I give it to him, he treated it just like that, a treasure. Ain't that something?" **ⓚ**

"Yeah, I guess so," Greg said.

"You *guess* so?" Lemon Brown's voice rose an octave[2] as he started to put his treasure back into the plastic. "Well, you got to guess, 'cause you sure don't know nothing. Don't know enough to get home when it's raining."

"I guess . . . I mean, you're right."

"You OK for a youngster," the old man said as he tied the strings around his leg, "better than those scalawags what come here looking for my treasure. That's for sure."

"You really think that treasure of yours was worth fighting for?" Greg asked.

---

2. **octave** (AHK tihv): musical term for the span of eight whole notes.

ⓙ Reading Focus **Retelling** Retell the events of Lemon Brown's past.

ⓚ Read and Discuss What do you learn about Lemon Brown's treasure?

"Against a pipe?"

"What else a man got 'cepting what he can pass on to his son, or his daughter, if she be his oldest?" Lemon Brown said. "For a big-headed boy, you sure do ask the fool-ishest questions."

Lemon Brown got up after patting his rags in place and looked out the window again.

"Looks like they're gone. You get on out of here and get yourself home. I'll be watch-ing from the window, so you'll be all right."

Lemon Brown went down the stairs behind Greg. When they reached the front door, the old man looked out first, saw the street was clear, and told Greg to scoot on home.

"You sure you'll be OK?" Greg asked.

"Now, didn't I tell you I was going to East St. Louis in the morning?" Lemon Brown asked. "Don't that sound OK to you?"

"Sure it does," Greg said. "Sure it does. And you take care of that treasure of yours."

"That I'll do," Lemon said, the wrinkles about his eyes suggesting a smile. "That I'll do." **L**

The night had warmed and the rain had stopped, leaving puddles at the curbs. Greg didn't even want to think how late it was. He thought ahead of what his father would say and wondered if he should tell him about Lemon Brown. He thought about it until he reached his stoop, and decided against it. Lemon Brown would be OK, Greg thought, with his memories and his treasure.

Greg pushed the button over the bell marked "Ridley," thought of the lecture he knew his father would give him, and smiled.

L **Read and Discuss** What has happened between the boy and the old man?

Applying Your Skills

Reading Standard 3.2 Evaluate the structural elements of the plot (e.g., sub-plots, parallel episodes, climax), the plot's development, and the way in which conflicts are (or are not) addressed and resolved.

The Treasure of Lemon Brown

Literary Response and Analysis

Reading Skills Focus
Quick Check

1. What does Lemon Brown reveal to Greg about his past?

Read with a Purpose

2. What is Lemon Brown's treasure? Why does it mean so much to him?

Reading Skills: Retelling

3. Review the chart you made as you read the story. Below the chart, describe the climax and resolution. How does the story end?

Characters	Conflicts	Complications (Main Events)
Greg	wants to play basketball	Needs to study; avoids going home to talk to dad

Climax:
Resolution:

Literary Skills Focus
Literary Analysis

4. **Evaluate** Some stories have **subplots,** or less important plots that relate to and can enrich the main plot. How is the story of Lemon Brown and his son a subplot? What is its relevance to the overall meaning of the story?

5. **Evaluate** Myers has said that one of his goals in writing is to "counter" values conveyed by television. What values do you think he means? If Myers asked you whether the plot of this story challenged the values on television, how would you respond?

Literary Skills: Conflict and Resolution

6. **Analyze** How does Lemon Brown resolve the conflict with the thugs? What surprised you about his actions during this episode?

7. **Interpret** What internal conflict has Greg resolved at the end of the story?

8. **Evaluate** In the **resolution** of a story, all the conflicts are usually addressed and resolved. What conflict at the beginning of the story does Myers leave unresolved at the end? Explain your opinion of this ending.

Literary Skills Review: Character

9. In what ways do you find the characters in this story credible? How does their behavior correspond to the way people act in real life? Use details from the text to support your opinion.

Writing Skills Focus
Think as a Reader/Writer

Use It in Your Writing Review the precise details of the setting that you recorded as you read. How do these details relate to the conflicts in the story? Write a two-paragraph essay in which you discuss the relevance of the setting in the text. How does the setting influence the way conflicts are addressed and resolved?

What Do You Think Now

What does Greg learn is important in life? How is what he learns also important to you?

The Treasure of Lemon Brown

Reading Standard 1.2 Understand the most important points in the history of the English language and use common word origins to determine the historical influences on English word meanings.

Vocabulary Development

History of the English Language: Latin Roots

Now you know what Lemon Brown's treasure really is. What about the word *treasure* itself? Where does that word, or any of the words we use, come from? If you speak English, about 60 percent of the words you use, including *treasure*, come from the Latin language.

Latin was spoken by the Romans. Roman civilization reached its height in the A.D. 100s and 200s. At that time , the Roman army conquered much of the Western world, including most of Europe and the Middle East as well as northern Africa. The Roman soldiers spoke Latin and spread their language around the world. In fact, Latin is the basis for all the Romance languages (French, Portuguese, Spanish, Italian, and Romanian). You could say that anyone who speaks any of these Romance languages is speaking a modern version of Latin.

Much of the English language comes from Latin, but English is not a Romance language. How did so much Latin get into it? Thanks to the Romans and later the Roman Catholic Church, the use of Latin spread. Just about every language in the Western world borrowed from it. Latin was the language of scholars for many centuries. There was one other event that resulted in the addition of thousands of Latin words to the English language: the Norman Conquest of England. In the year 1066, William the Conqueror, a Norman (from Normandy, in France) who spoke French, invaded England and became king. As a result, French—and through it, Latin —became a major influence on the development of English.

Your Turn

Study the following Latin words and their meanings. Then, match the Latin words to the Vocabulary words derived from them.

impromptu
tentatively
intently
probing
ominous

Latin Word	Meaning	Vocabulary Word
probare	test or examine	
tentare	feel; try	
ominosous	full of foreboding	
promere	bring out	
intendere	strain	

Language Coach

Latin Roots *Extemporaneous* is a synonym for *impromptu*. Both words come from Latin. *Extemporaneous* comes from *ex tempore*. *Tempore* is a form of the word *tempus,* the Latin word for "time." Work with a partner to think of other English words that come from *tempus*. What is the meaning of *tempus fugit*, a Latin phrase commonly used in English?

Academic Vocabulary

Talk About . . .
Evaluate the conclusion of "The Treasure of Lemon Brown." Explain which conflict is left unresolved, and analyze whether the story would be improved if every conflict were resolved.

Grammar Link
Nouns and Pronouns

Nouns are one of the basic building blocks of the English language. A **noun** is a word that is used to name a person, a place, a thing, or an idea.

Persons	Greg, Lemon Brown, street thugs
Places	Greg's front stoop, abandoned building
Things	couch, pipe, harmonica, flashlight
Ideas	fear, danger, love, sadness

Sometimes you can use a short word—a **pronoun**—in place of one or more nouns to avoid repetition.

Here is a sentence without pronouns:

When Lemon Brown crashed into the thugs, Lemon Brown scared the thugs away.

Here is the same sentence with pronouns:

When Lemon Brown crashed into the thugs, **he** scared **them** away.

The word that a pronoun stands for is called its **antecedent.** In the above sentences, *Lemon Brown* and *thugs* are the antecedents for the pronouns.

Your Turn

Rewrite the following sentences by replacing the repeated nouns with pronouns.

1. Greg wanted to play basketball because basketball was Greg's favorite sport.
2. Because Greg's father valued education, Greg's father wanted Greg to study harder.
3. The thugs attacked Lemon Brown to get Lemon Brown's treasure.

CHOICES

As you respond to the Choices, use these **Academic Vocabulary** words as appropriate: analyze, aspect, evaluate, relevance, structural.

REVIEW
Write a Scene

Partner Project With a classmate, write a scene with dialogue between Greg and his father that reveals and resolves their main conflict. Consider the following:

- What does Greg's father say in his lecture?
- How does Greg respond?
- Is there a resolution in this episode that will satisfy them both?

Perform the dialogue for your class.

CONNECT
Describe a Keepsake

Timed └Writing Lemon Brown's treasure is a keepsake, an object that has value as a remembrance. Write an essay describing a keepsake of your own. Imagine what its relevance might be to someone who found it. Organize your essay with a short introduction, body, and conclusion. Use precise details to help readers visualize the object.

EXTEND
Research the Blues

TechFocus Learn more about blues music by using the Internet to perform research. You might, for example, find out about the life of a musician or analyze the evolution of the guitar in blues music. Use presentation software to share your findings with the class.

Flowers for Algernon

by **Daniel Keyes**

What Do You Think?

When is knowledge power? When is ignorance bliss?

QuickWrite

Why might a person hesitate to tell a friend something upsetting? Write down your thoughts.

Reader/Writer Notebook

Use your **RWN** to complete the activities for this selection.

Reading Standard 3.2 Evaluate the structural elements of the plot (e.g., subplots, parallel episodes, climax), the plot's development, and the way in which conflicts are (or are not) addressed and resolved.

Literary Skills Focus

Subplots and Parallel Episodes A long story, such as the one that follows, will often include **subplots,** or minor plots that relate to the main conflict. A long story might also have **parallel episodes,** in which the writer repeats certain elements of the plot. You probably remember fairy tales that have three parallel episodes. A king, for example, might test his daughters three times to see if they are loyal to him. Watch for both subplots and parallel episodes as you read "Flowers for Algernon."

Literary Perspectives Read this story using the literary perspective described on page 33.

Reading Skills Focus

Retelling Using a strategy called Somebody Wanted But So will help you uncover the basic <u>structural</u> elements of plot, including the development of subplots and parallel episodes.

Into Action Use a chart like the one below to record the conflicts in the story. A long story like this one will require more than one chart to identify all the elements of its plot. Create a chart for the characters you meet in this part of the story, including doctors Strauss and Nemur, Miss Kinnian, even Algernon.

Somebody (Character)	Wanted (Goal or Desire)	But (Conflict)	So (Resolution)
Charlie	Wants to undergo surgery to increase his intelligence.		

Writing Skills Focus

Think as a Reader/Writer

Find It in Your Reading In this story, events unfold through a character's journal entries. Note how Keyes develops Charlie's character through Charlie's use of language as the plot develops.

Vocabulary

misled (mihs LEHD) *v.*: fooled; led to believe something false. *Joe and Frank misled Charlie into believing they were his friends.*

regression (rih GREHSH uhn) *n.*: return to an earlier or less advanced condition. *After its regression the mouse could no longer find its way through a maze.*

obscure (uhb SKYOOR) *v.*: hide. *He wanted to obscure the fact that he was losing his intelligence.*

deterioration (dih tihr ee uh RAY shuhn) *n.* used as *adj*: worsening; declining. *Charlie could predict mental deterioration syndromes by using his formula.*

introspective (ihn truh SPEHK tihv) *adj.*: looking inward. *Charlie was introspective about all the changes he went through.*

Language Coach

Related Words Which Vocabulary word above looks as if it is derived from the Latin verb *specere,* meaning "to see"? What other words do you know that contain the word part *–spec–*?

Learn It Online
Expand your story experience by visiting Literature Links at:

go.hrw.com   H8-31   **Go**

Daniel Keyes
(1927–   )

"Fascinated by . . . the Human Mind"

Born in Brooklyn, New York, Daniel Keyes says that he is "fascinated by the complexities of the human mind." In fact, he studied psychology so that he could create more believable characters in his stories.

Unhelpful "Advice"

When Keyes was looking for a publisher for "Flowers for Algernon," he was advised to change the ending of his story to a happy, "Hollywood" ending. Keyes refused. His decision proved to be a wise one. His story became famous around the world and was made into a novel, a play, a movie, and even a musical.

"When I went to Tokyo, they . . . brought me gifts, flowers, candy, letters, and I sat there thinking, 'I feel like a rock star.'"

Think About the Writer What might Keyes's refusal to change his story say about him?

Build Background

You will find terms dealing with psychology and science in "Flowers for Algernon." Here are some terms to know:

- **Rorschach** (RAWR shahk) **test:** psychological test in which people describe the images suggested to them by a series of inkblots. See page 37 for an example.

- **IQ:** short for *intelligence quotient;* a number that is meant to show how intelligent someone is. An IQ score is determined from an intelligence test.

- **hypothesis:** a theory to be proved. In the story the doctors' hypothesis is that they can improve intelligence through surgery.

Preview the Selection

In this story you'll meet **Charlie Gordon,** who undergoes experimental surgery to increase his intelligence. Charlie keeps a journal to record his progress and to share how the experiment affects his life.

CHARLY

Flowers for Algernon

by **Daniel Keyes**

Part 1

progris riport 1—martch 5 1965

Dr. Strauss says I shud rite[1] down what I think and evrey thing that happins to me from now on. I dont know why but he says its importint so they will see if they will use me. I hope they use me. Miss Kinnian says maybe they can make me smart. I want to be smart. My name is Charlie Gordon. I am 37 years old and 2 weeks ago was my brithday. I have nuthing more to rite now so I will close for today.

progris riport 2—martch 6

I had a test today. I think I faled it. and I think that maybe now they wont use me. What happind is a nice young man was in the room and he had some white cards with ink spillled all over them. He sed Charlie what do you see on this card. I was very

---

1. **shud rite:** should write. To understand Charlie's mis-spelled words, try sounding them out and reading the surrounding words for clues to the meaning.

Then I said if I had my glases I coud see better I usally only ware my glases in the movies or TV but I said they are in the closit in the hall. I got them. Then I said let me see that card agen I bet Ill find it now.

I tryed hard but I still coudnt find the picturs I only saw the ink. I told him maybe I need new glases. He rote somthing down on a paper and I got skared of faling the test. I told him it was a very nice inkblot with littel points all around the eges. He looked very sad so that wasnt it. I said please let me try agen. Ill get it in a few minits becaus Im not so fast somtimes. Im a slow reeder too in Miss Kinnians class for slow adults but I'm trying very hard.

He gave me a chance with another card that had 2 kinds of ink spilled on it red and blue.

He was very nice and talked slow like Miss Kinnian does and he explained it to me that it was a *raw shok*.[3] He said pepul see things in the ink. I said show me where. He said think. I told him I think a inkblot but that wasnt rite eather. He said what does it remind you—pretend something. I closd my eyes for a long time to pretend. I told him I pretned a fowntan pen with ink

skared even tho I had my rabits foot[2] in my pockit because when I was a kid I always faled tests in school and I spillled ink to.

I told him I saw a inkblot. He said yes and it made me feel good. I thot that was all but when I got up to go he stopped me. He said now sit down Charlie we are not thru yet. Then I dont remember so good but he wantid me to say what was in the ink. I dint see nuthing in the ink but he said there was picturs there other pepul saw some picturs. I coudnt see any picturs. I reely tryed to see. I held the card close up and then far away.

---

2. **rabits foot:** The hind foot of a rabbit is sometimes used as a good-luck charm.

3. **raw shok:** Charlie is trying to spell *Rorschach*.

leeking all over a table cloth. Then he got up and went out.

I dont think I passd the *raw shok* test. Ⓐ

progris report 3—martch 7

Dr Strauss and Dr Nemur say it dont matter about the inkblots. I told them I dint spill the ink on the cards and I couldn't see anything in the ink. They said that maybe they will still use me. I said Miss Kinnian never gave me tests like that one only spelling and reading. They said Miss Kinnian told that I was her bestist pupil in the adult nite scool becaus I tryed the hardist and I reely wantid to lern. They said how come you went to the adult nite scool all by yourself Charlie. How did you find it. I said I askd pepul and sumbody told me where I shud go to lern to read and spell good. They said why did you want to. I told them becaus all my life I wantid to be smart and not dumb. But its very hard to be smart. They said you know it will probly be tempirery. I said yes. Miss Kinnian told me. I dont care if it herts.

Later I had more crazy tests today. The nice lady who gave it me told me the name and I asked her how do you spellit so I can rite it in my progris riport. THEMATIC APPERCEPTION TEST. I dont know the frist 2 words but I know what *test* means. You got to pass it or you get bad marks. This test lookd easy becaus I coud see the picturs. Only this time she dint want me to tell her the picturs. That mixd me up. I said the man yesterday said I shoud tell him what

I saw in the ink she said that dont make no difrence. She said make up storys about the pepul in the picturs.

I told her how can you tell storys about pepul you never met. I said why shud I make up lies. I never tell lies any more becaus I always get caut.

She told me this test and the other one the raw-shok was for getting personalty. I laffed so hard. I said how can you get that thing from inkblots and fotos. She got sore and put her picturs away. I dont care. It was sily. I gess I faled that test too. Ⓑ

Later some men in white coats took me to a difernt part of the hospitil and gave me a game to play. It was like a race with a white mouse. They called the mouse Algernon. Algernon was in a box with a lot of twists and turns like all kinds of walls and they gave me a pencil and a paper with lines and lots of boxes. On one side it said START and on the other end it said FINISH. They said it was *amazed* and that Algernon and me had the same *amazed* to do. I dint see how we could have the same *amazed* if Algernon had a box and I had a paper but I dint say nothing. Anyway there wasnt time because the race started.

One of the men had a watch he was trying to hide so I wouldnt see it so I tryed not to look and that made me nervus.

Anyway that test made me feel worser than all the others because they did it over 10 times with difernt *amazeds* and Algernon won every time. I dint know that mice were so smart. Maybe thats because

---

Ⓐ **Read and Discuss** What situation has the author begun to develop?

Ⓑ **Read and Discuss** How does Charlie handle his latest test?

Algernon is a white mouse. Maybe white mice are smarter then other mice. **C**

progis riport 4—Mar 8

Their going to use me! Im so exited I can hardly write. Dr Nemur and Dr Strauss had a argament about it first. Dr Nemur was in the office when Dr Strauss brot me in. Dr Nemur was worryed about using me but Dr Strauss told him Miss Kinnian rekemmended me the best from all the people who she was teaching. I like Miss Kinnian becaus shes a very smart teacher. And she said Charlie your going to have a second chance. If you volenteer for this experament you mite get smart. They dont know if it will be perminint but theirs a chance. Thats why I said ok even when I was scared because she said it was an operashun. She said dont be scared Charlie you done so much with so little I think you deserv it most of all.

So I got scaird when Dr Nemur and Dr Strauss argud about it. Dr Strauss said I had something that was very good. He said I had a good *motor-vation*.[4] I never even knew I had that. I felt proud when he said that not every body with an eye-q of 68 had that thing. I dont know what it is or where I got it but he said Algernon had it too. Algernons *motor-vation* is the cheese they put in his box. But it cant be that because I didnt eat any cheese this week. **D**

Then he told Dr Nemur something I dint understand so while they were talking I wrote down some of the words.

He said Dr Nemur I know Charlie is not what you had in mind as the first of your new brede of intelek** (coudnt get the word) superman. But most people of his low ment** are host** and uncoop** they are usualy dull apath** and hard to reach. He has a good natcher hes intristed and eager to please.

Dr Nemur said remember he will be the first human beeng ever to have his intelijence trippled by surgicle meens.

Dr Strauss said exakly. Look at how well hes lerned to read and write for his low mentel age its as grate an acheve** as you and I lerning einstines therey of **vity[5] without help. That shows the intenss motor-vation. Its comparat** a tremen** achev** I say we use Charlie.

I dint get all the words and they were talking to fast but it sounded like Dr Strauss was on my side and like the other one wasnt.

Then Dr Nemur nodded he said all right maybe your right. We will use Charlie. When he said that I got so exited I jumped up and shook his hand for being so good to me. I told him thank you doc you wont be sorry for giving me a second chance. And I mean it like I told him. After the operashun Im gonna try to be smart. Im gonna try awful hard. **E**

---

4. **motor-vation:** motivation, the force or inner drive that makes someone want to do or accomplish something; here, Charlie's desire to learn.

5. **einstines therey of **vity:** theory of relativity, developed by Albert Einstein (1879–1955) and deals with matter, time, space, and energy.

C **Read and Discuss** What is the author hinting at here?

D **Reading Focus** **Retelling** What is the conflict between Dr. Strauss and Dr. Nemur?

E **Literary Perspectives** **Analyzing Credibility** Now that you have read this progress report, do you think Charlie will be a credible narrator? Why or why not?

progris ript 5—Mar 10

Im skared. Lots of people who work here and the nurses and the people who gave me the tests came to bring me candy and wish me luck. I hope I have luck. I got my rabits foot and my lucky penny and my horse shoe. Only a black cat crossed me when I was comming to the hospitil. Dr Strauss says dont be supersitis Charlie this is sience. Anyway Im keeping my rabits foot with me.

I asked Dr Strauss if Ill beat Algernon in the race after the operashun and he said maybe. If the operashun works Ill show that mouse I can be as smart as he is. Maybe smarter. Then Ill be abel to read better and spell the words good and know lots of things and be like other people. I want to be smart like other people. If it works perminint they will make everybody smart all over the wurld.

They dint give me anything to eat this morning. I dont know what that eating has to do with getting smart. Im very hungry and Dr Nemur took away my box of candy. That Dr Nemur is a grouch. Dr Strauss says I can have it back after the operashun. You cant eat befor a operashun . . .

Progress Report 6—Mar 15

The operashun dint hurt. He did it while I was sleeping. They took off the bandijis from my eyes and my head today so I can make a PROGRESS REPORT. Dr Nemur who looked at some of my other ones says I spell PROGRESS wrong and he told me how to spell it and REPORT too. I got to try and remember that.

I have a very bad memary for spelling. Dr Strauss says its ok to tell about all the things that happin to me but he says I shoud tell more about what I feel and what I think. When I told him I dont know how to think he said try. All the time when the bandijis were on my eyes I tryed to think. Nothing happened. I dont know what to think about. Maybe if I ask him he will tell me how I can think now that Im suppose to get smart. What do smart people think about. Fancy things I suppose. I wish I knew some fancy things alredy.

Progress Report 7—mar 19

Nothing is happining. I had lots of tests and different kinds of races with Algernon. I hate that mouse. He always beats me. Dr Strauss said I got to play those games. And he said some time I got to take those tests over again. Thse inkblots are stupid. And

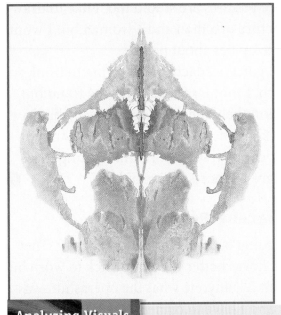

Analyzing Visuals   **Connecting to the Text** The image above is a Rorschach test. What do you see? Why do you think Charlie has difficulty with the test?

those pictures are stupid too. I like to draw a picture of a man and a woman but I wont make up lies about people.

I got a headache from trying to think so much. I thot Dr Strauss was my frend but he dont help me. He dont tell me what to think or when Ill get smart. Miss Kinnian dint come to see me. I think writing these progress reports are stupid too. **(F)**

Progress Report 8—Mar 23

Im going back to work at the factery. They said it was better I shud go back to work but I cant tell anyone what the operashun was for and I have to come to the hospitil for an hour evry night after work. They are gonna pay me mony every month for lerning to be smart.

Im glad Im going back to work because I miss my job and all my frends and all the fun we have there.

Dr Strauss says I shud keep writing things down but I dont have to do it every day just when I think of something or something speshul happins. He says dont get discoridged because it takes time and it happins slow. He says it took a long time with Algernon before he got 3 times smarter then he was before. Thats why Algernon beats me all the time because he had that operashun too. That makes me feel better. I coud probly do that *amazed* faster than a reglar mouse. Maybe some day Ill beat Algernon. Boy that would be something. So far Algernon looks like he mite be smart perminent.

Mar 25 (I dont have to write PROGRESS REPORT on top any more just when I hand it in once a week for Dr Nemur to read. I just have to put the date on. That saves time)

We had a lot of fun at the factery today. Joe Carp said hey look where Charlie had his operashun what did they do Charlie put some brains in. I was going to tell him but I remembered Dr Strauss said no. Then Frank Reilly said what did you do Charlie forget your key and open your door the hard way. That made me laff. Their really my friends and they like me.

Sometimes somebody will say hey look at Joe or Frank or George he really pulled a Charlie Gordon. I don't know why they say that but they always laff. This morning Amos Borg who is the 4 man at Donnegans used my name when he shouted at Ernie the office boy. Ernie lost a packige. He said Ernie for godsake what are you trying to be a Charlie Gordon. I dont understand why he said that. I never lost any packiges. **(G)**

Mar 28 Dr Strauss came to my room tonight to see why I dint come in like I was suppose to. I told him I dont like to race with Algernon any more. He said I dont have to for a while but I shud come in. He had a present for me only it wasnt a present but just for lend. I thot it was a little television but it wasnt. He said I got to turn it on when I go to sleep. I said your kidding why shud I turn it on when Im going to sleep. Who ever herd of a thing like that. But he said if I want to get smart I got to

---

(F) **Read and Discuss** | How has Charlie's spelling changed? What does this change indicate?

(G) **Literary Focus** | **Subplot** The author has introduced a new setting: Charlie's workplace. How do his co-workers behave?

do what he says. I told him I dint think I was going to get smart and he put his hand on my sholder and said Charlie you dont know it yet but your getting smarter all the time. You wont notice for a while. I think he was just being nice to make me feel good because I dont look any smarter.

Oh yes I almost forgot. I asked him when I can go back to the class at Miss Kinnians school. He said I wont go their. He said that soon Miss Kinnian will come to the hospitil to start and teach me speshul. I was mad at her for not comming to see me when I got the operashun but I like her so maybe we will be frends again. **H**

Mar 29 That crazy TV kept me up all night. How can I sleep with something yelling crazy things all night in my ears. And the nutty pictures. Wow. I dont know what it says when Im up so how am I going to know when Im sleeping.

Dr Strauss says its ok. He says my brains are lerning when I sleep and that will help me when Miss Kinnian starts my lessons in the hospitl (only I found out it isnt a

---

H **Read and Discuss** What does this conversation between Dr. Strauss and Charlie tell you?

hospitil its a labatory). I think its all crazy. If you can get smart when your sleeping why do people go to school. That thing I dont think will work. I use to watch the late show and the late late show on TV all the time and it never made me smart. Maybe you have to sleep while you watch it. ❶

PROGRESS REPORT 9—April 3

Dr Strauss showed me how to keep the TV turned low so now I can sleep. I dont hear a thing. And I still dont understand what it says. A few times I play it over in the morning to find out what I lerned when I was sleeping and I dont think so. Miss Kinnian says Maybe its another langwidge or something. But most times it sounds american. It talks so fast faster then even Miss Gold who was my teacher in 6 grade and I remember she talked so fast I coudnt understand her.

I told Dr Strauss what good is it to get smart in my sleep. I want to be smart when Im awake. He says its the same thing and I have two minds. Theres the *subconscious*[6] and the *conscious* (thats how you spell it). And one dont tell the other one what its doing. They don't even talk to each other. Thats why I dream. And boy have I been having crazy dreams. Wow. Ever since that night TV. The late late late late late show.

I forgot to ask him if it was only me or if everybody had those two minds.

(I just looked up the word in the dictionary Dr Strauss gave me. The word is *subconscious. adj. Of the nature of mental operations yet not present in consciousness; as, subconscious conflict of desires.*) Theres more but I still dont know what it means. This isnt a very good dictionary for dumb people like me.

Anyway the headache is from the party. My frends from the factery Joe Carp and Frank Reilly invited me to go with them to Muggsys Saloon for some drinks. I dont like to drink but they said we will have lots of fun. I had a good time.

Joe Carp said I shoud show the girls how I mop out the toilet in the factory and he got me a mop. I showed them and everyone laffed when I told that Mr Donnegan said I was the best janiter he ever had because I like my job and do it good and never come late or miss a day except for my operashun.

I said Miss Kinnian always said Charlie be proud of your job because you do it good.

---

6. **subconscious** (suhb KAHN shuhs): mental activity that takes place below the level of consciousness (KAHN shuhs nihs), or full awareness.

---

❶ Read and Discuss | Why does Dr. Strauss give Charlie the "crazy TV"? What is its purpose?

Everybody laffed and we had a good time and they gave me lots of drinks and Joe said Charlie is a card when hes potted. I dont know what that means but everybody likes me and we have fun. I cant wait to be smart like my best frends Joe Carp and Frank Reilly.

I dont remember how the party was over but I think I went out to buy a newspaper and coffe for Joe and Frank and when I came back there was no one their. I looked for them all over till late. Then I dont remember so good but I think I got sleepy or sick. A nice cop brot me back home. Thats what my landlady Mrs Flynn says.

But I got a headache and a big lump on my head and black and blue all over. I think maybe I fell but Joe Carp says it was the cop they beat up drunks some times. I don't think so. Miss Kinnian says cops are to help people. Anyway I got a bad headache and Im sick and hurt all over. I dont think Ill drink anymore. **Ⓙ**

April 6 I beat Algernon! I dint even know I beat him until Burt the tester told me. Then the second time I lost because I got so exited I fell off the chair before I finished. But after that I beat him 8 more times. I must be getting smart to beat a smart mouse like Algernon. But I dont *feel* smarter. **Ⓚ**

I wanted to race Algernon some more but Burt said thats enough for one day. They let me hold him for a minit. Hes not so bad. Hes soft like a ball of cotton. He blinks and when he opens his eyes their black and pink on the eges.

I said can I feed him because I felt bad to beat him and I wanted to be nice and make frends. Burt said no Algernon is a very specshul mouse with an operashun like mine, and he was the first of all the animals to stay smart so long. He told me Algernon is so smart that every day he has to solve a test to get his food. Its a thing like a lock on a door that changes every time Algernon goes in to eat so he has to lern something new to get his food. That made me sad because if he couldnt lern he would be hungry.

I dont think its right to make you pass a test to eat. How woud Dr Nemur like it to have to pass a test every time he wants to eat. I think Ill be frends with Algernon.

April 9 Tonight after work Miss Kinnian was at the laboratory. She looked like she was glad to see me but scared. I told her dont worry Miss Kinnian Im not smart yet and she laffed. She said I have confidence in you Charlie the way you struggled so hard to read and right better than all the others. At werst you will have it for a littel wile and your doing somthing for sience.

We are reading a very hard book. I never read such a hard book before. Its called *Robinson Crusoe* about a man who gets merooned on a dessert Iland. Hes smart and figers out all kinds of things so he can have a house and food and hes a good swimmer. Only I feel sorry because hes all alone and has no frends. But I think their must be somebody else on the iland

---

Ⓙ **Reading Focus** **Retelling** What has happened to Charlie?

Ⓚ **Literary Focus** **Subplot** How does this race differ from previous episodes? What does this race reveal about Charlie?

because theres a picture with his funny umbrella looking at footprints. I hope he gets a frend and not be lonely.

April 10 Miss Kinnian teaches me to spell better. She says look at a word and close your eyes and say it over and over until you remember. I have lots of truble with *through* that you say *threw* and *enough* and *tough* that you dont say *enew* and *tew*. You got to say *enuff* and *tuff*. Thats how I use to write it before I started to get smart. Im confused but Miss Kinnian says theres no reason in spelling.

Apr 14 Finished *Robinson Crusoe*. I want to find out more about what happens to him but Miss Kinnian says thats all there is. *Why*

Apr 15 Miss Kinnian says Im lerning fast. She read some of the Progress Reports and she looked at me kind of funny. She says Im a fine person and Ill show them all. I asked her why. She said never mind but I shoudnt feel bad if I find out that everybody isnt nice like I think. She said for a person who god gave so little to you done more then a lot of people with brains they never even used. I said all my frends are smart people but there good. They like me and they never did anything that wasnt nice. Then she got something in her eye and she had to run out to the ladys room.

Apr 16 Today, I lerned, the *comma*, this is a comma (,) a period, with a tail, Miss Kinnian, says its important, because, it makes writing better, she said, sombeody, coud lose, a lot of money, if a comma, isnt, in the, right place, I dont have, any money, and I dont see, how a comma, keeps you from losing it,

But she says, everybody, uses commas, so Ill use, them too,

Apr 17 I used the comma wrong. Its punctuation. Miss Kinnian told me to look up long words in the dictionary to lern to spell them. I said whats the difference if you can read it anyway. She said its part of your education so now on Ill look up all the words Im not sure how to spell. It takes a long time to write that way but I think Im remembering. I only have to look up once and after that I get it right. Anyway thats how come I got the word *punctuation* right. (Its that way in the dictionary). Miss Kinnian says a period is punctuation too, and there are lots of other marks to lern. I told her I thot all the periods had to have tails but she said no.

You got to mix them up, she showed? me" how. to mix! them(up,. and now; I can! mix up all kinds" of punctuation, in! my writing? There, are lots! of rules? to lern; but Im gettin'g them in my head.

One thing I? like about, Dear Miss Kinnian: (thats the way it goes in a business letter if I ever go into business) is she, always gives me' a reason" when—I ask. She's a gen'ius! I wish! I cou'd be smart" like, her; (Punctuation, is; fun!)

April 18 What a dope I am! I didn't even understand what she was talking about. I read the grammar book last night and it explanes the whole thing. Then I saw it was the same way as Miss Kinnian was trying to tell me, but I didn't get it. I got up in the middle of the night, and the whole thing straightened out in my mind. **L**

Miss Kinnian said that the TV working in my sleep helped out. She said I reached a plateau. Thats like the flat top of a hill.

After I figgered out how punctuation worked, I read over all my old Progress Reports from the beginning. Boy, did I have crazy spelling and punctuation! I told Miss Kinnian I ought to go over the pages and fix all the mistakes but she said, "No, Charlie, Dr. Nemur wants them just as they are. That's why he let you keep them after they were photostated, to see your own progress. You're coming along fast, Charlie."

That made me feel good. After the lesson I went down and played with Algernon. We don't race anymore.

April 20 I feel sick inside. Not sick like for a doctor, but inside my chest it feels empty like getting punched and a heartburn at the same time.

I wasn't going to write about it, but I guess I got to, because it's important. Today was the first time I ever stayed home from work.

Last night Joe Carp and Frank Reilly invited me to a party. There were lots of girls and some men from the factory. I remembered how sick I got last time I drank too much, so I told Joe I didn't want anything to drink. He gave me a plain Coke

---

L Read and Discuss | What does Charlie's ability to read and understand a grammar book indicate?

instead. It tasted funny, but I thought it was just a bad taste in my mouth.

We had a lot of fun for a while. Joe said I should dance with Ellen and she would teach me the steps. I fell a few times and I couldn't understand why because no one else was dancing besides Ellen and me. And all the time I was tripping because somebody's foot was always sticking out.

Then when I got up I saw the look on Joe's face and it gave me a funny feeling in my stomack. "He's a scream," one of the girls said. Everybody was laughing.

Frank said, "I ain't laughed so much since we sent him off for the newspaper that night at Muggsy's and ditched him."

"Look at him. His face is red."

"He's blushing. Charlie is blushing."

"Hey, Ellen, what'd you do to Charlie? I never saw him act like that before."

I didn't know what to do or where to turn. Everyone was looking at me and laughing and I felt naked. I wanted to hide myself. I ran out into the street and I threw up. Then I walked home. It's a funny thing I never knew that Joe and Frank and the others liked to have me around all the time to make fun of me.

Now I know what it means when they say "to pull a Charlie Gordon."

I'm ashamed. **Ⓜ**

PROGRESS REPORT 10

April 21 Still didn't go into the factory. I told Mrs. Flynn my landlady to call and tell Mr. Donnegan I was sick. Mrs. Flynn looks at me very funny lately like she's scared of me.

I think it's a good thing about finding out how everybody laughs at me. I thought about it a lot. It's because I'm so dumb and I don't even know when I'm doing something dumb. People think it's funny when a dumb person can't do things the same way they can.

Anyway, now I know I'm getting smarter every day. I know punctuation and I can spell good. I like to look up all the hard words in the dictionary and I remember them. I'm reading a lot now, and Miss Kinnian says I read very fast. Sometimes I even understand what I'm reading about, and it stays in my mind. There are times when I can close my eyes and think of a page and it all comes back like a picture.

Besides history, geography, and arithmetic, Miss Kinnian said I should start to learn a few foreign languages. Dr. Strauss gave me some more tapes to play while I sleep. I still don't understand how that conscious and unconscious mind works, but Dr. Strauss says not to worry yet. He asked me to promise that when I start learning college subjects next week I wouldn't read any books on psychology—that is, until he gives me permission.

I feel a lot better today, but I guess I'm still a little angry that all the time people were laughing and making fun of me because I wasn't so smart. When I become intelligent like Dr. Strauss says, with three times my I.Q. of 68, then maybe I'll be like

---

Ⓜ Reading Focus Retelling What happens when Charlie goes out with Joe and Frank?

everyone else and people will like me and be friendly.

I'm not sure what an I.Q. is. Dr. Nemur said it was something that measured how intelligent you were—like a scale in the drugstore weighs pounds. But Dr. Strauss had a big argument with him and said an I.Q. didn't weigh intelligence at all. He said an I.Q. showed how much intelligence you could get, like the numbers on the outside of a measuring cup. You still had to fill the cup up with stuff.

Then when I asked Burt, who gives me my intelligence tests and works with Algernon, he said that both of them were wrong (only I had to promise not to tell them he said so). Burt says that the I.Q. measures a lot of different things including some of the things you learned already, and it really isn't any good at all.

So I still don't know what I.Q. is except that mine is going to be over 200 soon. I didn't want to say anything, but I don't see how if they don't know *what* it is, or *where*

Ⓝ [Read and Discuss] Now that Charlie is becoming aware of his past limitations, how does he connect intelligence to the way people treat each other?

it is—I don't see how they know *how much* of it you've got.

Dr. Nemur says I have to take a *Rorschach Test* tomorrow. I wonder what *that* is.

April 22 I found out what a *Rorschach* is. It's the test I took before the operation—the one with the inkblots on the pieces of cardboard. The man who gave me the test was the same one.

So I still don't know what I.Q. is except that mine is going to be over 200 soon.

I was scared to death of those inkblots. I knew he was going to ask me to find the pictures and I knew I wouldn't be able to. I was thinking to myself, if only there was some way of knowing what kind of pictures were hidden there. Maybe there weren't any pictures at all. Maybe it was just a trick to see if I was dumb enough to look for something that wasn't there. Just thinking about that made me sore at him.

"All right, Charlie," he said, "you've seen these cards before, remember?"

"Of course I remember."

The way I said it, he knew I was angry, and he looked surprised. "Yes, of course. Now I want you to look at this one. What might this be? What do you see on this card? People see all sorts of things in these inkblots. Tell me what it might be for you—what it makes you think of."

I was shocked. That wasn't what I had expected him to say at all. "You mean there are no pictures hidden in those inkblots?"

He frowned and took off his glasses. "What?"

"Pictures. Hidden in the inkblots. Last time you told me that everyone could see them and you wanted me to find them too."

He explained to me that the last time he had used almost the exact same words he was using now. I didn't believe it, and I still have the suspicion that he misled me at the time just for the fun of it. Unless—I don't know any more—could I have been *that* feebleminded?

We went through the cards slowly. One of them looked like a pair of bats tugging at something. Another one looked like two men fencing with swords. I imagined all sorts of things. I guess I got carried away. But I didn't trust him any more, and I kept turning them around and even looking on the back to see if there was anything there I was supposed to catch. While he was making his notes, I peeked out of the corner of my eye to read it. But it was all in code that looked like this:

WF + A DdF-Ad orig. WF-A SF + obj

Vocabulary **misled** (mihs LEHD) *v.:* fooled; led to believe something false.

The test still doesn't make sense to me. It seems to me that anyone could make up lies about things that they didn't really see. How could he know I wasn't making a fool of him by mentioning things that I didn't really imagine? Maybe I'll understand it when Dr. Strauss lets me read up on psychology. **Ⓞ**

April 25 I figured out a new way to line up the machines in the factory, and Mr. Donnegan says it will save him ten thousand dollars a year in labor and increased production. He gave me a twenty-five-dollar bonus.

I wanted to take Joe Carp and Frank Reilly out to lunch to celebrate, but Joe said he had to buy some things for his wife, and Frank said he was meeting his cousin for lunch. I guess it'll take a little time for them to get used to the changes in me. Everybody seems to be frightened of me. When I went over to Amos Borg and tapped him on the shoulder, he jumped up in the air.

People don't talk to me much anymore or kid around the way they used to. It makes the job kind of lonely. **Ⓟ**

April 27 I got up the nerve today to ask Miss Kinnian to have dinner with me tomorrow night to celebrate my bonus.

At first she wasn't sure it was right, but I asked Dr. Strauss and he said it was okay. Dr. Strauss and Dr. Nemur don't seem to be getting along so well. They're arguing all the time. This evening when I came in to ask Dr. Strauss about having dinner with Miss Kinnian, I heard them shouting. Dr. Nemur was saying that it was *his* experiment and *his* research, and Dr. Strauss was shouting back that he contributed just as much, because he found me through Miss Kinnian and he performed the operation. Dr. Strauss said that someday thousands of neurosurgeons might be using his technique all over the world.

Dr. Nemur wanted to publish the results of the experiment at the end of this month. Dr. Strauss wanted to wait a while longer to be sure. Dr. Strauss said that Dr. Nemur was more interested in the Chair of Psychology at Princeton than he was in the experiment. Dr. Nemur said that Dr. Strauss was nothing but an opportunist who was trying to ride to glory on *his* coattails.

When I left afterwards, I found myself trembling. I don't know why for sure, but it was as if I'd seen both men clearly for the first time. I remember hearing Burt say that Dr. Nemur had a shrew of a wife who was pushing him all the time to get things published so that he could become famous. Burt said that the dream of her life was to have a big shot husband.

Was Dr. Strauss really trying to ride on his coattails?

April 28 I don't understand why I never noticed how beautiful Miss Kinnian really is. She has brown eyes and feathery brown hair that comes to the top of her neck. She's

---

Ⓞ **Literary Focus** Parallel Episodes Analyze Charlie's attitude toward lying in this episode compared to the last time he took the test. How has his attitude changed?

Ⓟ **Literary Perspectives** Analyzing Credibility How are Charlie's relationships changing? How does seeing these characters only through Charlie's eyes limit what you know about events?

only thirty-four! I think from the beginning I had the feeling that she was an unreachable genius—and very, very old. Now, every time I see her she grows younger and more lovely.

We had dinner and a long talk. When she said that I was coming along so fast that soon I'd be leaving her behind, I laughed.

"It's true, Charlie. You're already a better reader than I am. You can read a whole page at a glance while I can take in only a few lines at a time. And you remember every single thing you read. I'm lucky if I can recall the main thoughts and the general meaning."

"I don't feel intelligent. There are so many things I don't understand."

She took out a cigarette and I lit it for her. "You've got to be a *little* patient. You're accomplishing in days and weeks what it takes normal people to do in half a lifetime. That's what makes it so amazing. You're like a giant sponge now, soaking things in. Facts, figures, general knowledge. And soon you'll begin to connect them, too. You'll see how the different branches of learning are related. There are many levels, Charlie, like steps on a giant ladder that take you up higher and higher to see more and more of the world around you.

"I can see only a little bit of that, Charlie, and I won't go much higher than I am now, but you'll keep climbing up and up, and see more and more, and each step will open new worlds that you never even knew existed." She frowned. "I hope . . . I just hope to God—"

"What?"

"Never mind, Charles. I just hope I wasn't wrong to advise you to go into this in the first place."

I laughed. "How could that be? It worked, didn't it? Even Algernon is still smart."

We sat there silently for a while and I knew what she was thinking about as she watched me toying with the chain of my rabbit's foot and my keys. I didn't want to think of that possibility any more than elderly people want to think of death. I knew that this was only the beginning. I knew what she meant about levels because I'd seen some of them already. The thought of leaving her behind made me sad.

I'm in love with Miss Kinnian. **Q**

PROGRESS REPORT 11

April 30 I've quit my job with Donnegan's Plastic Box Company. Mr. Donnegan insisted that it would be better for all concerned if I left. What did I do to make them hate me so?

The first I knew of it was when Mr. Donnegan showed me the petition. Eight hundred and forty names, everyone connected with the factory, except Fanny Girden. Scanning the list quickly, I saw at once that hers was the only missing name. All the rest demanded that I be fired.

Joe Carp and Frank Reilly wouldn't talk to me about it. No one else would either,

---

Q **Literary Focus** **Subplot** What development has arisen in the relationship between Miss Kinnian and Charlie?

except Fanny. She was one of the few people I'd known who set her mind to something and believed it no matter what the rest of the world proved, said, or did—and Fanny did not believe that I should have been fired. She had been against the petition on principle and despite the pressure and threats she'd held out.

"Which don't mean to say," she remarked, "that I don't think there's something mighty strange about you, Charlie. Them changes. I don't know. You used to be a good, dependable, ordinary man—not too bright maybe, but honest. Who knows what you done to yourself to get so smart all of a sudden. Like everybody around here's been saying, Charlie, it's not right."

"But how can you say that, Fanny? What's wrong with a man becoming intelligent and wanting to acquire knowledge and understanding of the world around him?"

She stared down at her work and I turned to leave. Without looking at me, she said: "It was evil when Eve listened to the snake and ate from the tree of knowledge. It was evil when she saw that she was naked. If not for that none of us would ever have to grow old and sick, and die."

Once again now I have the feeling of shame burning inside me. This intelligence has driven a wedge between me and all the people I once knew and loved. Before, they laughed at me and despised me for my ignorance and dullness; now, they hate me for my knowledge and understanding. What in God's name do they want of me?

They've driven me out of the factory. Now I'm more alone than ever before . . . **Ⓡ**

Ⓡ **Literary Perspectives** **Analyzing Credibility** How are Charlie's tone and personality changing? Does he seem to be a more or less credible character?

April 30, 1965

Dear Mr. Donnegan:

We, the undersigned employees of Donnegan's Plastic Box Company, request that Charlie Gordon

49

Applying Your Skills

Reading Standard 3.2 Evaluate the structural elements of the plot (e.g., subplots, parallel episodes, climax), the plot's development, and the way in which conflicts are (or are not) addressed and resolved.

Flowers for Algernon, Part 1

Literary Response and Analysis

Reading Skills Focus

Quick Check

1. Why does Charlie want to be in the experiment?

2. Why does Dr. Strauss think Charlie would be a suitable subject for the experiment?

3. Who is Algernon? What does he have in common with Charlie?

4. What are some signs that Charlie's operation has been effective? How is he changing?

Reading Skills: Retelling

5. Look over your Somebody Wanted But So charts, and re-read the story events that you have included. This review will help you piece together the plot's development. Next, briefly describe the subplots you have found, noting conflicts and complications that are developing.

Literary Skills Focus

Literary Analysis

6. **Interpret** What does it mean "to pull a Charlie Gordon"?

7. **Evaluate** Early in the story, Dr. Strauss tells Dr. Nemur that Charlie's learning to read and write is as much of an achievement as their learning a difficult scientific theory without help (page 36). What does Dr. Strauss mean? Challenge or defend his statement.

8. **Compare and Contrast** Re-read Fanny's comments about the changes in Charlie (page 49). How are Charlie's experiences similar to those of Adam and Eve in the Bible? (Look especially at the entry for April 30. You may want to compare Charlie's description with the biblical account in Genesis 2:25–3:24.)

9. **Connect** Re-read the last few lines in Part 1. What do you think about people who dislike others who are different from them?

Literary Skills: Subplots and Parallel Episodes

10. **Analyze** Charlie takes a Rorschach test twice. How do these parallel episodes reveal what is happening to Charlie?

11. **Infer** A significant subplot in this story involves Charlie's relationship with Miss Kinnian. What have you learned about Charlie through this subplot?

Literary Skills Review: First-Person Point of View

12. **Extend** This story is told in the **first-person point of view,** in which one of the characters tells the story as "I" and readers know only what the character tells them. In "Flowers for Algernon," we experience everything through Charlie's eyes and see how he thinks and how he often misunderstands a situation. Choose one of Charlie's journal entries, and retell it from the point of view of one of the other characters, for example, Joe Carp for April 3 or Miss Kinnian for April 15.

Flowers for Algernon

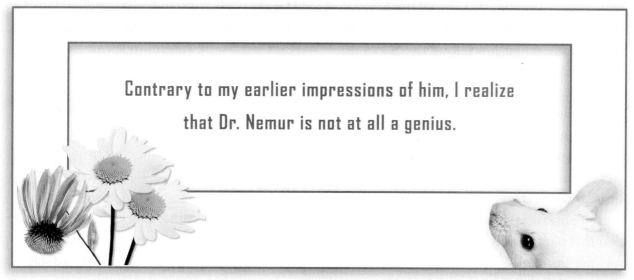

Contrary to my earlier impressions of him, I realize that Dr. Nemur is not at all a genius.

Part 2

May 15 Dr. Strauss is very angry at me for not having written any progress reports in two weeks. He's justified because the lab is now paying me a regular salary. I told him I was too busy thinking and reading. When I pointed out that writing was such a slow process that it made me impatient with my poor handwriting, he suggested that I learn to type. It's much easier to write now because I can type nearly seventy-five words a minute. Dr. Strauss continually reminds me of the need to speak and write simply so that people will be able to understand me.

I'll try to review all the things that happened to me during the last two weeks. Algernon and I were presented to the American Psychological Association sitting in convention with the World Psychological Association last Tuesday. We created quite a sensation. Dr. Nemur and Dr. Strauss were proud of us.

I suspect that Dr. Nemur, who is sixty—ten years older than Dr. Strauss—finds it necessary to see tangible results of his work. Undoubtedly the results of pressure by Mrs. Nemur.

Contrary to my earlier impressions of him, I realize that Dr. Nemur is not at all a genius. He has a very good mind, but it struggles under the specter of self-doubt. He wants people to take him for a genius. Therefore, it is important for him to feel that his work is accepted by the world. I believe that Dr. Nemur was afraid of further delay because he worried that someone else might make a discovery along these lines and take the credit from him.

Dr. Strauss on the other hand might be called a genius, although I feel that his

A **Read and Discuss** What does Dr. Strauss's request about writing and speaking simply tell you about Charlie's progress?

areas of knowledge are too limited. He was educated in the tradition of narrow specialization; the broader aspects of background were neglected far more than necessary—even for a neurosurgeon.

I was shocked to learn that the only ancient languages he could read were Latin, Greek, and Hebrew, and that he knows almost nothing of mathematics beyond the elementary levels of the calculus of variations. When he admitted this to me, I found myself almost annoyed. It was as if he'd hidden this part of himself in order to deceive me, pretending—as do many people, I've discovered—to be what he is not. No one I've ever known is what he appears to be on the surface.

Dr. Nemur appears to be uncomfortable around me. Sometimes when I try to talk to him, he just looks at me strangely and turns away. I was angry at first when Dr. Strauss told me I was giving Dr. Nemur an inferiority complex. I thought he was mocking me and I'm oversensitive at being made fun of.

How was I to know that a highly respected psychoexperimentalist like Nemur was unacquainted with Hindustani and Chinese? It's absurd when you consider the work that is being done in India and China today in the very field of his study.

I asked Dr. Strauss how Nemur could refute Rahajamati's attack on his method and results if Nemur couldn't even read them in the first place. That strange look on Dr. Strauss's face can mean only one of two things. Either he doesn't want to tell Nemur what they're saying in India, or else—and this worries me—Dr. Strauss doesn't know either. I must be careful to speak and write clearly and simply so that people won't laugh.

May 18 I am very disturbed. I saw Miss Kinnian last night for the first time in over a week. I tried to avoid all discussions of intellectual concepts and to keep the conversation on a simple, everyday level, but she just stared at me blankly and asked me what I meant about the mathematical variance equivalent in Dorbermann's Fifth Concerto.

When I tried to explain she stopped me and laughed. I guess I got angry, but I suspect I'm approaching her on the wrong level. No matter what I try to discuss with her, I am unable to communicate. I must review Vrostadt's equations on *Levels of Semantic Progression*. I find that I don't communicate with people much anymore. Thank God for books and music and things I can think about. I am alone in my apartment at Mrs. Flynn's boardinghouse most of the time and seldom speak to anyone. **Ⓑ**

May 20 I would not have noticed the new dishwasher, a boy of about sixteen, at the corner diner where I take my evening meals if not for the incident of the broken dishes.

They crashed to the floor, shattering and sending bits of white china under the

---

Ⓑ **Read and Discuss** | Charlie found it difficult to communicate with others before his operation. What new problem is hampering his efforts to connect with others?

tables. The boy stood there, dazed and frightened, holding the empty tray in his hand. The whistles and catcalls[1] from the customers (the cries of "Hey, there go the profits!" . . . "Mazel tov!"[2] . . . and "Well, *he*

didn't work here very long . . ." which invariably seem to follow the breaking of glass or dishware in a public restaurant) all seemed to confuse him.

When the owner came to see what the excitement was about, the boy cowered as if he expected to be struck and threw up his arms as if to ward off the blow.

"All right! All right, you dope," shouted the owner, "don't just stand there! Get the

---

1. **catcalls:** shouts and whistles made to express disapproval or ridicule, so called because people used to make noises like a cat's cry to show disapproval.
2. **mazel tov** (MAH zuhl tohv): Yiddish expression conveying "congratulations."

C **Literary Focus** **Parallel Episodes** How does the dishwasher's experience resemble episodes from Charlie's own life?

broom and sweep that mess up. A broom . . . a broom, you idiot! It's in the kitchen. Sweep up all the pieces."

The boy saw that he was not going to be punished. His frightened expression disappeared and he smiled and hummed as he came back with the broom to sweep the floor. A few of the rowdier customers kept up the remarks, amusing themselves at his expense.

"Here, sonny, over here there's a nice piece behind you . . ."

"C'mon, do it again . . ."

"He's not so dumb. It's easier to break 'em than to wash 'em . . ."

As his vacant eyes moved across the crowd of amused onlookers, he slowly mirrored their smiles and finally broke into an uncertain grin at the joke which he obviously did not understand.

I felt sick inside as I looked at his dull, vacuous smile, the wide, bright eyes of a child, uncertain but eager to please. They were laughing at him because he was mentally retarded.

And I had been laughing at him too.

Suddenly, I was furious at myself and all those who were smirking at him. I jumped up and shouted, "Shut up! Leave him alone!

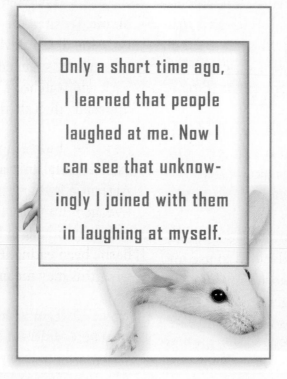

Only a short time ago, I learned that people laughed at me. Now I can see that unknowingly I joined with them in laughing at myself.

It's not his fault he can't understand! He can't help what he is! But for God's sake . . . he's still a human being!"

The room grew silent. I cursed myself for losing control and creating a scene. I tried not to look at the boy as I paid my check and walked out without touching my food. I felt ashamed for both of us.

How strange it is that people of honest feelings and sensibility, who would not take advantage of a man born without arms or legs or eyes—how such people think nothing of abusing a man born with low intelligence. It infuriated me to think that not too long ago I, like this boy, had foolishly played the clown.

And I had almost forgotten.

I'd hidden the picture of the old Charlie Gordon from myself because now that I was intelligent it was something that had to be pushed out of my mind. But today in looking at that boy, for the first time I saw what I had been. *I was just like him!*

Only a short time ago, I learned that people laughed at me. Now I can see that unknowingly I joined with them in laughing at myself. That hurts most of all. **D**

D **Read and Discuss** What discovery does Charlie make about himself in the diner?

I have often re-read my progress reports and seen the illiteracy, the childish naiveté,[3] the mind of low intelligence peering from a dark room, through the keyhole, at the dazzling light outside. I see that even in my dullness I knew that I was inferior, and that other people had something I lacked—something denied me. In my mental blindness, I thought that it was somehow connected with the ability to read and write, and I was sure that if I could get those skills I would automatically have intelligence too.

Even a feeble-minded man wants to be like other men.

A child may not know how to feed itself, or what to eat, yet it knows of hunger.

This then is what I was like. I never knew. Even with my gift of intellectual awareness, I never really knew.

This day was good for me. Seeing the past more clearly, I have decided to use my knowledge and skills to work in the field of increasing human intelligence levels. Who is better equipped for this work? Who else has lived in both worlds? These are my people. Let me use my gift to do something for them.

Tomorrow, I will discuss with Dr. Strauss the manner in which I can work in this area. I may be able to help him work out the problems of widespread use of the technique which was used on me. I have several good ideas of my own.

There is so much that might be done with this technique. If I could be made into a genius, what about thousands of others like myself? What fantastic levels might be achieved by using this technique on normal people? On *geniuses*?

There are so many doors to open. I am impatient to begin. **E**

Progress Report 12

May 23 It happened today. Algernon bit me. I visited the lab to see him as I do occasionally, and when I took him out of his cage, he snapped at my hand. I put him back and watched him for a while. He was unusually disturbed and vicious.

May 24 Burt, who is in charge of the experimental animals, tells me that Algernon is changing. He is less cooperative, he refuses to run the maze any more; general motivation has decreased. And he hasn't been eating. Everyone is upset about what this may mean. **F**

May 25 They've been feeding Algernon, who now refuses to work the shifting-lock problem. Everyone identifies me with Algernon. In a way we're both the first of our kind. They're all pretending that Algernon's behavior is not necessarily significant for me. But it's hard to hide the fact that some of the other animals who were used in this experiment are showing strange behavior.

Dr. Strauss and Dr. Nemur have asked me not to come to the lab anymore. I know what they're thinking but I can't accept it. I am going ahead with my plans to carry their research forward. With all due respect to

---

3. naiveté (nah eev TAY): simplicity; foolish innocence.

E **Literary Perspectives** Analyzing Credibility Do you find Charlie's transformation credible? Why or why not?

F **Read and Discuss** What is happening to Algernon?

both of these fine scientists, I am well aware of their limitations. If there is an answer, I'll have to find it out for myself. Suddenly, time has become very important to me.

May 29 I have been given a lab of my own and permission to go ahead with the research. I'm on to something. Working day and night. I've had a cot moved into the lab. Most of my writing time is spent on the notes which I keep in a separate folder, but from time to time I feel it necessary to put down my moods and my thoughts out of sheer habit.

I find the *calculus of intelligence* to be a fascinating study. Here is the place for the application of all the knowledge I have acquired. In a sense it's the problem I've been concerned with all my life.

May 31 Dr. Strauss thinks I'm working too hard. Dr. Nemur says I'm trying to cram a lifetime of research and thought into a few weeks. I know I should rest, but I'm driven on by something inside that won't let me stop. I've got to find the reason for the sharp regression in Algernon. I've got to know *if* and *when* it will happen to me.

Vocabulary **regression** (rih GREHSH uhn) *n.:* return to an earlier or less advanced condition.

June 4

LETTER TO DR. STRAUSS (*copy*)

Dear Dr. Strauss:

Under separate cover I am sending you a copy of my report entitled, "The Algernon-Gordon Effect: A Study of Structure and Function of Increased Intelligence," which I would like to have you read and have published.

As you see, my experiments are completed. I have included in my report all of my formulae, as well as mathematical analysis in the appendix. Of course, these should be verified.

Because of its importance to both you and Dr. Nemur (and need I say to myself, too?) I have checked and rechecked my results a dozen times in the hope of finding an error. I am sorry to say the results must stand. Yet for the sake of science, I am grateful for the little bit that I here add to the knowledge of the function of the human mind and of the laws governing the artificial increase of human intelligence.

I recall your once saying to me that an experimental *failure* or the *disproving* of a theory was as important to the advancement of learning as a success would be. I know now that this is true. I am sorry, however, that my own contribution to the field must rest upon the ashes of the work of two men I regard so highly.

Yours truly,
Charles Gordon
encl.: rept

June 5 I must not become emotional. The facts and the results of my experiments are clear, and the more sensational aspects of my own rapid climb cannot obscure the fact that the tripling of intelligence by the surgical technique developed by Drs. Strauss and Nemur must be viewed as having little or no practical applicability (at the present time) to the increase of human intelligence.

As I review the records and data on Algernon, I see that although he is still in his physical infancy, he has regressed mentally. Motor activity is impaired; there is a general reduction of glandular activity; there is an accelerated loss of coordination.

There are also strong indications of progressive amnesia. **G**

As will be seen by my report, these and other physical and mental deterioration syndromes can be predicted with statistically significant results by the application of my formula.

The surgical stimulus to which we were both subjected has resulted in an intensification and acceleration of all mental processes. The unforeseen development, which I have taken the liberty of calling the *Algernon-Gordon Effect*, is the logical extension of the entire intelligence speed-up. The hypothesis here proven may be described simply in the following terms: Artificially increased intelligence deteriorates at a rate of time directly proportional to the quantity of the increase.

I feel that this, in itself, is an important discovery.

G **Reading Focus** Retelling What changes is Algernon experiencing?

Vocabulary obscure (uhb SKYOOR) *v.*: hide.
deterioration (dih tihr ee uh RAY shuhn) *n.* used as *adj.*: worsening; declining.

As long as I am able to write, I will continue to record my thoughts in these progress reports. It is one of my few pleasures. However, by all indications, my own mental deterioration will be very rapid.

I have already begun to notice signs of emotional instability and forgetfulness, the first symptoms of the burnout. **Ⓗ**

June 10 Deterioration progressing. I have become absent-minded. Algernon died two days ago. Dissection shows my predictions were right. His brain had decreased in weight and there was a general smoothing out of cerebral convolutions as well as a deepening and broadening of brain fissures.[4]

I guess the same thing is or will soon be happening to me. Now that it's definite, I don't want it to happen.

I put Algernon's body in a cheese box and buried him in the backyard. I cried.

June 15 Dr. Strauss came to see me again. I wouldn't open the door and I told him to go away. I want to be left to myself. I have become touchy and irritable. I feel the darkness closing in. It's hard to throw off thoughts of suicide. I keep telling myself how important this introspective journal will be.

It's a strange sensation to pick up a book that you've read and enjoyed just a few months ago and discover that you don't

remember it. I remembered how great I thought John Milton was, but when I picked up *Paradise Lost* I couldn't understand it at all. I got so angry I threw the book across the room.

I've got to try to hold on to some of it. Some of the things I've learned. Oh, God, please don't take it all away.

June 19 Sometimes, at night, I go out for a walk. Last night I couldn't remember where I lived. A policeman took me home. I have the strange feeling that this has all happened to me before—a long time ago. I keep telling myself I'm the only person in the world who can describe what's happening to me.

June 21 Why can't I remember? I've got to fight. I lie in bed for days and I don't know who or where I am. Then it all comes back to me in a flash. Fugues of amnesia.[5] Symptoms of senility—second childhood. I can watch them coming on. It's so cruelly logical. I learned so much and so fast. Now my mind is deteriorating rapidly. I won't let it happen. I'll fight it. I can't help thinking of the boy in the restaurant, the blank expression, the silly smile, the people laughing at him. No—please—not that again . . .

June 22 I'm forgetting things that I learned recently. It seems to be following the classic pattern—the last things learned

---

4. **brain fissures** (FIHSH uhrz): grooves in the surface of the brain.

5. **fugues** (fyoogz) **of amnesia** (am NEE zhuh): temporary states of forgetfulness.

Ⓗ **Read and Discuss** What has Charlie learned about his condition?

are the first things forgotten. Or is that the pattern? I'd better look it up again. . . .

I re-read my paper on the *Algernon-Gordon Effect* and I get the strange feeling that it was written by someone else. There are parts I don't even understand.

Motor activity impaired. I keep tripping over things, and it becomes increasingly difficult to type.

June 23 I've given up using the typewriter completely. My coordination is bad. I feel that I'm moving slower and slower. Had a terrible shock today. I picked up a copy of an article I used in my research, Krueger's *Uber psychische Ganzheit*, to see if it would help me understand what I had done. First I thought there was something wrong with my eyes. Then I realized I could no longer read German. I tested myself in other languages. All gone. **❶**

June 30 A week since I dared to write again. It's slipping away like sand through my fingers. Most of the books I have are too hard for me now. I get angry with them because I know that I read and understood them just a few weeks ago.

I keep telling myself I must keep writing these reports so that somebody will know what is happening to me. But it gets harder to form the words and remember spellings. I have to look up even simple words in the dictionary now and it makes me impatient with myself.

Dr. Strauss comes around almost every day, but I told him I wouldn't see or speak to anybody. He feels guilty. They all do. But I don't blame anyone. I knew what might happen. But how it hurts.

July 7 I don't know where the week went. Todays Sunday I know becuase I can see through my window people going to church. I think I stayed in bed all week but I remember Mrs. Flynn bringing food to me a few times. I keep saying over and over Ive got to do something but then I forget or maybe its just easier not to do what I say Im going to do.

I think of my mother and father a lot these days. I found a picture of them with me taken at a beach. My father has a big ball under his arm and my mother is holding me by the hand. I dont remember them the way they are in the picture. All I remember is my father drunk most of the time and arguing with mom about money.

He never shaved much and he used to scratch my face when he hugged me. My mother said he died but Cousin Miltie said he heard his mom and dad say that my father ran away with another woman. When I asked my mother she slapped my face and said my father was dead. I dont think I ever

❶ **Reading Focus** Retelling What is happening to Charlie?

found out which was true but I don't care much. (He said he was going to take me to see cows on a farm once but he never did. He never kept his promises . . .) **J**

July 10 My landlady Mrs Flynn is very worried about me. She says the way I lay around all day and dont do anything I remind her of her son before she threw him out of the house. She said she doesn't like loafers. If Im sick its one thing, but if Im a loafer thats another thing and she wont have it. I told her I think Im sick.

I try to read a little bit every day, mostly stories, but sometimes I have to read the same thing over and over again because I dont know what it means. And its hard to write. I know I should look up all the words in the dictionary but its so hard and Im so tired all the time.

Then I got the idea that I would only use the easy words instead of the long hard ones. That saves time. I put flowers on Algernons grave about once a week. Mrs Flynn thinks Im crazy to put flowers on a mouses grave but I told her that Algernon was special.

July 14 Its sunday again. I dont have anything to do to keep me busy now because my television set is broke and I dont have any money to get it fixed. (I think I lost this months check from the lab. I dont remember)

I get awful headaches and asperin doesnt help me much. Mrs Flynn knows Im really sick and she feels very sorry for me. Shes a wonderful woman whenever someone is sick.

July 22 Mrs Flynn called a strange doctor to see me. She was afraid I was going to die. I told the doctor I wasnt too sick and that I only forget sometimes. He asked me did I have any friends or relatives and I said no I dont have any. I told him I had a friend called Algernon once but he was a mouse and we used to run races together. He looked at me kind of funny like he thought I was crazy.

He smiled when I told him I used to be a genius. He talked to me like I was a baby and he winked at Mrs Flynn. I got mad and chased him out because he was making fun of me the way they all used to.

July 24 I have no more money and Mrs Flynn says I got to go to work somewhere and pay the rent because I havent paid for over two months. I dont know any work but the job I used to have at Donnegans Plastic Box Company. I dont want to go back there because they all knew me when I was smart and maybe theyll laugh at me. But I don't know what else to do to get money.

July 25 I was looking at some of my old progress reports and its very funny but I cant read what I wrote. I can make out some of the words but they dont make sense.

Miss Kinnian came to the door but I said go away I dont want to see you. She cried and I cried too but I wouldnt let her in because I didn't want her to laugh at me. I told her I didn't like her any more. I told her I didnt want to be smart any more. Thats not true. I still love her and I still want to

---

J **Reading Focus** **Retelling** What details in the journal entry of July 7 suggest Charlie's increasing decline?

be smart but I had to say that so shed go away. She gave Mrs Flynn money to pay the rent. I dont want that. I got to get a job. **Ⓚ**

Please . . . please let me not forget how to read and write . . . **Ⓛ**

July 27 Mr Donnegan was very nice when I came back and asked him for my old job of janitor. First he was very suspicious but I told him what happened to me then he looked very sad and put his hand on my shoulder and said Charlie Gordon you got guts.

Everybody looked at me when I came downstairs and started working in the toilet sweeping it out like I used to. I told myself Charlie if they make fun of you dont get sore because you remember their not so smart as you once thot they were. And besides they were once your friends and if they laughed at you that doesnt mean anything because they liked you too.

One of the new men who came to work there after I went away made a nasty crack he said hey Charlie I hear your a very smart fella a real quiz kid. Say something intelligent. I felt bad but Joe Carp came over and grabbed him by the shirt and said leave him alone you lousy cracker or Ill break your

neck. I didn't expect Joe to take my part so I guess hes really my friend.

Later Frank Reilly came over and said Charlie if anybody bothers you or trys to take advantage you call me or Joe and we will set em straight. I said thanks Frank and I got choked up so I had to turn around and go into the supply room so he wouldnt see me cry. Its good to have friends. **Ⓜ**

Ⓚ **Literary Focus** **Subplot** Why does Charlie send Miss Kinnian away?

Ⓛ **Read and Discuss** What do Charlie's words "Please . . . please let me not forget how to read and write . . ." show you about his state of mind and what he's feeling?

Ⓜ **Literary Focus** **Subplot** What is the resolution of the subplot of Charlie's relationship with his co-workers?

July 28 I did a dumb thing today I forgot I wasnt in Miss Kinnians class at the adult center any more like I use to be. I went in and sat down in my old seat in the back of the room and she looked at me funny and she said Charles. I dint remember she ever called me that before only Charlie so I said hello Miss Kinnian Im redy for my lesin today only I lost my reader that we was using. She startid to cry and run out of the room and everybody looked at me and I saw they wasnt the same pepul who used to be in my class.

Then all of a suddin I rememberd some things about the operashun and me getting smart and I said holy smoke I reely pulled a Charlie Gordon that time. I went away before she come back to the room.

Thats why Im going away from New York for good. I dont want to do nothing like that agen. I dont want Miss Kinnian to feel sorry for me. Evry body feels sorry at the factery and I dont want that eather so Im going someplace where nobody knows that Charlie Gordon was once a genus and now he cant even reed a book or rite good.

Im taking a cuple of books along and even if I cant reed them Ill practise hard and maybe I wont forget every thing I lerned. If I try reel hard maybe Ill be a littel bit smarter then I was before the operashun. I got my rabits foot and my luky penny and maybe they will help me.

If you ever reed this Miss Kinnian dont be sorry for me Im glad I got a second chanse to be smart becaus I lerned a lot of things that I never even new were in this world and Im grateful that I saw it all for a littel bit. I dont know why Im dumb agen or what I did wrong maybe its becaus I dint try hard enuff. But if I try and practis very hard maybe Ill get a littl smarter and know what all the words are. I remember a littel bit how nice I had a feeling with the blue book that has the torn cover when I red it. Thats why Im gonna keep trying to get smart so I can have that feeling agen. Its a good feeling to know things and be smart. I wish I had it rite now if I did I would sit down and reed all the time. Anyway I bet Im the first dumb person in the world who ever found out somthing importent for sience. I remember I did somthing but I dont remember what. So I gess its like I did it for all the dumb pepul like me.

Good-by Miss Kinnian and Dr Strauss and evreybody. And P.S. please tell Dr Nemur not to be such a grouch when pepul laff at him and he woud have more frends. Its easy to make frends if you let pepul laff at you. Im going to have lots of frends where I go.

P.P.S. Please if you get a chanse put some flowrs on Algernons grave in the bakyard . . . **Ⓝ**

Ⓝ **Read and Discuss** How does Charlie's plan to leave New York reveal what he's thinking and feeling about his experience?

Applying Your Skills

Reading Standard 3.2 Evaluate the structural elements of the plot (e.g., sub-plots, parallel episodes, climax), the plot's develop-ment, and the way in which conflicts are (or are not) addressed and resolved.

Flowers for Algernon, Part 2
Literary Response and Analysis

Reading Skills Focus
Quick Check

1. At the beginning of Part 2, what conflicts is Charlie having with the doctors?

2. How does Charlie react when the boy in the diner drops the dishes?

3. What does Charlie's research reveal about the outcome of the experiment?

4. What are some of the signals that tell you that Charlie's mental state is declining?

5. At the end of the story, why does Charlie decide to leave New York?

Read with a Purpose

6. What has Charlie gained and lost by the end of the story? How does his loss affect him?

Reading Skills: Retelling

7. Review the charts you completed as you read the story. What complications prevent Charlie and other characters from getting what they want?

Literary Skills Focus
Literary Analysis

8. **Analyze** How does the author's use of Charlie's journal to tell his story influence the way we as readers understand Charlie's experience?

9. **Literary Perspectives** At the beginning of the story, Charlie's credibility as a narrator is affected by his intelligence. How does his credibility change as he becomes smarter? Explain which Charlie you found more trust-worthy—the original Charlie or the altered Charlie.

Literary Skills: Subplots and Parallel Episodes

10. **Analyze** What is the resolution of the subplot about Charlie and Miss Kinnian's relationship?

11. **Analyze** What parallel episodes in addition to the Rorschach tests can you find in the story? What relevance do the parallel episodes have to the plot's development?

Literary Skills Review: Resolution

12. **Extend** What do you think becomes of Charlie after the story ends? Why?

Writing Skills Focus
Think as a Reader/Writer

Use It in Your Writing Review your notes on the details Keyes uses to convey story events and the changes Charlie undergoes. Write a jour-nal entry about a remarkable event in your life. Include details that will make the events, and your evaluation of them, clear to your readers.

What Do You Think Now

In Charlie's case, was ignorance bliss? Decide whether he would have been better off if he had not had the operation.

Applying Your Skills

Flowers for Algernon

Reading Standard 1.2 Understand the most important points in the history of English language and use common word origins to determine the historical influences on English word meanings.

Vocabulary Development
History of the English Language

Digging into the Past Today's English developed over a long period of time and from many sources. The history of English can be divided into three periods: **Old English** (A.D. 450–1066), **Middle English** (1066–1485), and **Modern English** (1485 to the present).

Old English In the fifth century the Anglo-Saxons migrated from northern Europe to Britain. The Anglo-Saxons developed a new language, combining their old Germanic language and the Celtic language of the people native to Britain. Soon Vikings, from Scandinavia, invaded. Their language, Norse, was added to the language of Britain. We call this new language Old English. Here are three Old English words that survive today: *horse, night, wife.*

Middle English In the year 1066, William the Conqueror, from Normandy in France, conquered England. Soon French words were added to Old English. Latin also became an important influence on English because the French language developed from Latin. These borrowings from Anglo-Saxon, Norse, Latin, and French gave English the large, rich vocabulary it has today. Here are three words derived from French: *government, justice, literature.*

Modern English In 1485, Henry VII, the first Tudor king, came to the throne of England. The House of Tudor helped promote all things English—including the language. Printed books helped make it possible for all English people to speak, read, and write the same language.

You can find the history of a word by looking up its **etymology,** or origin, in a dictionary.

Your Turn

Use a dictionary to find the origin of each Vocabulary word at the right. Then, make a word map like the one below.

misled
regression
obscure
deterioration
introspective

> obscure
>
> | Derivation | OFr obscur < L obscurus, "covered over" |
> |---|---|
> | Meaning | verb, "to hide or conceal"; adjective, "not clear," "not easily understood" |

Language Coach

Word Origins Which two Vocabulary words share word origins with these words from Spanish? How can you tell?

introspectivo   deteriorar

Academic Vocabulary

Talk About . . .
Analyze the plot development of "Flowers for Algernon" with a partner. Discuss whether the writer adequately addresses and resolves Charlie's main conflict. Evaluate the effectiveness of the subplots and parallel episodes. How would the story change without them?

Learn It Online
To expand your vocabulary knowledge, visit Word Watch at:

 go.hrw.com   H8-64   Go

Reading Standard 3.2 Evaluate the structural elements of the plot (e.g., subplots, parallel episodes, climax), the plot's development, and the way in which conflicts are (or are not) addressed and resolved.

Grammar Link

Adjectives

What do the phrases *lively boy* and *feisty lion* have in common? Both include a noun modified by an adjective. An adjective is a word that describes a noun (such as *boy* or *lion*) or a pronoun (such as *she* or *them*). Adjectives typically answer one of the following questions: *What kind? Which one? How much* or *how many?* Examples of adjectives are underlined below.

What kind?	poor handwriting rowdy customers good mind
Which one (or ones)?	that boy those books any customer
How much or many?	both scientists a dozen times few pleasures

Your Turn

Identify the adjective(s) in each sentence or phrase below from "Flowers for Algernon."

1 ."... finds it necessary to see tangible results."
2. "Who else has lived in both worlds?"
3. "I put Algernon's body in a cheese box and buried him in the backyard."
4. "I looked at his dull, vacuous smile, the wide, bright eyes of a child ..."

Writing Applications Write three sentences of your own using three different types of adjectives: those answering *What kind? Which one(s)? How much* or *how many?*

CHOICES

As you respond to the Choices, use these **Academic Vocabulary** words as appropriate: analyze, aspect, evaluate, relevance, structural.

REVIEW

Analyze Conflict

Charlie Gordon faces several conflicts throughout "Flowers for Algernon." Write a brief essay in which you analyze the way Charlie's conflicts are resolved. Complete a chart like the one below before you write. Identify what Charlie wants at various points in the story.

Date	What Charlie Wants
March 5–April 18	
April 20–June 15	
June 19–July 28	

CONNECT

Analyze the Story

Timed Writing Although the outcome of the experiment was not good for Charlie, he experienced many new things. In a short essay, analyze the lesson or experience that was most important for him. Support your answer with evidence from the story.

EXTEND

Express an Opinion

Charlie writes at the end of the story, "Its easy to make frends if you let pepul laff at you." Write an essay in which you evaluate this statement. Explain whether or not you agree with it. Then explain why you believe your view is correct.

The Circuit

by **Francisco Jiménez**

What Do You Think?

When must you give up what you *want* to do for what you *have* to do?

QuickTalk

Military families, migrant workers, and show-business professionals must move frequently for their jobs. How might such moves affect the children in the family? Discuss your ideas with a partner.

Reader/Writer Notebook

Use your **RWN** to complete the activities for this selection.

Literary Skills Focus

Setting and Tone A writer's attitude about a place, event, or character is called **tone.** Tone is revealed through the writer's use of language. In describing a setting, a writer might use words that convey his love for the twisting streets of his neighborhood. The tone could be upbeat and positive. A second writer might use words that suggest hatred for the muddy fields and barnyard odors of the farm where she was born. The tone could be described as negative. Notice how Francisco Jiménez describes the places where he and his family picked crops in California. How does he feel about these settings? What tone does he convey?

Reading Skills Focus

Analyzing Details If you are having difficulty determining the tone of "The Circuit," consider the details that help you envision the setting. These details may contain positive or negative connotations that give you clues to the writer's attitude about the setting.

Details of Setting	Language and Tone
"Yes, it was that time of year. When I opened the front door to the shack, I stopped. Everything we owned was neatly packed in cardboard boxes. Suddenly I felt even more the weight of hours, days, weeks, and months of work." (page 70)	Words such as "everything we owned was neatly packed" and "weight of hours" convey a tone of sadness and acceptance.
"The garage was worn out by the years . . . The dirt floor, populated by earthworms, looked like a gray road map." (page 71)	

Writing Skills Focus

Think as a Reader/Writer

Find It in Your Reading Create a two-column chart in your *Reader/Writer Notebook*. In the first column, record the conflicts that Panchito and his family face. Record in the second column the place in which these conflicts develop.

Vocabulary

circuit (SUR kiht) *n.:* regular route of a job. *The family picked crops on a circuit.*

detect (dih TEHKT) *v.:* discover; notice. *He didn't detect any problems with the car.*

populated (PAHP yuh layt ihd) *v.* used as *adj.:* lived in. *The dirt floor, populated by worms, was badly in need of cleaning.*

drone (drohn) *n.:* continuous buzzing sound. *The insects' drone made the day seem hot.*

instinctively (ihn STIHNGK tihv lee) *adv.:* automatically. *Panchito instinctively hid when he saw the school bus.*

Language Coach

Related Words Some words have meanings that give you a clue to the meanings of other words. For example, the word *populated* is related to the word *popular.* Work with a partner or use a dictionary to find related words for at least two of the other Vocabulary words.

Learn It Online
Use Word Watch to improve your vocabulary at:

go.hrw.com   H8-67   **Go**

Francisco Jiménez
(1943–)

An Immigrant Success

Francisco Jiménez was born in Mexico and came to the United States when he was four years old. At the age of six, he started working in the fields. The crop cycle took his family all over Southern California. After many difficult years, Jiménez acquired U.S. citizenship and a doctoral degree in Latin American literature. Jiménez has won several awards for his short stories.

The Story of "The Circuit"

Jiménez writes:

> "'The Circuit' is an autobiographical short story based on my experiences as a child growing up in a family of migrant farm workers. The setting is the San Joaquin Valley, a rich agricultural area in California, where my family made a living working in the fields. . . .

> "I wrote the original version of 'The Circuit' in Spanish because it was the language in which the events I describe occurred. . . . Since Spanish was the dominant language during my childhood, I generally write about those experiences in Spanish."

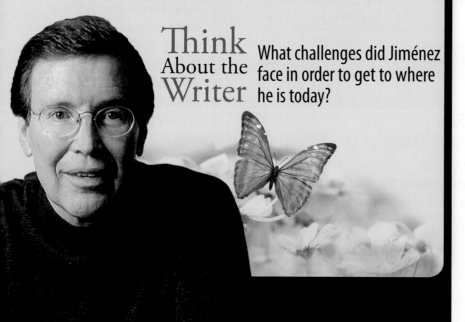

Think About the Writer What challenges did Jiménez face in order to get to where he is today?

Build Background

It was once common for young children to work at difficult, dangerous jobs. In the late 1800s an international movement to end child labor began. An important step toward restricting child labor in the United States was the Fair Labor Standards Act of 1938. This law made it illegal for children under sixteen to work during school hours in interstate commerce. Despite this and other laws, an estimated 300,000 children still plant, weed, and pick crops on commercial farms in the United States.

Preview the Selection

In this story a young boy named **Panchito** has to make sacrifices in order to help his family survive.

The Circuit
CAJAS DE CARTÓN[1]

by **Francisco Jiménez**

It was that time of year again. Ito, the strawberry sharecropper, did not smile. It was natural. The peak of the strawberry season was over, and the last few days the workers, most of them braceros,[2] were not picking as many boxes as they had during the months of June and July.

As the last days of August disappeared, so did the number of braceros. Sunday, only one—the best picker—came to work. I liked him. Sometimes we talked during our half-hour lunch break. That is how I found out he was from Jalisco,[3] the same state in Mexico my family was from. That Sunday was the last time I saw him.

When the sun had tired and sunk behind the mountains, Ito signaled us that it was time to go home. "Ya esora,"[4] he yelled in his broken Spanish. Those were the words I waited for twelve hours a day, every day, seven days a week, week after week. And the thought of not hearing them again saddened me.

As we drove home, Papá did not say a word. With both hands on the wheel, he stared at the dirt road. My older brother, Roberto, was also silent. He leaned his head back and closed his eyes. Once in a while he cleared from his throat the dust that blew in from outside.

---

1. **Cajas de cartón** (KAH hahs day kar TOHN): Cardboard Boxes. This is the original title of the story, which Jiménez wrote first in Spanish and later translated into English.
2. **braceros** (bruh SAIR ohs): Mexican farm laborers brought into the United States for limited time periods to harvest crops. *Bracero* comes from the Spanish word *brazo,* meaning "arm."

3. **Jalisco** (hah LEES koh).
4. **Ya esora** (ya ehs OH rah): *Ya es hora,* Spanish for "It's time."

A **Literary Focus** Tone What tone is conveyed in this paragraph? What words create this tone?

Vocabulary **circuit** (SUR kiht) *n.:* regular route of a job.

Yes, it was that time of year. When I opened the front door to the shack, I stopped. Everything we owned was neatly packed in cardboard boxes. Suddenly I felt even more the weight of hours, days, weeks, and months of work. I sat down on a box. The thought of having to move to Fresno and knowing what was in store for me there brought tears to my eyes. **Ⓑ**

That night I could not sleep. I lay in bed thinking about how much I hated this move.

A little before five o'clock in the morning, Papá woke everyone up. A few minutes later, the yelling and screaming of my little brothers and sisters, for whom the move was a great adventure, broke the silence of dawn. Shortly, the barking of the dogs accompanied them.

While we packed the breakfast dishes, Papá went outside to start the "Carcanchita." That was the name Papá gave his old '38 black Plymouth. He bought it in a used-car lot in Santa Rosa in the winter of 1949. Papá was very proud of his little jalopy. He had a right to be proud of it. He spent a lot of time looking at other cars before buying this one. When he finally chose the Carcanchita, he checked it thoroughly before driving it out of the car lot. He examined every inch of the car. He listened to the motor, tilting his head from side to side like a parrot, trying to detect any noises that spelled car trouble. After being satisfied with the looks and sounds of the car, Papá then insisted on knowing who the original owner was. He never did find out from the car salesman, but he bought the car anyway. Papá figured the original owner must have been an important man, because behind the rear seat of the car he found a blue necktie.

Papá parked the car out in front and left the motor running. "Listo,"[5] he yelled. Without saying a word, Roberto and I began to carry the boxes out to the car. Roberto carried the two big boxes and I carried the two smaller ones. Papá then threw the mattress on top of the car roof and tied it with ropes to the front and rear bumpers.

Everything was packed except Mamá's pot. It was an old, large galvanized pot[6] she had picked up at an army surplus store in Santa María the year I was born. The pot had many dents and nicks, and the more dents and nicks it acquired the more Mamá liked it. "Mi olla,"[7] she used to say proudly.

I held the front door open as Mamá carefully carried out her pot by both handles, making sure not to spill the cooked beans. When she got to the car, Papá reached out to help her with it. Roberto opened the rear car door and Papá gently placed it on the floor behind the front seat. All of us then climbed in. Papá sighed, wiped the sweat off his forehead with his sleeve, and said wearily: "Es todo."[8] **Ⓒ**

---

5. **listo** (LEES toh): Spanish for "ready."
6. **galvanized pot:** metal pot plated with zinc.
7. **mi olla** (mee OH yah): Spanish for "my pot."
8. **Es todo** (ehs TOH doh): Spanish for "That's all."

Ⓑ **Literary Focus** Setting What does the narrator's reaction tell you about the setting?

Ⓒ **Reading Focus** Analyzing Details What do you learn about Panchito's family from the description of the pot?

Vocabulary detect (dih TEHKT) *v.*: discover; notice.

As we drove away, I felt a lump in my throat. I turned around and looked at our little shack for the last time.

At sunset we drove into a labor camp near Fresno. Since Papá did not speak English, Mamá asked the camp foreman if he needed any more workers. "We don't need no more," said the foreman, scratching his head. "Check with Sullivan down the road. Can't miss him. He lives in a big white house with a fence around it."

When we got there, Mamá walked up to the house. She went through a white gate, past a row of rosebushes, up the stairs to the front door. She rang the doorbell. The porch light went on and a tall, husky man came out. They exchanged a few words. After the man went in, Mamá clasped her hands and hurried back to the car. "We have work! Mr. Sullivan said we can stay there the whole season," she said, gasping and pointing to an old garage near the stables.

The garage was worn out by the years. It had no windows. The walls, eaten by termites, strained to support the roof, full of holes. The dirt floor, populated by earthworms, looked like a gray road map.

That night, by the light of a kerosene lamp, we unpacked and cleaned our new home. Roberto swept away the loose dirt, leaving the hard ground. Papá plugged the holes in the walls with old newspapers and tin can tops. Mamá fed my little brothers and sisters. Papá and Roberto then brought in the mattress and placed it on the far corner of the garage. "Mamá, you and the little ones sleep on the mattress. Roberto,

Vocabulary **populated** (PAHP yuh layt ihd) *v.* used as *adj.*: lived in.

Migrant Farmworkers

Today when we think of farm work, we often think of machinery. Although machines such as tractors have made farm work easier, more than 85 percent of fruits and vegetables still have to be cared for or picked by hand. The bins of apples, peaches, and broccoli at your grocery store would be empty if migrant farmworkers hadn't carefully picked each one of them.

Who are the people picking your food? Most migrant farmworkers or their families come to the United States from Spanish-speaking countries. Every year, as soon as the first crop is ready to harvest, they leave their homes and go to work. When that crop is harvested, they move on to the crop that ripens next. Harvesting is hard and dangerous work, and most migrant farmworkers earn less than $7,500 a year. Today some states, governmental agencies, and other organizations are trying to address the needs of migrant farmworkers.

Ask Yourself
Why does the narrator dread the many moves his family's work demands?

Analyzing Visuals **Connecting to the Text** What feelings do you think the narrator experiences when he sees a bus like this coming down the road?

Panchito, and I will sleep outside under the trees," Papá said. **D**

Early next morning Mr. Sullivan showed us where his crop was, and after breakfast, Papá, Roberto, and I headed for the vineyard to pick.

Around nine o'clock the temperature had risen to almost one hundred degrees. I was completely soaked in sweat and my mouth felt as if I had been chewing on a handkerchief. I walked over to the end of the row, picked up the jug of water we had brought, and began drinking. "Don't drink too much; you'll get sick," Roberto shouted. No sooner had he said that than I felt sick to my stomach. I dropped to my knees and let the jug roll off my hands. I remained motionless with my eyes glued on the hot sandy ground. All I could hear was the drone of insects. Slowly I began to recover. I poured water over my face and neck and watched the dirty water run down my arms to the ground.

I still felt a little dizzy when we took a break to eat lunch. It was past two o'clock, and we sat underneath a large walnut tree that was on the side of the road. While we ate, Papá jotted down the number of boxes we had picked. Roberto drew designs on the ground with a stick. Suddenly I noticed Papá's face turn pale as he looked down the road. "Here comes the school bus," he whispered loudly in alarm. Instinctively, Roberto and I ran and hid in the vineyards. We did not want to get in trouble for not going to school. The neatly dressed boys about my age got off. They carried books under their arms. After they crossed the street, the bus drove away. Roberto and I came out from hiding and joined Papá. "Tienen que tener cuidado,"[9] he warned us.

After lunch we went back to work. The sun kept beating down. The buzzing insects,

9. **Tienen que tener cuidado** (tee EH nehn kay teh NAYR kwee DAH doh): Spanish for "You have to be careful."

D **Literary Focus** Setting <u>Analyze</u> the <u>relevance</u> of the setting in this passage. What problems has the new home created for the family?

Vocabulary **drone** (drohn) *n.:* continuous buzzing sound.
instinctively (ihn STIHNGK tihv lee) *adv.:* automatically.

the wet sweat, and the hot, dry dust made the afternoon seem to last forever. Finally the mountains around the valley reached out and swallowed the sun. Within an hour it was too dark to continue picking. The vines blanketed the grapes, making it difficult to see the bunches. **E**

"Vámonos,"[10] said Papá, signaling to us that it was time to quit work. Papá then took out a pencil and began to figure out how much we had earned our first day. He wrote down numbers, crossed some out, wrote down some more. "Quince,"[11] he murmured.

When we arrived home, we took a cold shower underneath a water hose. We then sat down to eat dinner around some wooden crates that served as a table. Mamá had cooked a special meal for us. We had rice and tortillas with carne con chile, my favorite dish.

The next morning I could hardly move. My body ached all over. I felt little control over my arms and legs. This feeling went on every morning for days until my muscles finally got used to the work. **F**

It was Monday, the first week of November. The grape season was over and I could now go to school. I woke up early that morning and lay in bed, looking at the stars and savoring[12] the thought of not going to work and of starting sixth grade for the first time that year. Since I could

not sleep, I decided to get up and join Papá and Roberto at breakfast. I sat at the table across from Roberto, but I kept my head down. I did not want to look up and face him. I knew he was sad. He was not going to school today. He was not going tomorrow, or next week, or next month. He would not go until the cotton season was over, and that was sometime in February. I rubbed my hands together and watched the dry, acid-stained skin fall to the floor in little rolls.

When Papá and Roberto left for work, I felt relief. I walked to the top of a small grade[13] next to the shack and watched the Carcanchita disappear in the distance in a cloud of dust.

Two hours later, around eight o'clock, I stood by the side of the road waiting for school bus number twenty. When it arrived, I climbed in. Everyone was busy either talking or yelling. I sat in an empty seat in the back.

When the bus stopped in front of the school, I felt very nervous. I looked out the bus window and saw boys and girls carrying books under their arms. I put my hands in my pant pockets and walked to the principal's office. When I entered, I heard a woman's voice say: "May I help you?" I was startled. I had not heard English for months. For a few seconds I remained speechless. I looked at the lady, who waited for an answer. My first instinct was to answer her in Spanish, but I held back. Finally, after struggling for English words, I managed to tell her that I wanted to enroll

---

10. **Vámonos** (VAH moh nohs): Spanish for "Let's go."
11. **quince** (KEEN say): Spanish for "fifteen."
12. **savoring** (SAY vuhr ihng): enjoying, as if tasting something delicious.

---

13. **grade:** here, hill.

E Reading Focus **Analyzing Details** What details help you see, hear, and feel the vineyard? What tone do these details convey?

F Read and Discuss What does the narrator reveal about the first day of work at the Sullivans' vineyard?

in the sixth grade. After answering many questions, I was led to my classroom.

Mr. Lema, the sixth-grade teacher, greeted me and assigned me a desk. He then introduced me to the class. I was so nervous and scared at that moment when everyone's eyes were on me that I wished I were with Papá and Roberto picking cotton. After taking roll, Mr. Lema gave the class the assignment for the first hour. "The first thing we have to do this morning is finish reading the story we began yesterday," he said enthusiastically. He walked up to me, handed me an English book, and asked me to read. "We are on page 125," he said politely. When I heard this, I felt my blood rush to my head; I felt dizzy. "Would you like to read?" he asked hesitantly. I opened the book to page 125. My mouth was dry. My eyes began to water. I could not begin. "You can read later," Mr. Lema said understandingly. **G**

For the rest of the reading period I kept getting angrier and angrier with myself. *I should have read*, I thought to myself.

During recess I went into the restroom and opened my English book to page 125. I began to read in a low voice, pretending I was in class. There were many words I did not know. I closed the book and headed back to the classroom.

Mr. Lema was sitting at his desk correcting papers. When I entered he looked up at me and smiled. I felt better. I walked up to him and asked if he could help me with the new words. "Gladly," he said.

The rest of the month I spent my lunch hours working on English with Mr. Lema, my best friend at school.

One Friday, during lunch hour, Mr. Lema asked me to take a walk with him to the music room. "Do you like music?" he asked me as we entered the building.

"Yes, I like corridos,"[14] I answered. He then picked up a trumpet, blew on it, and handed it to me. The sound gave me goose bumps. I knew that sound. I had heard it in many corridos. "How would you like to learn how to play it?" he asked. He must have read my face because before I could answer, he added: "I'll teach you how to play it during our lunch hours."

That day I could hardly wait to get home to tell Papá and Mamá the great news. As I got off the bus, my little brothers and sisters ran up to meet me. They were yelling and screaming. I thought they were happy to see me, but when I opened the door to our shack, I saw that everything we owned was neatly packed in cardboard boxes. **H**

---

14. **corridos** (kuhr REE dohs): Mexican folk ballads.

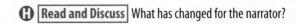

G **Literary Focus** Tone What words would you use to describe the tone of this paragraph?

H **Read and Discuss** What has changed for the narrator?

The Circuit

Literary Response and Analysis

Reading Skills Focus

Quick Check

1. Why does the family leave the shack near Ito's farm?
2. What are the family's new living conditions?
3. Why does the narrator, Panchito, consider Mr. Lema his best friend?

Read with a Purpose

4. How do you think Panchito will cope with having to move yet again?

Reading Skills: Analyzing Details

5. Review the notes you took while you read aloud. Add a row to the bottom of the chart to describe the writer's overall tone in "The Circuit."

Details of Setting	Language and Tone
"Yes, it was that time of year. When I opened the front door to the shack, . . .	Words such as . . .
Overall tone:	

Literary Skills Focus

Literary Analysis

6. **Draw Conclusions** What difficulties faced by migrant parents and their children does the text address? Support your answer with specific details from "The Circuit."
7. **Interpret** What relevance does the title have to the events in the story?
8. **Evaluate** Why do you think Jiménez ends the story so abruptly? Do you think this is an effective choice? Why or why not?

Literary Skills: Setting and Tone

9. **Analyze** What does the **setting** of this story tell you about the customs, foods, activities, clothing, and lifestyle of a migrant worker?
10. **Analyze** The narrator describes two settings in detail—the old garage the family lives in and Mr. Sullivan's vineyards. How would you describe the tone of these descriptions? How would the meaning of the story change if the writer chose a different tone?

Literary Skills Review: Plot

11. **Identify** Complete this time line to illustrate the development of the plot. State what happens to Panchito at each point in the time line.

June–July   Last days in August   November   December

Writing Skills Focus

Think as a Reader/Writer

Use it in Your Writing Review the chart you created in your *Reader/Writer Notebook* as you read. Write three paragraphs in which you analyze the relevance of the setting to the development of the plot of "The Circuit." How does the setting of the story contribute to the conflicts the characters face? How do the characters address and resolve these conflicts?

What Do **You Think Now** Explain whether it was more necessary for Panchito to get an education or to help his family.

The Circuit

Reading Standard 1.2 Understand the most important points in the history of the English language and use common word origins to determine the historical influences on English word meanings.

Vocabulary Development

Vocabulary Check

Answer the following questions.

circuit	
detect	
populated	
drone	
instinctively	

1. Why might a mail carrier's job be said to follow a **circuit**?
2. What should you do if you **detect** odd noises in a car's engine?
3. What might a garage nice enough to be **populated** by a family look like?
4. What does the **drone** of insects sound like? What is another sound that could be described as a drone?
5. Explain whether people who act **instinctively** are acting automatically or thoughtfully.

Spanish and English Words

English is made up of words from numerous languages. Some of these words became part of English long ago, and others have entered the language recently. Over time, thousands of Spanish words have become part of English. Some of them have changed from the original Spanish form. For instance, *rancho* has become *ranch* and *la reata* has become *lariat*. Other words, such as *patio* and *plaza*, have undergone slight changes in pronunciation, but not in spelling.

Spanish has contributed numerous proper nouns to English. In the sixteenth and seventeenth centuries, Spanish explorers gave Spanish names to mountains, rivers, lakes, and new settlements in North America. If you live in the Southwest, it is likely that some of the place names near you came from Spanish.

Your Turn

Copy this chart, and fill in the meanings of the Spanish names. Use a dictionary for reference.

Spanish Name	Meaning
Colorado	
Florida	
Los Angeles	
San Francisco	
Fresno	

Language Coach

Related Words Understanding related words can help you expand your vocabulary. Use a dictionary to find related words for the following words: *migrant, labor,* and *circuit*. Write the related words and their meanings in your *Reader/Writer Notebook*.

Academic Vocabulary

Talk About . . .

In a small group, assess the impact of hard work and a lack of education on the children of farmworkers. Then, brainstorm a list of services you think might be established to help these children. Allow your class to evaluate your ideas.

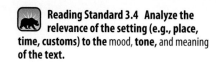

Reading Standard 3.4 Analyze the relevance of the setting (e.g., place, time, customs) to the mood, tone, and meaning of the text.

Grammar Link
Verbs

A **verb** is a word used to express action or a state of being. The verb's role in a sentence is to tell you something about the subject. Three types of verbs are **helping verbs, action verbs,** and **linking verbs**.

- A **helping verb** helps the main verb express action or a state of being. It does not stand alone. Some common helping verbs are *is, being, do, have, could.*

EXAMPLE Papá **was worried** about the school authorities. [The main verb is *worried*.]

- An **action verb** expresses physical action or mental action, such as *fly, jog, celebrate, regret*.

EXAMPLE The family **packed** their belongings.

- A **linking verb** connects the subject to a word or words that identify or describe the subject. Some common linking verbs are *am, seem, was, remain, feel*.

EXAMPLE The boy **felt** dizzy.

Your Turn

Fill in each blank below with a verb that fits the meaning of the sentence.

1. Only the best pickers _____ working on Sundays.
2. When the work was over, the family _____ to move to the next job.
3. She walked to the house and _____ the doorbell.
4. His father's face went white because he _____ so afraid.
5. They _____ dinner on a table of wooden crates.

CHOICES

As you respond to the Choices, use these **Academic Vocabulary** words as appropriate: analyze, aspect, evaluate, relevance, structural.

REVIEW
Describe a Setting

Write a brief descriptive essay about a place that is familiar to you. Include details that will appeal to your readers' senses. You will want them to see, hear, smell, and perhaps taste and touch the place you are describing. Be aware of your tone as you write your description. Choose words that will convey the relevance this setting has for you.

CONNECT
Express an Opinion

Timed Writing In the story, Panchito and his siblings do not have the same opportunities for education as most other children in the United States do. Write a brief essay in which you propose a solution to this problem. Support your ideas with details.

EXTEND
Research a Topic

Group Project Panchito has a deep desire for an education. What keeps some children from gaining an education? What percentage of children have to work instead of study? What impact does the limited education of some children have on a country? With a small group, research one aspect of this issue, and share your findings with your class.

Learn It Online
Use Internet links to expand your view of this story at:

go.hrw.com   H8-77   Go

The Inn of Lost Time

by **Lensey Namioka**

 What Do You Think? What is the most precious thing a person can wish for?

🕐 **QuickWrite**
Make a list of things in life that most people think are important. Then, number the list in order of importance to you.

Takachiho Mountain and Yufu Mountain (Yufu Mountain side) (Edo Period, c. 1808) by Tanomura Chikuden. Pair of hanging scrolls, color on silk (95.8 x 35.8). The Museum of the Imperial Collections, Sannomaru Schozokan.

Reader/Writer
Notebook

Reading Standard 3.2 Evaluate the structural elements of the plot (e.g., subplots, parallel episodes, climax), the plot's development, and the way in which conflicts are (or are not) addressed and resolved. **3.4 Analyze the** relevance of the setting (e.g., place, time, customs) to the mood, tone, and meaning of the text.

Literary Skills Focus

Setting and Mood Have you ever shivered through a movie that takes place in Antarctica or dripped with sweat while watching a desert scene? If so, you have experienced the power of the setting of a story. The **setting** is the time and place of a story. It also includes the customs and behaviors of people living in that time and place.

Setting can affect a story's **mood,** or atmosphere. If the story's setting is a rain-drenched, dismal day, for example, you can expect the story's mood to be gloomy. The writer may create a festive mood with a sunny day and the sound of laughter. Good writers create moods that are <u>relevant</u> to the setting of the story. They help us enter the actual world of the characters.

TechFocus Recall folk tales that you have heard as you read this story, which is based on a folk tale.

Reading Skills Focus

Sequence in Stories Most narratives tell story events in the time **sequence** in which they take place, one after the other. "The Inn of Lost Time" has a more complicated structure than most stories because it contains a frame story. Two other stories unfold within the frame story. Create a chart like the one below for each of the three stories. Complete the chart by recording the significant plot events of each story in "The Inn of Lost Time." A chart for the frame story has been started for you.

Frame Story:

A farmer tells his sons a bedtime story in which . . .	Event 2	Event 3

Writing Skills Focus

Think as a Reader/Writer

Find It in Your Reading The mysterious and historical meet in "The Inn of Lost Time." As you read, record in your *Reader/Writer Notebook* some of the descriptive words Lensey Namioka uses to create the haunting mood of "The Inn of Lost Time."

Language Coach

Oral Fluency Sometimes you can't tell how to pronounce English words. The last syllable of *chocolate,* for instance, does not sound like the word *late.* Instead, it's pronounced "liht." What Vocabulary word has an *–ate* ending? How is it pronounced?

Learn It Online
For a preview of this story, see the *PowerNotes* video introduction on:

| go.hrw.com | H8-79 | Go |

Lensey Namioka
(1929–   )

From Mathematician to Storyteller

Lensey Namioka was born in Beijing, China, and moved to the United States when she was a child. Before she became a writer, Namioka studied and taught math. However, she always loved telling stories, and eventually she began writing novels for young adults. Her award-winning novels have a wide range of settings, including China, Japan, and modern-day America. Her books explore many subjects—from growing up as an immigrant in America to medieval Japanese samurai culture.

A Rich Heritage

Namioka says, "For my writings, I draw heavily on my Chinese cultural heritage and on my husband's Japanese cultural heritage." A trip to her husband's hometown in Japan (where she visited a medieval castle on a hill with the name "Namioka") sparked her interest in Japanese feudal history.

> "I decided I liked being a writer
> better than being a mathematician."

Think About the Writer — What historical period captures Lensey Namioka's imagination?

Build Background

"The Inn of Lost Time" was written in modern times, but it is set in sixteenth-century Japan, when samurai, members of the warrior class, roamed the land. Lensey Namioka uses an age-old technique that is still popular today—the frame story, or story within a story. In fact, this story has *two* stories within it. One is an ancient Japanese folk tale that may remind you of "Rip Van Winkle," a popular American story in which a man sleeps for fifty years. The other is a tale about something that happened to one of the samurai.

Preview the Selection

Some of Namioka's most widely read stories, including "The Inn of Lost Time," recount the adventures of **Zenta** and **Matsuzo,** a pair of wandering samurai searching for work in long-ago Japan. In this story they stop for the night at a farmhouse, where Zenta tells a tale about a time he unraveled an intriguing mystery.

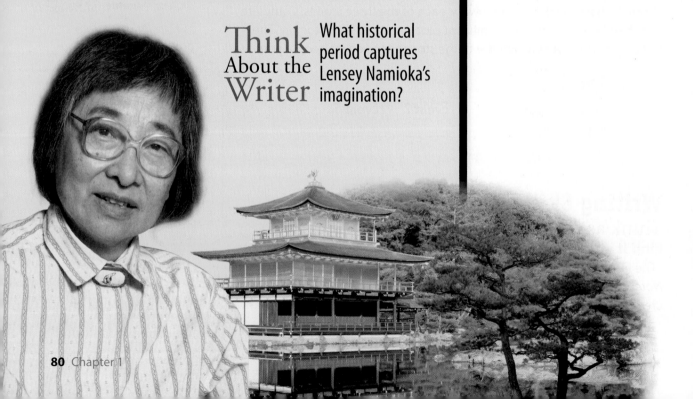

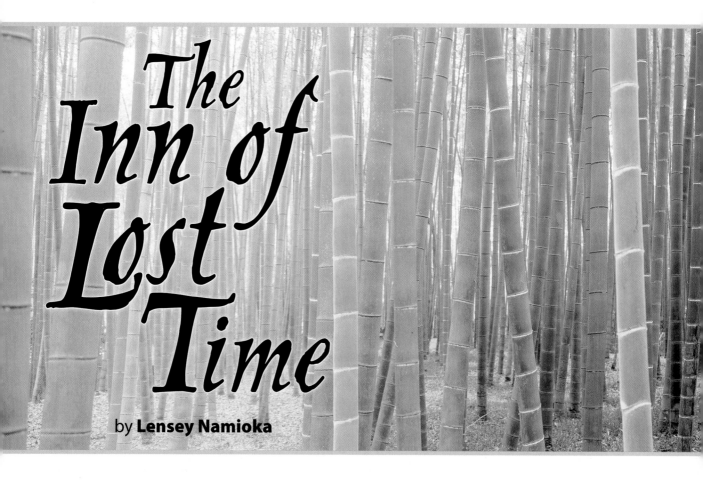

The Inn of Lost Time

by **Lensey Namioka**

"Will you promise to sleep if I tell you a story?" said the father. He pretended to put on a stern expression.

"Yes! Yes!" the three little boys chanted in unison. It sounded like a nightly routine.

The two guests smiled as they listened to the exchange. They were wandering ronin, or unemployed samurai, and they enjoyed watching this cozy family scene.

The father gave the guests a helpless look. "What can I do? I have to tell them a story, or these little rascals will give us no peace." Clearing his throat, he turned to the boys. "All right. The story tonight is about Urashima Taro."

Instantly the three boys became still. Sitting with their legs tucked under them, the three little boys, aged five, four, and three, looked like a descending row of stone statuettes. Matsuzo, the younger of the two ronin, was reminded of the wayside half-body statues of Jizo, the God of Travelers and Protector of Children.

Behind the boys the farmer's wife took

up a pair of iron chopsticks and stirred the ashes of the fire in the charcoal brazier.[1] A momentary glow brightened the room. The lean faces of the two ronin, lit by the fire, suddenly looked fierce and hungry.

The farmer knew that the two ronin were supposed to use their arms in defense of the weak. But in these troubled times, with the country torn apart by civil wars, the samurai didn't always live up to their honorable code.

Then the fire died down again and the subdued red light softened the features of the two ronin. The farmer relaxed and began his story. **Ⓐ**

The tale of Urashima Taro is familiar to every Japanese. No doubt the three little boys had heard their father tell it before—and more than once. But they listened with rapt attention.

Urashima Taro, a fisherman, rescued a turtle from some boys who were battering it with stones. The grateful turtle rewarded Taro by carrying him on his back to the bottom of the sea, where he

At the end of the story the boys were close to tears. Even Matsuzo found himself deeply touched.

lived happily with the Princess of the Undersea. But Taro soon became homesick for his native village and asked to go back on land. The princess gave him a box to take with him but warned him not to peek inside.

When Taro went back to his village, he found the place quite changed. In his home he found his parents gone, and living there was another old couple. He was stunned to learn that the aged husband was his own son, whom he had last seen as a baby! Taro thought he had spent only a pleasant week or two undersea with the princess. On land, seventy-two years had passed! His parents and most of his old friends had long since died.

Desolate, Taro decided to open the box given him by the princess. As soon as he looked inside, he changed in an instant from a young man to a decrepit old man of more than ninety. **Ⓑ**

At the end of the story the boys were close to tears. Even Matsuzo found himself deeply touched. He wondered why the farmer had told his sons such a poignant bedtime story. Wouldn't they worry all evening instead of going to sleep? **Ⓒ**

---

1. **brazier** (BRAY zhuhr): metal container that holds burning coals or charcoal, used to warm a room or cook food.

Ⓐ Read and Discuss What has the author told you so far?

Ⓑ Reading Focus Sequence in Stories Retell the events of the fisherman's story in the order they occur.

Ⓒ Literary Focus Mood How does the mood of the story affect its listeners?

Vocabulary desolate (DEHS uh liht) *adj.:* lonely; miserable.
poignant (POYN yuhnt) *adj.:* causing sadness or pain; touching.

But the boys recovered quickly. They were soon laughing and jostling each other, and they made no objections when their mother shooed them toward bed. Standing in order of age, they bowed politely to the guests and then lay down on the mattresses spread out for them on the floor. Within minutes the sound of their regular breathing told the guests that they were asleep.

Zenta, the older of the two ronin, sighed as he glanced at the peaceful young faces. "I wish I could fall asleep so quickly. The story of Urashima Taro is one of the saddest that I know among our folk tales."

The farmer looked proudly at his sleeping sons. "They're stout lads. Nothing bothers them much."

The farmer's wife poured tea for the guests and apologized. "I'm sorry this is only poor tea made from coarse leaves."

Zenta hastened to reassure her. "It's warm and heartening on a chilly autumn evening."

"You know what I think is the saddest part of the Urashima Taro story?" said Matsuzo, picking up his cup and sipping the tea. "It's that Taro lost not only his family and friends but a big piece of his life as well. He had lost the most precious thing of all: time."

The farmer nodded agreement. "I wouldn't sell even one year of my life for money. As for losing seventy-two years, no amount of gold will make up for that!" **D**

Zenta put his cup down on the floor and looked curiously at the farmer. "It's interesting that you should say that. I had an opportunity once to observe exactly how much gold a person was willing to pay for some lost years of his life." He smiled grimly. "In this case the man went as far as one gold piece for each year he lost."

"That's bizarre!" said Matsuzo. "You never told me about it."

"It happened long before I met you," said Zenta. He drank some tea and smiled ruefully. "Besides, I'm not particularly proud of the part I played in that strange affair."

"Let's hear the story!" urged Matsuzo. "You've made us all curious."

The farmer waited expectantly. His wife sat down quietly behind her husband and folded her hands. Her eyes looked intently at Zenta.

"Very well, then," said Zenta. "Actually, my story bears some resemblance to that of Urashima Taro. . . ." **E**

It happened about seven years ago, when I was a green, inexperienced youngster not quite eighteen years old. But I had had a good training in arms, and I was able to get a job as a bodyguard for a wealthy merchant from Sakai.

As you know, wealthy merchants are relatively new in our country. Traditionally the rich have been noblemen, landowners, and warlords with thousands of followers. Merchants, regarded as parasites in our society, are a despised class. But our civil wars have made people unusually mobile and

---

D **Literary Focus** Mood How has the mood changed since the farmer told his story?

E **Reading Focus** Sequence in Stories Explain the events of the frame story so far.

stimulated trade between various parts of the country. The merchants have taken advantage of this to conduct business on a scale our fathers could not imagine. Some of them have become more wealthy than a warlord with thousands of samurai under his command.

The man I was escorting, Tokubei, was one of this new breed of wealthy merchants. He was trading not only with outlying provinces but even with the Portuguese[2] from across the sea. On this particular journey he was not carrying much gold with him. If he had, I'm sure he would have hired an older and more experienced bodyguard. But if the need should arise, he could always write a message to his clerks at home and have money forwarded to him. It's important to remember this. **F**

The second day of our journey was a particularly grueling one, with several steep hills to climb. As the day was drawing to its close, we began to consider where we should spend the night. I knew that within an hour's walking was a hot-spring resort known to have several attractive inns.

But Tokubei, my employer, said he was already very tired and wanted to stop. He had heard of the resort and knew the inns there were expensive.

Wealthy as he was, he did not want to spend more money than he had to.

While we stood talking, a smell reached our noses, a wonderful smell of freshly cooked rice. Suddenly I felt ravenous. From the way Tokubei swallowed, I knew he was feeling just as hungry.

We looked around eagerly, but the area was forested and we could not see very far in any direction. The tantalizing smell seemed to grow and I could feel the saliva filling my mouth.

"There's an inn around here somewhere," muttered Tokubei. "I'm sure of it."

We followed our noses. We had to leave the well-traveled highway and take a narrow, winding footpath. But the mouthwatering smell of the rice and the vision of fluffy, freshly aired cotton quilts drew us on.

The sun was just beginning to set. We passed a bamboo grove, and in the low evening light the thin leaves turned into little golden knives. I saw a gilded[3] clump of bamboo shoots. The sight made me think of the delicious dish they would make when boiled in soy sauce.

We hurried forward. To our delight we soon came to a clearing with a thatched house standing in the middle. The fragrant smell of rice was now so strong that we were certain a meal was being prepared inside. **G**

---

2. **Portuguese:** The Portuguese were the first Europeans to reach Japan, arriving in 1543. Until they were expelled, in the 1630s, they traded extensively with the Japanese.

3. **gilded:** here, appearing to be coated with gold.

F **Literary Focus** Setting What do the details Zenta gives about his employer suggest about the setting of his story?

G **Literary Focus** Mood What mood does the description of the house and its surroundings create?

Vocabulary grueling (GROO uhl ihng) *adj.:* very tiring; demanding.

Analyzing Visuals

Connecting to the Text
How do these color choices help the artist convey the power of the samurai? In what way do the samurai in the story differ from this one?

The Actor Ichikawa Danjuro VII as a Samurai Warrior by Utagawa Kunisada. Surimono woodblock print.

Standing in front of the house was a pretty girl beaming at us with a welcoming smile. "Please honor us with your presence," she said, beckoning.

There was something a little unusual about one of her hands, but, being hungry and eager to enter the house, I did not stop to observe closely.

You will say, of course, that it was my duty as a bodyguard to be suspicious and to look out for danger. Youth and inexperience should not have prevented me from wondering why an inn should be found hidden away from the highway. As it was, my stomach growled, and I didn't even hesitate but followed Tokubei to the house.

Before stepping up to enter, we were given basins of water to wash our feet. As the girl handed us towels for drying, I saw what was unusual about her left hand: She had six fingers.

Tokubei had noticed it as well. When the girl turned away to empty the basins, he nudged me. "Did you see her left hand? She had—" He broke off in confusion as the girl turned around, but she didn't seem to have heard.

The Inn of Lost Time **85**

The inn was peaceful and quiet, and we soon discovered the reason why. We were the only guests. Again, I should have been suspicious. I told you that I'm not proud of the part I played.

Tokubei turned to me and grinned. "It seems that there are no other guests. We should be able to get extra service for the same amount of money." **H**

The girl led us to a spacious room which was like the principal chamber of a private residence. Cushions were set out for us on the floor and we began to shed our traveling gear to make ourselves comfortable.

The door opened and a grizzled-haired man entered. Despite his vigorous-looking face his back was a little bent, and I guessed his age to be about fifty. After bowing and greeting us, he apologized in advance for the service. "We have not always been innkeepers here," he said, "and you may find the accommodations lacking. Our good intentions must make up for our inexperience. However, to compensate for our inadequacies, we will charge a lower fee than that of an inn with an established reputation."

Tokubei nodded graciously, highly pleased by the words of our host, and the evening began well. It continued well when the girl came back with some flasks of wine, cups, and dishes of salty snacks.

While the girl served the wine, the host looked with interest at my swords.

From the few remarks he made, I gathered that he was a former samurai, forced by circumstances to turn his house into an inn.

Having become a bodyguard to a tight-fisted merchant, I was in no position to feel superior to a ronin-turned-innkeeper. Socially, therefore, we were more or less equal.

We exchanged polite remarks with our host while we drank and tasted the salty snacks. I looked around at the pleasant room. It showed excellent taste, and I especially admired a vase standing in the alcove. **I**

My host caught my eyes on it. "We still have a few good things that we didn't have to sell," he said. His voice held a trace of bitterness. "Please look at the panels of these doors. They were painted by a fine artist."

Tokubei and I looked at the pair of sliding doors. Each panel contained a landscape painting, the right panel depicting a winter scene and the left one the same scene in late summer. Our host's words were no idle boast. The pictures were indeed beautiful.

Tokubei rose and approached the screens for a closer look. When he sat down again, his eyes were calculating. No doubt he was trying to estimate what price the paintings would fetch. **J**

After my third drink I began to feel very tired. Perhaps it was the result of drinking on an empty stomach. I was

H **Literary Focus** Setting Analyze the details of this inn's setting. Which details seem comforting? Which details seem threatening?

I **Literary Focus** Mood What adjective would you use to describe the mood of this evening?

J Read and Discuss What is Zenta suggesting about Tokubei?

The Samurai

This story's main character, Zenta, is a samurai (SAM uh ry), a member of the warrior class in feudal Japan. The samurai were proud, disciplined warriors who led a life based on duty and sacrifice. They followed a code called Bushido, which required them to show absolute obedience and loyalty to their lords and to place their honor above anything else, including their own lives. The samurai class lost its privileges and began to die out when feudalism was abolished in Japan in 1871. You may be surprised to hear that these disciplined warriors produced many of Japan's famous arts, including the tea ceremony and flower arrangement.

One of the great movies of the twentieth century is *The Seven Samurai* (1954), directed by Akira Kurosawa. In the movie, set in the sixteenth century, a group of samurai who are looking for work hire themselves out to protect a village threatened by bandits. The movie has been called an "eastern western" because the seven samurai remind people of the heroic cowboys of American western movies.

Kojima Takanori Writing a Poem on a Cherry Tree, from the series Pictures of Flowers of Japan (1895) by Ogata Gekko. Woodblock print.

Ask Yourself

Do Zenta and Matsuzo seem to follow the ways and codes of the samurai? Explain.

---

glad when the girl brought in two dinner trays and a lacquered container of rice. Uncovering the rice container, she began filling our bowls.

Again I noticed her strange left hand with its six fingers. Any other girl would have tried to keep that hand hidden, but this girl made no effort to do so. If anything, she seemed to use that hand more than her other one when she served us. The extra little finger always stuck out from the hand, as if inviting comment.

The hand fascinated me so much that I kept my eyes on it and soon forgot to eat. After a while the hand looked blurry. And then everything else began to look blurry. The last thing I remembered was the sight of Tokubei shaking his head, as if trying to clear it.

When I opened my eyes again, I knew that time had passed, but not how much time. My next thought was that it was cold. It was not only extremely cold but damp.

I rolled over and sat up. I reached immediately for my swords and found them safe on the ground beside me. *On the ground?* What was I doing on the ground? My last memory was of staying at an inn with a merchant called Tokubei.

The thought of Tokubei put me into a panic. I was his bodyguard, and instead of watching over him, I had fallen asleep and had awakened in a strange place.

I looked around frantically and saw that he was lying on the ground not far from where I was. Had he been killed?

I got up shakily, and when I stood up, my head was swimming. But my sense of urgency gave some strength to my legs. I stumbled over to my employer and to my great relief found him breathing—breathing heavily, in fact.

When I shook his shoulder, he grunted and finally opened his eyes. "Where am I?" he asked thickly.

It was a reasonable question. I looked around and saw that we had been lying in a bamboo grove. By the light I guessed that it was early morning, and the reason I felt cold and damp was that my clothes were wet with dew. **K**

"It's cold!" said Tokubei, shivering and climbing unsteadily to his feet. He looked around slowly, and his eyes became wide with disbelief. "What happened? I thought we were staying at an inn!"

His words came as a relief. One of the possibilities I had considered was that I had gone mad and that the whole episode with the inn was something I had imagined. Now I knew that Tokubei had the same memory of the inn. I had not imagined it.

But why were we out here on the cold ground, instead of on comfortable mattresses in the inn?

"They must have drugged us and robbed us," said Tokubei. He turned and looked at me furiously. "A fine body-guard you are!"

There was nothing I could say to that. But at least we were both alive and unharmed. "Did they take all your money?" I asked.

Tokubei had already taken his wallet out of his sash and was peering inside. "That's funny! My money is still here!"

This was certainly unexpected. What did the innkeeper and his strange daughter intend to do by drugging us and moving us outside?

At least things were not as bad as we had feared. We had not lost anything except a comfortable night's sleep, although from the heaviness in my head I had certainly slept deeply enough—and long enough too. Exactly how much time had elapsed since we drank wine with our host?

All we had to do now was find the highway again and continue our journey. Tokubei suddenly chuckled. "I didn't even have to pay for our night's lodging!"

As we walked from the bamboo grove, I saw the familiar clump of bamboo shoots, and we found ourselves standing in the same clearing again. Before our eyes was the thatched house. Only it was somehow different. Perhaps things looked different in the daylight than at dusk.

But the difference was more than a change of light. As we approached the house slowly, like sleepwalkers, we saw that the thatching was much darker.

K **Reading Focus** Sequence in Stories Where are Zenta and Tokubei now? What details reveal this information?

On the previous evening the thatching had looked fresh and new. Now it was dark with age. Daylight should make things appear brighter, not darker. The plastering of the walls also looked more dingy. **L**

Tokubei and I stopped to look at each other before we went closer. He was pale, and I knew that I looked no less frightened. Something was terribly wrong. I loosened my sword in its scabbard.[4]

We finally gathered the courage to go up to the house. Since Tokubei seemed unable to find his voice, I spoke out. "Is anyone there?"

After a moment we heard shuffling footsteps and the front door slid open. The face of an old woman appeared. "Yes?" she inquired. Her voice was creaky with age.

What set my heart pounding with panic, however, was not her voice. It was the sight of her left hand holding on to the frame of the door. The hand was wrinkled and crooked with the arthritis of old age—and it had six fingers.

I heard a gasp beside me and knew that Tokubei had noticed the hand as well.

The door opened wider and a man appeared beside the old woman. At first I thought it was our host of the previous night. But this man was much younger, although the resemblance was strong. He carried himself straighter and his hair was black, while the innkeeper had been grizzled and slightly bent with age. **M**

"Please excuse my mother," said the man. "Her hearing is not good. Can we help you in some way?"

Tokubei finally found his voice. "Isn't this the inn where we stayed last night?"

The man stared. "Inn? We are not innkeepers here!"

"Yes, you are!" insisted Tokubei. "Your daughter invited us in and served us with wine. You must have put something in the wine!"

The man frowned. "You are serious? Are you sure you didn't drink too much at your inn and wander off?"

"No, I didn't drink too much!" said Tokubei, almost shouting. "I hardly drank at all! Your daughter, the one with six fingers on her hand, started to pour me a second cup of wine . . ." His voice trailed off, and he stared again at the left hand of the old woman.

"I don't have a daughter," said the man slowly. "My mother here is the one who has six fingers on her left hand, although I hardly think it polite of you to mention it."

When I opened my eyes again, I knew that time had passed, but not how much time.

---

4. **scabbard:** case for the blade of a sword.

L **Literary Focus** Setting How does this setting differ from the setting of the inn on the previous night?

M **Read and Discuss** What do these careful descriptions of the old woman and the man suggest?

"I'm getting dizzy," muttered Tokubei, and began to totter.

"I think you'd better come in and rest a bit," the man said to him gruffly. He glanced at me. "Perhaps you wish to join your friend. You don't share his delusion about the inn, I hope?"

"I wouldn't presume to contradict my elders," I said carefully. Since both

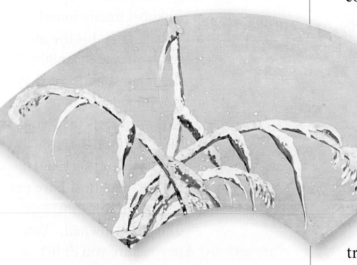

Snow-Laden Grasses by Ogata Kenzan (Edo Period). Fan; ink and color on paper (7 5/8 x 19 1/2 in).

Tokubei and the owner of the house were my elders, I wasn't committing myself. In truth, I didn't know what to believe, but I did want a look at the inside of the house.

The inside was almost the same as it was before but the differences were there when I looked closely. We entered the same room with the alcove and the pair of painted doors. The vase

I had admired was no longer there, but the doors showed the same landscapes painted by a master. I peered closely at the pictures and saw that the colors looked faded. What was more, the left panel, the one depicting a winter scene, had a long tear in one corner. It had been painstakingly mended, but the damage was impossible to hide completely. **N**

Tokubei saw what I was staring at and he became even paler. At this stage we had both considered the possibility that a hoax of some sort had been played on us. The torn screen convinced Tokubei that our host had not played a joke: The owner of a valuable painting would never vandalize it for a trivial reason.

As for me, I was far more disturbed by the sight of the sixth finger on the old woman's hand. Could the young girl have disguised herself as an old crone? She could put rice powder in her hair to whiten it, but she could not transform her pretty straight fingers into old fingers twisted with arthritis. The woman here with us now was genuinely old, at least fifty years older than the girl. **O**

It was this same old woman who finally gave us our greatest shock. "It's interesting that you should mention

---

N [Read and Discuss] What has happened?

O **Literary Focus** Mood Zenta observes details of his surroundings very carefully. Describe the mood they create.

an inn, gentlemen," she croaked. "My father used to operate an inn. After he died, my husband and I turned this back into a private residence. We didn't need the income, you see."

"Your . . . your . . . f-father?" stammered Tokubei.

"Yes," replied the old woman. "He was a ronin, forced to go into innkeeping when he lost his position. But he never liked the work. Besides, our inn had begun to acquire an unfortunate reputation. Some of our guests disappeared, you see."

Even before she finished speaking, a horrible suspicion had begun to dawn on me. Her *father* had been an innkeeper, she said, her father who used to be a ronin. The man who had been our host was a ronin-turned-innkeeper. Could this mean that this old woman was actually the same person as the young girl we had seen?

I sat stunned while I tried to absorb the implications. What had happened to us? Was it possible that Tokubei and I had slept while this young girl grew into a mature woman, got married, and bore a son, a son who was now an adult? If that was the case, then we had slept for fifty years!

The old woman's next words confirmed my fears. "I recognize you now! You are two of the lost guests from our inn! The other lost ones I don't remember so well, but I remember *you* because your disappearance made me so sad. Such a handsome youth, I thought; what a pity that he should have gone the way of the others!"

A high wail came from Tokubei, who began to keen[5] and rock himself back and forth. "I've lost fifty years! Fifty years of my life went by while I

Snow-Laden Pine Branches by Ogata Kenzan (Edo Period). Fan; ink and color on paper (7 5/8 x 19 7/16 in).

slept at this accursed inn!"

The inn was indeed accursed. Was the fate of the other guests similar to ours? "Did anyone else return as we did, fifty years later?" I asked.

The old woman looked uncertain and turned to her son. He frowned thoughtfully. "From time to time wild-looking people have come to us with stories similar to yours. Some of them

---

5. **keen:** wail.

went mad with the shock."

Tokubei wailed again. "I've lost my business! I've lost my wife, my young and beautiful wife! We had been married only a couple of months!"

A gruesome chuckle came from the old woman. "You may not have lost your wife. It's just that she's become an old hag like me!"

That did not console Tokubei, whose keening became louder. Although my relationship with my employer had not been characterized by much respect on either side, I did begin to feel very sorry for him. He was right: He had lost his world.

As for me, the loss was less traumatic. I had left home under extremely painful circumstances and had spent the next three years wandering. I had no friends and no one I could call a relation. The only thing I had was my duty to my employer. Somehow, someway, I had to help him.

"Did no one find an explanation for these disappearances?" I asked. "Perhaps if we knew the reason why, we might find some way to reverse the process."

The old woman began to nod eagerly. "The priestess! Tell them about the shrine priestess!"

"Well," said the man, "I'm not sure if it would work in your case. . . ."

"What? What would work?" demanded Tokubei. His eyes were feverish.

"There was a case of one returning guest who consulted the priestess at our local shrine," said the man. "She went into a trance and revealed that there was an evil spirit dwelling in the bamboo grove here. This spirit would put unwary travelers into a long, unnatural sleep. They would wake up twenty, thirty, or even fifty years later."

"Yes, but you said something worked in his case," said Tokubei.

The man seemed reluctant to go on. "I don't like to see you cheated, so I'm not sure I should be telling you this."

"Tell me! Tell me!" demanded Tokubei. The host's reluctance only made him more impatient.

"The priestess promised to make a spell that would undo the work of the evil spirit," said the man. "But she demanded a large sum of money, for she said that she had to burn some very rare and costly incense before she could begin the spell."

At the mention of money Tokubei sat back. The hectic[6] flush died down on his face and his eyes narrowed. "How much money?" he asked.

The host shook his head. "In my opinion the priestess is a fraud and makes outrageous claims about her powers. We try to have as little to do with her as possible."

---

6. **hectic:** feverish.

"Yes, but did her spell work?" asked Tokubei. "If it worked, she's no fraud!"

"At least the stranger disappeared again," cackled the old woman. "Maybe he went back to his own time. Maybe he walked into a river."

Tokubei's eyes narrowed further. "How much money did the priestess demand?" he asked again.

"I think it was one gold piece for every year lost," said the host. He hurriedly added, "Mind you, I still wouldn't trust the priestess."

"Then it would cost me fifty gold pieces to get back to my own time," muttered Tokubei. He looked up. "I don't carry that much money with me."

"No, you don't," agreed the host.

Something alerted me about the way he said that. It was as if the host knew already that Tokubei did not carry much money on him.

Meanwhile Tokubei sighed. He had come to a decision. "I do have the means to obtain more money, however. I can send a message to my chief clerk and he will remit the money when he sees my seal."

"Your chief clerk may be dead by now," I reminded him.

"You're right!" moaned Tokubei. "My business will be under a new man-

> *"My business will be under a new management and nobody will even remember my name!"*

agement and nobody will even remember my name!"

"And your wife will have remarried," said the old woman, with one of her chuckles. I found it hard to believe that the gentle young girl who had served us wine could turn into this dreadful harridan.[7]

"Sending the message may be a waste of time," agreed the host.

"What waste of time!" cried Tokubei. "Why shouldn't I waste time? I've wasted fifty years already! Anyway, I've made up my mind. I'm sending that message."

"I still think you shouldn't trust the priestess," said the host.

That only made Tokubei all the more determined to send for the money. However, he was not quite resigned to the amount. "Fifty gold pieces is a large sum. Surely the priestess can buy incense for less than that amount?"

"Why don't you try giving her thirty gold pieces?" cackled the old woman. "Then the priestess will send you back thirty years, and your wife will only be middle-aged." **ⓟ**

While Tokubei was still arguing with himself about the exact sum to send for, I decided to have a look at the bamboo grove. "I'm going for a walk," I

---

7. **harridan:** spiteful old woman.

ⓟ | Read and Discuss | What does this passage tell you?

announced, rising and picking up my sword from the floor beside me.

The host turned sharply to look at me. For an instant a faint, rueful smile appeared on his lips. Then he looked away.

Outside, I went straight to the clump of shoots in the bamboo grove. On the previous night—or what I perceived as the previous night—I had noticed that clump of bamboo shoots particularly, because I had been so hungry that I pictured them being cut up and boiled.

The clump of bamboo shoots was still in the same place. That in itself proved nothing, since bamboo could spring up anywhere, including the place where a clump had existed fifty years earlier. But what settled the matter in my mind was that the clump looked almost exactly the way it did when I had seen it before, except that every shoot was about an inch taller. That was a reasonable amount for bamboo shoots to grow overnight.

Overnight. Tokubei and I had slept on the ground here overnight. We had not slept here for a period of fifty years.

Young Servant Girl (detail) (19th century), series of Kabuki theatre, ukiyo-e print.

Once I knew that, I was able to see another inconsistency: the door panels with the painted landscapes. The painting with the winter scene had been on the *right* last night and it was on the *left* this morning. It wasn't simply a case of the panels changing places, because the depressions in the panel for the handholds had been reversed. In other words, what I saw just now was not a pair of paintings faded and torn by age. They were an entirely different pair of paintings. ⓞ

But how did the pretty young girl change into an old woman? The answer was that if the screens could be different ones, so could the women. I had seen one woman, a young girl, last night. This morning I saw a different woman, an old hag.

The darkening of the thatched roof? Simply blow ashes over the roof. The grizzled-haired host of last night could be the same man who claimed to be his grandson today. It would be a simple matter for a young man to put gray in his hair and assume a stoop.

And the purpose of the hoax? To make Tokubei send for fifty pieces of gold, of course. It was clever of the man to accuse the shrine priestess of fraud and pretend reluctance to let Tokubei send his message.

I couldn't even feel angry toward the man and his daughter—or mother, sister, wife, whatever. He could have killed me and taken my swords, which he clearly admired. Perhaps he was really a ronin and felt sympathetic toward another one.

When I returned to the house, Tokubei was looking resigned. "I've decided to send for the whole fifty gold pieces." He sighed.

"Don't bother," I said. "In fact, we should be leaving as soon as possible. We shouldn't even stop here for a drink, especially not of wine."

Tokubei stared. "What do you mean? If I go back home, I'll find everything changed!"

"Nothing will be changed," I told him. "Your wife will be as young and beautiful as ever."

"I don't understand," he said. "Fifty years . . ."

"It's a joke," I said. "The people here have a peculiar sense of humor, and they've played a joke on us."

Tokubei's mouth hung open. Finally he closed it with a snap. He stared at the host, and his face became first red and then purple. "You—you were trying to swindle me!" He turned furiously to me. "And you let them do this!"

"I'm not letting them," I pointed out. "That's why we're leaving right now."

"Are you going to let them get away with this?" demanded Tokubei. "They might try to swindle someone else!"

"They only went to this much trouble when they heard of the arrival of a fine

ⓞ **Literary Focus** Setting What details of setting provide clues to the mystery of the inn?

fat fish like you," I said. I looked deliberately at the host. "I'm sure they won't be tempted to try the same trick again." Ⓡ

"And that's the end of your story?" asked Matsuzo. "You and Tokubei just went away? How did you know the so-called innkeeper wouldn't try the trick on some other luckless traveler?"

Zenta shook his head. "I didn't know. I merely guessed that once the trick was exposed, they wouldn't take the chance of trying it again. Of course I thought about revisiting the place to check if the people there were leading an honest life."

"Why didn't you?" asked Matsuzo. "Maybe we could go together. You've made me curious about that family now."

"Then you can satisfy your curiosity," said Zenta, smiling. He held his cup out for more tea, and the farmer's wife came forward to pour.

Only now she used both hands to hold the pot, and for the first time Matsuzo saw her left hand. He gasped. The hand had six fingers.

"Who was the old woman?" Zenta asked the farmer's wife.

"She was my grandmother," she replied. "Having six fingers is something that runs in my family."

"And that's the end of your story?" asked Matsuzo.

At last Matsuzo found his voice. "You mean this is the very house you visited? This is the inn where time was lost?"

"Where we *thought* we lost fifty years," said Zenta. "Perhaps I should have warned you first. But I was almost certain that we'd be safe this time. And I see that I was right."

He turned to the woman again. "You and your husband are farmers now, aren't you? What happened to the man who was the host?"

"He's dead," she said quietly. "He was my brother, and he was telling you the truth when he said that he was a ronin. Two years ago he found work with another warlord, but he was killed in battle only a month later."

Matsuzo was peering at the pair of sliding doors, which he hadn't noticed before. "I see that you've put up the faded set of paintings. The winter scene is on the left side."

The woman nodded. "We sold the newer pair of doors. My husband said that we're farmers now and that people in our position don't need valuable paintings. We used the money to buy some new farm implements."

She took up the teapot again. "Would you like another cup of tea?" she asked Matsuzo.

Staring at her left hand, Matsuzo had a sudden qualm. "I—I don't think I want any more."

Everybody laughed. Ⓢ

Ⓡ **Reading Focus** Sequence in Stories How has the conflict in Zenta's story been addressed and resolved?

Ⓢ **Read and Discuss** Why do you think the author ends the story this way?

Applying Your Skills

Reading Standard 3.2 Evaluate the structural elements of the plot (e.g., subplots, parallel episodes, climax), the plot's development, and the way in which conflicts are (or are not) addressed and resolved. **3.4** **Analyze the relevance of the setting (e.g., place, time, customs) to the mood,** tone, **and meaning of the text.**

The Inn of Lost Time

Literary Response and Analysis

Reading Skills Focus

Quick Check

1. Where does the main story begin and end?
2. What happens in the old Japanese folk tale told by the farmer?
3. In Zenta's story, what do Zenta and his employer think has happened to them during the night they stay at the "inn of lost time"?
4. What do they discover later? What actually occurs?

Read with a Purpose

5. When did you solve the mystery? What clues give the deceivers away?

Reading Skills: Sequence in Stories

6. Review the charts you completed as you read "The Inn of Lost Time." Underneath the chart, identify the conflict of each story and discuss whether or not the conflict has been resolved.

Frame Story:

Conflict:
Resolution:

Literary Skills Focus

Literary Analysis

7. **Interpret** What is the connection between the inn in Zenta's story and the inn in the frame story? What surprises you about this aspect of the story? Explain.

8. **Infer** Why do you think the farmer's wife and her family changed their ways?

Literary Skills: Setting and Mood

9. **Analyze** How does the setting of the story affect the story's action? Why are details of setting (time, place, and customs) relevant to the meaning of this story? Think about how the story would change if any of these details were missing.
10. **Draw Conclusions** Describe the mood of the story. What aspects of the setting create this mood?

Literary Skills Review: Suspense

11. **Analyze** The uncertainty or anxiety that a reader feels about what will happen next is called **suspense.** Describe ways in which Lensey Namioka builds suspense in this tale.

Writing Skills Focus

Think as a Reader/Writer

Use It in Your Writing Namioka uses precise details in "The Inn of Lost Time" to create a believable and haunting picture of the past. Write a scene that takes place in another time and place of your choosing. Choose precise descriptive words that clearly establish the mood of this time and place.

What Do **You Think Now** Matsuzo calls time "the most precious thing of all." After reading this story, explain whether you agree or disagree with Matsuzo.

Applying Your Skills

The Inn of Lost Time

Reading Standard 1.3 Use word meanings within the appropriate context and show ability to verify those meanings by definition, restatement, example, comparison, or contrast.

Vocabulary Development
Verify Word Meanings

There are numerous ways to test and verify a word's meaning. You might restate the meaning of a word in slightly different terms or create comparisons to aid your comprehension. These strategies will help clarify your understanding of a word's meaning.

A word map will give you the ability to understand and use Vocabulary words in an appropriate context. Examine the word map below for the Vocabulary word **desolate.**

meanings of *desolate*	When might a person feel *desolate*?
• lonely • abandoned • run-down	• best friend moves away • difficult truth revealed • nothing to do on weekend

desolate

What words are antonyms of *desolate*?	What words are synonyms of *desolate*?
• cheerful • joyful	• miserable • wretched

Your Turn

Make a word map for each of the Vocabulary words from the list. Use your knowledge as you answer the questions below.

desolate
poignant
ruefully
grueling
traumatic

1. What is the opposite of a **desolate** mood?

2. The movie was **poignant**—it left me feeling incredibly _____.

3. What experience might lead someone to smile **ruefully**?

4. Our trip was very difficult. It became especially **grueling** when _____.

5. Name three historical events that would have been **traumatic** to experience.

Language Coach

Oral Fluency The *gn* letter combination can be pronounced in a number of ways. Look up the following words in a dictionary: *lasagna, campaign, signal.* Analyze the way each *gn* combination is pronounced. Match each word with the *gn* letter combination below to the word that contains the same sound.

6. lasagna
7. campaign
8. signal

a. ignite
b. complain
c. companion

Academic Vocabulary

Talk About . . .
<u>Analyze</u> the <u>structural</u> elements of "The Inn of Lost Time." What <u>aspects</u> of Zenta's story are similar to the story of Urashima Taro? How are the conflicts in each story addressed and resolved?

Grammar Link

Adverbs

Did you know that *not* and *here* are adverbs? Identifying and using adverbs correctly can be tricky because they do so many different jobs. Adverbs can tell *where, how, when*, and *to what extent*. They can modify verbs, other adverbs, and adjectives. Look at the examples below.

MODIFYING A VERB: Every night the three little boys listened **eagerly** to their father's stories.

MODIFYING AN ADVERB: The older ronin sighed **quite** wistfully.

MODIFYING AN ADJECTIVE: Tokubei was a **highly** successful merchant.

You can sometimes find multiple adverbs in a single sentence, as in the example below.

       where   *how*
EXAMPLE: Stepping **up** to enter, we were **quickly**

            to what extent
given basins of water to wash our feet **thoroughly.**

Your Turn

Complete each sentence with an adverb that answers the question in parentheses.

1. There was something a _____ unusual about one of her hands. (To what extent?)
2. The right panel showed a winter scene _____. (Where?)
3. Tokubei nodded _____ at our host. (How?)
4. I reached _____ for my swords. (When?)

CHOICES

As you respond to the Choices, use these **Academic Vocabulary** words as appropriate: analyze, aspect, evaluate, relevance, structural.

REVIEW

Analyze the Relevance of Setting

Imagine that "The Inn of Lost Time" took place in the United States today. What details of the setting (place, time, customs) would change? For instance, would Zenta still be a bodyguard? Consider other aspects of time, place, and customs that would change. Analyze the way these changes would affect the meaning of the text in a brief essay.

CONNECT

Present a Story

TechFocus A custom in medieval Japan was to gather and tell stories. Select a folk tale to make into a digital story or short video to share with your classmates. Bring the story to life with music, maps, photographs, and pictures.

EXTEND

Write to Persuade

Timed Writing Is it better to travel alone or with a friend, such as the samurai from the story? Write a short essay to convince others of your opinion. Structure your essay with an introduction stating your opinion, specific examples for support, and a conclusion.

Learn It Online
Add the sound of music to your story. Find out how at:

go.hrw.com   H8-99   **Go**

STOP THE SUN

by **Gary Paulsen**

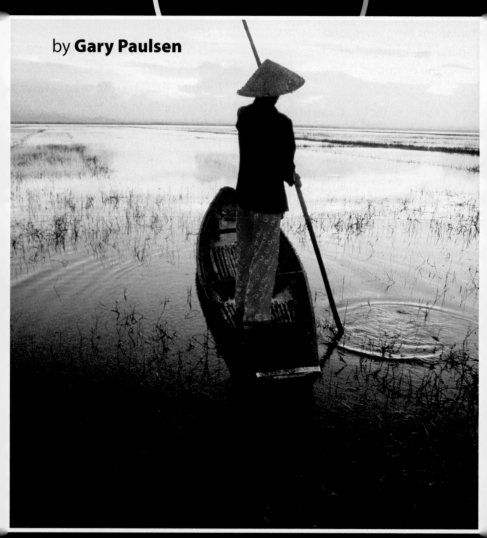

What drives your desire
to understand others?

 QuickTalk

Discuss why parents might shield a child from what they
experienced in wartime. Is withholding information a good

Reader/Writer
Notebook

Use your **RWN** to complete the activities
for this selection.

Reading Standard 3.4 **Analyze the
relevance of the setting (e.g., place,
time, customs) to the** mood, tone, and **meaning
of the text.**

Literary Skills Focus

Setting and a Text's Meaning **Theme** is the truth about life
revealed in a literary text. It is the **meaning** at the heart of a story. "Stop
the Sun" explores a son's struggle to understand his father, who fought
in the Vietnam War. The violent setting of the Vietnam War looms over
the action of "Stop the Sun." Read to discover how past actions in a hor-
rific setting affect the events and meaning of "Stop the Sun."

TechFocus As you read, list what a war veteran might want or need
when he or she returns home. Examples might be a new job or someone to talk to about the war experience.

Reading Skills Focus

Analyzing Story Details A story's theme, or meaning, is not usually
stated directly. Instead, you must <u>analyze</u> details from the story and consider what you know from real life to determine the meaning the author
wishes to convey. Ask yourself, "What idea about life does this story
<u>reveal</u>?"

Into Action Complete this chart to help you identify the significant
details of setting and <u>analyze</u> their influence on the theme of "Stop the
Sun."

> "Stop the Sun"
>
> | Details about the setting: | Terry's dad describes being attacked in a rice paddy in Vietnam. |
>
> | Setting's influence on theme: | |

Writing Skills Focus

Think as a Reader/Writer

Find It in Your Reading Writers sometimes repeat words and
phrases to emphasize important ideas. Record examples of
repetition in your *Reader/Writer Notebook*.

Language Coach

Word Study Some words have
different meanings depending on
the context in which they are used.
Which word on the list above also
means "remains of a decayed building"? How can you tell?

Learn It Online
Learn more about the author at:
go.hrw.com H8-102 Go

Gary Paulsen
(1939–)

A "Rough Run"

Because Gary Paulsen's father was an army officer, the family lived in several areas throughout the United States and in the Philippines. Paulsen calls his boyhood a "rough run." The longest period of time that Paulsen spent in one school was five months. "School was a nightmare," he says, "because I was unbelievably shy and terrible at sports. I had no friends, and teachers ridiculed me."

A Refuge

On a freezing day Paulsen found refuge at the public library. He recounts his experience there as a significant turning point:

> "I went in to get warm, and to my absolute astonishment the librarian walked up to me and asked if I wanted a library card. . . . When she handed me the card, she handed me the world. . . . I roared through [every book] she gave me and in the summer read a book a day."

A Run for Fun

As an adult Paulsen found a sport he enjoys: He races sled dogs in the Iditarod, a grueling race in Alaska.

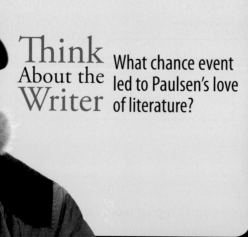

Think About the Writer What chance event led to Paulsen's love of literature?

Build Background

This story centers on a boy whose father suffers from "Vietnam syndrome," a term sometimes used to describe the post-traumatic stress disorder (PTSD) suffered by soldiers who served in Vietnam. This disorder causes anxiety, depression, and nightmares.

Preview the Selection

Terry Erickson, the main character of this story, struggles to understand and accept his father's unsettling and, at times, embarrassing behavior.

STOP THE SUN

by **Gary Paulsen**

Terry Erickson was a tall boy, 13, starting to fill out with muscle but still a little awkward. He was on the edge of being a good athlete, which meant a lot to him. He felt it coming too slowly, though, and that bothered him.

But what bothered him even more was when his father's eyes went away.

Usually it happened when it didn't cause any particular trouble. Sometimes during a meal his father's fork would stop halfway to his mouth, just stop, and there would be a long pause while the eyes went away, far away.

After several minutes his mother would reach over and take the fork and put it gently down on his plate, and they would go back to eating—or try to go back to eating—normally. **Ⓐ**

They knew what caused it. When it first started, Terry had asked his mother in private what it was, what was causing the strange behavior.

"It's from the war," his mother had said. "The doctors at the veterans' hospital call it the Vietnam syndrome."[1]

"Will it go away?"

"They don't know. Sometimes it goes away. Sometimes it doesn't. They are trying to help him."

"But what happened? What actually caused it?"

"I told you. Vietnam."

"But there had to be something," Terry persisted. "Something made him like that. Not just Vietnam. Billy's father was there, and he doesn't act that way."

"That's enough questions," his mother said sternly. "He doesn't talk about it, and I don't ask. Neither will you. Do you understand?"

"But, Mom."

"That's enough."

---

1. **Vietnam syndrome:** form of post-traumatic stress disorder.

Ⓐ **Read and Discuss** Why has the author begun the story by describing Terry's problem?

And he stopped pushing it. But it bothered him whenever it happened. When something bothered him, he liked to stay with it until he understood it, and he understood no part of this. **(B)**

Words. His father had trouble, and they gave him words like Vietnam syndrome. He knew almost nothing of the war, and when he tried to find out about it, he kept hitting walls. Once he went to the school library and asked for anything they might have that could help him understand the war and how it affected his father. They gave him a dry history that described French involvement, Communist involvement, American involvement. But it told him nothing of the war. It was all numbers, cold numbers, and nothing of what had *happened*. There just didn't seem to be anything that could help him.

Another time he stayed after class and tried to talk to Mr. Carlson, who taught history. But some part of Terry was embarrassed. He didn't want to say why he wanted to know about Vietnam, so he couldn't be specific.

"What do you want to know about Vietnam, Terry?" Mr. Carlson had asked. "It was a big war."

Terry had looked at him, and something had started up in his mind, but he didn't let it out. He shrugged. "I just want to know what it was like. I know somebody who was in it."

"A friend?"

"Yessir. A good friend."

Mr. Carlson had studied him, looking into his eyes, but didn't ask any other questions. Instead he mentioned a couple of books Terry had not seen. They turned out to be pretty good. They told about how it felt to be in combat. Still, he couldn't make his father be one of the men he read about. **(C)**

And it may have gone on and on like that, with Terry never really knowing any more about it except that his father's eyes started going away more and more often. It might have just gone the rest of his life that way except for the shopping mall.

It was easily the most embarrassing thing that ever happened to him.

It started as a normal shopping trip. His father had to go to the hardware store, and he asked Terry to go along.

When they got to the mall they split up. His father went to the hardware store, Terry to a record store to look at albums.

Terry browsed so long that he was late meeting his father at the mall's front door. But his father wasn't there, and Terry looked out to the car to make sure it was still in the parking lot. It was, and he supposed his father had just gotten busy, so he waited.

Still his father didn't come, and he was about to go to the hardware store to find him when he noticed the commotion. Or not a commotion so much as a sudden movement of people.

(B) Read and Discuss What does Terry think about his father's condition? What does he think about the way his mother is dealing with his father's condition?

(C) Reading Focus Analyzing Story Details How is Terry trying to understand his father? How successful are his attempts?

Vocabulary commotion (kuh MOH shuhn) *n.*: noisy confusion; disturbance.

Later, he thought of it and couldn't remember when the feeling first came to him that there was something wrong. The people were moving toward the hardware store and that might have been what made Terry suspicious.

There was a crowd blocking the entry to the store, and he couldn't see what they were looking at. Some of them were laughing small, nervous laughs that made no sense.

Terry squeezed through the crowd until he got near the front. At first he saw nothing unusual. There were still some people in front of him, so he pushed a crack between them. Then he saw it: His father was squirming along the floor on his stomach. He was crying, looking terrified, his breath coming in short, hot pants like some kind of hurt animal.

It burned into Terry's mind, the picture of his father down on the floor. It burned in and in, and he wanted to walk away, but something made his feet move forward. He knelt next to his father and helped the owner of the store get him up on his feet. His father didn't speak at all but continued to make little whimpering sounds, and they led him back into the owner's office and put him in a chair. Then Terry called his mother and she came in a taxi to take them home. Waiting, Terry sat in a chair next to his father, looking at the floor, wanting only for the earth to open and let him drop in a deep hole. He wanted to disappear. **ⓓ**

Words. They gave him words like Vietnam syndrome, and his father was

ⓓ Read and Discuss | What is happening with Terry's father?

Vietnam War

When Vietnam won its independence from France in 1954, it was split into two halves. When attempts to hold elections to choose a government for a united country failed, the communist North tried to unite the whole country under a communist regime. The United States supplied South Vietnam with weapons, troops, and other support, gradually increasing its involvement until by 1969 more than 500,000 U.S. military personnel were in Vietnam. Despite having superior technology and firepower, the United States was unable to defeat a guerrilla army fighting in its home territory. When President Richard Nixon took office in 1969, he began withdrawing U.S. troops. North Vietnam conquered the South, and by 1976, Vietnam had become a reunited country under communist rule.

Ask Yourself

What different insights into the war do this link and the short story offer?

crawling through a hardware store on his stomach.

When the embarrassment became so bad that he would cross the street when he saw his father coming, when it ate into him as he went to sleep, Terry realized he had to do something. He had to know this thing, had to understand what was wrong with his father.

When it came, it was simple enough at the start. It had taken some courage, more than Terry thought he could find. His father was sitting in the kitchen at the table and his mother had gone shopping. Terry wanted it that way; he wanted his father alone. His mother seemed to try to protect him, as if his father could break.

Terry got a soda out of the refrigerator and popped it open. As an afterthought, he handed it to his father and got another for himself. Then he sat at the table.

His father smiled. "You look serious."

"Well . . ."

It went nowhere for a moment, and Terry was just about to drop it altogether. It may be the wrong time, he thought, but there might never be a better one. He tightened his back, took a sip of pop.

"I was wondering if we could talk about something, Dad," Terry said.

His father shrugged. "We already did the bit about girls. Some time ago, as I remember it."

"No. Not that." It was a standing joke

Analyzing Visuals   Connecting to the Text

In what ways is this scene from Vietnam similar to and different from the places that haunt Terry's father?

between them. When his father finally got around to explaining things to him, they'd already covered it in school. "It's something else."

"Something pretty heavy, judging by your face."

"Yes."

"Well?"

I still can't do it, Terry thought. Things are bad, but maybe not as bad as they could get. I can still drop this thing.

"Vietnam," Terry blurted out. And he thought, there, it's out. It's out and gone.

"No!" his father said sharply. It was as if he had been struck a blow. A body blow.

"But, Dad."

"No. That's another part of my life. A bad part. A rotten part. It was before I met your mother, long before you. It has nothing to do with this family, nothing. No."

So, Terry thought, so I tried. But it wasn't over yet. It wasn't started yet.

"It just seems to bother you so much," Terry said, "and I thought if I could help or maybe understand it better. . . ." His words ran until he foundered, until he could say no more. He looked at the table, then out the window. It was all wrong to bring it up, he thought. I blew it. I blew it all up. "I'm sorry."

But now his father didn't hear him. Now his father's eyes were gone again, and a shaft of something horrible went through Terry's heart as he thought he had done this thing to his father, caused his eyes to go away.

"You can't know," his father said after a time. "You can't know this thing."

Terry said nothing. He felt he had said too much.

"This thing that you want to know— there is so much of it that you cannot know it all, and to know only a part is . . . is too awful. I can't tell you. I can't tell anybody what it was really like." **E**

It was more than he'd ever said about Vietnam, and his voice was breaking. Terry hated himself and felt he would hate himself until he was an old man. In one second he had caused such ruin. And all because he had been embarrassed. What difference did it make? Now he had done this, and he wanted to hide, to leave. But he sat, waiting, knowing that it wasn't done.

His father looked to him, through him, somewhere into and out of Terry. He wasn't in the kitchen anymore. He wasn't in the house. He was back in the green places, back in the hot places, the wet-hot places. **F**

"You think that because I act strange, that we can talk and it will be all right," his father said. "That we can talk and it will just go away. That's what you think, isn't it?"

Terry started to shake his head, but he knew it wasn't expected.

"That's what the shrinks say," his father continued. "The psychiatrists tell me that if I talk about it, the whole thing will go away. But they don't know. They weren't there. You

---

E **Reading Focus** Analyzing Story Details Why do you think Terry's father "can't tell anybody what it was really like"?

F **Read and Discuss** What is happening to Terry's father? What are the "green places, . . . the wet-hot places"?

Vocabulary **foundered** (FOWN duhrd) v.: broke down; failed.

ruin (ROO uhn) n.: great damage; devastation.

Connecting to the Text These pictures of Vietnamese rice paddies look peaceful, but how might they appear to a foreign soldier, at night, crossing this terrain?

weren't there. Nobody was there but me and some other dead people, and they can't talk because they couldn't stop the morning."

Terry pushed his soda can back and forth, looking down, frightened at what was happening. *The other dead people*, he'd said, as if he were dead as well. *Couldn't stop the morning.*

"I don't understand, Dad."

"No. You don't." His voice hardened, then softened again, and broke at the edges. "But see, see how it was. . . ." He trailed off, and Terry thought he was done. His father looked back down to the table, at the can

of soda he hadn't touched, at the tablecloth, at his hands, which were folded, inert on the table.

"We were crossing a rice paddy in the dark," he said, and suddenly his voice flowed like a river breaking loose. "We were crossing the paddy, and it was dark, still dark, so black you couldn't see the end of your nose. There was a light rain, a mist, and I was thinking that during the next break I would whisper and tell Petey Kressler how nice the rain felt, but of course I didn't know there wouldn't be a Petey Kressler."

Vocabulary **inert** (ihn URT) *adj.* : not moving; still.

He took a deep, ragged breath. At that moment Terry felt his brain swirl, a kind of whirlpool pulling, and he felt the darkness and the light rain because it was in his father's eyes, in his voice.

"So we were crossing the paddy, and it was a straight sweep, and then we caught it. We began taking fire from three sides, automatic weapons, and everybody went down and tried to get low, but we couldn't. We couldn't get low enough. We could never get low enough, and you could hear the rounds hitting people. It was just a short time before they brought in the mortars and we should have moved, should have run, but nobody got up, and after a time nobody *could* get up. The fire just kept coming and coming, and then incoming mortars, and I heard screams as they hit, but there was nothing to do. Nothing to do."

"Dad?" Terry said. He thought, maybe I can stop him. Maybe I can stop him before . . . before it gets to be too much. Before he breaks.

"Mortars," his father went on, "I hated mortars. You just heard them *wump* as they fired, and you didn't know where they would hit, and you always felt like they would hit your back. They swept back and forth with the mortars, and the automatic weapons kept coming in, and there was no radio, no way to call for artillery. Just the dark to hide in. So I crawled to the side and found Jackson, only he wasn't there, just part of his body, the top part, and I hid under it and waited, and waited, and waited.

"Finally the firing quit. But see, see how it was in the dark with nobody alive but me? I yelled once, but that brought fire again, so I shut up, and there was nothing, not even the screams." **ⓖ**

His father cried, and Terry tried to understand, and he thought he could feel part of it. But it was so much, so much and so strange to him.

"You cannot know this," his father repeated. It was almost a chant. "You cannot know the fear. It was almost dark, and I was the only one left alive out of 54 men, all dead but me, and I knew that the Vietcong[2] were just waiting for light. When the dawn came, 'Charley'[3] would come out and finish everybody off, the way they always did. And I thought if I could stop the dawn, just stop the sun from coming up, I could make it."

Terry felt the fear, and he also felt the tears coming down his cheeks. His hand went out across the table, and he took his father's hand and held it. It was shaking. **ⓗ**

"I mean I actually thought that if I could stop the sun from coming up, I could live. I made my brain work on that because it was all I had. Through the rest of the night in the rain in the paddy, I thought I could do it. I could stop the dawn." He took a deep breath. "But you can't, you know. You can't stop it from coming, and when I saw the gray light, I knew I was dead. It would just

---

2. **Vietcong:** South Vietnamese guerrillas who fought with support from North Vietnam.

3. **Charley:** term used by American soldiers to refer to the Vietcong.

ⓖ Literary Focus Setting and Meaning Terry's father suddenly provides several details about his war experience. What point is Paulsen making?

ⓗ Reading Focus Analyzing Story Details What does Terry's crying indicate? What is he learning from listening to his father?

Infantry Soldiers by Roger Blum.

be minutes, and the light would be full, and I just settled under Jackson's body, and hid."

He stopped, and his face came down into his hands. Terry stood and went around the table to stand in back of him, his hands on his shoulders, rubbing gently.

"They didn't shoot me. They came, one of them poked Jackson's body and went on and they left me. But I was dead. I'm still dead, don't you see? I died because I couldn't stop the sun. I died. Inside where I am—I died."

Terry was still in back of him, and he nodded, but he didn't see. Not that. He understood only that he didn't understand, and that he would probably never understand what had truly happened. And maybe his father would never be truly normal.

But Terry also knew that it didn't matter. He would try to understand, and the trying would have to be enough. He would try hard from now on, and he would not be embarrassed when his father's eyes went away. He would not be embarrassed no matter what his father did. Terry had knowledge now. Maybe not enough and maybe not all that he would need.

But it was a start. ❶

---

❶ **Literary Focus** Setting and Meaning What can you infer from the final paragraphs about the meaning of this story? What is the story saying about one person's efforts to understand another?

Applying Your Skills

Reading Standard 3.4 Analyze the relevance of the setting (e.g., place, time, customs) to the mood, tone, and meaning of the text.

Stop the Sun
Literary Response and Analysis

Reading Skills Focus
Quick Check

1. Why is Terry embarrassed by his father?
2. What steps does Terry take to better understand his father?

Read with a Purpose

3. What does Terry learn about his father's wartime experiences?

Reading Skills: Analyzing Story Details

4. Review the details you recorded on your chart. Then, add a row and write a sentence stating the story's **theme,** or meaning. Be sure to include the relevance of the setting in your statement.

Details of setting:

Setting's influence on theme:

Theme:

Literary Skills Focus
Literary Analysis

5. **Compare and Contrast** Terry and his mother support his father in different ways. What do these differences tell us about Terry and his mother?
6. **Interpret** What is the relevance of the story's title, "Stop the Sun"?
7. **Make Judgments** Evaluate whether or not Terry's decision to question his father is a good one. Explain whether Terry behaves admirably or should have confronted the situation differently.

Literary Skills: Setting and a Text's Meaning

8. **Analyze** How do past events affect present events in this story? Include examples from the text in your response.
9. **Interpret** What insight about life does Paulsen convey in "Stop the Sun"? What is the relevance of the Vietnam War to the mood, tone, and meaning of the text?

Literary Skills Review: Conflict

10. **Identify** Some **conflicts** are **external**—between characters or between a character and some outside force. Other conflicts are **internal**—within a character's mind. Identify one internal and one external conflict that Terry faces in "Stop the Sun." Analyze whether or not these conflicts are addressed and resolved.

Writing Skills Focus
Think as a Reader/Writer

Use It in Your Writing Review your notes on Paulsen's use of repetition in the story. Analyze the repeated words and phrases Paulsen uses. What important ideas do these repetitions illustrate?

What Do You Think Now Explain whether Terry's wish to understand his dad was worth the result.

Applying Your Skills

Stop the Sun

Vocabulary Development

Vocabulary Check

Answer the following questions. Include the bold-face Vocabulary word in your answer.

1. How would you respond if you heard a **commotion** in the school hallway?
2. If you heard a public speaker whose words **foundered,** what advice might you give?
3. What event might bring **ruin** to a country?
4. What might be the posture of an **inert** person?

Idioms

An **idiom** is an expression that means something beyond the literal meaning of its words. For example, if your friend's "heart is broken," you can infer the figurative meaning of the idiom. Your friend feels sad or had been disappointed in love.

A language's idioms can be confusing for non-native speakers because they are not consistent from language to language. For example, in English, if someone overreacts to a minor issue, you might say that person is "making a mountain out of a molehill." In German, however, you might say that person is "making an elephant out of a gnat."

Your Turn

Work in pairs to discuss and infer the meanings of the following idioms from "Stop the Sun."

1. "When he tried to find out about it, **he kept hitting walls.**"
2. "Terry was just about to **drop it** altogether."
3. "Something pretty **heavy,** judging by your face."

Language Coach

Word Study Each sentence below contains a boldface word followed by several definitions of that word. Choose the definition that best fits how the word is used in the sentence.

1. "His mother would reach over and take the fork and put it gently down on his **plate,** and they would go back to eating."
   a. dish
   b. illustration
   c. metal coating
2. "He was crying, looking terrified, his breath coming in short, hot **pants.**"
   a. trousers
   b. throbs
   c. gasps

Academic Vocabulary

Talk About . . .

Analyze the information Terry's father conveys about his experiences and feelings. What is the relevance of Terry's father repeating that Terry "cannot know" his experiences in Vietnam? Use the underlined Academic Vocabulary words in your discussion.

Learn It Online
Sharpen your word skills with *WordSharp* at:

go.hrw.com | H8-112 | Go

Grammar Link

Prepositions

Prepositions tell you how a noun or pronoun relates to another word. Notice how a change of preposition changes the meaning of the following sentence. The prepositions are boldface.

He wanted to talk **to** his father.
He wanted to talk **about** his father.
He wanted to talk **with** his father.
He wanted to talk **over** his father.
He wanted to talk **for** his father.

Your Turn

Complete the following sentences by choosing the appropriate preposition from the list below.

> around   after   by   next   in

1. He stayed _____ class and tried to talk to Mr. Carlson.
2. He knelt _____ to his father.
3. Terry called his mother, and she came _____ a taxi to take them home.
4. It was _____ the time that he met Terry's mother.
5. We were crossing a rice paddy _____ the dark.

CHOICES

As you respond to the Choices, use these **Academic Vocabulary** words as appropriate: analyze, aspect, evaluate, relevance, structural.

REVIEW

Discuss a Story's Meaning

Listening and Speaking Readers often have different interpretations of a story's **theme,** or overall meaning. Discuss with several classmates ideas about the meaning of "Stop the Sun." Remember to discuss the relevance of the setting to the meaning of the text. Each person should support his or her interpretation with details from the story and respect one another's points of view.

CONNECT

Write a Personal Essay

Timed └Writing Write a brief personal essay about an incident when you had difficulty understanding someone's behavior. Explain what the behavior was and what you did to comprehend it. Be sure to relate the relevance of the experience. Evaluate whether or not you made a discovery about yourself in the process.

EXTEND

Research Veterans' Support

TechFocus "Stop the Sun" addresses the effects of the Vietnam War on a young man's father. How have the veterans of more recent wars been affected by their experiences? Use reliable Internet resources to find out how people and organizations in the United States are supporting veterans. Then, create a PowerPoint presentation to share the results of your research with the class.

Comparing Plot and Setting

CONTENTS

 What Do You Think? Who are the people that help you find out what's important to you?

 QuickTalk
What customs do you know of that mark the passage into adulthood? Why do many cultures celebrate this important time?

Preparing to Read

The Medicine Bag / An Hour with Abuelo

 Reading Standard 3.2 Evaluate the structural elements of the plot (e.g., subplots, parallel episodes, climax), **the plot's development, and the way in which conflicts are (or are not) addressed and resolved. 3.4 Analyze the relevance of set-ting** (e.g., place, time, customs) **to the mood, tone,** and meaning **of the text.**

Literary Skills Focus

Plot and Setting The two stories that follow center on a character who takes an emotional journey that leads to a moment of recognition, or a realization about life. After this, the characters don't see themselves or their families the same way. The main character in each story struggles to resolve a conflict, but the setting of each story is different. The people living in these two places follow different customs.

Consider the <u>relevance</u> of the setting to each story's mood and each writer's tone. Recall that **mood** is the overall feeling of a work of literature, and **tone** is the writer's attitude toward a person, place, or event.

Reading Skills Focus

Comparing and Contrasting Complete a chart like the one below to compare and contrast the plot, setting, mood, and tone of each story. When you **compare,** you look for ways in which things that are alike. When you **contrast,** you look for ways in which things are different.

Comparing Stories		
	The Medicine Bag	An Hour with Abuelo
Plot development		
Setting and customs		
Mood		
Tone		

Writing Skills Focus

Think as a Reader/Writer

Use It in Your Writing Grandpa in "The Medicine Bag" describes several items that are important to him. You learn about a prized possession of Abuelo's in "An Hour with Abuelo." Record in your *Reader/Writer Notebook* the details that convey the significance of these objects.

Reader/Writer
Notebook
Use your **RWN** to complete the activities for these selections.

Vocabulary

The Medicine Bag

authentic (aw THEHN tihk) *adj.:* genuine. *Martin was proud of the authentic rawhide drum Grandpa had given him.*

fatigue (fuh TEEG) *n.:* exhaustion; tiredness. *Martin sensed Grandpa's fatigue during his visit.*

An Hour with Abuelo

recreation (rehk ree AY shuhn) *n.:* used as *adj.:* relaxation; amusement. *People listened to Abuelo read his stories in the recreation area.*

ignorant (IHG nuhr uhnt) *adj.:* without knowledge; uninformed. *Abuelo feared that the people from his village would be ignorant if he didn't teach them to read.*

Language Coach

Oral Fluency Many English words contain silent letters. Write the words *fatigue, tongue,* and *vaguely* in your *Reader/Writer Notebook.* Which letters are silent in these words? Use a dictionary if you need help.

Learn It Online
Take a look at the *PowerNotes* introduction to these stories on:

go.hrw.com   H8-115   **Go**

Virginia Driving Hawk Sneve

(1933–   )

Passing on the Heritage

Sneve began writing for young readers after she discovered inaccuracies regarding American Indians in books she was reading. She explains:

> "When I started writing for children, I did so with the specific purpose of informing my own children about their heritage and trying to correct some misconceptions about how they saw Indian people and how others thought about Indians."

Judith Ortiz Cofer

(1952–   )

"The Ultimate Goal"

Cofer was born in Hormigueros, Puerto Rico. Because her father was in the military, she spent her childhood moving back and forth between a village in Puerto Rico and an urban neighborhood in Paterson, New Jersey. She later received her master of arts degree in English and went on to teach at different schools, including the University of Georgia. She reveals:

> "It was a challenge not only to learn English, but to master it enough to teach it and—the ultimate goal—to write poetry in it."

Think About the Writer

What do Sneve and Cofer hope to achieve through their writing?

Preview the Selections

In "The Medicine Bag," you will meet **Martin,** who is getting a visit from his great-grandfather, Joe Iron Shell. In "An Hour with Abuelo," you will meet **Arturo,** who is visiting his grandfather in a nursing home.

The Medicine Bag

by **Virginia Driving Hawk Sneve**

Read with a Purpose
Read to discover what Martin learns from his grandfather.

Build Background
The passage into adulthood in some cultures and families is marked by a ritual such as the Jewish bar mitzvah or bat mitzvah ceremony or the Mexican American quinceañera. This is a story about a similar ritual for young people of an American Indian background.

My kid sister Cheryl and I always bragged about our Sioux grandpa, Joe Iron Shell. Our friends, who had always lived in the city and only knew about Indians from movies and TV, were impressed by our stories. Maybe we exaggerated and made Grandpa and the reservation sound glamorous, but when we'd return home to Iowa after our yearly summer visit to Grandpa, we always had some exciting tale to tell.

We always had some authentic Sioux article to show our listeners. One year Cheryl had new moccasins that Grandpa had made. On another visit he gave me a small, round, flat rawhide drum which was decorated with a painting of a warrior riding a horse. He taught me a real Sioux chant to sing while I beat the drum with a leather-covered stick that had a feather on the end. Man, that really made an impression.

We never showed our friends Grandpa's picture. Not that we were ashamed of him, but because we knew that the glamorous tales we told didn't go with the real thing. Our friends would have laughed at the picture, because Grandpa wasn't tall and stately like TV Indians. His hair wasn't in braids but hung in stringy gray strands on his neck, and he was old. He was our great-grandfather, and he didn't live in a tepee, but all by himself in a part log, part tar-paper shack on the Rosebud Reservation in South Dakota. So when Grandpa came to visit us, I was so ashamed and embarrassed I could've died. **Ⓐ**

There are a lot of yippy poodles and other fancy little dogs in our neighborhood, but they usually barked singly at the mailman from the safety of their own yards. Now it sounded as if a whole pack of mutts were barking together in one place.

I got up and walked to the curb to see what the commotion was. About a block

---

Ⓐ Read and Discuss | What do you learn about the narrator's feelings for Grandpa?

Vocabulary **authentic** (aw THEHN tihk) *adj.*: genuine.

away I saw a crowd of little kids yelling, with the dogs yipping and growling around someone who was walking down the middle of the street.

I watched the group as it slowly came closer and saw that in the center of the strange procession was a man wearing a tall black hat. He'd pause now and then to peer at something in his hand and then at the houses on either side of the street. I felt cold and hot at the same time as I recognized the man. "Oh, no!" I whispered. "It's Grandpa!"

I stood on the curb, unable to move even though I wanted to run and hide. Then I got mad when I saw how the yippy dogs were growling and nipping at the old man's baggy pant legs and how wearily he poked them away with his cane. "Stupid mutts," I said as I ran to rescue Grandpa.

When I kicked and hollered at the dogs to get away, they put their tails between their legs and scattered. The kids ran to the curb, where they watched me and the old man.

"Grandpa," I said, and felt pretty dumb when my voice cracked. I reached for his beat-up old tin suitcase, which was tied shut with a rope. But he set it down right in the street and shook my hand.

"Hau, Takoza, Grandchild," he greeted me formally in Sioux.

All I could do was stand there with the whole neighborhood watching and shake the hand of the leather-brown old man. I saw how his gray hair straggled from under his big black hat, which had a drooping feather in its crown. His rumpled black suit hung like a sack over his stooped frame. As he shook my hand, his coat fell open to expose a bright-red satin shirt with a beaded bolo tie[1] under the collar. His get-up wasn't out of place on the reservation, but it sure was here, and I wanted to sink right through the pavement. **B**

"Hi," I muttered with my head down. I tried to pull my hand away when I felt his bony hand trembling, and looked up to see fatigue in his face. I felt like crying. I couldn't think of anything to say, so I picked up Grandpa's suitcase, took his arm, and guided him up the driveway to our house.

Mom was standing on the steps. I don't know how long she'd been watching, but her hand was over her mouth and she looked as if she couldn't believe what she saw. Then she ran to us.

"Grandpa," she gasped. "How in the world did you get here?"

She checked her move to embrace Grandpa, and I remembered that such a display of affection is unseemly to the Sioux and would embarrass him.

"Hau, Marie," he said as he shook Mom's hand. She smiled and took his other arm.

As we supported him up the steps, the door banged open and Cheryl came bursting out of the house. She was all smiles and was so obviously glad to see Grandpa that I was ashamed of how I felt.

---

1. **bolo tie:** cord with a decorated fastening, worn as a necktie.

B **Literary Focus** **Plot** What internal conflicts does the narrator face when Grandpa arrives?

Vocabulary **fatigue** (fuh TEEG) *n.*: exhaustion; tiredness.

"Grandpa!" she yelled happily. "You came to see us!"

Grandpa smiled and Mom and I let go of him as he stretched out his arms to my ten-year-old sister, who was still young enough to be hugged. **C**

"Wicincala, little girl," he greeted her, and then collapsed.

He had fainted. Mom and I carried him into her sewing room, where we had a spare bed.

After we had Grandpa on the bed, Mom stood there helplessly patting his shoulder.

"Shouldn't we call the doctor, Mom?" I suggested, since she didn't seem to know what to do.

"Yes," she agreed, with a sigh. "You make Grandpa comfortable, Martin."

I reluctantly moved to the bed. I knew Grandpa wouldn't want to have Mom undress him, but I didn't want to, either. He was so skinny and frail that his coat slipped off easily. When I loosened his tie and opened his shirt collar, I felt a small leather pouch that hung from a thong² around his neck. I left it alone and moved to remove his boots. The scuffed old cowboy boots were tight and he moaned as I put pressure on his

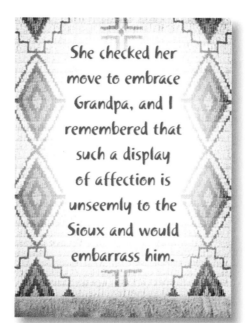

She checked her move to embrace Grandpa, and I remembered that such a display of affection is unseemly to the Sioux and would embarrass him.

___
2. **thong:** narrow strip of leather.

legs to jerk them off.

I put the boots on the floor and saw why they fit so tight. Each one was stuffed with money. I looked at the bills that lined the boots and started to ask about them, but Grandpa's eyes were closed again.

Mom came back with a basin of water. "The doctor thinks Grandpa is suffering from heat exhaustion," she explained as she bathed Grandpa's face. Mom gave a big sigh, "Oh hinh, Martin. How do you suppose he got here?"

We found out after the doctor's visit. Grandpa was angrily sitting up in bed while Mom tried to feed him some soup.

"Tonight you let Marie feed you, Grandpa," spoke my dad, who had gotten home from work just as the doctor was leaving. "You're not really sick," he said as he gently pushed Grandpa back against the pillows. "The doctor said you just got too tired and hot after your long trip."

Grandpa relaxed, and between sips of soup he told us of his journey. Soon after our visit to him Grandpa decided that he would like to see where his only living descendants lived and what our home was like. Besides, he admitted sheepishly, he was lonesome after we left. **D**

___

C **Reading Focus** Compare and Contrast How does each family member react to Grandpa's arrival? How are their reactions different?

D **Read and Discuss** What have you learned about Grandpa?

I knew everybody felt as guilty as I did—especially Mom. Mom was all Grandpa had left. So even after she married my dad, who's a white man and teaches in the college in our city, and after Cheryl and I were born, Mom made sure that every summer we spent a week with Grandpa.

I never thought that Grandpa would be lonely after our visits, and none of us noticed how old and weak he had become. But Grandpa knew and so he came to us. He had ridden on buses for two and a half days. When he arrived in the city, tired and stiff from sitting for so long, he set out, walking, to find us.

He had stopped to rest on the steps of some building downtown and a policeman found him. The cop, according to Grandpa, was a good man who took him to the bus stop and waited until the bus came and told the driver to let Grandpa out at Bell View Drive. After Grandpa got off the bus, he started walking again. But he couldn't see the house numbers on the other side when he walked on the sidewalk, so he walked in the middle of the street. That's when all the little kids and dogs followed him.

I knew everybody felt as bad as I did. Yet I was proud of this eighty-six-year-old man,

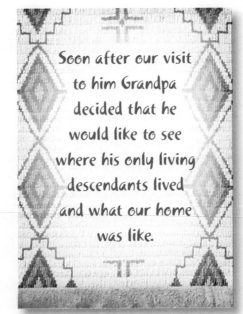

Soon after our visit to him Grandpa decided that he would like to see where his only living descendants lived and what our home was like.

who had never been away from the reservation, having the courage to travel so far alone.

"You found the money in my boots?" he asked Mom.

"Martin did," she answered, and roused herself to scold. "Grandpa, you shouldn't have carried so much money. What if someone had stolen it from you?"

Grandpa laughed. "I would've known if anyone tried to take the boots off my feet. The money is what I've saved for a long time—a hundred dollars—for my funeral. But you take it now to buy groceries so that I won't be a burden to you while I am here."

"That won't be necessary, Grandpa," Dad said. "We are honored to have you with us and you will never be a burden. I am only sorry that we never thought to bring you home with us this summer and spare you the discomfort of a long trip."

Grandpa was pleased. "Thank you," he answered. "But do not feel bad that you didn't bring me with you, for I would not have come then. It was not time." He said this in such a way that no one could argue with him. To Grandpa and the Sioux, he once told me, a thing would be done when

---

E **Literary Focus** **Plot** How does Grandpa's story of his journey change the way Martin sees him?

it was the right time to do it and that's the way it was.

"Also," Grandpa went on, looking at me, "I have come because it is soon time for Martin to have the medicine bag."

We all knew what that meant. Grandpa thought he was going to die and he had to follow the tradition of his family to pass the medicine bag, along with its history, to the oldest male child.

"Even though the boy," he said, still looking at me, "bears a white man's name, the medicine bag will be his."

I didn't know what to say. I had the same hot and cold feeling that I had when I first saw Grandpa in the street. The medicine bag was the dirty leather pouch I had found around his neck. "I could never wear such a thing," I almost said aloud. I thought of having my friends see it in gym class, at the swimming pool, and could imagine the smart things they would say. But I just swallowed hard and took a step toward the bed. I knew I would have to take it.

But Grandpa was tired. "Not now, Martin," he said, waving his hand in dismissal, "it is not time. Now I will sleep."

So that's how Grandpa came

Rawhide beaded pipe bag, Oglala Sioux.

to be with us for two months. My friends kept asking to come see the old man, but I put them off. I told myself that I didn't want them laughing at Grandpa. But even as I made excuses, I knew it wasn't Grandpa that I was afraid they'd laugh at.

Nothing bothered Cheryl about bringing her friends to see Grandpa. Every day after school started, there'd be a crew of giggling little girls or round-eyed little boys crowded around the old man on the patio, where he'd gotten in the habit of sitting every afternoon.

Grandpa would smile in his gentle way and patiently answer their questions, or he'd tell them stories of brave warriors, ghosts, animals, and the kids listened in awed silence. Those little guys thought Grandpa was great.

Finally, one day after school, my friends came home with me because nothing I said stopped them. "We're going to see the great Indian of Bell View Drive," said Hank, who was supposed to be my best friend. "My brother has seen him three times, so he oughta be well enough to see us."

When we got to my house, Grandpa was sitting on the

F **Literary Focus** Plot A conflict can occur when two people want different things. What does Martin want? What does Grandpa want?

patio. He had on his red shirt, but today he also wore a fringed leather vest that was decorated with beads. Instead of his usual cowboy boots he had solidly beaded moccasins on his feet that stuck out of his black trousers. Of course, he had his old black hat on—he was seldom without it. But it had been brushed and the feather in the beaded headband was proudly erect, its tip a brighter white. His hair lay in silver strands over the red shirt collar.

I stared just as my friends did and I heard one of them murmur, "Wow!"

Grandpa looked up and when his eyes met mine, they twinkled as if he were laughing inside. He nodded to me and my face got all hot. I could tell that he had known all along I was afraid he'd embarrass me in front of my friends.

"Hau, hoksilas, boys," he greeted, and held out his hand.

My buddies passed in a single file and shook his hand as I introduced them. They were so polite I almost laughed. "How, there, Grandpa," and even a "How do you do, sir."

"You look fine, Grandpa," I said

Sioux medicine man holding a medicine shield and wearing a bearclaw necklace.

as the guys sat on the lawn chairs or on the patio floor.

"Hanh, yes," he agreed. "When I woke up this morning, it seemed the right time to dress in the good clothes. I knew that my grandson would be bringing his friends."

"You guys want some lemonade or something?" I offered. No one answered. They were listening to Grandpa as he started telling how he'd killed the deer from which his vest was made.

Grandpa did most of the talking while my friends were there. I was so proud of him and amazed at how respectfully quiet my buddies were. Mom had to chase them home at suppertime. As they left, they shook Grandpa's hand again and said to me:

"Martin, he's really great!"

"Yeah, man! Don't blame you for keeping him to yourself."

"Can we come back?" **G**

But after they left, Mom said, "No more visitors for a while, Martin. Grandpa won't admit it, but his strength hasn't returned. He likes having company, but it tires him."

That evening Grandpa called me to his room before he went to sleep. "Tomorrow," he said, "when you come home, it will be time to give you the medicine bag."

I felt a hard squeeze from where my heart is supposed to be and was scared, but I answered, "OK, Grandpa." **H**

All night I had weird dreams about thunder and lightning on a high hill. From a distance I heard the slow beat of a drum.

When I woke up in the morning, I felt as if I hadn't slept at all. At school it seemed as if the day would never end and when it finally did, I ran home.

Grandpa was in his room, sitting on the bed. The shades were down and the place was dim and cool. I sat on the floor in front of Grandpa, but he didn't even look at me. After what seemed a long time, he spoke.

"I sent your mother and sister away. What you will hear today is only for a man's ears. What you will receive is only for a man's hands." He fell silent and I felt shivers down my back.

"My father in his early manhood," Grandpa began, "made a vision quest to find a spirit guide for his life. You cannot understand how it was in that time, when the great Teton Sioux were first made to stay on the reservation. There was a strong need for guidance from Wakantanka, the Great Spirit. But too many of the young men were filled with despair and hatred. They thought it was hopeless to search for a vision when the glorious life was gone and only the hated confines of a reservation lay ahead. But my father held to the old ways.

"He carefully prepared for his quest with a purifying sweat bath and then he went alone to a high butte[3] top to fast and pray. After three days he received his sacred dream—in which he found, after long

---

3. **butte:** steep, flat-topped hill standing alone on a plain.

G Read and Discuss What is Martin learning here?

H Reading Focus Comparing and Contrasting How has Martin's attitude about the medicine bag changed? Recall his thoughts about it from earlier in the story.

searching, the white man's iron. He did not understand his vision of finding something belonging to the white people, for in that time they were the enemy. When he came down from the butte to cleanse himself at the stream below, he found the remains of a campfire and the broken shell of an iron kettle. This was a sign which reinforced his dream. He took a piece of the iron for his medicine bag, which he had made of elk skin years before, to prepare for his quest.

"He returned to his village, where he told his dream to the wise old men of the tribe. They gave him the name Iron Shell, but neither did they understand the meaning of the dream. This first Iron Shell kept the piece of iron with him at all times and believed it gave him protection from the evils of those unhappy days.

"Then a terrible thing happened to Iron Shell. He and several other young men were taken from their homes by the soldiers and sent far away to a white man's boarding school. He was angry and lonesome for his parents and the young girl he had wed before he was taken away. At first Iron Shell resisted the teachers' attempts to change him and he did not try to learn. One day it was his turn to work in the school's blacksmith shop. As he walked into the place, he knew that his medicine had brought him there to learn and work with the white man's iron.

"Iron Shell became a blacksmith and worked at the trade when he returned to the reservation. All of his life he treasured the medicine bag. When he was old and I was a man, he gave it to me, for no one made the vision quest anymore." ❶

Grandpa quit talking and I stared in disbelief as he covered his face with his hands. His shoulders were shaking with quiet sobs and I looked away until he began to speak again.

"I kept the bag until my son, your mother's father, was a man and had to leave us to fight in the war across the ocean. I gave him the bag, for I believed it would protect him in battle, but he did not take it with him. He was afraid that he would lose it. He died in a faraway place."

Again Grandpa was still and I felt his grief around me.

"My son," he went on after clearing his throat, "had only a daughter and it is not proper for her to know of these things."

He unbuttoned his shirt, pulled out the leather pouch, and lifted it over his head. He held it in his hand, turning it over and over as if memorizing how it looked.

"In the bag," he said as he opened it and removed two objects, "is the broken shell of the iron kettle, a pebble from the butte, and a piece of the sacred sage."[4] He held the pouch upside down and dust drifted down.

"After the bag is yours, you must put a piece of prairie sage within and never open it again until you pass it on to your son." He replaced the pebble and the piece of

---

4. **sage:** plant with fragrant leaves.

❶ **Literary Focus** Setting and Mood Describe the time, place, and customs in Grandpa's story. What words would you use to describe the mood of his story?

iron and tied the bag.

I stood up, somehow knowing I should. Grandpa slowly rose from the bed and stood upright in front of me, holding the bag before my face. I closed my eyes and waited for him to slip it over my head. But he spoke.

"No, you need not wear it." He placed the soft leather bag in my right hand and closed my other hand over it. "It would not be right to wear it in this time and place, where no one will understand. Put it safely away until you are again on the reservation. Wear it then, when you replace the sacred sage."

Analyzing Visuals Connecting to the Text How does the subject of these portraits compare with your image of Martin's grandfather?

Chief Plenty Coups. Painted portraits of Crow leader Chief Plenty Coups through the years of his life—as a young brave, a famous chief, and a tribal elder.

Sioux Horses by Oscar Howe (Mazuha Hokshina, Yanktonai Sioux). Tempera on wove paper (8 1/4" x 10"). Museum purchase, 1937. Fred Jones Jr. Museum of Art, The University of Oklahoma, Norman.

Grandpa turned and sat again on the bed. Wearily he leaned his head against the pillow. "Go," he said, "I will sleep now."

"Thank you, Grandpa," I said softly, and left with the bag in my hands. **J**

That night Mom and Dad took Grandpa to the hospital. Two weeks later I stood alone on the lonely prairie of the reservation and put the sacred sage in my medicine bag. **K**

J Reading Focus Compare and Contrast How have Martin's attitudes toward his great-grandfather and his heritage changed since the beginning of the story?

K Literary Focus Plot How is Martin's internal conflict about the medicine bag addressed and resolved?

Applying Your Skills

Reading Standard 3.2 **Evaluate the structural elements of the plot** (e.g., subplots, parallel episodes, climax), **the plot's development, and the way in which conflicts are (or are not) addressed and resolved. 3.4 Analyze the relevance of the setting** (e.g., place, time, customs) **to the mood,** tone, and meaning **of the text.**

The Medicine Bag

Literary Response and Analysis

Reading Skills Focus
Quick Check

1. Use the following story map to outline the main elements of the story's plot.

> Characters: Settings:
>
> Conflict:
>
> Complications:
> 1.
> 2.
> 3.
> (add as many as you need)
>
> Climax:
>
> Resolution:

Read with a Purpose

2. What does Martin learn from his great-grand-father? What does he learn about himself?

✓ **Vocabulary Check**

3. What activities do you participate in that cause you **fatigue**?
4. How can you determine if a Native American relic is **authentic**?
5. Describe an instance when you **reluctantly** agreed to play a game.

Reading Skills: Compare and Contrast

6. Review the chart you completed as you read "The Medicine Bag." What moment of recognition changes Martin's life? How does the way he addresses and resolves his conflicts lead him to this realization?

Literary Skills Focus
Literary Analysis

7. **Analyze** Why is Martin ashamed of Grandpa at first? How do Martin's feelings change?
8. **Extend** How might Martin have felt about Grandpa if his friends had not been impressed by him? Explain.

Literary Skills: Plot and Setting

9. **Analyze** How is Martin's life different from Grandpa's? What problems, or conflicts, do these differences cause for Martin?
10. **Analyze** What is the relevance of the setting to the story's mood? How does the mood change as the plot develops?

Writing Skills Focus
Think as a Reader/Writer

Use It in Your Writing Review the notes you recorded on the items that are important to Grandpa. Write a brief essay in which you analyze why Grandpa considers these items significant. How does the history of these items affect Grandpa's feeling for them?

What Do You Think Now

What does Martin realize about his own life after hearing Grandpa's story of the medicine bag?

An Hour with Abuelo

by **Judith Ortiz Cofer**

Read with a Purpose

Read this story to discover the way Arturo's relationship with his grandfather changes.

Preparing to Read for this selection appears on page 115.

Build Background

Puerto Rico was ceded to the United States in 1898 at the end of the Spanish-American War. This transfer marked the beginning of a unique and often controversial relationship. The people of Puerto Rico are U.S. citizens, but Puerto Rico has a separate autonomous government.

Just one hour, *una hora*,[1] is all I'm asking of you, son." My grandfather is in a nursing home in Brooklyn, and my mother wants me to spend some time with him, since the doctors say that he doesn't have too long to go now. I don't have much time left of my summer vacation, and there's a stack of books next to my bed I've got to read if I'm going to get into the AP English class I want. I'm going stupid in some of my classes, and Mr. Williams, the principal at Central, said that if I passed some reading tests, he'd let me move up.

Besides, I hate the place, the old people's home, especially the way it smells like industrial-strength ammonia and other stuff I won't mention, since it turns my stomach. And really the abuelo[2] always has a lot of relatives visiting him, so I've gotten out of going out there except at Christmas, when a whole vanload of grandchildren are herded over there to give him gifts and a hug. We

Ⓐ

---

1. *una hora* (OO nah AWR ah): Spanish for "one hour."

2. **abuelo** (ahb WAY loh): Spanish for "grandfather."

Ⓐ **Literary Focus** Plot What conflict is hinted at in the opening paragraph?

all make it quick and spend the rest of the time in the recreation area, where they play checkers and stuff with some of the old people's games, and I catch up on back issues of *Modern Maturity*. I'm not picky, I'll read almost anything.

Anyway, after my mother nags me for about a week, I let her drive me to Golden Years. She drops me off in front. She wants me to go in alone and have a "good time" talking to Abuelo. I tell her to be back in one hour or I'll take the bus back to Paterson. She squeezes my hand and says, "*Gracias, hijo*,"[3] in a choked-up voice like I'm doing her a big favor. **Ⓑ**

---

3. *Gracias, hijo* (GRAH see ahs EE hoh): Spanish for "Thank you, son."

Ⓑ Reading Focus **Compare and Contrast** What similarities and differences do you see between this boy and Martin from "The Medicine Bag"? What similarities do you find in their situations?

I get depressed the minute I walk into the place. They line up the old people in wheelchairs in the hallway as if they were about to be raced to the finish line by orderlies who don't even look at them when they push them here and there. I walk fast to room 10, Abuelo's "suite." He is sitting up in his bed writing with a pencil in one of those old-fashioned black hardback notebooks. It has the outline of the island of Puerto Rico on it. I slide into the hard vinyl chair by his bed. He sort of smiles and the lines on his face get deeper, but he doesn't say anything. Since I'm supposed to talk to him, I say, "What are you doing, Abuelo, writing the story of your life?"

It's supposed to be a joke, but he answers, "Sí, how did you know, Arturo?"

Vocabulary **recreation** (rehk ree AY shuhn) *n.* used as *adj.*: relaxation; amusement.

His name is Arturo too. I was named after him. I don't really know my grandfather. His children, including my mother, came to New York and New Jersey (where I was born) and he stayed on the Island until my grandmother died. Then he got sick, and since nobody could leave their jobs to take care of him, they brought him to this nursing home in Brooklyn. I see him a couple of times a year, but he's always surrounded by his sons and daughters. My mother tells me that Don Arturo[4] had once been a teacher back in Puerto Rico, but had lost his job after the war. Then he became a farmer. She's always saying in a sad voice, "*Ay, bendito*![5] What a waste of a fine mind."

4. **Don:** "Don" is a title of respect, like "Mr."
5. *bendito* (behn DEE toh): Spanish for "bless him."

Then she usually shrugs her shoulders and says, "*Así es la vida.*" That's the way life is. It sometimes makes me mad that the adults I know just accept whatever crap is thrown at them because "that's the way things are." Not for me. I go after what I want.

Anyway, Abuelo is looking at me like he was trying to see inside my head, but he doesn't say anything. Since I like stories, I decide I may as well ask him if he'll read me what he wrote.

I look at my watch: I've already used up twenty minutes of the hour I promised my mother.

Abuelo starts talking in his slow way. He speaks what my mother calls book English. He taught himself from a dictionary, and his words sound stiff, like he's sounding them out in his head before he says them. With his children he speaks Spanish, and that funny book English with us grandchildren. I'm surprised that he's still so sharp, because his body is shrinking like a crumpled-up brown paper sack with some bones in it. But I can see from looking into his eyes that the light is still on in there. **C**

"It is a short story, Arturo. The story of my life. It will not take very much time to read it."

"I have time, Abuelo." I'm a little embarrassed that he saw me looking at my watch.

"Yes, hijo. You have spoken the truth. La verdad. You have much time."

Abuelo reads: "'I loved words from the beginning of my life. In the *campo*[6] where I was born one of seven sons, there were few

6. *campo* (KAHM poh): Spanish for "country."

C Read and Discuss What do you learn about Abuelo here?

books. My mother read them to us over and over: the Bible, the stories of Spanish conquistadors[7] and of pirates that she had read as a child and brought with her from the city of Mayagüez;[8] that was before she married my father, a coffee bean farmer; and she taught us words from the newspaper that a boy on a horse brought every week to her. She taught each of us how to write on a slate with chalks that she ordered by mail every year. We used those chalks until they were so small that you lost them between your fingers.

"'I always wanted to be a writer and a teacher. With my heart and soul I knew that I wanted to be around books all of my life. And so against the wishes of my father, who wanted all his sons to help him on the land, she sent me to high school in Mayagüez. For four years I boarded with a couple she knew. I paid my rent in labor, and I ate vegetables I grew myself. I wore my clothes until they were thin as parchment. But I graduated at the top of my class! My whole family came to see me that day. My mother brought me a beautiful *guayabera*, a white shirt made of the finest cotton and embroidered by her own hands. I was a happy young man.

"'In those days you could teach in a country school with a high school diploma.

So I went back to my mountain village and got a job teaching all grades in a little classroom built by the parents of my students.

"'I had books sent to me by the government. I felt like a rich man although the pay was very small. I had books. All the books I wanted! I taught my students how to read poetry and plays, and how to write them. We made up songs and put on shows for the parents. It was a beautiful time for me.

"'Then the war came, and the American President said that all Puerto Rican men would be drafted. I wrote to our governor and explained that I was the only teacher in the mountain village. I told him that the children would go back to the fields and grow up ignorant if I could not teach them their letters. I said that I thought I was a better teacher than a soldier. The governor did not answer my letter. I went into the U.S. Army.

---

7. **conquistadors** (kan KEES tah dohrz): any of the Spanish conquerors of Mexico, Peru, or other parts of America in the sixteenth century.
8. **Mayagüez** (mah yah GWES): port city in western Puerto Rico.

D **Literary Focus** Mood What mood does the description of Abuelo's past create? What is the role of the setting (time, place, customs) in creating this mood?

Vocabulary **ignorant** (IHG nuhr uhnt) *adj.:* without knowledge; uninformed.

"'I told my sergeant that I could be a teacher in the army. I could teach all the farm boys their letters so that they could read the instructions on the ammunition boxes and not blow themselves up. The sergeant said I was too smart for my own good, and gave me a job cleaning latrines. He said to me there is reading material for you there, scholar. Read the writing on the walls. I spent the war mopping floors and cleaning toilets.

"'When I came back to the Island, things had changed. You had to have a college degree to teach school, even the lower grades. My parents were sick, two of my brothers had been killed in the war, the others had stayed in Nueva York. I was the only one left to help the old people. I became a farmer. I married a good woman who gave me many good children. I taught them all how to read and write before they started school.'"

Abuelo then puts the notebook down on his lap and closes his eyes.

"*Así es la vida* is the title of my book," he says in a whisper, almost to himself. Maybe he's forgotten that I'm there.

For a long time he doesn't say anything else. I think that he's sleeping, but then I see that he's watching me through half-closed lids, maybe waiting for my opinion of his writing. I'm trying to think of something nice to say. I liked it and all, but not the title. And I think that he could've been a teacher if he had wanted to bad enough. Nobody is going to stop me from doing what I want with my life. I'm not going to let la vida get in my way. I want to discuss this with him, but the words are not coming into my head in Spanish just yet. I'm about to ask him why he didn't keep fighting to make his dream come true, when an old lady in hot-pink running shoes sort of appears at the door. **E**

She is wearing a pink jogging outfit too. The world's oldest marathoner, I say to myself. She calls out to my grandfather in a flirty voice, "Yoo-hoo, Arturo, remember what day this is? It's poetry-reading day in the rec room! You promised us you'd read your new one today."

I see my abuelo perking up almost immediately. He points to his wheelchair, which is hanging like a huge metal bat in the open closet. He makes it obvious that he wants me to get it. I put it together, and with Ms. Pink Running Shoes's help, we get him in it. Then he says in a strong deep voice I hardly recognize, "Arturo, get that notebook from the table, please."

I hand him another map-of-the-Island notebook—this one is red. On it in big letters it says, *Poemas De Arturo*.

I start to push him toward the rec room, but he shakes his finger at me.

"Arturo, look at your watch now. I believe your time is over." He gives me a wicked smile.

Then with her pushing the wheelchair—maybe a little too fast—they roll down the hall. He is already reading from his notebook, and she's making bird noises. I look at my watch and the hour *is* up, to the minute. I can't help but think that my abuelo has been timing *me*. It cracks me up. I walk slowly down the hall toward the exit sign. I want my mother to have to wait a little. I don't want her to think that I'm in a hurry or anything. **F**

E **Reading Focus** Compare and Contrast How does Arturo react to the story his grandfather tells him? In what ways is his reaction similar to Martin's reaction to his grandfather's story in "The Medicine Bag"?

F **Literary Focus** Plot How has Arturo addressed and resolved his conflict? In what ways has his attitude toward spending an hour with Abuelo changed?

Applying Your Skills

An Hour with Abuelo

Literary Response and Analysis

Reading Standard 3.2 Evaluate the structural elements of the plot (e.g., subplots, parallel episodes, climax), **the plot's development, and the way in which conflicts are (or are not) addressed and resolved. 3.4 Analyze the relevance of setting (e.g., place, time, customs) to the mood, tone,** and meaning **of the text.**

Reading Skills Focus
Quick Check

1. Use a story map like the one below to record the plot development of "An Hour with Abuelo."

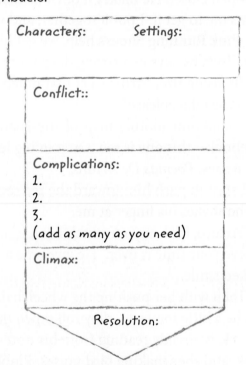

Characters: Settings:

Conflict::

Complications:
1.
2.
3.
(add as many as you need)

Climax:

Resolution:

Read with a Purpose

2. Describe Arturo's relationship with his grandfather at the beginning of the story. What causes the relationship to change?

✓ Vocabulary Check

3. What do you expect to find in a **recreation** area?
4. Why is being knowledgeable preferable to being **ignorant**?

Reading Skills: Comparing and Contrasting

5. Review the chart you completed as you read "An Hour with Abuelo." What moment of recognition changes Arturo's life? How does the way he addresses and resolves his conflict lead him to this realization?

6. Examine the ways in which Martin and Arturo resolve their conflicts. In what ways are the resolutions similar?

Literary Skills Focus
Literary Analysis

7. **Interpret** What does Arturo's grandfather mean when he says, "You have much time"?

8. **Analyze** Irony occurs when a situation turns out the opposite of the way you expect. Why is the ending of Arturo's visit with Abuelo ironic? What is surprising about the end of the story?

Literary Skills: Plot, Setting, Mood, and Tone

9. **Interpret** The **climax** of the story is the moment at which the outcome of a conflict is decided. What do you think is the climax of "An Hour with Abuelo"? Explain.

10. **Analyze** What words would you use to describe the mood of "An Hour with Abuelo"? Support your answer with at least three examples of words, images, and descriptions from the story that create the mood.

Writing Skills Focus
Think as a Reader/Writer

Use It in Your Writing In an essay, analyze the reasons why Abuelo prizes his notebook.

Wrap Up

Reading Standard 3.2 Evaluate the structural elements of the plot (e.g., subplots, parallel episodes, climax), **the plot's development, and the way in which conflicts are (or are not) addressed and resolved.** **3.4** Analyze the relevance of setting (e.g., **place, tone, customs**) to the mood, tone, and **meaning of the text.**

The Medicine Bag / An Hour with Abuelo

Writing Skills Focus
Writing a Comparison and Contrast Essay

Use it in Your Writing Write an essay in which you compare the plot and setting of "The Medicine Bag" and "An Hour with Abuelo." To help you plan your essay, review the chart you completed as you read each story. The chart will help you focus on key elements in the stories and how they are similar and how they are different.

Use the following outline to organize your essay:

I. Conflict
  A. Martin's feelings about his great-grandfather
  B. Arturo's feelings about his grandfather

II. Setting
  A. time, place, customs of "The Medicine Bag"
  B. time, place, customs of "An Hour with Abuelo"

III. Resolution
  A. What Martin learns from his great-grandfather
  B. What Arturo learns from his grandfather

What Do You Think Now How do other people help you learn about yourself? What can other people teach you?

CHOICES

As you respond to the Choices, use these **Academic Vocabulary** words as appropriate: analyze, aspect, evaluate, relevance, structural.

REVIEW
Compare Conflict and Resolution

Timed └ Writing Write a three-paragraph essay in which you compare the experiences of Martin from "The Medicine Bag" with those of Arturo in "An Hour with Abuelo." Analyze Martin's feelings for his great-grandfather and Arturo's feelings for his grandfather. Discuss the way the two characters resolve their conflicts with their grandfathers.

CONNECT
Write a Persuasive Essay

Both stories illustrate the need for traditions and meaningful rituals that help young people accept the duties of adult life. In what ways do young people today make the passage into adulthood? Do you think there should be other ways of helping young people to accept responsibilities? Do you believe these rituals are necessary? In a brief essay, explain your point of view.

EXTEND
Research a Culture

Group Activity With a small group, list everything you learned about Sioux customs and history. Then, brainstorm questions you still have about the Sioux. Use reference works and the Internet to explore the questions your group has. Share what you have learned in a presentation to the class.

Treatment, Scope, and Organization of Ideas

CONTENTS

 What Do You Think? How would thinking like a scientist change you?

 **QuickWrite**
List some of the ways that science has changed our lives, for better or for worse.

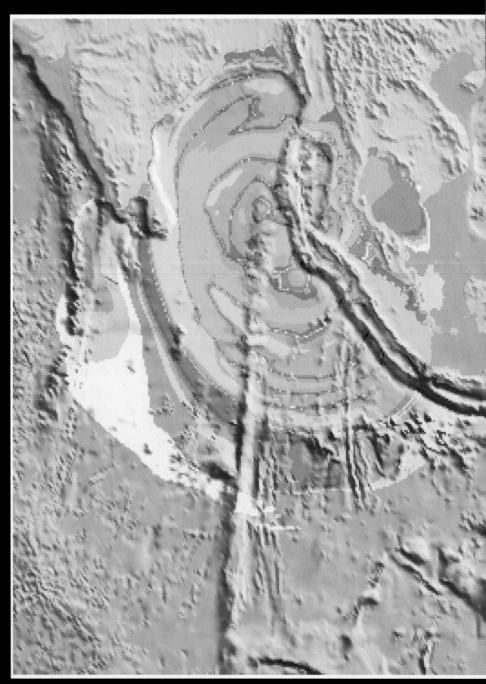

Tsunami two hours after earthquake.

Reading Standard 2.3 Find similarities and differences between texts in the treatment, scope, or organization of ideas.

Physical Science

Informational Text Focus

Treatment, Scope, and Organization of Ideas Anyone who wants to communicate or understand ideas on a subject needs to consider treatment, scope, and organization of ideas.

- **Treatment** refers to the particular way of dealing with or discussing a topic or idea. Treatment of the scientific method in a textbook, for example, would present a thorough, **objective** explanation of the subject that sticks to the facts and avoids opinions. A newspaper article on the same subject might include the writer's **subjective,** or personal, comments and opinions.
- **Scope** refers to the amount of information presented on a given topic. A treatment that covers many aspects of a topic is said to have a **broad** scope. A treatment that narrows the coverage of a topic is said to have a **limited** scope.
- **Organization** refers to the way information is arranged and presented. Writers use **text structures** to organize information. Common text structures include **enumeration,** or listing; **chronology**—sequence or time order—showing steps or events in the order in which they occur; **cause and effect,** or showing how one event causes another; and **comparison and contrast,** or showing how one thing is similar to or different from another.

You are about to read three texts that present information on the scientific method: a textbook, a newspaper article, and a magazine article. As you read the texts, look for similarities and differences in the treatment, organization, and scope of ideas.

Writing Skills Focus

Preparing for Timed Writing The way a writer organizes information can help that information make sense to you. As you read and discuss the textbook excerpt that follows, take notes in your *Reader/Writer Notebook* as you find information made clear due to its organization.

Reader/Writer
Notebook
Use your **RWN** to complete the activities for this selection.

Vocabulary

observation (ahb suhr VAY shuhn) *n.:* act of noticing. *Scientists can learn about glaciers by careful observation of their movements.*

hypothesis (hy PAHTH uh sihs) *n.:* possible explanation or answer. *Once a scientist has developed a hypothesis to attempt to answer a scientific question, he or she has to test the hypothesis.*

necessarily (nehs uh SAIR uh lee) *adv.:* unavoidably; in every case. *Conclusions based on only one experiment are not necessarily reliable or true.*

Language Coach

Prefixes *Hypothesis* comes from the Greek for "groundwork; foundation." Its Greek prefix, *hypo–,* means "under; beneath," and the root *tithenai* means "to place; to put." A **hypothesis** is the first educated guess that a scientist makes after performing many observations. Think of a hypothesis as forming the ground floor, the beginning of scientific study.

 Learn It Online
Take a closer look at comparing texts. Visit the interactive Reading Workshop on:

| go.hrw.com | H8-137 | Go |

Read with a Purpose

Read to examine the treatment, scope, and organization of ideas on scientific methods in three different texts.

Contents

UNIT 1 Introduction to Physical Science

CHAPTER 1

*Table of Contents This list of topics appears at the front of a book and shows the book's **scope** and **organization**.*

Ⓐ

Ⓐ **Informational Focus** Scope and Organization How would you describe the scope of this textbook? Explain how the information it presents is organized.

B Informational Focus **Scope and Organization** Why is it necessary to have a systematic organization when the scope of information is so broad and comprehensive?

Scientific Methods

Key Concept   Scientists use scientific methods to answer questions and to solve problems.

What You Will Learn

- Scientific methods are based on six steps, which may be followed in different ways based on the kind of question being asked.
- Scientific investigations begin with a question and proceed by forming a hypothesis and then testing it.
- Scientists use a variety of methods to analyze and report their data.

Why It Matters

Scientific methods provide a framework for conducting careful investigations and understanding the natural world.

Vocabulary

- scientific methods
- observation
- hypothesis
- data

READING STRATEGY

Graphic Organizer   In your **Science Journal**, create a Cause-and-Effect Map that shows the steps used in the scientific method.

Investigation and Experimentation
8.9.a Plan and conduct a scientific investigation to test a hypothesis.
8.9.b Evaluate the accuracy and reproducibility of data.
8.9.c Distinguish between variable and controlled parameters in a test.

*The sidebar called "What You Will Learn" **enumerates** the information presented in Section 2. What additional support does it offer readers?*

▶ Two scientists from the Massachusetts Institute of Technology (MIT) thought that studying penguins was a great way to improve ships! James Czarnowski (zahr NOW SKEE) and Michael Triantafyllou (tree AHN ti FEE loo) used scientific methods to develop *Proteus* (PROH tee uhs), the penguin boat. Can you imagine how and why they did that? In the next few pages, you will learn how these scientists used scientific methods to answer their questions. Scientific methods require knowledge and creativity. And they are very useful in answering some difficult questions.

What Are Scientific Methods?

Scientific methods are the ways in which scientists answer questions and solve problems. As scientists look for answers, they often use the same steps. But there is more than one way to use the steps. Look at **Figure 1.** This figure is an outline of the six steps on which scientific methods are based. Scientists may use all of the steps or just some of the steps during an investigation. They may even repeat some of the steps or do the steps in a different order. How they choose to use the steps depends on what works best to answer their question.   **C**

Figure 1   **Steps of Scientific Methods**

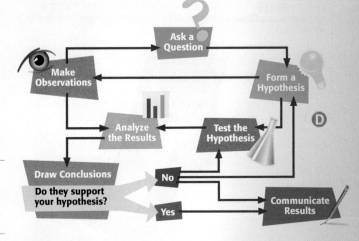

14   Chapter 1   The Nature of Physical Science

C **Read and Discuss**   What have you learned about the scientific method?

D **Informational Focus**   Treatment and Organization   What is the purpose of Figure 1? Compare its treatment and organization of ideas with the prose discussion of scientific methods.

Asking a Question

Asking a question helps focus the purpose of an investigation. Scientists often ask a question after making many observations. **Observation** is any use of the senses to gather information. Noting that the sky is blue or that a cotton ball feels soft is an observation. Measurements are observations that are made with tools. Observations can be made (and should be accurately recorded) at any point during an investigation. **E**

Standards Check In science, what is the purpose of asking questions?
🐻 8.9.a

A Real-World Question

Czarnowski and Triantafyllou, shown in **Figure 2,** are engineers—scientists who put scientific knowledge to practical use. Czarnowski was a graduate student at the Massachusetts Institute of Technology. He and Triantafyllou, his professor, worked together to observe boat propulsion (proh PUHL shuhn) systems. Then, they investigated how to make these systems work better. A propulsion system is what makes a boat move. Most boats have propellers to move them through the water.

Czarnowski and Triantafyllou began their investigation by studying the efficiency (e FISH uhn see) of boat propulsion systems. *Efficiency* compares energy output (the energy used to move the boat forward) with energy input (the energy supplied by the boat's engine). From their observations, Czarnowski and Triantafyllou learned that boat propellers are not very efficient.

Figure 2 *James Czarnowski (left) and Michael Triantafyllou (right) made observations about how boats work in order to develop Proteus.*

scientific methods (SIE uhn TIF ik METH uhdz) a series of steps followed to solve problems

observation (AHB zuhr VAY shuhn) the process of obtaining information by using the senses

---

E Read and Discuss│ What do "asking a question" and "observation" have to do with scientific methods?

Vocabulary **observation** (ahb suhr VAY shuhn) *n.:* act of noticing.

Figure 3 *Penguins use their flippers to "fly" underwater. As they pull their flippers toward their bodies, they push against the water, which propels them forward.*

hypothesis (hie PAHTH uh sis) a testable idea or explanation that leads to scientific investigation
<u>Wordwise</u> The prefix *hypo-* means "under." The root *thesis* means "proposition." Other examples are *hypodermic* and *hypoallergenic.*

The Importance of Boat Efficiency

Most boats that have propellers are only about 70% efficient. Boat efficiency is important because it saves many resources. Making only a small fraction of U.S. boats and ships just 10% more efficient would save millions of liters of fuel per year. Based on their observations and all of this information, Czarnowski and Triantafyllou were ready to ask a question: How can boat propulsion systems be made more efficient? This is a good example of a question that can start a scientific investigation because it is a question that can be answered by observation.

Forming a Hypothesis

Once you've asked your question and made observations, you are ready to form a hypothesis. A **hypothesis** is a possible explanation or answer to a question. You can use what you already know and what you have observed to form a hypothesis.

A good hypothesis is testable. In other words, information can be gathered or an experiment can be designed to test the hypothesis. A hypothesis that is not testable isn't necessarily wrong. But there is no way to show whether the hypothesis is right or wrong.

A Possible Answer from Nature

Czarnowski and Triantafyllou wanted to base their hypothesis on an example from nature. Czarnowski had made observations of penguins swimming. He observed how quickly and easily the penguins moved through the water. **Figure 3** shows how penguins propel themselves. Czarnowski also observed that penguins, like boats, have rigid bodies. These observations led to a hypothesis: A propulsion system that imitates the way that a penguin swims will be more efficient than a propulsion system that uses propellers.

16 Chapter 1 The Nature of Physical Science

F **Informational Focus** Scope How does including the examples shown in Figures 3 and 4 affect the scope of the discussion of the scientific method?

Vocabulary **hypothesis** (hy PAHTH uh sihs) *n.:* possible explanation or answer. **necessarily** (nehs uh SAIR uh lee) *adv.:* unavoidably; in every case.

Making Predictions

Before scientists test a hypothesis, they often predict what they think will happen when they test the hypothesis. Scientists usually state predictions in an if-then statement. The engineers at MIT might have made the following prediction: *If* two flippers are attached to a boat, *then* the boat will be more efficient than a boat powered by propellers.

Testing the Hypothesis

After you form a hypothesis, you must test it. You must find out if it is a reasonable answer to your question. Testing helps you find out if your hypothesis is pointing you in the right direction or if it is way off the mark. If your hypothesis is way off the mark, you may have to change it.

Controlled Experiments

A controlled experiment is a good way to test a hypothesis. A *controlled experiment* compares the results from a control group with the results from experimental groups. All factors remain the same except for one. The factors that are kept the same between the groups are called *controlled parameters*. These factors are held constant. The one factor that changes between the groups is called a *variable parameter*. The results will show the effect of the variable parameter.

Czarnowski and Triantafyllou thought the best way to test their hypothesis was to build a device to test. So, they built *Proteus*, the penguin boat, shown in **Figure 4.** It had flippers like a penguin so that the scientists could test their hypothesis.

Standards Check What is the difference between the controlled and the variable parameters in an experiment? 🐻**8.9.c** Ⓖ

Figure 4 Proteus, *a 3.4 m long and 50 cm wide specially built boat model, was used to test the "flippers" hypothesis.*

ⓐ *Proteus* has two flipperlike paddles, called *foils*. Both foils move out and then in, as the flippers of a penguin do.

ⓑ Two car batteries supply energy to the motors that drive *Proteus*'s flapping foils.

ⓒ A computer programs the number of times the foils flap per second.

ⓓ As the foils flap, they push water backward. The water pushes against the foils to propel the boat forward.

Ⓖ **Informational Focus** Treatment   Review the content of this page. Is the writing subjective or objective? How can you tell?

Applying Your Skills

Reading Standard 2.3 Find similarities and differences between texts in the treatment, scope, or organization of ideas.

Physical Science

Standards Review

Informational Text and Vocabulary

1. The textbook table of contents on pages 138–139 organizes information by

   A treatment.

   B chronology.

   C enumeration.

   D cause and effect.

2. In the scientific method, after making many observations, you might ask a question in order to limit, or narrow, the investigation's

   A subjectivity.

   B scope.

   C objectivity.

   D organization.

3. Which of the following might receive **subjective** treatment in a sidebar in the science textbook chapter?

   A an airplane based on a penguin's form

   B disabled students taught to swim with efficiency

   C "green" forms of energy used by U.S. Navy

   D a scientist's lifelong dream of working with ships

4. What do you use to make an *observation*?

   A your senses

   B your imagination

   C your hypotheses

   D your research

5. *Necessarily* means

   A certainly.

   B loudly.

   C unfriendly.

   D avoidably.

6. If you make a *hypothesis*, then you

   A avoid a dangerous situation.

   B analyze the results of an experiment.

   C solve one problem and create a new one.

   D come up with a possible solution.

Writing Skills Focus

Timed └Writing Which organizational features of the textbook excerpt did you find the most helpful? Give your reasons for your response.

What Do You Think Now

Explain which <u>aspect</u> of the scientific method might be most useful in your life.

NEWSPAPER ARTICLE
Preparing to Read

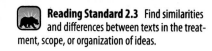

Reading Standard 2.3 Find similarities and differences between texts in the treatment, scope, or organization of ideas.

Hawaiian Teen Named Top Young Scientist

Informational Text Focus

Similarities and Differences in Treatment, Scope, and Organization of Ideas You are about to read a newspaper article that reports on an award-winning young scientist. Like the textbook you just read, the article includes references to the scientific method. As you read the article, compare and contrast the treatment, scope, and organization of ideas on the scientific method with those in the textbook.

The structure of a newspaper article provides a means for organizing information common to most news articles.

- The **headline** announces the topic of the article.
- The **byline** and **dateline** tell who wrote the article and when and where the information was reported.
- The **lead** is the sentence or paragraph that begins the article and presents the main idea of the story.

Into Action Read the following newspaper article, and then complete a chart like the one below.

	Textbook's Coverage of the Scientific Method	Newspaper Article's Coverage of the Scientific Method
Treatment		
Scope		
Organization		

Vocabulary

scholarship (SKAHL uhr shihp) *n.*: money given to help a student continue to study. *The winner of the science challenge receives a generous scholarship for college.*

competition (kahm puh TIHSH uhn) *n.*: contest. *In this competition the winner will be the student who creates the best science project.*

Language Coach

Suffixes When the suffix *–ship* is added to a noun, it creates another noun that means "the quality or state of" that noun. One definition of the Vocabulary word *scholarship* is "state of being a scholar." List at least three other words that contain the suffix *–ship*.

Writing Skills Focus

Preparing for **Timed ⌐Writing** In the following article, you'll find topics similar to those in the textbook excerpt: scientists; scientific method; desire to make the world a better place. The treatment, scope, and organization, though, are very different. As you read, think about whether different forms of writing are needed to address similar topics.

Reader/Writer Notebook

Use your **RWN** to complete the activities for this selection.

 Learn It Online

Learn more about the structure of newspaper articles using the interactive Reading Workshops at:

| go.hrw.com | H8-145 | Go |

HAWAIIAN TEEN NAMED TOP YOUNG SCIENTIST

from **Honolulu Advertiser**, October 27, 2006

Read with a Purpose
Read the following newspaper article to find out how it covers the scientific method.

Build Background
The Discovery Channel Young Scientist Challenge began in 1998. Each year, tens of thousands of middle school students enter science fairs around the country. After a semifinalist round, the best entries are selected to compete for the title of Top Young Scientist of the Year.

HONOLULU (AP) — A Hawaiian teen has won a $20,000 scholarship and the title America's Top Young Scientist of the Year.

"Right now, I'm more or less in shock," said Nolan Kamitaki, 14. "I was just happy to be in the national competition. I didn't expect this at all."

The Discovery Channel Young Scientist Challenge is for student grades 5 through 8. The winners were announced Wednesday.

Kamitaki is now a freshman at Waiakea High School. To get to the national competition in Washington, D.C., he first had to win his school science fair, district science fair and then state science fair.

He entered with a project analyzing the effect arsenic[1] in local soils has had on Big Island school children. He also competed against 40 finalists in a series of challenges at the National Institutes of Health.

"I tested for arsenic levels first in the soils of the Keaau and Hilo area, and I tested hair samples of students who attend nearby schools," Kamitaki said. "After reading newspaper

---

1. **arsenic:** a poisonous element.

A **Informational Focus** Organization What information do the headline, byline, and dateline provide? Why do you think newspaper articles use this method of organization?

Vocabulary **scholarship** (SKAHL uhr shihp) *n.:* money given to help a student continue to study.
competition (kahm puh TIHSH uhn) *n.:* contest.

articles, I realized there is a big problem with arsenic in the Keaau area where a hotel is about to be built. I decided if it is a problem for tourists, it is definitely a problem for kids who go to the schools there." **B**

Wayne Kamitaki is still having a hard time believing his son won. "He felt he had a chance, but we didn't want him to get too excited. The odds were difficult," he said. "We're so proud of him." The younger Kamitaki said he hasn't yet decided what he'd like to study in college, but he's leaning toward medicine or physics.

His father said he hopes his son's win will encourage other students in the islands. "He's from the public school system from Hawaii. Hawaii is such a small state and sometimes it is overlooked," he said. "Hopefully this shows people that Hawaii's kids can compete."

Maryland Teen Takes Second Place

A freshman at Montgomery Blair High School took second place in the Discovery Channel's Young Scientist Challenge for the science project he and a friend did at Robert Frost Middle School last year.

Jacob Hurwitz will get a $10,000 scholarship as a result. He and his partner Scott Yu presented their project called "Discombobulated,"[2] which took people with various education levels, family histories, and other factors and looked at their understanding of word permutations.[3]

The results, not surprisingly, indicated that those who attended preschool or whose parents went to college did better, while those who often missed class did the worst. **C**

---

2. **discombobulated** (dihs kuhm BAHB yuh lay tihd): slang term that means "very confused."

3. **permutations:** here, the different forms of related words, such as *perspective, respected, spectacles.*

B | Read and Discuss | How is the scientific method presented here?

C | Informational Focus | Similarities and Differences Compare the scope of this article with that of the textbook. Why would you expect to find more thorough coverage of the scientific method in the textbook?

Applying Your Skills

Reading Standard 2.3 Find similarities and differences between texts in the treatment, scope, or organization of ideas.

Hawaiian Teen Named Top Young Scientist

Standards Review

Informational Text and Vocabulary

1. Each of the following shows that the treatment of the newspaper article is more subjective than that of the textbook excerpt *except* that

   A the student scientist Kamitaki is directly quoted.

   B the young scientist's father gives his opinion.

   C Kamitaki tested students' hair for arsenic.

   D Kamitaki's response to winning was that he was in shock.

2. The newspaper article tries to cover all of these topics *except*

   A the "Discombobulated" project by Hurwitz and Yu.

   B Wayne Kamitaki's pride in his son.

   C a Hawaiian teen's $20,000 scholarship.

   D scientific method—the language of youth.

3. The newspaper article is different from the textbook excerpt because the article

   A provides personal history about subjects.

   B includes steps of the scientific method taken.

   C uses language the average adult can understand.

   D offers types of projects that could be copied.

4. A *competition* is a

   A strategy.

   B argument.

   C conquest.

   D contest.

5. The purpose of a *scholarship* is to help a student

   A get a work-study job.

   B pay for school costs.

   C take advanced placement courses.

   D prepare for studying.

Writing Skills Focus

Timed └Writing If the scope and treatment of the scientific method is broader and more objective in a textbook than in a newspaper, why do you think someone would and should write newspaper articles about the scientific method?

What Do You Think Now

How has thinking like a scientist changed Nolan Kamitaki's life? What other lives might his thinking have changed?

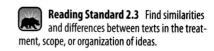

Reading Standard 2.3 Find similarities and differences between texts in the treatment, scope, or organization of ideas.

The Scientific Method

Informational Text Focus

Similarities and Differences in Treatment, Scope, and Organization of Ideas Before you read "The Scientific Method"—an article from the magazine *Current Science*—take a moment to notice the way it is structured. Its structure will help you understand how the writer organized the information. As you read the magazine article, compare and contrast the treatment, scope, and organization of ideas on the scientific method with those in the newspaper article and the textbook excerpt.

A magazine article may include the following features:

- a **headline** that announces the topic of the article
- **headings**—words or phrases (often printed in a different size or color in order to stand out) that break up the text into sections
- **illustrations**—photographs, drawings, maps, or other visuals that help you picture something described in an article. They may be accompanied by brief explanations called **captions**

Into Action After you read, complete a chart like the one below.

	Textbook's Coverage of the Scientific Method	Newspaper Article's Coverage of the Scientific Method	Magazine Article's Coverage of the Scientific Method
Treatment			
Scope			
Organization			

Vocabulary

formulated (FAWR myuh lay tihd) *v.:* formed in one's mind; developed. *Once she formulated her hypothesis, she could design an experiment to test it.*

correlate (KAWR uh layt) *v.:* show the connection between things. *It is important to correlate the results of your experiment to make sure that your cause and effect are related.*

verify (VEHR uh fy) *v.:* show to be true; confirm. *To verify the results of an experiment, you must repeat it and get the same results.*

Language Coach

Word Forms The Vocabulary words above are all verbs. *Formulation, correlation,* and *verification* are noun forms of the Vocabulary words. In your *Reader/Writer Notebook,* jot down the definitions of these noun forms in your own words. Consult a dictionary if you need help.

Writing Skills Focus

Preparing for **Timed ⌐Writing** This article follows sequential or **chronological** order. Notice the writer's use of **signal words,** such as *first, next, then* and *last,* which indicate chronological order.

Reader/Writer
Notebook
Use your **RWN** to complete the activities for this selection.

Learn It Online
There's more to words than just definitions. Get the whole story at:

go.hrw.com | H8-149 | **Go**

The Scientific Method

from Current Science

Read with a Purpose
Read the following magazine article to examine its coverage of the scientific method.

One of the ways that science differs from other branches of knowledge is that scientists follow their own special path of inquiry. That path is called the *scientific method*. The basic steps in the scientific method are as follows:

1. State the problem.

Often the first step in the scientific method involves simply noticing something—making an observation. For example, you have a friend who is very good at sports. Your friend also seems to have very fast reflexes—he or she responds very quickly when a ball or a puck is coming his or her way.

Could it be that having fast reflexes is what has made your friend a star athlete? In asking yourself that question, you have come up with a *research question*.

2. Gather information.

To answer your question, you might begin by gathering information on the subject from science books and journals. You might try to find out whether other scientists have explored the same question. You might also try to find out as much as you can about human reflexes and how best to test them.

A | **Informational Focus** Organization What information do the numbered headings provide?

3. Form a hypothesis.

Using all of the information you've gathered, you are then ready to suggest a possible solution to your problem in the form of a *hypothesis,* or an educated guess. In this case, you hypothesize that having fast reflexes determines a person's success at sports.

Once you've formulated your hypothesis, you must test it. You must find evidence that either supports or disproves your hypothesis.

B

4. Perform experiments.

In other words, you must perform an experiment. Experiments are performed according to specific directions. By following those directions, scientists can be confident that the information they uncover will clearly support or disprove the hypothesis.

For a study of human reflexes, you might perform a reaction-time test following these directions.

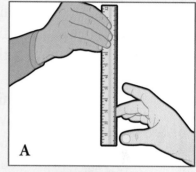

A

A. Hold one end of a ruler so that the other end is dangling between a subject's open thumb and middle finger. The 1-inch mark on the ruler should hang right between the subject's two open fingers.

B. Without warning, drop the ruler. The subject must catch the ruler between his or her two fingers.

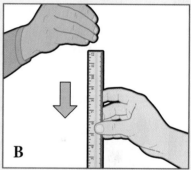

B

C. Note the spot where the subject caught the ruler. The lower the inch number at the point where the subject caught the ruler, the faster the subject's reaction time. Record the result.

C

Perform the reaction-time test on many subjects who are the same age but who have achieved different levels of athletic success. Some subjects will be top athletes; others will be average athletes; still others will be people who don't play sports well at all.

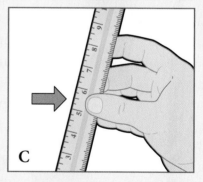

C

B [Read and Discuss] Compare the magazine article's description of the scientific method with the explanation in the newspaper article.

C [Informational Focus] **Treatment and Organization** What is the purpose of the illustrations labeled A, B, and C?

Vocabulary **formulated** (FAWR myuh lay tihd) *v.:* formed in one's mind; developed.

5. Record and analyze data.

Once all your subjects have been tested and you have recorded all your data, you must *analyze* the data. In this study, you will need to correlate your results. In other words, you will need to see whether there exists a match between the subjects' athletic ability and their individual scores on the ruler test. If the correlation is strong, you will find that top athletes did indeed have fast reaction times on the ruler test and poor athletes had slow reaction times on the ruler test.

6. Reach a conclusion.

With your evidence in hand, you can arrive at a *conclusion,* one that either supports or does not support the hypothesis. In this case, you might find, as many other scientists have found, that reaction time doesn't determine athletic achievement. **D**

7. Repeat the process.

In order to be satisfied that the data and your conclusion were accurate, you must verify the results—that is, repeat the experiment. Before other scientists accept your conclusion, they may repeat the experiment, too.

Even if scientists accept your conclusion, one answer inevitably leads to at least another question. In this case, you might want to find out whether fast reflexes are something a person is born with or whether they can be learned. The pursuit of scientific knowledge never ends.

D **Informational Focus** **Similarities and Differences** Compare the scope of this article with that of the newspaper article. Why might the magazine be better able to present this information than the newspaper?

Vocabulary **correlate** (KAWR uh layt) *v.:* show the connection between things. **verify** (VEHR uh fy) *v.:* show to be true; confirm.

MAGAZINE ARTICLE
Applying Your Skills

Reading Standard 2.3 Find similarities and differences between texts in the treatment, scope, or organization of ideas.

The Scientific Method
Standards Review

Informational Text and Vocabulary

1. Both the newspaper article and the magazine article are organized by headlines, illustrations, and

A headings.

B table of contents.

C chronology.

D enumeration.

2. The treatment of information in the magazine article is objective and instructional, whereas that in the newspaper article is

A stereotypical and negative.

B objective and humorous.

C biased and misleading.

D personal and inspirational.

3. What is the main pattern of organization in this magazine article?

A cause and effect

B chronology

C compare and contrast

D enumeration

4. To *verify* an answer means to

A compute it

B finish it

C prove it

D check it

5. When you *correlate* data, you show the information's

A connection.

B addition.

C logic.

D errors.

6. Read this sentence from the article:

Once you've <u>formulated</u> your hypothesis, you must test it.

In this sentence the word *formulated* means

A thought about.

B printed in detail.

C clearly expressed.

D experimented with.

Writing Skills Focus

Timed └Writing We all have step-by-step routines that we do each day: getting dressed, fixing breakfast, washing a load of clothes, and so on. Pick a simple action, and using the signal words that you wrote in your *Reader/Writer Notebook* from the magazine article, write at least five steps that you use to perform your action.

What Do You Think Now

How would you apply the scientific method to a challenge in your life? Explain your answer.

Writing Workshop

Short Story

Write with a Purpose

Write a short story for children, teenagers, or adults on the topic of your choice. Your **purpose** is to tell a clear, coherent story that will engage the attention of your **audience.**

A Good Short Story

- tells a clear, coherent story, using well-chosen details
- focuses on a conflict the characters must resolve
- includes a series of events that lead to a climax
- develops characters through specific action and relevant dialogue
- provides physical and background descriptions of characters and setting
- ends with a resolution of the climax
- reveals the significance of the events or the writer's attitude toward them

See page 162 for the complete rubric.

Reader/Writer Notebook

Use your **RWN** to complete the activities for this workshop.

Think as a Reader/Writer

You have read several enjoyable stories in this chapter. Here is your chance to stretch your imagination by writing a short story. Before you begin writing, read this excerpt from Francisco Jiménez's story "The Circuit."

> Mr. Lema was sitting at his desk correcting papers. When I entered he looked up at me and smiled. I felt better. I walked up to him and asked if he could help me with the new words. "Gladly," he said.
>
> The rest of the month I spent my lunch hours working on English with Mr. Lema, my best friend at school.
>
> One Friday, during lunch hour, Mr. Lema asked me to take a walk with him to the music room. "Do you like music?" he asked me as we entered the building.
>
> "Yes, I like corridos,"[1] I answered. He then picked up a trumpet, blew on it, and handed it to me. The sound gave me goose bumps. I knew the sound. I had heard it in many corridos. "How would you like to learn how to play it?" he asked. He must have read my face because before I could answer, he added: "I'll teach you how to play it during our lunch hours."

← Details of the setting help readers picture Mr. Lema at work.

← Readers learn about Mr. Lema through how the narrator reacts to him.

← Mr. Lema's actions and words show his thoughtfulness and kindness.

---

1. Corridos (kor REE dohs): Mexican folk ballads

Think About the Professional Model

With a partner, discuss the following questions about the model.

1. How do Mr. Lema's actions reveal what he is like as a person?
2. What does the reader learn about Mr. Lema from the narrator's reactions to him?

Writing Standard 1.2 Establish coherence within and among paragraphs through effective transitions, parallel structures, and similar writing techniques. **2.1 Write** biographies, autobiographies, **short stories**, or narratives: **a. Relate a clear, coherent incident, event, or situation by using well-chosen details. b. Reveal the significance of, or the writer's attitude about, the subject. c. Employ narrative and descriptive strategies (e.g., relevant dialogue, specific action, physical description, background description, comparison or contrast of characters).**

Prewriting

Choose an Idea for a Story

You write best about what you know well. Although a short story is a work of fiction, the characters and events should seem real. Even if you set your story in outer space in 2200, it will seem real to your readers if you use well-chosen details borrowed from the people and places you know. Look at the Idea Starters on the right for help in finding a topic.

Plan Your Story's Characters

Think of details about your characters until they seem real to you. Then, use narrative and descriptive strategies to make them come alive for your audience. Detailed physical descriptions help readers visualize the characters. Instead of simply describing your characters' personalities or motivations, however, try to reveal them through specific actions, relevant dialogue (dialogue that matches the situation), and the reactions of other characters. Make a list of your characters. Then, use a chart to organize the characteristics of each one.

Character	Appearance	Actions/Words	Other's Reactions
Martak	Wears futuristic clothing	Terminates his experiment regretfully	Supervisor treats him with respect

Plan Point of View

Who will narrate your story? Will it be the main character, using *I* or *me* as he or she narrates the story? Will it be a secondary character who watches the story unfold? Perhaps you would rather tell the story from the third-person point of view, using the pronouns *he* and *she* when you are discussing the characters.

Decide on a Setting

The description of the setting, where and when the story takes place, can give your readers a lot of information. The setting tells about the characters (a mansion indicates wealth) and can even cause the main conflict (a volcano erupts, causing everyone to flee). Ask yourself:

- Where and when does the story take place? Over how much time?
- What mood do you want your setting to evoke?
- Is the setting part of the conflict? What problems does it cause?

Idea Starters
- A middle-school student travels back in time.
- A lonely girl discovers a new side of herself.
- A star soccer player tries out for the school play.
- Two former friends compete for a prize.
- A boy and his computer get in trouble.

Peer Review

Share your chart with other students. Assess whether or not your characters are believable. What relevant dialogue, specific actions, and physical or background description might help bring each to life?

Your Turn _____

Get Started Use your **RWN** to take notes about the **characters** in your story. Also, write down your ideas about the **setting** of the story and the main **conflict** that occurs. Your notes will help you plan your short story.

 Learn It Online
To see how one writer met all the assignment criteria visit:

go.hrw.com   H8-155   **Go**

Think About Purpose and Audience

As you plan your story, keep in mind your **purpose** for writing and your **audience.** How will you make your story clear and coherent? What kind of story will engage the attention of your audience? Remember that your audience should also dictate the style of writing you use.

Develop a Plot

For your plot, plan four elements.

- A **conflict,** or struggle, which will be the basis of your story.
- A **series of related events** set in motion by the conflict.
- A **climax**, or most exciting point, when something happens that reveals how the conflict will turn out.
- A **resolution,** or ending showing how things work out.

Outline Your Plot

Here's one writer's **short story action plan**. Use an action plan like this one to outline the plot of your story.

Your Turn

Plan Your Plot To help you create your plot, make a **short story action plan.** Exchange action plans with a classmate. Think about what he or she says, and then revise your plan. In the "Beginning" section, the writer describes the characters and settings and introduces the conflict. In the "Middle" section, he or she shows the series of related events in time order and includes the climax of the story. In the "End" section, the writer tells how the conflict is resolved.

Short Story Action Plan

Beginning

Characters: Martak, a scientist observing an experiment; Johnny, a four-year-old boy building a sand castle; Martak's supervisor; Johnny's parents

Settings: (1) a laboratory in space; (2) the yard of a house in the evening

Introduction to Conflict: Martak, a scientist observing an "experiment," decides the experiment should end.

Middle

1. In lab: Martak observes an experiment and tells his supervisor that they should end it.
2. In yard: Johnny plays in a sandbox, building a sand castle.
3. In lab: Supervisor agrees to end experiment.
4. In yard: Johnny's mother calls him to come in.
5. Climax—on porch: Johnny sees a large star getting bigger. Johnny's parents scream.

End

6. In lab: Martak watches a sphere burning on his monitor.

Drafting

Follow Your Short Story Action Plan

Now that you've completed your action plan, it's time to bring your story to life. Using your outline as a guide, begin drafting. A framework for quick reference appears at the right. As you write, keep in mind the characteristics of a good short story, listed on page 154.

Craft a Strong Beginning

Your first sentence should catch the reader's attention. You may want to arouse your reader's curiosity by jumping immediately into the action.

Compare or Contrast Your Characters

A good way to highlight your characters' personalities is by showing them to be similar to or different from other characters. If your main character is adventurous but foolhardy, for example, you might have a timid friend try to talk her out of her plans.

Round Out the Ending

Show how characters are affected by the resolution of the conflict. Have they changed or learned something? Does your ending suggest an overall theme?

Framework for a Short Story

Introduction
- Use a strong first sentence that grabs the reader's attention.
- Introduce the characters and conflict.

Middle
- Create a series of events with rising action, leading toward a climax.

End
- Show how the conflict is resolved and how the characters are affected.

Grammar Link Using Active Voice

A verb in the **active voice** expresses an action done *by* the subject. A verb in the **passive voice** expresses an action done *to* its subject and always includes a form of the verb *be*. Using the active voice will help make your writing more direct and forceful. Although passive voice can be useful when you do not know (or don't want to say) who performed an action, the overuse of passive voice can make your writing sound weak and awkward. Here is an example from the student model.

Active voice: "I can't support the continued funding of Experiment 023681."
Passive voice: "The funding of this experiment should not be supported." (Who is responsible?)

.

Writing Tip

Unsure about how to craft a strong beginning to your story? Look to the experts: popular authors. Thumb through this textbook, and scan some story openings. Read the first few paragraphs, noting how the author starts the story.

Writing Tip

Remember that realistic dialogue can bring your characters to life.

Your Turn _____

Write Your Draft Following your **short story action plan,** write a draft of your story. Also, think about
- who tells the story
- how to develop characters and show action through dialogue

Peer Review

As the author of your story, you know it so well that it might be difficult to see what has been left out or left vague. A peer reviewer can tell you whether events in your story are confusing or whether more detail or transitions are needed. When you read someone else's story, first read for enjoyment. Then, re-read to offer the writer suggestions to improve the story. Use the chart to the right as you work with your partner.

Evaluating and Revising

Read the questions in the left column of the chart, and then use the tips in the middle to help you mark where revisions are needed. The right column suggests techniques to use to revise your draft.

Short Story: Guidelines for Content and Organization

Evaluation Questions	Tips	Revision Techniques
1. Does your story contain a well-developed plot?	**Place a check mark** next to each element: beginning, conflict, complications, climax, and resolution.	**Add** or **elaborate** on plot elements as necessary.
2. Are main characters complex and convincing? Are they shown as similar to or different from minor characters?	**Underline** character details, descriptions, and dialogue.	**Add** physical or background descriptions, relevant dialogue, and specific actions, if needed.
3. Does the story establish a clear setting and evoke a mood?	**Highlight** details about the setting and mood.	**Elaborate** on the setting, if necessary, by adding descriptive details.
4. Are events arranged in a coherent order? Are transitions used to make the order clear?	**Number** the major events. **Put a star** next to transitional expressions.	**Rearrange** events that are out of order. **Add** transitional words and phrases, if necessary, to show the order of events.
5. Is the point of view clear and consistent?	**Circle** pronouns that show whether the point of view is first or third person.	**Change** pronouns or details that shift the point of view.
6. Does the story reveal the writer's (your) attitude toward the events?	**Underline** clues that point to the tone of the story.	**Add** words, details, or sentences that clarify the writer's or narrator's attitude.

Read this student draft, and notice the comments on its strengths and suggestions for improvement at the right.

Experiment 023681

by Peter Leary, Athens Academy

"They're still regressing," said Martak, as he raised his head from the viewing screen, disappointment shadowing his face. "I can't support the continued funding of Experiment 023681. We have others which work much better."

"Very well," rumbled the deep voice of Martak's supervisor. "It's too bad, though. They seemed so promising."

"I know. Disappointing, isn't it?" commented Martak. "But living conditions are horrible, they insist on killing each other in these petty little things called 'wars,' and look at their life span: on the outside, ninety-five of their 'years'!"

"I agree. Permission granted to terminate Experiment 023681."

Johnny gazed on his mostly finished sand castle, feeling a four-year-old's pride. He knew it was getting dark, so he scooped quickly.

Martak looked at the small mass of swirling blues, greens, and whites on his monitor.

← The fact that the "experiment" is mysterious creates suspense. Dialogue conveys information about the setting, characters, and conflict.

← Suspense grows as another character and setting are introduced.

← The writer returns to the first setting.

MINI-LESSON ▶ **How to Use Relevant Dialogue to Advance the Plot**

Dialogue can be used not only to reveal character but also to advance the plot. Peter clarifies what happens after Martak is given permission to terminate his experiment by adding the following four lines to his revised draft of the story.

Peter's Revision of Paragraph Six

> Martak looked at the small mass of swirling blues, greens, and whites on his monitor.
> ∧He entered his access code.
> "Request?" questioned a tinny voice.
> "Terminate Experiment 023681."
> "Request confirmed. . . ."

Your Turn _____

Use Dialogue Read your draft, and then ask yourself,

- "Can I add dialogue that will reveal action?"
- "Does the dialogue that I have included advance the plot?"
- "Does the dialogue that I have included sound natural?"

Once you have answered these questions, make revisions to improve your draft.

Student Draft *continues*

The second setting and characters are further developed. →

"John, come in the house!" his mother shouted from the porch.

Johnny sighed and dropped his shovel as he trudged toward his house. He knew his mother meant it when she said, "John."

"I'm coming, Mom, he responded. Ambling to the porch, he glanced behind him at the sky. "Mommy, come look. There's a star that's getting bigger."

His mother screamed to come inside, away from the door and the windows. His dad screamed, "Invaders!" Johnny stood entranced by the light that now seemed to shine on his house.

The climax of the story is reached with its resolution now clear. →

Martak watched as the small, perfect sphere was engulfed in yellow flame. The flame slowly turned orange, then red, then finally settled into a black cloud, which died, leaving behind only dust. He sighed and turned to the next experiment.

MINI-LESSON ▶ How to Use Transitions and Parallel Structures to Advance the Plot

Peter does a good job of capturing his reader's interest. He can make his story even more interesting by adding suspense. To make your story clear and coherent, it is essential to include transitions that show the passage of time. Parallel actions can also be used to advance the plot. Peter adds to his draft a sentence showing the passage of time. He also moves the plot along by having the mother repeat her call.

Peter's Revision of Paragraph Eight

Johnny sighed and dropped his shovel as he trudged toward his house. He knew his mother meant it when she said, "John."

He looked up at the darkening sky and saw the first stars.
"Now, John," said his mother sternly.

"I'm coming, Mom, he responded. Ambling to the porch, he glanced behind him at the sky. "Mommy, come look. There's a star that's getting bigger."

Your Turn ———

Add Suspense Re-read your short story to see where you could increase suspense by emphasizing the passage of time. Work with a partner to check each other's revisions.

Proofreading and Publishing

Proofreading

Re-read your paper to see if the words you have chosen convey the mood and tone you want to establish. Then, correct any errors in spelling, punctuation, capitalization, and grammar before you prepare your final draft.

> ### Grammar Link Punctuating Dialogue
>
> Be careful that you use correct punctuation in dialogue, and pay special attention to end punctuation. To make it clear which words are part of the dialogue, or the character's actual words, Peter added punctuation in his final draft.
>
> "I'm coming, Mom," he responded. Ambling to the porch, he glanced
>
> behind him at the sky. "Mommy, come look. There's a star that's
>
> getting bigger."
>
> Notice how the quotation marks make clear just who is saying what. These punctuation marks make the final draft clearer.

Publishing

You might think about submitting your story to publications like these:

- your school's literary magazine
- an online literary magazine
- short story contests

If you decide to submit your story to a magazine for publication, write a letter to the editor. Include a brief summary of the story that will convince the editor to publish the story. Be sure to address the following points in your letter:

- Why is it important that your short story be published in this particular magazine?
- Why would magazine readers be interested in your short story?

Reflect on the Process
As you think about how you wrote your own short story, record answers to the following questions in your **RWN.**

1. How did writing a short story help you understand how short stories are put together?
2. How do you think writing your own story will help you in your reading?

● Proofreading Tip

It's helpful to have a classmate do a careful proofreading of your story. Ask the classmate to look out for errors in punctuation, especially in dialogue.

Your Turn _____

Proofread and Publish As you proofread, look closely to make sure that all your sentences have correct end punctuation. Also, make sure that quotation marks are placed correctly. Once you have corrected your draft, you can share it with your classmates or with an even wider audience.

Scoring Rubric

You can use the rubric below to evaluate your short story.

Narrative Writing	Organization and Focus	Sentence Structure	Conventions
4 • Provides a *thoroughly developed* plot line with: 1) beginning conflict 2) rising action 3) climax 4) resolution 5) point of view), *convincing characters*, and a definite setting. • Includes *appropriate* strategies (e.g., relevant dialogue, well-chosen details, narrow focus on a clear incident, event, or situation).	• *Clearly* addresses all of the writing tasks. • Demonstrates a *clear* understanding of purpose and audience. • Maintains a *consistent* point of view and smooth transitions. • *Effectively* creates settings evoking a strong mood.	• Includes sentence *variety*.	• Contains *few, if any,* errors in the conventions of the English language (grammar, punctuation, capitalization, spelling). These errors do **not** interfere with the reader's understanding of the writing.
3 • Provides an *adequately developed* plot line with: 1) beginning conflict 2) rising action 3) climax 4) resolution 5) point of view), *convincing* characters, and a *definite* setting. • Includes *appropriate* strategies (e.g., relevant dialogue, well-chosen details, narrow focus on a clear incident, event, or situation).	• Addresses *most* of the writing task • Demonstrates a *general* understanding of purpose and audience. • Maintains a *mostly consistent* point of view and *relatively smooth* transitions. • Creates *mostly effective* settings evoking a strong mood.	• Includes some sentence *variety*.	• Contains *some errors* in the conventions of the English language (grammar, punctuation, capitalization, spelling). These errors do **not** interfere with the reader's understanding of the writing.
2 • Provides a *minimally developed* plot line with some story elements, *somewhat convincing* characters, and a *minimally defined* setting. • *Attempts* to use appropriate strategies but with *minimal* effectiveness (e.g., *sometimes* relevant dialogue, details, focus on an incident, event or situation).	• Addresses *some* of the writing task • Demonstrates *little* understanding of purpose and audience. • Maintains an *inconsistent* point of view and *awkward* transitions that do not unify important ideas. • *Suggests* a setting with *limited* ability to evoke mood.	• Includes *little* sentence variety	• Contains *several errors* in the conventions of the English language (grammar, punctuation, capitalization, spelling). These errors **may** interfere with the reader's understanding of the writing.
1 • *Lacks* a developed plot line, convincing characters, and defined setting. • *Fails* to use appropriate strategies (e.g., relevant dialogue and well-chosen details).	• Addresses *only one* part of the writing task • Demonstrates *no* understanding of purpose and audience. • *Lacks* a point of view and transitions that unify important ideas. • *Lacks* a defined setting and *fails* to evoke mood.	• Includes *no* sentence variety.	• Contains *serious errors* in the conventions of the English language (grammar, punctuation, capitalization, spelling). These errors interfere with the reader's understanding of the writing.

Preparing for Timed Writing

Short Story

When responding to an on-demand prompt requiring a short story, use what you have learned from writing your own short story, the rubric, and the steps below.

Writing Standard 2.1 **Write** biographies, autobiographies, **short stories**, or narratives: **a. Relate a clear, coherent incident, event, or situation by using well-chosen details. b. Reveal the significance of, or the writer's attitude about, the subject. c. Employ narrative and descriptive strategies (e.g., relevant dialogue, specific action, physical description, background description, comparison or contrast of characters).**

Writing Prompt

Write a short story in which the main character or characters have to overcome an obstacle or conflict. Use precise details to describe the setting, and use relevant dialogue and specific action to create convincing characters. Write your story from a consistent point of view. Be sure to include a climax and resolution to the conflict.

Study the Prompt

Be sure to read the prompt carefully, and identify all parts of your task. Then, think of some story ideas based on your personal experience, stories you've read, or your own imagination. Choose the idea that you think will make the best story and that will appeal to your readers.

Tip: Spend about five minutes studying the prompt.

Plan Your Response

Once you understand your task and have settled on your story idea

- make notes about your main characters—how they look, how they talk, how they behave, and how others react to them
- record where and when the story occurs
- describe the main conflict of the story, and list the events that lead to the climax and resolution of the conflict
- decide whether the story will be told from a first-person or third-person point of view
- consider your attitude toward the story

Tip: Spend about fifteen minutes planning your response.

Respond to the Prompt

Using the notes you've just made, draft your short story. Follow these guidelines:

- In the introduction, get your readers' attention with interesting dialogue or by describing your characters in action. Set the scene with specific details.
- In the body of your story, relate the rising action—the events that lead to the climax, or high point, of the conflict. Make sure you present your events in a logical order. (Most short stories follow chronological order.)
- In the conclusion, resolve the story's conflict, showing how the characters are affected by its resolution.
- As you are writing, remember to use a consistent point of view.

Tip: Spend about twenty minutes writing your draft.

Improve Your Response

Revising Go back and check the prompt. Have you created convincing characters using relevant dialogue and specific action? Have they overcome an obstacle? Is your setting clear?

Proofreading Proofread your story to correct errors in grammar, spelling, punctuation, and capitalization. Make sure all of your edits are neat, and erase any stray marks.

Checking Your Final Copy Before your turn in your short story, read it one more time to catch any errors you may have missed.

Tip: Save five or ten minutes to improve your paper.

Listening & Speaking Workshop

Reciting a Literary Work

Speak with a Purpose

Organize and deliver an oral recitation to your class. As your classmates recite, practice listening and then analyze their presentations.

⬤ **Speaking Tip**

Practice, practice, practice

- Rehearse enough so that you can maintain almost constant eye contact with your audience.

- Look up the meaning and the pronunciation of any word you are unsure of.

- If you plan to stand before your audience, rehearse while standing.

- Deliver your presentation in front of a mirror. Then practice in front of family members or friends.

Reader/Writer Notebook

Use your **RWN** to complete the activities for this workshop.

Think as a Reader/Writer Reciting literary works—poems, plays, speeches, and short stories—and listening to the recitations of others can deepen your understanding of the works, sharpen your speaking skills, and improve your listening skills.

Choose and Prepare a Literary Work to Recite

Half the Battle

Choose a literary work that has the characteristics of good literature and is one you like and understand. It should give you the chance to use creative speaking techniques such as the **pace,** or speed, of your recitation; the **modulations,** or changes, in your voice to emphasize certain phrases or to communicate **tone; enunciation,** a clear and distinct voice; and the **facial expressions** and **gestures** you use to enhance the meaning for your audience. Follow these steps as you organize your preparation.

- **Study the piece for its meaning** Learn everything you can about the speaker—the voice—of the piece to determine the tone. Should your tone be happy or sad? sincere or sarcastic? excited or quiet?

- **Decide what impression you want to make on your audience with your recitation** Then focus your presentation on how you will make that impression. If you want your audience to feel compassion for a character, stress the elements that will be likely to enable that.

- **Prepare a reading script** Make a copy of the piece, typed and double-spaced, so you can write notes to guide you as you practice. Underline words you want to stress; describe a change in tone; note where a gesture will be; and write when to adjust the pace.

Here is part of one student's script for a recitation from an autobiography.

from "Stop the Sun" by Gary Paulsen	Delivery Notes
"We were crossing a rice paddy in the dark," he said, / and suddenly his voice flowed like a river breaking loose. / "We were crossing the paddy, and it was dark, still dark, so black you couldn't see the end of your nose."	Read slowly; pause slightly at /. Then read more quickly. Tone is serious; use use facial expression to convey "dark." Use pause to make eye contact. (Breathe; make eye contact; read quickly, but enunciate every word.)

Listening and Speaking Standard
1.1 Analyze oral interpretations of literature, including language choice and **delivery, and the effect of the interpretations on the listener. 1.3 Organize information to achieve particular purposes by matching the message,** vocabulary, **voice modulation, expression, and tone to the audience and purpose. 1.6** Use appropriate grammar, word choice, enunciation, and pace during formal presentations. **2.5 Recite poems, sections of speeches,** or dramatic soliloquies, **using voice modulation, tone, and gestures expressively to enhance the meaning.**

Listen to a Recitation

An Appreciative Listener

Listening to a recitation of a work of literature is an adventure in appreciative listening. To truly appreciate, you must analyze the selection as well as its presentation. Use suggestions in the chart below to analyze your classmates' literature choices and their recitations.

Just as you appreciate polite listeners and constructive criticism for your recitation, remember to be equally attentive as others recite and offer positive and useful feedback as you evaluate.

Analyze a Recitation

Before You Listen

- **Prepare** Ask yourself, What is the selection about? What is the title? Who is the author? What type of literature is it?
- **Predict** Make predictions about what you will hear.

As You Listen

- **Visualize and personalize** Picture what you hear and relate it to similar experiences or feelings you have had.
- **Record** Jot down notes, questions, and ideas you have as you listen.

After You Listen

- **Review** How did your predictions change as you listened?
- **Respond** How did the interpretation affect you? What did you feel as you listened? What did you like about the selection?
- **Identify and analyze** Which elements of literature did you hear— word choice, imagery, rhythm? What tone (or tones) did the author's word choices create? How did the literary elements contribute to its meaning?
- **Summarize** Write a brief summary of your overall reaction to the presentation, including an analysis of the speaker's delivery.
- **Evaluate** In your summary, determine the speaker's effectiveness in using the speaking techniques: pace, voice modulation, enunciation, facial expressions and gestures.
- **Reply** Be prepared to offer positive feedback to the speaker.

> ### A Good Recitation of a Literary Work
>
> - is selected from good literature.
> - has a typed and prepared script.
> - has been rehearsed thoroughly.
> - considers the literary elements of the selection.
> - employs appropriate speaking techniques: pace, voice modulation, tone, enunciation, and gestures.

Learn It Online
Bring your presentation to a wider audience. Use the Digital Storytelling mini-site at:

go.hrw.com   H8-165   **Go**

Literary Skills Review

Plot and Setting **Directions:** Read the passage. Then, answer each question that follows.

from The Cay by **Theodore Taylor**

In the novel The Cay, *Phillip, an eleven-year-old boy who is blind, is shipwrecked on a very small island, or cay, with a West Indian seaman named Timothy and a cat. Timothy dies while protecting Phillip during a hurricane. In this part of the story, Phillip is trying to make it on his own.*

The sun came out strong in the morning. I could feel it on my face. It began to dry the island, and toward noon, I heard the first cry of a bird. They were returning.

By now, I had taught myself to tell time, very roughly, simply by turning my head toward the direct warmth of the sun. If the angle was almost overhead, I knew it was around noon. If it was low, then of course, it was early morning or late evening.

There was so much to do that I hardly knew where to start. Get a campfire going, pile new wood for a signal fire, make another rain catchment for the water keg, weave a mat of palm fibers to sleep on. Then make a shelter of some kind, fish the hole on the reef, inspect the palm trees to see if any coconuts were left—I didn't think any could be up there—and search the whole island to discover what the storm had deposited. It was enough work for weeks, and I said to Stew Cat, "I don't know how we'll get it all done." But something told me I must stay very busy and not think about myself.

I accomplished a lot in three days, even putting a new edge on Timothy's knife by honing it on coral. I jabbed it into the palm nearest my new shelter, so that I would always know where it was if I needed it. Without Timothy's eyes, I was finding that in my world, everything had to be very precise; an exact place for everything.

On the fifth day after the storm, I began to scour the island to find out what had been cast up. It was exciting, and I knew it would take days or weeks to accomplish. I had made another cane and beginning with east beach, I felt my way back and forth, reaching down to touch everything that my cane struck; sometimes having to spend a long time trying to decide what it was that I held in my hands.

I found several large cans and used one of them to start the "time" can again, dropping five pebbles into it so that the reckoning would begin again from the night of the storm. I discovered an old broom, and a small wooden crate that would make a nice stool. I found a piece of canvas, and tried to think of ways to make pants from it, but I had no needle or thread.

Other than that, I found many shells, some bodies of dead birds, pieces of cork, and chunks of sponge, but nothing I could really put to good use.

It was on the sixth day after the storm, when I was exploring on south beach, that I heard the birds. Stew Cat was with me, as usual, and he growled when they first screeched. Their cries were angry, and I guessed that seven or eight might be in the air.

I stood listening to them; wondering what they were. Then I felt a beat of wing past my face, and an angry cry as the bird dived at me. I lashed out at it with my cane, wondering why they were attacking me.

Another dived down, screaming at me, and his bill nipped the side of my head. For a moment, I was confused, not knowing whether to run for cover under sea grape, or what was left of it, or try to fight them off with my cane. There seemed to be a lot of birds.

Then one pecked my forehead sharply, near my eyes, and I felt blood run down my face. I started to walk back toward camp, but had taken no more than three or four steps when I tripped over a log. I fell into the sand, and at the same time, felt a sharp pain in the back of my head. I heard a raging screech as the bird soared up again. Then another bird dived at me.

I heard Stew Cat snarling and felt him leap up on my back, his claws digging into my flesh. There was another wild screech, and Stew Cat left my back, leaping into the air.

His snarls and the wounded screams of the bird filled the stillness over the cay. I could hear them battling in the sand. Then I heard the death caw of the bird.

I lay still a moment. Finally, I crawled to where Stew Cat had his victim. I touched him; his body was rigid and his hair was still on edge. He was growling, low and muted.

Then I touched the bird. It had sounded large, but it was actually rather small. I felt the beak; it was very sharp.

Slowly, Stew Cat began to relax.

Wondering what had caused the birds to attack me, I felt around in the sand. Soon, my hand touched a warm shell. I couldn't blame the birds very much. I'd accidentally walked into their new nesting ground.

They were fighting for survival, after the storm, just as I was. I left Stew Cat to his unexpected meal and made my way slowly back to camp.

Literary Skills Review

Reading Standard 3.2 Evaluate the structural elements of the plot (e.g., subplots, parallel episodes, climax), the plot's development, and the way in which conflicts are (or are not) addressed and resolved. **3.4** Analyze the relevance of the setting (e.g., place, time, customs) to the mood, tone, and meaning of the text.

1. Which quotation reveals one of the boy's *main* conflicts involving his blindness?

   A "Everything had to be very precise; an exact place for everything."

   B "I found several large cans and used one of them to start the 'time' can again."

   C "The sun came out strong in the morning. I could feel it on my face."

   D "It was exciting, and I knew it would take days or weeks to accomplish."

2. Read this sentence from the third paragraph.

   > But something told me I must stay very busy and not think about myself.

   How does the setting of the story affect the meaning of this sentence?

   A Being alone on the deserted island, the boy must not despair and give up.

   B Because another hurricane might come soon, the boy must prepare quickly.

   C The boy hears voices in the wind and is afraid not to obey them.

   D The high tide is expected soon, and the new items may wash away.

3. The attack by the birds changes the story's mood from routine activity to

   A loneliness.

   B terror.

   C fluster.

   D anger.

4. Which of the following plot complications leads directly to the climax?

   A The boy wanders into a nesting area.

   B Trying to escape, the boy trips and is attacked.

   C Stew Cat climbs on the boy's back and leaps.

   D The boy crawls to Stew Cat and the dead bird.

5. At the end of the excerpt, the conflict is resolved as the boy

   A lets the cat eat the bird it killed.

   B realizes the birds were fighting for survival.

   C accepts his blindness and returns to camp.

   D decides to leave the eggs at the nesting area.

Timed Writing

6. The writer's tone toward this story is realistic and straightforward. Select three examples of adjectives used to describe the setting, and explain why you think that each represents the tone.

Informational Skills Review

Treatment, Scope and Organization of Ideas

Directions: Read the following two documents. Then, read and respond to the questions that follow.

Reading Standard 2.3
Find similarities and differences between texts in the treatment, scope, and organization of ideas.

Surrounded by Sound by  THE WORLD ALMANAC

A jet takes off from a nearby airport, its dull roar rattling your windows. *Woof!* A dog barks outside. All that noise is driving you crazy! The word *noise* comes from the Latin word *nausea,* meaning "seasickness"—a condition that causes distress. Sources of noise range from pets to construction equipment, stereos to leaf blowers. Noise is considered environmental pollution and is the number-one neighborhood complaint, ahead of crime, litter, and traffic, says a U.S. Census Bureau survey of more than 100 million households.

Hear This!

Long-term exposure to loud sounds harms hearing. Too-loud noise can damage the auditory nerve, which travels between the inner ear and brain. A person's hearing worsens as nerve endings die off. Exposure to loud sounds can also damage or destroy the sensory hair cells of the inner ear. About 28 million Americans have experienced hearing loss of some kind, according to the National Institutes of Health (NIH), and about one-third can blame—at least in part—noise.

How Loud Is Too Loud?

"If you have to raise your voice to be heard, the environment may be too loud for your ears," says researcher Sig Soli of the House Ear Institute. Prolonged exposure to sound above 85 decibels—the level of heavy city traffic—can cause gradual hearing loss, says the National Institute on Deafness and Other Communications Disorders. "The louder the sound, the less time it takes before your hearing is affected," Soli says.

Stressed Out by Sound

Noise pollution impairs concentration, says the World Health Organization. Even low-level noise can disturb sleep, cause headaches, increase blood pressure, interfere with digestion, and cause anxiety. How? Loud sounds can signal your body to activate its "fight or flight" response. Your body responds automatically, releasing adrenalin and other stress hormones into the bloodstream. Heart rate, blood pressure, and respiration increase; blood is redirected from the digestive tract to muscles and limbs. Excessive exposure may also contribute to stress-related conditions, such as chronic high blood pressure, ulcers, and migraine headaches, according to the Environmental Protection Agency.

Informational Skills Review CONTINUED

Sound Off on Noise!

**Dedicated to preventing noise pollution in our
Long Island Sound community**

Noise pollution is more than a nuisance— it's hazardous to your health!

Health Effects of Noise Pollution
- hearing loss
- buzzing or ringing in ears (tinnitus)
- impaired concentration
- interrupted sleep, sleep deprivation, fatigue
- high blood pressure, heart disease
- ulcers, migraine headaches

Sound Off on Noise! is a local volunteer organization whose goal is to raise awareness of the problem of noise in our neighborhoods. Its members work to preserve the quality of life on Long Island by

- **Educating the public** about noise pollution as a threat to human health and the environment. We display posters, distribute pamphlets, and host informational meetings.

- **Raising awareness through the media.** We send press releases to local television and radio outlets as well as to community newspapers.

- **Lobbying public officials** about the problem of noise pollution to enlist their support in addressing the issue.

- **Contacting agencies** such as local police departments, legislative councils, regulatory agencies, and the Federal Department of Environmental Protection.

- **Sponsoring free hearing screenings** at community events.

Noise pollution is everyone's problem—and responsibility. If you'd like more information about Sound Off on Noise!, please visit us on the Web at **www.soundoffonnoise.com.**

1. The organization of ideas in "Sound Off on Noise!" is mainly
   A in chronological order.
   B in point-by-point order.
   C by order of importance.
   D by cause and effect.

2. What is difference in scope between the two passages?
   A "Sound Off on Noise!" has a broad scope whereas "Surrounded by Sound" has a more limited scope.
   B "Surrounded by Sound" has a broad scope whereas "Sound Off on Noise!" has a more limited scope.
   C One is written about noise problems in New York whereas the other deals with California noise problems.
   D They disagree about battling noise pollution.

3. The treatment of noise pollution in the two passages is similar because both passages are
   A humorous.
   B positive.
   C angry.
   D serious.

4. Which idea is in "Surrounded by Sound" but is *not* in "Sound Off on Noise!"?
   A Noise pollution has a negative effect on neighborhoods.
   B Many Americans suffer from hearing loss.
   C Loud noises can be hazardous to people's health.
   D The word *noise* comes from the Latin word *nausea,* meaning "seasickness."

Timed Writing

5. What do you see as the main difference in **purpose** between the two passages? Do they complement each other, or present differing arguments? Explain, using details to support your ideas.

Vocabulary Skills Review

Synonyms   **Directions:** Choose the word that is the *best* synonym of each italicized word from the literary selections in this chapter.

1. If a body is *inert,* it is
   A twitching.
   B inactive.
   C inedible.
   D animated.

2. A *grueling* workout is a(n) _____ workout.
   A fatiguing
   B invigorating
   C healthful
   D grimy

3. *Detect* means the same as
   A run away.
   B insult.
   C locate.
   D bring.

4. To *obscure* a fault is to _____ it.
   A interpret
   B parade
   C fix
   D conceal

5. An *impromptu* celebration is
   A prepared.
   B organized.
   C important.
   D improvised.

6. If a document is *authentic,* it is
   A real.
   B authorized.
   C old.
   D signed.

7. An *ignorant* person is
   A misplaced
   B uninformed
   C disturbed
   D exhausted

Academic Vocabulary

Directions: Choose the word that is the *best* synonym of the Academic Vocabulary word.

8. To *evaluate* means to
   A evolve.
   B judge.
   C connect.
   D exercise.

9. If you *analyze* a short story, you _____ it.
   A dislike
   B retell
   C understand
   D examine

Writing Skills Review

Short Story **Directions:** Read the following passage from a short story. Then, answer each question that follows.

Writing Standard 2.1 **Write** biographies, autobiographies, **short stories**, or narratives: **a. Relate a clear, coherent incident, event, or situation by using well-chosen details. b. Reveal the significance of, or the writer's attitude about, the subject. c. Employ narrative and descriptive strategies (e.g., relevant dialogue, specific action, physical description, background description, comparison or contrast of characters).**

(1) Jesse nervously approached the front porch of his house and stopped before climbing the wooden steps to the front door. (2) His mother was probably in the kitchen preparing dinner. (3) His father wouldn't be home for another hour. (4) He knew his family's routine. (5) Wearily, Jesse slipped his backpack off and dropped it on the steps. (6) He froze in terror. (7) Inside the cover of his notebook, there was a letter addressed to his parents. (8) The letter was from the principal. (9) It said that Jesse had been caught plagiarizing a social studies report. (10) How was he going to face his parents?

---

1. Which words did the writer use to establish **setting?**

   A "the front porch of his house .. wooden steps to the front door."

   B "in the kitchen preparing dinner"

   C "He froze in terror."

   D "Inside the cover of his notebook, there was a letter addressed to his parents."

2. Which sentence is unnecessary and can be deleted?

   A sentence 4

   B sentence 7

   C sentence 8

   D sentence 9

3. A **cliché** is a phrase or expression that has been used so much that it loses its impact. Which sentence contains a cliché and should be rewritten?

   A sentence 2

   B sentence 3

   C sentence 6

   D sentence 8

4. What would be the best way to combine sentences 7 and 8?

   A Inside the cover of his notebook, there was a letter addressed to his parents and it was from the principal.

   B A letter that had been addressed to his parents and which was from the principal was inside the cover of his notebook.

   C A letter sent by the principal and addressed to his parents was inside the cover of his notebook.

   D Having been signed by the principal, a letter addressed to his parents was inside the cover of his notebook.

5. To develop this story, the writer should do all of the following *except*

   A add dialogue between characters.

   B provide a happy ending for all.

   C develop the internal and external conflicts.

   D bring events to a climax and resolution.

Read On

Fiction

Hatchet

Young Brian finds himself stranded alone in the Canadian wilderness after a plane crash. With only his wits and a hatchet to rely on for survival, Brian learns some memorable lessons about nature, growing up, and himself. Lovers of survival and adventure stories will find themselves engrossed in Gary Paulsen's Newbery Honor book *Hatchet.*

Ella Enchanted

On the day she was born, Ella received a gift from a fairy. However, Ella has never appreciated the gift because it is the gift of obedience. She has to do whatever anyone tells her to do. Gail Carson Levine's *Ella Enchanted,* a Newbery Medal winner, is a retelling of the Cinderella story. In this version, however, the heroine goes on a mission to change the way things are. Ella won't allow ogres, elves, or fairy godmothers to get in her way.

Ice Drift

When Alika and Sulu, two Inuit brothers, find themselves trapped on a floating island of ice in the Arctic, they must use all their knowledge and survival skills to stay alive. Alika, his little brother Sulu, and their dog Jamka must hunt for food, fend off polar bears, and endure the bitter subzero cold. *Ice Drift* by Theodore Taylor is a survival story that expertly weaves a gripping plot with a stark and deadly setting into a heart-pounding adventure.

Goodbye, Vietnam

One of the messages in the famous speech by Dr. Martin Luther King, Jr., is that freedom does not come easily for everyone; some people must face injustice and treachery before they can be free. You'll find a character determined to find freedom no matter how dire the situation in Gloria Whelan's *Goodbye, Vietnam.* Thirteen-year-old Mai and her family are forced to leave Vietnam for Hong Kong. The voyage is difficult, but they are determined to persevere so that they can eventually start a new life in the United States.

Nonfiction

Black Pioneers of Science and Invention

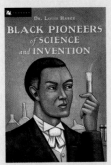

Many African Americans have made important contributions that have improved the lives of all Americans. Louis Haber tells the stories of fourteen such people in *Black Pioneers of Science and Invention*. Included are Benjamin Banneker, astronomer and surveyor; Granville T. Woods, inventor of many railroad improvements; George Washington Carver, chemist who discovered hundreds of uses for peanuts and other agricultural products; and more.

Samurai

Most people know that samurai were great warriors. Did you also know that in ancient Japan, samurai were the only people permitted to carry swords? In *Samurai*, Caroline Leavitt tells this warrior class's exciting story, spanning hundreds of years. Even though the age of the samurai came to an end when Japan opened its doors to the Western world, the spirit of these warriors has lasted into the present day. Beautiful illustrations complement this exciting work.

Farewell to Manzanar

In 1942, seven-year-old Jeanne Wakatsuki and her family were forced to leave their home and live in the Manzanar internment camp. Jeanne Wakatsuki Houston and James D. Houston's *Farewell to Manzanar* is the true story of a native-born American who grew up behind barbed wire in her own country during World War II.

Forensics

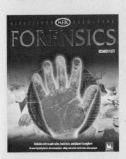

Forensics, or the science of crime investigation, is a popular topic on TV shows and movies. Read Richard Platt's overview of the subject to learn how forensics is really done. Topics such as ballistics, counterfeit money, DNA evidence, and identification of tsunami victims are explored and are illustrated with detailed color photos.

Learn It Online
Explore other novels and find tips for enjoying them at:

go.hrw.com   H8-175   Go

CHAPTER 2

Character

INFORMATIONAL TEXT FOCUS
Proposition and Support

 ## California Standards

Here are the Grade 8 standards you will work toward mastering in Chapter 2.

Word Analysis, Fluency, and Systematic Vocabulary Development
1.2 Understand the most important points in the history of English language and use common word origins to determine the historical influences on English word meanings.

Reading Comprehension (Focus on Informational Materials)
2.2 Analyze text that uses proposition and support patterns.

Literary Response and Analysis
3.3 Compare and contrast motivations and reactions of literary characters from different historical eras confronting similar situations or conflicts.

Writing Applications (Genres and Their Characteristics)
2.1 Write biographies, autobiographies, short stories, or narratives:
  a. Relate a clear, coherent incident, event, or situation by using well-chosen details.
  b. Reveal the significance of, or the writer's attitude about, the subject.
  c. Employ narrative and descriptive strategies (e.g., relevant dialogue, specific action, physical description, background description, comparison or contrast of characters).

"It is the ability to choose which makes us human."

—**Madeleine L'Engle**

What Do
You
Think

When do people stand up for what they believe in?

 Learn It Online
Take a different look at this chapter with *PowerNotes* online:

go.hrw.com | H8-177 | **Go**

Literary Skills Focus

by **Carol Jago**

How Do Characters Confront Conflict?

Most of us find other people fascinating. We are interested to see how others react to problems, disappointments, and temptations. Stories offer readers a window into worlds where all kinds of characters are in conflict. Without conflict, there is no story!

Motivation

We often wonder about people's **motivations**—the reasons that drive them to behave the way they do. In literature you often find clues to what makes people act as they do. You discover characters' motivations by observing what the characters say and the way they behave. Analyzing the motivations of characters confronting situations in a variety of works will help you recognize similarities and differences in the behavior of characters across the centuries. Analyzing motivation will also help you compare and contrast the ways in which literary characters react to conflicts.

Setting and Historical Context

The time and place in which the events in a text occur is called **setting.** Setting also includes the **customs** of the **era,** or long period of years, in which the text is set. When you consider the customs of an era in addition to time and place, you are looking at the historical context of the work.

Historical context refers to the social, political, economic, cultural, and intellectual beliefs popular during a particular time. For example, in this chapter, the poem "Barbara Frietchie" takes place within the historical context of the Civil War.

Characterization

Characters are the actors in a story. The way a writer creates characters is called **characterization.** There are two types. The simplest is **direct characterization.** When writers use this form of characterization, they tell you directly what a character is like. For example, in "Barbara Frietchie," John Greenleaf Whittier tells you exactly how brave Frietchie is.

> Bravest of all in Frederick town,
> She took up the flag the men hauled down
> from "Barbara Frietchie"
> by John Greenleaf Whittier

Most writers create a character using **indirect characterization.** They prefer to show their characters in situations and conflicts, allowing readers to decide for themselves what the character is like. They do this by letting you observe the character's actions, hear what the character says, and see how the character looks and dresses. In indirect characterization, the writer also tells you what the character is thinking and lets you observe how the character affects other people.

Following are five methods of indirect characterization:

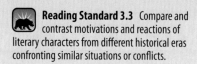

Reading Standard 3.3 Compare and contrast motivations and reactions of literary characters from different historical eras confronting similar situations or conflicts.

1. **Describing the appearance of a character** Frietchie is ninety years old.

> Up rose old Barbara Frietchie then,
> Bowed with her fourscore years and ten;
>
> from "Barbara Frietchie"
> by John Greenleaf Whittier

2. **Showing the character in action** Here Petry shows Harriet Tubman in action.

> Thus she forced them to go on. Sometimes she thought she had become nothing but a voice speaking in the darkness, cajoling, urging, threatening.
>
> from "Harriet Tubman: Conductor on the Underground Railroad" by Ann Petry

3. **Allowing you to hear the character speak** Here Tubman urges one in the group to continue the journey to Canada.

> She lifted the gun, aimed it at the despairing slave. She said, "Go on with us or die." The husky, low-pitched voice was grim.
>
> from "Harriet Tubman: Conductor on the Underground Railroad" by Ann Petry

4. **Revealing the character's thoughts and feelings** Here you learn Harriet Tubman's thoughts and fears.

> She knew moments of doubt, when she was half afraid and kept looking back over her shoulder, imagining that she heard the sound of pursuit.
>
> from "Harriet Tubman: Conductor on the Underground Railroad" by Ann Petry

5. **Showing how others react to the character**

> The people in the front of the crowd looked into my father's eyes and cried, "We will never forget you! We will see you again!"
>
> from "Passage to Freedom: The Sugihara Story" by Ken Mochizuki

Your Turn Analyze Characterization

Choose a character from a story you have read recently, and fill in a chart like the one below:

Character profile of_____

Method of Characterization	Story Details
Indirect Characterization	
Appearance	
Actions	
Words	
Thoughts	
Relationships with Others	
Direct Characterization	
What the Writer Says	

Learn It Online
Build your understanding using *PowerNotes* at:

go.hrw.com   H8-179   Go

Reading Skills Focus

by **Kylene Beers**

What Helps You Analyze Characters' Motivations?

Getting to know people is sometimes hard. You may wonder why they act the way they do, and it can take time to figure them out. The same is true for literary characters. When you want to analyze the motivations and reactions of literary characters, these strategies will help you make sense of why they do what they do.

Making Inferences

When you see your brother put a rain slicker into his school bag, what do you think is his motivation? If it looks cloudy outside, you may decide that he is going to protect himself from the rain. If it is a beautiful day, you may remember that he is going to wash cars after school to raise money for his scout troop. You make **inferences,** or educated guesses, based on your observations and your prior knowledge and experiences.

How to Make Inferences About Motivation

To make an inference about a character's motivations, combine the information the writer gives you with what you already know. As you read, keep these questions in mind.

- What does the writer tell you about how the character looks and acts? What do you know about people who look and act that way?
- What does the writer tell you about problems the character confronts? What do you know about similar situations?
- What does the writer tell you about the way people react to the character? What do such reactions usually tell you about a person?

Comparing and Contrasting

You can get to know the characters in a text better by considering the ways in which they are different from or similar to characters you have met in other texts. One exciting aspect of literature is that it can help you understand and appreciate the motivations and reactions of characters from eras other than the one in which you live today. As you read texts from different historical eras, compare the characters' motives and actions. How are their behaviors alike or different?

When you **compare** two characters, you look for ways in which they are alike. When you **contrast** them, you point out their differences. Organize your discoveries about the characters' similarities and differences in a Venn diagram like the one below. In the area where the circles overlap, list ways in which your characters are alike. In the outer parts of the circles, list qualities of the characters that are different.

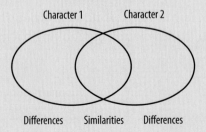

Character 1   Character 2

Differences   Similarities   Differences

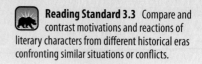

Reading Standard 3.3 Compare and contrast motivations and reactions of literary characters from different historical eras confronting similar situations or conflicts.

Making Connections

You have a wealth of knowledge to draw from because you have read stories, met people, and experienced or heard about world events. **Making connections** to what you know will enrich your understanding of the texts you read. You can read for deeper meaning by making three important types of connections to a text.

Text to Self Look for connections to your own life that help you put yourself in the story.

Text to Text Look for similarities between a new story and a familiar one.

Text to World Look for connections to similar situations or conflicts in your community and around the globe.

Connections Chart As you read about the characters in this chapter, use a chart like this one, based on "Passage to Freedom: The Sugihara Story," to connect to what you already know about similar situations.

Character:	Mr. Sugihara
Text to Self	I once protected someone who was being bullied, but I was scared I would become a target.
Text to Text	I know the story of Anne Frank, who faced a situation similar to that of the refugees Mr. Sugihara wants to help.
Text to World	I read about a man in Rwanda who saved many lives in spite of the threat to his own survival.

Your Turn Apply Reading Skills

Read the following passage from "The Circuit," by Francisco Jiménez, and then answer the questions below.

It was Monday, the first week of November. The grape season was over and I could now go to school. I woke up early that morning and lay in bed, looking at the stars and savoring the thought of not going to work and of starting sixth grade for the first time that year. Since I could not sleep, I decided to get up and join Papá and Roberto at breakfast. I sat at the table across from Roberto, but I kept my head down. I did not want to look up and face him. I knew he was sad. He was not going to school today. He was not going tomorrow, or next week, or next month. He would not go until the cotton season was over, and that was sometime in February. I rubbed my hands together and watched the dry, acid-stained skin fall to the floor in little rolls.

1. What can you infer about the narrator's feelings toward education?

2. Compare the situations of the narrator and his brother Roberto. How are they different? Why do you think they are different?

3. What connection to historical events or to other works of literature can you make?

> **Now go to the Skills in Action: Reading Model**

Learn It Online

For tips on applying reading strategies to longer works, visit:

go.hrw.com   H8-181   **Go**

Read with a Purpose Read to discover how a young girl confronts a difficult situation.

Build Background

This excerpt from an autobiography takes place in Sweden shortly after World War II. The narrator, a Polish Jewish girl, and her younger brother had been in Nazi concentration camps. There they both contracted tuberculosis, a serious lung disease. The children were rescued from the camps and taken to a sanitarium, an institution to which people are sent to recover from illness, in the Swedish countryside. The narrator has now recovered from her illness and is on her way to a shelter for Polish children in Stockholm, the capital of Sweden.

from
No Pretty Pictures: A Child of War

by **Anita Lobel**

It had been explained to me that I had recovered from my illness. I couldn't stay at a house for sick people anymore. When Herr[1] Nillson came to gather me up at the sanitarium, I had to accept that I was going with him alone. My brother was still sick. Lucky, I thought, to be allowed to stay for a little while longer at the sanitarium.

Herr Nillson was taking me to a shelter for Polish refugee kids. "You will like being with people from your own country again," he said. He must have sensed instantly that he had not reassured me. "It is a fine place," he said quietly. "You will see. And it is only temporary," he added. "Don't be frightened."

The trip to Stockholm had taken several hours. My recovery to good health was sending me into unwanted exile, but the journey did not feel like a deportation[2] or a flight. I loved sitting on a train with upholstered seats and watching the winter landscape rush by through the pristinely[3] polished window. In the January cold of Sweden there had been no possibility of sticking my head out an open window and letting the wind whip my face

Reading Focus

Making Inferences From Herr Nillson's soothing words to the narrator, you can infer his motivation for helping her. He is empathetic toward her and wants to improve her living situation.

Literary Focus

Characterization In this example of direct characterization, you learn from the narrator's words that she is not going to Stockholm willingly.

---

1. **Herr:** Swedish for "Mr."
2. **deportation:** forcible removal; banishment.
3. **pristinely:** here, to the point of perfect cleanliness.

Little Girl
by Felice Casorati.
©2010 Artists Rights Society
(ARS), New York/SIAE, Rome.

and hair. The hair that had grown to shoulder length and was as last braided into two thick, stubby braids. They were still too short. But there was no more concentration camp stubble to be ashamed of.

We came to a quiet street away from the tramways and neon lights. After a ride to the third floor in a small cage elevator, we stood in front of a door with a brass plaque with "A. Nillson" engraved on it. Herr Nillson rang the bell. The door was opened by a gaunt lady, in a prim white apron over a brown dress. Except that her gray hair was tightly wound into a bun and her head was not covered in a wimple, she made me think of a Benedictine nun. She curtsied to Herr Nillson. I curtsied to her. She took my little suitcase and my coat and scarf.

"If Miss Stina would be so kind," Herr Nillson said, "our young traveler will have some tea and sandwiches."

I was twelve years old that late January afternoon when I was ushered into A. Nillson's elegant apartment in Stockholm,

Literary Focus

Characterization The narrator uses indirect characterization to reveal Miss Stina's character. Miss Stina's appearance is stiff and proper.

Reading Focus

Making Connections The narrator and her experiences may remind you of other characters from history, movies, or books. Throughout history, many real and fictional characters have been forced to flee oppression.

Sweden. For seven years, in or out of danger, I had lived and slept in hovels[4] or public rooms with many other people. The convent. The concentration camp barracks. The sanitarium. Institutions. Since we had fled with Niania[5] away from Kraków,[6] I had not been in a private place where people had properly arranged tables and chairs and rugs and lamps. And servants.

"You may sit down," Herr Nillson smiled. In the beautiful sitting room I eased myself cautiously onto the edge of a wooden chair that stood by the door. There were pots with plants by the windows. There were lace curtains. Several paintings on twisted silk cords hung from moldings. There was a rug on the floor that made me think of the old kilim in my parents' apartment in Kraków. One whole wall was covered with books. I heard the sounds of piano music from somewhere in the building.

"No, sit here," Herr Nillson said, pointing to an elegant chair covered in a silky blue striped fabric.

I wished I had been a doll or a puppet. I wished someone would come and bend my arms and legs into the right angles so that I knew how to fit myself properly into the seat of the beautiful chair I had been asked to occupy. I had seen a movie one afternoon in the big hall in the sanitarium. It took place in France. The people moved and posed gracefully in splendid rooms. Ladies in gowns of silk sat on silk sofas and took little sips of tea out of pretty porcelain cups and delicate bites of little cakes. Gentlemen bowed and kissed the hands of the ladies.

Bunker beds, Stutthof concentration camp, Poland.

Reading Focus

Compare and Contrast The narrator in "The Circuit" also feels awkward when put in an unfamiliar situation—entering a new school. Unlike the narrator of this selection, though, he wishes he were somewhere else.

---

4. **hovels:** small, miserable dwellings; huts.
5. **Niania:** the children's nanny.
6. **Kraków:** city in Poland.

I knew my body was clean. There were no lice in my newly grown hair. Or in the seams of the skirt and blouse and sweater that had come out of a freshly donated bundle. When I carefully eased myself down onto the seat, I could feel my wool stockings pull around my thighs as the home-sewn garters with the buttons dug into my buttocks. I sat on Herr Nillson's silk chair, still fearing that shameful dirt would seep through. In my head there were echoes of the Nazis' shouts.

Herr Nillson sank easily into a large upholstered chair with curved arms.

Stina brought buttered bread and ham and tea on a tray. And cups and linen napkins. I took little bites of my sandwich and held my teacup as delicately as I could. I wanted to stay there with Herr Nillson forever.

Behind him I saw a half-opened door to a small room with a bed. Herr Nillson followed my gaze. "For tonight that is your room," he said. "Early tomorrow we will continue our journey." We both sipped from our teacups.

Herr Nillson told me about the work he did with refugees who had come to Sweden after the war. And about the interesting times I could expect at the Polish shelter and beyond. When it was time to go to bed, Herr Nillson took down a book from his crowded bookshelf. "This is for you," he said. "You may keep this."

Safely tucked in my suitcase were some catechism magazines that had been given out during Sunday school lessons at the sanitarium. And my miniature copy of the New Testament with pages thin and delicate and filled with beautiful pictures of the Holy Family, the gift from Sister Svea. Now I would add another book to my belongings. I thanked Herr Nillson for the volume of Selma Lagerlöf stories. I thanked the stern-looking Stina for the food. Everyone said, "*God natt.*"

Spring (detail) by Edvard Munch.
©2010 The Munch Museum/The Munch-Ellingsen Group/Artists Rights Society (ARS), NY.

Literary Focus

Motivation In identifying what motivates Herr Nillson to give the narrator a book, you might infer that books are important to him and that he wants to share something special with the narrator.

I went into my private room and closed the door. Tomorrow I was going to a place that would have no barbed wire around it. There would be no Nazis with guns. There would be no shooting. But again I would be living in an institution. Under the large soft bolster with my head on a pillow edged with lace, I fell asleep reading a tale by Selma Lagerlöf.

Read with a Purpose   How does the narrator react to her situation? What motivates those reactions?

MEET THE WRITER

Anita Lobel
(1934–   )

Anita Kempler Lobel was born into a prosperous Jewish family in Kraków, Poland. The comfortable life she and her brother lived came to a sudden end when Nazi forces invaded the country, in September 1939. At that point, Lobel's devoutly Catholic nanny, who had been with the family since Lobel was born, attempted to save the children from Nazi persecution by passing them off as her own. The trio spent five years moving from town to town, evading the authorities until they were finally captured. Anita and her brother spent time in several concentration camps, but they were eventually freed by Allied forces and brought to Sweden.

While living in Sweden, Lobel discovered her love of books and theater. She was also encouraged to pursue her interest in art. After miraculously reuniting with her parents and immigrating with them to New York, she studied art. Today, she is a writer and book illustrator with numerous awards to her name. About her life, she has said:

"I have always trusted that what I have become is an accumulation of what I have learned."

Think About the Writer   How does Lobel convey her feelings about books in *No Pretty Pictures: A Child of War*?

Reading Standard 3.3 Compare and contrast motivations and reactions of literary characters from different historical eras confronting similar situations or conflicts.

Into Action: Connections Chart

Practice making connections to the characters in *No Pretty Pictures* by completing a chart like the one below.

Character	
Text to Self	
Text to Text	
Text to World	

Talk About . . .

1. Discuss Anita Lobel's <u>reaction</u> to her situation. What factors from her past affect her <u>responses</u> to her new surroundings? Try to use each Academic Vocabulary word listed at the right in your response at least once.

Write About . . .

2. What can you tell about Herr Nillson's <u>motivation</u> for working with refugees from the way he interacts with the narrator?

3. Think about the narrator's <u>reaction</u> to the gift Herr Nillson gives her. How might this gift have helped her deal with her difficult situation?

Writing Skills Focus
Think as a Reader/Writer

In Chapter 2, you will read several stories with interesting characters. The Writing Skills Focus activities on the Preparing to Read pages will help you focus on the ways an author can reveal a character's personality. On the Applying Your Skills pages, you will have an opportunity to try out an author's techniques for yourself.

Academic Vocabulary for Chapter 2

Talking and Writing About Stories

Academic Vocabulary is the language you use to write and talk about literature. Use these words to discuss the characters in this chapter. The words are underlined throughout the chapter.

factor (FAK tuhr) *n.:* something that has an influence on something else. *Factors to consider when analyzing a character are his or her appearance, actions, and relationships.*

motivation (moh tuh VAY shuhn) *n.:* reasons behind a person's action or actions. *What is Herr Nillson's motivation for helping the refugee children?*

reaction (ree AK shuhn) *n.:* action in response to an influence or force. *Anita's reaction to leaving the sanitarium is both positive and negative.*

response (rih SPAHNS) *n.:* reply or reaction. *To learn more about a character, observe his or her response to a stressful event.*

Your Turn

Copy these Academic Vocabulary words into your *Reader/Writer Notebook,* and try to use them as you answer questions about the stories in the chapter.

Barbara Frietchie

by **John Greenleaf Whittier**

What Do **You Think?** How do people defend their beliefs?

QuickTalk

In a small group, discuss ways that people stand up for what they believe is right or just. Why are such people often regarded as heroes?

Reader/Writer Notebook

Use your **RWN** to complete the activities for this selection.

Literary Skills Focus

A Character's Character *How a person reacts to a challenge can be considered a test of character.* In that sentence, the word *character* means "a person's essential quality or personality." A person's character can be described as kind, self-centered, outgoing, honest, brave, selfish, and so on. The word *character* can also mean "a person in a story, play, or poem." In the following poem, the *character* Barbara Frietchie reveals her strength of *character* when she decides to stand up for her beliefs. In this chapter you will meet several characters from different historical eras who face similar challenges and tests of character.

Reading Skills Focus

Making Inferences Most of what you know about people—that a boy is shy or that a teacher is kind—is based on **inference,** an educated guess you make about someone or something. For example, you observe what people say or do and then infer what they are like. When you analyze a character, you make inferences based on your own experience and evidence from the text.

Into Action In an organizer such as the one below, make inferences about the character of Barbara Frietchie. As you read, write down details about her and details from your own experience. Add boxes as you need them. Then, below the chart, write at least one inference about Frietchie.

Facts about Barbara Frietchie	My knowledge/experience
Barbara Frietchie is 90 years old.	Most people didn't live that long in the 1860s.
Rebel soldiers are marching through her town.	

Inference:

Vocabulary

staff (staf) *n.:* pole. *Frietchie hung the flag from a staff outside her window.*

tread (trehd) *n.:* footstep. *The tread of the soldiers was echoed throughout the town.*

stirred (sturd) *v.:* affected deeply. *One woman's actions stirred the general's emotions.*

host (hohst) *n.:* army; large number. *The rebel host flooded the streets.*

Language Coach

Word Study Many words in English have more than one meaning. In fact, each of the vocabulary words above has more than one meaning. For example, *staff* can mean "group of employees." What other meanings do you know for *tread, stirred,* and *host*? Use a dictionary to help you.

Writing Skills Focus

Think as a Reader/Writer

Find It in Your Reading As you read, notice how Whittier conveys the drama and danger of the situation. Record in your *Reader/Writer Notebook* words and phrases that highlight the confrontation between Frietchie and the general.

 Learn It Online
Hear a professional actor read this poem. Visit the selection online at:

go.hrw.com   H8-189   **Go**

Learn It Online
Get more on the author's life at:
go.hrw.com H8-190 Go

John Greenleaf Whittier

(1807–1892)

"Barbara Frietchie Was No Myth"

John Greenleaf Whittier was born and raised on a farm in Haverhill, Massachusetts, where his Quaker family had lived since 1688. Whittier devoted most of his life to the antislavery movement. His poems reflect his dedication to freedom and justice and his deep religious faith. He was one of the hugely popular Fireside Poets, whose works sold the way best-selling novels do today. About "Barbara Frietchie," Whittier wrote:

> "This poem was written in strict conformity to the account of the incident as I had it from respectable and trustworthy sources. It has since been the subject of a good deal of conflicting testimony, and the story was probably incorrect in some of its details. It is admitted by all that Barbara Frietchie was no myth, but a worthy and highly esteemed gentlewoman, intensely loyal and a hater of the slavery rebellion, holding her Union flag sacred and keeping it with her Bible; that when the Confederates halted before her house and entered her dooryard, she denounced them in vigorous language, shook her cane in their faces, and drove them out; and when General Burnside's [a Union general] troops followed close upon Jackson's, she waved her flag and cheered them."

Build Background

This poem is set during the Civil War. In 1862, after defeating Union forces at the Second Battle of Bull Run, Confederate troops moved north into Maryland. Led by Generals Robert E. Lee and "Stonewall" Jackson, the troops marched into the town of Frederick. Lee and his men were expecting a warm welcome, but the people of Frederick were loyal to the Union. Whittier based "Barbara Frietchie" on these events.

Preview the Selection

In "Barbara Frietchie," you will meet a ninety-year-old woman named **Barbara Frietchie,** who bravely challenged a powerful general in order to uphold her beliefs.

Think About the Writer What personal values do you think led Whittier to write this poem?

Barbara Frietchie

by **John Greenleaf Whittier**

Up from the meadows rich with corn,
Clear in the cool September morn,

The clustered spires of Frederick stand
Green-walled by the hills of Maryland.

5 Round about them orchards sweep,
Apple and peach tree fruited deep,

Fair as the garden of the Lord
To the eyes of the famished rebel horde,°

On that pleasant morn of the early fall
10 When Lee marched over the mountain wall;

Over the mountains winding down,
Horse and foot, into Frederick town. **A**

Forty flags with their silver stars,
Forty flags with their crimson bars,
15 Flapped in the morning wind: the sun
Of noon looked down, and saw not one.

---

8. horde: crowd.

A Read and Discuss What have you learned about the time and place of this poem?

Up rose old Barbara Frietchie then,
Bowed with her fourscore years and ten;

Bravest of all in Frederick town,
20   She took up the flag the men hauled down

In her attic window the staff she set,
To show that one heart was loyal yet.   **B**

Up the street came the rebel tread,
Stonewall Jackson riding ahead.

25   Under his slouched hat left and right
He glanced; the old flag met his sight.

"Halt!"—the dust-brown ranks stood fast.
"Fire!"—out blazed the rifle blast.

It shivered the window, pane and sash;
30   It rent° the banner with seam and gash.

30. **rent:** tore; split.

Quick, as it fell, from the broken staff
Dame Barbara snatched the silken scarf.

She leaned far out on the windowsill,
And shook it forth with a royal will.

35   "Shoot, if you must, this old gray head,
But spare your country's flag," she said.   **C**
A shade of sadness, a blush of shame,
Over the face of the leader came;

B **Literary Focus** **Character** How does the speaker describe Barbara Frietchie here? Why does he call her "the bravest of all"?

C **Read and Discuss** What has happened?

Vocabulary   **staff** (staf) *n.:* pole.
tread (trehd) *n.:* footstep.

The nobler nature within him stirred
40 To life at that woman's deed and word;

"Who touches a hair of yon gray head
Dies like a dog! March on!" he said. **D**

All day long through Frederick street
Sounded the tread of marching feet:

45 All day long that free flag tossed
Over the heads of the rebel host.

Ever its torn folds rose and fell
On the loyal winds that loved it well;

And through the hill gaps sunset light
50 Shone over it with a warm good night.

Barbara Frietchie's work is o'er,
And the Rebel rides on his raids no more.

Honor to her! and let a tear
Fall, for her sake, on Stonewall's bier.°

55 Over Barbara Frietchie's grave,
Flag of Freedom and Union, wave!

Peace and order and beauty draw
Round thy symbol of light and law;

And ever the stars above look down
60 On thy stars below in Frederick town! **E**

Barbara Frietchie (1876) (detail) by
Dennis Malone Carter (1827–1881). Oil
on canvas (36 1/4" X 46 1/4").

Kirby Collection of Historical Paintings, Lafayette
College, Easton, Pennsylvania. Photo by Thomas
Kosa.

54. bier (bihr): coffin and the
platform on which it rests.
Stonewall Jackson died in 1863
after being wounded in battle.

D **Reading Focus** **Making Inferences** What inferences about Stonewall
Jackson's character can you make, based on his words here?

E **Read and Discuss** Now what do you know?

Vocabulary **stirred** (sturd) *v.*: affected deeply.
host (hohst) *n.*: army; large number.

Applying Your Skills

Reading Standard 3.3 Compare and contrast motivations and reactions of literary characters from different historical eras confronting similar situations or conflicts.

Barbara Frietchie

Literary Response and Analysis

Reading Skills Focus
Reading Check

1. **Paraphrase,** or restate in your own words, what happens in lines 25 to 42, which relate the most important actions in the poem.

2. In lines 55 and 56, the speaker addresses the flag. What does the speaker ask it to do?

Read with a Purpose

3. What deeds make Barbara Frietchie a memorable character?

Reading Skills: Making Inferences

4. In lines 15 and 16, something important happens, but you have to **infer** what it is. The speaker expects you to know, based on what he says next. What has happened by noontime in Frederick? Write your inference in a chart like the one below.

	My Inference
"Barbara Frietchie" lines 15–16	

Literary Skills Focus
Literary Analysis

5. **Identify** When writers use **allusions,** they refer to events, characters, or places in literature, history, or current events, and they expect you to understand what they are alluding to. What is the speaker alluding to in line 7, when he says the orchards of Maryland are as "fair as the garden of the Lord"?

6. **Connect** Whittier's comment in Meet the Writer suggests that the incident described in this poem might not have occurred exactly the way he tells it. How does that comment affect your response to the poem?

7. **Extend** Suppose Whittier were alive today. Who might make a good subject for his next poem? What situation or conflict would this character confront?

Literary Skills: Character

8. **Interpret** One definition of a hero is a person who does the right thing even though he or she has to act alone. Could this definition apply to Barbara Frietchie? to Stonewall Jackson? Consider the words and actions of these people in your responses.

Literary Skills Review: Plot

9. Review your paraphrase of the events that occur in lines 25 to 42. How is the conflict between Frietchie and Jackson resolved?

Writing Skills Focus
Think as a Reader/Writer

Use It in Your Writing Think about the person you cited in your response to question 7. Write a brief description of that person's situation or conflict. Use words and phrases that convey the drama of the moment.

 What Do You Think Now

Explain whether Barbara Frietchie's way of defending her beliefs was effective.

Applying Your Skills

Reading Standard 1.2 Understand the most important points in the history of English language and use common word origins to determine the historical influences on English word meanings.

Barbara Frietchie

Vocabulary Development

History of the English Language: Finding Our Roots

The written record of English dates back about fourteen hundred years, but the ancestry of English goes back much farther. Long ago, people living near the Caspian Sea (between what is now Asia and the Middle East) spoke a language we call Proto-Indo-European. (*Proto*– means "original or earliest." *Indo*– refers to India.)

These people were fighters, farmers, and herders, and they had an urge to travel. Eventually they took to their great four-wheeled carts and spread east through what are now Iran and India and west through Turkey and most of Europe.

As groups settled in different areas, their language changed into the languages we now call Persian, Hindi, Armenian, Sanskrit, Greek, Russian, Polish, Irish, Italian, French, Spanish, German, Dutch, Swedish, Norwegian—and English. All these languages share ancient roots and are called Indo-European.

Your Turn

Look up *staff* and *tread* in a dictionary to discover their **Indo-European (IE) roots.** Then, with a small group of classmates, try to figure out how each word's different meanings might have derived from its one root.

Language Coach

Multiple Meaning Words To practice using the multiple meanings of the Vocabulary words, fill in the blanks in the paragraph below with the appropriate word. Then, write sentences of your own, using another meaning of each word.

| staff |
| tread |
| stirred |
| host |

At daybreak the enemy ____, which was camped on the plain, ____ into action. The ____ of their massive formation could be heard for miles around as they marched to battle. On the hilltop the lieutenant proudly planted the ____ holding the company flag.

Academic Vocabulary

Talk About . . .
With a small group, discuss the <u>motivation</u> behind Barbara Frietchie's <u>response</u> to the rebel troops. What was she risking by speaking out about her beliefs?

Learn It Online
For action-packed vocabulary lessons, visit:

go.hrw.com H8-195 **Go**

Preparing to Read

from *Harriet Tubman*

CONDUCTOR ON THE UNDERGROUND RAILROAD

by **Ann Petry**

What Do **You Think** How much should a person sacrifice for freedom?

QuickTalk

How important is a person's individual freedom to a healthy society? Discuss with a partner how individual freedom shapes American society.

Harriet Tubman (c. 1945) by William H. Johnson. Oil on paperboard, sheet. 29 3/8" x 23 3/8" (73.5 cm x 59.3 cm).

Reader/Writer Notebook

Use your **RWN** to complete the activities for this selection.

Reading Standard 3.3 Compare and contrast motivations and reactions of literary characters from different historical eras confronting similar situations or conflicts.

Literary Skills Focus

Characters in a Biography When you read a **biography**—the story of someone's life written by another person—you get to know the real people in the story. You observe their **actions**—what they say and do. You think about their **motivations**—the reasons for their actions. You learn something about their values. You watch the way they interact with other people. You compare these characters with the people you know (or with other people you have read about). Soon you feel you know them.

Literary Perspectives Apply the literary perspective described on page 199 as you read this selection.

Reading Skills Focus

Making Connections Making personal connections to texts helps you read for deeper meaning. As you read, you can make connections between the text and yourself, another text, and the world.

Into Action Make connections as you read. The first row gives you an example. What other connections can you make to Harriet Tubman?

I can connect	to myself	to other texts	to situations in the world
Harriet Tubman		I read an article about Thomas Garrett and his work on the Underground Railroad.	
The conflict			
The resolution			

Writing Skills Focus

Think as a Reader/Writer

Find It in Your Reading Tubman and the fugitives from Maryland endure hardships along their journey to Canada. Record the words Petry uses to describe these hardships in your *Reader/Writer Notebook*.

Language Coach

Pronunciation English letters can often be pronounced in different ways. Sometimes the pronunciation of the letter *c* is soft (with an /s/ sound), and sometimes it is hard (with a /k/ sound). Practice saying aloud the words above that contain the letter *c* to hear the difference.

Learn It Online

Get a sneak peak at this story with the video introduction at:

go.hrw.com H8-197   **Go**

Learn It Online
Get more on the author's life at:
go.hrw.com H8-198 Go

Ann Petry
(1908–1997)

"A Message in the Story"

A native of Old Saybrook, Connecticut, Ann Petry was the granddaughter of a man who escaped from slavery on a Virginia plantation and went north by way of the Underground Railroad. She earned a Ph.D. in 1931 and worked as a pharmacist in her family's drugstore before moving to New York, where she became a writer of books for young people and adults. About her writing she said:

"My writing has, of course, been influenced by the books I've read but it has been much more influenced by the circumstances of my birth and my growing up, by my family. . . .

"We always had relatives visiting us. They added excitement to our lives. They brought with them the aura and the customs of a very different world. They were all storytellers, spinners of yarns. So were my mother and my father.

"Some of these stories had been handed down from one generation to the next, improved, embellished, embroidered. Usually there was a message in the story, a message for the young, a message that would help a young black child survive, help convince a young black child that black is truly beautiful."

Think About the Writer Petry grew up listening to stories. How might this have shaped the way she wrote?

Build Background

In the biblical Book of Exodus, Moses is chosen by God to lead the people of Israel out of slavery in Egypt. Moses takes his people on a long, perilous desert journey and leads them to the Promised Land. As you read this biography, look for reasons why Harriet Tubman was called the Moses of her people.

Preview the Selection

This excerpt from a biography relates how **Harriet Tubman** led a group of eleven people out of slavery in 1851. The fugitives traveled by night and slept by day, always on the alert and with the risk of capture constantly on their minds.

from

Harriet Tubman

CONDUCTOR ON THE UNDERGROUND RAILROAD

by **Ann Petry**

THE RAILROAD RUNS TO CANADA

Along the Eastern Shore of Maryland, in Dorchester County, in Caroline County, the masters kept hearing whispers about the man named Moses, who was running off slaves. At first they did not believe in his existence. The stories about him were fantastic, unbelievable. Yet they watched for him. They offered rewards for his capture.

They never saw him. Now and then they heard whispered rumors to the effect that he was in the neighborhood. The woods were searched. The roads were watched. There was never anything to indicate his whereabouts. But a few days afterward, a goodly number of slaves would be gone from the plantation. Neither the master nor the overseer had heard or seen anything unusual in the quarter.[1] Sometimes one or the other would vaguely remember having heard a whippoorwill call somewhere in the woods, close by, late at night. Though it was the wrong season for whippoorwills.

Sometimes the masters thought they had heard the cry of a hoot owl, repeated, and would remember having thought that the intervals between the low moaning cry were wrong, that it had been repeated four times in succession instead of three. There was never anything more than that to suggest

---

1. **quarter:** area in a plantation where enslaved blacks lived. It consisted of windowless, one-room cabins made of logs and mud.

Literary Perspectives

Use this perspective to understand characters in context.

Analyzing Historical Context When applying this perspective, you view a literary text within its historical context. Specifically, you notice historical information about the time in which the author wrote, about the time in which the text is set, and about the ways in which people of the period saw and thought about the world in which they lived. History, in this biography, refers to the social, political, economic, and cultural climate of the American South in the time period before the Civil War, when many African Americans were enslaved. As you read, use the questions in the text to guide you in using this perspective.

that all was not well in the quarter. Yet, when morning came, they invariably discovered that a group of the finest slaves had taken to their heels.  Ⓐ

Unfortunately, the discovery was almost always made on a Sunday. Thus a whole day was lost before the machinery of pursuit could be set in motion. The posters offering rewards for the fugitives could not be printed until Monday. The men who made a living hunting for runaway slaves were out of reach, off in the woods with their dogs and their guns, in pursuit of four-footed game, or they were in camp meetings saying their prayers with their wives and families beside them.

Harriet Tubman could have told them that there was far more involved in this matter of running off slaves than signaling the would-be runaways by imitating the call of a whippoorwill, or a hoot owl, far more involved than a matter of waiting for a clear night when the North Star was visible. Ⓑ

In December 1851, when she started out with the band of fugitives that she planned to take to Canada, she had been in the vicinity of the plantation for days, planning the trip, carefully selecting the slaves that she would take with her.

She had announced her arrival in the quarter by singing the forbidden spiritual[2]— "Go down, Moses, 'way down to Egypt Land"—singing it softly outside the door of a slave cabin, late at night. The husky voice was beautiful even when it was barely more than a murmur borne on the wind.

Once she had made her presence known, word of her coming spread from cabin to cabin. The slaves whispered to each other, ear to mouth, mouth to ear, "Moses is here." "Moses has come." "Get ready. Moses is back again." The ones who had agreed to go North with her put ashcake[3] and salt herring in an old bandanna, hastily tied it into a bundle, and then waited patiently for the signal that meant it was time to start.

There were eleven in this party, including one of her brothers and his wife. It was the largest group that she had ever conducted,

---

2. **forbidden spiritual:** Spirituals are religious songs, some of which are based on the biblical story of the Israelites' escape from slavery in Egypt. Plantation owners feared that the singing of certain spirituals might lead to rebellion.

3. **ashcake:** cornmeal bread baked in hot ashes.

Ⓐ **Read and Discuss** How has the author caught your interest?

Ⓑ **Literary Perspectives** **Historical Context** What historical information about this time period have you learned?

Vocabulary **fugitives** (FYOO juh tihvz) *n.:* people fleeing from danger or oppression.

but she was determined that more and more slaves should know what freedom was like.

She had to take them all the way to Canada. The Fugitive Slave Law[4] was no longer a great many incomprehensible words written down on the country's law books. The new law had become a reality. It was Thomas Sims, a boy, picked up on the streets of Boston at night and shipped back to Georgia. It was Jerry and Shadrach, arrested and jailed with no warning.   **C**

She had never been in Canada. The route beyond Philadelphia was strange to her. But she could not let the runaways who accompanied her know this. As they walked along, she told them stories of her own first flight; she kept painting vivid word pictures of what it would be like to be free.

But there were so many of them this time. She knew moments of doubt, when she was half afraid and kept looking back over her shoulder, imagining that she heard the sound of pursuit. They would certainly be pursued. Eleven of them. Eleven thousand dollars' worth of flesh and

Harriet Tubman (c. 1860s).

4. **Fugitive Slave Law:** harsh federal law passed in 1850 stating that fugitives who escaped from slavery to free states could be forced to return to their owners. As a result, those who escaped were safe only in Canada. The law also made it a crime for a free person to help fugitives or to prevent their return.

C **Literary Perspectives** **Historical Context** What do the names of captured fugitives add to your understanding of the Fugitive Slave Law?

Vocabulary **incomprehensible** (ihn kahm prih HEHN suh buhl) *adj.*: impossible to understand.

bone and muscle that belonged to Maryland planters. If they were caught, the eleven runaways would be whipped and sold South, but she—she would probably be hanged. **(D)**

They tried to sleep during the day but they never could wholly relax into sleep. She could tell by the positions they assumed, by their restless movements. And they walked at night. Their progress was slow. It took them three nights of walking to reach the first stop. She had told them about the place where they would stay, promising warmth and good food, holding these things out to them as an incentive to keep going.

When she knocked on the door of a farmhouse, a place where she and her parties of runaways had always been welcome, always been given shelter and plenty to eat, there was no answer. She knocked again, softly. A voice from within said, "Who is it?" There was fear in the voice.

She knew instantly from the sound of the voice that there was something wrong. She said, "A friend with friends," the password on the Underground Railroad.

The door opened, slowly. The man who stood in the doorway looked at her coldly, looked with unconcealed astonishment and fear at the eleven disheveled runaways who were standing near her. Then he shouted, "Too many, too many. It's not safe. My place was searched last week. It's not safe!" and slammed the door in her face.

She turned away from the house, frowning. She had promised her passengers food and rest and warmth, and instead of that, there would be hunger and cold and more walking over the frozen ground. Somehow she would have to instill courage into these eleven people, most of them strangers, would have to feed them on hope and bright dreams of freedom instead of the fried pork and corn bread and milk she had promised them. **(E)**

They stumbled along behind her, half dead for sleep, and she urged them on, though she was as tired and as discouraged as they were. She had never been in Canada, but she kept painting wondrous word pictures of what it would be like. She managed to dispel their fear of pursuit so that they would not become hysterical, panic-stricken. Then she had to bring some of the fear back, so that they would stay awake and keep walking though they drooped with sleep.

Yet, during the day, when they lay down deep in a thicket, they never really slept, because if a twig snapped or the wind sighed in the branches of a pine tree, they jumped to their feet, afraid of their own shadows, shivering and shaking. It was very cold, but they dared not make fires because someone would see the smoke and wonder about it.

She kept thinking, eleven of them. Eleven thousand dollars' worth of slaves. And she had to take them all the way to Canada.

(D) Reading Focus Making Connections What have you learned in social studies classes about the institution of slavery?

(E) Read and Discuss What has happened to Harriet Tubman and her group?

Vocabulary **incentive** (ihn SEHN tihv) *n.:* reason to do something; motivation.
dispel (dihs PEHL) *v.:* get rid of by driving away.

Sometimes she told them about Thomas Garrett, in Wilmington.[5] She said he was their friend even though he did not know them. He was the friend of all fugitives. He called them God's poor. He was a Quaker[6] and his speech was a little different from that of other people. His clothing was different, too. He wore the wide-brimmed hat that the Quakers wear.

She said that he had thick white hair, soft, almost like a baby's, and the kindest eyes she had ever seen. He was a big man and strong, but he had never used his strength to harm anyone, always to help people. He would give all of them a new pair of shoes. Everybody. He always did. Once they reached his house in Wilmington, they would be safe. He would see to it that they were.

She described the house where he lived, told them about the store where he sold shoes. She said he kept a pail of milk and a loaf of bread in the drawer of his desk so that he would have food ready at hand for any of God's poor who should suddenly appear before him, fainting with hunger. There was a hidden room in the store. A whole wall swung open, and behind it was a room where he could hide

---

5. **Wilmington:** city in Delaware.
6. **Quaker:** member of the Society of Friends, a religious group active in the movement to end slavery.

Harriet Tubman (left) with a group she helped escape from slavery.

fugitives. On the wall there were shelves filled with small boxes—boxes of shoes—so that you would never guess that the wall actually opened.

While she talked, she kept watching them. They did not believe her. She could tell by their expressions. They were thinking. New shoes, Thomas Garrett, Quaker, Wilmington—what foolishness was this? Who knew if she told the truth? Where was she taking them anyway? **F**

That night they reached the next stop—a farm that belonged to a German. She made the runaways take shelter behind trees at the edge of the fields before she knocked at the door. She hesitated before she approached the door, thinking, suppose that he too should refuse shelter, suppose—Then she thought, *Lord, I'm going to hold steady on to You and You've got to see me through*—and knocked softly.

She heard the familiar guttural voice say, "Who's there?"

She answered quickly, "A friend with friends."

He opened the door and greeted her warmly. "How many this time?" he asked.

"Eleven," she said and waited, doubting, wondering.

He said, "Good. Bring them in."

He and his wife fed them in the lamp-lit kitchen, their faces glowing as they offered food and more food, urging them to eat, saying there was plenty for everybody, have more milk, have more bread, have more meat.

They spent the night in the warm kitchen. They really slept, all that night and until dusk the next day. When they left, it was with reluctance. They had all been warm and safe and well-fed. It was hard to exchange the security offered by that clean, warm kitchen for the darkness and the cold of a December night. **G**

"Go On or Die"

Harriet had found it hard to leave the warmth and friendliness, too. But she urged them on. For a while, as they walked, they seemed to carry in them a measure of contentment; some of the serenity and the cleanliness of that big, warm kitchen lingered on inside them. But as they walked farther and farther away from the warmth and the light, the cold and the darkness entered into them. They fell silent, sullen, suspicious. She waited for the moment when some one of them would turn mutinous. It did not happen that night.

Two nights later, she was aware that the feet behind her were moving slower and slower. She heard the irritability in their voices, knew that soon someone would refuse to go on.

She started talking about William Still and the Philadelphia Vigilance Committee.[7] No one commented. No one asked any questions. She told them the story of William

---

7. **Philadelphia Vigilance Committee:** group that offered help to people escaping slavery. William Still, a free African American, was chairman of the committee.

F Read and Discuss How does Harriet keep her group going even when they are exhausted and afraid?

G Reading Focus Making Connections What characters in other texts have put themselves in danger to help others or to achieve an ideal? What was their <u>motivation</u>?

and Ellen Craft and how they escaped from Georgia. Ellen was so fair that she looked as though she were white, and so she dressed up in a man's clothing and she looked like a wealthy young planter. Her husband, William, who was dark, played the role of her slave. Thus they traveled from Macon, Georgia, to Philadelphia, riding on the trains, staying at the finest hotels. Ellen pretended to be very ill—her right arm was in a sling and her right hand was bandaged because she was supposed to have rheumatism.[8] Thus she avoided having to sign the register at the hotels, for she could not read or write. They finally arrived safely in Philadelphia and then went on to Boston.

No one said anything. Not one of them seemed to have heard her.

She told them about Frederick Douglass, the most famous of the escaped slaves, of his eloquence, of his magnificent appearance. Then she told them of her own first, vain effort at running away, evoking the memory of that miserable life she had led as a child, reliving it for a moment in the telling.

But they had been tired too long, hungry too long, afraid too long, footsore too long. One of them suddenly cried out in despair,

Analyzing Visuals **Connecting to the Text** What details in this picture of Ellen Craft hide her real identity?

"Let me go back. It is better to be a slave than to suffer like this in order to be free." **H**

She carried a gun with her on these trips. She had never used it—except as a threat. Now, as she aimed it, she experienced a feeling of guilt, remembering that time, years ago, when she had prayed for the death of Edward Brodas, the Master, and then, not too long afterward, had heard that

---

8. **rheumatism** (ROO muh tihz uhm): painful swelling and stiffness of the joints or muscles.

H **Literary Focus** **Characters in Biography** What is Tubman's motivation to continue to tell stories to the runaways? What response does one of the runaways make to her?

Vocabulary **eloquence** (EHL uh kwehns) *n.:* ability to write or speak gracefully.

Group going to the fields at James Hopkinson's plantation, c. 1862. Photographer: Henry P. Moore.

great wailing cry that came from the throats of the field hands, and knew from the sound that the Master was dead.

One of the runaways said again, "Let me go back. Let me go back," and stood still, and then turned around and said, over his shoulder, "I am going back."

She lifted the gun, aimed it at the despairing slave. She said, "Go on with us or die." The husky, low-pitched voice was grim.   ❶

He hesitated for a moment and then he joined the others. They started walking again. She tried to explain to them why none of them could go back to the plantation. If a runaway returned, he would turn traitor; the master and the overseer would force him to turn traitor. The returned slave would disclose the stopping places, the hiding places, the corn stacks they had used with the full knowledge of the owner of the farm, the name of the German farmer who had fed them and sheltered them. These people who had risked their own security to help runaways would be ruined, fined, imprisoned.

She said, "We got to go free or die. And freedom's not bought with dust."

---

❶ **Read and Discuss** What is happening between Harriet Tubman and the fugitives?

This time she told them about the long agony of the Middle Passage[9] on the old slave ships, about the black horror of the holds, about the chains and the whips. They too knew these stories. But she wanted to remind them of the long, hard way they had come, about the long, hard way they had yet to go. She told them about Thomas Sims, the boy picked up on the streets of Boston and sent back to Georgia. She said when they got him back to Savannah, got him in prison there, they whipped him until a doctor who was standing by watching said, "You will kill him if you strike him again!" His master said, "Let him die!" **J**

Thus she forced them to go on. Sometimes she thought she had become nothing but a voice speaking in the darkness, cajoling, urging, threatening. Sometimes she told them things to make them laugh; sometimes she sang to them and heard the eleven voices behind her blending softly with hers, and then she knew that for the moment all was well with them.

She gave the impression of being a short, muscular, indomitable woman who could never be defeated. Yet at any moment she was liable to be seized by one of those curious fits of sleep,[10] which might last for a few minutes or for hours.

Even on this trip, she suddenly fell asleep in the woods. The runaways, ragged, dirty, hungry, cold, did not steal the gun as they might have and set off by themselves or turn back. They sat on the ground near her and waited patiently until she awakened. They had come to trust her implicitly, totally. They, too, had come to believe her repeated statement, "We got to go free or die." She was leading them into freedom, and so they waited until she was ready to go on. **K**

Finally, they reached Thomas Garrett's house in Wilmington, Delaware. Just as Harriet had promised, Garrett gave them all new shoes, and provided carriages to take them on to the next stop.

By slow stages they reached Philadelphia, where William Still hastily recorded their names, and the plantations whence they had come, and something of the life they had led in slavery. Then he carefully hid what he had written, for fear it might be discovered.

---

9. **Middle Passage:** route traveled by ships carrying captured Africans across the Atlantic Ocean to the Americas. The captives endured the horrors of the Middle Passage crammed into holds, airless cargo areas below deck.

10. **fits of sleep:** Harriet's losses of consciousness were caused by a serious head injury that she had suffered as a teenager. Harriet had tried to protect someone else from punishment, and an enraged overseer threw a two-pound weight at her head.

J **Literary Perspectives** Historical Context In what ways do Tubman's stories reveal the customs and attitudes of this historical era?

K **Read and Discuss** What does this new detail about the gun reveal?

In 1872 he published this record in book form and called it *The Underground Railroad.* In the foreword to his book he said: "While I knew the danger of keeping strict records, and while I did not then dream that in my day slavery would be blotted out, or that the time would come when I could publish these records, it used to afford me great satisfaction to take them down, fresh from the lips of fugitives on the way to freedom, and to preserve them as they had given them." **L**

William Still, who was familiar with all the station stops on the Underground Railroad, supplied Harriet with money and sent her and her eleven fugitives on to Burlington, New Jersey.

Harriet felt safer now, though there were danger spots ahead. But the biggest part of her job was over. As they went farther and farther north, it grew colder; she was aware of the wind on the Jersey ferry and aware of the cold damp in New York. From New York they went on to Syracuse,[11] where the temperature was even lower.

In Syracuse she met the Reverend J. W. Loguen, known as "Jarm" Loguen. This was the beginning of a lifelong friendship. Both

> "We got to go free or die."

Harriet and Jarm Loguen were to become friends and supporters of Old John Brown.[12]

From Syracuse they went north again, into a colder, snowier city—Rochester. Here they almost certainly stayed with Frederick Douglass, for he wrote in his autobiography:

"On one occasion I had eleven fugitives at the same time under my roof, and it was necessary for them to remain with me until I could collect sufficient money to get them to Canada. It was the largest number I ever had at any one time, and I had some difficulty in providing so many with food and shelter, but, as may well be imagined, they were not very fastidious in either direction, and were well content with very plain food, and a strip of carpet on the floor for a bed, or a place on the straw in the barn loft."

Late in December 1851, Harriet arrived in St. Catharines, Canada West (now Ontario), with the eleven fugitives. It had taken almost a month to complete this journey.

---

11. **Syracuse:** city in central New York State.

12. **John Brown** (1800–1859): abolitionist (opponent of slavery) who was active in the Underground Railroad. In 1859, Brown led a raid on the federal arsenal at Harpers Ferry, then in Virginia, in hopes of inspiring a slave uprising. Federal troops overpowered Brown and his followers, and Brown was convicted of treason and hanged.

L **Literary Perspectives** **Historical Context** Think of all the events that have taken place. Does the journey's one-month duration surprise you?

Applying Your Skills

Reading Standard 3.3 Compare and contrast motivations and reactions of literary characters from different historical eras confronting similar situations or conflicts.

from Harriet Tubman: Conductor on the Underground Railroad
Literary Response and Analysis

Reading Skills Focus
Quick Check

1. List at least three facts you learned about the Underground Railroad. List at least five facts you learned about Harriet Tubman.

Read with a Purpose

2. How did Harriet Tubman manage to get all eleven slaves safely to Canada?

Reading Skills: Making Connections

3. Review the chart you completed as you read the text. List your strongest connections on a chart like the one below, and explain the reasons for your choices.

Text to Self	
Text to Text	
Text to World	

Literary Skills Focus
Literary Analysis

4. **Interpret** How is Tubman like Moses in the Bible? What is *her* Promised Land?

5. **Analyze** Why might Tubman, who was already free, risk her life to free others?

6. **Compare and Contrast** One definition of a hero is a person who does the right thing even though he or she might have to act alone. How might this definition apply to Harriet Tubman and to Barbara Frietchie (page 191)? What similar motivation did the two women share even though they faced situations in different historical eras?

7. **Literary Perspectives** What did you learn about the era in which this biography takes place? How did the **historical context** help you better understand the characters?

Literary Skills: Characters in Biography

8. **Interpret** What inferences can you make about the characters of Tubman, Garrett, and Still? What is their motivation to join together as conductors on the Underground Railroad?

9. **Literary Perspectives** What aspects of life in the 1850s made the fugitives' journey easier than it would have been in modern times? What aspects made it more difficult?

Literary Skills Review: Setting

10. **Analyze** What physical aspects of the journey north contribute to the hardships endured by the runaways?

Writing Skills Focus
Think as a Reader/Writer

Use It in Your Writing Write an entry for an imaginary diary kept by one of the runaways. Choose an incident from the biography, and use descriptive language to communicate the difficulty of the situation.

What Do **You Think Now**

How has reading this biography influenced your thoughts on the value of freedom?

Applying Your Skills

Reading Standard 1.2 Understand the most important points in the history of the English language and use common word origins to determine the historical influences on English word meanings.

from Harriet Tubman: Conductor on the Underground Railroad

Vocabulary Development

Vocabulary Check

Answer the following questions. Vocabulary words are in boldface.

1. What are some reasons a person might become a **fugitive**?
2. Is it easy to understand something that is **incomprehensible**?
3. What **incentive** did Harriet Tubman have to lead the slaves to freedom?
4. How did Tubman **dispel** the fears of the fugitives?
5. How might Frederick Douglass's **eloquence** have inspired Tubman?

Greek Roots and Affixes

The ancient Greek language helped shape many languages, including English. The Greek alphabet is the source of many of the letters we use today, and our practice of reading from left to right came from the Greek language.

One way Greek words entered the English language was through the Christian Church. English words like *monk, church,* and *prophet* have Greek origins. Another way was through the revival of interest in classical Greek texts during the Renaissance, beginning in the 1300s. Here are some Greek roots and their English derivatives.

Greek Root	Meaning	English Word
–oct–	eight	octagon
–bio–	life	biography
–dem–	people	democracy

Classical Greek is also a source for many English **affixes**—word parts added to a root to alter its meaning. Here are some common Greek affixes and their meanings:

Greek Affix	Meaning	English Word
anti–	opposing	antiwar
–ician	specialist in	technician
hyper–	over; excessive	hyperactive

Your Turn

Knowing the meanings of roots and affixes can help you define new words. Use the roots and affixes from the charts to answer these questions:

1. How does a person who is *antisocial* feel about being around people?
2. If something is a *biohazard,* would you want to be near it? Why or why not?
3. How might a *hypercritical* person act?
4. When might you need an *electrician*?
5. How many tentacles does an *octopus* have?

Language Coach

Roots Sort the words on the right into groups according to their roots, and write them in a chart like the one below. See if you can think of more words that share these roots.

autobiography
octave
democracy
octet
biosphere
demographics
biochemistry
octogenarian

Greek Root		
–oct–	–bio–	–dem–

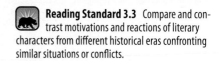

Reading Standard 3.3 Compare and contrast motivations and reactions of literary characters from different historical eras confronting similar situations or conflicts.

Grammar Link
Conjunctions

A **conjunction** is a word used to join words or groups of words. **Coordinating conjunctions,** such as those below, join words or groups of words used in the same way:

> and   but   or   nor   for   so   yet

EXAMPLE The stories about Moses were dramatic **and** moving. (*And* joins two adjectives.)

Correlative conjunctions are *pairs* of conjunctions that join words or groups of words used in the same way.

> both…and   either…or   neither…nor
> not only…but also   whether…or

EXAMPLE The slaveholder offered **either** a reward for the fugitives' captors **or** punishment for their helpers. (*Either . . . or* joins two nouns.)

Your Turn

Writing Applications The sentences below contain coordinating conjunctions. Rewrite the sentences using the correlative conjunctions given.

1. **neither . . . nor** His captors did not see or hear him.
2. **not only . . . but also** Harriet Tubman would help enslaved people and risk her own freedom.
3. **both . . . and** There were family members included in the party, her brother and his wife.
4. **whether . . . or** At the first stop the fugitives were not given food or shelter.

CHOICES

As you respond to the Choices, use these **Academic Vocabulary** words as appropriate: <u>factor</u>, <u>motivation</u>, <u>reaction</u>, <u>response</u>.

REVIEW
Compare and Contrast Motivations

Group Discussion Barbara Frietchie and Harriet Tubman are characters from different historical eras. In two paragraphs, compare and contrast these two characters. Consider the following questions: What is each woman's <u>motivation</u> to take action? What situation does each address? What are the outcomes of their actions? What was people's <u>reaction</u> to them in the past? Why are they still celebrated today?

CONNECT
Retell a Biography

Timed ⌙Writing Write a retelling of the biography of Harriet Tubman. In the first paragraph, include the title of the work, the author's name, and a general observation about the work. In the second paragraph, retell the important events covered in the biography.

EXTEND
Map an Escape

Group Project The fugitives discussed in this biography had an advantage over many others fleeing slavery: They were escaping from the northernmost slave state, Maryland. Work with a group to find out which states allowed slavery in 1851. Then, choose a location in one of those states, and draw a map showing a possible route to freedom. Research the Underground Railroad to see if there were any stops along your route.

PASSAGE TO FREEDOM:
THE SUGIHARA STORY

by **Ken Mochizuki**

The Hall of Names in the Yad Vashem Holocaust Memorial in Jerusalem.

What Do You Think

When is it more important to help others than to protect yourself?

QuickWrite

What advice would you give someone who had to choose between what he or she was told to do and what he or she thought was right?

Reader/Writer Notebook

Use your **RWN** to complete the activities for this selection.

Literary Skills Focus

Motivation What makes people do the things they do? In literature as in life, a person's **motivation,** or reason for acting a certain way, is not always clear. To analyze motivation as you read, ask yourself, "What clues tell me why the character did that?" Does each character's motivation become clearer to you as the text continues?

Reading Skills Focus

Comparing and Contrasting Characters Throughout history, people have had to respond to difficult situations. These situations have differed, depending on the time and place in which the people lived as well as on the culture and beliefs common during the period.

Into Action Consider the characters of Harriet Tubman and Chiune Sugihara. Compare their reactions to the challenges they face. Use a chart like the one below to help you.

	Harriet Tubman	Chiune Sugihara
Historical era	1851	World War II
Situation		
Conflict		
Motivation		

Vocabulary

diplomat (DIHP luh mat) *n.:* official who represents a country abroad. *A Japanese diplomat, Mr. Sugihara represents his country in Lithuania.*

refugees (rehf yuh JEEZ) *n.:* people who seek refuge, or safety, especially in another country. *The refugees desperately need to get out of Lithuania.*

superiors (suh PIHR ee uhrz) *n.:* people of higher rank. *The diplomat had to ask permission from his superiors.*

fate (fayt) *n.:* what becomes of someone or something. *The fate of the refugees is unknown.*

> Mr. Sugihara **(diplomat)**
> ↓
> needs permission from **superiors**
> ↓
> his actions affect **refugees' fate**

Writing Skills Focus

Think as a Reader/Writer

Find It in Your Reading The writer begins the story with the saying "The eyes tell everything about a person" and then uses images of people's eyes throughout the story. As you come across these descriptions, list them in your *Reader/Writer Notebook.*

TechFocus As you read, make a list of keywords for an Internet search to find out more about refugees in the world today.

Language Coach

Latin Roots The Vocabulary word *superiors* means "people of higher rank." It is derived from the Latin word *superus,* which means "that is above." Record the following words in your *Reader/Writer Notebook.* Use your knowledge of Latin roots to determine their meanings: *supermarket, superhuman,* and *superscript.*

Learn It Online

Increase your vocabulary with Word Watch at:

go.hrw.com H8-213   **Go**

Ken Mochizuki
(1954–)

One Person Can Make a Difference

Ken Mochizuki says that he wrote "Passage to Freedom" because he wanted to show that one person can make a difference in the world: Chiune Sugihara, the real-life subject of this story, issued about 6,000 visas to refugees. The descendants of those refugees now number more than 40,000.

Telling the Story

"Passage to Freedom" was Mochizuki's first try at writing historical fiction for young people. First, he gathered all the facts. Then, he had to figure out how he could tell the story. He decided to tell the story in the first-person point of view of a five-year-old boy, as if he were that boy himself.

Eliminating Stereotypes

Mochizuki, who was born in Seattle, Washington, speaks at schools about writing books for young people. He tries to challenge stereotypes by pointing out that although he has Japanese ancestry, his first language is English, he doesn't wear glasses or practice any martial arts, and as a student he wasn't particularly good at math.

Build Background

"Passage to Freedom" is a work of historical fiction. The story is fictional because the writer is narrating the story as if he were the family's eldest son, Hiroki Sugihara. The writer also invented some details and dialogue. The story is historical because it is based on real events and people. In fact, the real Hiroki Sugihara has written an afterword, which follows the selection.

Preview the Selection

In this story the narrator's father, **Mr. Sugihara,** must choose between what his government tells him to do and what his conscience tells him to do.

Think About the Writer How has Mochizuki shown that one person can make a difference?

Read with a Purpose Read to discover the risks a Japanese diplomat takes in a time of war.

PASSAGE TO FREEDOM:
THE SUGIHARA STORY

by **Ken Mochizuki**

There is a saying that the eyes tell everything about a person.

At a store, my father saw a young Jewish boy who didn't have enough money to buy what he wanted. So my father gave the boy some of his. That boy looked into my father's eyes and, to thank him, invited my father to his home.

That is when my family and I went to a Hanukkah[1] celebration for the first time. I was five years old. **A**

In 1940, my father was a diplomat representing the country of Japan. Our family lived in a small town in the small country called Lithuania. There was my father and mother, my Auntie Setsuko, my younger brother Chiaki, and my three-month-old baby brother, Haruki. My father worked in his office downstairs.

---

1. **Hanukkah** (HAH nu kah): Jewish festival celebrated in December.

In the mornings, birds sang in the trees. We played with girls and boys from the neighborhood at a huge park near our home. Houses and churches around us were hundreds of years old. In our room, Chiaki and I played with toy German soldiers, tanks, and planes. Little did we know that the real soldiers were coming our way.

Then one early morning in late July, my life changed forever. **B**

My mother and Auntie Setsuko woke Chiaki and me up, telling us to get dressed quickly. My father ran upstairs from his office.

"There are a lot of people outside," my mother said. "We don't know what is going to happen."

In the living room, my parents told my brother and me not to let anybody see us looking through the window. So, I parted

A **Literary Focus** Motivation What does this incident suggest about Mr. Sugihara and how he treats people?

Vocabulary **diplomat** (DIHP luh mat) *n.:* official who represents a country abroad.

B **Read and Discuss** What does the author tell you about the narrator and his family? What is the purpose of the sentence, "Then one early morning in late July, my life changed forever"?

the curtains a tiny bit. Outside, I saw hundreds of people crowded around the gate in front of our house.

The grown-ups shouted in Polish, a language I did not understand. Then I saw the children. They stared at our house through the iron bars of the gate. Some of them were my age. Like the grown-ups, their eyes were red from not having slept for days. They wore heavy winter coats—some wore more than one coat, even though it was warm outside. These children looked as though they had dressed in a hurry. But if they came from somewhere else, where were their suitcases?

"What do they want?" I asked my mother.

"They have come to ask for your father's help," she replied. "Unless we help, they may be killed or taken away by some bad men."

Some of the children held on tightly to the hands of their fathers, some clung to their mothers. One little girl sat on the ground, crying.

I felt like crying, too. "Father," I said, "please help them." **C**

My father stood quietly next to me, but I knew he saw the children. Then some of the men in the crowd began climbing over the fence. Borislav and Gudje, two young men who worked for my father, tried to keep the crowd calm. **D**

My father walked outside. Peering through the curtains, I saw him standing on the steps. Borislav translated what my father said: He asked the crowd to choose five people to come inside and talk.

My father met downstairs with the five men. My father could speak Japanese, Chinese, Russian, German, French, and English. At this meeting, everyone spoke Russian.

I couldn't help but stare out the window and watch the crowd, while downstairs, for two hours, my father listened to frightening stories. These people were refugees—people who ran away from their homes because, if they stayed, they would be killed. They were Jews from Poland, escaping from the Nazi soldiers who had taken over their country.

The five men had heard my father could give them visas—official written permission to travel through another country. The hundreds of Jewish refugees outside hoped to travel east through the Soviet Union and end up in Japan. Once in Japan, they could go to another country. Was it true? the men asked. Could my father issue these visas? If he did not, the Nazis would soon catch up with them.

My father answered that he could issue a few, but not hundreds. To do that, he would have to ask for permission from his government in Japan.

That night, the crowd stayed outside our house. Exhausted from the day's excitement, I slept soundly. But it was one of the worst nights of my father's life. He had to make a decision. If he helped these people, would he put our family in danger? If the Nazis found out, what would they do?

But if he did not help these people, they could all die. **E**

C **Literary Focus** Motivation What factors contributed to the boy's wish for his father to help the people?

Vocabulary refugees (rehf yuh JEEZ) *n.*: people who seek refuge, or safety, especially in another country.

D **Read and Discuss** What is happening now?

E **Reading Focus** Comparing and Contrasting Characters Compare the situation Sugihara faces with the situation Tubman confronts (page 199). What might Sugihara's reaction be?

Passage to Freedom: The Sugihara Story

"Passage to Freedom: The Sugihara Story" takes place in 1940, during the chaos of World War II. During this time, Nazi Germany was invading much of Western Europe and beginning its plan to rid Europe of Jewish people. Soviet Russia, at the time an ally of Germany, had invaded the small Baltic countries of Estonia, Latvia, and Lithuania, where this story takes place. It was not until more than a year later, on December 7, 1941, that Japan bombed Pearl Harbor and the United States entered the war.

The Jewish refugees from Poland in "Passage to Freedom" hope to travel east through the Soviet Union to Japan. Once in Japan, they hope to travel to other countries, where they will be safe.

Ask Yourself

Use the map above to trace the path the refugees would take. What qualities would a person need to survive such a journey?

My mother listened to the bed squeak as my father tossed and turned all night.

The next day, my father said he was going to ask his government about the visas. My mother agreed it was the right thing to do. My father sent his message by cable. Gudje took my father's written message down to the telegraph office.

I watched the crowd as they waited for the Japanese government's reply. The five representatives came into our house several times that day to ask if an answer had been received. Any time the gate opened, the crowd tried to charge inside.

Finally, the answer came from the Japanese government. It was "no." My father could not issue that many visas to Japan. For the next two days, he thought about what to do.

Hundreds more Jewish refugees joined the crowd. My father sent a second message to his government, and again the answer was "no." We still couldn't go outside. My little brother Haruki cried often because we were running out of milk.

I grew tired of staying indoors. I asked my father constantly, "Why are these people here? What do they want? Why do they have to be here? Who are they?"

My father always took the time to explain everything to me. He said the refugees needed his help, that they needed permission from him to go to another part of the world where they would be safe.

"I cannot help these people yet," he calmly told me. "But when the time comes, I will help them all that I can."

My father cabled his superiors yet a third time, and I knew the answer by the look in his eyes. That night, he said to my mother, "I have to do something. I may have to disobey my government, but if I don't, I will be disobeying God."

The next morning, he brought the family together and asked what he should do. This was the first time he ever asked all of us to help him with anything.

My mother and Auntie Setsuko had already made up their minds. They said we had to think about the people outside before we thought about ourselves. And that is what my parents had always told me—that I must think as if I were in someone else's place. If I were one of those children out there, what would I want someone to do for me?

I said to my father, "If we don't help them, won't they die?"

With the entire family in agreement, I could tell a huge weight was lifted off my father's shoulders. His voice was firm as he told us, "I will start helping these people."

Outside, the crowd went quiet as my father spoke, with Borislav translating.

"I will issue visas to each and every one of you to the last. So, please wait patiently."

The crowd stood frozen for a second. Then the refugees burst into cheers. Grown-ups embraced each other, and some reached to the sky. Fathers and mothers hugged their children. I was especially glad for the children.

My father opened the garage door and the crowd tried to rush in. To keep order, Borislav handed out cards with numbers. My

---

Vocabulary **superiors** (suh PIHR ee uhrz) *n.*: people of higher rank.

F Read and Discuss Why would the father feel a "huge weight" lifted from his shoulders when planning to disobey his government?

(opposite, left) Chiune Sugihara, c. 1937. (opposite, right) Polish Jewish refugees outside the Japanese consulate in Kaunas, Lithuania, waiting for visas from Sugihara. (near left) Reunion of Sugihara, left, and Zorach Warhaftig, Israeli citizen and Sugihara survivor, in Jerusalem, 1968.

Analyzing Visuals **Connecting to the Text** How do these photographs help you visualize the characters and events being described in this selection?

father wrote out each visa by hand. After he finished each one, he looked into the eyes of the person receiving the visa and said, "Good luck."

Refugees camped out at our favorite park, waiting to see my father. I was finally able to go outside.

Chiaki and I played with the other children in our toy car. They pushed as we rode, and they rode as we pushed. We chased each other around the big trees. We did not speak the same language, but that didn't stop us.

For about a month, there was always a line leading to the garage. Every day, from early in the morning till late at night, my father tried to write three hundred visas. He watered down the ink to make it last. Gudje and a young Jewish man helped out by stamping my father's name on the visas.

My mother offered to help write the visas, but my father insisted he be the only one, so no one else could get into trouble. So my mother watched the crowd and told my father how many were still in line.

One day, my father pressed down so hard on his fountain pen, the tip broke off. During that month, I only saw him late at night. His eyes were always red and he could hardly talk. While he slept, my mother massaged his arm, stiff and cramped from writing all day.

Soon my father grew so tired, he wanted to quit writing the visas. But my mother encouraged him to continue. "Many people are still waiting," she said. "Let's issue some more visas and save as many lives as we can." **G**

While the Germans approached from the west, the Soviets came from the east and took over Lithuania. They ordered my

G **Reading Focus** **Comparing and Contrasting Characters** Think about the situations Sugihara and Tubman (page 199) face. How do the <u>reactions</u> and support of others help them confront their conflict?

Passage to Freedom **219**

father to leave. So did the Japanese government, which reassigned him to Germany. Still, my father wrote the visas until we absolutely had to move out of our home. We stayed at a hotel for two days, where my father still wrote visas for the many refugees who followed him there.

Then it was time to leave Lithuania. Refugees who had slept at the train station crowded around my father. Some refugee men surrounded my father to protect him. He now just issued permission papers—blank pieces of paper with his signature.

As the train pulled away, refugees ran alongside. My father still handed permission papers out the window. As the train picked up speed, he threw them out to waiting hands. The people in the front of the crowd looked into my father's eyes and cried, "We will never forget you! We will see you again!"

I gazed out the train window, watching Lithuania and the crowd of refugees fade away. I wondered if we would ever see them again.

"Where are we going?" I asked my father.

"We are going to Berlin," he replied.

Chiaki and I became very excited about going to the big city. I had so many questions for my father. But he fell asleep as soon as he settled into his seat. My mother and Auntie Setsuko looked really tired, too.

Back then, I did not fully understand what the three of them had done, or why it was so important.

I do now. **H**

Afterword by Hiroki Sugihara

Each time that I think about what my father did at Kaunas, Lithuania, in 1940, my appreciation and understanding of the incident continues to grow. My father remained concerned about the fate of the refugees, and at one point left his address at the Israeli Embassy in Japan. Finally, in the 1960s, he started hearing from "Sugihara survivors," many of whom had kept their visas, and considered the worn pieces of paper to be family treasures.

In 1969, my father was invited to Israel, where he was taken to the famous Holocaust memorial, Yad Vashem. In 1985, he was chosen to receive the "Righteous Among Nations" Award from Yad Vashem. He was the first Japanese person to have been given this great honor.

In 1992, six years after his death, a monument to my father was dedicated in his birthplace of Yaotsu, Japan, on a hill that is now known as the Hill of Humanity. In 1994, a group of Sugihara survivors traveled to Japan to re-dedicate the monument in a ceremony that was attended by several high officials of the Japanese government. **I**

H **Literary Focus** Motivation Why were the Sugiharas' actions so important to themselves and others?

I **Read and Discuss** How has Mr. Sugihara been remembered?

Vocabulary **fate** (fayt) *n.*: what becomes of someone or something.

Applying Your Skills

Reading Standard 3.3 Compare and contrast motivations and reactions of literary characters from different historical eras confronting similar situations or conflicts.

Passage to Freedom

Literary Response and Analysis

Reading Skills Focus
Quick Check

1. **Plot** is a series of related events that occur in a story. Use a diagram like the one below to chart the plot of "Passage to Freedom."

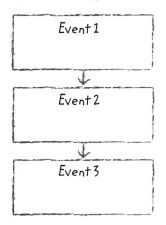

Read with a Purpose

2. What risks does Sugihara take to help the refugees?

Reading Skills: Comparing and Contrasting Characters

3. Complete the chart comparing Chiune Sugihara and Harriet Tubman. What comparisons can you make between the events that motivated them to take action?

	Harriet Tubman	Chiune Sugihara
Historical era	1851	World War II
Situation		
Conflict		
Motivation		

Literary Skills Focus
Literary Analysis

4. **Draw Conclusions** What values do Sugihara's actions teach his son?

5. **Analyze** In what ways does Sugihara's family support his actions? What impact does their behavior have on the success of his mission?

Literary Skills: Motivation

6. **Interpret** How do Sugihara's actions reveal his <u>motivation</u> to act? Explain whether his devotion to his cause falters or intensifies. Use examples from the text to support your reasoning.

Literary Skills Review: Conflict

7. **Analyze** List three **conflicts** (internal or external) in this story. Which conflict seems to be the main one?

Writing Skills Focus
Think as a Reader/Writer

Use It in Your Writing Look back at the images of eyes that you listed in your *Reader/Writer Notebook*. What do these images tell you about the people being described? Try writing some of your own images of eyes: the eyes of someone who is afraid, someone who is happy and excited, and someone who is angry.

 What Do You Think Now Have your thoughts about helping others versus protecting yourself changed? Why or why not?

Applying Your Skills

Passage to Freedom

Vocabulary Development

History of the English Language: Review

Here is a time line to help you review some highlights in the development of the English language.

Historic Event	Time Frame	Effect on the English Language
Tribes living near the Caspian Sea migrate to Europe and Asia.	c. third millennium B.C.	Proto-Indo-European gradually changes into many languages.
The Romans conquer most of Europe, North Africa, and the Middle East.	27 B.C.–A.D. 476	Latin, the language of Roman soldiers, influences the language of the Britons.
Anglo-Saxons arrive in Britain, driving out the Britons.	fifth century A.D.	The Germanic language of the Anglo-Saxons replaces the Celtic spoken by the Britons.
Saint Augustine arrives in Britain to do missionary work on behalf of the Roman Catholic Church.	A.D. 597	The Anglo-Saxons borrow many words from Latin, the language of the Roman Catholic Church.
Vikings from Scandinavia invade Britain.	end of the eighth century	Norse combines with the language of Britain to form what we now call Old English.
William the Conqueror, a Norman from France, conquers England.	1066	French and Latin influence the English language, and the period of Middle English begins.
William Caxton prints the first book in English.	1475	Written English reaches a great number of people.
Henry VII is crowned king of England.	1485	Henry VII promotes pride in all things English, including the language. The era of Modern English begins.
William Shakespeare is born.	1564	Shakespeare adds thousands of words and numerous phrases to the language.
Noah Webster publishes the *American Dictionary of the English Language.*	1828	Webster includes new American words and new meanings for older English words.
Americans move westward into territories originally settled by the Spanish.	middle of the nineteenth century	English-speaking Americans adopt many words of Spanish origin.
Science and technology advance at an unprecedented rate.	present	Use of English continues to spread around the world through the World Wide Web.

Your Turn

Use these words from the selection to solve the mystery-word questions below. You'll notice several of the historical influences listed in the time line on the previous page.

diplomat	refugees	superiors	fate	translate	monument

1. This word comes from the Latin preposition *super,* meaning "above; over." Similar words are found in Greek (*hyper*), Sanskrit (*upari*), Old Norse (*yfir*), and Old High German (*ubari*). It describes people who have a higher rank than another in an organization. What word is it? _____

2. This word is from Middle English, originally coming from the Latin verb *monere,* meaning "to remind." It describes an object whose purpose is to remind viewers of a significant event or person. Which word is it? _____

3. This word is from Middle English, derived from the Greek word *pheugein,* meaning "to flee." Today, it describes "people who flee their homes to avoid harm." What word is it? _____

4. This word can be traced back to Latin and from there to the Greek word *dipluoos,* meaning "double." Today, it describes an official who represents a country's interests while in other countries. What word is it? _____

5. This word comes from the Latin verb *ferre,* "to carry," and the preposition *trans*, "across." The word describes the process of "carrying across" information from one language to another. Which word is it? _____

6. This word is related to the Latin word *fatum,* which means "what had been spoken." It originally comes from the Greek word *phanai,* meaning "to say." Today, it means the circumstances that befall a person. What word is it? _____

Applying Your Skills

Reading Standard 1.3 Use word meanings within the appropriate context and show ability to verify those meanings by definition, **restatement,** example, comparison, or contrast.

Passage to Freedom

Vocabulary Development

Verifying Meanings by Restatement

Writers often help readers understand unfamiliar words by using definitions, examples, contrasts, and restatements. When you encounter an unfamiliar word, you can sometimes find a **restatement** in nearby words. For example, read this sentence from "Passage to Freedom."

> The five men had heard my father could give them visas—official written permission to travel through another country.

In this sentence the author restates the meaning of the word *visas*.

When you encounter unfamiliar words in your reading, look for such restatements to help you understand the words.

Your Turn

Complete the following sentences with restatements that clarify the meanings of the boldface Vocabulary words.

1. The narrator's father is a **diplomat,** someone who _____ .
2. The **refugees,** people who _____ , need his help.
3. Mr. Sugihara asks permission from his **superiors,** or _____ , several times.
4. The refugees' **fate**— _____ —is unknown.

Language Coach

Latin Roots and Suffixes The suffix *–ior* is a Latin suffix meaning "pertaining to" Adding *-ior* to the ends of some words can transform them into nouns that refer to a person. For example, the vocabulary word *superiors* is a combination of the Latin word *superus* and the suffix *–ior*. The word means "those of higher rank."

Use your knowledge of Latin roots and suffixes to answer the questions below.

1. The Latin word *videre* means "to see." Based on what you know, what does the word *supervisor* mean?
2. The Latin word *inferus* means "low" or "below." How would you describe someone who is *inferior*?

Academic Vocabulary

Talk About . . .

At the beginning of "Passage to Freedom," you learn the narrator's reaction to a young Jewish boy. Explain how this incident influences the events that follow.

Grammar Link

Direct and Indirect Objects

A **direct object** is a noun or pronoun that receives the action of a verb or shows the consequence of the action. A direct object tells *what* or *whom*.

EXAMPLE We read a **story.** (*Story* tells what was read.)

A **direct object** never follows a linking verb, since a linking verb—such as *become* or *is*—does not express action. Also, a direct object is never part of a prepositional phrase.

An **indirect object** is a noun or pronoun that comes between the verb and the direct object and tells *to what or whom* or *for what or whom the action is performed.*

EXAMPLE We read the **children** a story. (The *children* were read to.)

Linking verbs also do not have indirect objects, and indirect objects are never in a prepositional phrase.

Your Turn

Identify each boldface noun or pronoun as a direct or indirect object.

1. My father gave the **boy** some money.
2. Auntie Setsuko woke **me** up.
3. Our parents asked **us** our opinion; we agreed to help the refugees.
4. They rushed the **gate.**
5. The Sugihara survivors built my **father** a monument near his birthplace.

CHOICES

As you respond to the Choices, use these **Academic Vocabulary** words as appropriate: factor, motivation, reaction, response.

REVIEW

Compare Characters

In an essay, compare and contrast the characters of Barbara Frietchie, Harriet Tubman, and Chiune Sugihara. Be sure to address the way the historical era in which each person lived influenced the conflicts that the person faced. Use a chart like the one on page 213 to help you.

CONNECT

Make Character Judgments

Timed ⏲ Writing Imagine that you are Chiune Sugihara's superior. Do you think Sugihara should be punished for disobeying orders, or do you think he should be praised for saving lives? Use details from the text to support your position in a short persuasive essay.

EXTEND

Research Refugees

TechFocus Thousands of people live as refugees today. Working with two or three classmates, use credible Internet resources to prepare a report on one group of refugees. Look for answers to these questions using the keywords you collected as you read the story.

- From where did the refugees arrive?
- Why did they have to leave their homes?
- Where are they living now?
- What actions could be taken to help them?

Comparing and Contrasting Situations and Motivations

CONTENTS

Corina (detail) by Rose Freymuth-Frazier.
Courtesy, Ann Nathan Gallery, Chicago

What Do You Think

How do people make transitions into new circumstances?

 QuickWrite

Imagine making a transition in your life. Record thoughts about how you might feel in the first days and weeks.

Preparing to Read

Reading Standard 3.3 Compare and contrast motivations and reactions of literary characters from different historical eras confronting similar situations or conflicts.

Mrs. Flowers / A Shot at It

Literary Skills Focus

Situations and Motivations No matter what kind of story you read, real or imagined, you meet characters. You learn who they are, the battles they face, the actions they take, and their **motivations,** or reasons for behaving as they do.

You have probably heard the expression "Put yourself in my situation." A **situation** is the combination of all that is happening within the conditions that exist at a specific place and in a specific time. People often reveal their character—what they are made of—in hard times, when they face tough situations. People can also show their character in the way they live their everyday lives—especially in the way they treat other people.

Reading Skills Focus

Comparing and Contrasting Situations and Motivations As you read the two autobiographical accounts that follow, look for similarities and differences in the characters' situations and <u>motivations</u>.
Into Action Record details of the characters' situations and <u>motivations</u> in a chart like the one below.

Characters	Situation	Motivation
Mrs. Flowers and Marguerite		
Esmeralda and her teachers		

Writing Skills Focus
Think as a Reader/Writer

Find It in Your Reading Angelou and Santiago create detailed portraits of the people who help them through difficult situations. Record words and phrases that help you visualize these people.

Reader/Writer
Notebook
Use your **RWN** to complete the activities for these selections.

Vocabulary

Mrs. Flowers

benign (bih NYN) *adj.*: kindly; harmless. *Marguerite is comforted by Mrs. Flowers's benign smile.*

intolerant (ihn TAHL uhr uhnt) *adj.*: unwilling to accept something. *Mrs. Flowers was intolerant of rudeness.*

A Shot at It

mesmerized (MEHS muh ryzd) *v.* used as *adj.*: spellbound; hypnotized. *Mami, staring at the TV, was mesmerized by the actor's talent.*

impeccably (ihm PEHK uh blee) *adv.*: flawlessly. *The women who interviewed me were attractive, well-mannered, and impeccably dressed.*

petrified (PEHT ruh fyd) *adj.*: paralyzed with fear. *During the audition, Esmeralda grew petrified and couldn't speak.*

Language Coach
Word Study Words come into English from many sources. Some come from the name of a person. Which word above is derived from Franz Mesmer, an Austrian doctor whose studies led to the practice of hypnosis?

Maya Angelou
(1928–   )

"When You Get, Give"

Six feet tall, gracious, and commanding, Maya Angelou is as impressive a woman as Mrs. Flowers. She has been an actor, a teacher, a speaker, a civil rights worker and, above all, a writer. Her works include poems, plays, songs, screenplays, and newspaper and magazine articles, as well as four autobiographies. The selection "Mrs. Flowers" is from her autobiography *I Know Why the Caged Bird Sings*.

Angelou has influenced the lives of many young people, both in person and through her writing. She has said, "Black people say, when you get, give; when you learn, teach. As soon as that healing takes place, then we have to go out and heal somebody."

Esmeralda Santiago
(1948–   )

Living Two Lives

Born in Puerto Rico, Esmeralda Santiago was thirteen when her mother moved the family to Brooklyn, New York. Although the move from the island to the big city was initially terrifying, Santiago quickly adapted to the new language and way of life. Americanization brought good things to Santiago's life but also made her homesick for her Puerto Rican heritage. Her writing allows her to "get back to that feeling of Puertoricanness" she felt before moving to New York.

Think About the Writers

What types of life experiences do these writers share? How might their heritages and identities affect their writing?

Preview the Selections

In "Mrs. Flowers," a remarkable woman makes a strong impression on a young girl named **Marguerite** (mahr guhr EET).

In "A Shot at It," a fourteen-year-old girl named **Esmeralda Santiago** overcomes her struggle with a new language and poverty to pursue her goals with the help of her supportive teachers.

Mrs. Flowers

from I Know Why the Caged Bird Sings

by **Maya Angelou**

Read with a Purpose
Read this story to find out how a neighbor helps a young girl in need.

Build Background
"Mrs. Flowers" is from a volume of Maya Angelou's autobiography. When Angelou (born Marguerite Johnson) was a little girl, her parents separated. In the early 1930s she and her brother, Bailey, were sent to Stamps, Arkansas, to live with their grandmother (called Momma), who owned a general store. A year before meeting Mrs. Flowers, Marguerite had been violently assaulted by a friend of her mother's. Marguerite became depressed and withdrawn, and she stopped speaking.

For nearly a year, I sopped around the house, the Store, the school, and the church, like an old biscuit, dirty and inedible. Then I met, or rather got to know, the lady who threw me my first lifeline.

Mrs. Bertha Flowers was the aristocrat of Black Stamps. She had the grace of control to appear warm in the coldest weather, and on the Arkansas summer days it seemed she had a private breeze which swirled around, cooling her. She was thin without the taut look of wiry people, and her printed voile[1] dresses and flowered hats were as right for her as denim overalls for a farmer. She was our side's answer to the richest white woman in town.

Her skin was a rich black that would have peeled like a plum if snagged, but then no one would have thought of getting close enough to Mrs. Flowers to ruffle her dress, let alone snag her skin. She didn't encourage familiarity. She wore gloves too.

I don't think I ever saw Mrs. Flowers laugh, but she smiled often. A slow widening of her thin black lips to show even, small white teeth, then the slow effortless closing. When she chose to smile on me, I always wanted to thank her. The action was so graceful and inclusively benign.

She was one of the few gentlewomen I have ever known, and has remained throughout my life the measure of what a human being can be. **Ⓐ**

---

1. voile (voyl): thin, sheer fabric.

Ⓐ Read and Discuss What is the author conveying about Mrs. Flowers?

Vocabulary **benign** (bih NYN) *adj.*: kindly; harmless.

One summer afternoon, sweet-milk fresh in my memory, she stopped at the Store to buy provisions. Another Negro woman of her health and age would have been expected to carry the paper sacks home in one hand, but Momma said, "Sister Flowers, I'll send Bailey up to your house with these things."

She smiled that slow dragging smile, "Thank you, Mrs. Henderson. I'd prefer Marguerite, though." My name was beautiful when she said it. "I've been meaning to talk to her, anyway." They gave each other age-group looks. **B**

There was a little path beside the rocky road, and Mrs. Flowers walked in front swinging her arms and picking her way over the stones.

Mom and Dad (1944) by William H. Johnson. Oil on paperboard, 31" x 25 3/8" (78.7 x 64.5 cm).

She said, without turning her head, to me, "I hear you're doing very good schoolwork, Marguerite, but that it's all written. The teachers report that they have trouble getting you to talk in class." We passed the triangular farm on our left and the path widened to allow us to walk together. I hung back in the separate unasked and unanswerable questions.

"Come and walk along with me, Marguerite." I couldn't have refused even if I wanted to. She pronounced my name so nicely. Or more correctly, she spoke each word with such clarity that I was certain a foreigner who didn't understand English could have understood her.

"Now no one is going to make you talk—possibly no one can. But bear in

---

B **Literary Focus** Motivation What motivates Mrs. Flowers to ask to speak to Marguerite?

Little Sweet (1944) by William H. Johnson. Oil on paperboard. 28" x 22" (71.1 x 55.8 cm).

Analyzing Visuals

Connecting to the Text
Are these images similar to the way you picture Mrs. Flowers and Marguerite? Why or why not?

voice to infuse them with the shades of deeper meaning."

I memorized the part about the human voice infusing words. It seemed so valid and poetic.

She said she was going to give me some books and that I not only must read them, I must read them aloud. She suggested that I try to make a sentence sound in as many different ways as possible.

"I'll accept no excuse if you return a book to me that has been badly handled." My imagination boggled at the punishment I would deserve if in fact I did abuse a book of Mrs. Flowers's. Death would be too kind and brief. **C**

The odors in the house surprised me. Somehow I had never connected Mrs. Flowers with food or eating or any other common experience of common people. There must have been an outhouse, too, but my mind never recorded it.

mind, language is man's way of communicating with his fellow man and it is language alone which separates him from the lower animals." That was a totally new idea to me, and I would need time to think about it.

"Your grandmother says you read a lot. Every chance you get. That's good, but not good enough. Words mean more than what is set down on paper. It takes the human

C **Read and Discuss** | What is Mrs. Flowers doing?

The sweet scent of vanilla had met us as she opened the door.

"I made tea cookies this morning. You see, I had planned to invite you for cookies and lemonade so we could have this little chat. The lemonade is in the icebox."

It followed that Mrs. Flowers would have ice on an ordinary day, when most families in our town bought ice late on Saturdays only a few times during the summer to be used in the wooden ice cream freezers.

She took the bags from me and disappeared through the kitchen door. I looked around the room that I had never in my wildest fantasies imagined I would see. Browned photographs leered or threatened from the walls and the white, freshly done curtains pushed against themselves and against the wind. I wanted to gobble up the room entire and take it to Bailey, who would help me analyze and enjoy it.

"Have a seat, Marguerite. Over there by the table." She carried a platter covered with a tea towel. Although she warned that she hadn't tried her hand at baking sweets for some time, I was certain that like everything else about her the cookies would be perfect.

They were flat round wafers, slightly browned on the edges and butter-yellow in the center. With the cold lemonade they were sufficient for childhood's lifelong diet. Remembering my manners, I took nice little ladylike bites off the edges. She said she had made them expressly for me and that she had a few in the kitchen that I could take home to my brother. So I jammed one whole cake in my mouth and the rough crumbs scratched the insides of my jaws, and if I hadn't had to swallow, it would have been a dream come true.

As I ate she began the first of what we later called "my lessons in living." She said that I must always be intolerant of ignorance but understanding of illiteracy. That some people, unable to go to school, were more educated and even more intelligent than college professors. She encouraged me to listen carefully to what country people called mother wit. That in those homely sayings was couched the collective wisdom of generations. **Ⓓ**

> "It was the best of times, it was the worst of times. . . ." Her voice slid in and curved down through and over the words. She was nearly singing.

Ⓓ Read and Discuss | What does the author learn from Mrs. Flowers? What, in turn, is the author teaching you?

Vocabulary **intolerant** (ihn TAHL uhr uhnt) *adj.*: unwilling to accept something.

When I finished the cookies she brushed off the table and brought a thick, small book from the bookcase. I had read *A Tale of Two Cities* and found it up to my standards as a romantic novel. She opened the first page and I heard poetry for the first time in my life.

"It was the best of times, it was the worst of times. . . ." Her voice slid in and curved down through and over the words. She was nearly singing. I wanted to look at the pages. Were they the same that I had read? Or were there notes, music, lined on the pages, as in a hymn book? Her sounds began cascading gently. I knew from listening to a thousand preachers that she was nearing the end of her reading, and I hadn't really heard, heard to understand, a single word.

"How do you like that?"

It occurred to me that she expected a response. The sweet vanilla flavor was still on my tongue and her reading was a wonder in my ears. I had to speak.

I said, "Yes, ma'am." It was the least I could do, but it was the most also.

"There's one more thing. Take this book of poems and memorize one for me. Next time you pay me a visit, I want you to recite."

I have tried often to search behind the sophistication of years for the enchantment I so easily found in those gifts. The essence escapes but its aura[2] remains. To be

allowed, no, invited, into the private lives of strangers, and to share their joys and fears, was a chance to exchange the Southern bitter wormwood[3] for a cup of mead with Beowulf[4] or a hot cup of tea and milk with Oliver Twist. When I said aloud, "It is a far, far better thing that I do, than I have ever done . . ."[5] tears of love filled my eyes at my selflessness. **E**

On that first day, I ran down the hill and into the road (few cars ever came along it) and had the good sense to stop running before I reached the Store.

I was liked, and what a difference it made. I was respected not as Mrs. Henderson's grandchild or Bailey's sister but for just being Marguerite Johnson.

Childhood's logic never asks to be proved (all conclusions are absolute). I didn't question why Mrs. Flowers had singled me out for attention, nor did it occur to me that Momma might have asked her to give me a little talking-to. All I cared about was that she had made tea cookies for *me* and read to *me* from her favorite book. It was enough to prove that she liked me.

---

2. **aura** (AWR uh): feeling or mood that seems to surround something like a glow.

3. **wormwood:** bitter-tasting plant. Angelou is referring to the harshness of life for African Americans in the South at that time.

4. **Beowulf** (BAY uh wulf): hero of an Old English epic. During the period portrayed in the epic, people drank **mead,** a drink made with honey.

5. **"It is . . . ever done":** another quotation from Charles Dickens's *A Tale of Two Cities.* One of the characters says these words as he goes voluntarily to die in place of another man.

E **Reading Focus** Comparing and Contrasting

Motivation Compare Marguerite's previous <u>motivation</u> for reading with the motivation she expresses here. What has changed?

Applying Your Skills

Reading Standard 3.3 Compare and contrast motivations and reactions of literary characters from different historical eras confronting similar situations or conflicts.

Mrs. Flowers
Literary Response and Analysis

Reading Skills Focus
Quick Check

1. In a chart like the one below, fill in the main events of the narrative and the resolution. You should be able to find five key events.

Problem: _____

Event 1: _____

Event 2: _____

Event 3: _____

Event 4: _____

Event 5: _____

Resolution: _____

Read with a Purpose

2. In what ways does Mrs. Flowers help Marguerite?

Reading Skills: Comparing and Contrasting Situations and Motivations

3. Review the chart you created as you read. What motivates Mrs. Flowers to throw Marguerite a "lifeline"?

✅ Vocabulary Check

Complete the following sentences with the appropriate Vocabulary word.

| benign |
| intolerant |

4. Mrs. Flowers's _____ manner made Marguerite feel relaxed.

5. Mrs. Flowers is _____ of people who are careless with her belongings.

Literary Skills Focus
Literary Analysis

6. **Interpret** Find the only two words that Marguerite speaks. What do you think Angelou means when she writes, "It was the least I could do, but it was the most also" (p. 233)?

7. **Analyze** At the beginning of "Mrs. Flowers," Maya Angelou says that she "sopped around" until Mrs. Flowers threw her a "lifeline." What main idea does Angelou suggest here? Find some passages in the story that support this point she makes about her experience.

8. **Extend** What do you think Mrs. Flowers means when she tells Marguerite that she "must always be intolerant of ignorance but understanding of illiteracy"? Is that good advice for today? Draw on your own experience to support your answer.

Literary Skills: Situations and Motivations

9. **Analyze** How is Mrs. Flowers able to get Marguerite to speak? Discuss Marguerite's motivation for doing so. Use examples from the text to support your answer.

Writing Skills Focus
Think as a Reader/Writer

Use It in Your Writing Write a brief character sketch of someone who has a positive influence on a younger person. Your character may be real or fictional. Like Angelou, use detailed descriptions to reveal your character's nature.

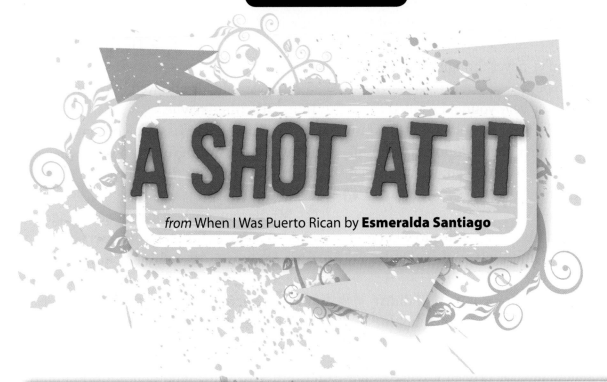

A SHOT AT IT

from When I Was Puerto Rican by **Esmeralda Santiago**

Read with a Purpose
Read this selection to find out if Esmeralda is accepted into the high school she hopes to attend.

Preparing to Read for this selection is on page 227.

Background
This selection is an excerpt taken from the final pages of Santiago's autobiography, *When I Was Puerto Rican*. New York City's High School of Performing Arts is a public school for students who want to pursue careers in theater, music, and dance.

Te conozco bacalao, aunque vengas disfrazao. I recognize you salted codfish, even if you're in disguise.

While Francisco[1] was still alive, we had moved to Ellery Street. That meant I had to change schools, so Mami walked me to P.S. 33, where I would attend ninth grade. The first week I was there I was given a series of tests that showed that even though I couldn't speak English very well, I read and wrote it at the tenth-grade level. So they put me in 9-3, with the smart kids.

One morning, Mr. Barone, a guidance counselor, called me to his office. He was short, with a big head and large hazel eyes under shapely eyebrows. His nose was long and round at the tip. He dressed in browns and yellows and often perched his tortoise-shell glasses on his forehead, as if he had another set of eyes up there.

"So," he pushed his glasses up, "what do you want to be when you grow up?"

"I don't know."

---

1. **Francisco:** Esmeralda's mother's suitor.

He shuffled through some papers. "Let's see here . . . you're fourteen, is that right?"

"Yes, sir."

"And you've never thought about what you want to be?"

When I was very young, I wanted to be a *jíbara*.[2] When I was older, I wanted to be a cartographer, then a topographer. But since we'd come to Brooklyn, I'd not thought about the future much. Ⓐ

"No, sir."

He pulled his glasses down to where they belonged and shuffled through the papers again.

"Do you have any hobbies?" I didn't know what he meant. "Hobbies, hobbies," he flailed his hands, as if he were juggling, "things you like to do after school."

"Ah, yes." I tried to imagine what I did at home that might qualify as a hobby. "I like to read."

He seemed disappointed. "Yes, we know that about you." He pulled out a paper and stared at it. "One of the tests we gave you was an aptitude test. It tells us what kinds of things you might be good at. The tests show that you would be good at helping people. Do you like to help people?"

I was afraid to contradict the tests. "Yes, sir."

"There's a high school we can send you where you can study biology and chemistry which will prepare you for a career in nursing."

I screwed up my face. He consulted the papers again.

"You would also do well in communications. Teaching maybe."

I remembered Miss Brown standing in front of a classroom full of rowdy teenagers, some of them taller than she was.

"I don't like to teach."

Mr. Barone pushed his glasses up again and leaned over the stack of papers on his desk. "Why don't you think about it and get back to me," he said, closing the folder with my name across the top. He put his hand flat on it, as if squeezing something out. "You're a smart girl, Esmeralda. Let's try to get you into an academic school so that you have a shot at college." Ⓑ

On the way home, I walked with another new ninth grader, Yolanda. She had been in New York for three years but knew as little English as I did. We spoke in Spanglish, a combination of English and Spanish in which we hopped from one language to the other depending on which word came first.

"*Te preguntó el* Mr. Barone, you know, *lo que querías hacer*[3] when you grow up?" I asked.

"*Sí, pero,* I didn't know. *¿Y tú?*"[4]

"*Yo tampoco.*[5] He said, *que* I like to help people. *Pero,* you know, *a mí no me gusta la*

---

2. *jíbara* (HEE bah rah): someone from the mountains of Puerto Rico; a peasant, but in this context it carries with it a certain romanticism.

3. *Te preguntó . . . hacer:* "He asked you . . . what you wanted to be."

4. *Sí, pero, . . . ¿Y tú?:* "Yes, but, . . . And you?"

5. *Yo tampoco:* "Me neither."

Ⓐ **Literary Skills** **Motivation** Why might Esmeralda have stopped thinking about the future? What does this tell you about her opinion of Brooklyn?

Ⓑ **Read and Discuss** What is Esmeralda experiencing?

View of Lower Manhattan from Brooklyn Heights by James Daugherty.

gente." When she heard me say I didn't like people much, Yolanda looked at me from the corner of her eye, waiting to become the exception.

By the time I said it, she had dashed up the stairs of her building. She didn't wave as she ducked in, and the next day she wasn't friendly. I walked around the rest of the day in embarrassed isolation, know-ing that somehow I had given myself away to the only friend I'd made at Junior High School 33. I had to either take back my words or live with the consequences of stat-ing what was becoming the truth. I'd never said that to anyone, not even to myself. It was an added weight, but I wasn't about to trade it for companionship. **C**

A few days later, Mr. Barone called me

C **Literary Skills** Situation What is Yolanda's reaction to Esmeralda's statement? Why does she have this response?

back to his office.

"Well?" Tiny green flecks burned around the black pupils of his hazel eyes.

The night before, Mami had called us into the living room. On the television "fifty of America's most beautiful girls" paraded in ruffled tulle dresses before a tinsel waterfall.

"Aren't they lovely?" Mami murmured, as the girls, escorted by boys in uniform, floated by the camera, twirled, and disappeared behind a screen to the strains of a waltz and an announcer's dramatic voice calling their names, ages, and states. Mami sat mesmerized through the whole pageant.

"I'd like to be a model," I said to Mr. Barone.

He stared at me, pulled his glasses down from his forehead, looked at the papers inside the folder with my name on it, and glared. "A model?" His voice was gruff, as if he were more comfortable yelling at people than talking to them. **D**

"I want to be on television."

"Oh, then you want to be an actress," in a tone that said this was only a slight improvement over my first career choice. We stared at one another for a few seconds. He pushed his glasses up to his forehead again and reached

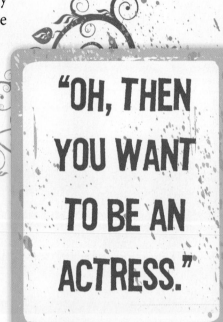

"OH, THEN YOU WANT TO BE AN ACTRESS."

for a book on the shelf in back of him. "I only know of one school that trains actresses, but we've never sent them a student from here."

Performing Arts, the write-up said, was an academic, as opposed to a vocational, public school that trained students wishing to pursue a career in theater, music, and dance.

"It says here that you have to audition." He stood up and held the book closer to the faint gray light coming through the narrow window high on his wall. "Have you ever performed in front of an audience?"

"I was announcer in my school show in Puerto Rico," I said. "And I recite poetry. There, not here."

He closed the book and held it against his chest. His right index finger thumped a rhythm on his lower lip. "Let me call them and find out exactly what you need to do. Then we can talk some more."

I left his office strangely happy, confident that something good had just happened, not knowing exactly what. **E**

"I'm not afraid . . . I'm not afraid . . . I'm not afraid." Every day I walked home from

---

D **Reading Skills** **Comparing and Contrasting Motivations** What motivates Esmeralda to choose this new career path? How might this motivation be different from what caused her in the past to want to be a cartographer or a topographer?

E **Read and Discuss** What just happened in the counselor's office?

Vocabulary **mesmerized** (MEHS muh ryzd) *v.* used as *adj.*: spellbound; hypnotized.

school repeating those words. The broad streets and sidewalks that had impressed me so on the first day we had arrived had become as familiar as the dirt road from Macún to the highway. Only my curiosity about the people who lived behind these walls ended where the façades of the buildings opened into dark hallways or locked doors. Nothing good, I imagined, could be happening inside if so many locks had to be breached to go in or step out.

It was on these tense walks home from school that I decided I had to get out of Brooklyn. Mami had chosen this as our home, and just like every other time we'd moved, I'd had to go along with her because I was a child who had no choice. But I wasn't willing to go along with her on this one.

"How can people live like this?" I shrieked once, desperate to run across a field, to feel grass under my feet instead of pavement.

"Like what?" Mami asked, looking around our apartment, the kitchen and living room crisscrossed with sagging lines of drying diapers and bedclothes.

"Everyone on top of each other. No room to do anything. No air."

"Do you want to go back to Macún, to live like savages, with no electricity, no toilets . . ."

"At least you could step outside every day without somebody trying to kill you." **F**

"Ay, Negi,⁶ stop exaggerating!"

---

6. **Negi:** Esmeralda's nickname.

F Literary Skills **Character** What does this reaction tell you about Esmeralda?

"I hate my life!" I yelled.

"Then do something about it," she yelled back.

Until Mr. Barone showed me the listing for Performing Arts High School, I hadn't known what to do. **G**

"The auditions are in less than a month. You have to learn a monologue, which you will perform in front of a panel. If you do well, and your grades here are good, you might get into the school."

Mr. Barone took charge of preparing me for my audition to Performing Arts. He selected a speech from *The Silver Cord,* a play by Sidney Howard, first performed in 1926, but whose action took place in a New York drawing room circa 1905.

"Mr. Gatti, the English teacher," he said, "will coach you. . . . And Mrs. Johnson will talk to you about what to wear and things like that."

I was to play Christina, a young married woman confronting her mother-in-law. I learned the monologue phonetically from Mr. Gatti. It opened with "You belong to a type that's very common in this country, Mrs. Phelps—a type of self-centered, self-pitying, son-devouring tigress, with unmentionable proclivities⁷ suppressed on the side."

"We don't have time to study the meaning of every word," Mr. Gatti said. "Just make sure you pronounce every word correctly."

---

7. **proclivities** (pruh KLIHV uh teez): tendencies.

G Read and Discuss What is on Esmeralda's mind?

Mrs. Johnson, who taught Home Economics, called me to her office.

"Is that how you enter a room?" she asked the minute I came in. "Try again, only this time, don't barge in. Step in slowly, head up, back straight, a nice smile on your face. That's it." I took a deep breath and waited. "Now sit. No, not like that. Don't just plop down. Float down to the chair with your knees together." She demonstrated, and I copied her. "That's better. What do you do with your hands? No, don't hold your chin like that; it's not ladylike. Put your hands on your lap, and leave them there. Don't use them so much when you talk."

I sat stiff as a cutout while Mrs. Johnson and Mr. Barone asked me questions they thought the panel at Performing Arts would ask.

"Where are you from?"

"Puerto Rico."

"No," Mrs. Johnson said, "Porto Rico. Keep your *r*'s soft. Try again."

"Do you have any hobbies?" Mr. Barone asked. Now I knew what to answer.

"I enjoy dancing and the movies."

"Why do you want to come to this school?"

Mrs. Johnson and Mr. Barone had worked on my answer if this question should come up.

"I would like to study at Performing Arts because of its academic program and so that I may be trained as an actress."

"Very good, very good!" Mr. Barone

rubbed his hands together, twinkled his eyes at Mrs. Johnson. "I think we have a shot at this."

"Remember," Mrs. Johnson said, "when you shop for your audition dress, look for something very simple in dark colors."

Mami bought me a red plaid wool jumper with a crisp white shirt, my first pair of stockings, and penny loafers. The night before, she rolled up my hair in pink curlers that cut into my scalp and made it hard to sleep. For the occasion, I was allowed to wear eye makeup and a little lipstick.

"You look so grown up!" Mami said, her voice sad but happy, as I twirled in front of her and Tata.[8]

"*Toda una señorita,*"[9] Tata said, her eyes misty.

We set out for the audition on an overcast January morning heavy with the threat of snow.

"Why couldn't you choose a school close to home?" Mami grumbled as we got on the train to Manhattan. I worried that even if I were accepted, she wouldn't let me go because it was so far from home, one hour each way by subway. But in spite of her complaints, she was proud that I was good enough to be considered for such a famous school. And she actually seemed excited that I would be leaving the neighborhood.

"You'll be exposed to a different class of people," she assured me, and I felt the force of her ambition without knowing exactly what she meant. **Ⓗ**

---

8. **Tata:** Esmeralda's grandmother.
9. *Toda una señorita:* "All a young lady should be."

Three women sat behind a long table in a classroom where the desks and chairs had been pushed against a wall. As I entered I held my head up and smiled, and then I floated down to the chair in front of them, clasped my hands on my lap, and smiled some more.

"Good morning," said the tall one with hair the color of sand. She was big boned and solid, with intense blue eyes, a generous mouth, and soothing hands with short fingernails. She was dressed in shades of beige from head to toe and wore no makeup and no jewelry except for the gold chain that held her glasses just above her full bosom. Her voice was rich, modulated, each word pronounced as if she were inventing it.

Next to her sat a very small woman with very high heels. Her cropped hair was pouffed around her face, with bangs brushing the tips of her long false lashes, her huge dark brown eyes were thickly lined in black all around, and her small mouth was carefully drawn in and painted cerise. Her suntanned face turned toward me with the innocent curiosity of a lively baby. She was dressed in black, with many gold chains around her neck, big earrings, several bracelets, and large stone rings on the fingers of both hands.

The third woman was tall, small boned, thin, but shapely. Her dark hair was pulled flat against her skull into a knot in back of her head. Her face was all angles and light, with fawnlike dark brown eyes, a straight nose, full lips painted just a shade pinker than their natural color. Silky forest green cuffs peeked out from the sleeves of her burgundy suit. Diamond studs winked from perfect earlobes.

Ⓗ [Read and Discuss] What is the plan for Esmeralda?

I had dreamed of this moment for several weeks. More than anything, I wanted to impress the panel with my talent, so that I would be accepted into Performing Arts and leave Brooklyn every day. And, I hoped, one day I would never go back.

But the moment I faced these three impeccably groomed women, I forgot my English and Mrs. Johnson's lessons on how to behave like a lady. In the agony of trying to answer their barely comprehensible questions, I jabbed my hands here and there, forming words with my fingers because the words refused to leave my mouth.

"Why don't you let us hear your monologue now?" the woman with the dangling glasses asked softly.

I stood up abruptly, and my chair clattered onto its side two feet from where I stood. I picked it up, wishing with all my strength that a thunderbolt would strike me dead to ashes on the spot.

"It's all right," she said. "Take a breath. We know you're nervous."

I closed my eyes and breathed deeply, walked to the middle of the room, and began my monologue.

"Ju bee lonh 2 a type dats berry cómo in dis kuntree, Meessees Felps. A type off selfcent red self pee tee in sun de boring tie gress wid on men shon ah ball pro klee bee tees on de side."

In spite of Mr. Gatti's reminders that I should speak slowly and enunciate every word, even if I didn't understand it, I recited my three-minute monologue in one minute flat.

The small woman's long lashes seemed to have grown with amazement. The elegant woman's serene face twitched with controlled laughter. The tall one dressed in beige smiled sweetly.

"Thank you, dear," she said. "Could you wait outside for a few moments?"

I resisted the urge to curtsy. The long hallway had narrow wainscotting halfway up to the high ceiling. Single bulb lamps hung from long cords, creating yellow puddles of light on the polished brown linoleum tile. A couple of girls my age sat on straight chairs next to their mothers, waiting their turn. They looked up as I came out and the door shut behind me. Mami stood up from her chair at the end of the hall. She looked as scared as I felt.

I HAD DREAMED OF THIS MOMENT.

Vocabulary impeccably (ihm PEHK uh blee) *adv.:* flawlessly.

"What happened?"

"Nothing," I mumbled, afraid that if I began telling her about it, I would break into tears in front of the other people, whose eyes followed me and Mami as we walked to the EXIT sign. "I have to wait here a minute."

"Did they say anything?"

"No. I'm just supposed to wait."

We leaned against the wall. Across from us there was a bulletin board with newspaper clippings about former students. On the ragged edge, a neat person had printed in blue ink, "P.A." and the year the actor, dancer, or musician had graduated. I closed my eyes and tried to picture myself on that bulletin board, with "P.A. '66" across the top.

The door at the end of the hall opened, and the woman in beige poked her head out.

"Esmeralda?"

"*Sí*, I mean, here." I raised my hand.

She led me into the room. There was another girl in there, whom she introduced as Bonnie, a junior at the school.

"Do you know what a pantomime is?" the woman asked. I nodded. "You and Bonnie are sisters decorating a Christmas tree."

Bonnie looked a lot like Juanita Marín, whom I had last seen in Macún four years earlier. We decided where the invisible Christmas tree would be, and we sat on the floor and pretended we were taking decorations out of boxes and hanging them on the branches.

My family had never had a Christmas tree, but I remembered how once I had helped Papi wind colored lights around the eggplant bush that divided our land from Doña Ana's. We started at the bottom and wound the wire with tiny red bulbs around and around until we ran out; then Papi plugged another cord to it and we kept going until the branches hung heavy with light and the bush looked like it was on fire.

Before long I had forgotten where I was,

and that the tree didn't exist and Bonnie was not my sister. She pretended to hand me a very delicate ball, and just before I took it, she made like it fell to the ground and shattered. I was petrified that Mami would come in and yell at us for breaking her favorite decoration. Just as I began to pick up the tiny fragments of non-existent crystal, a voice broke in. "Thank you." **❶**

Bonnie got up, smiled, and went out.

The elegant woman stretched her hand out for me to shake. "We will notify your school in a few weeks. It was very nice to meet you."

I shook hands all around then backed out of the room in a fog, silent, as if the pantomime had taken my voice and the urge to speak.

On the way home Mami kept asking what had happened, and I kept mumbling, "Nothing. Nothing happened," ashamed that, after all the hours of practice with Mrs. Johnson, Mr. Barone, and Mr. Gatti, after the expense of new clothes and shoes, after Mami had to take a day off from work to take me into Manhattan, after

all that, I had failed the audition and would never, ever, get out of Brooklyn. **❷**

Epilogue: One of These Days

El mismo jíbaro con diferente caballo.
Same jíbaro, different horse.

A decade after my graduation from Performing Arts, I visited the school. I was by then living in Boston, a scholarship student at Harvard University. The tall, elegant woman of my audition had become my mentor through my three years there. Since my graduation, she had married the school principal.

> "I REMEMBER YOUR AUDITION," SHE SAID.

"I remember your audition," she said, her chiseled face dreamy, her lips toying with a smile that she seemed, still, to have to control.

I had forgotten the skinny brown girl with the curled hair, wool jumper, and lively hands. But she hadn't. She told me that the panel had had to ask me to leave so that they could laugh, because it was so funny to see

---

❶ Literary Skills Comparing and Contrasting **Situations** How is Esmeralda's response to a challenging situation like or unlike that of Marguerite?

Vocabulary **petrified** (PEHT ruh fyd) *adj.*: paralyzed with fear.

❷ Read and Discuss What is all of this telling you about the audition?

a fourteen-year-old Puerto Rican girl jabbering out a monologue about a possessive mother-in-law at the turn of the century, the words incomprehensible because they went by so fast.

"We admired," she said, "the courage it took to stand in front of us and do what you did."

"So you mean I didn't get into the school because of my talent, but because I had chutzpah?"[10] We both laughed.

"Are any of your sisters and brothers in college?"

"No, I'm the only one, so far."

"How many of you are there?"

"By the time I graduated from high school there were eleven of us."

"Eleven!" She looked at me for a long time, until I had to look down. "Do you ever think about how far you've come?" she asked.

"No." I answered. "I never stop to think about it. It might jinx the momentum."

"Let me tell you another story, then," she said. "The first day of your first year, you were absent. We called your house. You said you couldn't come to school because you had nothing to wear. I wasn't sure if you were joking. I asked to speak to your mother, and you translated what she said. She needed you to go somewhere with her to interpret. At first you wouldn't tell me where, but then you admitted you were going to the welfare office. You were crying, and I had to assure you that you were not the only student in this school whose family received public assistance. The next day you were here, bright and eager. And now here you are, about to graduate from Harvard."

"I'm glad you made that phone call," I said.

"And I'm glad you came to see me, but right now I have to teach a class." She stood up, as graceful as I remembered. "Take care."

Her warm embrace, fragrant of expensive perfume, took me by surprise. "Thank you," I said as she went around the corner to her classroom.

I walked the halls of the school, looking for the room where my life had changed. It was across from the science lab, a few doors down from the big bulletin board where someone with neat handwriting still wrote the letters "P.A." followed by the graduating year along the edges of newspaper clippings featuring famous alumni.

"P.A. '66," I said to no one in particular. "One of these days." **Ⓚ**

---

10. **chutzpah:** brazenness; daring boldness (Yiddish slang).

Ⓚ **Read and Discuss** What is the author letting you know in the epilogue?

Applying Your Skills

Reading Standard 3.3 Compare and contrast motivations and reactions of literary characters from different historical eras confronting similar situations or conflicts.

A Shot at It

Literary Response and Analysis

Reading Skills Focus
Quick Check

1. In a chart like the one below, fill in the main events and resolution of the narrative. You should be able to find five key events.

Problem:

Event 1:

Event 2:

Event 3:

Event 4:

Event 5:

Resolution:

Read with a Purpose

2. What surprised you about Esmeralda's acceptance into the high school?

Reading Skills: Comparing and Contrasting Situations and Motivations

3. What motivated Esmeralda's teachers to help her succeed? How is her situation similar to Marguerite's in "Mrs. Flowers"? In what way is the help that both girls receive a "lifeline"?

✔ Vocabulary Check

Match the Vocabulary words with their definitions.

4. **mesmerized**   a. very scared
5. **impeccably**   b. under a spell
6. **petrified**   c. perfectly

Literary Skills Focus
Literary Analysis

7. **Infer** What is Esmeralda's motivation to audition for the High School of Performing Arts?

8. **Evaluate** What do Esmeralda's coaches try to teach her? What is Esmeralda's reaction? Explain.

9. **Analyze** As an adult, Esmeralda finds out why she was accepted to the High School of Performing Arts. What does she find out? What **theme,** or idea about life, is suggested by this piece of information?

Literary Skills: Situations and Motivations

10. **Compare** What life experiences do Esmeralda and Marguerite have in common? How do these experiences serve as motivation for their actions?

11. **Compare and Contrast** Each of the autobiographies involves a relationship between a younger person and an older person. What similarities do you find in these relationships? What differences do you find?

Writing Skills Focus
Think as a Reader/Writer

Use It in Your Writing Write about a time when somebody helped you in some way—singling you out for attention or making you feel liked and respected for being yourself. Use precise descriptions to portray the person's character and include his or her motivation for helping you.

Reading Standard 3.3 Compare and contrast motivations and reactions of literary characters from different historical eras confronting similar situations or conflicts.

Mrs. Flowers / A Shot at It

Writing Skills Focus
Write a Comparison-and-Contrast Essay

Each of these works describes a childhood experience of feeling like an outsider and receiving assistance from a caring adult. What adult perspectives are offered in each work? How are they similar, and how are they different? Reexamine these two stories, and write a comparison-and-contrast essay in which you

- compare and contrast the characters' situations, <u>motivations</u>, and actions
- look for ways in which the stories' characters experience similar and different situations
- evaluate the stories' **themes,** or the insights that the stories convey about life

Use an outline such as this one to organize your essay:

I. Introduction and thesis statement
II. Body of essay
   A. Characters' situations
   B. Similarities and differences in characters' <u>response</u> to experience
   C. Comparison of story themes
III. Summary and conclusion

Revise your writing to clarify your ideas and remove unnecessary details. Proofread your essay to eliminate errors in spelling, grammar, and punctuation.

What Do **You Think Now** Both works discuss important life transitions. How have your opinions about dealing with them changed after doing this reading?

CHOICES

As you respond to the Choices, use these **Academic Vocabulary** words as appropriate: <u>factor</u>, <u>motivation</u>, <u>reaction</u>, <u>response</u>.

REVIEW
Write a Thank-You Letter

In both "Mrs. Flowers" and "A Shot at It," a young person is helped to make a transition into a new phase of her life. Imagine that you are Marguerite or Esmeralda. Write a letter thanking either Mrs. Flowers or one of the teachers for his or her help. Be sure to address the specific <u>factors</u> you think led the older person to decide to help you.

CONNECT
Write in Another Genre

"Mrs. Flowers" comes from Maya Angelou's autobiography *I Know Why the Caged Bird Sings.* Angelou's descriptions of Mrs. Flowers are warm and vibrant, bringing to life the real person who helped Angelou during a difficult period. Maya Angelou is also a poet. Try borrowing some of Angelou's vivid imagery to write a poem that reveals Mrs. Flowers's character to your readers.

EXTEND
Design a Web Profile

TechFocus Would you still be essentially the same person if you had grown up in New York City in the early 1960s? in Arkansas in the 1930s? Choose a time and place in history, and put yourself there. Design a Web profile of yourself that describes a day of your life then and there. You may want to include illustrations or other visuals.

Proposition and Support

CONTENTS

What does it
take to be a
good citizen?

 **QuickWrite**

Imagine that your community is going to give a
Citizen of the Year award. Make a list of qualities
that you think a good citizen should have.

Reading Standard 2.2 Analyze text that uses proposition and support patterns.

Don't Know Much About Liberty / Left Out in '08

Informational Text Focus

Proposition and Support You are going to read two informational texts in which the writer presents a **proposition,** or a controlling idea or opinion, and supports the proposition with reasons. The **support** may be in the form of facts, statistics, examples, and expert opinions.

Recognizing Support

A proposition can be supported with the following evidence:
- **facts**—true details, including results of research or surveys
- **statistics**—facts in number form
- **examples**—specific instances that illustrate reasons or facts
- **expert opinions**—quotations from experts in a given subject area.

Into Action Complete a chart like the one below for each article. First, identify the proposition of each article. Then, record examples of the types of support you discover as you read.

Proposition: _____

Type of Support	Example
Fact	
Statistic	"Twenty-two percent could name all five."
Example	
Expert Opinion	

Writing Skills Focus

Preparing for Timed Writing As you read, record in your *Reader/Writer Notebook* the ways in which support is being signaled. An expert opinion might begin with a description of the speaker's background. A statistic might be stated as "More than two thirds."

Reader/Writer
Notebook
Use your **RWN** to complete the activities for these selections.

Vocabulary

Don't Know Much About Liberty

majority (muh JAWR uh tee) *n.:* larger part of something. *A majority of the voters chose the youngest candidate.*

minority (muh NAWR uh tee) *n.:* smaller part of something. *A minority of the people voted for someone else.*

Left Out in '08

suffrage (SUHF rihj) *n.:* right to vote. *Women in the United States did not have suffrage until 1920.*

Language Coach

Words and Their Derivations The following words are derived from the Latin word *minor,* which means "small." Define the following words and check your answers in a dictionary. How does your knowledge of the Latin word *minor* give you a clue to each word's meaning?

> minimize
> miniature
> minimal

Learn It Online
To read more articles like this one, go to the interactive reading workshops at:

go.hrw.com | H8-249 | **Go**

Read with a Purpose Read this article to learn about the rights guaranteed by the First Amendment.

Don't Know Much About ★★★ LIBERTY ★★★

Americans Are Clueless When It Comes to the First Amendment

from Weekly Reader Senior

Illustrations by Chris Murphy.

When it comes to the First Amendment, most Americans don't know their rights from their wrongs!

Only one in 1,000 Americans can list all five freedoms protected by the First Amendment to the U.S. Constitution, according to a recent survey. (Just in case you're one of those 999 people who can't, the rights are freedom of religion, freedom of speech, freedom of the press, freedom of assembly, and freedom to petition.) **Ⓐ**

One in seven people could name one of the five First Amendment freedoms, and one in five people could name two, according to the McCormick Tribune Freedom Museum in Chicago, which sponsored the survey.

Although Americans failed the First Amendment pop quiz, they passed the Bart Simpson section of the survey with flying colors. More than half of the respondents could name at least two of the main characters of *The Simpsons*. Twenty-two percent could name all five. **Ⓑ**

Ⓐ Informational Focus Proposition and Support In your own words, state the proposition in the first sentence, and describe how it is supported in the second sentence.

Ⓑ Informational Focus Proposition and Support What statistics in these two paragraphs support the writer's proposition?

Those findings made Gene Policinski, executive director of the First Amendment Center, want to eat his shorts (as Bart Simpson would say). "These are such basic freedoms, and they're in our lives every day," he told *Senior Edition*. "All we have to do is look around." **C**

No matter how old you are or what state you live in, you exercise First Amendment freedoms every day, Policinski says. When you turn on the television, you can choose the show you want to watch. If you disagree with a law, you can write a letter to your state representative. If you don't like something the government is doing, you can say so without getting in trouble. **D**

That's exactly what the nation's founders hoped to achieve when they ratified, or approved, the Bill of Rights in 1791. The Bill of Rights is the first 10 amendments to the Constitution. The founders wanted Americans to have control over their daily lives and a say in how the government is run.

Here's why the founders included each freedom:

The Five Freedoms of the First Amendment

1 Freedom of religion

The Colonists came to America in search of religious freedom. They wanted to worship without fear of punishment. The nation's founders included this clause to make sure Congress could neither establish a national religion nor stop people from practicing their chosen religion.

2 Freedom of speech

The Colonists' rocky relationship with Great Britain made them determined to prevent their new government from abusing its power. This clause ensures that the government can't stop people from saying almost anything they want to say—even if it's unpopular or critical of the president.

C **Informational Focus** Support Why might quoting Policinski help support the writer's proposition?

D **Informational Focus** Support What type of support does Policinski provide?

3 Freedom of the press

The nation's founders feared that if the government controlled the nation's newspapers, it could violate the Constitution without anyone finding out. This clause allows U.S. newspapers, magazines, and other media to report on whatever they want, as long as they don't print false information or invade people's privacy.

4 Freedom of assembly

Majority may rule in the United States, but the nation's founders wanted to make sure minority voices were still heard. This clause gives Americans the right to protest or parade publicly in support of any cause—no matter how controversial—as long as they do it peacefully.

5 Freedom to petition the government for a redress of grievances

The Colonists started the American Revolution (1775–1783) because they had little voice in Great Britain's government. This clause requires that the government listen to what citizens have to say, whether it be through letter writing or lawsuits. **E**

Read with a Purpose What did you learn about your First Amendment rights?

E **Read and Discuss** What do the reasons behind these freedoms tell you about life without them and how they came about?

Vocabulary **majority** (muh JAWR uh tee) *n.:* larger part of something.
minority (muh NAWR uh tee) *n.:* smaller part of something.

Applying Your Skills

Don't Know Much About Liberty

Standards Review

Informational Text and Vocabulary

1. What is the **proposition** of the writer of this magazine article?

  A The Bill of Rights is an essential political document.

  B U.S. citizens should memorize their First Amendment freedoms.

  C Americans were better citizens one hundred years ago than they are today.

  D U.S. citizens would be better citizens if they knew their rights.

2. All of the following types of reasons are used to **support** the article's proposition *except*

  A statistics.

  B anecdotes.

  C expert opinions.

  D examples.

3. Which of the following is a **statistic** used to support the writer's proposition?

  A "when it comes to the First Amendment"

  B "The Bill of Rights is the first 10 amendments."

  C "One in seven people could name one of the five First Amendment freedoms."

  D "although Americans failed the First Amendment pop quiz"

4. Which is *not* an **example** used by Policinski in the article?

  A You can choose the television show you want to watch.

  B You can write about laws you disagree with.

  C We all use these rights every day.

  D You can say you dislike what the government is doing.

5. If a group held the *majority* of positions, that group

  A had fewer positions than any other's.

  B had more positions than any other's.

  C won each election held.

  D ratified its own laws.

6. The opposite of *minority* is

  A the greater quantity.

  B less than half.

  C the better quality.

  D the lesser quantity.

Writing Skills Focus

Timed └Writing Find one of each kind of support used in the magazine article "Don't Know Much About Liberty," and describe how the support is signaled by the writer.

What Do You Think Now

Even though you're not old enough to vote, how might you work on becoming a better citizen now?

Read with a Purpose
Read the following selection to analyze a proposition put forth in the *Los Angeles Times*.

Build Background
People become U.S. citizens in several ways. First, anyone born in the United States or a territory it controls is a citizen. People born in a foreign country are U.S. citizens if at least one parent is a U.S. citizen. Foreign-born people whose parents are not citizens must move to the United States to become naturalized citizens. . . .

Only two differences between naturalized and native-born citizens exist. Naturalized citizens can lose their citizenship, and *they cannot become president or vice president.* Many famous Americans have been naturalized citizens, including scientist Albert Einstein and former secretary of state Madeleine Albright.

from Holt's United States History: Independence to 1914

Left Out in '08

Arnold Schwarzenegger can't run for president because the founding fathers didn't want a foreign king.

Los Angeles, CA, Jan. 14, 2007 — THE GOVERNOR OF the nation's largest state was reelected in a landslide in November [2006], even though his Republican Party is a minority in California. He works with Democrats in a way that offers the rest of the country a model of much-needed bipartisanship.[1] To kick off his second term, he has proposed the most ambitious healthcare and environmental reforms in the country, and he is also committed to a massive reconstruction of the state's infrastructure. **Ⓐ**

Yet, oddly enough, Gov. Arnold Schwarzenegger is not on the list of potential presidential candidates in 2008.

Why? Because the founders were worried in the 18th century that our fledgling nation might go the way of Poland and be overtaken by a foreign monarchy. Hence the constitutional qualifier that only "natural-born citizens" are eligible for the presidency of the United States.

In their wisdom, however, the Constitution's authors adopted a mechanism for the nation's founding document to be amended. Amendments should be undertaken sparingly, we agree, but it's a good thing that slavery was done away

---

1. **bipartisanship:** cooperation and agreement between two major parties.

Ⓐ | Read and Discuss | What is your impression of Arnold Schwarzenegger?

with and that suffrage has been expanded.

And now that we can all rest assured that no foreign monarch is going to move into the White House, it's long past due for this nation of immigrants to amend the Constitution to allow naturalized Americans to aspire[2] to the presidency. This is precisely the type of defining issue—what it means to be American—that the amendment process was designed to address. **B**

Think about it. Someone could come to the U.S. at the age of two from Britain or China or Peru, become a citizen, join the military, win a Medal of Honor, cure cancer—but that person would still not be "good enough" for the White House.

2. **aspire:** have a strong desire to achieve something.

Vocabulary **suffrage** (SUHF rihj) *n.:* right to vote.

B **Informational Focus** Proposition and Support
What is the proposition of this article?

One of the exceptional qualities of this meritocratic[3] nation of immigrants is its sense of possibility. Americans like to tell their kids that they can be anything they want to be when they grow up—including president. But for millions of patriotic Americans, the Constitution says otherwise. The idea of citizenship only as a birthright is a decidedly foreign notion. And the idea that voters cannot elect as their leader a naturalized citizen is decidedly undemocratic.

That's why California's representatives in Washington should support a constitutional amendment. If the United States is a nation of immigrants, California is a state of immigrants. And California leaders who want to hold on to the eighteenth century prohibition against naturalized citizens running for the presidency are not doing a very good job representing their constituents.

3. **meritocratic:** having a system based on intellectual or academic achievement.

Read with a Purpose   Explain whether the writer adequately supports the proposition.

C **Informational Focus** **Proposition and Support**
List at least three examples of support for the proposition.

Applying Your Skills

Reading Standard 2.2 Analyze text that uses proposition and support patterns.

Left Out in '08
Standards Review

Informational Text and Vocabulary

1. What is the **proposition** of the writer of this newspaper article?

 A Arnold Schwarzenegger would make a good president.

 B Naturalized citizens should be allowed to vote for president.

 C The Constitution should be amended so that naturalized citizens can run for president.

 D California congressional leaders do not represent their voters.

2. To **support** the proposition that Arnold Schwarzenegger is a good governor, the writer uses

 A facts.

 B statistics.

 C expert opinions.

 D definitions.

3. Which statement from the newspaper article **supports** the proposition that the Constitution should be amended to allow naturalized citizens to run for president?

 A "No foreign monarch is going to move into the White House."

 B "Suffrage has been expanded."

 C "Slavery was done away with."

 D "The Constitution's authors adopted a mechanism."

4. Naturalized citizens can do all of the following *except*

 A join the military.

 B cure cancer.

 C win a Medal of Honor.

 D win the election.

5. A fight for *suffrage* is a fight for

 A relief from pain.

 B voting rights.

 C amendments.

 D women's rights.

Writing Skills Focus

Timed ∟Writing The writer describes the American quality of a "sense of possibility" in the second-to-last paragraph. Describe what you think the writer means by that and whether you think it is fair that some citizens are prevented from becoming president.

 What Do You Think Now

How might it help all citizens if naturalized citizens got the right to run for president?

Writing Workshop

Autobiographical Narrative

Write with a Purpose

Write an autobiographical narrative about a significant experience in your life. Include well-chosen details as you tell what happened, and explain why this experience continues to be meaningful to you. Your **purpose** for writing is to entertain your **audience** by sharing a meaningful event.

A Good Autobiographical Narrative

- focuses on a single, coherent incident
- is told from the first-person point of view
- relates events in a clear order, usually chronological
- includes transitions that help readers follow the events
- includes well-chosen details, relevant dialogue, and specific actions
- makes clear what the experience means to the writer

See page 266 for complete rubric.

Reader/Writer Notebook

Use your **RWN** to complete the activities for this workshop.

Think as a Reader/Writer
In this chapter, you've noted techniques writers use, and you've also practiced some of those techniques. Now it's time to relate an experience of your own. A good autobiographical narrative not only tells what happened but reveals why the incident is significant to the writer. To get started, read this excerpt from "A Shot at It" by Esmeralda Santiago.

One morning, Mr. Barone, a guidance counselor, called me to his office. He was short, with a big head and large hazel eyes under shapely eyebrows. His nose was long and round at the tip. He dressed in browns and yellows and often perched his tortoiseshell glasses on his forehead, as if he had another set of eyes up there.

← Well-chosen details allow the reader to picture the character.

"So," he pushed his glasses up, "what do you want to be when you grow up?"

"I don't know."

He shuffled through some papers. "Let's see here … you're fourteen, is that right?"

"Yes, sir."

"And you've never thought about what you want to be?"

← Relevant dialogue advances the action.

When I was very young I wanted to be a jibara [someone from the mountains of Puerto Rico]. When I was older, I wanted to be a cartographer, then a topographer. But since we'd come to Brooklyn, I'd not thought about the future much.

"No, sir."

He pulled his glasses down to where they belonged and shuffled through the papers again.

"Do you have any hobbies?" I didn't know what he meant. "Hobbies, hobbies," he flailed his hands, as if he were juggling, "things you like to do after school."

← The writer reveals her unspoken thoughts.

← Physical description makes the narrative come alive.

Think About the Professional Model
With a partner, discuss the following questions about the model.

1. What did you learn about the two characters from their dialogue?

2. Why do you think the experience was significant to the writer?

Writing Standard 1.6 Revise writing for word choice; appropriate organization; consistent point of view; and transitions between paragraphs, passages, and ideas. **2.1** Write biographies, autobiographies, short stories, or narratives: **a. Relate a clear, coherent incident, event, or situation by using well-chosen details. b. Reveal the significance of, or the writer's attitude about, the subject. c. Employ narrative and descriptive strate-**gies (e.g., relevant dialogue, specific action, physical description, background description, comparison or contrast of characters).

Prewriting

Choose a Topic

Use the Idea Starters in the margin to help you recall some memorable experiences that you enjoy telling people about. Ask yourself the following questions about each experience on your list:

- What specific details, such as sights, sounds, smells, and sensations, do I remember about the experience?
- What does the incident reveal about me or about someone else?
- What was my attitude toward the events then? What is it now?
- Why does this experience continue to be significant to me?
- Why might reading about it be important or interesting for someone else?
- Am I comfortable sharing my thoughts about the incident with my readers?

Gather Details

As you decide what situation you would like to write about, gather the details that you want to include. Ask yourself these *5 W-How?* questions:

- *Who* was involved in the incident, and what did the people involved say?
- *What* happened, and in what order did events occur?
- *When* did I have this experience?
- *Where* did the events happen?
- *Why* did the events happen? What set them in motion?
- *How* did I feel about the incident at the time, and how do I feel now?
- *How* do I want my readers to feel about my experience?

To be sure that you recall the details clearly and coherently, create a chart of events like the one below:

Time	Experience	Details
when I was 13	I was the only middle school student to become a varsity cross-country runner.	I dedicated myself to running; I easily passed the older racers.

Idea Starters

- a childhood adventure
- going to a family reunion
- my first day of middle school
- winning or losing a big game
- attending a birthday party

Your Turn _____

Get Started Making notes in your **RWN,** decide on a specific experience to write about. Then, use a chart like the one on the left to gather details about the experience. Your notes and chart will help you plan your autobiographical narrative.

 Learn It Online
An interactive graphic organizer can help you generate and organize ideas. Try one at:

go.hrw.com   H8-259   **Go**

Think About Audience and Purpose

Before you begin your draft, think about your **audience** and about your **purpose** for writing. This will help you decide what details to include and what ideas to emphasize. Jot down answers to the following questions:

- Who will read my narrative? Will it be read by my classmates? my teacher? my family? What information will they need to understand my story?
- Why am I writing about this experience? Do I want to make my audience laugh—or cry? Do I want them to understand something about me or about the world we live in?

Plan Your Narrative

What will you include in your autobiographical narrative? Use an outline like the one below to help you plan your personal narrative.

> **Plan for an Autobiographical Narrative**
> Write what the experience means to you: _____
> **Introduction** _____
> **Body** (Order of events):
>   **1.** _____
>   **2.** _____
>   **3.** _____
>   **4.** _____
> **Conclusion** _____

Here is one writer's outline for an autobiographical narrative. Use this model to help you create your own plan.

> *Autobiographical Narrative*
> This experience was significant to me because I learned that the most important thing is to do your best.
> **Introduction:** "This is going to be the year for me," I thought.
> **Body:**
>   1. I prepared to win the first race by training hard, so that I would make the varsity team.
>   2. In the race, I ran as fast as I could, and only one runner kept up.
>   3. The other runner at first fell behind but caught up with me at the end.
>   4. I won a varsity letter and met my goal.
> **Conclusion:** Proud of myself, I thought, "I did my best this year, and next year I'll do even better."

Peer Review

Share your completed plan with a peer. Ask your peer to offer concrete suggestions for improving your plans for your autobiographical narrative.

Your Turn _____

Plan Your Narrative To help you decide what to include in your autobiographical narrative, make a **personal narrative plan.** Then review your plan, asking yourself which details you should emphasize and which you could add to make your narrative more effective. Remember to keep in mind your **purpose** and **audience.**

Drafting

Keep Point of View Consistent

In an autobiographical narrative you'll use the **first-person point of view** pronouns (*I, me, my*) to refer to yourself. Be sure to use your natural voice—the words and phrases you would use when telling the story to your friends. Your **tone** helps reveal your attitude about your topic.

Use Relevant Dialogue

A good rule for writing stories and narratives is "Show don't tell." One way to do this is, instead of simply describing what is happening, to show what is going on through dialogue. In her autobiographical narrative, Esmeralda Santiago uses dialogue that not only reveals what the two characters are like but also moves the action along. You also have to think about when not to use dialogue, as Santiago does when she tells us what she is thinking but does not say aloud.

> **Framework for an Autobiographical Narrative**
>
> **Introduction**
> - Begin with an engaging first sentence.
> - Include details about when and where the incident took place.
>
> **Body**
> - Relay the order of events using well-chosen details, specifications, and relevant dialogue.
> - Include your thoughts and feelings as the events unfold.
>
> **Conclusion**
> - Reveal why the experience is meaningful.

Grammar Link Punctuating Dialogue

When you write an autobiographical narrative, be sure to punctuate your dialogue correctly. Study the following sentence from "A Shot at It."

"So," he pushed his glasses up, "what do you want to be when you grow up?"

- Use quotation marks around the words that are actually spoken.
- Put closing quotation marks outside punctuation (commas, periods, question marks, exclamation marks).

Here are two examples:

"You're new here, aren't you?" Marta said. "Let me help you find your homeroom."

"You know you can do it," the coach exhorted on the day of the big game, "so get out there and give it your all!"

● Writing Tip

When you write dialogue, remember to begin a new paragraph each time you change speakers.

Your Turn _____

Write Your Draft After creating your framework, use it to help you write a draft of your narrative. Think about the following questions as you write your draft:

- What **tone** should I use in my narrative?
- Did my use of dialogue bring the incident to life?
- Have I punctuated my dialogue correctly?

Peer Review

Work with a partner and review each other's drafts. Answer each question on the chart to the right to see how you could improve your drafts. Be sure to take notes about what your partner suggests.

Evaluating and Revising

Read the questions in the left column of the chart, and use the tips in the middle column to make revisions to your autobiographical narrative. The right column suggests techniques that you can use to revise your draft.

Autobiographical Narrative: Guidelines for Content and Organization

Evaluation Questions	Tips	Revision Techniques
1. Have you related a clear, coherent incident?	**Put stars** next to details that show when and where the experience happened.	**Add** details about where and when the event took place.
2. Have you used the first-person point of view consistently?	**Check** that you consistently tell the story from your own point of view.	**Change** any third-person pronouns to first-person pronouns, as necessary.
3. Are events organized clearly in chronological order?	**Number the events.** Check that the sequence shows the actual order of events.	**Rearrange** events in the order in which they occurred. **Add** transitions to link events.
4. Have you included well-chosen descriptive details?	**Highlight** sensory details. In the margin, note which senses the sensory details appeal to.	**Elaborate** with sensory details, if necessary. **Delete** irrelevant details.
5. Is your dialogue relevant to your purpose?	**Put a star** next to dialogue that reveals character. **Put a check** next to dialogue that advances the action.	**Add** dialogue that reveals character and advances the action. **Delete** irrelevant dialogue.
6. Does your narrative include specific actions?	**Circle** each specific action.	**Add** actions that will make your narrative come alive.
7. Does your narrative reveal why the incident is significant to you—and perhaps to your audience?	**Underline** details that show why the experience is meaningful.	**Add** a statement that explains the significance of the incident, if necessary.

Read this student's draft, the comments on its structure, and some suggestions for how the narrative could be made even stronger.

Today Is the Day

by Alex Bloom, Gray Middle School

"This is going to be the year for me," I thought. To achieve the standards I set for myself, I worked out every spare minute. As the season progressed, I focused even more on my running, securing a position on the school's track team. But I wanted more. Determined to be the only varsity cross-country runner from middle school, I pushed myself the extra mile. I made running part of my daily routine. I drank, ate, and slept running. I was determined to be prepared to win the first race of the year.

← The student's first-person **point of view** is established right away and maintained throughout the narrative.

Bang! The race began. "I can do this," I thought. I quickly passed most of the racers from the other teams, putting myself in the front of the pack. My hair blew from side to side in the wind, and my uniform was no longer neat. I sped past the rest of the racers, leaving them behind. Only one runner stayed with me throughout the race. We flew around every turn with speed and precision, competing, challenging each other. He fell back as I powered up the hill, I moved ahead, gaining distance. I turned into the final corner.

← Well-chosen details bring the race to life.

← The chronological order of the events is clear.

MINI-LESSON ▶ **How to Add Descriptive Details**

Notice that Alex's description of the race doesn't really help readers picture it. Alex might add details to the second paragraph to make the descriptions even more clear to the reader.

Alex's Revision of Paragraph Two

Bang! The race began. "I can do this," I thought. I quickly passed most

of the racers from the other teams, putting myself in the front of the

pack. My *long* hair blew from side to side in the wind, and my *bright red* uniform

was no longer neat. *drenched in sweat.* I sped past the rest of the racers, leaving them

behind. Only one runner *, a gangly freshman,* stayed with me throughout the race.

Your Turn _____

Add Details Read your draft and then ask yourself: What specific details and descriptive information would help my readers picture events better?

Student Draft *continues*

After writing the **climax** of the narrative, Alex reflects on what it means.

> I stepped carefully on the uneven surface, hoping not to twist my ankle. "I want to win this race," I thought. I used every bit of energy left in my exhausted body, but the other runner suddenly appeared right behind me. I guess you could call it a photo finish because we crossed the finish line neck and neck, but he won by inches. Then it hit me. It didn't matter if I won or not because I tried my hardest.

The final sentence of the narrative helps reveal the significance of Alex's experience.

> The season ended. An awards ceremony was held in the school cafeteria. The coach called everybody's name, and then he finally called mine. "This is the moment," I thought. "This is the moment of truth." I received a varsity letter, reaching the goal I had set. I was also named the Outstanding Middle School Runner of the Year. Proud of myself, I thought, "I did my best this year, and next year I'll do even better."

MINI-LESSON ▶ **How to Add Transitions**

In the final paragraph of his draft, Alex jumps from the end of the season to an awards ceremony. Then, he describes the coach calling "everybody's name." Alex does not use transitions to connect these ideas, and the sentences seem choppy. How can Alex describe what happened and make the passage of time clear? Transitions will help.

Alex revised the paragraph, adding transitions to show the passage of time and to connect the ideas. Transitions are written in blue.

Alex's Draft of Paragraph Four

> The season ended. An awards ceremony was held in the school cafeteria. The coach called everybody's name, and then he finally called mine.

Alex's Revision of Paragraph Four

> After many more races, ⟨I was excited when I went to the⟩
>   ⋏The season ended. An awards ceremony ~~was held~~ in the school
> later that month. Soon
> cafeteria. ⋏The coach called everybody's name, and then he finally
>
> called mine.

Your Turn _____

Add Transitions Read your draft and then ask yourself:

- Does each sentence flow logically from one idea to another?
- What transitional words, phrases, or sentences should I add to make my ideas flow more logically?

Proofreading and Publishing

Proofreading

Re-read your autobiographical narrative, and look for errors in grammar, usage, spelling, and punctuation. Make sure that you have used commas correctly in any series of verbs or verb phrases.

Proofreading Partners Trade papers with a partner to proofread each other's work and discuss any possible changes. Then, prepare your final copy to share with your audience.

Grammar Link **Fixing Run-on Sentences**

As you read over your narrative, be sure that you have a period at the end of every complete thought. In the second paragraph of his draft, Alex's writing was not clear because he had a run-on sentence. To fix the run-on sentence, Alex needed to fix the punctuation.

> He fell back as I powered up the hill. I moved ahead, gaining distance.

Notice how Alex separated the run-on sentence into two complete sentences simply by changing the comma to a period.

Publishing

Share your autobiographical narrative with your audience. Here are some ways to share your essay:

- Give a copy of your narrative to friends, family members, and classmates. If you wish, add photographs or illustrations to your narrative.
- Read your narrative aloud to a group.

Reflect on the Process
Thinking about how you wrote your autobiographical narrative will help you in other writing that you'll do. In your **RWN,** make notes about what you learned and answer the following questions:

1. How did writing an autobiographical narrative help you to better understand how you feel about your experience or what the significance of the incident might be?
2. What techniques did you use to convey the importance of your experience to your readers?

Proofreading Tip

Reading your narrative aloud may help you catch errors that you do not see when scanning the page. As you read aloud, pay attention to places where you stumble over phrases. There might be punctuation errors that you need to correct. Also pay attention to places where one thought runs into another. These might be run-on sentences that each need to end with a period.

Your Turn _____

Proofread and Publish Take time to proofread your work. Check to be sure you have fixed any run-on sentences. Also, correct any errors in punctuating a series of verbs. Some places where you could submit your work are

- an online literary magazine
- your personal Web page
- a class anthology

Scoring Rubric

You can use one of the rubrics below to evaluate your autobiographical narrative from the Writing Workshop or your response to the on-demand prompt on the next page.

Autobiographical Narrative Writing	Organization and Focus	Sentence Structure	Conventions
4 • Provides a *thoroughly developed* narrative with a clear, coherent incident, event, or situation. • Includes *appropriate* strategies (e.g., relevant dialogue, specific action, physical description, and background description).	• *Clearly* addresses all of the writing tasks. • Demonstrates a *complete and specific* understanding of purpose and audience. • Maintains a *consistent* point of view and *clear* transitions. • *Effectively* reveals the significance of, or the writer's attitude about, the subject.	• Includes sentence *variety*.	• Contains *few, if any,* errors in the conventions of the English language (grammar, punctuation, capitalization, spelling). These errors do **not** interfere with the reader's understanding of the writing.
3 • Provides an *adequately developed* narrative with a clear, coherent incident, event, or situation. • Includes *mostly appropriate* strategies (e.g., relevant dialogue, specific action, physical description, and background description).	• Addresses most of the writing task • Demonstrates a *general* understanding of purpose and audience. • Maintains a *mostly consistent* point of view and *relatively clear* transitions. • For the most part *effectively* reveals the significance of, or the writer's attitude about, the subject.	• Includes some sentence *variety*.	• Contains *some errors* in the conventions of the English language (grammar, punctuation, capitalization, spelling). These errors do **not** interfere with the reader's understanding of the writing.
2 • Provides a *minimally developed* narrative with a *somewhat clear,* coherent incident, event, or situation. • *Attempts* to use appropriate strategies but with *minimal effectiveness* (e.g., relevant dialogue, specific action, physical description, and background description).	• Addresses *some* of the writing task • Demonstrates *little* understanding of purpose and audience. • Maintains an *inconsistent* point of view and *awkward* transitions that do not unify important ideas. • *Suggests* the significance of, or the writer's attitude about, the subject but with *limited* success.	• Includes *little* sentence variety	• Contains *several errors* in the conventions of the English language (grammar, punctuation, capitalization, spelling). These errors **may** interfere with the reader's understanding of the writing.
1 • Lacks a developed narrative with a clear, coherent incident, event, or situation. • Fails to use appropriate strategies (e.g., relevant dialogue, specific action, physical description, and background description).	• Addresses *only one* part of the writing task • Demonstrates *no understanding* of purpose and audience. • *Lacks* a point of view and transitions that unify important ideas. • *Does not convey* the significance of, or the writer's attitude about, the subject.	• Includes *no* sentence variety.	• Contains *serious errors* in the conventions of the English language (grammar, punctuation, capitalization, spelling). These errors interfere with the reader's understanding of the writing.

Preparing for **Timed Writing**

Autobiographical Narrative

When responding to a prompt asking you to write an autobiographical narrative, use what you have learned from this chapter's Writing Workshop, the rubric on page 266, and the steps below.

Writing Standard 2.1 Write biographies, **autobiographies,** short stories, or narratives: **a. Relate a clear, coherent incident, event, or situation by using well-chosen details. b. Reveal the significance of, or the writer's attitude about, the subject. c. Employ narrative and descriptive strategies (e.g., relevant dialogue, specific activities, physical description, background description,** comparison or contrast of characters.

Writing Prompt
Write an autobiographical narrative in which you relate a clear, coherent incident. Use well-chosen details, specific actions, and relevant dialogue to describe the events, and let readers know why the experience is still significant for you.

Study the Prompt
Be sure to read the prompt carefully, and identify all parts of your task. Circle or underline key instructional words: *autobiographical, narrative, coherent, details, actions, dialogue, experience, significant*. Re-read the prompt to make sure you understand your task.

Note that your narrative should not only describe the events of this incident but also the meaning the experience had for you.
Tip: Spend about five minutes studying the prompt.

Plan Your Response
First, think of some personal experiences that you feel comfortable writing about. Choose the most meaningful of those experiences as the subject of your narrative. Once you have settled on your subject, take notes on the following:

- specific details that you remember about the events
- what the incident reveals about you or someone else
- why the experience is still important to you

Tip: Spend about fifteen minutes planning your response.

Respond to the Prompt
Using the notes you've just made, draft your narrative. Follow these guidelines:

- In the introduction, grab the reader's attention with an interesting opener, and set the scene with well-chosen descriptive details.
- In the body of your narrative, relate the events in chronological order, using dialogue wherever relevant.
- In the conclusion, state why the incident is meaningful to you.
- Remember to use a consistent first-person point of view.

Tip: Spend about twenty minutes writing your draft.

Improve Your Response
Revising Go back to the key aspects of the prompt. Have you used descriptive details and relevant dialogue? Have you used transitions to guide the reader?

Proofreading Take a few minutes to proofread your narrative to correct errors in grammar, spelling, punctuation, and capitalization. Make sure that all of your edits are neat, and erase any stray marks.

Checking Your Final Copy Before you turn in your autobiographical narrative, read it one more time to catch any errors that you may have missed. You'll be glad that you took the extra time for one final review.

Tip: Save ten minutes to improve your paper.

Delivering an Autobiographical Narrative

Speak with a Purpose

Adapt your written autobiographical narrative into an oral narrative. After you have practiced delivering your narrative, present it to your class.

Think as a Reader/Writer Good stories aren't always fiction. They can be true stories, or narratives, about experiences that someone has had. A story about something that you did, or that happened to you, can reveal more than just the facts of the experience. As you deliver your narrative, you can express why the story is relevant to you—and perhaps to your audience as well. In this workshop you will turn a true story about yourself, an autobiographical narrative, into an oral presentation.

Adapt Your Autobiographical Narrative

Make It Interesting

Tell your story so that you will capture your audience's attention. Remember, your audience is listening to your autobiographical narrative, not reading it, so they have only one chance to understand what you are saying. Use these tips to develop an enjoyable oral presentation.

- **Background Information** Include extra information your listeners might need to understand your narrative.
- **Realistic Dialogue** Try to re-create the actual words of the people involved in the events, as well as the <u>motivation</u> behind the words.
- **Specific Action** Describe events directly and clearly.
- **Word Choice** Use precise nouns to describe people, settings, and things. Use active verbs, ones that express either physical or mental activity (as opposed to *be* verbs such as *is, were, am,* and *been*).
- **Descriptive Details** Select words and phrases that appeal to one or more of the five senses—sight, hearing, touch, taste, and smell.
- **Organization** Tell your story in chronological order. Use transitions to help listeners follow your story.
- **Conclusion** Sum up your story by sharing with listeners why your experience was memorable, fun, scary, or eye-opening.

Streamline

Look back at your written autobiographical narrative and consider what you can exclude. Remember that some words are necessary for readers but not for listeners.

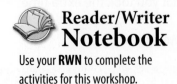

Reader/Writer Notebook

Use your **RWN** to complete the activities for this workshop.

Listening and Speaking Standard 1.3 Organize information to achieve particular purposes by matching the message, vocabulary, **voice modulation, expression, and tone** to the audience and purpose.

2.1 Deliver narrative presentations (e.g., biographical, **autobiographical): a.** Relate a clear, coherent incident, event, or situation by using well-chosen details. **b.** Reveal the significance of, and the subject's attitude about, the incident, event, or situation. **c.** Employ narrative and descriptive strategies (e.g., relevant dialogue, specific action, physical description, background description, comparison or contrast of characters).

Deliver Your Autobiographical Narrative

Engage Your Audience

Acting out information, rather than depending solely on your words, is an effective—and often more interesting—way to communicate an idea. **Verbal techniques,** the manner in which you use your voice, and **nonverbal techniques,** the manner in which you use your body, can help you communicate your purpose, feelings, and message. For example, instead of telling your audience that someone is angry, you can show them by using **facial expressions** (such as scowling or glaring) or **voice modulation** (raising the pitch of your voice to a shrill level, or changing the tone of your voice to sound irritated).

Verbal Techniques	Nonverbal Techniques
Volume No matter how loudly or softly you speak, be sure your audience can understand you.	**Facial Expressions** Smiling or frowning, looking puzzled or surprised can help you convey your meaning.
Pace Speak fast enough not to bore your listeners and slowly enough that they can follow your presentation.	**Gestures** Pointing, reaching, or banging can add emphasis to what you say, but be careful not to gesture needlessly.
Pitch Qualities of pitch, or modulation—such as high, low, voice, musical, or rumbling—can help clarify your meaning.	**Posture** Whether you stand straight or slouch can influence the way your audience reacts to what you say.
Tone Your attitude toward what you are saying, such as amused, angry, or serious, should be clear from the tone of your voice.	**Appearance** You may want to dress more formally for a serious presentation but wear casual clothes for a humorous one.
Enunciation Say each word clearly and precisely. Be sure not to slur words or drop word endings.	**Eye Contact** Make eye contact with your audience members frequently. This will make them feel that you are speaking to each of them personally.

Try, Try Again

The best way to feel comfortable and prepared in front of an audience is to be well rehearsed. Review the tips on practicing on page 164.

Note It

To avoid finding yourself tongue-tied when you present your autobiographical narrative, jot down some notes. Your notes should be brief and easy to read so that you can glance at them without losing eye contact with your audience.

A Presentation of a Good Autobiographical Narrative

- focuses on a single, clear, and important event
- provides insight into the speaker's attitude about the incident
- reveals the significance of the narrative to the speaker
- re-creates dialogue of the people involved
- contains descriptive details that allow listeners to visualize the people, settings, and action in the situation.
- includes extra background information, if needed

⬤ Speaking Tip

To improve your speaking, be your own listener. When you practice, use an audio or video recorder to capture the delivery of your autobiographical narrative. Take note of <u>factors</u>, such as where you should speed up or slow down, when you can make eye contact, and how gestures or other nonverbal techniques might be helpful. Also note where you might pause for effect—you might also have to pause for your audience's reaction.

Learn It Online
Bring your presentation to a wider audience. Use the *Digital Storytelling* mini-site at:

go.hrw.com   H8-269   **Go**

Character   **Directions:** Read the two passages. Then, answer each question that follows.

Survival on the Atlantic
from Adrift: Seventy-Six Days Lost at Sea by **Steven Callahan**

The author of this passage was on a boat that sank off the coast of Africa. He survived on a life raft that had only three pounds of food and one gallon of fresh water. No one had ever lasted more than a month under these conditions, but he crossed the Atlantic Ocean and was rescued after almost eleven weeks.

The sea lies flat. Clouds sit motionless in the sky as if glued there. The sun beats down, roasting my arid[1] body. The working still[2] may provide just enough water to carry me the three hundred miles to the shipping lanes. The wind has turned. The lanes somehow always seem to be three hundred miles away. As I succumb[3] to drowsiness, fantasies of being picked up by a ship and lying in the cool green grass by the pond at my parents' house race through my head.

The shaking of the raft jerks me from my stupor.[4] I look down. A flat, gray, round-headed beast scrapes its hide across the bottom as it lazily swings around for another bite. It's incredible that the dorados and triggers[5] have not fled the shark at all! Instead, they collect closely around it. I think they have invited him for tea. "Come over to our place and have a taste of this big black crumpet."[6] He slowly swims around to the stern and slides under. Rolling over, belly up, he bites one of the ballast pockets,[7] quaking the raft with his convulsive[8] ten-foot torso. Bless the pockets. He might tear a hole in the floor, but that shouldn't damage the tubes, at least not yet. Should I take a shot and risk losing the spear?

He cruises out in front of me just below the surface. I thrust, and the steel strikes his back. It is like hitting stone. With one quick stroke he slithers away, not in any particular hurry. I watch for a long time

---

1. **arid:** dry.
2. **still:** here, mechanism for purifying water.
3. **succumb:** give way; yield.
4. **stupor:** daze; trance.

5. **dorados and triggers:** kinds of fish.
6. **crumpet:** type of pastry often served with tea in England.
7. **ballast pockets:** sections of the raft holding weights to keep the raft stable.
8. **convulsive:** shaking.

before collapsing, craving water more than ever.

I thought that the fish would scatter and give me notice of a shark's approach, but now I know that I cannot trust them to warn me of danger. I worry about the gas bottle and line that inflated the raft and that lie under the bottom tube. If that link is bitten through, will the whole raft deflate? Will the bottle lure the sharks to bite the tube from which it hangs? Worry, worry, worry. It is apprehension[9] that beds with me each night and apprehension that awakens me each day. As darkness comes and I drift off to sleep, I long to be in a place with no anxieties. How repetitious and simple my desires have become.

The raft is lifted and thrown to the side as if kicked by a giant's boot. A shark's raking skin scrapes a squeak from it as I leap from slumber. "Keep off the bottom!" I yell at myself as I pull the cushion and sleeping bag close to the opening. I perch as lightly as possible upon it. Peering into the night, I grasp the spear gun. He's on the other side. I must wait until he comes to the opening. A fin breaks the water in a quick swirl of phosphorescent[10] fire and darts behind the raft, circling in to strike again. A flicker of light in the black sea shows me he is below, and I jab with a splash. Nothing. The splash may entice[11] him to attack more viciously. Again the fin cuts the surface. The shark smashes into the raft with a rasping blow. I strike at the flicker. Hit! The water erupts, the dark fin shoots out and around and then is gone. Where is he? My heart's pounding breaks the silence. It beats across the still black waters to the stars. I wait.

Gulping a half pint of water, I rearrange my bed so that at the first bump I can be ready at the entrance. Hours pass before I drift again into uneasy sleep.

For two days the going is slow under the baking sky. I go fourteen or fifteen miles each twenty-four hours. Hunger wrenches my insides. My mouth burns. But the still produces twenty ounces of water a day. I begin to rebuild my stock while drinking one pint for each arc of the sun. The calm is also good for visibility. Should a ship pass, the glowing orange canopy will be more easily spot-

---

9. **apprehension:** worry; dread.

10. **phosphorescent:** like light given off without heat.
11. **entice:** tempt; lure.

Literary Skills Review CONTINUED

ted. However, sharks also visit more frequently in calm weather. The shipping lanes lie over two weeks to the west at this pace. For hours I pore over the chart, estimating minimum and maximum time and distance to rescue.

In my thirteen days adrift, I have eaten only three pounds of food. My stomach is in knots, but starvation is more subtle than simply increasing pain. My movements are slower, more fatiguing. The fat is gone. Now my muscles feed on themselves. Visions of food snap at me like whips. I feel little else.

Several triggerfish swim up from astern[12] as the breeze builds. They come up broadside. Once again I aim and fire. The spear strikes and drives through. I yank the impaled[13] fish aboard. Its tight round mouth belches a clicking croak. Its eyes roll wildly. The stiff, rough body can only flap its fins in protest. Food! Lowering my head I chant, "Food, I have food." My eyes fill with tears. I weep for my fish, for me, for the state of my desperation. Then I feed on its bitter meat.

The evening skies of my seventy-fifth day are smudged with clouds migrating westward. A drizzle falls, barely more than a fog, but any amount of saltless moisture causes me to jump into action. For two hours I swing my plastic buckets through the air, collecting a pint and a half. My catchment[14] systems will do the trick.

As long as the waves are not too large, I do not worry about capsizing, so I curl up and sleep against the bow. These days it takes so long to choke out the pain and fall asleep. When I do, it is only an hour or less before a sharp stab from a wound or sore awakens me.

I arise to survey the black waters, which occasionally flash with phosphorescent lines from a breaking wave or the flight of a fish. A soft glow looms just to the south of dead ahead. And there, just to the north, is another. A fishing fleet? They do not move. My god, these are no ships! It is the nighttime halo of land that I detect! Standing, I glimpse a flip of light from the side. A lighthouse beam, just over the horizon, sweeps a wide bar of light like a club beating out a rhythm—flash, pause, flash-flash, rest; flash, pause, flash-flash. It is land. "Land!" I shout. "Land ho!" I'm dancing up and down, flinging my arms about, as if hugging an invisible companion. I can't believe it!

---

12. **astern:** at the back of the raft.
13. **impaled:** pierced or fixed on something pointed.

14. **catchment:** collecting of water, especially rainfall.

from the Odyssey by Homer

retold by **Robin Lister**

A sudden tempest whipped up the sea. Clinging to the mast I looked up to see great Zeus[1] himself burst out of the clouds with an arm raised high above his head. In the next instant his arm came down and hurled his dreaded thunderbolt straight at our ship. The vessel exploded, and those men not killed by the blast were drowned.

I alone survived. But it seemed that I had only been saved for a more horrible end. I had clung to the mast as the ship broke up around me and it kept me afloat in the seething water. The storm soon abated,[2] but our old friend, the southeasterly wind, now returned to drive me back toward the grim straits of Scylla and Charybdis.[3] All through the night that same wind blew, and when morning came I saw the dreaded cliffs ahead of me. Before I knew it, I was racing toward the smaller cliff. I was only feet away when the water began to churn. Charybdis was sucking her whirlpool in.

I clung to the mast and shut my eyes. There was nothing I could do. Seconds later the far end was sucked down with such violence that I was catapulted[4] high up into the branches of the fig tree that grows out of the cliff.

Now I could see right down to the bottom of the whirlpool, where the hideous monster lay. Her vast tentacles swirled the water around, and her bulbous, octopus eyes stared greedily up, waiting for me to fall. But I held on and waited, for one hour, then another, and still she sucked the whirlpool in. Finally, Charybdis could hold it in no longer, and with a great gush the undigested contents of her belly flew into the air around me. As soon as the water had settled I dived and swam furiously away from the cliff. The mast was floating in the middle of the straits, and I managed to grab hold of it once more. Now I was within reach of the cruel Scylla, but Zeus must have been watching over me; a powerful current carried me out of the straits before she sensed that I was there.

---

1. **Zeus:** chief of the Greek gods.
2. **abated:** lessened in force.
3. **Scylla and Charybdis:** two mythical monsters on either side of a narrow waterway.

---

4. **catapulted:** thrown; hurled.

For nine days and nights I drifted with the currents. They took me around the southeast headland of Thrinacia,[5] but although I was parched and hungry I dared not set foot on those fateful shores again. Then the currents carried me slowly westward, further and further away from my long-lost home. On the tenth morning I was finally washed up on an unknown shore. I was too weak to move, and my throat too dry to utter a sound. I lay on the burning sand, beneath the cruel sun, waiting to die.

Then I must have passed out, because Calypso told me later that she had found me lying on the beach, unconscious and half-dead. She dragged me back to her cavern of marble and gold, and nursed me back to life. I opened my eyes to see the lovely nymph[6] staring down at me, her braided hair falling toward my face. She had laid me on a bed of the softest down, covered my burned, cracked skin with cold wet cloths, and poured cool spring water between my parched lips. I tried to speak, but no words came. She placed a finger over my mouth and smiled her lovely smile. I gazed at her in wonder until I fell into a deep sleep.

---

5. **Thrinacia:** island where the sun god Helios keeps his cattle.

---

6. **nymph:** minor nature goddess.

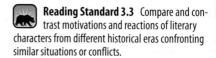

Reading Standard 3.3 Compare and contrast motivations and reactions of literary characters from different historical eras confronting similar situations or conflicts.

1. Both the narrator in "Survival on the Atlantic" and the narrator in the *Odyssey* react to their situation by
   A hanging on to a ship's mast.
   B catching fish for food.
   C facing dangerous sea creatures.
   D alerting passing ships.

2. Read this sentence from "Survival on the Atlantic," and note the narrator's use of irony when faced with danger.

   > "Come over to our place and have a taste of this big black crumpet."

   Which quote from the *Odyssey* reflects its narrator's use of irony in the face of danger?
   A "our old friend, the southeasterly wind"
   B "Charybdis was sucking her whirlpool in."
   C "It kept me afloat in the seething water."
   D "The currents carried me slowly westward."

3. The narrator of "Survival on the Atlantic" determines where he is at sea by studying charts. The narrator of the *Odyssey* determines where he is by
   A recognizing the coast line.
   B reading the stars at night.
   C rowing with oars.
   D using ancient tools, such as sextants.

4. Compared with the narrator in "Survival on the Atlantic," the narrator in the *Odyssey* survived *mostly* because he was
   A a more experienced sailor.
   B a luckier man.
   C more prepared.
   D physically stronger.

5. Read this phrase from the *Odyssey*.

   > ". . . away from my long-lost home."

   Which quote from "Survival on the Atlantic" shares the motivation of the one above?
   A "It is the nighttime halo of land."
   B "'Land!' I shout. 'Land ho!' I'm dancing."
   C "Keep off the bottom."
   D "fantasies of lying . . . by the pond at my parents' house"

6. Each of the following reactions by the narrator of "Survival on the Atlantic" sets him in the modern age *except*
   A "I worry about the gas bottle and line."
   B "Will the whole raft deflate?"
   C "I swing my plastic buckets through the air."
   D "'Food, I have food.' My eyes fill with tears."

Timed Writing

7. Both narrators face a similar conflict. Identify each character's conflict and his reaction to it. Explain how the reaction leads to the resolution of the excerpt. Finally, state the common resolution to the conflict.

Informational Skills Review

Proposition and Support   **Directions:** Read the

selection below. Then, answer each question that follows.

Dear Councilman Duane:

More and more minors are smoking. When teens smoke, many problems arise. Something needs to be done to prove to minors that smoking is a bad thing. I am writing this letter to you in hopes that you will take steps to end this big problem.

Many problems develop when teenagers smoke. When teens smoke, laws are broken. Merchants break laws by intentionally selling cigarettes to minors. Teenage smokers damage their bodies permanently by smoking. Cigarettes cause addictions; even when teens want to quit, they often find they can't. Smoking can even affect a teenager's schooling. If a teenager needs a cigarette badly, he or she may ditch school to get one.

To help stop this problem, the city council could start a campaign against teenage smoking. You could make sure that schools with the sixth grade and older have a required class about the hazards of smoking, especially before the legal age. You could sponsor contests in each school for the best "Don't Smoke" posters, poems, essays, and stories. You could put the winners' posters and writing up around New York City. An educational campaign aimed at young teenagers would definitely help solve the problem of smoking by minors.

Some teenagers think, "It's my body; I can do what I want with it." Most smoking teenagers haven't fully matured emotionally. That means that what they believe now can change drastically in the following three to ten years of their lives. Therefore, as adults they may seriously regret decisions they made as teenagers.

Thank you for listening to my thoughts on this matter. I appreciate it and hope that you can do something to end the dilemma. Teenagers need to stop smoking, and you, as a person in power, can help them understand that it isn't all right to smoke.

—Hannah Fleury
St. Luke's School
New York, New York

1. Which of the following sentences states the letter writer's proposition?

   A "Even when teens want to quit, they often find they can't."

   B "Teenagers think, 'It's my body; I can do what I want with it.'"

   C "Something needs to be done to prove to minors that smoking is a bad thing."

   D "Most smoking teenagers haven't fully matured emotionally."

2. Which of the following statements from the letter is an opinion?

   A "Cigarettes cause addictions."

   B "More and more minors are smoking."

   C "When teens smoke, many problems arise."

   D "Something needs to be done to prove to minors that smoking is a bad thing."

3. To keep students from smoking, the author suggests all of the following *except* a(n)

   A required class.

   B fine for smoking.

   C school contest.

   D educational campaign.

4. Which of the following sentences does *not* offer support for the letter writer's main idea?

   A "When teens smoke, laws are broken."

   B "Cigarettes cause addictions."

   C "Smoking can even affect a teenager's schooling."

   D "Teenagers need to stop smoking."

5. The letter writer uses all of the following supports for her argument *except*

   A facts.

   B opinions.

   C anecdotes.

   D statistics.

6. The conclusion of this letter

   A restates the proposition.

   B is a call to action.

   C both of the above

   D none of the above

Timed Writing

7. What is the letter writer's purpose for writing this essay? Do you think she is successful? Explain.

Vocabulary Skills Review

Synonyms **Directions:** Choose the word or phrase that is the *best* synonym of each italicized word.

1. An *incentive* is a(n)
   A motivation.
   B opening.
   C incident.
   D protection.

2. At work, your *superiors* are your
   A co-workers.
   B assistants.
   C bosses.
   D employees.

3. An *incomprehensible* speech is
   A insolvable.
   B flowery.
   C not believable.
   D not understandable.

4. If an animal is *petrified,* it is
   A terrified.
   B poisonous.
   C obstinate.
   D conspicuous.

5. *Stirred* means
   A rooted.
   B silenced.
   C excited.
   D stiffened.

6. To *dispel* is to
   A assemble.
   B drive away.
   C distribute.
   D bring forth.

7. A *fugitive* is a(n)
   A boundary.
   B outburst.
   C departure.
   D escapee.

8. A man who is *impeccably* dressed is dressed
   A perfectly.
   B sloppily.
   C hastily.
   D fancily.

Academic Vocabulary

Answer the following questions about the Academic Vocabulary words from this chapter.

9. Another term for *factor* is
   A reason.
   B response.
   C component.
   D fabrication.

10. Your *reactions* are your
    A desires.
    B responses.
    C reasons.
    D behaviors.

Writing Skills Review

Writing Standard 2.1 **Write** biographies, **autobiographies**, short stories, or narratives.

Autobiographical Narrative **Directions:** Read the following passage from a short story. Then, answer each question that follows.

(1) It was a cool October evening as I stood backstage all dressed up in my black leotard and tights with a gold-sequined belt. (2) My hair was pulled back in a bun, and a strong flowery smell of hair spray wafted around me. (3) My brother had teased me and called my outfit "silly," but I felt beautiful. (4) I was seven years old, and I knew that my first dance performance would be perfect. (5) I had eaten spaghetti, my favorite meal, for dinner. (6) As I pranced proudly onto the stage and into the hot, bright stage lights, I swelled with confidence. (7) Just as I neared my position on stage, my enthusiasm interfered with my footing, and I tripped. (8) On my knees on the stage floor, I could hear my brother's distinctive laugh and feel the heat rushing to my face. (9) I remembered my dance teacher's advice: "If you make a mistake, keep smiling and move on." (10) I held my tears and jumped up from the floor like a graceful ballerina. (11) I wouldn't let a little fall stop me from enjoying my night in the spotlight.

1. Which of the following additions would *best* help the writer develop the ideas introduced in this paragraph?

   A description of the main character's mother

   B description of the main character's expressions

   C description of the actions of the other dancers

   D description of the car ride to the performance

2. Which of the following sentences is *least* necessary for the paragraph's coherence?

   A sentence 2

   B sentence 3

   C sentence 5

   D Sentence 7

3. What should the writer add to this paragraph or to a later passage to make the autobiographical narrative complete?

   A a reflection on the importance of this event

   B an explanation of the history of dance recitals

   C a description of the dance's choreography

   D a summary of the events leading up to the fall

4. The tone of this story would *best* be described as a mixture of

   A anger and confidence.

   B confidence and sadness.

   C confusion and sadness.

   D embarrassment and confidence.

Fiction

The Clay Marble

Twelve-year-old Dara and her family flee war-torn Cambodia and find a haven at the refugee camp of Nong Chan. In *The Clay Marble* by Minfong Ho, Dara makes a new friend, Jantu, and for a short while their lives are peaceful. When the war brings chaos to the camp, however, Dara is separated from her family and Jantu. Now she must find the courage to reunite with the people she loves.

North by Night: A Story of the Underground Railroad

Katherine Ayres's *North by Night: A Story of the Underground Railroad* is composed of fictional journal entries and letters written by sixteen-year-old Lucy Spenser. Lucy has been helping fugitives from slavery reach Canada for four years. When one of the fugitives dies while giving birth to a baby, Lucy is faced with a difficult decision.

Call Me María

When María moves with her father from Puerto Rico to New York, she finds the two worlds couldn't be more different. *Call Me María* by Judith Ortiz Cofer uses a mixture of prose, letters, and poems to describe María's experiences adjusting to life in a new country, speaking a new language, and making new friends.

The Call of the Wild

In Jack London's classic adventure story *The Call of the Wild,* Buck is a house pet who is stolen from his comfortable home and forced into service as a sled dog in the Alaskan wilderness. As he struggles to adapt to his new surroundings, Buck learns to draw on his instincts to survive among brutal owners and fierce competition.

Nonfiction

The Story of My Life

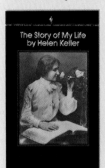

When she was nineteen months old, Helen Keller was left blind and deaf by an illness. As she grew older, however, she was determined to read and write. In *The Story of My Life,* Keller writes about her refusal to give up in the face of unthinkable adversity. The book includes letters and personal records that will lead readers to a greater understanding of her life.

Freedom's Children

What was it like to walk through angry, violent mobs to integrate an all-white school? to be arrested for refusing to give up a seat on a bus? In *Freedom's Children,* Ellen Levine presents oral histories by African Americans who as children or teenagers were involved in the civil rights movement of the 1950s and 1960s.

Rescue: The Story of How Gentiles Saved Jews in the Holocaust

The Holocaust was a terrifying and tragic period for Jews and others targeted by the Nazi regime. Yet all over Europe, non-Jews risked their lives to save neighbors and friends from the death camps. In *Rescue: The Story of How Gentiles Saved Jews in the Holocaust,* Milton Meltzer tells of their heroism.

Lives of the Musicians

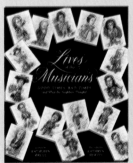

Are you a slob? Well, so was Beethoven. Is your favorite color red? It was also Mozart's favorite. In *Lives of the Musicians,* Kathleen Krull shares fascinating facts and tidbits from the lives of twenty famous musicians. Revealing funny gossip and detailing the musicians' quirky behavior, Krull brings the humanity back to our musical heroes. Hewitt's engaging art provides a perfect counterpoint to the text.

 Learn It Online
Upgrade your understanding of novels.
Visit *NovelWise* at:

go.hrw.com H8-281 **Go**

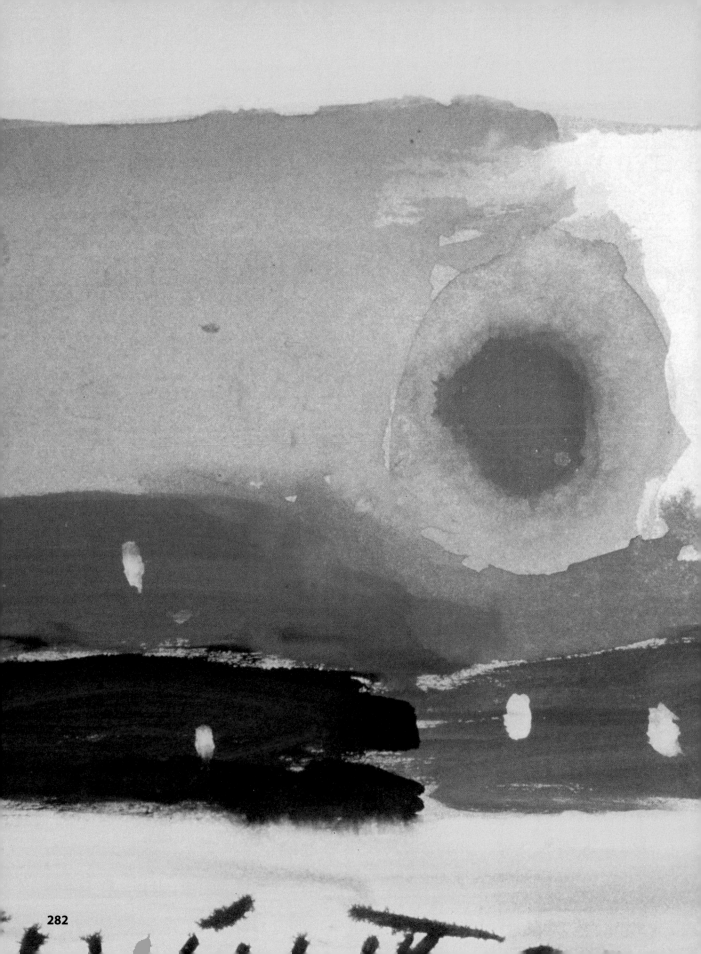

CHAPTER 3

Theme

INFORMATIONAL TEXT FOCUS

Treatment, Scope, and Organization of Ideas

 California Standards
Here are the grade 8 standards that you will work toward mastering in Chapter 3.

Word Analysis, Fluency, and Systematic Vocabulary Development
1.3 Use word meanings within the appropriate context and show ability to verify those meanings by definition, restatement, example, comparison, or contrast.

Reading Comprehension (Focus on Informational Materials)
2.3 Find similarities and differences between texts in the treatment, scope, or organization of ideas.

Literary Response and Analysis
3.5 Identify and analyze recurring themes (e.g., good versus evil) across traditional and contemporary works.

Writing Applications (Genres and Their Characteristics)
2.4 Write persuasive compositions:
  a. Include a well-defined thesis (i.e., one that makes a clear and knowledgeable judgment).
  b. Present detailed evidence, examples, and reasoning to support arguments, differentiating between facts and opinions.
  c. Provide details, reasons, and examples, arranging them effectively by anticipating and answering reader concerns and counterarguments.

"In spite of everything, I still believe that people are really good at heart."

—**Anne Frank**

What Do **You Think** How can we do the best with what we're given?

Watercolor (1944) by Nelly Silvínová, age 12. Theresienstadt Concentration Camp, Terezin, Czechoslovakia. The artist died before her thirteenth birthday.
©Jewish Museum in Prague

 **Learn It Online**
Find graphic organizers online to help you read:

| go.hrw.com | H8-283 | **Go** |

Literary Skills Focus

by **Carol Jago**

What Are Recurring Themes?

A story can be rich in a number of ways—in the strength of its plot, the authenticity of its characters, or the power of its language. What lends a story importance—what makes you remember a story long after you've read it—is often its theme, or the central idea about life, around which all the other elements of the story revolve.

Theme

Truths About Life A story usually affects you because it has taught you something. A story that has meaning beyond the people and events on its pages—a meaning you can take to heart and apply to yourself—is a story that changes your life. This deeper meaning is called **theme.**

A theme will often emerge naturally from the work as it progresses and from the writer's beliefs about life. A writer who believes that a single mistake can haunt a person forever, for example, will write one kind of story. Someone who believes that learning from one's mistakes and moving on is what matters most will write another kind. You, the reader, discover a truth about life as you share the characters' experiences. At the end of the story, the characters' discoveries become your discoveries as well.

Traditional or Contemporary? Theme is at the heart of every story, whether the work is traditional or contemporary. **Traditional works** are the myths, folk tales, stories, and poems passed on by word of mouth, often over many centuries. In this chapter, "The People Could Fly" is an example of a traditional folk tale. It is retold by a contemporary writer, Virginia Hamilton.

> They say the people could fly. Say that long ago in Africa, some of the people knew magic.
>
> from "The People Could Fly"
> by Virginia Hamilton

Contemporary works are works written in the twentieth and twenty-first centuries. Some scholars say that contemporary works are those written after 1960. In this chapter, "In Response to Executive Order 9066" is an example of a contemporary work.

> I am a fourteen-year-old girl with bad spelling / and a messy room. If it helps any, I will tell you / I have always felt funny using chopsticks / and my favorite food is hot dogs.
>
> from "In Response to Executive Order 9066" by Dwight Okita

Theme: What Does It Mean? Plot answers the question "What happens?" Theme answers the question "What does it mean?" A story's theme is often difficult to state. In fact, no two readers will state a theme in exactly the same way.

Nevertheless, in a good story, theme is always there. Theme is what the writer *means* by the whole story.

Theme is stated in a sentence. The subject, or topic, of a story can be stated in a phrase ("growing up"). A theme says something about the subject ("Growing up can be a painful but comical experience"). Think of the folk tale "Sleeping Beauty." You may be struck by the magic of the kiss that wakes a princess from a hundred-year nap, but that's only plot. The theme of that story is the revelation that love has the power to awaken even the coldest and deadest of hearts.

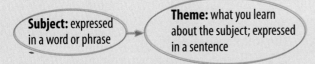

Subject: expressed in a word or phrase → **Theme:** what you learn about the subject; expressed in a sentence

Recurring Themes

Have you ever noticed that different stories seem to have the same messages? People all over the world and through time share the same dreams and fears. They long for a vision of life that gives meaning to their own existence. They long for heroes who will rescue them in times of danger. They long for a good life and for someone to love. It is not surprising, then, that people all over the world tell the same stories—more or less.

Characters vary and settings differ, but themes recur. The same themes, called **universal themes** or **recurring themes,** can be found in traditional works, such as ancient myths, folk tales from around the world, and great dramas, and in contemporary works, such as short stories published today, movies, and even TV shows.

As you read more and more, you will notice how the history of literature can be seen as an ongoing dialogue about a number of important recurring themes. For generations people have written texts about the pursuit of love, about the conflict between good and evil, and about the meaning of existence. These are just a few of the ideas that writers have taken up from all who have written before them. By comparing the way a theme is treated across time by different writers, you will learn about life and about literature.

Your Turn Analyze Recurring Themes

How many times have you read a story or seen a movie with these themes?

- Things may not always be what they seem.
- Wishes can have surprising consequences.
- You should treasure the good in your life.
- The gift of love can change a person.

To begin your exploration of recurring themes, study the list of themes above. Then, think of traditional and contemporary works you have studied or read on your own. Think also of movies, plays, and TV shows you have seen. With a group of classmates, brainstorm titles of works that reflect those themes. Record your titles in a chart like the one below.

Theme	Titles
Things may not always be what they seem.	"The Inn of Lost Time" "An Hour with Abuelo"
Wishes can have surprising consequences.	"Those Three Wishes" "Flowers for Algernon"

Learn It Online
To learn more about literary elements in novels, check out *NovelWise* at:

go.hrw.com H8-285 **Go**

Reading Skills Focus

by **Kylene Beers**

What Skills Help You Analyze Recurring Themes?

When asked to state the theme of a story, you may think, "Isn't keeping track of the characters and events enough?" Yet once you are able to state a story's theme in your own words, you will have truly absorbed the meaning of the story—and will be the wiser for it.

Finding the Theme

Like the truths we discover in real life, themes in traditional and contemporary works can be complicated, open to interpretation, and sometimes difficult to put into words. Analyzing these literary elements will help you identify a work's theme:

The Title A story's title sometimes hints at its theme. "The People Could Fly," for example, suggests an exceptional feat. Consider why the writer chose this title. It may be a clue to the story's theme.

The Characters The main characters generally change in the course of the story. What they discover could have meaning to other people's lives—including your own. Look at the example in the next column.

> Of one thing I was sure. The wire fence was real. I no longer had the right to walk out of it. It was because I had Japanese ancestors. It was also because some people had little faith in the ideas and ideals of democracy.
>
> from "Camp Harmony"
> by Monica Sone

Conflict What scenes or passages in the story address the main conflict? What revelation about life might the passage below suggest?

> The folks were full of misery, then. Got sick with the up and down of the sea. So they forgot about flyin when they could no longer breathe the sweet scent of Africa.
>
> from "The People Could Fly"
> by Virginia Hamilton

The Resolution Think about the way problems or conflicts in the story are resolved. Does the resolution give you an idea about what the story means?

> But Toby just laughed. Say he threw back his head and said, "Hee, hee! Don't you know who I am? Don't you know some of us in the field?" He said it to their faces. "We are ones who fly!"
>
> from "The People Could Fly"
> by Virginia Hamilton

Considering these literary elements will help you formulate a theme statement.

Making Generalizations

A **generalization** is a broad statement that extends your observations and experiences to a larger understanding. You make generalizations after considering many specific details. For instance, you may have read works about people finding freedom in America. You might generalize: *America offers a refuge for all people fleeing oppression.* However, to be **valid,** or true, your generalization must apply to every member of a group. You may discover that some people did not find freedom from oppression in America. You might say the following to make your generalization valid: *America offers a refuge for many people fleeing oppression.*

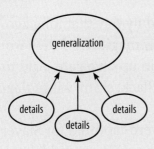

Making Generalizations About Theme

When you make a statement about the theme of a story or recurring themes across traditional and contemporary works, you are making a generalization. You use details from works as the basis of a broad statement about life. To make a statement about recurring themes, consider the following:

- the way conflicts are addressed and resolved
- discoveries made by the main character
- similarities between other traditional and contemporary works
- how the story relates to your own experiences

Making Inferences

Writers rarely state the themes of their works directly. It is up to you to make an **inference,** or educated guess, about what the theme might be. To make inferences about the theme of a literary work, analyze details from the text, and connect what the text says to what you already know.

What the text says	My connections	Inference on theme
Miep tries to comfort Mr. Frank.	My friends encourage me when I face hard times.	A considerate, caring friend tries to help in times of suffering.

A chart like this will also be helpful as you analyze recurring themes. Think about how a story's characters and conflicts are similar to those that you've read about in other stories or novels.

Your Turn   Apply Reading Skills

1. With a partner, brainstorm a short list of movie titles. Choose three titles, and explain how they hint at the movies' themes.

2. Choose a story you have read from this book, and make a generalization based on what one of the characters learns.

Now go to the Skills in Action: Reading Model

Learn It Online

For a visual approach to learning, try the *PowerNotes* version of this lesson at:

go.hrw.com   H8-287   **Go**

Read with a Purpose   Read the folk tale to discover how some people escaped from slavery.

The People Could Fly

by **Virginia Hamilton**

Build Background

This African American folk tale is set in the days of plantation slavery but begins "long ago in Africa," when "some of the people knew magic" and "flew like blackbirds." Hamilton based this story on actual myths and legends.

They say the people could fly. Say that long ago in Africa, some of the people knew magic. And they would walk up on the air like climbin up on a gate. And they flew like blackbirds over the fields. Black, shiny wings flappin against the blue up there.

Then, many of the people were captured for Slavery. The ones that could fly shed their wings. They couldn't take their wings across the water on the slave ships. Too crowded, don't you know.

The folks were full of misery, then. Got sick with the up and down of the sea. So they forgot about flyin when they could no longer breathe the sweet scent of Africa.

Say the people who could fly kept their power, although they shed their wings. They kept their secret magic in the land of slavery. They looked the same as the other people from Africa who had been comin over, who had dark skin. Say you couldn't tell anymore one who could fly from one who couldn't.

One such who could was an old man, call him Toby. And standin tall, yet afraid, was a young woman who once had wings. Call her Sarah. Now Sarah carried a babe tied to her back. She trembled to be so hard worked and scorned.

The slaves labored in the fields from sunup to sundown. The owner of the slaves callin himself their Master. Say he was a hard lump of clay. A hard, glinty coal. A hard rock pile, wouldn't be moved. His Overseer on horseback pointed out the slaves who were slowin down. So the one called Driver cracked his whip over the slow ones to make them move faster. That whip was a slice-open cut of pain. So they did move faster. Had to.

Sarah hoed and chopped the row as the babe on her back slept.

Say the child grew hungry. That babe started up bawlin too loud. Sarah couldn't stop to feed it. Couldn't stop to soothe and quiet it down. She let it cry. She didn't want to. She had no heart to croon to it.

Reading Focus

Making Generalizations
From the way Sarah's situation is described, you can make the generalization that slavery had debilitating, damaging, and terrifying effects on people. Even babies were subjected to this harsh treatment.

"Keep that thing quiet," called the Overseer. He pointed his finger at the babe. The woman scrunched low. The Driver cracked his whip across the babe anyhow. The babe hollered like any hurt child, and the woman fell to the earth.

The old man that was there, Toby, came and helped her to her feet.

"I must go soon," she told him.

"Soon," he said.

Sarah couldn't stand up straight any longer. She was too weak. The sun burned her face. The babe cried and cried, "Pity

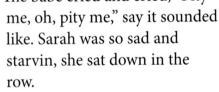

me, oh, pity me," say it sounded like. Sarah was so sad and starvin, she sat down in the row.

"Get up, you black cow," called the Overseer. He pointed his hand, and the Driver's whip snarled around Sarah's legs. Her sack dress tore into rags. Her legs bled onto the earth. She couldn't get up.

Toby was there where there was no one to help her and the babe.

"Now, before it's too late," panted Sarah. "Now, Father!"

"Yes, Daughter, the time is come," Toby answered. "Go, as you know how to go!"

He raised his arms, holdin them out to her. "Kum . . . yali, kum buba tambe," and more magic words, said so quickly, they sounded like whispers and sighs.

The young woman lifted one foot on the air. Then the other. She flew clumsily at first, with the child now held tightly in her arms. Then she felt the magic, the African mystery. Say she rose just as free as a bird. As light as a feather.

Reading Focus

Making Inferences Though the writer does not specifically say so, you can infer from the details in the text that Sarah is going to fly to freedom.

The Overseer rode after her, hollerin. Sarah flew over the fences. She flew over the woods. Tall trees could not snag her. Nor could the Overseer. She flew like an eagle now, until she was gone from sight. No one dared speak about it. Couldn't believe it. But it was, because they that was there saw that it was.

Say the next day was dead hot in the fields. A young man slave fell from the heat. The Driver come and whipped him. Toby come over and spoke words to the fallen one. The words of ancient Africa once heard are never remembered completely. The young man forgot them as soon as he heard them. They went way inside him. He got up and rolled over on the air. He rode it awhile. And he flew away.

Another and another fell from the heat. Toby was there. He cried out to the fallen and reached his arms out to them. "Kum kunka yali, kum . . . tambe!" Whispers and sighs. And they too rose on the air. They rode the hot breezes. The ones flyin were black and shinin sticks, wheelin above the head of the Overseer. They crossed the rows, the fields, the fences, the streams, and were away.

"Seize the old man!" cried the Overseer. "I heard him say the magic *words*. Seize him!"

The one callin himself Master come runnin. The Driver got his whip ready to curl around old Toby and tie him up. The slaveowner took his hip gun from its place. He meant to kill old, black Toby.

Reading Focus

Find the Theme Toby has resolved his conflict with the figures who keep him enslaved. The way the conflict is resolved may be a clue to the story's theme.

But Toby just laughed. Say he threw back his head and said, "Hee, hee! Don't you know who I am? Don't you know some of us in this field?" He said it to their faces. "We are ones who fly!"

And he sighed the ancient words that were a dark promise.

He said them all around to the others in the field under the whip, ". . . buba yali . . . buba tambe. . . ."

There was a great outcryin. The bent backs straighted up. Old and young who were called slaves and could fly joined hands. Say like they would ring-sing. But they didn't shuffle in a circle. They didn't sing. They rose on the air. They flew in a flock that was black against the heavenly blue. Black crows or black shadows. It didn't matter, they went so high. Way above the plantation, way over the slavery land. Say they flew away to *Free-dom.*

And the old man, old Toby, flew behind them, takin care of them. He wasn't cryin. He wasn't laughin. He was the seer. His gaze fell on the plantation where the slaves who could not fly waited.

"Take us with you!" Their looks spoke it but they were afraid to shout it. Toby couldn't take them with him. Hadn't the time to teach them to fly. They must wait for a chance to run.

"Goodie-bye!" The old man called Toby spoke to them, poor souls! And he was flyin gone.

So they say. The Overseer told it. The one called Master said it was a lie, a trick of the light. The Driver kept his mouth shut.

The slaves who could not fly told about the people who could fly to their children. When they were free. When they sat close before the fire in the free land, they told it. They did so love firelight and *Free-dom,* and tellin.

They say that the children of the ones who could not fly told their children. And now, me, I have told it to you.

Read with a Purpose How did the people escape slavery?

MEET THE WRITER

Virginia Hamilton
(1936–2002)

"The Horrors of Slavery"

Hamilton grew up in Yellow Springs, Ohio, an Underground Railroad stop where her grandfather had settled after escaping from slavery in Virginia. Hamilton became a celebrated writer of books for children and young adults, including the award-winning folk tale collection *The People Could Fly: American Black Folktales.* She writes

"'The People Could Fly' is one of the most extraordinary, moving tales in black folklore. It almost makes us believe that the people *could* fly. There are numerous separate accounts of flying Africans and slaves in black folk tale literature. Such accounts are often combined with tales of slaves disappearing. A plausible explanation might be the slaves running away from slavery, slipping away while in the fields or under cover of darkness. In code language murmured from one slave to another, 'Come fly away!' might have been the words used. Another explanation is the wish-fulfillment motif."

"'The People Could Fly' is a . . . powerful testament to the millions of slaves who never had the opportunity to 'fly' away. They remained slaves, as did their children. 'The People Could Fly' was first told and retold by those who had only their imaginations to set them free."

Think About the Writer: How might her grandfather's life experiences have influenced Hamilton's work?

SKILLS IN ACTION
Wrap Up

Reading Standard 3.5 Identify and analyze recurring themes (e.g., good versus evil) across traditional and contemporary works.

Into Action: Finding the Theme

Review "The People Could Fly," and fill in the literary elements in the chart below. Write a theme statement for "The People Could Fly" in the center oval.

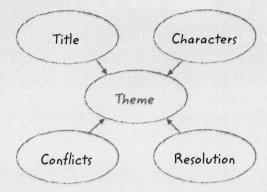

Talk About . . .

1. With a partner, discuss the theme of the story. What does the story say about slavery and freedom? Try to use each Academic Vocabulary word listed at the right in your discussion.

Write About . . .

Use the underlined Academic Vocabulary words as you answer the following questions about "The People Could Fly."

2. Why is the detail that African Americans lost their wings on slave ships <u>significant</u> to the meaning of the story?

3. How do literary elements make the theme of "The People Could Fly" <u>evident</u>?

4. What <u>insight</u> about freedom does Hamilton reveal in "The People Could Fly"? What other <u>traditional</u> or <u>contemporary</u> works that you have read reveal similar truths about freedom?

Writing Skills Focus
Think as a Reader/Writer

Find It in Your Reading Writing Skills Focus activities on the Preparing to Read pages will show you ways writers use literary elements to reveal theme in their works. The Applying Your Skills pages will offer you opportunities to analyze and practice the authors' techniques.

Academic Vocabulary for Chapter 3

Talking and Writing About Theme

Academic Vocabulary is the language you use to write and talk about literature. Use these words to discuss the stories you read. The words are underlined throughout the chapter.

contemporary (kuhn TEHM puh rehr ee) *adj.*: in the style of present time; modern. *Contemporary works often share a theme with works written long ago.*

evident (EHV uh duhnt) *adj.*: clear. *Themes of literary works are made evident through the ways writers use literary elements.*

insight (IHN syt) *n.*: understanding; wisdom. *Virginia Hamilton has keen insight into the problems enslaved people faced.*

significant (sihg NIHF uh kuhnt) *adj.*: meaningful; important. *Focusing on significant details can help you find the theme.*

traditional (truh DIHSH uh nuhl) *adj.*: handed down, usually by word of mouth. *"The People Could Fly" is one of many traditional stories that address the issue of slavery.*

Your Turn

Copy each Academic Vocabulary word into your *Reader/Writer Notebook*. Then, use each word in a paragraph about "The People Could Fly."

The Diary of Anne Frank

by **Frances Goodrich** and **Albert Hackett**

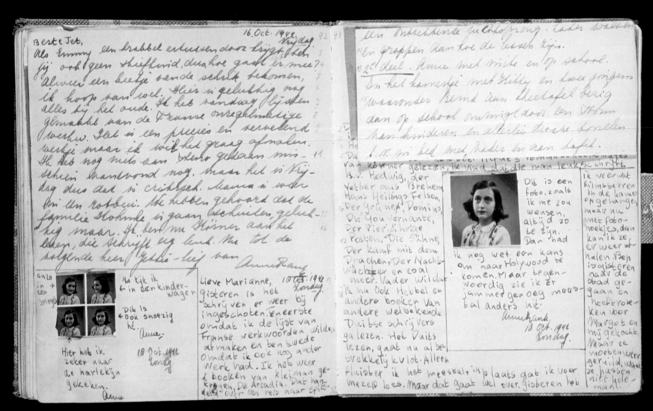

Pages from Anne Frank's diary, written in 1942.

What Do You Think?

How do people find the strength to endure terrifying experiences?

QuickTalk

In a small group, discuss an instance when you each had to do something you didn't want to do, yet made the best of it. What skills did you draw on to make your situation tolerable?

Reader/Writer
Notebook
Use your **RWN** to complete the
activities for this selection.

Literary Skills Focus

Theme The general idea or <u>insight</u> about human existence that is revealed in a literary work is called its **theme.** Most works of literature have more than one theme. A long work, such as *The Diary of Anne Frank,* reveals many different themes. Be attentive to the themes that emerge as you experience with the characters the terror of hiding from enemies. Note also themes that may recur throughout other works of literature. You may notice themes in this <u>contemporary</u> work that are similar to themes in <u>traditional</u> works, such as "The People Could Fly."

Literary Perspectives As you read this play, apply the literary perspective described on page 303.

Reading Skills Focus

Finding the Theme Writers rarely state themes directly. It is up to you to find the theme of a work by analyzing its literary elements, such as conflict and character. Use a chart like the one below to organize the literary elements in the play and to discover what they reveal about the play's themes.

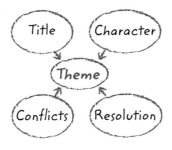

Writing Skills Focus
Think as a Reader/Writer

Find It in Your Reading A play consists of **dialogue,** or conversations between two or more characters. As you read, make notes about what the dialogue reveals about the characters' issues and concerns. How do their attitudes change as the drama progresses?

Vocabulary

conspicuous (kuhn SPIHK yoo uhs) *adj.:* noticeable. *The Nazis required Jews to wear a conspicuous yellow Star of David.*

indignantly (ihn DIHG nuhnt lee) *adv.:* with anger caused by something felt to be unjust. *Anne indignantly claimed that she had not been rude.*

tyranny (TIHR uh nee) *n.:* absolute power used unjustly. *The tyranny of the Nazis caused many Jewish families to flee.*

ostentatiously (ahs tehn TAY shuhs lee) *adv.:* in a showy way. *Mrs. Van Daan ostentatiously wore a fur coat in July.*

forlorn (fawr LAWRN) *adj.:* abandoned and lonely. *Without her friends, Anne felt forlorn.*

Language Coach

Suffixes The suffix *—ly* usually signals that a word is an adverb. Adverbs describe *how, where, when,* or *to what extent.* Which two Vocabulary words above are adverbs? Use each one in a sentence.

Learn It Online
For a preview of this play, see the video introduction on:

 go.hrw.com | H8-295 | **Go**

Frances Goodrich
(1890–1984)

Albert Hackett
(1900–1995)

Together Onstage and Off

Authors Frances Goodrich and Albert Hackett both began their careers in the theater as actors. They began writing plays and screenplays together and were married soon after. Working at desks facing in opposite directions in the same room, they would each write a version of a scene, then read and comment on the other's version before revising the script. In this way, Goodrich and Hackett created the scripts for many light-hearted movies, including *Easter Parade, Father of the Bride,* and *It's a Wonderful Life.*

The Making of a Masterpiece

The Diary of Anne Frank, a work totally unlike Goodrich and Hackett's other writing, is considered their masterpiece. They spent ten days in Amsterdam before they wrote the play, visiting the Secret Annex and questioning Otto Frank on his memories. It took them two years and eight drafts to complete the play, which opened on Broadway in 1955 to great acclaim. The play won a Pulitzer Prize in 1956 and has since been performed countless times in countries around the world.

Think About the Writers Why do you think the writers put so much effort into this play?

Preview the Selection

Anne Frank and her family fled the Nazis in 1942 and went into hiding. Each day they lived in fear of being discovered and deported to a concentration camp. During her time in hiding, Anne Frank kept a diary in which she described the events of daily life and expressed her feelings and ideas. Her once-private words became public after the end of World War II and have since inspired millions of readers and audiences around the world.

This play is based on the events Anne described and even includes some passages from the diary.

Build Background

*I hope I shall be able to confide in you com-
pletely, as I have never been able to do in
anyone before, and I hope that you will be a
great support and comfort to me.*

Anne Frank, 1942.

So begins the diary of a thirteen-year-old
Jewish girl named Anne Frank. Anne's diary
opens in 1942 with stories of boyfriends,
parties, and school life. It closes two years
later, just days before Anne is captured and
imprisoned in a Nazi concentration camp.

Anne Frank was born in Frankfurt,
Germany, in 1929. When she was four years
old, her family immigrated to Amsterdam,
the Netherlands, to escape the anti-Jewish
measures being introduced in Germany. Otto
Frank, Anne's father, managed a company
in Amsterdam that sold pectin, a substance
used in making jams and jellies. Anne and
her older sister, Margot, enjoyed a happy,
carefree childhood until May 1940, when
the Netherlands capitulated (surrendered)
to the invading German army. Anne wrote
in her diary about the Nazi occupation that
followed:

*After May 1940, good times rapidly fled:
first the war, then the capitulation, followed
by the arrival of the Germans, which is
when the sufferings of us Jews really began.
Anti-Jewish decrees followed each other in
quick succession. Jews must wear a yellow
star, Jews must hand in their bicycles, Jews
are banned from trains and are forbidden
to drive. Jews are only allowed to do their
shopping between three and five o'clock and
then only in shops which bear the placard
"Jewish shop." Jews must be indoors by eight*
*o'clock and cannot even sit in their own gar-
dens after that hour. Jews are forbidden to
visit theaters, cinemas, and other places of
entertainment. Jews may not take part in
public sports. Swimming baths, tennis courts,
hockey fields, and other sports grounds are
all prohibited to them. Jews may not visit
Christians. Jews must go to Jewish schools,
and many more restrictions of a similar kind.*

*So we could not do this and were for-
bidden to do that. But life went on in
spite of it all.*

Soon, however, the situation in the
Netherlands grew worse. As in other
German-occupied countries, the Nazis
began rounding up Jews and transporting
them to concentration camps and death
camps, where prisoners died from overwork,
starvation, or disease, or were murdered in
gas chambers. Escaping Nazi-occupied territory became nearly impossible. Like many

(left) Nazis arresting Jewish families in the Warsaw Ghetto, Poland, 1943.

Occupied Europe in 1942
Germany and Germany Occupied
Germany Allies and Dependents
Neutral Countries
Allied Countries

Analyzing Visuals **Connecting to the Text** What do the photo and map reveal about the Franks' situation?

other Jews trapped in Europe at the time, Anne and her family went into hiding to avoid capture. Others were not so lucky, as Anne knew:

Countless friends and acquaintances have gone to a terrible fate. Evening after evening the green and gray army lorries [trucks] trundle past. The Germans ring at every front door to inquire if there are any Jews living in the house. If there are, then the whole family has to go at once. If they don't find any, they go on to the next house. No one has a chance of evading them unless one goes into hiding. Often they go around with lists and only ring when they know they can get a good haul. Sometimes they let them off for cash—so much per head. It seems like the slave hunts of olden times. . . . In the evenings when it's dark, I often see rows of good, innocent people accompanied by crying children, walking on and on, in the charge of a couple of these chaps, bullied and knocked about

until they almost drop. No one is spared—old people, babies, expectant mothers, the sick— each and all join in the march of death.

The Frank family and four other Jews lived for more than two years hidden in a few cramped rooms (now known as the Secret Annex) behind Mr. Frank's office and warehouse. In August 1944, the Nazi police raided their hiding place and sent all eight of its occupants to concentration camps. Of the eight, only Otto Frank survived. Anne died of typhus in a camp in Germany called Bergen-Belsen. She was fifteen years old.

When she began her diary, Anne didn't intend to show it to anyone unless she found a "real friend." Through its dozens of translations and the stage adaptation you are about to read, Anne's diary has found her generations of friends all over the world.

June 12: Anne Frank is born in Frankfurt, Germany.

1929

1930 to 1932

The National Socialist German Workers' (Nazi) Party begins its rise to power. The Nazis proclaim the superiority of the German "master race" and blame Jews for the German defeat in World War I and for the troubled economy.

Adolf Hitler

The Franks decide to leave Germany to escape Nazi persecution. While Mr. Frank looks for a new home in Amsterdam, the Netherlands, the rest of the family stays with relatives in Aachen, Germany.

1933

January 30: The Nazi Party leader, Adolf Hitler, becomes chancellor (head of the government) of Germany.

March 10: The first concentration camp is established by the Nazis at Dachau, Germany.

April: The Nazis pass their first anti-Jewish law, banning the public employment of Jews.

Anne with her father at Miep Santrouschitz and Jan Gies's wedding.

1934

1935

September 15: The Nuremberg Laws are passed, denying Jews German citizenship and forbidding marriage between Jews and non-Jews.

1936

October 25: Germany and Italy form an alliance (the Axis).

Summer: The Van Pels family (called the Van Daans in Anne's diary) flee Germany for the Netherlands.

1937

December 8: Fritz Pfeffer (called Albert Dussel in Anne's diary) flees Germany for the Netherlands.

1938

March 12–13: The German army invades and annexes Austria.

September 29: The Munich Agreement, granting Germany the right to annex part of Czechoslovakia, is drafted and signed by representatives of France, Great Britain, Italy, and Germany.

November 9–10: Kristallnacht (Night of the Broken Glass). Led by the SS, the Nazi special police, Germans beat and kill Jews, loot Jewish stores, and burn synagogues.

Anne playing with her friend Sanne Ledermann in Amsterdam
The Granger Collection, New York.

ANNE FRANK'S LIFE

Anne, second from left, with friends on her tenth birthday.
The Granger Collection, New York.

June 12: Anne receives a diary for her thirteenth birthday.

July 6: The Franks go into hiding after Margot receives an order to appear for deportation to a labor camp in Germany. The Van Pels family joins them one week later.

November 16: Fritz Pfeffer becomes the eighth occupant of the Secret Annex.

August 4: Nazi police raid the Secret Annex; the occupants are sent to concentration camps.

September: Mr. Van Pels dies in Auschwitz.

December 20: Fritz Pfeffer dies in Neuengamme.

Anne's mother, Edith Frank, dies in Auschwitz. Three weeks later Otto Frank is freed when Auschwitz is liberated by the Soviet army. Anne and Margot die in Bergen-Belsen a few weeks before British soldiers liberate the camp. Peter Van Pels dies in Mauthausen. Mrs. Van Pels dies in Theresienstadt.

WORLD EVENTS

1939

March: Germany invades and occupies most of Czechoslovakia.

September 1: Germany invades Poland; World War II begins. France and Great Britain declare war on Germany two days later.

1940

Spring: Germany invades Denmark, Norway, the Netherlands, Belgium, Luxembourg, and France.

September 27: Japan joins the Axis.

1941

June 22: Germany invades the Soviet Union.

December: The United States enters the war on the side of the Allied nations (including Great Britain, the Soviet Union, and other countries) after Japan attacks the U.S. naval base at Pearl Harbor in Hawaii.

1942

January: The "Final Solution" is secretly announced at a conference of Nazi officials: Europe's Jews are to be "exterminated," or murdered. Construction of death camps begins in Poland. Millions of people (Jews and non-Jews) will die in those camps.

1943

1944

June 6: D-day. Allied forces land in Normandy, in northern France, and launch an invasion of Western Europe.

1945

May 8: The war in Europe ends with Germany's unconditional surrender to the Allies.

Bombing of Nagasaki.

September 2: Japan surrenders after the United States drops atomic bombs on the Japanese cities of Hiroshima and Nagasaki. World War II ends one week later.

Read with a Purpose Read this play to discover how Anne Frank's wartime experiences affect her views of the world.

The Diary of Anne Frank

by **Frances Goodrich** and **Albert Hackett**

CHARACTERS

Occupants of the Secret Annex:

Anne Frank

Margot Frank, her older sister

Mr. Frank, their father

Mrs. Frank, their mother

Peter Van Daan

Mr. Van Daan, his father

Mrs. Van Daan, his mother

Mr. Dussel, a dentist

Workers in Mr. Frank's Business:

Miep Gies,[1] a young Dutchwoman

Mr. Kraler,[2] a Dutchman

Setting: Amsterdam, the Netherlands, July 1942 to August 1944; November 1945.

ACT ONE
SCENE 1

The scene remains the same throughout the play. It is the top floor of a warehouse and office building in Amsterdam, Holland. The sharply peaked roof of the building is outlined against a sea of other rooftops stretching away into the distance. Nearby is the belfry of a church tower, the Westertoren, whose carillon[3] *rings out the hours. Occasionally faint sounds float up from below: the voices of children playing in the street, the tramp of marching feet, a boat whistle from the canal.*[4]

---

1. **Miep Gies** (meep khees).
2. **Kraler** (KRAH luhr).
3. **carillon** (KAR uh lahn): set of bells, each of which produces a single tone.
4. **canal:** artificial waterway. Amsterdam, which was built on soggy ground, has more than one hundred canals, built to help drain the land. The canals are used like streets for boats.

Connecting to the Text How can this view of the stage help you visualize the play?

Stage scene showing the Secret Annex in a 1997 stage production of *The Diary of Anne Frank*.
© Joan Marcus.

The three rooms of the top floor and a small attic space above are exposed to our view. The largest of the rooms is in the center, with two small rooms, slightly raised, on either side. On the right is a bathroom, out of sight. A narrow, steep flight of stairs at the back leads up to the attic. The rooms are sparsely furnished, with a few chairs, cots, a table or two. The windows are painted over or covered with makeshift blackout curtains. In the main room there is a sink, a gas ring for cooking, and a wood-burning stove for warmth.

The room on the left is hardly more than a closet. There is a skylight in the sloping ceiling. Directly under this room is a small, steep stairwell, with steps leading down to a door. This is the only entrance from the building below. When the door is opened, we see that it has been concealed on the outer side by a bookcase attached to it.

The curtain rises on an empty stage. It is late afternoon, November 1945.

The rooms are dusty, the curtains in rags. Chairs and tables are overturned. **Ⓐ**

The door at the foot of the small stairwell swings open. MR. FRANK comes up the steps into view. He is a gentle, cultured European in his middle years. There is still a trace of a German accent in his speech.

He stands looking slowly around, making a supreme effort at self-control. He is weak, ill. His clothes are threadbare.

Ⓐ Read and Discuss | Stage directions are unique to written plays. They provide information to readers, actors, and directors. How might these different groups respond to the stage directions?

After a second he drops his rucksack on the couch and moves slowly about. He opens the door to one of the smaller rooms and then abruptly closes it again, turning away. He goes to the window at the back, looking off at the Westertoren as its carillon strikes the hour of six; then he moves restlessly on.

From the street below we hear the sound of a barrel organ and children's voices at play. There is a many-colored scarf hanging from a nail. MR. FRANK *takes it, putting it around his neck. As he starts back for his rucksack, his eye is caught by something lying on the floor. It is a woman's white glove. He holds it in his hand and suddenly all of his self-control is gone. He breaks down crying.*

We hear footsteps on the stairs. MIEP GIES *comes up, looking for* MR. FRANK. MIEP *is a Dutchwoman of about twenty-two. She wears a coat and hat, ready to go home. She is pregnant. Her attitude toward* MR. FRANK *is protective, compassionate.*

Miep. Are you all right, Mr. Frank?

Mr. Frank (*quickly controlling himself*). Yes, Miep, yes.

Miep. Everyone in the office has gone home. . . . It's after six. (*Then, pleading*) Don't stay up here, Mr. Frank. What's the use of torturing yourself like this?

Mr. Frank. I've come to say goodbye. . . . I'm leaving here, Miep.

Miep. What do you mean? Where are you going? Where?

Mr. Frank. I don't know yet. I haven't decided.

Miep. Mr. Frank, you can't leave here! This is your home! Amsterdam is your home. Your business is here, waiting for you. . . . You're needed here. . . . Now that the war is over, there are things that . . .

Mr. Frank. I can't stay in Amsterdam, Miep. It has too many memories for me. Everywhere, there's something . . . the house we lived in . . . the school . . . that street organ playing out there. . . . I'm not the person you used to know, Miep. I'm a bitter old man. (*Breaking off*) Forgive me. I shouldn't speak to you like this . . . after all that you did for us . . . the suffering . . .

Miep. No. No. It wasn't suffering. You can't say we suffered. (*As she speaks, she straightens a chair which is overturned.*)

Mr. Frank. I know what you went through, you and Mr. Kraler. I'll remember it as long as I live. (*He gives one last look around.*) Come, Miep. (*He starts for the steps, then remembers his rucksack, going back to get it.*)

Literary Perspectives

The following perspective will help you relate to and understand this play.

Analyzing Responses to Literature Your response to a work of literature is shaped by your ideas and experiences. You may have strong feelings about characters or situations you recognize from your own life or from other literary works. You may also make connections to what you know about the history of the times. The way a writer develops literary elements, such as plot, setting, and theme, will influence the way you respond to a literary work as well. As you read *The Diary of Anne Frank*, combine what you know about World War II and the holocaust with details presented in the play to better appreciate the seriousness of the Franks' and Van Daans' situation. Also use your knowledge of human nature to enrich your understanding of the characters' motivation and human nature. As you read, questions in the text will guide you in using this perspective.

Miep (*hurrying up to a cupboard*). Mr. Frank, did you see? There are some of your papers here. (*She brings a bundle of papers to him.*) We found them in a heap of rubbish on the floor after . . . after you left.

Mr. Frank. Burn them. (*He opens his rucksack to put the glove in it.*)

Miep. But, Mr. Frank, there are letters, notes . . .

Mr. Frank. Burn them. All of them.

Miep. Burn this? (*She hands him a paper-bound notebook.*)

Mr. Frank (*quietly*). Anne's diary. (*He opens the diary and begins to read.*) "Monday, the sixth of July, nineteen forty-two." (*To* MIEP) Nineteen forty-two. Is it possible, Miep? . . .

Anne's desk in the Anne Frank House Museum in Amsterdam, set up to look as it did when she and her family hid there.

Only three years ago. (*As he continues his reading, he sits down on the couch.*) "Dear Diary, since you and I are going to be great friends, I will start by telling you about myself. My name is Anne Frank. I am thirteen years old. I was born in Germany the twelfth of June, nineteen twenty-nine. As my family is Jewish, we emigrated to Holland when Hitler came to power."

[*As* MR. FRANK *reads on, another voice joins his, as if coming from the air. It is* ANNE's *voice.*] **Ⓑ**

Mr. Frank and Anne's Voice. "My father started a business, importing spice and herbs. Things went well for us until nineteen forty. Then the war came, and the Dutch capitulation, followed by the arrival of the Germans. Then things got very bad for the Jews."

[MR. FRANK's *voice dies out.* ANNE's *voice continues alone. The lights dim slowly to darkness. The curtain falls on the scene.*]

Anne's Voice. You could not do this and you could not do that. They forced Father out of his business. We had to wear yellow stars.[5] I had to turn in my bike. I couldn't go to a Dutch school anymore. I couldn't go to the movies or ride in an automobile or even on a streetcar, and a million other things. But somehow we children still managed to have

---

5. **yellow stars:** The Nazis ordered all Jews to sew a large Star of David (a six-pointed star) on their outer clothing so that they could be easily recognized as Jews.

Ⓑ **Read and Discuss** A voice-over is an element of some plays. How might hearing Anne without seeing her affect an audience watching the play?

fun. Yesterday Father told me we were going into hiding. Where, he wouldn't say. At five o'clock this morning Mother woke me and told me to hurry and get dressed. I was to put on as many clothes as I could. It would look too suspicious if we walked along carrying suitcases. It wasn't until we were on our way that I learned where we were going. Our hiding place was to be upstairs in the building where Father used to have his business. Three other people were coming in with us . . . the Van Daans and their son Peter . . . Father knew the Van Daans but we had never met them . . . **C**

[*During the last lines the curtain rises on the scene. The lights dim on.* ANNE's *voice fades out.*]

SCENE 2

It is early morning, July 1942. The rooms are bare, as before, but they are now clean and orderly.

MR. VAN DAAN, *a tall, portly man in his late forties, is in the main room, pacing up and down, nervously smoking a cigarette. His clothes and overcoat are expensive and well cut.*

MRS. VAN DAAN *sits on the couch, clutching her possessions: a hatbox, bags, etc. She is a pretty woman in her early forties. She wears a fur coat over her other clothes.*

PETER VAN DAAN *is standing at the window of the room on the right, looking down at* the street below. *He is a shy, awkward boy of sixteen. He wears a cap, a raincoat, and long Dutch trousers, like plus fours.*[6] *At his feet is a black case, a carrier for his cat.*

The yellow Star of David is conspicuous *on all of their clothes.*

Mrs. Van Daan (*rising, nervous, excited*). Something's happened to them! I know it!
Mr. Van Daan. Now, Kerli!
Mrs. Van Daan. Mr. Frank said they'd be here at seven o'clock. He said . . .
Mr. Van Daan. They have two miles to walk. You can't expect . . .
Mrs. Van Daan. They've been picked up. That's what's happened. They've been taken . . .

[MR. VAN DAAN *indicates that he hears someone coming.*]

Mr. Van Daan. You see?

[PETER *takes up his carrier and his school bag, etc., and goes into the main room as* MR. FRANK *comes up the stairwell from below.* MR. FRANK *looks much younger now. His movements are brisk, his manner confident. He wears an overcoat and carries his hat and a small cardboard box. He crosses to the* VAN DAANS, *shaking hands with each of them.*]

---

6. **plus fours:** baggy trousers that end in cuffs just below the knees.

C Read and Discuss How have the writers captured your interest in what will happen next?

Vocabulary conspicuous (kuhn SPIHK yoo uhs) *adj.:* noticeable.

Mr. Frank. Mrs. Van Daan, Mr. Van Daan, Peter. (*Then, in explanation of their lateness*) There were too many of the Green Police[7] on the streets . . . we had to take the long way around.

[*Up the steps come* MARGOT FRANK, MRS. FRANK, MIEP (*not pregnant now*), *and* MR. KRALER. *All of them carry bags, packages, and so forth. The Star of David is conspicuous on all of the* FRANKS' *clothing.* MARGOT *is eighteen, beautiful, quiet, shy.* MRS. FRANK *is a young mother, gently bred, reserved. She, like* MR. FRANK, *has a slight German accent.* MR. KRALER *is a Dutchman, dependable, kindly.*

As MR. KRALER *and* MIEP *go upstage to put down their parcels,* MRS. FRANK *turns back to call* ANNE.]

Mrs. Frank. Anne?

[ANNE *comes running up the stairs. She is thirteen, quick in her movements, interested in everything, mercurial[8] in her emotions. She wears a cape and long wool socks and carries a school bag.*] Ⓓ

Mr. Frank (*introducing them*). My wife, Edith. Mr. and Mrs. Van Daan (MRS. FRANK *hurries over, shaking hands with them.*) . . . their son, Peter . . . my daughters, Margot and Anne.

[ANNE *gives a polite little curtsy as she shakes* MR. VAN DAAN'S *hand. Then she immediately*

starts off on a tour of investigation of her new home, going upstairs to the attic room.

MIEP *and* MR. KRALER *are putting the various things they have brought on the shelves.*]

Mr. Kraler. I'm sorry there is still so much confusion.

Mr. Frank. Please. Don't think of it. After all, we'll have plenty of leisure to arrange everything ourselves.

Miep (*to* MRS. FRANK). We put the stores of food you sent in here. Your drugs are here . . . soap, linen here.

Mrs. Frank. Thank you, Miep.

Miep. I made up the beds . . . the way Mr. Frank and Mr. Kraler said. (*She starts out.*) Forgive me. I have to hurry. I've got to go to the other side of town to get some ration books[9] for you.

Mrs. Van Daan. Ration books? If they see our names on ration books, they'll know we're here.

Mr. Kraler. There isn't anything . . . ⎫
Miep. Don't worry. Your names won't be on them. (*As she hurries out*) I'll be up later. ⎬ *Together*
⎭

Mr. Frank. Thank you, Miep.

Mrs. Frank (*to* MR. KRALER). It's illegal, then, the ration books? We've never done anything illegal.

Mr. Frank. We won't be living here exactly according to regulations.

---

7. **Green Police:** Nazi police, who wore green uniforms.
8. **mercurial** (muhr KYOOR ee uhl): changeable.

9. **ration books:** books of stamps or coupons issued by the government during wartime. People could purchase scarce items, such as food, clothing, and gasoline, only with these coupons.

Ⓓ [Read and Discuss] This is Anne's first appearance on stage. What do you learn about Anne?

[*As* MR. KRALER *reassures* MRS. FRANK, *he takes various small things, such as matches and soap, from his pockets, handing them to her.*]

Mr. Kraler. This isn't the black market,[10] Mrs. Frank. This is what we call the white market . . . helping all of the hundreds and hundreds who are hiding out in Amsterdam.

[*The carillon is heard playing the quarter-hour before eight.* MR. KRALER *looks at his watch.* ANNE *stops at the window as she comes down the stairs.*]

Anne. It's the Westertoren!
Mr. Kraler. I must go. I must be out of here and downstairs in the office before the workmen get here. (*He starts for the stairs leading out.*) Miep or I, or both of us, will be up each day to bring you food and news and find out what your needs are. Tomorrow I'll get you a better bolt for the door at the foot of the stairs. It needs a bolt that you can throw yourself and open only at our signal. (*To* MR. FRANK) Oh . . . You'll tell them about the noise?
Mr. Frank. I'll tell them.
Mr. Kraler. Goodbye, then, for the moment. I'll come up again, after the workmen leave.
Mr. Frank. Goodbye, Mr. Kraler.
Mrs. Frank (*shaking his hand*). How can we thank you?

[*The others murmur their goodbyes.*]

Mr. Kraler. I never thought I'd live to see the

---

10. **black market:** place or system for buying and selling goods illegally, without ration stamps.

Westerkerk, the church in Amsterdam whose bell Anne hears.

day when a man like Mr. Frank would have to go into hiding. When you think—

[*He breaks off, going out.* MR. FRANK *follows him down the steps, bolting the door after him. In the interval before he returns,* PETER *goes over to* MARGOT, *shaking hands with her. As* MR. FRANK *comes back up the steps,* MRS. FRANK *questions him anxiously.*]

Mrs. Frank. What did he mean, about the noise?
Mr. Frank. First let us take off some of these clothes.

[*They all start to take off garment after garment. On each of their coats, sweaters, blouses, suits, dresses is another yellow Star of David.* MR. *and* MRS. FRANK *are underdressed quite simply. The others wear several things: sweaters, extra dresses, bathrobes, aprons, nightgowns, etc.]*

Mr. Van Daan. It's a wonder we weren't arrested, walking along the streets . . . Petronella with a fur coat in July . . . and that cat of Peter's crying all the way.

Anne (*as she is removing a pair of panties*). A cat?

Mrs. Frank (*shocked*). Anne, please!

Anne. It's all right. I've got on three more.

[She pulls off two more. Finally, as they have all removed their surplus clothes, they look to MR. FRANK, *waiting for him to speak.]* **E**

Mr. Frank. Now. About the noise. While the men are in the building below, we must have complete quiet. Every sound can be heard down there, not only in the workrooms but in the offices too. The men come at about eight-thirty and leave at about five-thirty. So, to be perfectly safe, from eight in the morning until six in the evening we must move only when it is necessary, and then in stockinged feet. We must not speak above a whisper. We must not run any water. We cannot use the sink or even, forgive me, the w.c.[11] The pipes go down through the workrooms. It would be heard. No trash . . . (MR. FRANK *stops abruptly as he hears the sound of marching feet from the street below. Everyone is motionless, paralyzed with fear.* MR. FRANK

---

11. **w.c.**: short for "water closet," or toilet.

goes quietly into the room on the right to look down out of the window. ANNE *runs after him, peering out with him. The tramping feet pass without stopping. The tension is relieved.* MR. FRANK, *followed by* ANNE, *returns to the main room and resumes his instructions to the group.*) . . . No trash must ever be thrown out which might reveal that someone is living up here . . . not even a potato paring. We must burn everything in the stove at night. This is the way we must live until it is over, if we are to survive. **F**

[There is silence for a second.]

Mrs. Frank. Until it is over.

Mr. Frank (*reassuringly*). After six we can move about . . . we can talk and laugh and have our supper and read and play games . . . just as we would at home. (*He looks at his watch.*) And now I think it would be wise if we all went to our rooms, and we settled before eight o'clock. Mrs. Van Daan, you and your husband will be upstairs. I regret that there's no room for Peter. But he will be here, near us. This will be our common room, where we'll meet to talk and eat and read like one family.

Mr. Van Daan. And where do you and Mrs. Frank sleep?

Mr. Frank. This room is also our bedroom.

Mrs. Van Daan. That isn't right. We'll sleep here and you take the room upstairs. ⎫

Mr. Van Daan. It's your place. ⎬ *Together*

Mr. Frank. Please. I've thought ⎭

E Reading Focus **Finding the Theme** Characters in a drama reveal themselves through their actions as well as words. What do Anne's actions reveal about her character?

F Literary Perspectives **Analyze Responses** What do Mr. Frank's rules tell you about the characters' situation during World War II?

this out for weeks. It's the best arrangement. The only arrangement.

Mrs. Van Daan (*to* MR. FRANK). Never, never can we thank you. (*Then, to* MRS. FRANK) I don't know what would have happened to us, if it hadn't been for Mr. Frank.

Mr. Frank. You don't know how your husband helped me when I came to this country . . . knowing no one . . . not able to speak the language. I can never repay him for that. (*Going to* MR. VAN DAAN) May I help you with your things?  **G**

Mr. Van Daan. No. No. (*To* MRS. VAN DAAN) Come along, liefje.[12]

Mrs. Van Daan. You'll be all right, Peter? You're not afraid?

Peter (*embarrassed*). Please, Mother.

[*They start up the stairs to the attic room above.* MR. FRANK *turns to* MRS. FRANK.]

Mr. Frank. You too must have some rest, Edith. You didn't close your eyes last night. Nor you, Margot.

Anne. I slept, Father. Wasn't that funny? I knew it was the last night in my own bed, and yet I slept soundly.

Mr. Frank. I'm glad, Anne. Now you'll be able to help me straighten things in here. (*To* MRS. FRANK *and* MARGOT) Come with me. . . . You and Margot rest in this room for the time being. (*He picks up their clothes, starting for the room on the right.*)

Mrs. Frank. You're sure . . . ? I could help. . . . And Anne hasn't had her milk . . .

___
12. **liefje** (LEEF hyuh): Dutch for "little dear one."

Margot and Anne in the stage production. © Joan Marcus.

Mr. Frank. I'll give it to her. (*To* ANNE *and* PETER) Anne, Peter . . . it's best that you take off your shoes now, before you forget. (*He leads the way to the room, followed by* MARGOT.)

Mrs. Frank. You're sure you're not tired, Anne?

Anne. I feel fine. I'm going to help Father.

Mrs. Frank. Peter, I'm glad you are to be with us.

Peter. Yes, Mrs. Frank.

[MRS. FRANK *goes to join* MR. FRANK *and* MARGOT.

During the following scene MR. FRANK *helps* MARGOT *and* MRS. FRANK *to hang up*

G | **Read and Discuss** What do these details about Mr. Frank and the Van Daans tell you about them?

their clothes. Then he persuades them both to lie down and rest. The VAN DAANS, *in their room above, settle themselves. In the main room* ANNE *and* PETER *remove their shoes.* PETER *takes his cat out of the carrier.*]

Anne. What's your cat's name?

Peter. Mouschi.[13]

Anne. Mouschi! Mouschi! Mouschi! (*She picks up the cat, walking away with it. To* PETER) I love cats. I have one . . . a darling little cat. But they made me leave her behind. I left some food and a note for the neighbors to take care of her. . . . I'm going to miss her terribly. What is yours? A him or a her?

Peter. He's a tom. He doesn't like strangers. (*He takes the cat from her, putting it back in its carrier.*)

Anne (*unabashed*). Then I'll have to stop being a stranger, won't I? Is he fixed?

Peter (*startled*). Huh?

Anne. Did you have him fixed?

Peter. No.

Anne. Oh, you ought to have him fixed—to keep him from—you know, fighting. Where did you go to school?

Peter. Jewish Secondary.

Anne. But that's where Margot and I go! I never saw you around.

Peter. I used to see you . . . sometimes . . .

Anne. You did?

Peter. . . . in the schoolyard. You were always in the middle of a bunch of kids. (*He*

takes a penknife from his pocket.)

Anne. Why didn't you ever come over?

Peter. I'm sort of a lone wolf. (*He starts to rip off his Star of David.*)

Anne. What are you doing?

Peter. Taking it off.

Anne. But you can't do that. They'll arrest you if you go out without your star.

[*He tosses his knife on the table.*]

Peter. Who's going out? Ⓟ

Anne. Why, of course! You're right! Of course we don't need them anymore. (*She picks up his knife and starts to take her star off.*) I wonder what our friends will think when we don't show up today?

Peter. I didn't have any dates with anyone.

Anne. Oh, I did. I had a date with Jopie to go and play ping-pong at her house. Do you know Jopie de Waal?[14]

Peter. No.

Anne. Jopie's my best friend. I wonder what she'll think when she telephones and there's no answer? . . . Probably she'll go over to the house. . . . I wonder what she'll think . . . we left everything as if we'd suddenly been called away . . . breakfast dishes in the sink . . . beds not made . . . (*As she pulls off her star, the cloth underneath shows clearly the color and form of the star.*) Look! It's still there! (PETER *goes over to the stove with his star.*) What're you going to do with yours?

---

13. **Mouschi** (MOO shee).

14. **Jopie de Waal** (YOH pee duh VAHL).

Ⓟ **Read and Discuss** What do Peter's words and actions tell you about him?

Peter. Burn it.

Anne (*she starts to throw hers in, and cannot*). It's funny, I can't throw mine away. I don't know why.

Peter. You can't throw . . . ? Something they branded you with . . . ? That they made you wear so they could spit on you?

Anne. I know. I know. But after all, it is the Star of David, isn't it?

[*In the bedroom, right,* MARGOT *and* MRS. FRANK *are lying down.* MR. FRANK *starts quietly out.*]

Peter. Maybe it's different for a girl.

[MR. FRANK *comes into the main room.*]

Mr. Frank. Forgive me, Peter. Now let me see. We must find a bed for your cat. (*He goes to a cupboard.*) I'm glad you brought your cat. Anne was feeling so badly about hers. (*Getting a used small wash-tub*) Here we are. Will it be comfortable in that?

Peter (*gathering up his things*). Thanks.

Mr. Frank (*opening the door of the room on the left*). And here is your room. But I warn you, Peter, you can't grow anymore. Not an inch, or you'll have to sleep with your feet out of the skylight. Are you hungry?

Peter. No.

I've never had a diary. And I've always longed for one.

Mr. Frank. We have some bread and butter.

Peter. No, thank you.

Mr. Frank. You can have it for luncheon then. And tonight we will have a real supper . . . our first supper together.

Peter. Thanks. Thanks. (*He goes into his room. During the following scene he arranges his possessions in his new room.*)

Mr. Frank. That's a nice boy, Peter.

Anne. He's awfully shy, isn't he?

Mr. Frank. You'll like him, I know.

Anne. I certainly hope so, since he's the only boy I'm likely to see for months and months.

[MR. FRANK *sits down, taking off his shoes.*]

Mr. Frank. Annele,[15] there's a box there. Will you open it?

[*He indicates a carton on the couch.* ANNE *brings it to the center table. In the street below, there is the sound of children playing.*]

Anne (*as she opens the carton*). You know the way I'm going to think of it here? I'm going to think of it as a boardinghouse. A very peculiar summer boardinghouse, like the one that we— (*She breaks off as she pulls out some photographs.*) Father! My movie stars! I was wondering where they were! I was

15. **Annele** (AHN uh luh): Yiddish for "little Anne" (like "Annie").

🅘 **Literary Focus** Theme Conflict in a drama may occur between two characters or within a character's mind. What conflict does Anne feel here? What theme might the conflict suggest?

Anne and her father in the stage production. © Joan Marcus.

father.) I've never had a diary. And I've always longed for one. (*She looks around the room.*) Pencil, pencil, pencil, pencil. (*She starts down the stairs.*) I'm going down to the office to get a pencil.

Mr. Frank. Anne! No! (*He goes after her, catching her by the arm and pulling her back.*)

Anne (*startled*). But there's no one in the building now.

Mr. Frank. It doesn't matter. I don't want you ever to go beyond that door.

Anne (*sobered*). Never . . . ? Not even at nighttime, when everyone is gone? Or on Sundays? Can't I go down to listen to the radio?

Mr. Frank. Never. I am sorry, Anneke.[17] It isn't safe. No, you must never go beyond that door.

[*For the first time* ANNE *realizes what "going into hiding" means.*]

Anne. I see.

Mr. Frank. It'll be hard, I know. But always remember this, Anneke. There are no walls, there are no bolts, no locks that anyone can put on your mind. Miep will bring us books. We will read history, poetry, mythology. (*He gives her the glass of milk.*) Here's your milk. (*With his arm about her, they go over to the couch, sitting down side by side.*) As a matter of fact, between us, Anne, being here has certain advantages for you. For instance, you remember the battle you had with your mother the other day on the subject of over-

looking for them this morning . . . and Queen Wilhelmina![16] How wonderful!

Mr. Frank. There's something more. Go on. Look further. (*He goes over to the sink, pouring a glass of milk from a thermos bottle.*)

Anne (*pulling out a pasteboard-bound book*). A diary! (*She throws her arms around her*

---

16. **Queen Wilhelmina** (vihl hehl MEE nah) (1880–1962): queen of the Netherlands from 1890 to 1948.

17. **Anneke** (AHN uh kuh): another affectionate nickname for Anne.

shoes? You said you'd rather die than wear overshoes? But in the end you had to wear them? Well now, you see, for as long as we are here, you will never have to wear overshoes! Isn't that good? And the coat that you inherited from Margot, you won't have to wear that anymore. And the piano! You won't have to practice on the piano. I tell you, this is going to be a fine life for you! **J**

[ANNE'S *panic is gone.* PETER *appears in the doorway of his room, with a saucer in his hand. He is carrying his cat.*]

Peter. I . . . I . . . I thought I'd better get some water for Mouschi before . . .
Mr. Frank. Of course.

[*As he starts toward the sink, the carillon begins to chime the hour of eight. He tiptoes to the window at the back and looks down at the street below. He turns to* PETER, *indicating in pantomime that it is too late.* PETER *starts back for his room. He steps on a creaking board. The three of them are frozen for a minute in fear. As* PETER *starts away again,* ANNE *tiptoes over to him and pours some of the milk from her glass into the saucer for the cat.* PETER *squats on the floor, putting the milk before the cat.* MR. FRANK *gives* ANNE *his fountain pen and then goes into the room at the right. For a second* ANNE *watches the cat; then she goes over to the center table and opens her diary.*

In the room at the right, MRS. FRANK *has sat up quickly at the sound of the caril-*

lon. MR. FRANK *comes in and sits down beside her on the settee,[18] his arm comfortingly around her.*

Upstairs, in the attic room, MR. *and* MRS. VAN DAAN *have hung their clothes in the closet and are now seated on the iron bed.* MRS. VAN DAAN *leans back, exhausted.* MR. VAN DAAN *fans her with a newspaper.*

ANNE *starts to write in her diary. The lights dim out; the curtain falls.*

In the darkness ANNE'S *voice comes to us again, faintly at first and then with growing strength.*]

Anne's Voice. I expect I should be describing what it feels like to go into hiding. But I really don't know yet myself. I only know it's funny never to be able to go outdoors . . . never to breathe fresh air . . . never to run and shout and jump. It's the silence in the nights that frightens me most. Every time I hear a creak in the house or a step on the street outside, I'm sure they're coming for us. The days aren't so bad. At least we know that Miep and Mr. Kraler are down there below us in the office. Our protectors, we call them. I asked Father what would happen to them if the Nazis found out they were hiding us. Pim[19] said that they would suffer the same fate that we would. . . . Imagine! They know this, and yet when they come up here, they're always cheerful and gay, as if there were nothing in the world to bother them. . . . Friday, the

---

18. **settee (seh TEE): small couch.**
19. **Pim:** family nickname for Mr. Frank.

---

twenty-first of August, nineteen forty-two. Today I'm going to tell you our general news. Mother is unbearable. She insists on treating me like a baby, which I loathe. Otherwise things are going better. The weather is . . . **Ⓚ**

[*As* ANNE'*s voice is fading out, the curtain rises on the scene.*]

SCENE 3

It is a little after six o'clock in the evening, two months later.

MARGOT *is in the bedroom at the right, studying.* MR. VAN DAAN *is lying down in the attic room above.*

The rest of the "family" is in the main room. ANNE *and* PETER *sit opposite each other at the center table, where they have been doing their lessons.* MRS. FRANK *is on the couch.* MRS. VAN DAAN *is seated with her fur coat, on which she has been sewing, in her lap. None of them are wearing their shoes.*

Their eyes are on MR. FRANK, *waiting for him to give them the signal which will release them from their day-long quiet.* MR. FRANK, *his shoes in his hand, stands looking down out of the window at the back, watching to be sure that all of the workmen have left the building below.*

After a few seconds of motionless silence, MR. FRANK *turns from the window.*

Mr. Frank (*quietly, to the group*). It's safe now. The last workman has left.

[*There is an immediate stir of relief.*]

Anne (*her pent-up energy explodes*). WHEE!
Mrs. Frank (*startled, amused*). Anne!
Mrs. Van Daan. I'm first for the w.c.

[*She hurries off to the bathroom.* MRS. FRANK *puts on her shoes and starts up to the sink to prepare supper.* ANNE *sneaks* PETER'*s shoes from under the table and hides them behind her back.* MR. FRANK *goes into* MARGOT'*s room.*]

Mr. Frank (*to* MARGOT). Six o'clock. School's over.

[MARGOT *gets up, stretching.* MR. FRANK *sits down to put on his shoes. In the main room* PETER *tries to find his.*]

Peter (*to* ANNE). Have you seen my shoes?
Anne (*innocently*). Your shoes?
Peter. You've taken them, haven't you?
Anne. I don't know what you're talking about.
Peter. You're going to be sorry!
Anne. Am I?

[PETER *goes after her.* ANNE, *with his shoes in her hand, runs from him, dodging behind her mother.*]

Mrs. Frank (*protesting*). Anne, dear!
Peter. Wait till I get you!
Anne. I'm waiting! (PETER *makes a lunge for her. They both fall to the floor.* PETER *pins her down, wrestling with her to get the shoes.*) Don't! Don't! Peter, stop it. Ouch!

Ⓚ **Read and Discuss** What do you discover in this scene?

Mrs. Frank. Anne! . . . Peter!

[*Suddenly* PETER *becomes self-conscious. He grabs his shoes roughly and starts for his room.*]

Anne (*following him*). Peter, where are you going? Come dance with me.

Peter. I tell you I don't know how.

Anne. I'll teach you.

Peter. I'm going to give Mouschi his dinner.

Anne. Can I watch?

Peter. He doesn't like people around while he eats.

Anne. Peter, please.

Peter. No!

[*He goes into his room.* ANNE *slams his door after him.*]

Mrs. Frank. Anne, dear, I think you shouldn't play like that with Peter. It's not dignified.

Anne. Who cares if it's dignified? I don't want to be dignified.

[MR. FRANK *and* MARGOT *come from the room on the right.* MARGOT *goes to help her mother.* MR. FRANK *starts for the center table to correct* MARGOT'S *school papers.*]

Mrs. Frank (*to* ANNE). You complain that I don't treat you like a grown-up. But when I do, you resent it.

Anne. I only want some fun . . . someone to laugh and clown with. . . . After you've sat still all day and hardly moved, you've got to have some fun. I don't know what's the matter with that boy.

Mr. Frank. He isn't used to girls. Give him a little time.

Anne. Time? Isn't two months time? I could cry. (*Catching hold of* MARGOT) Come on, Margot . . . dance with me. Come on, please.

Margot. I have to help with supper.

Anne. You know we're going to forget how to dance. . . . When we get out, we won't remember a thing.

[*She starts to sing and dance by herself.* MR. FRANK *takes her in his arms, waltzing with her.* MRS. VAN DAAN *comes in from the bathroom.*] ⓛ

Mrs. Van Daan. Next? (*She looks around as she starts putting on her shoes.*) Where's Peter?

Anne (*as they are dancing*). Where would he be!

Mrs. Van Daan. He hasn't finished his lessons, has he? His father'll kill him if he catches him in there with that cat and his work not done. (MR. FRANK *and* ANNE *finish their dance. They bow to each other with extravagant formality.*) Anne, get him out of there, will you?

Anne (*at* PETER'S *door*). Peter? Peter?

Peter (*opening the door a crack*). What is it?

Anne. Your mother says to come out.

Peter. I'm giving Mouschi his dinner.

Mrs. Van Daan. You know what your father says. (*She sits on the couch, sewing on the lining of her fur coat.*)

ⓛ **Literary Focus** **Theme** How does Anne keep her attitude positive? What theme about life might Anne's attitude express?

The Diary of Anne Frank, Act One **315**

Peter. For heaven's sake, I haven't even looked at him since lunch.

Mrs. Van Daan. I'm just telling you, that's all.

Anne. I'll feed him.

Peter. I don't want you in there.

Mrs. Van Daan. Peter!

Peter (*to* ANNE). Then give him his dinner and come right out, you hear?

[*He comes back to the table.* ANNE *shuts the door of* PETER's *room after her and disappears behind the curtain covering his closet.*]

Mrs. Van Daan (*to* PETER). Now is that any way to talk to your little girlfriend?

Peter. Mother . . . for heaven's sake . . . will you please stop saying that?

Mrs. Van Daan. Look at him blush! Look at him!

Peter. Please! I'm not . . . anyway . . . let me alone, will you? Ⓜ

Mrs. Van Daan. He acts like it was something to be ashamed of. It's nothing to be ashamed of, to have a little girlfriend.

Peter. You're crazy. She's only thirteen.

Mrs. Van Daan. So what? And you're sixteen. Just perfect. Your father's ten years older than I am. (*To* MR. FRANK) I warn you, Mr. Frank, if this war lasts much longer, we're going to be related and then . . .

Mr. Frank. Mazel tov![20]

Mrs. Frank (*deliberately changing the conversation*). I wonder where Miep is. She's usually so prompt.

---

20. **mazel tov** (MAH zuhl tohv): Yiddish expression meaning "congratulations."

[*Suddenly everything else is forgotten as they hear the sound of an automobile coming to a screeching stop in the street below. They are tense, motionless in their terror. The car starts away. A wave of relief sweeps over them. They pick up their occupations again.* ANNE *flings open the door of* PETER's *room, making a dramatic entrance. She is dressed in* PETER's *clothes.* PETER *looks at her in fury. The others are amused.*]

Anne. Good evening, everyone. Forgive me if I don't stay. (*She jumps up on a chair.*) I have a friend waiting for me in there. My friend Tom. Tom Cat. Some people say that we look alike. But Tom has the most beautiful whiskers, and I have only a little fuzz. I am hoping . . . in time . . .

Peter. All right, Mrs. Quack Quack!

Anne (*outraged—jumping down*). Peter! Ⓝ

Peter. I heard about you . . . how you talked so much in class they called you Mrs. Quack Quack. How Mr. Smitter made you write a composition . . . "'Quack, quack,' said Mrs. Quack Quack."

Anne. Well, go on. Tell them the rest. How it was so good he read it out loud to the class and then read it to all his other classes!

Peter. Quack! Quack! Quack . . . Quack . . . Quack . . .

[ANNE *pulls off the coat and trousers.*]

Anne. You are the most intolerable, insufferable boy I've ever met!

Ⓜ **Literary Perspectives** Analyzing Responses What do you know about teenagers that helps you understand Peter's reaction?

Ⓝ **Reading Focus** Finding the Theme What do Anne's actions suggest about her character? Why is Peter so upset with her?

[*She throws the clothes down the stairwell.* PETER *goes down after them.*]

Peter. Quack, quack, quack!

Mrs. Van Daan (*to* ANNE). That's right, Anneke! Give it to him!

Anne. With all the boys in the world . . . why I had to get locked up with one like you! . . .

Peter. Quack, quack, quack, and from now on stay out of my room!

[*As* PETER *passes her,* ANNE *puts out her foot, tripping him. He picks himself up and goes on into his room.*]

Mrs. Frank (*quietly*). Anne, dear . . . your hair. (*She feels* ANNE's *forehead.*) You're warm. Are you feeling all right?

Anne. Please, Mother. (*She goes over to the center table, slipping into her shoes.*)

Mrs. Frank (*following her*). You haven't a fever, have you?

Anne (*pulling away*). No. No.

Mrs. Frank. You know we can't call a doctor here, ever. There's only one thing to do . . . watch carefully. Prevent an illness before it comes. Let me see your tongue.

Anne. Mother, this is perfectly absurd.

Mrs. Frank. Anne, dear, don't be such a baby. Let me see your tongue. (*As* ANNE *refuses,* MRS. FRANK *appeals to* MR. FRANK.) Otto . . . ?

Mr. Frank. You hear your mother, Anne.

[ANNE *flicks out her tongue for a second, then turns away.*]

Peter in the stage production. © Joan Marcus.

Mrs. Frank. Come on—open up! (*As* ANNE *opens her mouth very wide*) You seem all right . . . but perhaps an aspirin . . .

Mrs. Van Daan. For heaven's sake, don't give that child any pills. I waited for fifteen minutes this morning for her to come out of the w.c.

Anne. I was washing my hair!

Mr. Frank. I think there's nothing the matter with our Anne that a ride on her bike or a visit with her friend Jopie de Waal wouldn't cure. Isn't that so, Anne?

[MR. VAN DAAN *comes down into the room. From outside we hear faint sounds of bombers going over and a burst of ack-ack.*][21] **O**

_____

21. **ack-ack:** slang for "antiaircraft gunfire."

O Read and Discuss | Why did the writers include these sound effects? How might an audience respond to them?

Mr. Van Daan. Miep not come yet?

Mrs. Van Daan. The workmen just left, a little while ago.

Mr. Van Daan. What's for dinner tonight?

Mrs. Van Daan. Beans.

Mr. Van Daan. Not again!

Mrs. Van Daan. Poor Putti! I know. But what can we do? That's all that Miep brought us.

[MR. VAN DAAN *starts to pace, his hands behind his back.* ANNE *follows behind him, imitating him.*]

Anne. We are now in what is known as the "bean cycle." Beans boiled, beans en casserole, beans with strings, beans without strings . . .

[PETER *has come out of his room. He slides into his place at the table, becoming immediately absorbed in his studies.*]

Mr. Van Daan (*to* PETER). I saw you . . . in there, playing with your cat.

Mrs. Van Daan. He just went in for a second, putting his coat away. He's been out here all the time, doing his lessons.

Mr. Frank (*looking up from the papers*). Anne, you got an "excellent" in your history paper today . . . and "very good" in Latin.

Anne (*sitting beside him*). How about algebra?

Mr. Frank. I'll have to make a confession. Up until now I've managed to stay ahead of you in algebra. Today you caught up with me. We'll leave it to Margot to correct.

Anne. Isn't algebra vile, Pim!

Mr. Frank. Vile!

Margot (*to* MR. FRANK). How did I do?

Anne (*getting up*). Excellent, excellent, excellent, excellent!

Mr. Frank (*to* MARGOT). You should have used the subjunctive here . . .

Margot. Should I? . . . I thought . . . look here . . . I didn't use it here . . .

[*The two become absorbed in the papers.*]

Anne. Mrs. Van Daan, may I try on your coat?

Mrs. Frank. No, Anne.

Mrs. Van Daan (*giving it to* ANNE). It's all right . . . but careful with it. (ANNE *puts it on and struts with it.*) My father gave me that the year before he died. He always bought the best that money could buy.

Anne. Mrs. Van Daan, did you have a lot of boyfriends before you were married?

Mrs. Frank. Anne, that's a personal question. It's not courteous to ask personal questions.

Mrs. Van Daan. Oh, I don't mind. (*To* ANNE) Our house was always swarming with boys. When I was a girl, we had . . .

Mr. Van Daan. Oh, God. Not again!

Mrs. Van Daan (*good-humored*). Shut up! (*Without a pause, to* ANNE. MR. VAN DAAN *mimics* MRS. VAN DAAN, *speaking the first few words in unison with her.*) One summer we had a big house in Hilversum. The boys came buzzing round like bees around a jam pot. And when I was sixteen! . . . We were wearing our skirts very short those days and I had good-looking legs. (*She pulls up her skirt, going to* MR. FRANK.) I still have 'em. I may not be as pretty as I used to be, but I still have my legs. How about it, Mr. Frank? Ⓟ

Ⓟ **Reading Focus** **Finding the Theme** What do you learn about Mrs. Van Daan's character from these lines of dialogue?

Mr. Van Daan. All right. All right. We see them.

Mrs. Van Daan. I'm not asking you. I'm asking Mr. Frank.

Peter. Mother, for heaven's sake.

Mrs. Van Daan. Oh, I embarrass you, do I? Well, I just hope the girl you marry has as good. (*Then, to* ANNE) My father used to worry about me, with so many boys hanging round. He told me, if any of them gets fresh, you say to him . . . "Remember, Mr. So-and-So, remember I'm a lady."

Anne. "Remember, Mr. So-and-So, remember I'm a lady." (*She gives* MRS. VAN DAAN *her coat.*)

Mr. Van Daan. Look at you, talking that way in front of her! Don't you know she puts it all down in that diary?

Mrs. Van Daan. So, if she does? I'm only telling the truth!

[ANNE *stretches out, putting her ear to the floor, listening to what is going on below. The sound of the bombers fades away.*]

Mrs. Frank (*setting the table*). Would you mind, Peter, if I moved you over to the couch?

Anne (*listening*). Miep must have the radio on.

[PETER *picks up his papers, going over to the couch beside* MRS. VAN DAAN.]

Mr. Van Daan (*accusingly, to* PETER). Haven't you finished yet?

Peter. No.

Mr. Van Daan. You ought to be ashamed of yourself.

Peter. All right. All right. I'm a dunce. I'm a hopeless case. Why do I go on?

Mrs. Van Daan. You're not hopeless. Don't talk that way. It's just that you haven't any-one to help you, like the girls have. (*to* MR. FRANK) Maybe you could help him, Mr. Frank?

Mr. Frank. I'm sure that his father . . . ?

Mr. Van Daan. Not me. I can't do anything with him. He won't listen to me. You go ahead . . . if you want.

Mr. Frank (*going to* PETER). What about it, Peter? Shall we make our school coeducational?

Mrs. Van Daan (*kissing* MR. FRANK). You're an angel, Mr. Frank. An angel. I don't know why I didn't meet you before I met that one there. Here, sit down, Mr. Frank . . . (*She forces him down on the couch beside* PETER.) Now, Peter, you listen to Mr. Frank.

Mr. Frank. It might be better for us to go into Peter's room.

[PETER *jumps up eagerly, leading the way.*]

Mrs. Van Daan. That's right. You go in there, Peter. You listen to Mr. Frank. Mr. Frank is a highly educated man.

> All right. All right.
> I'm a dunce.
> I'm a hopeless
> case.

[*As* MR. FRANK *is about to follow* PETER *into his room,* MRS. FRANK *stops him and wipes the lipstick from his lips. Then she closes the door after them.*]

Anne (*on the floor, listening*). Shh! I can hear a man's voice talking.

Mr. Van Daan (*to* ANNE). Isn't it bad enough here without your sprawling all over the place?

[ANNE *sits up.*]

Mrs. Van Daan (*to* MR. VAN DAAN). If you didn't smoke so much, you wouldn't be so bad-tempered.

Mr. Van Daan. Am I smoking? Do you see me smoking?

Mrs. Van Daan. Don't tell me you've used up all those cigarettes.

Mr. Van Daan. One package. Miep only brought me one package.

Mrs. Van Daan. It's a filthy habit anyway. It's a good time to break yourself.

Mr. Van Daan. Oh, stop it, please.

Mrs. Van Daan. You're smoking up all our money. You know that, don't you?

Mr. Van Daan. Will you shut up? (*During this,* MRS. FRANK *and* MARGOT *have studiously kept their eyes down. But* ANNE, *seated on the floor, has been following the discussion interestedly.* MR. VAN DAAN *turns to see her staring up at him.*) And what are you staring at?

Anne. I never heard grown-ups quarrel before. I thought only children quarreled.

Mr. Van Daan. This isn't a quarrel! It's a discussion. And I never heard children so rude before.

Anne (*rising,* indignantly). *I,* rude!

Mr. Van Daan. Yes!

Mrs. Frank (*quickly*). Anne, will you get me my knitting? (ANNE *goes to get it.*) I must remember, when Miep comes, to ask her to bring me some more wool.

Margot (*going to her room*). I need some

Q **Read and Discuss** How would you describe the Van Daans' relationship?

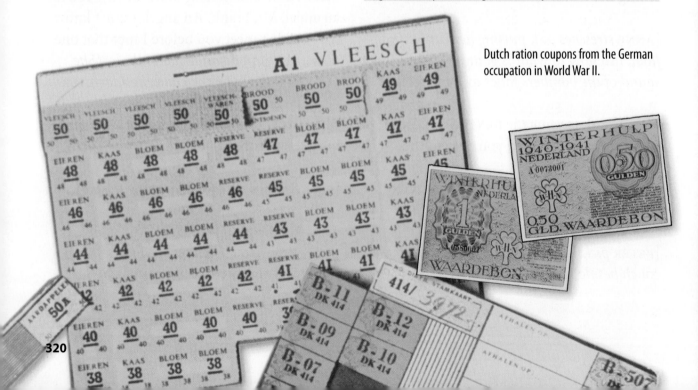

Dutch ration coupons from the German occupation in World War II.

hairpins and some soap. I made a list. (*She goes into her bedroom to get the list.*)

Mrs. Frank (*to* ANNE). Have you some library books for Miep when she comes?

Anne. It's a wonder that Miep has a life of her own, the way we make her run errands for us. Please, Miep, get me some starch. Please take my hair out and have it cut. Tell me all the latest news, Miep. (*She goes over, kneeling on the couch beside* MRS. VAN DAAN.) Did you know she was engaged? His name is Dirk, and Miep's afraid the Nazis will ship him off to Germany to work in one of their war plants. That's what they're doing with some of the young Dutchmen . . . they pick them up off the streets—

Mr. Van Daan (*interrupting*). Don't you ever get tired of talking? Suppose you try keeping still for five minutes. Just five minutes.

[*He starts to pace again. Again* ANNE *follows him, mimicking him.* MRS. FRANK *jumps up and takes her by the arm up to the sink and gives her a glass of milk.*]

Mrs. Frank. Come here, Anne. It's time for your glass of milk.

Mr. Van Daan. Talk, talk, talk. I never heard such a child. Where is my . . . ? Every evening it's the same, talk, talk, talk. (*He looks around.*) Where is my . . . ?

Mrs. Van Daan. What're you looking for?

Mr. Van Daan. My pipe. Have you seen my pipe?

Mrs. Van Daan. What good's a pipe? You haven't got any tobacco.

Mr. Van Daan. At least I'll have something to hold in my mouth! (*Opening* MARGOT'S *bedroom door*) Margot, have you seen my pipe?

Margot. It was on the table last night.

[ANNE *puts her glass of milk on the table and picks up his pipe, hiding it behind her back.*]

Mr. Van Daan. I know. I know. Anne, did you see my pipe? . . . Anne!

Mrs. Frank. Anne, Mr. Van Daan is speaking to you.

Anne. Am I allowed to talk now?

Mr. Van Daan. You're the most aggravating. . . . The trouble with you is, you've been spoiled. What you need is a good old-fashioned spanking.

Anne (*mimicking* MRS. VAN DAAN). "Remember, Mr. So-and-So, remember I'm a lady." (*She thrusts the pipe into his mouth, then picks up her glass of milk.*)

Mr. Van Daan (*restraining himself with difficulty*). Why aren't you nice and quiet like your sister Margot? Why do you have to show off all the time? Let me give you a little advice, young lady. Men don't like that kind of thing in a girl. You know that? A man likes a girl who'll listen to him once in a while . . . a domestic girl, who'll keep her house shining for her husband . . . who loves to cook and sew and . . .   **ℝ**

Anne. I'd cut my throat first! I'd open my veins! I'm going to be remarkable! I'm going to Paris . . .

Mr. Van Daan (*scoffingly*). Paris!

ℝ | **Read and Discuss** | What is the conflict between Anne and Mr. Van Daan?

Anne. . . . to study music and art.

Mr. Van Daan. Yeah! Yeah!

Anne. I'm going to be a famous dancer or singer . . . or something wonderful.

[*She makes a wide gesture, spilling the glass of milk on the fur coat in* MRS. VAN DAAN'S *lap.* MARGOT *rushes quickly over with a towel.* ANNE *tries to brush the milk off with her skirt.*]

Mrs. Van Daan. Now look what you've done . . . you clumsy little fool! My beautiful fur coat my father gave me . . .

Anne. I'm so sorry.

Mrs. Van Daan. What do you care? It isn't yours. . . . So go on, ruin it! Do you know what that coat cost? Do you? And now look at it! Look at it!

Anne. I'm very, very sorry.

Mrs. Van Daan. I could kill you for this. I could just kill you!

[MRS. VAN DAAN *goes up the stairs, clutching the coat.* MR. VAN DAAN *starts after her.*]

Mr. Van Daan. Petronella . . . liefje! Liefje! . . . Come back . . . the supper . . . come back!

Mrs. Frank. Anne, you must not behave in that way.

Anne. It was an accident. Anyone can have an accident.

Mrs. Frank. I don't mean that. I mean the answering back. You must not answer back. They are our guests. We must always show the greatest courtesy to them. We're all living under terrible tension. (*She stops as*

MARGOT *indicates that* MR. VAN DAAN *can hear. When he is gone, she continues.*) That's why we must control ourselves. . . . You don't hear Margot getting into arguments with them, do you? Watch Margot. She's always courteous with them. Never familiar. She keeps her distance. And they respect her for it. Try to be like Margot.

Anne. And have them walk all over me, the way they do her? No, thanks!

Mrs. Frank. I'm not afraid that anyone is going to walk all over you, Anne. I'm afraid for other people, that you'll walk on them. I don't know what happens to you, Anne. You are wild, self-willed. If I had ever talked to my mother as you talk to me . . .

Anne. Things have changed. People aren't like that anymore. "Yes, Mother." "No, Mother." "Anything you say, Mother." I've got to fight things out for myself! Make something of myself! **Ⓢ**

Mrs. Frank. It isn't necessary to fight to do it. Margot doesn't fight, and isn't she . . . ?

Anne (*violently rebellious*). Margot! Margot! Margot! That's all I hear from everyone . . . how wonderful Margot is . . . "Why aren't you like Margot?"

Margot (*protesting*). Oh, come on, Anne, don't be so . . .

Anne (*paying no attention*). Everything she does is right, and everything I do is wrong! I'm the goat around here! . . . You're all against me! . . . And you worst of all!

[*She rushes off into her room and throws herself down on the settee, stifling her sobs.* MRS. FRANK *sighs and starts toward the stove.*]

Ⓢ **Literary Focus** **Theme** Why are Anne's comments significant? What themes do these comments suggest?

Mrs. Frank (*to* MARGOT). Let's put the soup on the stove . . . if there's anyone who cares to eat. Margot, will you take the bread out? (MARGOT *gets the bread from the cupboard.*) I don't know how we can go on living this way. . . . I can't say a word to Anne . . . she flies at me . . .

Margot. You know Anne. In half an hour she'll be out here, laughing and joking.

Mrs. Frank. And . . . (*She makes a motion upward, indicating the* VAN DAANS.) . . . I told your father it wouldn't work . . . but no . . . no . . . he had to ask them, he said . . . he owed it to him, he said. Well, he knows now that I was right! These quarrels! . . . This bickering!

Margot (*with a warning look*). Shush. Shush.

[*The buzzer for the door sounds.* MRS. FRANK *gasps, startled.*]

Mrs. Frank. Every time I hear that sound, my heart stops!

Margot (*starting for* PETER'S *door*). It's Miep. (*She knocks at the door.*) Father?

[MR. FRANK *comes quickly from* PETER'S *room.*]

Mr. Frank. Thank you, Margot. (*As he goes down the steps to open the outer door*) Has everyone his list?

Margot. I'll get my books. (*Giving her*

Anne and Mrs. Van Daan in the stage production. © Joan Marcus.

mother a list) Here's your list. (MARGOT *goes into her and* ANNE'S *bedroom on the right.* ANNE *sits up, hiding her tears, as* MARGOT *comes in.*) Miep's here.

[MARGOT *picks up her books and goes back.* ANNE *hurries over to the mirror, smoothing her hair.*]

Mr. Van Daan (*coming down the stairs*). Is it Miep?

Margot. Yes. Father's gone down to let her in.

Mr. Van Daan. At last I'll have some cigarettes!

Mrs. Frank (*to* MR. VAN DAAN). I can't tell you how unhappy I am about Mrs. Van Daan's coat. Anne should never have touched it.

Mr. Van Daan. She'll be all right.

Mrs. Frank. Is there anything I can do?

Mr. Van Daan. Don't worry.

[*He turns to meet* MIEP. *But it is not* MIEP *who comes up the steps. It is* MR. KRALER, *followed by* MR. FRANK. *Their faces are grave.* ANNE *comes from the bedroom.* PETER *comes from his room.*]

Mrs. Frank. Mr. Kraler!

Mr. Van Daan. How are you, Mr. Kraler?

Margot. This is a surprise.

Mrs. Frank. When Mr. Kraler comes, the sun begins to shine.

Mr. Van Daan. Miep is coming?

Mr. Kraler. Not tonight. (MR. KRALER *goes to* MARGOT *and* MRS. FRANK *and* ANNE, *shaking hands with them.*)

Mrs. Frank. Wouldn't you like a cup of coffee? . . . Or, better still, will you have supper with us?

Mr. Frank. Mr. Kraler has something to talk over with us. Something has happened, he says, which demands an immediate decision.

Mrs. Frank (*fearful*). What is it?

[MR. KRALER *sits down on the couch. As he talks he takes bread, cabbages, milk, etc., from his briefcase, giving them to* MARGOT *and* ANNE *to put away.*]

Mr. Kraler. Usually, when I come up here, I try to bring you some bit of good news. What's the use of telling you the bad news when there's nothing that you can do about it? But today something has happened. . . Dirk . . . Miep's Dirk, you know, came to me just now. He tells me that he has a Jewish friend living near him. A dentist. He says he's in trouble. He begged me, could I do anything for this man? Could I find him a hiding place? . . . So I've come to you. . . . I know it's a terrible thing to ask of you, living as you are, but would you take him in with you?

Mr. Frank. Of course we will.

Mr. Kraler (*rising*). It'll be just for a night or two . . . until I find some other place. This happened so suddenly that I didn't know where to turn.

Mr. Frank. Where is he?

Mr. Kraler. Downstairs in the office.

Mr. Frank. Good. Bring him up.

Mr. Kraler. His name is Dussel[22] . . .

Mr. Frank. Dussel. . . . I think I know him.

Mr. Kraler. I'll get him.

[*He goes quickly down the steps and out.* MR. FRANK *suddenly becomes conscious of the others.*]

---

22. **Dussel** (DOOS uhl).

> Mr. Kraler has something to talk over with us. Something has happened.

Mr. Frank. Forgive me. I spoke without consulting you. But I knew you'd feel as I do.

Mr. Van Daan. There's no reason for you to consult anyone. This is your place. You have a right to do exactly as you please. The only thing I feel . . . there's so little food as it is . . . and to take in another person . . .

[PETER *turns away, ashamed of his father.*]

Mr. Frank. We can stretch the food a little. It's only for a few days.

Mr. Van Daan. You want to make a bet?

Mrs. Frank. I think it's fine to have him. But, Otto, where are you going to put him? Where?

Peter. He can have my bed. I can sleep on the floor. I wouldn't mind.

Mr. Frank. That's good of you, Peter. But your room's too small . . . even for you.

Anne. I have a much better idea. I'll come in here with you and Mother, and Margot can take Peter's room and Peter can go in our room with Mr. Dussel.

Margot. That's right. We could do that.

Mr. Frank. No, Margot. You mustn't sleep in that room . . . neither you nor Anne. Mouschi has caught some rats in there. Peter's brave. He doesn't mind.

Anne. Then how about *this?* I'll come in here with you and Mother, and Mr. Dussel can have my bed.

Mrs. Frank. No. No. *No!* Margot will come in here with us and he can have her bed. It's the only way. Margot, bring your things in here. Help her, Anne.

[MARGOT *hurries into her room to get her things.*]

Anne (*to her mother*). Why Margot? Why can't I come in here?

Mrs. Frank. Because it wouldn't be proper for Margot to sleep with a. . . . Please, Anne. Don't argue. Please.

[ANNE *starts slowly away.*]

Mr. Frank (*to* ANNE). You don't mind sharing your room with Mr. Dussel, do you, Anne?

Anne. No. No, of course not.

Mr. Frank. Good. (ANNE *goes off into her bedroom, helping* MARGOT. MR. FRANK *starts to search in the cupboards.*) Where's the cognac?[23]

Mrs. Frank. It's there. But, Otto, I was saving it in case of illness.

Mr. Frank. I think we couldn't find a better time to use it. Peter, will you get five glasses for me?

[PETER *goes for the glasses.* MARGOT *comes out of her bedroom, carrying her possessions, which she hangs behind a curtain in the main room.* MR. FRANK *finds the cognac and pours it into the five glasses that* PETER *brings him.* MR. VAN DAAN *stands looking on sourly.* MRS. VAN DAAN *comes downstairs and looks around at all the bustle.*]

Mrs. Van Daan. What's happening? What's going on?

Mr. Van Daan. Someone's moving in with us.

Mrs. Van Daan. In here? You're joking.

Margot. It's only for a night or two . . . until

---

23. **cognac** (KOHN yak): type of brandy (distilled wine).

Mr. Kraler finds him another place.

Mr. Van Daan. Yeah! Yeah!

🅣

[MR. FRANK *hurries over as* MR. KRALER *and* DUSSEL *come up.* DUSSEL *is a man in his late fifties, meticulous, finicky . . . bewildered now. He wears a raincoat. He carries a briefcase, stuffed full, and a small medicine case.*]

Mr. Frank. Come in, Mr. Dussel.

Mr. Kraler. This is Mr. Frank.

Dussel. Mr. Otto Frank?

Mr. Frank. Yes. Let me take your things. (*He takes the hat and briefcase, but* DUSSEL *clings to his medicine case.*) This is my wife, Edith . . . Mr. and Mrs. Van Daan . . . their son, Peter . . . and my daughters, Margot and Anne.

[DUSSEL *shakes hands with everyone.*]

Mr. Kraler. Thank you, Mr. Frank. Thank you all. Mr. Dussel, I leave you in good hands. Oh . . . Dirk's coat.

[DUSSEL *hurriedly takes off the raincoat, giving it to* MR. KRALER. *Underneath is his white dentist's jacket, with a yellow Star of David on it.*]

Dussel (*to* MR. KRALER). What can I say to thank you . . . ?

Mrs. Frank (*to* DUSSEL). Mr. Kraler and Miep. . . . They're our lifeline. Without them we couldn't live.

Mr. Kraler. Please. Please. You make us seem very heroic. It isn't that at all. We simply don't like the Nazis. (*To* MR. FRANK, *who offers him a drink*) No, thanks. (*Then, going on*) We

don't like their methods. We don't like . . .

Mr. Frank (*smiling*). I know. I know. "No one's going to tell us Dutchmen what to do with our damn Jews!"

Mr. Kraler (*to* DUSSEL). Pay no attention to Mr. Frank. I'll be up tomorrow to see that they're treating you right. (*To* MR. FRANK) Don't trouble to come down again. Peter will bolt the door after me, won't you, Peter?

Peter. Yes, sir.

Mr. Frank. Thank you, Peter. I'll do it.

Mr. Kraler. Good night. Good night.

Group. Good night, Mr. Kraler. We'll see you tomorrow. (*Etc., etc.*)

[MR. KRALER *goes out with* MR. FRANK. MRS. FRANK *gives each one of the "grown-ups" a glass of cognac.*]

Mrs. Frank. Please, Mr. Dussel, sit down.

[DUSSEL *sinks into a chair.* MRS. FRANK *gives him a glass of cognac.*]

Dussel. I'm dreaming. I know it. I can't believe my eyes. Mr. Otto Frank here! (*To* MRS. FRANK) You're not in Switzerland, then? A woman told me. . . . She said she'd gone to your house . . . the door was open, everything was in disorder, dishes in the sink. She said she found a piece of paper in the wastebasket with an address scribbled on it . . . an address in Zurich.[24] She said you must have escaped to Zurich.

---

24. **Zurich** (ZUR ihk): Switzerland's largest city. Because Switzerland remained neutral during World War II, many refugees sought safety there.

🅣 **Read and Discuss** How does Mr. Van Daan feel now?

Anne. Father put that there purposely . . . just so people would think that very thing!

Dussel. And you've been *here* all the time?

Mrs. Frank. All the time . . . ever since July.

[ANNE *speaks to her father as he comes back.*]

Anne. It worked, Pim . . . the address you left! Mr. Dussel says that people believe we escaped to Switzerland.

Mr. Frank. I'm glad. . . . And now let's have a little drink to welcome Mr. Dussel. (*Before they can drink,* DUSSEL *bolts his drink.* MR. FRANK *smiles and raises his glass.*) To Mr. Dussel. Welcome. We're very honored to have you with us.

Mrs. Frank. To Mr. Dussel, welcome.

[*The* VAN DAANS *murmur a welcome. The "grown-ups" drink.*]

Mrs. Van Daan. Um. That was good.

Mr. Van Daan. Did Mr. Kraler warn you that you won't get much to eat here? You can imagine . . . three ration books among the seven of us . . . and now you make eight.

[PETER *walks away, humiliated. Outside, a street organ is heard dimly.*]

Dussel (*rising*). Mr. Van Daan, you don't realize what is happening outside that you should warn me of a thing like that. You don't realize what's going on. . . . (*As* MR. VAN DAAN *starts his characteristic pacing,* DUSSEL *turns to speak to the others.*) Right here in Amsterdam every day hundreds of Jews disappear. . . . They surround a block and search house by house. Children come home from school to find their parents gone. Hundreds are being deported[25] . . . people that you and I know . . . the Hallensteins . . . the Wessels . . .

Mrs. Frank (*in tears*). Oh, no. No!

Dussel. They get their call-up notice . . . come to the Jewish theater on such and such a day and hour . . . bring only what you can carry in a rucksack. And if you refuse the call-up notice, then they come and drag you from your home and ship you off to Mauthausen. The death camp!

Mrs. Frank. We didn't know that things had got so much worse.

Dussel. Forgive me for speaking so.

---

25. **deported:** forcibly sent away (here, to concentration camps and death camps).

The call-up document that was issued when Jews in Amsterdam were ordered to depart for work or concentration camps. It states what they can bring and when they must leave.

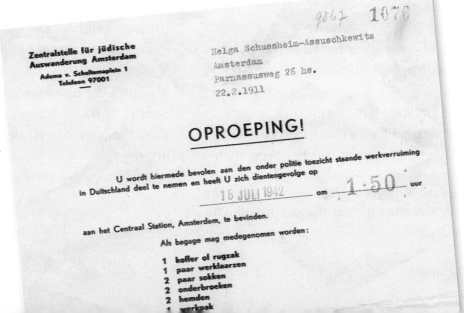

Anne (*coming to* DUSSEL). Do you know the de Waals? . . . What's become of them? Their daughter Jopie and I are in the same class. Jopie's my best friend.

Dussel. They are gone.

Anne. Gone?

Dussel. With all the others.

Anne. Oh, no. Not Jopie!

[*She turns away, in tears.* MRS. FRANK *motions to* MARGOT *to comfort her.* MARGOT *goes to* ANNE, *putting her arms comfortingly around her.*]

Mrs. Van Daan. There were some people called Wagner. They lived near us . . . ?

Mr. Frank (*interrupting, with a glance at* ANNE). I think we should put this off until later. We all have many questions we want to ask. . . . But I'm sure that Mr. Dussel would like to get settled before supper.

Dussel. Thank you. I would. I brought very little with me.

Mr. Frank (*giving him his hat and briefcase*). I'm sorry we can't give you a room alone. But I hope you won't be too uncomfortable. We've had to make strict rules here . . . a schedule of hours . . . We'll tell you after supper. Anne, would you like to take Mr. Dussel to his room?

Anne (*controlling her tears*). If you'll come with me, Mr. Dussel? (*She starts for her room.*)

Dussel (*shaking hands with each in turn*). Forgive me if I haven't really expressed my gratitude to all of you. This has been such

a shock to me. I'd always thought of myself as Dutch. I was born in Holland. My father was born in Holland, and my grandfather. And now . . . after all these years . . . (*He breaks off.*) If you'll excuse me.

[DUSSEL *gives a little bow and hurries off after* ANNE. MR. FRANK *and the others are subdued.*]

Anne (*turning on the light*). Well, here we are.

[DUSSEL *looks around the room. In the main room* MARGOT *speaks to her mother.*]

Margot. The news sounds pretty bad, doesn't it? It's so different from what Mr. Kraler tells us. Mr. Kraler says things are improving.

U **Read and Discuss** How might the news about Jopie and her family effect the audience? How does the action on stage affect that response?

Anne and Mr. Dussel in the stage production. © Joan Marcus.

Mr. Van Daan. I like it better the way Kraler tells it.

[*They resume their occupations, quietly.* PETER *goes off into his room. In* ANNE'S *room,* ANNE *turns to* DUSSEL.]

Anne. You're going to share the room with me.

Dussel. I'm a man who's always lived alone. I haven't had to adjust myself to others. I hope you'll bear with me until I learn.

Anne. Let me help you. (*She takes his briefcase.*) Do you always live all alone? Have you no family at all?

Dussel. No one. (*He opens his medicine case and spreads his bottles on the dressing table.*)

Anne. How dreadful. You must be terribly lonely.

Dussel. I'm used to it.

Anne. I don't think I could ever get used to it. Didn't you even have a pet? A cat, or a dog?

Dussel. I have an allergy for fur-bearing animals. They give me asthma.

Anne. Oh, dear. Peter has a cat.

Dussel. Here? He has it here?

Anne. Yes. But we hardly ever see it. He keeps it in his room all the time. I'm sure it will be all right.

Dussel. Let us hope so. (*He takes some pills to fortify himself.*)

Anne. That's Margot's bed, where you're going to sleep. I sleep on the sofa there. (*Indicating the clothes hooks on the wall*) We cleared these off for your things. (She goes over to the window.) The best part about this room . . . you can look down and see a bit of the street and the canal. There's a houseboat . . . you can see the end of it . . . a bargeman lives there with his family. . . . They have a baby and he's just beginning to walk and I'm so afraid he's going to fall into the canal someday. I watch him . . .

Dussel (*interrupting*). Your father spoke of a schedule.

Anne (*coming away from the window*). Oh,

yes. It's mostly about the times we have to be quiet. And times for the w.c. You can use it now if you like.

Dussel (*stiffly*). No, thank you.

Anne. I suppose you think it's awful, my talking about a thing like that. But you don't know how important it can get to be, especially when you're frightened. . . . About this room, the way Margot and I did . . . she had it to herself in the afternoons for studying, reading . . . lessons, you know . . . and I took the mornings. Would that be all right with you?

Dussel. I'm not at my best in the morning.

Anne. You stay here in the mornings, then. I'll take the room in the afternoons.

Dussel. Tell me, when you're in here, what happens to me? Where am I spending my time? In there, with all the people?

Anne. Yes.

Dussel. I see. I see.

Anne. We have supper at half past six.

Dussel (*going over to the sofa*). Then, if you don't mind . . . I like to lie down quietly for ten minutes before eating. I find it helps the digestion.

Anne. Of course. I hope I'm not going to be too much of a bother to you. I seem to be able to get everyone's back up.

[DUSSEL *lies down on the sofa, curled up, his back to her.*]

Dussel. I always get along very well with children. My patients all bring their children to me, because they know I get on well with them. So don't you worry about that.

[ANNE *leans over him, taking his hand and shaking it gratefully.*]

Anne. Thank you. Thank you, Mr. Dussel.

[*The lights dim to darkness. The curtain falls on the scene.* ANNE's *voice comes to us, faintly at first and then with increasing power.*]

Anne's Voice. . . . And yesterday I finished Cissy Van Marxvelt's latest book. I think she is a first-class writer. I shall definitely let my children read her. Monday, the twenty-first of September, nineteen forty-two. Mr. Dussel and I had another battle yesterday. Yes, Mr. Dussel! According to him, nothing, I repeat . . . nothing is right about me . . . my appearance, my character, my manners. While he was going on at me, I thought . . . sometime I'll give you such a smack that you'll fly right up to the ceiling! Why is it that every grown-up thinks he knows the way to bring up children? Particularly the grown-ups that never had any. I keep wishing that Peter was a girl instead of a boy. Then I would have someone to talk to. Margot's a darling, but she takes everything too seriously. To pause for a moment on the subject of Mrs. Van Daan. I must tell you that her attempts to flirt with Father are getting her nowhere. Pim, thank goodness, won't play. **ⓥ**

[*As she is saying the last lines, the curtain rises on the darkened scene.* ANNE's *voice fades out.*]

ⓥ **Literary Focus** **Theme** How is the group responding to the new circumstances? What theme might this reaction suggest?

Applying Your Skills

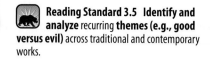

Reading Standard 3.5 Identify and analyze recurring themes (e.g., good versus evil) across traditional and contemporary works.

The Diary of Anne Frank, Act One, Scenes 1–3

Literary Response and Analysis

Reading Skills Focus
Quick Check

1. Describe Anne Frank. What is she like? At first, what is her attitude toward going into hiding?

Read with a Purpose

2. When does Anne begin to understand what going into hiding means? How is life in the Secret Annex different from life outside?

Reading Skills: Finding the Theme

3. **Identify**. List the ten characters in the play, and choose three adjectives to describe each one. Use a chart like the one below to list their traits.

Character	Character Traits
Anne	hopeful
Peter	awkward
Mr. Frank	

Literary Skills Focus
Literary Analysis

4. **Compare and Contrast** Describe Mr. Frank's and Mr. Van Daan's contrasting reactions to the news of Mr. Dussel's arrival.

5. **Analyze** How do you describe Anne and Peter's attitudes toward their families? What aspects of their attitudes surprise you? Support your response with examples from the text and from your own experiences.

6. **Interpret** What does Mrs. Frank mean by her comment to Anne: "You complain that I don't treat you like a grown-up. But when I do, you resent it" (page 315)?

7. **Analyze** A **flashback** interrupts a story to take you back to earlier times and events. Most of this play is told in an extended flashback, framed by the opening and closing scenes. Where in Scene 1 does the flashback begin? What do you learn about the characters and their basic situation before the flashback begins?

8. **Analyze** Sounds from outside the Secret Annex play an important part in the play. Some represent ordinary life in the city. Others are reminders of dangers outside. List four sounds from the play and explain your responses to them.

9. **Literary Perspectives** What is the hardest part of life in the Secret Annex? How do elements of the drama express how difficult it is?

Literary Skills: Theme

10. **Interpret** Mr. Frank tells Anne, "There are no walls, there are no bolts, no locks that anyone can put on your mind" (page 312). What **theme,** or truth about life, might this statement reveal?

Literary Skills Review: Conflict

11. **Analyze** List the conflicts that have developed among the characters by the end of Scene 3. Why are these conflicts dangerous for the characters? What other conflicts do you think might arise?

SCENE 4

It is the middle of the night, several months later. The stage is dark except for a little light which comes through the skylight in PETER'S *room.*

    Everyone is in bed. MR. *and* MRS. FRANK *lie on the couch in the main room, which has been pulled out to serve as a makeshift double bed.*

    MARGOT *is sleeping on a mattress on the floor in the main room, behind a curtain stretched across for privacy. The others are all in their accustomed rooms.*

    From outside we hear two drunken soldiers singing "Lili Marlene." A girl's high giggle is heard. The sound of running feet is heard coming closer and then fading in the distance. Throughout the scene there is the distant sound of airplanes passing overhead.

    A match suddenly flares up in the attic. We dimly see MR. VAN DAAN. *He is getting his bearings. He comes quickly down the stairs and goes to the cupboard where the food is stored. Again the match flares up, and is as quickly blown out. The dim figure is seen to steal back up the stairs.* Ⓐ

    There is quiet for a second or two, broken only by the sound of airplanes and running feet on the street below. Suddenly, out of the silence and the dark, we hear ANNE *scream.*

Anne (*screaming*). No! No! Don't . . . don't take me!

[She moans, tossing and crying in her sleep. The other people wake, terrified. DUSSEL *sits up in bed, furious.]*

Dussel. Shush! Anne! Anne, for God's sake, shush!

Anne (*still in her nightmare*). Save me! Save me!

[She screams and screams. DUSSEL *gets out of bed, going over to her, trying to wake her.]*

Dussel. For God's sake! Quiet! Quiet! You want someone to hear?

[In the main room MRS. FRANK *grabs a shawl and pulls it around her. She rushes in to* ANNE, *taking her in her arms.* MR. FRANK *hurriedly gets up, putting on his overcoat.* MARGOT *sits up, terrified.* PETER'S *light goes on in his room.]*

Mrs. Frank (*to* ANNE, *in her room*). Hush, darling, hush. It's all right. It's all right. (*Over her shoulder, to* DUSSEL) Will you be kind enough to turn on the light, Mr. Dussel? (*Back to* ANNE) It's nothing, my darling. It was just a dream.

[DUSSEL turns on the light in the bedroom. MRS. FRANK *holds* ANNE *in her arms. Gradually* ANNE *comes out of her nightmare, still trembling with horror.* MR. FRANK *comes into the room, and goes quickly to the window, looking out to be sure that no one outside has heard* ANNE'S *screams.* MRS. FRANK *holds* ANNE, *talking softly to her. In the main room*

Ⓐ **Read and Discuss** What is Mr. Van Daan doing in the first few moments of the scene? How might his actions create complications later?

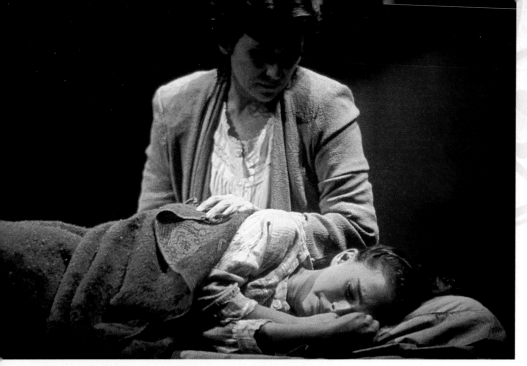

Anne and her mother in the stage production. ©Joan Marcus.

MARGOT *stands on a chair, turning on the center hanging lamp. A light goes on in the* VAN DAANS' *room overhead.* PETER *puts his robe on, coming out of his room.*] **B**

Dussel (*to* MRS. FRANK, *blowing his nose*). Something must be done about that child, Mrs. Frank. Yelling like that! Who knows but there's somebody on the streets? She's endangering all our lives.
Mrs. Frank. Anne, darling.
Dussel. Every night she twists and turns. I don't sleep. I spend half my night shushing her. And now it's nightmares!

[MARGOT *comes to the door of* ANNE's *room, followed by* PETER. MR. FRANK *goes to them, indicating that everything is all right.* PETER *takes* MARGOT *back.*]

Mrs. Frank (*to* ANNE). You're here, safe, you see? Nothing has happened. (*To* DUSSEL) Please, Mr. Dussel, go back to bed. She'll be herself in a minute or two. Won't you, Anne?
Dussel (*picking up a book and a pillow*). Thank you, but I'm going to the w.c. The one place where there's peace!

[*He stalks out.* MR. VAN DAAN, *in underwear and trousers, comes down the stairs.*]

Mr. Van Daan (*to* DUSSEL). What is it? What happened?
Dussel. A nightmare. She was having a nightmare!
Mr. Van Daan. I thought someone was murdering her.
Dussel. Unfortunately, no.

B Reading Focus **Finding the Theme** How do the other characters respond to Anne's cries? What does each character's reaction suggest about him or her?

[*He goes into the bathroom.* MR. VAN DAAN *goes back up the stairs.* MR. FRANK, *in the main room, sends* PETER *back to his own bedroom.*]

Mr. Frank. Thank you, Peter. Go back to bed.

[PETER *goes back to his room.* MR. FRANK *follows him, turning out the light and looking out the window. Then he goes back to the main room, and gets up on a chair, turning out the center hanging lamp.*]

Mrs. Frank (*to* ANNE). Would you like some water? (ANNE *shakes her head.*) Was it a very bad dream? Perhaps if you told me . . . ?
Anne. I'd rather not talk about it.
Mrs. Frank. Poor darling. Try to sleep, then. I'll sit right here beside you until you fall asleep. (*She brings a stool over, sitting there.*)
Anne. You don't have to.
Mrs. Frank. But I'd like to stay with you . . . very much. Really.
Anne. I'd rather you didn't.
Mrs. Frank. Good night, then. (*She leans down to kiss* ANNE. ANNE *throws her arm up over her face, turning away.* MRS. FRANK, *hiding her hurt, kisses* ANNE'S *arm.*) You'll be all right? There's nothing that you want?
Anne. Will you please ask Father to come.
Mrs. Frank (*after a second*). Of course, Anne dear. (*She hurries out into the other room.* MR. FRANK *comes to her as she comes in.*) Sie verlangt nach Dir![1]
Mr. Frank (*sensing her hurt*). Edith, Liebe, schau . . .[2]

Mrs. Frank. Es macht nichts! Ich danke dem lieben Herrgott, dass sie sich wenigstens an Dich wendet, wenn sie Trost braucht! Geh hinein, Otto, sie ist ganz hysterisch vor Angst.[3] (*As* MR. FRANK *hesitates*) Geh zu ihr.[4] (*He looks at her for a second and then goes to get a cup of water for* ANNE. MRS. FRANK *sinks down on the bed, her face in her hands, trying to keep from sobbing aloud.* MARGOT *comes over to her, putting her arms around her.*) She wants nothing of me. She pulled away when I leaned down to kiss her.
Margot. It's a phase. . . . You heard Father. . . . Most girls go through it . . . they turn to their

---

1. **Sie . . . Dir:** German for "She's asking for you."
2. **Liebe, schau:** "Dear, look."

3. **Es . . . Angst:** "It doesn't matter! I thank the dear Lord that she turns at least to you when she needs comfort! Go to her, Otto, she's completely hysterical with fear."
4. **Geh zu ihr:** "Go to her."

Mr. Frank. Something to quiet you.

[*She takes it and drinks the water. In the main room* MARGOT *turns out the light and goes back to her bed.*]

Mr. Frank (*to* ANNE). Do you want me to read to you for a while?

Anne. No. Just sit with me for a minute. Was I awful? Did I yell terribly loud? Do you think anyone outside could have heard?

Mr. Frank. No. No. Lie quietly now. Try to sleep.

Anne. I'm a terrible coward. I'm so disappointed in myself. I think I've conquered my fear . . . I think I'm really grown-up . . . and then something happens . . . and I run to you like a baby. . . . I love you, Father. I don't love anyone but you.

Mr. Frank (*reproachfully*). Annele!

Anne. It's true. I've been thinking about it for a long time. You're the only one I love.

Mr. Frank. It's fine to hear you tell me that you love me. But I'd be happier if you said you loved your mother as well. . . . She needs your help so much . . . your love . . .

Anne. We have nothing in common. She doesn't understand me. Whenever I try to explain my views on life to her, she asks me if I'm constipated.

Mr. Frank. You hurt her very much just now. She's crying. She's in there crying.

Anne. I can't help it. I only told the truth. I didn't want her here . . . (*Then, with sudden change*) Oh, Pim, I was horrible, wasn't I? And the worst of it is, I can stand off and

fathers at this age . . . they give all their love to their fathers.

Mrs. Frank. You weren't like this. You didn't shut me out.

Margot. She'll get over it. . . .

[*She smoothes the bed for* MRS. FRANK *and sits beside her a moment as* MRS. FRANK *lies down. In* ANNE'S *room* MR. FRANK *comes in, sitting down by* ANNE. ANNE *flings her arms around him, clinging to him. In the distance we hear the sound of ack-ack.*]

Anne. Oh, Pim. I dreamed that they came to get us! The Green Police! They broke down the door and grabbed me and started to drag me out the way they did Jopie.

Mr. Frank. I want you to take this pill.

Anne. What is it?

look at myself doing it and know it's cruel and yet I can't stop doing it. What's the matter with me? Tell me. Don't say it's just a phase! Help me.

Mr. Frank. There is so little that we parents can do to help our children. We can only try to set a good example . . . point the way. The rest you must do yourself. You must build your own character. **C**

Anne. I'm trying. Really I am. Every night I think back over all of the things I did that day that were wrong . . . like putting the wet mop in Mr. Dussel's bed . . . and this thing now with Mother. I say to myself, that was wrong. I make up my mind, I'm never going to do that again. Never! Of course, I may do something worse . . . but at least I'll never do *that* again! . . . I have a nicer side, Father . . . a sweeter, nicer side. But I'm scared to show it. I'm afraid that people are going to laugh at me if I'm serious. So the mean Anne comes to the outside and the good Anne stays on the inside, and I keep on trying to switch them around and have the good Anne outside and the bad Anne inside and be what I'd like to be . . . and might be . . . if only . . . only . . .

[*She is asleep.* MR. FRANK *watches her for a moment and then turns off the light, and starts out. The lights dim out. The curtain falls on the scene.* ANNE'*s voice is heard, dimly at first and then with growing strength.*]

Anne's Voice. . . . The air raids[5] are getting worse. They come over day and night. The noise is terrifying. Pim says it should be music to our ears. The more planes, the sooner will come the end of the war. Mrs. Van Daan pretends to be a fatalist.[6] What will be, will be. But when the planes come over, who is the most frightened? No one else but Petronella! . . . Monday, the ninth of November, nineteen forty-two. Wonderful news! The Allies have landed in Africa. Pim says that we can look for an early finish to the war. Just for fun, he asked each of us what was the first thing we wanted to do when we got out of here. Mrs. Van Daan longs to be home with her own things, her needlepoint chairs, the Bechstein piano her father gave her . . . the best that money could buy. Peter would like to go to a movie. Mr. Dussel wants to get back to his dentist's drill. He's afraid he is losing his touch. For myself, there are so many things . . . to ride a bike again . . . to laugh till my belly aches . . . to have new clothes from the skin out . . . to have a hot tub filled to overflowing and wallow in it for hours . . . to be back in school with my friends . . . **D**

[*As the last lines are being said, the curtain rises on the scene. The lights dim on as* ANNE'*s voice fades away.*]

---

5. **air raids:** Allied aircraft conducted air raids, or bombing attacks on ground targets, in the Netherlands because the country was occupied by the Germans.

6. **fatalist** (FAY tuh lihst): person who believes that all events are determined by fate and therefore cannot be prevented or affected by people's actions.

C Literary Focus **Theme** What larger idea might Mr. Frank's words express?

D Read and Discuss What is Anne talking about?

SCENE 5

It is the first night of the Hanukkah[7] celebration. MR. FRANK *is standing at the head of the table on which is the menorah.[8] He lights the shamas, or servant candle, and holds it as he says the blessing. Seated, listening, are all of the "family," dressed in their best. The men wear hats;* PETER *wears his cap.*

Mr. Frank (*reading from a prayer book*). "Praised be Thou, oh Lord our God, Ruler of the universe, who has sanctified us with Thy commandments and bidden us kindle the Hanukkah lights. Praised be Thou, oh Lord our God, Ruler of the universe, who has wrought wondrous deliverances for our fathers in days of old. Praised be Thou, oh Lord our God, Ruler of the universe, that Thou has given us life and sustenance and brought us to this happy season." (MR. FRANK *lights the one candle of the menorah as he continues.*) "We kindle this Hanukkah light to celebrate the great and wonderful deeds wrought through the zeal with which God filled the hearts of the heroic Maccabees, two thousand years ago. They fought against indifference, against tyranny and oppression, and they restored our Temple to us. May these lights remind us that we should ever look to God, whence cometh our help." Amen. (*Pronounced "oh-mayn"*)
All. Amen.

[MR. FRANK *hands* MRS. FRANK *the prayer book.*]

Mrs. Frank (*reading*). "I lift up mine eyes unto the mountains, from whence cometh my help. My help cometh from the Lord who made heaven and earth. He will not suffer thy foot to be moved. He that keepeth thee will not slumber. He that keepeth Israel doth neither slumber nor sleep. The Lord is thy keeper. The Lord is thy shade upon thy right hand. The sun shall not smite thee by day, nor the moon by night. The Lord shall keep thee from all evil. He shall keep thy soul. The Lord shall guard thy going out and thy coming in, from this time forth and forevermore."[9] Amen.
All. Amen.

[MRS. FRANK *puts down the prayer book and goes to get the food and wine.* MARGOT *helps her.* MR. FRANK *takes the men's hats and puts them aside.*]

Dussel (*rising*). That was very moving.
Anne (*pulling him back*). It isn't over yet!
Mrs. Van Daan. Sit down! Sit down!

---

7. **Hanukkah** (HAH noo kah): joyous eight-day Jewish holiday, usually falling in December, celebrating the rededication of the holy Temple in Jerusalem in 164 B.C. The Temple had been taken over by the Syrians, who had conquered Jerusalem. The Maccabee family led the Jews in a successful rebellion against the Syrians and retook the Temple.
8. **menorah** (muh NOH ruh): Hebrew for "lamp." Mr. Frank is lighting a menorah that holds nine candles: eight candles, one for each of the eight nights of Hanukkah, and the shamas, the candle used to light the others.

---

9. Mrs. Frank is reading Psalm 121 from the Bible.

Vocabulary **tyranny** (TIHR uh nee) *n.:* absolute power used unjustly.

Anne distributing presents in the stage production. ©Joan Marcus.

Anne. There's a lot more, songs and presents.
Dussel. Presents?
Mrs. Frank. Not this year, unfortunately.
Mrs. Van Daan. But always on Hanukkah everyone gives presents . . . everyone!
Dussel. Like our St. Nicholas's Day.[10]

[*There is a chorus of no's from the group.*]

Mrs. Van Daan. No! Not like St. Nicholas! What kind of a Jew are you that you don't know Hanukkah?
Mrs. Frank (*as she brings the food*). I remember particularly the candles. . . . First, one, as we have tonight. Then, the second night, you light two candles, the next night three . . . and so on until you have eight candles burning. When there are eight candles, it is truly beautiful.
Mrs. Van Daan. And the potato pancakes.
Mr. Van Daan. Don't talk about them!
Mrs. Van Daan. I make the best latkes[11] you ever tasted!
Mrs. Frank. Invite us all next year . . . in your own home.
Mr. Frank. God willing!
Mrs. Van Daan. God willing.
Margot. What I remember best is the presents we used to get when we were little . . . eight days of presents . . . and each day they got better and better.
Mrs. Frank (*sitting down*). We are all here, alive. That is present enough.
Anne. No, it isn't. I've got something. . . .

---

10. **St. Nicholas's Day:** December 6; Christian holiday celebrated in the Netherlands and elsewhere on its eve, December 5, when small gifts are given.

11. **latkes** (LAHT kuhz): potato pancakes, a traditional Hanukkah food.

(*She rushes into her room, hurriedly puts on a little hat improvised from the lampshade, grabs a satchel bulging with parcels, and comes running back.*) **E**

Mrs. Frank. What is it?

Anne. Presents!

Mrs. Van Daan. Presents!

Dussel. Look!

Mr. Van Daan. What's she got on her head?

Peter. A lampshade!

Anne (*she picks out one at random*). This is for Margot. (*She hands it to* MARGOT, *pulling her to her feet.*) Read it out loud.

Margot (*reading*).

You have never lost your temper.
You never will, I fear,
You are so good.
But if you should,
Put all your cross words here.

(*She tears open the package.*) A new crossword puzzle book! Where did you get it?

Anne. It isn't new. It's one that you've done. But I rubbed it all out, and if you wait a little and forget, you can do it all over again.

Margot (*sitting*). It's wonderful, Anne. Thank you. You'd never know it wasn't new.

[*From outside we hear the sound of a streetcar passing.*]

Anne (*with another gift*). Mrs. Van Daan.

Mrs. Van Daan (*taking it*). This is awful . . . I haven't anything for anyone . . . I never thought . . .

Mr. Frank. This is all Anne's idea.

Mrs. Van Daan (*holding up a bottle*). What is it?

Anne. It's hair shampoo. I took all the odds and ends of soap and mixed them with the last of my toilet water.[12]

Mrs. Van Daan. Oh, Anneke!

Anne. I wanted to write a poem for all of them, but I didn't have time. (*Offering a large box to* MR. VAN DAAN) Yours, Mr. Van Daan, is *really* something . . . something you want more than anything. (*As she waits for him to open it*) Look! Cigarettes!

Mr. Van Daan. Cigarettes!

Anne. Two of them! Pim found some old pipe tobacco in the pocket lining of his coat . . . and we made them . . . or rather, Pim did.

Mrs. Van Daan. Let me see . . . Well, look at that! Light it, Putti! Light it.

[MR. VAN DAAN *hesitates.*]

Anne. It's tobacco, really it is! There's a little fluff in it, but not much.

[*Everyone watches intently as* MR. VAN DAAN *cautiously lights it. The cigarette flares up. Everyone laughs.*]

Peter. It works!

Mrs. Van Daan. Look at him.

Mr. Van Daan (*spluttering*). Thank you, Anne. Thank you.

---

12. **toilet water:** cologne.

E **Literary Focus** **Theme** Anne remains generous and conscientious even under these circumstances. What <u>insight</u> might the playwright be sharing by describing her behavior?

[ANNE *rushes back to her satchel for another present.*]

Anne (*handing her mother a piece of paper*). For Mother, Hanukkah greeting. (*She pulls her mother to her feet.*)
Mrs. Frank (*she reads*).

Here's an IOU that I promise to pay.
Ten hours of doing whatever you say.
Signed, Anne Frank.

(MRS. FRANK, *touched, takes* ANNE *in her arms, holding her close.*)
Dussel (*to* ANNE). Ten hours of doing what you're told? *Anything* you're told?
Anne. That's right.
Dussel. You wouldn't want to sell that, Mrs. Frank?
Mrs. Frank. Never! This is the most precious gift I've ever had! **🅕**

[*She sits, showing her present to the others.* ANNE *hurries back to the satchel and pulls out a scarf, the scarf that* MR. FRANK *found in the first scene.*]

Anne (*offering it to her father*). For Pim.
Mr. Frank. Anneke . . . I wasn't supposed to have a present! (*He takes it, unfolding it and showing it to the others.*)
Anne. It's a muffler . . . to put round your neck . . . like an ascot, you know. I made it myself out of odds and ends. . . . I knitted it in the dark each night, after I'd gone to bed. I'm afraid it looks better in the dark!
Mr. Frank (*putting it on*). It's fine. It fits me perfectly. Thank you, Annele.

[ANNE *hands* PETER *a ball of paper with a string attached to it.*]

Anne. That's for Mouschi.
Peter (*rising to bow*). On behalf of Mouschi, I thank you.
Anne (*hesitant, handing him a gift*). And . . . this is yours . . . from Mrs. Quack Quack. (*As he holds it gingerly in his hands*) Well . . . open it. . . . Aren't you going to open it?
Peter. I'm scared to. I know something's going to jump out and hit me.
Anne. No. It's nothing like that, really.
Mrs. Van Daan (*as he is opening it*). What is it, Peter? Go on. Show it.
Anne (*excitedly*). It's a safety razor!
Dussel. A what?
Anne. A razor!
Mrs. Van Daan (*looking at it*). You didn't make that out of odds and ends.
Anne (*to* PETER). Miep got it for me. It's not new. It's secondhand. But you really do need a razor now.
Dussel. For what?
Anne. Look on his upper lip . . . you can see the beginning of a moustache.
Dussel. He wants to get rid of that? Put a little milk on it and let the cat lick it off.
Peter (*starting for his room*). Think you're funny, don't you.
Dussel. Look! He can't wait! He's going in to try it!
Peter. I'm going to give Mouschi his present! (*He goes into his room, slamming the door behind him.*)
Mr. Van Daan (*disgustedly*). Mouschi, Mouschi, Mouschi.

🅕 Read and Discuss | How has Anne's attitude toward her mother changed?

[*In the distance we hear a dog persistently barking.* ANNE *brings a gift to* DUSSEL.]

Anne. And last but never least, my roommate, Mr. Dussel.

Dussel. For me? You have something for me? (*He opens the small box she gives him.*)

Anne. I made them myself.

Dussel (*puzzled*). Capsules! Two capsules!

Anne. They're earplugs!

Dussel. Earplugs?

Anne. To put in your ears so you won't hear me when I thrash around at night. I saw them advertised in a magazine. They're not real ones. . . . I made them out of cotton and candle wax. Try them. . . . See if they don't work. . . . See if you can hear me talk . . .

Dussel (*putting them in his ears*). Wait now until I get them in . . . so.

Anne. Are you ready?

Dussel. Huh?

Anne. Are you ready?

Dussel. Good God! They've gone inside! I can't get them out! (*They laugh as* DUSSEL *jumps about, trying to shake the plugs out of his ears. Finally he gets them out. Putting them away*) Thank you, Anne! Thank you!

Mr. Van Daan. A real Hanukkah! ⎫
Mrs. Van Daan. Wasn't it cute of her? ⎪
⎬ *Together*
Mrs. Frank. I don't know when she did it. ⎪
Margot. I love my present. ⎭

Anne (*sitting at the table*). And now let's have the song, Father . . . please . . . (*To* DUSSEL) Have you heard the Hanukkah song, Mr. Dussel? The song is the whole thing! (*She*

Menorah lit for Hanukkah.

sings) "Oh, Hanukkah! Oh, Hanukkah! The sweet celebration . . ."

Mr. Frank (*quieting her*). I'm afraid, Anne, we shouldn't sing that song tonight. (*To* DUSSEL) It's a song of jubilation, of rejoicing. One is apt to become too enthusiastic.

Anne. Oh, please, please. Let's sing the song. I promise not to shout!

Mr. Frank. Very well. But quietly, now . . . I'll keep an eye on you and when . . .

[*As* ANNE *starts to sing, she is interrupted by* DUSSEL, *who is snorting and wheezing.*]

Dussel (*pointing to* PETER). You . . . You! (PETER *is coming from his bedroom, ostentatiously holding a bulge in his coat as if he were holding his cat, and dangling* ANNE's *present before it.*) How many times . . . I told you . . . Out! Out!

Mr. Van Daan (*going to* PETER). What's the matter with you? Haven't you any sense? Get that cat out of here.

Peter (*innocently*). Cat?

Mr. Van Daan. You heard me. Get it out of here!

Peter. I have no cat.

Vocabulary **ostentatiously** (ahs tehn TAY shuhs lee) *adv.*: in a showy way.

[*Delighted with his joke, he opens his coat and pulls out a bath towel. The group at the table laugh, enjoying the joke.*]

Dussel (*still wheezing*). It doesn't need to be the cat . . . his clothes are enough . . . when he comes out of that room . . .

Mr. Van Daan. Don't worry. You won't be bothered anymore. We're getting rid of it.

Dussel. At last you listen to me. (*He goes off into his bedroom.*)

Mr. Van Daan (*calling after him*). I'm not doing it for you. That's all in your mind . . . all of it! (*He starts back to his place at the table.*) I'm doing it because I'm sick of seeing that cat eat all our food.

Peter. That's not true! I only give him bones . . . scraps . . .

Mr. Van Daan. Don't tell me! He gets fatter every day! Damn cat looks better than any of us. Out he goes tonight!

Peter. No! No!

Anne. Mr. Van Daan, you can't do that! That's Peter's cat. Peter loves that cat.

Mrs. Frank (*quietly*). Anne.

Peter (*to* MR. VAN DAAN). If he goes, I go.

Mr. Van Daan. Go! Go!

Mrs. Van Daan. You're not going and the cat's not going! Now please . . . this is Hanukkah . . . Hanukkah . . . this is the time to celebrate. . . . What's the matter with all of you? Come on, Anne. Let's have the song.

Anne (*singing*).

Oh, Hanukkah!
Oh, Hanukkah!
The sweet celebration.

Mr. Frank (*rising*). I think we should first blow out the candle . . . then we'll have something for tomorrow night.

Margot. But, Father, you're supposed to let it burn itself out.

Mr. Frank. I'm sure that God understands shortages. (*Before blowing it out*) "Praised be Thou, oh Lord our God, who hast sustained us and permitted us to celebrate this joyous festival."　　　　　**G**

[*He is about to blow out the candle when suddenly there is a crash of something falling below. They all freeze in horror, motionless. For a few seconds there is complete silence.* MR. FRANK *slips off his shoes. The others noiselessly follow his example.* MR. FRANK *turns out a light near him. He motions to* PETER *to turn off the center lamp.* PETER *tries to reach it, realizes he cannot, and gets up on a chair. Just as he is touching the lamp, he loses his balance. The chair goes out from under him. He falls. The iron lampshade crashes to the floor. There is a sound of feet below running down the stairs.*]　　**H**

Mr. Van Daan (*under his breath*). God Almighty! (*The only light left comes from the Hanukkah candle.* DUSSEL *comes from his room.* MR. FRANK *creeps over to the stairwell and stands listening. The dog is heard barking excitedly.*) Do you hear anything?

Mr. Frank (*in a whisper*). No. I think they've gone.

Mrs. Van Daan. It's the Green Police. They've found us.

Mr. Frank. If they had, they wouldn't have left. They'd be up here by now.

G [Read and Discuss] How do the playwrights introduce conflict and suspense in this scene?

H [Read and Discuss] What complication is introduced here?

Mrs. Van Daan. I know it's the Green Police. They've gone to get help. That's all. They'll be back!

Mr. Van Daan. Or it may have been the Gestapo,[13] looking for papers . . .

Mr. Frank (*interrupting*). Or a thief, looking for money.

Mrs. Van Daan. We've got to do something. . . . Quick! Quick! Before they come back.

Mr. Van Daan. There isn't anything to do. Just wait.

[MR. FRANK *holds up his hand for them to be quiet. He is listening intently. There is complete silence as they all strain to hear any sound from below. Suddenly* ANNE *begins to sway. With a low cry she falls to the floor in a faint.* MRS. FRANK *goes to her quickly, sitting beside her on the floor and taking her in her arms.*]

Mrs. Frank. Get some water, please! Get some water!

[MARGOT *starts for the sink.*]

Mr. Van Daan (*grabbing* MARGOT). No! No! No one's going to run water!

Mr. Frank. If they've found us, they've found us. Get the water. (MARGOT *starts again for the sink.* MR. FRANK, *getting a flashlight*) I'm going down.

[MARGOT *rushes to him, clinging to him.* ANNE *struggles to consciousness.*]

Margot. No, Father, no! There may be someone there, waiting. . . . It may be a trap!

------

13. **Gestapo** (guh STAH poh): Nazi secret police.

Mr. Frank. This is Saturday. There is no way for us to know what has happened until Miep or Mr. Kraler comes on Monday morning. We cannot live with this uncertainty.

Margot. Don't go, Father!

Mrs. Frank. Hush, darling, hush. (MR. FRANK *slips quietly out, down the steps, and out through the door below.*) Margot! Stay close to me.

[MARGOT *goes to her mother.*]

Mr. Van Daan. Shush! Shush!

[MRS. FRANK *whispers to* MARGOT *to get the water.* MARGOT *goes for it.*]

Mrs. Van Daan. Putti, where's our money? Get our money. I hear you can buy the Green Police off, so much a head. Go upstairs quick! Get the money!

Mr. Van Daan. Keep still!

Mrs. Van Daan (*kneeling before him, pleading*). Do you want to be dragged off to a concentration camp? Are you going to stand there and wait for them to come up and get you? Do something, I tell you!

Mr. Van Daan (*pushing her aside*). Will you keep still!

[*He goes over to the stairwell to listen.* PETER *goes to his mother, helping her up onto the sofa. There is a second of silence; then* ANNE *can stand it no longer.*]

Anne. Someone go after Father! Make Father come back!

Peter (*starting for the door*). I'll go.

Mr. Van Daan. Haven't you done enough?

[*He pushes* PETER *roughly away. In his anger against his father* PETER *grabs a chair as if to hit him with it, then puts it down, burying his face in his hands.* MRS. FRANK *begins to pray softly.*]

Anne. Please, please, Mr. Van Daan. Get Father.
Mr. Van Daan. Quiet! Quiet!

[ANNE *is shocked into silence.* MRS. FRANK *pulls her closer, holding her protectively in her arms.*]

Mrs. Frank (*softly, praying*). "I lift up mine eyes unto the mountains, from whence cometh my help. My help cometh from the Lord who made heaven and earth. He will not suffer thy foot to be moved. . . . He that keepeth thee will not slumber . . ."

[*She stops as she hears someone coming. They all watch the door tensely.* MR. FRANK *comes quietly in.* ANNE *rushes to him, holding him tight.*]

Mr. Frank. It was a thief. That noise must have scared him away.
Mrs. Van Daan. Thank God.
Mr. Frank. He took the cash box. And the radio. He ran away in such a hurry that he didn't stop to shut the street door. It was swinging wide open. (*A breath of relief sweeps over them.*) I think it would be good to have some light.
Margot. Are you sure it's all right?
Mr. Frank. The danger has passed. (MARGOT *goes to light the small lamp.*) Don't be so terrified, Anne. We're safe.

Dussel. Who says the danger has passed? Don't you realize we are in greater danger than ever?
Mr. Frank. Mr. Dussel, will you be still! (MR. FRANK *takes* ANNE *back to the table, making her sit down with him, trying to calm her.*)
Dussel (*pointing to* PETER). Thanks to this clumsy fool, there's someone now who knows we're up here! Someone now knows we're up here, hiding!
Mrs. Van Daan (*going to* DUSSEL). Someone knows we're here, yes. But who is the someone? A thief! A thief! You think a thief is going to go to the Green Police and say . . . "I was robbing a place the other night and I heard a noise up over my head?" You think a thief is going to do that?
Dussel. Yes. I think he will. ❶
Mrs. Van Daan (*hysterically*). You're crazy! (*She stumbles back to her seat at the table.* PETER *follows protectively, pushing* DUSSEL *aside.*)
Dussel. I think someday he'll be caught and then he'll make a bargain with the Green Police . . . if they'll let him off, he'll tell them where some Jews are hiding!

[*He goes off into the bedroom. There is a second of appalled silence.*]
Mr. Van Daan. He's right.
Anne. Father, let's get out of here! We can't stay here now. . . . Let's go . . .
Mr. Van Daan. Go! Where?
Mrs. Frank (*sinking into her chair at the table*). Yes. Where?
Mr. Frank (*rising, to them all*). Have we lost

---

❶ **Literary Focus** **Theme** How are the characters behaving toward one another? What theme does this part of the scene convey?

all faith? All courage? A moment ago we thought that they'd come for us. We were sure it was the end. But it wasn't the end. We're alive, safe. (MR. VAN DAAN *goes to the table and sits.* MR. FRANK *prays*) "We thank Thee, oh Lord our God, that in Thy infinite mercy Thou hast again seen fit to spare us." (*He blows out the candle, then turns to* ANNE.) Come on, Anne. The song! Let's have the song! (*He starts to sing.* ANNE *finally starts falteringly to sing, as* MR. FRANK *urges her on. Her voice is hardly audible at first.*)

Anne (*singing*).

Oh, Hanukkah! Oh, Hanukkah!
The sweet . . . celebration . . .

[*As she goes on singing, the others gradually join in, their voices still shaking with fear.* MRS. VAN DAAN *sobs as she sings.*]

Group.

Around the feast . . . we . . . gather
In complete . . . jubilation . . .
Happiest of sea . . . sons
Now is here.
Many are the reasons for good cheer.

[DUSSEL *comes from the bedroom. He comes over to the table, standing beside* MARGOT, *listening to them as they sing.*]

Together
We'll weather
Whatever tomorrow may bring.

Anne in the stage production. ©Joan Marcus.

[*As they sing on with growing courage, the lights start to dim.*]

So hear us rejoicing
And merrily voicing
The Hanukkah song that we sing.
Hoy!

[*The lights are out. The curtain starts slowly to fall.*]

Hear us rejoicing
And merrily voicing
The Hanukkah song that we sing.

[*They are still singing as the curtain falls.*] **(K)**

Curtain

Applying Your Skills

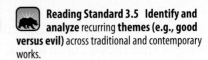

Reading Standard 3.5 **Identify** and **analyze** recurring **themes (e.g., good versus evil)** across traditional and contemporary works.

The Diary of Anne Frank, Act One, Scenes 4–5

Literary Response and Analysis

Reading Skills Focus

Quick Check

1. What are the characters doing in Scene 5?
2. What happens at the end of Scene 5?

Read with a Purpose

3. How does Anne's view of the world change in Scenes 4–5? Support your answer with examples from the play.

Reading Skills: Finding the Theme

4. Go back to the list of characters you made after you read Scenes 1–3. Explain which adjectives, if any, you would change.

Literary Skills Focus

Literary Analysis

5. **Analyze** How does Anne's nightmare in Scene 4 cause tensions to escalate within the household?
6. **Speculate** Imagine that you are watching this play in a theater. What questions do you have as the curtain comes down on Act One? What do you predict will happen in Act Two?
7. **Compare and Contrast** How does the Hanukkah celebration contrast with the harsh reality outside the hiding place? How would you describe the way the characters feel? What causes their feelings to change?

8. **Extend** Characters in literature, like people in real life, sometimes take courage from a speech or a song. How do the families take courage at the end of Scene 5? What other episodes in plays or movies (or in real life) can you think of in which people facing danger summon up courage from a speech or a song? Explain.
9. **Literary Perspectives** Describe the **reversal**—the sudden change in the characters' fortunes—that occurs in Scene 5. What impact does that plot event have on the audience?

Literary Skills: Theme

10. **Interpret** A **theme** is a general idea or insight about life as revealed in a work of literature. In drama, the theme can often be discovered in the characters' actions or dialogue. What theme is revealed in Anne's conversation with her father at the end of Scene 4?

Literary Skills Review: Character

11. **Analyze** Anne is a **dynamic character**—a character who changes during the play. How does her generosity to Peter and Mrs. Frank show that she has changed?

ACT TWO

SCENE 1

In the darkness we hear ANNE's *voice, again reading from the diary.*

Anne's Voice. Saturday, the first of January, nineteen forty-four. Another new year has begun and we find ourselves still in our hiding place. We have been here now for one year, five months, and twenty-five days. It seems that our life is at a standstill. Ⓐ

[*The curtain rises on the scene. It is late afternoon. Everyone is bundled up against the cold. In the main room* MRS. FRANK *is taking down the laundry, which is hung across the back.* MR. FRANK *sits in the chair down left, reading.* MARGOT *is lying on the couch with a blanket over her and the many-colored knitted scarf around her throat.* ANNE *is seated at the center table, writing in her diary.* PETER, MR. *and* MRS. VAN DAAN, *and* DUSSEL *are all in their own rooms, reading or lying down.*

As the lights dim on, ANNE's *voice continues, without a break.*]

Anne's Voice. We are all a little thinner. The Van Daans' "discussions" are as violent as ever. Mother still does not understand me. But then I don't understand her either. There is one great change, however. A change in myself. I read somewhere that girls of my age don't feel quite certain of themselves. That they become quiet within and begin to think of the miracle that is taking place in their bodies. I think that what is happening to me is so wonderful . . . not only what can be seen, but what is taking place inside. Each time it has happened, I have a feeling that I have a sweet secret. (*We hear the chimes and then a hymn being played on the carillon outside.*) And in spite of any pain, I long for the time when I shall feel that secret within me again.

[*The buzzer of the door below suddenly sounds. Everyone is startled.* MR. FRANK *tiptoes cautiously to the top of the steps and listens. Again the buzzer sounds, in* MIEP's *V-for-victory signal.*[1]]

Mr. Frank. It's Miep!

[*He goes quickly down the steps to unbolt the door.* MRS. FRANK *calls upstairs to the* VAN DAANS *and then to* PETER.]

Mrs. Frank. Wake up, everyone! Miep is here! (ANNE *quickly puts her diary away.* MARGOT *sits up, pulling the blanket around her shoulders.* DUSSEL *sits on the edge of his bed, listening, disgruntled.* MIEP *comes up*

---

1. **V-for-victory signal:** three short rings and one long ring, Morse code for the letter *V*, the Allied symbol for victory.

Ⓐ **Read and Discuss** More than a year has elapsed since the end of Act One. How has life for the characters changed, according to the voice-over?

the steps, followed by MR. KRALER. *They bring flowers, books, newspapers, etc.* ANNE *rushes to* MIEP, *throwing her arms affectionately around her.*) Miep . . . and Mr. Kraler. . . . What a delightful surprise!

Mr. Kraler. We came to bring you New Year's greetings.

Mrs. Frank. You shouldn't . . . you should have at least one day to yourselves. (*She goes quickly to the stove and brings down teacups and tea for all of them.*)

Anne. Don't say that, it's so wonderful to see them! (*Sniffing at* MIEP's *coat*) I can smell the wind and the cold on your clothes.

Miep (*giving her the flowers*). There you are. (*Then to* MARGOT, *feeling her forehead*) How are you, Margot? . . . Feeling any better?

Margot. I'm all right.

Anne. We filled her full of every kind of pill so she won't cough and make a noise.

[*She runs into her room to put the flowers in water.* MR. *and* MRS. VAN DAAN *come from upstairs. Outside there is the sound of a band playing.*]

Mrs. Van Daan. Well, hello, Miep. Mr. Kraler.

Mr. Kraler (*giving a bouquet of flowers to* MRS. VAN DAAN). With my hope for peace in the New Year.

Peter (*anxiously*). Miep, have you seen Mouschi? Have you seen him anywhere around?

Miep. I'm sorry, Peter. I asked everyone in the neighborhood had they seen a gray cat. But they said no. **Ⓑ**

[MRS. FRANK *gives* MIEP *a cup of tea.* MR. FRANK *comes up the steps, carrying a small cake on a plate.*]

Mr. Frank. Look what Miep's brought for us!

Mrs. Frank (*taking it*). A cake!

Mr. Van Daan. A cake! (*He pinches* MIEP's *cheeks gaily and hurries up to the cupboard.*) I'll get some plates.

[DUSSEL, *in his room, hastily puts a coat on and starts out to join the others.*]

Mrs. Frank. Thank you, Miepia. You shouldn't have done it. You must have used all of your sugar ration for weeks. (*Giving it to* MRS. VAN DAAN) It's beautiful, isn't it?

Mrs. Van Daan. It's been ages since I even saw a cake. Not since you brought us one last year. (*Without looking at the cake, to* MIEP) Remember? Don't you remember, you gave us one on New Year's Day? Just this time last year? I'll never forget it because you had "Peace in nineteen forty-three" on it. (*She looks at the cake and reads*) "Peace in nineteen forty-four!"

Miep. Well, it has to come sometime, you know. (*As* DUSSEL *comes from his room*) Hello, Mr. Dussel.

Mr. Kraler. How are you?

Mr. Van Daan (*bringing plates and a knife*). Here's the knife, liefje. Now, how many of us are there?

Miep. None for me, thank you.

Mr. Frank. Oh, please. You must.

Miep. I couldn't.

Ⓑ Read and Discuss What has happened to Mouschi?

Mr. Kraler (with hat) and Mr. Frank converse in the stage production. © Joan Marcus.

Mr. Van Daan. Good! That leaves one . . . two . . . three . . . seven of us.

Dussel. Eight! Eight! It's the same number as it always is!

Mr. Van Daan. I left Margot out. I take it for granted Margot won't eat any.

Anne. Why wouldn't she!

Mrs. Frank. I think it won't harm her.

Mr. Van Daan. All right! All right! I just didn't want her to start coughing again, that's all.

Dussel. And please, Mrs. Frank should cut the cake.

Mr. Van Daan. What's the difference?

Mrs. Van Daan. It's not Mrs. Frank's cake, is it, Miep? It's for all of us.

} *Together*

Dussel. Mrs. Frank divides things better.

Mrs. Van Daan (*going to* DUSSEL). What are you trying to say?

Mr. Van Daan. Oh, come on! Stop wasting time!

} *Together*

Mrs. Van Daan (*to* DUSSEL). Don't I always give everybody exactly the same? Don't I?

Mr. Van Daan. Forget it, Kerli.

Mrs. Van Daan. No. I want an answer! Don't I?

Dussel. Yes. Yes. Everybody gets exactly the same . . . except Mr. Van Daan always gets a little bit more.

[MR. VAN DAAN *advances on* DUSSEL, *the knife still in his hand*.]

Mr. Van Daan. That's a lie!

[DUSSEL *retreats before the onslaught of the* VAN DAANS.] Ⓒ

Mr. Frank. Please, please! (*Then, to* MIEP) You see what a little sugar cake does to us? It goes right to our heads!

Mr. Van Daan (*handing* MRS. FRANK *the knife*). Here you are, Mrs. Frank.

Mrs. Frank. Thank you. (*Then, to* MIEP, *as she goes to the table to cut the cake*) Are you sure you won't have some?

Miep (*drinking her tea*). No, really, I have to go in a minute.

[*The sound of the band fades out in the distance.*]

Peter (*to* MIEP). Maybe Mouschi went back to our house . . . they say that cats . . . Do you ever get over there . . . ? I mean . . . do you suppose you could . . . ?

Miep. I'll try, Peter. The first minute I get, I'll try. But I'm afraid, with him gone a week . . .

Dussel. Make up your mind, already someone has had a nice big dinner from that cat!

[PETER *is furious, inarticulate. He starts toward* DUSSEL *as if to hit him.* MR. FRANK *stops him.* MRS. FRANK *speaks quickly to ease the situation.*]

Mrs. Frank (*to* MIEP). This is delicious, Miep!

Mrs. Van Daan (*eating hers*). Delicious!

Mr. Van Daan (*finishing it in one gulp*). Dirk's in luck to get a girl who can bake like this!

Miep (*putting down her empty teacup*). I have to run. Dirk's taking me to a party tonight.

Anne. How heavenly! Remember now what everyone is wearing and what you have to eat and everything, so you can tell us tomorrow.

Miep. I'll give you a full report! Goodbye, everyone!

Mr. Van Daan (*to* MIEP). Just a minute. There's something I'd like you to do for me. (*He hurries off up the stairs to his room.*)

Mrs. Van Daan (*sharply*). Putti, where are you going? (*She rushes up the stairs after him, calling hysterically.*) What do you want? Putti, what are you going to do?

Miep (*to* PETER). What's wrong?

Peter (*his sympathy is with his mother*). Father says he's going to sell her fur coat. She's crazy about that old fur coat.

Dussel. Is it possible? Is it possible that anyone is so silly as to worry about a fur coat in times like this?

Peter. It's none of your darn business . . . and if you say one more thing . . . I'll, I'll take you and I'll . . . I mean it . . . I'll . . .

[*There is a piercing scream from* MRS. VAN DAAN, *above. She grabs at the fur coat as* MR. VAN DAAN *is starting downstairs with it.*]

Mrs. Van Daan. No! No! No! Don't you dare take that! You hear? It's mine! (*Downstairs* PETER *turns away, embarrassed, miserable.*) My father gave me that! You didn't give it to me. You have no right. Let go of it . . . you hear?

Ⓒ **Literary Focus** **Theme** What has caused the conflicts among the characters to escalate since the end of Act One? What insight about life do these conflicts reveal?

[MR. VAN DAAN *pulls the coat from her hands and hurries downstairs.* MRS. VAN DAAN *sinks to the floor, sobbing. As* MR. VAN DAAN *comes into the main room, the others look away, embarrassed for him.*]

Mr. Van Daan (*to* MR. KRALER). Just a little—discussion over the advisability of selling this coat. As I have often reminded Mrs. Van Daan, it's very selfish of her to keep it when people outside are in such desperate need of clothing. . . . (*He gives the coat to* MIEP.) So if you will please to sell it for us? It should fetch a good price. And by the way, will you get me cigarettes. I don't care what kind they are . . . get all you can. **D**

Miep. It's terribly difficult to get them, Mr. Van Daan. But I'll try. Goodbye.

> My father gave me that! You didn't give it to me. You have no right.

[*She goes.* MR. FRANK *follows her down the steps to bolt the door after her.* MRS. FRANK *gives* MR. KRALER *a cup of tea.*]

Mrs. Frank. Are you sure you won't have some cake, Mr. Kraler?

Mr. Kraler. I'd better not.

Mr. Van Daan. You're still feeling badly? What does your doctor say?

Mr. Kraler. I haven't been to him.

Mrs. Frank. Now, Mr. Kraler! . . .

Mr. Kraler (*sitting at the table*). Oh, I tried.

But you can't get near a doctor these days . . . they're so busy. After weeks I finally managed to get one on the telephone. I told him I'd like an appointment . . . I wasn't feeling very well. You know what he answers . . . over the telephone . . . "Stick out your tongue!" (*They laugh. He turns to* MR. FRANK *as* MR. FRANK *comes back.*) I have some contracts here . . . I wonder if you'd look over them with me . . .

Mr. Frank (*putting out his hand*). Of course.

Mr. Kraler (*he rises*). If we could go downstairs . . . (MR. FRANK *starts ahead;* MR. KRALER *speaks to the others.*) Will you forgive us? I won't keep him but a minute. (*He starts to follow* MR. FRANK *down the steps.*)

Margot (*with sudden foreboding*). What's happened? Something's happened! Hasn't it, Mr. Kraler?

[MR. KRALER *stops and comes back, trying to reassure* MARGOT *with a pretense of casualness.*]

Mr. Kraler. No, really. I want your father's advice . . .

Margot. Something's gone wrong! I know it!

Mr. Frank (*coming back, to* MR. KRALER). If it's something that concerns us here, it's better that we all hear it.

Mr. Kraler (*turning to him, quietly*). But . . . the children . . . ?

D Read and Discuss | Why does Mr. Van Daan decide to sell the coat?

Mr. Frank. What they'd imagine would be worse than any reality.

[*As* MR. KRALER *speaks, they all listen with intense apprehension.* MRS. VAN DAAN *comes down the stairs and sits on the bottom step.*]

Mr. Kraler. It's a man in the storeroom . . . I don't know whether or not you remember him . . . Carl, about fifty, heavyset, nearsighted. . . . He came with us just before you left.

Mr. Frank. He was from Utrecht?

Mr. Kraler. That's the man. A couple of weeks ago, when I was in the storeroom, he closed the door and asked me . . . "How's Mr. Frank? What do you hear from Mr. Frank?" I told him I only knew there was a rumor that you were in Switzerland. He said he'd heard that rumor too, but he thought I might know something more. I didn't pay any attention to it . . . but then a thing happened yesterday . . . He'd brought some invoices to the office for me to sign. As I was going through them, I looked up. He was standing staring at the bookcase . . . your bookcase. He said he thought he remembered a door there . . . Wasn't there a door there that used to go up to the loft? Then he told me he wanted more money. Twenty guilders[2] more a week. **E**

Mr. Van Daan. Blackmail!

Mr. Frank. Twenty guilders? Very modest blackmail.

Mr. Van Daan. That's just the beginning.

_____

2. **guilders** (GIHL duhrz): Dutch money.

Dussel (*coming to* MR. FRANK). You know what I think? He was the thief who was down there that night. That's how he knows we're here.

Mr. Frank (*to* MR. KRALER). How was it left? What did you tell him?

Mr. Kraler. I said I had to think about it. What shall I do? Pay him the money? . . . Take a chance on firing him . . . or what? I don't know.

Dussel (*frantic*). For God's sake, don't fire him! Pay him what he asks . . . keep him here where you can have your eye on him.

Mr. Frank. Is it so much that he's asking? What are they paying nowadays?

Mr. Kraler. He could get it in a war plant. But this isn't a war plant. Mind you, I don't know if he really knows . . . or if he doesn't know.

Mr. Frank. Offer him half. Then we'll soon find out if it's blackmail or not.

Dussel. And if it is? We've got to pay it, haven't we? Anything he asks we've got to pay!

Mr. Frank. Let's decide that when the time comes.

Mr. Kraler. This may be all my imagination. You get to a point, these days, where you suspect everyone and everything. Again and again . . . on some simple look or word, I've found myself . . .

[*The telephone rings in the office below.*]

Mrs. Van Daan (*hurrying to* MR. KRALER). There's the telephone! What does that mean, the telephone ringing on a holiday?

_____

E **Literary Perspectives** **Analyze Responses** What complication does Mr. Kraler introduce? How does it add to the suspense?

The United States Holocaust Memorial Museum

In 1978, more than thirty years after the end of World War II, President Jimmy Carter asked a committee led by the Holocaust survivor and author Elie Wiesel to suggest ways in which the victims of the Holocaust could be honored. The committee called for the construction of a memorial museum in Washington, D.C. In 1985, participants in a ground-breaking ceremony for the United States Holocaust Memorial Museum buried on the National Mall, near the Lincoln Memorial and the Washington Monument, two small containers of ashes and dirt from concentration camps. Opened in 1993, the museum serves both as a memorial to the Holocaust's victims and a reminder of the dangers of genocide—the mass killing of a people—that still exists in the world today. Since 1993, more than 25 million people have visited the museum.

Ask Yourself

What quotations from Anne Frank's diary would you include in an exhibit in the Holocaust Museum?

Mr. Kraler. That's my wife. I told her I had to go over some papers in my office . . . to call me there when she got out of church. (*He starts out.*) I'll offer him half, then. Goodbye . . . we'll hope for the best!

[*The group call their goodbyes halfheartedly.* MR. FRANK *follows* MR. KRALER *to bolt the door below. During the following scene,* MR. FRANK *comes back up and stands listening, disturbed.*]

Dussel (*to* MR. VAN DAAN). You can thank your son for this . . . smashing the light! I tell you, it's just a question of time now. (*He goes to the window at the back and stands looking out.*)

Margot. Sometimes I wish the end would come . . . whatever it is.

Mrs. Frank (*shocked*). Margot!

[ANNE *goes to* MARGOT, *sitting beside her on the couch with her arms around her.*]

Margot. Then at least we'd know where we were.

Mrs. Frank. You should be ashamed of yourself! Talking that way! Think how lucky we are! Think of the thousands dying in the war, every day. Think of the people in concentration camps.

Anne (*interrupting*). What's the good of that? What's the good of thinking of misery when you're already miserable? That's stupid!

Mrs. Frank. Anne!

[*As* ANNE *goes on raging at her mother,* MRS. FRANK *tries to break in, in an effort to quiet her.*]

Anne. We're young, Margot and Peter and I! You grown-ups have had your chance! But look at us. . . . If we begin thinking of all the horror in the world, we're lost! We're trying to hold on to some kind of ideals . . . when everything . . . ideals, hopes . . . everything is being destroyed! It isn't our fault that the world is in such a mess! We weren't around when all this started! So don't try to take it out on us! (*She rushes off to her room, slamming the door after her. She picks up a brush from the chest and hurls it to the floor. Then she sits on the settee, trying to control her anger.*)

Mr. Van Daan. She talks as if we started the war! Did we start the war? (*He spots* ANNE'S cake. *As he starts to take it,* PETER *anticipates him.*)

Peter. She left her cake. (*He starts for* ANNE'S *room with the cake. There is silence in the main room.* MRS. VAN DAAN *goes up to her room, followed by* MR. VAN DAAN. DUSSEL *stays looking out the window.* MR. FRANK *brings* MRS. FRANK *her cake. She eats it slowly, without relish.* MR. FRANK *takes his cake to* MARGOT *and sits quietly on the sofa beside her.* PETER *stands in the doorway of* ANNE'S *darkened room, looking at her, then makes a little movement to let her know he is there.* ANNE *sits up quickly, trying to hide the signs of her tears.* PETER *holds out the cake to her.*) You left this.

Anne (*dully*). Thanks.

[PETER *starts to go out, then comes back.*]

Peter. I thought you were fine just now. You know just how to talk to them. You know just how to say it. I'm no good . . . I never can think . . . especially when I'm mad. . . . That

F **Reading Focus** Finding the Theme Why do you think Margot's and Anne's views differ from their mother's?

Anne's room in the Anne Frank Museum, Amsterdam.

Dussel . . . when he said that about Mouschi . . . someone eating him . . . all I could think is . . . I wanted to hit him. I wanted to give him such a . . . a . . . that he'd . . . That's what I used to do when there was an argument at school. . . . That's the way I . . . but here. . . . And an old man like that . . . it wouldn't be so good.

Anne. You're making a big mistake about me. I do it all wrong. I say too much. I go too far. I hurt people's feelings. . . .

[DUSSEL *leaves the window, going to his room.*]

Peter. I think you're just fine. . . . What I want to say . . . if it wasn't for you around here, I don't know. What I mean . . .

[PETER *is interrupted by* DUSSEL'S *turning on the light.* DUSSEL *stands in the doorway, startled to see* PETER. PETER *advances toward him forbiddingly.* DUSSEL *backs out of the room.* PETER *closes the door on him.*]

Anne. Do you mean it, Peter? Do you really mean it?
Peter. I said it, didn't I?
Anne. Thank you, Peter! **G**

[*In the main room* MR. *and* MRS. FRANK *collect the dishes and take them to the sink, washing them.* MARGOT *lies down again on the couch.* DUSSEL, *lost, wanders into* PETER'S *room and takes up a book, starting to read.*]

Peter (*looking at the photographs on the wall*). You've got quite a collection.

Anne. Wouldn't you like some in your room? I could give you some. Heaven knows you spend enough time in there . . . doing heaven knows what . . .
Peter. It's easier. A fight starts, or an argument . . . I duck in there.
Anne. You're lucky, having a room to go to. His Lordship is always here. . . . I hardly ever get a minute alone. When they start in on me, I can't duck away. I have to stand there and take it.
Peter. You gave some of it back just now.
Anne. I get so mad. They've formed their opinions . . . about everything . . . but we . . . we're still trying to find out. . . . We have problems here that no other people our age have ever had. And just as you think you've solved them, something comes along and bang! You have to start all over again.
Peter. At least you've got someone you can talk to.
Anne. Not really. Mother . . . I never discuss anything serious with her. She doesn't understand. Father's all right. We can talk about everything . . . everything but one thing. Mother. He simply won't talk about her. I don't think you can be really intimate with anyone if he holds something back, do you?
Peter. I think your father's fine.
Anne. Oh, he is, Peter! He is! He's the only one who's ever given me the feeling that I have any sense. But anyway, nothing can take the place of school and play and friends of your own age . . . or near your age . . . can it?
Peter. I suppose you miss your friends and all.

G [Read and Discuss] How has Anne and Peter's relationship changed since Act One?

Anne. It isn't just . . . (*She breaks off, staring up at him for a second.*) Isn't it funny, you and I? Here we've been seeing each other every minute for almost a year and a half, and this is the first time we've ever really talked. It helps a lot to have someone to talk to, don't you think? It helps you to let off steam.

Peter (*going to the door*). Well, any time you want to let off steam, you can come into my room.

Anne (*following him*). I can get up an awful lot of steam. You'll have to be careful how you say that.

Peter. It's all right with me.

Anne. Do you mean it?

Peter. I said it, didn't I?

[*He goes out.* ANNE *stands in her doorway looking after him. As* PETER *gets to his door, he stands for a minute looking back at her. Then he goes into his room.* DUSSEL *rises as he comes in, and quickly passes him, going out. He starts across for his room.* ANNE *sees him coming and pulls her door shut.* DUSSEL *turns back toward* PETER'S *room.* PETER *pulls his door shut.* DUSSEL *stands there, bewildered, forlorn.*

The scene slowly dims out. The curtain falls on the scene. ANNE'S *voice comes over in the darkness . . . faintly at first and then with growing strength.*]

Anne's Voice. We've had bad news. The people from whom Miep got our ration books have been arrested. So we have had

to cut down on our food. Our stomachs are so empty that they rumble and make strange noises, all in different keys. Mr. Van Daan's is deep and low, like a bass fiddle. Mine is high, whistling like a flute. As we all sit around waiting for supper, it's like an orchestra tuning up. It only needs Toscanini[3] to raise his baton and we'd be off in the "Ride of the Valkyries."[4] Monday, the sixth of March, nineteen forty-four. Mr. Kraler is in the hospital. It seems he has ulcers. Pim says we are his ulcers. Miep has to run the business and us too. The Americans have landed on the southern tip of Italy. Father looks for a quick finish to the war. Mr. Dussel is waiting every day for the warehouse man to demand more money. Have I been skipping too much from one subject to another? I can't help it. I feel that spring is coming. I feel it in my whole body and soul. I feel utterly confused. I am longing . . . so longing . . . for everything . . . for friends . . . for someone to talk to . . . someone who understands . . . someone young, who feels as I do . . . **Ⓗ**

[*As these last lines are being said, the curtain rises on the scene. The lights dim on.* ANNE'S *voice fades out.*]

---

3. **Toscanini** (tahs kuh NEE nee): Arturo Toscanini (1867–1957), a famous orchestra conductor.

4. **"Ride of the Valkyries"** (val KIHR eez): lively piece of music from an opera by the German composer Richard Wagner (1813–1883).

Ⓗ Literary Focus **Theme** What insight about life is evident in this passage from Anne's diary?

Vocabulary **forlorn** (fawr LAWRN) *adj.:* abandoned and lonely.

SCENE 2

It is evening, after supper. From outside we hear the sound of children playing. The "grown-ups," with the exception of MR. VAN DAAN, *are all in the main room.* MRS. FRANK *is doing some mending.* MRS. VAN DAAN *is reading a fashion magazine.* MR. FRANK *is going over business accounts.* DUSSEL, *in his dentist's jacket, is pacing up and down, impatient to get into his bedroom.* MR. VAN DAAN *is upstairs working on a piece of embroidery in an embroidery frame.*

In his room PETER *is sitting before the mirror, smoothing his hair. As the scene goes on, he puts on his tie, brushes his coat and puts it on, preparing himself meticulously for a visit from* ANNE. *On his wall are now hung some of* ANNE's *motion picture stars.*

In her room ANNE *too is getting dressed. She stands before the mirror in her slip, trying various ways of dressing her hair.* MARGOT *is seated on the sofa, hemming a skirt for* ANNE *to wear.*

In the main room DUSSEL *can stand it no longer. He comes over, rapping sharply on the door of his and* ANNE's *bedroom.*

Anne (*calling to him*). No, no, Mr. Dussel! I am not dressed yet. (DUSSEL *walks away, furious, sitting down and burying his head in his hands.* ANNE *turns to* MARGOT.) How is that? How does that look?
Margot (*glancing at her briefly*). Fine.
Anne. You didn't even look.
Margot. Of course I did. It's fine.
Anne. Margot, tell me, am I terribly ugly?
Margot. Oh, stop fishing.

Anne. No. No. Tell me.
Margot. Of course you're not. You've got nice eyes . . . and a lot of animation, and . . .
Anne. A little vague, aren't you?

[*She reaches over and takes a brassiere out of* MARGOT's *sewing basket. She holds it up to herself, studying the effect in the mirror. Outside,* MRS. FRANK, *feeling sorry for* DUSSEL, *comes over, knocking at the girls' door.*]

Mrs. Frank (*outside*). May I come in?
Margot. Come in, Mother.
Mrs. Frank (*shutting the door behind her*). Mr. Dussel's impatient to get in here.
Anne (*still with the brassiere*). Heavens, he takes the room for himself the entire day.
Mrs. Frank (*gently*). Anne, dear, you're not going in again tonight to see Peter?
Anne (*dignified*). That is my intention.
Mrs. Frank. But you've already spent a great deal of time in there today.
Anne. I was in there exactly twice. Once to get the dictionary, and then three quarters of an hour before supper.
Mrs. Frank. Aren't you afraid you're disturbing him?
Anne. Mother, I have some intuition.
Mrs. Frank. Then may I ask you this much, Anne. Please don't shut the door when you go in.
Anne. You sound like Mrs. Van Daan! (*She throws the brassiere back in* MARGOT's *sewing basket and picks up her blouse, putting it on.*)
Mrs. Frank. No. No. I don't mean to suggest anything wrong. I only wish that you wouldn't expose yourself to criticism . . . that you wouldn't give Mrs. Van Daan the opportunity to be unpleasant.

Anne. Mrs. Van Daan doesn't need an opportunity to be unpleasant!

Mrs. Frank. Everyone's on edge, worried about Mr. Kraler. This is one more thing . . .

Anne. I'm sorry, Mother. I'm going to Peter's room. I'm not going to let Petronella Van Daan spoil our friendship.

[MRS. FRANK *hesitates for a second, then goes out, closing the door after her. She gets a pack of playing cards and sits at the center table, playing solitaire. In* ANNE's *room* MARGOT *hands the finished skirt to* ANNE. *As* ANNE *is putting it on,* MARGOT *takes off her high-heeled shoes and stuffs paper in the toes so that* ANNE *can wear them.*]

Margot (*to* ANNE). Why don't you two talk in the main room? It'd save a lot of trouble. It's hard on Mother, having to listen to those remarks from Mrs. Van Daan and not say a word.

Anne. Why doesn't she say a word? I think it's ridiculous to take it and take it.

Margot. You don't understand Mother at all, do you? She can't talk back. She's not like you. It's just not in her nature to fight back.

Anne. Anyway . . . the only one I worry about is you. I feel awfully guilty about you. (*She sits on the stool near* MARGOT, *putting on* MARGOT's *high-heeled shoes.*)

Margot. What about?

Anne. I mean, every time I go into Peter's room, I have a feeling I may be hurting you. (MARGOT *shakes her head.*) I know if it were me, I'd be wild. I'd be desperately jealous, if it were me.

Margot. Well, I'm not.

Anne. You don't feel badly? Really? Truly? You're not jealous?

Margot. Of course I'm jealous . . . jealous that you've got something to get up in the morning for. . . . But jealous of you and Peter? No. ⓘ

[ANNE *goes back to the mirror.*]

Anne. Maybe there's nothing to be jealous of. Maybe he doesn't really like me. Maybe I'm just taking the place of his cat . . . (*She picks up a pair of short white gloves, putting them on.*) Wouldn't you like to come in with us?

Margot. I have a book.

[*The sound of the children playing outside fades out. In the main room* DUSSEL *can stand it no longer. He jumps up, going to the bedroom door and knocking sharply.*]

Dussel. Will you please let me in my room!

Anne. Just a minute, dear, dear Mr. Dussel. (*She picks up her mother's pink stole and adjusts it elegantly over her shoulders, then gives a last look in the mirror.*) Well, here I go . . . to run the gantlet.[5] (*She starts out, followed by* MARGOT.)

Dussel (*as she appears—sarcastic*). Thank you so much.

---

5. **run the gantlet** (GAWNT liht): proceed while under attack from both sides.

ⓘ **Reading Focus** Finding the Theme What does this scene reveal about the relationship between the two sisters? How are their characters similar? How are they different?

[DUSSEL *goes into his room.* ANNE *goes toward* PETER's *room, passing* MRS. VAN DAAN *and her parents at the center table.*]

Mrs. Van Daan. My God, look at her! (ANNE *pays no attention. She knocks at* PETER's *door.*) I don't know what good it is to have a son. I never see him. He wouldn't care if I killed myself. (PETER *opens the door and stands aside for* ANNE *to come in.*) Just a minute, Anne. (*She goes to them at the door.*) I'd like to say a few words to my son. Do you mind? (PETER *and* ANNE *stand waiting.*) Peter, I don't want you staying up till all hours tonight. You've got to have your sleep. You're a growing boy. You hear?
Mrs. Frank. Anne won't stay late. She's going to bed promptly at nine. Aren't you, Anne?
Anne. Yes, Mother . . . (*To* MRS. VAN DAAN) May we go now?
Mrs. Van Daan. Are you asking me? I didn't know I had anything to say about it.
Mrs. Frank. Listen for the chimes, Anne dear.

[*The two young people go off into* PETER's *room, shutting the door after them.*]
Mrs. Van Daan (*to* MRS. FRANK). In my day it was the boys who called on the girls. Not the girls on the boys.
Mrs. Frank. You know how young people like to feel that they have secrets. Peter's room is the only place where they can talk.
Mrs. Van Daan. Talk! That's not what they called it when I was young.

[MRS. VAN DAAN *goes off to the bathroom.* MARGOT *settles down to read her book.* MR. FRANK *puts his papers away and brings a chess game to the center table. He and* MRS. FRANK *start to play. In* PETER's *room,* ANNE *speaks to* PETER, *indignant, humiliated.*]

Anne. Aren't they awful? Aren't they impossible? Treating us as if we were still in the nursery.

[*She sits on the cot.* PETER *gets a bottle of pop and two glasses.*]

Peter. Don't let it bother you. It doesn't bother me.
Anne. I suppose you can't really blame them . . . they think back to what *they* were like at our age. They don't realize how much more advanced we are. . . . When you think what wonderful discussions we've had! . . . Oh, I forgot. I was going to bring you some more pictures.
Peter. Oh, these are fine, thanks.
Anne. Don't you want some more? Miep just brought me some new ones.
Peter. Maybe later. (*He gives her a glass of pop and, taking some for himself, sits down facing her.*)
Anne (*looking up at one of the photographs*). I remember when I got that. . . . I won it. I bet Jopie that I could eat five ice-cream cones. We'd all been playing ping-pong. . . . We used to have heavenly times . . . we'd finish up with ice cream at the Delphi or the Oasis, where Jews were allowed . . . there'd always be a lot

> They don't realize how much more advanced we are.

of boys . . . we'd laugh and joke. . . . I'd like to go back to it for a few days or a week. But after that I know I'd be bored to death. I think more seriously about life now. I want to be a journalist . . . or something. I love to write. What do you want to do?

Peter. I thought I might go off someplace . . . work on a farm or something . . . some job that doesn't take much brains.

Anne. You shouldn't talk that way. You've got the most awful inferiority complex.

Peter. I know I'm not smart.

Anne. That isn't true. You're much better than I am in dozens of things . . . arithmetic and algebra and . . . well, you're a million times better than I am in algebra. (*With sudden directness*) You like Margot, don't you? Right from the start you liked her, liked her much better than me.

Peter (*uncomfortably*). Oh, I don't know.

[*In the main room* MRS. VAN DAAN *comes from the bathroom and goes over to the sink, polishing a coffeepot.*]

Anne. It's all right. Everyone feels that way. Margot's so good. She's sweet and bright and beautiful and I'm not.

Peter. I wouldn't say that.

Anne. Oh, no, I'm not. I know that. I know quite well that I'm not a beauty. I never have been and never shall be.

Peter. I don't agree at all. I think you're pretty.

Anne. That's not true!

Peter. And another thing. You've changed . . . from at first, I mean.

Anne. I have?

Peter. I used to think you were awful noisy.

Anne. And what do you think now, Peter? How have I changed?

Peter. Well . . . er . . . you're . . . quieter.

[*In his room* DUSSEL *takes his pajamas and toilet articles and goes into the bathroom to change.*]

Anne. I'm glad you don't just hate me.

Peter. I never said that.

Anne. I bet when you get out of here, you'll never think of me again.

Peter. That's crazy.

Anne. When you get back with all of your friends, you're going to say . . . now what did I ever see in that Mrs. Quack Quack.

Peter. I haven't got any friends.

Anne. Oh, Peter, of course you have. Everyone has friends.

Peter. Not me. I don't want any. I get along all right without them.

Anne. Does that mean you can get along without me? I think of myself as your friend.

Peter. No. If they were all like you, it'd be different.

[*He takes the glasses and the bottle and puts them away. There is a second's silence and then* ANNE *speaks, hesitantly, shyly.*]

Anne. Peter, did you ever kiss a girl?

Peter. Yes. Once.

Anne (*to cover her feelings*). That picture's crooked. (PETER *goes over, straightening the photograph.*) Was she pretty?

🄹 **Read and Discuss** Why do you think Anne asks Peter about his feelings for Margot?

Peter. Huh?

Anne. The girl that you kissed.

Peter. I don't know. I was blindfolded. (*He comes back and sits down again.*) It was at a party. One of those kissing games.

Anne (*relieved*). Oh. I don't suppose that really counts, does it?

Peter. It didn't with me.

Anne. I've been kissed twice. Once a man I'd never seen before kissed me on the cheek when he picked me up off the ice and I was crying. And the other was Mr. Koophuis, a friend of Father's, who kissed my hand. You wouldn't say those counted, would you?

Peter. I wouldn't say so.

Anne. I know almost for certain that Margot would never kiss anyone unless she was engaged to them. And I'm sure too that Mother never touched a man before Pim. But I don't know . . . things are so different now. . . . What do you think? Do you think a girl shouldn't kiss anyone except if she's engaged or something? It's so hard to try to think what to do, when here we are with the whole world falling around our ears and you think . . . well . . . you don't know what's going to happen tomorrow and . . . What do you think?

Peter. I suppose it'd depend on the girl. Some girls, anything they do's wrong. But others . . . well . . . it wouldn't necessarily be wrong with them. (*The carillon starts to strike nine o'clock.*) I've always thought that when two people . . .

Anne. Nine o'clock. I have to go.

Peter. That's right.

Anne (*without moving*). Good night.

Peter and Anne in the stage production. © Joan Marcus.

[*There is a second's pause; then* PETER *gets up and moves toward the door.*]

Peter. You won't let them stop you coming?

Anne. No. (*She rises and starts for the door.*) Sometime I might bring my diary. There are so many things in it that I want to talk over with you. There's a lot about you.

Peter. What kind of thing?

Anne. I wouldn't want you to see some of it. I thought you were a nothing, just the way you thought about me.

Peter. Did you change your mind, the way I changed my mind about you?

Anne. Well. . . . You'll see . . .

[*For a second* ANNE *stands looking up at* PETER, *longing for him to kiss her. As he makes no move, she turns away. Then suddenly* PETER *grabs her awkwardly in his arms, kissing her on the cheek.* ANNE *walks out dazed. She stands for a minute, her back to the people in the main room. As she regains her poise, she goes to her mother and father and* MARGOT, *silently kissing them. They murmur their good nights to her. As she is about to open her bedroom door, she catches sight of* MRS. VAN DAAN. *She goes quickly to her, taking her face in her hands and kissing her, first on one cheek and then on the other. Then she hurries off into her room.* MRS. VAN DAAN *looks after her and then looks over at* PETER's *room. Her suspicions are confirmed.*]

Mrs. Van Daan (*she knows*). Ah hah!

[*The lights dim out. The curtain falls on the scene. In the darkness* ANNE's *voice comes, faintly at first and then with growing strength.*]

Anne's Voice. By this time we all know each other so well that if anyone starts to tell a story, the rest can finish it for him. We're having to cut down still further on our meals. What makes it worse, the rats have been at work again. They've carried off some of our precious food. Even Mr. Dussel wishes now that Mouschi was here. Thursday, the twentieth of April, nineteen forty-four. Invasion fever is mounting every day. Miep tells us

that people outside talk of nothing else. For myself, life has become much more pleasant. I often go to Peter's room after supper. Oh, don't think I'm in love, because I'm not. But it does make life more bearable to have someone with whom you can exchange views. No more tonight. P.S. . . . I must be honest. I must confess that I actually live for the next meeting. Is there anything lovelier than to sit under the skylight and feel the sun on your cheeks and have a darling boy in your arms? I admit now that I'm glad the Van Daans had a son and not a daughter. I've outgrown another dress. That's the third. I'm having to wear Margot's clothes after all. I'm working hard on my French and am now reading *La Belle Nivernaise.*[6] **Ⓚ**

[*As she is saying the last lines, the curtain rises on the scene. The lights dim on as* ANNE's *voice fades out.*]

SCENE 3

It is night, a few weeks later. Everyone is in bed. There is complete quiet. In the VAN DAANS' *room a match flares up for a moment and then is quickly put out.* MR. VAN DAAN, *in bare feet, dressed in underwear and trousers, is dimly seen coming stealthily down the stairs and into the main room, where* MR. *and* MRS. FRANK *and* MARGOT *are sleeping. He goes to the food safe and again lights a match. Then he cautiously opens the safe, taking out a half*

---

6. *La Belle Nivernaise* (nee VEHR nehz): children's story by Alphonse Daudet (1840–1897).

Ⓚ | Read and Discuss | What has changed within the household?

loaf of bread. As he closes the safe, it creaks. He stands rigid. MRS. FRANK *sits up in bed. She sees him.* **L**

Mrs. Frank (*screaming*). Otto! Otto! Komme schnell![7]

[*The rest of the people wake, hurriedly getting up.*]

Mr. Frank. Was ist los? Was ist passiert?[8]

[DUSSEL, *followed by* ANNE, *comes from his room.*]

Mrs. Frank (*as she rushes over to* MR. VAN DAAN). Er stiehlt das Essen![9]
Dussel (*grabbing* MR. VAN DAAN). You! You! Give me that.
Mrs. Van Daan (*coming down the stairs*). Putti . . . Putti . . . what is it?
Dussel (*his hands on* MR. VAN DAAN'S *neck*). You dirty thief . . . stealing food . . . you good-for-nothing . . .
Mr. Frank. Mr. Dussel! For God's sake! Help me, Peter!

[PETER *comes over, trying, with* MR. FRANK, *to separate the two struggling men.*]

Peter. Let him go! Let go!

---

7. **Komme schnell:** German for "Come quickly."
8. **Was . . . passiert:** "What's going on? What happened?"
9. **Er . . . Essen:** "He is stealing the food."

[DUSSEL *drops* MR. VAN DAAN, *pushing him away. He shows them the end of a loaf of bread that he has taken from* MR. VAN DAAN.]

Dussel. You greedy, selfish . . . !

[MARGOT *turns on the lights.*]

Mrs. Van Daan. Putti . . . what is it?

[*All of* MRS. FRANK'S *gentleness, her self-control, is gone. She is outraged, in a frenzy of indignation.*]

Mrs. Frank. The bread! He was stealing the bread!
Dussel. It was you, and all the time we thought it was the rats!
Mr. Frank. Mr. Van Daan, how could you!
Mr. Van Daan. I'm hungry.
Mrs. Frank. We're all of us hungry! I see the children getting thinner and thinner. Your own son Peter . . . I've heard him moan in his sleep, he's so hungry. And you come in the night and steal food that should go to them . . . to the children!
Mrs. Van Daan (*going to* MR. VAN DAAN *protectively*). He needs more food than the rest of us. He's used to more. He's a big man.

[MR. VAN DAAN *breaks away, going over and sitting on the couch.*]

Mrs. Frank (*turning on* MRS. VAN DAAN). And you . . . you're worse than he is! You're a mother, and yet you sacrifice your child to this man . . . this . . . this . . .

L **Reading Focus** **Finding the Theme** What new conflict has arisen? How might this conflict affect the play's theme?

Mr. Frank. Edith! Edith!

[MARGOT *picks up the pink woolen stole, putting it over her mother's shoulders.*]

Mrs. Frank (*paying no attention, going on to* MRS. VAN DAAN). Don't think I haven't seen you! Always saving the choicest bits for him! I've watched you day after day and I've held my tongue. But not any longer! Not after this! Now I want him to go! I want him to get out of here!

Mr. Frank. Edith!
Mr. Van Daan. Get out of here? ⎫
Mrs. Van Daan. What do you mean? ⎬ *Together*
Mrs. Frank. Just that! Take your things and get out! Ⓜ
Mr. Frank (*to* MRS. FRANK). You're speaking in anger. You cannot mean what you are saying.
Mrs. Frank. I mean exactly that!

[MRS. VAN DAAN *takes a cover from the* FRANKS' *bed, pulling it about her.*]

Mr. Frank. For two long years we have lived here, side by side. We have respected each other's rights . . . we have managed to live in peace. Are we now going to throw it all away? I know this will never happen again, will it, Mr. Van Daan?
Mr. Van Daan. No. No.
Mrs. Frank. He steals once! He'll steal again!

[MR. VAN DAAN, *holding his stomach, starts for the bathroom.* ANNE *puts her arms around him, helping him up the step.*]

Mr. Frank. Edith, please. Let us be calm. We'll all go to our rooms . . . and afterwards we'll sit down quietly and talk this out . . . we'll find some way . . .
Mrs. Frank. No! No! No more talk! I want them to leave!
Mrs. Van Daan. You'd put us out, on the streets?
Mrs. Frank. There are other hiding places.
Mrs. Van Daan. A cellar . . . a closet. I know. And we have no money left even to pay for that.
Mrs. Frank. I'll give you money. Out of my own pocket I'll give it gladly. (*She gets her purse from a shelf and comes back with it.*)
Mrs. Van Daan. Mr. Frank, you told Putti you'd never forget what he'd done for you when you came to Amsterdam. You said you could never repay him, that you . . .
Mrs. Frank (*counting out money*). If my husband had any obligation to you, he's paid it, over and over.
Mr. Frank. Edith, I've never seen you like this before. I don't know you.
Mrs. Frank. I should have spoken out long ago.
Dussel. You can't be nice to some people.
Mrs. Van Daan (*turning on* DUSSEL). There would have been plenty for all of us, if *you* hadn't come in here!
Mr. Frank. We don't need the Nazis to destroy us. We're destroying ourselves. Ⓝ

Ⓜ **Reading Focus** **Finding the Theme** What does this sudden change in attitude suggest about Mrs. Frank's character? What might Anne and the audience learn about her from her outburst?

Ⓝ **Read and Discuss** What does Mr. Frank's comment add to the scene?

[*He sits down, with his head in his hands.* MRS. FRANK *goes to* MRS. VAN DAAN.]

Mrs. Frank (*giving* MRS. VAN DAAN *some money*). Give this to Miep. She'll find you a place.

Anne. Mother, you're not putting *Peter* out. Peter hasn't done anything.

Mrs. Frank. He'll stay, of course. When I say I must protect the children, I mean Peter too.

[PETER *rises from the steps where he has been sitting.*]

Peter. I'd have to go if Father goes.

[MR. VAN DAAN *comes from the bathroom.*

MRS. VAN DAAN *hurries to him and takes him to the couch. Then she gets water from the sink to bathe his face.*]

Mrs. Frank (*while this is going on*). He's no father to you . . . that man! He doesn't know what it is to be a father!

Peter (*starting for his room*). I wouldn't feel right. I couldn't stay.

Mrs. Frank. Very well, then. I'm sorry.

Anne (*rushing over to* PETER). No, Peter! No! (PETER *goes into his room, closing the door after him.* ANNE *turns back to her mother, crying.*) I don't care about the food. They can have mine! I don't want it! Only don't send them away. It'll be daylight soon. They'll be caught . . .

Margot (*putting her arms comfortingly around* ANNE). Please, Mother!

Mrs. Frank. They're not going now. They'll stay here until Miep finds them a place. (*To* MRS. VAN DAAN) But one thing I insist on! He must never come down here again! He must never come to this room where the food is stored! We'll divide what we have . . . an equal share for each! (DUSSEL *hurries over to get a sack of potatoes from the food safe.* MRS. FRANK *goes on, to* MRS. VAN DAAN) You can cook it here and take it up to him.

[DUSSEL *brings the sack of potatoes back to the center table.*]

Margot. Oh, no. No. We haven't sunk so far that we're going to fight over a handful of rotten potatoes.

Dussel (*dividing the potatoes into piles*). Mrs. Frank, Mr. Frank, Margot, Anne, Peter, Mrs. Van Daan, Mr. Van Daan, myself . . . Mrs. Frank . . .   ⓞ

[*The buzzer sounds in* MIEP's *signal.*]

Mr. Frank. It's Miep! (*He hurries over, getting his overcoat and putting it on.*)

Margot. At this hour?

Mrs. Frank. It is trouble.

Mr. Frank (*as he starts down to unbolt the door*). I beg you, don't let her see a thing like this!

Dussel (*counting without stopping*) . . . Anne, Peter, Mrs. Van Daan, Mr. Van Daan, myself . . .

Margot (*to* DUSSEL). Stop it! Stop it!

Dussel. . . . Mr. Frank, Margot, Anne, Peter, Mrs. Van Daan, Mr. Van Daan, myself, Mrs. Frank . . .

Mrs. Van Daan. You're keeping the big ones for yourself! All the big ones. . . . Look at the size of that! . . . And that! . . .

[DUSSEL *continues with his dividing.* PETER, *with his shirt and trousers on, comes from his room.*]

Margot. Stop it! Stop it!

[*We hear* MIEP's *excited voice speaking to* MR. FRANK *below.*]

Miep. Mr. Frank . . . the most wonderful news! . . . The invasion[10] has begun!

Mr. Frank. Go on, tell them! Tell them!

[MIEP *comes running up the steps, ahead of* MR. FRANK. *She has a man's raincoat on over her nightclothes and a bunch of orange-colored flowers in her hand.*]

Miep. Did you hear that, everybody? Did you hear what I said? The invasion has begun! The invasion!

[*They all stare at* MIEP, *unable to grasp what she is telling them.* PETER *is the first to recover his wits.*]

---

10. **the invasion:** On June 6, 1944, Allied forces landed in Normandy, a region of northern France, to launch a military campaign against the Germans.

ⓞ **Literary Perspectives** **Analyzing Responses** Compare this conflict to others that have occurred among the characters throughout the play. What similarities and differences do you see?

Peter. Where?
Mrs. Van Daan. When? When, Miep?
Miep. It began early this morning . . .

[*As she talks on, the realization of what she has said begins to dawn on them. Everyone goes crazy. A wild demonstration takes place.* MRS. FRANK *hugs* MR. VAN DAAN.]

Mrs. Frank. Oh, Mr. Van Daan, did you hear that?

[DUSSEL *embraces* MRS. VAN DAAN. PETER *grabs a frying pan and parades around the room, beating on it, singing the Dutch national anthem.* ANNE *and* MARGOT *follow him, singing, weaving in and out among the excited grown-ups.* MARGOT *breaks away to take the flowers from* MIEP *and distribute them to everyone. While this pandemonium is going on,* MRS. FRANK *tries to make herself heard above the excitement.*]

Mrs. Frank (*to* MIEP). How do you know?
Miep. The radio . . . The BBC![11] They said they landed on the coast of Normandy! Ⓟ
Peter. The British?
Miep. British, Americans, French, Dutch, Poles, Norwegians . . . all of them! More than

> Did you hear what I said? The invasion has begun!

four thousand ships! Churchill[12] spoke, and General Eisenhower![13] D-day, they call it!
Mr. Frank. Thank God, it's come!
Mrs. Van Daan. At last!
Miep (*starting out*). I'm going to tell Mr. Kraler. This'll be better than any blood transfusion.
Mr. Frank (*stopping her*). What part of Normandy did they land, did they say?
Miep. Normandy . . . that's all I know now . . . I'll be up the minute I hear some more! (*She goes hurriedly out.*)
Mr. Frank (*to* MRS. FRANK). What did I tell you? What did I tell you?

[MRS. FRANK *indicates that he has forgotten to bolt the door after* MIEP. *He hurries down the steps.* MR. VAN DAAN, *sitting on the couch, suddenly breaks into a convulsive sob. Everybody looks at him, bewildered.*]

Mrs. Van Daan (*hurrying to him*). Putti! Putti! What is it? What happened?
Mr. Van Daan. Please. I'm so ashamed.

[MR. FRANK *comes back up the steps.*]

Dussel. Oh, for God's sake!

---

11. **BBC:** British Broadcasting Corporation. People listened to the BBC, illegally, for news of the war that was more accurate than what German-controlled broadcasters offered.

12. **Churchill:** Sir Winston Churchill (1874–1965), British prime minister during World War II.

13. **General Eisenhower:** Dwight D. Eisenhower (1890–1969), commander of the Allied forces in western Europe. He later became president of the United States (1953–1961).

Ⓟ **Literary Perspectives** Analyzing Responses   How does your knowledge of World War II influence your response to this news?

Mrs. Van Daan. Don't, Putti.

Margot. It doesn't matter now!

Mr. Frank (*going to* MR. VAN DAAN). Didn't you hear what Miep said? The invasion has come! We're going to be liberated! This is a time to celebrate! (*He embraces* MRS. FRANK *and then hurries to the cupboard and gets the cognac and a glass.*)

Mr. Van Daan. To steal bread from children!

Mrs. Frank. We've all done things that we're ashamed of.

Anne. Look at me, the way I've treated Mother . . . so mean and horrid to her.

Mrs. Frank. No, Anneke, no.

[ANNE *runs to her mother, putting her arms around her.*]

Anne. Oh, Mother, I was. I was awful.

Mr. Van Daan. Not like me. No one is as bad as me!

Dussel (*to* MR. VAN DAAN). Stop it now! Let's be happy!

Mr. Frank (*giving* MR. VAN DAAN *a glass of cognac*). Here! Here! Schnapps![14] L'chaim![15]

[MR. VAN DAAN *takes the cognac. They all watch him. He gives them a feeble smile.* ANNE *puts up her fingers in a V-for-victory sign. As* MR. VAN DAAN *gives an answering V sign, they are startled to hear a loud sob from behind them. It is* MRS. FRANK, *stricken with remorse. She is sitting on the other side of the room.*]

---

14. **schnapps** (shnahps) *n.*: strong liquor.
15. **l'chaim** (luh HAH yihm): Hebrew toast meaning "to life."

Mrs. Frank (*through her sobs*). When I think of the terrible things I said . . .

[MR. FRANK, ANNE, *and* MARGOT *hurry to her, trying to comfort her.* MR. VAN DAAN *brings her his glass of cognac.*]

Mr. Van Daan. No! No! You were right!

Mrs. Frank. That I should speak that way to you! . . . Our friends! . . . Our guests! (*She starts to cry again.*)

Dussel. Stop it, you're spoiling the whole invasion!

[*As they are comforting her, the lights dim out. The curtain falls.*]

Anne's Voice (*faintly at first and then with growing strength*). We're all in much better spirits these days. There's still excellent news of the invasion. The best part about it is that I have a feeling that friends are coming. Who knows? Maybe I'll be back in school by fall. Ha, ha! The joke is on us! The warehouse man doesn't know a thing and we are paying him all that money! . . . Wednesday, the second of July, nineteen forty-four. The invasion seems temporarily to be bogged down. Mr. Kraler has to have an operation, which looks bad. The Gestapo have found the radio that was stolen. Mr. Dussel says they'll trace it back and back to the thief, and then, it's just a matter of time till they get to us. Everyone is low. Even poor Pim can't raise their spirits. I have often been downcast myself . . . but never in despair. I can shake off everything if I write. But . . . and that is the great question . . . will I ever be able to write well? I want to so much. I want to go on living even after

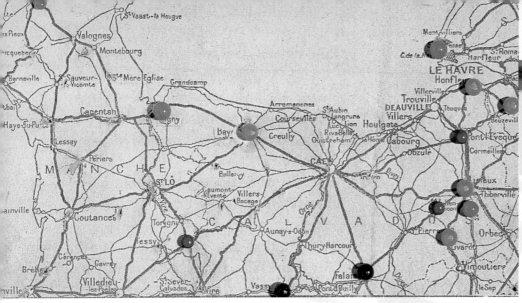
Map that Otto Frank kept to record Allied troop movements, 1944.

Analyzing Visuals

Connecting to the Text
Why might Mr. Frank keep a map showing troop movements during the war?

my death. Another birthday has gone by, so now I am fifteen. Already I know what I want. I have a goal, an opinion. **Ⓠ**

[*As this is being said, the curtain rises on the scene, the lights dim on, and* ANNE's *voice fades out.*]

SCENE 4

It is an afternoon a few weeks later. . . . Everyone but MARGOT *is in the main room. There is a sense of great tension.*

   Both MRS. FRANK *and* MR. VAN DAAN *are nervously pacing back and forth.* DUSSEL *is standing at the window, looking down fixedly at the street below.* PETER *is at the center table, trying to do his lessons.* ANNE *sits opposite him, writing in her diary.* MRS. VAN DAAN *is seated on the couch, her eyes on* MR. FRANK *as he sits reading.*

   The sound of a telephone ringing comes from the office below. They all are rigid, listening tensely. DUSSEL *rushes down to* MR. FRANK.

Dussel. There it goes again, the telephone! Mr. Frank, do you hear?
Mr. Frank (*quietly*). Yes. I hear.
Dussel (*pleading, insistent*). But this is the third time, Mr. Frank! The third time in quick succession! It's a signal! I tell you it's Miep, trying to get us! For some reason she can't come to us and she's trying to warn us of something!
Mr. Frank. Please. Please.
Mr. Van Daan (*to* DUSSEL). You're wasting your breath.
Dussel. Something has happened, Mr. Frank. For three days now Miep hasn't been

Ⓠ Literary Focus Theme What theme does Anne's attitude suggest?

and not a man at work. (*He rushes back to* MR. FRANK, *pleading with him, almost in tears.*) I tell you Mr. Kraler's dead. That's the only explanation. He's dead and they've closed down the building, and Miep's trying to tell us!

Mr. Frank. She'd never telephone us.

Dussel (*frantic*). Mr. Frank, answer that! I beg you, answer it!

Mr. Frank. No.

Mr. Van Daan. Just pick it up and listen. You don't have to speak. Just listen and see if it's Miep.

Dussel (*speaking at the same time*). For God's sake . . . I ask you.

Mr. Frank. No. I've told you, no. I'll do nothing that might let anyone know we're in the building.

Peter. Mr. Frank's right.

Mr. Van Daan. There's no need to tell us what side you're on.

Mr. Frank. If we wait patiently, quietly, I believe that help will come.

[*There is silence for a minute as they all listen to the telephone ringing.*]

Dussel. I'm going down. (*He rushes down the steps.* MR. FRANK *tries ineffectually to hold him.* DUSSEL *runs to the lower door, unbolting it. The telephone stops ringing.* DUSSEL *bolts the door and comes slowly back up the steps.*) Too late. **Ⓡ**

[MR. FRANK *goes to* MARGOT *in* ANNE'S *bedroom.*]

(above) Movable bookcase, which hid the stairs to the Secret Annex.
(left) Movable bookcase with one of the Franks' Dutch helpers.

to see us! And today not a man has come to work. There hasn't been a sound in the building!

Mrs. Frank. Perhaps it's Sunday. We may have lost track of the days.

Mr. Van Daan (*to* ANNE). You with the diary there. What day is it?

Dussel (*going to* MRS. FRANK). I don't lose track of the days! I know exactly what day it is! It's Friday, the fourth of August. Friday,

Ⓡ **Reading Focus** Finding the Theme How is Anne's reaction to this complication different from the reactions of other characters? How has Anne changed over the course of the play?

Mr. Van Daan. So we just wait here until we die.

Mrs. Van Daan (*hysterically*). I can't stand it! I'll kill myself! I'll kill myself!

Mr. Van Daan. For God's sake, stop it!

[*In the distance, a German military band is heard playing a Viennese waltz.*]

Mrs. Van Daan. I think you'd be glad if I did! I think you want me to die!

Mr. Van Daan. Whose fault is it we're here? (MRS. VAN DAAN *starts for her room. He follows, talking at her.*) We could've been safe somewhere . . . in America or Switzerland. But no! No! You wouldn't leave when I wanted to. You couldn't leave your things. You couldn't leave your precious furniture.

Mrs. Van Daan. Don't touch me!

[*She hurries up the stairs, followed by* MR. VAN DAAN. PETER, *unable to bear it, goes to his room.* ANNE *looks after him, deeply concerned.* DUSSEL *returns to his post at the window.* MR. FRANK *comes back into the main room and takes a book, trying to read.* MRS. FRANK *sits near the sink, starting to peel some potatoes.* ANNE *quietly goes to* PETER'S *room, closing the door after her.* PETER *is lying face down on the cot.* ANNE *leans over him, holding him in her arms, trying to bring him out of his despair.*]

Anne. Look, Peter, the sky. (*She looks up through the skylight.*) What a lovely, lovely day! Aren't the clouds beautiful? You know what I do when it seems as if I couldn't stand being cooped up for one more minute? I *think* myself out. I think myself on a walk in the park where I used to go with Pim. Where the jonquils and the crocuses and the violets grow down the slopes. You know the most wonderful part about *thinking* yourself out? You can have it any way you like. You can have roses and violets and chrysanthemums all blooming at the same time. . . . It's funny . . . I used to take it all for granted . . . and now I've gone crazy about everything to do with nature. Haven't you?

Peter. I've just gone crazy. I think if something doesn't happen soon . . . if we don't get out of here . . . I can't stand much more of it!

Anne (*softly*). I wish you had a religion, Peter.

Peter. No, thanks! Not me!

Anne. Oh, I don't mean you have to be Orthodox[16] . . . or believe in Heaven and Hell and Purgatory and things . . . I just mean some religion . . . it doesn't matter what. Just to believe in something! When I think of all that's out there . . . the trees . . . and flowers . . . and sea gulls . . . When I think of the dearness of you, Peter . . . and the goodness of the people we know . . . Mr. Kraler, Miep, Dirk, the vegetable man, all risking their lives for us every day. . . . When I think of these good things, I'm not afraid anymore . . . I find myself, and God, and I . . .

[PETER *interrupts, getting up and walking away.*]

Peter. That's fine! But when I begin to think, I get mad! Look at us, hiding out for two years. Not able to move! Caught here like . . .

---

16. **Orthodox:** Orthodox Jews strictly observe Jewish law.

The Frank family in the stage production, ready to depart. ©Joan Marcus.

waiting for them to come and get us . . . and all for what?

Anne. We're not the only people that've had to suffer. There've always been people that've had to . . . sometimes one race . . . sometimes another . . . and yet . . .

Peter. That doesn't make me feel any better!

Anne (*going to him*). I know it's terrible, trying to have any faith . . . when people are doing such horrible. . . . But you know what I sometimes think? I think the world may be going through a phase, the way I was with Mother. It'll pass, maybe not for hundreds of years, but someday. . . . I still believe, in spite of everything, that people are really good at heart. Ⓢ

Peter. I want to see something now . . . not a

thousand years from now! (*He goes over, sitting down again on the cot.*)

Anne. But, Peter, if you'd only look at it as part of a great pattern . . . that we're just a little minute in the life . . . (*She breaks off.*) Listen to us, going at each other like a couple of stupid grown-ups! Look at the sky now. Isn't it lovely? (*She holds out her hand to him.* PETER *takes it and rises, standing with her at the window looking out, his arms around her.*) Someday, when we're outside again, I'm going to . . .

[*She breaks off as she hears the sound of a car, its brakes squealing as it comes to a sudden stop. The people in the other rooms also become aware of the sound. They listen tensely. Another car roars up to a screeching*

Ⓢ **Literary Focus** **Theme** How can Anne believe this after all she has endured? What theme does this statement suggest?

stop. ANNE *and* PETER *come from* PETER'S *room.* MR. *and* MRS. VAN DAAN *creep down the stairs.* DUSSEL *comes out from his room. Everyone is listening, hardly breathing. A doorbell clangs again and again in the building below.* MR. FRANK *starts quietly down the steps to the door.* DUSSEL *and* PETER *follow him. The others stand rigid, waiting, terrified.*

In a few seconds DUSSEL *comes stumbling back up the steps. He shakes off* PETER'S *help and goes to his room.* MR. FRANK *bolts the door below and comes slowly back up the steps. Their eyes are all on him as he stands there for a minute. They realize that what they feared has happened.* MRS. VAN DAAN *starts to whimper.* MR. VAN DAAN *puts her gently in a chair and then hurries off up the stairs to their room to collect their things.* PETER *goes to comfort his mother. There is a sound of violent pounding on a door below.*]

Mr. Frank (*quietly*). For the past two years we have lived in fear. Now we can live in hope.

[*The pounding below becomes more insistent. There are muffled sounds of voices, shouting commands.*]

Men's Voices. Aufmachen! Da drinnen! Aufmachen! Schnell! Schnell! Schnell![17] (*Etc., etc.*)

---

17. **Aufmachen . . . Schnell:** German for "Open up! You in there! Open up! Quickly! Quickly! Quickly!"

🅣 **Read and Discuss** | What has happened?

[*The street door below is forced open. We hear the heavy tread of footsteps coming up.* MR. FRANK *gets two school bags from the shelves and gives one to* ANNE *and the other to* MAR-GOT. *He goes to get a bag for* MRS. FRANK. *The sound of feet coming up grows louder.* PETER *comes to* ANNE, *kissing her goodbye; then he goes to his room to collect his things. The buzzer of their door starts to ring.* MR. FRANK *brings* MRS. FRANK *a bag. They stand together, waiting. We hear the thud of gun butts on the door, trying to break it down.*

ANNE *stands, holding her school satchel, looking over at her father and mother with a soft, reassuring smile. She is no longer a child, but a woman with courage to meet whatever lies ahead.*

The lights dim out. The curtain falls on the scene. We hear a mighty crash as the door is shattered. After a second ANNE'S *voice is heard.*]

Anne's Voice. And so it seems our stay here is over. They are waiting for us now. They've allowed us five minutes to get our things. We can each take a bag and whatever it will hold of clothing. Nothing else. So, dear Diary, that means I must leave you behind. Goodbye for a while. P.S. Please, please, Miep, or Mr. Kraler, or anyone else. If you should find this diary, will you please keep it safe for me, because someday I hope . . . 🅣

[*Her voice stops abruptly. There is silence. After a second the curtain rises.*]

SCENE 5

It is again the afternoon in November 1945. The rooms are as we saw them in the first scene. MR. KRALER *has joined* MIEP *and* MR. FRANK. *There are coffee cups on the table. We see a great change in* MR. FRANK. *He is calm now. His bitterness is gone. He slowly turns a few pages of the diary. They are blank.*

Mr. Frank. No more. (*He closes the diary and puts it down on the couch beside him.*)

Miep. I'd gone to the country to find food. When I got back, the block was surrounded by police . . .

Mr. Kraler. We made it our business to learn how they knew. It was the thief . . . the thief who told them.

[MIEP *goes up to the gas burner, bringing back a pot of coffee.*]

Mr. Frank (*after a pause*). It seems strange to say this, that anyone could be happy in a concentration camp. But Anne was happy in the camp in Holland where they first took us. After two years of being shut up in these rooms, she could be out . . . out in the sunshine and the fresh air that she loved.

Miep (*offering the coffee to* MR. FRANK). A little more?

Mr. Frank (*holding out his cup to her*). The news of the war was good. The British and Americans were sweeping through France. We felt sure that they would get to us in time. In September we were told that we were to be shipped to Poland. . . . The men to one camp. The women to another. I was sent to Auschwitz. They went to Belsen. In January we were freed, the few of us who were left. The war wasn't yet over, so it took us a long time to get home. We'd be sent here and there behind the lines where we'd be safe. Each time our train would stop . . . at a siding or a crossing . . . we'd all get out and go from group to group . . . Where were you? Were you at Belsen? At Buchenwald? At Mauthausen? Is it possible that you knew my wife? Did you ever see my husband? My son? My daughter? That's how I found out about my wife's death . . . of Margot, the Van Daans . . . Dussel. But Anne . . . I still hoped. . . . Yesterday I went to Rotterdam. I'd heard of a woman there. . . . She'd been in Belsen with Anne . . . I know now. **ⓤ**

[*He picks up the diary again and turns the pages back to find a certain passage. As he finds it, we hear* ANNE's *voice.*]

Anne's Voice. In spite of everything, I still believe that people are really good at heart.

[MR. FRANK *slowly closes the diary.*]

Mr. Frank. She puts me to shame.

[*They are silent.*]

Curtain

ⓤ ⌷Read and Discuss⌷ The part of a play that tells what happens to all the characters is called the resolution. According to Mr. Frank, what has happened to them all?

Applying Your Skills

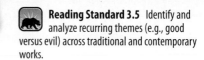

Reading Standard 3.5 Identify and analyze recurring themes (e.g., good versus evil) across traditional and contemporary works.

The Diary of Anne Frank, Act Two, Scenes 1–5

Literary Response and Analysis

Reading Skills Focus
Quick Check

1. What does Mr. Van Daan do in Act Two, Scene 3 that increases tension in the Secret Annex?

Read with a Purpose

2. What is Anne's view of the world at the end of Act Two? Support your response with examples from the play.

Reading Skills: Finding the Theme

3. Review the chart you completed as you read the play. What themes did you find? What literary elements helped you find the themes?

Literary Skills Focus
Literary Analysis

4. **Evaluate** In Act One, Scene 4, Mr. Frank tells Anne, "You must build your own character" (page 336). Explain whether you think Anne has done this by the end of the play.

5. **Make Judgments** Comment on Anne's statement, "In spite of everything, I still believe that people are really good at heart" (page 374). Explain whether you agree with her statement, in light of what happened to her and her family.

6. **Analyze** Anne says, "I want to go on living even after my death" (pages 368–369). How has her wish come true?

7. **Literary Perspectives** What do you think is the main conflict in the play? Is it the conflict between the occupants of the Secret Annex and the Nazis, or is it something else? Support your answer with details from the text.

Literary Skills: Theme

8. **Analyze** What theme is suggested by the conflict between the characters and the Nazis? Support your response with reasons.

9. **Interpret** In Act Two, Scene 3, Mr. Frank says, "We don't need the Nazis to destroy us. We're destroying ourselves." What theme about humanity is suggested by that remark?

10. **Compare and Contrast** What does this play reveal about humanity's need for freedom? Explain why this insight represents a recurring theme. Consider in your response how the play's theme relates to another work, such as "The People Could Fly" or another traditional or contemporary work.

Literary Skills Review: Climax

11. **Analyze** The **climax** of a play is its moment of greatest tension, the point at which the conflict is about to be resolved. What is the play's climax? How did you feel at that moment?

Writing Skills Focus
Think as a Reader/Writer

Use It in Your Writing Review the notes you took on dialogue as you read. What does the dialogue reveal about the characters' issues and concerns? Write a brief essay exploring how dialogue reveals the way characters' attitudes changed most over the course of the play.

 What Do You Think Now How have the characters' behaviors affected your ideas on how to confront difficult situations?

Applying Your Skills

The Diary of Anne Frank

Vocabulary Development

Verify Word Meanings: Contrast

One way to discover the meaning of an unfamiliar word is to look for **contrast clues** that show how a word is unlike another word. Words that signal contrast include *although, but, yet, however, in contrast, instead, not,* and *unlike.*

For example, you can guess that the meaning of the word *inarticulate* is "unable to speak" from the contrast clue in the following sentence:

Peter became *inarticulate* when he was angry, **but** Anne always **found plenty to say.**

Your Turn

Complete the following sentences with the correct Vocabulary word. Contrast clues are boldface in the passages.

conspicuous
indignantly
tyranny
ostentatiously
forlorn

1. Mr. Van Daan's desire for food was _____, **but** the other characters kept their hunger pangs **well hidden.**

2. The Nazis exercised great _____ over the Dutch people; **however,** in the Secret Annex, the characters demonstrated great **tolerance and respect** toward each other.

3. Mrs. Van Daan _____ showed off her fur; **in contrast,** Mrs. Frank **modestly** covered herself with a shawl.

4. Anne often left the room _____ after hearing critical comments from Mr. Van Daan, **unlike** Margot, who responded **calmly** to criticism.

5. **Instead** of feeling _____ in the concentration camp, Anne at first felt **overjoyed** at being outside after so many months indoors.

Language Coach

Suffixes Notice the suffix *–ly* that appears in the Vocabulary words *indignantly* and *ostentatiously*. This suffix indicates the words are adverbs. When you remove the suffix, you create adjectives.

Write two sentences using the adjectives *indignant* and *ostentatious*. For additional practice using the suffix *–ly,* add it to the adjectives *conspicuous* and *forlorn*. Then, use these newly formed adverbs in sentences of your own.

Academic Vocabulary

Talk About ...

With a partner, discuss how the realities of World War II and the Holocaust are <u>significant</u> to the events in *The Diary of Anne Frank*.

- Which historic events are <u>evident</u> during the play?

- What <u>insight</u> about life can you discern from the details that connect world history to personal lives?

- What themes in the play do you recognize from other <u>contemporary</u> or <u>traditional</u> works?

Learn It Online
Focus on vocabulary with *Word Sharp*:

go.hrw.com   H8-376   **Go**

Grammar Link

Conjunctions

A conjunction is a word used to join words or groups of words. Coordinating conjunctions join words or groups of words used in the same way.

and	but	or	nor	for	so	yet

EXAMPLE Mr. Frank is Anne **and** Margot's father. [*And* joins two nouns.]

Correlative conjunctions are pairs of conjunctions that join words or groups of words used in the same way.

both . . . and	either . . . or	neither . . . nor
not only . . . but also	whether . . . or	

EXAMPLE Anne can **either** hide in relative safety **or** move freely and risk capture. [*Either . . . or* joins two verbs.]

Your Turn

Writing Applications The sentences below contain coordinating conjunctions. Rewrite the sentences, using the correlative conjunctions given.

1. **both . . . and** The families hiding in the attic included the Franks and the Van Daans.
2. **not only . . . but also** The Franks fled Hitler in Germany and in Holland.
3. **either . . . or** Each day Miep or Mr. Kraler brought food up to the attic.
4. **neither . . . nor** During the day, those in the attic could not run water or speak above a whisper.

CHOICES

As you respond to the Choices, use these **Academic Vocabulary** words as appropriate: <u>contemporary</u>, <u>evident</u>, <u>insight</u>, <u>significant</u>, <u>traditional</u>.

REVIEW
Analyze the Themes

Review the theme chart you completed. In an essay, analyze the effect a literary element had on a theme. Think about the way a character changes over the course of the play, or the way people in the household address their conflicts. Why are these literary elements <u>significant</u> to the truth that the play reveals about life?

CONNECT
Describe a Tradition

Timed ∟Writing The characters take comfort in celebrating Hanukkah, the Jewish festival of lights. What <u>traditions</u> or celebrations bring you and your loved ones together? Write a brief description of one tradition or celebration.

EXTEND
Report on the Holocaust

Research Project How do memories of the Holocaust continue to affect the world today? Using Internet and print sources in a library, research either the work of the Anne Frank Foundation or the creation of the U.S. Holocaust Memorial Museum in Washington, D.C. Write a brief report on what you learn.

Learn It Online
Tell your story in a whole new way. Try digital storytelling—we'll show you how on:

go.hrw.com   H8-377   **Go**

Preparing to Read

from *The Diary of a Young Girl*

Anne Frank (2007) by Keith Mayerson. Oil on linen (38" by 40"). Courtesy of the Brett Shaheen Gallery.

What Do
You
Think

What qualities do you think help people prevail—grow stronger—during hard times?

QuickWrite
Record some qualities Anne shows in the play that you think helped her endure during her time in the Secret Annex.

Reader/Writer
Notebook

Use your **RWN** to complete the
activities for this selection.

Reading Standard 3.5 **Identify and
analyze** recurring **themes (e.g., good
versus evil) across** traditional and **contemporary
works.**

Literary Skills Focus

Conflict and Character Most stories, whether real or fictional,
revolve around characters facing conflict. As characters address and
resolve conflicts, you gain <u>insight</u> into their hopes, fears, strengths,
and weaknesses. As you read the following diary entries, consider the
way Anne Frank addresses her conflict in a time of war. What theme is
revealed as you read?

TechFocus As you read these diary entries, think about what you
might want to say in a modern form of a diary: a blog.

Reading Skills Focus

Comparing and Contrasting Characters Works of literature
are often based on historical events. The play *The Diary of Anne Frank* is
inspired by the real-life experiences that Anne Frank records in *The Diary
of a Young Girl*. As you read Anne's diary, you will recognize characters
and conflicts. You might, however, notice differences in the way Anne
portrays herself versus the way she is portrayed in the drama. A different
theme, or truth about life, may become <u>evident</u> as a result.

Into Action Use a chart like the one below to compare the way characters are portrayed in both works.

	Anne's Thoughts	Anne's Feelings
The Diary of Anne Frank		
The Diary of a Young Girl		

Writing Skills Focus
Think as a Reader/Writer

Find It in Your Reading Diaries are usually written for personal
use, but some may be works of literature. Record in your *Reader/Writer
Notebook* specific, carefully chosen words that Anne Frank uses to
express her thoughts and her feelings.

Vocabulary

liberation (lihb uh RAY shuhn) *n.:*
release from imprisonment or
enemy occupation. *When the troops
withdrew, the city celebrated its
liberation.*

cherished (CHEHR ihsht) *v.* used as
adj.: valued; well loved. *Her ideals
are her most cherished possession
because they give meaning to her
life.*

Language Coach

Latin Roots The English language
has developed over time from many
languages. Latin is one of the most
influential languages on English. The
Vocabulary word *liberation* is derived
from the Latin word *liber*, which
means "free." Other English words,
including *liberty*, are derived from
this Latin word.

Note that in Latin, *liber* has two
meanings. It also means "book."
Words such as *library* are derived
from this Latin word.

Learn It Online
Master these words. Visit Word Watch at:

go.hrw.com   H8-379   **Go**

from
The Diary of a Young Girl

by **Anne Frank**

Wednesday, 3 May, 1944

. . . Since Saturday we've changed over, and have lunch at half past eleven in the mornings, so we have to last out with one cupful of porridge; this saves us a meal. Vegetables are still very difficult to obtain; we had rotten boiled lettuce this afternoon. Ordinary lettuce, spinach, and boiled lettuce, there's nothing else. With these we eat rotten potatoes, so it's a delicious combination! **Ⓐ**

As you can easily imagine, we often ask ourselves here despairingly: "What, oh, what is the use of the war? Why can't people live peacefully together? Why all this destruction?"

The question is very understandable, but no one has found a satisfactory answer to it so far. Yes, why do they make still more gigantic planes, still heavier bombs, and, at the same time, prefabricated[1] houses for reconstruction? Why should millions be spent daily on the war and yet there's

---

1. **prefabricated:** constructed in pieces for easy shipment and assembly.

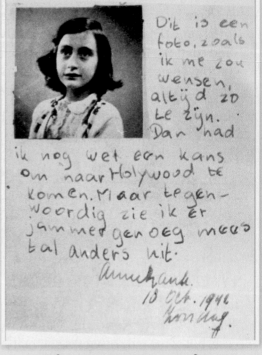

⬉ Anne at age 10 ⬈

Ⓐ **Read and Discuss** Anne includes specific details in this paragraph. What impression does she give you?

not a penny available for medical services, artists, or poor people?

Why do some people have to starve while there are surpluses rotting in other parts of the world? Oh, why are people so crazy?

I don't believe that the big men, the politicians and the capitalists alone, are guilty of the war. Oh no, the little man is just as guilty; otherwise the peoples of the world would have risen in revolt long ago! There's in people simply an urge to destroy, an urge to kill, to murder and rage, and until all mankind, without exception, undergoes a great change, wars will be waged, everything that has been built up, cultivated, and grown will be destroyed and disfigured, after which mankind will have to begin all over again. **B**

I have often been downcast, but never in despair; I regard our hiding as a dangerous adventure, romantic and interesting at the same time. In my diary I treat all the privations[2] as amusing. I have made up my mind now to lead a different life from other girls and, later on, different from ordinary housewives. My start has been

Anne in 1939

so very full of interest, and that is the sole reason why I have to laugh at the humorous side of the most dangerous moments.

I am young and I possess many buried qualities; I am young and strong and am living a great adventure; I am still in the midst of it and can't grumble the whole day long. I have been given a lot: a happy nature, a great deal of cheerfulness and strength. Every day I feel that I am developing inwardly, that the liberation is drawing nearer,

---

2. **privations:** lack of necessities.

B **Literary Focus** **Conflict and Character** What do Anne's thoughts reveal about how the war is affecting her?

Vocabulary **liberation** (lihb uh RAY shuhn) *n.*: release from imprisonment or enemy occupation.

and how beautiful nature is, how good the people are about me, how interesting this adventure is! Why, then, should I be in despair?

Yours,
Anne

Saturday, 15 July, 1944

. . . "For in its innermost depths youth is lonelier than old age." I read this saying in some book and I've always remembered it, and found it to be true. Is it true, then, that grown-ups have a more difficult time here than we do? No. I know it isn't. Older people have formed their opinions about everything and don't waver before they act. It's twice as hard for us young ones to hold our ground and maintain our opinions in a time when all ideals are being shattered and destroyed, when people are showing their worst side and do not know whether to believe in truth and right and God.

Anyone who claims that the older ones have a more difficult time here certainly doesn't realize to what extent our problems weigh down on us, problems for which we are probably much too young but which thrust themselves upon us continually, until, after a long time, we think we've found a solution, but the solution doesn't seem able to resist the facts which reduce it to nothing again. That's the difficulty in these times: Ideals, dreams, and cherished hopes rise within us, only to meet the horrible truth and be shattered. **C**

It's really a wonder that I haven't dropped all my ideals, because they seem so absurd and impossible to carry out. Yet I keep them, because in spite of everything I still believe that people are really good at heart. I simply can't build up my hopes on a foundation consisting of confusion, misery, and death. I see the world gradually being turned into a wilderness, I hear the ever approaching thunder, which will destroy us too, I can feel the sufferings of millions, and yet, if I look up into the heavens, I think that it will all come right, that this cruelty too will end, and that peace and tranquility will return again.

In the meantime, I must uphold my ideals, for perhaps the time will come when I shall be able to carry them out. **D**

Yours,
Anne

C Reading Focus **Comparing and Contrasting** How is Anne's attitude in this entry different from that in the previous entry?

D Read and Discuss How does this passage fit in with what you know about Anne?

Vocabulary **cherished** (CHEHR ihsht) *v.* used as *adj.:* valued; well loved.

Applying Your Skills

from The Diary of a Young Girl

Literary Response and Analysis

Reading Skills Focus
Quick Check

1. How does Anne describe herself in the first entry?

Read with a Purpose

2. In what ways does the character revealed in the excerpts from Anne's diary surprise you?

Reading Skills: Comparing and Contrasting Characters

3. Review the chart you completed comparing Anne's character in the play and in the diary. Decide whether Anne's character in the play captures the real Anne or lacks important aspects of Anne's personality. What can a play accomplish that a diary cannot? What can a diary tell you that a play cannot?

✔ Vocabulary Check

4. What **cherished** possession can help you through a difficult time?
5. Why do people yearn for **liberation** from oppression?

Literary Skills Focus
Literary Analysis

6. **Connect** Dramatic irony is created when the reader knows something a character does not know. What do you know as you read Anne's diary that Anne does not know? How does having this <u>insight</u> make you feel?

7. **Analyze** There is no evidence in Anne's diary that Mr. Van Daan stole food. The playwrights may have invented this incident for dramatic effect. What is your opinion of such changes in fiction that is based on real events?

Literary Skills: Conflict and Character

8. **Interpret** What internal conflict does Anne address in the second diary entry? How does she resolve this conflict?

9. **Evaluate** In the first entry, Anne writes, "There's in people simply an urge to destroy, an urge to kill, to murder and rage. . . ." In the second entry, she says that "in spite of everything I still believe that people are really good at heart." How do you think Anne was able to reconcile these contradictory opinions?

Literary Skills Review: Theme

10. **Analyze** What theme is revealed in the diary? Consider the way conflicts are resolved and the way Anne's character is represented. In what ways is this theme similar to or different from the theme of the play?

Writing Skills Focus
Think as a Reader/Writer

Use It in Your Writing Review the words Anne uses to describe herself. Write a profile of yourself or someone else. Like Anne, choose your words and phrases carefully to give the reader a precise picture of the person you are describing.

Camp Harmony

from Nisei Daughter *by* **Monica Sone**

In Response to Executive Order 9066

by **Dwight Okita**

In March (1943) by Hisako Hibi. Gift of Ibuki Hibi Lee, Japanese American National Museum (96.601.14)

What Do You Think

How do people react when they are forced to leave home?

 QuickWrite

What would you take if you had to leave home and you only one small suitcase? What would you find hard to

Reader/Writer Notebook

Use your **RWN** to complete the activities for these selections.

Literary Skills Focus

Recurring Themes Because **themes** are general <u>insights</u> about human experience, they have been repeated again and again in literature throughout the ages. For instance, a theme such as *Good can triumph over evil* can be found in <u>traditional</u> folk tales as well as in <u>contemporary</u> novels. As you read the following selections, look for themes you recognize from other works, including *The Diary of Anne Frank*.

TechFocus As you read the autobiography and poem, think of a scene you could depict using an online storyboard program.

Reading Skills Focus

Making Generalizations A **generalization** is a broad statement based on several particular situations. When you make a generalization, you combine evidence in texts with what you already know to make a universal statement on a topic.

Into Action In a chart like the one below, record similarities you find in the experiences of Anne Frank and Monica Sone. Then, make generalizations about the conditions shared by some groups of people during World War II.

Details from Anne Frank's diary	Details from "Camp Harmony"	Generalization
The family lives in a cramped, hidden room.	The internment camp housing is primitive.	People were forced to live away from home and in terrible conditions.

Writing Skills Focus
Think as a Reader/Writer

Find It in Your Reading As you read "Camp Harmony," notice how the author uses transitions to move from one part of her story to the next. Which transitional words and phrases show the passage of time? Which show the relationship between ideas? List these transitions in your *Reader/Writer Notebook*.

Language Coach
Derivations The English word *vigil* derives from the same word in Latin. In Latin, *vigil* means "awake." How does this meaning connect to the English meaning shown in the Vocabulary list above?

Learn It Online
Hear a professional actor read these selections at:

go.hrw.com   H8-385   Go

Monica Sone
(1919–   )

A Child of Two Worlds

Born in Seattle, Washington, Monica Sone is a native-born American whose parents were from Japan. While living in Camp Harmony, Sone wrote several letters to a friend describing the living conditions in the camp. Her friend saved these and one day showed them to an editor at Little, Brown and Co. The editor was interested and asked Sone to consider writing a book about her camp experiences. Sone's autobiography, *Nisei Daughter*, was published in 1953. It was the first book about the internment camps written by an internee.

Dwight Okita
(1958–   )

Controversial Issues in a Charming Style

Dwight Okita frequently looks to events from his own life as material for his poetry. His parents had to report to an internment camp for Japanese Americans during World War II, a traumatic event that inspired "In Response to Executive Order 9066."

Okita does not shy away from controversial social and political issues, but he maintains a light, charming style that has made his writing popular with American readers. *Crossing with the Light,* the collection that features "In Response to Executive Order 9066," was published in 1992.

Think About the Writers

What might personal retellings such as those of Sone's reveal that Okita's poetry might not?

Build Background

In 1942, many thousands of Japanese Americans living on the West Coast were sent to internment camps. They had committed no crime, but the United States had gone to war with Japan. Executive Order 9066 made their confinement legal. Ironically, many of the evacuated families had sons or brothers serving with the U.S. Army in the war overseas. Most of the 120,000 Japanese Americans detained spent three years behind barbed wire.

Preview the Selections

In this excerpt from her autobiography, **Monica Sone** tells about her family's experience in Camp Harmony, an internment camp to which her family, as Japanese Americans, were forced to relocate.

In the poem "In Response to Executive Order 9066," written in letter format, the **fourteen-year-old speaker** addresses the U.S. authorities about her internment.

Camp Harmony

from **Nisei Daughter**

by **Monica Sone**

When our bus turned a corner and we no longer had to smile and wave, we settled back gravely in our seats. Everyone was quiet except for a chattering group of university students, who soon started singing college songs. A few people turned and glared at them, which only served to increase the volume of their singing. Then suddenly a baby's sharp cry rose indignantly above the hubbub. The singing stopped immediately, followed by a guilty silence. Three seats behind us, a young mother held a wailing red-faced infant in her arms, bouncing it up and down. Its angry little face emerged from multiple layers of kimonos, sweaters, and blankets, and it, too, wore the white pasteboard tag[1] pinned to its blanket. A young man stammered out an apology as the mother gave him a wrathful look. She hunted frantically for a bottle of milk in a shopping bag, and we all relaxed when she had found it.

We sped out of the city southward along beautiful stretches of farmland, with dark, newly turned soil. In the beginning we devoured every bit of scenery which flashed past our window and admired the massive-muscled workhorses plodding along the edge of the highway, the rich burnished copper color of a browsing herd of cattle, the vivid spring green of the pastures, but eventually the sameness of the country landscape palled[2] on us. We tried to sleep to escape from the restless anxiety which kept bobbing up to the surface of our minds. I awoke with a start when the bus filled with excited buzzing. A small group of straw-hatted Japanese farmers stood by the highway, waving at us. I felt a sudden warmth toward them, then a twinge of pity. They would be joining us soon. Ⓐ

---

1. **white pasteboard tag:** All Japanese American families registering for evacuation were given numbered tags to wear and to attach to their luggage. Monica's family became number 10710.

2. **palled:** became boring or tiresome.

Ⓐ **Read and Discuss** What has the author told you so far?

About noon we crept into a small town. Someone said, "Looks like Puyallup, all right." Parents of small children babbled excitedly, "Stand up quickly and look over there. See all the chick-chicks and fat little piggies?" One little city boy stared hard at the hogs and said tersely, "They're bachi—dirty!"

Our bus idled a moment at the traffic signal, and we noticed at the left of us an entire block filled with neat rows of low shacks, resembling chicken houses. Someone commented on it with awe, "Just look at those chicken houses. They sure go in for poultry in a big way here." Slowly the bus made a left turn, drove through a wire-fence gate, and to our dismay, we were inside the oversized chicken farm. The bus driver opened the door, the guard stepped out and stationed himself at the door again. Jim, the young man who had shepherded us into the buses, popped his head inside and sang out, "OK, folks, all off at Yokohama, Puyallup."

We stumbled out, stunned, dragging our bundles after us. It must have rained hard the night before in Puyallup, for we sank ankle deep into gray, glutinous[3] mud. The receptionist, a white man, instructed us courteously, "Now, folks, please stay together as family units and line up. You'll be assigned your apartment." **B**

We were standing in Area A, the mammoth parking lot of the state fairgrounds.

---

3. **glutinous:** sticky; gluey.

B **Reading Focus** **Making Generalizations** Using the details in these paragraphs and what you already know, what generalization can you make about conditions in the internment camps?

Vocabulary **tersely** (TURS lee) *adv.:* briefly and clearly; without unnecessary words.

A family on the way to a Japanese internment camp.

Analyzing Visuals

Connecting to the Text What might these evacuees be thinking? What detail in the photo stands out the most?

There were three other separate areas, B, C, and D, all built on the fairgrounds proper, near the baseball field and the racetracks. This camp of army barracks was hopefully called Camp Harmony.

We were assigned to apartment 2–I–A, right across from the bachelor quarters. The apartments resembled elongated,[4] low stables about two blocks long. Our home was one room, about eighteen by twenty feet, the size of a living room. There was one small window in the wall opposite the one door. It was bare except for a small, tinny wood-burning stove crouching in the center. The flooring consisted of two-by-fours laid directly on the earth, and dandelions were already pushing their way up through the cracks. Mother was delighted when she saw their shaggy yellow heads. "Don't anyone pick them. I'm going to cultivate them."

Father snorted, "Cultivate them! If we don't watch out, those things will be growing out of our hair."

Just then Henry stomped inside, bringing the rest of our baggage. "What's all the excitement about?"

We stumbled out, stunned.

Sumi replied laconically,[5] "Dandelions." Henry tore off a fistful. Mother scolded, "Arra! Arra! Stop that. They're the only beautiful things around here. We could have a garden right in here."

"Are you joking, Mama?"

I chided Henry, "Of course she's not. After all, she has to have some inspiration to write poems, you know, with all the 'nari keri's.'[6] I can think of a poem myself right now:
Oh, Dandelion, Dandelion,
Despised and uprooted by all,
Dance and bob your golden heads
For you've finally found your home
With your yellow fellows, nari keri, amen!"

Henry said, thrusting the dandelions in Mother's black hair, "I think you can do ten times better than that, Mama."

Sumi reclined on her sea bag[7] and fretted, "Where do we sleep? Not on the floor, I hope."

---

4. **elongated:** lengthened.
5. **laconically:** with few words; briefly.
6. **nari keri's:** referring to a phrase used to end many Japanese poems, meant to convey wonder and awe.
7. **sea bag:** large canvas bag like the ones sailors use to carry their personal belongings. Each person was allowed to bring only one sea bag of bedding and two suitcases of clothing to the internment camps.

C **Literary Focus** **Recurring Themes** What kind of person does Mrs. Sone seem to be? Which characters in *The Diary of Anne Frank* display similar traits?

Japanese Internment Camps

Immediately after the declaration of Executive Order 9066 in February 1942, the U.S. government constructed internment camps in parts of Arkansas, California, Arizona, Colorado, Idaho, Washington, Utah, and Wyoming. By August 1942, most of the Japanese Americans in the western part of the country were imprisoned in these camps. Over half of these internees were children. Internees faced many difficulties. The physical environment was often harsh, the food was bad, and the people had little or no privacy. Traditional family structure and discipline were hard to maintain. Released in 1945, at the end of World War II, internees returned home to find their property stolen and their livelihoods gone. More than forty years later they received an apology and compensation from the U.S. government.

Ask Yourself
What hardships did Sone face while forced to live in an internment camp?

Family awaiting transportation to Manzanar, 1942 (detail). Photographer: Dorothea Lange.

"Stop worrying," Henry replied disgustedly.

Mother and Father wandered out to see what the other folks were doing and they found people wandering in the mud, wondering what other folks were doing. Mother returned shortly, her face lit up in an ecstatic smile, "We're in luck. The latrine is right nearby. We won't have to walk blocks."

We laughed, marveling at Mother who could be so poetic and yet so practical. Father came back, bent double like a wood-cutter in a fairy tale, with stacks of scrap lumber over his shoulder. His coat and trouser pockets bulged with nails. Father dumped his loot in a corner and explained, "There was a pile of wood left by the car-penters and hundreds of nails scattered loose. Everybody was picking them up, and I hustled right in with them. Now maybe we can live in style, with tables and chairs." **D**

The block leader knocked at our door and announced lunchtime. He instructed us to take our meal at the nearest mess hall. As I untied my sea bag to get out my pie plate, tin cup, spoon, and fork, I realized I was hungry. At the mess hall we found

D | Read and Discuss | What do you find out about the family's apartment?

a long line of people. Children darted in and out of the line, skiing in the slithery mud. The young stood impatiently on one foot, then the other, and scowled, "The food had better be good after all this wait." But the issei[8] stood quietly, arms folded, saying very little. A light drizzle began to fall, coating bare black heads with tiny sparkling raindrops. The chow line inched forward.

Lunch consisted of two canned sausages, one lob of boiled potato, and a slab of bread. Our family had to split up, for the hall was too crowded for us to sit together. I wandered up and down the aisles, back and forth along the crowded tables and benches, looking for a few inches to squeeze into. A small issei woman finished her meal, stood up, and hoisted her legs modestly over the bench, leaving a space for one. Even as I thrust myself into the breach, the space had shrunk to two inches, but I worked myself into it. My dinner companion, hooked just inside my right elbow, was a baldheaded, gruff-looking issei man who seemed to resent nestling at mealtime. Under my left elbow was a tiny, mud-spattered girl. With busy, runny nose, she

> The hall was too crowded for us to sit together.

was belaboring her sausages, tearing them into shreds and mixing them into the potato gruel which she had made with water. I choked my food down. **Ⓔ**

We cheered loudly when trucks rolled by, distributing canvas army cots for the young and hardy, and steel cots for the older folks. Henry directed the arrangement of the cots. Father and Mother were to occupy the corner nearest the woodstove.

In the other corner, Henry arranged two cots in an L shape and announced that this was the combination living room–bedroom area, to be occupied by Sumi and myself. He fixed a male den for himself in the corner nearest the door. If I had had my way, I would have arranged everyone's cots in one neat row, as in Father's hotel dormitory.

We felt fortunate to be assigned to a room at the end of the barracks, because we had just one neighbor to worry about. The partition wall separating the rooms was only seven feet high, with an opening of four feet at the top, so at night, Mrs. Funai next door could tell when Sumi was still sitting up in bed in the dark, putting her hair up. "Mah, Sumi-chan," Mrs. Funai would say through the plank wall, "are you curling your hair tonight, again? Do you put it up every

---

8. **issei:** Japanese who immigrated to North America. Issei were forbidden by law to become U.S. citizens.

Ⓔ **Reading Focus** Making Generalizations What generalization about human nature can you make based on the actions described here?

Vocabulary **breach** (breech) *n.*: opening.

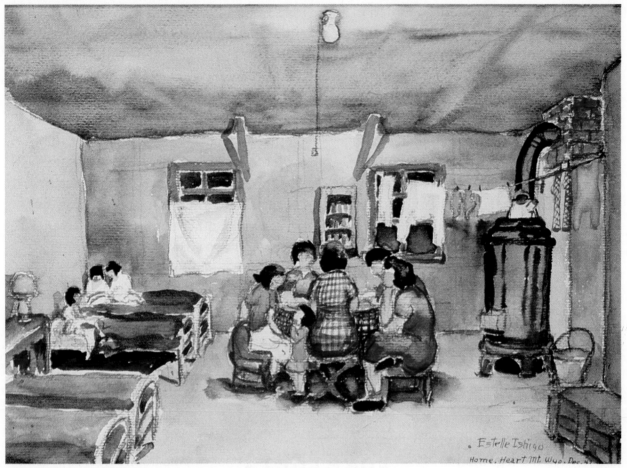

Home, Heart Mountain (December 1942) by Estelle Ishigo. Watercolor painting.

night?" Sumi would put her hands on her hips and glare defiantly at the wall. **F**

The block monitor, an impressive nisei[9] who looked like a star tackle, with his crouching walk, came around the first night to tell us that we must all be inside our room by nine o'clock every night. At ten o'clock, he rapped at the door again, yelling, "Lights out!" and Mother rushed to turn the light off not a second later.

Throughout the barracks, there was a medley[10] of creaking cots, whimpering infants, and explosive night coughs. Our attention was riveted on the intense little woodstove, which glowed so violently

---

9. **nisei:** native U.S. or Canadian citizen born to Japanese immigrant parents.

10. **medley:** jumble; mixture.

F **Literary Focus** **Recurring Themes** What does this detail of everyday life reveal about people's behavior under trying circumstances? What details in *The Diary of Anne Frank* reveal this recurring theme?

Vocabulary **riveted** (RIHV iht ihd) *v.* used as *adj.:* fastened; held firmly.

I feared it would melt right down to the floor. We soon learned that this condition lasted for only a short time, after which it suddenly turned into a deep freeze. Henry and Father took turns at the stove to produce the harrowing[11] blast which all but singed our army blankets but did not penetrate through them. As it grew quieter in the barracks, I could hear the light patter of rain. Soon I felt the *splat! splat!* of raindrops digging holes into my face. The dampness on my pillow spread like a mortal bleeding, and I finally had to get out and haul my cot toward the center of the room. In a short while, Henry was up. "I've got multiple leaks, too. Have to complain to the landlord first thing in the morning." **G**

All through the night I heard people getting up, dragging cots around. I stared at our little window, unable to sleep. I was glad Mother had put up a makeshift curtain on the window, for I noticed a powerful beam of light sweeping across it every few seconds. The lights came from high towers placed around the camp, where guards with tommy guns kept a twenty-four-hour vigil. I remembered the wire fence encircling us, and a knot of anger tightened in my breast. What was I doing behind a fence, like a criminal? If there were accusations to be made, why hadn't I been given a fair trial? Maybe I wasn't considered an American anymore. My citizenship wasn't real, after all. Then what was I? I was certainly not a citizen of Japan, as my parents were. On second thought, even Father and Mother were more alien residents of the United States than Japanese nationals, for they had little tie with their mother country. In their twenty-five years in America, they had worked and paid their taxes to their adopted government as any other citizen.

Of one thing I was sure. The wire fence was real. I no longer had the right to walk out of it. It was because I had Japanese ancestors. It was also because some people had little faith in the ideas and ideals of democracy. They said that after all these were but words and could not possibly ensure loyalty. New laws and camps were surer devices. I finally buried my face in my pillow to wipe out burning thoughts and snatch what sleep I could. **H**

> I stared at our little window, unable to sleep.

---

11. **harrowing:** extremely distressing.

G [Read and Discuss] What have you learned about life at Camp Harmony?

H [Reading Skills] **Making Generalizations** Considering the selection as a whole, particularly these comments, and what you already know, what generalization can you make about how war affects people's attitudes and behavior toward one another?

Vocabulary vigil (VIHJ uhl) *n.*: watch.

In Response to Executive Order 9066:
All Americans of Japanese Descent Must Report to Relocation Centers

by **Dwight Okita**

Dear Sirs:
Of course I'll come. I've packed my galoshes
and three packets of tomato seeds. Denise
    calls them
"love apples." My father says where we're going
5   they won't grow.

I am a fourteen-year-old girl with bad spelling
and a messy room. If it helps any, I will tell you
I have always felt funny using chopsticks
and my favorite food is hot dogs.
10   My best friend is a white girl named Denise—
we look at boys together. She sat in front of me
all through grade school because of our names:
O'Connor, Ozawa. I know the back of Denise's head
    very well.
I tell her she's going bald. She tells me I copy on tests.
15   We're best friends.

I saw Denise today in Geography class.
She was sitting on the other side of the room.
"You're trying to start a war," she said, "giving secrets away
to the Enemy. Why can't you keep your big mouth shut?"
20   I didn't know what to say.
I gave her a packet of tomato seeds
and asked her to plant them for me, told her
when the first tomato ripened
she'd miss me.

Ⓐ Literary Focus **Recurring Themes** What recurring theme can you infer
from these lines? How does the poem's expression of this theme compare to one found
in *The Diary of Anne Frank*?

Applying Your Skills

Reading Standard 3.5 Identify and analyze recurring themes (e.g., good versus evil) **across** traditional and **contemporary** works.

Camp Harmony/In Response to Executive Order 9066

Literary Response and Analysis

Reading Skills Focus
Quick Check

1. Write a one-paragraph **retelling,** or short restatement, of the main events in "Camp Harmony."

2. Briefly retell the main events in "In Response to Executive Order 9066."

Read with a Purpose

3. How do Sone and her family react to their new situation? How does the speaker in the poem react?

Reading Skills: Making Generalizations

4. Re-read the generalizations you made about the experiences shared by some groups of people during World War II. Which generalizations can be applied more broadly to all people who have been involved in a war?

Details from "Camp Harmony"	Details from Anne Frank's diary	Generalization
The internment camp housing is primitive.	The family lives in a cramped, hidden room.	People were forced to live away from home and in terrible conditions.

Literary Skills Focus
Literary Analysis

5. **Evaluate** Sone says her camp "was hopefully called Camp Harmony" (page 389). What is ironic about the name of the camp? Support your answer with evidence from the text.

6. **Identify** What details in Okita's poem show that the speaker feels she is a true American? How is the speaker betrayed by a friend?

7. **Evaluate** Sone says she was imprisoned "because some people had little faith in the ideas and ideals of democracy" (page 393). What does she mean? Explain whether you agree or disagree with her statement.

Literary Skills: Recurring Themes

8. **Connect** In her text, Sone's anger over the internment and her newly created doubts about her identity are evident. How does Sone's reaction to her situation compare to that of Anne Frank in *The Diary of Anne Frank*?

Literary Skills Review: Setting

9. **Analyze** The **setting** of a story is the time and place in which the story takes place. In "Camp Harmony," why does Sone describe the setting at length? Why is the setting significant to the narrative?

Writing Skills Focus
Think as a Reader/Writer

Use It in Your Writing Write a brief autobiographical essay about an important day in your life. Be sure to use transitional words and phrases to clarify how the details you include are related.

What Do You Think Now

What is surprising about the internees' reactions to their situation?

Reading Standard 1.3 Use word meanings within the appropriate context and show ability to verify those meanings by definition, **restatement**, example, comparison, or contrast.

Camp Harmony / In Response to Executive Order 9066

Vocabulary Development

Verify Word Meanings: Restatement

In your reading, you probably come across words whose meanings you think you know, but you are not quite sure about. How can you verify their meanings? One strategy is to look at a word's **context**—the words and sentences that surround it—for clues.

One type of context clue is **restatement,** a rephrasing of a word in more familiar terms. For example, if you were unfamiliar with the word *resourceful,* you could probably make a good guess about its meaning by noting the restatement, which appears in boldface in this sentence:

> The resourceful internees were **able to think of ways to deal with their situation.** They collected scraps of wood to make furniture.

Your Turn

Rewrite the following sentences to include restatements of the boldface Vocabulary words. Your restatements can be in the same sentence or in an additional sentence. Circle your restatement.

tersely
breach
riveted
vigil

1. One little boy stared at the hogs and said **tersely,** "Dirty."
2. Guards with tommy guns kept a constant **vigil** around the prison camp.
3. The narrator thrust herself into the tiny **breach** between two people sitting on the bench.
4. The family's eyes were **riveted** on the stove.

Language Coach

Related Words When you learn a new word, pay attention to related words that are **derived** from, or come from, the same root, such as *hazard* and *hazardous*. Write down and define two words that derive from the same root as the following words from the selection:

> emerged (page 387)
> quarters (page 389)
> instructed (page 390)

Referring to a dictionary may be helpful.

Academic Vocabulary

Talk About . . .

In a small group, discuss your reactions to injustice. Consider these questions:

1. What examples of injustice are evident in your community?
2. What contemporary examples have you observed on television?
3. How significant do you consider the problem to be worldwide?
4. What insights do you have about how to end injustice?

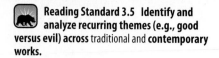

Grammar Link
Direct and Indirect Objects

A **direct object** is a noun or pronoun that receives the action of a verb or that shows the result of the action. A direct object tells *what* or *whom*.

EXAMPLE We read a **story.** (*Story* tells what was read.)

A direct object never follows a linking verb, since a linking verb—such as *become* or *is*—does not express action. Also, a direct object is never part of a prepositional phrase.

An **indirect object** is a noun or pronoun that comes between the verb and the direct object and tells *to what* or *to whom* or *for what* or *for whom* the action is performed.

EXAMPLE We read the **children** a story. (The *children* were read to.)

Linking verbs also do not have indirect objects, and indirect objects are never in a prepositional phrase.

Your Turn

Identify each boldface noun or pronoun as a direct or indirect object.

1. The young mother held an **infant** in her arms.
2. I recited a **poem** for mother.
3. The glowing woodstove gave **us** warmth.
4. Henry handed his **mother** a flower for her hair.
5. She handed her **friend** a packet of seeds.

CHOICES

As you respond to the Choices, use these **Academic Vocabulary** words as appropriate: <u>contemporary</u>, <u>evident</u>, <u>insight</u>, <u>significant</u>, <u>traditional</u>.

REVIEW
Comparing Themes

Here are two theme statements:
- *Innocent people often bear the burden of blame for things they did not do.*
- *In a struggle with the state, individuals are often helpless victims.*

Choose one of those themes, and discuss how it is revealed in "Camp Harmony," in "In Response to Executive Order 9066," and in another story you've read or movie or TV show you have watched. How are the treatments of the theme similar, and how are they different?

CONNECT
Compose a Persuasive Letter

Timed ⌐Writing Write a letter to President Franklin D. Roosevelt, persuading him to cancel Executive Order 9066. Make your case, supporting your argument with details from the text as well as from your own observations of life.

EXTEND
Create a Graphic Story

TechFocus Use graphics to retell a scene from Sone's autobiography or Okita's poem. Choose an event to depict. Then, use an online storyboard program to draw the scene in three or four panels, with short descriptions underneath. Include dialogue balloons as needed.

Analyzing Recurring Themes

Newly sworn-in U.S. citizens at a naturalization ceremony.

CONTENTS

What Do You Think

What does the American Dream mean to you?

 QuickWrite

Why do many people move to the United States? Discuss your ideas with a small group of classmates, and write down your group's top three reasons.

Preparing to Read

Reading Standard 3.5 Identify and analyze recurring themes (e.g., good versus evil) across traditional and contemporary works.

The New Colossus / Refugee in America / The First Americans

Literary Skills Focus

Recurring Themes: The American Dream The promise of freedom and equality has long inspired waves of immigrants to come to the United States in search of the American Dream. These people have struggled for years to gain equality and attain their dreams. The first immigrants from England to settle in North America, in the 1600s, dreamed of establishing a society where they could experience religious freedom. In the 1800s, millions of Europeans poured through the open doors of America. These often desperately poor and persecuted people dreamed of a society where their children would not be judged by their language or religion. At the same time, millions of people who came to the United States from Africa were being held in slavery. They dreamed of living in freedom, without fearing oppression because of their skin color.

Reading Skills Focus

Finding Recurring Themes After you read the three texts that follow, you'll compare their views of the American Dream. Study the key aspects of the American Dream on page 400. Decide which aspects are reflected in each selection.

Comparing Expressions of the American Dream

	Expressions of the American Dream
"The New Colossus"	
"Refugee in America"	
"The First Americans"	

Writing Skills Focus

Think as a Reader/Writer

Find It in Your Reading As you read, note examples of words and phrases that evoke a strong emotional response.

Reader/Writer
Notebook

Use your **RWN** to complete the activities for these selections.

Vocabulary

The New Colossus

yearning (YURN ihng) v. used as adj.: longing for; wanting badly. *The immigrants, yearning for a better life, took a risk and moved to the United States.*

teeming (TEEM ihng) adj.: full (in this case, of people); crowded. *The teeming lower deck of the ship was full of people.*

The First Americans

patriots (PAY tree uhts) n.: people who love and support their country. *Patriots will often fly a flag to show their love of country.*

wholesome (HOHL suhm) adj.: good for the mind and spirit. *The authors want wholesome explanations of American Indian life taught in school.*

Language Coach

Word Origins *Whole* in *wholesome* comes from the Old English word *hál*, meaning "whole." Other words with this same origin are *holy*, *healthy*, and *heal*. With a partner, discuss how the idea of wholeness exists in these other words.

Learn It Online
Improve your vocabulary skills with Word Watch at:
go.hrw.com   H8-399   Go

Learn It Online

Learn more about Hughes at:

go.hrw.com H8-400 Go

Emma Lazarus
(1849–1887)

"Mother of Exiles"

Emma Lazarus was born into a wealthy family in New York City. From an early age, Lazarus studied the classics and foreign languages. Her first collection of poetry was published when she was a teenager. After reading an article by Lazarus in support of Jewish refugees from Russia, the Statue of Liberty committee asked her to write a poem for the statue's pedestal. The result was the powerful sonnet "The New Colossus."

Langston Hughes
(1902–1967)

In his autobiography *The Big Sea* (1940), Hughes describes his writing process:

"There are seldom many changes in my poems, once they're down. Generally, the first two or three lines come to me from something I'm thinking about, or looking at, or doing, and the rest of the poem (if there is to be a poem) flows from those first few lines, usually right away. If there is a chance to put the poem down then, I write it down. If not, I try to remember it until I get to a pencil and paper; for poems are like rainbows: They escape you quickly."

For more about Langston Hughes, see page 638.

Think
About the
Writers

What surprises you about Hughes's writing process?

Preview the Selections

In "The New Colossus" the speaker of the poem compares an ancient Greek statue to the Statue of Liberty.

In "Refugee in America" the speaker of the poem discusses racial prejudice.

"The First Americans," a speech presented to the mayor of Chicago in 1927, sought to reform the stereotypes of American Indians found in textbooks and classes, asking that they present a full and fair history of the "First Americans."

Key Aspects of the American Dream

- America offers endless opportunity to those willing to work hard.

- People can find freedom in America.

- All Americans are equal under the law.

- Americans respect one another and celebrate their differences as well as their similarities.

- America offers a refuge for people fleeing oppression.

The New Colossus

by **Emma Lazarus**

Read with a Purpose

Read this poem to discover how one writer compares the Statue of Liberty with the ancient statue of the Colossus.

Build Background

In 1886, the Statue of Liberty, a gift from France to the United States, was erected in New York Harbor. In 1903, a poem by Emma Lazarus called "The New Colossus" was engraved on a bronze plaque that was placed inside the pedestal of the statue. The title of the poem refers to the Colossus, a huge bronze (or brazen) statue of the Greek god Helios that towered over the harbor of the Greek city of Rhodes from 280 to 225 B.C.

Not like the brazen giant of Greek fame,
With conquering limbs astride from land to land;
Here at our sea-washed, sunset gates shall stand
A mighty woman with a torch, whose flame
5 Is the imprisoned lightning, and her name
Mother of Exiles. From her beacon-hand **A**
Glows world-wide welcome; her mild eyes command
The air-bridged harbor that twin cities frame.
"Keep, ancient lands, your storied pomp[1]!" cries she
10 With silent lips. "Give me your tired, your poor,
Your huddled masses yearning to breathe free,
The wretched refuse[2] of your teeming shore.
Send these, the homeless, tempest-tost[3] to me.
I lift my lamp beside the golden door!" **B**

---

1. **pomp:** splendor; magnificence.
2. **refuse** (REHF yoos): something useless or unwanted.
3. **tempest-tost:** upset by storm. *Tempest* here refers to other hardships as well.

A Read and Discuss What is the poet talking about here? What is she saying about the two statues?

B Literary Focus Recurring Themes What aspect of the American Dream is suggested by the words Lazarus attributes to the Statue of Liberty?

Vocabulary **yearning** (YURN ihng) *v.* used as *adj.:* longing for; wanting badly.
teeming (TEEM ihng) *adj.:* full (in this case, of people); crowded.

Applying Your Skills

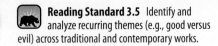

Reading Standard 3.5 Identify and analyze recurring themes (e.g., good versus evil) across traditional and contemporary works.

The New Colossus

Literary Response and Analysis

Reading Skills Focus
Quick Check

1. In lines 3-8, how does the speaker describe the statue that stands at New York's "gates"?

2. According to lines 9-14, what does the statue seem to say?

3. Whom is the statue talking to? What line tells you?

Read with a Purpose

4. What do you think is Lazarus's intent in comparing the "old Colossus" with the new one?

Reading Skills: Finding Recurring Themes

5. Think about what the poem, particularly the statue's words to people coming to the United States, reveals about the American Dream. In the chart below, write down what the poem says about that dream.

	Expressions of the American Dream
"The New Colossus"	

✓ Vocabulary Check

Fill in the blanks with the correct Vocabulary word.

> yearning   teeming

6. The Statue of Liberty welcomes the _____ masses from other lands, those who are _____ to find a better life.

Literary Skills Focus
Literary Analysis

7. **Interpret** In the late 1800s, immigrants from Europe poured into America. What do you think the statue means when she tells these countries to keep their "storied pomp"? Explain your interpretation.

8. **Extend** The statue calls the people coming to American "huddled masses." What do you think they long for?

9. **Analyze** How does Lazarus's use of **personification** (giving human traits to something nonhuman) affect your understanding of what the Statue of Liberty represents?

Literary Skills: Recurring Themes

10. **Interpret** What do the statue's words to people coming to the United States reveal about the American dream? What do the words suggest about the poem's theme? What symbols does Lazarus use to make her message evident?

Writing Skills Focus
Think as a Reader/Writer

Use It in Your Writing Look back at your notes in your *Reader/Writer Notebook*. What words and phrases evoked the strongest emotions in you? Write a paragraph in which you explain why these examples are significant. What ideas do you connect with the words?

REFUGEE IN AMERICA

by **Langston Hughes**

Read with a Purpose

Read this poem to see how its speaker feels about the American dream of freedom and liberty.

Preparing to Read for this selection is on page 399.

Build Background

This poem about the American Dream was written around 1943, before the Civil Rights Movement of the 1950s and 1960s. The Civil Rights Movement led to increased liberties for African Americans. For example, the Civil Rights Act of 1964 made discrimination based on race, religion, or national origin illegal. The Voting Rights Act of 1965 was designed to stop tactics used to keep African Americans from voting.

There are words like *Freedom*
Sweet and wonderful to say.
On my heart-strings freedom sings
All day everyday.

There are words like *Liberty*
That almost make me cry.
If you had known what I knew
You would know why.

A Literary Focus Recurring
Themes What is a refugee? What does the title suggest about this poem's theme?

B Read and Discuss What does the speaker want you to understand?

Applying Your Skills

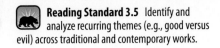

Reading Standard 3.5 Identify and analyze recurring themes (e.g., good versus evil) across traditional and contemporary works.

Refugee in America
Literary Response and Analysis

Reading Skills Focus
Read with a Purpose

1. What words does the speaker use to describe the word *freedom* in stanza 1?

2. What happens to the speaker when he hears the word *liberty*?

Reading Skills: Finding Recurring Themes

3. In the chart that follows, write down your answers to these questions:

   - Which aspects of the American Dream does the speaker of this poem refer to?
   - What does he think America promises us?
   - What does he think about the way America has kept that promise?

   Add any other ideas you have about the way the poem comments on the American Dream. After you respond to the next selection, your chart will be complete with details from all three texts.

	Expressions of the American Dream
"The New Colossus"	
"Refugee in America"	

Literary Skills Focus
Literary Analysis

4. **Interpret** The word *refugee* typically refers to a displaced person or someone without a country. The title of this poem suggests that the speaker sees himself as a refugee. Why does the speaker consider himself a refugee in his own country?

5. **Analyze** The speaker has different reactions to two words that mean nearly the same thing. Do you see any differences in meaning between the words *freedom* and *liberty*? Explain.

6. **Interpret** What do you think the speaker means by the words "If you had known what I knew / You would know why"?

Literary Skills: Recurring Themes

7. **Interpret** One aspect of the American Dream is a belief in freedom, equality, and respect for all people. What recurring theme does this poem convey about the American Dream?

Writing Skills Focus
Think as a Reader/Writer

Use It in Your Writing Which words or phrases in this poem made a strong impression on you? Choose a word or phrase from the poems, and write your own poem that explores some ideas you associate with that word or phrase.

THE FIRST AMERICANS

The Grand Council Fire of American Indians

December 1, 1927

Read with a Purpose

Read this speech to find out how some American Indians felt about their portrayal in textbooks.

Preparing to Read for this selection is on page 399.

Build Background

In 1927, an organization called the Grand Council Fire of American Indians sent a group of representatives from the Chippewa, Ottawa, Navajo, Sioux, and Winnebago peoples to address the mayor of Chicago. Their goal was to persuade him that American Indians should be more fairly and accurately represented in textbooks and classrooms. Mayor William Hale Thompson, who had been reelected just a month before the council met with him, had campaigned on the slogan "America First." (Thompson opposed U.S. involvement in world affairs and claimed that the British government influenced the U.S. government's policies.) "The First Americans" comments on this and other patriotic slogans of the time, which excluded many Americans from the American Dream.

To the mayor of Chicago:
You tell all white men "America First." We believe in that. We are the only ones, truly, that are one hundred percent. We therefore ask you, while you are teaching schoolchildren about America First, teach them truth about the First Americans. **Ⓐ**

We do not know if school histories are pro-British, but we do know that they are unjust to the life of our people—the American Indian. They call all white victories battles and all Indian victories massacres.

The battle with Custer[1] has been taught to schoolchildren as a fearful massacre on our part. We ask that this, as well as other incidents, be told fairly. If the Custer battle was a massacre, what was Wounded Knee?[2]

---

1. **battle with Custer:** the Battle of the Little Bighorn, which took place in 1876 in what is now Montana. General George A. Custer (1839–1876) led an attack on an American Indian village and was killed along with all of his troops by Sioux and Cheyenne forces.

2. **Wounded Knee:** Wounded Knee Creek, in South Dakota, was the site of a battle in 1890 between U.S. soldiers and Sioux whom they had captured. The U.S. soldiers killed about two hundred Sioux men, women, and children.

Ⓐ **Read and Discuss** What does the slogan "America First" mean to the Grand Council? What does it mean to the mayor? (See Build Background.)

Ben Nighthorse Campbell, a Colorado congressman (1992–2004) and a Northern Cheyenne chief.

History books teach that Indians were murderers—is it murder to fight in self-defense? Indians killed white men because white men took their lands, ruined their hunting grounds, burned their forests, destroyed their buffalo. White men penned[3] our people on reservations, then took away the reservations. White men who rise to protect their property are called patriots—Indians who do the same are called murderers.

---

3. **penned:** confined or enclosed. (A pen is a fenced area where animals are kept.)

White men call Indians treacherous—but no mention is made of broken treaties on the part of the white man. White men say that Indians were always fighting. It was only our lack of skill in white man's warfare that led to our defeat. An Indian mother prayed that her boy be a great medicine man rather than a great warrior. It is true that we had our own small battles, but in the main we were peace loving and home loving. **B**

White men called Indians thieves—and yet we lived in frail skin lodges and needed no locks or iron bars. White men

Vocabulary   patriots (PAY tree uhts) *n.:* people who love and support their country.

B **Reading Focus** Finding Recurring Themes
Compare this speaker's concerns with those of the speaker in Hughes's poem. How are their situations different? How are they similar?

call Indians savages. What is civilization? Its marks are a noble religion and philosophy, original arts, stirring music, rich story and legend. We had these. Then we were not savages, but a civilized race.

We made blankets that were beautiful, that the white man with all his machinery has never been able to duplicate. We made baskets that were beautiful. We wove in beads and colored quills designs that were not just decorative motifs but were the outward expression of our very thoughts. We made pottery—pottery that was useful, and beautiful as well. Why not make schoolchildren acquainted with the beautiful handicrafts in which we were skilled? Put in every school Indian blankets, baskets, pottery.

We sang songs that carried in their melodies all the sounds of nature—the running of waters, the sighing of winds, and the calls of the animals. Teach these to your children that they may come to love nature as we love it.

We had our statesmen—and their oratory[4] has never been equaled. Teach the children some of these speeches of our people, remarkable for their brilliant oratory.

---

4. **oratory** (AWR uh tawr ee): skill in public speaking; the art of public speaking.

We played games—games that brought good health and sound bodies. Why not put these in your schools? We told stories. Why not teach schoolchildren more of the wholesome proverbs and legends of our people? Tell them how we loved all that was beautiful. That we killed game only for food, not for fun. Indians think white men who kill for fun are murderers. **G**

Tell your children of the friendly acts of Indians to the white people who first settled here. Tell them of our leaders and heroes and their deeds. Tell them of Indians such as Black Partridge, Shabbona, and others who many times saved the people of Chicago at great danger to themselves. Put in your history books the Indian's part in the World War. Tell how the Indian fought for a country of which he was not a citizen, for a flag to which he had no claim, and for a people that have treated him unjustly.

The Indian has long been hurt by these unfair books. We ask only that our story be told in fairness. We do not ask you to overlook what we did, but we do ask you to understand it. A true program of America First will give a generous place to the culture and history of the American Indian.

We ask this, Chief, to keep sacred the memory of our people.

G Read and Discuss | What would history books' including examples of American Indian weavings, baskets, songs, speeches, games, and heroic actions show readers?

Vocabulary   wholesome (HOHL suhm) *adj.:* good for the mind and spirit.

Applying Your Skills

The First Americans

Literary Response and Analysis

Reading Skills Focus
Quick Check

1. What is the intent of this speech?
2. What does the council recommend that children be taught? Why?

Read with a Purpose

3. How do the speakers feel about their portrayal in textbooks?

Reading Skills: Finding Recurring Themes

4. In the chart below, write down how this speech reflects the American Dream. Be sure to consider the information presented in the box on page 400. You'll use your finished chart, including the notes you added after reading "The New Colossus" and "Refugee in America," to plan an essay comparing views on the American Dream expressed in these three texts.

	Expressions of the American Dream
"The New Colossus"	
"Refugee in America"	
"The First Americans"	

✓ Vocabulary Check

Include the boldface Vocabulary words in your answers to the questions below. Refer to a dictionary if you need help.

5. What actions might **patriots** take?
6. What is an example of a **wholesome** food?

Literary Skills Focus
Literary Analysis

7. **Analyze** A **stereotype** is a fixed idea about a group of people; for example, the statement "Athletes are not intellectual" reflects a stereotype. Stereotypes are often offensive. What stereotypes about American Indians does the speaker address in this speech?

8. **Infer** What can you infer from the fact that a council had to be formed to request that positive aspects of Native American life be included in history books?

9. **Extend** This speech was delivered in 1927. Which of its suggestions, if any, have been put into effect? Explain.

10. **Connect** The writers of the speech mention the importance of appreciating their peoples' blankets, pottery, and other handicrafts. How can art be a symbol of a culture?

Literary Skills: Recurring Themes

11. **Analyze** Most works reveal themes about more than one topic. What theme does "The First Americans" reveal about each of the following topics:

- history
- education
- citizenship

Writing Skills Focus
Think as a Reader/Writer

Use It in Your Writing Think of an issue about which you feel strongly. Write a short persuasive essay to convince others to agree with your view. Try to include language that will evoke an emotional response from your readers.

Reading Standard 3.5 Identify and analyze recurring themes (e.g., good versus evil) across traditional and contemporary works.

The New Colossus / Refugee in America / The First Americans

Writing Skills Focus
Writing a Comparison-Contrast Essay

Write an essay of four paragraphs comparing views of the American Dream expressed in "The New Colussus," "Refugee in America," and "The First Americans." To find points of comparison for your essay, review the chart you filled in after you read each selection. Also check the box on page 400 that lists aspects of the American Dream.

Organize your essay in the following way:

Paragraph 1: Explain how "The New Colussus" reflects the American Dream.

Paragraph 2: Explain how "Refugee in America" reflects the American Dream.

Paragraph 3: Explain how "The First Americans" reflects the American Dream.

Paragraph 4: Describe your response, whether positive or negative, to one of the selections.

Ask yourself the following questions as you revise your essay.

- Did I state my main idea clearly?
- Did I include details and examples that support my main points?
- Is the organization of my essay easy to follow, with transitional words or phrases for clarity?

What Do **You Think Now** How have these selections affected your impression of the American Dream?

CHOICES

As you respond to the Choices, use these **Academic Vocabulary** words as appropriate: contemporary, evident, insight, significant, traditional.

REVIEW
Evaluate Theme

Timed ⏲ Writing Review the chart you completed as you read the three selections. Which selection's expression of the American Dream is most similar to your own ideas? Write a paragraph in which you explain why you agree with the selection's insights.

CONNECT
Present an Oral Reading

Listening and Speaking Prepare "The New Colossus" or "Refugee in America" for an oral presentation. Before you begin, copy the selection onto a piece of paper. Note the punctuation marks that indicate where you should pause briefly and where you should come to a complete stop. Use your voice to express your interpretation of the poem.

EXTEND
Create a Web Site

TechFocus Using history texts and reliable Internet sites, research the Statue of Liberty's history. Create a Web site for your findings, including text, pictures, and sound files.

Treatment, Scope, and Organization of Ideas

Visitors to the Auschwitz Museum in Poland view photographs of people who were killed by the Nazis.

CONTENTS

What Do
You
Think ? **How do historical tragedies continue to shape the world we live in?**

 QuickTalk

With a small group of classmates, discuss a recent large-scale tragedy that you've seen on the news or read about. How did it affect you? How will memories of it affect future generations?

MAGAZINE ARTICLE
Preparing to Read

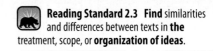

Reading Standard 2.3 Find similarities and differences between texts in **the** treatment, scope, or **organization of ideas**.

A Tragedy Revealed: A Heroine's Last Days

Informational Text Focus

Comparing Organizational Patterns Recognizing how a writer of an informational text has organized his or her ideas will help you understand what you read. Writers may not use the same organizational pattern throughout an entire text. Pay attention to where and why the pattern of organization changes for important clues to the writer's ideas. Here are some of the organizational patterns you will find in this article.

- **chronological,** or **sequential, order**—putting events or steps in the order in which they occur; also called **time order.**
- **order of importance**—presenting supporting details in order of least to most important or from most to least important.
- **logical order**—arranging into related groups so that their connections are clear. For example, a movie review may discuss the plot, then characters, then the soundtrack.

Into Action This article contains a **chronological** account of what happened to Anne Frank and the other residents of the Secret Annex after their arrest by the Gestapo. Draw a time line that shows what Ernst Schnabel discovered. Start with 1942 and end with March 1945. Use a format like the one shown below.

Time Line of Events

1942   1945
| |
Franks
forced into
hiding in the
Netherlands

Writing Skills Focus

Preparing for Timed ⌐Writing As you read, think about Anne's statement that "people are really good at heart." Record your thoughts in your *Reader/Writer Notebook*.

Reader/Writer
Notebook

Use your **RWN** to complete the activities for this selection.

Language Coach

Oral Fluency Because most of the Vocabulary words have many syllables, they may seem hard to pronounce. Use the pronunciation guide in parentheses to sound out each word. The capital letters indicate which syllable gets the most stress.

Learn It Online

Learn more about organizational patterns online at:

go.hrw.com | H8-411 | Go

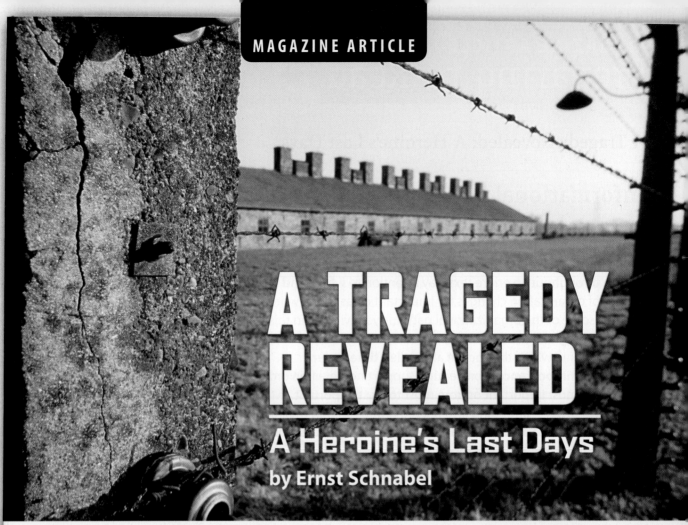

A TRAGEDY REVEALED

A Heroine's Last Days

by Ernst Schnabel

Close-up of the barbed-wire fence at the Auschwitz-Birkenau concentration camp.

Read with a Purpose

Read this article to find out what happened to Anne Frank after she was taken prisoner.

L ast year in Amsterdam I found an old reel of movie film on which Anne Frank appears. She is seen for only ten seconds and it is an accident that she is there at all.

The film was taken for a wedding in 1941, the year before Anne Frank and seven others went into hiding in their "Secret Annex." It has a flickering, Chaplinesque[1] quality, with people popping suddenly in and out of doorways, the nervous smiles and hurried waves of the departing bride and groom.

Then, for just a moment, the camera seems uncertain where to look. It darts to the right, then to the left, then whisks up a wall, and into view comes a window crowded with people waving after the departing automobiles. The camera swings

1. **Chaplinesque** (chap lih NEHSK): like the old silent movies starring Charlie Chaplin (1889–1977).

farther to the left, to another window. There a girl stands alone, looking out into space. It is Anne Frank.

Just as the camera is about to pass on, the child moves her head a trifle. Her face flits more into focus, her hair shimmers in the sun. At this moment she discovers the camera, discovers the photographer, discovers us watching seventeen years later, and laughs at all of us, laughs with sudden merriment and surprise and embarrassment all at the same time.

I asked the projectionist to stop the film for a moment so that we could stand up to examine her face more closely. The smile stood still, just above our heads. But when I walked forward close to the screen, the smile ceased to be a smile. The face ceased to be a face, for the canvas screen was granular and the beam of light split into a multitude of tiny shadows, as if it had been scattered on a sandy plain. **Ⓐ**

Anne Frank, of course, is gone too, but her spirit has remained to stir the conscience of the world. Her remarkable diary has been read in almost every language. I have seen a letter from a teenaged girl in Japan who says she thinks of Anne's Secret Annex as her second home. And the play based on the diary has been a great success wherever it is produced. German audiences, who invariably greet the final curtain of *The Diary of Anne Frank* in stricken silence, have jammed the theaters in what seems almost a national act of penance.

Last year I set out to follow the fading trail of this girl who has become a legend. The trail led from Holland to Poland and back to Germany, where I visited the moss-grown site of the old Bergen-Belsen concentration camp at the village of Belsen and saw the common graves shared by Anne Frank and thirty thousand others. I interviewed forty-two people who knew Anne or who survived the ordeal that killed her. Some had known her intimately in those last tragic months. In the recollections of others she appears only for a moment. But even these fragments fulfill a promise. They make explicit a truth implied in the diary. As we somehow knew she must be, Anne Frank, even in the most frightful extremity, was indomitable. **Ⓑ**

The known story contained in the diary is a simple one of human relationships, of the poignant maturing of a perceptive girl who is thirteen when her diary begins and only fifteen when it ends. It is a story without violence, though its background is the most dreadful act of violence in the history of man, Hitler's annihilation of six million European Jews.

In the summer of 1942, Anne Frank, her father, her mother, her older sister, Margot, and four others were forced into hiding during the Nazi occupation of Holland. Their

---

Ⓐ **Informational Focus** Organization In your own words, describe how Schnabel uses order of importance to describe Anne's appearance in the film.

Ⓑ **Read and Discuss** What point about Anne Frank is the author making?

Vocabulary annihilation (uh ny uh LAY shuhn) *n*.: complete destruction.

refuge was a tiny apartment they called the Secret Annex, in the back of an Amsterdam office building. For twenty-five months the Franks, the Van Daan family, and later a dentist, Albert Dussel,[2] lived in the Secret Annex, protected from the Gestapo[3] only by a swinging bookcase which masked the entrance to their hiding place and by the heroism of a few Christians who knew they were there. Anne Frank's diary recounts the daily pressures of their cramped existence: the hushed silences when strangers were in the building, the diminishing food supply, the fear of fire from the incessant Allied air raids, the hopes for an early invasion, above all the dread of capture by the pitiless men who were hunting Jews from house to house and sending them to concentration camps. Anne's diary also describes with sharp insight and youthful humor the bickerings, the wounded pride, the tearful reconciliations of the eight human beings in the Secret Annex. It tells of Anne's wishes for the understanding of her adored father, of her despair at the gulf between her mother and herself, of her tremulous and growing love for young Peter Van Daan.

The actual diary ends with an entry for August 1, 1944, in which Anne Frank, addressing her imaginary friend Kitty, talks of her impatience with her own unpredictable personality. The stage version goes further: It attempts to reconstruct something of the events of August 4, 1944, the day the Secret Annex was violated and its occupants finally taken into a captivity from which only one returned.

What really happened on that August day fourteen years ago was far less dramatic than what is now depicted on the stage. The automobiles did not approach with howling sirens, did not stop with screaming brakes in front of the house on the Prinsengracht canal in Amsterdam. No rifle butt pounded against the door until it reverberated, as it now does in the theater every night somewhere in the world. The truth was, at first, that no one heard a sound. **C**

It was midmorning on a bright summer day. In the hidden apartment behind the secret bookcase there was a scene of relaxed domesticity. The Franks, the Van Daans, and Mr. Dussel had finished a poor breakfast of ersatz[4] coffee and bread. Mrs. Frank and Mrs. Van Daan were about to clear the table. Mr. Van Daan, Margot Frank, and Mr. Dussel were resting or reading. Anne Frank was very likely at work on one of the short stories she often wrote when she was not busy with her diary or her novel. In Peter Van Daan's tiny attic room Otto Frank was

---

2. **Van Daan . . . Dussel:** In her diary, Anne made up names. The Van Daans were really named Van Pels, and Albert Dussel was really Fritz Pfeffer.

3. **Gestapo** (guh STAH poh): Nazi secret police force, known for its use of terror.

4. **ersatz** (ehr ZAHTS): artificial. Regular coffee was unavailable because of severe wartime shortages.

C **Informational Focus** Organization   What three accounts is Schnabel comparing in this paragraph and in the preceding one?

Analyzing Visuals **Connecting to the Text** What might it have been like to hide in the midst of a busy city such as this?

Front of Anne Frank House, Amsterdam, the Netherlands.

chiding the eighteen-year-old boy for an error in his English lesson. "Why, Peter," Mr. Frank was saying, "you know that *double* is spelled with only one *b*."

In the main part of the building four other people, two men and two women, were working at their regular jobs. For more than two years these four had risked their lives to protect their friends in the hide-out, supplied them with food, and brought them news of a world from which they had disappeared. One of the women was Miep, who had just got married a few months earlier. The other was Elli, a pretty typist of twenty-three. The men were Kraler and Koophuis,[5]

middle-aged spice merchants who had been business associates of Otto Frank's before the occupation. Mr. Kraler was working in one office by himself. Koophuis and the two women were in another.

I spoke to Miep, Elli, and Mr. Koophuis in Amsterdam. The two women had not been arrested after the raid on the Secret Annex. Koophuis had been released in poor health after a few weeks in prison, and

---

5. **Kraler and Koophuis:** The author continues to use Anne's made-up names. Kraler and Koophuis were really named Victor Kugler and Johannes Kleiman.

Kraler, who now lives in Canada, had eventually escaped from a forced labor camp.

Elli, now a mother, whose coloring and plump good looks are startlingly like those of the young women painted by the Dutch masters,[6] recalled: "I was posting entries in the receipts book when a car drove up in front of the house. But cars often stopped, after all. Then the front door opened, and someone came up the stairs. I wondered who it could be. We often had callers. Only this time I could hear that there were several men. . . ."

Miep, a delicate, intelligent, still young-looking woman, said: "The footsteps moved along the corridor. Then a door creaked, and a moment later the connecting door to Mr. Kraler's office opened, and a fat man thrust his head in and said in Dutch: 'Quiet. Stay in your seats.' I started and at first did not know what was happening. But then, suddenly, I knew."

Mr. Koophuis is now in very poor health, a gaunt, white-haired man in his sixties. He added: "I suppose I did not hear them because of the rumbling of the spice mills in the warehouse. The fat man's head was the first thing I knew. He came in and planted himself in front of us. 'You three stay here, understand?' he barked. So we stayed in the office and listened as someone else went upstairs, and doors rattled, and then there were footsteps everywhere. They searched the whole building." **D**

Mr. Kraler wrote me this account from Toronto: "A uniformed staff sergeant of the Occupation Police[7] and three men in civilian clothes entered my office. They wanted to see the storerooms in the front part of the building. All will be well, I thought, if they don't want to see anything else. But after the sergeant had looked at everything, he went out into the corridor, ordering me again to come along. At the end of the corridor they drew their revolvers all at once and the sergeant ordered me to push aside the bookcase and open the door behind it. I said: 'But there's only a bookcase there!' At that he turned nasty, for he knew everything. He took hold of the bookcase and pulled. It yielded and the secret door was exposed. Perhaps the hooks had not been properly fastened. They opened the door and I had to precede them up the steps. The policemen followed me. I could feel their pistols in my back. I was the first to enter the Franks' room. Mrs. Frank was standing at the table. I made a great effort and managed to say: 'The Gestapo is here.'" **E**

Otto Frank, now sixty-eight, has remarried and lives in Switzerland. Of the eight who lived in the Secret Annex, he is the

---

6. **Dutch masters:** seventeenth-century painters, including Rembrandt, Frans Hals (frahns hahls), and Jan Vermeer (yahn vuhr MEHR).

7. **Occupation Police:** police organized by the German forces while they occupied the Netherlands.

D [Informational Focus] Organization Schnabel presents Mr. Frank's account last. What organizational pattern is he using in this section?

E [Read and Discuss] What is happening here? What mood has been created by these accounts?

only survivor. A handsome, soft-spoken man of obviously great intelligence, he regularly answers correspondence that comes to him about his daughter from all over the world. He recently went to Hollywood for consultation on the movie version of *The Diary of Anne Frank*. About the events of that August morning in 1944 Mr. Frank told me: "I was showing Peter Van Daan his spelling mistakes when suddenly someone came running up the stairs. The steps creaked, and I started to my feet, for it was morning, when everyone was supposed to be quiet. But then the door flew open and a man stood before us holding his pistol aimed at my chest.

"In the main room the others were already assembled. My wife and the chil-dren and Van Daans were standing there with raised hands. Then Albert Dussel came in, followed by another stranger. In the middle of the room stood a uniformed policeman. He stared into our faces.

"'Where are your valuables?' he asked. I pointed to the cupboard where my cash box was kept. The policeman took it out. Then he looked around and his eye fell on the leather briefcase where Anne kept her diary and all her papers. He opened it and shook everything out, dumped the contents on the floor so that Anne's papers and notebooks and loose sheets lay scattered at our feet. No one spoke, and the policeman didn't even glance at the mess on the floor as he put our valuables into the briefcase and closed it. He asked us whether we had

The common living room, dining room, and room of the Van Pels family in the Anne Frank House.

any weapons. But we had none, of course. Then he said, 'Get ready.'"

Who betrayed the occupants of the Secret Annex? No one is sure, but some suspicion centers on a man I can only call M., whom the living remember as a crafty and disagreeable sneak. He was a warehouse clerk hired after the Franks moved into the building, and he was never told of their presence. M. used to come to work early in the mornings, and he once found a locked briefcase which Mr. Van Daan had carelessly left in the office, where he sometimes worked in the dead of night. Though Kraler claimed it was his own briefcase, it is possible the clerk suspected. Little signs lead to bigger conclusions. In the course of the months he had worked in the building, M. might have gathered many such signs: the dial on the office radio left at BBC[8] by nocturnal listeners, slight rearrangements in the office furniture, and, of course, small inexplicable sounds from the back of the building.

M. was tried later by a war crimes court, denied everything, and was acquitted. No one knows where he is now. I made no effort to find him. Neither did I search out Silberthaler, the German police sergeant who made the arrest. The betrayers would have told me nothing. **F**

Ironically enough, the occupants of the Secret Annex had grown optimistic in the last weeks of their self-imposed confinement. The terrors of those first nights had largely faded. Even the German army communiqués[9] made clear that the war was approaching an end. The Russians were well into Poland. On the Western front Americans had broken through at Avranches and were pouring into the heart of France. Holland must be liberated soon. In her diary Anne Frank wrote that she thought she might be back in school by fall.

Now they were all packing. Of the capture Otto Frank recalled: "No one wept. Anne was very quiet and composed, only just as dispirited as the rest of us. Perhaps that was why she did not think to take along her notebooks, which lay scattered about on the floor. But maybe she too had the premonition that all was lost now, everything, and so she walked back and forth and did not even glance at her diary."

As the captives filed out of the building, Miep sat listening. "I heard them going," she said, "first in the corridor and then down the stairs. I could hear the heavy boots and the footsteps, and then the very light footsteps of Anne. Through the years she had taught herself to walk so softly that you

---

8. **BBC:** British Broadcasting Corporation.

9. **communiqués** (kuh myoo nih KAYZ): official bulletins.

F **Read and Discuss** What theory does Schnabel present here?

Vocabulary **inexplicable** (ihn ihk SPLIHK uh buhl) *adj.:* unable to be explained.
premonition (prehm uh NIHSH uhn) *n.:* feeling that something will happen.

could hear her only if you knew what to listen for. I did not see her, for the office door was closed as they all passed by."

At Gestapo headquarters the prisoners were interrogated only briefly. As Otto Frank pointed out to his questioners, it was unlikely, after twenty-five months in the Secret Annex, that he would know the whereabouts of any other Jews who were hiding in Amsterdam.

The Franks, the Van Daans, and Dussel were kept at police headquarters for several days, the men in one cell, the women in the other. They were relatively comfortable there. The food was better than the food they had had in the Secret Annex and the guards left them alone.

Suddenly, all eight were taken to the railroad station and put on a train. The guards named their destination: Westerbork, a concentration camp for Jews in Holland, about eighty miles from Amsterdam. Mr. Frank said: "We rode in a regular passenger train. The fact that the door was bolted did not matter very much. We were together and had been given a little food for the journey. We were actually cheerful. Cheerful, at least, when I compare that journey to our next. We had already anticipated the possibility that we might not remain in Westerbork to the end. We knew what was happening to Jews in Auschwitz. But weren't the Russians already deep into Poland? We hoped our luck would hold.

"As we rode, Anne would not move from the window. It was summer outside. Meadows, stubble fields, and villages flew by. The telephone wires along the right of way curved up and down along the windows. After two years it was like freedom for her. Can you understand that?"

Among the names given me of survivors who had known the Franks at Westerbork was that of a Mrs. de Wiek, who lives in Apeldoorn, Holland. I visited Mrs. de Wiek in her home. A lovely, gracious woman, she told me that her family, like the Franks, had been in hiding for months before their capture. She said: "We had been at Westerbork three or four weeks when the word went around that there were new arrivals. News of that kind ran like wildfire through the camp, and my daughter Judy came running to me, calling, 'New people are coming, Mama!'

"The newcomers were standing in a long row in the mustering square,[10] and one of the clerks was entering their names on a list. We looked at them, and Judy pressed close against me. Most of the people in the camp were adults, and I had often wished for a

> **Who betrayed the occupants of the Secret Annex? No one is sure.**

---

10. **mustering square:** place of assembly for inspection and roll call.

young friend for Judy, who was only fifteen. As I looked along the line, fearing I might see someone I knew, I suddenly exclaimed, 'Judy, see!'

"In the long line stood eight people whose faces, white as paper, told you at once that they had been hiding and had not been in the open air for years. Among them was this girl. And I said to Judy, 'Look, there is a friend for you.'

"I saw Anne Frank and Peter Van Daan every day in Westerbork. They were always together, and I often said to my husband, 'Look at those two beautiful young people.'

"Anne was so radiant that her beauty flowed over into Peter. Her eyes glowed and her movements had a lilt to them. She was very pallid at first, but there was some-

(above) A women's barracks in the Auschwitz-Birkenau concentration camp. (right) The personal effects forced from the people deported to Auschwitz around 1945, covering the train tracks leading to the camp's entrance.

Analyzing Visuals

Connecting to the Text
How do you think Anne and Peter could be considered beautiful in such oppressive conditions?

thing so attractive about her frailty and her expressive face that at first Judy was too shy to make friends.

"Anne was happy there, incredible as it seems. Things were hard for us in the camp. We 'convict Jews' who had been arrested in hiding places had to wear blue overalls with a red bib and wooden shoes. Our men had their heads shaved. Three hundred people lived in each barracks. We were sent to work at five in the morning, the children to a cable workshop and the grown-ups to a shed where we had to break up old batteries and salvage the metal and the carbon rods. The food was bad, we were always kept on the run, and the guards all screamed 'Faster, faster!' But Anne was happy. It was as if she had been liberated. Now she could see new people and talk to them and could laugh. She could laugh while the rest of us thought nothing but: Will they send us to the camps in Poland? Will we live through it?

"Edith Frank, Anne's mother, seemed numbed by the experience. She could have been a mute. Anne's sister Margot spoke little and Otto Frank was quiet too, but his was a reassuring quietness that helped Anne and all of us. He lived in the men's barracks, but once when Anne was sick, he came over to visit her every evening and would stand beside her bed for hours, telling her stories. Anne was so like him. When another child, a twelve-year-old boy named David, fell ill, Anne stood by his bed and talked to him. David came from an Orthodox family, and he and Anne always talked about God." **G**

Anne Frank stayed at Westerbork only three weeks. Early in September a thousand of the "convict Jews" were put on a freight train, seventy-five people to a car. Brussels fell to the Allies, then Antwerp, then the Americans reached Aachen. But the victories were coming too late. The Franks and their friends were already on the way to Auschwitz, the camp in Poland where four million Jews died.

Mrs. de Wiek was in the same freight car as the Franks on that journey from Westerbork to Auschwitz. "Now and then when the train stopped," she told me, "the SS guards[11] came to the door and held out their caps and we had to toss our money and valuables into the caps. Anne and Judy sometimes pulled themselves up to the small barred window of the car and described the villages we were passing through. We made the children repeat the addresses where we could meet after the war if we became separated in the camp. I remember that the Franks chose a meeting place in Switzerland.

"I sat beside my husband on a small box. On the third day in the train, my husband suddenly took my hand and said, 'I want to thank you for the wonderful life we have had together.'

"I snatched my hand away from his, crying, 'What are you thinking about? It's not over!'

---

11. **SS guards:** Nazi special police, who ran the concentration camps.

G **Read and Discuss** What information does Mrs. de Wiek give about the Franks?

"But he calmly reached for my hand again and took it and repeated several times, 'Thank you. Thank you for the life we have had together.' Then I left my hand in his and did not try to draw it away."

On the third night, the train stopped, the doors of the car slid violently open, and the first the exhausted passengers saw of Auschwitz was the glaring searchlights fixed on the train. On the platform, kapos (criminal convicts who were assigned to positions of authority over the other prisoners) were running back and forth shouting orders. Behind them, seen distinctly against the light, stood the SS officers, trimly built and smartly uniformed, many of them with huge dogs at their sides. As the people poured out of the train, a loudspeaker roared, "Women to the left! Men to the right!"

Mrs. de Wiek went on calmly: "I saw them all as they went away, Mr. Van Daan and Mr. Dussel and Peter and Mr. Frank. But I saw no sign of my husband. He had vanished. I never saw him again.

"'Listen!' the loudspeaker bawled again. 'It is an hour's march to the women's camp. For the children and the sick there are trucks waiting at the end of the platform.'

"We could see the trucks," Mrs. de Wiek said. "They were painted with big red crosses. We all made a rush for them.

> "Thank you. Thank you for the life we have had together."

Who among us was not sick after those days on the train? But we did not reach them. People were still hanging on to the backs of the trucks as they started off. Not one person who went along on that ride ever arrived at the women's camp, and no one has ever found any trace of them."

Mrs. de Wiek, her daughter, Mrs. Van Daan, Mrs. Frank, Margot, and Anne survived the brutal pace of the night march to the women's camp at Auschwitz. Next day their heads were shaved; they learned that the hair was useful as packing for pipe joints in U-boats.[12] Then the women were put to work digging sods of grass, which they placed in great piles. As they labored each day, thousands of others were dispatched with maniacal efficiency in the gas chambers, and smoke rising from the stacks of the huge crematoriums[13] blackened the sky.

Mrs. de Wiek saw Anne Frank every day at Auschwitz. "Anne seemed even more beautiful there," Mrs. de Wiek said, "than she had at Westerbork. Of course her long hair was gone, but now you could see that her beauty was in her eyes, which seemed to grow bigger as she grew thinner. Her gaiety had vanished, but she was still alert and

---

12. **U-boats:** submarines.
13. **crematoriums** (kree muh TAWR ee uhmz): furnaces in which prisoners' bodies were cremated (burned to ashes).

The Blind of Theresienstadt by Leo Haas. Watercolor.

sweet, and with her charm she sometimes secured things that the rest of us had long since given up hoping for.

"For example, we each had only a gray sack to wear. But when the weather turned cold, Anne came in one day wearing a suit of men's long underwear. She had begged it somewhere. She looked screamingly funny with those long white legs but somehow still delightful.

"Though she was the youngest, Anne was the leader in her group of five people. She also gave out the bread to everyone in the barracks and she did it so fairly there was none of the usual grumbling.

"We were always thirsty at Auschwitz, so thirsty that at roll call we would stick out our tongues if it happened to be raining or snowing, and many became sick from bad water. Once, when I was almost dead because there was nothing to drink, Anne suddenly came to me with a cup of coffee. To this day I don't know where she got it.

"In the barracks many people were dying, some of starvation, others of weakness and despair. It was almost impossible not to give up hope, and when a person gave up, his face became empty and dead. The Polish woman doctor who had been caring for the sick said to me, 'You will pull through. You still have your face.'

"Anne Frank, too, still had her face, up to the very last. To the last also she was moved by the dreadful things the rest of us had somehow become hardened to. Who bothered to look when the flames shot up into the sky at night from the crematoriums? Who was troubled that every day new people were being selected and gassed? Most of us were beyond feeling. But not Anne. I can still see her standing at the door and looking down the camp street as a group of naked Gypsy girls were driven by on their way to the crematorium. Anne watched them going and cried. And she also cried when we marched past the Hungarian children who had been waiting half a day in the rain in front of the gas chambers. And Anne nudged me and said, 'Look, look! Their eyes!' Anne cried. And you cannot imagine how soon most of us came to the end of our tears." **Ⓗ**

Late in October the SS selected the healthiest of the women prisoners for work in a munitions factory in Czechoslovakia. Judy de Wiek was taken from her mother, but Anne and her sister Margot were rejected because they had contracted scabies.[14] A few days later there was another selection for shipment from Auschwitz. Stripped, the women waited naked for hours on the mustering ground outside the barracks. Then, one by one, they filed into the barracks, where a battery of powerful lights had been set up and an SS doctor waited to check them over. Only those able to stand a trip and do hard work were being chosen for this new shipment, and many of

the women lied about their age and condition in the hope that they would escape the almost certain death of Auschwitz. Mrs. de Wiek was rejected and so was Mrs. Frank. They waited, looking on.

"Next it was the turn of the two girls, Anne and Margot," Mrs. de Wiek recalled. "Even under the glare of that light Anne still had her face, and she encouraged Margot, and Margot walked erect into the light. There they stood for a moment, naked and shaven-headed, and Anne looked at us with her unclouded face, looked straight and stood straight, and then they were approved and passed along. We could not see what was on the other side of the light. Mrs. Frank screamed, 'The children! Oh, God!'" **Ⓘ**

The chronicle of most of the other occupants of the Secret Annex ends at Auschwitz. Mrs. Frank died there of malnutrition two months later. Mr. Frank saw Mr. Van Daan marched to the gas chambers. When the SS fled Auschwitz before the approaching Russians in January 1945, they took Peter Van Daan with them. It was bitter cold and the roads were covered with ice and Peter Van Daan, Anne Frank's shy beloved, was never heard of again.

From Auschwitz, Mr. Dussel, the dentist, was shipped to a camp in Germany, where he died. Only Otto Frank remained there alive until liberation. Anne Frank and Mrs. Van Daan and Margot had been selected for shipment to Bergen-Belsen.

Last year I drove the 225 miles from

---

14. **scabies:** skin disease that causes severe itching.

Ⓗ **Read and Discuss** What is your impression of Anne as she is presented here?

Ⓘ **Read and Discuss** What does Mrs. de Wiek mean when she says that Anne "still had her face"?

Amsterdam to Belsen and spent a day there walking over the heath.[15] The site of the old camp is near the city of Hannover, in the state of Lower Saxony. It was June when I arrived, and lupine was in flower in the scrubland.

My guide first showed me the cemetery where fifty thousand Russian prisoners of war, captured in one of Hitler's great early offensives, were buried in 1941. Next to them is a cemetery for Italians. No one knows exactly whether there are three hundred or three thousand in that mass grave.

About a mile farther we came to the main site of the Bergen-Belsen camp. Amid the low growth of pine and birches many large rectangular patches can be seen on the heath. The barracks stood on these, and between them the worn tracks of thousands of bare feet are still visible. There are more mass graves nearby, low mounds overgrown with heath grass or new-planted dwarf pines. Boards bearing the numbers of the dead stand beside some mounds, but others are unmarked and barely discernible. Anne Frank lies there.

The train that carried Anne from Auschwitz to Belsen stopped at every second station because of air raids. At Bergen-Belsen there were no roll calls, no organization, almost no sign of the SS.

---

15. **heath** (heeth): area of open wasteland covered with low-growing plants.

A memorial stands at one of several mass graves at the site of the former Nazi concentration camp, Bergen-Belsen, in Belsen, Germany. The inscription reads "Here Rest 1,000 Dead, April 1945."

Prisoners lived on the heath without hope. The fact that the Allies had reached the Rhine encouraged no one. Prisoners died daily—of hunger, thirst, sickness.

The Auschwitz group had at first been assigned to tents on the Bergen-Belsen heath, tents which, one survivor recalls, gave an oddly gay, carnival aspect to the camp. One night that fall a great windstorm brought the tents crashing down, and their occupants were then put in wooden barracks. Mrs. B. of Amsterdam remembered about Anne: "We lived in the same block and saw each other often. In fact, we had a party together at Christmastime. We had saved up some stale bread, and we cut this up and put onions and boiled cabbage on the pieces. Over our feast we nearly forgot our misery for a few hours. We were almost happy. I know that it sounds ghastly now, but we really were a little happy in spite of everything."

One of Anne Frank's dearest childhood friends in Amsterdam was a girl named Lies Goosens.[16] Lies is repeatedly mentioned in the diary. She was captured before the Franks were found in the Secret Annex, and Anne wrote of her great fears for the safety of her friend. Now the slim and attractive wife of an Israeli army officer, Lies lives in Jerusalem. But she was in Bergen-Belsen in February 1945, when she heard that a group of Dutch Jews had been moved into the

Anne Frank (second from left) with a group of friends. The Granger Collection, New York.

next compound.

Lies said, "I waited until night. Then I stole out of the barracks and went over to the barbed wire which separated us from the newcomers. I called softly into the darkness, 'Is anyone there?'

"A voice answered, 'I am here. I am Mrs. Van Daan.'

"We had known the Van Daans in Amsterdam. I told her who I was and asked whether Margot or Anne could come to the fence. Mrs. Van Daan answered in a breathless voice that Margot was sick but that Anne could probably come and that she would go look for her.

"I waited, shivering in the darkness. It took a long time. But suddenly I heard a voice: 'Lies? Lies? Where are you?'

"I ran in the direction of the voice, and

___
16. **Lies Goosens** (lees KOH sihns).

then I saw Anne beyond the barbed wire. She was in rags. I saw her emacitated, sunken face in the darkness. Her eyes were very large. We cried and cried as we told each other our sad news, for now there was only the barbed wire between us, nothing more, and no longer any difference in our fates.

"But there was a difference after all. My block still had food and clothing. Anne had nothing. She was freezing and starving. I called to her in a whisper, 'Come back tomorrow. I'll bring you something.'

"And Anne called across, 'Yes, tomorrow. I'll come.'

"I saw Anne again when she came to the fence on the following night," Lies continued. "I had packed up a woolen jacket and some zwieback[17] and sugar and a tin of sardines for her. I called out, 'Anne, watch now!' Then I threw the bundle across the barbed wire.

"But I heard only screams and Anne crying. I shouted, 'What's happened?' And she called back, weeping, 'A woman caught it and won't give it to me.' Then I heard rapid footsteps as the woman ran away. Next night I had only a pair of stockings and zwieback, but this time Anne caught it."

In the last weeks at Bergen-Belsen, as Germany was strangled between the Russians and the Western Allies, there was almost no food at all. The roads were blocked, the railroads had been bombed, and the SS commander of the camp drove around the district trying unsuccessfully to requisition supplies. Still, the crematoriums worked night and day. And in the midst of the starvation and the murder there was a great epidemic of typhus.

Both Anne and Margot Frank contracted the disease in late February or early March of 1945. Margot lay in a coma for several days. Then, while unconscious, she somehow rolled from her bed and died. Mrs. Van Daan also died in the epidemic.

The death of Anne Frank passed almost without notice. For Anne, as for millions of others, it was only the final anonymity, and I met no one who remembers being with her in that moment. So many were dying. One woman said, "I feel certain she died because of her sister's death. Dying is easy for anyone left alone in a concentration camp." Mrs. B., who had shared the pitiful Christmastide feast with Anne, knows a little more: "Anne, who was very sick at the time, was not informed of her sister's death. But a few days later she sensed it and soon afterward she died, peacefully."

Three weeks later British troops liberated Bergen-Belsen. **J**

Miep and Elli, the heroic young women who had shielded the Franks for two years, found Anne's papers during the week after the police raid on the Secret Annex. "It

---

17. **zwieback** (ZWEE bahk): sweetened bread that is sliced and toasted after it is baked.

Vocabulary **emaciated** (ih MAY shee ay tihd) *v.* used as *adj.*: extremely thin, as from starvation.

J [Read and Discuss] Now what has happened?

was terrible when I went up there," Miep recalled. "Everything had been turned upside down. On the floor lay clothes, papers, letters, and school notebooks. Anne's little wrapper hung from a hook on the wall. And among the clutter on the floor lay a notebook with a red-checked cover. I picked it up, looked at the pages, and recognized Anne's handwriting."

Elli wept as she spoke to me: "The table was still set. There were plates, cups, and spoons, but the plates were empty, and I was so frightened I scarcely dared take a step. We sat down on the floor and leafed through all the papers. They were all Anne's, the notebooks and the colored duplicate paper from the office too. We gathered all of them and locked them up in the main office.

"A few days later M. came into the office, M. who now had the keys to the building. He said to me, 'I found some more stuff upstairs,' and he handed me another sheaf of Anne's papers. How strange, I thought, that *he* should be the one to give these to me. But I took them and locked them up with the others."

Miep and Elli did not read the papers they had saved. The red-checked diary, the office account books into which it over-flowed, the 312 tissue-thin sheets of colored paper filled with Anne's short stories and the beginnings of a novel about a young girl who was to live in freedom—all these were kept in the safe until Otto Frank finally returned to Amsterdam alone. Thus Anne Frank's voice was preserved out of the millions that were silenced. No louder than a child's whisper, it speaks for those millions and has outlasted the raucous shouts of the murderers, soaring above the clamorous voices of pass-ing time. **L**

Anne Frank, about age 12, c. 1941.

Thus Anne Frank's voice was preserved out of the millions that were silenced.

Read with a Purpose What did you learn about Anne's final days?

K **Read and Discuss** Elli says that she thought it strange that M. should be the one to give her some of Anne's papers. Why would that be strange?

L **Informational Focus** **Organization** What order of importance do the details in the final paragraph reflect?

Vocabulary raucous (RAW kuhs) *adj.*: loud and rough.

Applying Your Skills

A Tragedy Revealed: A Heroine's Last Days

Standards Review

Informational Text and Vocabulary

1. What overall organizational pattern does Mrs. de Wiek's account follow?

A sequential order

B logical order

C order of importance

D question and answer

2. Which of the following shows a contrast between the play about Anne Frank and this article?

A "Anne had nothing. She was freezing and starving."

B "the hushed silences when strangers were in the building"

C "the dread of capture by the pitiless men who were hunting Jews"

D "Their refuge was a tiny apartment they called the Secret Annex."

3. As people retell their memories in direct quotations in the article, the organizational pattern *most* often used is

A logical.

B problem-solution.

C question-answer.

D sequential.

4. A synonym of *annihilation* is

A vaccination.

B extinction.

C construction.

D expectation.

5. *Premonition* means

A preparation.

B devastation.

C initial.

D forewarning.

6. If behavior is *inexplicable,* it is

A condensed.

B indistinct.

C undefinable.

D institutional.

7. An *emaciated* dog looks as if it is

A escaping.

B barking.

C sneaking.

D starving.

Writing Skills Focus

Timed ⌐Writing Now that you've read Schnabel's article, how do you feel about Anne's statement that "people are really good at heart." In a paragraph, explain whether your reading of the article tends to support or contradict Anne's belief. Look at your notes for ideas.

What Do **You Think Now** Why is it important to keep alive memories of the Holocaust and other great tragedies?

Applying Your Skills

A Tragedy Revealed: A Heroine's Last Days

Vocabulary Development

Vocabulary Check

Answer the following questions.

1. What has happened to a city that has experienced **annihilation**?

2. Explain whether you have watched a television show that discussed **inexplicable** events.

3. Explain why you might stay inside if you have a **premonition** that it might rain.

4. If someone is not **emaciated,** how might you describe him?

5. If you are in a library, why might a **raucous** person disturb you?

Connotations

Connotations are the feelings associated with a word, feelings that go beyond its strict dictionary definition, or **denotation.** Often, connotations show shades of meaning or intensity.

Your Turn

Complete the chart below. Place the symbol "+" in the center column if the word on the right seems stronger than the word from "A Tragedy Revealed" on the left. Use "−" if it seems weaker. Use a dictionary for help.

indomitable		strong
refuge		shelter
reconciliations		agreements
dispirited		hopeless
clamorous		loud

Language Coach

Suffixes Suffixes can sometimes make nouns out of verbs, adjectives, and even other nouns. Review the words from the selection in the chart below to see the way suffixes make nouns out of different parts of speech. Then, think of one or two words that use each suffix.

selection word	suffix	new word
frail (adj.)	−ty	frailty
content (adj.)	−ment	contentment
survive (v.)	−or	survivor
hero (n.)	−ism	heroism
Enter (v.)	−y	entry

Academic Vocabulary

Write About . . .

Think of another historical figure whose "spirit has remained to stir the conscience of the world." Describe in a paragraph the lasting influence this person has had. Include details that convey why this figure is significant.

ESSAY / PERSONAL NARRATIVE
Preparing to Read

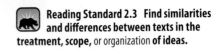

Reading Standard 2.3 Find similarities and differences between texts in the treatment, scope, or organization of ideas.

Walking with Living Feet

Informational Text Focus

Treatment and Scope Writings on the Holocaust take many forms. The **treatment** of their ideas is also varied. For example, writings such as memoirs have a **subjective** treatment, containing personal feelings and **biased,** or one-sided, opinions. Subjective details allow you to understand more fully the emotional experiences of the writers. Other writings, such as histories, are usually treated objectively, based on fact. An **objective,** or balanced, treatment presents all sides of a subject so that you can draw your own conclusions.

Texts about the Holocaust also have different **scopes,** or coverage of topics and ideas. For example, a history of the Nazi's treatment of the Jewish people might have a **broad** scope, whereas an essay about a specific prison camp will have a more **narrow** scope.

Into Action Use a chart like the one below to help you identify the treatment and scope of the previous informational selection and the following one.

A Tragedy Revealed	Walking with Living Feet
Treatment: both subjective and objective	Treatment:
Subjective detail:	Detail:
Objective detail: Their refuge was a tiny apartment they called the Secret Annex.	Detail:
Scope:	Scope:

Writing Skills Focus

Preparing for Timed Writing As you read, make notes in your *Reader/Writer Notebook* when you find that the writer's treatment of ideas is subjective and when it is objective. Also record instances of broad scope and of narrow scope. Then write details from the text that support your choices.

Reader/Writer
Notebook
Use your **RWN** to complete the activities for this selection.

Vocabulary

hysterically (hihs TEHR uh klee) *adv.:* in an uncontrolled or wild manner. *When she thought about the horrors of the Holocaust, she began crying hysterically.*

barracks (BAR ehks) *n.:* large buildings or groups of buildings in which many people live. *At the Nazi concentration camps, Jews were forced to live in crowded barracks.*

compressed (kuhm PREHST) *v.:* constricted; stifled, as if squeezed. *She felt as if the gas chamber compressed her lungs, as if she could no longer breathe.*

Language Coach

Affixes The word *press* has many meanings, such as "push," "squeeze," "force," "urge," and "emphasize." When you add a prefix, as in *compress,* you create a word with a new meaning. Think about how prefixes change the meaning of *press* in the words *depression, impress, oppressive,* and *repression.* How do the different suffixes change the meanings? Consult a dictionary if you need help.

Learn It Online
Expand your vocabulary with Word Watch at:

go.hrw.com	H8-431	Go

Walking with Living Feet

by **Dara Horn,** Millburn High School
Millburn, New Jersey

Read with a Purpose
Read this selection to learn how one teenager responded to a visit to a concentration camp in Poland.

I had a very unusual fifteenth birthday. During my birthday week, at the end of April, I was traveling with five thousand high school students from around the world, visiting concentration camps in Poland. I learned more there than I learned during my entire life in school; once I stepped out of a gas chamber, I became a different person. When I turned fifteen, I discovered that no matter how much you read about the Holocaust, nothing can ever be like seeing it with your own eyes. The day after my fifteenth birthday was the turning point of my life. I was at Majdanek, one of the largest Nazi concentration camps. And I will never forget it. **A**

Majdanek has been left exactly as it was when it was in use, so intact that if it were to be "plugged in," it could start gassing people tomorrow.

I stood in a gas chamber there, at Majdanek. I saw the blue stains of Zyklon B streaking the ceilings and walls, the poison used to kill the people who were crushed into this tiny, gray cement room. I could see how their fingers had scraped off the white paint, trying to escape. The cement floor that I sat on was cold and clammy; the air in the room seemed made of chills. When I first sat down, I did not notice, but soon those chilling waves were seeping into my skin, like so many tiny fingers trying to pull at my nerves and make my bones quiver. All around me, kids were crying hysterically, yet the chills that rankled the air around me hadn't reached my mind, and I could not

---

A **Informational Focus** Treatment Explain whether this first paragraph indicates a subjective or an objective treatment of the topic.

Vocabulary **hysterically** (hihs TEHR uh klee) *adv.:* in an uncontrolled or wild manner.

feel. I hated myself for it. Anger, fear, pain, and shock—I could have felt all of those and more, but instead I felt nothing. That void was far worse: All the other emotions around me showed the presence of human hearts, but I was almost not there at all. I wanted to feel; I hated the guilt I had at my lack of reaction as much as I hated what happened there. Only my squirming skin could attest to my surroundings, and the crawling air made my lungs tighten. I wished I could cry, but I couldn't break down my mental blockade. Why? **B**

The camp of Majdanek extends for miles, but one of the worst things about it is that it's right in a town, almost a city, called Lublin. There are actually houses right next to the barbed wire, the fence with its thorns that stabbed my frightened eyes, enough to separate a universe. The people of that city would have had to be dead not to notice the death which struck daily, right behind their backyards, where I saw children playing. People marched through Lublin from the train station, entered through the same barbed wire gate that I did, and left through the chimney. Nobody in Lublin noticed, because if they had,

their fate would have been the same. And today the camp's long gray, barn-like barracks still extend forever, in endless rows, the sky a leaden weight blocking the colors that grace free life. Gray is the color of hell.

Inside each of the barracks is a new horror. Some are museum exhibits, with collections of people's toothbrushes (they were told that they were being "relocated" and to bring one suitcase, the contents of which were confiscated) and people's hair. All of the walls in one barracks are covered with people's hats, hanging in rows. But the worst were the shoes.

About five of the barracks are filled with nothing but the shoes of some of the people who were killed there—over 850,000 pairs. In one barracks, I sat on a platform about five feet off the ground, and surrounding it was an ocean of shoes, five feet deep. In the gas chamber I could not feel, but in that room filled with shoes, my mental blockade cracked. The photographs meant nothing to me, the history lessons and names and numbers were never strong enough. But here each shoe is different, a different size and shape: a high heel, a sandal, a baby's shoe so

---

B Read and Discuss What question is the writer asking herself?

Vocabulary **barracks** (BAR ehks) *n.*: large buildings or groups of buildings in which many people live.

tiny that its owner couldn't have been old enough to walk, and shoes like mine. Each pair of those shoes walked a path all its own, guided its owner through his or her life and to all of their deaths. Thousands and thousands of shoes, each pair different, each pair silently screaming someone's murdered dreams. No book can teach me what I saw there with my own eyes!

Shoes taken from prisoners at the Auschwitz concentration camp.

I glanced at my own shoe, expecting it to be far different from those in that ocean of death, and my breath caught in my throat as I saw that my shoe seemed to be almost the same style as one, no, two, three, of the shoes I saw; it seemed as if every shoe there was my shoe. I touched the toe of one nearby and felt its dusty texture, certain that mine would be different. But as I touched my own toe, tears welled in my eyes as my fingers traced the edges of my dusty, living shoes. Eight hundred and fifty thousand pairs of shoes, but now I understood: They weren't numbers; they were people.

Soon I was crying, but for some-one else: for the child whose mother's sandals rested on that pile, for the woman whose husband's shoes swam motionless in that sea, like the tears that streaked my face, for the girl whose best friend's slippers were buried in that ocean of grayness and silence. I was lost to the shoes there. I wished I could throw my shoes into that pile, to grasp and feel each shoe, to jump into the sea of shoes, to become a part of it, to take it with me. I wanted to add my own shoes to that ocean, but all I could leave there were my salty tears. My feet clumped on the wooden platform as I left, and I had never been more conscious of how my shoes fit my living feet. **C**

C Informational Focus Scope What does the author's focus on shoes show about the scope of the essay?

At the very end of the camp was another gas chamber and the crematorium, its smokestack jutting through the leaden sky. This gas chamber did not have the blue poison stains that streaked the walls in the one I saw first, or maybe it did: The only light in that cement room was from dozens of memorial candles. It was too dark to see. The air inside was damp and suffocating, like a burial cave, and yet the air was savagely alive. It crawled down my neck and compressed me as the walls and ceiling seemed to move closer. No words can express how it felt to step out of that gas chamber alive, wearing my living shoes.

And I saw the crematorium where the corpses were burned, ovens shaped to fit a person. As I touched the brick furnaces with trembling fingers, my tears froze in my eyes and I could not cry. It was here that I felt my soul go up in flames, leaving me an empty shell.

Majdanek reeks of death everywhere. Even the reminders and signs of life that exist in a cemetery, like a footprint or rustling leaves, are absent here, every image of life erased. Even the wind does not ruffle the grass, which never used to grow here because the prisoners would eat it. But in the crematorium, I felt something I cannot express. No words exist to describe how I felt. It was someone else's nightmare, a nightmare that turned real before I even noticed it. It was a stark and chilling reality that struck me there, standing where people were slaughtered and burned, and my mind simply stopped. Have you ever been to Planet Hell? My people are numbers here, struck from a list and sent out the chimney, their children's bodies roasting. And I was there. You cannot visit this planet through any film or book; photographs cannot bring you here. Planet Hell is beyond the realm of tears. This is why I could not cry.

I left the camp. How many people, who had walked in those 850,000 pairs of shoes, once dreamed of doing what I had just done? And did they, too, forget how to cry?

In Israel I planted a tree with soil I had taken from concentration camps. In the soil were white specks, human bone ash. I am fifteen years old, and I know I can never forget.

Read with a Purpose How does this essay add to your understanding of Anne Frank?

Vocabulary **compressed** (kuhm PREHST) *v.:* constricted; stifled, as if squeezed.

Applying Your Skills

Reading Standard 2.3 Find similarities and differences between texts in the treatment, scope, or organization of ideas.

A Tragedy Revealed / Walking with Living Feet

Standards Review

Informational Text and Vocabulary

1. Which of the following statements about the **scope** of the two selections is *not* true?

  A "Walking with Living Feet" has a broader scope than "A Tragedy Revealed."

  B "A Tragedy Revealed" has a broader scope than "Walking with Living Feet."

  C The scope of "A Tragedy Revealed" is broad because it describes many events.

  D "Walking with Living Feet" has a narrow scope because it describes one event.

2. What is the main difference in the **treatment** of the two pieces?

  A "Walking with Living Feet" is more detailed than "A Tragedy Revealed."

  B "Walking with Living Feet" discusses a more painful event than "A Tragedy Revealed."

  C "Walking with Living Feet" is objective, whereas "A Tragedy Revealed" is subjective.

  D "Walking with Living Feet" is subjective, whereas "A Tragedy Revealed" is both subjective and objective.

3. Which statement accurately describes a similarity between the article and the essay?

  A Both texts focus on the causes of a war.

  B Both texts focus on a girl's experiences.

  C Both texts call for changes in society.

  D Both texts present details about the operation of gas chambers.

4. To laugh *hysterically* means to laugh

  A viciously.

  B frantically.

  C loudly.

  D angrily.

5. A soldier's *barracks* is his

  A canteen.

  B company.

  C dormitory.

  D headquarters.

6. A synonym for *compressed* is

  A contracted.

  B forged.

  C distorted.

  D clean.

Writing Skills Focus

Timed ⌐Writing Using your notes from your *Reader/Writer Notebook,* write one paragraph describing the ideas the writer treats objectively and with broad scope. Write a second paragraph describing the ideas she looks at subjectively and with a narrow view. Use examples of her details in your descriptions.

What Do **You Think Now?**

How do historical tragedies continue to shape our world view?

Vocabulary Development

✓ Vocabulary Check

1. Describe what life would be like if you lived in a **barracks.**
2. If you are laughing **hysterically,** what might you sound like?
3. If you are **compressed** in an elevator, how are you feeling?

Context Clues

In the following passages from this essay, context clues for the boldface words are in italic type. Use the context clues to identify the meaning of each boldface word.

1. "The cement floor that I sat on was *cold* and **clammy;** *the air in the room seemed made of chills." Clammy* means
   a. cold and damp.
   b. warm and damp.
   c. flooded.
   d. rough.

2. "Anger, fear, pain, and shock—I could have felt all of those and more, but instead *I felt nothing.* That **void** was far worse." *Void* means
   a. pit.
   b. vista.
   c. space.
   d. emptiness.

3. "I wished I could cry, but I couldn't *break down* my mental **blockade.**" *Blockade* means
   a. barrier.
   b. bombardment.
   c. agony.
   d. illness.

Language Coach

Context Clues The boldface words from the selection have different meanings when they are used in other contexts. Try to answer these questions.

1. How would a cave explorer use the word **clammy**?
2. How would a physicist use the word **void**?
3. How would a naval officer use the word **blockade**?

Academic Vocabulary

Write About . . .
Write a paragraph in which you discuss the main idea of "Walking with Living Feet." How does the writer make the significance of the idea <u>evident</u>?

Writing Workshop

Persuasive Writing

Write with a Purpose

Write a persuasive essay supporting your position on an important issue. Your **purpose** is to explain your point of view and give your audience good reasons to agree with you. Take into account the concerns of your **audience,** which may include teachers, parents, or local newspaper readers.

A Good Persuasive Essay

- includes a coherent thesis
- supports its argument with detailed evidence, examples, and reasoning, based on both research and original ideas
- differentiates between fact and opinion
- is clearly organized and presents a consistent point of view
- anticipates and answers readers' concerns and counter-arguments
- includes a clear, well-supported conclusion

See page 446 for complete rubric.

Reader/Writer Notebook

Use your **RWN** to complete the activities for this workshop.

Think as a Reader/Writer
In your daily conversations you often find yourself explaining and defending your ideas. In this workshop you'll write an essay in which you present an opinion and try to persuade others to agree with you. Before you begin, read these excerpts from Dr. Martin Luther King, Jr.'s, powerful "I Have a Dream" speech (pages 773–774), delivered on August 28, 1963, in Washington, D.C.

> I say to you today, my friends, that in spite of the difficulties and frustrations of the moment I still have a dream. It is a dream deeply rooted in the American Dream.
>
> I have a dream that one day this nation will rise up and live out the true meaning of its creed: "We hold these truths to be self-evident; that all men are created equal."
>
> I have a dream that one day on the red hills of Georgia the sons of former slaves and the sons of former slave owners will be able to sit down together at the table of brotherhood.
>
> I have a dream that one day even the state of Mississippi, a desert state sweltering with the heat of injustice and oppression, will be transformed into an oasis of freedom and justice.
>
> I have a dream that my four little children will one day live in a nation where they will not be judged by the color of their skin but by the content of their character. . . .
>
> When we let freedom ring, . . . we will be able to speed up that day when all God's children . . . will be able to join hands and sing . . . "Free at last! Free at last! Thank God almighty, we are free at last!"

← King acknowledges his **audience's** feelings.

← The quotation from the U.S. Declaration of Independence both defines and supports King's position.

King gives other examples that further define his
← position.

← He makes an **emotional appeal** and a **call to action.**

Think About the Professional Model
With a partner, discuss the following questions about the model.

1. What opinion does King support in this speech? How does he support this opinion in this excerpt?
2. What was King's purpose for writing? Explain whether he achieved it.

Writing Standard 1.1 Create compositions that establish a controlling impression, have a coherent thesis, and end with a clear and well-supported conclusion. **1.3** Support theses or conclusions with analogies, paraphrases, quotations, opinions from authorities, comparisons, and similar devices. **1.5** Achieve an effective balance between researched information and original ideas. **2.4** Write persuasive compositions: a. Include a well-defined thesis (i.e., one that makes a clear and knowledgeable judgment). b. Present detailed evidence, examples, and reasoning to support arguments, differentiating between facts and opinions. c. Provide details, reasons, and examples, arranging them effectively by anticipating and answering reader concerns and counterarguments.

Prewriting

Choose a Topic

When choosing a topic to write about, look for an issue that is both controversial and important to many other people. An **issue** is a subject about which people disagree. Brainstorm issues with a partner or small group. Then, evaluate possible ideas by completing a chart like the one below. Finally, choose an issue that you feel strongly about.

Topic or Issue	Argument on One Side	Argument on the Other Side
Leash laws in local parks	Dogs should have time to run and play off leash.	Dogs off leash can bite other dogs and children.
Starting a paper recycling program at our school	Recycling is important to avoid waste, save trees, and save the planet.	Recycling is too much trouble, too expensive, and takes up too much space.

Write a Thesis Statement

Once you have chosen an issue that you feel strongly about, it is time to write your **thesis statement,** in which you clearly state your opinion. A well-defined thesis is one that makes a clear and knowledgeable judgment. Thesis statements for the issues in the chart above might be:

• Dogs should be allowed time to run off leash in the city parks.

• We need to start a paper-recycling program at our school.

Support Your Position

The key to successful persuasion is developing a strong argument. Once you have stated your thesis and considered your purpose and audience, your task is to develop at least three strong reasons to support your position. Then, jot down the evidence that supports each reason. A proposition can be supported with the following types of evidence:

• **facts**—including the results of research and surveys

• **statistics**—facts in number form

• **examples**—specific instances that illustrate reasons or facts

• **anecdotes**—brief stories, such as personal experiences

• **definitions**

• **opinions from experts**—especially with direct quotations

Idea Starters

Think about current controversies in these areas:

• neighborhood changes, such as a new mall or park

• school dress code

• extended school year

• limits on Internet access

• leash laws for dogs

• making "volunteer" work mandatory

Peer Review

Ask a partner to review your three best ideas. Ask which idea your partner thinks would make the most interesting essay. You might also ask your partner's opinion on each issue. If you find that you and your partner disagree on one, consider choosing that topic. Your goal could be to change your partner's mind.

Your Turn _____

Get Started Make a list of issues in your **RWN.** Then, make a chart to evaluate the issues. After reviewing the chart, choose the best issue for your essay.

Next, write a **thesis statement.** Make sure your thesis tells both your issue and your position.

 Learn It Online

An interactive graphic organizer can help you organize your ideas. Try the persuasive planner at:

go.hrw.com   H8-439   **Go**

Writing Tip

You can use comparisons and analogies to help your audience understand how you see things. **Comparisons,** which show how things are alike, can take many forms. Here is a straightforward comparison: *Recycling paper and using public transportation are both effective ways to help the environment.* An **analogy** is a comparison made between two things to show how they are alike: *Recycling is much like fighting fires: both require great perseverance and both save trees.*

Your Turn

Plan Your Essay In your **RWN**, list three reasons your reader should support your position. Write down the evidence that supports each reason. Be sure your support is based on facts rather than opinions.

Differentiate Between Fact and Opinion

When you look for evidence to support your position, be sure to distinguish between fact and opinion. A fact is something that can be proved true by direct observation or by checking with a reliable source. An opinion is a belief or an attitude that cannot be proved true or false. An opinion can be considered valid, however, if it can be supported by facts.

FACT: Dogs need exercise to stay healthy.

This statement is a fact that can be verified by checking with a veterinarian.

OPINION: Dogs love to play with other dogs.

This statement is an opinion. We cannot prove all dogs' feelings.

VALID OPINION: Many dogs enjoy playing with other dogs.

We still cannot prove dogs' feelings, but this opinion can be supported by the observation of numerous dogs playing with other dogs.

Be sure to support your argument with as much evidence as possible, including facts and valid opinions.

Taking Notes

Here are some tips for taking notes as you research evidence to support your position.

- Put notes from different sources on separate index cards or sheets of paper, or in separate computer files.
- Use short phrases. You don't have to write full sentences.
- Use your own words unless you find material you want to quote. If you quote an author's exact words, put quotation marks around them.
- Include in your notes opinions from experts and analogies (or comparisons to more familiar topics or situations) as well as your own original ideas.
- Take notes from a variety of sources, including those with different perspectives, or opinions, on your topic.

Think About Audience and Purpose

As you plan your persuasive essay, keep your audience and purpose in mind. Your **audience** is members of your school community or readers of your local newspaper. Your **purpose** is to convince your readers to agree with you on your topic and perhaps to inspire them to take action.

Drafting

Organize and Draft Your Essay

Use a framework like this to organize and draft your essay. Consider arranging your reasons in order of importance. You can present the most important reason first and follow with less important reasons, or begin with the least important reason and build up to the most important one.

Elaborate on Your Ideas

You can elaborate on your ideas by defining words that your readers may not know, explaining the way a piece of evidence supports a reason, adding evidence such as an example or a quote from an expert, or using an analogy or a comparison to illustrate an idea.

End with a Bang

Conclude your argument with a well-supported conclusion. Restate your opinion clearly and summarize your reasons. You might end your essay forcefully with a **call to action.** Ask your audience to take a specific action, such as voting a certain way or joining a volunteer group.

Framework for a Persuasive Essay

Introduction
- Engaging beginning
- Well-defined thesis statement

Body
- Reason #1 and supporting evidence
- Reason #2 and supporting evidence
- Reason #3 and supporting evidence
- additional reasons and evidence, as appropriate

Conclusion
- Restatement of position
- Summary of reasons
- Closing statement and call to action, if appropriate

Grammar Link Avoiding Run-on Sentences

Your persuasive essay will be more effective if your ideas are clearly expressed. Writing about a topic you care about could lead you to create a **run-on sentence**—two or more complete thoughts that are run together as if they were one complete sentence. Avoid this problem while you draft by thinking about the idea you want to express in each sentence. Here are two strategies.

Write Two Sentences Instead of One
Run-on Sentence: We could save over one hundred trees a year, we should start today.
Correct: We could save over one hundred trees a year. **We** should start today.

Write a Sentence with a Comma and a Conjunction
Run-on Sentence: Our school uses about six tons of paper a year we could reduce that amount.
Correct: Our school uses about six tons of paper a year, **but** we could reduce that amount.

● Writing Tip

Remember that some of your readers may not agree with your position on the issue. You need to address their concerns, or counterarguments, by showing you understand their views. You don't have to agree with the counterargument, just indicate you're aware of it.

Your Turn _____

Draft Your Essay Using the Framework for a Persuasive Essay above, create an outline. Then, using your outline and the tips for A Good Persuasive Essay (page 438), write your first draft. As you write, think about these questions:
- What tone can you use to appeal to your audience?
- Have you provided strong support for your position?
- Have you arranged your reasons, details, and examples effectively?

Peer Review

As you read your partner's persuasive essay, think about the issue presented. Did reading the draft change your opinion about the issue? Why or why not? Are there any important aspects of the topic that the writer left out? Are there counterarguments the writer has not addressed? Discuss with your partner ways the argument could be strengthened.

Evaluating and Revising

Read the questions in the left column of the chart, and then use the tips in the middle column to help you make revisions to your essay. The right column suggests techniques you can use to revise your draft.

Persuasive Essay: Guidelines for Content and Organization

Evaluation Questions	Tips	Revision Techniques
1. Does your introduction contain a coherent and well-defined thesis?	**Circle** the sentence or sentences that state the issue and your position.	**Add** a thesis statement or **revise** your statement for clarity.
2. Are the paragraphs in the essay arranged effectively?	**Number** the paragraphs in order of importance.	**Rearrange** the paragraphs if necessary.
3. Have you provided reasons and evidence to support your opinion?	**Put a star** next to each reason, and **highlight** your evidence.	**Add** reasons, or add an example, statistic, anecdote, comparison, or expert opinion to support a reason, if needed.
4. Have you addressed counterarguments?	**List** any counterarguments that have not been addressed.	**Answer** any unaddressed reader concerns.
5. Have you differentiated between fact and opinion?	**Underline** all the facts in your paper. **Circle** all the opinions.	**Cut** any lines of argument that do not support your position.
6. Does your conclusion restate your opinion and summarize your reasons? Is there a call to action?	**Underline** the restatement, the summary, and the call to action.	**Replace** opinions with facts where possible or support your opinions with facts to make them valid.

Read this student draft, and notice the comments on its strengths as well as suggestions on how it could be improved.

Letter to the School Board

by Teresa Lacey, Franklin Middle School

Distinguished Members of the School Board:

I am in favor of the proposed requirement that eighth-graders spend fifteen hours during the school year volunteering to help the elderly.

One reason this would be a good idea is that it would be a learning experience. Students could learn how to work with and relate to older people.

Another reason I think this rule would be magnificent is that it is a good way to help others. Eighth-graders can help people who cannot do things themselves. Students could do yard work, housework, run errands, or just spend time with the elderly so they would not be alone.

Teresa's **thesis statement** clearly states the issue and position.

Teresa's first **reason** is presented and explained.

Her second **reason** is presented and followed by specific examples.

MINI-LESSON > How to Include Evidence and Emotional Appeals

In persuasive writing, reasons must be fully supported with **evidence** (for instance, **examples, facts, anecdotes, statistics, definitions, expert opinions**). **Emotional appeals** are also an effective way to persuade your audience. Teresa reviewed her draft and added a personal anecdote that presents logical evidence. She also changed several words to make the project sound exciting. Notice how the new paragraph supports Teresa's **thesis.**

Teresa's Revision of Paragraph Two

One reason this would be a good idea is that it would be a learning experience. Students could learn how to work with and relate to older people. My mother works at a nursing home, so I have had the opportunity to help her in the summer. I have learned to help with the residents there by playing games or walking with them, or by reading aloud to them. But it's not just a one-way street! The people there have taught me lessons about getting through tough times and about friendship. I love hearing the stories they tell about their lives.

Your Turn _____

Include Strong Support Read your draft and then ask yourself:

- Have I fully supported each of my reasons with sufficient and strong support?

If your answer is no, look for additional facts, statistics, examples, anecdotes, definitions, expert opinion, analogies, or comparisons to bolster your argument.

Student Draft *continues*

Finally, I think just spending at least fifteen hours a school year with the elderly would improve students' people skills. Students would learn to talk to and relate to others. They would learn how to be less shy, too. In a recent *Time* magazine poll, sixty percent of people becoming nurses in care homes said they learned how to talk to residents and their families more confidently.

For all these reasons, I believe the proposed requirement for volunteering would make a good rule. I hope that you will consider my reasons and vote to accept the proposed requirement.

Teresa includes **statistics from an authoritative source** to back up her claim.

She concludes with a restatement of her position and a direct **call to action**.

MINI-LESSON ▶ **How to Address Counterarguments**

Anticipating an objection your audience might raise to your opinion can be very persuasive. When Teresa was reviewing her draft, her partner had one comment: "I already have so much to do, how could I possibly add in volunteering to my busy schedule?"

Teresa thought about the question. She decided to include a **counterargument** and her response in her essay. To do this, Teresa decided on the strongest response to a concern about the time volunteering might take. She argues that volunteering could not be as time consuming as readers expect. She added this paragraph immediately before her conclusion.

Teresa's Revision before the conclusion

⌃Some students might argue that they already have too much work to do. It's true that we have many obligations, but the proposal is for just 15 hours per school year. If those hours are spread out over nine months, it works out to less than two hours a month. The benefits to both students and community residents would be worth a little rescheduling.

For all these reasons, I believe the proposed requirement for volunteering would make a good rule. I hope that you will consider my reasons and vote to accept the proposed requirement.

Your Turn _____

Addressing Counterarguments
Consider how readers might respond to your opinions. Ask yourself the following questions:

- What are some of the objections that readers might raise to your ideas?
- How can you respond to these arguments?

Look for a place in your essay where you might address possible counterarguments. If you have already done so, check that your appeals are as persuasive as possible.

Proofreading and Publishing

Proofreading

Look for errors you may have introduced when cutting and moving material. Also, be sure that you have documented your evidence and double-checked examples, statistics, names, and quotations. When you are done, exchange your essay with a partner. Read your partner's essay once for grammatical errors and then once again for spelling errors.

Grammar Link Placing Modifiers

Place modifying words, phrases, and clauses as near as possible to the words they modify.

Misplaced Modifier: <u>When she is on a leash</u>, the owner controls the dog. (Is the owner leashed?)
Revision: The owner controls the dog <u>when she is on the leash</u>. (The clause modifies *dog*.)

Misplaced Modifier: <u>Securely fenced and clean</u>, people can let their dogs play freely in the park. (The adjectives cannot logically modify anything in this sentence.)
Revision: People can let their dogs play freely in the <u>securely fenced and clean</u> park. (The missing noun *park* is added.)

Publishing

Here are some suggestions on how you might share your persuasive essay with a larger audience.

- Submit your essay as a letter to the editor at a school or community newspaper.
- Post your essay on an Internet bulletin board where your audience is likely to read it.

Reflect on the Process In your **RWN,** write short responses to the questions below.

1. How do you think your essay could have been more convincing to your audience?

2. In what way did your essay achieve your purpose for writing?

3. How did addressing possible counterarguments help you better understand an opposing viewpoint?

● **Proofreading Tip**

Take a break before you proofread your essay. If you go right from revising to proofreading, you might be tired and overly familiar with your words. As a result, you might miss some obvious errors. After a short break, your brain will be clear and ready to catch mistakes.

Your Turn _____
Proofread and Publish
Proofread your essay for grammar, mechanics, and usage mistakes. Pay special attention to placement of modifiers. Publish your essay for your audience. As you reflect on the process, write your responses in your **RWN.**

Scoring Rubric

You can use the rubric below to evaluate your persuasive essay.

	Persuasive Writing	Organization and Focus	Sentence Structure	Conventions
4	• Presents *detailed* evidence, examples, and reasoning to *authoritatively* support arguments, *clearly* differentiating between fact and opinion. • Arranges details, reasons, and examples *effectively*, by anticipating and *convincingly* addressing readers' concerns.	• *Clearly* addresses all parts of the writing task. • Demonstrates a *clear* understanding of purpose and audience. • Maintains a *consistent* focus and organizational structure. • Provides a *well-defined* thesis, a *coherent* introduction, and a *clear, well-supported* conclusion.	• Includes sentence *variety* (e.g. simple, complex, compound-complex).	• Contains *few, if any,* errors in the conventions of the English language (grammar, punctuation, capitalization, spelling). These errors do **not** interfere with the reader's understanding of the writing.
3	• Presents evidence, examples, and reasoning to support arguments, differentiating between fact and opinion. • Addresses readers' concerns.	• Addresses most of the writing task. • Demonstrates a *general* understanding of purpose and audience. • Maintains a *mostly consistent* focus and organizational structure. • Provides a thesis and *clear* introduction and conclusion or explanations.	• Includes some sentence *variety* (e.g. simple, complex, compound-complex).	• Contains *some errors* in the conventions of the English language (grammar, punctuation, capitalization, spelling). These errors do **not** interfere with the reader's understanding of the writing.
2	• Presents *vague* evidence to support arguments, *without* differentiating between fact and opinion. • *May* address readers' concerns.	• Addresses *some* of the writing task. • Demonstrates *little* understanding of purpose and audience. • Maintains an *inconsistent* focus and/or organizational structure. • Suggests a thesis and *attempts* an introduction and conclusion.	• Includes *little* sentence variety.	• Contains *several errors* in the conventions of the English language (grammar, punctuation, capitalization, spelling). These errors **may** interfere with the reader's understanding of the writing.
1	• *Fails* to provide evidence. • *Fails* to address readers' concerns.	• Addresses *only one or no* part of the writing task. • Demonstrates *no* understanding of purpose and audience. • *Lacks* a focus and organizational structure. • *Lacks* a thesis, introduction, and/or conclusion.	• Includes *no* sentence variety.	• Contains *serious errors* in the conventions of the English language (grammar, punctuation, capitalization, spelling). These errors interfere with the reader's understanding of the writing.

Persuasive Essay

When responding to a prompt, use what you've learned from your reading, writing your persuasive essay, and studying the rubric on page 446. Use the steps below to develop a response to the following prompt.

Writing Standard 2.4 Write persuasive compositions: a. Include a well-defined thesis (i.e., one that makes a clear and knowledgeable judgment). b. Present detailed evidence, examples, and reasoning to support arguments, differentiating between facts and opinions. c. Provide details, reasons, and examples, arranging them effectively by anticipating and answering reader concerns and counterarguments.

Writing Prompt

Students have many choices when deciding how to spend their time after school in extracurricular activities. Write an essay persuading a friend to join the activity that you enjoy the most. Convince your friend with strong reasons and persuasive appeals.

Study the Prompt

Begin by reading the prompt carefully. Circle or underline key words: *extracurricular activities, after school, enjoy.*

The word *convince* tells you to use a *persuasive* approach in your essay. You will explain *why* you enjoy the activity and more important, why your friend will enjoy it. Your reasons must appeal to your audience.

Tip: Spend about five minutes studying the prompt.

Plan Your Response

Make a list of extracurricular activities and think about which one would appeal to your friend. Possible activities might include exercising, working with others, or volunteering.

Ask yourself why your friend might enjoy the activity. Decide on two or three reasons to support the position that your friend should join you in this extracurricular activity. Use examples and anecdotes, or brief stories, to support each reason.

Plan your reasons so that the most persuasive reason is presented last to end your essay as strongly as possible.

Tip: Spend about ten minutes planning your response.

Respond to the Prompt

Start writing, even if you are unsure of how to begin. The most important thing is to get your ideas on paper.

One way to begin this essay is to describe the extracurricular activity as if you are participating in it. Make the description of it appealing and fun with specific details; then invite your friend to join. Use one reason for each body paragraph to convince your friend to join you in the activity. Remember to appeal to what your friend enjoys and values with specific examples and anecdotes. You can conclude with a brief scenario about the two of you enjoying the activity together.

Tip: Spend about twenty minutes writing your persuasive essay.

Improve Your Response

Revising Go back to the key aspects of the prompt. Did you fully describe what the activity is and what it involves? Does your essay provide reasons to convince your reader that joining you in the activity is a good idea? Have you added specific examples and anecdotes to make the essay more convincing? Did you invite your friend to join? If not, add these elements to your essay.

Proofreading Take a few minutes to proofread your essay to correct errors in grammar, spelling, punctuation, and capitalization. Make sure all your edits are neat and the paper is legible.

Checking Your Final Copy Before you turn your essay in, read it one more time to catch any errors you may have missed.

Tip: Save ten minutes to improve your paper.

Delivering a Persuasive Presentation

Speak with a Purpose

Adapt your persuasive essay into a persuasive presentation. Rehearse your presentation, and then present it to your class.

Think as a Reader/Writer Speaking to persuade and writing to persuade are similar skills in many ways. However, to give an effective speech, you will need to do much more than read a persuasive essay directly from the page; you will need to deliver the most important points in a solid presentation that will grab the attention of your audience.

Adapt Your Essay

Consider Your Audience, Message, and Purpose

As you prepare to change your essay into a speech, keep in mind these three questions:

- To whom will you be speaking (**audience**)?
- How might you adjust your content depending on this audience (**message**)?
- What will you need to do to achieve your goal (**purpose**), that is persuading your audience that your opinion is right?

For example, the purpose of your essay might have been to persuade your teachers to create an art gallery in the school's hallway. Perhaps you gave evidence that viewing art improves student participation in class. Suppose you are delivering your speech to your classmates. You may need to supply different supporting evidence to convince fellow students that supplying art for the hallway gallery will be good for them.

Organize Your Presentation

To make sure your speech is **coherent,** or easily understood, be certain that all your ideas are clearly related, given in an order that makes sense, and connected with **transitional words** and **phrases.**

Once you have identified which pieces of support from your essay you intend to keep and which need to be changed, you can start organizing your speech notes. The first step in organizing is to write brief sentences and phrases about important points on note cards. Once you have your points listed on note cards, number them in the order you want to present them. Arrange your support—your **reasons** and **evidence**—in order of importance. Begin your speech with the strongest reason for your opinion to get your audience's attention, or end with your strongest reason to leave a powerful impression. Conclude your speech with a **call to action** that tells the audience what they can do about the issue.

Speaking Tip

Make your speech memorable. Look for opportunities to replace dull, vague words with lively, **precise language.** Include **sensory details**—words and phrases that appeal to the five senses—use **colorful modifiers** and the **active voice**.

Speaking Tip

Persuading your audience won't be possible if they can't follow what you're saying. Make sure your audience understands exactly what you mean by providing definitions of new and unfamiliar words as you use them.

Reader/Writer Notebook

Use your **RWN** to complete the activities for this workshop.

Listening and Speaking Standard
1.3 Organize information to achieve particular purposes by matching the message, vocabulary, voice modulation, expression, and tone to the audience and purpose. **1.5** Use precise language, action verbs, sensory details, appropri-ate and colorful modifiers, and the active rather than the passive voice in ways that enliven oral presentations. **2.4** Deliver persuasive presentations: **a.** Include a well-defined thesis (i.e., one that makes a clear and knowledgeable judgment). **b.** Differentiate fact from opinion and support arguments with detailed evidence, exam-ples, and reasoning. **c.** Anticipate and answer listener concerns and counterarguments effectively through the inclusion and arrangement of details, reasons, examples, and other elements. **d.** Main-tain a reasonable tone.

Deliver Your Speech

Since the purpose of your presentation is to persuade others, your delivery, or the way you give the speech, is critical. To ensure that your speech runs smoothly, practice giving it more than once. Keep the fol-lowing suggestions in mind as you practice:

- **If possible, practice in front of an audience** so that you can get used to speaking in front of a group.
- **Practice using your note cards** just as you will use them on the day of your speech.
- **Use a timer or watch** to ensure that you stay within the time limit you have been given.
- **Finally, review the evaluation guidelines below.** Knowing how your audience will be evaluating your presentation will help you prepare.

Guidelines for Evaluating a Persuasive Presentation

Content

What is the purpose of the speech? Paraphrase the speaker's purpose.

What is the topic? Paraphrase the speaker's point of view on the topic. Does the speaker clearly state his or her opinion?

Which reasons are convincing and which are not? Are they supported?

Delivery

Describe the speaker's tone. Is it conversational or does it sound too formal?

Does the speaker speak loudly and slowly enough?

How often does the speaker make eye contact with the audience?

How do the speaker's nonverbal messages (such as gestures and facial expressions) match the verbal message? Are any of the gestures distracting? In what way are they distracting?

Credibility (Believability)

What is the speaker's bias? How do you know?

What facts has the speaker used to support his or her opinion?

Does the speaker have unsupported opinions? What are they?

A Good Persuasive Speech

- is tailored to listeners' backgrounds and interests
- has a clear message and purpose, and convincing support
- is coherent, with clearly connected ideas
- uses transitional words and phrases for clarity
- uses precise language, sensory details, colorful modifiers and the active voice
- uses verbal and nonverbal cues to reinforce the message of the speech
- has a conclusion summarizing the message and including a call to action

 Speaking Tip

Remember that you are the creator of your speech, and you can modify it to respond to audience feedback, if neces-sary. Some modifications you can make are to spend more or less time on a point, add some humor, or speak more loudly.

Learn It Online
Pictures, cartoons, graphs and charts can make your speech stand out. See how on *MediaScope* at:

go.hrw.com | H8-449 | Go

Literary Skills Review

Theme   Directions: Read the two stories. Then answer each question that follows.

The Dog and the Wolf by **Aesop** (sixth century B.C.)

One cold and snowy winter the Wolf couldn't find enough to eat. She was almost dead with hunger when a House Dog happened by.

"Ah, cousin," said the Dog, "you are skin and bones. Come, leave your life of roaming and starving in the forest. Come with me to my master and you'll never go hungry again."

"What will I have to do for my food?" said the Wolf.

"Not much," said the House Dog. "Guard the property, keep the Fox from the henhouse, protect the children. It's an easy life."

That sounded good to the Wolf, so the Dog and the Wolf headed to the village. On the way the Wolf noticed a ring around the Dog's neck where the hair had been rubbed off.

"What's that?" she asked.

"Oh, it's nothing," said the Dog. "It's just where the collar is put on at night to keep me chained up. I'm used to it."

"Chained up!" exclaimed the Wolf, as she ran quickly back to the forest.

Better to starve free than to be a well-fed slave.

The Puppy by **Aleksandr Solzhenitsyn** (twentieth century)

translated by **Michael Glenny**

In our backyard a boy keeps his little dog Sharik chained up, a ball of fluff shackled since he was a puppy.

One day I took him some chicken bones that were still warm and smelt delicious. The boy had just let the poor dog off his lead to have a run round the yard. The snow there was deep and feathery; Sharik was bounding about like a hare, first on his hind legs, then on his front ones, from one corner of the yard to the other, back and forth, burying his muzzle in the snow.

He ran towards me, his coat all shaggy, jumped up at me, sniffed the bones—then off he went again, belly-deep in the snow.

I don't need your bones, he said. Just give me my freedom. . . .

1. Both the House Dog and Sharik
   A are chained at times.
   B run away from home.
   C are starving.
   D hate their masters.

2. What do both the Wolf and Sharik want more than food?
   A love
   B friends
   C security
   D freedom

3. Which quotation points to a recurring theme for both stories?
   A "Just give me my freedom."
   B "Sharik was bounding about like a hare."
   C "the collar is put on at night."
   D "sniffed the bones—then off he went"

4. Read the moral from the end of "The Dog and the Wolf."

Better to starve free than to be a well-fed slave.

   Which quotation from "The Puppy" *most* closely matches the moral's meaning?
   A "Sniffed the bones—then off he went again, belly-deep."
   B "I don't need your bones, he said. Just give me my freedom."
   C "The boy had just let the poor dog off his lead to have a run round the yard."
   D "Sharik was bounding about like a hare, first on his hind legs."

5. Although the writers live 2,600 years apart, their shared ideas support each of the following recurring themes *except*
   A It is human to want freedom.
   B Food can be more important than freedom.
   C We learn about ourselves when we tell stories about animals.
   D Slavery has proved impossible to erase.

6. Which of the following is a theme found in *both* "The Dog and the Wolf" and "The Puppy"?
   A Slavery is worse than hunger any day.
   B Some freedoms are worth giving up in order to gain safety.
   C Sometimes people think they are free when they really aren't.
   D The weak have to rely on the strong for protection.

Timed Writing

7. What theme do the fable from ancient Greece and the story from the communist U.S.S.R. have in common?

Informational Skills Review

Treatment, Scope, and Organization of Ideas

Directions: Read these articles, and answer the questions that follow.

The Cook Legacy by **John Robson**

Captain James Cook is a name known and recognized throughout the world. Like Christopher Columbus and Marco Polo, Cook was an explorer whose fame continued long after his death. Almost every year, new books celebrate his voyages and achievements. A replica of the *Endeavour* sails to international ports, drawing huge numbers of visitors, while museums in various countries house collections of materials associated with his voyages and host exhibits celebrating his achievements.

Surely one of the greatest explorers, sailors, surveyors, and mapmakers of all time, James Cook raised the art of marine exploration to a new level. When he sailed into the Pacific Ocean in 1769, that vast expanse of water was only partly known. Nevertheless, using the knowledge he gained from crisscrossing its waters many times over the next twelve years, Cook produced a map that we can recognize today. Unlike earlier sailors, Cook knew exactly where he was and skillfully and quickly made charts that showed where he had been. He also had a knack for finding islands in the vast ocean. Like someone playing pinball, Cook seemed to bounce from tiny island to tiny island.

Of equal interest is what he did not find. To disprove the existence of a great southern continent, Cook sailed farther south than any of his predecessors. The first to cross the Antarctic Circle, he sailed in extreme cold among the icebergs and in dense fog. In doing so, he showed that the continent, if it existed at all, would be too harsh to inhabit.

On his third voyage, Cook helped prove that a Northwest Passage through the North American continent, south of 65 degrees north, was not possible. The cold and ice north of Alaska and Canada had finally stopped Cook as he sailed north through the Bering Strait, and it would take ships that were larger and stronger than his to get through this area.

Cook's three voyages can be regarded as the first scientific voyages. The work of the naturalists (Joseph Banks, Daniel Solander, and Johann and Georg Forster), the astronomers (Charles Green, William Wales, and William Bayly), the artists (Sydney Parkinson, Herman Sporing, William Hodges, and John Webber), and Cook himself ensured that the voyages would be remembered for more than just the sailing. The specimens brought back to Europe, the collection of charts, drawings, and paintings, and the descriptions of people, places, and events combined to produce a treasury of information still being used today.

Cook's dealings with the people of the Pacific were good, but not perfect. Sadly, he died in Hawaii after one confrontation. Until that time, however, relations had been friendly, and Cook genuinely regretted every death that resulted from contact with visiting Europeans. Cook's descriptions, and those of his colleagues, provide us with great insight into the lives of Pacific Islanders who had had no previous contact with foreigners.

In dealing with his own men, Cook was strict but fair. Their health was a major concern, and Cook was an early advocate of a good diet and cleanliness. His insistence on fresh food at every opportunity and on making sure that the crew washed both their clothes and themselves ensured that few men became sick or died. Cook set standards that others soon followed.

In the early 1800s, a Russian explorer named a group of scattered islands in the Pacific after Cook. Nearly 200 years later, the people of the Cook Islands voted to retain that name and not replace it with a Polynesian one. Similarly, mountains, towns, inlets, and other geographical features around the world have been named for him.

In the 1990s, the United States government recognized the role of Cook in the history of exploration by naming two space shuttles for ships that he took to the Pacific. The *Discovery* and the *Endeavour* shuttles are two additional examples of how the achievements of Captain James Cook continue to be celebrated throughout the world.

An Air of Duty and Discipline

by **Barbara Krasner-Khait**

Captain James Cook made the importance of discipline clear to his men. As crew members of the *Endeavour* prepared to sail in August 1768, he read them the 36 clauses of the Articles of War, many of which dealt with discipline and punishment.

If any man disobeyed Cook's orders, he would be subjected to a dozen lashes with a whip for each violation. Crew members were forced to witness the punishment so they would not make the same mistake.

Cook's insistence on duty and discipline served the voyage well in time of crisis. When the *Endeavour* sustained heavy damage on Australia's Great Barrier Reef in June 1770, botanist Joseph Banks was impressed by the men's cheerfulness as they banded together to preserve the ship. He was also surprised that given the grueling work they had to do, they did not disobey. Banks attributed this to the "cool and steady conduct of the officers," no doubt a tribute to Cook's style of leadership.

Cook did not tolerate theft, whether the culprits were members of his own crew or natives. Once, for example, when some food was stolen on board, Cook cut the crew's meat allowance in half until the thief came forward.

Cook's disciplinary actions changed noticeably on the third voyage, however. Some could not understand his new policies, but perhaps the long voyages were taking their toll.

Cook had fallen ill on both his second and his third voyages and showed signs of tiredness. As a result, his relationship with his men and with Pacific Islanders seems to have been affected. On one occasion, at Moorea,° natives stole a goat from the ship. Cook's officers and men reluctantly followed disciplinary orders. According to midshipman Gilbert, they "burnt in all 20 Houses & 18 large War Canoes . . ." and ". . . neither tears nor entreaties could move Cook. He seem'd to be very rigid in the performance of his order . . . I can't well account for Capt Cook's proceedings on this occasion; as they were so very different from his conduct in like cases in his former voyages."

Although Cook ran a tight ship and was stern while at sea, he would sometimes relax and talk with his men while on shore,

---

° **Moorea:** island in French Polynesia, located near Tahiti.

forgetting for a time that he was their commander. Some men loved him for the hard discipline; others did not. Some adored him and considered him a father figure; others considered him a tyrant. There is no doubt, however, that the air of duty and discipline aboard Cook's ships contributed to the success of the voyages.

---

1. Which statement accurately describes a similarity between the two magazine articles?

   A Each emphasizes his harsh discipline.

   B Each describes his illnesses.

   C Each gives accounts of his voyages.

   D Each tells of future ships named after his.

2. Which of the following statements about the scope of the two articles is *not* true?

   A "The Cook Legacy" has a broader scope than "An Air of Duty and Discipline."

   B "An Air of Duty and Discipline" has a broader scope than "The Cook Legacy."

   C "An Air of Duty and Discipline" has a more narrow scope because it focuses on one topic.

   D The scope of "The Cook Legacy" is broader because it describes many events.

3. What is the *main* difference in the treatment of the two pieces?

   A "An Air of Duty and Discipline" is more detailed than "The Cook Legacy."

   B "An Air of Duty and Discipline" is biased, whereas "The Cook Legacy" is balanced.

   C "An Air of Duty and Discipline" is objective, whereas "The Cook Legacy" is biased.

   D "The Cook Legacy" discusses a more disturbing topic than "An Air of Duty and Discipline."

4. The *main* organizational pattern of "The Cook Legacy" is

   A enumeration.

   B cause and effect.

   C order of importance.

   D logical order.

5. Which of the following statements from "The Cook Legacy" *best* describes its treatment?

   A "one of the greatest explorers, sailors, surveyors, and mapmakers of all time"

   B "When he sailed into the Pacific Ocean in 1769"

   C "A Russian explorer named a group of scattered islands after Cook."

   D "Almost every year, new books celebrate his voyages and achievements."

Timed Writing

6. Re-read the last paragraph of "An Air of Duty and Discipline" and the last paragraph of "The Cook Legacy." Based on these two closing paragraphs, explain which article you think gives a more objective treatment of the topic. Provide details from both articles to support your choice.

Vocabulary Skills Review

Synonyms   **Directions:** Choose the word or phrase that is the *best* synonym of each italicized word.

1. People who oppose *tyranny* fight against
   A justice.
   B oppression.
   C monsters.
   D racism.

2. When someone is *forlorn,* he or she feels
   A weary.
   B unhappy.
   C satisfied.
   D peaceful.

3. A person who speaks *indignantly* speaks
   A shyly.
   B humorously.
   C playfully.
   D angrily.

4. When you celebrate *liberation,* you celebrate
   A creation.
   B destruction.
   C intelligence.
   D freedom.

5. A *tersely* worded letter is
   A brief.
   B clear.
   C rambling.
   D explanatory.

6. A *conspicuous* flaw is
   A discolored.
   B natural.
   C faint.
   D obvious.

7. A *cherished* object is
   A valued.
   B misplaced.
   C disregarded.
   D refurbished.

8. When you hold a *vigil,* you
   A rest.
   B watch.
   C eat.
   D read.

9. A *teeming* room is
   A warm.
   B loud.
   C crowded.
   D empty.

Academic Vocabulary

Direction: Choose the *best* synonym for the italicized Academic Vocabulary word.

10. Something that is *evident* is
    A obvious.
    B dubious.
    C outrageous.
    D tenuous.

Writing Skills Review

Persuasive Essay **Directions:** Read the following passage. Then, answer each question that follows.

Writing Standard 2.4 Write persuasive compositions: a. Include a well-defined thesis (i.e., one that makes a clear and knowledgeable judgment). b. Present detailed evidence, examples, and reasoning to support arguments, differentiating between facts and opinions. c. Provide details, reasons, and examples, arranging them effectively by anticipating and answering reader concerns and counterarguments.

(1) Although more American students are getting high school diplomas than at any other time in the past, the high school dropout rate is still too high. (2) Various estimates place the dropout rate between 12 and 25 percent. (3) The unemployment rate for high school dropouts is greater than that for graduates. (4) Dropping out of high school reduces one's options for work. (5) Also, the jobs available to a person without a degree may be less stable. (6) People believe students who already have jobs do not need a diploma. (7) However, with a diploma, students can earn more and choose from a greater number of jobs. (8) A diploma gives students a bright, shining future filled with opportunities. (9) To help "at risk" students stay in school, we need to consider a range of proposals. (10) We need to offer career counseling to students. (11) Second, we should provide stimulating, quality education that will give students incentives to complete their schooling. (12) And third, we must get parents more involved in school programs and policies.

1. Which title would *best* fit this persuasive essay?

  A The Problem of Unemployment

  B At-Risk High School Students

  C Decrease the Dropout Rate

  D Career Counseling Helps

2. In sentence 6, the author provides a

  A topic sentence.

  B supporting fact.

  C solution.

  D counterargument.

3. Sentence 7 is an example of

  A supporting evidence.

  B a detail.

  C an emotional appeal.

  D a call to action.

4. Which transitional word would make sentence 10 clearer?

  A first

  B finally

  C last

  D because

5. In this essay, the author includes all of the following *except* a(n)

  A thesis.

  B conclusion.

  C argument.

  D body.

Read On

Fiction

Journey Home

As World War II comes to a close, Yuki Sakane and her family are finally released from an internment camp and allowed to return home to Berkeley, California. However, the Sakanes quickly find that Berkeley has changed. Because of the war, former friends and other residents have become suspicious of returning Japanese Americans. Yuki and her family try to overcome this hostility in Yoshiko Uchida's novel *Journey Home*.

Number the Stars

How far would you go to save a friend's life? In the 1990 Newbery Medal winner by Lois Lowry, *Number the Stars*, Annemarie Johansen and Ellen Rosen, best friends living in peaceful Copenhagen, Denmark, don't concern themselves with questions like this—until the Nazis come for Ellen.

A Gathering of Days

In Joan W. Blos's *A Gathering of Days*, teenager Catherine Hall receives a journal in which she chronicles an eventful time of her life. Beginning in 1830, Catherine learns about racial prejudice from a man fleeing slavery, loses a close friend, and assumes greater responsibility on her family's New Hampshire farm as she journeys toward adulthood.

The Friends

You know her: the new kid in class no one wants for a friend. In *The Friends* by Rosa Guy, the new girl is Phyllisia Cathy, and she is from the West Indies. The only person who will befriend her is Edith, a Harlem-born girl trying to keep her family together despite the hardships of poverty.

Nonfiction

Behind Barbed Wire

After the bombing of Pearl Harbor, Japanese Americans were forced to abandon their homes and businesses and live in internment camps. Families were guarded twenty-four hours a day by armed soldiers. Japanese Americans were essentially stripped of their human and civil rights. In *Behind Barbed Wire*, Daniel S. Davis describes the many difficulties they faced during World War II and the courage they showed in making a new start when they were finally released from the camps.

We Are Witnesses: Five Diaries of Teenagers Who Died in the Holocaust

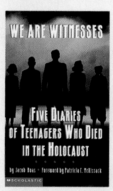

Jacob Boas looks at excerpts from the diaries of five teenagers who lived during World War II. Although they lived in different countries, each received a death sentence under Hitler's reign of terror. *We Are Witnesses: Five Diaries of Teenagers Who Died in the Holocaust* shows how the teenagers dealt with the worst kind of pain and oppression.

The Upstairs Room and The Journey Back

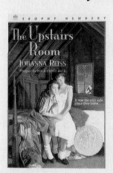

In the Netherlands during World War II, Anne and Margot Frank went into hiding with their parents. At the same time, another pair of sisters escaped to the country to live through the war with a Dutch family in their farmhouse. *The Upstairs Room* and its sequel, *The Journey Back,* tell the true story of Johanna Reiss and her sister Sini.

Zlata's Diary: A Child's Life in Wartime Sarajevo

Zlata Filipovic was just a girl when the war in Bosnia started. She chronicles those dark days with a unique voice and poetic sensibility. An international bestseller when it was first released, Filipovic's diary has been compared to the diary of Anne Frank in its poignancy and portrayal of a childhood lost to war.

Learn It Online
Explore other novels and find tips for choosing, reading, and studying words at:

go.hrw.com   H8-459   **Go**

Heart flowers (20th century)
by St. Pierre. Haitian art.

Style

INFORMATIONAL TEXT FOCUS
Evaluating a Summary

 California Standards
Here are the Grade 8 standards that you will work toward mastering in Chapter 4.

Word Analysis, Fluency, and Systematic Vocabulary Development
1.1 Analyze idioms, analogies, metaphors, and similes to infer the literal and figurative meanings of phrases.

Reading Comprehension (Focus on Informational Materials)
2.4 Compare the original text to a summary to determine whether the summary accurately captures the main ideas, includes critical details, and conveys the underlying meaning.

Literary Response and Analysis
3.6 Identify significant literary devices (e.g., metaphor, symbolism, dialect, irony) that define a writer's style and use those elements to interpret the work.

Writing Applications (Genres and Their Characteristics)
2.2 Write responses to literature:
  a. Exhibit careful reading and insight in their interpretations.
  b. Connect the student's own responses to the writer's techniques and to specific textual references.
  c. Draw supported inferences about the effects of a literary work on its audience.
  d. Support judgments through references to the text, other works, other authors, or to personal knowledge.

"Could it think, the heart would stop beating."

—**Fernando Pessoa**

What Do
**You
Think** Which is better—acting from the mind or from the heart?

Learn It Online
Find out more about the authors in this chapter at the Writers' Lives site online:

go.hrw.com | H8-461 | **Go**

Literary Skills Focus

by **Carol Jago**

How Do You Define a Writer's Style?

When you hear the word *style*, you may immediately think of the way your friends dress or the way a baseball player swings a bat. A person's style is created by *how* he or she does something— such as wearing clothes or playing a sport. You can define a writer's style by identifying the way he or she uses language.

Style

Every writer has a style, though some styles are more distinctive and easily recognized than others. Dr. Seuss's poetry, for example, is known for its regular rhythm, rhyme patterns, and invented words. Most writers do not deliberately create a specific style. Rather, their style evolves through the choices they make when they put words on a page. Their decisions eventually determine their style.

Figurative Language

Perhaps the most important part of any writer's style is the use of **figurative language**—language based on some sort of comparison that is not literally true. Figurative language includes many **literary devices,** such as metaphor, simile, personification, imagery, irony, and symbolism.

Figures of speech Expressions that are not literally true but that suggest similarities between usually unrelated things are called **figures of speech.** They almost always involve some sort of imaginative comparison between seemingly unlike things. Metaphors, similes, and personification are the most common figures of speech.

Metaphors compare unlike things directly, without using a specific word of comparison.

> The wind was a thousand souls dying.
>
> from "The Dragon"
> by Ray Bradbury

Similes compare two unlike things using a word of comparison, such as *like*, *than*, *as*, or *resembles*.

> Feeling like two birds in the gray sky, McDunn and I sent the light touching out, red, then white, then red again, to eye the lonely ships.
>
> from "The Fog Horn"
> by Ray Bradbury

Personification speaks of a nonhuman or inanimate thing as if it has human or lifelike qualities.

> [T]he high tower was cold, the light was coming and going, and the Fog Horn was calling and calling through the raveling mist.
>
> from "The Fog Horn"
> by Ray Bradbury

Reading Standard 3.6 Identify significant literary devices (e.g., metaphor, symbolism, dialect, irony) that define a writer's style and use those elements to interpret the work.

Writers try to create fresh figures of speech to help you see everyday things in new ways.

Imagery Language that creates word pictures and appeals to your senses is called **imagery.** Images make you feel as if you are seeing (or hearing, touching, tasting, or smelling) what the writer is describing. The poet John Greenleaf Whittier helps you experience the start of a New England blizzard with this image: "The sun that brief December day / Rose cheerless over hills of gray."

Irony Another aspect of writers' style is irony. **Irony** occurs when what actually happens is not the same as what you expect to happen.

Verbal irony occurs when you say one thing and mean something else. For example, a friend might say, "That's just great," in a disgusted tone, and you know she means that it isn't great at all.

Situational irony is a situation that turns out to be just the opposite of what you would expect; for example, the butcher's son is a vegetarian.

Dramatic irony occurs when you know something that a character doesn't know; for example, you don't want the heroine to go down the dark hall because you know she'll find danger there.

Symbolism People, places, or events that have meaning in themselves but also stand for something else are called **symbols.** For example, Moby-Dick is a white whale hunted by Captain Ahab in the novel *Moby-Dick,* but he is also a symbol of the evil all of humanity encounters. In everyday life you encounter many symbols. They are called public symbols because everyone knows what they mean: A skull and crossbones symbolizes poison; a dove carrying an olive branch symbolizes peace.

Dialect Another literary device writers use to appeal to your senses (in this case, hearing) is dialect. **Dialect** is a way of speaking that is characteristic of a particular place or group of people. Reading "Y'all come back now" tells you the character is likely to be from the South. Writers often include dialect to convey a clear sense of time and place.

Your Turn

Read this passage from Ray Bradbury's "The Fog Horn" (page 532), and explain which statement below correctly describes its style, citing examples from the passage.

> Out there in the cold water, far from land, we waited every night for the coming of the fog, and it came, and we oiled the brass machinery and lit the fog light up in the stone tower. Feeling like two birds in the gray sky, McDunn and I sent the light touching out, red, then white, then red again, to eye the lonely ships. And if they did not see our light, then there was always our Voice, the great deep cry of our Fog Horn shuddering through the rags of mist to startle the gulls away like decks of scattered cards and make the waves turn high and foam.

Statement of Style 1	Statement of Style 2
The writer uses imagery to create a playful tone about a serious subject.	Repetition and vivid imagery help describe a bleak setting.

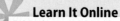

Learn It Online
To learn how to use these literary elements in longer works, visit *NovelWise* at:

go.hrw.com   H8-463   **Go**

Reading Skills Focus

by **Kylene Beers**

What Reading Skills Help You Interpret Style?

In order to determine a writer's style, you look for the literary devices the writer uses. Just identifying these devices isn't enough, though. To understand a story fully, you need to interpret those elements of style. Paraphrasing and analyzing details can help you begin this process.

Paraphrasing

When you **paraphrase,** you restate a text in your own words. A paraphrase is different from a retelling, in which you restate only the most important points. Any time you paraphrase, you should include all the information that is in the original.

Paraphrasing helps you understand difficult lines of poetry and sentences written in an old-fashioned or unfamiliar style. Paraphrasing also helps you appreciate an author's style. When you compare your paraphrase with the original, you will be able to see differences in style.

Compare this passage from Edgar Allan Poe's "The Tell-Tale Heart," along with a paraphrase.

Original Text	Paraphrase
His fears had been ever since growing upon him. He had been trying to fancy them causeless but could not.	He had been getting more scared since then. He told himself not to worry, but he could not stop.

You can easily see that the original text is written in formal language and gives you a strong feeling for the narrator's voice. The paraphrase is written in everyday English and tells you little about the narrator.

Analyzing Details

Analyzing details can help you understand what you read. Such analysis helps you follow a plot, visualize a setting, understand characters, and figure out a theme. Analyzing details can also help you appreciate an author's style.

Examine the details in this passage from Ray Bradbury's "The Fog Horn." Consider the length and complexity of Bradbury's sentences. Also, look for figures of speech, strong images, and the level of vocabulary he uses.

> It was a cold night, as I have said; the high tower was cold, the light coming and going, and the Fog Horn calling and calling raveling mist.
>
> from "The Fog Horn"
> by Ray Bradbury

Besides giving you a precise picture of working in the lighthouse, the passage also reveals aspects of the author's style. Ray Bradbury uses long sentences with occasional figures of speech ("like two birds in the gray sky"). He also uses repetition (coming/came, fog) as he sets the scene for this story.

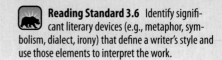

Reading Standard 3.6 Identify significant literary devices (e.g., metaphor, symbolism, dialect, irony) that define a writer's style and use those elements to interpret the work.

Reading Aloud

You have probably been asked to **read aloud** by your teacher to demonstrate understanding or fluency—the smoothness with which you read. Reading aloud can also be fun. For example, you may read aloud dialogue from stories to hear the characters' conversation. Reading aloud can also enable you to hear what the author's style sounds like.

"The Tell-Tale Heart" has no dialogue. The story consists of a long monologue delivered by the narrator to an unspecified "you." However, reading passages from the story aloud can give you clues to the narrator's personality and to the author's style. What do you learn about Edgar Allan Poe's style from reading this passage aloud?

> Ha! Would a madman have been so wise as this? And then, when my head was well in the room, I undid the lantern cautiously—oh, so cautiously—cautiously (for the hinges creaked)—I undid it just so much that a single thin ray fell upon the vulture eye.
>
> from "The Tell-Tale Heart"
> by Edgar Allan Poe

You might notice, as you gasp for breath, that Poe uses long sentences. By having the narrator repeat himself and add parenthetical (or side) comments, Poe also shows that the narrator is—at the very least—highly agitated. You might also notice that Poe uses words that make the passage sound rather weird and scary ("madman," "hinges creaked," and "vulture eye").

Drawing Conclusions

A conclusion is your final thought or judgment about something. To **draw conclusions** about an author's style, consider details from the text, and decide how they contribute to the style.

Your Turn

Read the following passage aloud. Then, answer the questions below.

> So I'm strolling down Broadway breathing out and breathing in on counts of seven, which is my lucky number, and here comes Gretchen and her sidekicks: Mary Louise, who used to be a friend of mine when she first moved to Harlem from Baltimore and got beat up by everybody till I took up for her on account of her mother and my mother used to sing in the same choir. . . .
>
> from "Raymond's Run"
> by Toni Cade Bambara

1. What details of Bambara's style do you notice? What conclusions can you draw from them?

2. Paraphrase the passage, and compare your paraphrase with the original.

> **Now go to the Skills in Action: Reading Model**

Learn It Online
Learn with graphics. Use the *PowerNotes* version of this lesson at:

go.hrw.com   H8-465   Go

Build Background

The mother in the following story refers to the tragic opera *Madama Butterfly* by Giacomo Puccini. In the opera a U.S. naval officer stationed in Japan marries a young Japanese woman, Butterfly, and then returns to the United States. She waits faithfully for him, with their child, for years. After he returns to Japan with an American wife, Butterfly commits suicide.

Read with a Purpose Read to discover a mother's advice.

A SMART COOKIE

from
The House on Mango Street

by **Sandra Cisneros**

Reading Focus

Analyzing Details Notice how Cisneros omits quotation marks to set off dialogue. This aspect of Cisneros's style makes the story seem less formal; it also makes you curious to read the story.

Literary Focus

Symbolism Madame Butterfly can be seen as a symbol for passive women who depended on men.

Dialect Read this paragraph aloud to hear the mother's voice and dialect.

I could've been somebody, you know? my mother says and sighs. She has lived in this city her whole life. She can speak two languages. She can sing an opera. She knows how to fix a TV. But she doesn't know which subway train to take to get downtown. I hold her hand very tight while we wait for the right train to arrive.

She used to draw when she had time. Now she draws with a needle and thread, little knotted rosebuds, tulips made of silk thread. Someday she would like to go to the ballet. Someday she would like to see a play. She borrows opera records from the public library and sings with velvety lungs powerful as morning glories.

Today while cooking oatmeal she is Madame Butterfly until she sighs and points the wooden spoon at me. I could've been somebody, you know? Esperanza, you go to school. Study hard. That Madame Butterfly was a fool. She stirs the oatmeal. Look

Analyzing Visuals **Viewing and Interpreting** What quotation from the story might make an appropriate caption for this photo? Why?

at my comadres.[1] She means Izaura whose husband left and Yolanda whose husband is dead. Got to take care all your own, she says shaking her head.

Then out of nowhere:

Shame is a bad thing, you know. It keeps you down. You want to know why I quit school? Because I didn't have nice clothes. No clothes, but I had brains.

Yup, she says disgusted, stirring again. I was a smart cookie then.

1. **comadres** (koh MAH drays): Spanish for "close female friends" (literally, a child's mother and godmother).

Read with a Purpose What advice does the mother offer? Why does she give this advice?

Sandra Cisneros
(1954–)

A Daughter's Independence

Like Esperanza, the narrator of *The House on Mango Street,* Sandra Cisneros grew up in a Mexican American family in Chicago. The only daughter in a family of seven children, she often felt as if she had "seven fathers." Her father expected her to take on a traditional female role in adult life. Instead, she chose an artist's path, developing a voice that speaks for generations of Mexican American women.

Her Own Style

Cisneros is known for her strong, precise, and colorful style. She often bases her stories on her own experiences and family history. Her bicultural upbringing also heavily influences her style. Cisneros often includes Spanish in her English prose. She writes:

> "I know how much of a role Spanish plays, even when I write in English. If you take [*The House on*] *Mango Street* and translate it, it's Spanish. The syntax, the sensibility, the diminutives, the way of looking at inanimate objects. . . . Incorporating the Spanish, for me, allows me to create new expressions in English. . . ."

Think About the Writer What qualities do you think enabled Cisneros to follow her own path?

Reading Standard 3.6 Identify significant literary devices (e.g., metaphor, symbolism, dialect, irony) that define a writer's style and use those elements to interpret the work.

Into Action: Analyzing Details to Determine Author's Style

Review "A Smart Cookie" and look for details that reveal Cisneros's writing style. Write the details in the left column of a chart like the one below. In the right column, write the name of the literary device that describes the detail.

Story Detail	Literary Device

Talk About . . .

1. With a partner, discuss how Cisneros's use of figures of speech and irony define her style. Try to use each Academic Vocabulary word listed at the right in your discussion.

Write About . . .

Use the underlined Academic Vocabulary words in your answers to the following questions about "A Smart Cookie."

2. What literary <u>devices</u> does Cisneros use to convey the theme of the story?

3. Which details from the text help you to <u>interpret</u> Cisneros's feelings toward education?

Writing Skills Focus
Think as a Reader/Writer

In Chapter 4 the Writing Skills Focus activities on the Preparing to Read pages will guide you in recognizing elements of each writer's style. On the Applying Your Skills pages, you will have opportunities to use these elements in your own writing.

Academic Vocabulary for Chapter 4

Talking and Writing About Style

Academic Vocabulary is the language you use to talk and write about literature. Use the following words to discuss the selections you read in this chapter. These words are underlined throughout the chapter.

critical (KRIHT uh kuhl) *adj.:* 1. crucial; of greatest importance. *A good summary of a text includes all the critical information and leaves out the minor details.* 2. expressing judgment of the merits and faults of a literary or artistic work. *The language arts class performed a critical review of three of Ray Bradbury's works.*

device (dih VYS) *n.:* method used to produce a specific effect. *The author uses such literary devices as similes and metaphors to help her readers visualize the motion.*

distinctive (dihs TIHNGK tihv) *adj.:* special; different from others. *A distinctive style, not one that is bland or clichéd, is an indication of a fine writer.*

interpret (ihn TUR priht) *v.:* decide the intended meaning of something. *Readers combine their own knowledge with what they read when they interpret the meaning of a work.*

Your Turn

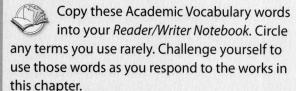

Copy these Academic Vocabulary words into your *Reader/Writer Notebook*. Circle any terms you use rarely. Challenge yourself to use those words as you respond to the works in this chapter.

The Tell-Tale Heart

by **Edgar Allan Poe**

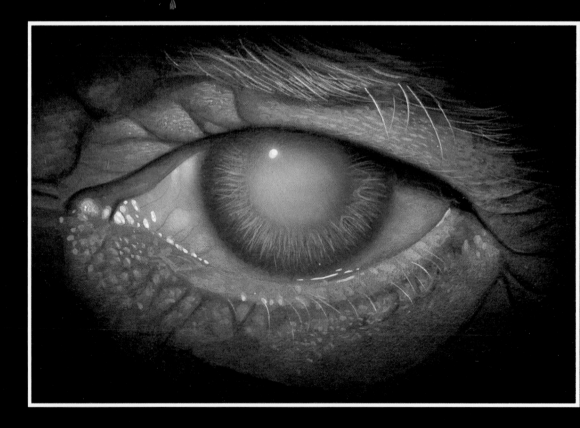

What Do You Think?

How do you decide if someone is trustworthy?

 QuickTalk

What is the difference between a lie and a delusion? Share your ideas with your classmates. Refer to a dictionary, if necessary.

 **Reader/Writer Notebook**

Use your **RWN** to complete the activities for this selection.

Reading Standard 3.6 Identify significant literary devices (e.g., metaphor, symbolism, dialect, **irony**) that define a writer's style and use those elements to interpret the work.

Literary Skills Focus

Narrator When you read a story, you rely on the **narrator**—the person telling the story—to let you know what is happening. What do you do if you cannot trust the narrator? As you begin reading this story, decide whether or not the narrator is a reliable source of information.

Irony Much of the horror in this story comes from Poe's skillful use of **irony,** a contrast between expectation and reality. There are three kinds:

- **Verbal irony** occurs when you say the opposite of what you mean.
- **Situational irony** occurs when something happens that is the opposite of what you expect.
- **Dramatic irony** occurs when you know something a character doesn't.

Literary Perspectives Apply the literary perspective described on page 473 as you read this story.

Reading Skills Focus

Paraphrasing a Text **Paraphrasing,** or restating the text in your own words, can help you unlock the meaning of complicated or confusing text. Paraphrasing can also help you recognize and interpret the literary devices that define a writer's style.

Into Action As you read the story, record complex or confusing sentences in a chart like the one below. Paraphrase each sentence, and compare yours with the original. Were there any you were not able to paraphrase? Which style elements become more noticeable?

Original Sentence	My Paraphrase
"Hearken! and observe how healthily—how calmly I can tell you the whole story."	Listen and you'll learn how I can tell you my story in a calm and healthy way.

Writing Skills Focus
Think as a Reader/Writer

Find It in Your Reading As you read, write down words or phrases that you feel best represent Poe's distinctive style.

Vocabulary

vexed (vehkst) *v.:* disturbed; annoyed. *The old man's eye vexed the narrator.*

audacity (aw DAS uh tee) *n.:* boldness. *Impressed with his own audacity, the narrator smiled.*

vehemently (VEE uh muhnt lee) *adv.:* forcefully; passionately. *He talked more vehemently, but he couldn't drown out the sound.*

gesticulations (jehs TIHK yuh LAY shuhnz) *n.:* energetic movements. *The narrator's violent gesticulations did not disturb the calm police officers.*

derision (dih RIHZH uhn) *n.:* contempt; ridicule. *Most of all, the narrator hated the smiling derision of the police.*

Language Coach

Style: Punctuation and Italics In this story, Poe uses these techniques that define his unique style:

Italic type—used to show that a word is emphasized.
Dash—used to show an abrupt change in thought.
Exclamation point—used to indicate strong feeling.

Watch for italics, dashes, and exclamation points in the story. Read passages out loud to feel the full impact of Poe's famous style.

Learn It Online
Learn more about Poe at:
go.hrw.com H8-472 Go

Edgar Allan Poe
(1809–1849)

Orphaned and Penniless

Born in Boston, Edgar Allan Poe was the son of traveling actors. His father deserted the family when Poe was a baby, and his mother died before his third birthday. Poe was taken in by the wealthy Allan family of Richmond, Virginia, and given a first-class education. At the age of twelve, he had already written enough poems (mainly love poems to girls he knew) to fill a book. By the time he was twenty, he had published two volumes of poetry.

Poe constantly argued with his foster father, John Allan, about money. Allan eventually broke all ties with Poe, leaving Poe penniless. In 1831, Poe moved in with his aunt, Maria Clemm, and her children in Baltimore. He married his young cousin Virginia Clemm five years later.

Celebrated and Poor

Poe became as celebrated for his tales of horror and mystery as for his poetry. He made very little money from his writing. One of his most famous poems, "The Raven," earned him only about fifteen dollars. He seemed to live on the brink of disaster. His wife's death from tuberculosis in 1847 brought on a general decline in his physical and emotional health. He was found very ill in a Baltimore tavern on a rainy day in 1849; he died four days later of unknown causes.

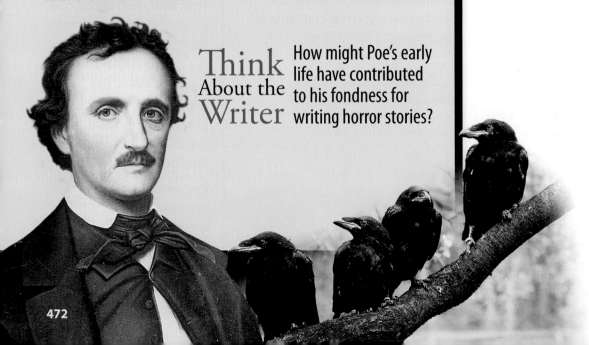

Think About the Writer How might Poe's early life have contributed to his fondness for writing horror stories?

Build Background

Edgar Allan Poe is often credited with having invented the modern horror or suspense story. Many of the familiar elements from today's horror movies are found in this story—fury, murder, blood, and madness.

As both a critic and an author, Poe felt that prose writing should express a focused truth about human existence. He expressed his truths in the horror or suspense genre, but he was also one of the first writers to explore science fiction and detective styles.

Preview the Selection

In this story an unnamed narrator describes why he is offended by a certain old man and what he plans to do about it.

Read with a Purpose As you read this famous short story, determine whether the narrator is or is not sane.

The Tell-Tale Heart

by **Edgar Allan Poe**

rue!—nervous—very, very dreadfully nervous I had been and am; but why *will* you say that I am mad? The disease had sharpened my senses—not destroyed—not dulled them. Above all was the sense of hearing acute. I heard all things in the heaven and in the earth. I heard many things in hell. How, then, am I mad? Hearken! and observe how healthily—how calmly I can tell you the whole story. **Ⓐ**

It is impossible to say how first the idea entered my brain; but once conceived, it haunted me day and night. Object[1] there was none. Passion there was none. I loved the old man. He had never wronged me. He had never given me insult. For his gold I had no desire. I think it was his eye! Yes, it was this!

One of his eyes resembled that of a vulture—a pale blue eye, with a film over it. Whenever it fell upon me, my blood ran cold; and so by degrees—very gradually—I made up my mind to take the life of the old man and thus rid myself of the eye forever. **Ⓑ**

Literary Perspectives

Use this perspective to help you analyze Poe's distinctive style.

Analyzing an Author's Techniques To understand a writer's style, you analyze his or her techniques. That means you consider how word choices contribute to the tone and mood; you appreciate the sensory images; you interpret the figures of speech and their impact; you notice the symbolism of important objects or places; and you distinguish the different types of irony in the work. As you read, respond to the questions in the text, which will guide you in using this perspective.

---

1. **object** (AHB jehkt): purpose or goal.

Ⓐ **Literary Focus** Narrator How does the style of this paragraph suggest the narrator's extreme nervousness? Consider Poe's word choice and punctuation as you respond.

Ⓑ **Reading Focus** Paraphrasing Paraphrase the final sentence of this paragraph. What has the narrator decided to do?

Now this is the point. You fancy me mad. Madmen know nothing. But you should have seen *me*. You should have seen how wisely I proceeded—with what caution—with what foresight—with what dissimulation[2] I went to work! I was never kinder to the old man than during the whole week before I killed him. And every night, about midnight, I turned the latch of his door and opened it—oh, so gently! And then, when I had made an opening sufficient for my head, I put in a dark lantern, all closed, closed, so that no light shone out, and then I thrust in my head. Oh, you would have laughed to see how cunningly I thrust it in! I moved it slowly—very, very slowly, so that I might not disturb the old man's sleep. It took me an hour to place my whole head within the opening so far that I could see him as he lay upon his bed. Ha! Would a madman have been so wise as this? And then, when my head was well in the room, I undid the lantern cautiously—oh, so cautiously—cautiously (for the hinges creaked)—I undid it just so much that a single thin ray fell upon the vulture eye. And this I did for seven long nights—every night just at midnight—but I found the eye always closed; and so it was impossible to do the work; for it was not the old man who vexed me, but his Evil Eye. And every morning, when the day broke, I went boldly into the chamber and spoke courageously to him, calling him by name in a hearty tone and inquiring how he had passed the night. So you see he would have been a very profound[3] old man, indeed, to suspect that every night, just at twelve, I looked in upon him while he slept.

Upon the eighth night I was more than usually cautious in opening the door. A watch's minute hand moves more quickly than did mine. Never before that night had I *felt* the extent of my own powers—of my sagacity.[4] I could scarcely contain my feelings of triumph. To think that there I was, opening the door, little by little, and he not even to dream of my secret deeds or thoughts. I fairly chuckled at the idea; and perhaps he heard me; for he moved on the bed suddenly, as if startled. Now you may think that I drew back—but no. His room was as black as pitch with the thick darkness (for the shutters were close fastened, through fear of robbers), and so I knew that he could not see the opening of the door, and I kept pushing it on steadily, steadily. **C**

I had my head in, and was about to open the lantern, when my thumb slipped upon the tin fastening, and the old man sprang up in the bed, crying out—"Who's there?"

I kept quite still and said nothing. For a whole hour I did not move a muscle, and in

---

2. **dissimulation** (dih sihm yuh LAY shuhn): disguising of intentions or feelings. (Look for a similar word at the end of the story.)

3. **profound** (pruh FOWND): having great intellectual depth and insight.

4. **sagacity** (suh GAS uh tee): intelligence and good judgment.

C **Literary Focus** **Irony** Why is it ironic that the old man feared robbers? What type of irony is this?

Vocabulary **vexed** (vehkst) *v.*: disturbed; annoyed.

The illustrations for this selection are from a short movie based on "The Tell-Tale Heart."

the meantime I did not hear him lie down. He was still sitting up in the bed listening—just as I have done, night after night, hearkening to the deathwatches[5] in the wall. **D**

Presently I heard a slight groan, and I knew it was the groan of mortal terror. It was not a groan of pain or of grief—oh, no!—it was the low, stifled sound that arises from the bottom of the soul when overcharged with awe. I knew the sound well. Many a night, just at midnight, when all the world slept, it has welled up from my own bosom, deepening, with its dreadful echo, the terrors that distracted me. I say I knew it well. I knew what the old man felt, and pitied him, although I chuckled at heart. I knew that he had been lying awake ever since the first slight noise, when he had turned in the bed. His fears had been ever since growing upon him. He had been

trying to fancy them causeless but could not. He had been saying to himself—"It is nothing but the wind in the chimney—it is only a mouse crossing the floor," or "It is merely a cricket which has made a single chirp." Yes, he had been trying to comfort himself with these suppositions; but he had found all in vain. *All in vain;* because Death, in approaching him, had stalked with his black shadow before him and enveloped the victim. And it was the mournful influence of the unperceived shadow that caused him to feel—although he neither saw nor heard—to *feel* the presence of my head within the room. **E**

When I had waited a long time, very patiently, without hearing him lie down, I resolved to open a little—a very, very little crevice in the lantern. So I opened it—you cannot imagine how stealthily, stealthily—until, at length, a single dim ray, like the thread of the spider, shot from out the crevice and full upon the vulture eye.

5. **deathwatches:** beetles that burrow into wood and make tapping sounds, which some people believe are a sign of approaching death.

D | Read and Discuss | What mood is the author establishing here?

E | Literary Focus | Narrator What can you infer about the narrator from this paragraph?

It was open—wide, wide open—and I grew furious as I gazed upon it. I saw it with perfect distinctness—all a dull blue, with a hideous veil over it that chilled the very marrow in my bones; but I could see nothing else of the old man's face or person, for I had directed the ray, as if by instinct, precisely upon the damned spot. **F**

And now have I not told you that what you mistake for madness is but overacuteness of the senses?—now, I say, there came to my ears a low, dull, quick sound, such as a watch makes when enveloped in cotton. I knew *that* sound well too. It was the beating of the old man's heart. It increased my fury, as the beating of a drum stimulates the soldier into courage.

But even yet I refrained[6] and kept still. I scarcely breathed. I held the lantern motionless. I tried how steadily I could maintain the ray upon the eye. Meantime the hellish tattoo[7] of the heart increased. It grew quicker and quicker and louder and louder every instant. The old man's terror *must* have been extreme! It grew louder, I say, louder every moment!—do you mark me well? I have told you that I am nervous: So I am. And now at the dead hour of the night, amid the dreadful silence of that old house, so strange a noise as this excited me to uncontrollable terror. Yet for some minutes longer I refrained and stood still. But the beating grew louder, louder! I thought the heart must burst. And now a new anxiety seized me—the sound would be heard by a neighbor! The old man's hour had come! With a loud yell, I threw open the lantern and leaped into the room. He shrieked once—once only. In an instant I dragged him to the floor and pulled the heavy bed over him. I then smiled gaily to find the deed so far done. But, for many minutes, the heart beat on with a muffled sound. This, however, did not vex me; it would not be heard through the wall. At length it ceased. The old man was dead. I removed the bed and examined the corpse. Yes, he was stone, stone dead. I placed my hand upon the heart and held it there many minutes. There was no pulsation. He was stone dead. His eye would trouble me no more. **G**

If still you think me mad, you will think so no longer when I describe the wise precautions I took for the concealment of the body. The night waned,[8] and I worked hastily but in silence. First of all I dismembered the corpse. I cut off the head and the arms and the legs.

I then took up three planks from the flooring of the chamber and deposited all between the scantlings.[9] I then replaced the boards so cleverly, so cunningly, that no human eye—not even *his*—could have detected anything wrong. There was nothing to wash out—no stain of any kind—no blood spot whatever. I had been too wary for that. A tub had caught all—ha! ha!

When I had made an end of these labors, it was four o'clock—still dark as midnight.

---

6. refrained (rih FRAYND): held back.

7. tattoo: steady beat.

8. waned (waynd): gradually drew to a close.

9. scantlings: small beams of wood.

F Reading Focus **Paraphrasing** Paraphrase this paragraph.

G Read and Discuss How has the narrator solved his problem?

As the bell sounded the hour, there came a knocking at the street door. I went down to open it with a light heart—for what had I *now* to fear? There entered three men, who introduced themselves, with perfect suavity,[10] as officers of the police. A shriek had been heard by a neighbor during the night; suspicion of foul play had been aroused; information had been lodged at the police office, and they (the officers) had been deputed[11] to search the premises.

I smiled—for *what* had I to fear? I bade the gentlemen welcome. The shriek, I said, was my own in a dream. The old man, I mentioned, was absent in the country.

---

10. **suavity** (SWAH vuh tee): smoothness; politeness.
11. **deputed** (dih PYOOT uhd): appointed.

I took my visitors all over the house. I bade them search—search *well*. I led them, at length, to *his* chamber. I showed them his treasures, secure, undisturbed. In the enthusiasm of my confidence, I brought chairs into the room and desired them *here* to rest from their fatigues, while I myself, in the wild **audacity** of my perfect triumph, placed my own seat upon the very spot beneath which reposed the corpse of the victim. **H**

The officers were satisfied. My *manner* had convinced them. I was singularly at ease. They sat, and while I answered cheerily, they chatted of familiar things. But, ere long, I felt myself getting pale and wished them gone. My head ached, and I fancied a ringing in my ears; but still they sat and still chatted. The ringing became more distinct—it

H **Literary Perspectives** Analyzing Techniques What word choices create the narrator's confident tone in this paragraph?

Vocabulary **audacity** (aw DAS uh tee) *n.*: boldness.

continued and became more distinct: I talked more freely to get rid of the feeling: but it continued and gained definitiveness—until, at length, I found that the noise was *not* within my ears.

No doubt I now grew *very* pale—but I talked more fluently and with a heightened voice. Yet the sound increased—and what could I do? It was *a low, dull, quick sound—much such a sound as a watch makes when enveloped in cotton.* I gasped for breath—and yet the officers heard it not. I talked more quickly—more vehemently; but the noise steadily increased. I arose and argued about trifles, in a high key and with violent gesticulations, but the noise steadily increased. Why *would* they not be gone? I paced the floor to and fro with heavy strides, as if excited to fury by the observation of the men—but the noise steadily increased. Oh God! what *could* I do? I foamed—I raved—I swore! I swung the chair upon which I had been sitting and grated it upon the boards, but the noise arose over all and continually increased. It grew louder—louder—*louder*! And still the men chatted pleasantly, and smiled. Was it possible they heard not? Almighty God!—no, no! They heard!—they suspected!—they *knew!*—they were making a mockery of my horror!—this I thought, and this I think. But anything was better than this agony! Anything was more tolerable than this derision! I could bear those hypocritical smiles no

longer! I felt that I must scream or die!—and now—again!—hark! louder! *louder!* louder! louder!—

"Villains!" I shrieked, "dissemble no more! I admit the deed!—tear up the planks!—here, here!—it is the beating of his hideous heart!"

---

❶ **Literary Perspectives** **Analyzing Techniques**
What literary <u>devices</u> does the author use to show that the narrator is becoming more and more agitated?

❶ **Read and Discuss** How do things turn out for the narrator?

Applying Your Skills

Reading Standard 3.6 Identify significant literary devices (e.g., metaphor, symbolism, dialect, **irony**) that define a writer's style and use those elements to interpret the work.

The Tell-Tale Heart
Literary Response and Analysis

Reading Skills Focus
Quick Check

1. What <u>distinctive</u> quality of the old man's eye makes the narrator hate it so much?
2. How does the narrator kill the old man?
3. Why does the narrator finally admit his guilt?

Read with a Purpose

4. Is the narrator mad or very clever? Find support for both theories based on his thoughts and actions.

Reading Skills: Paraphrasing a Text

5. Look back at your paraphrase chart. What does comparing Poe's text with your paraphrases teach you about Poe's style? Write your answer in a chart like the one below.

Original Sentence	My Paraphrase

What I learned: _____

Literary Skills Focus
Literary Analysis

6. **Speculate** What is your explanation for the "heartbeat" noise that drives the narrator to confess? (Make sure you know the meaning of *tell-tale*.)
7. **Analyze** The overall feeling in a story is called **mood.** How would you describe the mood of this story? What details does Poe use to create that mood?
8. **Literary Perspectives** What literary <u>devices</u> does Poe use to build tension and increase the impact of the story?

9. **Interpret** The **narrator** keeps claiming to be sane, but you become more and more certain that he is insane. What details in the story indicate that the narrator is insane?

Literary Skills: Irony

10. **Infer** There is a strong sense of dramatic irony in this story. What do you know that the narrator doesn't?
11. **Analyze** How does Poe's use of irony help create a sense of horror and suspense?

Literary Skills Review: Climax

12. **Analyze** The story's final paragraph builds to a kind of mad **climax,** the point of highest emotional tension in a story. How does Poe use words and punctuation to create tension—and even the rhythm of a heartbeat?

Writing Skills Focus
Think as a Reader/Writer

Use It in Your Writing Poe wrote that every word in a story should help create a "single overwhelming impression." How well has he done that in "The Tell-Tale Heart"? In a paragraph, describe the story's impact on you. Mention at least three striking details that help to create this impact.

 What Do You Think Now

How can you tell if the narrator of "The Tell-Tale Heart" is telling the truth? What parts of his story are true or imagined?

The Tell-Tale Heart

Vocabulary Development

Synonyms

A significant aspect of Poe's style in "The Tell-Tale Heart" is his word choice. The more words you know how to use, the more interesting your own writing will be. A good way to expand your vocabulary is to learn **synonyms**—words with similar meanings—for both familiar and unfamiliar words. To locate synonyms, use a dictionary, a **thesaurus** (a dictionary of synonyms, which can also be found on your computer's software), or a **synonym finder.**

Your Turn

Find synonyms for all of the Vocabulary words in the box. Then, for each Vocabulary word, write two sentences of your own, one using the Vocabulary word, and another using a synonym.

> vexed
> audacity
> vehemently
> gesticulations
> derision

Analyze Figures of Speech

A **figure of speech** is a word or phrase that describes one thing in terms of another and is not meant to be understood as literally true.

Your Turn

Each boldface phrase below contains a figure of speech from the story. State what two things are being compared in each sentence. Then, explain what each figure of speech means.

1. The narrator says the old man's **eye resembled that of a vulture.**
2. He says the eye makes his **blood run cold.**
3. He is moving in a **room as black as pitch.**

4. The heartbeat causes fury in the narrator the way **the beating of a drum stimulates the soldier into courage.**

Language Coach

Style: Punctuation and Italics Poe's words and sentence structures are two of the elements that define his style. His style is made up of other elements too—notably italic type, dashes, and exclamation points. To understand what Poe is doing, study specific examples from the story.

- Read the first sentence of "The Tell-Tale Heart" aloud. Then, discuss what the exclamation point, the dashes, and the italics add to the sentence. How does the sentence's meaning change without them?
- Find two other sentences in the story that contain italics, dashes, and/or an exclamation point. Explain what these punctuation marks add to each sentence.

Academic Vocabulary

Write About . . .

Write a critical response to the story. Discuss whether you liked it, disliked it, or (if possible) weren't affected much one way or the other. Include references to Poe's use of specific literary devices in your response.

Grammar Link

Phrases

Nearly every sentence you read, write, and speak contains at least one phrase. A **phrase** is a group of related words that is used as a single part of speech and does not contain a verb and the verb's subject. There are many kinds of phrases:

Prepositional phrases can act as adjectives or adverbs.

PREPOSITIONAL PHRASE I heard all things **in heaven and earth**.

Participial phrases act as adjectives.

PARTICIPIAL PHRASE His room was **black, resembling pitch**.

Appositive phrases explain or identify key nouns.

APPOSITIVE PHRASE It was the old man, **who never suspected me**, whom I was determined to kill.

Using phrases to add information to your writing helps you avoid writing short, choppy sentences.

Your Turn

Writing Applications Combine the pairs of sentences below by adding the boldface phrases to the first sentence of each pair. There may be more than one way to revise the sentences.

1. I opened the door very slowly. I opened the door **little by little**.
2. The old man was in bed. He was **fast asleep**.
3. I went about my crime carefully. I am **a completely sane man**.
4. He was groaning from the bottom of his soul. He was **fearing for his life**.

CHOICES

As you respond to the Choices, use these **Academic Vocabulary** words as appropriate: critical, device, distinctive, interpret.

REVIEW
Analyze the Use of Irony

Timed ⓛ **Writing** In "The Tell-Tale Heart," dramatic irony increases and intensifies the suspense. Identify two examples of dramatic irony in the story, and explain in a brief essay how they create suspense. How does this use of irony define Poe's style?

CONNECT
Write a Police Report

Imagine that you are one of the police officers responding to the neighbor's call. Write a report to be filed after you return to the station. Explain what you found when you arrived on the scene. Include descriptions of the suspect's appearance and of your impressions. When did the suspect's behavior begin to strike you as odd?

EXTEND
Phrases

Group Activity "The Tell-Tale Heart" was made into a movie in 1960. With several classmates, plan a remake. Who would you cast? When would the movie take place? What costumes would the characters wear? Share your ideas with the class.

Learn It Online
Expand your view of this story at:

go.hrw.com   H8-481   Go

RAYMOND'S RUN

by **Toni Cade Bambara**

What Do **You** **Think** What does a person need to do to gain respect?

🕐 QuickWrite

Respecting a person means seeing him or her clearly and valuing what you see. Write a paragraph about a time when you gained new respect for someone. What helped you see the person more clearly?

Reader/Writer Notebook

Use your **RWN** to complete the activities for this selection.

Reading Standard 3.6 Identify significant literary devices (e.g., metaphor, symbolism, **dialect**, irony) **that define a writer's style and use those elements to interpret the work**.

Literary Skills Focus

Style: Dialect When you read this story, you hear Squeaky's own true voice—her dialect. A **dialect** is a way of speaking that is characteristic of a certain geographical area or a certain group of people. Dialect can involve special pronunciations, vocabulary, and grammar. In "Raymond's Run," Toni Cade Bambara captures the voice of her characters by having them speak in a dialect used in 1970s Harlem, a neighborhood in New York City.

Style: Allusions An **allusion** is a reference to something in current events, on TV, in history, in literature, and so on. When writers use allusions, they expect readers to understand what they are referring to. Allusions usually refer to an aspect of culture that people share—literature, history, mythology, sports, and so on. Sometimes allusions can become dated. Footnotes in this story explain some allusions that may be unfamiliar to you.

Reading Skills Focus

Analyzing Style: Literary Devices This story's main character, Squeaky, speaks in dialect and uses allusions. These and other details help create Squeaky's voice.

Into Action Use a chart to record and analyze details from the text. Identify the types of literary devices (irony, figurative language, dialect) that Bambara uses.

Story Details	Literary Device
"And a lot of smart mouths got lots to say about that too. . . ."	dialect
"The big kids call me Mercury. . . ."	

Writing Skills Focus

Think as a Reader/Writer

Find It in Your Reading The story's main character is memorable. As you read, note in your *Reader/Writer Notebook* some of the funny observations she makes.

TechFocus As you read, think about how you might use video and digital technology to portray the story's characters.

Language Coach

Dialect Have you ever heard a Midwest accent or a Southern drawl? Each region of the United States has its own dialect, or way of speaking English, that sets it apart from other regions. Some cities have their own dialects as well. A dialect usually involves distinct ways of pronouncing many words. A dialect also contains special vocabulary. In some parts of the country, groceries are carried in a *bag*, while in others they are carried in a *sack*. Grammar also differs. In a Brooklyn dialect, a person might say *youse* instead of the standard *you* when referring to two or more people; a Southerner might say *you-all* or *y'all*. Watch for instances of special pronunciation, vocabulary, and grammar in "Raymond's Run."

Learn It Online
Use *PowerNotes* for more help at:

go.hrw.com | H8-483 | **Go**

Learn It Online

Learn more about Bambara at:

go.hrw.com H8-484 Go

Toni Cade Bambara
(1939–1995)

Voices of Her Childhood

Toni Cade Bambara grew up in New York City, where "Raymond's Run" takes place. Her writing draws on the voices of her childhood—the street-corner speechmakers, barbershop storytellers, and performers at Harlem's legendary Apollo Theater.

Stories from the Imagination

The author's stories, however, come from Bambara's imagination.

> "It does no good to write autobiographical fiction, cause the minute the book hits the stand here comes your mama screamin how could you. . . . So I deal in straight-up fiction myself, cause I value my family and friends, and mostly cause I lie a lot anyway."

A New Name

Toni Cade Bambara adopted the name Bambara from a signature on a sketchbook she found in her great-grandmother's trunk. The Bambara are a people of northwestern Africa known for their skill in woodcarving.

Think About the Writer What does Bambara's decision to adopt a new last name suggest about her?

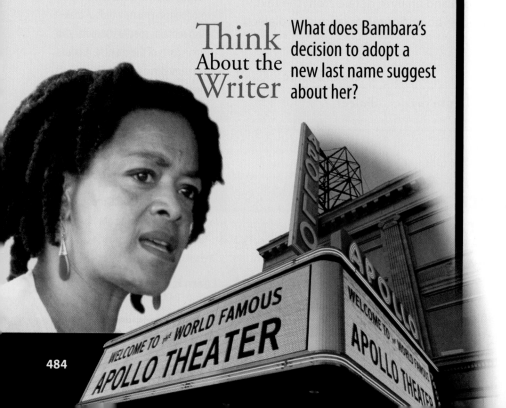

Build Background

"Raymond's Run" is set in Harlem, a neighborhood in New York City. From about 1900 to 1925, many African Americans moved to Harlem from the South. During the 1920s, the neighborhood was the center of an outpouring of writing, music, and art that became known as the Harlem Renaissance. In later decades, economic conditions in Harlem deteriorated. More recently the area has enjoyed revitalization.

Preview the Selection

The main character of this story, a girl called **Squeaky,** has never lost a race. This year, however, she faces stiff competition when a newcomer, **Gretchen,** enters the May Day race.

RAYMOND'S RUN

by **Toni Cade Bambara**

I don't have much work to do around the house like some girls. My mother does that. And I don't have to earn my pocket money by hustling; George runs errands for the big boys and sells Christmas cards. And anything else that's got to get done, my father does. All I have to do in life is mind my brother Raymond, which is enough.

Sometimes I slip and say my little brother Raymond. But as any fool can see he's much bigger and he's older too. But a lot of people call him my little brother cause he needs looking after cause he's not quite right. And a lot of smart mouths got lots to say about that too, especially when George was minding him. But now, if anybody has anything to say to Raymond, anything to say about his big head, they have to come by me. And I don't play the dozens[1] or believe in standing around with somebody in my face doing a lot of talking. I much rather just knock you down and take my chances even if I am a little girl with skinny arms and a squeaky voice, which is how I got the name Squeaky. And if things get too rough, I run. And as anybody can tell you, I'm the fastest thing on two feet. **Ⓐ**

There is no track meet that I don't win the first-place medal. I used to win the twenty-yard dash when I was a little kid in kindergarten. Nowadays, it's the fifty-yard dash. And tomorrow I'm subject to run the quarter-meter relay all by myself and come in first, second, and third. The big kids call me Mercury[2] cause I'm the swiftest thing in the neighborhood. Everybody knows that—except two people who know better, my father and me. He can beat me to Amsterdam Avenue with me having a two-fire-hydrant head start and him running with his hands in his pockets and whistling. But that's private information. Cause

---

1. **play the dozens:** slang for "trade insults."

2. **Mercury:** in Roman mythology, messenger of the gods, known for his speediness.

Ⓐ Read and Discuss In what ways does Squeaky's personality suit her job of taking care of her brother Raymond?

can you imagine some thirty-five-year-old man stuffing himself into PAL[3] shorts to race little kids? So as far as everyone's concerned, I'm the fastest and that goes for Gretchen, too, who has put out the tale that she is going to win the first-place medal this year. Ridiculous. In the second place, she's got short legs. In the third place, she's got freckles. In the first place, no one can beat me and that's all there is to it.

I'm standing on the corner admiring the weather and about to take a stroll down Broadway so I can practice my breathing exercises, and I've got Raymond walking on the inside close to the buildings, cause he's subject to fits of fantasy and starts thinking he's a circus performer and that the curb is a tightrope strung high in the air. And sometimes after a rain he likes to step down off his tightrope right into the gutter and slosh around getting his shoes and cuffs wet. Then I get hit when I get home. Or sometimes if you don't watch him he'll dash across traffic to the island[4] in the middle of Broadway and give the pigeons a fit. Then I have to go behind him apologizing to all the old people sitting around trying to get some sun and getting all upset with the pigeons fluttering around them, scattering their newspapers and upsetting the waxpaper lunches in their laps. So I keep Raymond on the inside of me, and he plays like he's driving a stagecoach which is OK by me so long as

I'M SERIOUS ABOUT MY RUNNING AND I DON'T CARE WHO KNOWS IT.

he doesn't run me over or interrupt my breathing exercises, which I have to do on account of I'm serious about my running, and I don't care who knows it. **Ⓑ**

Now some people like to act like things come easy to them, won't let on that they practice. Not me. I'll high-prance down 34th Street like a rodeo pony to keep my knees strong even if it does get my mother uptight so that she walks ahead like she's not with me, don't know me, is all by herself on a shopping trip, and I am somebody else's crazy child. Now you take Cynthia Procter for instance. She's just the opposite. If there's a test tomorrow, she'll say something like, "Oh, I guess I'll play handball this afternoon and watch television tonight," just to let you know she ain't thinking about the test.

3. **PAL:** Police Athletic League.
4. **island:** traffic island, a car-free area in the middle of the street.

Ⓑ **Reading Focus** Analyzing Style What details does Squeaky reveal to help you understand how difficult it is to watch Raymond?

Or like last week when she won the spelling bee for the millionth time, "A good thing you got 'receive,' Squeaky, cause I would have got it wrong. I completely forgot about the spelling bee." And she'll clutch the lace on her blouse like it was a narrow escape. Oh, brother. But of course when I pass her house on my early morning trots around the block, she is practicing the scales on the piano over and over and over and over. Then in music class she always lets herself get bumped around so she falls accidentally on purpose onto the piano stool and is so surprised to find herself sitting there that she decides just for fun to try out the ole keys. And what do you know—Chopin's[5] waltzes just spring out of her fingertips and she's the most surprised thing in the world. A regular prodigy. I could kill people like that. I stay up all night studying the words for the spelling bee. And you can see me any time of day practicing running. I never walk if I can trot, and shame

on Raymond if he can't keep up. But of course he does, cause if he hangs back someone's liable to walk up to him and get smart, or take his allowance from him, or ask him where he got that great big pumpkin head. People are so stupid sometimes. **C**

So I'm strolling down Broadway breathing out and breathing in on counts of seven, which is my lucky number, and here comes Gretchen and her sidekicks: Mary Louise, who used to be a friend of mine when she first moved to Harlem from Baltimore and got beat up by everybody till I took up for her on account of her mother and my mother used to sing in the same choir when they were young girls, but people ain't grateful, so now she hangs out with the new girl Gretchen and talks about me like a dog; and Rosie, who is as fat as I am skinny and has a big mouth where Raymond is concerned and is too stupid to know that there is not a big deal of difference between herself and Raymond and that she can't afford to throw stones. So they are steady coming up Broadway and I see right away that it's going to be one of those

---

5. **Chopin's:** Frédéric François Chopin (SHOH pan) (1810–1849), Polish composer and pianist.

Vocabulary **prodigy** (PRAHD uh jee) *n.:* child with exceptional talent.

C **Literary Focus** Dialect What nonstandard words and grammar does Squeaky use in this paragraph? How does this make the character <u>distinctive</u>?

Dodge City scenes[6] cause the street ain't that big and they're close to the buildings just as we are. First I think I'll step into the candy store and look over the new comics and let them pass. But that's chicken and I've got a reputation to consider. So then I think I'll just walk straight on through them or even over them if necessary. But as they get to me, they slow down. I'm ready to fight, cause like I said I don't feature a whole lot of chit-chat, I much prefer to just knock you down right from the jump and save everybody a lotta precious time. **Ⓓ**

---

6. **Dodge City scenes:** showdowns such as those in the television western *Gunsmoke*, which was set in Dodge City, Kansas. In a typical scene a marshal and an outlaw face off with pistols on an empty street.

"You signing up for the May Day races?" smiles Mary Louise, only it's not a smile at all. A dumb question like that doesn't deserve an answer. Besides, there's just me and Gretchen standing there really, so no use wasting my breath talking to shadows.

"I don't think you're going to win this time," says Rosie, trying to signify[7] with her hands on her hips all salty, completely forgetting that I have whupped her behind many times for less salt than that.

"I always win cause I'm the best," I say straight at Gretchen who is, as far as I'm concerned, the only one talking in this ventriloquist-dummy routine. Gretchen smiles, but it's not a smile, and I'm thinking

---

7. **signify:** slang for "act boastful or insult someone."

Ⓓ **Literary Focus** **Dialect and Allusions** Squeaky speaks in dialect and uses allusions ("can't afford to throw stones" and "those Dodge City scenes"). How do these details help you understand and enjoy Squeaky's character?

Vocabulary **reputation** (rehp yuh TAY shuhn) *n.*: the way others see a person.

Analyzing Visuals **Connecting to the Text** How does the body language of these girls capture the attitudes of the characters in the story?

that girls never really smile at each other because they don't know how and don't want to know how and there's probably no one to teach us how, cause grown-up girls don't know either. Then they all look at Raymond who has just brought his mule team to a standstill. And they're about to see what trouble they can get into through him.

"What grade you in now, Raymond?"

"You got anything to say to my brother, you say it to me, Mary Louise Williams of Raggedy Town, Baltimore."

"What are you, his mother?" sasses Rosie.

"That's right, Fatso. And the next word out of anybody and I'll be their mother too." So they just stand there and Gretchen shifts from one leg to the other and so do they. Then Gretchen puts her hands on her hips and is about to say something with her freckle-face self but doesn't. Then she walks around me looking me up and down but keeps walking up Broadway, and her sidekicks follow her. So me and Raymond smile at each other and he says, "Gidyap" to his team and I continue with my breathing exercises, strolling down

"I ALWAYS WIN CAUSE I'M THE BEST."

Broadway toward the iceman on 145th with not a care in the world cause I am Miss Quicksilver[8] herself. **E**

I take my time getting to the park on May Day because the track meet is the last thing on the program. The biggest thing on the program is the May Pole dancing, which I can do without, thank you, even if my mother thinks it's a shame I don't take part and act like a girl for a change. You'd think my mother'd be grateful not to have to make me a white organdy dress with a big satin sash and buy me new white baby-doll shoes that can't be taken out of the box till the big day. You'd think she'd be glad her daughter ain't out there prancing around a May Pole getting the new clothes all dirty and sweaty and trying to act like a fairy or a flower or whatever you're supposed to be when you should be trying to be yourself, whatever that is, which is, as far as I am concerned, a poor black girl who really can't afford to buy shoes and a new dress you only wear once a lifetime cause it won't fit next year.

---

8. **quicksilver:** another name for mercury, a silver-colored liquid metal that flows rapidly.

E [Read and Discuss] What does this scene with the three girls add to what you know about Squeaky?

I was once a strawberry in a Hansel and Gretel pageant when I was in nursery school and didn't have no better sense than to dance on tiptoe with my arms in a circle over my head doing umbrella steps and being a perfect fool just so my mother and father could come dressed up and clap. You'd think they'd know better than to encourage that kind of nonsense. I am not a strawberry. I do not dance on my toes. I run. That is what I am all about. So I always come late to the May Day program, just in time to get my number pinned on and lay in the grass till they announce the fifty-yard dash. **F**

I put Raymond in the little swings, which is a tight squeeze this year and will be impossible next year. Then I look around for Mr. Pearson, who pins the numbers on. I'm really looking for Gretchen if you want to know the truth, but she's not around. The park is jam-packed. Parents in hats and corsages and breast-pocket handkerchiefs peeking up. Kids in white dresses and light-blue suits. The parkees unfolding chairs and chasing the rowdy kids from Lenox[9] as if they had no right to be there. The big guys with their caps on backwards, leaning against the fence swirling the basketballs on the tips of their fingers, waiting for all these crazy people to clear out the park so they can play. Most of the kids in my class are carrying bass drums and glockenspiels[10] and flutes. You'd think they'd put in a few bongos or something for real like that. **G**

Then here comes Mr. Pearson with his clipboard and his cards and pencils and whistles and safety pins and fifty million other things he's always dropping all over the place with his clumsy self. He sticks out in a crowd because he's on stilts. We used to call him Jack and the Beanstalk to get him mad. But I'm the only one that can outrun him and get away, and I'm too grown for that silliness now.

"Well, Squeaky," he says, checking my name off the list and handing me number seven and two pins. And I'm thinking he's got no right to call me Squeaky, if I can't call him Beanstalk.

"Hazel Elizabeth Deborah Parker," I correct him and tell him to write it down on his board.

"Well, Hazel Elizabeth Deborah Parker, going to give someone else a break this year?" I squint at him real hard to see if he is seriously thinking I should lose the race on purpose just to give someone else a break. "Only six girls running this time," he continues, shaking his head sadly like it's my fault all of New York didn't turn out

9. **Lenox:** Lenox Avenue, a major street in Harlem.

10. **glockenspiels** (GLAHK uhn speelz): musical instruments with flat metal bars that are struck with small hammers and produce bell-like sounds. Glockenspiels are often used in marching bands.

F **Literary Focus** Dialect Why do you think Bambara writes "didn't have no better sense" (instead of *didn't have any better sense*)?

G **Read and Discuss** How do Squeaky's descriptions of May Pole dancing, acting as a strawberry in a play, and commentary on the people in the park on May Day add to your image of her?

in sneakers. "That new girl should give you a run for your money." He looks around the park for Gretchen like a periscope in a submarine movie. "Wouldn't it be a nice gesture if you were . . . to ahhh . . ."

I give him such a look he couldn't finish putting that idea into words. Grown-ups got a lot of nerve sometimes. I pin number seven to myself and stomp away, I'm so burnt. And I go straight for the track and stretch out on the grass while the band winds up with "Oh, the Monkey Wrapped His Tail Around the Flag Pole," which my teacher calls by some other name. The man on the loudspeaker is calling everyone over to the track and I'm on my back looking at the sky, trying to pretend I'm in the country, but I can't, because even grass in the city feels hard as sidewalk, and there's just no pretending you are anywhere but in a "concrete jungle" as my grandfather says. **H**

The twenty-yard dash takes all of two minutes cause most of the little kids don't know no better than to run off the track or run the wrong way or run smack into the fence and fall down and cry. One little kid, though, has got the good sense to run straight for the white ribbon up ahead so he wins. Then the second-graders line up for the thirty-yard dash and I don't even bother to turn my head to watch cause Raphael Perez always wins. He wins before he even begins by psyching the runners, telling them they're going to trip on their shoelaces and fall on their faces or lose their shorts or something, which he doesn't really have to do since he is very fast, almost as fast as I am. After that is the forty-yard dash which I used to run when I was in first grade. Raymond is hollering from the swings cause he knows I'm about to do my thing cause the man on the loudspeaker has just announced the fifty-yard dash, although

H **Read and Discuss** What do you learn about Squeaky from her remarks about Mr. Pearson and other grown-ups? How do you think she feels when she makes her last remark?

he might just as well be giving a recipe for angel food cake cause you can hardly make out what he's sayin for the static. I get up and slip off my sweat pants and then I see Gretchen standing at the starting line, kicking her legs out like a pro. Then as I get into place I see that ole Raymond is on line on the other side of the fence, bending down with his fingers on the ground just like he knew what he was doing. I was going to yell at him but then I didn't. It burns up your energy to holler.

Every time, just before I take off in a race, I always feel like I'm in a dream, the kind of dream you have when you're sick with fever and feel all hot and weightless. I dream I'm flying over a sandy beach in the early morning sun, kissing the leaves of the trees as I fly by. And there's always the smell of apples, just like in the country when I was little and used to think I was a choo-choo train, running through the fields of corn and chugging up the hill to the orchard. And all the time I'm dreaming this, I get lighter and lighter until I'm flying over the beach again, getting blown through the sky like a feather that weighs nothing at all. But once I spread my fingers in the dirt and crouch over the Get on Your Mark, the dream goes and I am solid again and am telling myself, Squeaky you must win, you must win, you are the fastest thing in the world, you can even beat your father up Amsterdam if you really try. And then I feel my weight coming back just behind my knees then down to my feet then into the earth and the pistol shot explodes in my blood and

I am off and weightless again, flying past the other runners, my arms pumping up and down and the whole world is quiet except for the crunch as I zoom over the gravel in the track. I glance to my left and there is no one. To the right, a blurred Gretchen, who's got her chin jutting out as if it would win the race all by itself. And on the other side of the fence is Raymond with his arms down to his side and the palms tucked up behind him, running in his very own style, and it's the first time I ever saw that and I almost stop to watch my brother Raymond on his first run. But the white ribbon is bouncing toward me and I tear past it, racing into the distance till my feet with a mind of their own start digging up footfuls of dirt and brake me short. Then all the kids standing on the side pile on me, banging me on the back and slapping my head with their May Day programs, for I have won again and everybody on 151st Street can walk tall for another year. **❶**

"In first place . . ." the man on the loud-speaker is clear as a bell now. But then he pauses and the loudspeaker starts to whine. Then static. And I lean down to catch my breath and here comes Gretchen walking back, for she's overshot the finish line too, huffing and puffing with her hands on her hips taking it slow, breathing in steady time like a real pro and I sort of like her a little for the first time. "In first place . . ." and then three or four voices get all mixed up on the loudspeaker and I dig my sneaker into the grass and stare at Gretchen who's staring back, we both wondering just who did win. I can hear old Beanstalk argu-ing with the man on the loudspeaker and then a few others running their mouths about what the stopwatches say. Then I hear Raymond yanking at the fence to call me and I wave to shush him, but he keeps rattling the fence like a gorilla in a cage like in them gorilla movies, but then like a dancer or something he starts climbing up nice and easy but very fast. And it occurs to me, watching how smoothly he climbs hand over hand and remembering how he looked running with his arms down to his side and with the wind pulling his mouth back and his teeth showing and all, it occurred to me that Raymond would make a very fine runner. Doesn't he always keep up with me on my trots? And he surely knows how to breathe in counts of seven cause he's always doing it at the dinner

---

❶ Literary Focus **Dialect** What kind of language does the author use in this paragraph? Why do you think she doesn't use dialect?

table, which drives my brother George up the wall. And I'm smiling to beat the band cause if I've lost this race, or if me and Gretchen tied, or even if I've won, I can always retire as a runner and begin a whole new career as a coach with Raymond as my champion. After all, with a little more study I can beat Cynthia and her phony self at the spelling bee. And if I bugged my mother, I could get piano lessons and become a star. And I have a big rep[11] as the baddest thing around. And I've got a roomful of ribbons and medals and awards. But what has Raymond got to call his own? **J**

So I stand there with my new plans, laughing out loud by this time as Raymond jumps down from the fence and runs over with his teeth showing and his arms down to the side, which no one before him has quite mastered as a running style. And by the time he comes over I'm jumping up and down so glad to see him—my brother Raymond, a great runner in the family tradition. But of course everyone thinks I'm jumping up and down because the men on the loudspeaker have finally gotten themselves together and compared notes and are announcing "In first place—Miss Hazel Elizabeth Deborah Parker." (Dig that.) "In second place—Miss Gretchen P. Lewis." And I look over at Gretchen wondering what the "P" stands for. And I smile. Cause she's good, no doubt about it. Maybe she'd like to help me coach Raymond; she obviously is serious about running, as any fool can see. And she nods to congratulate me and then she smiles. And I smile. We stand there with this big smile of respect between us. It's about as real a smile as girls can do for each other, considering we don't practice real smiling every day, you know, cause maybe we too busy being flowers or fairies or strawberries instead of something honest and worthy of respect . . . you know . . . like being people. **K**

---

11. **rep:** slang for "reputation." People often create slang by clipping off parts of words.

J **Read and Discuss** How does Squeaky's new plan connect to what you already know about her?

K **Literary Focus** **Dialect** What parts of this paragraph show Squeaky's special way of talking?

Applying Your Skills

Reading Standard 3.6 Identify significant literary devices (e.g., metaphor, symbolism, **dialect,** irony) **that define a writer's style and use those elements to interpret the work**.

Raymond's Run
Literary Response and Analysis

Reading Skills Focus
Quick Check

1. Explain why taking care of Raymond is not an easy job. How does Squeaky protect him?
2. What does Squeaky decide to do for Raymond?

Read with a Purpose

3. How do you think Squeaky's new discovery will change her life?

Reading Skills: Analyzing Details

4. Review your chart containing details about Bambara's writing style. Add a row at the bottom to describe Bambara's overall writing style.

Story Details	Literary Device
"And a lot of smart mouths got lots to say about that too...."	dialect

Bambara's overall writing style:

Literary Skills Focus
Literary Analysis

5. **Interpret** What do you think is the most important conflict in this story? Why?
6. **Analyze** Explain whether Squeaky is very different from the girls she describes in the story. Cite details to support your answer.
7. **Infer** Why do you think Squeaky and Gretchen smile at each other after the race?
8. **Evaluate** Would you have called this story "Raymond's Run"? Defend Bambara's choice, or invent a new title and explain why you think it's better.

Literary Skills: Dialect and Allusion

9. **Analyze** What does the use of dialect in this story reveal about its narrator and the time and place in which she lives? How would your interpretation of the story change if it had been written without dialect?
10. **Identify** What do Squeaky's allusions reveal about her interests and education? Support your answer with details from the text.

Literary Skills Review: Theme

11. **Analyze** Squeaky realizes something important during the race. What does Squeaky's new outlook reveal about the story's **theme,** or insight about life?

Writing Skills Focus
Think as a Reader/Writer

Use It in Your Writing Create a character who has a distinctive way of expressing himself or herself. For example, he or she might speak in a dialect, use exclamations, or exaggerate. Write a paragraph in which your character, in a distinct voice, tells about his or her talent.

What Do You Think Now

After reading the story, what qualities do you think are most worthy of respect?

Applying Your Skills

Reading Skill 1.1 Analyze idioms, analogies, metaphors, and similes to infer the literal and figurative meaning of phrases.

Raymond's Run

Vocabulary Development

Vocabulary Check

Use the Vocabulary words to answer the questions below.

prodigy
reputation

1. If you could choose to be a **prodigy** at anything, what would you choose?
2. What kind of **reputation** do you strive for?

Figures of Speech

In "Raymond's Run," Squeaky speaks in a colorful way, using lots of slang. The slang terms are often based on **metaphors,** in which one thing is compared to another. She also sprinkles her language with **similes,** in which she compares one thing to another using such words as *like, as, than,* and *resembles.* In addition, Squeaky uses an **analogy,** a comparison of two things, when she reveals her state of mind before the race by comparing it to a dream about flying.

Your Turn

Identify each boldface figure of speech that follows as a metaphor or a simile. Then, explain the comparison made in each one.

1. Squeaky prances down the street **like a rodeo pony** to keep her knees strong.
2. Squeaky gets angry when people ask Raymond where he got that great big **pumpkin head.**
3. She says that Mr. Pearson looks around the park **like a periscope in a submarine movie.**

4. Re-read the analogy that Squeaky makes comparing her state of mind before the race to flying (page 492). Then, write an analogy of your own. Open your analogy with words like these: "Playing football is like . . ." or "Reading a good story is like . . ."

Language Coach

Dialect In a dialect, words can have special meaning, pronunciation, or spelling. What do you think the italicized words in the following sentence from "Raymond's Run" mean? "'I don't think you're going to win this time,' says Rosie, trying to *signify* with her hands on her hips *all salty,* completely forgetting that I have *whupped* her behind many times for less *salt* than that" (page 488). Rewrite the sentence as someone in your neighborhood would say it.

Academic Vocabulary

Talk About . . .
About midway through the story, Squeaky says, "you should be trying to be yourself, whatever that is . . ." How do you <u>interpret</u> this statement? Explain whether or not you agree with her.

Grammar Link

Clauses

Clauses are the main building blocks of sentences. Every clause has a subject and a verb. Some clauses can stand by themselves as a simple sentence. We call these **independent clauses.** Other clauses cannot stand alone because they do not express a complete thought. These are called **subordinate clauses,** and they must be combined with other clauses, words, or phrases to make sense.

EXAMPLE I don't have much work to do around the house. *[The entire sentence is an independent clause.]*

EXAMPLE Because I don't have much work to do around the house *[This clause is a subordinate clause. Although it has a subject and verb, it cannot stand by itself as a complete sentence.]*

Your Turn

Writing Applications Create sentences using the subordinate clauses below as a base. Each new sentence you create should be about "Raymond's Run."

1. that I don't win the first-place medal
2. and sometimes after it rains
3. like things come easy to them
4. is the May Pole dancing

CHOICES

As you respond to the Choices, use these **Academic Vocabulary** words as appropriate: <u>critical</u>, <u>device</u>, <u>distinctive</u>, <u>interpret</u>.

REVIEW
Define a Writer's Style

Re-read Bambara's biography on page 484. Then, in a paragraph, discuss your impression of Bambara's writing style. Consider how she uses dialect to establish both her own <u>distinctive</u> voice and that of her main character, Squeaky.

CONNECT
Write a Contrast Essay

Timed ⏲ Writing In "Raymond's Run," Squeaky does her best to win a race and, as a result of her effort, sees the people around her more clearly. How does she now view Raymond and Gretchen? Write a brief essay contrasting her previous views with her new perceptions.

EXTEND
Portray a Character

TechFocus Plan a digital narrative in which you portray one of the characters in the story— Squeaky, Raymond, Gretchen. Begin by choosing a character. Then, create a storyboard of your video. What would the character most like to show or explain to a viewer? Use your imagination, but try to use some of the story's details about the setting and characters.

Learn It Online
Find a storyboard template at the Digital Storytelling site online:

go.hrw.com | H8-497 | **Go**

MY MOTHER PIECED QUILTS

by **Teresa Palomo Acosta**

Sweater / Suéter

by **Alberto Forcada**

Reader/Writer
Notebook

Use your **RWN** to complete the
activities for these selections.

Reading Standard 3.6 Identify
significant literary devices (e.g.,
metaphor, **symbolism**, dialect, irony) **that
define a writer's style and use those
elements to interpret the work.**

Literary Skills Focus

Symbolism A **symbol** is a person, a place, a thing, or an event that
stands for something beyond itself. Some symbols are traditional and
common to a culture. We understand them because people have agreed
on their meaning. For example, a blindfolded woman holding scales has
come to symbolize justice.

In literature, however, symbols are created by individual writers,
and must be <u>interpreted</u> by the readers. Here is what the writer Gary
Soto says about symbols in poetry: "Each word in a poem is very important and is chosen very carefully to convey just the right meaning. For
example, the word *tree* might stand for more than a tree in an orchard.
It might symbolize life itself, or it might symbolize the strength of your
grandfather or your father."

Reading Skills Focus

Reading Poetry Poetry is written in lines—some long and some very
short. Some poets use punctuation in their lines, while others do not.
When you read a poem that does not use punctuation, you have to read
the lines as thought units. That means that you do not come to a stop at
the end of every line. You have to see if the sense of the line carries over
to the next line.

Into Action As you read each poem, fill in a chart like the one below
with thought units. Add rows to your charts as needed.

My Mother Pieced Quilts	
1st thought unit	they were meant as covers in winter
2nd thought unit	

Writing Skills Focus
Think as a Reader/Writer

Find It in Your Reading Teresa Palomo Acosta includes lists of
things in her poem. As you read, note in your *Reader/Writer Notebook*
the lists of objects or images that are grouped together.

Vocabulary

**My Mother Pieced
Quilts**

frayed (frayd) *adj.*: worn away; unraveled. *Frayed pieces of fabric are
finished into a quilt.*

somber (SAHM buhr) *adj.*: dark; melancholy. *She grew somber, thinking
about the funeral.*

taut (tawt) *adj.*: pulled tight. *The taut
thread holds the quilt together.*

Language Coach

**Language Conventions Proper
nouns** name specific people, places,
and things. In English, proper nouns
are capitalized. Teresa Palomo
Acosta, however, deliberately begins
proper nouns, such as *January,
October, Michigan, Santa Fe,* and
Easter, with lowercase letters in her
poem. After you've read the poem,
think about why she made that
choice.

Learn It Online
Develop your vocabulary skills with Word Watch:

| go.hrw.com | H8-499 | **Go** |

Teresa Palomo Acosta
(1949–   )

A Love of Poetry
Teresa Palomo Acosta grew up in McGregor, Texas, and began writing poetry when she was just sixteen. She published her first poem in 1976. As a teenager she enjoyed European and early American poetry. Later she was inspired by African American and Mexican American poetry. She has been involved in various projects to promote Latino literature and is the co-author of the book *Las Tejanas: 300 Years of History*.

Alberto Forcada
(1969–   )

The Dreams of Children
The poems of Alberto Forcada that appear in *Despertar (Awaking)*—"Suéter" is one of them—describe the dreams and fantasies of children. Forcada has a degree in philosophy from the National University of Mexico. His poems have been collected in three books and have been published in magazines such as *De Polanco para Polanco,* which serves a neighborhood in Mexico City.

Think About the Writers Forcada's poem is about a sweater, but it represents a larger meaning. What everyday item would you choose to write about?

Build Background
Piecing a quilt means sewing together pieces of fabric to create a bed cover. Usually the scraps of fabric are stitched together to form a pattern. Some quilts follow a traditional pattern, while others are unique.

Wedding ring, American quilt (detail) (c. 1930). Cotton patchwork.

Preview the Selections
In "My Mother Pieced Quilts" the speaker tells you about the associations she makes with the patchwork in her mother's quilts.

In "Sweater" the speaker asks his grandmother for more than a garment to keep himself warm.

MY MOTHER PIECED QUILTS

by **Teresa Palomo Acosta**

they were just meant as covers
in winters
as weapons
against pounding january winds

5   but it was just that every morning I awoke to these
october ripened canvases
passed my hand across their cloth faces
and began to wonder how you pieced
all these together
these strips of gentle communion cotton and flannel
10   nightgowns
wedding organdies
dime store velvets Ⓐ

Ⓐ **Literary Focus** **Symbolism** What might the different types of fabric listed here symbolize?

how you shaped patterns square and oblong and round
positioned

15 balanced
then cemented them
with your thread
a steel needle
a thimble

20 how the thread darted in and out
galloping along the frayed edges, tucking them in
as you did us at night
oh how you stretched and turned and rearranged
your michigan spring faded curtain pieces

25 my father's santa fe work shirt
the summer denims, the tweeds of fall   **Ⓑ**

Ⓑ **Read and Discuss** What is Acosta illustrating for you as she lists different fabrics, shapes, and clothing types?

Vocabulary **frayed** (frayd) *adj.:* worn away; unraveled.

in the evening you sat at your canvas
—our cracked linoleum floor the drawing board
me lounging on your arm
30 and you staking out the plan:
whether to put the lilac purple of easter against the red
        plaid of winter-going-
into-spring
whether to mix a yellow with blue and white and
        paint the
corpus christi noon when my father held your hand
35 whether to shape a five-point star from the
somber black silk you wore to grandmother's funeral

Vocabulary **somber** (SAHM buhr) *adj.:* dark; melancholy.

Crazy patchwork quilt (c. 1875).

Analyzing Visuals

Connecting to the Text
How do you picture the
mother's quilts?

you were the river current
carrying the roaring notes . . .
forming them into pictures of a little boy reclining
40 a swallow flying
you were the caravan master at the reins
driving your threaded needle artillery across the
      mosaic cloth bridges
delivering yourself in separate testimonies° **C**

oh mother you plunged me sobbing and laughing
45 into our past
into the river crossing at five
into the spinach fields
into the plainview cotton rows
into tuberculosis wards
50 into braids and muslin dresses
sewn hard and **taut** to withstand the thrashing of
      twenty-five years

stretched out they lay
armed/ready/shouting/celebrating

knotted with love
55 the quilts sing on

---

43. testimonies: declarations. For example, people make
testimonies of faith or of love.

C **Read and Discuss** Acosta uses phrases such as "river current," "caravan master," and "driving your needle" to describe her mother's quilting. What do these phrases tell you about the mother and the way Acosta views her?

Vocabulary **taut** (tawt) *adj.:* pulled tight.

Sweater

by **Alberto Forcada**
translated by **Judith Infante**

Grandmother,
I'm cold;
can you knit me
some wrinkles? Ⓐ

Ⓐ **Read and Discuss** What is the
speaker really saying here?

Suéter

por **Alberto Forcada**

Abuela,
tengo frío;
téjeme a mí también
unas arrugas.

Applying Your Skills

Reading Standard 3.6 Identify significant literary devices (e.g., metaphor, **symbolism**, dialect, irony) **that define a writer's style and use those elements to interpret the work.**

My Mother Pieced Quilts / Sweater/Suéter
Literary Response and Analysis

Reading Skills Focus
Read with a Purpose

1. Why are the quilts in "My Mother Pieced Quilts" more than just "covers"?

2. Why does the speaker of "Sweater" want wrinkles?

Reading Skills: Reading Poetry

3. Review your charts, and think about the ideas each poem expresses. Then, decide what **theme,** or insight about life, comes through in each poem. Add a theme statement to each chart.

My Mother Pieced Quilts

1st thought unit	they were meant as covers in winter
2nd thought unit	
Poem's theme:	

✓ Vocabulary Check

Match each Vocabulary word with its definition.

4. **frayed**   a. pulled tight
5. **somber**   b. worn away; unraveled
6. **taut**   c. dark; melancholy

Literary Skills Focus
Literary Analysis

7. **Identify** A figure of speech that gives something inanimate human qualities is called **personification.** List three or more examples of personification in Acosta's poem.

8. **Interpret** To what does the speaker in "Sweater" compare the sweater? Would this comparison be appropriate if the poem had been addressed to his sister? Why or why not?

9. **Compare** In line 6 of "My Mother Pieced Quilts," the speaker refers to the quilts as "ripened canvases." What associations can you make between what her mother does and what a painter of pictures might do?

Literary Skills: Symbolism

10. **Interpret** What do you think the quilts symbolize for the speaker of "My Mother Pieced Quilts"?

11. **Interpret** Why do you think Forcada titled his poem "Sweater"? What might the sweater symbolize?

Literary Skills Review: Imagery

12. **Analyze** Re-read lines 44–51 of Acosta's poem. Based on the images presented, how do you think the speaker feels about the past?

Writing Skills Focus
Think as a Reader/Writer

Use It in Your Writing Look back at the lists you recorded in your *Reader/Writer Notebook*. Now, write a paragraph about an object that is significant to you. Like Acosta, use the form of a list to create a rich description.

 **What Do You Think Now** Why do some ordinary objects, such as quilts and sweaters, evoke strong meanings?

Vocabulary Development

More on Metaphors

Metaphors are an important part of everyday speech. They make our language colorful and fun. They are even more essential to poetry. It would be unusual to find a poem without at least one metaphor in it.

Your Turn

The following statements refer to metaphors in "My Mother Pieced Quilts." For each statement, tell what is being compared to what. Then, explain how the metaphor works—what is the poet saying about the quilts and the quilter in each metaphor? In some cases you will have to use your imagination. The first one has been completed for you.

1. Quilts were meant as <u>weapons against pounding january winds</u>.

   Answer: Quilts are compared to weapons. The metaphor means that the quilts protect the sleeper against the cold winds of January, just as weapons may protect someone from harm.

2. Quilts are <u>october ripened canvases</u>.

3. The quilter is said to have <u>cemented</u> the quilt pieces with her thread.

4. The thread is described as <u>galloping along the frayed edges</u>.

5. The speaker says the quilt maker was <u>the river current / carrying the roaring notes</u>.

6. The speaker says the quilt maker was <u>the caravan master at the reins / driving your threaded needle artillery across the mosaic cloth bridges</u>.

7. The quilts are said to be <u>armed/ready/shouting/celebrating</u>.

Language Coach

Precise Language What's the difference between a *chair* and a *rocker*? What about *loud* and *roaring*? Every language contains both general and precise words. Precise nouns and adjectives help a writer create a specific setting. Precise verbs and adverbs can make the action clear. Because poems are short, every word in them is important. Therefore, poets use the most precise, specific language they can to convey their message. Re-read "My Mother Pieced Quilts," looking for examples of precise words and phrases. Write the words you find in your *Reader/Writer Notebook*.

Academic Vocabulary

Talk About . . .

Think about the poems you just read. How successful was the main literary <u>device</u>, the use of symbols, in conveying the writers' messages? With a partner, state your opinion of the writers' <u>distinctive</u> styles. Which poem do you prefer? Why?

Learn It Online
For action-packed vocabulary lessons, visit:

go.hrw.com | H8-507 | Go

A word is dead
by **Emily Dickinson**

The Word/La palabra
by **Manuel Ulacia**

What Do You Think? When do words appeal to your mind? When might they appeal to your heart?

QuickWrite
Discuss an instance when you experienced the power of words, such as reading a poem that changed your thinking.

Reader/Writer Notebook

Use your **RWN** to complete the activities for these selections.

Reading Standard 3.6 Identify significant literary devices (e.g., metaphor, symbolism, dialect, irony) **that define a writer's style and use those elements to interpret the work.**

Literary Skills Focus

Figures of Speech Some of the most significant literary <u>devices</u> writers use to convey meaning are called figures of speech. **Figures of speech** are expressed as comparisons and are not literally true. The three most common figures of speech follow:

- A **metaphor** directly compares two very different things. *The moon was a golden coin high in the sky.*
- A **simile** compares two things using a word or phrase of comparison such as *like, as, such as, than,* or *resembles. The moon looked like a golden coin high in the sky.*
- **Personification** describes a nonhuman or inanimate thing as if it were human and behaved as if it were alive. *The moon smiled down from high in the sky.*

Reading Skills Focus

Reading Aloud Reading a poem aloud more than once will help you understand the poem. You will appreciate the poet's use of literary <u>devices</u> and sound effects and will be fully prepared to <u>interpret</u> a poem and analyze the writer's style.

Into Action Use a chart like the one below to track what you discover as you read each poem aloud.

	A word is dead
1st reading (early impression)	This is a simple poem about words.
2nd reading (study elements of style)	
3rd reading (my interpretation)	

Writing Skills Focus

Think as a Reader/Writer

Find It in Your Reading Record the literary <u>devices</u>, including figures of speech, that the poets use in their writing in your *Reader/Writer Notebook*.

Language Coach

Language Conventions When reading poetry, be aware that poets often omit punctuation marks in their poems. Look at the following stanza from "A word is dead."

> A word is dead
> When it is said,
> Some say.

When you read the stanza, think of it as if it had the following punctuation:

> "A word is dead
> when it is said,"
> some say.

As you read the poems that follow, try repunctuating them to help you understand their meaning.

Learn It Online
Listen to these poems at:

go.hrw.com   H8-509   Go

Learn It Online

Learn more about Dickinson at:

go.hrw.com H8-510 Go

Emily Dickinson
(1830–1886)

"Letter to the World"

Although today Emily Dickinson is one of the most respected poets in the world, her work was almost completely unknown during her lifetime. Dickinson led an extremely private life in her family home in Amherst, Massachusetts. After she died, her sister Lavinia discovered the poems—almost eighteen hundred of them—that Dickinson had gathered into hand-made booklets. Dickinson said that her poems were her "letter to the world" that never wrote to her.

Manuel Ulacia
(1954–2001)

Professor and Poet

Manuel Ulacia studied both architecture and literature. He went on to become a professor at Yale University and also taught at Mexico City's Universidad Autónoma. In addition to writing his own poetry, Ulacia studied and wrote about the work of his mentor, Octavio Paz, a Nobel Prize–winning Latin American poet and essayist.

Think About the Writers Dickinson led a private life; Ulacia taught at universities. What do they have in common?

Preview the Selections

In "A word is dead" the speaker contrasts her beliefs about language with what other people think.

In "The Word" the speaker uses comparisons to describe a word.

A word is dead

by **Emily Dickinson**

A word is dead
When it is said,
Some say.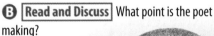

I say it just
Begins to live
That day. **Ⓑ**

Ⓐ **Reading Focus** **Read Aloud** Read the first stanza aloud slowly. Who is expressing an opinion? What is this opinion?

Ⓑ **Read and Discuss** What point is the poet making?

The Word

by **Manuel Ulacia**
translated by **Jennifer Clement**

comes out from the pen
like a rabbit from a magician's hat
astronaut who knows itself alone
and weightless suspended on a line
in space **Ⓒ**

Ⓒ **Literary Focus** **Figures of Speech**
To what does the speaker compare words? What do these comparisons tell you about words?

La palabra

por **Manuel Ulacia**

sale de la pluma
como el conejo del sombrero de un mago
astronauta que se sabe sola y sin peso
suspendida en una línea
en el espacio

Sketch of a Rabbit (c. 1900–1925)
by Seiho Takeuchi.

Applying Your Skills

Reading Standard 3.6 Identify significant literary devices (e.g., metaphor, symbolism, dialect, irony) **that define a writer's style and use those elements to interpret the work.**

A word is dead / The Word / La palabra

Literary Response and Analysis

Reading Skills Focus
Read with a Purpose

1. What surprising ideas about words do these poems convey?

Reading Skills: Read Aloud

2. If you know Spanish, read the original text of Ulacia's poem aloud. Does it use rhyme? What is your evaluation of its translation into English?

Literary Skills Focus
Literary Analysis

3. **Interpret** In Dickinson's poem, what do people believe happens when a word is spoken? What does the speaker say happens?

4. **Interpret** In "The Word," to what is a word compared? What do these comparisons suggest?

5. **Make Judgments** Explain whether you agree with Dickinson's and Ulacia's points of view about words.

6. **Extend** Name a word that seems "alive" to you. Why does it seem so?

7. **Extend** A children's rhyme goes "Sticks and stones / Can break my bones / But names can never hurt me." How do you think Dickinson would respond to that saying? What is your opinion of it?

Literary Skills: Figures of Speech

8. **Interpret** Dickinson uses personification when she says that a word "begins to live." How do you interpret this phrase? How might a word begin to "live" after it is spoken?

9. **Interpret** What do the similes in lines 2–4 of Ulacia's poem make you see?

Literary Skills Review: Imagery

10. **Analyze** Language that appeals to the senses of sight, hearing, touch, taste, or smell is called **imagery.** In Ulacia's poem, to which sense does the image of a rabbit coming out of a magician's hat appeal? To which senses does the image of an astronaut "weightless suspended on a line in space" appeal? How do these images help you interpret the meaning of the poem?

Writing Skills Focus
Think as a Reader/Writer

Use It in Your Writing Look back at the literary devices you recorded in your *Reader/Writer Notebook*. Write a paragraph in which you compare and contrast the way Dickinson and Ulacia use literary devices with the way Teresa Palomo Acosta or Alberto Forcada uses them (pages 501–505). How does the use of literary devices define each writer's style? What makes each poet's style distinctive?

What Do You Think Now

What appealed to you most in these two poems?

Vocabulary Development
Metaphors, Similes, and Personification

The most common figures of speech are metaphors, similes, and personification. **Metaphors** directly compare two unlike things. **Similes** compare two unlike things but use a word or phrase such as *like, than, as, such as,* or *resembles* to introduce the comparison. **Personification** gives human or lifelike qualities or behavior to something that is not human.

Your Turn

The following lines are from well-known poems. Each line includes a figure of speech. Determine whether each quotation uses a metaphor, a simile, or personification. Infer the meaning of each phrase by stating what is being compared.

1. "'Hope' is the thing with feathers"
   —Emily Dickinson

2. "I wandered lonely as a cloud"
   —William Wordsworth

3. "The road was a ribbon of moonlight"
   —Alfred Noyes

4. "O my Luve is like a red, red rose"
   —Robert Burns

5. "I hear America singing . . ."
   —Walt Whitman

6. "The sea is a hungry dog, / Giant and gray. / He rolls on the beach all day."
   —James Reeves

7. "The fog comes / on little cat feet"
   —Carl Sandburg

8. "I stepped on the toe / Of an unemployed hoe. / It rose in offense / And struck me a blow . . ." —Robert Frost

Language Coach
Language Conventions Manuel Ulacia deliberately leaves out words and phrases in "The Word." Re-read the poem once more, and mentally fill in the words that are missing. Explain whether filling in these words helped you <u>interpret</u> the poem.

Academic Vocabulary

Talk About . . .
Emily Dickinson is known for her <u>distinctive</u> style. How is her poetry different from other poetry you have encountered? Discuss these questions with a classmate.

Learn It Online
For action-packed vocabulary lessons, visit
go.hrw.com   H8-513   **Go**

Author Study: Ray Bradbury

CONTENTS

DESTINATION

Ray Bradbury gives the keynote address at the grand opening of the Allied Signal Challenger Learning Center, California State Dominguez Hill Campus, California.

What Do You Think
How can writing help you share your beliefs with others?

QuickWrite
How do people express their ideas about life and the world? Write for a few minutes about the ways in which musicians, writers, and artists share their ideas with others.

Preparing to Read

from Ray Bradbury Is on Fire! / The Flying Machine / The Dragon / The Fog Horn

Literary Skills Focus

Style Ray Bradbury is one of the best-loved writers of our time. His stories are marked by the fantastic, the mysterious, and the magical. Bradbury's stories are somewhat like old fables—they always contain a powerful message or lesson.

Bradbury has a <u>distinctive</u> style full of literary <u>devices</u>. For example, he uses **irony** (a contrast between expectation and reality) to enliven his plots, **symbolism** (people, places, or events that have meaning in themselves and also stand for something else) to enhance his themes, and **personification** (a figure of speech in which a nonhuman or inanimate thing acts as if it has human or lifelike qualities) to enrich his writing.

Reading Skills Focus

Drawing Conclusions A **conclusion** is the final idea or judgment you come to after you've considered the evidence. You will be learning about Bradbury's life and reading three of his stories. From this, you will be able to draw conclusions about Bradbury's style.

Into Action To draw conclusions about Bradbury's style, consider details from the text, and decide how they contribute to his style. Use a chart like the one below to help you keep track of the details.

Irony	Symbolism	Personification	Metaphors

Writing Skills Focus
Think as a Reader/Writer

Find It in Your Reading **Figures of speech** are words or phrases that create a comparison between two unlike things. Record the **similes** (comparisons using *like, as,* or *resembles*) and **metaphors** (direct comparisons) that help bring Bradbury's fantasies to life.

Reader/Writer
Notebook

Use your **RWN** to complete the activities for these selections.

Language Coach

Oral Fluency In English words that begin with *wr–*, such as *write*, the initial *w* is silent. Which Vocabulary word above falls into this category? How is it pronounced? Make a list of five other words that begin with the letter combination *wr–*.

Learn It Online
Watch the video introduction at:

go.hrw.com | H8-515 | **Go**

Learn more about Bradbury at:

go.hrw.com H8-516 Go

Ray Bradbury
(1920–   )

A Writer at Heart

At the age of twelve, Ray Bradbury wrote his first short stories in pencil on brown wrapping paper. He's been writing stories—and novels, poems, plays, and screenplays—ever since. Bradbury is famous for his work ethic. In more than seventy years of writing, he has published more than six hundred works. Bradbury moves effortlessly between past, present, and future. The settings of his works range from Mars and Venus to Ireland and Green Town, a fictional town based on his birthplace, Waukegan, Illinois. Whatever he is writing about, Bradbury's stories often express his belief that advances in science and technology should never come at the expense of human beings.

Encouraging Others

Bradbury has also explored the realm of nonfiction. One of his notable works of nonfiction is *Zen in the Art of Writing,* a collection of essays that captures the complete joy Bradbury experiences whenever he writes. In this book he encourages aspiring writers to view writing as an exciting venture:

Think About the Writer

What qualities do you think help to make Ray Bradbury such a successful writer?

Key Elements of Bradbury's Writing

Settings are strange and mysterious places, a combination of fantasy and reality. The past, the present, and the future may blend together in a single story.

Plots are often built around conflicts between characters and powerful forces. Characters may confront monsters, the sinister side of technology, or tyranny.

Messages often focus on our fascination with and our fear of technology. These messages often celebrate heroism and individual freedoms.

"Writing is supposed to be difficult, agonizing, a dreadful exercise, a terrible occupation. But, you see, my stories have led me through my life. They shout, I follow. They run up and bite me on the leg—I respond by writing down everything that goes on during the bite. When I finish, the idea lets go and runs off."

from RAY BRADBURY IS ON FIRE!

by **James Hibberd**

Read with a Purpose

Read these selections to discover Bradbury's views on technology and its impact on human beings.

Today Bradbury continues to criticize modern innovations, putting him in the seemingly contradictory position of being a sci-fi writer who's also a technophobe.[1] He famously claims to have never driven a car (Bradbury finds accident statistics appallingly unacceptable; he witnessed a deadly car accident as a teen). He is scornful of the Internet (telling one reporter it's "a big scam" by computer companies) and ATMs (asking, "Why go to a machine when you can go to a human being?") and computers ("A computer is a typewriter," he says. "I have two typewriters, I don't need another one"). **A**

Ray Bradbury typing on a typewriter.

By mocking the electronic shortcuts and distracting entertainment that replace human contact and active thinking, Bradbury shows his science-fiction label is misplaced. He cares little for science or its fictions. The author of more than thirty books, six hundred short stories,

---

1. **technophobe:** person with a fear or dislike of advanced or complex technology.

A **Reading Focus** **Drawing Conclusions** What is Bradbury's attitude toward technology?

Vocabulary **contradictory** (kahn truh DIHK tuhr ee) *adj.*: in disagreement; opposing.

and numerous poems, essays, and plays, Bradbury is a consistent champion of things human and real. There is simply no ready label for a writer who mixes poetry and mythology with fantasy and technology to create literate tales of suspense and social criticism; no ideal bookstore section for the author whose stories of rockets and carnivals and Halloween capture the fascination of twelve-year-olds, while also stunning adult readers with his powerful prose and knowing grasp of the human condition.

One secret to Bradbury's lifelong productivity is that his play and his work are the same. When asked, "How often do you write?" Bradbury replies, "Every day of my life—you got to be in love or you shouldn't do it."

. . . When I phoned his Los Angeles home for a 9:00 A.M. interview, Bradbury was thoughtful and cranky, and told me he'd already written a short story.

JAMES HIBBERD. **What makes a great story?**

RAY BRADBURY. If you're a storyteller, that's what makes a great story. I think the reason my stories have been so successful is that I have a strong sense of metaphor. . . . I grew up on Greek myths, Roman myths, Egyptian myths, and the Norse Eddas. So when you have influences like that, your metaphors are so strong that people can't forget them. **Ⓑ**

JAMES HIBBERD. **You've been critical of computers in the past. But what about programs that aid creativity? Do you think using a word processor handicaps a writer?**

Ⓑ **Literary Focus** Style How have ancient myths influenced Bradbury's style?

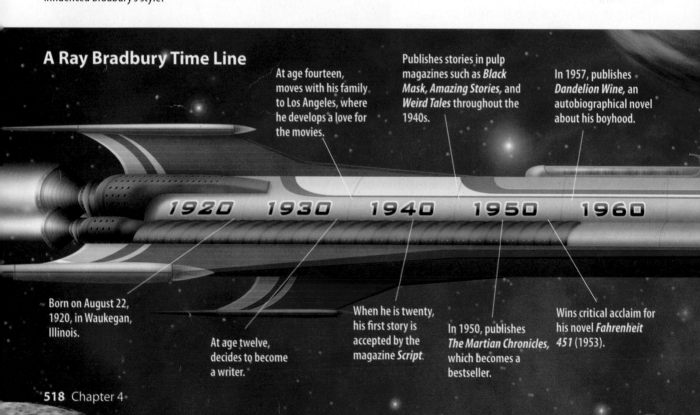

A Ray Bradbury Time Line

At age fourteen, moves with his family to Los Angeles, where he develops a love for the movies.

Publishes stories in pulp magazines such as *Black Mask, Amazing Stories,* and *Weird Tales* throughout the 1940s.

In 1957, publishes *Dandelion Wine,* an autobiographical novel about his boyhood.

1920   1930   1940   1950   1960

Born on August 22, 1920, in Waukegan, Illinois.

At age twelve, decides to become a writer.

When he is twenty, his first story is accepted by the magazine *Script.*

In 1950, publishes *The Martian Chronicles,* which becomes a bestseller.

Wins critical acclaim for his novel *Fahrenheit 451* (1953).

RAY BRADBURY. There is no one way of writing. Pad and pencil, wonderful. Typewriter, wonderful. It doesn't matter what you use. In the last month I've written a new screenplay with a pad and pen. There's no one way to be creative. Any old way will work. . . .

JAMES HIBBERD. What's an average workday like for you?

RAY BRADBURY. Well, I've already got my work done. At 7:00 A.M., I wrote a short story.

JAMES HIBBERD. How long does that usually take?

RAY BRADBURY. Usually about a morning. If an idea isn't exciting you shouldn't do it. I usually get an idea around 8 o'clock in the morning, when I'm getting up, and by noon it's finished. And if it isn't done quickly you're

going to begin to lie. So as quickly as you can, you emotionally react to an idea. That's how I write short stories. They've all been done in a single morning when I felt passionately about them. . . .  **C**

JAMES HIBBERD. There's so much competition for a young person's attention nowadays. For the record, why is reading still important?

RAY BRADBURY. Are you kidding? You can't have a civilization without that, can you? If you can't read and write you can't think. Your thoughts are dispersed if you don't know how to read and write. You've got to be able to look at your thoughts on paper and discover what a fool you were. . . . **D**

C [Read and Discuss] What is Bradbury saying about his manner of working?

D [Reading Focus] Drawing Conclusions What is the value of reading for Bradbury?

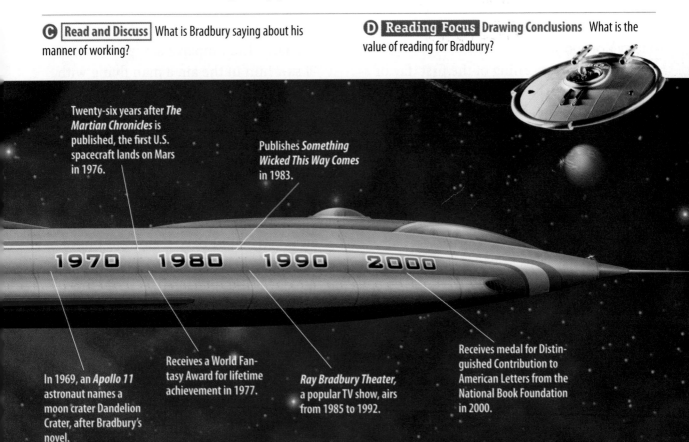

Twenty-six years after *The Martian Chronicles* is published, the first U.S. spacecraft lands on Mars in 1976.

Publishes *Something Wicked This Way Comes* in 1983.

1970　1980　1990　2000

In 1969, an *Apollo 11* astronaut names a moon crater Dandelion Crater, after Bradbury's novel.

Receives a World Fantasy Award for lifetime achievement in 1977.

Ray Bradbury Theater, a popular TV show, airs from 1985 to 1992.

Receives medal for Distinguished Contribution to American Letters from the National Book Foundation in 2000.

The Flying Machine

by **Ray Bradbury**

Read with a Purpose Read this story to learn what happens when a man invents a flying machine.

Preparing to Read for this selection is on page 515.

Build Background

Ray Bradbury says he tells tales to warn people about dangers in the world around them. You are about to read a fairy tale–like story that takes place in the distant past. As you read, think about how this story connects to our world today.

In the year A.D. 400, the Emperor Yuan held his throne by the Great Wall of China, and the land was green with rain, readying itself toward the harvest, at peace, the people in his dominion[1] neither too happy nor too sad.

Early on the morning of the first day of the first week of the second month of the new year, the Emperor Yuan was sipping tea and fanning himself against a warm breeze when a servant ran across the scarlet and blue garden tiles, calling, "Oh, Emperor, Emperor, a miracle!"

"Yes," said the Emperor, "the air *is* sweet this morning."

"No, no, a miracle!" said the servant, bowing quickly.

"And this tea is good in my mouth, surely that is a miracle."

_____

1. **dominion:** country; territory.

"No, no, Your Excellency."

"Let me guess then—the sun has risen and a new day is upon us. Or the sea is blue. *That* now is the finest of all miracles."

"Excellency, a man is flying!"

"What?" The Emperor stopped his fan.

"I saw him in the air, a man flying with wings. I heard a voice call out of the sky, and when I looked up, there he was, a dragon in the heavens with a man in its mouth, a dragon of paper and bamboo, colored like the sun and the grass."

"It is early," said the Emperor, "and you have just wakened from a dream."

"It is early, but I have seen what I have seen! Come, and you will see it too."

"Sit down with me here," said the Emperor. "Drink some tea. It must be a strange thing, if it is true, to see a man fly. You must have time to think of it, even as I must have time to pre-

Ⓐ **Literary Focus** **Style** What literary <u>device</u> does Bradbury use in his description of the flying man?

pare myself for the sight."

They drank tea.

"Please," said the servant at last, "or he will be gone."

The Emperor rose thoughtfully. "Now you may show me what you have seen." Ⓑ

They walked into a garden, across a meadow of grass, over a small bridge, through a grove of trees, and up a tiny hill.

"There!" said the servant.

The Emperor looked into the sky.

And in the sky, laughing so high that you could hardly hear him laugh, was a man; and the man was clothed in bright papers and reeds to make wings and a beautiful yellow tail, and he was soaring all about like the largest bird in a universe of birds, like a new dragon in a land of ancient dragons.

The man called down to them from high in the cool winds of morning. "I fly, I fly!"

The servant waved to him. "Yes, *yes!*"

The Emperor Yuan did not move. Instead he looked at the Great Wall of China now taking shape out of the farthest mist in the green hills, that splendid snake of stones which writhed with majesty across the entire land. That wonderful wall which had protected them for a timeless time from enemy hordes[2] and preserved peace for years without number. He saw the town, nestled to itself by a river and a road and a hill, beginning to waken.

---

2. **hordes:** moving crowds.

Ⓑ [Read and Discuss] What is the author suggesting about this emperor and his people?

Vocabulary **writhed** (rythd) *v*.: twisted and turned.

Analyzing Visuals **Connecting to the Text**
What qualities of this Chinese nobleman are similar to those of the emperor in the story?

Ancestor Portrait (Late 17th or early 18th century). Chinese school. Ink and color on silk.

"Tell me," he said to his servant, "has anyone else seen this flying man?"

"I am the only one, Excellency," said the servant, smiling at the sky, waving.

The Emperor watched the heavens another minute and then said, "Call him down to me."

"Ho, come down, come down! The Emperor wishes to see you!" called the servant, hands cupped to his shouting mouth.

The Emperor glanced in all directions while the flying man soared down the morning wind. He saw a farmer, early in his fields, watching the sky, and he noted where the farmer stood.

The flying man alit with a rustle of paper and a creak of bamboo reeds. He came proudly to the Emperor, clumsy in his rig, at last bowing before the old man.

"What have you done?" demanded the Emperor.

"I have flown in the sky, Your Excellency," replied the man.

"What *have* you done?" said the Emperor again.

"I have just told you!" cried the flier.

"You have told me nothing at all." The Emperor reached out a thin hand to touch the pretty paper and the birdlike keel of the apparatus. It smelled cool, of the wind.

"Is it not beautiful, Excellency?"

"Yes, too beautiful."

"It is the only one in the world!" smiled the man. "And I am the inventor."

"The *only* one in the world?"

"I swear it!"

"Who else knows of this?"

"No one. Not even my wife, who would think me mad with the sun. She thought I was making a kite. I rose in the night and walked to the cliffs far away. And when the morning breezes blew and the sun rose, I gathered my courage, Excellency, and leaped from the cliff. I flew! But my wife does not know of it."

"Well for her, then," said the Emperor. "Come along." **C**

They walked back to the great house. The sun was full in the sky now, and the smell of the grass was refreshing. The Emperor, the servant, and the flier paused within the huge garden.

The Emperor clapped his hands. "Ho, guards!"

The guards came running.

"Hold this man."

The guards seized the flier.

"Call the executioner," said the Emperor.

"What's this!" cried the flier, bewildered. "What have I done?" He began to weep, so that the beautiful paper apparatus rustled.

"Here is the man who has made a certain machine," said the Emperor, "and yet asks us what he has created. He does not know himself. It is only necessary that he create, without knowing why he has done so, or what this thing will do."

The executioner came running with a sharp silver ax. He stood with his naked, large-muscled arms ready, his face covered with a serene white mask.

"One moment," said the Emperor. He turned to a nearby table upon which sat a machine that he himself had created. The

---

C | Read and Discuss | What does the conversation between the emperor and the flying man tell you about the emperor's thoughts?

Vocabulary   **serene** (suh REEN) *adj.:* calm; undisturbed.

Blue and Green Landscapes by Li Qing.

Emperor took a tiny golden key from his own neck. He fitted his key to the tiny, delicate machine and wound it up. Then he set the machine going.

The machine was a garden of metal and jewels. Set in motion, the birds sang in tiny metal trees, wolves walked through miniature forests, and tiny people ran in and out of sun and shadow, fanning themselves with miniature fans, listening to tiny emerald birds, and standing by impossibly small but tinkling fountains.

"Is *it* not beautiful?" said the Emperor. "If you asked me what I have done here, I could answer you well. I have made birds sing, I have made forests murmur, I have set people to walking in this woodland, enjoying the leaves and shadows and songs. That is what I have done."

"But, oh, Emperor!" pleaded the flier, on his knees, the tears pouring down his face. "I have done a similar thing! I have found beauty. I have flown on the morning wind. I have looked down on all the sleeping houses and gardens. I have smelled the sea and even *seen* it, beyond the hills, from my high place. And I have soared like a bird; oh, I cannot say how beautiful it is up there, in the sky, with the wind about me, the wind blowing me here like a feather, there like a fan, the way the sky smells in the morning! And how free one feels! *That* is beautiful, Emperor, that is beautiful too!"

"Yes," said the Emperor sadly, "I know it must be true. For I felt my heart move with you in the air and I wondered: What is it like? How does it feel? How do the distant pools look from so high? And how my houses and servants? Like ants? And how the distant towns not yet awake?"

"Then spare me!"

"But there are times," said the Emperor, more sadly still, "when one must lose a little beauty if one is to keep what little beauty one already has. I do not fear you, yourself, but I fear another man."

"What man?"

"Some other man who, seeing you, will build a thing of bright papers and bamboo like this. But the other man will have an evil face and an evil heart, and the beauty will be gone. It is this man I fear."

"Why? Why?"

"Who is to say that someday just such a man, in just such an apparatus of paper and reed, might not fly in the sky and drop huge stones upon the Great Wall of China?" said the Emperor. **(D)**

No one moved or said a word.

"Off with his head," said the Emperor.

The executioner whirled his silver ax.

"Burn the kite and the inventor's body and bury their ashes together," said the Emperor.

The servants retreated to obey.

The Emperor turned to his hand-servant, who had seen the man flying. "Hold your tongue. It was all a dream, a most sorrowful and beautiful dream. And that farmer in the distant field who also saw, tell him it would pay him to consider it only a vision. If ever the word passes around, you and the farmer die within the hour."

"You are merciful, Emperor."

"No, not merciful," said the old man. Beyond the garden wall he saw the guards burning the beautiful machine of paper and reeds that smelled of the morning wind. He saw the dark smoke climb into the sky. "No, only very much bewildered and afraid." He saw the guards digging a tiny pit wherein to bury the ashes. "What is the life of one man against those of a million others? I must take solace from that thought." **(E)**

He took the key from its chain about his neck and once more wound up the beautiful miniature garden. He stood looking out across the land at the Great Wall, the peaceful town, the green fields, the rivers and streams. He sighed. The tiny garden whirred its hidden and delicate machinery and set itself in motion; tiny people walked in forests, tiny faces loped through sun-speckled glades in beautiful shining pelts, and among the tiny trees flew little bits of high song and bright blue and yellow color, flying, flying, flying in that small sky.

"Oh," said the Emperor, closing his eyes, "look at the birds, look at the birds!"

(D) | Read and Discuss | What kind of person is the emperor? Why does he demand to see the flying man?

(E) | Read and Discuss | What does the emperor mean by "What is the life of one man against those of a million others?"

Vocabulary **solace** (SAHL ihs) *n.*: comfort.

Applying Your Skills

Reading Standard 3.6 Identify significant literary devices (e.g., metaphor, symbolism, dialect, irony) that define a writer's style and use those elements to interpret the work.

from **Ray Bradbury Is on Fire! /**
The Flying Machine

Literary Response and Analysis

Reading Skills Focus
Quick Check

1. According to the interview, what does Bradbury believe is necessary for civilization?

2. What does the emperor in "The Flying Machine" say are miracles? What does the servant say is a miracle?

Read with a Purpose

3. Based on these selections, what surprises you about Bradbury's attitudes toward technology?

Reading Skills: Drawing Conclusions

4. You have read a biography, an interview, and one of Bradbury's short stories. What conclusions can you draw about Bradbury's writing style based on the details you recorded in your chart?

Irony	Symbolism	Personification	Metaphors

✔ Vocabulary Check

Match the Vocabulary words with their definitions.

5. **serene**   a. opposing
6. **writhed**   b. comfort
7. **contradictory**   c. peaceful
8. **solace**   d. twisted

Literary Skills Focus
Literary Analysis

9. **Explain** In "Ray Bradbury Is on Fire!" what does the interviewer find ironic about calling Bradbury a science fiction writer?

10. **Interpret** Discuss the two inventions in "The Flying Machine." Why does the emperor see beauty only in his own invention?

11. **Analyze** Explain how the following messages are supported by the the story.
    • The beauty of nature is a precious resource.
    • New technology can inspire fear.

12. **Extend** Discuss Bradbury's belief that distracting entertainment can interfere with active thinking. How do you interpret his idea? What examples from current society might Bradbury have in mind?

Literary Skills: Style

13. **Analyze** The emperor fears that the flying machine will be used for evil purposes. What inventions have been used for both good and harmful purposes in our own world? What might the flying machine **symbolize**?

Writing Skills Focus
Think as a Reader/Writer

Use It in Your Writing Refer to your list of figures of speech that Bradbury uses in this story. Then, write four or five sentences of your own using figurative language to describe an event or an unusual setting.

Here is what Ray Bradbury has said about "The Dragon":

It is hard to talk about "The Dragon" without giving away its secret, telling you the surprise. So all I can talk about is the boy I was that became the young man who thought about, and the older man who wrote, this story. I loved dinosaurs from the age of five, when I saw the film *The Lost World,* filled with prehistoric monsters. I became even more enamored with these beasts when at age thirteen, *King Kong* fell off the Empire State and landed on me in the front row of the Elite Theater. I never recovered. Later, I met and became friends with Ray Harryhausen, who built and film-animated dinosaurs in his garage when we were both eighteen. We dedicated our lives to these monsters, to dragons in all their shapes and forms. Simultaneously, we loved airplanes, rocket ships, trolley cars, and trains. From this amalgam of loves came our lives and careers. We wound up doing *The Beast from 20,000 Fathoms* as our first film. Not very good, but a beginning. He went on to *Mighty Joe Young* and I to *Moby Dick* and its great sea-beast. When I was in my thirties I wrote "The Dragon" and combined two of these loves. You'll have to read the story to find out which ones. Read on.

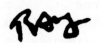

Chinese lacquered art with dragon representation.

THE DRAGON

by **Ray Bradbury,** adapted by **Vicente Segrelles**

Read with a Purpose Read the next two stories to see what happens when the past meets the present.

Preparing to Read for this selection is on page 515.

A

B

A **Literary Focus** **Style** Interpret the metaphor "The wind was a thousand souls dying."

B **Read and Discuss** What information has the author given you in these four panels?

C Read and Discuss | How do the illustrations help build suspense?

The Dragon **529**

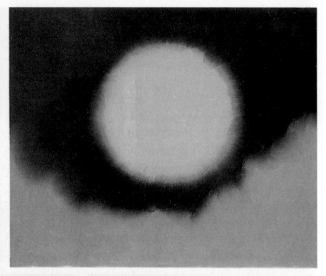

LORD HAVE MERCY!

THE LANCE STRUCK THE UNLIDDED YELLOW EYE, BUCKLED, TOSSED THE MAN THROUGH THE AIR.

THE BLACK BRUNT OF ITS SHOULDER SMASHED THE REMAINING HORSE AND RIDER A HUNDRED FEET AGAINST THE SIDE OF A BOULDER. THE DRAGON'S WAIL BECAME A SHRIEK. THERE WAS FIRE ALL ABOUT.

D

D Read and Discuss What has happened to the knights?

E **Reading Focus** **Drawing Conclusions** What attitudes and beliefs of Bradbury's are revealed in this story?

The Fog Horn

by **Ray Bradbury**

Read with a Purpose Read this story to learn the effect of a fog horn.

Preparing to Read for this selection is on page 515.

Out there in the cold water, far from land, we waited every night for the coming of the fog, and it came, and we oiled the brass machinery and lit the fog light up in the stone tower. Feeling like two birds in the gray sky, McDunn and I sent the light touching out, red, then white, then red again, to eye the lonely ships. And if they did not see our light, then there was always our Voice, the great deep cry of our Fog Horn shuddering through the rags of mist to startle the gulls away like decks of scattered cards and make the waves turn high and foam. Ⓐ

"It's a lonely life, but you're used to it now, aren't you?" asked McDunn.

"Yes," I said. "You're a good talker, thank the Lord."

"Well, it's your turn on land tomorrow," he said, smiling, "to dance the ladies and drink gin."

"What do you think, McDunn, when I leave you out here alone?"

"On the mysteries of the sea." McDunn lit his pipe. It was a quarter past seven of a cold November evening, the heat on, the light switching its tail in two hundred directions, the Fog Horn bumbling in the high throat of the tower. There wasn't a town for

---

Ⓐ **Literary Focus** Style How does the narrator personify the fog horn?

a hundred miles down the coast, just a road which came lonely through dead country to the sea, with few cars on it, a stretch of two miles of cold water out to our rock, and rare few ships.

"The mysteries of the sea," said McDunn thoughtfully. "You know, the ocean's the most confounded big snowflake ever? It rolls and swells a thousand shapes and colors, no two alike. Strange. One night, years ago, I was here alone, when all of the fish of the sea surfaced out there. Something made them swim in and lie in the bay, sort of trembling and staring up at the tower light going red, white, red, white across them so I could see their funny eyes. I turned cold. They were like a big peacock's tail, moving out there until midnight. Then, without so much as a sound, they slipped away, the million of them was gone. I kind of think maybe, in some sort of way, they came all those miles to worship. Strange. But think how the tower must look to them, standing seventy feet above the water, the God-light flashing out from it, and the tower declaring itself with a monster voice. They never came back, those fish, but don't you think for a while they thought they were in the Presence?"

I shivered. I looked out at the long gray lawn of the sea stretching away into nothing and nowhere.

"Oh, the sea's full." McDunn puffed his pipe nervously, blinking. He had been nervous all day and hadn't said why. "For all our engines and so-called submarines, it'll be ten thousand centuries before we set foot on the real bottom of the sunken lands, in the fairy kingdoms there, and know *real*

terror. Think of it, it's still the year 300,000 Before Christ down under there. While we've paraded around with trumpets, lopping off each other's countries and heads, they have been living beneath the sea twelve miles deep and cold in a time as old as the beard of a comet." **B**

"Yes, it's an old world."

"Come on. I got something special I been saving up to tell you."

We ascended the eighty steps, talking and taking our time. At the top, McDunn switched off the room lights so there'd be no reflection in the plate glass. The great eye of the light was humming, turning easily in its oiled socket. The Fog Horn was blowing steadily, once every fifteen seconds.

"Sounds like an animal, don't it?" McDunn nodded to himself. "A big lonely animal crying in the night. Sitting here on the edge of ten billion years called out to the Deeps, I'm here, I'm here, I'm here. And the Deeps do answer, yes, they do. You been here now for three months, Johnny, so I better prepare you. About this time of year," he said, studying the murk and fog, "something comes to visit the lighthouse."

"The swarms of fish like you said?"

"No, this is something else. I've put off telling you because you might think I'm daft. But tonight's the latest I can put it off, for if my calendar's marked right from last year, tonight's the night it comes. I won't go into detail, you'll have to see it yourself. Just sit down there. If you want, tomorrow you can pack your duffel and take the motorboat in to land and get your car parked there at the dinghy pier on the cape and drive on

---

B **Read and Discuss** What is McDunn describing?

back to some little inland town and keep your lights burning nights. I won't question or blame you. It's happened three years now, and this is the only time anyone's been here with me to verify it. You wait and watch." **C**

Half an hour passed with only a few whispers between us. When we grew tired of waiting, McDunn began describing some of his ideas to me. He had some theories about the Fog Horn itself.

"One day many years ago a man walked along and stood in the sound of the ocean on a cold sunless shore and said, "We need a voice to call across the water, to warn ships. I'll make one. I'll make a voice like all of time and all of that fog that ever was; I'll make a voice that is like an empty bed beside you all night long, and like an empty house when you open the door, and like trees in autumn with no leaves. A sound like the birds flying south, crying, and a sound like November wind and the sea on the hard, cold shore. I'll make a sound that's so alone that no one can miss it, that whoever hears it will weep in their souls, and hearths will seem warmer, and being inside will seem better to all who hear it in the distant towns. I'll make me a sound and an apparatus and they'll call it a Fog Horn and whoever hears it will know the sadness of eternity and the briefness of life." **D**

The Fog Horn blew.

"I made up that story," said McDunn quietly, "to try to explain why this thing keeps coming back to the lighthouse every year. The Fog Horn calls it, I think, and it comes. . . ."

"But—" I said.

"Sssst!" said McDunn. "There!" He nodded out to the Deeps.

Something was swimming toward the lighthouse tower.

It was a cold night, as I have said; the high tower was cold, the light coming and going, and the Fog Horn calling and calling through the raveling mist. You couldn't

C **Read and Discuss** What is McDunn saying here?

D **Literary Focus** Style McDunn uses a string of figures of speech to help you imagine the sound of the fog horn. To what does he compare it?

see far and you couldn't see plain, but there was the deep sea moving on its way about the night earth, flat and quiet, the color of gray mud, and here were the two of us alone in the high tower, and there, far out at first, was a ripple, followed by a wave, a rising, a bubble, a bit of froth. And then, from the surface of the cold sea came a head, a large head, dark-colored, with immense eyes, and then a neck. And then—not a body—but more neck and more! The head rose a full forty feet above the water on a slender and beautiful dark neck. Only then did the body, like a little island of black coral and shells and crayfish, drip up from the subterranean.[1] There was a flicker of tail. In all, from head to tip of tail, I estimated the monster at ninety or a hundred feet.

I don't know what I said. I said something.

"Steady, boy, steady," whispered McDunn.

"It's impossible!" I said.

"No, Johnny, *we're* impossible. *It's* like it always was ten million years ago. *It* hasn't changed. It's *us* and the land that've changed, become impossible. *Us!*"

It swam slowly and with a great dark majesty out in the icy waters, far away. The fog came and went about it, momentarily erasing its shape. One of the monster eyes caught and held and flashed back our immense light, red, white, red, white, like a disk held high and sending a message in primeval[2] code. It was as silent as the fog through which it swam.

"It's a dinosaur of some sort!" I crouched down, holding to the stair rail.

"Yes, one of the tribe."

"But they died out!"

"No, only hid away in the Deeps. Deep, deep down in the deepest Deeps. Isn't *that* a word now, Johnny, a real word, it says so much: the Deeps. There's all the coldness and darkness and deepness in a

---

1. **subterranean** (suhb tuh RAY nee uhn): underground.

2. **primeval** (pry MEE vuhl): of the earliest times; ancient.

E **Reading Focus** Drawing Conclusions What conclusions can you draw about Bradbury's views on humanity?

word like that."

"What'll we do?"

"Do? We got our job, we can't leave. Besides, we're safer here than in any boat trying to get to land. That thing's as big as a destroyer and almost as swift."

"But here, why does it come here?"

The next moment I had my answer.

The Fog Horn blew.

And the monster answered.

A cry came across a million years of water and mist. A cry so anguished and alone that it shuddered in my head and my body. The monster cried out at the tower. The Fog Horn blew. The monster roared again. The Fog Horn blew. The monster opened its great toothed mouth and the sound that came from it was the sound of the Fog Horn itself. Lonely and vast and far away. The sound of isolation, a viewless sea, a cold night, apartness. That was the sound. **F**

"Now," whispered McDunn, "do you know why it comes here?"

I nodded.

"All year long, Johnny, that poor monster there lying far out, a thousand miles at sea, and twenty miles deep maybe, biding its time, perhaps it's a million years old, this one creature. Think of it, waiting a million years; could *you* wait that long? Maybe it's the last of its kind. I sort of think that's true. Anyway, here come men on land and build this lighthouse, five years ago. And set up their Fog Horn and sound it and sound it out toward the place where you bury yourself in sleep and sea memories of a world where there were thousands like yourself, but now you're alone, all alone in a world not made for you, a world where you have to hide.

"But the sound of the Fog Horn comes and goes, comes and goes, and you stir from the muddy bottom of the Deeps, and your eyes open like the lenses of two-foot

---

F **Literary Focus** Style What is distinctive about Bradbury's style in this paragraph?

cameras and you move, slow, slow, for you have the ocean sea on your shoulders, heavy. But that Fog Horn comes through a thousand miles of water, faint and familiar, and the furnace in your belly stokes up, and you begin to rise, slow, slow. You feed yourself on great slakes of cod and minnow, on rivers of jellyfish, and you rise slow through the autumn months, through September when the fogs started, through October with more fog and the horn still calling you on, and then, late in November, after pressurizing yourself day by day, a few feet higher every hour, you are near the surface and still alive. You've got to go slow; if you surfaced all at once you'd explode. So it takes you all of three months to surface, and then a number of days to swim through the cold waters to the lighthouse. And there you are, out there, in the night, Johnny, the biggest monster in creation. And here's the lighthouse calling to you, with a long neck like your neck sticking way up out of the water, and a body like your body, and, most important of all, a voice like your voice. Do you understand now, Johnny, do you understand?" **G**

The Fog Horn blew.

The monster answered.

I saw it all, I knew it all—the million years of waiting alone, for someone to come back who never came back. The million years of isolation at the bottom of the sea, the insanity of time there, while the skies cleared of reptile-birds, the swamps dried on the continental lands, the sloths and saber-tooths had their day and sank in tar pits, and men ran like white ants upon the hills.

The Fog Horn blew.

"Last year," said McDunn, "that creature swam round and round, round and round, all night. Not coming too near, puzzled, I'd say. Afraid, maybe. And a bit angry after coming all this way. But the next day, unexpectedly, the fog lifted, the sun came out fresh, the sky was as blue as a painting. And the monster swam off away from the heat and the silence and didn't come back. I suppose it's been brooding on it for a year now, thinking it over from every which way."

The monster was only a hundred yards off now, it and the Fog Horn crying at each other. As the lights hit them, the monster's eyes were fire and ice, fire and ice.

"That's life for you," said McDunn. "Someone always waiting for someone who never comes home. Always someone loving some thing more than that thing loves them. And after a while, you want to destroy whatever that thing is, so it can't hurt you no more." **H**

The monster was rushing at the lighthouse.

The Fog Horn blew.

"Let's see what happens," said McDunn.

He switched the Fog Horn off.

The ensuing minute of silence was so intense that we could hear our hearts pounding in the glassed area of the tower, could hear the slow greased turn of the light.

G | Read and Discuss | What is McDunn explaining?

H | Reading Focus | Drawing Conclusions How does McDunn describe life? What does this say about Bradbury's views?

The monster stopped and froze. Its great lantern eyes blinked. Its mouth gaped. It gave a sort of rumble, like a volcano. It twitched its head this way and that, as if to seek the sounds now dwindled off into the fog. It peered at the lighthouse. It rumbled again. Then its eyes caught fire. It reared up, threshed the water, and rushed at the tower, its eyes filled with angry torment.

"McDunn!" I cried. "Switch on the horn!"

McDunn fumbled with the switch. But even as he flicked it on, the monster was rearing up. I had a glimpse of its gigantic paws, fishskin glittering in webs between the finger-like projections, clawing at the tower. The huge eyes on the right side of its anguished head glittered before me like a caldron into which I might drop, screaming. The tower shook. The Fog Horn cried; the monster cried. It seized the tower and gnashed at the glass, which shattered in upon us.

McDunn seized my arm. "Downstairs!"

The tower rocked, trembled, and started to give. The Fog Horn and the monster roared. We stumbled and half fell down the stairs. "Quick!"

We reached the bottom as the tower buckled down toward us. We ducked under the stairs into the small stone cellar. There were a thousand concussions as the rocks rained down; the Fog Horn stopped

abruptly. The monster crashed upon the tower. The tower fell. We knelt together, McDunn and I, holding tight, while our world exploded.

Then it was over, and there was nothing but darkness and the wash of the sea on the raw stones.

That and the other sound.

"Listen," said McDunn quietly. "Listen."

We waited a moment. And then I began to hear it. First a great vacuumed sucking of air, and then the lament, the bewilderment, the loneliness of the great monster, folded over and upon us, above us, so that the sickening reek of its body filled the air, a stone's thickness away from our cellar. The monster gasped and cried. The tower was gone. The light was gone. The thing that had called to it across a million years was gone. And the monster was opening its mouth and sending out great sounds. The sounds of a Fog Horn, again and again. And ships far at sea, not finding the light, not seeing anything, but passing and hearing late that night, must've thought: There it is, the lonely sound, the Lonesome Bay horn. All's well. We've rounded the cape.

And so it went for the rest of that night.

The sun was hot and yellow the next afternoon when the rescuers came out to dig us from our stoned-under cellar. **❶**

"It fell apart, is all," said Mr. McDunn gravely. "We had a few bad knocks from the waves and it just crumbled." He pinched my arm.

There was nothing to see. The ocean was calm, the sky blue. The only thing was a great algaic stink from the green matter that covered the fallen tower stones and the shore rocks. Flies buzzed about. The ocean washed empty on the shore.

The next year they built a new lighthouse, but by that time I had a job in the little town and a wife and a good small warm house that glowed yellow on autumn nights, the doors locked, the chimney puffing smoke. As for McDunn, he was master of the new lighthouse, built to his own specifications, out of steel-reinforced concrete. "Just in case," he said.

The new lighthouse was ready in November. I drove down alone one evening late and parked my car and looked across the gray waters and listened to the new horn sounding, once, twice, three, four times a minute far out there, by itself.

The monster?

It never came back.

"It's gone away," said McDunn. "It's gone back to the Deeps. It's learned you can't love anything too much in this world. It's gone into the deepest Deeps to wait another million years. Ah, the poor thing! Waiting out there, and waiting out there, while man comes and goes on this pitiful little planet. Waiting and waiting."

I sat in my car, listening. I couldn't see the lighthouse or the light standing out in Lonesome Bay. I could only hear the Horn, the Horn, the Horn. It sounded like the monster calling.

I sat there wishing there was something I could say. **❿**

---

❶ Read and Discuss | What has happened?

❿ Reading Focus Drawing Conclusions Have your impressions about Bradbury's attitude toward technology changed?

Applying Your Skills

Reading Standard 3.6 Identify significant literary devices (e.g., metaphor, symbolism, dialect, irony) that define a writer's style and use those elements to interpret the work.

The Dragon / The Fog Horn

Literary Response and Analysis

Reading Skills Focus

Quick Check

1. Who are the main characters in "The Dragon"? What problem do they face?

2. In "The Fog Horn," why is the monster drawn to the fog horn?

Read with a Purpose

3. In "The Dragon," what happens when people and creatures from the past encounter modern technology?

4. What happens after McDunn switches off the fog horn? Why does it happen?

Reading Skills: Drawing Conclusions

5. Refer to the chart of details you made. What conclusions about Bradbury's writing style can you draw based on these details?

Irony	Symbolism	Personification	Metaphors

My Conlusions: _____

Literary Skills Focus

Literary Analysis

6. **Interpret** Now that you know the dragon's real identity, what do the following descriptions in "The Dragon" refer to: (1) his "unlidded yellow eye"; (2) "his breath like white gas"?

7. **Analyze** Explain which of these messages you think Bradbury conveys in "The Dragon."

- Our machines are as powerful as the mythical dragons of old.

- It is heroic to fight against monsters, even when these monsters are not real.

- People of earlier times would see our lives as full of terrifying dangers.

8. **Extend** Connect McDunn's statement about "the sadness of eternity and the briefness of life" (page 534) to the creature's agony. How does the anguish the monster suffers relate to those who earn their living from the sea and those who wait for the seafarers to return home?

Literary Skills: Style

9. **Connect** In his interview with James Hibberd, Bradbury expresses his impressions of technology and human civilization. Explain how these concerns are reflected in "The Dragon" and "The Fog Horn."

Writing Skills Focus

Think as a Reader/Writer

Use It in Your Writing Bradbury uses **similes,** or comparisons using *like* or *as,* to help you imagine the sound of a fog horn (page 534). In a short paragraph, describe a different sound using as many similes as you can think of. Read your description aloud to a partner, and see if he or she can guess what the sound is.

Wrap Up

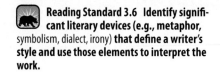 **Reading Standard 3.6** Identify significant literary devices (e.g., metaphor, symbolism, dialect, irony) **that define a writer's style and use those elements to interpret the work.**

Author Study: Ray Bradbury

Writing Skills Focus
Think as a Reader/Writer

Style After reading the stories in this Author Study, you now know that many of Bradbury's stories reflect his fascination with human society, monsters, and fantasy and reality. His stories also concern the costs and benefits of modern civilization, and the positive and negative effects of technology.

Write a three-paragraph essay in which you consider the messages in Bradbury's stories and how those messages reflect his own attitudes.

- In the essay's first paragraph, introduce your topic and state what you see as Bradbury's main concerns.

- In the second paragraph, write about how Bradbury's concerns are reflected in the short stories you have read. Be sure to discuss his use of literary devices. Support your ideas by citing details from the texts.

- In the last paragraph, draw a conclusion about how Bradbury's ideas relate to his fiction.

Evaluation Guidelines
An effective essay contains—
✓ a clearly stated topic
✓ main ideas that are supported with details
✓ a clear and logical organization
✓ a thought-provoking conclusion

 **What Do You Think Now** Bradbury shares his ideas through writing. In what other ways can you share your ideas and beliefs with the world?

CHOICES

As you respond to the Choices, use these **Academic Vocabulary** words as appropriate: critical, device, distinctive, interpret.

REVIEW
Analyze Metaphor

Timed ○ Writing In the interview on page 517, Bradbury talks about his use of **metaphor.** In an essay, show how Bradbury uses metaphors in the stories you have read. Be sure to quote passages that include metaphors and discuss how these passages affect the way you interpret the work.

CONNECT
Create a Graphic Story

Partner Activity Choose another short story by Bradbury or a short story in this book. With a partner, design a graphic version of the story. Most graphic stories are created by a writer and an artist working together. The writer usually divides the story into panels and creates a script. Then, the artist takes over and illustrates the story. You and your partner can share the writing and illustrating or split the tasks.

EXTEND
Paint an Online World

TechFocus Using painting software, create a fantasy world of your own. Will your world exist in the past, future, alternate present, or an imaginary universe? What will your setting look like? Who will live there—people, animals, robots? What impression will it make on visitors? Share your fantasy world with others.

Evaluating a Summary

Paddle steamboat on the Mississippi River, in modern-day New Orleans.

CONTENTS

What does it take to make a good idea work?

QuickWrite
Write down a major technological invention developed in your lifetime. What need did it fill? What impact has it had on your life?

Preparing to Read

Reading Standard 2.4 Compare the original text to a summary to determine whether the summary accurately captures the main ideas, includes critical details, and conveys the underlying meaning.

Steam Rising: The Revolutionary Power of Paddleboats / Summaries of "Steam Rising"

Informational Text Focus

Evaluating a Summary Writing a good summary of an informational text is not easy. You have to restate the main ideas, include critical details, and sum up the underlying meaning of the text. A summary's purpose is to give you a brief overview of an article. If the summary is not clear, though, you won't understand the basics of the article. Here is how to create a meaningful summary of an informational text:

- Open with the article's **title** and **author.**
- State the **topic** of the article.
- State the **main ideas,** in the **order** in which they occur in the article.
- Include important **supporting details** (people, places, dates).
- Include quotation marks around words from the text that are quoted exactly.

Into Action Use a chart like the one below to evaluate the summaries of "Steam Rising: The Revolutionary Power of Paddleboats."

Summary	Title and Author	Topic	Main Ideas in Order	Supporting Details
#1				
#2				

Writing Skills Focus

Preparing for Timed ⌐Writing As you read "Steam Rising," note which details are most important for a general understanding of the topic. These details support the main ideas and should be included in an effective summary; less important details should be excluded. You will use these details to write a summary.

Vocabulary

antiquated (AN tuh kway tihd) *adj.:* old-fashioned. *The steamboat is antiquated technology by today's standards.*

prototype (PROH tuh typ) *n.:* first or original model of something. *After seeing the prototype, the investors were willing to fund the building of steamboats.*

monopoly (muh NAHP uh lee) *n.:* total control over a particular business. *No one else could make money from steamboats because Fulton had a monopoly on them.*

Language Coach

Context Clues Sometimes writers give clues to a word's meaning within a passage or sentence. Read this sentence: *Although it was very popular in the past, the steamboat is an old, antiquated form of travel.* How do the clues shown below help you understand what *antiquated* means?

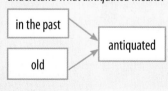

in the past → antiquated ← old

Reader/Writer
Notebook
Use your **RWN** to complete the activities for these selections.

Learn It Online
To increase your understanding of summaries, go to the interactive Reading Workshop at:

go.hrw.com H8-543   Go

STEAM RISING

THE REVOLUTIONARY POWER OF PADDLEBOATS

by  THE WORLD ALMANAC

*"S-t-e-a-m-boat a-comin'!" and the scene changes! . . .
all in a twinkling the dead town is alive and moving.
Drays, carts, men, boys, all go hurrying from many
quarters to a common center, the wharf.*

—from *Life on the Mississippi,* by Mark Twain

In the days when paddle steamboats filled the Mississippi River, the famed author Mark Twain served as a cub pilot. He wrote about that experience and his love of steamboats in *Life on the Mississippi.* Today, modern tourists still take these antiquated vessels along U.S. waterways, such as the Columbia River. Travel writers advertise the charms of these trips: the closeness of the riverbank towns, the lull of the running water, and the feeling of time set apart.   Ⓐ

ECONOMIC NEED

The steamboat was not invented for pleasure, however. The vessel was developed to help move the country along economically. Before paddle steamboats, travel from Louisville,

---

Ⓐ **Read and Discuss**   What do you learn about the steamboat's impact on people, both in the past and the present?

Vocabulary   **antiquated** (AN tuh kway tihd) *adj.:* old-fashioned.

Kentucky, to New Orleans, Louisiana, was a four-month project. After their invention, the Industrial Revolution was able to move full steam ahead.

Paddle steamboats are created specifically for inland water runs. A giant paddlewheel is built into the back or side of a flat-bottomed boat, which can navigate shallow waters. Steam rising from wood- or coal-fired boilers turns the wheel. Their design is basic, but their invention revolutionized travel and transport.

Colonial American leaders long recognized the need to power boats with something more predictable than sails, which are at the mercy of the wind. They knew they needed boats capable of traveling upriver. In 1784, the inventor James Rumsey talked with George Washington about such a vessel. John Fitch, of Connecticut, tinkered with the idea of a steamboat as early as 1785. In 1790, he and his partner Henry Voight sent a prototype between Philadelphia and Trenton, New Jersey. But they could not raise the funds needed to build a steamboat line.   Ⓑ

ROBERT FULTON

Robert Fulton gets credit for creating the first "efficient" steamboat. Fulton hailed from Lancaster, Pennsylvania. As a boy, he spent time in mechanics' shops.

There he discovered his talent for drawing. He trained in art in Philadelphia as a teen and then traveled to England, where he was introduced to science and became interested in solving engineering problems. His early ideas included a canal system created on an incline, which would end the need for locks, and a submarine. He had no takers for those ideas, but in 1802, with backing from the U.S. ambassador to France, Robert R. Livingston, Fulton successfully sent a paddle steamboat up a French river. The rest is history.

Along with financial support, Livingston had political steam to offer. The U.S. patent system[1] was not well developed at that point; to profit from their creations, inventors and their backers lobbied[2] politicians for state rights. Livingston was able to obtain a monopoly on New York waterways by promising that Fulton's steamboat could travel at four miles per hour. Fulton sealed the deal by building the *Clermont,* which ran from New York City to Albany at almost five miles per hour. The vessel allowed manufacturers to send raw materials and finished goods to their destinations more quickly, and Fulton became a rich man.

---

1. **U.S. patent system:** system that grants an inventor exclusive rights to manufacture an invention for a limited amount of time.
2. **lobbied** (LAHB eed): influenced lawmakers.

Ⓑ **Informational Focus** Summary What is the main idea of this section, "Economic Need"?

Vocabulary **prototype** (PROH tuh typ) *n.:* first or original model of something.
monopoly (muh NAHP uh lee) *n.:* total control over a particular business.

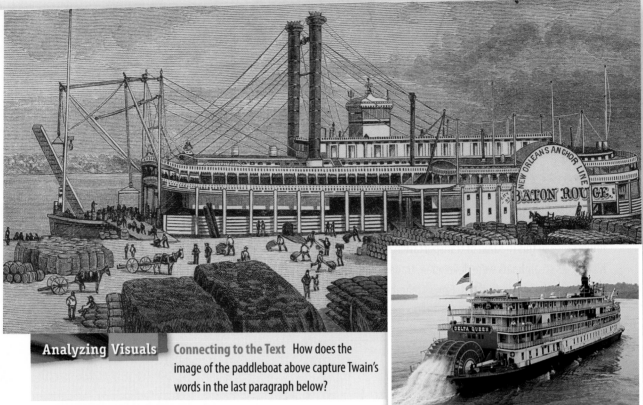

Analyzing Visuals **Connecting to the Text** How does the image of the paddleboat above capture Twain's words in the last paragraph below?

"The Baton Rouge" illustration from Mark Twain's *Life on the Mississippi*. Boston; James R. Osgood and Company, 1833. Frontispiece image.

Delta Queen riverboat on the Mississippi.

RIVER COMMERCE **C**

Early steamboats were inefficient and sometimes dangerous. But engineers learned from mistakes and improved their design. In addition, Congress authorized funding for major improvements along the Mississippi and Ohio rivers, which encouraged the development of waterway engineering. These factors, along with industrial growth, contributed to the steamboat's rapid rise. In 1814, records show, 21 steamboats visited New Orleans. By 1833, that number had grown to more than 1,200.

By the 1850s, when Twain was working on the river, paddleboats had become fancy affairs. "And the [*City of Baton Rouge*] boat IS a rather handsome sight, too," he wrote in *Life on the Mississippi,* going on to describe gingerbread trim atop the pilothouse, shiny white railings, and the flapping flag. These vessels had come to define the Mississippi, the principal U.S. waterway. Until railroads crisscrossed the country in the 1870s, nothing replaced the great U.S. steamboat, and in many ways, nothing ever has. **D**

Read with a Purpose
What steps would you take to begin a clear and concise summary of this article?

C | **Informational Focus** Summary Give an example of a supporting detail you would include in a summary of this section, "River Commerce."

D | **Read and Discuss** What is the main point of this article?

SUMMARIES OF "STEAM RISING: THE REVOLUTIONARY POWER OF PADDLEBOATS"

Summary #1

"Steam Rising" outlines the development of the U.S. paddle steamboat: its design, its inventors, and the importance of this method of transportation in national history. As steamboats were developed, trade along the country's waterways increased. Fancy steamboats plowed up and down the Mississippi in the 1850s, delivering goods and people to places far and wide. "Steam Rising" is about paddle steamboats and how important they are to people who love boats. Admirers of this unique method of travel and transport still exist today. Mark Twain, the famous U.S. author, said it best: "And the boat is a rather handsome sight, too." **E**

Summary #2

"Steam Rising: The Revolutionary Power of Paddleboats" by World Almanac describes the invention, development, and impact of the steam-powered paddleboat. Steamboat technology played a major role in America's Industrial Revolution. Colonial Americans understood the importance of using America's waterways for travel and to transport materials in order to make the economy run more efficiently. As early as 1784, inventors were working on ideas for a steamboat that would be able to travel upstream. Building such a vessel was expensive, however, and funds were not easy to find.

Robert Fulton gets credit for making the first working model of a steamboat, paddling up a French river in 1802. Fulton was from Lancaster, Pennsylvania. He discovered a love of drawing early in life, and after studying science, he applied his talents to solving engineering problems. With both financial and political aid from U.S. ambassador Robert R. Livingston, Fulton was able to build and patent his steamboat designs. Fulton's steamboats allowed manufacturers to deliver their products more quickly and ultimately made Fulton rich. **F**

Steamboat designs evolved, becoming safer and more efficient as well as more attractive. These improvements, along with government improvements to America's rivers, allowed the steamboat to blossom. By 1833, records show that 1,200 steamboats visited New Orleans alone. Until the advent of the railroads, the steamboat played an important role in the U.S. economy. **G**

E **Informational Focus** Evaluating a Summary
What important information is missing in the first sentence of Summary #1?

F **Informational Focus** Evaluating a Summary
Explain whether all the details in Summary #2 support the article's main idea.

G **Read and Discuss** What do these summaries show you?

Reading Standard 2.4 Compare the original text to a summary to determine whether the summary accurately captures the main ideas, includes critical details, and conveys the underlying meaning.

Steam Rising: The Revolutionary Power of Paddleboats / Summaries of "Steam Rising"

Standards Review

Informational Text and Vocabulary

1. What critical **supporting detail** from the article does the first summary omit?

   A James Rumsey talked to George Washington about creating a steamboat.

   B Robert Fulton was the creator of the first effective steamboat.

   C The *Clermont* paddled from New York City to Albany at almost five miles per hour.

   D The Mississippi River was the principal U.S. waterway.

2. The second **summary** differs from the first summary in that it

   A includes a quotation.

   B provides more supporting details.

   C states an opinion.

   D uses Fulton's personal letters as a source.

3. Which feature of an effective **summary** is missing from the first summary but included in the second?

   A the full title and author

   B the main idea

   C some supporting details

   D a quotation

4. If someone calls a piece of furniture *antiquated,* he or she means that it is

   A attractive.

   B contemporary.

   C out-of-date.

   D expensive.

5. Which of the following words is a synonym for *prototype*?

   A original

   B patent

   C exclusive

   D current

6. A *monopoly* gives a person

   A the right to influence lawmakers.

   B a guaranteed income.

   C a portion of profits from an invention.

   D exclusive control over something.

Writing Skills Focus

Timed └Writing Which details in the article did you identify as most important? Create an outline of the original article that shows the details you would include in a summary.

What Do **You Think Now**

What did you learn from this article about how a new idea can be made to work?

Writing Workshop

Response to Literature

Write with a Purpose

Write an essay in response to a piece of literature that you have read. Your **purpose** is to exhibit careful reading and insight in your interpretation of the work. Your **audience** is your classmates, who may or may not have read the work.

Think as a Reader/Writer

The most common type of response to literature is generally found in the book review pages of newspapers and magazines. The purpose of these reviews is to evaluate books so that others can decide whether or not to read them. Another type of response is a literary essay that analyzes elements of the work, such as plot, characters, and/or theme.

Before you write your own response to literature, read this excerpt from a review of a book entitled *The Best of Ray Bradbury*. The review was written and posted on the Internet by Jason Sacks.

> Ray Bradbury is one of the finest writers of science fiction and fantasy literature. His stories are taught in high school and college literature classes throughout the English-speaking world. He allowed EC Comics to adapt several of his stories in their science fiction comics in the 1950s. That series was unjustly ignored during the comics bust, but now it is back with a collection of some of the finest adaptations from that series.
>
> Mark Chiarello's adaptation of "A Piece of Wood" uses color in a spectacular way to illuminate the story of two men talking about a weapon that could forever end war. And Gibbons's take on "Come Into My Cellar" uses the artist's traditional comics style to great effect, wonderfully conveying the banality of his characters' lives through use of small panels that seem to be just slightly askew.
>
> This book is the ideal gift for a science fiction fan who is interested in comics. The worst of these stories are unmemorable; the best are wonderful examples of what happens when master creators play with each others' ideas.

The reviewer identifies the **author** *and adds* **background facts**.

The reviewer states his **thesis**.

The reviewer supports his judgment through **references** *to the text.*

The reviewer infers the effect of the book on its audience and supports his inference.

A Good Response to Literature

- presents a coherent thesis
- exhibits careful reading
- includes insightful interpretations
- analyzes the writer's techniques
- refers to the text and other works, other authors, or personal knowledge
- infers the effects of the work on its audience
- ends with a clear and well-supported conclusion

See page 558 for complete rubric.

Reader/Writer Notebook

Use your **RWN** to complete the activities for this workshop.

Think About the Professional Model

With a partner, discuss the following questions about the model.

1. What is the writer's controlling impression, or overall tone of the review?

2. How does the writer support his thesis with references to the text?

Writing Standard 1.1 Create compositions that establish a controlling impression, have a coherent thesis, and end with a clear and well-supported conclusion. **2.2** Write responses to literature. a. Exhibit careful reading and insight in their interpretations. b. Connect the student's own responses to the writer's techniques and to specific textual references. c. Draw supported inferences about the effects of a literary work on its audience. d. Support judgments through references to the text, other works, other authors, or to personal knowledge.

Prewriting

Choose a Literary Work

Which literary work will you be writing about? If your teacher hasn't assigned one, choose a work that you feel strongly about. Once you know which piece of literature you will be writing about, write down this information:

- title of the work (with correct spelling, capitalization, and punctuation)
- author (include the full name)
- genre, or type of work (short story, poem, novel, mystery, biography)
- date of publication (if available)

Respond to the Work

Think about how you responded to the work as you were reading it. Then, write down your reactions.

- What kind of reactions did you have as your read? Did you laugh? cry?
- Was the plot exciting? suspenseful? slow moving? dull? realistic? unrealistic?
- Were the characters static? dynamic? unique? ordinary? believable? unbelievable?
- What techniques did the writer use to cause your reactions? imagery? figurative language? symbolism? irony? dialect?
- How does the work relate to other works? to your personal knowledge?

Think About Audience and Purpose

Before you begin writing, think about who will read your review and what they will need to know. Also, identify your **purpose** for writing and how you want your writing to affect your **audience.**

Details About My Audience	What Is My Purpose?
• students • my age • may not have read work	• interpret the work • evaluate the work • recommend the work

Idea Starters

- Respond to story in your textbook.
- Respond to your favorite novel.
- Respond to the latest book in a popular series.
- Respond to a biography of a person you admire.

● Writing Tip

As you begin, think about what makes the work unique. Start by answering questions like these:

- Is the work like anything else you've read?
- How did the work surprise you?
- What else has the author written?
- Who was your favorite character?
- What kind of reader would enjoy this work?

Your Turn _____

Get Started Make notes in your **RWN** describing a piece of literature you will write about and your overall response to the work. Then, answer the questions on this page to expand on your responses to the literature. Your notes will help you plan your essay.

 Learn It Online
Need help organizing your essay? Use the interactive graphic organizer at:

go.hrw.com | H8-551 | Go

Writing Tip

Writing Tip

When you write about literature, you should tell your reader what the work is about without retelling the story. Remember that some readers of your essay will have already read the work, but those who have not yet read it will want to discover surprises on their own.

Organize Your Ideas

To help plan what you will write, organize your ideas in an outline. Your response to literature should include the following:

- **Introduction:** Start with an engaging opening. Make sure to identify the type of work you're covering, the title, and the author. Introduce your main idea in a coherent thesis statement.
- **Body:** Here you can present your interpretations and judgments. Support your opinions through references to the text—such as short quotations—as well as to other works, other authors, and personal knowledge.
- **Conclusion:** As you finish your response, you may want to point out the effect of the work on its audience. You can also explain whether you would recommend this work, and to whom. Finally, end with a clear, well-supported conclusion.

Here's an example of one writer's plan. You can use it as a model.

> ### Introduction
>
> **Engaging Opening:** "The best way to stop arguments is to get people to eat peanut butter sandwiches. They can't talk."
> **Work and Author:** "Scout's Honor" by Avi
> **Type of Work:** short story
> **Main Theme of Work:** Friendship and courage can help people endure difficult circumstances.
> **My General Reaction:** positive
>
> ### Body
>
> **Interpretations and Judgments:** The boys learn that admitting they are not as tough as the others takes more courage than going on.
> **Examples:** The umbrella example shows the bonds of friendship.
> **Short Quotes:** Max: "Naw. I wanted to quit but I wasn't tough enough to do it." Horse: "You saying I'm the one who's tough? I hate roughing it!"
>
> ### Conclusion
>
> **Recommendations:** I would recommend this story to my classmates and peers.
> **Closing Statement:** Restate the theme of the story—that is, the importance of friendship, courage, and honor.

Your Turn

Plan Your Review Before writing your response to literature, make a plan for its **introduction, body,** and **conclusion.** Share your plan with a classmate, and consider using his or her feedback to make changes to your plan.

Drafting

Follow Your Plan

Using your plan as a guide, draft your response to your chosen piece of literature. As you write, keep in mind the characteristics of a good response to literature, described on page 550. The framework at the right provides a quick reference for you as you draft.

Use Examples From the Text

To help your readers understand the points you make, you should cite examples from the text. Notice that in his review of *The Best of Ray Bradbury*, Jason Sacks tells his readers exactly how a particular illustration adds to the story.

> . . . .Gibbons's take on "Come Into My Cellar" uses the artist's traditional comics style to great effect, wonderfully conveying the banality of his characters' lives through use of small panels that seem to be just slightly askew.

Framework for Response to Literature

Introduction
- Begin with an engaging opening.
- Supply the author's name and the work's title and genre.
- Offer a clear, coherent thesis.

Body
- Give your interpretations and judgments.
- Support them with references to the text.

Conclusion
- Give recommendations.
- Offer a clear, well-supported conclusion.

Grammar Link Pronouns and Referents

When writing a response to literature, you will be referring to characters, text passages, the author, and so on. Whenever you use a **pronoun** to stand for a **noun,** make sure the pronoun's **referent** (the noun that the pronoun stands for) is clear. Look at the example from the professional model to see how to make referents clear.

> <u>Ray Bradbury</u> is one of the finest writers of science fiction and fantasy literature. <u>His</u> stories are taught in high school and college literature classes throughout the English-speaking world. <u>He</u> allowed EC Comics to adapt several of <u>his</u> stories in their science fiction comics in the 1950s.

Because the writer mentions Bradbury in the first sentence, the *His* in the second sentence and the *he* and *his* in the third sentence are clear.

Writing Tip

You may want to quote passages from the work to help explain your response to the literature. Introduce the quoted material so that your reader knows where the quotation comes from, and enclose any quoted material between quotation marks. Remember to keep your quotations as short as possible. Quote just enough of a passage to illustrate your point, and then explain to your reader why the quote is important.

Your Turn _____

Write Your Draft Using the plan that you created, write a draft of your review. Think about these questions:

- What **examples** from the literary work can I include?
- What passages, if any, should I quote in the review?
- Are all my **pronoun referents** clear?

Peer Review

Using the chart at the right, you can help your partner give you useful feedback and suggestions by mentioning the kinds of questions you have about your draft.

- Is there a point in your draft that you think might need to be clarified? Direct your partner's attention to that point.
- Do you think you might need to expand your draft? Ask your partner where you might say more about an example or add another point.
- Are there questions on the Evaluating and Revising chart that you are not sure you've addressed in your essay? Point these out to your partner.

Evaluating and Revising

Read the questions in the left column of the chart, and then use the tips in the middle column to help you make revisions to your essay. The right column suggests techniques you can use to revise your draft.

Response to Literature: Guidelines for Content and Organization

Evaluation Questions	Tips	Revision Techniques
1. Does your introduction grab the reader's attention?	**Put a star** next to your thesis statement.	**Add** an interesting fact about the author or a striking quote from the work.
2. Have you supplied necessary information: the title, the genre, and the author's full name?	**Circle** the title, the genre, and author's name.	**Double-check** the correct spelling of the author's name and the title of the work.
3. Have you written a clear, coherent thesis statement?	**Put a star** next to the word or phrase that names the theme.	**Rewrite** your statement to make it more clear, if needed.
4. Does your draft exhibit careful reading and insight in your interpretation?	**Underline** points that you think are especially insightful.	**Add** more thoughtful analyses of the work, if necessary.
5. Have you shown how the writer's techniques contributed to your responses?	**Highlight** sentences that refer to the writer's style and techniques.	**Add** sentences that explain the role of the author's style and techniques.
6. Have you supported your judgments with references to the text?	**Put a check** next to each detail or quotation from the text.	**Add** details or quotations from the text wherever such support is needed.
7. Have you written recommendations and a clear, well-supported conclusion?	**Circle** your recommendations. **Draw a box** around your conclusion.	**Add** a recommendation for the reader and a clear statement of your conclusion, if needed.

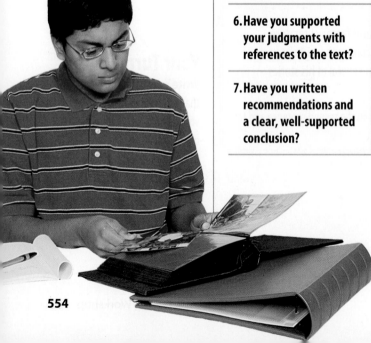

Read this student's draft, and notice the comments on its structure and suggestions for how the response could be improved.

More Than Just Camping

by Jenna Galper, Paradise Canyon Elementary

"The best way to stop arguments is to get people to eat peanut butter sandwiches. They can't talk." The narrator learns this lesson in Avi's short story "Scout's Honor." The narrator and his two friends must go on an overnight hike in the country to progress a level in Boy Scouts. The three boys use friendship, courage, and honor to guide them through their first camping trip.

The narrator, Horse, and Max share a special friendship. You can tell that throughout the story. No matter where they are or how bad the circumstances are, the boys still express their friendship and have fun.

→ Jenna opens with an engaging **quote,** identifies the **title, author,** and **genre,** describes the basic **plot** situation, and states a coherent **thesis,** or main idea.

→ Jenna supports her thesis with an **example** from the text of the characters' friendship.

MINI-LESSON ▶ **How to Elaborate with Textual References**

Jenna's second paragraph makes a point about the boys' helping each other, but she doesn't support her point with references to the story. She can use a specific incident from the story to illustrate the point about the boys' friendship. Making reference to the incident with the umbrella provides support. She concludes this addition with a comment on how this incident relates to the boys' friendship. Here is how Jenna revised the second paragraph of her response.

Jenna's Revision to Paragraph Two

The narrator, Horse, and Max share a special friendship. ~~You can tell throughout the story.~~ For example, when they are crossing the George Washington Bridge in the pouring rain, the narrator puts up his umbrella, with him in the middle and Horse and Max on either side. Max and Horse are still getting wet, so the narrator closes his umbrella and they all get equally soaked. If the three boys hadn't had such a great friendship, the narrator would have let his friends get soaked while he stayed dry in the middle. No matter where they are or how bad the circumstances are, the boys still express their special bond of friendship and have fun.

Your Turn

Use Textual References Read your draft, and then ask yourself, "What specific textual references from the work would help to illustrate my points?"

Student Draft *continued*

Jenna supports her **thesis** with an **example** of the way the characters have fun.

> Another example of their outstanding bond is when, despite being cold and tired, the boys still found a way to have fun—FOOD FIGHT! No matter where they are, the narrator, Max, and Horse can always find a way to express their special bond and have fun.

Dialogue from the text brings the example to life.

> When the boys finally give up on their trip, the narrator is the first to admit that he isn't as tough as the other guys. Max responds by saying, "Naw. I wanted to quit but I wasn't tough enough to do it." Horse makes a fist and demands, "You saying I'm the one who's tough? I hate roughing it!" The boys realize that it takes more courage to admit that they aren't as tough as the others than it does to pretend that they are.

Jenna supports her thesis with a **reference** to the text showing the characters' sense of honor.

> The friends share a great understanding of honor and what it means. The boys promise each other that they won't tell the scout leader that they left early. They clasp hands, and the narrator says two simple words that sum up the whole story: "Scout's Honor."

Jenna sums up by restating her **thesis.**

> The three friends learn much more than just camping. They learn lessons they will never forget.

MINI-LESSON **How to Write an Effective Conclusion**

In her draft, Jenna ends with a vague closing statement. What lessons do the friends learn? Were these lessons the theme of Avi's story? Jenna decides to improve her draft by restating the theme of the short story and linking it back to the title and author in her own words.

Jenna's Revision of Paragraph Six

> In Avi's short story "Scout's Honor," three boys go into the country to learn new skills and earn a badge in Boy Scouts. However,
>   life
> The three friends learn much more than just camping. They learn les-
> can take with them forever: friendship, courage, and honor.
> sons they will never forget.

Your Turn _____

Write an Effective Conclusion With a partner, look over the **conclusion** of your review. If your conclusion is vague or weak, one way you can improve it by using your own words to restate the **theme** of the work.

Proofreading and Publishing

Proofreading

Re-read your essay for errors in grammar, usage, and punctuation. Re-read your essay again to look for repetitive sentence structures. Then, vary your sentence structures to add interest to your essay. Finally, prepare your final copy to share with your audience.

Grammar Link **Varying Sentence Structure**

Be careful to avoid using the same sentence structure too often. In one of the last paragraphs, Jenna decides she has begun too many sentences with a noun. To vary her sentence structure and add emphasis, Jenna adds an introductory phrase to one of the sentences.

> *Above all else, the*
> ~~The~~ friends share a great understanding of honor and what it means. The boys promise each other that they won't tell the scout leader that they left early. They clasp hands . . . ."

Publishing

Here are some ways to share your response to literature:

- Submit your essay to your school paper.
- E-mail your essay to a friend who you think will enjoy the work you wrote about.
- Submit your response to an online bookstore that publishes customer reviews.
- Post your work on your personal Web page or the author's Web page.

Reflect on the Process
In your **RWN,** note what you learned while writing your response to literature. Then, answer the following questions:

1. How did writing about the literary work lead you to a better understanding or appreciation of it?

2. Was the tone of your response to literature knowledgeable yet friendly? How might you adjust your tone if you were writing this response for a different audience?

3. What new techniques or ideas about literary analysis did you learn in this workshop? How might you apply these techniques to analyzing other forms of literature?

Proofreading Tip
Exchange essays with a classmate, and take time to read each other's responses carefully. Ask your classmate to read your draft for repetition in sentence structure and for punctuation errors. Is there a place where he or she would change your original sentence structure to add variety?

Your Turn
Proofread and Publish As you are proofreading, look carefully at whether you begin too many sentences in a row with a noun or an article. Where appropriate, add introductory phrases or rearrange the word order to vary your sentence structure. When your draft is ready, share it with others.

Scoring Rubric

You can use the rubric below to evaluate your response to literature.

	Literary Response Writing	Organization and Focus	Sentence Structure	Conventions
4	• Exhibits *careful* reading and includes *insightful* interpretations. • Analyzes the writer's technique *clearly*, supported *consistently* by examples from the text, other works, other authors, and/or personal knowledge. • Connects personal responses *unambiguously* to writer's technique and to specific textual references. • Draws *supported* inferences about the effects of the literary work on its audience.	• *Clearly* addresses all parts of the writing task. • Demonstrates a *clear* understanding of purpose and audience. • Shows *effective* organization *throughout*, with *smooth* transitions. • Focuses *consistently* on a *coherent* thesis. • Provides a *clear* introduction and a *well-supported* conclusion.	• Includes sentence *variety* (e.g. simple, complex, compound-complex).	• Contains *few*, if any, errors in the conventions of the English language (grammar, punctuation, capitalization, spelling). These errors do **not** interfere with the reader's understanding of the writing.
3	• Exhibits *mostly careful* reading and includes *relatively insightful* interpretations. • Analyzes the writer's technique *somewhat clearly*, supported *inconsistently* by examples from the text, other works, other authors, and/or personal knowledge. • Connects personal responses *relatively clearly* to writer's technique and to specific textual references. • Draws *partly supported* inferences about the effects of the literary work on its audience.	• Addresses most of the writing task. • Demonstrates a *general* understanding of purpose and audience. • Shows *effective* organization throughout, with *minor* lapses. • Focuses on a *coherent* thesis, with *minor* distractions. • Provides a *relatively* clear introduction and a *partially supported* conclusion.	• Includes some sentence *variety* (e.g. simple, complex, compound-complex).	• Contains *some errors* in the conventions of the English language (grammar, punctuation, capitalization, spelling). These errors do **not** interfere with the reader's understanding of the writing.
2	• Exhibits *some attention* to reading and includes *few* interpretations. • Analyzes the writer's technique *unclearly*, *rarely* supported by examples from the text, other works, other authors, and/or personal knowledge. • Connects personal responses *ambiguously* to writer's technique and to textual references. • Draws *few* inferences about the effects of the literary work on its audience.	• Addresses *some* of the writing task. • Demonstrates *little* understanding of purpose and audience. • Shows *some* organization, with *noticeable gaps* in the logical flow of ideas. • Includes some *loosely related* ideas that *distract* from the writer's focus. • *Suggests* an introduction and conclusion.	• Includes *little* sentence variety.	• Contains *several errors* in the conventions of the English language (grammar, punctuation, capitalization, spelling). These errors *may* interfere with the reader's understanding of the writing.
1	• Exhibits *no* attention to reading and includes *unclear* interpretations. • Analyzes the writer's technique *minimally*, *without* examples from the text, other works, other authors, and/or personal knowledge. • *May not* include personal responses or connect them to writer's technique and to textual references. • Draws *no* inferences about the effects of the literary work on its audience.	• Addresses *only one or no* part of the writing task. • Demonstrates *no* understanding of purpose and audience. • *Lacks* focus and organization. • *Lacks* an introduction, and/or conclusion.	• Includes *no* sentence variety.	• Contains *serious errors* in the conventions of the English language (grammar, punctuation, capitalization, spelling). These errors interfere with the reader's understanding of the writing.

Preparing for Timed Writing

Response to Literature

When responding to a prompt, use what you've learned from your reading, writing your response to literature, and studying the rubric on page 558. Use the steps below to develop a response to the following prompt.

Writing Standard 2.2 Write responses to literature. a. Exhibit careful reading and insight in their interpretations. b. Connect the student's own responses to the writer's techniques and to specific textual references. c. Draw supported inferences about the effects of a literary work on its audience. d. Support judgments through references to the text, other works, other authors, or to personal knowledge.

Writing Prompt

Write a response to literature in which you evaluate a book or other literary selection that you know well. Your response should encourage your audience—fellow students—to either read or not read the work. Provide details from the text to support your opinions.

Study the Prompt

Read the prompt carefully, and identify all parts of your task. You must choose a book or other literary selection for your response. Your **response** must make your **opinions** clear. It must also provide several **details** from the text to support your opinions.

Tip: Spend about five minutes studying the prompt.

Plan Your Response

First, think of some books, stories, or poems that you have read recently. Then, choose the piece of literature that you know best. Once you have settled on your subject, jot down the following:

- the work's title, author, genre (novel, short story, poem) and the date of publication
- your reactions to the work
- what your readers need to know about the work
  Your response will state your overall opinion of the work, but because your time is limited, you may want to focus on one or two elements that support your opinion. For example, if you thought the selection was depressing, you might focus on the author's use of gloomy images or settings.

Tip: Spend about ten minutes planning your response.

Respond to the Prompt

Using the notes you've just made, draft your response to literature. It may help to follow these guidelines:

- In the introduction, get your readers' attention with an engaging opening. Provide the title, author, and type of work; a clear thesis statement or your general reaction to the work.
- In the body of your response, use examples and short quotations from the text to support your opinions.
- In the conclusion, say whether you recommend the work.
  Tip: Spend about twenty minutes writing your draft.

Improve Your Response

Revising Go back to the key aspects of the prompt. Did you identify the work? Did you state your thesis clearly? Did you support your thesis?

Proofreading Take a few minutes to proofread your response to correct errors in grammar, spelling, punctuation, and capitalization. Make sure all your edits are neat, and erase any stray marks.

Checking Your Final Copy Before you turn in your response, read it one last time to catch any errors you may have missed.

Tip: Save ten minutes to improve your response.

Delivering an Oral Response to Literature

Think as a Reader/Writer When you write a response to literature, such as an evaluation of a novel, you do not receive immediate feedback. You cannot gauge your audience's comprehension and appropriately adjust your approach. When you deliver a speech, however, you can adjust your presentation for maximum impact. You also have more delivery tools at your disposal. You can use your voice, face, and hands to create a lively, clear presentation.

Adapt Your Response

Organize Your Presentation

An effective oral response to a piece of literature includes

- **a well-supported, insightful interpretation of the work.** Show your knowledge, and familiarize your audience with your topic.
- **a response to the writer's technique.** Include specific textual references that illustrate how the writer chose and arranged the words in the work.
- **infers the effects of a literary work.** Provide textual support for your inference of the work's effects on its intended audience.

As you consider what to include in your speech, consider your audience. Detemine what will interest them most. Decide the order in which to present your main ideas, and be sure to follow a coherent pattern of organization.

Organization of an Oral Review	
Introduction	Grab your audience's attention. Introduce the work by title and author, and give a brief preview of your main points. State your thesis in a way that conveys your judgment of the work.
Body	Logically develop your thesis. Support your judgment primarily through references to the text, but also refer to other works of literature, to other authors, or to personal knowledge.
Conclusion	Restate your thesis, and make sure your judgment is clear. Tell your audience how you believe the work will affect its readers.

Reader/Writer Notebook

Use your **RWN** to complete the activities for this workshop.

Listening and Speaking Standard **1.1** Analyze oral interpretations of literature, including language choice and delivery, and the effect of the interpretations on the readers. **1.4 Prepare a speech outline based upon a chosen pattern or organization, which generally includes an introduction; transitions,** previews, and summaries; **a logically developed body; and an effective conclusion. 1.6 Use appropriate** grammar, **word choice, enunciation, and pace during formal presentations. 2.2** Deliver oral responses to literature: a. Interpret a reading and provide insight. b. Connect the students' own responses to the writer's techniques and to specific textual references. c. Draw supported inferences about the effects of a literary work on its audience. d. Support judgments through references to the text, other works, other authors, or personal knowledge.

Rehearse and Deliver Your Response

Put Yourself in the Audience's Shoes

You should not deliver your oral response to literature without rehearsing. You should practice delivering your presentation two or three times. As you rehearse, be sure to consider the effect your response will have on your audience. Keep the following questions in mind as you practice.

✓ Are my **word choices** appropriate for my audience? Are there any technical terms I need to define? Is my vocabulary too simple or too advanced for my listeners?

✓ Am I enunciating clearly so that everyone can understand what I am saying? **Enunciation** refers to the distinctness of the sounds you make when you speak. Good enunciation is clear and precise. Poor enunciation often causes words to be slurred or word endings to be left off.

✓ Does the **pace** of my delivery sound unhurried, yet not so slow as to lull my listeners to sleep?

Ask for Feedback

Practice delivering your oral response two or three times in front of your family or friends. As you practice, keep in mind the questions you answered above. After you have rehearsed your presentation, ask for feedback. Was anything you said confusing? Were your examples interesting, and did they support your points well? Use the feedback to rework your presentation as necessary.

Be Prepared

Prepare notecards to use as you give your presentation. Make your notes brief and clear so that they help you remember what you need to say. Do not simply to read them to the class. Arrange your notecards in the order in which you want to present your ideas.

A Good Oral Response

- offers a clear interpretation of and provides original insight to the literary work.
- chooses a pattern of organization with an introduction, body, and conclusion
- describes the writer's techniques
- offers supported inferences on the way a work affects the audience
- supports judgments with references to the text, other works, other authors, or personal knowledge
- uses fitting word choice, clear enunciation, and appropriate pace.

 Speaking Tip

As you deliver your oral presentation in class, pay attention to the audience's **nonverbal responses**, or body language. If your audience members seem distracted, pick up the pace or move on to another point. If audience members look puzzled you may want to clarify your point.

 Learn It Online

Turn your response into a multimedia presentation. Find out how at MediaScope online:

go.hrw.com | H8-561 | Go

Listening and Speaking Workshop **561**

Literary Skills Review

Style   **Directions:** Read the following selection. Then, read and respond to the questions that follow.

Gil's Furniture Bought and Sold

by **Sandra Cisneros**

There is a junk store. An old man owns it. We bought a used refrigerator from him once, and Carlos sold a box of magazines for a dollar. The store is small with just a dirty window for light. He doesn't turn the lights on unless you got money to buy things with, so in the dark we look and see all kinds of things, me and Nenny. Tables with their feet upside-down and rows and rows of refrigerators with round corners and couches that spin dust in the air when you punch them and a hundred T.V.'s that don't work probably. Everything is on top of everything so the whole store has skinny aisles to walk through. You can get lost easy.

The owner, he is a black man who doesn't talk much and sometimes if you didn't know better you could be in there a long time before your eyes notice a pair of gold glasses floating in the dark. Nenny who thinks she is smart and talks to any old man, asks lots of questions. Me, I never said nothing to him except once when I bought the Statue of Liberty for a dime.

But Nenny, I hear her asking one time how's this here and the man says, This, this is a music box, and I turn around quick thinking he means a *pretty* box with flowers painted on it, with a ballerina inside. Only there's nothing like that where this old man is pointing, just a wood box that's old and got a big brass record in it with holes. Then he starts it up and all sorts of things start happening. It's like all of a sudden he let go a million moths all over the dusty furniture and swan-neck shadows and in our bones. It's like drops of water. Or like marimbas only with a funny little plucked sound to it like if you were running your fingers across the teeth of a metal comb.

And then I don't know why, but I have to turn around and pretend I don't care about the box so Nenny won't see how stupid I am. But Nenny, who is stupider, already is asking how much and I can see her fingers going for the quarters in her pants pocket.

This, the old man says shutting the lid, this ain't for sale.

1. Which of the following images is a metaphor for the junk-shop owner?
   A the Statue of Liberty
   B the music box
   C a pair of gold glasses
   D a broken television

2. Cisneros uses dialect to do all of the following *except*
   A to make the characters believable.
   B to give the characters a unique voice.
   C to make fun of the characters.
   D to show readers how the characters speak to one another.

3. The narrator of this story says, "It's like all of a sudden he let go a million moths all over the dusty furniture and swan-neck shadows and in our bones." She uses these figures of speech to describe
   A how dirty the store is.
   B how creepy she thinks insects are.
   C the animal puppets in the store.
   D the magical sound of the music box.

4. When the narrator says that the music is "like drops of water," she means that it feels
   A calming.
   B biting.
   C refreshing.
   D cold.

5. In this story the music box might be a symbol for
   A the unsold furniture.
   B the power of beauty in our lives.
   C a child's fear of scary places.
   D the experience of going shopping.

6. When the narrator says that Nenny is "stupider" than she is, she is using verbal irony. What she really means is that
   A Nenny is not ashamed to like the music box.
   B she is angry because Nenny has some money.
   C Nenny is not as smart as the narrator is.
   D she is embarrassed to be seen with Nenny.

7. The situational irony in this story results from the fact that
   A the girls are in an uncomfortable situation.
   B the girls find beauty in a junk store.
   C the junk store is dirty and crowded.
   D the junk store is full of moths.

Timed Writing

8. Based on details in this short story, what can you conclude about the author's style? Write a few sentences, citing details from the story to support your response.

Informational Skills Review

Evaluating a Summary   **Directions:** Read the selection. Then, answer each question that follows.

Native Hoops by

The Native Stars basketball team is part of a year-round athletic program in Arizona for Native American girls in grades 7 through 12. Players from in and around Phoenix take part. From August to October, the girls prepare for their school tryouts. Through March, they play on their school teams, and when the school season ends, they compete together in Native American summer tournaments. The program is designed to build the girls' confidence—and to help talented players break through barriers to achieve national success.

Basketball, known there as "rez ball," has long been part of life on Native American reservations. The problem is that even the best players are not seen much outside the reservation boundaries. Consequently, Native Americans have yet to break into the NBA or WNBA.

To help Native American athletes get past these limitations, people like Coach Everett Largo of the Native Stars are stepping forward with special programs. "I'm just trying to help these young Native Americans who come out here to the city," says the coach. "A lot of times when they come off the reservations, they kind of hold back. On the reservation it's more laid back. It's quiet. The urban world is fast and very competitive."

Professional teams and business leaders have recognized the problem, too. The Native American Basketball Invitational (NABI) tournament was started in 2003 by sponsors that include the Phoenix Suns and the Arizona Diamondbacks. The event draws high-level U.S. and Canadian teams and large crowds.

Another major competition, the Lori Piestewa National Native American Games, was begun in 2003 as well. Piestewa, a Hopi, was killed in Iraq—the first Native American woman to die in the U.S. military. The annual games held in her honor include competitions in basketball, softball, volleyball, and track and field.

The Native Stars attended the Piestewa games for the first time in 2006, earning good reviews all around. This year, as always, the girls are working hard to prepare for summer tournaments like NABI. "It [is] neat to play with the best of the best," says Native Star Paula Martinez, a Pascua Yaqui Indian. "Yeah, we [have] wins and losses, but it [is] great," says teammate Danielle Explain, a Navajo. "You can also get your game better by watching others play."

Summary

In this article the author describes the importance of basketball to young Native Americans and the programs and tournaments in which they participate. Basketball is a common sport on Native American reservations, but no Native Americans have played in the NBA or WNBA. Because of this, several programs have been developed to raise the confidence of these players and the profile of Native American athletes around the nation. These include training programs, such as the Native Stars girls' basketball team in Phoenix, Arizona, and competitions, such as the Native American Basketball Invitational (NABI) and the Lori Piestewa tournament, which also includes basketball, softball, volleyball, and track and field.

1. Which passage from the summary is *not* an important **supporting** detail and could be omitted?

   A "the author describes the importance of basketball"

   B "Basketball is a common sport on Native American reservations"

   C "no Native Americans have played in the NBA or WNBA"

   D "which also includes basketball, softball, volleyball, and track and field"

2. What missing information would be important to include in the summary?

   A a list of other sports played on reservations

   B a quotation from the team's coach

   C the article's title and source

   D the ages of the basketball players

3. What is the main idea of both the article and the summary?

   A Basketball has long been a popular sport on Native American reservations.

   B Programs have been developed to help young Native American basketball players achieve national success.

   C A tournament is named after the first Native American woman to die in Iraq.

   D The Native Stars have attended two important tournaments.

Timed Writing

4. Identify two or three essential elements of a good summary. Cite examples from the summary above.

Vocabulary Skills Review

Synonyms   **Directions:** Choose the *best* synonym for each of the italicized words below.

1. Another word for *derision is*
   A contempt.
   B hostility.
   C disgust.
   D negligence.

2. Another term for *vehemently* is
   A with anger.
   B with sadness.
   C with authority.
   D with passion.

3. A *prodigy* is a person with
   A reluctance.
   B arrogance.
   C talent.
   D poise.

4. Another term for *contradictory* is
   A revealing.
   B opposing.
   C cursory.
   D positive.

5. A *serene* place is
   A unique.
   B destroyed.
   C unknown.
   D exposed.

6. *Somber* means
   A gloomy.
   B healthy.
   C gray.
   D remembered.

7. Another term for *taut* is
   A thick.
   B shameful.
   C humbled.
   D stretched.

Academic Vocabulary

Directions: Choose the *best* synonym for each of the italicized Academic Vocabulary words below.

8. Artwork that is *distinctive* is
   A unique.
   B exciting.
   C instinctual.
   D beautiful.

9. When you *interpret* another person's actions, you are making a(n)
   A mistake.
   B narrative.
   C inference.
   D theme.

Writing Skills Review

Response to Literature **Directions:** Read the following passage from a book review. Then, answer each question that follows.

Writing Standard 2.2 Write responses to literature. a. Exhibit careful reading and insight in their interpretations. b. Connect the student's own responses to the writer's techniques and to specific textual references. c. Draw supported inferences about the effects of a literary work on its audience. d. Support judgments through references to the text, other works, other authors, or to personal knowledge.

(1) In *Red Scarf Girl,* Ji-li Jiang not only writes a compelling autobiography, she makes the history of the Communist Chinese Cultural Revolution come alive for her readers. (2) The story takes place in Communist China. (3) Her story begins in 1966, when she was twelve years old. (4) Always an excellent student, Ji-li Jiang is shocked to discover that her talent will not be enough for her to get ahead in the new Communist society. (5) She is at a disadvantage because her deceased grandfather had been a wealthy landlord, something that is looked down upon. (6) Many terrible things happen to Ji-li Jiang and her family. (7) Terrible things happen to many innocent people in China at this time. (8) I recommend this book to anyone who would like to meet an interesting girl growing up in difficult times and to anyone who would like to learn about Chinese history.

---

1. Which transitional word or phrase would add clarity to the first sentence?

  A but also

  B because

  C and so

  D nevertheless

2. Which sentence contains the thesis, or main idea, of the essay?

  A sentence 1

  B sentence 3

  C sentence 6

  D sentence 8

3. This passage could be improved by

  A providing stronger opinions.

  B adding examples from the story text.

  C combining sentences.

  D giving background information about communism.

4. What would be the best way to combine sentences 6 and 7?

  A Many terrible things happen to Ji-li Jiang's family, and many terrible things happen to other innocent people in China at this time.

  B Many terrible things happen to innocent people in China at this time, including Ji-li Jiang and her family.

  C Ji-li Jiang and her family suffered terribly at that time in China, along with other innocent people.

  D Other innocent people in China at this time had terrible things happen to them and to Ji-li Jiang and her family.

Read On

For Independent Reading

Fiction

River Rats

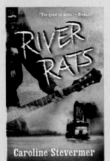

Imagine if paddleboats became as important in the future as they were in the nineteenth century. In *River Rats*, Caroline Stevermer tells the story of a postnuclear future in which a group of orphan kids travels up and down the Mississippi River on a sturdy paddleboat. As tough and challenging as their life on the river is, it's better than trying to survive on the dangerous and savage shore.

Roll of Thunder, Hear My Cry

Eight-year-old Cassie Logan does not understand the startling actions of white landowners in Depression-era Mississippi. Over the course of a year, she learns another lesson—why her family is desperately fighting to hold onto the land they call home. In *Roll of Thunder, Hear My Cry*, Mildred Taylor tells a story of pride and courage that all families can learn from.

Out of the Dust

While dust storms are devastating her family's Oklahoma farm in 1934, Billie Jo finds joy only in playing the piano. Then a terrible accident takes that joy away and changes Billie Jo's life forever. *Out of the Dust*, Karen Hesse's Newbery Medal–winning novel, tells the story of Billie Jo's coming to terms with her struggles and misfortunes. The story is told through a series of free-verse poems written in everyday language.

A Christmas Carol

During his lifetime, Charles Dickens was known for his acts of charity. Perhaps that aspect of Dickens's character inspired his holiday classic *A Christmas Carol*. Ebenezer Scrooge, a bitter, selfish old man, is unmoved by the holiday season. With the help of three Christmas spirits, he is able to change the course of his life and discover the joys of giving and receiving.

568 Chapter 4

Nonfiction

There Comes a Time: The Struggle for Civil Rights

The civil rights movement was one of the most important chapters in American history, yet it is often confusing to people because of its great scale. In *There Comes a Time: The Struggle for Civil Rights*, Milton Meltzer gives an overview of African Americans' struggle for equality. The penetrating writing is accompanied by many riveting photographs, which eloquently capture the energy of the movement.

Savion: My Life in Tap

A superstar in the world of tap dancing, Savion Glover combines hip style, grace, innovation, and virtuosity. In *Savion: My Life in Tap*, we see the dancer's journey from child prodigy to bona fide tap master. Glover describes his influences, struggles, and triumphs, emphasizing his goal of making tap dancing an art form with worldwide popularity.

Travels with Charley

By the time John Steinbeck turned fifty-eight, he had written the classic American novels *Of Mice and Men* and *The Grapes of Wrath*. He continued his career by writing *Travels with Charley* about his journey across the country. With his French poodle, Charley, by his side, Steinbeck encountered fascinating aspects of America in the 1960s.

Black Hands, White Sails

In *Black Hands, White Sails*, Patricia C. and Fredrick L. McKissack bring attention to the African Americans who worked in the whaling industry from colonial times until the nineteenth century. Some became shipowners and captains, while others played key roles in the Civil War and the Underground Railroad.

Learn It Online
Master your knowledge of novels. Learn tips for studying novels with *NovelWise* at:

go.hrw.com | H8-569 | **Go**

CHAPTER **5**

Poetry

" The poetry and the songs that you are supposed to write, I believe are in your heart. You just have to open up your heart and not be afraid to get them out."

—**Judy Collins**

What Do
You
Think

How important is it that we express our feelings?

Learn It Online
Listen to the poems in this chapter online at:

go.hrw.com   H8-571   **Go**

Literary Skills Focus

by **Carol Jago**

What Are the Characteristics of Poetry?

Have you ever read the song lyrics before playing a new CD? The words need music to bring them to life. Poetry is different. The words in a good poem create their own music.

Sounds of Poetry

The English poet Samuel Taylor Coleridge once defined poetry as "the best words in their best order." Read aloud these opening lines from a famous poem:

> Listen my children, and you shall hear
> Of the midnight ride of Paul Revere,
> On the eighteenth of April, in Seventy-five;
> Hardly a man is now alive
> Who remembers that famous day and year.
>
> from "Paul Revere's Ride"
> by Henry Wadsworth Longfellow

All Longfellow gave us were words on a page, and yet more than a century after he wrote them down, the music still comes through. How did he do it?

"I think that I shall never see, a poem as lovely as a bee, flea, sea, ski, plea, key . . ."

Rhythm If words can create the haunting music of a poem, **rhythm**—the repetition of stressed and unstressed syllables—provides the poem's beat. Like many other languages, English is accented: Certain syllables get a stronger beat than other syllables. The beat of a poem comes from the patterns made by the stressed and unstressed syllables. If you say a few English words aloud, you'll hear the beat built into them: MOUN-tain, be-CAUSE, Cin-cin-NAT-i. Say your name aloud, and notice its beat.

Read aloud this **elegy**—a poem that mourns someone who has died. Listen to the way your voice rises and falls as you pronounce the stressed and unstressed syllables.

> This lovely flower fell to seed;
> Work gently, sun and rain;
> She held it as her dying creed
> That she would grow again.
>
> "For My Grandmother"
> by Countee Cullen

A regular pattern of stressed and unstressed syllables is called **meter.** You probably stressed the words this way (ˊ indicates a stressed syllable; ˇ indicates an unstressed syllable):

˘ ˊ ˘ ˊ ˘ ˊ ˘ ˊ
This lovely flower fell to seed.

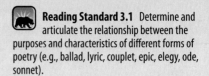

Reading Standard 3.1 Determine and articulate the relationship between the purposes and characteristics of different forms of poetry (e.g., ballad, lyric, couplet, epic, elegy, ode, sonnet).

Rhyme The chiming effect of **rhyme** adds to the music of a poem. Most rhymes in poetry are **end rhymes.** In "For My Grandmother" the end rhymes are *seed* and *creed,* and *rain* and *again* (pronounced the old-fashioned way: uh GAYN). When the two rhyming lines are consecutive, they're called a **couplet.** Here is a couplet with end rhymes that are spelled differently—*moan* and *bone*—but they rhyme:

> Well, he seemed so low that I couldn't say
>   no; then he says with a sort of moan:
> "It's the cursèd cold, and it's got right hold
>   till I'm chilled clean through to the
>   bone."
>> from "The Cremation of Sam McGee"
>> by Robert W. Service

Rhymes can also occur within lines; these are called **internal rhymes.** In the lines above, *low* and *no*, and *cold* and *hold* are internal rhymes. These rhymes are all **exact rhymes.** Many modern poets prefer approximate rhymes (also called near rhymes, off rhymes, imperfect rhymes, or slant rhymes). **Approximate rhymes** are sounds that are similar but not exactly the same, like *fellow* and *follow* or *cat* and *catch.* In this example from Chapter 2, *staff* and *scarf* are approximate rhymes:

> Quick, as it fell, from the broken staff
> Dame Barbara snatched the silken scarf.
>> from "Barbara Frietchie"
>> by John Greenleaf Whittier

Some people think approximate rhymes sound less artificial than exact rhymes, more like everyday speech. Some poets use approximate rhymes because they feel that all the good exact rhymes have already been used too many times.

Repetition Poets also make music in their poems by using repetition. Repeating sentence patterns will create rhythm, as in these lines by Walt Whitman:

> I hear America singing, the varied carols
>   I hear,
> Those of mechanics, each one singing his
>   as it should be blithe and strong,
> The carpenter singing his as he measures
>   his plank or beam,
> The mason singing his as he makes ready
>   for work, or leaves off work,
>> from "I Hear America Singing"
>> by Walt Whitman

Poets also use repetition of sounds. Note all the /th/ and /h/ sounds as you read aloud these lines:

> There wasn't a breath in that land of death,
>   and I hurried, horror-driven
>> from "The Cremation of Sam McGee"
>> by Robert E. Service

This is **alliteration** (uh lit uhr AY shun), the repetition of consonant sounds in several words that are close together. When vowel sounds are repeated, as in *breath* and *death*, it is called **assonance** (AS uh nuhns).

Onomatopoeia The line from Service's poem, quoted in the left column, also includes an example of **onomatopoeia** (ahn oh maht oh PEE uh), which is the use of words with sounds that imitate or suggest their meaning—such as *moan.* Doesn't *sizzle* sound like bacon frying on the griddle? How about *snap, crackle,* or *pop*? Words like these help poets bring sound and sense together.

Poetic Devices

Poems appeal to our emotions and imagination as well as to our sense of reason. To achieve this effect, poets use poetic devices such as these:

Imagery We are drawn into the experience of the poem through the poet's use of **imagery,** or language that appeals to our senses. The following example appeals to our senses of touch, sight, and hearing:

> If our eyes we'd close, then the lashes froze
> till sometimes we couldn't see;
> It wasn't much fun, but the only one to
> whimper was Sam McGee.
>> from "The Cremation of Sam McGee"
>> by Robert W. Service

Symbols A **symbol** is something that has meaning in itself and also stands for something else. In "For My Grandmother," which appears on page 572, the flower has meaning as a plant that blooms and produces seed, but it also represents Countee Cullen's grandmother. Some symbols in literature are obvious, and some are fresh and subtle. Here are some common, or universal, symbols you will probably recognize:

| flag / country | dove / peace | 4-leaf clover / good luck |

Figures of Speech **Figures of speech** are words or phrases that describe one thing in terms of another and are not meant to be understood as literally true. **Similes** compare two unlike things using words such as *like, as, than,* and *resembles.* When you say, "He is as stubborn as a mule," you are using a simile. In this simile, the cold weather is compared to a nail:

> Talk of your cold! through the parka's fold
> it stabbed like a driven nail.
>> from "The Cremation of Sam McGee"
>> by Robert W. Service

A **metaphor** makes a comparison without using a connecting word. If you said, "He is such a stubborn mule," you'd be using a metaphor. When poets carry a metaphor over several lines, it is called an **extended metaphor.** "O Captain! My Captain!" contains an extended metaphor in which President Abraham Lincoln is compared to the captain of a ship.

> My Captain does not answer, his lips are pale and still,
>> from "O Captain! My Captain!"
>> by Walt Whitman

Personification is a particular kind of metaphor in which a nonhuman or inanimate thing is described as if it had human or lifelike qualities. In this example, grim melancholy, or sadness, sits on a large group of people watching a ballgame.

> So upon that stricken multitude grim melancholy sat,
>> from "Casey at the Bat"
>> by Ernest Lawrence Thayer

Reading Standard 3.1 Determine and articulate the relationship between the purposes and characteristics of different forms of poetry (e.g., ballad, lyric, couplet, epic, elegy, ode, sonnet).

Forms of Poetry

Most people can recognize a poem when they see it. Poems usually consist of **lines** instead of sentences and present ideas in **stanzas** instead of paragraphs. There are exceptions to every rule, and poems exist in many forms.

Narrative Poems Simply put, the purpose of a **narrative poem** is to tell a story. "Paul Revere's Ride" relates a famous incident that took place during the American Revolution. "Barbara Frietchie" describes a woman's courageous actions during the Civil War.

Ballads A **ballad** tells a story, often about love, betrayal, or death, in a songlike form. The characteristics of a ballad include a regular, steady rhythm, a simple rhyme pattern, and a refrain. These characteristics make ballads easy to memorize so they can be sung aloud. "The Dying Cowboy" is a traditional ballad.

Epics **Epics** are long narrative poems about the mighty deeds of a great hero. The hero's purpose is to embody the important values of the society or culture he comes from. (The heroes of epics have—so far—all been male.)

Lyric Poems **Lyric poems** usually do not tell a story. Instead, they are written to express the personal thoughts and feelings of a **speaker,** the voice talking to you in a poem. In "Birdfoot's Grampa", the speaker expresses feelings about people and nature.

Sonnets A **sonnet** is a fourteen-line lyric poem that follows strict rules of structure, meter, and rhyme. "On the Grasshopper and the Cricket" is a traditional sonnet.

Odes **Odes** are long lyric poems traditionally written to celebrate a famous person or a lofty idea. Today, many odes, such as "Ode to Thanks," are written to celebrate ordinary things.

Elegies An **elegy** is a poem of mourning, usually for someone who has died. "O Captain! My Captain!" is an elegy for the slain president Abraham Lincoln.

Free-Verse Many poets today prefer to work in **free verse.** With free verse, they do not have to write in meter or a regular rhyme scheme. Instead, they try to capture the sound of everyday speech. Free-verse poems do include other elements of poetry, such as rhythm, imagery, figures of speech, and alliteration. "I Hear America Singing" is a free-verse poem.

Your Turn Analyze Poetry

Read this poem by W. S. Merwin, and answer the questions below.

> Your absence has gone through me
> Like thread through a needle.
> Everything I do is stitched with its color.
> "Separation" by W. S. Merwin

1. What form of poetry is "Separation"? How can you tell?
2. What figures of speech does it contain?
3. What examples of alliteration can you find in the poem?

Learn It Online
To find out more about poetic devices and types of poetry, use *PowerNotes* at:

go.hrw.com   H8-575   **Go**

Reading Skills Focus

by **Kylene Beers**

What Skills Help You Understand Poetry?

Robert Frost said that a poem "begins in delight and ends in wisdom." As you read a poem, you will recognize its rhythms, rhymes, images, and comparisons and the story or experience it shares. By the end you will often find a wisdom that touches you.

Reading a Poem

Poems are meant to be enjoyed as well as analyzed. Here are some strategies for accomplishing both goals.

Read the poem aloud. After you've read the poem twice silently, read it aloud. Each poem has its own sound, which you can hear more distinctly by reading it aloud. Punctuation serves an especially essential purpose in poetry. As you read, stop only when there is a punctuation mark. Pause briefly at commas and dashes, and a little longer at periods. Don't stop just because you've come to the end of a line.

Pay attention to each word. Poets often use few words, so each word is carefully chosen. Look up any unfamiliar words. The shorter the poem, the more meaningful each word is likely to be—as in this short poem by Alberto Forcada, from Chapter 4:

> Grandmother,
> I'm cold;
> can you knit me
> some wrinkles?
> "Sweater" by Alberto Forcada

Pay attention to the title. Sometimes the meaning of the poem is stated or hinted at in the title. If you did not know the poem by Forcada was titled "Sweater," you might not fully comprehend the poem.

Read the poem for pleasure. Poems are not written to torment you. Even the most serious poem, written to express the deepest emotion, involves a kind of play. Poets play with words, sounds, rhythms, and rhymes. Then, you play a game with the poet as you determine the meaning or feeling of the poem. See if you can picture this beautiful scene described in the opening stanzas of "Barbara Frietchie" from Chapter 2.

> Up from the meadows rich with corn,
>   Clear in the cool September morn,
>
> The clustered spires of Frederick stand
>   Green-walled by the hills of Maryland.
>
> Round about them orchards sweep,
>   Apple and peach tree fruited deep.
>   from "Barbara Frietchie"
>   by John Greenleaf Whittier

Re-reading

A key strategy for understanding a poem—and enjoying it—is **re-reading.** You will understand some poems right away, but you will want to re-read them to enjoy their music. You will probably have no trouble following the story of "Paul Revere's Ride," but reading it several times, especially out loud, will help you appreciate characteristics such as its rhymes and its rhythm.

When you re-read a complex poem, think about each word and the feelings it evokes. These feelings are clues to the poem's meaning.

Paraphrasing

Another useful strategy for understanding a poem is paraphrasing. When you paraphrase, you restate a line, sentence, or stanza in your own words. You also explain the meaning of figures of speech that appear in the poem. Poets sometimes use **inversion**—that is, they put parts of their sentences in reverse order from what you are used to. When you paraphrase, you put the sentence into a familiar order. See for instance, this line from "On the Grasshopper and the Cricket" by John Keats.

> The poetry of earth is ceasing never:
> from "On the Grasshopper and the
> Cricket" by John Keats

You might paraphrase the line as "The earth's poetry never ends." You'll have to read the poem to understand what "the poetry of earth" is.

Retelling

Retelling a poem can help you understand what you are reading. In a good **retelling** of a poem, you state in your own words what the poet describes.

Many poems are written in **stanzas**, groups of consecutive lines that form a single unit of meaning. Therefore, the end of a stanza is a good place to pause and retell what you have read to check your comprehension.

Your Turn   Apply Reading Skills

Read this opening stanza from "Ode to Thanks":

> Thanks to the word
> that says *thanks!*
> Thanks to *thanks,*
> word
> that melts
> iron and snow!
> > from "Ode to Thanks"
> > by Pablo Neruda

1. Read the stanza aloud several times. Then, paraphrase it.

2. What does the figure of speech "word that melts iron and snow" mean?

3. Why do you think the poet puts the word *thanks* in italics?

> Now go to the Skills in
> Action: Reading Model

Learn It Online
Try the *PowerNotes* version of this lesson:

go.hrw.com   H8-577   **Go**

Read with a Purpose Read these two poems to discover the writers' messages.

Riding Lesson

by **Henry Taylor**

I learned two things
from an early riding teacher.
He held a nervous filly°
in one hand and gestured
5   with the other, saying, "Listen.
Keep one leg on one side,
the other leg on the other side,
and your mind in the middle."
He turned and mounted.
10   She took two steps, then left
the ground, I thought for good.
But she came down hard, humped
her back, swallowed her neck,
and threw her rider as you'd
15   throw a rock. He rose, brushed
his pants and caught his breath,
and said, "See that's the way
to do it. When you see
they're gonna throw you, get off."

3. **filly:** young female horse.

Introduction to Poetry

by **Billy Collins**

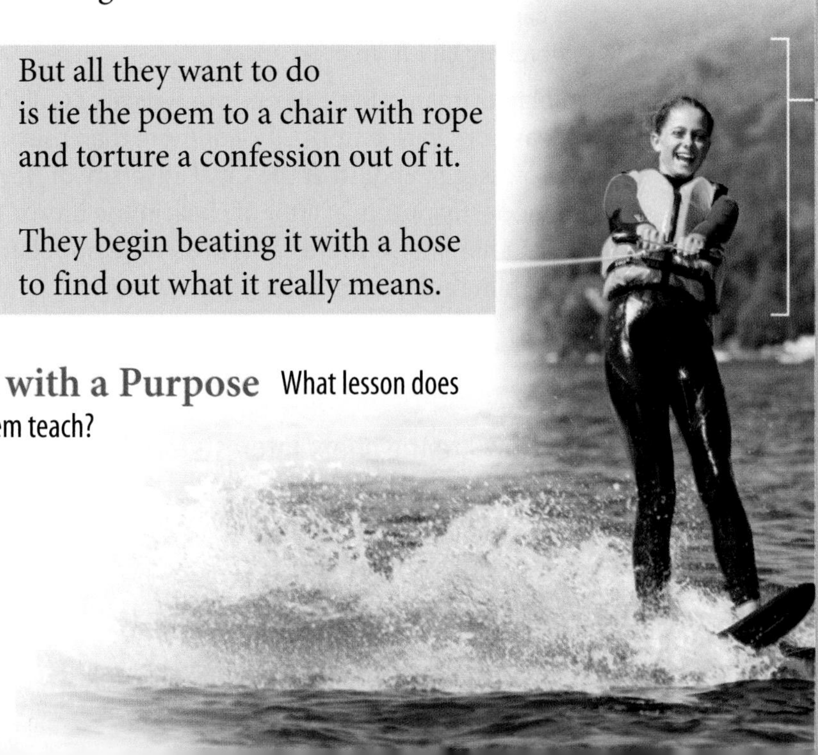

Reading Focus

Reading a Poem The title and first line suggest that the speaker's purpose is to teach a lesson on poetry.

I ask them to take a poem
and hold it up to the light
like a color slide

or press an ear against its hive.

5   I say drop a mouse into a poem
and watch him probe his way out,

Literary Focus

Figures of Speech The poet uses a simile to compare reading a poem to examining a color slide. In later lines the poem is also compared, through metaphor, to a hive, a maze, a room, and a body of water.

or walk inside the poem's room
and feel the walls for a light switch.

I want them to water-ski
10   across the surface of a poem
waving at the author's name on the shore.

But all they want to do
is tie the poem to a chair with rope
and torture a confession out of it.

15   They begin beating it with a hose
to find out what it really means.

Literary Focus

Figures of Speech The poet uses personification in a startling way in lines 12–16.

Read with a Purpose What lesson does each poem teach?

MEET THE WRITERS

Henry Taylor
(1942–   )

Pulitzer Prize WINNER

A Lover of Horses

Pulitzer Prize–winning poet Henry Taylor grew up in rural Virginia, where his father was a dairy farmer. Although Taylor decided at an early age not to follow in his father's footsteps, he was strongly influenced by his surroundings. He says:

> "Horses, in fact, were central to my life until I was in my early twenties; my sisters and I had various ponies and horses around the place, showing in small local horse and pony shows, and generally being as horsy as we could be. . . . Many of my poems draw heavily on that experience."

Billy Collins
(1941–   )

U.S. Poet Laureate WINNER

A "Lifter of Chalk"

When Billy Collins was named poet laureate of the United States in 2001, he said:

> "It came completely out of the blue, like a soft-wrecking ball from outer space."

Surprising and playful images like this one are typical of Collins's poetry. Collins was born in New York City. For more than thirty years, he has been a professor of English at the City University of New York—or, as he modestly puts it, a "lifter of chalk in the Bronx." His poetry has brought him many awards as well as wide popularity. Some have called him the most popular poet in America.

Think About the Writers

How are the poets' interests in real life reflected in their poems?

SKILLS IN ACTION
Wrap Up

Reading Standard 3.1 Determine and articulate the relationship between the purposes and characteristics of different forms of poetry (e.g., ballad, lyric, couplet, epic, elegy, ode, sonnet).

Into Action: Forms and Characteristics of Poetry

Choose either "Riding Lesson" or "Introduction to Poetry" and complete a chart like the one below. First, determine the forms and characteristics of each poem. Then explain your interpretation of the poem.

Title of Poem: _____

Form of poetry: _____

Characteristics of poetry: _____

Interpretation: _____

Talk About . . .

1. With a partner who has chosen the same poem as you, discuss your interpretation of the poem. Refer to your chart for ideas, and try to use the Academic Vocabulary words listed at the right in your discussion.

Write About . . .

Use the underlined Academic Vocabulary words in your answers to the following questions. Definitions of the terms appear to the right.

2. How do the underlined associations you made while reading "Riding Lesson" help you understand the poem?

3. Explain Billy Collins's intent in suggesting that his students "walk inside the poem's room / and feel the walls for a light switch."

4. Articulate the characteristics of free verse and of lyric poems.

Writing Skills Focus
Think as a Reader/Writer

You will find many types of poems in Chapter 5. The Writing Skills Focus activities on the Preparing to Read pages will guide you in understanding each poet's techniques. On the Applying Your Skills pages, you will have opportunities to practice these techniques in your own writing.

Academic Vocabulary for Chapter 5

Talking and Writing About Poetry

Academic Vocabulary is the language you use to write and talk about literature. Use these words to discuss the poetry in this chapter. The words are underlined throughout the chapter.

articulate (ahr TIHK yuh layt) *v.:* clearly express in words. *Each reader may articulate a different response to a poem.*

associations (uh soh see AY shuhnz) *n.:* connections in the mind between different things. *To understand a poem, you may have to consider your own associations to the words and images.*

characteristics (kar ihk tuh RIHS tihks) *n.:* qualities or features of something. *Poems written in a specific form have distinguishing characteristics.*

intent (ihn TEHNT) *n.:* purpose; plan; aim. *The intent of a lyric poem is to share an idea or emotion.*

Your Turn

Copy these Academic Vocabulary words into your *Reader/Writer Notebook*. Now, think of one of your favorite songs. Use each Academic Vocabulary word in a sentence that explains why the song appeals to you.

Preparing to Read

Blue Riot (detail) by TAFA. Oil on canvas (30" x 40"). Courtesy of the artist.

Reader/Writer
Notebook

Use your **RWN** to complete the
activities for this selection.

Valentine for Ernest Mann /
Birdfoot's Grampa

Literary Skills Focus

Lyric Poems Some poems tell stories, while others express the personal feelings of the speaker. Poems that express feelings and do not tell stories are called **lyric poems.** Lyric poems are usually short, and they imply—rather than state directly—a single, strong emotion.

The word *lyric* comes from the word *lyre*, which refers to a stringed instrument that is like a small harp. In ancient Greece, people used to recite poetry to the strumming of a lyre. (At poetry readings today, music is still sometimes used to set the beat or create atmosphere.)

Reading Skills Focus

Reading a Poem The first time you read a poem, don't worry about identifying literary elements; just enjoy! Then, read the poem again, paying closer attention to its individual parts, such as its title, word choice, and punctuation.

Into Action As you read a poem, record the way it affects you each time you read it in a chart like this one.

Valentine for Ernest Mann	Birdfoot's Grampa
First reading: I like the speaker's conversational tone. The valentine was a real surprise.	First reading:
Second reading:	Second reading:

Writing Skills Focus
Think as a Reader/Writer

Find It in Your Reading These poems use imagery to help you see ordinary things in a new way. **Images** appeal to your senses of sight, smell, touch, hearing, or taste. As you read these poems, list at least three sensory images from each poem in your *Reader/Writer Notebook*.

Vocabulary

Valentine for Ernest Mann

spirit (SPIHR iht) *n.*: courage; liveliness. *Asking a famous poet to write you a poem shows spirit.*

drifting (DRIHF tihng) *v.* used as *adj.*: being carried along as if by a current of air or water. *We can catch beautiful, poetic images drifting throughout our lives.*

Language Coach

Connotations Words have two kinds of meanings: **denotations,** or definitions you find in a dictionary, and **connotations,** or the feelings and associations the words bring forth. Think about the word *spirit*, listed above. What connotations does that word evoke?

Learn It Online
To observe a good reader in action, visit:

go.hrw.com	H8-583	Go

Learn It Online

Learn more about Bruchac at:

go.hrw.com   H8-584   **Go**

Naomi Shihab Nye
(1952–   )

Finding Poetry in the Familiar

Naomi Shihab Nye often runs workshops in schools to help students find the poetry hidden in their imaginations. She is inspired by everyday activities and tasks. In her poems, Nye makes the tiniest details exceptional and wonderful. She once said:

> "Familiar sights, sounds, smells have always been my necessities. Let someone else think about future goals and professional lives! I will keep track of the bucket and the hoe . . . and clouds drifting in from the horizon."

For more information about Naomi Shihab Nye, see page 814.

Joseph Bruchac
(1942–   )

When You Least Expect Them

Joseph Bruchac was born in Saratoga Springs, New York, and raised there by his grandmother and grandfather, who was a member of the Abenaki people. Bruchac studied wildlife conservation in college. Today he is a well-known editor, publisher, poet, and collector of folk tales. He says that "Birdfoot's Grampa" describes a lesson he was taught "in the way most good lessons come to you—when you least expect them."

Think
About the Writers

What does each poet believe poetry can express?

Preview the Selections

In "Valentine for Ernest Mann" the speaker responds to someone who has asked for a poem.

The speaker of "Birdfoot's Grampa" is frustrated when his grandfather seems to pay too much attention to toads.

Read with a Purpose Read this poem to discover its surprising message.

Valentine for Ernest Mann

by **Naomi Shihab Nye**

You can't order a poem like you order a taco.
Walk up to the counter, say, "I'll take two"
and expect it to be handed back to you
on a shiny plate.

Still, I like your spirit.
Anyone who says, "Here's my address,
write me a poem," deserves something in reply.
So I'll tell a secret instead:
poems hide. In the bottoms of our shoes,
they are sleeping. They are the shadows
drifting across our ceilings the moment
before we wake up. What we have to do
is live in a way that lets us find them. **A**

A **Literary Focus** **Lyric Poem** What idea does the poet articulate?

Vocabulary **spirit** (SPIHR iht) *n.:* courage; liveliness.
drifting (DRIHF tihng) *v.* used as *adj.:* being carried along as if by a current of air or water.

Once I knew a man who gave his wife
15 two skunks for a valentine.
He couldn't understand why she was crying.
"I thought they had such beautiful eyes."
And he was serious. He was a serious man
who lived in a serious way. Nothing was ugly
20 just because the world said so. He really
liked those skunks. So, he re-invented them
as valentines and they became beautiful.
At least, to him. And the poems that had been hiding
in the eyes of skunks for centuries
25 crawled out and curled up at his feet.

Maybe if we re-invent whatever our lives give us
we find poems. Check your garage, the odd sock
in your drawer, the person you almost like, but not quite.
And let me know. **Ⓑ**

Ⓑ [Read and Discuss] How does the skunk story connect to the way the poet views
the origins and development of poetry?

BIRDFOOT'S GRAMPA

by **Joseph Bruchac**

The old man
must have stopped our car
two dozen times to climb out
and gather into his hands
5   the small toads blinded
by our lights and leaping,
live drops of rain.   **A**

The rain was falling,
a mist about his white hair
10   and I kept saying
you can't save them all
accept it, get back in
we've got places to go.

But, leathery hands full
15   of wet brown life,
knee deep in the summer
roadside grass,
he just smiled and said
they have places to go to
20   *too.*   **B**

A Read and Discuss What is the grandfather doing?

B Literary Focus Lyric Poem The speaker and the grandfather have different ideas about what is important. What idea do you think the poem articulates?

Applying Your Skills

Reading Standard 3.1 Determine and articulate the relationship between the purposes and characteristics of different forms of poetry (**e.g.,** ballad, **lyric,** couplet, epic, elegy, ode, sonnet).

Valentine for Ernest Mann / Birdfoot's Grampa
Literary Response and Analysis

Reading Skills Focus
Read with a Purpose

1. What does "Valentine for Ernest Mann" say about where poems hide? What is important to Birdfoot's Grampa?

Reading Skills: Reading a Poem

2. Complete the chart below if you haven't done so already. Then, describe what you noticed about each poem the second time you read it that you hadn't noticed in the first reading.

Birdfoot's Grampa	Valentine for Ernest Mann
First reading:	First reading:
Second reading:	Second reading:

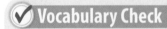

✓ Vocabulary Check

Match each Vocabulary word with its definition.
3. **spirit**   **a.** floating
4. **drifting**   **b.** courage

Literary Skills Focus
Literary Analysis

5. **Analyze** In the first stanza of "Valentine for Ernest Mann," the poet uses a **simile.** What two very different things is she comparing? What is she saying about poems by using this simile?

6. **Interpret** In the second stanza of "Valentine for Ernest Mann," the poet **personifies** poems. What human characteristics does she give poems? What is she telling you about poems by using this figure of speech?

7. **Interpret** The second stanza of "Valentine for Ernest Mann" also includes a **metaphor.** What are compared to poems? What does this metaphor tell you about poems?

8. **Analyze** Why does the speaker talk about the man and the skunk in the third stanza of "Valentine for Ernest Mann"? (What associations does the speaker make between skunks and poetry?)

9. **Extend** Many people, like Birdfoot's Grampa, believe that their actions can make a difference. Think of someone who has acted on that belief. What was the intent of the person's actions? What were the results of his or her actions?

Literary Skills: Lyric Poems

10. **Classify** What are the characteristics of lyric poetry? Why are these poems lyrics? Support your answer with details from these poems.

Literary Skills Review: Theme

11. What do both poems suggest is essential in life?

Writing Skills Focus
Think as a Reader/Writer

Use It in Your Writing Follow Nye's advice, and try to find a lyric poem in your life. Write a lyric poem that uses sensory images to help readers view something apparently ordinary in a new way.

What Do You Think Now

Have the poems changed your idea of beauty? Why might you see skunks and toads in a different way?

Vocabulary Development

Metaphors, Similes, and Personification

The most common figures of speech are metaphors, similes, and personification. **Metaphors** directly compare two unlike things. **Similes** also compare two unlike things but use the words *like, than, as,* or *resembles* to introduce the comparison. **Personification** gives human or lifelike qualities or behavior to nonhuman things.

Your Turn

The following lines from famous poems include figures of speech. Decide if each quotation uses a metaphor, a simile, or personification. (Watch out: Personification is a type of metaphor.) Then, tell what two things are being compared, and infer the meaning of each comparison.

1. " 'Hope' is the thing with feathers" —Emily Dickinson

2. "I wandered lonely as a cloud" —William Wordsworth

3. "The road was a ribbon of moonlight" —Alfred Noyes

4. "I hear America singing . . ." —Walt Whitman

5. "The sea is a hungry dog, / Giant and gray. / He rolls on the beach all day." —James Reeves

6. "The fog comes / on little cat feet" —Carl Sandburg

7. "I stepped on the toe / Of an unemployed hoe. It rose in offense / And struck me a blow...."
   —Robert Frost

Language Coach

Connotations Connotations are the feelings associated with a word, feelings that go beyond its strict dictionary definition, or **denotation**. Often connotations show variations in meaning or intensity.

Use the symbol "+" if the word on the right seems stronger than the numbered Vocabulary word on the left. Use a "–" sign if it seems weaker. Use a dictionary for help (Try this exercise with a partner. You may not agree on the answers.)

8. **spirit** __   zeal __

9. **drifting** __   floating __

10. **reinvented** __   re-create __

Academic Vocabulary

Talk About . . .

Discuss the <u>characteristics</u> of "Valentine for Ernest Mann" and "Birdfoot's Grampa" with a partner. Then, <u>articulate</u> your ideas about the meanings of the poems.

Cupolas (1909) by Wassily Kandinsky. Oil on cardboard (33 ½" x 45 ¹¹⁄₁₆").
© 2007 Artist Rights Society (ARS), New York/ADAGP, Paris.

CONTENTS

What Do **You Think** How do people express their beliefs and emotions?

 QuickTalk

In a small group, discuss ways that people express themselves. For example, how do people stand up to authority? How do they make requests?

Reader/Writer
Notebook
Use your **RWN** to complete the
activities for this selection.

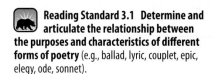

Reading Standard 3.1 Determine and
articulate the relationship between
the purposes and characteristics of different
forms of poetry (e.g., ballad, lyric, couplet, epic,
elegy, ode, sonnet).

Paul Revere's Ride

Literary Skills Focus

Narrative Poem A narrative poem is a form of poetry that tells a
story. The poem you are about to read tells about a historical event.

Rhythm People love rhythm—the rhythm of music, of dance, and of
language. Rhythm is not only pleasing to the ear; it also affects the way
we feel. A slow rhythm can make us feel sad or dreamy. A fast rhythm
can make us feel like dancing. Rhythm is as essential to language as it is
to music. In language, rhythm is the rise and fall of the voice, produced
by stressed and unstressed syllables. When the sounds occur in a
particular pattern, we call it meter.

"Paul Revere's Ride" is written with a strong meter. Notice, when you
read it aloud, how the meter sounds like a galloping horse: da da DUM
da da DUM da da DUM da da DUM. The story of Paul Revere has been
told many times and in many different ways, but this poem is the most
famous version of what happened on that fateful night. What makes
people remember this poem is its rhythm.

Reading Skills Focus

Paraphrasing When you paraphrase a text, you restate it in your own
words. A paraphrase restates all the information in the original, unlike a
summary, which retells only the most important points.

Into Action Stop to paraphrase the difficult lines of poems. Keep track
of your paraphrases in a chart like this one.

Paul Revere's Ride	My Paraphrase
lines 1-3	Listen, and I will tell you all about Paul Revere's famous midnight ride that took place on April 18, 1775.
lines	

Writing Skills Focus
Think as a Reader/Writer
Find It in Your Reading As you read, notice the poet's
use of images that appeal to the senses. Record examples of
Longfellow's images and the effect those images have on you.

Language Coach

Word Choice In "Paul Revere's
Ride," the poet creates memorable
images by using precise descriptions,
such as *muffled phantom ship, somber rafters,* and *hurrying hoofbeats.*
Each image not only suggests a picture but also indicates a feeling. For
each of the following nouns, use one
or two adjectives to create a precise
image. Try to suggest not only a picture or idea but also a feeling.

1. storm
2. carnival
3. roar
4. desert
5. star

Learn It Online
Find out more about "Paul Revere's Ride" through the
PowerNotes introduction at:

go.hrw.com	H8-591	Go

Learn It Online
Learn more about Longfellow at:
go.hrw.com H8-592 Go

Henry Wadsworth Longfellow
(1807–1882)

A Poet of American History

If you had gone to school a hundred years ago, you and all your friends would probably be able to recite by heart several of the poems of Henry Wadsworth Longfellow. Born in Portland, Maine, Longfellow became the most popular poet of his day. Many of his poems, such as *Evangeline* (1847), *The Song of Hiawatha* (1855), and *The Courtship of Miles Standish* (1858), were inspired by people and events in American history. As "Paul Revere's Ride" shows, Longfellow believed that one person's actions could make a difference. In an early piece of verse, he wrote:

"Lives of great men all remind us

We can make our lives sublime.

And, departing, leave behind us

Footprints on the sand of time."

Build Background

In April of 1775, the British wanted to arrest two Americans who were calling for armed resistance to England. The British also wanted to destroy a supply of arms being stored in Concord. The next day armed volunteers known as minutemen, who had been alerted to the British army's presence by Paul Revere, William Dawes, and Samuel Prescott, confronted the British at Lexington and Concord. These were the first battles of the American Revolution.

Preview the Selection

In "Paul Revere's Ride," you will read Longfellow's account of how **Paul Revere** warned his fellow citizens that the British forces were coming.

Think About the Writer

What values do you think Longfellow held dear?

Paul Revere's Ride

by **Henry Wadsworth Longfellow**

> ### Read with a Purpose
> Read the following poem to learn about Paul Revere's memorable actions.

Listen, my children, and you shall hear
Of the midnight ride of Paul Revere,   **A**
On the eighteenth of April, in Seventy-five;
Hardly a man is now alive
5   Who remembers that famous day and year.

He said to his friend, "If the British march
By land or sea from the town tonight,
Hang a lantern aloft in the belfry° arch
Of the North Church tower as a signal light—
10 One, if by land, and two, if by sea;
And I on the opposite shore will be,
Ready to ride and spread the alarm
Through every Middlesex village and farm,
For the country folk to be up and to arm."   **B**

15 Then he said, "Good night!" and with muffled oar
Silently rowed to the Charlestown shore,

---

8. belfry (BEHL free): steeple of a church where bells are hung.

A **Literary Focus** **Rhythm** The rhythm of this poem reflects its subject—a long, fast ride on horseback. Clap out the first two lines of the stanza. What <u>associations</u> does the rhythm evoke?

B **Read and Discuss** What is Revere's plan?

Just as the moon rose over the bay,
Where swinging wide at her moorings° lay
The Somerset, British man-of-war;
20   A phantom ship, with each mast and spar°
Across the moon like a prison bar,
And a huge black hulk, that was magnified
By its own reflection in the tide.

Meanwhile, his friend, through alley and street,   **C**
25   Wanders and watches with eager ears,
Till in the silence around him he hears
The muster° of men at the barrack door,
The sound of arms, and the tramp of feet,
And the measured tread of the grenadiers,°
30   Marching down to their boats on the shore.

Then he climbed the tower of the Old North Church,
By the wooden stairs, with stealthy tread,
To the belfry chamber overhead,   **D**
And startled the pigeons from their perch
35   On the somber rafters, that round him made
Masses and moving shapes of shade—
By the trembling ladder, steep and tall,
To the highest window in the wall,
Where he paused to listen and look down
40   A moment on the roofs of the town,
And the moonlight flowing over all.

Beneath, in the churchyard, lay the dead,
In their night encampment on the hill,
Wrapped in silence so deep and still
45   That he could hear, like a sentinel's° tread,

18. moorings: cables holding a ship in place so that it doesn't float away.

20. mast and spar: poles supporting a ship's sails.

27. muster: assembly; gathering.

29. grenadiers (grehn uh DIHRZ): foot soldiers who carry and throw grenades.

45. sentinel's (SEHN tuh nuhlz): guard's.

C **Literary Focus** Narrative Poem The poet begins this stanza with the transitional word *Meanwhile*. The stanza before begins with *Then*. Why might you find transitions in a narrative poem?

D **Reading Focus** Paraphrasing Paraphrase what Revere's friend did at the church tower (lines 31–33).

A statue of a minuteman in Lexington, Massachusetts.

Revere's Ride and the American Revolution

Paul Revere's famous ride succeeded in forestalling the planned raid on Boston by the British. One reason the British planned to raid Concord was to arrest two Americans who were calling for armed resistance against England. The British also wanted to destroy a supply of arms located in Concord. The day after Revere's ride, armed volunteers known as minutemen confronted the British at Lexington and Concord. These were the first battles of the American Revolution. The war lasted for eight years, until September 3, 1783, when the Treaty of Paris was signed and the United States was recognized as an independent country.

Ask Yourself

What might have happened had Revere and his friends failed to warn people of the British advance?

> The watchful night wind, as it went
> Creeping along from tent to tent,
> And seeming to whisper, "All is well!"
> A moment only he feels the spell
> 50 Of the place and the hour, and the secret dread
> Of the lonely belfry and the dead;
> For suddenly all his thoughts are bent
> On a shadowy something far away,
> Where the river widens to meet the bay—
> 55 A line of black that bends and floats
> On the rising tide, like a bridge of boats. **E**
>
> Meanwhile, impatient to mount and ride,
> Booted and spurred, with a heavy stride
> On the opposite shore walked Paul Revere.
> 60 Now he patted his horse's side,
> Now gazed at the landscape far and near,
> Then, impetuous, stamped the earth,

E | Read and Discuss | What is the speaker telling you?

Vocabulary **impetuous** (ihm PEHCH u uhs) *adj.*: impulsive; eager.

And turned and tightened his saddle girth;
But mostly he watched with eager search
65 The belfry tower of the Old North Church,
As it rose above the graves on the hill,
Lonely and spectral° and somber and still.
And lo! as he looks, on the belfry's height
A glimmer, and then a gleam of light!
70 He springs to the saddle, the bridle he turns,
But lingers and gazes, till full on his sight
A second lamp in the belfry burns!   **F**

A hurry of hoofs in a village street,
A shape in the moonlight, a bulk in the dark,
75 And beneath, from the pebbles, in passing, a spark
Struck out by a steed flying fearless and fleet:
That was all! And yet, through the gloom and the light,
The fate of a nation was riding that night;
And the spark struck out by that steed, in his flight,
80 Kindled the land into flame with its heat.   **G**

He has left the village and mounted the steep,
And beneath him, tranquil and broad and deep,
Is the Mystic, meeting the ocean tides;
And under the alders° that skirt its edge,
85 Now soft on the sand, now loud on the ledge,
Is heard the tramp of his steed as he rides.

It was twelve by the village clock,
When he crossed the bridge into Medford town.
He heard the crowing of the cock,
90 And the barking of the farmer's dog,
And felt the damp of the river fog,
That rises after the sun goes down.

67. spectral: ghostly.

84. alders (AWL duhrz): shrubs and trees of the birch family.

F | Read and Discuss | What has happened?

G | Literary Focus | Rhythm Re-read lines 73–80. Here, the action is at full speed. What association can you make between the rhythm and the action?

Analyzing Visuals **Connecting to the Text** In what ways does this famous depiction of Paul Revere's ride echo the drama of the poem?

It was one by the village clock,
When he galloped into Lexington.
95 He saw the gilded weathercock°
Swim in the moonlight as he passed,
And the meetinghouse windows, blank and bare,
Gaze at him with a spectral glare,
As if they already stood aghast
100 At the bloody work they would look upon.

95. weathercock: weathervane made to look like a rooster (cock). Weathervanes indicate the direction in which the wind is blowing.

Vocabulary **aghast** (uh GAST) *adj.:* shocked; horrified.

It was two by the village clock,
When he came to the bridge in Concord town.
He heard the bleating of the flock,
And the twitter of birds among the trees,
105 And felt the breath of the morning breeze
Blowing over the meadows brown.
And one was safe and asleep in his bed
Who at the bridge would be first to fall,
Who that day would be lying dead,
110 Pierced by a British musket ball.

You know the rest. In the books you have read,
How the British Regulars fired and fled—
How the farmers gave them ball for ball,
From behind each fence and farmyard wall,
115 Chasing the redcoats down the lane,
Then crossing the fields to emerge again
Under the trees at the turn of the road,
And only pausing to fire and load.   **H**

So through the night rode Paul Revere;
120 And so through the night went his cry of alarm
To every Middlesex village and farm—
A cry of defiance and not of fear,
A voice in the darkness, a knock at the door,
And a word that shall echo forevermore!
125 For, borne on the night wind of the Past,
Through all our history, to the last,
In the hour of darkness and peril and need,
The people will waken and listen to hear
The hurrying hoofbeats of that steed,
130 And the midnight message of Paul Revere.   **I**

H **Reading Focus** **Paraphrasing** Paraphrase this stanza's
description of the battle of Lexington and Concord.

I **Read and Discuss** What message is Longfellow trying to convey to
readers?

Applying Your Skills

Reading Standard 3.1 Determine and articulate the relationship between the purposes and characteristics of different forms of poetry (e.g., ballad, lyric, couplet, elegy, ode, sonnet).

Paul Revere's Ride

Literary Response and Analysis

Reading Skills Focus

Quick Check

1. A narrative poem relates a series of events, just as a short story does. Trace the main events of Revere's ride, as it is described in lines 81–102.

Read with a Purpose

2. Why is it appropriate that people remember what Paul Revere did?

Reading Skills: Paraphrasing

3. If you haven't done so already, paraphrase the final lines of "Paul Revere's Ride" to understand the poem's message.

	My Paraphrase
Paul Revere's Ride lines 125–130	

✓ Vocabulary Check

Fill in the blanks with the correct Vocabulary words.

impetuous   aghast

4. The townspeople were _____ that a British army was coming. Revere, always _____, was ready to act.

Literary Skills Focus

Literary Analysis

5. **Interpret** What does the poet mean when he says, "The fate of a nation was riding that night" (line 78)? What does he mean by saying that the spark struck by the horse's hoof "kindled the land into flame" (line 80)?

6. **Infer** What do you think the word or words are "that shall echo forevermore" (line 124)? Write what Revere might have said as he knocked on each door.

7. **Connect** What other figures from history or living today have rallied their people with cries "of defiance and not of fear" (line 122)?

Literary Skills: Narrative Poetry and Rhythm

8. **Identify** Read aloud the first stanza. Mark its stressed and unstressed syllables to indicate its **meter.** (Review the marks on page 572.) Notice that the poet varies the pattern to avoid monotony. One thing that never varies is the stress on the last syllable of each line.

Literary Skills Review: Theme

9. **Analyze** Why does the poet believe that "in the hour of darkness and peril and need," Americans will remember Paul Revere's message? Articulate the significance you think this story has today.

Writing Skills Focus

Think as a Reader/Writer

Use It in Your Writing Choose one of the people you identified in response to question 7. Create a short narrative poem about that person and the actions he or she has taken. Next to the narrative details, list examples of imagery you would add to your poem.

 What Do You Think Now
What was the effect of Paul Revere expressing his beliefs?

Applying Your Skills

Reading Standard 1.1 Analyze idioms, analogies, metaphors, and similes **to infer the literal and figurative meanings of phrases**.

Paul Revere's Ride

Vocabulary Development

Using Figures of Speech

If you look carefully, you'll begin to find poetic techniques used in everyday language.

Directions: Read the following statements, and then answer the questions below.

1. *"Reporters peppered the president with questions."*
   A What is the literal meaning of this statement?
   B What is the statement's figurative meaning?

2. *"The worldly and the wise will watch for good buys."*
   A Which words rhyme in this advertising blurb?
   B Which words form alliteration?

3. *"When the going gets tough, the tough get going."*
   A What two meanings of the word *tough* does this saying depend on?
   B Where does this saying use alliteration?

Directions: Answer the questions that follow.

4. The Colts, Bears, Cubs, Red Wings, and Rams are all effective names of popular sports teams. Think of five mammals or birds or insects that would be inappropriate names for sports teams.

5. Many towns, states, and rivers in the United States have American Indian names that are figures of speech. Use a dictionary to find out what these names mean in their original language. Explain which meaning surprises you most.
   A Aztec
   B Chicago
   C Shenandoah
   D Omaha
   E Yosemite
   F Missouri

Language Coach

Word Choice Poets sometimes order phrases in a way that doesn't seem natural. Take "I on the opposite shore will be" in line 11. "I will be on the opposite shore" might be the order you would expect. When poets write in meter, they sometimes reorder words or phrases to maintain the poem's rhythm. Look at line 49 for similar wording. Why might the poet have chosen to order the phrases as he did?

Preparing to Read

**Reading Standard 3.1** Determine and articulate the relationship between the purposes and characteristics of different forms of poetry (e.g., ballad, lyric, couplet, epic, elegy, ode, sonnet).

The Cremation of Sam McGee / The Dying Cowboy

Reader/Writer Notebook

Use your **RWN** to complete the activities for these selections.

Literary Skills Focus

Ballads A **ballad** is a song or a songlike poem that tells a story, usually about lost love, betrayal, or death. Ballads usually use simple language and a great deal of repetition. Most ballads have **refrains,** or repeated words, phrases, lines, or groups of lines. Their simple, regular meters and rhyme patterns make them easy to memorize. All these characteristics make them fun to sing or read aloud. The most famous ballads were passed on orally for many years before they were written down. The authors are unknown, and the songs were changed as they were handed down. That's why most popular ballads come in many versions.

Exaggeration "The Cremation of Sam McGee" is a **tall tale**—an exaggerated, far-fetched story that is obviously untrue but told as if it were fact. **Exaggerations,** which stretch the truth about as high and wide as it will go, are used in tall tales for humor.

Literary Perspectives Apply the literary perspective described on page 609 as you read "The Dying Cowboy."

Reading Skills Focus

Retelling Narrative poems such as ballads usually tell a story. In a good **retelling** of a narrative poem, you identify the main characters, relate the main events in order, and explain how the poem ends.

Into Action Many narrative poems are written in **stanzas**—groups of consecutive lines that form a single unit. After reading each stanza of the poems, record your retelling of each stanza in a chart.

Poem: The Cremation of Sam McGee

Stanza Number	Events
1	The speaker tells us that the poem will be about the night he cremated Sam McGee.
2	

Writing Skills Focus

Think as a Reader/Writer

Find It in Your Reading Note the poets' use of **imagery,** language that appeals to the senses. How does the imagery enliven the stories?

Robert W. Service
(1874–1958)

"A Story Jack London Never Got"

Born in Lancashire, England, Robert W. Service immigrated to Canada in his early twenties. After traveling along the Canadian Pacific coast, he took a job with a bank and was transferred to the Yukon Territory. He wrote his most popular poems there, including "The Cremation of Sam McGee." The poem was inspired by a story Service heard at a party where he was feeling awkward and out of place:

> "I was staring gloomily at a fat fellow across the table. . . . Suddenly he said, 'I'll tell you a story Jack London never got.' Then he spun a yarn of a man who cremated his pal. It had a surprise climax which occasioned much laughter. I did not join, for I had a feeling that here was a decisive moment of destiny. I still remember how a great excitement usurped me. Here was a perfect ballad subject. The fat man who ignored me went his way to bankruptcy, but he had pointed me the road to fortune."

Service left the party and spent the next six hours wandering through the frozen woods, verses in his head. When he went to bed, the poem was complete; he didn't even put it on paper until the next day.

Think About the Writer
What detail about Service's background is most surprising to you?

Build Background
The Cremation of Sam McGee

In the 1890s, thousands of fortune hunters rushed north, braving bitter cold and deep snow. Gold had been found in northwestern Canada, in the Klondike region of the Yukon Territory. The town of Dawson, at the center of the region, became the Yukon's capital.

Like many other gold seekers, Sam McGee is unprepared for the Klondike's seven-month winter, when the temperature sometimes falls as low as minus sixty-eight degrees Fahrenheit. This poem tells his story. (*Cremation* means burning a body to ashes.)

The Dying Cowboy

Ballads like this one were sung by cowboys in the American West. This ballad is based on an eighteenth-century Irish tune and is the basis of the famous blues song "St. James Infirmary." The ballad also provided the title and the haunting theme music for *Bang the Drum Slowly,* a movie about the death of a young baseball player.

Preview the Selections

The two ballads you are about to read are both about men who die before their time. Each man asks a friend to honor his last request. The main characters of the poems are **Sam McGee** in "The Cremation of Sam McGee" and simply **a handsome young cowboy** in "The Dying Cowboy."

The Cremation of Sam McGee

by **Robert W. Service**

There are strange things done in the midnight sun
*   By the men who moil° for gold;*
The Arctic trails have their secret tales
*   That would make your blood run cold;*
5 *The Northern Lights have seen queer sights,*
*   But the queerest they ever did see*
Was that night on the marge° of Lake Lebarge
*   I cremated Sam McGee.* **Ⓐ**

2. moil: labor.

7. marge: edge.

Now Sam McGee was from Tennessee, where the cotton
    blooms and blows.
Why he left his home in the South to roam 'round the
10   Pole, God only knows.
He was always cold, but the land of gold seemed to hold
    him like a spell;
Though he'd often say in his homely way that he'd
    "sooner live in hell." **Ⓑ**

On a Christmas Day we were mushing our way over the
    Dawson trail.
Talk of your cold! through the parka's fold it stabbed like
    a driven nail.

Ⓐ Read and Discuss What has the poet told you so far?

Ⓑ Reading Focus Retelling Retell the information in this stanza.

15 If our eyes we'd close, then the lashes froze till sometimes
         we couldn't see;
   It wasn't much fun, but the only one to whimper was
         Sam McGee.

   And that very night, as we lay packed tight in our robes
         beneath the snow,
   And the dogs were fed, and the stars o'erhead were
         dancing heel and toe,
   He turned to me, and "Cap," says he, "I'll cash in this
         trip, I guess;
   And if I do, I'm asking that you won't refuse my last
20   request."

   Well, he seemed so low that I couldn't say no; then he
         says with a sort of moan:
   "It's the cursèd cold, and it's got right hold till I'm chilled
         clean through to the bone.
   Yet 'tain't being dead—it's my awful dread of the icy
         grave that pains;
   So I want you to swear that, foul or fair, you'll cremate
         my last remains."

   A pal's last need is a thing to heed, so I swore I would
25   not fail;
   And we started on at the streak of dawn; but God! he
         looked ghastly pale.
   He crouched on the sleigh, and he raved all day of his
         home in Tennessee;
   And before nightfall a corpse was all that was left of Sam
         McGee.

C | **Read and Discuss** | Why is cremation important to Sam McGee?

604

There wasn't a breath in that land of death, and
    I hurried, horror-driven,
With a corpse half hid that I couldn't get rid, because of
30   a promise given;
It was lashed to the sleigh, and it seemed to say: "You
    may tax your brawn and brains,
But you promised true, and it's up to you to cremate
    those last remains."

Now a promise made is a debt unpaid, and the trail has
    its own stern code.
In the days to come, though my lips were dumb, in my
    heart how I cursed that load.
In the long, long night, by the lone firelight, while the
35   huskies, round in a ring,
Howled out their woes to the homeless snows—O God!
    how I loathed the thing. **D**

D **Literary Focus** **Exaggeration** What is the purpose of the exaggerations
in these stanzas?

Vocabulary **tax** (taks) *v.:* here, burden; strain.
loathed (lohthd) *v.:* hated.

And every day that quiet clay seemed to heavy and
      heavier grow;
And on I went, though the dogs were spent and the grub
      was getting low;
The trail was bad, and I felt half mad, but I swore I
      would not give in;
And I'd often sing to the hateful thing, and it hearkened°
40   with a grin.

Till I came to the marge of Lake Lebarge, and a derelict°
      there lay;
It was jammed in the ice, but I saw in a trice it was called
      the "Alice May."
And I looked at it, and I thought a bit, and I looked at
      my frozen chum;
Then "Here," said I, with a sudden cry, "is my cre-ma-
      tor-ium." **E**

Some planks I tore from the cabin floor, and I lit the
45   boiler fire;
Some coal I found that was lying around, and I heaped
      the fuel higher;
The flames just soared, and the furnace roared—such a
      blaze you seldom see;
And I burrowed a hole in the glowing coal, and I stuffed
      in Sam McGee.

Then I made a hike, for I didn't like to hear him sizzle so;
And the heavens scowled, and the huskies howled, and
50   the wind began to blow.
It was icy cold, but the hot sweat rolled down my cheeks,
      and I don't know why;
And the greasy smoke in an inky cloak went streaking
      down the sky.

E Read and Discuss How is the speaker handling McGee's death?

Vocabulary spent (spehnt) *adj.:* worn-out.

606

I do not know how long in the snow I wrestled with
    grisly° fear;
But the stars came out and they danced about ere again
    I ventured near;
I was sick with dread, but I bravely said: "I'll just take a
55   peep inside.
I guess he's cooked, and it's time I looked"; . . . then the
    door I opened wide.

And there sat Sam, looking cool and calm, in the heart
    of the furnace roar;
And he wore a smile you could see a mile, and he said:
    "Please close that door.
It's fine in here, but I greatly fear you'll let in the cold
    and storm—
Since I left Plumtree, down in Tennessee, it's the first
60   time I've been warm." **F**

There are strange things done in the midnight sun
    By the men who moil for gold;
The Arctic trails have their secret tales
    That would make your blood run cold;
65 *The Northern Lights have seen queer sights,*
    But the queerest they ever did see
Was that night on the marge of Lake Lebarge
    I cremated Sam McGee. **G**

53. grisly (GRIHZ lee): here, caused by something horrible.

F **Literary Focus** **Ballad** What is the climax of this story?

G **Read and Discuss** Why has the poet chosen to end the poem by repeating its beginning?

607

The Dying Cowboy

traditional American ballad

As I rode out by Tom Sherman's barroom,
As I rode out so early one day,
'Twas there I espied a handsome young cowboy,
All dressed in white linen, all clothed for the grave.

The Bronco Buster (1910)
by Frederic Remington.

5   "I see by your outfit that you are a cowboy,"
These words he did say as I boldly stepped by.
"Come sit down beside me and hear my sad story,
For I'm shot in the breast and I know I must die.   **Ⓐ**

"Then beat your drum slowly and play your fife lowly,
10   And play the dead march as you carry me along,
And take me to the graveyard and throw the sod o'er me,
For I'm a young cowboy and I know I've done wrong. **Ⓑ**

"'Twas once in the saddle I used to go dashing,
'Twas once in the saddle I used to go gay,
15   But I first took to drinking and then to card playing,
Got shot in the body and I'm dying today.

"Let sixteen gamblers come handle my coffin,
Let sixteen young cowboys come sing me a song,
Take me to the green valley and lay the sod o'er me,
20   For I'm a poor cowboy and I know I've done wrong.

Ⓐ **Read and Discuss** What have you learned so far?

Ⓑ **Reading Focus** Retelling   What information does this stanza present?

"Go bring me back a cup of cool water
To cool my parched lips," this cowboy then said.
Before I returned, his soul had departed
And gone to his Maker—the cowboy lay dead.

25   We swung our ropes slowly and rattled our spurs lowly,
And gave a wild whoop as we carried him on,
For we all loved our comrade, so brave, young and handsome,
We all loved our comrade, although he'd done wrong.   **C**

C **Literary Perspectives** Analyzing Archetypes How is this cowboy
similar to cowboys you have read about in other stories?

Vocabulary **comrade** (KAHM rad) *n.:* companion; friend; associate.

Literary Perspectives

The following perspective will help you analyze the ballad you have just read.

Analyzing Archetypes The word *archetype* means a recognizable pattern in
literature. Stories, symbols, themes, and characters can be archetypes. Archetypal
characters, such as the trickster or the rebel-hero, capture some basic aspect of
human experience. In this ballad, you will meet another archetype: the cowboy.
Even if you are unfamiliar with "The Dying Cowboy," you will notice that the
cowboy in the ballad shares character traits with other characters you have read
about or seen in television and movies. Like most other cowboys, the cowboy in
"The Dying Cowboy" is physically appealing and rides a horse. Notice other details
about this cowboy that make him a universal type. As you read, answer the
questions in the text, which will guide you in using this perspective.

Applying Your Skills

Reading Standard 3.1 Determine and articulate the relationship between the purposes and characteristics of different forms of poetry (e.g., ballad, lyric, couplet, epic, elegy, ode, sonnet).

The Cremation of Sam McGee /
The Dying Cowboy

Literary Response and Analysis

Reading Skills Focus
Read with a Purpose

1. What last request does each speaker fulfill?

Reading Skills: Retelling

2. Complete the charts you began while reading. Then, add a row to each chart and write a short retelling of each ballad.

Poem: The Creation of Sam McGee

Stanza Number	Events
1	
2	

Retelling:

✓ Vocabulary Check

Match each Vocabulary word with its synonym.

3. **loathed**   a. tired
4. **tax**   b. friend
5. **spent**   c. hated
6. **comrade**   d. burden

Literary Skills Focus
Literary Analysis

7. **Identify** List two or three images from "The Cremation of Sam McGee" that help you picture the frozen landscape or feel the cold.

8. **Infer** Based on the language he uses to describe Sam McGee and his actions, what does the speaker think of Sam?

9. **Literary Perspectives** In what ways is the dying cowboy timeless? How might the archetype of the lone cowboy be represented in a modern story?

Literary Skills: Ballad and Exaggeration

10. **Analyze** How does the use of exaggeration contribute to the humorous mood of "The Cremation of Sam McGee"? Cite at least two examples in your response.

11. **Analyze** Review the characteristics of ballads on page 601. Then, use these characteristics to compare, point by point, "The Cremation of Sam McGee" with "The Dying Cowboy." Which poem is closer to the traditional ballad form?

Literary Skills Review: Character

12. **Analyze** In "The Dying Cowboy," what trait of the dying cowboy is repeated? Why do you think this trait is emphasized?

Writing Skills Focus
Think as a Reader/Writer

Use It in Your Writing How does the use of imagery bring the ballads to life? What feelings do the images evoke? Explain, and give examples.

What Do You Think Now

What ideas about life are these poems expressing?

Preparing to Read

from **Beowulf / Casey at the Bat**

Reader/Writer Notebook

Use your **RWN** to complete the activities for these selections.

Literary Skills Focus

Epic An **epic** is a long narrative poem written in formal, elegant language that tells about a series of quests undertaken by a great hero. In ancient epics, such as *Beowulf,* this hero is a warrior who embodies the values cherished by the culture that recites the epic.

The oldest stories in the world are epics. In ancient Mesopotamia around 2000 B.C., people told the epic of the hero Gilgamesh. In ancient Greece around 500 B.C., children learned values by studying the *Iliad* and the *Odyssey*. In Anglo-Saxon England around A.D. 700, bards told the story of Beowulf, who saved a kingdom from two swamp monsters.

Mock-Heroic Epic "Casey at the Bat" is a **mock-heroic epic** that imitates the old epic tales, but in a humorous way. Instead of capturing the values of a culture, the intent of a mock epic is to be comical. A mock epic treats a trivial subject in a grand manner. For example, instead of a warrior, we have a small-town baseball player, and instead of the epic poet's elegant language, we have the language of sports.

Reading Skills Focus

Retelling Retelling the information described in a narrative poem can help you understand what you are reading. In a good **retelling,** you identify the main characters and most important details.

Into Action Pause after reading two or three lines of each poem. In a chart like the one below, record your retelling of each sentence group.

Poem: Beowulf	Retelling
lines 1–8	Beowulf greets the king and tells him where he is from and that he has had a glorious past. Beowulf has heard about Grendel and that the Herot mead hall is empty.

Writing Skills Focus
Think as a Reader/Writer

Find It in Your Reading Heroic actions call for strong active verbs to describe them. As you read, record in your *Reader/Writer Notebook* the verbs that tell about Beowulf's and Casey's actions.

Vocabulary

from **Beowulf**

purge (purj) *v.:* get rid of something harmful. *Beowulf wanted to purge the monsters from the kingdom.*

scorn (skawrn) *n.:* obvious disrespect or dislike for someone or something. *The monsters feel scorn for the Danes.*

Casey at the Bat

defiance (dih FY uhns) *n.:* willingness to fight; rebellious feelings. *Full of defiance, Casey sneered at the pitcher.*

Language Coach

Formal Language In "Casey at the Bat," Thayer uses formal, elegant language rarely used to describe a baseball game. For example, he says *spheroid* instead of *baseball*. List one or two less formal "translations" for each of the following italicized phrases from the poem:

1. "A sickly silence fell upon the *patrons of the game*."
2. "... the leather-covered sphere came hurtling through the air."

Learn It Online
Listen to professional actors read these poems at:

go.hrw.com H8-611 **Go**

Ernest Lawrence Thayer

(1863–1940)

Secret Author

When the journalist Ernest Lawrence Thayer submitted "Casey at the Bat" to the *San Francisco Examiner* in 1888, he had no idea it would become the most famous baseball poem ever written. In fact, he didn't even sign his own name to his work, choosing instead to use a nickname, Phin.

Surprise Success

Shortly after the poem appeared in the California newspaper, a copy was given to a vaudeville entertainer named William De Wolf Hopper, who was about to appear in a Baseball Night performance in New York. He went onstage and recited it; the audience went wild. Hopper went on to make a successful career of touring the country reciting "Casey at the Bat."

Undesired Attention

Despite the poem's popularity, Thayer considered it badly written and for years would not admit authorship. When he was finally identified as the author, he refused to take money for the poem's many reprintings.

"All I ask is never to be reminded of it again."

Think About the Writer What can you infer about the author from his reaction to his poem's success?

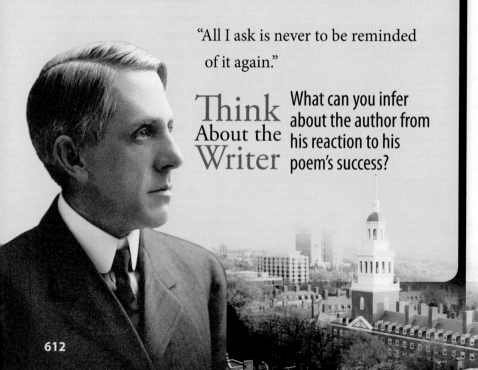

Build Background

Beowulf is considered the first great work of English literature. The poem was handed down orally for many generations and has an unknown author. Since it was originally written in Old English, which is very different from the English used today, the epic has been translated into Modern English many times.

First page of *Beowulf* (10th century).

Preview the Selections

In the excerpt from the epic poem, **Beowulf,** a warrior from the land of the Geats (in Scandinavia), has arrived at the court of **Hrothgar,** a Danish king. Beowulf gives his credentials; that is, he tells the king why he should be chosen to face **Grendel,** a huge monster who has been devouring Hrothgar's followers. Beowulf is speaking to King Hrothgar in the section that follows.

In "Casey at the Bat" by Ernest Lawrence Thayer, you will meet **Casey**—the star baseball player of Mudville—who plans to turn around the game for his losing team.

from

Beowulf

translated by
Burton Raffel

"Hail, Hrothgar!
Higlac is my cousin° and my king; the days
Of my youth have been filled with glory. Now Grendel's
Name has echoed in our land: Sailors
5 Have brought us stories of Herot, the best
Of all mead-halls,° deserted and useless when the moon
Hangs in skies the sun had lit,
Light and life fleeing together. Ⓐ
My people have said, the wisest, most knowing
10 And best of them, that my duty was to go to the Danes'
Great King. They have seen my strength for themselves,
Have watched me rise from the darkness of war,
Dripping with my enemies' blood. I drove
Five great giants into chains, chased
15 All of that race from the earth. I swam

2. cousin: any relative. Higlac is Beowulf's uncle and his king.

6. mead-halls: Mead is a drink made from honey, water, yeast, and malt. The hall was a central gathering place where warriors could feast, listen to a bard's stories, and sleep in safety.

Ⓐ **Reading Focus** **Retelling** What problem does Beowulf describe in lines 1–8?

Gundestrup caldron (1st century B.C.E.).

In the blackness of night, hunting monsters
Out of the ocean, and killing them one
By one; death was my errand and the fate
They had earned. Now Grendel and I are called
20   Together, and I've come. Grant me, then,
Lord and protector of this noble place,
A single request! I have come so far,
Oh shelterer of warriors and your people's loved friend,
That this one favor you should not refuse me—
25   That I, alone and with the help of my men,
May purge all evil from this hall. I have heard, **B**
Too, that the monster's scorn of men
Is so great that he needs no weapons and fears none.
Nor will I. My lord Higlac
30   Might think less of me if I let my sword
Go where my feet were afraid to, if I hid
Behind some broad linden shield:° My hands
Alone shall fight for me, struggle for life
Against the monster. God must decide
35   Who will be given to death's cold grip. **C**

---

32. linden shield: shield made from wood of the linden tree.

B **Literary Focus** **Epic Poem** Look at lines 20–26. What words or phrases are especially formal or elegant? What "favor" does Beowulf hope for?

C **Read and Discuss** What is Beowulf saying here?

Vocabulary **purge** (purj) *v.:* get rid of something harmful.
scorn (skawrn) *n.:* obvious disrespect or dislike for someone or something.

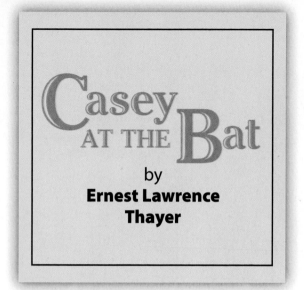

The Patrons of the Game

Illustrations by Dan Sayre Groesbeck (1912).

Casey AT THE Bat

by
Ernest Lawrence Thayer

The outlook wasn't brilliant for the Mudville nine that day;
The score stood four to two, with but one inning more to play;
And so, when Cooney died at first, and Burrows did the same,
A sickly silence fell upon the patrons of the game.

5   A straggling few got up to go in deep despair. The rest
Clung to the hope which springs eternal in the human breast;
They thought, if only Casey could but get a whack, at that,
They'd put up even money now, with Casey at the bat.

But Flynn preceded Casey, as did also Jimmy Blake,
10   And the former was a pudding, and the latter was a fake;
So upon that stricken multitude grim melancholy sat,
For there seemed but little chance of Casey's getting to the bat.   **Ⓐ**

But Flynn let drive a single, to the wonderment of all,
And Blake, the much-despised, tore the cover off the ball;
15   And when the dust had lifted, and they saw what had occurred,
There was Jimmy safe on second, and Flynn a-hugging third.

Ⓐ **Reading Focus** **Retelling** What is happening so far? What is the crowd thinking?

There was Blakey safe on Second

Mighty Casey was Advancing to the Bat

Then from the gladdened multitude went up a joyous yell;
It bounded from the mountaintop, and rattled in the dell;
It struck upon the hillside, and recoiled upon the flat;
20   For Casey, mighty Casey, was advancing to the bat.   **B**

There was ease in Casey's manner as he stepped into his place;
There was pride in Casey's bearing, and a smile on Casey's face;
And when, responding to the cheers, he lightly doffed his hat,
No stranger in the crowd could doubt 'twas Casey at the bat.

25   Ten thousand eyes were on him as he rubbed his hands with dirt;
Five thousand tongues applauded when he wiped them on his shirt;
Then while the writhing pitcher ground the ball into his hip,
Defiance gleamed in Casey's eye, a sneer curled Casey's lip.   **C**

B **Reading Focus** **Retelling** What is happening in the game now?

C **Literary Focus** **Mock-Heroic Poem** What heroic language does the speaker use to describe Casey and the crowd?

Vocabulary **defiance** (dih FY uhns) *n.:* willingness to fight; rebellious feelings.

A Sneer Curled Casey's Lip

"Strike one" the Umpire Said

And now the leather-covered sphere came hurtling through the air,
30 And Casey stood a-watching it in haughty grandeur there;
Close by the sturdy batsman the ball unheeded sped.
"That ain't my style," said Casey. "Strike one," the umpire said.

From the benches, black with people, there went up a muffled roar,
Like the beating of the storm waves on a stern and distant shore;
35 "Kill him! Kill the umpire!" shouted someone on the stand;
And it's likely they'd have killed him had not Casey raised his hand.

With a smile of Christian charity great Casey's visage shone;
He stilled the rising tumult; he bade the game go on;
He signaled to the pitcher, and once more the spheroid flew;
40 But Casey still ignored it, and the umpire said, "Strike two." **Ⓓ**

Ⓓ **Read and Discuss** What does this stanza tell you about Casey as a person and
a player?

CaseyWouldn't let that Ball go by again

By the Force of Casey's Blow

"Fraud!" cried the maddened thousands, and the echo answered, "Fraud!"
But a scornful look from Casey, and the audience was awed;
They saw his face grow stern and cold, they saw his muscles strain,
And they knew that Casey wouldn't let that ball go by again.

45 The sneer is gone from Casey's lips, his teeth are clenched in hate,
He pounds with cruel violence his bat upon the plate;
And now the pitcher holds the ball, and now he lets it go,
And now the air is shattered by the force of Casey's blow. **E**

Oh! somewhere in this favored land the sun is shining bright;
50 The band is playing somewhere, and somewhere hearts are light;
And somewhere men are laughing, and somewhere children shout,
But there is no joy in Mudville—mighty Casey has struck out! **F**

E Literary Focus **Mock-Heroic Poem** What is Casey's quest? Why is he considered a hero?

F Read and Discuss What just happened? Discuss the irony—the unexpected outcome—of the poem's ending.

Applying Your Skills

Reading Standard 3.1 Determine and articulate the relationship between the purposes and characteristics of different forms of poetry (e.g., ballad, lyric, couplet, **epic**, elegy, ode, sonnet).

from Beowulf / Casey at the Bat

Literary Response and Analysis

Reading Skills Focus
Read with a Purpose

1. How do Beowulf and Casey plan to remedy their situations?

Reading Skills: Retelling

2. Once you have finished reading these poems, review your retelling charts. Use your retellings to write a one-paragraph summary of each poem.

Poem: Beowulf	Retelling
lines 1–8	Beowulf greets the king and tells him where he is from and that he has had a glorious past. Beowulf has heard about Grendel and that the Herot mead hall is empty.

✓ Vocabulary Check

Match the Vocabulary words with their definitions.

3. **purge**   a. obvious dislike
4. **scorn**   b. rebellious feelings
5. **defiance**   c. get rid of

Literary Skills Focus
Literary Analysis

6. **Compare and Contrast** Beowulf has come to Herot, the great hall of King Hrothgar, where he expects to perform mighty deeds. Casey is expected to perform his mighty deeds in a baseball stadium. Underline the similarities and differences between the two settings.

7. **Evaluate** "Casey at the Bat" is said to be the most famous baseball poem ever written. Explain whether or not you feel it deserves such an honor.

8. **Compare** What associations can you make between Casey and sports stars of today? Support your ideas with details from the poem.

Literary Skills: Epic and Mock-Heroic Poems

9. **Analyze** List three characteristics of epic poetry that you find in *Beowulf*.

10. **Analyze** Epic heroes embody the values that their society holds dear—traits like courage, humility, generosity, and selflessness. What values do you think Casey embodies? Explain whether these values are especially American.

Literary Skills Review: Characterization

11. **Compare and Contrast** Beowulf is a typical epic hero in that he is enormously strong and comes to save a kingdom. Find places where Casey seems like a great epic hero. Then, compare and contrast the heroes.

Writing Skills Focus
Think as a Reader/Writer

Use It in Your Writing Using strong, active verbs, write a short paragraph about a heroic action you have witnessed.

What Do **You Think Now** How do you respond to people who express great confidence in themselves?

Vocabulary Development

Analyzing Idioms

An **idiom** is an expression that is specific to a certain language and cannot be understood by looking at the literal meanings of the individual words. For example, the literal meaning of the expression "to fall in love" doesn't make any sense. Like many idioms, this one implies a comparison. The experience of love can be so overwhelming that it is like falling down to the ground. The idiom might also suggest that being in love is like falling into a trap, although not necessarily an unpleasant one.

Your Turn

1. What is the literal meaning of the phrase "to stand up for"? What is its idiomatic meaning? What comparison is implied in the idiom?
2. Identify the meanings of each of the following idioms. Check a dictionary if necessary. Which ones suggest comparisons?
   A to stand on your own two feet
   B to stand a chance
   C to stand by
   D to stand to reason
   E to stand up to

Academic Vocabulary

Talk About . . .
Thayer's <u>intent</u> in "Casey at the Bat" is to make readers laugh by treating something trivial in a lofty, grand manner. With a partner, discuss whether or not the humor in the poem is successful.

Analyzing Metaphors: Mixed Metaphors

If two or more metaphors are used together, the images suggested by them must be consistent and logical, or a **mixed metaphor** results. For example, when a poet writes of life as a voyage on stormy seas, we expect further images to be consistent: The voyage of life ends "in a safe harbor" or "on the shores of an unknown island." If the poet says that life is a voyage on stormy seas that brings us to a "crash landing in the jungle," we realize that the poet has lost control of the metaphor.

Your Turn

Since metaphors are common in speech, people tend to mix them without thinking. Explain what is inconsistent about the following metaphors:

1. That snake-in-the-grass is barking up the wrong tree.
2. The House subcommittee has a lot of bottlenecks to iron out of the budget.

Language Coach

Formal Language To elevate his language, Thayer often uses fancy words in "Casey at the Bat." Record a simpler word or phrase that Thayer might have used for each of the following italicized phrases below.

1. Then from the *gladdened multitude* went up a *joyous yell.*
2. *There was ease in Casey's manner* as he stepped into his place.
3. He signaled to the pitcher and once more the *spheroid flew.*

CONTENTS

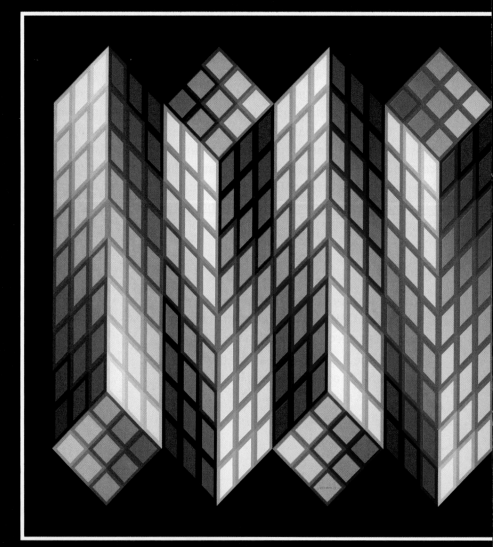

Toroni-Nagy (1969) by Victor Vasarely.
© Artists Rights Society (ARS), New York/ADAGP, Paris.

 What Do You Think?

Why are poems a useful form for expressing emotions such as joy, grief, and wonder?

 QuickWrite

What means of communication would you use to express emotions of joy, grief, or wonder? Record your notes.

Reader/Writer Notebook

Use your **RWN** to complete the activities for this selection.

On the Grasshopper and the Cricket

Literary Skills Focus

Sonnet A **sonnet** is a fourteen-line poem that is usually written in **iambic pentameter. Iambic** refers to verse in which an unstressed syllable is followed by a stressed syllable. **Pentameter** is verse with five stressed beats in every line.

‿ ´/‿ ´/‿ ´/‿ ´/‿ ´
The poetry of earth is never dead

Keats's poem is written in the **Italian sonnet** (also called Petrarchan sonnet) form, in which he makes a main point in the first eight lines and responds to the point in the last six lines.

Another sonnet form, called the **English sonnet,** or **Shakespearean sonnet,** is made up of three units with four lines in each one. Each unit expresses related ideas. Two rhymed lines (called a **couplet**) articulate the main points of the poem.

Reading Skills Focus

Form and Meaning Knowing the form of a poem helps you determine its meaning. You know that "On the Grasshopper and the Cricket" is a sonnet written in the Italian form. That means you can divide it into two chunks of meaning. Look in the first eight lines for a problem, a question, or an idea. Then, see how the final six lines resolve the problem, answer the question, or comment on the idea.

Writing Skills Focus

Think as a Reader/Writer

Find It in Your Reading This poem is filled with imagery that appeals to the senses of sight, touch, and hearing. As you read, make a list of these images in your *Reader/Writer Notebook*.

> **Language Coach**
> **Inverted Word Order** Why do poets sometimes order words in a way that doesn't seem natural? Take "increasing ever" in line 12 of "On the Grasshopper and the Cricket." "Ever increasing" might be the word order you would expect.
>
> When poets write in iambic pentameter, they alternate unstressed and stressed syllables in each line. Changing "increasing ever" to "ever increasing" would destroy the rhythm of iambic pentameter.
>
> As you read the poem, notice another example of inverted word order in line 9. Why might the poet have ordered the words as he did?

Learn It Online
Use *PowerNotes* to help you learn visually at:

| go.hrw.com | H8-623 | Go |

John Keats
(1795–1821)

From Medical School to Poetry

When Keats wrote "On the Grasshopper and the Cricket," he had only begun to write sonnets. He had trained to be a doctor for six years and had passed his examinations to practice medicine, but he disliked surgery. He really wanted to become a poet. Keats did indeed become a poet, one of the greatest in the English language.

A Short, Tragic Life

Keats's short life was filled with tragedy. When he was eight, his father died in an accident. His mother died of tuberculosis when Keats was fourteen. Keats's beloved brother Tom died of tuberculosis in 1818. Shortly afterward, Keats himself began to show signs of the disease. He had fallen in love with a young woman named Fanny Brawne, but he knew that his illness would keep them from marrying. Even though he was dying, Keats continued to write poems of such beauty and depth of meaning that they are still read and admired today.

"Beauty is truth, truth beauty,"—that is all
Ye know on earth, and all ye need to know.

Think About the Writer How might appreciating the beauty in life have helped Keats during difficult times?

John Keats (detail) (c. 1822)
by William Hinton, after Joseph Severn.
Oil on canvas (30" x 25").
National Portrait Gallery, London.

Build Background

"On the Grasshopper and the Cricket" was written as the result of a sonnet-writing contest that John Keats had with another poet, his friend Leigh Hunt. Snug indoors on a winter's night in 1816, the two poets heard the chirping of a cricket. Hunt challenged Keats to see which of them could write the better sonnet on the subject of the grasshopper and the cricket—within fifteen minutes.

Preview the Selection

This sonnet compares the songs of the grasshopper and the cricket. Notice when each insect sings.

ON THE
Grasshopper
AND THE
Cricket

by **John Keats**

Huts at Walberswick, Suffolk by Christine McKechnie. Collage and watercolor on paper.

The poetry of earth is never dead:
    When all the birds are faint with the hot sun,
    And hide in cooling trees, a voice will run   **A**
From hedge to hedge about the new-mown mead;°
5 That is the Grasshopper's—he takes the lead
In summer luxury—he has never done
With his delights; for when tired out with fun
He rests at ease beneath some pleasant weed.
The poetry of earth is ceasing never:
10   On a lone winter evening, when the frost
    Has wrought a silence, from the stove there shrills
The Cricket's song, in warmth increasing ever,
    And seems to one in drowsiness half lost,
      The Grasshopper's among some grassy hills.   **B**

---

4. mead: meadow.

A Literary Focus Sonnet Which syllables in line 3 are stressed? How do you know this line is written in iambic pentameter?

B Read and Discuss How does the poem clarify the line "The poetry of earth is never dead"?

Applying Your Skills

Reading Standard 3.1 Determine and articulate the relationship between the purposes and characteristics of different forms of poetry (e.g., ballad, lyric, couplet, epic, elegy, ode, **sonnet**).

On the Grasshopper and the Cricket
Literary Response and Analysis

Reading Skills Focus
Read with a Purpose

1. How do the grasshopper and the cricket keep "the poetry of earth" alive?

Reading Skills: Form and Meaning

Complete a chart like the one below, and use it to help you answer the questions on this page.

Sonnet's Form or Structure	Meaning
Octave (first eight lines) expresses an idea	
Sestet (final six lines) comments on the idea	

2. **Interpret** In this Italian sonnet, Keats describes two poets of the natural world. Who is the poet of summer in the first eight lines? Who is the poet of winter in the last six lines?

3. **Analyze** In this sonnet, Keats makes points about several elements of life: nature, sound and silence, the heat of summer (and life), and the cold of winter (and death). Articulate in your own words *one* point that the poet makes in the first eight lines of the sonnet. What point, related to the first one you mentioned, does he make in the last six lines?

Literary Skills Focus
Literary Analysis

4. **Identify** What common words does Keats use to describe the hot, sleepy feeling of a summer day? What words does he use to describe his sleepy winter evening?

5. **Interpret** Which line of the poem echoes the first line? How do the changed words affect the meaning?

Literary Skills: Sonnet

6. **Analyze** Review the characteristics of a sonnet as described on page 623. Which of those elements do you find in "On the Grasshopper and the Cricket"?

Literary Skills Review: Tone

7. **Analyze** The attitude a writer takes toward the subject, characters, and audience is called **tone**. Tone is revealed through the writer's word choice. How would you describe the tone of "On the Grasshopper and the Cricket"? Cite specific words from the poem that create the tone.

Writing Skills Focus
Think as a Reader/Writer

Use It in Your Writing Look back at the images you listed in your *Reader/Writer Notebook*. Choose two images that are particularly striking to you. Explain which sense the image appeals to and why you found it effective.

What Do You Think Now

What feelings about life does Keats express through the sonnet?

Preparing to Read

Ode to Thanks

Reader/Writer Notebook

Use your **RWN** to complete the activities for this selection.

Literary Skills Focus

Ode An **ode** celebrates, in elegant language, one person or thing. For centuries, poets imitated this long, complex poetic form, which originated in ancient Greece. Over the centuries, odes have been written to nightingales, Greek vases, autumn, melancholy, joy, solitude, and winners in the Olympic Games. Although today's odes are looser in form, the intent of odes is still the same: to celebrate a single person or thing. The Chilean poet Pablo Neruda has written several books of odes, most of which celebrate ordinary objects and everyday experiences.

Reading Skills Focus

Paraphrasing When you **paraphrase** a writer's text, you restate it in your own words. Paraphrasing poems as you read them can help you comprehend the writer's message. Units of thought in poems often extend over several lines of poetry.

Into Action As you read this poem, identify its units of thought. Then, consider what each one means. Use a chart like the one below to record your paraphrases.

Ode to Thanks	Paraphrase
Stanza 1 Unit of thought: lines 1–6	Say thanks to the word "thanks." The word "thanks" has special power.
Stanza 2 Unit of thought:	

> **Language Coach**
>
> **Language Conventions: Text Styles** Note that in this poem, italic type—*type that is slanted like this*—means that Neruda is talking about the word *thanks* rather than actually thanking something (in which case, he uses regular type).
>
> Skim the poem. What other words are in italic type? Why do you think they are italicized?

Writing Skills Focus
Think as a Reader/Writer

Find It in Your Reading In this poem, Neruda uses several **metaphors**—comparisons between two unlike things that do not use connecting words, such as *like* or *as*. In your *Reader/Writer Notebook*, list three metaphors Neruda uses in the poem. Note what he is comparing and what the figurative meaning of the metaphor might be.

Learn It Online
Listen to a professional reading of this poem at:

| go.hrw.com | H8-627 | **Go** |

Learn It Online
Learn more about Neruda at:
go.hrw.com H8-628 Go

Pablo Neruda
(1904–1973)

A Man of the World

Pablo Neruda was born and died in his beloved Chile, but he lived many years of his life abroad. Sometimes he was a diplomat representing his country, and sometimes he lived in political exile. In 1971, Neruda won the Nobel Prize in literature. Today, Neruda is considered by many to be the most influential Latin American poet of the twentieth century.

A Poet for Everyone

Neruda was only in his twenties when he first became famous for his love poems. In his odes, Pablo Neruda gave up a complex, formal style and adopted a plainer one, using simple words and short lines so that his poems could be enjoyed by all people.

> "I wanted to describe many things that had been sung and said over and over again. My intention was to start like the boy chewing on his pencil, setting to work on his composition assignment about the sun, the blackboard, the clock, or the family."

Think About the Writer From the information above, what can you infer about Neruda's attitude toward life?

Preview the Selection

The speaker in "Ode to Thanks" expresses his gratitude for the word *thanks,* while reflecting on all the good that this one simple word produces.

Read with a Purpose Read this poem to discover the power of one little word.

Ode to Thanks

by **Pablo Neruda**

translated by **Ken Krabbenhoft**

Thanks to the word
that says *thanks!*
Thanks to *thanks,*
word
5   that melts
iron and snow!

The world is a threatening place
until
thanks
10   makes the rounds
from one pair of lips to another,
soft as a bright
feather
and sweet as a petal of sugar,
15   filling the mouth with its sound
or else a mumbled
whisper.   **Ⓐ**
Life becomes human again:
it's no longer an open window.
20   A bit of brightness
strikes into the forest,
and we can sing again beneath the leaves.
Thanks, you're the medicine we take
to save us from
25   the bite of scorn.   **Ⓑ**

Ⓐ **Read and Discuss** What point is the poet making about the word *thanks?*

Ⓑ **Literary Focus** **Ode** How does the poet celebrate the power of *thanks* in lines 18–25?

Your light brightens the altar of harshness.
Or maybe
a tapestry
known
30 to far distant peoples.
Travelers
fan out
into the wilds,
and in that jungle
35 of strangers,
merci°
rings out
while the hustling train
changes countries,
40 sweeping away borders,
then *spasibo*°
clinging to pointy
volcanoes, to fire and freezing cold,
or *danke,*° yes! and *gracias,*° and
45 the world turns into a table:
a single word has wiped it clean,
plates and glasses gleam,
silverware tinkles,
and the tablecloth is as broad as a plain. **C**

50 Thank you, *thanks,*
for going out and returning,
for rising up
and settling down.
We know, *thanks,*
55 that you don't fill every space—
you're only a word—
but
where your little petal
appears
60 the daggers of pride take cover,
and there's a penny's worth of smiles.

36. *merci* (mehr SEE):
French for "thanks."

41. *spasibo* (spa SEE buh):
Russian for "thanks."

44. *danke* (DAHNG kuh):
German for "thanks." ***gracias***
(GRAH see ahs): Spanish for
"thanks."

C **Read and Discuss** What is the poet saying about the power
of *thanks* in lines 31–49?

Applying Your Skills

Reading Standard 3.1 Determine and articulate the relationship between the purposes and characteristics of different forms of poetry (e.g., ballad, lyric, couplet, epic, elegy, **ode,** sonnet).

Ode to Thanks

Literary Response and Analysis

Reading Skills Focus
Read with a Purpose

1. Why is the word *thanks* so powerful?

Reading Skills: Paraphrasing

2. Review the chart you made while you read. Then, add a row to the chart and write down the insight about life Neruda conveys in this poem.

"Ode to Thanks"	What it means to me
Stanza 1 Unit of thought: lines 1–6	Say thanks to "thanks." The word "**thanks**" has special power.

Insight about life:

Literary Skills Focus
Literary Analysis

3. **Interpret** What do you think the speaker means when he says in lines 3–6 that *thanks* "melts iron and snow"?

4. **Interpret** What does the speaker compare thanks to in lines 12–15? How is a thank-you like these things?

5. **Analyze** According to lines 45–49, the word *thanks* turns the world into a table. How is thanking someone like setting a beautiful table for dinner?

6. **Interpret** In lines 58–61, what does the speaker say the word *thanks* does to pride? How do these words celebrate *thanks*?

7. **Extend** Neruda makes a point that a small word, *thanks,* sends a powerful message. What other "simple" words carry powerful messages and associations?

Literary Skills: Ode

8. **Analyze** Review the characteristics of an ode on page 627. How is "Ode to Thanks" similar to classical odes? How is it different? Cite details to support your answer.

Literary Skills Review: Repetition

9. **Analyze** Poets often use repetition for both sound and sense. How do the many uses of the word *thanks* add to the meaning of the poem? How do the repeated structures of the phrases create rhythm in lines 12–14 and 51–53?

Writing Skills Focus
Think as a Reader/Writer
Use It in Your Writing Review the metaphors Neruda uses in his ode. Now, choose a person, place, or thing you would like to celebrate, and write an ode. Your purpose is to express strong, positive feelings about many aspects of your subject. Include at least two metaphors in your ode.

 What Do You Think Now

How could writing an ode help you express your feelings?

Preparing to Read

O Captain! My Captain!

Reading Standard 3.1 Determine and articulate the relationship between the purposes and characteristics of different forms of poetry (e.g., ballad, lyric, couplet, epic, **elegy**, ode, sonnet).

Reader/Writer Notebook

Use your **RWN** to complete the activities for this selection.

Literary Skills Focus

Elegy and Extended Metaphor An **elegy** (EHL uh jee) is a poem of mourning. Most elegies are about someone who has died. "O Captain! My Captain!" mourns the tragic death of President Abraham Lincoln. Whitman's elegy includes an **extended metaphor**, a comparison that is extended through several lines or even an entire poem. As you read, decide who the captain really is and what the ship represents.

Reading Skills Focus

Paraphrasing When you **paraphrase,** you restate all of the text in your own words. A paraphrase is unlike a retelling, which covers only major points. Paraphrasing can help you understand difficult poems, especially ones that use **inversion,** the reversal of the normal word order of a sentence. Look for the subject and verb to help you paraphrase sentences with inversion.

Into Action Use a chart to paraphrase complicated sentences or phrases. An example that includes inversion is shown below.

Text from Poem	My Paraphrase
"O the bleeding drops of red, / Where on the deck my Captain lies, / Fallen cold and dead."	Oh, the blood is on the deck where my dead captain lies.

Writing Skills Focus

Think as a Reader/Writer

Find It in Your Reading Many poets use repetition to add emphasis and rhythm to their writing. Look for instances of repeated words and phrases in "O Captain! My Captain!" Note them in your *Reader/Writer Notebook*.

Vocabulary

weathered (WEHTH uhrd) *v.*: survived; came through safely. *The crew weathered the storm and returned to port.*

mournful (MAWRN fuhl) *adj.*: full of deep sadness. *The mournful speaker is upset about his fallen captain.*

poem's speaker

- **weathered** the storm with the captain as leader
- is **mournful** as he sees the welcoming crowd on the shore

Language Coach

Word Forms and Origins Which word on the Vocabulary list also appears in two other forms in the Literary Skills Focus section? If you chose *mournful*, you're right. The English word *mourn*, built on the Indo-European root *mer*, means "remember." How does knowing the meaning of this Indo-European root give you a clue to the meaning of the word *mournful*? In what way is mourning a remembrance?

Learn It Online

Increase your word knowledge with Word Watch at:

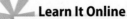 go.hrw.com H8-632   **Go**

Walt Whitman
(1819–1892)

A Colorful Character
Walt Whitman, who was born in Long Island, New York, was never interested in being like everyone else. He dressed and behaved in a manner all his own. According to one story, Whitman once drove a horse-drawn carriage along Broadway, in New York City, reciting Shakespeare at the top of his lungs.

Leaves of Grass
Whitman was a determined and talented writer. When he couldn't find a publisher for his book of poems, *Leaves of Grass*, he published the book himself in 1855. He even wrote his own reviews. The poems in the book embrace and celebrate all aspects of the United States and its people.

A Criticized Masterpiece
Leaves of Grass is now recognized as a masterpiece, but that wasn't always so. Many readers criticized Whitman's poems because they were about common people and experiences and because they were written in free verse instead of in rhyme and meter. Undeterred, Whitman continued adding poems to *Leaves of Grass* and publishing new editions of the book until he died. It is now one of the best-loved books in American literature.

"An American bard at last!"

Think About the Writer Based on this information, what three adjectives would you use to describe Whitman? Why?

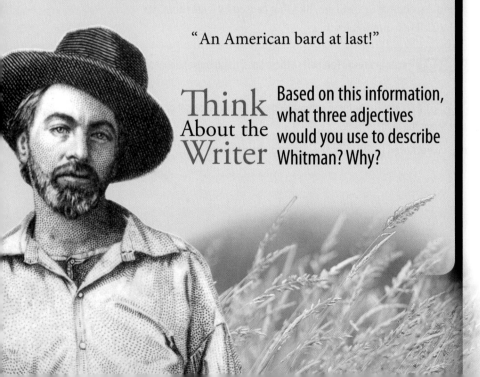

Build Background
Walt Whitman lived in Washington, D.C., during the Civil War, where he worked as a government clerk and war correspondent and also served as a volunteer nurse. He cared for thousands of wounded soldiers who filled the nearby military hospitals.

The Saturday before Abraham Lincoln's second inauguration, Whitman attended a reception at the White House. On inauguration day, March 4, 1865, Whitman twice saw Lincoln pass by in his carriage. He commented that the president "looked very much worn and tired; the lines, indeed, of vast responsibilities, intricate questions, and demands of life and death, cut deeper than ever upon his dark brown face; yet all the old goodness, tenderness, sadness, and canny shrewdness, underneath the furrows."

Lincoln was assassinated on April 14, 1865, just a month after Whitman saw him on inauguration day. Although the Civil War was over, the difficult job of healing the country had just begun.

Preview the Selection
In this poem, the speaker—a sailor on a ship returning from a perilous journey—tries to encourage his captain to rise up and see the adoring crowds who are celebrating and waiting for him at the port.

O CAPTAIN! MY CAPTAIN!

by **Walt Whitman**

O Captain! my Captain! our fearful trip is done,
The ship has weathered every rack,° the prize we sought is won,   **Ⓐ**
The port is near, the bells I hear, the people all exulting,°
While follow eyes the steady keel, the vessel grim and daring;
5   But O heart! heart! heart!
            O the bleeding drops of red,
                Where on the deck my Captain lies,
                    Fallen cold and dead.   **Ⓑ**

O Captain! my Captain! rise up and hear the bells;
10   Rise up—for you the flag is flung—for you the bugle trills,
For you bouquets and ribboned wreaths—for you the shores a-crowding,
For you they call, the swaying mass, their eager faces turning;

---

2. **rack**: here, violent change or disorder, like that caused by a storm.
3. **exulting** (ehg ZUHLT ihng): rejoicing.

Ⓐ Reading Focus Paraphrasing Paraphrase these lines, using conventional word order.

Ⓑ Literary Focus Elegy The purpose of most elegies is to express regret or sorrow. What is the speaker mourning in these lines?

Vocabulary **weathered** (WEHTH uhrd) v.: survived; came through safely.

Here Captain! dear father!
   The arm beneath your head!
15   It is some dream that on the deck,
       You've fallen cold and dead.

My Captain does not answer, his lips are pale and still,
My father does not feel my arm, he has no pulse nor will,
The ship is anchored safe and sound, its voyage closed and done,
20 From fearful trip the victor° ship comes in with object won:
   Exult O shores, and ring O bells!
     But I with mournful tread,
       Walk the deck my Captain lies,
         Fallen cold and dead. **C**

20. victor: winning; triumphant.

C | Read and Discuss | What does this stanza tell you about the captain?

Vocabulary   **mournful** (MAWRN fuhl) *adj.:* full of deep sadness.

Applying Your Skills

Reading Standard 3.1 Determine and articulate the relationship between the purposes and characteristics of different forms of poetry (e.g., ballad, lyric, couplet, epic, elegy, ode, sonnet).

O Captain! My Captain!

Literary Response and Analysis

Reading Skills Focus
Read with a Purpose

1. How does the speaker feel about his captain?

Reading Skills: Paraphrasing

2. Review the paraphrases in the chart you began on page 632. Then, use a chart like the one below to express the meaning of each stanza. Finally, state the meaning of the poem as a whole.

Stanza 1 Meaning	Stanza 2 Meaning	Stanza 3 Meaning	Meaning of Poem

✓ Vocabulary Check

Match each Vocabulary word with its definition.

3. **mournful**   a. full of sorrow
4. **weathered**   b. survived

Literary Skills Focus
Literary Analysis

5. **Analyze** Repetition is one <u>characteristic</u> of this elegy. What line is repeated at the end of each stanza? Why is the situation it describes **ironic;** that is, what is unexpected about the victorious return of the ship's captain?

6. **Interpret** The poet uses a metaphor in lines 13 and 18. What is the metaphor, and how does it enhance the sadness of the poem?

7. **Interpret** In line 20, the poet says, "From fearful trip the victor ship comes in with object won." If the ship is a metaphor for the country, what "trip" has the country made? What "object" has it won?

Literary Skills: Elegy and Extended Metaphor

8. **Analyze** "O Captain! My Captain!" is built on an extended metaphor. What clues tell you that the captain is Abraham Lincoln and that the ship stands for the United States?

9. **Analyze** The <u>intent</u> of Whitman's elegy is to mourn the death of Lincoln. What <u>characteristics</u> of the poem reflect both Whitman's and the nation's grief over Lincoln's death?

Literary Review Skills: Rhyme and Meter

10. **Analyze** How does the use of a strong meter and regular rhyme (or near-rhyme) scheme affect the poem's power and meaning? What emotions do these sound effects evoke?

Writing Skills Focus
Think as a Reader/Writer

Use It in Your Writing Review your list of examples of repetition. Consider Whitman's <u>intent</u> in repeating these words. How does Whitman use repetition to emphasize his purpose and evoke the sadness he is feeling? Write a short analysis of how Whitman uses repetition in the poem.

 What Do You Think Now

How might Whitman's poetic expression of sadness have helped others who read or heard his poem?

Preparing to Read

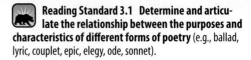

Reading Standard 3.1 Determine and articulate the relationship between the purposes and characteristics of different forms of poetry (e.g., ballad, lyric, couplet, epic, elegy, ode, sonnet).

I Hear America Singing / I, Too

Reader/Writer Notebook

Use your **RWN** to complete the activities for these selections.

Literary Skills Focus

Free Verse A **free-verse** poem does not follow a regular rhyme scheme or meter. Without a strict pattern to follow, poets writing free verse must rely on their own sense of balance and measure. Poets writing free verse may use the following poetic devices:

- **Alliteration:** repetition of consonant sounds (**s**now **s**piraling)
- **Repetition:** the recurrence of words and phrases
- **Imagery:** language that evokes sensations of sight, sound, smell, taste, and touch
- **Figures of speech:** language based on comparisons, such as metaphors, similes, and personification
- **Rhythm:** the musical quality produced by the repetition of stressed and unstressed syllables or the repetition of other sound patterns

Reading Skills Focus

Reading Aloud One way to hear the difference between a free-verse poem and some of the other forms of poetry you have studied is to read those two poems aloud. For example, you might want to compare the rhythm and rhyme in "O Captain! My Captain!" to "I Hear America Singing."

Into Action After you have read these poems aloud once or twice, record examples of the following poetic devices.

Alliteration	Repetition	Imagery	Figures of Speech
singing . . . strong . . . songs			America is singing

Language Coach

Word Study The speakers in the poems that follow both talk about "singing."

The word *sing* has many meanings, some of which appear in the dictionary entry below. Read through these definitions of the verb *sing*.

sing (sihng) *v.:* **1.** to make music with the voice. **2.** to make pleasant musical sounds (Birds were *singing* in the trees.) **3.** to make a humming, whistling, or buzzing sound (I heard the kettle *sing*.) **4.** to shout out or proclaim. **5.** slang: to inform about or tell on.

As you read the poems, think about the ways the poets talk about singing. What differences, if any, do you find in the meaning of the word as it is used in those poems?

Writing Skills Focus
Think as a Reader/Writer

Find It in Your Reading Record in your *Reader/Writer Notebook* images from the poems that evoke strong emotional associations.

Learn It Online
Listen to professional actors read these poems at:

go.hrw.com   H8-637   **Go**

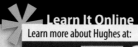
Learn It Online
Learn more about Hughes at:
go.hrw.com H8-638 Go

Walt Whitman
(1819–1892)

For a biography of Walt Whitman, see page 633.

Langston Hughes
(1902–1967)

A Chance Meeting of Poets

Born in Joplin, Missouri, Langston Hughes began writing poetry in his early teens. As a young man, he traveled around the world and held many jobs, including teacher, clerk, deck-hand, and flower salesman. One day in 1925, Hughes discovered that the famous poet Vachel Lindsay was staying at the Washington, D.C., hotel where Hughes was working as a bus-boy. Hughes left some of his poems beside Lindsay's dinner plate. That night, Lindsay read them aloud at a poetry reading, announcing that he had discovered a great new poet. The next day, Hughes received national publicity.

A Commitment to Justice and Strength

Hughes believed in writing for everyday people, those who "are not too important to themselves or the community, or too well fed, or too learned to watch the lazy world go round." From his grandmother, he learned strength and determination. In his autobiography, he wrote:

> "Nobody cried in my grandmother's stories. They worked, or schemed, or fought. . . . Something about my grandmother's stories (without her ever having said so) taught me the uselessness of crying about anything."

Think About the Writers

How might Hughes's varied jobs and experiences have helped him write poems?

Build Background

"I Hear America Singing"

Walt Whitman was the first American poet to use free verse. Today many poets write in free verse, so we take it for granted. In Whitman's day, however, people were used to poems written in "poetic" language, which used strict rhyme schemes and meters. These people were shocked by Whitman's sprawling lines and use of slang. In time many critics came to feel that Walt Whitman was the first and greatest poet to "give voice" to America. "I Hear America Singing" offers a good example of why they came to think so.

"I, Too"

"I, Too" was written by Langston Hughes in response to "I Hear America Singing" by Walt Whitman. While Whitman's poem is a celebration of the American worker, Hughes's poem points out the injustices felt by African Americans. When Hughes wrote this poem in 1924, segregation and discrimination were the norm in the United States.

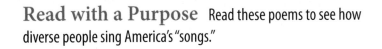

I HEAR AMERICA SINGING

by **Walt Whitman**

I hear America singing, the varied carols I hear,
Those of mechanics, each one singing his as it should be
 blithe and strong,
The carpenter singing his as he measures his plank or
 beam,
The mason singing his as he makes ready for work, or
 leaves off work,  **A**
5 The boatman singing what belongs to him in his boat,
 the deckhand singing on the steamboat deck,
The shoemaker singing as he sits on his bench, the hatter
 singing as he stands,
The woodcutter's song, the plowboy's on his way in the
 morning, or at noon intermission or at sundown,
The delicious singing of the mother, or of the young wife
 at work, or of the girl sewing or washing,
Each singing what belongs to him or her and to none
 else,
10 The day what belongs to the day—at night the party of
 young fellows, robust, friendly,
Singing with open mouths their strong melodious
 songs. **B**

A **Literary Focus** **Free Verse** What literary device does Whitman use in these lines to create a sense of rhythm?

B **Read and Discuss** What picture is Whitman painting for us?

Sit In (2005) by Gil Mayers.
Collage.

I, TOO

by **Langston Hughes**

I, too, sing America.

I am the darker brother.
They send me to eat in the kitchen
When company comes,
5   But I laugh,
And eat well,
And grow strong.   **A**

Tomorrow,
I'll sit at the table
10   When company comes.
Nobody'll dare
Say to me,
"Eat in the kitchen,"
Then.

15   Besides,
They'll see how beautiful I am
And be ashamed—

I, too, am America.   **B**

A Read and Discuss What have you learned about the speaker?

B Literary Focus Free Verse What metaphor appears in the poem's last line? What two things are being compared?

Applying Your Skills

Reading Standard 3.1 Determine and articulate the relationship between the purposes and characteristics of different forms of poetry (e.g., ballad, lyric, couplet, epic, elegy, ode, sonnet).

I Hear America Singing / I, Too
Literary Response and Analysis

Reading Skills Focus
Read with a Purpose

1. What might Whitman mean when he talks of "Each [person] singing what belongs to him or her and to none else?" What does Hughes mean when he says "I, too, sing America"?

Reading Skills: Reading Aloud

2. Review the entries in the chart you began on page 637. Then, write a statement that describes how reading aloud helped you identify sound devices and recognize the <u>characteristics</u> of free verse.

Literary Skills Focus
Literary Analysis

3. **Analyze** How do all the descriptions of working people connect to the title "I Hear America Singing"? What do these descriptions have in common?

4. **Make Judgments** Explain whether the singers in Whitman's poem sing about sad things or about poor working conditions. Explain whether Whitman is making working life in the nineteenth century too pretty.

5. **Interpret** "I, Too" was written in response to "I Hear America Singing." Whitman's poem is a celebration of the American worker. What does Hughes's poem celebrate?

Literary Skills: Free Verse

6. **Analyze** Explain how "I Hear America Singing" and "I, Too" reflect the <u>characteristics</u> of free verse.

7. **Analyze** The poems you just read are **free-verse** poems—they do not have a regular rhyme scheme or meter. They do, however, use repetition to create **rhythm.** In each poem, find examples of repeated words, lines, and sentence patterns. Use a chart like this one to help you gather details.

Examples of Repetition	My Notes
"singing his as he"	

Literary Skills Review: Symbol

8. **Interpret** A **symbol** is a person, place, thing, or event that stands for something beyond itself. What do you think the kitchen and the table symbolize in Hughes's poem? Explain your response.

Writing Skills Focus
Think as a Reader/Writer

Use It in Your Writing Look back at the images you noted in your *Reader/Writer Notebook.* What <u>associations</u> do these images evoke for you? Write a paragraph in which you describe the mood, or emotional effect, of each poem. Use the images you noted to support your interpretations.

What Do You Think Now

What different attitudes do the two poets express in these poems?

Vocabulary Development

Word Study: Multiple Meanings

Many English words have more than one meaning. Some words can even be used as different parts of speech. Look at the following example:

The **cycle** of semesters continues every year.
The author wrote a **cycle** of poems.
The stars **cycle** through the heavens.
The riders **cycle** madly to the finish line.

Cycle is used as a noun in the first two sentences; in the final two, *cycle* is used as a verb.

Your Turn

The first two words below are from "I Hear America Singing"; the last word is from "I, Too." Write down each word's meaning in the poem. Then, use a dictionary to determine the word's other possible meanings.

	Meaning in Poem	Other Meanings
leaves (line 4)		
intermission (line 7)		
company (line 4)		

Academic Vocabulary

Talk About . . .

Get together with a partner and <u>articulate</u> your interpretation of one of the poems in this chapter. Analyze whether the poet's <u>intent</u> is for the poem to have more than one meaning.

CHOICES

As you respond, use these **Academic Vocabulary** words as appropriate: <u>articulate</u>, <u>associations</u>, <u>characteristics</u>, <u>intent</u>.

REVIEW
Compare Two Poems

Timed ⏱Writing Choose two poems from this section. Write a two-paragraph essay in which you compare and contrast the poets' purposes and the <u>characteristics</u> of the form of each poem. For example, you may compare and contrast Keats's sonnet with Whitman's elegy.

CONNECT
Recite a Poem

Listening and Speaking Which poem from this section was most striking to you? Choose a poet, and check out a collection of his or her poems from a library. Find another work from the poet, and recite it for your class. Introduce your poem first. Then, <u>articulate</u> your interpretation of its meaning.

EXTEND
Write a Free-Verse Poem

Write a free-verse poem about sounds you hear during your day. Structure your poem the way Walt Whitman structured his—as a list. Build your sentences so that most of them have the same structure—just as Whitman does. Describe the sounds you hear or include your feelings about the "songs." Be sure to use images that will evoke the sounds for your reader.

Learn It Online
Sharpen your knowledge of multiple-meaning words with the online Interactive Vocabulary Tutor at:

go.hrw.com   H8-643   **Go**

Writing Workshop

Technical Documents

Write with a Purpose

Write a technical document in which you explain how to design a system, operate a tool or a machine, or follow the bylaws of an organization. Your **purpose** is to explain how to complete a multistep process. Your **audience** is classmates or others who are not familiar with the process you will explain.

A Good Technical Document

- encourages the reader
- provides a clear sequence of steps
- gives all the information necessary for success
- uses formatting, such as bulleted lists and font styles, to help the reader
- anticipates readers' questions or difficulties

See page 654 for complete rubric.

Reader/Writer Notebook

Use your **RWN** to complete the activities for this workshop.

Think as a Reader/Writer

Reading directions can be confusing and frustrating. Why couldn't the writer be clear? If you have ever tried to explain something complicated in writing, you know that it can be difficult to communicate exactly what you want your reader to understand. However, good writer can create a technical document that is clear and well organized. Before you write your own technical document, notice how Dennis Coello gives clear information in the opening of his article "Fix a Flat," originally published in *Boys' Life* magazine.

> Flat tires are part of bicycling. But fixing a flat is easy. You will need:
> - two tire levers (small tools used to pry the tire from the rim)
> - a six-inch crescent wrench (if your wheels aren't quick-release)
> - a tube repair kit
> - an air pump
>
> Most flats are in the rear. Removing the rear wheel from the bike is more difficult than removing the front one, but it's easy once you know how.
>
> First, **shift the chain onto the smallest freewheel cog.** Remove the brake cable by pressing both brake pads toward the wheel so you can easily lift the loose end from its housing in the brake lever.
>
> Next, **put the bike on its back.** Flip the quick-release lever or use the crescent wrench to loosen both axle nuts. Take the derailleur body (the mechanism that moves the chain from sprocket to sprocket) and pull it back toward you. Then, **lift the chain and remove the wheel.**

← The **introduction** encourages the audience to read on.

← Using **a bulleted list** helps the reader to quickly see what tools are needed.

← Using **boldface print** helps the reader understand the basic instruction.

← **Transition words** such as *first, next,* and *then* make the sequence of steps clear.

Think About the Professional Model

With a partner, discuss the following questions about the model.

1. How does Coello encourage readers to think they can fix flats?

2. How does Coello's writing style match his purpose for writing?

Writing Standards 1.2 Establish coherence within and among paragraphs through effective transitions, parallel structures, and similar writing techniques. **2.6** Write technical documents: a. Identify the sequence of activities needed to design a system, operate a tool, or explain the bylaws of an organization. b. Include all the factors and variables that need to be considered c. Use formatting techniques (e.g., headings, differing fonts) to aid comprehension.

Prewriting

Choose a Topic

A technical document can explain any process, from putting on a play or operating a dishwasher to training a dog to sit and stay. For this assignment, however, focus on explaining the steps needed to (1) design a system, (2) operate a tool or machine, or (3) follow the bylaws of an organization. Examples of designing a system could include planning a scientific experiment or creating a blog or Web page on the Internet. Some tools or machines you might write about are DVD players, power drills, or MP3 music players. You could describe the by-laws of a club you belong to at school or of a government organization you research on the Internet. Think about systems or devices you use every day at school or at home. Consider processes that you feel confident doing. It might be something that you have already taught someone else how to do.

Note the Details

Concentrate on the details you need to communicate to your audience. The chart below shows specific details that an effective technical document will include.

Essential Information	Details
Topic	What is the task, tool, or bylaws you will explain?
Materials Needed	What does your reader need to complete the process successfully?
Steps	What are the steps, in order, that your reader must follow?
Factors	Are there any conditions that might affect the outcome? Do you need to provide any warnings about safety?
Variables	Your reader won't have exactly the same equipment and conditions you have. How can you make sure your technical document will apply to a variety of situations?
Questions	What are some questions your audience will probably have about the process?

Idea Starters

For help in coming up with ideas, think about these questions:

- What kinds of systems have you already designed? Did you ever come up with a new way of doing something? Who might benefit from knowing about your system?
- What kind of tools or machines do you operate often? Which are you comfortable using?
- What organizations do you belong to? How do their bylaws affect the meetings or operations of the group? How are the bylaws useful?

Peer Review

If possible, teach a partner part of the process in person. Notice which steps are difficult, and pay careful attention to questions your partner asks. Take notes about how you will address these questions in your technical document.

Your Turn _____

Get Started Brainstorm topics for your technical document in your **RWN.** Choose a topic that is interesting and that you feel comfortable explaining. Then, create a detail chart like the one shown on this page. Answer the questions and take notes about each category of detail.

Learn It Online
See how one writer met all the assignment criteria. Use an interactive writer's model at:

go.hrw.com   H8-645   **Go**

Writing Tip

Think about the words your audience may not know that relate to your topic. **Jargon** is specialized vocabulary used in a particular field. For example, a sailor uses the terms *jib, keel,* and *mainstay* to describe parts of a boat.

What jargon might you use in your document? You might decide to eliminate jargon by stating the same information in simpler words. If you must include jargon, be sure to give your readers a clear definition of any unfamiliar terms.

Think About Audience and Purpose

When you have been given the job of writing a technical document, your **purpose** is to give readers the benefit of expert knowledge that you have and they need. Ask yourself these questions to think about **the audience** who will read your technical document and what they will need to know to be successful.

- Why might someone be reading this document?
- What might readers already know about your topic?
- What will they need to know before they begin this process?
- What kind of format might help them follow your directions?

Technical Document Plan

Use an outline like the one below to plan your technical document. Note that the introduction and conclusion of many technical documents are fairly short. The key information and explanations appear in the body.

Introduction

- What tool, task, or bylaws will I explain? _____
- What results can my readers expect? _____
- What encouragement can I provide to reassure my readers? _____ _____

Body

- What materials are needed? _____
- What are the steps of the process in order? _____
- What possible difficulties do my readers need to anticipate? _____ _____
- How can I help my readers avoid common mistakes? _____ _____

Conclusion

- What can I tell my readers about why the process is important? _____ _____
- What are the possible rewards of the process? _____

Your Turn _____

Create an Organized Outline
In your **RWN,** create an outline like the one on this page. Briefly note the information you will include in the introduction, body, and conclusion of your technical document. Be sure to include any necessary details from your detail chart.

Drafting

Follow Your Plan

Use your outline from page 646 and the framework at the right to draft your technical document.

Format Your Document

The way you format your document can make a big difference in how successful your reader is in completing his or her task. Use boldface and italic type to draw your reader's attention to the key words or steps.

When you are writing about a number of steps that must be done in the proper order, it is important to make the sequence of steps clear. One way to help your reader follow the steps correctly is to use a bulleted list. You might also choose to create a numbered list like the one below.

Step 1. Shift the chain onto the smallest freewheel cog.
Step 2. Remove the brake cable.
Step 3. Put the bike on its back.

Framework for a Technical Document

Introduction
- Clearly state your purpose for writing.
- Explain what you will be teaching your readers to do, and then give them an idea of how you will present the information.
- Encourage readers to keep reading.

Body
- Provide a list of tools and supplies your reader will need.
- Provide a sequence of steps or a list of tips, depending on the type of instructions you are giving.
- Give a warning about any difficult part of the process.

Conclusion
- State the end result that your reader will have achieved.

◉ Writing Tip

Remember that your readers are more likely to pay attention to your instructions if you use a friendly and encouraging tone.

Grammar Link Using Precise Language

You probably know a lot about the topic you are going to write about and could give a lot of information about it. When you are writing technical documents, however, you want your instructions to be as precise as possible. As you create your draft, try to put yourself in your reader's shoes and identify any steps in your document that might be confusing. One way to avoid confusion is to use precise language. Look at the following examples of vague and precise language.

Vague Language	Precise Language
• Loosen the nuts with the wrench. • Take the wheel off the bike.	• Use the crescent wrench to loosen both axle nuts. • Lift the chain, and remove the wheel.

Your Turn _____

Draft Your Document Using the notes in your detail chart from page 645 and your framework, create your first draft. Also, think about:

- any jargon you'll need to define
- the tone you will use in your writing. Will it be formal or informal? Why?
- how to give your audience the confidence they need to successfully follow your explanation.

Technical Documents

● Writing Tip

Format your bylaws in a way that makes them easy to read. You may want to use capital letters or boldface type to distinguish articles and sections as in the student draft that begins on this page.

Format Your Bylaws

Bylaws are technical documents that outline the rules for governing a group, club, or organization. Like other technical documents, bylaws describe a process to be followed. However, bylaws have a format that is different from other technical documents and that includes a specific vocabulary for its headings.

The heading for each section of a list of bylaws is called an **article,** and articles are numbered using Roman numerals. For example, the first heading of your bylaws is likely to be: *ARTICLE I: NAME.*

Framework for Bylaws of an Organization
• **Name** of the organization
• **Objectives** of the organization
• **Membership** eligibility and requirements
• **Officers**—titles, eligibility, requirements, and procedures for elections
• **Meetings**—locations and times
• **Amendments**—steps to revise the bylaws once they are written

Under each article, you write the specific rules, or laws. Each rule is called a **section,** and each section is numbered using Arabic numerals. For example, the rule stating the name of the organization might be: *Section 1. The name of the organization shall be the Buenos Amigos Club.*

The framework above lists information that is usually included in bylaws. Each boldface term should be an individual article in your formatted document.

Read the student draft, by Pedro Morales from Sacramento, of bylaws for a student club and notice the comments on its strengths as well as suggestions on how it could be improved.

Student Draft

The writer uses the correct headings for bylaws and formats them in a way that makes them clear for the reader. →

ARTICLE I: NAME

Section 1. The name of the organization shall be the Buenos Amigos Club.

ARTICLE II: OBJECTIVES

Section 1. The primary club objective will be to provide volunteer services to the community and to the school.

Section 2. Other objectives are to develop leadership and teamwork skills.

ARTICLE III: MEMBERSHIP

Section 1. Students in grades six through eight may apply for membership.

Section 2. Membership will be terminated after four unexcused absences.

ARTICLE IV: OFFICERS

Section 1. Officers will be president, vice-president, secretary, and reporter.

Section 2. Duties of Officers:

- President—to run meetings, represent the club, and call special meetings.
- Vice-President—to stand in for and assist the president as needed.
- Secretary—to record and file meeting minutes and club records.
- Reporter—to submit the club's plans and achievements to newspapers.

← The duties of each officer are specified in a **bulleted list.**

Section 3. Eligibility:

- Officer candidates must maintain a B average, display satisfactory conduct, and have no unexcused absences.
- Officers may be re-elected to office.

Section 4. Elections and term of office:

- New officers shall be elected by majority vote at the last spring meeting.
- Officers will serve for one year.

ARTICLE V: MEETINGS

Section 1. The club will meet Tuesdays at 3:15 in the cafeteria.

ARTICLE VI: AMENDMENTS

Section 1. Two thirds of the members present must vote to change, or amend, these bylaws.

← **Sections** of each article are clearly marked.

Section 2. All members must be notified before a vote to amend bylaws.

MINI-LESSON ▶ **How to Include All Factors and Variables**

In writing bylaws it is especially important to consider any **factors** and **variables** that might apply to your group. For example, if your club collects dues, your bylaws should state what the dues are, when they will be collected, and how they will be used. When Pedro looked at his draft, he realized that in Article V: Meetings, he had not accounted for the fact that this was a school club. He added a section to cover this variable.

Pedro's Revision of Article V

ARTICLE V: MEETINGS

Section 1. The club will meet Tuesdays at 3:15 in the cafeteria.

∧ *Section 2. The club will meet only during the school year and only when school is in session.*

Peer Review

Working with a partner, review your drafts and take notes. Imagine yourself performing the steps described. (Ask your partner to read your work in the same way.) Answering each question in this chart can help you figure out where and how your drafts could be improved.

Evaluating and Revising

Read the questions in the left column of the chart, and then use the tips in the middle column to help you make revisions to your document. The right column suggests techniques you can use to revise your draft.

Technical Document: Guidelines for Content and Organization

Evaluation Questions	Tips	Revision Techniques
1. Does your introduction encourage your audience to continue reading?	**Underline** a sentence that encourages your reader.	**Insert** a sentence that puts your audience at ease or will make them curious.
2. Does your document include a list of necessary supplies?	**Put a star** next to each item in the list.	**Indent** your list, and **add** a bullet before each item.
3. Is the sequence of your steps clear? Have you used clear, direct language?	**Circle** all your numbers or transition words. **Highlight** unclear language.	**Add** numbers or words like *first, then,* and *next.* **Revise** confusing or unclear language.
4. Does your draft include formatting that aids comprehension?	**Draw a box** around the most important sentences.	**Use** boldface type to draw your reader's attention to these sentences.
5. Have you explained the results of the process you are writing about?	**Put a check mark** beside sentences that describe the results your reader can expect.	**Add** sentences that tell your reader what to expect.
6. Have you included a warning about any difficult parts of the process?	**Bracket** any sentences that caution your reader.	**Add** a sentence that warns your reader of a possible difficulty.

Read this student draft, and notice the comments on its strengths as well as suggestions on how it could be improved.

Guide to Cell Phones
by Sadie Aikman, Abiding Word Lutheran School

Operating a cell phone is a simple task. No matter how many "special features" it has, it serves one purpose: to make and receive calls.

Dialing a number is easy. Simply push the corresponding numbers that match the person's phone number and press the green button on either the left or right side of the keypad (depending on which model you own). To hang up, just press the red button on the other side.

← Notice that Sadie **encourages the reader** by saying that using a cell phone is a "simple task."

← Sadie uses **clear, direct language** to explain each step.

MINI-LESSON ▸ **How to Write an Engaging Introduction**

Sadie has offered encouragement to her readers in the introduction to her technical document. At the same time, she needs to add a more engaging introduction to her technical document so she can catch readers' attention and keep them reading. Since cell phones are a part of everyone's life, Sadie can draw upon that familarity to write a more interesting beginning to her technical document.

Sadie's Revision of Paragraph Two

Most teens can't wait to get their first cell phone. They deliberate for hours about what cover and color to choose: red, white, and blue American flag; school colors and mascot; or polka dots. Then they have to choose the all important ring: their favorite song, school fight song, or something silly like a lullaby. These decisions are time-consuming, but actually learning to use a cell phone is not. ∧ Operating a cell phone is a simple task. No matter how many "special features" it has, it serves one purpose: to make and receive calls.

Your Turn _____

Write an Engaging Introduction Read your draft, and then ask yourself:

- Have I engaged my readers with an interesting beginning?
- What details can I add to keep their attention?

Consider adding details that will encourage readers and capture their interest.

Student Draft *continues*

Sadie warns readers that this part of the process might be more difficult. →

To add a contact to your phone is a little more complicated. Go to your menu screen and scroll over to "Contacts." Press "OK," and another screen should come up. Scroll down to "Add Contact" and press "OK." It will ask you to insert the name of the person you wish to add; just look down at your keypad, and the letters will be listed. You will have to insert the number. Just press "OK," and you're done! You now have a contact in your phone.

Sadie presents the steps in the **order** they must be followed. →

To change your ring tone, volume, wallpaper, etc., you go back to your menu screen and find "settings." Push "OK," and a screen will come up giving the things that you can change. Scroll down to the icon that represents what you want to change. Press "OK," and follow the directions.

Sadie's document has a clear **conclusion**. →

Congratulations! You have successfully programmed your phone to your liking.

MINI-LESSON ▶ **Using Transition Words to Show Sequence**

Sadie's partner became confused when trying to follow the directions for adding a contact. Sadie decided to add **transition words,** such as *first, then, again,* and *afterward,* to make the order of the steps clear.

Sadie's Revision to Paragraph Three

To add a contact to your phone is a little more complicated. *First,* Go to your menu screen and scroll over to "Contacts." *Next,* Press "OK," and another screen should come up. *Then,* Scroll down to "Add Contact" and press "OK" *again*.

It will ask you to insert the name of the person you wish to add; just look down at your keypad, and the letters will be listed. *Afterward* You will have to insert the number. Just press "OK," and you're done! You now have a contact in your phone.

Your Turn _____

Use Transition Words to Show Sequence With a partner, review your draft for steps that must be followed in a specific sequence. Ask your partner to identify areas where a transition word might make your document easier to follow.

Proofreading and Publishing

Proofreading

When you have finished your draft, review your document for errors in spelling, grammar, usage, and punctuation. Then, be sure that the steps in the process you are writing about are in the correct order.

> ### Grammar Link Using Commas Correctly
>
> You should make it easy for readers to follow your thoughts as they read your technical document. Using commas correctly after transitional words or phrases will help you show the transition from one step or idea to the next. Look at the following examples:
>
> #### Example 1
> First go to your menu screen and scroll over to "Contacts." Next press "OK" and another screen should come up.
>
> #### Example 2
> First, go to your menu screen and scroll over to "Contacts." Next, press "OK," and another screen should come up.
>
> In the second example, the commas make the sequence clear so that the reader doesn't have to go back and re-read the instructions. When you are proofreading your document, check to see that you have correctly used commas to indicate sequence.

Publishing

Here are some suggestions on how you might share your technical document with a larger audience.

- Compile a class "how-to" manual. Ask writers if they want to add illustrations to their articles. Choose a title and design a cover.
- Post your work on an Internet site.

Reflect on the Process In your **RWN,** write short responses to the following questions:

1. What did you learn about clear writing by creating a technical document? What did you learn about the process you explained?

2. How did your document improve during revision? Which change do you think had the greatest impact?

● Proofreading Tip

A small error in a technical document could create serious problems for readers. Double check any numbers, statistics, or specific details to make sure you have given the correct information.

Your Turn _____

Proofread and Publish

Proofread your draft to eliminate errors. As you proofread, check that you have used correct punctuation. Then, make a final copy of your technical document and publish it.

Scoring Rubric

You can use the rubric below to evaluate your technical document.

	Technical Document	Organization and Focus	Sentence Structure	Conventions
4	• Provides an *extremely clear* sequence of activities. • Explains each step of the process *thoroughly,* using examples and *detailed* instructions. • Includes a *comprehensive* list of all factors, variables, and information that needs to be considered. • *Consistently* anticipates readers' questions and /or difficulties.	• *Clearly* addresses all parts of the writing task. • Demonstrates a *clear* understanding of purpose and audience. • Establishes *coherent* writing within and among paragraphs through *effective* transitions, parallel structures, and similar writing techniques. • Uses *clear* and *appropriate* formatting techniques to aid user comprehension.	• Includes sentence *variety* (e.g. simple, complex, compound-complex).	• Contains *few, if any, errors* in the conventions of the English language (grammar, punctuation, capitalization, spelling). These errors do **not** interfere with the reader's understanding of the writing.
3	• Provides a *clear* sequence of activities. • Explains each step of the process *adequately,* with a mixture of *general* and *specific* instructions. • Includes a *mostly complete* list of all factors, variables, and information that need to be considered. • Anticipates readers' questions and /or difficulties.	• Addresses most of the writing task. • Demonstrates a *general* understanding of purpose and audience. • Establishes *mostly coherent* writing within and among paragraphs through *mostly effective* transitions. • Uses *relatively clear* and *mostly appropriate* formatting techniques to aid user comprehension.	• Includes some sentence *variety* (e.g. simple, complex, compound-complex).	• Contains *some errors* in the conventions of the English language (grammar, punctuation, capitalization, spelling). These errors do **not** interfere with the reader's understanding of the writing.
2	• Provides an *adequate,* though *occasionally unclear* sequence of activities. • Explains the process with *uneven* elaboration. • Includes an *incomplete* list of all factors, variables, and information that need to be considered. • May *occasionally* anticipate readers' questions and /or difficulties.	• Addresses *some* of the writing task. • Demonstrates *little* understanding of purpose and audience. • Establishes *somewhat coherent* writing within and among paragraphs through *somewhat effective* transitions. • Uses *often unclear* and *sometimes inappropriate* formatting techniques.	• Includes *little* sentence variety.	• Contains *several errors* in the conventions of the English language (grammar, punctuation, capitalization, spelling). These errors **may** interfere with the reader's understanding of the writing.
1	• Provides an *unclear* sequence of activities, if at all. • Develops the explanation in only a *minimal* way, if at all. • *Fails* to provide a list of all factors, variables, and information that need to be considered. • *Fails* to anticipate readers' questions and /or difficulties.	• Addresses *only one or no* part of the writing task. • Demonstrates *no* understanding of purpose and audience. • Demonstrates *neither* coherent writing, *nor* effective transitions. • Uses *unclear* formatting techniques, if at all.	• Includes *no* sentence variety.	• Contains *serious errors* in the conventions of the English language (grammar, punctuation, capitalization, spelling). These errors interfere with the reader's understanding of the writing.

Preparing for Timed Writing

Technical Directions

Writing Standard 2.6 Write technical documents. a. Identify the sequence of activities needed to design a system, operate a tool, or explain the bylaws of an organization. b. Include all the factors and variables that need to be considered. c. Use formatting techniques (e. g., headings, differing fonts) to aid comprehension.

When responding to a prompt, use what you've learned from your reading, writing your technical document, and studying the rubric on page 654. Use the steps below to develop a technical document.

Writing Prompt

Write a technical document in which you explain how to operate a tool or machine or how to complete a multistep process. Make sure you explain each step clearly and completely and that you arrange the steps in a clear order. Also include any materials needed.

Study the Prompt

Be sure to read the prompt and identify all parts of the task. You must give directions for using a tool or completing a multistep process. It is important that your directions are written for someone who has no experience with the tool or the process. You must also explain each step carefully.

Tip: Spend about five minutes studying the prompt.

Plan Your Response

Think of a tool that you know how to use very well or a tool you use often. Make sure the process or tool requires several steps. Try to select a process that will interest your readers. Once you understand your task and have settled on your subject:

- write down what background information your readers will need before they start
- record the steps in your process, in the order in which they will be completed
- think about any materials needed for the process
- think about the best format for presenting your process

  Tip: Spend about twenty minutes planning your response.

Respond to the Prompt

Using the notes you've just made, draft your essay. Follow these guidelines:

- Begin with a brief introduction, encouraging your readers to follow your directions.
- The main part of your document should list the steps in order for completing the process or using the tool. Warn readers of potential problems, and tell them what results to expect. Consider using bulleted or numbered lists to make the steps clear.
- In the conclusion, point out the usefulness of your process or tool.

  Tip: Spend about twenty minutes writing your draft.

Improve Your Response

Revising Go back to the key aspects of the prompt. Are your directions clearly organized? Are your process steps connected by clear transitional phrases? Have you included all necessary information?

Proofreading Take a few minutes to proofread your essay to correct errors in grammar, spelling, punctuation, and capitalization. Make sure all your edits are neat, and erase any stray marks.

Checking Your Final Copy Before you turn in your directions, read them one more time to catch any errors you may have missed. You'll be glad you gave your best effort.

Tip: Save ten minutes to improve your paper.

Listening & Speaking Workshop

Evaluating the Credibility of a Speaker

Listen with a Purpose

In this workshop you will learn to evaluate the credibility of a speaker delivering a persuasive speech.

Think as a Reader/Writer To evaluate a speaker's credibility, you have to consider not only the words that you hear but also the source of the information. Who is delivering the speech? Is it possible that the speaker has a bias or a hidden agenda? When you evaluate the credibility of a speaker, you should keep all of these questions in mind.

Evaluate Credibility

Before you evaluate a speech, keep in mind that most persuasive speakers have a **bias,** or a strong leaning toward a particular point of view. A speaker who reveals the reasons for his or her bias can seem more credible than one who does not. A speaker who does not reveal a bias may have a **hidden agenda**—a secret reason for speaking. For example, a speaker trying to convince classmates to establish an art gallery in the hallways may not tell his audience that he is really trying to make sure his artwork is displayed.

Listen Carefully

To evaluate a speech effectively, you must listen carefully. As you listen, take notes on the speaker's content, delivery, and credibility by answering the questions in the chart below.

Content	✗ What is the purpose of the speech? Paraphrase it.
	✗ What is the topic? Paraphrase the speaker's point of view. Does the speaker clearly state his or her opinion?
	✗ Which reasons are convincing and which are not? How are the reasons supported?
Delivery	✗ Is the speaker's tone conversational or too formal?
	✗ Does the speaker speak loudly and slowly enough?
	✗ How often does the speaker make eye contact with the audience?
	✗ How do the speaker's nonverbal messages (such as gestures or facial expressions) match the verbal message?
Credibility	✗ What is the speaker's bias? How do you know?
	✗ What facts has the speaker used to support the opinion?
	✗ Does the speaker have unsupported opinions? What are they?

Reader/Writer
Notebook

Use your **RWN** to complete the activities for this workshop.

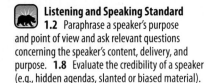

Listening and Speaking Standard
1.2 Paraphrase a speaker's purpose and point of view and ask relevant questions concerning the speaker's content, delivery, and purpose. **1.8** Evaluate the credibility of a speaker (e.g., hidden agendas, slanted or biased material).

Examine Evidence and Support

A good persuasive speech is built on strong support. One way to build a strong persuasive speech is to appeal to listeners' common sense by making a logical appeal. A speaker who makes a **logical appeal** uses reasons and evidence to support an opinion, including facts, statistics, anecdotes, examples, and expert opinions. When evaluating the credibility of a speaker, determine whether he or she offers logical support for the opinions presented. If the speech does not offer you information to think over but appeals to your emotions in order to convince you of something, the speaker may not be credible.

Ask Relevant Questions

After listening to a persuasive speech, the audience will often have a chance to ask the speaker any questions they have. A question-and-answer session is an excellent opportunity to evaluate the credibility of a speaker.

To help evaluate the credibility of the speaker, ask **relevant questions**—ones that relate to the speaker's topic. Your questions should address the content of the speech, the speaker's delivery, and the overall purpose. You might ask for clarification of the speaker's points or ask for the speaker to provide further support of his or her opinions. You can also ask questions that will help you discover whether or not the speaker has any biases or hidden agendas.

A student listening to a speech that supported the creation of an art gallery in the hallways asked the following questions:

Content	"Could you explain what you meant when you said all students deserve a place to hang their artwork?"
Delivery	"From your tone, I could tell that the art teacher is also excited about the students' art. Will she support the creation of a student gallery?"
Credibility	"I understand your main point to be that the empty hall needs brightening up, and the student gallery is the best use of the space. Am I correct?"

A Credible Speaker

- clearly states his or her point of view
- uses logical appeals to support his or her point of view
- reveals the reasons behind any bias
- does not have a hidden agenda for speaking on the topic

● Listening Tip

Before audience members can accept a speaker's opinion, they must see the speaker as **credible,** or believable. To build credibility, speakers should tell the audience why the issue he or she is sharing is important. An honest explanation will help the audience understand the speaker's motives.

Learn It Online
Learn more about recognizing bias at the MediaScope mini-site:

go.hrw.com | H8-657 | **Go**

Literary Skills Review

Poetry **Directions:** Answer each question that follows.

1. Homer's great stories of the heroes of the Trojan War, the *Iliad* and the *Odyssey;* the ancient Mesopotamian story of the hero-king Gilgamesh; and the story of the warrior Beowulf, who saves a people from monsters—all of these are called

   A ballads.

   B epics.

   C lyrics.

   D elegies.

2. If you were reading a serious poem written to mourn someone who has died, you would be reading

   A an ode.

   B an epic.

   C a lyric.

   D an elegy.

3. A ballad, a songlike poem that usually tells a sad story, uses a steady rhythm, a simple rhyme pattern, and a refrain. These elements help to make it

   A appear to be more sorrowful.

   B easier to memorize.

   C sound singsong when read.

   D become a series of related events.

4. Within a strict structure, rhyme, and meter, a sonnet

   A poses a question, then responds to it.

   B lists the qualities of a person, then mourns him or her.

   C tells the events of a story, then reaches a conclusion.

   D narrates the feats of a famous hero.

5. Which of the following phrases is the *best* example of a simple meter?

   A "Come on out into the sunlight"

   B "milly befriended a stranded star"

   C "So quiet, so quiet, he scarcely snores."

   D "Abuelito who throws coins like rain"

6. If you read a poem called "Ode to the West Wind," you could expect a

   A poem that was lighthearted and humorous.

   B mournful song with a refrain.

   C sad poem about someone who died.

   D poem that celebrates its topic.

7. Read this short poem by Langston Hughes, and answer the questions that follow.

   > O God of dust and rainbows help
   > us see
   > That without dust the rainbow
   > would not be.

   This is a lyric poem because it

   A has five stressed beats in every line.

   B is about the many deeds of a great hero.

   C tells a story by relating a series of events.

   D expresses the feelings of the speaker.

8. In the Hughes poem above, the rhyme could *best* be described as

   A free verse.

   B a couplet.

   C meter.

   D approximate rhyme.

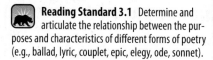

Reading Standard 3.1 Determine and articulate the relationship between the purposes and characteristics of different forms of poetry (e.g., ballad, lyric, couplet, epic, elegy, ode, sonnet).

9. Read these famous lines from the Bible, and answer the questions that follow.

> To every thing there is a season,
> And a time to every purpose under the heaven:
> A time to be born, and a time to die;
> A time to plant, and a time to pluck up that which is planted.
> —Ecclesiastes 3:1–2

Which of the following comments about these lines is correct?

A The lines are in free verse.

B The lines are in couplets.

C The lines are a ballad.

D The lines are written in strict meter.

10. By repeating the phrase "a time to" the writer emphasizes its

A refrain and its free verse.

B lyricism and its meter.

C importance and its rhythm.

D subject and its rhyme.

11. Read the following poem, and answer the questions that follow. (Be sure to count the number of lines in the poem. Also, note that "*D.R.*" in line 6 means "Dominican Republic.")

> I've heard said that among the eskimos
> there are over a hundred words for snow:
> the soft kind, the hard-driving kind, the roll
> a snowball kind: snow being such a force
> 5 in their lives, it needs a blizzard of words.
> In my own D.R. we have many rains:
> the sprinkle, the shower, the hurricane,
> the tears, the many tears for our many dead.
> I've asked around and find that in all tongues
> 10 there are at least a dozen words for talk:
> the heart-to-heart, the chat, the confession,
> the juicy gossip, the quip, the harangue—
> no matter where we're from we need to talk
> about snow, rain, about being human.
> —Julia Alvarez

The last six lines of Alvarez's poem

A finishes the story from the first eight lines.

B uses a refrain in the first eight lines.

C responds to an idea in the first eight lines.

D changes the idea in the first eight lines.

continued on next page

Literary Skills Review

Reading Standard 3.1 Determine and articulate the relationship between the purposes and characteristics of different forms of poetry (e.g., ballad, lyric, couplet, epic, elegy, ode, sonnet).

12. In line 5 of Alvarez's poem on page 659, the **metaphor** "blizzard of words" compares a snowstorm to

  A the great need for words about snow.

  B well-worded weather reports about snow.

  C humans' great need to talk with one another.

  D the damage of a hurricane.

13. Alvarez's sonnet form here is different from the classic Italian sonnet form because Alvarez writes

  A in the twentieth century.

  B without rhyme or meter.

  C about her feelings.

  D with humor.

14. Compare the Hughes poem from item 7 with this Alvarez poem. The poems share each of the following features *except*

  A speaker's feelings.

  B examples from nature.

  C rhyme and meter.

  D imagery.

Timed Writing

15. List at least four elements of poetry. Then, describe what all poems have in common.

16. Choose three forms of poetry from this list of seven:

- ballad
- couplet
- elegy
- epic
- lyric
- ode
- sonnet

Then, determine two characteristics of each form and write two or three sentences comparing and contrasting the purposes of each form.

Vocabulary Skills Review

Synonyms   **Directions:** Choose the word or phrase that is the best synonym of each italicized word.

1. A *mournful* expression is
   A unreadable.
   B beaming.
   C joyous.
   D sad.

2. To *tax* a person is to
   A support him.
   B scold him.
   C burden him.
   D scorn him.

3. A *comrade* is a
   A friend.
   B competitor.
   C soldier.
   D sibling.

4. An object that is *loathed* is
   A unusable.
   B hated.
   C tolerated.
   D worn.

5. When you *purge* something, you
   A store it.
   B clean it.
   C organize it.
   D empty it.

6. An *impetuous* child is
   A impatient.
   B rude.
   C insincere.
   D disagreeable.

7. A *spent* animal is
   A dignified.
   B exhausted.
   C overworked.
   D eager.

8. The *aghast* teacher is
   A proud.
   B complimentary.
   C tired.
   D astonished.

Academic Vocabulary

Directions: Choose the best synonym for the italicized Academic Vocabulary word.

9. The *characteristics* of a poem are its
   A purposes.
   B consequences.
   C qualities.
   D messages.

Poetry

In the Eyes of the Cat

You will gain an appreciation of Japanese poetry in *In the Eyes of the Cat.* The editor and illustrator Demi has selected short poems about animals, from the gnat to the monkey, and has arranged them according to the seasons. The illustrations, which are as important as the poems, at times burst with colors and at other times are subdued with the pastel colors of fall and winter. The intricate artwork, along with the fine translations, help make this a thoroughly enjoyable book for all readers.

You Come Too

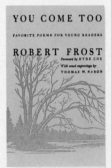

Discover some of the best of Robert Frost's poetry in *You Come Too.* In this collection for readers of all ages, you'll encounter poems such as "Christmas Tree," "Hyla Brook," and his famous, inviting title poem. Frost brings to life the trees, mountains, cliffs, dirt roads, old fences, grassy fields, and abandoned houses of his beloved New England. Reading his work, you'll have the sense that you are there—deep in the woods or at the edge of a babbling brook.

Canto Familiar

Gary Soto, the well-known writer for young adults, celebrates the experience of growing up in a Mexican American community in *Canto Familiar.* Many of these touching poems focus on everyday tasks, such as washing dishes or ironing clothes. Soto lovingly and humorously captures childhood in this collection. Artist Annika Nelson supplements the writing with beautiful, original woodcut illustrations.

This Same Sky: A Collection of Poems from Around the World

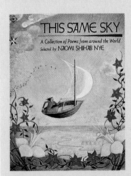

In her anthology, *This Same Sky: A Collection of Poems from Around the World,* Naomi Shihab Nye offers up a large assortment of poems from countries in the Middle East, Asia, Africa, India, and South and Central America. Like the variety of the poems' origins, the subject matter varies greatly and includes musings on language, nature, childhood, and politics. The collection is a great resource for kids and parents alike.

Nonfiction

Island of Hope: The Story of Ellis Island and the Journey to America

Dramatic firsthand stories and evocative archival photographs combine to bring the Ellis Island experience to life in Martin Sandler's *Island of Hope: The Story of Ellis Island and the Journey to America*. Both the joys and miseries of the immigration process are captured in this historic account. Sandler also gives an overview of the immigrants' lives after they were finally settled in America.

Lincoln: A Photobiography

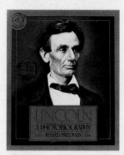

Russell Freedman's *Lincoln: A Photobiography* takes an intimate look at the man who has been called our greatest president. Freedman writes about Abraham Lincoln's childhood, his legendary debates with Stephen Douglas, and his struggles as president during the years of the Civil War. The photographs and text of this Newbery Medal winner are complemented by illustrations and historical documents.

A Great and Glorious Game

Baseball was more than a game to A. Bartlett Giamatti; each game was a drama that gave insight into the American character. *A Great and Glorious Game* collects some of Giamatti's writings about the game he loved, from the time he was a literature professor at Yale University through the period when he served as commissioner of baseball.

The Harlem Renaissance

In *The Harlem Renaissance*, Veronica Chambers looks back at a special time in American history. During the 1920s, African American musicians such as Duke Ellington, writers such as Zora Neale Hurston, and painters such as William H. Johnson produced visionary art. Their work continues to influence American culture and society to this day.

CHAPTER 6

Reading for Life

 California Standards

Here are the grade 8 standards you will work toward mastering in Chapter 6.

Reading Comprehension (Focus on Informational Materials)

2.1 Compare and contrast the features and elements of consumer materials to gain meaning from documents (e.g., warranties, contracts, product information, instruction manuals).

2.5 Understand and explain the use of a complex mechanical device by following technical directions.

2.6 Use information from a variety of consumer, workplace, and public documents to explain a situation or decision and to solve a problem.

Writing Applications (Genres and Their Characteristics)

2.5 Write documents related to career development, including simple business letters and job applications:
  a. Present information purposefully and succinctly and meet the needs of the intended audience.
  b. Follow the conventional format for the type of document (e.g., letter of inquiry, memorandum).

"Problems can become opportunities when the right people come together."

—Robert Redford

What Do **You** Think

How can we solve the problems we face in daily life?

The start of a 2,500-mile solar-powered car race between Austin, Texas, and Calgary, Canada, in 2005.

 Learn It Online

Find graphic organizers to help you as you read:

| go.hrw.com | H8-665 | **Go** |

Informational Skills Focus

by **Carol Jago**

What Types of Documents Will I Read in Real Life?

Imagine you want to see a movie. Besides finding the time and place, you might want to read reviews, learn about the cast, and reserve seats. You'll read many types of informational documents throughout your life that can help you either explain a situation or decision or solve a problem.

Workplace Documents

You may hold a variety of jobs in the next thirty years. The job you volunteer for at age thirteen will probably be very different from the one you accept at age forty. Whether you are taking orders at a restaurant or giving orders to a staff of a thousand, your job will likely require that you read for information. That information is important when it is related to your profession. The **workplace documents** you will read serve two basic functions: communication and instruction.

Communication E-mails, memorandums (memos), and reports tell you about upcoming meetings, changes in policy, and other crucial information you need to know in order to do your job. Letters of application and résumés will help you find a job.

Instruction Employee manuals specify what is expected of you on the job. User guides teach you how to operate the equipment you will use in the office.

Public Documents

Public documents contain information about public agencies and community groups. These documents can address voting issues, health concerns, and many other subjects. These reports explain situations, decisions, responsibilities, schedules, occasions, and interesting events. You might use public documents if you work with a government agency, school, park, or library. Public documents inform people about what is happening in their community, city, state, nation, and even on the planet.

THE REAL-LIFE READING AND COMPREHENSION TEST...

CAUTION DRY PAINT

8-20 Ucomics.com/nonsequitur

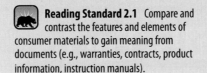

Reading Standard 2.1 Compare and contrast the features and elements of consumer materials to gain meaning from documents (e.g., warranties, contracts, product information, instruction manuals).

2.5 Understand and explain the use of a complex mechanical device by following technical directions. **2.6** Use information from a variety of consumer, workplace, and public documents to explain a situation or decision and to solve a problem.

Consumer Documents

A **consumer** is someone who buys something or uses something another person buys. That covers just about everyone: you, your friends—even a baby. The things consumers buy fall into two basic categories: goods and services.

Some goods, such as magazines or bananas, are simple to use. More complicated goods may not be easy to use. Suppose you buy a computer. You might need some information to get the computer up and running. Therefore, the computer package will include **consumer documents** containing features and elements to help you set up and operate your computer. The documents also define legal rights and responsibilities—yours, those of the company that made the computer, and those of the company that sold it to you.

- **Product information** on the box or label tells you if an item is really the one you want. Is the shirt washable? Does the CD player have the features you want? Read the details given to find out.
- **Contracts** specify exactly what services are and are not provided. Contracts are generally binding once they are signed by you, your parent or guardian, or both. Read carefully before signing a contract.
- **Warranties** guarantee that a product will work for a specified period of time. They also explain what happens if it doesn't work properly and what you have to do to receive a refund or service.
- **Instruction manuals** tell you how to set up and use a product. If you break the product because you didn't read the instructions carefully, you will be responsible for the damage.
- **Technical directions** give precise technical information about installing, assembling, and operating a product.

Technical Directions

Directions are helpful for many activities. You may need to follow directions when you cook, dance, exercise, play sports, sing, or play music. You follow **technical directions** when you install, assemble, or operate a scientific, mechanical, or electronic device. If you skip a step or perform one step out of order, the device may not work or may even break, so read the directions carefully. When following technical directions for using a complex device, it is a good idea to

- read the directions all the way through before you begin
- check off the steps one by one as you complete them
- compare your work with the diagrams and drawings provided for each step

---

Your Turn   Analyze Documents

In your *Reader/Writer Notebook,* write four headings at the top of two pages: Workplace Documents and Public Documents on one page and Consumer Documents and Technical Directions on the other page. Under each heading, list all the relevant documents that you might need to use sometime soon. Put check marks next to any you have already used or can find in your home or classroom. Add items (and check marks) as you think of more documents and as you read the documents in this chapter.

Learn It Online
Try the *PowerNotes* version of this lesson on:

| go.hrw.com | H8-667 | Go |

Reading Skills Focus

by **Kylene Beers**

What Skills Help You Understand Documents?

What do you do when you want to see your favorite team play a game? You look up the schedule, ticket prices, and routes to the stadium. Basically, you read public and consumer documents. You'll want to find the information you need quickly. Here are some skills that will help you navigate documents that provide an explanation or find a solution to a problem.

Previewing

Before you read a public, consumer, or workplace document, you should check to see if it has the information you need. A good way to find out is by previewing the text. To **preview** a text, first glance over the document quickly, without reading every word. Pay attention to heads and subheads. They give essential information, as do charts, lists, and illustrations. Follow these tips for previewing a text:

Tips for Previewing Documents

1. If the text has numbered steps, picture someone telling you, "First, do this. Next, do that."

2. Look for heads and subheads. They usually introduce a new topic.

3. Watch for boldface and italic type. Special type treatments signal key words and ideas.

4. You can often find information you are looking for in bulleted or numbered lists.

5. Look at graphics such as maps or charts. They give you additional information.

Skimming and Scanning

Skimming and scanning can also help you find the information you need in a document. To skim and scan, you read parts of the text quickly. Then, when you find what you need, you can slow down and read carefully.

Skimming is looking at a document quickly. You read the title, heads, and subheads. Then, you read the first line or two of each paragraph.

Scanning is looking for the particular information you want. You search for boldface key words and phrases or other important details that relate to your topic.

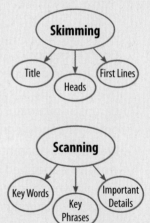

Reading Standard 2.1 Compare and contrast the features and elements of consumer materials to gain meaning from documents (e.g., warranties, contracts, product information, instruction manuals). **2.5** Understand and explain the use of a complex mechanical device by following technical directions. **2.6** Use information from a variety of consumer, workplace, and public documents to explain a situation or decision and to solve a problem.

Understanding Graphics

A good place to find information about a document is in its accompanying graphics. **Graphics** include graphs, tables, maps, cartoons, and illustrations. The titles or captions of these graphics can often lead you to the information you need.

Tables list information in categories. Facts are put in horizontal rows and vertical columns. You choose a category at the top or on the left side that interests you and read down or across to find the information. Here is an example of a table:

Types of Graphics	
Tables	put information into categories
Graphs	show relationships
Illustrations	show what is being described
Maps	show geographical areas

Graphs show relationships between things. Two common types are line graphs and bar graphs. You have probably seen line graphs that depict how the economy is doing, like the one in this cartoon:

"At times like this, I wish I were a poet."

Following Sequence

Writers of instruction manuals put the information they present in **sequence**—they list the steps in the process they are describing in the logical order in which you must complete them. Following the sequence of steps in the instruction manuals will enable you to use of a variety of mechanical devices.

Your Turn Apply Reading Skills

1. What strategy would you use if you were looking for key statements in a consumer document?

2. Why is it important to follow directions in a sequence when you install a printer for your computer?

3. Preview the text below. Then, explain what you think the document will be about.

   Did You Know?

   - In our city there are 165,000 licensed dogs.

   - The city devotes a total of 10 acres to leash-free dog areas.

   - Eastside Leash-Free Dog Park accommodates 2,000 dogs per week on its 1-acre site.

   Now go to the Skills in Action: Reading Model

 Learn It Online
Need help reading informational texts? Check out the interactive Reading Workshops on:

| go.hrw.com | H8-669 | **Go** |

Build Background

The Global Positioning System (GPS) uses satellite signals to find the location, speed, and direction of a receiver. GPS was first developed by the United States Department of Defense for military use. GPS is now used in a wide range of consumer products, from cell phones to cars. The documents here are consumer documents.

Read with a Purpose Read to learn what is involved in acquiring a GPS device.

GPS DOCUMENTS

by

The Browns recently vacationed in New York and rented a car with a Global Positioning System (GPS) receiver. They found the device to be very useful, so when they returned home to Indiana, they discussed buying one for their daughter, Nidia. She was attending college in California and had an internship that required extensive traveling. Soon after, their son Eric, an eighth grader, saw the following advertisement in a newspaper and pointed it out to his parents.

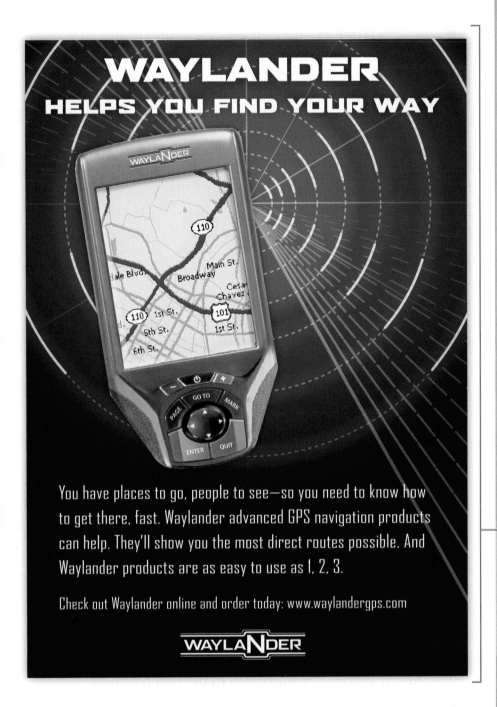

WAYLANDER
HELPS YOU FIND YOUR WAY

You have places to go, people to see—so you need to know how to get there, fast. Waylander advanced GPS navigation products can help. They'll show you the most direct routes possible. And Waylander products are as easy to use as 1, 2, 3.

Check out Waylander online and order today: www.waylandergps.com

WAYLANDER

The Browns did their homework, comparing several GPS products. In the end, they did decide to buy a Waylander for Nidia based on the price and consumer reports. They ordered the unit over the Internet and had it delivered to her directly. When it arrived, Nidia excitedly looked over the instructions, beginning with the table of contents.

Reading Model

Previewing When previewing the table of contents, you learn about the features of the instruction manual.

HOW TO USE YOUR WAYLANDER
CONTENTS

Reading Focus

Scanning If you have problems with your GPS device, scanning the table of contents tells you that troubleshooting advice can be found at the end of the manual, on page 130.

Nidia had a basic idea about the way GPS units work, but the list of unfamiliar terms in the table of contents made her realize there was plenty she needed to learn. So she sat down in her favorite chair to read through the instructions. The introduction discussed satellite systems and gave an overview. Nidia then zeroed in on the instructions for operation. After reading "How Does It Work?" she moved on to the chapter called "The Keypad."

Nidia activated her unit and tried to use it while reviewing the manual. She was all thumbs at first—or at least she felt that way. She hit MARK when she meant to hit PAGE. Then she got the hang of it. After a little practice, she put the unit down and continued reading. When she shifted in her chair, some papers fell out of the manual. One of them was an extended warranty.

THE KEYPAD

Your keypad is not much larger than the face of a watch. Smaller buttons surround the bigger key button in the center, which provides four directions, displayed by arrows. When your unit has been activated, the display above the buttons shows a series of screens, called pages. On each page are specific functions.

To cycle through the pages, use POWER, PAGE, and QUIT:

1. **Power.** Press the POWER button. Hold for two seconds.
2. **Status.** A welcome will appear, followed by the status page.
3. **Location.** Press PAGE. Information about your location will appear.
4. **Map Data.** Press PAGE again to see map data.
5. **Navigation Information.** Press PAGE again for navigation information.
6. **Menu Commands.** Press PAGE again to see the menu commands.
7. **Return.** Hit QUIT when you want to rotate pages backward.
8. **End.** Press the POWER button again to turn the unit off.

The buttons on your keypad help you perform various functions:

 POWER turns the unit on and off.

 ARROWS on the center key button help you change selections on the screens.

 PAGE provides map and navigation information.

 ENTER confirms entries and allows you to enter data in highlighted screens.

 GO TO sets a course for a destination you select.

 MARK stores a current location in a log for later reference.

 QUIT sends you back to a previous page. It will back you out of functions. It clears data entry or restores a data field's previous value.

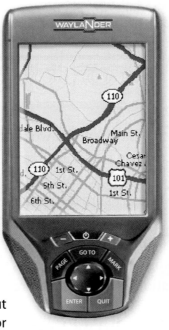

Informational Text Focus

Technical Directions These technical directions include a numbered list of steps to follow.

Reading Focus

Understanding Graphics These illustrations of the GPS device and its buttons help you understand the technical directions above.

Informational Text Focus

Consumer Documents When using a consumer document, such as this warranty, read it very carefully, and follow the directions exactly. Unlike the instruction manual, it explains how to extend your warranty, not how to use the unit.

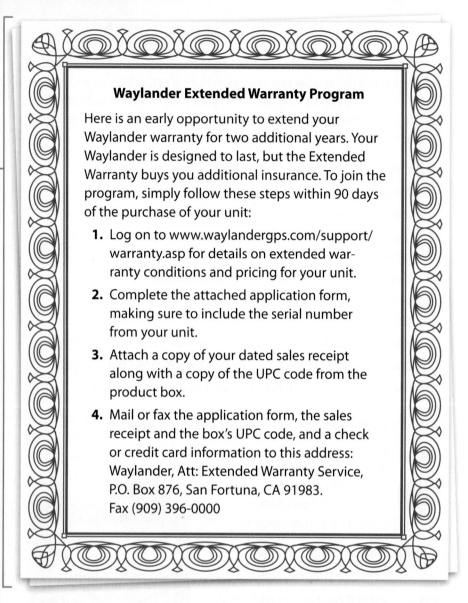

Waylander Extended Warranty Program

Here is an early opportunity to extend your Waylander warranty for two additional years. Your Waylander is designed to last, but the Extended Warranty buys you additional insurance. To join the program, simply follow these steps within 90 days of the purchase of your unit:

1. Log on to www.waylandergps.com/support/warranty.asp for details on extended warranty conditions and pricing for your unit.

2. Complete the attached application form, making sure to include the serial number from your unit.

3. Attach a copy of your dated sales receipt along with a copy of the UPC code from the product box.

4. Mail or fax the application form, the sales receipt and the box's UPC code, and a check or credit card information to this address: Waylander, Att: Extended Warranty Service, P.O. Box 876, San Fortuna, CA 91983. Fax (909) 396-0000

Nidia knew she would have to balance the likelihood of needing a repair against the cost of the extended warranty and the cost of the unit. Because she didn't know the cost of the unit, she wasn't sure if it made sense to purchase the extension. Nidia called her parents, who told her that an extended warranty had been offered free as part of a promotion. She had done the right thing by calling. It always makes sense to have as much information as possible before making an important decision.

Read with a Purpose What documents are involved in purchasing a GPS device?

Reading Standard 2.1 Compare and contrast the features and elements of consumer materials to gain meaning from documents (e.g., warranties, contracts, product information, instruction manuals).

Reading Standard 2.6 Use information from a variety of consumer, workplace, and public documents to explain a situation or decision and to solve a problem.

Into Action: Reading for Information

In a chart like the one below, give examples of each text feature and explain how you were able to use each text feature to help you understand the GPS documents.

Informational Text Feature	Examples and Explanations
Headings	
Graphics	
Numbered lists	

Talk About . . .

1. Discuss with a partner the similarities and differences between the GPS documents. Try to use each Academic Vocabulary word listed at the right at least once in your discussion.

Write About . . .

Answer the following questions about the GPS documents. For definitions of the underlined Academic Vocabulary words, see the column at the right.

2. Why should you follow complex technical directions in the correct order?

3. What critical information does the page from the keypad chapter (page 673) give you?

4. Specify the elements you would expect to find in a warranty.

Writing Skills Focus
Think as a Reader/Writer

Find It In Your Reading The Writing Skills Focus activities on the Preparing to Read pages guide you in recognizing how each type of document delivers information. On the Applying Your Skills pages, you will monitor your understanding of these document types.

Academic Vocabulary for Chapter 6

Talking and Writing About Informational Documents

Academic Vocabulary is the language you use to write and talk about what you read. Use these words to discuss the informational documents you read in this chapter. The words are underlined throughout the chapter.

complex (kuhm PLEHKS) *adj.*: complicated; difficult to understand. *Before operating a complex device, be sure to read the directions.*

critical (KRIHT ih kuhl) *adj.*: vital; very important. *It is critical to pay attention to all items in a warranty.*

elements (EHL uh muhnts) *n.*: parts of which things are made up. *Before purchasing an expensive item, be sure you understand the elements of its warranty in case the item breaks.*

specify (SPEHS uh fy) *v.*: mention or describe in detail; give as a condition. *When signing up with an Internet service provider, be sure to specify which service you are choosing.*

Your Turn

Copy the Academic Vocabulary words into your *Reader/Writer Notebook*. Then, use each word correctly in a sentence.

Using Information to Solve a Problem

CONTENTS

What Do **You** Think? How do we solve problems that affect an entire community?

QuickWrite

What improvements would you like to see in your community? You might consider a town pool or new traffic signs, for example. Record your ideas.

DOCUMENTS
Preparing to Read

Reading Standard 2.6 Use information from a variety of consumer, workplace, and public documents to explain a situation or decision and to solve a problem.

Skateboard Park Documents / Leash-Free Dog Run Documents

Informational Text Focus

Using Information from Documents to Solve a Problem Getting accurate information is <u>critical</u> when you need to solve a problem. You may gather information from a variety of sources, including **workplace documents,** such as memos, e-mails, and reports; **public documents,** such as schedules, government publications, and Web sites; and **consumer documents,** such as contracts, advertisements, and manuals. In the following pages you'll find documents that concern problems faced by communities. Pretend you are a member of these communities. The annotations beside some documents show the type of critical thinking you might do to understand the situation. Once you get all the facts, you'll be able to find the best solution.

Reading Skills Focus

Previewing When you **preview** material, you look over text you are about to read to find out what lies ahead. You may begin by noticing headings and subheadings.

Into Action To complete a preview chart, list each document you will read, explain what it is, and describe the topic it covers.

Title/Description	Kind of Document	Topic
Memorandum	workplace document from the Parks Department	issues regarding the new skateboard park: need, liability, cost, location
The City Beat	public document: newspaper column	

Writing Skills Focus

Preparing for **Timed Writing** Use the information in these documents to form opinions about the skateboard park and the dog run.

Reader/Writer
Notebook
Use your **RWN** to complete the activities for these selections.

Language Coach

Prefixes A **prefix** is a word part added to the front of a word. The prefixes *en–* and *em–* mean "to cause to be." Which Vocabulary word contains one of these prefixes? How does the prefix affect the meaning of the word?

Learn It Online
To learn more about analyzing forms of writing, visit *MediaScope* at:

go.hrw.com   H8-677   **Go**

Skateboard Park Documents

Read with a Purpose Read these workplace, public, and consumer documents to solve a skateboarding problem.

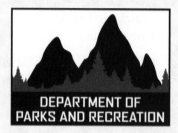

DEPARTMENT OF PARKS AND RECREATION

MEMORANDUM

From: A. Longboard, Assistant Director of Parks and Recreation

To: J. Cool, Director of Parks and Recreation

Re: Establishment of a Permanent Skateboard Park

> *The Parks and Recreation Department is thinking about building a skateboard park.*

CRITICAL ISSUES

> *There is a clear need: 7,000+ skaters, no existing park, complaints, tickets. What about injuries?*

A. Need. Ten percent of the families in this city, about seven thousand households, include at least one skateboarder. The city provides no designated space for skateboarding. Police reports show that citations for illegal skating are rising every month. This problem is particularly acute in downtown areas, leading to complaints from businesses. The nearest public skateboard park is twenty miles to the east in Mogul, where illegal skating dropped sharply when its park opened last year.

B. Liability.[1] California AB 1296 states that persons who skateboard on public property are expected to know that it is a potentially dangerous sport. They cannot sue the city, county, or state for their injuries as long as the city has passed an ordinance[2] requiring

> *Looks as if skateboarders cannot sue the city. Will the city keep kids safe, though?*

- helmet, kneepads, and elbow pads for skaters
- clear and visible signs warning citizens of this requirement

---

1. **liability** (ly uh BIHL uh tee): legal responsibility.
2. **ordinance** (AWR duh nuhns): law; rule.

Vocabulary **potentially** (poh TEHN shuh lee) *adv.:* possibly.

- citations for skaters who violate the ordinance

Such an ordinance was enacted by our city council on July 15, 2008. Therefore, building a skateboard park would not pose a liability risk.

Looks as if we could afford it.

C. Cost. Local groups have raised half the necessary $140,000. The Parks and Recreation Department's budget can fund the other half. Costs will be minimal—only inspection for damage and yearly maintenance.

D. Location. The city already owns two sites:

Site 1: Automobile safety issues? Neighbors' complaints? What's on that site now?

- 1.3 acres of the park area between 180th Avenue and 360th Drive, bordered by Drab Street and Grinding Drive, two heavily used thoroughfares. On two sides of the park are neighborhood houses.

Site 2: No busy street or neighbors. Close to paramedics. Better choice.

- 2.1 acres in the 15-acre sports park at Ramp and Spin avenues. This site is set back from heavily traveled roads but still offers excellent access and visibility from service roads within the park. It is also three-tenths of a mile from the fire station and paramedic aid. There are no residential neighborhoods bordering the complex. **B**

A **Read and Discuss** Given the information presented here, how could you describe the need for establishing a skateboard park?

B **Informational Focus** **Using Information** How do the two proposed sites compare?

The City Beat

by N. PARKER

A lively debate occurred at last Tuesday's packed city council meeting on the subject of whether to establish a skateboard park. Mayor Gridlock made a few opening remarks and then turned the microphone over to J. Cool, Director of Parks and Recreation. Mr. Cool read from portions of a report prepared by his staff, who had investigated the need for and the liability, risks, cost, and possible location of a park. Several members of the community spoke.

A packed meeting? Looks as if there's a lot of interest.

K. Skater said, "Skateboarding is a challenging sport. It's good for us. But right now we have no place to skate, and so kids are getting tickets for illegal skating. Lots of people say it's too dangerous, but that's not true. Kids get hurt in every sport, but you can make it a lot less dangerous for us if you give us a smooth place to practice. Still, we skaters have to be responsible and only take risks we can handle. That teaches us a lot."

The right space would cut risks. Sports help kids learn to judge their strengths and limitations.

D. T. Merchant remarked, "I am a store owner downtown. These skaters use our curbs and handrails as their personal skating ramps. They threaten pedestrians and scare people. If we build them an alternative, I believe most will use it. Then the police can concentrate on the few who break the rules."

Merchants need relief. Illegal skating is unsafe for everyone. Park may reduce police time spent citing skaters.

G. Homeowner had this to say: "Skaters are illiterate bums. They think safety gear means thick hair gel. They have no respect. They will disturb my neighborhood all night long with their subhuman noise.

This guy really hates site 1.

I would like to remind the city council—I pay taxes and I vote. A skateboard park? Not in my backyard!"

F. Parent: "My son is an outstanding citizen. He is respectful and well behaved. He also lives to skateboard. This city has placed my son at risk by failing to give him a safe place to skate. If we were talking about building a basketball court, nobody would think twice before agreeing. I'm a voter too, and I expect the city council to be responsive to the needs of *all* citizens."

> Safety again. Good point.

Finally, S. B. Owner said, "I am the owner of the Skate Bowl. Skateboarding is not a fad. It is here to stay. You may not like the way some skaters act or look, but I know them all. They're great kids. Seems like most of the good folks here tonight are worried about safety. So here's what I propose: I will sell all safety gear at my store at 50 percent off. That's less than it costs me, folks. All that you parents have to do is fill out the emergency information card for your skater and return it to me. I'll see that the information is entered in a database that paramedics, hospital workers, and police officers can access. I'll also make sure that everyone who comes to my store knows what the Consumer Product Safety Commission says: "'Kids who want to skate are going to skate. Let's help them skate safely.'" **C**

> Affordable safety gear, emergency contacts, consumer education—I think I'll write a letter in support of this idea.

Mr. Owner's proposal was met with a standing ovation. Plans to move ahead with the new skateboard park project will be put to a formal vote at next month's regular session.

> It looks as if this could pass. Now they will have to decide where to put the park.

C **Informational Focus** Using Information
Specify how the information in the article different from the information in the memo.

Vocabulary **proposal** (pruh POHZ uhl) *n.*: suggestion.

50%OFF   **50%OFF**

DISCOUNT COUPON FOR

S. B. OWNER'S

SKATE BOWL

This coupon entitles bearer,

_____

to **50 PERCENT OFF**   **D**
the regular list price on all helmets,
kneepads, and elbow pads.

Discount does not extend to shoes, padded clothing, boards, trucks,
stickers, or any other equipment. Discount does not include state or
local sales tax. Discount is not good in combination with any other
discount or coupon. Bearer must show photo identification, such as
a school ID or a yearbook photograph.   **E**

_Read the fine
print. Not all
protective items
are reduced in
price. Kids will
need a photo ID
too._

D Reading Focus Previewing   What is the purpose of this coupon?
E Informational Focus Using Information   Why is it important to read the
fine print on this coupon?

Excerpts from

Consumer Product Safety Commission: Document 93

Approximately 26,000 persons go to hospital emergency rooms each year for skateboarding-related injuries. Several factors—lack of protective equipment, poor board maintenance, and irregular riding surfaces—are involved in these accidents.

> *Board maintenance? Nobody ever thinks about that.*

Who gets injured. Six of every ten skateboard injuries happen to children under fifteen years of age. Skateboarders who have been skating for less than a week suffer one third of the injuries; riders with a year or more of skating experience have the next highest number of injuries.

> *Let's hold beginner safety classes.*

Injuries to first-time skateboarders are, for the most part, caused by falls. Experienced riders suffer injuries mostly when they fall after their skateboards strike rocks and other irregularities in the riding surface, or when they attempt difficult stunts. **F**

Environmental hazards. Irregular surfaces account for more than half the skateboarding injuries caused by falls. Before riding, skateboarders should check the surface for holes, bumps, rocks, and debris. Areas set aside for skateboarding generally have smoother riding surfaces. Skateboarding in the street can result in collisions with cars, causing serious injury or even death. **G**

> *This section certainly supports the need to build a park and then inspect it regularly. It also supports arguments for site 2.*

The skateboard. Before using their boards, riders should check them for hazards, such as loose, broken, or cracked parts; sharp edges; slippery top surfaces; and wheels with nicks and cracks. Serious defects should be corrected by a qualified repair person.

> *Let's hold yearly skateboard checkup clinics.*

Protective gear. Protective gear—such as slip-resistant, closed shoes, helmets, and specially designed padding—may not fully protect skateboarders from fractures, but its use is recommended because such gear can reduce the number and severity of injuries.

The protective gear currently on the market is not subject to federal performance standards, and so careful selection by consumers is necessary. In a helmet,

> *Kids grow quickly. Parents need to be alert to changes in fit.*

F **Informational Focus** **Using Information** What ideas or opinions from the other documents can be supported with these statistics?

G **Read and Discuss** Why is the information in the Consumer Safety Commission document significant for solving the skateboarding problem?

Vocabulary **hazards** (HAZ uhrdz) *n.*: dangers; things that can cause danger.

look for proper fit and a chin strap; make sure the helmet does not block the rider's vision and hearing. Body padding should fit comfortably. If it is tight, it can restrict circulation and reduce the skater's ability to move freely. Loose-fitting padding, on the other hand, can slip off or slide out of position.

Source: U.S. Consumer Product Safety Commission, Washington, D.C. 20207

Read with a Purpose Now that you've read these documents, how would you solve the skateboarding problem?

DOCUMENTS

Applying Your Skills

Reading Standard 2.6 Use information from a variety of consumer, workplace, and public documents to explain a situation or decision and to solve a problem.

Skateboard Park Documents

Standards Review

Informational Text and Vocabulary

1. The **memorandum** gives information about

A the benefits of opening a skateboard park.

B the reasons against building a skateboard park.

C a proposal for developing a skateboard park.

D the history of the old skateboard park.

2. Which document presents all sides of the issue to help you solve the skateboarding problem?

A the advertisement

B the memorandum

C the Consumer Product Safety Commission document

D the newspaper article

3. The Consumer Product Safety document tries to do all of these *except*

A interest readers in taking up skateboarding.

B convince readers to take steps to avoid injury.

C offer readers examples of potential skateboard hazards.

D explain the importance of wearing protective gear.

4. Another word for *hazards* is

A faults.

B dangers.

C arguments.

D worries.

5. If a problem is *potentially* serious, it is

A very serious.

B not at all serious.

C definitely serious.

D possibly serious.

6. Someone who presents a *proposal* gives a

A suggestion.

B summary.

C reaction.

D prediction.

Writing Skills Focus

Timed └Writing If you lived in this community, would you support the new skateboard park? Where would you decide to build it? Use a graphic organizer like the one below to explain the benefits and drawbacks of each site. Then, write a letter to the city council explaining your opinion. Cite information from the skateboard park documents to support your position.

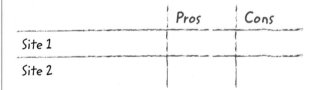

	Pros	Cons
Site 1		
Site 2		

What Do **You Think Now** Which document was most helpful in explaining the community's problem?

Leash-Free Dog Run Documents

Read with a Purpose Read these public, workplace, and consumer documents to learn about the problems they address.

File   Edit   View   Favorites   Tools   Help

Back   Forward   Stop   Refresh   Home   Search   Favorites   History   Mail   Print

Address   http://www.sp.com/home   Go

SouthPaws   Home   Volunteer   Join   Shop   Forum

Welcome to the SouthPaws Web site. SouthPaws is a not-for-profit group dedicated to creating and maintaining a leash-free space on the south side of our city for its 165,000 canine (that's dog) citizens. Please consider joining our 3,300+ members. Your membership fees are tax-deductible and will help give our dogs their own space! If you are interested in volunteering, please check out <u>Volunteer Want Ads</u>. You might want to consider purchasing SouthPaws T-shirts, sweats, caps, or leashes as a gift or for yourself. All proceeds support SouthPaws. **Ⓐ**

What's New?

Congratulations and thank you to the hundreds of volunteers who gathered signatures on the SouthPaws petition. All that hard work last spring paid off! The residents of our city have voted to establish a park or a beach where our dogs can run unleashed. This space will be jointly funded by the city and SouthPaws donations. SouthPaws volunteers will supervise the space during daylight hours and will be empowered to ticket dog owners who do not observe cleanup and safety rules. We will have one trial year after the space officially opens to prove that the idea works. Now we need your help more than ever. **Ⓑ**

Ⓐ **Read and Discuss** What problem has the writer explained to you?

Ⓑ **Informational Focus** **Using Information** Where will the organization get the money for the proposed dog run?

	🐾 PRO	🐾 CON
CAMEO PARK	• is centrally located • has convenient access roads • has street parking	• will incur high maintenance costs • is smallest, at 1.2 residential acres • is now a popular family park • may lead nearby residents to object to noise, nuisances
ROCKY POINT BEACH	• is little used • consists of 5 nonresidential acres • has ample parking • will incur low start-up and maintenance costs	• is inconveniently located • has non-sand beach; smooth but potentially slippery rocks
MAIN BEACH	• is centrally located • consists of 7.3 nonresidential acres • has sand beach	• is heavily used all year • may cause conflicts with businesses • has limited, costly parking • will require 24-hour security and maintenance staffing • will incur high maintenance costs

Ⓒ

The most likely locations for the dog run are described above. Click **here** to cast your vote in our survey. **Ⓓ**

Ⓒ **Reading Focus** **Previewing** What information is contained in these bulleted lists?

Ⓓ **Read and Discuss** Explain whether or not the design of this page is clear and effective.

🌐 Internet

 1111 South P Street ❁ South City, CA 90123

December 12, 2008

Ms. T. Wagger
Director of Parks and Recreation
2222 Central Avenue
South City, CA 90123

Dear Ms. Wagger,

SouthPaws members would like you to take their concerns into account when choosing the site of the proposed dog run. Here they are, in order of importance:

1. Space. Healthy dogs need ample space in which to run. The park needs to be large enough for a fair number of dogs to run around in it without colliding with one another. Ample size will minimize the possibility of dogfights.

2. Conflicts. A site that is already popular for sports, family activities, or tourism will likely be a problem.

3. Site. Our research shows that dog beaches are preferable to dog parks. Dogs are hard on park grass, which quickly turns to mud in rainy weather. Sand or shells can be brushed off a dog, but mud requires a bath. Dog beaches are also easier to supervise and clean.

Thank you for working with us to find a solution that is in the best interests of the most people. We are looking forward to meeting with you next week. **E**

Sincerely,

A. K. Nine

A. K. Nine
Chairperson, SouthPaws Site Committee **F**

E Read and Discuss What is the purpose of this letter?

F Informational Focus Using Information How might the writer's connection with the SouthPaws Site Committee affect the information presented in this letter?

Vocabulary **ample** (AM puhl) *adj.*: as much as is needed; enough.

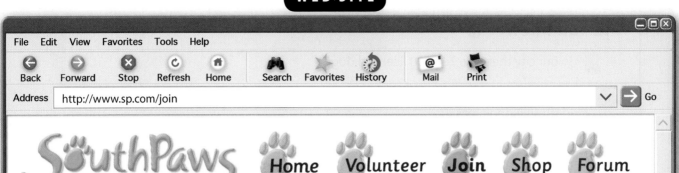

File　Edit　View　Favorites　Tools　Help

Back　Forward　Stop　Refresh　Home　Search　Favorites　History　Mail　Print

Address　http://www.sp.com/join　Go

SouthPaws
Home　Volunteer　Join　Shop　Forum

SouthPaws Membership Information

Annual Tax-Deductible Membership Fees

Basic: $15 per year; entitles you to newsletter and voting rights

Deluxe: $25 per year; entitles you to the above plus one T-shirt or cap

Sponsor: $100 per year; entitles you to all of the above plus discounted dog-obedience classes and merchandise from local merchants

Benefactor: $250 per year; entitles you to all of the above plus your name on our Dog Walk of Fame **Ⓖ**

Membership in SouthPaws makes a great gift. Print out a membership application, complete it, and mail it with your donation.

Don't want to join? Then how about making a donation? We appreciate contributions in any amount.

> **Ⓖ Informational Focus** Using Information
> How does the information about membership fees add to your understanding of the situation?

SouthPaws

Did You Know?

 In our city there are 165,000 licensed dogs.

The city devotes a total of 10 acres to leash-free dog areas.

 The city devotes 1,050 acres to softball, 1,040 acres to golf, and 287 acres to tennis.

 Eastside Leash-Free Dog Park accommodates 2,000 dogs per week on its 1-acre site.

New!

Help SouthPaws while you tell the world about your best friend. Buy a brick in the new Dog Walk of Fame. Your pet's name and a short message will be inscribed. Be sure to provide your pet's name, your name, and your message (up to 45 characters). (Available to SouthPaws members only; $50 per pet's name.)

H Reading Focus Previewing What kinds of information do you find in this section?

I Read and Discuss What point is the writer making? How do the facts on the Web page support this point?

Read with a Purpose What problems do these documents address?

 Internet

Applying Your Skills

Reading Standard 2.6 Use information from a variety of consumer, workplace, and public documents to explain a situation or decision and to solve a problem.

Leash-Free Dog Run Documents
Standards Review

Informational Text and Vocabulary

1. The decision to build the dog run was made by

A the city council.

B Parks and Recreation.

C SouthPaws.

D voters.

2. The purpose of the **Web site** is to offer

A an opinion on which site is best.

B a comparison of the sites.

C the name of the site most voters chose.

D all the possible locations in town.

3. The purpose of the **business letter** is to

A convince the Parks Department to build a dog run.

B tell the Parks Department which site is best.

C share concerns about a dog run site.

D state the requirements for choosing a site.

4. What information appears on the first Web page that does not appear in the letter?

A the name of the city agency involved in the park's creation

B a list of all the sites being considered

C a reason why increasing the size of the park will reduce fighting

D reasons why beach areas are easier to maintain than grassy areas

5. The site that *best* meets the needs and concerns of SouthPaws members is

A Cameo Park.

B Rocky Point Beach.

C Main Beach.

D none of the above.

6. Another word for *ample* is

A controversial.

B narrow.

C lacking.

D enough.

Writing Skills Focus

Timed └Writing What decision did you make about the location of the dog run? Write a brief opinion statement that expresses your decision. Use critical information from the Leash-Free Dog Run documents to explain your decision.

What Do You Think Now

What do these documents say about effective ways to solve problems affecting an entire community?

Comparing Consumer Materials

CONTENTS

What Do **You** Think? What questions should you ask when you are shopping for a product?

 QuickWrite

Think of something you might want to purchase, such as a bicycle or an MP3 player. How do you decide which kind to buy? Record your ideas.

Reading Standard 2.1 Compare and contrast the features and elements of consumer materials to gain meaning from documents (e.g., warranties, contracts, product information, instruction manuals).

WarpSpeedNet Documents / SweetPlayer Documents

Informational Text Focus

Elements and Features of Consumer Documents What has two wheels, pedals to make it go, and handles for steering the front wheel? A _____. That was easy to figure out because the question names a bicycle's most basic elements. You want a bicycle that stands out in your crowd. You want features that make it unique. Bicycles have common elements as well as special features. So do consumer documents. The **elements** of consumer materials define what the document is—warranty, contract, product information, or instructional manual. The **features** are what make consumer materials unique. For example, all contracts detail what you are giving and what you are receiving by signing. You can't have a contract without those two elements. The notes in the margins will help you when you compare and contrast the elements and features of the consumer materials that follow.

Reading Skills Focus

Skimming and Scanning These techniques can help you gain meaning from complex consumer documents. **Skim** to get a general idea of the information included. **Scan** to look for specific information. Use headings, boldface terms, and graphics to help locate information.

Into Action Use a chart like this one as you skim and scan to compare and contrast the elements and features of consumer materials.

Document	Skimming	Scanning
Advertisement	It's an ad for an Internet service provider.	The ad does not give exact prices.
Service Agreement		

Writing Skills Focus

Preparing for Timed ⌐Writing As you read the advertisement, note which details are the most clear and helpful.

Reader/Writer Notebook

Use your **RWN** to complete the activities for these selections.

WarpSpeedNet Documents

Read with a Purpose Read these consumer documents to learn what subscribing to high-speed internet service involves.

Choosing a High-Speed Internet Service Provider

Juan's family's phone line is always busy because everyone uses the Internet. They decide it is time to subscribe to high-speed Internet access. They see the product information in this advertisement.

Element—*description of selling points.*
Features—*no equipment to buy, speedy, convenient.*

Element—*enticements to buy.*
Features—*free installation, money-back guarantee, short-term offer.*

Element—*contact information.*

Element—*limitations.*
Features—*is not available everywhere, does not work with all computers, has expiration date.*

WarpSpeedNet

You Get What You Want—Now.

Only WarpSpeedNet provides all the cable equipment and services you need for a lightning-fast Internet connection through your home computer. Never wait again to dial in, log on, or connect. WarpSpeedNet is always on, always ready to go. You'll never be disconnected in the middle of a download again! **A**

WarpSpeedNet is point-and-click easy to use. Get weather reports now, news now, Web shopping now, music now, games now. Anything the World Wide Web offers, WarpSpeedNet brings to you—now!

CALL DURING THE NEXT TWO WEEKS TO RECEIVE FREE INSTALLATION AND A RISK-FREE 30-DAY MONEY-BACK GUARANTEE.

Call now and mention priority code RIW.
1-555-WarpNet

Service subject to availability in your area. Offer good in South and North County areas only. Minimum computer system requirements apply. Offer expires 12/31/10. **B**

A **Reading Focus** **Skimming** How can skimming—reading quickly—help you understand the product information contained in this advertisement?

B **Informational Focus** **Consumer Documents** Why do you think product limitations, an element of some ads, are usually presented in tiny type?

Vocabulary **disconnected** (dihs kuh NEHK tihd) *v.*: not connected; cut off; separated.

Reading a Service Agreement Juan's family decides to give WarpSpeedNet a try. They live in South County, meet the minimum computer system requirements, and call within the two-week deadline. They are now entitled to everything the company promised: free installation, thirty-day money-back trial, and all the necessary cable equipment. They also receive some important consumer documents. Let's take a look at some of those documents, beginning with this **contract.**

WarpSpeedNet

Service Agreement ©

1. Equipment

A. Equipment includes rental of cable modem and necessary connections to permit use of one (1) computer with WarpSpeedNet service.

B. WarpSpeedNet will install equipment. Subscriber will grant company reasonable access to install, inspect, repair, maintain, or disconnect the equipment. Refusal to do so may result in discontinued service.

C. Cable equipment remains the property of WarpSpeedNet. Upon termination of service, equipment shall be returned in original condition, ordinary wear and tear excepted.

2. Charges

A. Subscriber agrees to pay for the monthly service subscribed to, including charges for installation, in advance. Monthly charges are set forth on a separate price list and are subject to change.

B. Subscribers who discontinue service will be required to pay all due and past-due charges. If the subscriber reconnects service, a charge will apply.

C. If cable equipment is lost, damaged, or stolen, subscriber must pay $300 to WarpSpeedNet for replacement. Ⓓ

_____
Company representative signature and date

_____
Subscriber signature and date

ment—services that Juan's family eives).
tures—equipment one computer, allation, and up.

Element—costs (what Juan's family pays).
Features—payments per agreement, including all fees, charges, and replacement costs.

Element—signatures (no contract is valid without them).

© **Read and Discuss** What are three responsibilities of the subscriber?

Ⓓ **Informational Focus** **Consumer Documents** Compare and contrast the elements of the contract with the advertisement on page 694. Name one way in which they are similar and one way in which they are different.

Vocabulary **discontinued** (dihs kuhn TIHN yood) *v.* used as *adj.*: not continued; stopped; ended.

Reading an Instruction Manual Juan's family also receives an **instruction manual.** Let's review it.

Welcome to

WarpSpeedNet ⓔ

Element—table of contents.

ⓔ **Reading Focus Scanning** How does scanning—looking for specific information—help you locate information on modem lights in this instruction manual?

Cable Modem Lights

There are four lights on the front of your cable modem.

1. POWER ●POWER	**STEADY GREEN:** Power is on.
2. CABLE ○POWER ●CABLE ○PC ○DATA	**STEADY GREEN:** Cable is ready to use. **FLASHING RED-GREEN:** Cable is setting up connection. Wait. **FLASHING RED:** Connection has a problem. See Troubleshooting, page 33. **NO LIGHT:** There is no cable connection. Call for service.
3. COMPUTER LINK ○POWER ○CABLE ●PC ○DATA	**STEADY GREEN:** Connection is working. **FLASHING RED:** There is a connection problem. See Troubleshooting, page 33. **NO LIGHT:** Computer has been turned off or disconnected.
4. DATA ●DATA	**FLASHING LIGHT:** Modem is sending or receiving data. **F**

Element—
explanation of product.
Features—
specific meaning of each light.

F **Informational Focus** **Consumer Documents** How might <u>elements</u> of the instruction manual help you understand the meaning of the lights on the cable modem?

Reading a Warranty If the cable modem doesn't work, what can Juan's family do? Let's check the warranty. A **warranty** tells you when, how, and for how long you can get your money back. WarpSpeedNet's warranty offers a refund if the equipment fails during the first year. But that doesn't really apply to Juan's family. Can you figure out why? (Hint: Go back and read the contract.)

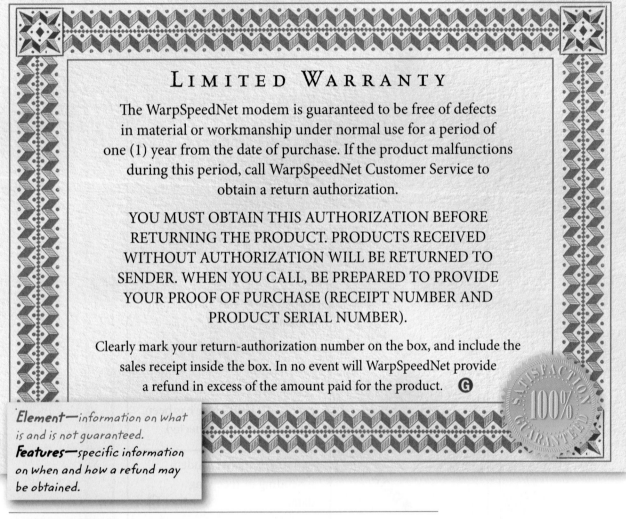

LIMITED WARRANTY

The WarpSpeedNet modem is guaranteed to be free of defects in material or workmanship under normal use for a period of one (1) year from the date of purchase. If the product malfunctions during this period, call WarpSpeedNet Customer Service to obtain a return authorization.

YOU MUST OBTAIN THIS AUTHORIZATION BEFORE RETURNING THE PRODUCT. PRODUCTS RECEIVED WITHOUT AUTHORIZATION WILL BE RETURNED TO SENDER. WHEN YOU CALL, BE PREPARED TO PROVIDE YOUR PROOF OF PURCHASE (RECEIPT NUMBER AND PRODUCT SERIAL NUMBER).

Clearly mark your return-authorization number on the box, and include the sales receipt inside the box. In no event will WarpSpeedNet provide a refund in excess of the amount paid for the product. **G**

Element—information on what is and is not guaranteed.
Features—specific information on when and how a refund may be obtained.

G [Read and Discuss] How are the <u>elements</u> of the contract on page 695 similar to an element of the warranty?

Vocabulary **authorization** (aw thuhr uh ZAY shuhn) *n.:* official permission.

Read with a Purpose What did the family learn about subscribing to a high-speed Internet service?

Reading Standard 2.1 Compare and contrast the features and elements of consumer materials to gain meaning from documents (e.g., warranties, contracts, product information, instruction manuals).

WarpSpeedNet Documents
Standards Review

Informational Text and Vocabulary

1. Important elements of the WarpSpeedNet and all **advertisements** include
   - **A** an enticement to buy and contact information.
   - **B** a discount offer for the first individuals to call.
   - **C** an Internet address and a toll-free phone number.
   - **D** a description of how to use the product.

2. According to the **contract,** subscribers agree to all of the following *except*
   - **A** pay WarpSpeedNet a fee for lost equipment.
   - **B** allow WarpSpeedNet to install equipment.
   - **C** return equipment to WarpSpeedNet after service ends.
   - **D** notify WarpSpeedNet about defective equipment.

3. While the purpose of the advertisement is to persuade you to buy a product, the purpose of the **instruction manual** is to
   - **A** lay out the responsibilities of the Warp-SpeedNet company.
   - **B** describe how to install, use, and maintain the cable equipment.
   - **C** explain why you should buy the cable service.
   - **D** provide all the information you need to make your purchasing decision.

4. If you have *authorization*, you have
   - **A** an error in your understanding.
   - **B** curiosity about an issue.
   - **C** official permission to do something.
   - **D** the ability to write clearly.

5. Something that has been *disconnected* is
   - **A** cut off.
   - **B** not appropriate.
   - **C** thrown away.
   - **D** acted upon.

6. If a project is *discontinued*, it is
   - **A** reduced.
   - **B** not perfect.
   - **C** not easy.
   - **D** stopped.

Writing Skills Focus

Timed └Writing Compose a paragraph that critiques the advertisement you read. Specify which elements are most helpful and which are least helpful. Which features do you think are fair, unfair, or misleading? Use information from the document to explain your decisions.

What Do
You
Think
Now

What have you learned about making smart consumer decisions?

SweetPlayer Documents

Read with a Purpose Read these consumer documents to determine their purpose.

Choosing an MP3 Player Now Juan is ready to use that high-speed modem. His first stop? MP3s and fast downloads! MP3 is an audio format, a software code that turns sounds into information a computer can understand. MP3 squeezes good sound quality into a small package. The sound-size combination makes MP3 the most popular audio format used today. Juan checks out the rules for downloading MP3s on the Internet.

IS IT LEGAL?

The Internet is full of music. You can get your favorite hit in MP3 format with a single click. It's easy, it's free—and it could be illegal. Many music sites contain music that someone has digitally copied from a CD and then placed where other people can download it. It's a convenient and popular practice, but it is not legal. So what is legal?

1. You may rip tracks from a CD you own to a computer as long as they are for your own use and not for the use of other people.

2. You may download free promotional tracks. This is an increasingly popular way for artists to introduce their work to you. Free and promotional tracks are clearly marked, usually under the heading "Free Music." There are often CDs for sale by the artist, too. Watch

out, though. If a friend wants the same track, he or she will have to download it. It is not legal for you to copy a CD you downloaded from the Internet.

3. You may buy the track for your own use. Many sites, including those of more and more record companies, are now offering songs for sale in this manner.

Rule of thumb: If the way in which music is to be downloaded doesn't fit any of the three situations described above, the process probably isn't legal. When in doubt, check the copyright notice on the site. **Ⓐ**

Ⓐ **Read and Discuss** What <u>critical</u> information about downloading music is contained in this box?

🌐 Internet

Reading an Advertisement Juan can't wait to start listening to music on the family's computer. He needs the right software and has narrowed his search to a product called SweetPlayer—but which version should he get? Let's look at the Internet advertisement.

SWEET PLAYER

HOME   PLAYER   MP3   RADIO   ABOUT US

SWEETPLAYER
THE BEST FREE MP3 PLAYER

Try it for 30 days, risk free.*

SWEETPLAYER

SweetPlayer gives you:

- fast and easy one-click downloading of MP3 files
- access to any of 2,500+ Web radio stations
- sound close to CD quality, with 128 Kbps data rate

And for a *limited time* you get SweetPlayer Deluxe for the introductory price of $19.95 (suggested retail price $29.95).** **B**

DOWNLOAD NOW

SWEETPLAYER *Deluxe*

SweetPlayer Deluxe offers all the features of SweetPlayer; plus it

- creates, edits, and organizes play lists
- rips CDs to MP3 files quickly and easily
- provides 256 Kbps, which deliver CD-quality sound
- personalizes your look with a choice of 100+ skins

DOWNLOAD NOW

*After 30 days, software will require an activation code. Upon receipt of payment, purchaser will be sent the activation code by e-mail, fax, or U.S. mail. **C**

**Special offer ends 6/15/10.

B **Reading Focus** **Scanning** Scan this advertisement to learn how much SweetPlayer Deluxe costs.

C **Informational Focus** **Consumer Documents** How is the placement of this information similar to the fine print in the WarpSpeedNet product information?

Following Download Directions Juan clicks on the button to download SweetPlayer Deluxe. The following downloading directions appear on the screen:

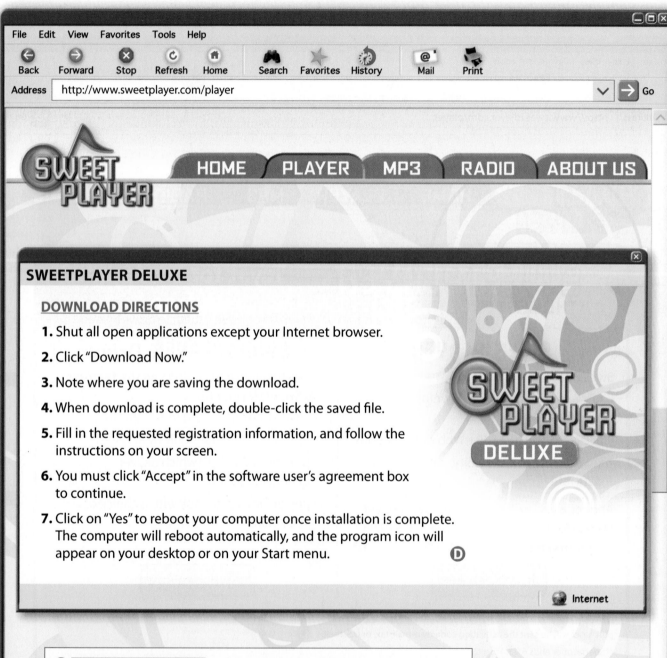

File   Edit   View   Favorites   Tools   Help

Back   Forward   Stop   Refresh   Home   Search   Favorites   History   Mail   Print

Address   http://www.sweetplayer.com/player   Go

SWEET PLAYER

HOME   PLAYER   MP3   RADIO   ABOUT US

SWEETPLAYER DELUXE

DOWNLOAD DIRECTIONS

1. Shut all open applications except your Internet browser.

2. Click "Download Now."

3. Note where you are saving the download.

4. When download is complete, double-click the saved file.

5. Fill in the requested registration information, and follow the instructions on your screen.

6. You must click "Accept" in the software user's agreement box to continue.

7. Click on "Yes" to reboot your computer once installation is complete. The computer will reboot automatically, and the program icon will appear on your desktop or on your Start menu. **D**

SWEET PLAYER DELUXE

Internet

D **Informational Focus** **Consumer Documents** Contrast these download directions with those of the instruction manual on pages 696–697. What is different about how the information is organized?

Reading a Software User's Agreement Even though he plans to click "Accept," Juan reads the software user's agreement carefully. (Remember that a user agreement is a form of **contract.**) It is long and complicated. Here are the parts that grab Juan's attention:

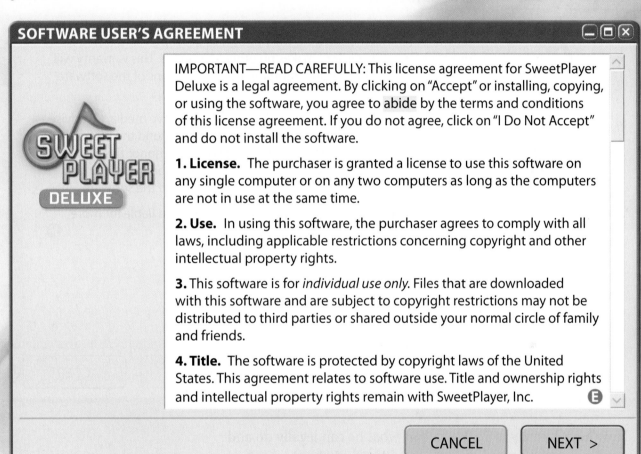

SOFTWARE USER'S AGREEMENT

IMPORTANT—READ CAREFULLY: This license agreement for SweetPlayer Deluxe is a legal agreement. By clicking on "Accept" or installing, copying, or using the software, you agree to abide by the terms and conditions of this license agreement. If you do not agree, click on "I Do Not Accept" and do not install the software.

1. License. The purchaser is granted a license to use this software on any single computer or on any two computers as long as the computers are not in use at the same time.

2. Use. In using this software, the purchaser agrees to comply with all laws, including applicable restrictions concerning copyright and other intellectual property rights.

3. This software is for *individual use only*. Files that are downloaded with this software and are subject to copyright restrictions may not be distributed to third parties or shared outside your normal circle of family and friends.

4. Title. The software is protected by copyright laws of the United States. This agreement relates to software use. Title and ownership rights and intellectual property rights remain with SweetPlayer, Inc. **E**

CANCEL   NEXT >

E **Informational Focus** Consumer Documents What would happen if Juan let a friend borrow this software?

Vocabulary **abide** (uh BYD) (with *by*) *v.:* accept and follow.

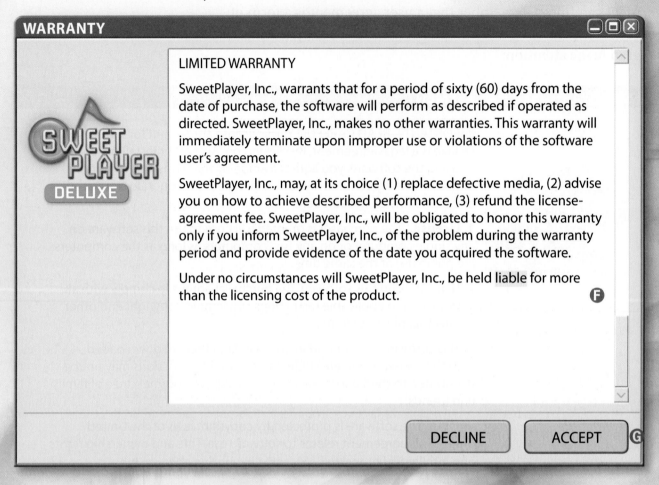

Reading a Limited Warranty Before clicking "Accept,"
Juan also reads the warranty.

WARRANTY

LIMITED WARRANTY

SweetPlayer, Inc., warrants that for a period of sixty (60) days from the date of purchase, the software will perform as described if operated as directed. SweetPlayer, Inc., makes no other warranties. This warranty will immediately terminate upon improper use or violations of the software user's agreement.

SweetPlayer, Inc., may, at its choice (1) replace defective media, (2) advise you on how to achieve described performance, (3) refund the license-agreement fee. SweetPlayer, Inc., will be obligated to honor this warranty only if you inform SweetPlayer, Inc., of the problem during the warranty period and provide evidence of the date you acquired the software.

Under no circumstances will SweetPlayer, Inc., be held liable for more than the licensing cost of the product. **F**

DECLINE   ACCEPT **G**

Now Juan is ready to go. He knows what he can legally do and what the company must legally provide. He clicks "Accept."

F **Informational Focus** Consumer Documents Explain whether the features of the SweetPlayer warranty are similar to those of the WarpSpeedNet warranty on page 698.

G **Read and Discuss** When Juan accepts the warranty, what does that mean?

Vocabulary **liable** (LY uh buhl) *adj.*: legally responsible.

Read with a Purpose What is the purpose of these consumer documents?

CONSUMER DOCUMENTS
Applying Your Skills

Reading Standard 2.1 Compare and contrast the features and elements of consumer materials to gain meaning from documents (e.g., warranties, contracts, product information, instruction manuals).

SweetPlayer Documents
Standards Review

Informational Text and Vocabulary

1. The "Accept" button on the **software user's agreement** takes the place of a

A description of services.

B catalog of equipment.

C feature of a warranty.

D signature on a contract.

2. The SweetPlayer download **instructions** are similar to an **instructional manual** because both

A include terms of an agreement.

B explain how to do something.

C persuade you to purchase a product.

D detail costs and services.

3. The **advertisement** and the **software user's agreement** are alike in that they both

A offer important information about the product.

B entice the reader to buy the product.

C discuss legal terms and conditions of use.

D tell the buyer how to get a refund.

4. The **software user's agreement** and the **warranty** are different in that the first

A describes the product, while the second describes the company.

B is a legal document, while the second is not.

C outlines mainly what the seller must do, while the second outlines mainly what the buyer must do.

D outlines mainly what the buyer must do, while the second outlines mainly what the seller must do.

5. If you are *liable* for something, you are

A responsible for it.

B unhappy with it.

C not connected with it.

D limited by it.

6. When a writer encourages people to *abide* by a law, she wants readers to

A challenge the law.

B rewrite the law.

C follow the law.

D shorten the law.

Writing Skills Focus

Timed └Writing Write a short essay that specifies the benefits and risks of skimming these complex consumer documents. List two examples of how skimming is helpful and two examples of how it can be harmful.

What Do You Think Now

After reading these documents, what questions would you ask before making a major purchase?

Following Technical Directions

CONTENTS

What Do You Think?

How can following instructions help you in your daily life?

 QuickWrite

List a task that instructions helped you complete. Which directions did you follow exactly? Which did you follow loosely?

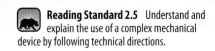

Reading Standard 2.5 Understand and explain the use of a complex mechanical device by following technical directions.

Guide to Computers

Informational Text Focus

Technical Directions Many products come with instruction manuals that explain how the product works. The manuals also outline basic parts and functions and <u>specify</u> the steps to assemble or operate the product. When the product is a scientific, electronic, or mechanical device, these instructions are called **technical directions.** If you skip steps or perform them out of order, the device may not work. You can understand and explain the use of a <u>complex</u> mechanical device by following technical directions. These directions often contain

- a parts list or glossary of <u>critical</u> terms that you'll need to know
- illustrations, diagrams, and photos that show key steps
- clearly labeled instructions that appear in a logical sequence

Reading Skills Focus

Understanding Graphics Instruction manuals may include illustrations, diagrams, and photos. These visual elements—often called **figures**—can help you understand what is being described.

Into Action As you read the following texts, note what types of figures are provided and what type of information they convey.

	What the Graphics Tell Me
Photos	
Diagrams	
Illustrations	

Writing Skills Focus

Preparing for Timed ∟Writing As you read, notice how the steps in the technical directions follow a logical progression. Write down any questions you have about <u>elements</u> that are unclear or steps that seem to be out of sequence.

Reader/Writer
Notebook
Use your **RWN** to complete the activities for this selection.

Vocabulary

functions (FUHNGK shuhnz) *n.:* uses; purposes. *A computer's many functions include calculating data and storing information.*

corresponding (kawr uh SPAHN dihng) *adj.:* matching; equivalent. *Be careful to plug the cable into the corresponding outlet.*

secure (sih KYUR) *v.:* fix firmly in place. *Be sure to secure the cord firmly in the port on the back of the computer.*

Language Coach

Multiple-Meaning Words When you read technical documents, you might come across words that have more than one meaning. For example, *functions* can be a noun meaning "events" and a verb meaning "works." What is another meaning of *functions*? Consider the Vocabulary word *secure*. What other meanings does this word have?

Learn It Online
Do pictures help you learn? Try the *PowerNotes* lesson at:

go.hrw.com | H8-707 |

GUIDE TO COMPUTERS

Figure 1 *Believe it or not, this MP3 player contains a computer!*

Read with a Purpose
Read to understand how to operate a complex mechanical device.

WHAT IS A COMPUTER?

Did a computer help you wake up this morning? You might think of a computer as something you use to send e-mails or surf the Internet, but computers are around you all the time. Computers are in alarm clocks, cars, phones, and even MP3 players. An MP3 player, like the one in **Figure 1,** allows you to build your own music lists and carry thousands of songs with you wherever you go.

A **computer** is an electronic device that performs tasks by processing and storing information. A computer performs a task when it is given a command and has the instructions necessary to carry out that command. Computers do not operate by themselves, or "think."

Basic Functions
The basic functions a computer performs are shown in **Figure 2.** The information you give to a computer is called *input.* Downloading songs onto your MP3 player or setting your alarm clock is a type of input. To perform a task, a computer processes the input, changing it to a desired form. Processing could mean adding a list of numbers, executing a drawing, or even moving a piece of equipment. Input doesn't have to be processed immediately; it can be stored until it is needed. Computers store information in their *memory.* For example, your MP3 player stores the songs you have chosen to input. It can then process this stored information by playing the songs you request. *Output* is the final result of the task performed by the computer. The output of an MP3 player is the music you hear when you put on your headphones! **(A)**

(A) **Read and Discuss** What point is the author making here?

Vocabulary **functions** (FUHNGK shuhnz) *n.:* uses; purposes.

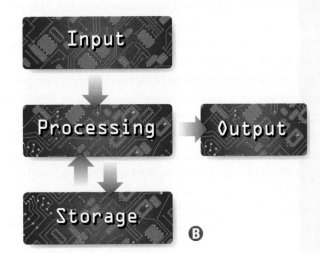

Figure 2 *The Functions of a Computer*

COMPUTER HARDWARE

For each function of a computer, there is a corresponding part of the computer where that function occurs. *Hardware* refers to the parts, or equipment, that make up a computer. As you read about each piece of hardware, refer to **Figure 3.**

Input Devices

An *input device* is a piece of hardware that feeds information to the computer. You can enter information into a computer by using a keyboard, mouse, scanner, digitizing pad and pen, or digitizing camera—or even your own voice!

Central Processing Unit

A computer performs tasks within an area called the *central processing unit,* or CPU. In a personal computer, the CPU is a microprocessor. Input goes through the CPU for immediate processing or for storage in memory. The CPU is where the computer does calculations, solves problems, and executes the instructions given to it. Some computers now come with two—or more—CPUs to process information more effectively.

B **Reading Focus** **Understanding Graphics** What do the arrows in this diagram indicate?

Vocabulary **corresponding** (kawr uh SPAHN dihng) *adj.:* matching; equivalent.

Memory

Information can be stored in the computer's memory until it is needed. CD-ROMs, DVDs, and flash drives inserted into a computer and hard disks inside a computer have memory to store information. Two types of memory are *ROM* (read-only memory) and *RAM* (random-access memory).

ROM is permanent. It handles functions such as computer start-up, maintenance, and hardware management. ROM normally cannot be added to or changed, and it cannot be lost when the computer is turned off. On the other hand, RAM is temporary. It stores information only while that information is being used. RAM is sometimes called working memory. The more RAM a computer has, the more information can be input and the more powerful the computer is.

Figure 3 *Computer Hardware* **C**

Keyboard

Modem

Mouse

CPU

RAM

ROM

CD/DVD drive

Hard disk

C **Reading Focus** **Understanding Graphics** How does this graphic help you understand the components of a computer?

Output Devices

Once a computer performs a task, it shows the results of the task on an *output device*. Monitors, printers, and speaker systems are all examples of output devices.

Modems

One piece of computer hardware that serves as an input device as well as an output device is a *modem*. Modems allow computers to communicate. One computer can input information into another computer over a telephone or cable line as long as each computer has its own network connection. In this way, modems permit computers to "talk" with other computers. **Ⓓ**

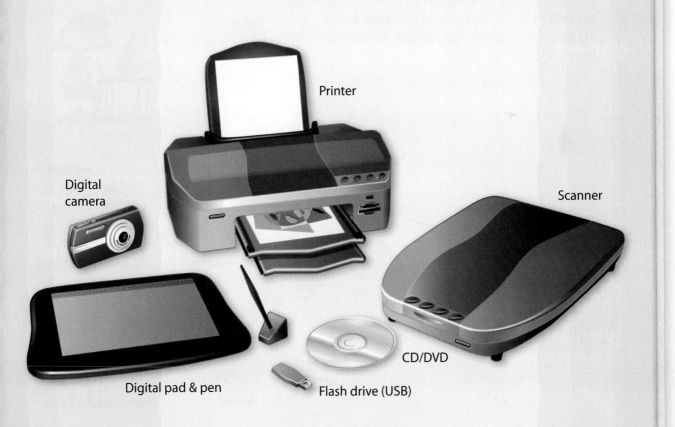

Printer

Digital camera

Scanner

Digital pad & pen

CD/DVD

Flash drive (USB)

Ⓓ **Read and Discuss** What does this section say about the computer's hardware?

THE INTERNET—A GLOBAL NETWORK

Thanks to high-speed connections and computer software, it is possible to connect many computers and allow them to communicate with one another. That's what the **Internet** is—a huge computer network consisting of millions of computers that can all share information with one another. **Ⓔ**

How the Internet Works

Computers can connect to one another on the Internet by using a modem to dial into an Internet service provider, or ISP. A home computer connects to an ISP over a phone or cable line. A school, business, or other group can connect all of its computers to form a local area network (LAN). Then, a single network connection can be used to connect the LAN to an ISP. As depicted in **Figure 4,** ISPs are connected globally by satellite. And that's how computers go global!

Figure 4 *Through a series of connections like these, every computer on the Internet can store information.*

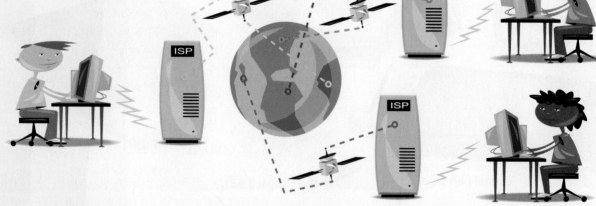

Ⓔ | Read and Discuss | What is the purpose of the Internet?

HOW TO SET UP A DESKTOP COMPUTER

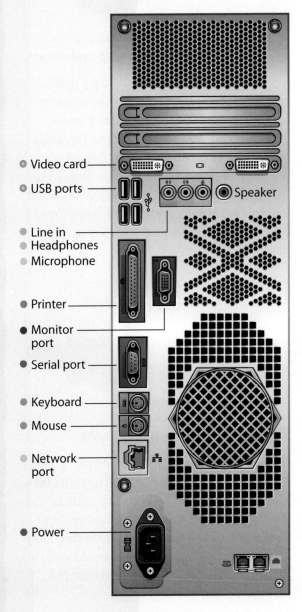

- Video card
- USB ports
- Line in
- Headphones
- Microphone
- Printer
- Monitor port
- Serial port
- Keyboard
- Mouse
- Network port
- Power

Speaker

Figure 5 *Computer Connections*

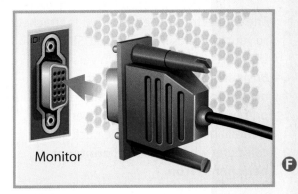

Monitor

❿

STEP 1 Connect the monitor to the computer.

The monitor has two cords. One cord, the **monitor interface cable,** lets the computer communicate with the monitor. The monitor cable connects to the video port (the port designated for monitors) at the back of the computer. The connector on this cord is a plug with pins in it; the pins correspond to holes in the video port on the computer. This cable probably has screws to secure the connection. The other cord is the **monitor's power cord,** which plugs into a wall outlet or **surge protector,** a plug-in device that protects electronic equipment from high-voltage electrical surges (see Step 5).

---

❿ **Reading Focus** **Understanding Graphics**
How are the two graphics on this page different? What is the purpose of each?

Vocabulary **secure** (sih KYUR) *v.:* fix firmly in place.

USB

STEP 2 Connect the printer to the computer.

The connector on the cable that is attached to your printer is most likely a USB cable. USB ports (USB stands for Universal Serial Bus) can accept any device with a USB connector. Connect one end to the back of your printer. Then connect the other end to an available USB port on the back of your computer where you see a **printer** or **peripherals icon.**

Keyboard/mouse

STEP 3 Connect the keyboard and mouse.

Look at the **connector** on the cord that is attached to the keyboard or mouse. If this connector is round, plug the cord into a matching port on the back of the computer. If the connector on the cord is flat, plug it into any available USB port. (See Step 2 illustration.) If you are using a cordless keyboard or mouse, connect it to the computer by following the manufacturer's technical directions.

Network

STEP 4 Connect the modem to the computer by using a network cable.

Connect the **network cable** to the network port on the back of your computer. Connect the other end of the network cable to your modem. As long as you have an active Internet connection, the software should automatically detect that you are connected to the Internet when your computer starts.

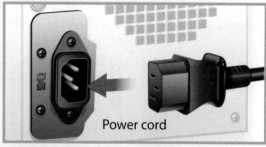

Power cord

STEP 5 Connect the power cords.

The **power cord** is a three-pronged, grounded cord that you attach to your computer. First, attach one end of the power cord to the computer; then, plug the other end of the cord into a **surge protector.** Plug the surge protector into a grounded wall outlet. Turn on the monitor and then the computer, and you are ready to go! **ⓖ**

ⓖ Informational Focus Technical Directions
Why are diagrams and text both included in these directions?

Read with a Purpose What is the purpose of this document?

TECHNICAL DIRECTIONS
Applying Your Skills

Reading Standard 2.5 Understand and explain the use of a complex mechanical device by following technical directions.

Guide to Computers
Standards Review

Informational Text and Vocabulary

1. The purpose of these **technical directions** is to
  A convince you to buy a new computer.
  B establish legal responsibility for a computer.
  C describe how to install a computer.
  D explain the possible uses of a computer.

2. Figure 3 gives information about
  A MP3 setups.
  B a computer's hardware.
  C steps to avoid.
  D output devices.

3. According to these **directions,** when should you connect the modem to your computer?
  A before you connect anything else
  B after you hook up the monitor
  C before you connect the power cords
  D after you connect the keyboard and mouse

4. The purpose of a modem is to
  A protect the computer from power surges.
  B let the computer communicate with the monitor.
  C store information only while that information is being used.
  D allow computers to communicate.

5. Another word for *functions* is
  A breakdowns.
  B circuits.
  C purposes.
  D reasons.

6. What are *corresponding* parts?
  A parts that match or fit together
  B parts that use electrical current
  C parts that are connected to the Internet
  D parts that are broken or not working

7. If a plug is *secure,* it is
  A connected to the Internet.
  B firmly attached.
  C waterproof.
  D very powerful.

Writing Skills Focus

Timed Writing Think of something you know how to do well that involves a technical device. Write a list of instructions that explains how to do the skill you chose. The task could be operating a familiar device, such as a DVD or MP3 player. If you are unable to think of a particular task you are familiar with, find instructions for operating a technical device, and compose a new list of instructions in your own words.

What Do You Think Now? What new ideas do you have about the role directions play in daily life?

Writing Workshop

Writing for Career Development

Write with a Purpose

Write a letter addressed to someone who is in charge of a business, a school, or another organization or institution. Your **purpose** is to communicate a clear, important message. Your **audience** is the person who will receive the letter.

Then, write a memorandum with the **purpose** of following up on the information in the business letter.

A Good Business Letter

- follows the format for business letters
- is purposeful and succinct
- maintains a friendly but formal tone
- uses the addressee's title and is suited to its audience
- states the purpose, or main idea, early in the letter
- is grammatically correct and free of spelling errors

A Good Memo

- follows the format for a memo
- is brief and to the point

See page 724 for complete rubric.

Reader/Writer Notebook

Use your **RWN** to complete the activities for this workshop.

Think as a Reader/Writer You will probably have to write business letters and memos (short for "memorandums") at some point in your career development. To succeed, you will need to know how to write them well. Here is a sample business letter and a follow-up memo:

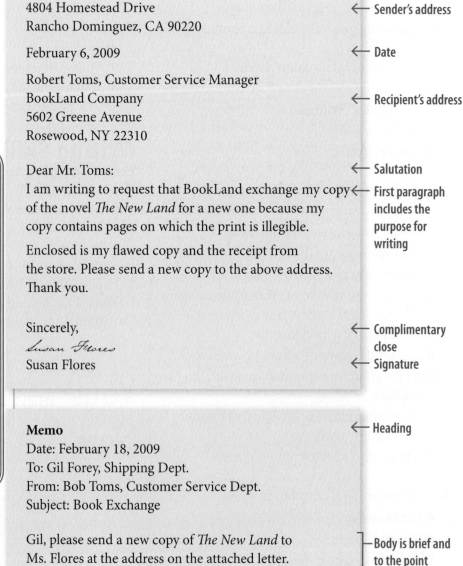

4804 Homestead Drive
Rancho Dominguez, CA 90220

← Sender's address

February 6, 2009

← Date

Robert Toms, Customer Service Manager
BookLand Company
5602 Greene Avenue
Rosewood, NY 22310

← Recipient's address

Dear Mr. Toms:

← Salutation

I am writing to request that BookLand exchange my copy of the novel *The New Land* for a new one because my copy contains pages on which the print is illegible.

← First paragraph includes the purpose for writing

Enclosed is my flawed copy and the receipt from the store. Please send a new copy to the above address. Thank you.

Sincerely,
Susan Flores
Susan Flores

← Complimentary close
← Signature

Memo
Date: February 18, 2009
To: Gil Forey, Shipping Dept.
From: Bob Toms, Customer Service Dept.
Subject: Book Exchange

← Heading

Gil, please send a new copy of *The New Land* to Ms. Flores at the address on the attached letter.

← Body is brief and to the point

Writing Standard 1.6 Revise writing for word choice; appropriate organization; consistent point of view; and transitions between paragraphs, passages, and ideas. 2.5 Write documents related to career development, including simple business letters and job applications: a. Present information purposefully and succinctly and meet the needs of the intended audience. b. Follow the conventional format for the type of document (e.g., letter of inquiry, memorandum).

Think About the Professional Model

With a partner, discuss the following questions about the model:

1. What was the purpose of this letter? Did this letter fulfill that purpose?

2. How would you describe the tone of the letter?

3. What makes the tone of the memo slightly different?

Prewriting

Choose a Topic

Think about the kinds of situations that might call for a business letter. Usually, the topic of a business letter is of some importance and is treated seriously. Read the Idea Starters at the right, and use your imagination to supply the details for each situation.

Think About Your Audience and Purpose

Take some time to think about the **purpose** for writing your letter. Are you making a request? suggesting something new? expressing your satisfaction—or dissatisfaction—with a product or a situation? What do you want to see happen? Before you begin writing your letter, draft a simple statement of purpose in your **RWN.**

Considering your **audience** when you are writing a business letter is also important. Remember that you are writing to this person because you think that he or she has the power or ability to give you a job, produce your new invention, financially support your team, refund your money, or change the way something happens. Fill in a chart like the one below to help you think about your audience.

What are the values and the interests of the audience?	What are the audience's worries and concerns?	What concerns do you have in common?	What questions will your audience have?

Addresses and Titles

Before you send a business letter, you should be sure that the addresses—your address and your recipient's address—are correct. You also need to be sure that you use the correct title for the person you are writing to.

Idea Starters

Here are some situations that might call for a business letter:

- applying for a job
- expressing your opinion about a product
- proposing a new program for an organization
- requesting information about a company
- asking a business to sponsor your baseball team

Your Turn _____

Get Started Choose a topic for your business letter, and draft a **statement of purpose.** Then, to help you think about your **audience,** fill in a chart like the one at the left in your **RWN.** You'll also need to confirm that you have the proper title and address for the recipient of your letter.

 Learn It Online
To see how one writer structured a business letter, use the interactive writer's model at:

go.hrw.com   H8-717   Go

Kinds of Business Letters

Business letters generally fall into five categories. Determining the kind of letter you are writing will help you meet the needs of your intended audience. Which category does your letter fall into?

- **Letters of inquiry** request information or an answer.
- **Job application letters** express your interest in a particular job and tell an employer why you are suited to that job.
- **Letters of complaint** explain a problem and request a response that will solve the problem.
- **Letters of commendation** are usually written to let an employee's supervisor know that the employee has done a good job.
- **Thank-you letters** are written directly to the person who has done something you appreciate.

Outline and Format Your Letter

Use the outline below to help you format and organize the information in your business letter.

Business Letter Outline
Heading
Date, with month spelled out
Recipient's Address
Salutation
or greeting, followed by a colon
Body
Paragraph 1: Purpose (why you are writing the letter).
Paragraph 2: Information relevant to your goal, including questions and information about your background.
Paragraph 3: Express appreciation to the recipient in advance for taking the time to take action on your request.
Closing
followed by a comma
Signature
handwritten
sender's name, typed out

Your Turn

Create an Outline In your **RWN,** prepare an outline for your business letter. Think carefully about the body of your letter. Make sure you include all the necessary background information and ask any questions that are necessary for achieving your goal. Identify what you want your letter's recipient to do.

Drafting

Draft Your Letter

Use the outline on page 718 and the framework at the right as guides for drafting your letter. Remember to stay focused on what you want your letter to accomplish—your purpose in writing the letter. Also, keep in mind your audience's values and concerns.

> **Framework for Body of a Business Letter**
>
> **Introduction**
> - State your purpose for writing.
>
> **Body**
> - Include background information.
> - Ask questions.
>
> **Conclusion**
> - Express appreciation to the recipient.

Consider Your Tone

When you speak to a person who is in a position of authority—your school principal, for instance—you are careful to maintain a respectful tone and speak more formally than you do with your friends. Your tone of voice when you speak reflects your attitude. When you write, your choice of words and the way you write about your subject give your writing its tone. The tone of your business letter reflects your attitude toward the subject you are writing about and meets the needs of your intended audience. All business letters should be written in a formal style and tone. They should not include sentence fragments or slang.

The Memo

The term *memo* comes from the longer word *memorandum*. Both terms come from the same root as the word *memory*. In general, the purpose of a business memo is to remind the audience of something or to point something out quickly and simply. Memos are generally sent to people who work with the writer. Because the sender and the receiver know each other, a memo might be slightly less formal than a business letter.

Grammar Link Use Formal Language

In both business letters and memos, replace slang and informal language with a formal style to maintain a respectful tone.

Informal Language	Revision
Hi, Ms. Santoro! (The informality is not appropriate in a business letter.)	Dear Ms. Santoro: (Replace the informal greeting with the standard salutation.)
Thanks! (Avoid using exclamation points in business letters.)	Thanks for your help. (Slight informality can be appropriate for some audiences.)
I think your new product is really cool. (The slang term "cool" is not appropriate.)	I think your new product works remarkably well. (Replace slang with formal language.)

Writing Tip

Here are a few things to keep in mind when you are writing a business letter:
- Use a formal form of address.
- If you do not know the name of the person to whom you are writing, you may use the salutation "To Whom It May Concern," followed by a colon.
- Use a standard complimentary close such as "Sincerely" followed by a comma.
- Sign your full name.
- Type your full name below your signature.

Your Turn _____

Write Your Draft Following the outline, write a draft of your business letter. Be sure your letter
- clearly states your purpose for writing
- is written in a formal tone
- contains all the elements of a business letter (including the date, both your and the recipient's addresses, a salutation, and a closing)
- includes a clear statement of purpose

Peer Review

Exchange letters with a writing partner. Ask your partner to read the letter as if it were addressed to him or her. Ask how well he or she thinks your audience will receive the letter.

Then, ask your writing partner if your memo is clear and to the point. Use the chart at the right as your guide.

Evaluating and Revising

Read the questions in the left-hand column of the chart and then use the tips in the middle column to help you make revisions to your letter or memo. In the right-hand column you'll find techniques you can use to revise your draft.

Business Letter and Memo: Guidelines for Content and Organization

Evaluation Questions	Tips	Revision Techniques
1. Is your purpose stated clearly?	**Underline** the sentence or sentences that state your main point.	**Add** a statement that makes clear your purpose for writing.
2. Have you written succinctly and to the point?	**Circle** any information that does not support your purpose in writing.	**Delete** any unnecessary information.
3. Have you chosen a tone that is appropriate for your audience?	**Put a star** next to instances of casual phrasing or slang.	**Replace** overly informal word choices with more formal words.
4. Have you included all the necessary background information?	**Draw a box** around the part of your letter that includes background information.	**Elaborate** by adding explanations and addressing reader's concerns.
5. Have you followed the standard business letter and memo formats?	**Label** each section of your letter and memo, and **circle** the correct punctuation.	**Add** any missing parts of the letter and memo, and **correct** punctuation.
6. Have you checked your letter for grammar, punctuation, and spelling errors?	**Circle** any problems that you find.	**Correct** any problems you find.

Read this student's draft and note the comments about its strengths and suggestions on how it could be improved.

Student Draft

March 2, 2009

Henry Diaz, Director
Camp Sunset
10902 Sunset Road
Tampa, FL 33601

Dear Mr. Diaz:

For the last five years, I have attended Camp Sunset as a camper, moving from Novice status when I was eight years old to my current rank as Camper II. Now at age 13, I am ready to use my experience to serve as a counselor for boys age 8-10 in the Pioneer section of Camp Sunset. My completed application for the position is attached.

I have learned the routines and programs of Camp Sunset: the safety procedures for swimming and hiking, the opportunities for public service, and the creativity of the crafts programs. In addition, my five years as a Boy Scout have prepared me for the job as a counselor at Camp Sunset. I have earned badges in Leadership and Community Service involving supervision of younger scouts. A letter of recommendation from my Scout Master, Gerald Fisher, is attached.

I would make a totally awesome counselor! Take a look at my application!

Yours truly,

Cedric Kinney
Cedric Kinney

← Cedric has included the proper information in the **date** and **recipient's address.**

← Here, Cedric **introduces** himself to his audience.

The **body** of Cedric's letter provides **support** for his application for the position of
← camp counselor.

← For most of the letter, Cedric maintains a **serious tone** that is suitable for an application for a position of responsibility.

MINI-LESSON **How to Keep Your Tone Consistent**

When Cedric reviewed the draft of his letter he noticed a shift in tone in his last paragraph. Here is his revision:

Cedric's Revision of the Last Paragraph

~~I would make a totally awesome counselor! Take a look at my application!~~ I am eager to apply my experiences as a camper and as a Scout to the job of camp counselor. Please consider my application.

Your Turn _____

Maintain a Serious Tone

Review your letter to be sure that you have not made word choices that are too informal for the situation. Eliminate slang that you might use in writing to a close friend, but that is not appropriate here.

Student Draft *continues*

Memo
To: Phil Stevens
From: Cedric Kinney, Counselor

Hey, Phil!
In response to your request for an RSVP: 20 campers from my group will attend the Bon Voyage party. I hope that we will have good weather on that day. Some campers have expressed concern about the possibility of rain.

Cedric is missing information from the **heading** of his memo.

Cedric strays from the **main point** of his memo here.

MINI-LESSON ▸ **How to Revise and Format Your Memo**

The person or people who receive a memo expect the information in the heading to be presented in a specific order so that they can read it quickly. Cedric needed to reformat the head of his memo and eliminate the unnecessary—and too informal—salutation.

The body of a memo should be succinct and to the point. Cedric added non-essential information about his hopes for good weather and neglected essential information about the total number of people attending his party. He corrected both problems in his revision.

Cedric's Revision

Memo
Date: August 22, 2009
To: Phil Stevens, Camp Coordinator
From: Cedric Kinney, Counselor
Subject: RSVP for Bon Voyage Party

~~Hey, Phil!~~
In response to your request for an RSVP: 20 campers from my group will attend the Bon Voyage party. ~~I hope that we will have good weather on that day. Some campers have expressed concern about the possibility of rain.~~
In addition, 14 parents will also be coming to the festivities.

Your Turn _____

Be Succinct but Complete Keep your memo succinct, but do not neglect to include information that your audience needs. Ask yourself these questions as you edit your memo:

- Have I included all of the essential information?
- Have I eliminated unnecessary and distracting details?

Proofreading and Publishing

Proofreading

You have revised your business letter and your memo. Now it is time to polish them, eliminating any errors that might distract your readers. Edit your letter and your memo to correct any misspellings, punctuation errors, and problems in sentence structure.

> ### Grammar Link Formatting Your Letter Properly
>
> If you follow the conventional format of a business letter, your reader will take the letter more seriously. Use one of the following styles to format your business letter:
>
>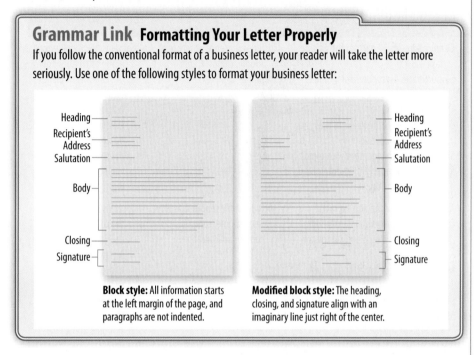
>
> **Block style:** All information starts at the left margin of the page, and paragraphs are not indented.
>
> **Modified block style:** The heading, closing, and signature align with an imaginary line just right of the center.

Publishing

Now it is time to publish your letter and memo to a wider audience. Here are some ways to share your documents:

- Do you know someone who writes and reads business letters and memos in his or her work? Give your documents to that person and ask for feedback.

- E-mail your documents to a friend, and ask him or her to reply as if your friend were the person addressed in the letter and memo.

Reflect on the Process
In your **RWN,** write a short response to the following questions:

1. Why do you think it is important to proofread business letters and memos?

2. What might a carefully prepared document suggest to you, as the recipient, about the writer?

Proofreading Tip
You will want the business letters and memos you write to be free of errors. Ask three peers to join a proofreading circle with you. Circulate your letters and memos so that three readers will review each letter and memo for errors.

Writing Tip
When writing a business letter, use only one side of unlined, full-size (8½" x 11") white paper. Type or word-process your letter, or use your best handwriting, using blue or black ink; single-space your letter. If the body contains more than one paragraph, leave a blank line between paragraphs.

Your Turn _____
Proofread and Publish
Proofread your letter and your memo, eliminating all errors in word choice, grammar, punctuation, and spelling. Be sure that you have followed the conventional format for business letters and memos.

Scoring Rubric

You can use the rubric below to evaluate your writing for career development, such as a business letter, memo, or job application.

Writing for Career Development	Organization and Focus	Sentence Structure	Conventions
4 • *Consistently* follows the proper format for the particular type of writing. • Presents information *purposefully* and *succinctly*. • Presents ideas that are *meaningful* and *insightful*, supported with *fully elaborated* explanations and *specific* examples.	• *Clearly* addresses all parts of the writing task. • Demonstrates a *clear* understanding of purpose, stating it early in the correspondence. • *Consistently* meets the needs of the intended audience. • Shows *focused* engagement with topic. • Shows *effective* organization throughout, with *clear* transitions.	• Includes sentence *variety* (e.g., simple, complex, compound-complex).	• Contains *few, if any,* errors in the conventions of the English language (grammar, punctuation, capitalization, spelling). These errors do **not** interfere with the reader's understanding of the writing.
3 • Follows the proper format for the particular type of writing, with *minor* lapses. • Presents information *relatively clearly*. • Presents ideas that are *mostly meaningful*, supported with a mixture of *general* and *specific* examples.	• Addresses *most* of the writing task. • Demonstrates a *general* understanding of purpose, stating it early in the correspondence. • Meets the needs of the intended audience. • Shows engagement with topic. • Shows *relatively effective* organization, with *minor* lapses.	• Includes *some* sentence *variety* (e.g., simple, complex, compound-complex).	• Contains *some errors* in the conventions of the English language (grammar, punctuation, capitalization, spelling). These errors do **not** interfere with the reader's understanding of the writing.
2 • *Inconsistently* follows the proper format for the particular type of writing. • Presents information, though often *unclearly*. • Presents ideas that may be *routine* and *predictable*, supported with *uneven* elaboration.	• Addresses *some* of the writing task. • Demonstrates a *general* understanding of purpose. • Meets the needs of the intended audience. • Shows *some* engagement with topic. • Shows *some* organization, with *noticeable gaps* in the logical flow of ideas.	• Includes *little* sentence variety.	• Contains *several errors* in the conventions of the English language (grammar, punctuation, capitalization, spelling). These errors **may** interfere with the reader's understanding of the writing.
1 • *Fails* to follow the proper format. • *Lacks* necessary information. • Presents *simplistic, unclear,* or *illogical* ideas, developed in only a *minimal* way, if at all.	• Addresses *only one or no* part of the writing task. • Demonstrates *no* understanding of purpose or audience. • *Fails* to show engagement with topic. • *Lacks* focus and organization.	• Includes *no* sentence variety.	• Contains *serious errors* in the conventions of the English language (grammar, punctuation, capitalization, spelling). These errors interfere with the reader's understanding of the writing.

Preparing for **Timed Writing**

Job Application

When responding to a prompt, use what you have learned from your reading, writing your business letter, and studying the rubric on page 724. Use the steps below to develop a response to the following prompt.

Writing Standard 2.5 Write documents related to career development, including simple business letters and job applications: a. Present information purposefully and succinctly and meet the needs of the intended audience. b. Follow the conventional format for the type of document (e. g., letter of inquiry, memorandum).

Writing Prompt

Write a business letter in which you apply for a job at a business or organization. Make sure you use the conventional business letter format.

Study the Prompt

Begin by reading the prompt carefully. Circle or underline key instructional words: *apply, job, business, organization, format*. Reread the prompt to make sure you understand your task.

Remember that a business letter is different from a personal letter in both content and style. The prompt is reminding you to use the business letter format. You must think back to what you have learned to use the correct style.

Tip: Spend about five minutes studying the prompt.

Plan Your Response

Think of a job you might like to do. Make sure it is something you have some qualifications for doing. Once you understand your task and have settled on your topic:

- identify the business or organization you'll be addressing
- write down your request for the job.
- record your qualifications for the job
- list the parts of a standard business letter that you'll need to include.

Tip: Spend about fifteen minutes planning your response to the prompt.

Respond to the Prompt

Begin writing your letter using the notes you've just made. You can start with the actual body of the letter and add the other elements (date, addresses, salutation) later. It may help to follow these guidelines:

- In the heading of your letter, include the date and recipient's address. If you choose to include your address, list it above that of the recipient.
- In the body, include a formal salutation, introduction and statement of purpose, support, and conclusion.
- In the closing, include a complimentary close (such as *Sincerely*), your signature, and your typed full name.

As you are writing, remember to use formal language and a respectful tone.

Tip: Spend about twenty minutes writing your draft.

Improve Your Response

Revising Go back to the key aspects of the prompt. Did you use the standard business letter format? Does your letter make clear your request?

Proofreading Take a few minutes to proofread your letter to correct errors in grammar, spelling, punctuation, and capitalization. Make sure all your edits are neat, and erase any stray marks.

Checking Your Final Copy Before you turn your letter in, read it one more time to catch any errors you may have missed.

Tip: Save ten minutes to improve your paper.

Media Workshop

Interpreting and Evaluating Visual Representations

View with a Purpose

In this workshop you will learn to interpret and evaluate media images. You will learn how to identify techniques used by illustrators, photographers, and graphic artists and explain the ways media images can be used to persuade viewers.

Think as a Reader/Writer

When you look at a photograph of yourself, you don't see the *real* you, but a representation of you. In fact, all media images are representations of reality that can shape people's ideas about the world. People who create these images make conscious choices about what an image will show and how it will show it. Therefore, the image reflects the point of view of the person who created it.

Interpret Visual Images

Content

The **content** of an image is what it shows—everything included in the image. The way an image maker chooses to present a subject is the most significant choice he or she will make. For example, the photographer who photographs the president tripping over an electrical cable will communicate a very different message than the one who shoots a posed portrait of the president.

Color

Image makers use **color** to create interest or to establish a mood. To create interest, an illustrator may use color to highlight the most important part of an image. A photographer may use a computer to color one part of a black-and-white photo to make it stand out.

Light and Shadow

An image maker may carefully place shadows in a work to make a subject look frightening or dramatic or romantic. Using plenty of light with few shadows can make the subject look real or approachable.

Point of View, or Angle

The angle at which you see the subject of an image can affect your impression. For example, seeing a photograph of a person taken from above makes the person look small and vulnerable. Photographing the same person from a low angle looking up makes the person look large and powerful, and perhaps even intimidating.

Media Tip

To create mood, illustrators may use cool colors, such as blues and greens, to make viewers feel more relaxed, or warm colors, such as reds and yellows, to make viewers feel energized.

Reader/Writer Notebook

Use your **RWN** to complete the activities for this workshop.

Listening and Speaking Standard

1.9 Interpret and evaluate the various ways in which visual image makers (e.g., graphic artists, illustrators, news photographers) communicate information and affect impressions and opinions.

Medium

A **medium** is the means by which an image is created. All images makers use the techniques just described, but media still have their own characteristics and techniques. For example, the persuasive power of photographs lies in our belief that "photographs do not lie"—that they show reality. However, as a photograph is being taken, the photographer can, under the right circumstances, use camera angles or lighting to alter the reality of the situation to suit a persuasive purpose. Even after developing a photo, a photographer can **crop,** or cut out, an unwanted part of a scene. Computer techniques make it easy to alter photographs, so today photographs may, indeed, lie.

Evaluate Visual Images

To interpret an evaluate a media image, consider the following:

General Questions	• Who created the image? Do I know of a bias this source has—either positive or negative feelings toward the subject? Does this bias affect the message? • For what purpose was this image created?
Questions About Content	• What impression do I get from the image about its subject? What opinion does the image maker wish to convey? • How is this version of reality similar to or different from what I know from my own experience? • What may have been left out of the image?
Questions About Color	• Is the image black-and-white, color, or both? • What mood do the color choices create? What parts of the image stand out because of color? Why might these parts be important?
Questions About Light and Shadow	• Is the light in the image even, or are there shadows? • What mood do the light and shadows create? Do shadows make the subject seem frightening or dramatic? What message does this send?
Questions About Point of View	• At what angle do I see the subject? A direct angle? an angle above the subject? a low angle? • What impression of the subject does the angle give me? Does the subject seem powerful? vulnerable?

Media Tip

The plural of *medium* is **media,** a term often applied to television, radio, newspapers, and the Internet.

Your Turn _____

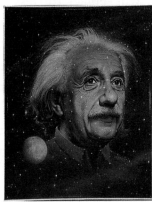

If you had seen only one of these portraits, how would you feel about Albert Einstein? What opinion would you have of this scientist and of his life's work? Use the questions in the chart at the left as you consider your response.

✳ Learn It Online

Learn more about interpreting and evaluating visual representations at the *MediaScope* mini-site:

go.hrw.com | H8-727 | **Go**

Informational Skills Review

Analyzing Documents   **Directions:** Read the following documents. Then, read and respond to the questions that follow.

All Channels Newsletter

April 20, 2007, Vol. 6, Issue 4

Going Digital:
What's Your IQ on DTV?

"What transition to DTV?" In a recent consumer survey, participants were asked if they had heard of the upcoming transition to digital television (DTV) broadcasting. More than half reported that they had seen, read, or heard no information about the changeover. Yet this major change is scheduled for February 17, 2009.

After that date, digital broadcasting will replace the less efficient analog method. DTV signals will be sent from local transmitters to homes. Analog TVs will no longer receive signals. To continue broadcast service, analog households have three options:

- Buy a TV with an HDTV (high definition television) tuner, which receives programming in several digital formats.
- Buy a converter box for each analog TV in the home. Such devices convert digital signals into analog form.
- Pay for cable or satellite services. Cable and satellite companies provide signal conversion.

Nearly 20 million U.S. households rely on over-the-air television signals, so if they do not make plans beforehand, their TVs will go dark. Given this scenario, an immediate, national educational program is needed. Toward that end, legislation on consumer education has been proposed in the House of Representatives.

Instructions for Using Your New HDTV Cable Converter Box
To view HDTV, follow these steps
(the first includes an important safety precaution):

1. Read all steps before connecting to the power source. DO NOT plug the converter box into the power outlet right away.

2. Connect the cable from the wall into the connector marked CABLE IN on the back of your converter box.

3. Connect the HDTV set to your VCR, following specific diagrams for stereo and nonstereo models. If there is no VCR, connect the set directly to the cable box.

4. Now plug the converter into the wall outlet. Wait until the clock on the converter box shows the correct time.

5. Press POWER on the converter box. Wait until the cable signal loads. This can take up to 10 minutes.

6. Turn to channel 99 for remote control programming. Select "Video Input" to view HDTV programming on the set.

LIMITED WARRANTY

Grant's TVs warrants this HDTV Cable Converter Box ("Product") against defects in material or workmanship as follows:

LABOR: For a period of one (1) year from the date of purchase, if this Product is determined to be defective, Grant's TVs will repair or replace the Product.

PARTS: Grant's TVs will supply, at no charge, new or rebuilt replacements in exchange for defective parts for a period of one (1) year.

ACCESSORIES: Parts and labor for all accessories are for one (1) year. (See other side for contact information and address.)

1. These HDTV documents (newsletter, instruction manual, warranty) are intended primarily to explain a situation to a
   A consumer.
   B cable company.
   C manufacturer.
   D salesperson.

2. The newsletter explains
   A the efficiency of DTV.
   B the 2009 switch to DTV.
   C buying converter boxes.
   D paying for satellite service.

3. The HDTV warranty covers
   A damage due to an accident.
   B damage due to adjustments.
   C damage due to defective parts.
   D damage due to misuse.

4. The newsletter and the instructions are alike in that both
   A explain how to install HDTV.
   B are legal documents.
   C explain terms and conditions.
   D give information about a product.

5. If your new HDTV converter box is broken, which document would you use to solve the problem?
   A technical directions
   B warranty
   C newsletter
   D converter box

Timed Writing

6. Imagine you had to show a neighbor how to switch from analog TV to digital TV. What documents might provide the clearest explanation? In two sentences, explain how you might help the neighbor.

Vocabulary Skills Review

Reading Standard 1.3 Use word meanings within the appropriate **context** and show ability to verify those meanings by definition, restatement, example, comparison, or contrast.

Context Clues **Directions:** Use context clues to determine the meaning of each italicized word or phrase in the following sentences.

1. "By clicking on the Accept button, you agree to *abide by* the rules explained in this license agreement." In this sentence, *abide by* means to

   A understand.

   B read.

   C share.

   D follow.

2. "According to the legal agreement, the company is not *liable* if a person gets hurt while using the product." In this sentence, *liable* means

   A sympathetic.

   B responsible.

   C happy.

   D flexible.

3. "Avalanches occasionally happen; people who ski in the wilderness are *potentially* making a dangerous choice." In this sentence, *potentially* means

   A definitely.

   B possibly.

   C suddenly.

   D rarely.

4. "The students took a *proposal* to the principal to offer free ice cream in the lunchroom next year." In this sentence, a *proposal* is a(n)

   A argument.

   B invitation.

   C problem.

   D suggestion.

5. "Uneven or broken sidewalks can be safety *hazards* for skateboarders." In this sentence, *hazards* are

   A dangers.

   B inconveniences.

   C challenges.

   D skills.

6. "'Input' and 'Output' are two *functions* that make the computer run smoothly." In this sentence, *functions* means

   A names.

   B uses.

   C bugs.

   D plans.

Academic Vocabulary

Directions: Use context clues to determine the meaning of the italicized Academic Vocabulary.

7. "It is *critical* to follow directions when assembling a product so that it will work properly." In this sentence, *critical* means

   A helpful.

   B unhelpful.

   C important.

   D unnecessary.

8. "Limitations of a product may be hidden when the organization of an advertisement is *complex*." In this sentence, *complex* means

   A stylish.

   B complicated.

   C muddled.

   D persuasive.

Writing Skills Review

Writing Standard 2.5 Write documents related to career development, including simple business letters and job applications: a. Present information purposefully and succinctly and meet the needs of the intended audience. b. Follow the conventional format for the type of document (e. g., letter of inquiry, memorandum).

Business Documents **Directions:** Read the following memo. Then, answer each question that follows.

(1) To: John Kilas, Varsity Basketball Coach
(2) From: Fred Williams, Headmaster
(3) Re: Awards Ceremony

(4) John, congratulations on another winning season! (5) You and the team have made this school extremely proud. (6) You have led one of the city's best basketball teams to another championship. (7) You've also nurtured another group of student athletes who understand the importance of an education. (8) My son, Toby, especially enjoyed the game against Wooter in which our team came back from 25 points down to win. (9) In honor of all these accomplishments, the school would like to host a celebratory awards ceremony, honoring all of the players and coaches. (10) At your earliest convenience, would you please send me a list of all the players with their names correctly spelled so we can order the awards? (11) Congratulations again!

1. Which of the following should be included in the heading of this memorandum?
   A   a return address
   B   a signature
   C   the date
   D   the sender's country

2. Which sentence could be deleted as unnecessary?
   A   sentence 2
   B   sentence 7
   C   sentence 8
   D   sentence 9

3. Which sentences could be combined by adding the transitions *not only* and *but*?
   A   sentences 4 and 5
   B   sentences 6 and 7
   C   sentences 8 and 9
   D   sentences 10 and 11

4. The memo's use of repetition in sentences 4 and 11
   A   is unnecessary.
   B   should be eliminated.
   C   clarifies a point.
   D   adds emphasis.

Magazines

Cobblestone

Each issue of *Cobblestone* focuses on an important aspect of the history of the United States. You might read about a historic figure such as Robert E. Lee, a famous event such as the California gold rush, or an important document such as the Bill of Rights. There has even been an issue dedicated to American cartoons! *Cobblestone* brings history to life with informative feature stories, engaging activities, and riveting photographs.

National Geographic Kids

In *National Geographic Kids* magazine you will read reports on developments in technology and features on exotic animals. You'll find Kids Did It!, profiles of young people who are making impressive achievements in science, sports, and music. Check out its Web site at www.nationalgeographic.com/kids.

Cricket

Cricket magazine has been capturing the imaginations of kids for more than twenty-five years. In a typical issue you'll find folk tales, poetry, biographies, and just about any other style of writing you can think of. *Cricket* also features word games, story contests, and plenty of compelling illustrations.

Muse

Muse gets you to question the world around you and to wonder how and why things work the way they do. The articles (many of which are written by experts) cover a range of topics having to do with art, science, and history. There are also nine cartoon Muses (like the nine Muses in Greek mythology) who appear in the margins of each issue and add a little humor by making comments and cracking jokes.

Web Sites

4Kids

The team of teachers, artists, writers, students, and technology experts at *4Kids* has put together an award-winning Web site that provides an easy, fun, and unique learning environment. The Web site points the way toward some of the best sites in all subjects for learning on the Internet. *4Kids* also has a section that answers your questions about technology and even a page with online video games. To see all these features and more, visit www.4kids.org.

Kids' Castle

Kids' Castle is an online magazine developed by *Smithsonian* magazine. You will discover a variety of worlds inside: air and space, history, the arts, animals, science, and personalities. Click on the history link, and you might learn the story behind postage stamps. Follow the sports links, and you could learn about vintage baseball leagues, where the rules of the game were different from those of today. That's just the beginning. For more, log on to www.kidscastle.si.edu.

MidLink

MidLink, an online magazine, fosters creativity in students around the globe through international poetry exchanges. Kids also build Web sites on topics such as favorite authors, historic landmarks, and camping experiences. With its links to sites on social studies, science, and more, *MidLink* can also serve as a research tool. You'll find *MidLink* at www.ncsu.edu/midlink.

NASA Kids

Have you ever wanted the inside scoop on outer space? Now you can find it on the Web at kids.msfc.nasa.gov. You'll discover a three-dimensional map of the solar system, biographical pieces about astronauts, and information on how NASA keeps track of all of its spacecraft. The site is also loaded with games, and it even features an art gallery.

CHAPTER 7

Expository Critique

California Standards

Here are the grade 8 standards you will work toward mastering in Chapter 7:

Reading Comprehension (Focus on Informational Materials)
2.7 Evaluate the unity, coherence, logic, internal consistency, and structural patterns of text.

Writing Applications (Genres and Their Characteristics)
2.3 Write research reports:
  a. Define a thesis.
  b. Record important ideas, concepts, and direct quotations from significant information sources and paraphrase and summarize all perspectives on the topic, as appropriate.
  c. Use a variety of primary and secondary sources and distinguish the nature and value of each.
  d. Organize and display information on charts, maps, and graphs.

" Get the facts, or the facts will get you. When you get them, get them right, or they will get you wrong."

—**Dr. Thomas Fuller**

What Do
You
Think

How do you judge the ideas you encounter in text?

Learn It Online
Learn more about expository critique at:

go.hrw.com	H8-735	Go

Informational Text Focus

by **Carol Jago**

What Is Expository Critique?

How do you evaluate informational materials? When you read to learn about a subject, it is critical to consider how the information is presented. Is the proposal coherently and logically presented? Has the writer offered convincing and consistent supporting evidence? How does the structure of the text support its purpose? Good readers are always on the lookout for clues to evaluate what they read.

Critiquing Texts

A critic's job is to **critique**, or critically evaluate, analyze, and judge. Food critics visit restaurants, tasting dishes from a menu to rate the chef. Consumer critics test-drive cars to determine the best buys. Music critics evaluate new releases to help listeners decide what to purchase.

All of these critics use a set of **criteria** for making their judgments. When critiquing a dessert, a food critic might use taste, appearance, and calories as criteria for judging a slice of triple strawberry cake with chocolate topping. Cars are often judged on the basis of safety, price, and style. A music critic might evaluate a recording based on its lyrics, beat, and performance.

Evaluating Expository Texts

Expository texts are texts that explain. They usually present information about complicated material to readers. When expository texts are well-written, they clarify a complex issue or process. When you analyze and evaluate expository texts, consider the following criteria:

1. Unity
2. Coherence
3. Logic
4. Internal Consistency
5. Structural Patterns

Criteria for Expository Critique

Unity	All the elements of the expository text are arranged to contribute to the whole.
Coherence	All the elements of the expository text hold together in an orderly fashion.
Logic	All the elements of the expository text are sensible and correct.
Internal Consistency	All the elements of the expository text are connected and in agreement with one another.
Structural Pattern	The format of the expository text—the way it presents information.

1. **Unity** When a text has **unity,** all of its details support the text's main idea or proposal. In a unified passage, each sentence relates to a single topic. Study the example below. Notice that the passage's unity is disrupted when a sentence about wood is introduced.

Lacking Unity	Unified
Today the most important sources of energy are oil and coal. Oil, however, is becoming scarce and more expensive. **Wood is not a practical source of energy.** Coal is difficult to mine and dirty when burned.	Today the most important sources of energy are oil and coal. Oil, however, is becoming scarce and more expensive. Coal is difficult to mine and dirty when burned.

2. **Coherence** An expository text has **coherence** (koh HIHR uhns) when all of its elements hold together and can be clearly understood. Transitional words and phrases help readers connect sentences and ideas, as in the coherent passage below.

Lacking Coherence	Coherent
The National Park Service administers parks, monuments, historical sites, and recreational spots in all parts of the United States. **[Transition needed.]** The service must provide for the comfort and safety of the millions of visitors who come to the parks every year.	The National Park Service administers parks, monuments, historical sites, and recreational spots in all parts of the United States. **In addition,** the service must provide for the comfort and safety of the millions of visitors who come to the parks every year.

3. **Logic** Correct reasoning is called **logic.** Logical texts present statements supported by reasons, evidence, and examples. The logical text below contains an example that specifically supports a statement.

Illogical	Logical
As the season advances, other mysterious comings and goings take place. Where the whales came from or by what route no one knows.	As the season advances, other mysterious comings and goings take place. **Whales suddenly appear off the coastal banks where the shrimplike krill are spawning.** Where the whales came from or by what route no one knows.

4. **Internal Consistency** If a text is logical and coherent, it has **internal consistency.** Consistency is essential because unimportant or disconnected details distract readers and disrupt the logic of the text.

Inconsistent	Consistent
A company is offering to broadcast messages into space. For a fee, the company will send your message to any of the planets in your solar system. **Wow, what would you say?** For an additional fee, the company will assist you in writing a message.	A company is offering to broadcast messages into space. For a fee, the company will send your message to any of the planets in your solar system. For an additional fee, the company will assist you in writing a message.

5. **Structural Patterns** Most expository texts are organized according to one or more of these structural patterns:

- **chronological order:** time order—steps or events presented in the order they occur.
- **order of importance:** more important information precedes less important information.
- **comparison and contrast:** information is arranged by similarities and differences.
- **classification:** information is sorted into groups. All the items in a group are related.
- **proposition and support:** a proposal is supported by evidence such as facts, statistics, and quotations.

Your Turn Critique Expository Text

Explain whether this passage contains logic and coherence: "In 1989, a huge earthquake shook San Francisco. The earthquake hit during a World Series game between the San Francisco Giants and the Oakland A's. These teams had never met in the playoffs before. Oakland, however, had won the series in the 1970s."

Learn It Online
Learn more about expository critique at:

go.hrw.com   H8-737   **Go**

Reading Skills Focus

by **Kylene Beers**

What Skills Help You Critique Expository Text?

Expository texts can be challenging to read and difficult to understand without background knowledge. Good readers don't let these challenges get them down. They know how to tackle an expository text and how to learn from it.

Determining the Main Idea

When grappling with an informational text, your first task is to determine the writer's main idea. The **main idea** is the writer's most important point, opinion, or message. Occasionally the main idea is directly stated. More often, you have to find it yourself. Use these tips to discover main ideas in informational materials:

- Look for direct statements the writer makes.
- Analyze headings or other formatting.
- You will often find the main idea at the beginning of the text. A text's structural pattern may point to the main idea.
- Look for significant supporting details.
- Try to put the main idea in your own words.

In the example below, the writers state the main idea and support it with consistent details.

> While some will have questions about the mayor's motives or disagree with an apology, there is no question that the despicable institution of slavery is part of our nation's legacy. Slaves were first brought to this country in 1619, one year before the pilgrims landed at Plymouth Rock . . .
>
> *from* "Apologies for Past Actions Are Still Appropriate Today"

Evaluating Evidence

Writers use **evidence,** or clear, specific reasons, to support their main ideas. Look for these types of evidence in expository texts:

- **facts**—statements that can be proved true
- **statistics**—facts presented in number form
- **quotations**—comments from people who are experts in a field

Not all evidence is created equal. Look for evidence that undermines or detracts from the effectiveness of the writer's argument. The following are types of weak evidence:

- **bias:** the tendency to favor one person, group, or issue over another
- **stereotyping:** an oversimplified, inaccurate generalization of a group
- **inadequate support:** vague, unreliable reasons, including unsupported opinions
- **faulty reasoning:** reasoning that is not logical or that is false or flawed
- **irrelevant information:** support that has nothing to do with the main topic.

To grapple with informational materials, you will need to be a textual detective.

Recognizing Author's Intent and Tone

As you read expository texts, be aware of the author's **intent,** or purpose. Sometimes writers give you information; "Lewis and Clark: Into the Unknown" in this chapter is written to inform. Other writers want to persuade you to take action; for example, in a speech written in 1852, Frederick Douglass encourages listeners to reject slavery in "What to the Slave Is the Fourth of July?"

An author's intent directly affects a work's tone. **Tone** is the writer's attitude toward his or her subject. Credible expository texts have a serious, reasonable tone. You should question the credibility of expository texts that have a highly emotional or angry tone.

Word choice has a powerful effect on the tone of informational materials. For example, a literary critic adopts a serious tone when saying that a story is "well crafted." If the writer said "That story rocked!" the tone of the review would be casual and you might question the writer's credibility.

Word Choice	Words to describe tone
"This is our **hope.** This is the **faith** with which I return to the South."	sincere; encouraging
". . . why may not B snatch the same **argument,** and **prove equally** that he may enslave A."	persuasive; logical
"On **March 10, 1804,** Lewis and Clark attended the ceremony that made the Louisiana Purchase **official**."	straightforward; informative

Evaluating Logic, Coherence, and Consistency

Read these two expository texts about the story "The Treasure of Lemon Brown" (page 17):

Text 1: Lemon Brown is a homeless person; he could not have been a good blues player. I once knew someone who played the harmonica really well. He had red hair and was on my baseball team. I think homeless people should be given a place to stay so that they all don't have to sleep on the sidewalk. Lemon Brown should get a job so he could get an apartment.

Text 2: The character of Lemon Brown reminds us of the humanity of homeless people. They are not misfits who embarrass us by sleeping on our sidewalks or begging for change. Before their problems left them with no place to live, they too had jobs and families. We should always remember that they are individuals with ideas, opinions, and a life history. We should treat them with concern and respect.

Your Turn Apply Reading Skills

Using the information in the chart, critique the logic, coherence, and consistency of the two texts about Lemon Brown.

Text 1	Text 2
Illogical: statements are not supported by reasons	Logical: statements are supported by evidence in the text
Incoherent: writer jumps from one idea to another without connecting them	Coherent: writer uses transitional phrase to connect ideas when necessary
Inconsistent: sentences are unrelated to one another and do not focus on one idea.	Consistent: passage centers on why homeless people deserve respect.

Now go to the Skills in Action: Reading Model

Galaxies

from **Holt Physical Science**

Key Concept Galaxies contain billions of stars and have different shapes.

What You Will Learn

- The three types of galaxies are spiral galaxies, elliptical galaxies, and irregular galaxies.
- Galaxies are composed of stars, planetary systems, nebulas, and star clusters.
- Looking at distant galaxies reveals what young galaxies looked like.

Reading Focus

Author's Intent and Tone The author's intent is to provide information. Simple vocabulary and short, direct sentences convey a serious, straightforward tone.

Why It Matters

The structure and composition of galaxies give clues to the structure and composition of the universe.

Vocabulary

- galaxy

READING STRATEGY

Graphic Organizer In your **Science Journal,** make a Comparison Table that compares various characteristics of the different types of galaxies.

Informational Focus

Expository Critique Writers of expository texts include graphics and other features to give a text coherence.

8.4.a Students know galaxies are clusters of billions of stars and may have different shapes. **8.4.b** Students know that the Sun is one of many stars in the Milky Way galaxy and that stars may differ in size, temperature, and color.

▶ Large groups of stars, dust, and gas are called **galaxies.** Galaxies come in a variety of sizes and shapes. The largest galaxies contain more than a trillion stars. Astronomers don't count the stars, of course. They estimate how many sun-sized stars a galaxy contains by studying the size and brightness of the galaxy.

Figure 1 Types of Galaxies

Spiral Galaxy
The Andromeda galaxy is a spiral galaxy that looks similar to what our galaxy, the Milky Way, is thought to look like.

Types of Galaxies

The light from individual stars in another galaxy comes to Earth from so far away that the light blurs together. From Earth, other galaxies look cloudy and have a spiral shape, a round or oval shape, or no definite shape. Astronomers **classify** a galaxy as a spiral, elliptical, or irregular galaxy according to its shape. They also **classify** a galaxy by the energy that it emits or by the rate of star formation.

Spiral Galaxies

When someone says the word *galaxy*, most people probably think of a spiral galaxy. *Spiral galaxies,* such as the Andromeda galaxy, shown in **Figure 1,** have a bulge at the center and spiral arms. The spiral arms are made up of gas, dust, and new stars that have formed in these dense regions of gas and dust.

The Milky Way

The galaxy in which we live is a spiral galaxy called the *Milky Way.* The Milky Way consists of about 200 billion stars, including the sun. The sun is located about two-thirds of the way between the center of the galaxy and the galaxy's edge. From Earth, the edge of the Milky Way is seen as a bright band of stars that cuts across the night sky.

Elliptical Galaxies

Because most elliptical galaxies are round or oval, they can be thought of as "cosmic snowballs," as **Figure 1** shows. However, some elliptical galaxies are slightly flattened, but not as much as spiral galaxies are. Unlike spiral galaxies, whose gas clouds are still forming stars, elliptical galaxies seem to have stopped making new stars more than 10 billion years ago. Elliptical galaxies are among the largest galaxies in the universe. They can contain up to 5 trillion stars! Evidence suggests that many large elliptical galaxies form by the merging of smaller galaxies.

Informational Focus

Expository Critique This expository text uses the structural pattern of **classification**. The writers sort information according to the different types of galaxies. Information about spiral galaxies is presented first.

Informational Focus

Expository Critique The text has internal consistency because each sentence in this section focuses on details about the Milky Way galaxy.

Reading Focus

Evaluating Evidence Writers of science textbooks include facts, statistics, and other reliable information.

Elliptical Galaxy
Unlike the Milky Way, the galaxy known as M87, an elliptical galaxy, has no spiral arms.

Irregular Galaxy
The Large Magellanic Cloud, an irregular galaxy, is located within our galactic neighborhood.

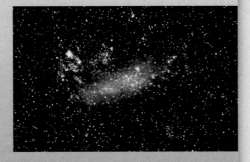

Reading Model

Irregular Galaxies

Irregular galaxies are galaxies that have no definite shape. The smallest irregular galaxies have only about 10 million stars. The largest irregular galaxies can contain several billion stars. Irregular galaxies form new stars slowly. Some irregular galaxies form when galaxies collide.

The Milky Way is consuming a pair of nearby irregular galaxies called the **Magellanic Clouds.** The Large Magellanic Cloud is shown in **Figure 1.** It is located about 190,000 light-years from Earth and is visible by eye from the southern hemisphere.

Informational Focus

Determining the Main Idea
Heads and subheads contain clues to the main ideas of sections of a textbook. Notice that the main idea of this section is stated in the first sentence.

QUICK LAB

Modeling Galaxies

 8.4.a

1. Fill a **medium mixing bowl** two-thirds full of **water**.

2. Place **1 tsp of colored glitter** in the center of the bowl.

3. Use your fingers or a **large stirring spoon** to rapidly swirl the water in the bowl.

4. What kind of pattern does the glitter form?

5. What type of galaxy does the glitter model?

Read with a Purpose How did specific text features help you understand the information about galaxies?

SKILLS IN ACTION
Wrap Up

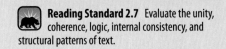

Reading Standard 2.7 Evaluate the unity, coherence, logic, internal consistency, and structural patterns of text.

Into Action: Expository Critique

Evaluate the excerpt from *Holt Physical Science* in a chart like the one below. First, identify and evaluate the text's unity and its structural patterns. Then, analyze the text's <u>coherence</u>, logic, and <u>consistency</u>. Finally, state your overall critique of the text.

"Galaxies" from Holt Physical Science
What are the text's structural patterns? How is the structure unified?
What makes the text coherent, logical, and consistent?
My critique:

Talk About . . .

1. With a partner, discuss the techniques writers use to create <u>coherence</u>, logic, and <u>consistency</u> in a text. Try to use each Academic Vocabulary word listed on the right at least once in your discussion.

Write About . . .

Answer the following questions about "Galaxies" from *Holt Physical Science*. For definitions of the underlined Academic Vocabulary words, see the column on the right.

2. Why is "Galaxies" from *Holt Physical Science* considered an <u>expository</u> text?

3. Explain whether the use of heads and subheads add to the <u>coherence</u> and <u>consistency</u> of the text.

4. Why is a set of criteria useful when you <u>critique</u> a text?

Writing Focus
Think as a Reader/Writer

The Writing Skills Focus activities in Chapter 7 will give you opportunities to evaluate and <u>critique</u> authors' explorations of a variety of topics.

Academic Vocabulary for Chapter 7

Talking and Writing About Expository Critique

Academic Vocabulary is the language you use to talk and write about texts. Use these words to discuss the expository texts you read in this chapter. The words are underlined throughout the chapter.

coherence (koh HIHR uhns) *n.:* clarity; logical connection. *A text has coherence when its main ideas are clearly supported by details.*

consistency (kuhn SIHS tuhn see) *n.:* uniformity; regularity. *Consistency of tone is crucial when a writer is crafting a convincing argument.*

critique (krih TEEK) *v.:* judge the quality of. *Use criteria when you critique an informational text.*

expository (ehk SPAHZ uh tawr ee) *adj.:* containing an explanation. *Readers regularly consult expository texts when they are looking for information.*

Your Turn

Copy the Academic Vocabulary words into your *Reader/Writer Notebook*. Explain each in your own words.

Evaluating Logic, Coherence, and Structural Patterns

The Discovery Expedition (2003) retraces the route of Lewis and Clark's expedition. The photographs that accompany this selection were taken during the reenactment of Lewis and Clark's historic journey.

CONTENTS

What Do **You** Think? How do you evaluate articles about the past?

QuickWrite
How much do you know about the country you live in? Record five facts about the history and geography of the United States.

MAGAZINE ARTICLE
Preparing to Read

Reading Standard 2.7 Evaluate the unity, **coherence, logic,** internal consistency, and structural patterns **of text.**

Lewis and Clark: Into the Unknown

Informational Text Focus

Logic and Coherence **Logic** means correct reasoning. To be logical, the main ideas in a text should be supported by reasons, evidence, and examples. (In a long piece of writing, the writer develops a main idea over many paragraphs.) Statements are *illogical* if the evidence does *not* support what is being said. The statement "Lincoln's presidency was impressive because he was tall" is illogical.

A text is **coherent** when all of its sentences and paragraphs flow smoothly from one to the next. The ideas in a coherent article have a clear relationship to one another. Consider the following statements: "Lincoln was elected president in 1860. One year later, the Civil War began." These sentences have <u>coherence</u> because they are connected chronologically by the phrase *one year later*.

Into Action Use a chart like the one below to <u>critique</u> "Lewis and Clark: Into the Unknown." How effectively does the writer convey the main idea?

Lewis and Clark: Into the Unknown

What is the main idea?

What details support the main idea?

How thoroughly is the main idea developed?

My critique:

Writing Skills Focus

Preparing for Timed Writing Writers give texts <u>coherence</u> by using transitional words to connect sentences and ideas. Record in your *Reader/Writer Notebook* five instances where writers use transitional words to link ideas.

Reader/Writer
Notebook
Use your **RWN** to complete the activities for this selection.

Language Coach

Transitional Words Transitional words help readers follow the <u>coherence</u> of a text by connecting sentences and ideas. If you pay attention to transitional words, you may understand text more easily. The following list shows ways writers use them.

- to connect ideas in time order: *first, next, before, when, while*
- to connect ideas in space: *above, among, below, in, near, next to*
- to connect ideas in order of importance: *more important, then, last*
- to compare ideas: *also, and, another, just as, like, similarly*
- to contrast ideas: *although, but, however*

 Learn It Online
Reinforce your understanding of this lesson with a multimedia presentation at:

go.hrw.com | H8-745 | **Go**

Lewis and Clark: INTO THE UNKNOWN

Meriwether Lewis (1807)
by Charles Willson Peale.

by **THE WORLD ALMANAC**

William Clark
by Charles Willson Peale.

Read with a Purpose

Read this article to learn why Thomas Jefferson wanted to explore a huge part of the country.

Build Background

In 1800, Spain made a secret agreement giving France control of a large area of North American land known as the Louisiana Territory. When the United States learned of this arrangement, in 1801, politicians knew that this land was strategically important. It contained the key commercial port of New Orleans as well as the mouth of the Mississippi River. In 1803, the United States decided to buy this land from France, paying about three cents per acre for 828,000 square miles of land. This sale, known as the Louisiana Purchase, doubled the size of the United States.

A ll the vast, unknown land beyond the great river—what did it look like? What strange animals might be living there? Could prehistoric creatures still exist in such a place? In 1802, these questions were on the mind of America's third president, Thomas Jefferson. The "great river," the Mississippi, formed the western boundary of the United States. Little was known about the land beyond.

Jefferson believed westward expansion was in the country's best interest, so the United States **negotiated** with France for the huge land tract between the Mississippi River and the Rocky Mountains. Meanwhile, the president wanted Americans to get excited about this **acquisition**—the Louisiana Purchase—and about the West. A successful expedition across the continent, he thought, might create that kind of "buzz." **A**

A **Informational Focus** **Logic** What example supports the statement that Jefferson thought westward expansion was a good idea?

Vocabulary **negotiated** (nih GOH shee ayt ihd) *v.*: came to an agreement through discussion; talked.
acquisition (ak wuh ZIHSH uhn) *n.*: something purchased or gained.

U.S. explorers would bring back information. They would talk to native peoples, explaining the shift in power and creating goodwill. Most important, they might discover the long-hoped-for Northwest Passage: a continuous water—rather than land—route from the Atlantic to the Pacific oceans. **Ⓑ**

Analyzing Visuals

Connecting to the Text
Look closely at the map. How is the map of the United States different now?

FORMING THE CORPS

Not only did Jefferson need someone brave and resourceful to lead the expedition, but he also needed to trust him. He chose Meriwether Lewis, his personal secretary. First, the president sent Lewis to Philadelphia to study with experts to ready him for the trip. Since there would be no doctors in the wilderness, Lewis needed to know medicine. Similarly, he had to understand celestial navigation (steering by the stars), botany (plant science), and zoology (animal science).

Ⓑ Informational Focus **Logic** What statement in the second paragraph of the article do these reasons support?

Lewis was enthusiastic about the challenge. He did not want to go it alone. He asked his former army comrade and friend William Clark to be co-commander. Then, in 1803, the two headed down the Ohio River toward St. Louis on the Mississippi, along with York, an enslaved person who had been with Clark since childhood. They recruited and trained nearly four dozen men as members of their Corps of Discovery, along with a dog named Seaman.

STRANGE PLACES AND NEW FACES

On March 10, 1804, Lewis and Clark attended the St. Louis ceremony that made the Louisiana Purchase official. Then in late spring, their assembled group started up the Missouri River in boats. As they passed the seven-house cluster of La Charette on May 25, Charles Floyd, one of the corps, noted in his journal that it was "the last settlement of whites on this river." From then on, almost everyone the Corps encountered was American Indian. **C**

The explorers knew it would be impossible to get across the continent without help—or at least acceptance—from American Indians. Therefore, Lewis and Clark sought meetings with native peoples along the way. The explorers found many native peoples welcoming but had difficulties with a few.

Contemporary illustration of the original Lewis and Clark expedition.

WELCOME ADDITIONS

In late October, the explorers began building a winter fort near a large community of Mandan and Hidatsa Indians in what is now North Dakota. During their stay at Fort Mandan, Lewis and Clark learned that horses were needed to cross the mountains. The native peoples told them the Shoshone might provide the animals, if they could strike a bargain.

C **Informational Focus** **Logic** What statement does the quotation from Charles Floyd support?

Vocabulary **corps** (kawr) *n.*: group of people with special training; a military unit.

Lewis and Clark found a Shoshone woman to help with these negotiations: Sacagawea, who had been captured by the Hidatsa years earlier. Lewis and Clark hired her and her husband, Toussaint Charbonneau, a French Canadian fur trapper, as translators. When the corps set out in spring, they and their infant son, Jean Baptiste, went along.

Sacagawea's ability to speak Shoshone was, indeed, a great benefit. She was able to procure horses and provide aid in many ways. The native groups the explorers encountered were sometimes fearful and suspicious of them. When they saw Sacagawea and her little son, however, they felt more at ease. Surely the explorers weren't a war party—not with a young woman and baby. **D**

To the Pacific

The Corps of Discovery faced incredible obstacles. They had run-ins with grizzly bears and shot their canoes through rapids so treacherous that local American Indians stared in disbelief. At one point, they spent a month making a portage° around a waterfall. They lost their way in the Bitterroot Mountains and nearly starved.

The expedition found no Northwest Passage—the dreamed-of water route across the continent. Nevertheless, they did discover the new country's rich western assets. They named locations and landmarks and described 178 plants and 122 animals that had been previously unknown. With courage, intelligence, and luck, the Corps of Discovery made it all the way to what is today Oregon—and home again—to tell their remarkable tale. **E**

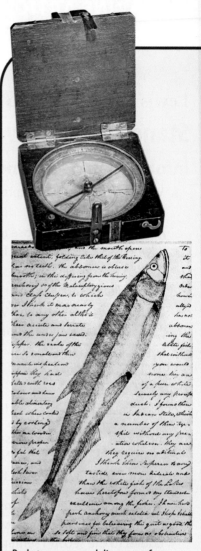

Pocket compass and diary page from Lewis and Clark expedition.

°**portage:** act of carrying boats from one place to another overland in order to bypass sections of a waterway that cannot be navigated.

Read with a Purpose What goals did Lewis and Clark's expedition achieve?

D **Informational Focus** Coherence What contrasting ideas does the transitional word *however* make clear?

E **Read and Discuss** How did things turn out for the explorers?

MAGAZINE ARTICLE
Applying Your Skills

Reading Standard 2.7 **Evaluate the** unity, **coherence, logic,** internal consistency, and structural patterns **of text.**

Lewis and Clark: Into the Unknown

Standards Review

Informational Text and Vocabulary

1. Which statement *best* expresses the **main idea** of the article?

A Meriwether Lewis chose an excellent crew who were well prepared for the trip.

B The Corps of Discovery took two years to complete its travels.

C The Corps explored new Western lands and brought back valuable information.

D Sacajawea translated for the explorers and helped provide safety.

2. Read these two sentences from the article.

The "great river," the Mississippi, formed the western boundary of the United States. Little was known about the land beyond.

Which of the following transitional words or phrases would *most* improve **coherence** if added to the second sentence?

A at that time

B on the other hand

C then

D similarly

3. Which statement would *most* improve the **coherence** of the last paragraph?

A The Corps of Discovery mapped huge sections of the new U.S. territory.

B Although the Corps did not accomplish all of its goals, it was still a great success.

C Despite the best efforts of its crew, the Corps failed in many ways.

D The Corps could not find a water route between the Atlantic and Pacific oceans.

4. Which of the following statements does *not* support the idea that Lewis was a good choice for leader?

A President Jefferson trusted Lewis.

B He studied necessary areas of knowledge.

C He recruited and trained almost fifty men.

D He knew he wouldn't need a co-leader.

5. Another term for *acquisition* is

A territory.

B exploration.

C addition.

D adventure.

6. If you have *negotiated* a deal, you have

A bargained.

B purchased.

C translated.

D argued.

7. A *corps* usually includes

A water that can be navigated.

B decisions made by a leader.

C traveling equipment.

D members with specific skills.

Writing Skills Focus

Timed └Writing Use the chart you created while reading to critique this article. Explain whether or not the main idea was adequately presented, and evaluate the logic and coherence of the author's writing.

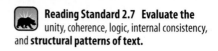

Reading Standard 2.7 Evaluate the unity, coherence, logic, internal consistency, and **structural patterns of text.**

Lewis and Clark Revisited

Informational Text Focus

Structural Patterns of Text Imagine that "Lewis and Clark: Into the Unknown" began by describing Lewis and Clark's dealings with Sacagawea. After that, it mentioned Lewis and Clark's background information. Finally, it discussed Jefferson's enthusiasm for westward expansion. A careful reader would <u>critique</u> such a text harshly because it had no discernible structural pattern.

As it is written, "Lewis and Clark: Into the Unknown" has a clear structural pattern. It is organized in **chronological order,** or the order in which the events occurred. As a result, you are able to identify the writer's main ideas and identify reasons why Lewis and Clark are important historical figures. "Lewis and Clark Revisited" uses a different structural pattern: **compare-and-contrast.** This structural pattern supports the meaning of the text because "Lewis and Clark Revisited" discusses the similarities and differences between Lewis and Clark's exhibition and a historical reenactment of the events.

Into Action Use a chart like the one below to <u>critique</u> "Lewis and Clark Revisited." Why is the compare-and-contrast structural pattern an effective way of presenting the essential ideas of the text?

Lewis and Clark Revisited

What is the main idea?
What details support the main idea?
How well is the main idea developed?
How effective is the author's use of structural patterns?
My critique:

Writing Skills Focus

Preparing for Timed ⌐Writing As you read these selections, look for transitional words that signal that ideas are being compared or contrasted.

Reader/Writer
Notebook

Use your **RWN** to complete the activities for this selection.

Vocabulary

commemorate (kuh MEHM uh rayt) *v.:* honor the memory of. *This event is planned to commemorate the anniversary of Lewis and Clark's journey.*

mimicking (MIHM ihk ihng) *v.* used as *adj.:* imitating; copying. *The travelers are mimicking the conditions of the original journey.*

resembles (rih ZEHM buhlz) *v.:* admitted; acknowledged. *The modern boat resembles one of the canoes that traveled down the Mississippi two hundred years ago.*

Language Coach

Spelling Patterns For some words that end in *c,* you should add a *k* before adding an ending. For example, *panic* becomes *panicked,* and *garlic* becomes *garlicky.* The vocabulary word *mimicking* reflects this spelling pattern. Pay attention to the *k* to help you pronounce these words correctly.

Learn It Online
Delve into vocabulary using Word Watch at:

| go.hrw.com | H8-751 | **Go** |

LEWIS AND CLARK REVISITED

by  THE WORLD ALMANAC

Read with a Purpose
Read this article to learn how a modern group of adventurers followed in the footsteps of Lewis and Clark.

Build Background
The following article compares a historical reenactment, or re-creation of a historical event, to the actual historical event. Some reenactments focus on a specific event, such as a battle or an expedition. Other reenactments try to create an accurate portrait of a past period, such as the Middle Ages or Colonial America. All reenactments create a living history, bringing the past to life for both the participants and audiences. A viewing public can enjoy reenactments by visiting them in person, reading about them in magazines, or following Internet updates on them.

Discovery Expedition members David Cain (left) and Payton "Bud" Clark, great-, great-, great-grandson of William Clark.

President Thomas Jefferson's directions to Meriwether Lewis more than 200 years ago were clear: Find and map "the most direct & practicable" waterway to the Pacific, share the country's intentions with people along the way, and then record your findings. When Lewis and the rest of the Corps of Discovery stepped forth to explore the Louisiana Territory, however, most details about the terrain[1] and its waterways were murky or unknown.

To commemorate the bicentennial[2] of that courageous expedition, the Army Corps of Engineers facilitated a "journey of rediscovery," named the Discovery Expedition. Starting in 2003, as many as 177 participants, many of them retired military men and women, traveled the well-known Lewis and Clark trail. Around ten reenactors stayed with it from start to finish. **Ⓐ**

While Lewis and Clark had a diplomatic and economic mission, the reenactors' goals were primarily symbolic and educational. In Lewis and Clark's time, two-thirds of the U.S. population lived within 50 miles of the Atlantic. Now, Americans are spread across the land from sea to sea, details about the trail are available on the Internet, and the "reenactment" was just that, a kind of theater acted out by dedicated history buffs.

STARTING OUT

Organizers of the Discovery Expedition took pains to be authentic but made concessions to time. Lewis, for instance, traversed the Ohio River with a keelboat using oars, poles, sails, or ropes for cordelling (pulling a boat along a waterway from the shore). However, in the reenactment, "Lewis" had a motor powering his craft. **Ⓑ**

The bicentennial crew had supplies mimicking the originals'—within reason. Lewis and Clark brought medicines of the day, including "Rush's Pills," which had explosive powder and mercury in the mix. The first explorers smeared themselves with tallow and bear grease to fight mosquitoes.

Lewis and Clark made their first winter camp in Camp Wood, Illinois. Because the Mississippi has moved eastward, reenactors had to place their replica camp two miles from the original site. The original Corps of Discovery did not spend the cold months in video conferences with schools around the nation, as Discovery Expedition "explorers" did. Those on the modern trek ate venison and salt pork for authenticity but also enjoyed pizza and doughnuts donated by visitors.

---

1. **terrain:** surface features of land.
2. **bicentennial:** two-hundredth anniversary.

Ⓐ Read and Discuss What has the author told you so far about the Discovery Expedition?

Ⓑ Informational Focus Structural Patterns Which words in this paragraph signal a contrast?

Vocabulary **commemorate** (kuh MEHM uh rayt) *v.*: honor the memory of.
mimicking (MIHM ihk ihng) *v.*: used as *adj.*: imitating; copying.

ENCOUNTERS ALONG THE WAY

Lewis and Clark met friendly American Indians and adopted some of their ways, including abandoning their military uniforms for buckskin clothing, buffalo robes, and moccasins. The Mandan and Hidatsa peoples helped them pass the winter at Fort Mandan, providing maps for the trek ahead. But other groups threatened the expedition.

The reenactors heard just an echo of that: the Oto and Missouri chiefs welcomed them, for instance, as did the Omaha. The Yankton Sioux held a mock council in Nebraska. However, the Lakota came out in protest, saying that the journey opened "old wounds" about the government's treatment of them after the expedition.   **C**

CHANGES TO THE LAND

The land only vaguely resembles the old countryside. On the one hand, the Missouri River stretch called the Missouri Breaks, wrote reporter Anthony Brandt, "still looks almost exactly as Lewis and Clark found it 200 years ago." On the other hand, the river system has changed dramatically. For example, numerous dams and irrigation projects have left marks, as have agricultural and industrial pollution.

Forests of the Rockies, Cascades, and coastal ranges have been heavily cut and logged. There were 20 million acres of old-growth forest in Oregon and Washington. Now there are 2.3 million, according to Water Planet.

C **Informational Focus** **Structural Patterns** How does the author organize information presented in this section?

Vocabulary **resembles** (rih ZEHM buhlz) *v.:* looks like.

Analyzing Visuals

Connecting to the Text
How similar are these pictures of the Discovery Expedition reenactment to your perception of the original expedition?

Lewis and Clark recorded encounters with wildlife, including 40 grizzly kills. Today, these bears are endangered. There were as many as 100,000 grizzlies from the Great Plains to the Pacific. Now they number about 1,000.

When the original travelers tasted salmon for the first time at the Columbia River, Clark drew a picture of the free-running fish. Estimates place the fishes' population then at 30 million. Today it is closer to 300,000. **Ⓓ**

Ⓓ Read and Discuss How does this information add to what you have already learned about the two expeditions?

A LONGER HUMAN REACH

The original crew completed their journey in September 1806, in St. Louis. In their day, that city's population was about 1,000. Today, wrote Brandt upon return, "that's fewer than attend a lot of high school football games."

Lewis and Clark returned with crucial knowledge about the United States and its inhabitants. The bicentennial crew, like the originals, accomplished much of what they set out to do—they renewed excitement about this pivotal trek in our country's history. **Ⓔ**

MAPS THEN AND NOW

The mapmaking tools of Lewis and Clark's time were the octant and the sextant, which determined longitude and latitude when the operator fixed them on the sun, the moon, or a star. Mapmakers marked space by using surveying tools that measured quarter miles. On water, nautical miles were measured by throwing a chain ahead in the water and noting the time taken to meet it.

Today, mapmaking has gone high tech. Satellites photograph sections of the earth, and computers analyze the sections. Maps are created by layering the information digitally. Satellites in global positioning systems can locate a position using beamed signals.

Analyzing Visuals

Connecting to the Text
How are the Great Falls of the Missouri River in Montana different today (below) from when Lewis and Clark visited them (above)?

Ⓔ Informational Focus Structural Patterns   Explain whether the compare and contrast structural pattern was effective in this article.

Read with a Purpose
How was the modern expedition similar to that of Lewis and Clark?

Reading Standard 2.7 Evaluate the unity, coherence, logic, internal consistency, and **structural patterns of text.**

Lewis and Clark Revisited

Standards Review

Informational Text and Vocabulary

1. Which statement *best* expresses the **main idea** of the article?

A The reenactors have great respect for the Corps of Discovery.

B The reenactors copied the Lewis and Clark trip, using nineteenth and twenty-first century resources.

C If Lewis and Clark could have followed the reenactors' example, their trip would have been more successful.

D The reenactors' trip failed, whereas the Lewis and Clark expedition succeeded.

2. According to the section "Encounters Along the Way," the reenactors were welcomed by some American Indians. In **contrast,** the

A Lakota protested the modern explorers.

B Oto and Missouri chiefs greeted them.

C Hidatsa helped them through the winter.

D modern men began wearing buckskin.

3. Each subheading in the article introduces

A comparisons and contrasts.

B causes and effects.

C positives and negatives.

D an order of importance.

4. Both expeditions

A developed new mapmaking techniques.

B discovered previously unknown plants.

C employed the same number of people.

D traveled the same route from Missouri to Oregon.

5. Another term for *mimicking* is

A liking.

B imitating.

C sounding.

D running.

6. If a man *resembles* his father, he

A is offended by him.

B dislikes him.

C looks like him.

D worries him.

7. If a speaker *commemorates* a historic event, she

A honors the event.

B ignores the event.

C satisifies the event.

D recites at the event.

Writing Skills Focus

Timed └Writing Choose one of the sections of the article. State its **main idea;** then in a paragraph, explain how the author effectively conveys the main idea by using the structural pattern.

What Do You Think Now

How might participating in a reenactment help you become a more informed citizen?

Evaluating Structural Patterns

Anthony Hopkins in a scene from Steven Spielberg's film *Amistad* (1997).

CONTENTS

What can mistakes of the past teach us today?

 QuickTalk
What actions can a nation take to correct injustices? Discuss this issue with a small group of classmates.

Preparing to Read

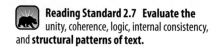

Reading Standard 2.7 Evaluate the unity, coherence, logic, internal consistency, and **structural patterns of text.**

Fragment on Slavery, 1854 / *from* What to the Slave Is the Fourth of July? / Apologies for Past Actions Are Still Appropriate Today

Informational Text Focus

Structural Patterns of Text: Proposition and Support

People are always trying to convince you of something—from what to buy to what to think to how to act. What they are trying to convince you of is called the **proposition.** The evidence they use is called the **support.** "Eat your vegetables (proposition) because they are good for you (support)." You will now read three selections that use this structural pattern. In "Fragment on Slavery, 1854," Lincoln uses the proslavery argument of his time to argue *against* it. How effective is this argument?

Into Action Make and complete a chart like the one below to <u>critique</u> each of the selections that follow. A chart for "Fragment on Slavery, 1854" has been started for you.

Fragment on Slavery, 1854

What is the author's proposition?
He asks whether the argument <u>for</u> slavery be used <u>against</u> slavery.

How does the author support the proposition?
He systematically refutes reasons for slavery.

How well is the argument developed?

What structural patterns does the author use?
Proposition and support

My critique:

Writing Skills Focus

Preparing for Timed ⌐Writing As you read, locate and record at least three ways each author focuses and clarifies the argument.

Reader/Writer
Notebook

Use your **RWN** to complete the activities for these selections.

Vocabulary

from **What to the Slave Is the Fourth of July?**

denounce (dih NOWNS) *v.*: speak against. *We must denounce all forms of injustice.*

perpetuate (puhr PEHCH oo ayt) *v.*: cause to continue. *We are opposed to anything that can perpetuate injustice.*

conceded (kuhn SEED ihd) *v.*: admitted; acknowledged. *We conceded the point; we did not need to argue.*

hypocrisy (hih PAHK ruh see) *n.*: false show of virtue or goodness. *His hypocrisy is obvious because he says one thing and does the opposite.*

Apologies for Past Actions Are Still Appropriate Today

despicable (DEHS pih kuh buhl) *adj.*: hateful; detested. *The institution of slavery is a despicable part of America's past.*

Language Coach

Word Origins The Latin root *cedere* means "to go." Look for the word in the list above that contains this word root. Many other English words are also built on this root. Here are some examples:

Word	Meaning
recede	go back
antecedent	something that comes before
exceed	go beyond

Read with a Purpose

Read to discover the proposition at the heart of each of the following selections.

Build Background

Abraham Lincoln, the U.S. president from 1861 to 1865, presided over the country during the American Civil War, in which Northern states and Southern states fought over the institution of slavery, among other issues. In 1863, Lincoln signed the Emancipation Proclamation, which freed all American slaves in the Southern states. Lincoln struggled with the political reality of slavery throughout his career. Some of his earliest writings on the practice date from the 1830s, years before he became president.

Fragment on Slavery, 1854

by Abraham Lincoln

If A can prove, however conclusively, that he may of right enslave B—why may not B snatch the same argument, and prove equally that he may enslave A?

You say A is white, and B is black. It is color, then, the lighter having the right to enslave the darker? Take care. By this rule you are to be slave to the first man you meet with a fairer skin than your own. **A**

You do not mean color exactly? You mean the whites are intellectually the superior of the blacks and, therefore, have the right to enslave them? Take care again. By this rule, you are to be slave to the first man you meet with an intellect superior to your own.

But, say you, it is a question of interest; and, if you can make it your interest, you have the right to enslave another. Very well. And if he can make it his interest, he has the right to enslave you. **B**

A **Informational Focus** What proposition does Lincoln present in this paragraph? Why is it unusual?

B **Read and Discuss** How do paragraphs 2–4 relate to paragraph 1? What pattern does each of these paragraphs follow? What variation is introduced in the final paragraph?

Read with a Purpose
Restate Lincoln's argument in your own words.

Abraham Lincoln (1860) by George Peter Alexander Healy.

from
What to the Slave Is the Fourth of July?

by Frederick Douglass

Build Background

Frederick Douglass was raised in slavery in Maryland. Although it was illegal in Maryland for a slave to be educated, Douglass managed to learn to read. After escaping slavery, Douglass became a passionate speaker against the institution. His speeches were so well written that some people doubted that a former slave could express himself so well. As a result, Douglass decided to write his autobiography in 1845. Because he revealed the name of his former owner in it, Douglass had to leave the country. When he came back from Europe, he bought his freedom and launched a newspaper dedicated to the antislavery cause. He delivered this speech on July 5, 1852, in Rochester, New York.

Frederick Douglass (c. 1844) attributed to Elisha Hammond. Oil on canvas 69.9 x 57.1 cm.

Fellow citizens, pardon me, and allow me to ask, why am I called upon to speak here today? What have I or those I represent to do with your national independence? Are the great principles of political freedom and of natural justice, embodied in that Declaration of Independence, extended to us? And am I, therefore, called upon to bring our humble offering to the national altar, and to confess the benefits, and express devout gratitude for the blessings resulting from your independence to us? . . .

Fellow citizens, above your national, tumultuous joy, I hear the mournful wail of millions, whose chains, heavy and grievous yesterday, are today rendered more intolerable by the jubilant shouts that reach them. . . .

My subject, then, fellow citizens, is "American Slavery." I shall see this day and its popular characteristics from the slave's point of view. Standing here, identified with the American bondman,[1] making his wrongs mine, I do not hesitate to declare, with all my soul, that the character and conduct of this nation never looked blacker to me than on this Fourth of July. **(A)**

. . . I will, in the name of humanity, which is outraged, in the name of liberty, which is fettered,[2] in the name of the Constitution and the Bible, which are disregarded and trampled upon, dare to call in question and to denounce, with all the emphasis I can command, everything that serves to perpetuate slavery—the

---

1. **bondman:** someone who is enslaved.
2. **fettered** (FEHT uhrd): in chains.

(A) Informational Focus Proposition and Support What is Douglass's subject in this speech? What opinion does he express in this paragraph?

Vocabulary **denounce** (dih NOWNS) *v.:* speak against.
perpetuate (puhr PEHCH oo ayt) *v.:* cause to continue.

Analyzing Visuals

Connecting to the Text
What is happening in this image? How does it relate to the ideas in Douglass's speech?

great sin and shame of America! "I will not equivocate[3]—I will not excuse." I will use the severest language I can command, and yet not one word shall escape me that any man, whose judgment is not blinded by prejudice, or who is not at heart a slave-holder, shall not confess to be right and just. . . . **B**

What point in the anti-slavery creed[4] would you have me argue? On what branch of the subject do the people of this country need light? Must I undertake to prove that the slave is a man? That point is conceded already. Nobody doubts it. The slave-holders themselves acknowledge it in the enactment of laws for their government. They acknowledge it when they punish disobedience on the part of the slave. There are seventy-two crimes in the State of Virginia, which, if committed by a black man (no matter how ignorant he be), subject him to the punishment of death; while

only two of these same crimes will subject a white man to like punishment.

What is this but the acknowledgment that the slave is a moral, intellectual, and responsible being? The manhood of the slave is conceded. It is admitted in the fact that Southern statute books are covered with enactments, forbidding, under severe fines and penalties, the teaching of the slave to read and write. When you can point to any such laws in reference to the beasts of the field, then I may consent to argue the manhood of the slave. When the dogs in your streets, when the fowls of the air, when the cattle on your hills, when the fish of the sea, and the reptiles that crawl, shall be unable to distinguish the slave from a brute, then I will argue with you that the slave is a man! **C**

For the present it is enough to affirm the equal manhood of the Negro race. Is it not astonishing that, while we are plowing, planting, and reaping, using all kinds of mechanical tools, erecting houses, constructing bridges, building ships, working in metals of brass,

---

3. **equivocate** (ih KWIHV uh kayt): speak vaguely; try to mislead by speaking indirectly.
4. **creed:** belief.

B **Informational Focus** Proposition and Support
What is Douglass's proposition in this speech?

C **Read and Discuss** What key idea unifies this paragraph?

Vocabulary **conceded** (kuhn SEED ihd) *v.:* admitted; acknowledged.

iron, copper, silver, and gold; that while we are reading, writing, and ciphering,[5] acting as clerks, merchants, and secretaries, having among us lawyers, doctors, ministers, poets, authors, editors, orators, and teachers; that we are engaged in all the enterprises common to other men—digging gold in California, capturing the whale in the Pacific, feeding sheep and cattle on the hillside, living, moving, acting, thinking, planning, living in families as husbands, wives, and children, and above all, confessing and worshipping the Christian God, and looking hopefully for life and immortality beyond the grave—we are called upon to prove that we are men?

Would you have me argue that man is entitled to liberty? That he is the rightful owner of his own body? You have already declared it. Must I argue the wrongfulness of slavery? Is that a question for republicans?[6] Is it to be settled by the rules of logic and argumentation, as a matter beset with great difficulty, involving a doubtful application of the principle of justice, hard to understand? How should I look today in the presence of Americans, dividing and subdividing a discourse, to show that men have a natural right to freedom, speaking of it relatively and positively, negatively and affirmatively? To do so would be to make myself ridiculous, and to offer an insult to your understanding. There is not a man beneath the canopy of heaven who does not know that slavery is wrong for him. **D**

---

5. **ciphering** (SY fuhr ihng): doing arithmetic.
6. **republicans:** citizens who believe in the elected government, a republic.

What! Am I to argue that it is wrong to make men brutes, to rob them of their liberty, to work them without wages, to keep them ignorant of their relations to their fellow men, to beat them with sticks, to flay their flesh with the lash, to load their limbs with irons, to hunt them with dogs, to sell them at auction, to sunder[7] their families, to knock out their teeth, to burn their flesh, to starve them into obedience and submission to their masters? Must I argue that a system thus marked with blood and stained with pollution is wrong? No—I will not. I have better employment for my time and strength than such arguments would imply. . . .

At a time like this, scorching irony, not convincing argument, is needed. Oh! had I the ability, and could I reach the nation's ear, I would today pour out a fiery stream of biting ridicule, blasting reproach, withering sarcasm, and stern rebuke. For it is not light that is needed, but fire; it is not the gentle shower, but thunder. We need the storm, the whirlwind, and the earthquake. The feeling of the nation must be quickened; the conscience of the nation must be roused; the propriety[8] of the nation must be startled; the hypocrisy of the nation must be exposed; and its crimes against God and man must be denounced. . . . **E**

---

7. **sunder:** drive apart; separate.
8. **propriety** (pruh PRY uh tee): sense of correct behavior.

Read with a Purpose
What is the most effective part of Douglass's argument?

D **Read and Discuss** Why does Douglass say about freedom in this paragraph?

E **Informational Focus** Proposition and Support
How does Douglass conclude the speech? What comparisons does he make to express his point?

Vocabulary **hypocrisy** (hih PAHK ruh see) *n.*: false show of virtue or goodness.

What to the Slave Is the Fourth of July? **763**

Applying Your Skills

Reading Standard 2.7 Evaluate the unity, coherence, logic, **internal consistency, and structural patterns of text.**

Fragment on Slavery, 1854 / What to the Slave Is the Fourth of July?

Standards Review

Informational Text and Vocabulary

1. What is Lincoln's basic **proposition** in "Fragment on Slavery, 1854"?

   A Slavery can be proven to be just.

   B Slavery is an oppressive institution.

   C White people could be held in slavery.

   D Reasons in favor of slavery do not hold up.

2. Lincoln **supports** his proposition in "Fragment on Slavery, 1854" by

   A arguing against his opponents' reasons.

   B posing questions based on his opponents' reasons.

   C drawing conclusions based on predictions.

   D giving statistics to show slavery is immoral.

3. What **proposition** does Douglass support in his speech?

   A Slavery is immoral and unjust.

   B Virginia is a slave state.

   C It is illegal for slaves to learn to read.

   D Everyone honors the Fourth of July.

4. If added to Douglass's speech, which of these topics about enslaved people would break the speech's **internal consistency?**

   A the right to earn wages

   B the harshness of punishment

   C the way to escape

   D the desire to learn

5. The proposition-and-support **structural pattern** within each selection helps

   A set up a comparison.

   B provide unity and coherence.

   C present sequential information.

   D classify information into groups.

6. If you *denounce* a law, you

   A support it.

   B condemn it.

   C overturn it.

   D speak about it.

7. To *perpetuate* an action, you

   A start it.

   B stop it.

   C explain it.

   D keep it going.

8. A synonym for *conceded* is

   A accepted.

   B stopped.

   C proved.

   D denied.

Writing Skills Focus

Timed └Writing In a paragraph, critique the use of logic in the proposition and support structural pattern in either Lincoln's text or Douglass's speech.

What Do You Think Now? How did the institution of slavery affect the people living in the 1800s?

Apologies for Past Actions Are Still Appropriate TODAY

by The Macon Telegraph

FEB. 21, 2007, MACON, GEORGIA—The mayor of Macon has issued an executive order apologizing for the city's role in the institution of slavery. According to the 1830 U.S. Census, Bibb County had a population of 7,154, of which 2,988 were slaves. In 1830, Georgia had a population of 516,823, and of those, 217,531 were slaves. Two states, Kentucky and South Carolina, had more slaves than free persons. Mississippi's white population outnumbered the slave population by less than 5,000. **A**

While some will have questions about the mayor's motives or disagree with an apology, there is no question that the despicable institution of slavery is part of our nation's legacy.

Slaves were first brought to this country in 1619, one year before the pilgrims landed at Plymouth Rock, and whatever our country's fortunes are, the backbone of those fortunes rested on the economic shoulders of slave labor.

It's easy to wonder in 2007 how this country, founded on freedom, could have stood for such an institution. Certainly, it was a different time. Thankfully, civilization has progressed to the point of recognizing each individual's intrinsic value, and we have come to understand the true meaning of "We hold these truths to be self-evident, that all men are created equal, that they are endowed by their Creator with certain unalienable Rights."

A **Informational Focus** Proposition and Support
Explain what these statistics add to this paragraph.

Vocabulary **despicable** (DEHS pih kuh buhl) *adj.*: hateful; detested.

Monument (by sculptor Ed Dwight) to the Underground Railroad, on Detroit's riverfront.

With that said, why do some Americans have so much trouble dealing with historical records that lead to the conclusion that an apology for slavery is not only warranted but necessary? Though slavery was ended with the 13th Amendment to the Constitution, the effects of hundreds of years of servitude still live on in a race of people who were enslaved simply on the basis of their skin color. Those who feel absolved of responsibility by saying they had nothing to do with slavery should look around. They are enjoying today the white privileges that were etched in law only to be recently erased; the ultimate affirmative action program[1] of which they are beneficiaries. **B**

In the scope of things, the mayor's apology may mean little to the city, but it could mean a lot to him. That's OK. Each government entity has to examine its own history before taking such a step. In Maine, Indiana, Massachusetts, New Hampshire and Ohio, the slave population, according to the census, was in the single digits. Vermont didn't have a single slave, but in a city where the African-American population is 62.5 percent, it is more than likely the slaves that inhabited the area are the ancestors of many present-day residents.

Issuing an official apology and recognizing the contributions of slaves can have a cathartic[2] effect, not only for the descendants of slaves, but for the descendants of slave owners—some of whom are still living in the area, too. **C**

2. **cathartic** (kuh THAHR tihk): causing relief from emotional tensions.

1. **affirmative action program:** plan that aims to correct past discrimination by giving preference to members of certain groups, such as African Americans, Native Americans, or women.

Read with a Purpose
What is the proposition of this editorial?

B Read and Discuss Why does the article mention the Constitution here?

C Informational Focus Proposition and Support Explain whether this statement is supported by evidence in the text.

Applying Your Skills

Apologies for Past Actions Are Still Appropriate Today

Standards Review

Informational Text and Vocabulary

1. The *Macon Telegraph* editorial **proposes** that the mayor's apology for slavery

   A will damage his career.

   B is the right thing to do.

   C has nothing to do with residents today.

   D is meaningless.

2. To support its **proposition,** the *Macon Telegraph* editorial uses all of the following *except*

   A facts.

   B anecdotes.

   C logical reasoning.

   D statistics.

3. Which of following provides **support** for the argument that an apology for slavery is still relevant today?

   A Vermont didn't have a single slave.

   B In 1830, Georgia had a population of 516,823.

   C Descendants of slaves and slaveholders are still alive.

   D Slavery is an immoral and unjust institution.

4. Which sentence could be added to the first paragraph without destroying its **unity**?

   A The states of Louisiana and Alabama also counted high percentages of slaves to free persons.

   B The population of immigrants living in Georgia was not counted separately.

   C The 1830 U.S. Census counted the population of the entire nation.

   D Today Macon is home to a great number of African American people.

5. Each of the following is an example of **logical evidence** used in this editorial except

   A the editor's feelings.

   B population statistics.

   C quotations from the Constitution.

   D historical facts.

6. If something is *despicable,* it is

   A in the past.

   B illegal.

   C debatable.

   D horrible.

Writing Skills Focus

Timed └Writing Review the charts you created while reading these three texts. Critique the text you find most or least impressive. Support your opinion with examples from the text.

What Do You Think Now Has your understanding of how slavery continues to affect the United States changed after reading this selection? Explain.

CONTENTS

Dr. Martin Luther King, Jr. delivers his
"I Have a Dream" speech on the steps of
the Lincoln Memorial in Washington, D.C.
during the 1963 March on Washington.

What Do You Think?

What does the idea of freedom mean to you?

QuickWrite

Lincoln and King use the idea of freedom to inspire their listeners.
How have you seen freedom addressed in other works? Discuss
with a partner.

SPEECHES
Preparing to Read

Reading Standard 2.7 Evaluate the unity, coherence, logic, internal consistency, and structural patterns of text.

The Gettysburg Address / *from* I Have a Dream

Informational Text Focus

Structural Patterns: Refrain Like poets, good speakers appeal to our sense of hearing. One way that they do this is by using refrains, which create echoes in listeners' ears. A refrain is a repeated sound, word, phrase, line, or group of lines. Refrains are used to build rhythm, create internal <u>consistency</u>, and emphasize important messages.

As you study "The Gettysburg Address" and "I Have a Dream," pay attention to the tone of each selection. **Tone** is the writer's attitude toward his or her subject. Both Lincoln and King use a consistent tone throughout their speeches. The details they include and words they repeat affect your understanding of the text. Think of words you would use to describe each writer's tone as you read the selections.

Into Action Use a chart like the one below to <u>critique</u> the two selections. A chart for "The Gettysburg Address" has been started for you.

The Gettysburg Address

What is the author's main idea?

What details support the main idea?

How well is the main idea developed?

What structural patterns does the author use?

My critique:

Writing Skills Focus

Preparing for Timed └Writing As you read these selections, record in your *Reader/Writer Notebook* examples of words and phrases that King and Lincoln have chosen to repeat.

Reader/Writer
Notebook
Use your **RWN** to complete the activities for these selections.

Vocabulary

The Gettysburg Address

detract (dih TRACT) *v.*: take away from; make less important. *Lincoln believes that nothing people say can add to or detract from the sacrifices made at Gettysburg.*

nobly (NOH blee) *adv.*: in a manner that is excellent or heroic. *Lincoln honors the brave men who died nobly for freedom and equality.*

I Have a Dream

creed (kreed) *n.*: statement of belief or principles. *Dr. King developed a creed of nonviolence.*

oasis (oh AY sihs) *n.*: place or thing offering relief. *A land of equality for all races would be an oasis after years in a desert of racism.*

Language Coach

Word Origins The Vocabulary word *creed* comes from the Latin word *credo*, which means "I believe." Other derivatives of this word include *credible* and *credit*. How would you explain the relationship between these words and the Latin word *credo*?

Abraham Lincoln
(1809–1865)

A Wartime President

When he was a boy, Abraham Lincoln rarely went to school. He was interested in learning, however, and eventually taught himself law. He entered the field of politics and was elected president in 1860, during a period of crisis that quickly erupted into war between the Northern and Southern states. In 1863, during the Civil War, he issued the Emancipation Proclamation. This proclamation led to the adoption of the Thirteenth Amendment to the Constitution, which outlawed slavery.

When war broke out, Lincoln was determined to keep the Union together. He did not live to see his country reunited, however. He was shot by an assassin in a theater in Washington, D.C.

Dr. Martin Luther King, Jr.
(1929–1968)

A National Leader

Dr. Martin Luther King, Jr., was a Baptist minister from Atlanta, Georgia, and a national leader in the civil rights movement. He faced violence and arrest while spreading his message of nonviolent resistance. He believed that the racism and segregation he witnessed daily could be overcome without using further violence. He became known for his powerful voice and eloquent message.

In 1964, four years before he was assassinated in Memphis, Tennessee, King was awarded the Nobel Peace Prize.

Think About the Writers
What vision did Lincoln and King share?

Preview the Selections

At his address at Gettysburg, **Abraham Lincoln** expresses his vision of American democracy while commemorating the soldiers who were killed in the Battle of Gettysburg during the Civil War.

In "I Have a Dream," a speech delivered in August 1963, **Dr. Martin Luther King, Jr.,** expresses his hopes for the future of race relations and inspires a nation.

Read with a Purpose

Read this speech to learn how Lincoln honored those who sacrificed their lives.

Build Background

The Battle of Gettysburg, which took place in Pennsylvania in 1863, was a turning point in the Civil War. After the bloody three-day battle, 51,000 soldiers on both sides were dead, wounded, or missing. On November 19, 1863, part of the battlefield was dedicated as a military cemetery. President Lincoln gave the following short address at the dedication ceremony.

The Gettysburg Address

by **Abraham Lincoln**

An artist's depiction of Abraham Lincoln delivering the Gettysburg Address.

November 19, 1863

Four score and seven years[1] ago our fathers brought forth on this continent a new nation, conceived[2] in liberty, and dedicated to the proposition that all men are created equal. **Ⓐ**

Now we are engaged in a great civil war, testing whether that nation, or any nation so conceived and so dedicated, can long endure. We are met on a great battlefield of that war. We have come to dedicate a portion of that field, as a final resting place for those who here gave their lives that that nation might live. It is altogether fitting and proper that we should do this. **Ⓑ**

But, in a larger sense, we cannot dedicate—we cannot consecrate[3]—we cannot hallow[4]—this ground.

---

1. **four score and seven years:** eighty-seven years.
2. **conceived:** developed.
3. **consecrate:** set apart as sacred or holy.
4. **hallow:** make holy.

Ⓐ **Read and Discuss** What event does Lincoln refer to here?

Ⓑ **Informational Focus** **Tone** What words would you use to describe Lincoln's tone?

The brave men, living and dead, who struggled here, have consecrated it, far above our poor power to add or detract. The world will little note nor long remember what we say here, but it can never forget what they did here. It is for us the living, rather, to be dedicated here to the unfinished work which they who fought here have thus far so nobly advanced. It is rather for us to be here dedicated to the great task remaining before us—that from these honored dead we take increased devotion to that cause for which they gave the last full measure of devotion—that we here highly resolve that these dead shall not have died in vain—that this nation, under God, shall have a new birth of freedom—and that government of the people, by the people, for the people, shall not perish from the earth. **C**

C **Informational Focus** **Refrain** What words does Lincoln repeat at the end of the speech? What key idea does this repetition emphasize?

Vocabulary **detract** (dih TRAKT) *v.*: take away from; make less important. **nobly** (NOH blee) *adv.*: in a manner that is excellent or heroic.

Read with a Purpose
How does Lincoln honor those who have sacrificed their lives?

A statue in Gettysburg, Pennsylvania.

from I Have a Dream

by **Dr. Martin Luther King, Jr.**

Read with a Purpose

Read this speech to discover what Dr. Martin Luther King, Jr., envisioned America could and should be.

Preparing to Read for this selection is on page 769.

Build Background

On August 28, 1963, more than 200,000 Americans of all races and from all over the country took part in a march in Washington, D.C., to demand full equality for African Americans. Late in the day, Dr. Martin Luther King, Jr., rose to speak. What follows is a portion of his deeply moving speech.

August 28, 1963

I say to you today, my friends, that in spite of the difficulties and frustrations of the moment I still have a dream. It is a dream deeply rooted in the American Dream.

I have a dream that one day this nation will rise up and live out the true meaning of its creed: "We hold these truths to be self-evident; that all men are created equal."

I have a dream that one day on the red hills of Georgia the sons of former slaves and the sons of former slave owners will be able to sit down together at the table of brotherhood. **Ⓐ**

I have a dream that one day even the state of Mississippi, a desert state sweltering with the heat of injustice and oppression, will be transformed into an oasis of freedom and justice.

I have a dream that my four little children will one day live in a nation where they will not be judged by the color of their skin but by the content of their character.

I have a dream today.

I have a dream that one day every valley shall be exalted,[1] every hill and mountain shall be made low, the rough places will be made plain, and the crooked places will be made straight, and the glory of the Lord shall be revealed, and all flesh shall see it together. **Ⓑ**

This is our hope. This is the faith with which I return to the South. With this faith

---

1. **exalted** (ehg ZAWL tihd): raised; lifted up.

Ⓐ Informational Focus **Tone** What words would you use to describe the tone of this speech so far?

Ⓑ Informational Focus **Refrain** What patterns of repetition can you find so far? What idea is being emphasized?

Vocabulary **creed** (kreed) *n.:* statement of belief or principles.
oasis (oh AY sihs) *n.:* place or thing offering relief.

Annual Martin Luther King, Jr. march in Raleigh, N.C., in 2007.

we will be able to hew out of the mountain of despair a stone of hope. With this faith we will be able to transform the jangling discords of our nation into a beautiful symphony of brotherhood. With this faith we will be able to work together, to pray together, to struggle together, to go to jail together, to stand up for freedom together, knowing that we will be free one day. **C**

This will be the day when all of God's children will be able to sing with new meaning "My country 'tis of thee, sweet land of liberty, of thee I sing. Land where my fathers died, land of the pilgrim's pride, from every mountainside, let freedom ring."

And if America is to be a great nation, this must become true. So let freedom ring from the prodigious[2] hilltops of New Hampshire. Let freedom ring from the mighty mountains of New York. Let freedom ring from the heightening Alleghenies of Pennsylvania!

Let freedom ring from the snowcapped Rockies of Colorado!

Let freedom ring from the curvaceous peaks of California!

But not only that; let freedom ring from Stone Mountain of Georgia!

Let freedom ring from Lookout Mountain of Tennessee!

Let freedom ring from every hill and molehill of Mississippi. From every mountainside, let freedom ring.

When we let freedom ring, when we let it ring from every village and every hamlet, from every state and every city, we will be able to speed up that day when all of God's children, black men and white men, Jews and Gentiles, Protestants and Catholics, will be able to join hands and sing in the words of the old Negro spiritual, "Free at last! Free at last! Thank God almighty, we are free at last!" **D**

Read with a Purpose
What is King's vision for America?

---

2. **prodigious** (pruh DIHJ uhs): huge; amazing.

C Read and Discuss What is King saying about freedom?

D Informational Focus Refrain What words does King repeat in the paragraphs on this page? What does the repetition add to the speech?

Applying Your Skills

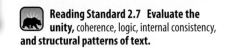
The Gettysburg Address / *from* I Have a Dream

Standards Review

Informational Text and Vocabulary

1. Unity exists in the Gettysburg Address because *all* of its ideas are related to the need

  A to struggle to preserve the ideals of liberty and democracy.

  B to deliver speeches at battlefields.

  C for soldiers to believe in what they fight for.

  D to end the American Civil War.

2. Read this sentence from Lincoln's speech.

> But in a larger sense, we cannot dedicate—we cannot consecrate— we cannot hallow—this ground.

In the sentence above, Lincoln repeats the **refrain** "we cannot" for

  A chronological order.

  B internal consistency.

  C classification.

  D problem-solution pattern.

3. Which statement *best* expresses the **main idea** of King's "I Have a Dream" speech?

  A You must be willing to suffer to achieve your goals.

  B The coming of equality will save all Americans.

  C Freedom and equality will come for all Americans.

  D Protesting without violence is the best way to get a point heard.

4. Which of the following sentences could be added to the "I Have a Dream" speech without destroying its **unity**?

  A I have a dream that one day we will conquer disease.

  B I have a dream that one day the evil on earth will be punished by the good.

  C I have a dream that one day we will eliminate world hunger.

  D I have a dream that one day we will live in a world without prejudice and hate.

5. Another term for *detract* is

  A diminish.

  B request.

  C resolve.

  D endure.

6. A *creed* is a(n)

  A attack.

  B plan.

  C question.

  D belief.

Writing Skills Focus

Timed ⌴Writing Review your list of repeated phrases from the speeches. Analyze the way these phrases and the writer's key ideas are related. Then, write a paragraph in which you critique the internal consistency of each speech.

What Do You Think Now

Why is the presentation of freedom in these speeches effective?

Writing Workshop

Research Report

Write with a Purpose

Write a research report about a historical subject. Your **audience** will include your teacher, classmates, and other students at your school. Your **purpose** is to convey unbiased factual information on your chosen subject.

A Good Research Report

- presents a coherent and well-defined thesis
- includes ideas, concepts, and direct quotations from reliable sources
- uses a variety of primary and secondary sources
- paraphrases or summarizes appropriate perspectives on the topic, as appropriate
- organizes information on charts, maps, and graphs
- ends by summarizing ideas or drawing an overall conclusion
- includes references and a Works Cited list

See page 784 for complete rubric.

Reader/Writer Notebook

Use your **RWN** to complete the activities for this workshop.

Think as a Reader/Writer Research often begins with a question about a subject that interests you or that you have a certain theory about. The success of your **research report** depends on carefully selecting evidence from sources to support your **thesis,** or main idea. Read the following excerpt from a report that began with a question the writer had about African American soldiers in World War II.

World War II brings many heroic images to mind. People may think of Rosie the Riveter or the Iwo Jima statue of six Marines. One lesser-known story, though, is the heroism of African American soldiers in World War II. The 761st Tank Battalion proved that African Americans could serve their country with excellence and bravery.

⟵ The controlling idea, or **thesis,** of the report is stated clearly.

When the war began in the late 1930s, African Americans made up only a small part of the army. The armed forces were segregated, or separated, by race. . . . In 1940, the U.S. Congress passed the Selective Training and Service Act, which included these words, "there shall be no discrimination against any person on account of race or color" (qtd. in Pfeifer 13–14).The act led to the creation of black combat units, including the 761st Tank Battalion (Pfeifer 22).

⟵ Background on the topic is presented.

⟵ A historical document is quoted and the source cited.

In October 1944, the battalion joined General George S. Patton's Third Army in Europe. According to the writer Catherine Reef, Patton told the soldiers, "I would never have asked for you if you weren't good. I have nothing but the best in my Army" (qtd. in Reef 51).

⟵ A phrase signals the introduction of a quote from a source.

Think About the Model

With a partner, discuss the following questions about the model:

1. How would you describe the organization of the first paragraph?

2. How does the quote in the last paragraph support the writer's thesis?

Writing Standards 1.1 Create compositions that establish a controlling impression, have a coherent thesis, and end with a clear and well-supported conclusion. **1.4 Plan and conduct multiple-step information searches by using computer networks** and modems. **1.5** Achieve an effective balance between researched information and original ideas. **2.3** Write research reports: a. Define a thesis. b. Record important ideas, concepts, and direct quotations from significant information sources and paraphrase and summarize all perspectives on the topic, as appropriate. c. Use a variety of primary and secondary sources and distinguish the nature and value of each. d. Organize and display information on charts, maps, and graphs.

Prewriting

Choose a Subject

Brainstorm a list of possible historical figures or events to research. Perhaps you are considering the history of basketball as your subject. You cannot hope to cover the entire history of the sport in your report. You need to narrow your broad subject to a manageable one, one that you can research and then say something significant about in the time you have for the assignment.

Broad Subject	Narrow Subject	Narrower Subject
history of basketball	important basketball players	Michael Jordan

Narrow Your Research

For example, if you chose the basketball player Michael Jordan as your subject, you might ask this question: *What made Michael Jordan an important player in basketball history?*

Think About Purpose and Audience

When planning your research report, keep your purpose and audience in mind. Your **purpose** in expository, or informative, writing is to present factual information about your subject. Your **audience** includes your teacher, classmates, and other students at your school who will read your report.

Gather Sources

Use at least three sources of information for your report. To find sources, plan and conduct a multi-step search on the Internet or in your library catalog, which will help you keep your search focused. Search library catalogs by title, author, subject, or keyword. When you find items you want, write down the title, author, and call number, the code of numbers and letters that locates items on library shelves. On the Internet use a search engine, a software tool that finds information on the Web. Just enter a search term, or keyword and the search engine will return a list of pertinent Web pages. Whenever possible, use **primary sources** (first-hand accounts), such as diaries and letters. **Secondary sources** are interpretations of primary materials. They include encyclopedia entries, newspaper articles, and documentaries. Check subheadings to get an idea for an aspect of your subject to research. Posing a question can also help guide your work.

Idea Starters

Here are some examples of the kinds of people or events that you might research and write about:

- a great musician of the past
- an early governor of your state
- early space exploration
- an important discovery in medicine
- the history of your favorite game
- a major weather event, such as a flood, hurricane, or blizzard

Writing Tip

Use your answers to the following questions to help limit the scope of your research:

- How did the individual or event change the world?
- How did the individual contribute to or affect a moment in history?
- Why is the historical event important and memorable?
- Why should we continue to think about this historical person or event?

Your Turn _____

Get Started Making notes in your **RWN,** choose a subject and narrow your focus. Then, begin gathering information about your topic.

Learn It Online
Use an interactive writer's model to take another look at writing reports:

go.hrw.com | H8-777 | Go

Evaluate Sources

Before you begin taking notes from your sources, evaluate each source to determine whether it is factual, up-to-date, and trustworthy. Answer these questions:

- Is the source nonfiction?
- Is the information current? Does it include recent thinking or research on this historical subject?
- Is the source trustworthy? Is the author an expert in the field? If the source is a Web site, does the address end in *.org, .edu,* or *.gov?*

Prepare a notecard for each source. Accurately record the title of the source, the author, the city in which it was published, the name of the publisher, and the year of publication. Give each source a number.

Take Notes on Your Information

Record each fact, idea, or concept you might want to use on a separate index card. Include all perspectives on your topic (including original ideas you may have). Summarize or paraphrase the information by restating it in your own words. Then, record the source number and the number of the page on which you found the information. If you want to use a direct quotation, copy it word for word and put quotation marks around it in your notes and in your report. Remember that you will need to cite your sources.

Write a Thesis Statement

Your **thesis statement** tells what the point of the research report will be. It usually appears in your introductory paragraph. Your thesis should state both the topic of your paper and the most important conclusion you've drawn from your research. What do you want your audience to understand about your topic after they have read your report? The answer to this question is your thesis.

Outline Your Report

Organize important information and supporting details in an outline. Sort your notes into several major categories; then, divide them further into subtopics, each to be developed into a full paragraph. Decide how you will organize the information in your report—by order of importance or in chronological (time) order—and record your plan.

Use Graphic Aids

Wherever possible, organize and display your information in graphic form. Graphic aids such as charts, maps, and graphs will help your reader grasp important information quickly and clearly.

● Writing Tip

Remember the different ways you can take notes from your sources:

- **paraphrase**: restate the information in your own words
- **summarize**: state the main ideas in the source
- **quote**: write down the quotation or information word-for-word, using quotation marks

Your Turn _____

Organize Information Finish gathering and evaluating your sources. Decide which facts and ideas you will use in your report, and take notes on the source of each. Then, outline your report in your **RWN** in preparation for drafting.

Drafting

Follow the Writer's Framework

The Framework of a Research Report to the right outlines how to draft an effective report. As you write, keep in mind the characteristics of a good research report (page 776). You may need to rearrange your ideas or add new ones. Or, you may have to take out or add new information. Keep referring to your notes, and go back to your sources when necessary. You can expand your draft by interpreting the information you have gathered. Ask yourself, "Why is the information important?"

Write an Introduction

The main purpose of the research report's introduction is to introduce the subject and to state the thesis, but a good introduction will also entice your audience. Some writers like to begin by drafting their introduction, whereas others prefer to write the introduction after the rest of the paper. Do what works best for you.

Framework of a Research Report

Introduction
- Arouses reader's interest, clearly identifies the subject of report, and states the thesis

Body
- Discusses each main idea in one or more paragraphs and supports each main idea with facts, examples, and quotations

    Idea #1

    Idea #2

    Idea #3

Conclusion
- Summarizes or restates main idea(s) and draws conclusions

Works Cited List
- Lists sources alphabetically

Writing Tip

When you use sources in your writing, you need to guard against plagiarism. Your original ideas clearly don't require a source. However, using another writer's words without crediting the source or presenting another writer's ideas as your own is **plagiarism,** or literary theft. Taking careful notes as you research will help you avoid this serious problem.

Writing Tip

For a complete version of a research paper, log on to the Interactive Student Edition at go.hrw.com and go to page 776.

Grammar Link Using Transitional Words and Phrases

When you use chronological order to talk about an event or a person's life, you organize the information according to the order in which things happened in time. You can help your reader stay oriented by using **transitional words** and **phrases** to connect ideas chronologically both within and between paragraphs. Here is a list of common words and phrases that indicate sequence in time:

first	next	before	then	when	while	meanwhile	at last	finally

Unclear	Clear
The musicians play a tune. The pianist plays it in double time. The bass player changes the harmony. The musicians come together in a return to the original tune.	*First,* the musicians play a tune. *Then,* the pianist plays it in double time. *Meanwhile,* the bass player changes the harmony. *Finally,* the musicians come together in a return to the original tune.

Reference Note For more transitional words and phrases, see the Handbook section.

Your Turn

Draft Your Report Using your framework and source notes, create your first draft. Consider writing your introduction after you've drafted the rest of your paper. When writing a chronological report, use transitional words and phrases in your writing to help your reader understand the order in which events occurred.

Peer Review

Working with a partner, review your draft. Answer each question in the chart to the right to locate where and how your drafts could be improved. As you discuss your papers, be sure to take notes about each other's suggestions.

Evaluating and Revising

Read the questions in the left-hand column of the chart, and then use the tips in the middle column to help you make revisions to your research report. The right-hand column suggests techniques you can use to revise your draft.

Research Report: Guidelines for Content and Organization

Evaluation Questions	Tips	Revision Techniques
1. Does your introduction clearly state your topic and include a coherent thesis?	**Put stars** next to your statements of the report's topic and thesis.	**State** the topic clearly and **add** a well-defined thesis, if needed.
2. Does your draft include original ideas as well as significant information to support your thesis?	**Highlight** each important fact, idea, concept, and direct quotation.	**Add** additional supporting information, if necessary.
3. Have you paraphrased or summarized all perspectives on the topic?	**Number** each different perspective on your topic.	**Include** a different perspective, if appropriate.
4. Have you used at least three reliable sources? Are they both primary and secondary sources?	**Circle** your references. **Evaluate** the reliability of each source and **identify** it as primary or secondary.	**Add** information from additional reliable primary and secondary sources, if needed.
5. Have you organized and displayed information in graphic form?	**Highlight** each chart, map, or graph.	**Show** your information in graphic form, where possible.
6. Does your final paragraph adequately sum up your overall findings, or conclusions?	**Put a check mark** next to the conclusion, or final statement.	If your final statement is unclear, **revise** it for clarity.
7. Have you included all quotations and other necessary information on your Works Cited list?	**Put a check mark** beside each piece of information necessary in a citation.	**Add** sources to the Works Cited list, if needed.

Read this student draft; note the comments on its strengths as well as suggestions on how the draft could be improved.

The Greatest Basketball Player in U.S. History

by Tito Onesto, Talent Middle School

Michael "Air" Jordan is the greatest basketball player of all time because he's a phenomenal athlete with a unique combination of grace, speed, power, and an unquenchable competitive desire. Michael Jordan single-handedly redefined the words "NBA superstar."

← Tito states his **thesis:** Jordan was a uniquely great player.

Players like Robert Parish and Larry Bird played for the Boston Celtics. They are big names in basketball too. Michael Jordan wasn't always a big name. He was cut from his high school varsity team as a sophomore, which made him practice for hours, day after day. Jordan eventually made the varsity team and led the Lanley High School Buccaneers to the North Carolina State Championship.

← He begins by giving **background** in **chronological order.**

He accepted a basketball scholarship to the University of North Carolina. As a freshman, Jordan made the winning shot in the 1982 NCAA Championship game against the Georgetown Hoyas and future NBA rival Patrick Ewing. "That made Mike Jordan into Michael Jordan," stated James and Delores Jordan after the game-winning shot (Lovitt 68).

← Tito **quotes** experts on Jordan's playing.

MINI-LESSON ▶ **How to Keep Your Focus**

At the beginning of his second paragraph, Tito strays too far from his topic. He simply deletes the first two sentences in that paragraph and improves the focus of his report. He then decides to add a quote from the subject of the report in order to support his point that Jordan had an "unquenchable competitive desire."

Tito's Revision of Paragraph Two

~~Players like Robert Parish and Larry Bird played for the Boston Celtics. They are big names in basketball too.~~ Michael Jordan wasn't always a big name. He was cut from his high school varsity team as a sophomore, which made him practice for hours, day after day. *"When I was working out and I got tired and figured I ought to stop, I'd close my eyes and see that list without my name on it," Jordan said, "and it usually got me going again" (Lovitt 68).* Jordan eventually made the varsity team and led the Lanley High School Buccaneers to the North Carolina State Championship.

Your Turn

Edit Distracting Material As you review your draft, ask yourself whether each point is relevant to your thesis. If you have included information that may distract your reader from your main point, cross out the unnecessary material.

Student Draft *continues*

Jordan was drafted third overall in the 1984 draft by the Chicago Bulls. He averaged 28.8 points, 6.5 rebounds, 5.9 assists, and 2.4 steals per game that rookie season, but it was cut short because of a foot injury in the third game. Michael Jordan's team, the Bulls of Chicago, managed to make the NBA playoffs, but they didn't win, eventually losing to the eventual NBA championship winning team, the Celtics of Boston. Even though the Chicago Bulls got killed in that series, it is remembered because Michael Jordan dropped 63 points, setting an NBA record. "He was God disguised as Michael Jordan," stated Larry Bird after Jordan's 63-point performance (Lovitt 82). After that season, Michael Jordan was considered among the best in the league.

Michael Jordan is considered the greatest basketball player in NBA history because of his career accomplishments: six NBA Championships, five-time NBA Most Valuable Player, ten-time Scoring Champ, ten-time All-NBA first team, Rookie of the Year, All-Star Dunk Contest Champion, NCAA National Champion with North Carolina in 1982, and two-time Olympic Gold Medalist. Surely, there will never be another basketball player like Michael Jordan.

Works Cited

Lovitt, Chip. Michael Jordan: Basketball's Best. New York: Scholastic, Inc., 2002.
"Michael Jordan's Biography." 23Jordan (2006): 1–4. Online. Internet. 26
    February 2006. Available <http://www.23jordan.com/bio1.htm>.
Reed, William F. "Jordan, Michael. "World Book Online Reference Center. 2007.
    Online. Internet. 26 February 2007. Available <http://
    worldbookonline.com/wb/Article?id=ar290875&st=michael+jordan>.

Tito **quotes** another expert in the field.

He closes with a well-supported **conclusion.**

Tito includes a **list of cited works** and properly formats each of his sources.

MINI-LESSON ▶ **How to Eliminate Wordiness**

When Tito read an earlier draft, he realized that he was using far too many words that did not add any information, interest, or elegance to his report. He edited his work for wordiness.

Tito's Revision of Paragraph Four

~~Michael Jordan's team, the~~ The Bulls ~~of Chicago,~~ managed to make the

NBA playoffs, but they ~~didn't win, eventually losing~~ lost to the eventual NBA

~~championship winning team, the Celtics of Boston~~ champions, Boston Celtics.

Your Turn _____

Eliminate Wordiness Read your draft, and ask yourself if there are places where you have used several words when you could have used one. Edit your draft by taking out any redundancies and unnecessary repetitions of words or ideas.

Proofreading and Publishing

Proofreading

You have revised your research report, and now it is time to polish it, eliminating any errors that might distract your readers. Edit your work to correct any misspellings and errors in punctuation or sentence structure.

Grammar Link **Using Capitalization and Punctuation**

Following the rules for **capitalization** and **punctuation** will help make your report more readable for your audience. Use capital letters to mark the beginnings of sentences, proper nouns, and the most important words in titles. Use end mark punctuation to indicate the end of a sentence.

Incorrect:	Correct:
The popular magazine time contains an article about the history of Basketball did you know that the Sport was first played in springfield, a city in massachusetts	The popular magazine *Time* contains an article about the history of basketball. Did you know that the sport was first played in Springfield, a city in Massachusetts?

Publishing

Now it is time to publish your research report. Here are some ways to share your work:

- Is there a team or club at your school that might be interested in your subject? Give the coach or club president a copy.

- Did you write your research report because you became interested in something you learned in another class? Ask the teacher of that class if you can give a multimedia presentation on your research. Use presentation software to prepare, and include audio and visual materials where appropriate.

Reflect on the Process
In your **RWN,** write a short response to each of the following questions:

1. What was the most interesting fact you learned from your research?

2. Which part of the process went well for you, and where did you have trouble? What would you do differently the next time you write a report?

3. Did your ideas about the topic change? What else would you like to learn about the topic?

● **Proofreading Tip**

Take the time to carefully proofread the Works Cited section of your report. Remember that all the required punctuation marks help your reader access this information. After you have proofread your own work, exchange reports with a peer, and ask him or her to pay special attention to the punctuation in your Works Cited list.

Your Turn
Proofread and Publish

Proofread your report for instances of wordiness. Make every sentence convey its idea in as concise a manner as possible. Also, be sure that you have followed the rules of capitalization and punctuation throughout your report, including the Works Cited section. Finally, share your work with others.

Scoring Rubric

You can use the rubric below to evaluate your research report.

Research Report Writing	Organization and Focus	Sentence Structure	Conventions
4 • Provides a *thoroughly defined* thesis that is *appropriately* narrow in focus. • Records *appropriate* ideas, concepts, and direct quotations from reliable sources. • Uses and *identifies correctly* both primary and secondary sources. • Makes *excellent* use of charts, maps, and graphs. • Demonstrates *advanced ability* to locate and use information in print and electronic texts.	• *Clearly* addresses all of the writing tasks. • Demonstrates a *clear* understanding of purpose and audience. • Maintains a *consistent* point of view and *smooth* transitions. • Includes an *entirely complete* and *consistently* formatted Works Cited list. • Uses *thoroughly appropriate* formatting (margins, tabs, spacing, etc.).	• Includes sentence *variety*.	• Contains *few, if any,* errors in the conventions of the English language (grammar, punctuation, capitalization, spelling). These errors do **not** interfere with the reader's understanding of the writing.
3 • Provides a *defined* thesis that is narrow in focus. • Records *mostly appropriate* ideas, concepts, and direct quotations from reliable sources. • Uses and identifies primary and secondary sources. • Makes *good* use of charts, maps, and graphs. • Demonstrates *ability* to locate and use information in print and electronic texts.	• Addresses most of the writing task. • Demonstrates a *general* understanding of purpose and audience. • Maintains a *mostly consistent* point of view and *usually smooth* transitions. • Includes a *mostly complete* and *properly* formatted Works Cited list. • Uses *mostly appropriate* formatting (margins, tabs, spacing, etc.).	• Includes some sentence *variety*.	• Contains *some errors* in the conventions of the English language (grammar, punctuation, capitalization, spelling). These errors do **not** interfere with the reader's understanding of the writing.
2 • Provides a *somewhat defined* thesis that is narrow in focus. • Records *sometimes appropriate* ideas, concepts, and direct quotations from reliable sources. • Uses and *sometimes* identifies primary and secondary sources. • Makes *an attempt* to use charts, maps, and graphs. • Demonstrates *limited ability* to locate and use information in print and electronic texts.	• Addresses *some* of the writing task. • Demonstrates *little* understanding of purpose and audience. • Maintains an *inconsistent* point of view and *awkward* transitions. • Includes an *incomplete* and *inconsistently* formatted Works Cited list. • Demonstrates *inconsistent use of appropriate* formatting.	• Includes *little* sentence variety.	• Contains *several errors* in the conventions of the English language (grammar, punctuation, capitalization, spelling). These errors **may** interfere with the reader's understanding of the writing.
1 • *Lacks* a defined thesis that is narrow in focus. • *Fails* to record appropriate ideas, concepts, and direct quotations from reliable sources. • *Fails* to use and identify primary and secondary sources. • *Fails* to use charts, maps, and graphs. • *Fails* to locate and use information in print and electronic texts.	• Addresses *only one* part of the writing task. • Demonstrates *no* understanding of purpose and audience. • *Lacks* a point of view and transitions. • *Lacks* a Works Cited list. • *Lacks* an understanding of appropriate formatting.	• Includes *no* sentence variety.	• Contains *serious errors* in the conventions of the English language (grammar, punctuation, capitalization, spelling). These errors interfere with the reader's understanding of the writing.

Preparing for **Timed Writing**

Informative Essay

When responding to the prompt, use what you've learned from your reading, writing your research report, and studying the rubric on page 784. Use the steps below to develop a response to the following prompt.

Writing Prompt

Being respected is a quality that most of us would like to earn. In an essay, explain how a person gains the respect of others. Be sure to use supporting evidence to back up your points. You may use examples from your own experience or from people you have observed.

Study the Prompt

Begin by reading the prompt carefully. Circle or underline key words: *explain, respect, earn,* and *quality*.

Your purpose is to explain how a person earns other people's respect. What have you observed that leads to respect? Make a list of actions or aspects that you can illustrate with examples.
Tip: Spend about five minutes studying the prompt.

Plan Your Response

Review your list and choose two to four actions or aspects that you can explain with examples. Be sure that your points do not overlap. For example, if you think of "loyalty" as an aspect of earning respect, list "always sticks with me" as a supporting detail, not as another aspect. Then you will need to clarify what the person did to demonstrate loyalty and earn respect.

Look at your list of points. What do they have in common? Choose a common idea to connect ideas about how respect is earned. That idea becomes your **thesis statement.**
Tip: Spend about ten minutes planning your response.

Respond to the Prompt

Using your thesis and your notes, draft your essay: Follow these guidelines:

- Begin your essay with an introduction. A creative way to begin is with a brief anecdote, or story, that illustrates respect. The introduction must include your thesis statement.

- The body of the essay should address each aspect or action in a logical order. Remember that your supporting points about earning respect must relate to the thesis of your essay. Support each point with specific examples.

- In the conclusion, restate your thesis and reflect on the way a person can earn respect.
  Tip: Spend about twenty minutes writing your draft.

Improve Your Response

Revising Go back to the key aspects of the prompt. Does your essay explain how you feel a person earns respect? Have you used specific examples? Are all aspects and actions connected to your thesis?

Proofreading Take a few minutes to proofread your essay to correct errors in grammar, spelling, punctuation, and capitalization. Make sure your edits are neat, and erase any stray marks.

Checking Your Final Copy Before you turn in your essay, read it one more time to catch any errors you may have missed or to make any finishing touches.

Listening & Speaking Workshop

Giving and Listening to a Research Presentation

Think as a Reader/Writer When preparing a written expository, or informative, report, you develop your thesis and decide on the best way to convey your research findings to your reader. When preparing a research presentation, you keep the same focus in mind; however, you also need to consider the specific needs of the listening audience.

Adapt Your Research Report

All of the work that you put into writing your report will put you a step ahead when you are preparing your oral presentation. You will however, need to adjust the information to keep it interesting for your audience.

- **Think about the purpose and occasion as you make decisions about word choice and delivery.** Are you giving an informal speech, or is your speech part of a formal evaluation? The grammar and tone of a formal speech should be serious. Avoid casual language. On the other hand, if you are speaking at an informal occasion, it's a good idea to make sure that your speech doesn't sound overly academic. Choose words and phrases that will put your listeners at ease. Include paraphrases or summaries of various viewpoints, or perspectives, on your topic.

- **Limit your speech to your report's major ideas and to the evidence you need to clarify and support those ideas.** Read through a copy of your original report and highlight the thesis statement and most important points you made. Be sure to highlight those major points in your speech. If necessary, cut your least important points, and narrow your support to only the strongest evidence, examples, and elaboration. As you adapt your report, be sure that your presentation shares information from a variety of primary and secondary sources. Remember to keep information that tells your audience what sources you used for the information in your speech.

- **Adjust your word choice.** Think about who will be listening to your presentation. Your audience should be able to easily understand your ideas and learn from your speech. Define terms with which your audience will be unfamiliar. At the same time, use precise nouns and verbs for vivid description.

Listening and Speaking Standard 1.2 Paraphrase a speaker's purpose and point of view and **ask relevant questions concerning the speaker's** content, **delivery,** and purpose. **1.4** Prepare a speech outline based upon a chosen pattern of organization, which generally includes an introduction; transitions, previews, and summaries; a logically developed body; and an effective conclusion. **1.6** Use appropriate grammar, word choice, enunciation, and pace during formal presentations. **1.7** Use audience feedback (e.g., verbal and nonverbal cues). **1.8.** Evaluate the credibility of a speaker (e.g., hidden agendas, slanted or biased material). **2.3** Deliver research presentations: a. Define a thesis. b. Record important ideas, concepts, and direct quotations from significant information sources and paraphrase and summarize all relevant perspectives on the topic, as appropriate. c. Use a variety of primary and secondary sources and distinguish the nature and value of each. d. Organize and record information on charts, maps, and graphs.

Deliver Your Research Presentation

Use Verbal Techniques

Use an effective **rate** and **volume** for your audience—avoid speaking too quickly, too slowly, too loudly, or too softly. Use your voice to emphasize key points, and be sure not to rush through your presentation. Make sure to **enunciate** each word, clearly distinguishing one word from another.

Use Nonverbal Techniques

Pay attention to the wordless communication you are sending—use natural facial expressions and gestures. Also, add clarity and interest to your presentation by using well-chosen visuals (such as charts, graphs, presentation software, audio clips, and the like). Graphics should focus on one main image and a few details. They should be uncluttered and have lettering and images large enough to be seen clearly from the back of the room.

Evaluate a Presentation

As you listen to and view a classmate's research presentation, evaluate the content and delivery by writing down your answers to the following questions. These evaluation notes will be helpful to the speaker the next time he or she prepares to give a presentation.

- **Organization** How well is the presentation organized? Do the ideas flow logically, and are they clearly connected? Do you understand all of the ideas presented?

- **Description** How vivid is description in the presentation? What precise nouns, verbs, and modifiers does the speaker use?

- **Credibility** Is the speaker credible? For example, is the information presented in a balanced way? If so, how does the speaker include other viewpoints? Or, do you think the author has hidden agendas or is presenting biased material? Explain why you think so.

- **Use of Visuals** How appropriate and effective is the use of visual resources? How do the visual resources relate to the topic and clarify the ideas given in the presentation?

- **Delivery** How was the speaker's delivery? Did he or she speak loudly, slowly, and clearly enough for you to understand the presentation? How well did the presentation keep your attention? What suggestions for improvement can you offer the speaker for the next time he or she delivers a presentation?

Speaking Tip

While you are giving your presentation, pay close attention to your audience. **Nonverbal feedback,** such as confused looks, or **verbal feedback,** such as questions, can be a sign that you need to adjust your presentation. You might need to speak more slowly, more loudly, or to repeat important ideas.

Speaking Tip

In order to deliver a strong presentation, practice it until you feel you know it backward and forward. If possible, rehearse your presentation in the same location that you will be giving it.

Listening Tip

Sometimes you may find a speaker's mannerisms or personality distracting or even a little off-putting. Even so, try to focus harder on what the speaker is saying—if you don't pay attention, you may miss something truly interesting.

Reader/Writer Notebook

Use your **RWN** to complete the activities for this workshop.

Informational Skills Review

Expository Critique **Directions:** Read the selection. Then, answer each question that follows.

In EXTREME Culture Shock!

by **World Almanac**

Extreme sports takes familiar athletics and gives them a new twist or an extra push to the edge. Roller skating becomes aggressive in-line skating. Traditional skiing gives way to speed skiing, at more than 125 miles per hour.

From BMX racing to "up skiing," high-adrenaline sports have gone from obscurity to popularity, exerting influence on popular culture along the way. First, a daring athlete has a will to push the limits. Second, inventiveness is sparked among followers. Marketers sell new concepts inspired by extreme sports, using nontraditional advertising. Then, the mainstream catches on. In this way the energy of X-sports pioneers can influence the larger population, carrying with it new models of speaking, dressing, and acting.

Sports historians trace this rebel mind-set and its trend-setting ability to the 1950s, when masses of young people on the West Coast became surfers. The creation of smaller, cheaper cars allowed young men and women to chase waves along the coast, flaunting their independence from mainstream culture. Surfing hit the American market like a giant wave. Within a decade, the daring and individualistic extreme sport of surfing was making money not only for those selling boards and baggy shorts, but for people making movies about surfers and for anyone selling a product that could help someone look like a surfer.

In 1965, the "snurfer" was introduced: a surfboard for snow. Ten years later, straps were added—and snowboards filled traditional ski hills. In 1985, less than 10 percent of ski areas allowed snowboarders. Now there are more boarders than skiers on the slopes.

Compared with traditional athletes, such as basketball players, extreme-sports competitors place less emphasis on team games and group practice. Typically, X-athletes take an individual sport such as skateboarding and apply their ingenuity and defiance to it. These athletes challenge the forces of nature more than one another.

Heroes among extreme-sports fans are athletes like Tony Hawk, a skateboarder who turned pro at 14, is a popular video-

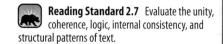

Reading Standard 2.7 Evaluate the unity, coherence, logic, internal consistency, and structural patterns of text.

game avatar, and has his own clothing line. He has a rebel image, as opposed to a conventional baseball or football team player's.

The extreme-sport mind-set has not stopped at the U.S. border. South Africa welcomed a hotel chain that celebrates extreme sports activities, and the first extreme sports club opened in Kyrgyzstan. The X-Games, first held in 1995, attracted competitors from around the world. Like its marketing in the States, global sales around X-sports are *extreme*!

---

1. In this article, which structural pattern does the writer use to explain the development of extreme sports?

  A order of importance

  B chronological order

  C comparison and contrast

  D proposition and support

Read the following sentence from the article.

> The energy of X-sports pioneers can influence the larger population, carrying with it new ways of speaking, dressing, and acting.

2. Which main idea does this sentence support?

  A X-athletes today are more influential than traditional athletes.

  B In the 1950s, many people on the West Coast became surfers.

  C Inventive athletes are highly valued in extreme sports.

  D Extreme sports are rapidly gaining popularity.

3. Which sentence could be added to paragraph 5 without destroying its unity?

  A Tony Hawk is one athlete famous for his creativity.

  B Some of the tricks skateboarders perform seem as if they defy laws of gravity.

  C While a team player has to conform, the X-athlete can explore individuality.

  D However, team games will always be more popular.

4. Since Tony Hawk is a hero to extreme sports fans, it is logical that he

  A is an American.

  B turned pro at age 14.

  C has his own clothing company.

  D has a rebellious image.

Timed Writing

5. Suppose that you wanted to write an essay about the differences between a popular basketball player and an extreme sports star. Explain which structural pattern you would use to organize your essay and why that pattern would be effective.

Vocabulary Skills Review

Synonyms **Directions:** Choose the best synonym for the italicized word in each sentence.

1. *Despicable* means
   A horrible.
   B supreme.
   C irritable.
   D unforgiveable.

2. An *acquisition* is a(n)
   A work of art.
   B communication.
   C profit.
   D obtainment.

3. Another term for *creed* is
   A refusal.
   B belief.
   C distraction.
   D impulse.

4. To *commemorate* is to
   A honor.
   B control.
   C frustrate.
   D contribute.

5. Another term for *detract* is
   A retain.
   B belittle.
   C present.
   D conflict.

6. *Conceded* means
   A argued.
   B uttered.
   C admitted.
   D defined.

7. To *denounce* is to
   A order.
   B deplete.
   C urge.
   D condemn.

8. To *perpetuate* is to
   A motivate.
   B open.
   C sustain.
   D imply.

Academic Vocabulary

Directions: Choose the correct definition for each italicized Academic Vocabulary word from this chapter.

9. When you *critique* something, you
   A evaluate it.
   B dislike it.
   C comprehend it.
   D connect it.

10. If a text has *consistency,* it has
    A integrity.
    B gravity.
    C uniformity.
    D quality.

Writing Skills Review

Research Report   **Directions:** Read this passage from a research report. Then, answer each question that follows.

Writing Standard 2.3   Write research reports: a. Define a thesis. b. Record important ideas, concepts, and direct quotations from significant information sources and paraphrase and summarize all perspectives on the topic, as appropriate. c. Use a variety of primary and secondary sources and distinguish the nature and value of each. d. Organize and display information on charts, maps, and graphs.

(1) Some parasites make their hosts behave strangely. (2) A kind of wasp can make a spider build a home for the wasp's larva. (3) According to *Nature* magazine,[1] the wasp stings the spider to paralyze it and then lays an egg on the spider's abdomen. (4) After the larva hatches, it feeds on the living spider's blood. (5) Then, the larva injects a chemical into the spider that makes the spider spin a special kind of web, one very different from its usual web. (6) In a BBC News Online article,[2] Dr. William Eberhard, a scientist who studies these insects, calls it "the ideal web from the wasp-larva point of view" because it provides "a very solid and durable support." (7) When the web is finished, the larva kills and eats the spider, and then builds its cocoon in the spider's last web. (8) As scientist Fritz Vollrath comments in a Discovery.com article,[3] "The irony is that the poor thing that fed this larva builds it a little shelter as its last act. (9) It makes a gruesome fairy tale."

1. Watson, Isabelle. "Hymenoptera and Parasitism." *Nature*, Vol. 65, Issue 12, December 2006, pp. 78–92.
2. Hidalgo, Roberto. "Surprising Behavior in the Insect World," BBC News Online 25 June 2007. 20 Jan 2008. HYPERLINK "http://www.bbc" http://www.bbc.org/news/2007/June25/hidalgo.html.
3. "Taking Over: Parasites and Their Hosts." *Discovery* 29 March 2007: 1–4. 22 Jan 2007. Available WWW: http://www.discovery.com/creatures/parasites.html.

1. Which of the following would be the *best* thesis statement for this research report?
   A There are many types of parasites found all over the world.
   B A parasite is an organism that can provide some benefits to its host.
   C After the larva hatches, it feeds on the living spider's blood.
   D Some parasites make their hosts behave in surprising ways.

2. Which transition might be added to the beginning of sentence 2 to improve clarity?
   A By the way,
   B On the other hand,
   C For example,
   D As a result,

3. The sources mentioned in this passage come from
   A print and online media.
   B radio and television news.
   C the Internet.
   D scientific journals.

4. The references for this report include
   A every source written on the topic.
   B sources the writer considered important.
   C all sources cited in the report.
   D all sources the writer could find.

Read On

For Independent Reading

Fiction

The Glory Field

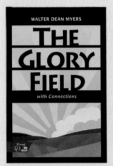

In *The Glory Field,* Walter Dean Myers covers 250 years in the lives of an African American family. From their beginnings in Africa to the end of segregation in America, the members of the Lewis family have always supported one another despite the challenges they faced. Can they persuade one lost relative in modern-day New York City to return to their South Carolina home?

Behind Rebel Lines

Determined to be a member of the Union army, Emma Edmonds presents herself as a man named Franklin Thompson and enlists as a private. Seymour Reit details her adventures in *Behind Rebel Lines.* When Edmonds is sent across Confederate lines to spy, she learns military secrets and how hard it is to be a soldier, no matter what side you are fighting for.

Little Women

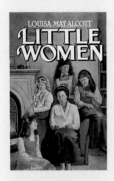

In Louisa May Alcott's *Little Women,* readers are introduced to Meg, Jo, Beth, and Amy March, four sisters who are growing up in Massachusetts during the Civil War. This classic American story about familial love has been a favorite of readers for more than a century. The book has been adapted into a movie four times.

The Captain's Dog: My Journey with the Lewis and Clark Tribe

We all have read about history from a human's point of view, but what about a dog's point of view? In *The Captain's Dog,* Roland Smith takes us inside the mind of Captain Lewis's dog, named Seaman. As Lewis and Clark embark on their adventure across America, Seaman shares his own account of the beautiful country, the harsh conditions, and the trailblazing spirit that changed the United States.

Nonfiction

The Boys' War

Grizzled men were not the only soldiers who fought in the American Civil War. Many teenagers signed up to fight for both the Union and the Confederate armies. In *The Boys' War*, Jim Murphy tells of the excitement the young soldiers felt as they embarked on this new experience and the horror they felt when they came face to face with the grim reality of war.

To Be a Slave

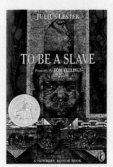

In *To Be a Slave,* a Newbery Honor book written by Julius Lester, men and women who lived through slavery tell their stories in their own words. Readers who want to learn more about this subject should also read Lester's *Long Journey Home,* an uplifting sequel that details six true stories of freedom.

Sacajawea

As a translator, peacemaker, caretaker, and guide, Sacajawea was indispensable to the success of the Lewis and Clark expedition. By many accounts, the whole undertaking would have failed without the aid of this famous American Indian. In *Sacajawea,* Joseph Bruchac provides a firsthand look at the journey through the alternating viewpoints of Sacajawea and William Clark.

The Flight of Red Bird: The Life of Zitkala-Sa

When Gertrude Bonnin was eight years old, she was removed from a Sioux reservation and placed in a boarding school in Indiana. She resisted when her instructors tried to make her renounce her customs. Instead she renamed herself Zitkala-Sa (Red Bird). As an adult, she made people aware of the harsh treatment American Indians were enduring. Doreen Rappaport tells this brave woman's story in *The Flight of Red Bird: The Life of Zitkala-Sa.*

CHAPTER 8

Literary Criticism: A Biographical Approach

California Standards
Here are the Grade 8 Standards you will work toward mastering in Chapter 8.

Word Analysis, Fluency, and Systematic Vocabulary Development
1.2 Understand the most important points in the history of English language and use common word origins to determine the historical influences on English word meanings.

Literary Response and Analysis
3.7 Analyze a work of literature, showing how it reflects the heritage, traditions, attitudes, and beliefs of its author. (Biographical approach)

Writing Applications (Genres and Their Characteristics)
2.1 Write biographies, autobiographies, short stories, or narratives:
   a. Relate a clear, coherent incident, event, or situation by using well-chosen details.
   b. Reveal the significance of, or the writer's attitude about, the subject.
   c. Employ narrative and descriptive strategies (e.g., relevant dialogue, specific action, physical description, background description, comparison or contrast of characters).

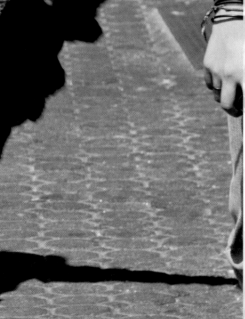

" Nothing which has entered into our experience is ever lost."

—William Ellery Channing

What Do You Think

How do the things we have experienced in our lives continue to affect us?

Literary Skills Focus

by **Carol Jago**

What Is a Biographical Approach to Literary Criticism?

Imagine that you and a friend have come from seeing the latest comedy by a writer/director whose other movies you have liked. Your friend says about the director: "Have you noticed that the villains in his movies are always high-school athletes? I heard he hated sports as a kid and this is his way of getting back at the guys who teased him." You may not have realized it, but your friend was engaging in biographical criticism.

What Is Literary Criticism?

To engage in **literary criticism,** you must analyze, evaluate, or respond to a piece of literature, using evidence from the text to support your claims. There are many "lenses" through which you can view a work of fiction. You can view a book or movie through the lens of feminist criticism, noting whether the work treats women in a balanced way or presents them as stereotypes. You can use the lens of historical criticism, looking at the work as a product of its particular historical period.

Biographical Approach The **biographical approach** to literary criticism, or **biographical criticism,** is an examination of the way a writer's work reflects his or her background, experiences, and beliefs.

When you use a biographical approach in literary criticism, you need to know something about the writer's biography, or life story. From researching facts about the writer—including interviews and quotations—you can start to understand the writer's **heritage,** or background, as well as his or her traditions, attitudes, and beliefs.

The Author's Life and Beliefs

Although writers' lives often influence their subject matter, fiction is not autobiography. Characters are not identical with their authors, though they may reflect their authors' heritage and beliefs. Many of Gary Soto's stories and poems take place in the Mexican American neighborhood where he grew up, but not everything he writes about actually happened to him, nor is he exactly like his characters.

Writers use their knowledge of situations, people, and emotions to create realistic characters and scenes. However, they also use their imaginations. Gary Paulsen was not stranded alone in the Canadian wilderness when he was thirteen, but his adult adventures training sled dogs in Alaska and running the Iditarod helped him understand his main character's fight for survival in *Hatchet*.

There are also limits to the idea that writers should write only about what they know. In Laurence Yep's science fiction novel *Sweetwater*, none of the main characters is Asian, like the author. Some aren't even human! Yet, Yep is writing about what he knows—the fear we all feel in the face of the unknown.

Tips for Using the Biographical Approach

1. Do not assume that a fictional character, especially one who narrates the story and speaks as "I," is the writer.

2. When you wonder if something in a work reflects the writer's heritage or background, check a biography of the writer to be sure your hunch is correct.

3. Be specific in citing connections between the work and the writer's life. Don't assume that, because the main characters in the writer's works tend to be rebels or outsiders, that the writer must be a rebel. Sometimes writers like to write about the kinds of people they wish they had been.

4. Do not ignore the part played by the writer's imagination. Do not assume that every realistic detail in the story is based on fact. A good writer does not have to be a man in order to write about male characters, nor a police officer to write about crime.

Supporting Biographical Criticism

Poor literary criticism begins and ends with remarks like these: "I hated it." "I was a little bored." "It was great." When you are taking a biographical approach to literary criticism, you have to support every claim you make with details from the text and with facts about the writer's life. Here is an example of an appropriate biographical criticism of a novel. The criticism works because the writer researched facts about the life of author Sandra Cisneros and tells us *specifically* how the novel reflects those facts of the writer's life.

The House on Mango Street by Sandra Cisneros is shaped by the writer's own experiences growing up in a Mexican American family in a Chicago barrio. The house in the book's title probably refers to the house the Cisneros family purchased when Sandra was young; Sandra hated the house because she thought it was ugly and old. In the same way, the girl in the novel hates the house her family has moved into, which is also in a Chicago barrio.

The main character, Esperanza (for "hope"), a determined but sensitive little girl, is clearly based on Cisneros herself. Esperanza uses writing as a way of escaping Mango Street in her imagination. Sandra Cisneros actually did escape her neighborhood by writing successful books.

There is another similarity: The women on Mango Street, including Esperanza, are dominated by men. Some of the women characters in the novel seem never to leave their homes. In the same way, Cisneros fought to be independent of the men who dominated her own life. She was the only girl in a family of seven children.

Your Turn   Use the Biographical Approach

Choose one of the following stories from this book: "The Treasure of Lemon Brown" by Walter Dean Myers (page 17) or "An Hour with Abuelo" by Judith Ortiz Cofer (page 128). Read the selection as well as the accompanying author biography. Discuss how the work reflects the writer's heritage, traditions, attitudes, and beliefs.

Learn It Online
To understand the role of literary elements in novels, visit *NovelWise* at:

go.hrw.com   H8-797   **Go**

Reading Skills Focus

by **Kylene Beers**

What Strategies Help You with Biographical Criticism?

I once asked a class what they could tell me about the author after they finished a story. After a long silence, a student named Adam said, "I didn't read anything about the author. I just read the story." Adam was right in one way, but he was also wrong. As a critical reader, you can consider a writer's life experiences as you respond to and analyze a text. The strategies of making connections, re-reading, taking notes, and drawing conclusions can help you take a biographical approach to literary criticism.

Making Connections

Biographical criticism requires that you go beyond the text to make connections to the writer's life. This means that you need to know some key facts about the writer's biography, or life story. If you plan to do biographical criticism of a work, you'll probably want to do extra research. Go beyond simply learning the writer's ethnic background and where he or she was born and lived; try to find out what kind of childhood he or she had, what the important events in his or her life have been, and what he or she believes in and cares about. (Interviews and quotations are good sources of information.) Then, as you read, you will be able to make valid connections between the writer's life and his or her work.

To make connections between a writer and his or her work, you might want to create an "Author Fact Sheet" like the following:

Author Fact Sheet

Author:	Gary Paulsen
Best-Known Works:	*Hatchet, The River, Brian's Winter, Dogsong*
What He Writes About:	Teenagers—usually boys—on their own, forced to face challenges
Facts About Paulsen	• **heritage:** born in Minnesota; he writes about activities of the region, such as trapping, sledding, hunting, fishing • **experiences:** left home at fourteen; took part in Iditarod dog sled race in Alaska • **attitudes:** seems to love to challenge himself physically; great respect for nature and the outdoors • **beliefs:** thinks kids have strength and resourcefulness; stories show kids taking care of themselves

Try making and keeping such fact sheets on your favorite writers—those whose books you read on your own, as well as any writers you enjoy from this book.

Re-Reading

Taking a biographical approach to literary criticism is a bit like being a detective; when you have the facts about the writer's life, you'll want to look carefully for clues in the text to see if you can find connections. Get in the habit of re-reading text, especially in order to locate passages that seem to link to the writer's own life. If you know, for example, that a writer lived in poverty during her childhood, you will want to go back carefully over passages in a story or poem that detail a character's impoverished circumstances.

Taking Notes

As you re-read a work, take careful notes. Remember that you are looking for details from the story that relate to experiences in the writer's life. Use a chart like the one below to record key details about an author's life and note the ways you see the author's life reflected in the work.

	Details in Biography	Details in Text
Places lived		
Family background		
Important experiences		
Career		
Beliefs/attitudes		

Drawing Conclusions

A conclusion is a final judgment that you draw, or arrive at, after considering all you have learned. As you gather details from your reading, you will be drawing conclusions about the relationship between the text and the writer's life. Be sure to draw conclusions that make sense and that you can defend. One student who read "The Medicine Bag" by Virginia Driving Hawk Sneve (page 117) concluded that the story was not based on the writer's experiences because "The story is narrated by a boy named Martin, although the author is a woman." Another student, having done his research, correctly came to the conclusion that the story "is based on an experience that the writer had with a visit from an elderly relative who lived on the Sioux reservation, although the writer has made up many details."

Your Turn Apply Reading Skills

In the index to this book, locate the poem "In Response to Executive Order 9066" by Dwight Okita. Read the poem and the biography of Okita, and take notes. Then, discuss with a partner the connection between the poem and Okita's own experiences, and state the conclusion that you have drawn.

> **Now go to the Skills in Action: Reading Model**

Learn It Online
Try the PowerNotes version of this lesson at:
go.hrw.com   H8-799   Go

Read with a Purpose Read to discover how a writer's background is reflected in his poem.

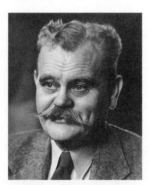

That New England Spirit:
The Life of Robert P. Tristram Coffin

Robert P. Tristram Coffin was born in 1892 on a saltwater farm in Brunswick, Maine. He identified himself "a New Englander by birth, by bringing up, by spirit." Coffin enjoyed growing up in rural Maine so much that as an adult he bought the red-brick schoolhouse he had attended, preserving the old schoolhouse in honor of his childhood. Coffin went on from the red-brick schoolhouse to Bowdoin College and Princeton University, and in 1920 he was named a Rhodes Scholar. He taught for years at Wells College in New York and at Bowdoin College in his beloved Maine.

A popular speaker, Coffin, in the last years of his life, gave about a thousand lectures or readings. In 1936 he won a Pulitzer Prize for a book of poetry called *Strange Holiness*.

A Cheerful Depiction of the Good in the World

Coffin's writings provide a cheerful depiction of the good in the world. Coffin himself once defined poetry as "saying the best one can about life."

"A good many of my poems," he said, "are such combinations of good things, I find. . . . I am proud to see that sometimes I have been able to reach out and bring things together in a poem that are as far apart as the east is from the west: The living and the dead, love and hate in lonely women in a big house, cruelty and beauty in a hawk, life and death in deer and hounds, and the light of a match and the light behind the sun, when my father leaned over me in my illness once, when I was a child, in the dead of night."

Coffin died in 1955 in Portland, Maine.

The Secret Heart

by **Robert P. Tristram Coffin**

Across the years he could recall
His father one way best of all.

In the stillest hour of night
The boy awakened to a light.

5   Half in dreams, he saw his sire
With his great hands full of fire.

The man had struck a match to see
If his son slept peacefully.

He held his palms each side the spark
10 His love had kindled in the dark.

Literary Focus

Biographical Criticism The poet said that he defines poetry as "saying the best one can about life." This poem about a father's love for his son, and his son's recognition of that love—inspired by an actual event in the writer's life—fulfills the poet's idealistic goals.

Reading Focus

Re-Reading Starting with line 11, carefully re-read the lines to make sure you are clear about the two hearts being discussed. One heart is formed by the shape of the father's hands holding the match; the other heart is the "hidden" heart, the father's unspoken love and tenderness for his son, briefly illuminated by the match.

His two hands were curved apart
In the semblance of a heart.

He wore, it seemed to his small son,
A bare heart on his hidden one,

15   A heart that gave out such a glow
No son awake could bear to know.

It showed a look upon a face
Too tender for the day to trace.

One instant, it lit all about,
20   And then the secret heart went out.

But it shone long enough for one
To know that hands held up the sun.

Reading Focus

Drawing Conclusions In the biographical article, Coffin mentioned "the light of a match and the light behind the sun, when my father leaned over me in my illness once, when I was a child, in the dead of night." The careful reader will recognize this imagery and will draw the conclusion that this poem probably is drawn from the poet's experience with his father.

Read with a Purpose How are details from the poet's biography reflected in the poem's message?

SKILLS IN ACTION
Wrap Up

Reading Standard 3.7 Analyze a work of literature, showing how it reflects the heritage, traditions, attitudes, and beliefs of its author. (Biographical approach)

Into Action: Taking Notes

Complete a chart like the following with notes about the poem "The Secret Heart" and the way it reflects the writer's life and attitudes.

Detail in Poem	Connection to Writer's Life	How Writer's Attitude is Reflected

Talk About . . .

1. **Homophones** (HAHM uh fohnz) are words that sound alike but are spelled differently and have different meanings. The word *sun* is used in line 22. What other word in the poem does *sun* sound like? Think about these two words and then discuss the different meanings you can give to the last line of the poem. Try to use some of the Academic Vocabulary words listed at the right in your criticism.

Write About . . .

2. In a paragraph, analyze this poem through the lens of the biographical approach to literary criticism. First, discuss the writer's approach to poetry, as revealed in the short biography. Then, analyze the character of the poet's father based on details in the poem. What is significant about the fact that the heart is "secret"? In your analysis, think about the traditions the poet honors. What values do you think his father passed on to him, and what will he pass on to his own children? Finally, indicate how the poem reflects the writer's attitudes toward life and poetry.

Writing Skills Focus
Think as a Reader/Writer

In this chapter the Writing Skills Focus activities on the Preparing to Read pages will help you approach each text through the lens of biographical criticism—that is, you will learn how to read the texts in relationship to the life of each writer.

Academic Vocabulary for Chapter 8

Talking and Writing About Biographical Criticism

Academic Vocabulary is the language you use to write and talk about literature. Use these words, which are underlined throughout the chapter, to discuss the selections you read.

approach (uh PROHCH) *n.*: method or style of doing something. *Coffin's approach reflects his belief that poetry means "saying the best one can about life."*

attitude (AT uh tood) *n.*: way of thinking about or viewing something. *Coffin's attitude toward life was optimistic.*

criticism (KRIHT uh sihz uhm) *n.*: analysis and judgment of a work's strengths and weaknesses. *An effective biographical criticism requires that you know key facts about an author's life.*

tradition (truh DIHSH uhn) *n.*: custom, belief, or way of doing things that is handed down, as in families. *The traditions of his small New England town were important to the poet.*

Your Turn

Copy the Academic Vocabulary words into your *Reader/Writer Notebook*. Practice using these Academic Vocabulary words as you talk and write about the selections in this chapter.

Preparing to Read

"Out, Out—"

by **Robert Frost**

What Do You Think

In what different ways can people respond to tragic events?

QuickWrite

Write a few sentences about the various ways people you have observed respond to tragedies in your community or on the news. Explain how some people respond lovingly or supportively to such events.

Reader/Writer Notebook

Use your **RWN** to complete the activities for this selection.

Reading Standard 3.7 Analyze a work of literature, showing how it reflects the heritage, traditions, attitudes, and beliefs of its author. (Biographical approach)

Literary Skills Focus

Biographical Criticism Some writers are so influenced by everyday life in the place they live that they use that world in poem after poem and in story after story. These writers create people and scenes that have strong connections to people and scenes they know well. When you read their works, you get not only a sense of a specific place but also a sense of the writer's <u>attitude</u> toward the place and its people. When you examine a text to find out how it relates to the writer's life experiences and attitudes, you are using **biographical criticism.**

Reading Skills Focus

Taking Notes/Re-Reading In order to compare a text with details in the writer's life, take notes as you read both the text and the writer's biography. Re-read both texts to be sure you have noted all the possible biographical connections.

Into Action As you read the biography of Robert Frost and the poem that follows it, use a chart like the one below to record the specific ways that Frost's own life seems to be reflected in the text.

	Details in Biography	Details in Text
Places lived		
Family background		
Important experiences		
Work/career		
Beliefs/attitudes		

Writing Skills Focus

Think as a Reader/Writer

Find It in Your Reading You can tell from this poem that Frost knew what it was like to use a buzz saw—and knew the danger of such work. As you read, use your *Reader/Writer Notebook* to note how Frost describes the buzz saw—how it sounds and how it acts.

Language Coach

Metaphors A **metaphor** is a figure of speech which compares one thing to something very different from it. Metaphors, unlike similes, do not use a specific word of comparison, such as *like* or *as*. Instead, metaphors make their comparisons directly, often by linking two unlike things with the verb *is*:
Life is a dream. My brother is a rock. Hope is a sunrise.

The title of this poem comes from a famous speech by Macbeth in Shakespeare's play of that name. Macbeth has just heard of his wife's death, and he speaks bitterly of the shortness of life, saying, "Out, out, brief candle! / Life's but a walking shadow. . . ." The speech continues with several metaphors about life.

Learn It Online
Listen to a professional actor read this poem at:

go.hrw.com | H8-805 | Go

Robert Frost

(1874–1963)

A Slow Start

Winner of four Pulitzer Prizes for Poetry, Robert Frost was for many years the best-known poet in the United States. When he read his poem "The Gift Outright" at John F. Kennedy's inauguration in 1961, Frost was the first poet to read a poem at a presidential inauguration. His fame did not come quickly or easily, however. In 1912, after the deaths of two of his children, he and his family moved to England, and it was there that Frost met with his first success, finding a publisher for his first two collections of poetry. By the time Frost returned to the United States, in 1915, publishers were interested in his work.

An American Icon

Although born in San Francisco, Frost was raised in New England, and once he returned to the United States he lived and worked in New Hampshire and Vermont. This farmer, teacher, lecturer, and poet soon became a kind of "national poet," or "voice of the people." His themes are suggested by his famous definition of poetry:

"A poem begins as a lump in the throat, a sense of wrong, a homesickness, a lovesickness."

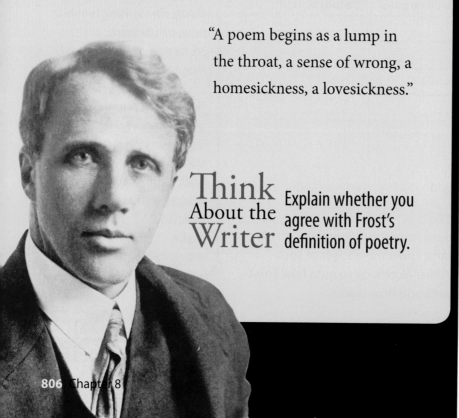

Think About the Writer Explain whether you agree with Frost's definition of poetry.

Build Background

The title of this famous poem is an **allusion**—a reference to another literary work or a work in another field, such as science, history, psychology, or mythology. This title's allusion is to a famous speech by the title character in Shakespeare's tragic play *Macbeth*. In the play, Macbeth has just heard of his wife's death, and he speaks bitterly of the shortness of life:

"Out, out, brief candle!
Life's but a walking shadow, a poor
    player
That struts and frets his hour upon the
    stage,
And then is heard no more. It is a tale
Told by an idiot, full of sound and
    fury,
Signifying nothing."

Preview the Selection

In "Robert Frost: The New England Poet," you will learn details of Robert Frost's life. In "Out, Out," the **speaker** tells the story of a tragic accident that occurs when an unnamed **boy** in rural Vermont is called to supper as he is cutting wood.

ROBERT FROST: The New England Poet

> **Read with a Purpose** Read this biography to discover what inspired Robert Frost's poem "Out, Out—."

Robert Frost lived in New England for most of his life and found his subjects in the landscapes and people of that area, especially in New Hampshire and Vermont. The plain speech and everyday subjects of his poems disguise their complex thoughts.

Frost once wrote that a subject for poetry "should be common in experience and uncommon in books. . . . It should have happened to everyone but it should have occurred to no one before as material."

He drew on the events that occurred around him for his subjects. For example, Frost based the poem "Out, Out—" on an article in the *Littleton Courier,* a New Hampshire newspaper. The article, entitled "Sad Tragedy at Bethlehem," appeared in the March 31, 1901, issue. It read as follows:

Raymond Fitzgerald a Victim of Fatal Accident

Raymond Tracy Fitzgerald, one of the twin sons of Michael G. and Margaret Fitzgerald of Bethlehem, died at his home Thursday afternoon, March 24, as the result of an accident by which one of his hands was badly hurt in a sawing machine. The young man was assisting in sawing up some wood in his own dooryard [yard] with a sawing machine and accidentally hit the loose pulley, causing the saw to descend upon his hand, cutting and lacerating it badly. Raymond was taken into the house and a physician was immediately summoned, but he died very suddenly from the effects of the shock, which produced heart failure. . . . **(A)**

In his poems, Frost tried to depict the sounds of New Englanders' speech. He deliberately used the everyday language he heard in conversations with farmers. Frost wrote about his fascination with speech:

"I have sought only those words I had met up with as a boy in New Hampshire, working on farms during the summer vacations. I listened to the men with whom I worked and found that I could make out their conversation as they talked together out of earshot, even when I had not plainly heard the words they spoke. When I started to carry their conversation over into poetry, I could hear their voices." **(B)**

Given Frost's feelings about the importance of the spoken word, it is not surprising that he liked to "say" rather than to recite his poetry. However, Frost never read "Out, Out—" (page 808) in public because he felt it was "too cruel."

(A) Read and Discuss What do you think the poem "Out, Out—" will be about?

(B) Literary Focus Biographical Criticism How does Frost describe the dialogue in his poems? What can you infer about the poet from that description?

Vocabulary **summoned** (SUHM uhnd) *v.*: called; requested to come.
recite (rih SYT) *v.*: present a memorized text orally, often in a formal manner.

OUT, OUT—

by **Robert Frost**

> **Read with a Purpose** Read this poem to discover the way it reflects the writer's life experiences.

The buzz saw snarled and rattled in the yard
And made dust and dropped stove-length sticks of
    wood,
Sweet-scented stuff when the breeze drew across it.
And from there those that lifted eyes could count
5 Five mountain ranges one behind the other
Under the sunset far into Vermont. **Ⓐ**
And the saw snarled and rattled, snarled and rattled,
As it ran light, or had to bear a load.
And nothing happened: day was all but done.
10 Call it a day, I wish they might have said
To please the boy by giving him the half hour
That a boy counts so much when saved from work.

Ⓐ **Literary Focus** **Biographical Criticism** What is the setting of this poem? Did Frost live somewhere similar? Explain.

His sister stood beside them in her apron
To tell them "Supper." At the word, the saw,
15   As if to prove saws knew what supper meant,
Leaped out at the boy's hand, or seemed to leap—
He must have given the hand. However it was,
Neither refused the meeting. But the hand!
The boy's first outcry was a rueful laugh,
20   As he swung toward them holding up the hand,
Half in appeal, but half as if to keep
The life from spilling. Then the boy saw all—
Since he was old enough to know, big boy
Doing a man's work, though a child at heart—
25   He saw all spoiled. "Don't let him cut my hand off—
The doctor, when he comes. Don't let him, sister!"   **B**
So. But the hand was gone already.
The doctor put him in the dark of ether.°
He lay and puffed his lips out with his breath.
30   And then—the watcher at his pulse took fright.
No one believed. They listened at his heart.
Little—less—nothing!—and that ended it.
No more to build on there. And they, since they
Were not the one dead, turned to their affairs.   **C**

---

28. ether (EE thuhr): chemical compound used as an
anesthetic.

B | Read and Discuss | What has happened to the boy?

C | Reading Focus | Taking Notes What connections do you see
between this poem and Frost's biography? What notes would you take?

Vocabulary **rueful** (ROO fuhl) *adj.:* regretful.
appeal (uh PEEL) *n.:* plea or call for help or sympathy.

Applying Your Skills

Reading Standard 3.7 Analyze a work of literature, showing how it reflects the heritage, traditions, attitudes, and beliefs of its author. (Biographical approach)

Out, Out—

Literary Response and Analysis

Reading Skills Focus
Quick Check

1. What causes the boy's death?

2. How do the people around the dying boy respond to his death?

Read with a Purpose

3. What details did Frost make up and add to the news story of the boy's death?

Reading Skills: Taking Notes/ Re-Reading

4. Complete the chart you worked on (page 805) as you read the poem. Then, formulate a statement in which you explain how "Out, Out—" shows a connection with Frost's New England heritage. What does the poem indicate about his <u>attitude</u> toward the people there?

Literary Skills Focus
Literary Analysis

5. **Interpret** Re-read the explanation of the poem's title on page 806. In the speech from the play, what is Macbeth comparing life to? Why do you think Frost called his poem "Out, Out—"?

6. **Infer** What do lines 10–12 suggest about the speaker and what he wishes had happened?

7. **Interpret** Look at Frost's definition of poetry in the biography on page 806. What does he reveal about his approach to poetry? Where do you think this poem began: as a lump in the throat, a sense of wrong, a homesickness, or a lovesickness? Explain.

8. **Analyze** Frost did many poetry readings, but he said he never read "Out, Out—" in public because it was "too cruel." Explain whether you agree with Frost's comment.

Literary Skills: Biographical Criticism

9. **Draw Conclusions** "Out, Out—" ends with a surprising observation delivered in a matter-of-fact tone. What does this ending reveal about Frost's <u>attitude</u> toward life and his beliefs about human nature?

Literary Skills Review: Onomatopoeia and Personification

10. **Analyze** The use of words that actually sound like what they mean is called **onomatopoeia**. (The word *buzz* itself is an example of onomatopoeia.) What words in lines 1 and 7 imitate the sounds made by a buzz saw? What words in line 14–18 **personify** the saw—make it seem like a person? What is the effect of these elements on the poem?

Writing Skills Focus
Think as a Reader/Writer
Use It in Your Writing Describe a tool or mechanical device, using words that help readers hear its sounds and visualize its behavior. Try to personify the tool or mechanical device—describe it as if it is a person or an animal.

 What Do You Think Now

How do you feel about the family's reaction to the tragedy? Explain.

✔ Vocabulary Check

Be sure you can justify your answers to these questions.

1. If someone is **rueful** about a situation, is the person regretful or confused?
2. Rue is a very bitter plant. How does this help explain the meaning of **rueful**?
3. The boy in the poem stretched out his hand as if in **appeal** to the people standing there. Explain whether he was saying goodbye or pleading for help or sympathy.
4. Based on the definition of **appeal** given in the Vocabulary list, how would you explain what a lawyer is doing when he or she makes an appeal to a higher court?

Language Coach

Metaphors Metaphors, like other figures of speech, are useful to writers, who use them to pack a great deal of meaning into just a few words. Refer to the quotation from the play *Macbeth* on page 806 to answer the following questions.

1. Write down and explain the four metaphors used in this quotation to describe life. Include the metaphor in line 1: What is the "brief candle"?
2. Shakespeare's metaphors emphasize the shortness of life and its meaninglessness. They reflect the feelings of the character Macbeth at the time of his wife's death. There are more positive ways you can describe life. Create four metaphors of your own describing life as something positive and meaningful. Start each one this way: "Life is . . ."

CHOICES

As you respond to the Choices, use these **Academic Vocabulary** words as appropriate: approach, attitude, criticism, tradition.

REVIEW
"Out, Out—" in Performance

Group Project Even though Frost never read this poem to audiences, give it a try yourself. With a group, plan an oral presentation of "Out, Out—." First, determine how many speakers you will need. Second, appoint a director. As you rehearse your reading, try it out in front of a selected audience and ask for feedback. Consider the possibility of using props and music to accompany the reading.

CONNECT
Another News Story

Look at news sources (newspapers, Internet) and locate a story that you think you could write a poem about. It could be a sad, happy, surprising, mysterious, or even humorous story. Write your poem in the conversational, matter-of-fact style used by Frost, and do not worry about rhyme. You may wish to add your own details the way Frost did.

EXTEND
The Public Poet

TechFocus Use the resources on the Internet and in other reference sources to prepare an oral presentation of Robert Frost as a "public poet": one who speaks as the voice of the people of his time. In your presentation, include further details from Frost's biography; Frost's reading at the inauguration of John F. Kennedy in 1961; and the U.S. Senate's resolution honoring Frost on his seventy-fifth birthday.

HAMADI

by **Naomi Shihab Nye**

The Musicians (1995) by Zahi Khamis. Acrylic on paper. www.PalestinianArt.com; www.ZahiArt.com

What Do
You
Think

What can the experiences of people who are different from us teach us about our own lives?

🕐 **QuickWrite**

Think of a friend who is different from you. Write for a few minutes about what this friend has taught you.

Reader/Writer
Notebook

Use your **RWN** to complete the activities for this selection.

Reading Standard 3.7 Analyze a work of literature, showing how it reflects the heritage, traditions, attitudes, and beliefs of its author. (Biographical approach)

Literary Skills Focus

Biographical Criticism Writers typically write about things they care deeply about and know well. If a poet spent his whole life in Central Texas, the images in his poetry might be inspired by the Hill Country there. To examine the ways in which Naomi Shihab Nye's life may have influenced the characters, settings, and concerns of "Hamadi," carefully read Meet the Writer on the next page as well as the story itself.

Reading Skills Focus

Making Connections/Re-Reading When you think that a detail in a story or poem might be drawn from an experience in the writer's life, or that it might reflect an <u>attitude</u> or conviction of the writer, re-read the text and the author biography carefully. When you come across statements or quotations that seem especially important, note whether these passages reveal something about the writer's attitudes or concerns.

Into Action Use the organizer below to record details in "Hamadi" that might connect to something in the writer's own life or reveal something about the writer's beliefs, concerns, or <u>traditions</u>. Be sure to re-read the text and the biography carefully.

Details in Text/Key Statements	Details in Biography
Susan's family had lived in Jerusalem.	Nye lived in Jerusalem.
"Believe anything can happen."	Reflects Nye's philosophy?

Writing Skills Focus

Think as a Reader/Writer

Find It in Your Reading As you read this story, notice how the writer creates the character of Hamadi. Sometimes she describes what he is doing, other times what he is wearing or what he says. Sometimes she tells us how people respond to him. As you read, use your *Reader/Writer Notebook* to record some of the details Nye uses to bring Hamadi to life.

Vocabulary

tedious (TEE dee uhs) *adj.:* boring. *Susan prepares family recipes, even though the work is tedious.*

archaic (ahr KAY ihk) *adj.:* very old or old-fashioned. *Mr. Hamadi's stately manners seem archaic.*

vaguely (VAYG lee) *adv.:* unclearly. *Because of her shyness, Tracy only vaguely mumbles a hello.*

inquiring (ihn KWYR ihng) *v.:* looking for answers; asking. *By inquiring about the people around him, Mr. Hamadi shows that he cares.*

Language Coach

Greek Roots *Archaios* is a Greek word meaning "old." Which word in the list above comes from *archaios?* The word *archaeology* also comes from the word *archaios.* What does *archaeology* mean?

Learn It Online
Improve your comprehension and understanding of words at:

| go.hrw.com | H8-813 | **Go** |

Naomi Shihab Nye
(1952–   )

The Makings of a Writer

Naomi Shihab Nye was born in St. Louis, Missouri. Her American mother read her poetry aloud, and her Palestinian father told her stories of his homeland. As a child, Nye read constantly. Her love of reading led naturally to writing. She is best known as a poet, but she also writes fiction for children and young adults.

A Sampling of Cultures

When Nye was a teenager, her family returned to Jerusalem, where she completed a year of high school and immersed herself in the culture of her father's homeland. From Jerusalem, her family moved to San Antonio, Texas, a city with a rich Latino culture. Nye absorbed this culture from her neighbors and still lives in an inner-city San Antonio neighborhood.

In an interview, Nye once talked about her Palestinian grandmother, an elderly woman who had endured many losses in her lifetime. Despite all her troubles, she said to her granddaughter before she died: "I never lost my peace inside."

"I hope that my characters are brave and strong. I want them to use their voices. I want young people to be reminded, always, that voices are the best tools we have."

Think About the Writer What details in the biography suggest that Nye values cultural connections?

Preview the Selection

The main character in this story is **Susan,** an American high school student. Susan's father was born in Palestine; her mother was born in America. **Saleh Hamadi,** a friend of Susan's father, is a Palestinian who has lived in America for years.

Old Jerusalem, Israel.

HAMADI

by **Naomi Shihab Nye**

> "It takes two of us to discover truth:
> one to utter it and one to understand it."
> KAHLIL GIBRAN, *Sand and Foam*

Susan didn't really feel interested in Saleh Hamadi until she was a freshman in high school carrying a thousand questions around. Why this way? Why not another way? Who said so and why can't I say something else? Those brittle women at school in the counselor's office treated the world as if it were a yardstick and they had tight hold of both ends.

Sometimes Susan felt polite with them, sorting attendance cards during her free period, listening to them gab about fingernail polish and television. And other times she felt she could run out of the building yelling. That's when she daydreamed about Saleh Hamadi, who had nothing to do with any of it. Maybe she thought of him as escape, the way she used to think about the Sphinx at Giza[1] when she was younger. She would picture the golden Sphinx sitting quietly in the desert with sand blowing around its face, never changing its expression. She would think of its wry, slightly crooked mouth and how her grandmother looked a little like that as she waited for her bread to bake in the old village north of Jerusalem.[2] Susan's family had lived in Jerusalem for three years before she was ten and drove out to see her grandmother every weekend. They would find her patting fresh dough between her hands, or pressing cakes of dough onto the black rocks in the *taboon,* the rounded old oven outdoors. Sometimes she moved her lips as she worked. Was she praying? Singing a secret song? Susan had never seen her grandmother rushing.

Now that she was fourteen, she took long walks in America with her father down by

---

1. **Sphinx at Giza:** Giza is a city in Egypt, where there is a giant statue of a sphinx, a mythological creature with the body of a lion and a human head.

2. **Jerusalem:** major city of the Middle East.

the drainage ditch at the end of their street. Pecan trees shaded the path. She tried to get him to tell stories about his childhood in Palestine. She didn't want him to forget anything. She helped her American mother complete tedious kitchen tasks without complaining—rolling grape leaves around their lemony rice stuffing, scrubbing carrots for the roaring juicer. Some evenings when the soft Texas twilight pulled them all outside, she thought of her far-away grandmother and said, "Let's go see Saleh Hamadi. Wouldn't he like some of that cheese pie Mom made?" And they would wrap a slice of pie and drive downtown. Somehow he felt like a good substitute for a grandmother, even though he was a man. **Ⓐ**

Usually Hamadi was wearing a white shirt, shiny black tie, and a jacket that reminded Susan of the earth's surface just above the treeline on a mountain—thin, somehow purified. He would raise his hands high before giving advice.

"It is good to drink a tall glass of water every morning upon arising!" If anyone doubted this, he would shake his head. "Oh Susan, Susan, Susan," he would say.

He did not like to sit down, but he wanted everyone else to sit down. He made Susan sit on the wobbly chair beside the desk and he made her father or mother sit in the saggy center of the bed. He told them people should eat six small meals a day.

They visited him on the sixth floor of the Traveler's Hotel, where he had lived so long nobody could remember him ever traveling. Susan's father used to remind him of the apartments available over the Victory Cleaners, next to the park with the fizzy pink fountain, but Hamadi would shake his head, pinching kisses at his spartan[3] room. "A white handkerchief spread across a tabletop, my two extra shoes lined by the wall, this spells 'home' to me, this says 'mi casa.' What more do I need?"

Hamadi liked to use Spanish words. They made him feel expansive, worldly. He'd learned them when he worked at the fruits and vegetables warehouse on Zarzamora Street, marking off crates of apples and avocados on a long white pad. Occasionally he would speak Arabic, his own first language, with Susan's father and uncles, but he said it made him feel too sad, as if his mother might step into the room at any minute, her arms laden with fresh mint leaves. He had come to the United States on a boat when he was eighteen years old and he had never been married. "I married books," he said. "I married the wide horizon."

"What is he to us?" Susan used to ask her father. "He's not a relative, right? How did we meet him to begin with?"

Susan's father couldn't remember. "I think we just drifted together. Maybe we

---

3. **spartan:** simple; not luxurious.

Ⓐ **Literary Focus** Biographical Criticism What details here reflect personal incidents from Nye's own life?

Vocabulary **tedious** (TEE dee uhs) *adj.*: repetitive; boring.

Analyzing Visuals

Connecting to the Text
How does the man in the photograph compare to your impressions of Hamadi?

met at your uncle Hani's house. Maybe that old Maronite[4] priest who used to cry after every service introduced us. The priest once shared an apartment with Kahlil Gibran[5] in New York—so he said. And Saleh always says he stayed with Gibran when he first got off the boat. I'll bet that popular guy Gibran has had a lot of roommates he doesn't even know about."

---

4. **Maronite:** The Maronite Church is in Lebanon and is part of the Eastern Catholic Church.
5. **Kahlil Gibran** (kah LEEL jih BRAHN) (1883–1931): Lebanese writer who wrote about religious and philosophical topics. One of his most famous books written in English is *The Prophet.*

Susan said, "Dad, he's dead."

"I know, I know," her father said.

Later Susan said, "Mr. Hamadi, did you really meet Kahlil Gibran? He's one of my favorite writers." Hamadi walked slowly to the window of his room and stared out. There wasn't much to look at down on the street—a bedraggled flower shop, a boarded-up tavern with a hand-lettered sign tacked to the front, GONE TO FIND JESUS. Susan's father said the owners had really gone to Alabama.

Hamadi spoke patiently. "Yes, I met brother Gibran. And I meet him in my heart every day. When I was a young

Hamadi **817**

man—shocked by all the visions of the new world—the tall buildings—the wild traffic—the young people without shame—the proud mailboxes in their blue uniforms—I met him. And he has stayed with me every day of my life."

"But did you really meet him, like in person, or just in a book?"

He turned dramatically. "Make no such distinctions, my friend. Or your life will be a pod with only dried-up beans inside. Believe anything can happen."

Susan's father looked irritated, but Susan smiled. "I do," she said. "I believe that. I want fat beans. If I imagine something, it's true, too. Just a different kind of true." **B**

Susan's father was twiddling with the knobs on the old-fashioned sink. "Don't they even give you hot water here? You don't mean to tell me you've been living without hot water?"

On Hamadi's rickety desk lay a row of different "Love" stamps issued by the post office.

"You must write a lot of letters," Susan said.

"No, no, I'm just focusing on that word," Hamadi said. "I particularly like the globe in the shape of a heart," he added.

"Why don't you take a trip back to your village in Lebanon?" Susan's father asked. "Maybe you still have relatives living there."

Hamadi looked pained. "'Remembrance is a form of meeting,' my brother Gibran says, and I do believe I meet with my cousins every day."

"But aren't you curious? You've been gone so long! Wouldn't you like to find out what has happened to everybody and everything you knew as a boy?" Susan's father traveled back to Jerusalem once each year to see his family.

"I would not. In fact, I already know. It is there and it is not there. Would you like to share an orange with me?" **C**

His long fingers, tenderly peeling. Once when Susan was younger, he'd given her a lavish ribbon off a holiday fruit basket and expected her to wear it on her head. In the

---

B **Literary Focus** **Biographical Criticism** How might this conversation about books and imagination connect with Nye's own feelings about reading?

C **Reading Focus** **Re-reading** What do Hamadi and Susan's father think about returning to their homeland?

car, Susan's father said, "Riddles. He talks in riddles. I don't know why I have patience with him." Susan stared at the people talking and laughing in the next car. She did not even exist in their world.

Susan carried *The Prophet* around on top of her English textbook and her Texas history. She and her friend Tracy read it out loud to one another at lunch. Tracy was a junior—they'd met at the literary magazine meeting where Susan, the only freshman on the staff, got assigned to do proofreading. They never ate in the cafeteria; they sat outside at picnic tables with sack lunches, whole wheat crackers and fresh peaches. Both of them had given up meat.

Tracy's eyes looked steamy. "You know that place where Gibran says, 'Hate is a dead thing. Who of you would be a tomb?'"

Susan nodded. Tracy continued. "Well, I hate someone. I'm trying not to, but I can't help it. I hate Debbie for liking Eddie and it's driving me nuts."

"Why shouldn't Debbie like Eddie?" Susan said. "*You* do."

Tracy put her head down on her arms. A gang of cheerleaders walked by giggling. One of them flicked her finger in greeting.

"In fact, we *all* like Eddie," Susan said. "Remember, here in this book—wait and I'll find it—where Gibran says that loving teaches us the secrets of our hearts and that's the way we connect to all of Life's heart? You're not talking about liking or loving, you're talking about owning." **D**

Tracy looked glum. "Sometimes you remind me of a minister."

Susan said, "Well, just talk to me someday when *I'm* depressed."

Susan didn't want a boyfriend. Everyone who had boyfriends or girlfriends seemed to have troubles. Susan told people she had a boyfriend far away, on a farm in Missouri, but the truth was, boys still seemed like cousins to her. Or brothers. Or even girls.

A squirrel sat in the crook of a tree, eyeing their sandwiches. When the end-of-lunch bell blared, Susan and Tracy jumped—it always seemed too soon. Squirrels were lucky; they didn't have to go to school.

Susan's father said her idea was ridiculous: to invite Saleh Hamadi to go Christmas caroling with the English Club. "His English is archaic, for one thing, and he won't know *any* of the songs."

"How could you live in America for years and not know 'Joy to the World' or 'Away in a Manger'?"

"Listen, I grew up right down the road from 'Oh Little Town of Bethlehem' and I still don't know a single verse." **E**

D **Reading Focus** Making Connections What quotations from Gibran seem to be important in the story?

E **Reading Focus** Making Connections What does Susan's father mean by this remark?

Vocabulary archaic (ar KAY ihk) *adj.*: out of date; old-fashioned.

"I want him. We need him. It's boring being with the same bunch of people all the time."

So they called Saleh and he said he would come—"thrilled" was the word he used. He wanted to ride the bus to their house, he didn't want anyone to pick him up. Her father muttered, "He'll probably forget to get off." Saleh thought "caroling" meant they were going out with a woman named Carol. He said, "Holiday spirit—I was just reading about it in the newspaper."

Susan said, "Dress warm."

Saleh replied, "Friend, my heart is warmed simply to hear your voice."

All that evening Susan felt light and bouncy. She decorated the coffee can they would use to collect donations to be sent to the children's hospital in Bethlehem. She had started doing this last year in middle school, when a singing group collected $100 and the hospital responded on exotic onion-skin stationery that they were "eternally grateful."

Her father shook his head. "You get something into your mind and it really

> Saleh replied, "Friend, my heart is warmed simply to hear your voice."

takes over," he said. "Why do you like Hamadi so much all of a sudden? You could show half as much interest in your own uncles."

Susan laughed. Her uncles were dull. Her uncles shopped at the mall and watched TV. "Anyone who watches TV more than twelve minutes a week is uninteresting," she said.

Her father lifted an eyebrow.

"He's my surrogate[6] grandmother," she said. "He says interesting things. He makes me think. Remember when I was little and he called me The Thinker? We have a connection." She added, "Listen, do you want to go too? It's not a big deal. And Mom has a *great* voice. Why don't you both come?"

A minute later her mother was digging in the closet for neck scarves, and her father was digging in the drawer for flashlight batteries.

Saleh Hamadi arrived precisely on time, with flushed red cheeks and a sack of dates stuffed in his pocket. "We may need suste-

---

6. **surrogate:** used as a substitute for something else.

nance on our journey." Susan thought the older people seemed quite giddy as they drove down to the high school to meet the rest of the carolers. Strands of winking lights wrapped around their neighbors' drainpipes and trees. A giant Santa tipped his hat on Dr. Garcia's roof.

Her friends stood gathered in front of the school. Some were smoothing out song sheets that had been crammed in a drawer or cabinet for a whole year. Susan thought holidays were strange; they came, and you were supposed to feel ready for them. What if you could make up your own holidays as you went along? She had read about a woman who used to have parties to celebrate the arrival of fresh asparagus in the local market. Susan's friends might make holidays called Eddie Looked at Me Today and Smiled.

Two people were alleluia-ing in harmony. Saleh Hamadi went around the group formally introducing himself to each person and shaking hands. A few people laughed silently when his back was turned. He had stepped out of a painting, or a newscast, with his outdated long overcoat, his clunky old man's shoes and elegant manners.

Susan spoke more loudly than usual. "I'm honored to introduce you to one of my best friends, Mr. Hamadi."

"Good evening to you," he pronounced musically, bowing a bit from the waist.

What could you say back but "Good evening, sir." His old-fashioned manners were contagious.

They sang at three houses that never opened their doors. **F**

They sang "We Wish You a Merry Christmas" each time they moved on. Lisa had a fine, clear soprano. Tracy could find the alto harmony to any line. Cameron and Elliot had more enthusiasm than accuracy. Lily, Rita, and Jeannette laughed every time they said a wrong word and fumbled to find their places again. Susan loved to see how her mother knew every word of every verse without looking at the paper, and how her father kept his hands in his pockets and seemed more interested in examining people's mailboxes or yard displays than in trying to sing. And Saleh Hamadi—what language was he singing in? He didn't even seem to be pronouncing words, but humming deeply from his throat. Was he saying, "Om"? Speaking Arabic? Once he caught her looking and whispered, "That was an Aramaic word that just drifted into my mouth—the true language of the Bible, you know, the language Jesus Christ himself spoke." **G**

By the fourth block their voices felt tuned up and friendly people came outside to listen. Trays of cookies were passed around and dollar bills stuffed into the little can. Thank you, thank you. Out of the

---

F **Reading Focus** Re-reading How do Hamadi's good manners and kindness contrast with the way people in three houses respond to the singers?

G **Reading Focus** Making Connections How is Nye connecting the carols sung in an American suburb with ancient Palestine?

dark from down the block, Susan noticed Eddie sprinting toward them with his coat flapping, unbuttoned. She shot a glance at Tracy, who pretended not to notice. "Hey, guys!" shouted Eddie. "The first time in my life I'm late and everyone else is on time! You could at least have left a note about which way you were going." Someone slapped him on the back. Saleh Hamadi, whom he had never seen before, was the only one who managed a reply. "Welcome, welcome to our cheery group!"

Eddie looked mystified. "Who is this guy?"

Susan whispered, "My friend."

Eddie approached Tracy, who read her song sheet intently just then, and stuck his face over her shoulder to whisper, "Hi." Tracy stared straight ahead into the air and whispered "Hi" vaguely, glumly. Susan shook her head. Couldn't Tracy act more cheerful at least?

They were walking again. They passed a string of blinking reindeer and a wooden snowman holding a painted candle.

Eddie fell into step beside Tracy, murmuring so Susan couldn't hear him anymore. Saleh Hamadi was flinging his arms up high as he strode. Was he power walking? Did he even know what power

Vocabulary **vaguely** (VAYG lee) adv.: unclearly.

walking was? Between houses, Susan's mother hummed obscure songs people hardly remembered: "What Child Is This?" and "The Friendly Beasts."

Lisa moved over to Eddie's other side. "I'm *so excited* about you and Debbie!" she said loudly. "Why didn't she come tonight?"

Eddie said, "She has a sore throat."

Tracy shrank up inside her coat.

Lisa chattered on. "James said we should make our reservations *now* for dinner at the Tower after the Sweetheart Dance, can you believe it? In December, making a reservation for February? But otherwise it might get booked up!"  **H**

Saleh Hamadi tuned into this conversation with interest; the Tower was downtown, in his neighborhood. He said, "This sounds like significant preliminary planning! Maybe you can be an international advisor someday." Susan's mother bellowed, "Joy to the World!" and voices followed her, stretching for notes. Susan's father was gazing off into the sky. Maybe he thought about all the refugees in camps in Palestine far from doorbells and shutters. Maybe he thought about the horizon beyond Jerusalem when he was a boy, how it seemed to be inviting him, "Come over, come over." Well, he'd come all the way to the other side of the world, and

---

H Read and Discuss | How does the writer feel about Lisa? Explain.

now he was doomed to live in two places at once. To Susan, immigrants seemed bigger than other people, and always slightly melancholy. They also seemed doubly interesting. Maybe someday Susan would meet one her own age. **Ⓘ**

Two thin streams of tears rolled down Tracy's face. Eddie had drifted to the other side of the group and was clowning with Cameron, doing a tap dance shuffle. "While fields and floods, rocks, hills and plains, repeat the sounding joy, repeat the sounding joy . . ." Susan and Saleh Hamadi noticed her. Hamadi peered into Tracy's face, inquiring, "Why? Is it pain? Is it gratitude? We are such mysterious creatures, human beings!"

Tracy turned to him, pressing her face against the old wool of his coat, and wailed. The song ended. All eyes were on Tracy and this tall, courteous stranger who would never in a thousand years have felt comfortable stroking her hair. But he let her stand there, crying, as Susan stepped up firmly on the other side of Tracy, putting her arms around her friend. And Hamadi said something Susan would remember years later, whenever she was sad herself, even after college, a creaky anthem sneaking back into her ear, "We go on. On and on. We don't stop where it hurts. We turn a corner. It is the reason why we are living. To turn a corner. Come, let's move." **Ⓙ**

Above them, in the heavens, stars lived out their lonely lives. People whispered, "What happened? What's wrong?" Half of them were already walking down the street. **Ⓚ**

Ⓘ **Reading Focus** **Making Connections** How might Susan's thoughts about her father and Palestine connect with details from Nye's life?

Vocabulary **inquiring** (ihn KWYR ihng) *v.:* looking for answers; asking.

Ⓙ **Read and Discuss** What do you think of Hamadi's statement?

Ⓚ **Literary Focus** **Biographical Criticism** What key experience from Nye's life seems to be reflected in this story?

Reading Standard 3.7 Analyze a work of literature, showing how it reflects the heritage, traditions, attitudes, and beliefs of its author. (Biographical approach)

Hamadi

Literary Response and Analysis

Reading Skills Focus
Quick Check

1. What is Mr. Hamadi's connection to Susan's family?

2. What impact does Mr. Hamadi have on Susan?

Read with a Purpose

3. How does Mr. Hamadi affect the people around him? Support your answer with examples from the story.

Reading Skills: Making Connections/ Re-Reading

4. Refer to the chart you made while you were reading and re-reading this story. Put an asterisk beside each detail that seems to make an important connection to Nye's life. Put asterisks beside three quotations from the story that seem important.

Literary Skills Focus
Literary Analysis

5. **Interpret** How does the quotation, "It takes two of us to discover truth: one to utter it and one to understand it" relate to the story?

6. **Analyze** How would you describe Mr. Hamadi's character—is he a happy man or a sad man? What do you think Mr. Hamadi represents to Susan?

7. **Analyze** Find three story details that help you understand the essence of Susan's character. How would you describe her character?

8. **Analyze** Why do you think the writer included the relationship triangle involving Tracy, Eddie, and Debbie in the story?

9. **Extend** Susan thinks that everyone who has boyfriends or girlfriends seems to have troubles. Explain whether or not you agree.

10. **Infer** What does Susan value most? Support your opinion with facts from the story.

11. **Evaluate** Explain whether you find the behavior of the characters in this story to be believable.

Literary Skills: Biographical Criticism

12. What traditions and attitudes of Nye's do you think are reflected in the story? How might Nye's heritage have influenced her choice of subject matter?

Literary Skills Review: Setting

13. **Setting** refers to the time and place of a story. Setting includes details like food and customs, as well as descriptions of a place. There are two contrasting settings in this story. What are they? How are they different?

Writing Skills Focus
Think as a Reader/Writer

Use It in Your Writing In "Hamadi," Nye develops the character of Hamadi by telling what he wears, what he says, what he does, and how other people respond to him. Think of someone you like or admire. In a paragraph, recreate that character by describing the person's appearance, words, actions and effect on other people.

What Do You Think Now How does this story make the point that most people have similar fears and dreams?

Applying Your Skills

Reading Standard 1.2 Understand the most important points in the history of the English language and use common word origins to determine the historical influences on English word meanings.

Hamadi

Vocabulary Development

Etymology

Languages are not invented overnight; they develop over time. **Etymology** is the study of how languages develop. When you study etymology, you discover that each word has a history of its own. A look in your dictionary will help you discover a word's past. For each entry in a dictionary, you'll find an abbreviated word history. For example, look at the bracketed portion of the entry for *gratitude* which follows. (The symbol < means "derived from" or "came from.")

gratitude (GRAT uh tood) *n.* [Fr < ML *gratitudo* < L *gratus,* pleasing] thankfulness.

The abbreviation *Fr* stands for *French, ML* for *Middle Latin,* and *L* for *Latin.* The words in italics, *gratitudo* and *gratus,* are the original words, in Middle Latin and Latin, that *gratitude* came from. Note the meaning of *gratus:* "pleasing." How are *pleasing* and *thankfulness* related?

Your Turn

Look up each Vocabulary word in a dictionary. In your *Reader/Writer Notebook,* write the "ancestor word" each Vocabulary word has come from. Then write down the meaning of the ancestor word.

EXAMPLE: *tedious;* Ancestor word: Latin *taedet,* meaning "it disgusts or offends."

> tedious
> archaic
> vaguely
> inquiring

Language Coach

Word Origins Just as people may have lots of relatives—siblings, parents, grandparents, aunts, uncles, and cousins—words have relatives too. It's not unusual for ten or more words to spring from a common root.

The cluster below shows three word families. See if you can add one more word to each of these word families by including one of the Vocabulary words in the box on the left.

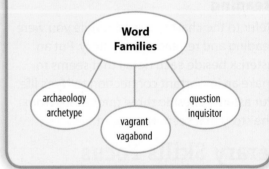

Academic Vocabulary

Write About . . .

In a paragraph, describe Naomi Shihab Nye's attitude toward her characters in this story. How does she seem to view the traditions of her character Hamadi? If you were writing a biographical criticism of this story, what elements of Nye's biography would you be sure to cite? Use the underlined Academic Vocabulary words in your response.

Grammar Link
Subject-Verb Agreement

In a sentence the verb should always agree in number with the subject. If the subject is singular, the verb should be singular. If the subject is plural, the verb should be plural.

Singular Verbs	Plural Verbs
comes, helps, does, is	come, help, do, are

EXAMPLES: **He rides** the bicycle. [The singular verb *rides* agrees with the singular subject *He*.]

Most **children love** ice cream. [The plural verb *love* agrees with the plural subject *children*.]

The **thought** of bats **scares** me. [The singular verb *scares* agrees with the singular subject *thought*.]

Your Turn

Choose the form of the verb in parentheses that agrees with the subject in the sentence.

1. Susan (think, thinks) little of their ideas.
2. Sometimes she (move, moves) her lips as she works.
3. People should (eat, eats) six small meals a day.
4. Hamadi (like, likes) to use Spanish words.
5. The students (want, wants) to collect donations for a children's hospital.

Writing Applications Write a short paragraph using the following words: *Susan, Hamadi, love,* and *family*. Check each sentence to be sure your verbs all agree in number with your subjects.

CHOICES

As you respond to the Choices, use these **Academic Vocabulary** words as appropriate: approach, attitude, criticism, tradition.

REVIEW
Write a Biographical Criticism

Timed └Writing The biography of Naomi Shihab Nye on page 814 suggests that her attitude toward life involves valuing cultural connections. In one or two paragraphs, explain how the story "Hamadi" illustrates this attitude.

CONNECT
Write a "Fish-Out-of-Water" Story

In "Hamadi," Mr. Hamadi is like a "fish out of water" when he goes caroling with the English Club. Think about a time when you were a fish out of water. In a one-page essay, describe the situation and the way it made you feel. Be sure to contrast your actions with the behavior of everyone else in the group.

EXTEND
Conduct an Interview

Interview someone from a culture that is different from yours. Ask the following questions. Take notes and listen carefully and respectfully.

- Where are your parents from, and how did they come here?
- What are your favorite foods and activities?
- What do you like best about school? least?

Read your notes back to your subject to be sure you have recorded the answers accurately. Have you discovered any common ground with this person?

A Retrieved Reformation

by **O. Henry**

What Do You Think

Everyone makes mistakes. When is it a good idea to give someone a second chance?

 QuickWrite

Think about a situation in which a person might be given a second chance. What might the person learn from that experience?

Reader/Writer
Notebook

Use your **RWN** to complete the activities for this selection.

Reading Standard 3.7 Analyze a work of literature, showing how it reflects the heritage, traditions, **attitudes, and beliefs of its author. (Biographical approach)**

Literary Skills Focus

Biographical Criticism When you examine a text to see if the writer's life and experiences are reflected in it, you are using the **biographical approach** to **literary criticism.** In the case of this story, your curiosity would be raised right away: the story is about a man released from prison, and O. Henry spent some time in prison. What other connections are there between the story and O. Henry's life? How does the story reveal O. Henry's feelings about prison and about what happens to a man in prison? What other <u>attitudes</u> does the author reveal in this story?

TechFocus As you read, imagine what it might be like to conduct a video interview with someone like Jimmy Valentine. What would you want to know about how his mind works?

Reading Skills Focus

Drawing Conclusions When you do biographical <u>criticism</u>, you compare a literary text with information about the author's heritage, <u>traditions</u>, <u>attitudes</u>, and beliefs. To follow this approach, you consider all the evidence and then **draw conclusions,** or make final judgments, about the relationship between the author's life and the text.

Into Action In a chart like the one below, record details from the text and from the writer's biography. Then, draw conclusions about how they relate.

Details in Text	Details in Biography	My Conclusions

Writing Skills Focus

Think as a Reader/Writer

Find It in Your Reading O. Henry is known for writing endings with interesting, unexpected twists. As you read, use your *Reader/Writer Notebook* to record what you expect to happen in the story based on the way it begins. Then, record what actually happens. Explain whether you are surprised by the ending.

Vocabulary

rehabilitate (ree huh BIHL uh tayt) *v.*: restore to good standing. *The prison warden hopes Jimmy will rehabilitate himself.*

clemency (KLEHM uhn see) *n.*: mercy. *Well-behaved prisoners may receive clemency in the form of shorter sentences.*

elusive (ih LOO sihv) *adj.*: hard to catch. *The safecracker was elusive; the detectives found it difficult to catch him.*

anguish (ANG gwihsh) *n.*: emotional pain, great fear. *Annabel's eyes were full of anguish as she thought of her niece trapped in the safe.*

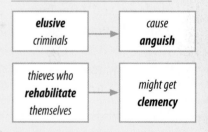

Language Coach

Oral Fluency With a partner, take turns reading aloud the example sentences for each Vocabulary word. If you have difficulty pronouncing any of the vocabulary words, refer to the pronunciation guides provided.

Learn It Online
For a preview of this story, see the video introduction at:

go.hrw.com   H8-829   **Go**

O. Henry
(1862–1910)

Learn It Online
Get more on the author's life at:
go.hrw.com H8-830 Go

A Tragic Love Story

William Sidney Porter, who later changed his name to O. Henry, was brought up in Greensboro, North Carolina. At age twenty, he went to Texas. Eventually he settled in Austin, where he led an active social life. He fell deeply in love with Athol Estes, who was seventeen and deathly ill from tuberculosis. The couple eloped, and Porter began working as a bank teller. When he was accused (perhaps unjustly) of embezzling money from the bank, he fled to Central America, planning to send for his family when he was settled. Athol could not travel, however, and news of his wife's illness brought Porter back to Austin—knowing that he would be arrested when he arrived. He was sentenced to five years in prison. Some people believe he took his pen name from the name of a prison guard, Orrin Henry.

Stories Everywhere

Porter moved to New York City after his wife died. Some of his most famous stories are set in that city, including "The Gift of the Magi" and "After Twenty Years." About the sources for his hundred stories, O. Henry said:

> "There are stories in everything. I've got some of my best yarns from park benches, lampposts, and newspaper stands."

Think About the Writer How might O. Henry's personal experiences have affected his choice of plots and characters?

Build Background

O. Henry based the character of Jimmy Valentine—the criminal with a heart—on a safecracker (a person who can open safes, such as those in bank vaults) he met in prison. The story was later made into a Broadway play called *Alias Jimmy Valentine.*

Preview the Selection

Jimmy Valentine is a career criminal and an expert safecracker who, at the beginning of this story, is released from prison. **Ben Price** is the detective who is soon hot on Valentine's trail.

A Retrieved Reformation

by **O. Henry**

guard came to the prison shoeshop, where Jimmy Valentine was assiduously[1] stitching uppers, and escorted him to the front office. There the warden handed Jimmy his pardon, which had been signed that morning by the Governor. Jimmy took it in a tired kind of way. He had served nearly ten months of a four-year sentence. He had expected to stay only about three months, at the longest. When a man with as many friends on the outside as Jimmy Valentine had is received in the "stir," it is hardly worthwhile to cut his hair. Ⓐ

"Now, Valentine," said the warden, "you'll go out in the morning. Brace up, and make a man of yourself. You're not a bad fellow at heart. Stop cracking safes, and live straight."

"Me?" said Jimmy, in surprise. "Why, I never cracked a safe in my life."

"Oh, no," laughed the warden. "Of course not. Let's see, now. How was it you happened to get sent up on that Springfield job? Was it because you wouldn't prove an alibi for fear of compromising somebody in extremely high-toned society? Or was it simply a case of a mean old jury that had it in for you? It's always one or the other with you innocent victims."

"Me?" said Jimmy, still blankly virtuous. "Why, warden, I never was in Springfield in my life!"

"Take him back, Cronin!" smiled the warden, "and fix him with outgoing clothes. Unlock him at seven in the morning, and let him come to the bullpen.[2] Better think over my advice, Valentine." Ⓑ

At a quarter past seven on the next morning Jimmy stood in the warden's outer office. He had on a suit of the villainously fitting, ready-made clothes and a pair of the stiff, squeaky shoes that the state furnishes to its discharged compulsory[3] guests.

---

1. **assiduously** [uh SIHJ yoo uhs lee]: steadily and busily.

2. **bullpen:** a barred room where prisoners are held temporarily.
3. **compulsory:** forced.

Ⓐ **Literary Focus** Biographical Criticism What details in this first paragraph suggest a similarity to the writer's own life?

Ⓑ **Read and Discuss** What does the conversation between Jimmy and the warden tell you about Jimmy?

THE SATURDAY EVENING POST

By The House of KUPPENHEIMER

The Beaufort

YOU will recognize the Beaufort as one of the pronounced style hits of the season. It stands for a group of advanced Kuppenheimer Models that offer the young man a wide range of choice and an opportunity to express his individuality. Prices $20 to $45. Write for our Book "Styles for Men."

HOUSE OF KUPPENHEIMER
Chicago

Copyright 1917, The House of Kuppenheimer

Analyzing Visuals Connecting to the Text

How does the man in this advertisement compare with your mental image of Jimmy Valentine?

The clerk handed him a railroad ticket and the five-dollar bill with which the law expected him to rehabilitate himself into good citizenship and prosperity. The warden gave him a cigar, and shook hands. Valentine, 9762, was chronicled on the books, "Pardoned by Governor," and Mr. James Valentine walked out into the sunshine.

Disregarding the song of the birds, the waving green trees, and the smell of the flowers, Jimmy headed straight for a restaurant. There he tasted the first sweet joys of liberty in the shape of a broiled chicken and a bottle of white wine— followed by a cigar a grade better than the one the warden had given him. From there he proceeded leisurely to the depot. He tossed a quarter into the hat of a blind man sitting by the door and boarded his train. Three hours set him down in a little town near the state line. He went to the café of one Mike Dolan and shook hands with Mike, who was alone behind the bar.

"Sorry we couldn't make it sooner, Jimmy, me boy," said Mike. "But we had that protest from Springfield to buck against, and the governor nearly balked. Feeling all right?"

"Fine," said Jimmy. "Got my key?"

He got his key and went upstairs, unlocking the door of a room at the rear. Everything was just as he had left it. There on the floor was still Ben Price's collar button that had been torn from that eminent detective's shirt band when they had overpowered Jimmy to arrest him.

Vocabulary **rehabilitate** (ree huh BIHL uh tayt) *v.*: restore to good standing.

Pulling out from a wall a folding bed, Jimmy slid back a panel in the wall and dragged out a dust-covered suitcase. He opened this and gazed fondly at the finest set of burglar's tools in the East. It was a complete set, made of specially tempered steel, the latest designs in drills, punches, braces and bits, jimmies, clamps, and augers,[4] with two or three novelties invented by Jimmy himself, in which he took pride. Over nine hundred dollars they had cost him to have made at ———, a place where they make such things for the profession.

In half an hour Jimmy went downstairs and through the café. He was now dressed in tasteful and well-fitting clothes and carried his dusted and cleaned suitcase in his hand.

"Got anything on?" asked Mike Dolan genially.

"Me?" said Jimmy, in a puzzled tone. "I don't understand. I'm representing the New York Amalgamated Short Snap Biscuit Cracker and Frazzled Wheat Company."

This statement delighted Mike to such an extent that Jimmy had to take a seltzer and milk on the spot. He never touched "hard" drinks. **C**

A week after the release of Valentine, 9762, there was a neat job of safe burglary done in Richmond, Indiana, with no clue to the author. A scant eight hundred dollars was all that was secured. Two weeks after

that a patented, improved, burglarproof safe in Logansport was opened like a cheese to the tune of fifteen hundred dollars, currency; securities and silver untouched. That began to interest the rogue-catchers. Then an old-fashioned bank safe in Jefferson City became active and threw out of its crater an eruption of bank notes amounting to five thousand dollars. The losses were now high enough to bring the matter up into Ben Price's class of work. By comparing notes, a remarkable similarity in the methods of the burglaries was noticed. Ben Price investigated the scenes of the robberies, and was heard to remark:

"That's Dandy Jim Valentine's autograph. He's resumed business. Look at that combination knob—jerked out as easy as pulling up a radish in wet weather. He's got the only clamps that can do it. And look how clean those tumblers were punched out! Jimmy never has to drill but one hole. Yes, I guess I want Mr. Valentine. He'll do his bit next time without any short-time or clemency foolishness." **D**

Ben Price knew Jimmy's habits. He had learned them while working on the Springfield case. Long jumps, quick getaways, no confederates,[5] and a taste for good society—these ways had helped Mr. Valentine to become noted as a successful dodger of retribution.[6] It was given out that

---

4. **drills . . . augers** (AW guhrz): tools for working with metal.

5. **confederates:** accomplices, or fellow criminals.
6. **retribution** (reht ruh BYOO shuhn): punishment.

C **Reading Focus** Drawing Conclusions What is O. Henry's attitude toward Jimmy? What details support your answer?

D **Read and Discuss** What is Jimmy doing now?

Vocabulary **clemency** (KLEHM uhn see) *n.:* mercy.

Ben Price had taken up the trail of the elusive cracksman, and other people with burglarproof safes felt more at ease.

One afternoon Jimmy Valentine and his suitcase climbed out of the mail hack[7] in Elmore, a little town five miles off the railroad down in the blackjack country of Arkansas. Jimmy, looking like an athletic young senior just home from college, went down the board sidewalk toward the hotel.

A young lady crossed the street, passed him at the corner, and entered a door over which was the sign "The Elmore Bank." Jimmy Valentine looked into her eyes, forgot what he was, and became another man. She lowered her eyes and colored slightly. Young men of Jimmy's style and looks were scarce in Elmore. **E**

Jimmy collared a boy that was loafing on the steps of the bank as if he were one of the stockholders, and began to ask him questions about the town, feeding him dimes at intervals. By and by the young lady came out, looking royally unconscious of the young man with the suitcase, and went her way.

"Isn't that young lady Miss Polly Simpson?" asked Jimmy, with specious guile.[8]

"Naw," said the boy. "She's Annabel Adams. Her pa owns this bank. What'd you come to Elmore for? Is that a gold watch chain? I'm going to get a bulldog. Got any more dimes?" **F**

Jimmy went to the Planters' Hotel, registered as Ralph D. Spencer, and engaged a room. He leaned on the desk and declared his platform[9] to the clerk. He said he had come to Elmore to look for a location to go into business. How was the shoe business, now, in the town? He had thought of the shoe business. Was there an opening?

The clerk was impressed by the clothes and manner of Jimmy. He, himself, was something of a pattern of fashion to the thinly gilded[10] youth of Elmore, but now he perceived his shortcomings. While trying to figure out Jimmy's manner of tying his four-in-hand,[11] he cordially gave information.

Yes, there ought to be a good opening in the shoe line. There wasn't an exclusive shoe store in the place. The dry goods and general stores handled them. Business in all lines was fairly good. Hoped Mr. Spencer would decide to locate in Elmore. He would find it a pleasant town to live in, and the people very sociable.

Mr. Spencer thought he would stop over in the town a few days and look over the situation. No, the clerk needn't call the boy. He would carry up his suitcase, himself; it was rather heavy.

---

7. **mail hack:** horse-drawn carriage used to carry mail from one town to another.
8. **with specious** (SPEE shuhs) **guile** (gyl): in a tricky way that appears to be innocent.

9. **platform:** here, intentions, or plans.
10. **thinly gilded:** only seeming to be well-dressed. To be gilded is to be covered with a layer of gold.
11. **four-in-hand:** a necktie.

E Reading Focus Drawing Conclusions What could the detail about Jimmy's response to the young lady reveal about O. Henry's feeling about the power of love?

F Read and Discuss What is happening now? What do Jimmy's encounters with people on the street tell you about him?

Vocabulary elusive (ih LOO sihv) *adj.*: hard to catch.

STYLE BOOK—FALL & WINTER
S. D. BROADHURST CO.
Mt. Olive, N. C.
1919 1920

Peters DIAMOND BRAND SHOES

Peters Shoe Co's Diamond Brand St. Louis

Peters DIAMOND BRAND SHOES

Socially he was also a success and made many friends. And he accomplished the wish of his heart. He met Miss Annabel Adams and became more and more captivated by her charms.

At the end of a year the situation of Mr. Ralph Spencer was this: he had won the respect of the community, his shoe store was flourishing, and he and Annabel were engaged to be married in two weeks. Mr. Adams, the typical, plodding country banker, approved of Spencer. Annabel's pride in him almost equaled her affection. He was as much at home in the family of Mr. Adams and that of Annabel's married sister as if he were already a member. **G**

One day Jimmy sat down in his room and wrote this letter, which he mailed to the safe address of one of his old friends in St. Louis:

Mr. Ralph Spencer, the phoenix[12] that arose from Jimmy Valentine's ashes—ashes left by the flame of a sudden and alterative attack of love—remained in Elmore and prospered. He opened a shoe store and secured a good run of trade.

12. **phoenix** (FEE nihks): bird in ancient Egyptian mythology. It was believed that the phoenix burned itself up and that from its ashes a new bird arose.

Dear Old Pal:

I want you to be at Sullivan's place, in Little Rock, next Wednesday night, at nine o'clock. I want you to wind up some little matters for me. And, also, I want to make you a present of my little kit of tools. I know you'll be glad to get them—you couldn't duplicate the lot for a thousand dollars. Say, Billy, I've quit

G **Read and Discuss** How are things looking for Jimmy?

the old business—a year ago. I've got a nice store. I'm making an honest living, and I'm going to marry the finest girl on earth two weeks from now. It's the only life, Billy—the straight one. I wouldn't touch a dollar of another man's money now for a million. After I get married I'm going to sell out and go West, where there won't be so much danger of having old scores brought up against me. I tell you, Billy, she's an angel. She believes in me; and I wouldn't do another crooked thing for the whole world. Be sure to be at Sully's, for I must see you. I'll bring along the tools with me.

Your old friend,

Jimmy **H**

On the Monday night after Jimmy wrote this letter, Ben Price jogged unobtrusively into Elmore in a livery buggy.[13] He lounged about town in his quiet way until he found out what he wanted to know. From the drugstore across the street from Spencer's shoe store, he got a good look at Ralph D. Spencer.

"Going to marry the banker's daughter, are you, Jimmy?" said Ben to himself, softly. "Well, I don't know!"

The next morning Jimmy took breakfast at the Adamses'. He was going to Little Rock that day to order his wedding suit and buy something nice for Annabel. That would be the first time he had left town since he came to Elmore. It had been more than a year now since those last professional "jobs," and he thought he could safely venture out.

After breakfast quite a family party went downtown together—Mr. Adams, Annabel, Jimmy, and Annabel's married sister with her two little girls, aged five and nine. They came by the hotel where Jimmy still boarded, and he ran up to his room and brought along his suitcase. Then they went on to the bank. There stood Jimmy's horse and buggy and Dolph Gibson, who was going to drive him over to the railroad station.

All went inside the high, carved oak railings into the banking room—Jimmy included, for Mr. Adams' future son-in-law was welcome anywhere. The clerks were pleased to be greeted by the good-looking, agreeable young man who was going to marry Miss Annabel. Jimmy set his suitcase down. Annabel, whose heart was bubbling with happiness and lively youth, put on Jimmy's hat and picked up the suitcase. "Wouldn't I make a nice drummer?"[14] asked Annabel. "My! Ralph, how heavy it is! Feels like it was full of gold bricks."

"Lot of nickel-plated shoehorns in there," said Jimmy, coolly, "that I'm going to return. Thought I'd save express charges by taking them up. I'm getting awfully economical." **I**

The Elmore Bank had just put in a new safe and vault. Mr. Adams was very

---

13. **livery buggy:** hired horse and carriage.

14. **drummer:** here, a traveling salesperson.

H [Reading Focus] Drawing Conclusions What motivates Jimmy to write this letter? What could this reveal about O. Henry's attitude toward love?

I [Read and Discuss] Now what has happened? Why is Jimmy's suitcase so heavy?

proud of it and insisted on an inspection by everyone. The vault was a small one, but it had a new patented door. It fastened with three solid steel bolts thrown simultaneously with a single handle, and had a time lock. Mr. Adams beamingly explained its workings to Mr. Spencer, who showed a courteous but not too intelligent interest. The two children, May and Agatha, were delighted by the shining metal and funny clock and knobs.

While they were thus engaged, Ben Price sauntered in and leaned on his elbow, looking casually inside between the railings. He told the teller that he didn't want anything; he was just waiting for a man he knew.

Suddenly there was a scream or two from the women and a commotion. Unperceived by the elders, May, the nine-year-old girl, in a spirit of play had shut Agatha in the vault. She had then shot the bolts and turned the knob of the combination as she had seen Mr. Adams do.

The old banker sprang to the handle and tugged at it for a moment. "The door can't be opened," he groaned. "The clock hasn't been wound nor the combination set."

Agatha's mother screamed again, hysterically.

Jealousy (detail) (1892) by Tihamer Margitay.

"Hush!" said Mr. Adams, raising his trembling hand. "All be quite for a moment. Agatha!" he called as loudly as he could. "Listen to me." During the following silence they could just hear the faint sound of the child wildly shrieking in the dark vault in a panic of terror.

"My precious darling!" wailed the mother. "She will die of fright! Open the door! Oh, break it open! Can't you men do something?"

"There isn't a man nearer than Little Rock who can open that door," said Mr. Adams, in a shaky voice. "Spencer, what shall we do? That child—she can't stand it long in there. There isn't enough air, and, besides, she'll go into convulsions[15] from fright." **J**

Agatha's mother, frantic now, beat the door of the vault with her hands. Somebody wildly suggested dynamite. Annabel turned to Jimmy, her large eyes full of anguish, but not yet despairing. To a woman nothing seems quite impossible to the powers of the man she worships.

"Can't you do something, Ralph—*try*, won't you?"

He looked at her with a queer, soft smile on his lips and in his keen eyes.

"Annabel," he said, "give me that rose you are wearing, will you?"

Hardly believing that she heard him aright, she unpinned the bud from the bosom of her dress, and placed it in his hand. Jimmy stuffed it into his vest pocket, threw off his coat, and pulled up his shirt sleeves. With that act Ralph D. Spencer passed away, and Jimmy Valentine took his place. **K**

"Get away from the door, all of you," he commanded, shortly.

He set his suitcase on the table, and opened it out flat. From that time on he

_____
15. **convulsions:** shaking fits.

seemed to be unconscious of the presence of anyone else. He laid out the shining, queer implements swiftly and orderly, whistling softly to himself as he always did when at work. In a deep silence and immovable, the others watched him as if under a spell.

In a minute Jimmy's pet drill was biting smoothly into the steel door. In ten minutes—breaking his own burglarious record—he threw back the bolts and opened the door.

Agatha, almost collapsed, but safe, was gathered into her mother's arms.

Jimmy Valentine put on his coat, and walked outside the railings toward the front door. As he went he thought he heard a far-away voice that he once knew call "Ralph!" But he never hesitated.

At the door a big man stood somewhat in his way.

"Hello, Ben!" said Jimmy, still with his strange smile. "Got around at last, have you? Well, let's go. I don't know that it makes much difference, now."

And then Ben Price acted rather strangely.

"Guess you're mistaken, Mr. Spencer," he said. "Don't believe I recognize you. Your buggy's waiting for you, ain't it?"

And Ben Price turned and strolled down the street. **L**

_____

J | Read and Discuss | What is happening? What crisis has been created?

K | Read and Discuss | What does this sentence mean?

L | Literary Focus | **Biographical Criticism** What details in the story do you think reflect O. Henry's own life and <u>attitudes</u>?

Vocabulary **anguish** (ANG gwihsh) *n.*: emotional pain.

Applying Your Skills

Reading Standard 3.7 Analyze a work of literature, showing how it reflects the heritage, traditions, **attitudes, and beliefs** of its author. (Biographical approach)

A Retrieved Reformation
Literary Response and Analysis

Reading Skills Focus
Quick Check

1. Who is Ben Price, and what is his opinion of Jimmy?

2. What decision does Ben Price make at the end of the story?

Read with a Purpose

3. What critical decision does Jimmy Valentine make when Agatha gets locked in the safe? What risk is he taking, and what does this tell you about him?

Reading Skill: Drawing Conclusions

4. Review the chart you completed as you read "A Retrieved Reformation." What connections did you discover between O. Henry's life and his work? Support your response with details from the story.

Literary Skills Focus
Literary Analysis

5. **Interpret** At what point in the story did you realize that Jimmy Valentine had given up his life of crime?

6. **Infer** What can you infer about the type of person Ben Price is when he lets Jimmy go?

7. **Make Judgments** Explain whether you believe Ben Price made the right decision at the end of the story.

8. **Extend** Explain whether you believe that Jimmy has truly reformed and given up stealing for good. Support your response with details from the story.

Literary Skills: Biographical Criticism

9. Refer to the chart you made as you read in order to draw conclusions for the biographical basis of this story.

- What details in the story seem to reflect specific experiences in O. Henry's life?

- What details might reflect O. Henry's attitudes toward prison?

- What details might reflect O. Henry's personal beliefs about redemption and the power of love?

Literary Skills Review: Conflict

10. **Interpret** A struggle between two or more forces is a **conflict. External conflict** occurs between a character and another character or force; **internal conflict** occurs inside a character's mind. What is the external conflict in this story? What is the internal conflict?

Writing Skills Focus
Think as a Reader/Writer

Use It in Your Writing Review the notes you made in your *Reader/Writer Notebook* about the surprise ending to this story. Think about what you expected to happen and what actually did happen. Then, write an idea for a brief story of your own with a surprise twist. You might even try extending O. Henry's story and introducing yet another twist to it.

What Do **You Think Now** How has reading "A Retrieved Reformation" changed your ideas about giving people chances?

Applying Your Skills

Reading Standard 1.2 Understand the most important points in the history of the English language and use common word origins to determine the historical influences on English word meanings.

A Retrieved Reformation

Vocabulary Development

Influences on English

The histories of English words can give us a glimpse of the history of the English-speaking peoples themselves. Thousands of words that we use every day have come into English from other languages. Some countries have tried to prevent foreign words from entering their languages. English, however, has always been like a giant sponge, absorbing words from every group with which it comes in contact. The Vocabulary words in "A Retrieved Reformation" all come from Latin.

- **rehabilitate** L *re–*, "again," + L *habilitare*, "make suitable"
- **clemency** L *clemens*, "merciful"
- **elusive** L *elusus*, "trick, fool"
- **anguish** L *angustia*, "tightness, distress"

Your Turn

Match each Vocabulary word with a related word that springs from the same Latin word.

> rehabilitate
> anguish
> elusive
> clemency

1. **rehabilitate** a. clement
2. **anguish** b. elude
3. **elusive** c. anger
4. **clemency** d. habit

Language Coach

Oral Fluency People in many professions, such as newscasters and actors, need to be able to speak fluently and clearly. To do that, they practice speaking aloud. With a partner, take turns reading the following "news item" aloud as if you were a television anchor reporting the event. Remember to refer to the pronunciations of the words on page 829 if you need help.

News Item:

Following a period of good behavior, Jasper "Fingers" Johnson was shown **clemency** and released from prison one year into his sentence. Sadly, the criminal was unable to **rehabilitate** himself, and he returned to his old ways, stealing pianos. Despite law enforcement's best efforts, "Fingers" remains **elusive.** His relatives wait with **anguish,** unsure of the fate that lies in store for Johnson once he is finally recaptured.

Academic Vocabulary

Talk About . . .
With a partner, discuss what <u>attitudes</u> toward human behavior the author reveals through this story. What general <u>approach</u> to life do you think O. Henry took, especially after his own brushes with the law?

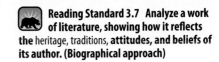
Grammar Link
Correct Placement of Modifiers

A **modifier** is a word or phrase that describes or limits the meaning of another word or phrase. Always place modifiers as close as possible to the word or words they modify, or tell about. A modifier that is too far from what it modifies is misplaced, and your reader could become confused. Look at this example.

> *Exhausted,* dancing was the last thing on Kevin's mind.

Since the modifier *exhausted* is closest to *dancing,* it appears to modify *dancing* instead of the word it should modify: *Kevin.* Let's try the sentence again.

> Dancing was the last thing on *exhausted* Kevin's mind.

Your Turn

Rewrite each sentence below by placing the misplaced modifier as close as possible to the word it should modify.

1. He was now dressed and carried his suitcase in his hand tastefully.
2. Price was waiting for a man he knew patiently.
3. The child's mother pounded her hands against the safe, panicked.

Writing Applications Now, write three sentences of your own about the story you have just read, using correctly placed modifiers.

CHOICES

As you respond to the Choices, use these **Academic Vocabulary** words: approach, attitude, criticism, tradition.

REVIEW
Evaluate a Character

Timed ∟Writing Write a brief essay evaluating Jimmy's character, using details from the story and from O. Henry's life as support. In your conclusion, explain whether you find him to be a believable, or credible, character and whether you think his character reflects O. Henry's attitudes or beliefs.

CONNECT
Conduct an Interview

TechFocus Imagine interviewing Jimmy Valentine about his life of crime. Write at least three questions you would ask him and what you imagine his responses would be. Choose two classmates to play the roles of Jimmy and his interviewer, and create a slideshow or short video presentation of the interview.

EXTEND
Pitch a Television Series

Group Project Imagine that this story is the first episode in a new television series, *The Life and Times of Jimmy Valentine.* Develop an outline for the series, explaining its basic premise (what it will be about) and describing the plots of the first few episodes. "Pitch" your ideas to the class, and ask if they would watch the show.

Learn It Online
Create an impressive multimedia presentation! Visit the *MediaScope* mini-site at:

go.hrw.com | H8-841 | Go

Writing Workshop

Biographical Narrative

Write with a Purpose

Write a biographical narrative that makes the personality of your subject come alive. Your **purpose** is to express your feelings and thoughts about your subject and explain why the subject is important to you. Your **audience** may include your teacher and classmates, family and friends.

A Good Biographical Narrative

- brings the subject to life
- includes concrete details about the subject's appearance, behavior, and background
- relates specific incidents that reveal the subject's personality
- communicates the significance of the subject to the writer

See page 850 for complete rubric.

Reader/Writer Notebook

Use your **RWN** to complete the activities for this workshop.

Think as a Reader/Writer

Our thoughts and actions are often shaped by those of others. We've all known people who are important to us. In this workshop you will create a portrait, a biography, of one of those people. A biography is a true story about someone else's life. Before you write, read the excerpt below from Maya Angelou's *I Know Why the Caged Bird Sings,* in which she portrays an important adult from her childhood.

> For nearly a year, I sopped around the house, the Store, the school, and the church, like an old biscuit, dirty and inedible. Then I met, or rather got to know, the lady who threw me my first lifeline.
>
> Mrs. Bertha Flowers was the aristocrat of Black Stamps. She had the grace of control to appear warm in the coldest weather, and on the Arkansas summer days it seemed she had a private breeze which swirled around, cooling her. She was thin without the taut look of wiry people, and her printed voile dresses and flowered hats were as right for her as denim overalls for a farmer. . . .
>
> I don't think I ever saw Mrs. Flowers laugh, but she smiled often. A slow widening of her thin black lips to show even, small white teeth, then the slow effortless closing. When she chose to smile on me, I always wanted to thank her. The action was so graceful and inclusively benign.
>
> I didn't question why Mrs. Flowers had singled me out for attention, nor did it occur to me that Momma might have asked her to give me a little talking-to. All I cared about was that she had made tea cookies for *me* and read to *me* from her favorite book. It was enough to prove that she liked me.

← The writer states Mrs. Flowers's importance in her life.

← Specific details about Mrs. Flowers's appearance and behavior reveal her character.

← The end makes clear the writer's feelings.

Think About the Professional Model

With a partner, discuss the following questions about the model:

1. Why does the author start by describing her own mental state?

2. What does the description of Mrs. Flowers tell us about her character?

 **Writing Standard 1.2 Establish coherence within and among paragraphs** through effective transitions, parallel structures, and similar writing techniques. **1.6 Revise writing for word choice**; appropriate organization; consistent point of view; and transitions between paragraphs, passages and ideas. **2.1 Write biographies,** autobiographies, short stories, or narratives: **a. Relate a clear, coherent incident, event, or situation by using well-chosen details. b. Reveal the significance of, or the** writer's attitude about, the subject. **c. Employ narrative and descriptive strategies (e.g., relevant dialogue, specific action, physical description, background description, comparison or contrast of characters).**

Prewriting

Choose a Subject

Your first step in writing your biographical narrative is to choose a subject. Ask yourself these questions:

- Whom do I know well?
- Which of these people have shaped my life in some way?
- Which of these people would I feel comfortable writing about?

Explore Your Imagination

Here is another idea to help you come up with a subject for your biography. Brainstorm the most memorable times in your life—times you were happiest, saddest, proudest, most worried, most relieved, and so on. Was someone with you at the time? What influence did that person have on you? Make a list of memorable times and the people they involved. From the list, pick the person you most want to write about.

Think About Purpose and Audience

As you begin planning your biographical narrative, keep your purpose and your audience in mind. Your **purpose** is to bring to life to the character of someone significant to you and to explain their importance in your life.

Your **audience** is an individual or group of individuals who will read your narrative, most probably your teacher and classmates. To focus on your audience, answer the following questions:

- Who is my audience?
- What information does my audience already know about my subject?
- What does my audience need to know to fully understand my subject?
- How can I make my feelings about my subject clear to my audience?

Idea Starters

- someone you love
- someone you want to be like
- someone who makes you angry or sad or joyful
- someone who helped you learn an important lesson
- someone you helped

Your Turn _____

Get Started Making notes in your **RWN**, choose a person you want to write about. Answer the questions about **audience** on this page. Keep your **purpose** in mind as you write your notes. Write a short statement explaining how this person has influenced you.

 Learn It Online
An interactive graphic organizer can help you generate and organize ideas. Try one at:

go.hrw.com   H6-843   **Go**

Writing Tip
To gather details about your subject's appearance, try sketching—or imagine that you're sketching—your subject. What specific posture, clothing, and facial expression will you sketch? What setting will your sketch show?

What Your Subject Means to You

You may be able to say exactly why this person is so important in your life, or you may just know you feel strongly about him or her. At this point it doesn't matter. Look over your notes, and think about these questions:

- Have I learned something important from this person?
- How has my life changed because of this person?
- What would my life be like without this person?

Then, in a sentence or two, state what your subject means to you. What you write here may be the heart of your biographical narrative. But no matter where you begin, you'll want to tell about what this person is like, what this person has done, and why he or she is significant in your life.

Bring Your Subject to Life

In order to bring your subject fully to life you'll need to portray both external and internal characteristics. Here are some narrative and descriptive strategies that can help you:

- relate coherent incidents using well-chosen details
- include specific actions that reveal your subject's character
- include relevant dialogue spoken by your subject
- use physical descriptions of your setting and subject's appearance
- add background descriptions that highlight your subject's qualities
- compare and contrast your subject with other people
- make clear the significance of your subject in your life

Creating an Outside/Inside Chart can help you organize your thoughts. See how the chart could be used to organize information about the character of Mrs. Flowers and her relationship to the writer.

Your Turn _____

Create an Outside/Inside Chart

Before writing your biographical narrative, create a chart to compile details about your subject's appearance, actions, qualities, and relationship with you. Share your chart with a classmate and ask whether he or she gets a clear picture of your subject from the details in your chart. Consider whether or not you need to include more details or different information about your subject based on the feedback from your classmate.

Outside	
Appearance	thin; wears printed voile dresses and flowered hats; has small white teeth
Specific Actions	moves gracefully; doesn't laugh but smiles a lot; recites from books; makes cookies; gives gifts
Inside	
Inner Qualities	controlled; benign; thoughtful
Our Relationship	my lifeline; gives me attention; likes me; encourages me

Drafting

Follow the Writer's Framework
Look over your notes. Mark the sections you think are the most important. Be sure you include details that describe your subject's appearance and personality. As you draft, expect to make discoveries—to learn more about how your subject is unique and how he or she has influenced you. Use the Framework for a Biographical Narrative to provide a quick reference as you write your draft.

Framework for a Biographical Narrative

Introduction
- sparks the reader's curiosity
- shows your subject in action
- mentions an interesting detail

Body
- describes your subject's qualities
- illustrates with stories of shared experiences
- provides other specific details

Conclusion
- tells what your subject means to you

Shape and Organize
Look over your notes and decide which of the following would be the most coherent way to organize your biography:

a. **Chronology.** You can use chronological order, or time order, and tell the story of a single event, a single day, or a series of incidents in your subject's life.
b. **Features.** You can organize your description by different features of your subject's appearance and personality. Notice how Maya Angelou discusses different aspects of Mrs. Flowers's personality on page 842.
c. **Comparison/contrast.** You can compare and contrast your subject with yourself or with one or more other people, showing how your subject is unique.

Grammar Link Using Precise Verbs
Precise verbs can help readers clearly see the subject of your biographical narrative. Notice the use of precise verbs in this excerpt from "Mrs. Flowers."

> Her skin was a rich black that would have **peeled** like a plum if it **snagged,**
>
> but then no one would have thought of getting close enough to Mrs. Flowers to
>
> **ruffle** her dress, let alone **snag** her skin.

Choose precise verbs to bring the subject of your biographical narrative to life.

Writing Tip
To catch your readers' interest right away with a strong beginning, try one of the following ideas:
- Show your subject in action.
- Quote something meaningful your subject said.
- Mention an interesting fact or detail.
- Ask an intriguing question about your subject.
- Describe a funny incident.

Your Turn _____
Write Your Draft Using the notes you gathered and the **Writer's Framework,** write a draft of your biographical narrative. Be sure to think about
- sparking the audience's curiosity
- using specific details to describe your subject's appearance and actions
- telling what your subject means to you

Biographical Narrative

Peer Review

Working with a peer, go over the chart at the right. Then, review your draft. Answer each question in this chart to locate where and how your draft could be improved. Be sure to take notes on what you and your partner discuss. You can refer to your notes as you revise your draft.

Evaluating and Revising

Read the questions in the left column of the chart, and then use the tips in the middle column to help you make revisions to your essay. The right column suggests techniques you can use to revise your draft.

Biographical Narrative: Guidelines for Content and Organization

Evaluation Question	Tip	Revision Technique
1. Does the introduction spark the audience's curiosity?	**Underline** the questions, quote, interesting fact or detail, funny incident, or action that would interest the audience.	If needed, **add** an attention-grabber to the beginning of the narrative.
2. Does the narrative create a clear description of its subject?	**Put a star** next to the concrete details describing the subject's appearance, behavior, and background.	**Add** details if necessary.
3. Does the narrative include incidents or events that illustrate the subject's personality?	**Circle** accounts of specific incidents and events that show the subject's personality.	**Add** incidents as needed. **Elaborate** on the incidents by adding details or explaining their meaning.
4. Does the conclusion communicate why the subject is important to the writer?	**Put a check mark** next to the sentence(s) that explain the subject's significance to the writer.	**Add** a conclusion that clearly expresses why the subject is important to the writer.

Read this student draft and notice the comments on its strengths and suggestions about how it could be improved.

An Awesome Lady

by Kelsey Peterson

What's not to love about someone who's gentle and kind, who knows you better than you know yourself, and who offers you sweet words like "I love you" every day? Sound like someone you know? For me, this is my mother, the very person I admire and treasure more than the sun itself. If you ever gave me the option to hang out with her all day or spend time with anyone else in the entire world, she'd make the cut. I know I sound all sentimental and sappy, but I can't help it! My mom and I are what my generation likes to call "tight." Not even the bonds with my closest comrades can rival my relationship with my mom. She knows all that there is to know about me, and for being who she is, I look up to her. Put simply, she's just an awesome lady.

← The beginning grabs the reader's attention by posing a question.

← Kelsey states her mother's significance in her life.

MINI-LESSON ▶ **How to Elaborate with Specific Action**

Kelsey makes the point that she admires her mother. She can strengthen this point by describing specific actions of her mother.

Kelsey's Revision of Paragraph One

She knows all that there is to know about me, and for being who she is, I look up to her. ∧ *For example, one of the things I most admire is the fact that my mother has never shied away from a challenge. She has demonstrated that if you work hard you can achieve your dreams. When others told Mom that raising two kids and putting herself through law school was impossible, she just smiled and plugged away. While working full time as a legal secretary she managed to get her law degree, take care of me and my brother, and share a few laughs along the way.* Put simply, she's just an awesome lady.

Your Turn _____

Strengthen Your Narrative

Read your draft and then ask yourself these questions:

- What details in my draft can be strengthened by adding specific events?
- What do the specific actions tell me about my subject?

Well-chosen details about the mother's behavior help reveal her character.

My mom is also one of the wisest people I've ever met if there's ever something that's troubling me, she's always there to offer helpful advice. My mom's the kind of person who has seen it all before. Nothing ever scares her. Someday, I hope to become as strong a person as she is.

All in all, since she's the one that I admire and love the most, I'd choose to spend a day with my mom over anyone. We're extremely close, she knows everything about me, and basically, she's my hero. On top of all that, she also has a great sense of humor. You can't find a better deal than that anywhere else, that's for sure.

MINI-LESSON ▸ **How to Clearly Communicate the Importance of Your Subject**

Kelsey's final paragraph repeats her feelings of love and admiration for her mother. To strengthen her conclusion, she could more clearly communicate why her mother is important to her.

Kelsey's Revision of Paragraph Three

All in all, since she's the one that I admire and love the most, I'd choose to spend a day with my mom over anyone. We're extremely close, she knows everything about me, and basically, she's my hero. ∧ *Most importantly, my mother has shown me the kind of woman I want to grow into. Her example has provided me with life lessons I know will serve me for the rest of my life.* On top of all of that, she also has a great sense of humor. You can't find a better deal than that anywhere else, that's for sure.

Your Turn _____

Communicating Your Subject's Importance With a partner, review your narrative. Ask your partner to explain why your subject is important. Use your partner's feedback to evaluate whether or not you need to add more information about the importance of your subject.

Proofreading and Publishing

Check your work carefully for mistakes in spelling, grammar, and punctuation. If you're using a computer, proofread a printout of your work. Mistakes are harder to spot on screen.

Proofreading Tip

Have three different peers read your composition, each one focusing on only one potential problem area: spelling, punctuation, or sentence structure. Use each reader's suggestions to improve your essay.

> ### Grammar Link Run-On Sentences
>
> A run-on sentence is actually two or more sentences run together into one. In run-ons, thoughts that should be separate and clear become one confusing blur.
>
> **Run-on**
> My mom is also one of the wisest people I've ever met if there's ever something that's troubling me, she's always there to offer helpful advice.
>
> It's often hard to tell where one idea in a run-on ends and the next one begins. One way to correct a run-on is to make it into two separate sentences. Add a period at the proper point to bring the ideas in these sentences back into focus:
>
> **Correct**
> My mom is also one of the wisest people I've ever met. If there's ever something that's troubling me, she's always there to offer helpful advice.

Publishing

If possible, read your work (or send it) to the person who inspired it and to others who know your subject. Or you might submit it to your school newspaper or literary magazine. As a class, consider making a bulletin-board display of your biographies with photographs of the subjects.

Reflect on the Process

In your **RWN,** write short responses to these questions:

1. What discoveries did I make about myself or about my relationship with the person I wrote about?
2. What was the hardest part about writing this biography?
3. What's my favorite part of this biography, and why?

Your Turn _____
Proofread and Publish

Exchange your biographical narrative with a classmate's. Act as the proofreader of your partner's paper. Circle any run-on sentences you find, and suggest a correction for each. Exchange papers again, and decide for yourself how you will correct the run-ons your partner found in your paper. When your draft is ready, share it with others.

Scoring Rubric

You can use the rubric below to evaluate your biographical narrative.

Biographical Narrative Writing	Organization and Focus	Sentence Structure	Conventions
4 • Provides a *thoroughly developed* narrative with a clear, coherent incident, event, or situation. • Includes *appropriate* strategies (e.g., relevant dialogue, specific action, physical description, and background description).	• *Clearly* addresses all of the writing tasks. • Demonstrates a *complete and specific* understanding of purpose and audience. • Maintains a *consistent* point of view and *clear* transitions. • *Effectively* reveals the significance of, or the writer's attitude about, the subject.	• Includes sentence *variety*.	• Contains *few, if any,* errors in the conventions of the English language (grammar, punctuation, capitalization, spelling). These errors do **not** interfere with the reader's understanding of the writing.
3 • Provides an *adequately developed* narrative with a clear, coherent incident, event, or situation. • Includes *mostly appropriate* strategies (e.g., relevant dialogue, specific action, physical description, and background description).	• Addresses *most* of the writing task. • Demonstrates a *general* understanding of purpose and audience. • Maintains a *mostly consistent* point of view and *relatively clear* transitions. • For the most part, *effectively* reveals the significance of, or the writer's attitude about, the subject.	• Includes *some* sentence variety.	• Contains *some errors* in the conventions of the English language (grammar, punctuation, capitalization, spelling). These errors do **not** interfere with the reader's understanding of the writing.
2 • Provides a *minimally developed* narrative with a *somewhat clear,* coherent incident, event, or situation. • *Attempts* to use appropriate strategies but with *minimal effectiveness* (e.g., relevant dialogue, specific action, physical description, and background description).	• Addresses *some* of the writing task. • Demonstrates *little* understanding of purpose and audience. • Maintains an *inconsistent* point of view and *awkward* transitions that do not unify important ideas. • *Suggests* the significance of, or the writer's attitude about, the subject but with *limited* success.	• Includes *little* sentence variety.	• Contains *several errors* in the conventions of the English language (grammar, punctuation, capitalization, spelling). These errors **may** interfere with the reader's understanding of the writing.
1 • *Lacks* a developed narrative with a clear, coherent incident, event, or situation. • *Fails* to use appropriate strategies (e.g., relevant dialogue, specific action, physical description, and background description).	• Addresses *only one* part of the writing task. • Demonstrates *no understanding* of purpose and audience. • *Lacks* a point of view and transitions that unify important ideas. • *Does not convey* the significance of, or the writer's attitude about, the subject.	• Includes *no* sentence variety.	• Contains *serious errors* in the conventions of the English language (grammar, punctuation, capitalization, spelling). These errors interfere with the reader's understanding of the writing.

Preparing for Timed ⏲ Writing

Biographical Narrative

When responding to a prompt asking you to write a biographical narrative, use what you have learned from this chapter's Writing Workshop and the rubric on page 850.

Writing Standard 2.1 Write biographies, autobiographies, short stories, or narratives: **a. Relate a clear, coherent incident, event, or situation by using well-chosen details. b. Reveal the significance of, or the writer's attitude about, the subject. c. Employ narrative and descriptive strategies (e. g., relevant dialogue, specific action, physical description, background description, comparison or contrast of characters).**

Writing Prompt

Write a biographical narrative in which you relate a clear, coherent incident. Use well-chosen details, specific actions, and relevant dialogue to describe the events and reveal the subject's character.

Study the Prompt

Be sure to read the prompt carefully, and identify all parts of your task. Circle or underline key instructional words: *biographical, narrative, coherent, details, actions, dialogue, character.* Re-read the prompt to make sure you understand your task. Note that your narrative should not only describe the events of this incident but also reveal aspects of the subject's character.

Tip: Spend about five minutes studying the prompt.

Plan Your Response

First, think of a person in your life whom you know well or a historical or public figure about whom you know enough information to write an essay. Make sure you have specific knowledge of at least one incident that reveals the person's character. Once you have settled on your subject, take notes on the following:

- specific details about the events
- what the incident reveals about the subject
- your point of view on the subject

Tip: Spend about fifteen minutes planning your response.

Respond to the Prompt

Using the notes you've just made, draft your narrative. Follow these guidelines:

- In the introduction, grab the reader's attention with an interesting opener, and set the scene with well-chosen descriptive details.
- In the body of the narrative, relate the events in chronological order, using dialogue wherever relevant.
- In the conclusion, make a direct statement about the subject's character.
- Remember to use a consistent point of view.

Tip: Spend about twenty minutes writing your draft.

Improve Your Response

Revising Go back to the key aspects of the prompt. Did you provide descriptive details and relevant dialogue? Do you need to add transitions or improve your word choices?

Proofreading Take a few minutes to proofread your narrative to correct errors in grammar, spelling, punctuation, and capitalization. Make sure that all of your edits are neat, and erase any stray marks.

Checking Your Final Copy Before you turn in your biographical narrative, read it one more time to catch any errors that you may have missed. You'll be glad that you took the extra time for one final review.

Tip: Save ten minutes to improve your paper.

Listening & Speaking Workshop

Delivering a Biographical Narrative

Speak with a Purpose

Adapt your biographical narrative into an oral narrative. After you have practiced delivering your narrative, present it to the class.

Think as a Reader/Writer Most of us tell true stories about ourselves. However, you can also tell stories about another person's true experiences. You will learn how by delivering a biographical narrative about someone important or special to you. In your presentation, you'll use narrative and descriptive strategies and a clear pattern of organization to create an accurate portrait of your subject.

Adapt Your Personal Narrative

Send a Message

As you develop your biographical presentation, consider the message you want to express about your subject. Be sure to include details that reveal your attitude to your biographical subject. For example, if your subject has fought through adversity to achieve success, you will want to include details that convey a hopeful message.

Use Narrative and Descriptive Strategies

Use the following list of narrative and descriptive strategies to employ as you develop a biographical presentation.

- Use **background description** to give listeners information they need to understand the subject of your biographical narrative.
- **Comparing and contrasting characters** in your narrative is useful. You may want to convey the importance of a mentor figure to your subject by describing ways in which they are similar.
- Include **relevant dialogue,** the actual words of the people involved in the events, to reveal your subject's attitude toward incidents, events, and situations.
- By relating your subject's **specific actions,** you will relate incidents, events, and situations in a clear, coherent way.
- Use **physical descriptions,** including precise nouns and adjectives and action verbs, to enliven your oral presentation.

Organize

Prepare an informal outline of the events you wish to relate in your biographical presentation. It is usually best to organize your biographical narrative in chronological order. Conclude your narrative with a summary of why your subject is significant to you.

Reader/Writer Notebook

Use your **RWN** to complete the activities for this workshop.

Listening and Speaking Standard 1.5
Use precise language, action verbs, sensory details, appropriate and colorful modifiers, and the active rather than the passive voice **in ways that enliven oral presentations. 1.6 Use appropriate** grammar, **word choice,** enunciation, and pace during formal presentations. **2.1 Deliver narrative presentations (e.g., biographical,** autobiographical): **a. Relate a clear, coherent incident, event, or situation by using well-chosen details. b. Reveal the significance** of, and the subject's attitude about, the incident, event, or situation. c. Employ narrative and descriptive strategies (e.g., relevant dialogue, specific action, physical description, background description, comparison or contrast of characters).

Deliver Your Biographical Narrative

Find Your Voice

Remember to use **nonverbal techniques** to communicate ideas in a biographical narrative effectively. For example, if you are describing your subject receiving a notable award, you might use a facial expression, such as a broad smile, to convey your admiration. You can also use **verbal techniques,** such as changing the tone of your voice and adjusting your **modulation,** or pitch, to sound impressed.

Practice using your body and voice to communicate your message. For example, practice telling your story several different ways. Think about how your presentation changes if you use a soft voice or a loud voice. Match your voice to the mood you are trying to create for the audience and to the events you are trying to relate. If your biographical narrative has a happy ending, make sure the tone and expression of your voice matches that happiness.

Practice, Practice

Practice delivering your presentation in front of a mirror. Then, try to rehearse in front of friends or a family member. Consider their ideas to make your presentation effective. Keep these hints in mind to deliver an effective biographical narrative:

- **Speak loudly** enough for everyone to hear you. The volume of your voice may sound unnaturally loud to you, but people sitting in the back of the room will appreciate it.
- Speak at an appropriate **pace,** neither too slowly nor too quickly.
- In addition to speaking loudly and slowly, be sure to **enunciate** clearly. Do not slur words or end words abruptly.
- Maintain **eye contact** with your audience.
- Notice reactions, especially **nonverbal cues,** in your audience. If they seem bored, it might be because they cannot hear you. If they nod or smile, then you can feel comfortable that you are speaking clearly and effectively.

A Good Delivery of a Biographical Narrative

- reveals the significance of the subject to the speaker
- employs relevant dialogue, specific action, physical description, and background description
- follows a clear pattern of organization
- matches voice modulation, facial expression, and tone to the audience and purpose
- holds listeners' attention through verbal and nonverbal techniques

 Speaking Tip

When you deliver your narrative orally, listeners only have one opportunity to hear what you have to say. Be sure to include transition words as you deliver your biographical narrative. Since most biographical narratives are told in chronological order, words such as *first, next, then,* and *after* are appropriate for inclusion.

 Learn It Online
Graphics can make your speech more compelling. See how on *MediaScope:*

| go.hrw.com | H8-853 | Go |

Literary Skills Review

Literary Criticism   **Directions:** Read the story. Then, answer each question that follows.

Just Enough Is Plenty: A Hanukkah Tale

by **Barbara Diamond Goldin**

This excerpt is taken from a story that takes place in nineteenth-century Poland, during Hanukkah, the Jewish Festival of Lights, which usually begins in December. Hanukkah celebrates the rededication of the Temple in Jerusalem in 165 B.C. Another Jewish holiday, Purim, mentioned in the first paragraph, is a spring festival that honors Queen Esther.

Malka's family lived in a village in Poland. They were poor, but not so poor. They had candles for the Sabbath, noisemakers for Purim, and spinning tops for Hanukkah.

Mama was busy preparing for tonight, the first of the eight nights of Hanukkah. She peeled onions and grated potatoes for the latkes, the potato pancakes.

Malka's younger brother Zalman carved a dreidel, a spinning top.

"This dreidel will spin the fastest of all," he boasted.

Papa was working long hours in his tailor shop so they could buy more food for the holiday. More potatoes, more onions, more flour, more oil.

For on the first night of Hanukkah, Malka's family always invited many guests. But this year only Aunt Hindy and Uncle Shmuel were coming to visit.

"Only two guests?" Malka asked. "Last year, we had so many guests that Papa had to put boards over the pickle barrels to make the table big enough."

"That was last year," Mama said gently. "This year has not been a good one for Papa in the shop. People bring him just a little mending here, a little mending there. He cannot afford to buy new material to sew fancy holiday dresses and fine suits."

"But it's Hanukkah," Malka reminded Mama.

Mama patted Malka's shoulder. "Don't worry, Malkaleh. We know how to stretch. We're poor, but not so poor. Now go. Ask Papa if he has a few more coins. I need more eggs for the latkes."

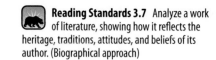

Reading Standards 3.7 Analyze a work of literature, showing how it reflects the heritage, traditions, attitudes, and beliefs of its author. (Biographical approach)

Meet the Writer

When she wrote this story, Barbara Diamond Goldin was a preschool teacher and storyteller who lived with her husband and two children in Northampton, Massachusetts. Three of her grandparents came from Poland. It was only in doing research for this book that she learned how they probably lived before coming to America. Perhaps this fictional story could be their true story!

1. The setting, a village in Poland, *best* reflects the author's heritage because
   A Poland is where she was born.
   B most of her grandparents came from Poland.
   C many Poles immigrated to America.
   D Poland was once the home of many Jews.

2. Read these sentences from the story.

   > They were poor, but not so poor. They had candles for the Sabbath, noisemakers for Purim, and spinning tops for Hanukkah.

   The comparison of the family's finances with their possessions indicates that the author believes in
   A observing religion.
   B cooking dinners.
   C family parties.
   D making money.

3. Read these sentences from the story.

   > Mama patted Malka's shoulder. "Don't worry, Malkaleh. We know how to stretch."

   These lines indicate the author's attitude toward
   A receiving presents.
   B enjoying a festival.
   C the value of working hard.
   D a caring family.

4. The author's family traditions can be seen in each of the following examples *except*
   A the celebration of Hanukkah.
   B the family's poverty.
   C a spinning top called a dreidel.
   D noisemakers for Purim.

Timed Writing

5. How does this story excerpt reflect the author's heritage, traditions, attitudes, and beliefs? Support your response with examples from the introduction, the story, and the biography.

Vocabulary Skills Review

Synonyms   **Directions:** Choose the word or phrase that is the best synonym for each italicized word.

1. A leader who grants a prisoner *clemency* offers
   A   weakness.
   B   mercy.
   C   pride.
   D   anger.

2. If something is *archaic,* it is
   A   wooden.
   B   expensive.
   C   outdated.
   D   strong.

3. To feel *anguish* is to feel
   A   boredom.
   B   energized.
   C   misery.
   D   amused.

4. A *tedious* story is
   A   confusing.
   B   heartwarming.
   C   boring.
   D   surprising.

5. If a friend is *inquiring* about you, she is
   A   gossiping.
   B   asking.
   C   thinking.
   D   worrying.

6. When you *rehabilitate* something, you
   A   replace it.
   B   research it.
   C   restore it.
   D   remember it.

7. If you are wearing a *rueful* expression, you look
   A   unhappy.
   B   excited.
   C   bored.
   D   amused.

8. An *elusive* idea is
   A   agreeable to a group.
   B   a cause of unhappiness.
   C   one that is uncommon.
   D   difficult to grasp.

Academic Vocabulary

Choose the word or phrase that is the *best* synonym for the italicized Academic Vocabulary word.

9. Another word for *tradition* is
   A   holiday.
   B   custom.
   C   history.
   D   kindness.

Writing Skills Review

Biographical Narrative

Directions: Read the following paragraph from a student's narrative. Then, answer the questions that follow.

 Writing Standard 2.1 Write biographies, autobiographies, short stories, or narratives: **a. Relate a clear, coherent incident, event, or situation by using well-chosen details. b. Reveal the significance of, or the writer's attitude about, the subject. c. Employ narrative and descriptive strategies (e. g., relevant dialogue, specific action, physical description, background description, comparison or contrast of characters).**

(1) Before I got to know him, I never imagined that the head librarian at the town library would become my friend. (2) His appearance really frightened me. (3) I was also afraid of the school-crossing guard. (4) One day I was having trouble finding a book I wanted to use for an assignment and I needed help. (5) "He's going to grumble and be unhelpful," I thought as I approached his desk, but to my surprise, he greeted me warmly and helped me find the book I needed. (6) While finding the book with me, the librarian told me that he was also a fan of mystery novels, as he knew I was from the books I'd borrowed. (7) I was shocked that he remembered my book preferences and that he was so friendly. (8) I was reminded of an old saying: Don't judge a book by its cover.

1. To portray the setting of the passage more specifically, the writer could
   A relate the look of the library's neighborhood.
   B describe the librarian's desk.
   C describe the writer's own desk at home.
   D explain the school assignment the writer needs to complete.

2. Which character description would support the idea in sentence 2?
   A The librarian works on the weekends, so I see him every time I go to the library.
   B He has a cheerful smile and places colorful flowering plants around his desk.
   C He has a photograph of his wife and children on his desk.
   D His shaggy hair framed a creased face that scowled uninvitingly.

3. Which sentence could be eliminated and not change the meaning of the passage?
   A Sentence 1
   B Sentence 3
   C Sentence 6
   D Sentence 7

4. Which of the following narrative techniques did the writer use in sentence 5?
   A imagery
   B sensory details
   C dialogue
   D metaphor

5. The word that *best* describes the writer's attitude toward his subject is
   A admiration
   B fright
   C friendship
   D surprise

Fiction

Habibi

Liyana, a 14-year-old Arab American living in St. Louis, is used to the American way of life. So when her father, a native Palestinian, decides to move the family back to Jerusalem, she is confronted with a very different culture. Set among a backdrop of Jerusalem's markets, political clashes, and a profound sense of history, Naomi Shihab Nye's *Habibi* is the story of a girl trying to balance her American instincts with the lifestyle of her new home.

King of Shadows

Nat Field is thrilled when he is cast in a school production of Shakespeare's *A Midsummer Night's Dream*. The drama troupe travels to London to perform at a re-creation of the famous Globe Theatre. In twenty-first-century London, Nat falls ill, sleeps fitfully, and awakens to find himself transported back 400 years to Shakespeare's time! Not only that, but he still must act in the play, which is now directed by the famous bard himself.

Bud, Not Buddy

Bud—not Buddy—has gotten bad treatment in orphanages and foster homes, so he runs off in search of his father. Bud does not know his father but suspects that he is a member of the famous jazz band the Dusky Devastators of the Depression. Bud finds both adventure and trouble during his search in *Bud, Not Buddy*. This heartwarming and hilarious novel by Christopher Paul Curtis won a Newbery Medal.

Join In: Multiethnic Short Stories

Join In: Multiethnic Short Stories is a collection that pays homage to the American teenage experience. The stories are written by authors from varying ethnic backgrounds: Japanese, Cuban, Chinese, African American, Puerto Rican, and more. Although the stories are from different perspectives, they all speak to the ups and downs of teenage life—friends, tests, music, sports, and love.

Nonfiction

Within Reach: My Everest Story

Imagine crossing three-hundred-foot crevasses, climbing up glaciers, and trekking so high that you need an oxygen tank to breathe. Such is the Everest experience. Now imagine doing it all at age sixteen! That's what Mark Pfetzer did in 1996; he became the youngest person to reach 26,000 feet on Mount Everest. Mark describes his unique childhood and gives a first-hand account of the 1996 Everest tragedy in his exciting book, *Within Reach: My Everest Story*.

Princess Ka'iulani: Hope of a Nation, Heart of a People

More than a hundred years ago Hawaii was an independent territory that the United States was anxious to acquire. However, Hawaii's seventeen-year-old Princess Ka'iulani cherished her country's independence. In *Princess Ka'iulani: Hope of a Nation, Heart of a People,* Sharon Linnéa describes the princess's struggle with the U.S. government and even with members of her own family.

A Frontier Fort on the Oregon Trail

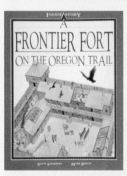

In *A Frontier Fort on the Oregon Trail,* Scott Steedman and Mark Bergin look at the way people lived in the Old West. Bergin's detailed illustrations present a typical day in the life of a soldier, a homemaker, and a trapper. Steedman fleshes out the illustrations with helpful text, including an explanation of how a cabin and a fort were built on the nineteenth-century U.S. frontier.

Pioneer Girl: Growing Up on the Prairie

Although living on the prairie could be physically and mentally grueling, Grace McCance loved it. Andrea Warren documents McCance's life on the Nebraska prairie in *Pioneer Girl: Growing Up on the Prairie.* Even when blizzards or thunderstorms damaged their land, Grace and her family found a way to survive, and even to triumph.

Resource Center

Reading Matters Strategy Lessons by Kylene Beers

Reading Standard 3.2 Evaluate the structural elements of the plot (e.g., subplots, parallel episodes, climax), the plot's development, and the way in which conflicts are (or are not) addressed and resolved.

Strategy Lesson 1
How Do I Find a Plot's Structure?

Somebody Wanted But So

The Downfall of an Egg

Notice the plot structure of this simple story as you read. Humpty Dumpty sat on a wall. Humpty, who was afraid of heights to begin with, had never wanted to sit on that wall. As a result of losing his bet to Jack—his bet about jumping over the candlestick (Jack cleared the candle, but Humpty didn't)—he had to sit there for an hour. That wouldn't have been hard to do if Humpty weren't an egg and therefore oval shaped.

While Humpty was trying to stay balanced on the wall, Mr. B. B. Wolf, at the other end of the village, had just finished a tasty snack of pork chops. "Ah," thought Wolf, "if only I had some eggs. Nothing beats pork chops and eggs." [A problem is introduced: Wolf wants an egg.] He liked his idea so much that he let out a tremendous howl. Back at the wall, Humpty heard the howl. It startled him so much that he began wobbling. He teetered off the edge of the wall and landed—splat—on the ground. [Two major events occur.]

The king's men were out patrolling that morning, looking for some sheep. The sheep, it was rumored, had been lost because the Little Blue Boy had fallen asleep while tending them. When the king's men came across the broken Humpty, they tried to put him back together but had no luck. [This is the climax of the story.] Then they saw Jack lurking nearby. When they asked him why a good egg like Humpty had been up on a wall, Jack told them about the bet. He was arrested for reckless endangerment of an egg. [The resolution of the story starts here.] The king's men completely forgot about the sheep, so the Little Blue Boy slept on. Wolf decided to skip the eggs and go for some cookies that a little girl was carrying in her basket.

> **Allusions** An allusion is a reference to someone or something in history, literature, sports, politics—something the writer feels the reader will recognize. In addition to the big allusion to "Humpty Dumpty," this story alludes to four other children's stories. The allusions are to "Jack Be Nimble," "The Three Little Pigs," "Little Boy Blue," and "Little Red Riding Hood."

Understanding Plot Structure

"The Downfall of an Egg" is a simple story, but when you have a story with sub-plots, keeping track of the main plot structure can be difficult.

For help identifying the basic structural elements of a plot, use a strategy called **Somebody Wanted But So.** First, jot down those four words on a piece of paper (see below). Next, write the main character's name under the heading "Somebody." Then, under the heading "Wanted," write down what the character wants. In the "But" column, write down what prevents the character from getting what he or she wants. In the "So" column, write the story's resolution. When you're finished, you'll have one sentence. It might take more Somebody Wanted But So statements to cover the entire plot. If so, just use a word like *then* or *later* or *but* or *therefore*—whichever one makes sense—to connect the statements.

Somebody	Wanted	But	So
Humpty	wanted to win the bet with Jack	but he lost,	so he had to sit on the wall for an hour.

Somebody	Wanted	But	So
Humpty	wanted to stay balanced on the wall though that was hard for an ovoid	but a loud howl startled him,	so he fell and splattered.

Now, ask yourself if there's information about the plot that didn't show up in those two sentences. If you answer yes, write another SWBS statement.

Your Turn   Find a Plot's Structure

1. Review the stories in Chapter 1. Reduce one of them to the Somebody Wanted But So framework. You might try "The Treasure of Lemon Brown" (page 17) or "Flowers for Algernon" (page 33). You might also try one of the **subplots** in "Flowers for Algernon."

2. The **climax** of a story is its most exciting moment—the moment when the outcome of the conflict is determined. On your SWBS chart, circle the climax. Then, compare your charts in class. Readers won't always agree.

Strategy Lesson 2

How Do I Analyze the Relevance of Setting?

If . . . Then . . .

Where Am I?

Suppose you are the director of a movie, but you have only three lines of the script. Here are the three lines:

Actor One. You're late.

Actor Two. I'm sorry.

Actor One. It doesn't matter.

At this point you can't give the actors much direction on how to say the lines. You don't know if Actor One is angry or not or if Actor Two is really sorry or not. There's a lot you don't know because you don't even know where this conversation takes place. So, let's add some settings:

1. an empty church decorated for a wedding

2. a football field during a neighborhood afternoon pickup game

3. a football field during the Super Bowl

4. a busy airport

Now you've got some help in deciding what the problem might be. What does each setting suggest the play might be about? What problem could be connected to one of these settings? Is there a setting in which it really doesn't matter that Actor Two is late? Is there a setting in which Actor One actually does think it matters that Actor Two is late? As the director, show your actors how you want the lines said in each setting. How does their tone change as their setting changes?

What you can quickly see in this short exercise is that place makes a difference. As writers change their settings, plots or problems may also change.

Setting includes many details having to do with place and time. Setting can affect things like what food the characters eat, where they live, what values they hold. It can affect how they dress, where they work, and where they vacation. Setting can even tell you what books your characters read (if any) and what hopes they have.

Changing Places

To understand the power of a setting, think about what would happen if you changed it. Think in terms of **If . . . Then. . . .** For example, if the setting is the early 1900s in Pittsburgh, then what happens if I change the setting to the early 3000s? If the setting is downtown Los Angeles, then what happens if I change it to a beach in Maine? If the setting is an ocean liner, then what happens if I change it to a rocket ship?

Setting and Mood

The setting of a story strongly affects its mood. A story set in a dark cave or in a place where the sun shines only a few months per year would probably not make you feel very cheerful. A sunny garden creates feelings of pleasure and freedom. A dungeon creates feelings of doom and entrapment.

Your Turn Analyze the Relevance of Setting

Below are two conversations. Read both conversations, and choose the one you like better. Then, describe three different settings and place the characters and their dialogue in each setting. How does a change in setting change the scene?

Choice 1

Character One:	You stole it.
Character Two:	Was that a good idea?
Character One:	Who said you could do that?

Choice 2

Character One:	I'll go last.
Character Two:	No, I'll go last.
Character One:	No, I insist. I'll go last.

Before you describe your setting, gather your details in a diagram like the one below:

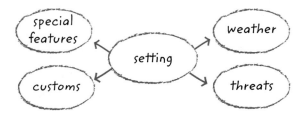

Strategy Lesson 3

How Do I Compare and Contrast Characters?

Semantic Differential Scales

Scales. There are fish scales, piano scales, and the scales of justice. Your skin can be dry and scaly, you can scale a fence, and you can weigh fruit on the scales in the grocery store. You can also use scales to compare characters. This special character-comparing scale is called a **semantic differential scale.** It can help you when you are comparing the traits of two or more characters or people.

Semantic Differential Scales

Semantic differential scales sound complex, but they are not. The word *semantic* refers to meanings of words. The word *differential* has to do with differences. To make a scale, simply place words that are opposite in meaning at opposite ends of a scale, like this:

kind _____ mean

Then, think of a person (say, your brother or sister), and decide where you'd place that person on this scale. If the person is kind, put a mark above the word *kind.* If the person is pretty mean, put your mark on the other end of the scale, as close to the word *mean* as you want it to be. Next, think of a second person (maybe your best friend), and rate that person on the same scale—using a different color ink. Notice how the scale helps you see at a glance how those two people are alike or different.

When You Read

When you are reading, you can easily make semantic differential scales in your *Reader/Writer Notebook.* As you think about the characters, make marks on the scales to remind you of the qualities they reveal. You'll probably notice that characters change. A character who is timid at the beginning of a story might be bold at the end. You can compare two or more characters on the same scale by using a different color ink for each character.

The key to a good scale is the words you choose for your comparisons. Brainstorming a list of qualities with a partner or group will help you find your words.

Here's a list of words you might use to create your scales:

Examples of Character Traits

brave/fearful	kind/mean
compassionate/cruel	loyal/disloyal
curious/indifferent	obedient/disobedient
optimistic/pessimistic	fair/unfair
powerful/weak	reliable/unreliable
forgiving/unforgiving	selfless/selfish
generous/stingy	sincere/insincere
happy/unhappy	truthful/untruthful
joyful/sad	wise/foolish

Your Turn   Compare and Contrast Characters

Think about Abraham Lincoln and Dr. Martin Luther King, Jr., well-known leaders who lived at different times in history, each associated with human rights. Now, decide where you'd place each of them on the following semantic differential scales. (If you prefer, select two contemporary leaders you know something about, and put them on the scales.)

powerful _____ weak

brave _____ fearful

compassionate _____ cruel

Strategy Lesson 4

How Do I Analyze Recurring Themes?

Most Important Word

Recurring Themes

The more you read, the more you'll discover that certain themes show up repeatedly in literary works. These are called **recurring themes.** *Recurring* simply means "happening over and over again." Here's a list of some themes that have been expressed in literature for thousands of years:

- Innocence has the power to conquer evil.

- Nature renews itself, just as people can renew themselves.

- Love endures.

- People will forever search for freedom.

- The power of imagination can transform the world.

- Heroism can come from unexpected sources.

- Our dreams of a perfect world often end in disappointment.

To see how themes can recur over time, think about Daniel Defoe's *Robinson Crusoe* (published in 1719) and Gary Paulsen's *Hatchet* (published in 1987). In both stories, a castaway must survive in a wilderness. Each castaway survives his quest. Each one creates in the wilderness a kind of human home. Each emerges from the wilderness a wiser person. The theme of both stories has to do with what we learn about ourselves when all the trappings of civilization are taken from us. From this quest to survive, we learn truths about ourselves.

Most Important Word

To identify themes, you can use a strategy called **Most Important Word.** With this strategy, you decide which word from the text you think is the most important word (or words—there can be more than one). Here are some of the rules:

- Don't use a character's name.
- Look for a word that is often used; that is used at a key point in the story, as in the climax; or that is used at the beginning and then again at the end.
- Think about how the word relates to the characters, setting, conflict, and resolution of the story.

Here's an example of how the most important word helped a reader identify theme:

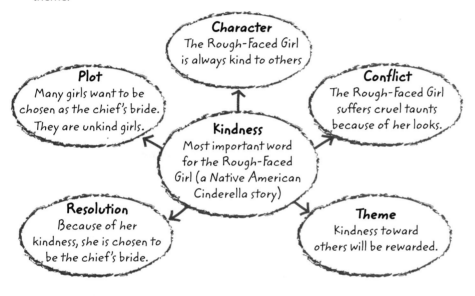

Character
The Rough-Faced Girl is always kind to others

Plot
Many girls want to be chosen as the chief's bride. They are unkind girls.

Conflict
The Rough-Faced Girl suffers cruel taunts because of her looks.

Kindness
Most important word for the Rough-Faced Girl (a Native American Cinderella story)

Resolution
Because of her kindness, she is chosen to be the chief's bride.

Theme
Kindness toward others will be rewarded.

Your Turn   Analyze Recurring Themes

Fill out a chart like the one that follows. Write down the titles of two books you have read that show similar themes. Then, briefly state the way the theme is handled in each book.

Display your charts in class.

Theme	
Story 1	
Story 2	

Reading Standard 3.6 Identify significant literary devices (e.g., metaphor, symbolism, dialect, irony) that define a writer's style and use those elements to interpret the work.

Strategy Lesson 5

How Do I Interpret a Literary Work?

Logographic Clues

Writers use devices that help you interpret their works. For instance, a writer might have a character speak in a **dialect** to tell something about that character's education or background. A writer might use **symbolism** to deepen your understanding of a text. Imagine, for example, a scene in which a character sees a rainbow in the sky—that rainbow could symbolize hope. A writer might also use **metaphors** to provide clues to the text's deeper meaning. A character who is described as "prickly as a cactus" is a character who causes trouble. A writer might even make a point by using **irony**—a contrast between what you expect to happen and what really happens. You'd probably feel a sense of irony if you read a story about a Great Dane who runs away from a mouse.

Spotting Literary Devices

All those literary devices can help you interpret the text only if you can (1) identify them and (2) keep up with them! Lots of activities in this book help you identify literary devices. On the side of this page, you'll find a quick review of those devices. Once you identify those literary devices, look closely at the way they are used. How do they help you interpret a character, a plot, a theme?

One way of keeping literary devices straight in your mind is by using logographic (lawg uh GRAF ihk) clues. The word *logographic* simply means "a picture that stands for a word." (*Graph* is from a Greek word for "writing," and *logo* is from *logos,* a Greek word for "word.") Logographic clues are little picture clues that you can use to highlight something in a text.

Significant Literary Devices

metaphor: a direct comparison of two unlike things. *The boy was a thorn in my side.*

simile: a comparison of two unlike things using the word *like, as, than,* or *resembles. The boy was* like *a thorn in my side.*

personification: animals or inanimate objects talked about as if they were human or alive. *The wind danced through the branches of the tree.*

The best logographic clues are the ones you create yourself. A few suggested clues appear below. Use clues like these to mark the literary devices you come across. Many readers draw the little pictures on sticky notes and place the notes next to the places in the text where the literary devices appear. You might want to do that.

Metaphor . . . .

Simile . . . .

Personification . . . .

Symbolism . . . .

Irony . . . .

Dialect . . . .

Your Turn Interpret a Literary Work

Read "Raymond's Run" (page 485), looking for places where Toni Cade Bambara uses **irony** and **dialect** to give you insight into the characters. As you read, use your logographic clues on sticky notes to pinpoint those places where irony and dialect are used. When you've finished reading the story, look back at examples of the dialect you've marked. What does Miss Hazel Elizabeth Deborah Parker's word choice tell you about her? What tone of voice do you hear when Squeaky speaks? Now, look at your irony markers. What does the irony tell you about Squeaky and her dreams?

More Literary Devices

symbolism: the use of an object or an event that functions as itself but also stands for something broader than itself. In these lines from an old song, the rainbow is used as a symbol of hope: *God gave Noah the rainbow sign: no more water; the fire next time.*

irony: a contrast between what is expected to happen and what actually happens. *The runner called Speedy lost the race.*

dialect: a way of speaking that is characteristic of a certain region or group of people. Compare *That is like so totally cool* with *I think that is most appropriate.*

Reading Standard 3.1 Determine and articulate the relationship between the purposes and characteristics of different forms of poetry (e.g., ballad, lyric, couplet, epic, elegy, ode, sonnet)

Strategy Lesson 6

How Do I Analyze Forms of Poetry?

Text Reformulation

When the president of the United States invites dignitaries from other countries to dinner, he doesn't send a handwritten note that says "Y'all come." When you invite friends to go out for pizza, you don't send an engraved invitation that requests the honor of their presence. In other words, the form of an invitation matches the situation. In a book on manners, you'll find that different types of invitations even have different names. There's the formal (engraved), the semiformal (printed), the informal (handwritten), and the casual (phone call or e-mail). With each type you'll find that not only does the form change but the language that's used also changes. A formal invitation may request an RSVP (that's an abbreviation for the French term that means "respond if you please"), while your casual phone call might conclude with "Wanna go?"

The Poet's "Book of Manners"

Poets also have different forms to choose from as they write their poems.

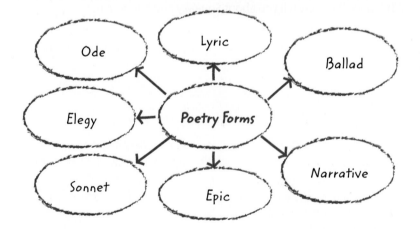

Poets choose a form that best helps them say what they want to say.

Forms of Poetry		
Form	**Purpose**	**Example**
Ballad	a simple song or songlike poem with a refrain. A ballad tells a story, usually a tragedy or an adventure.	"The Cremation of Sam McGee"
Narrative	a poem that tells a story	"Paul Revere's Ride"
Epic	a very long, complex narrative poem that reflects the values of a whole society and focuses on a hero's quest to win something of great value	*Beowulf*
Lyric	a poem, usually short, that expresses the feelings of the poet instead of telling a story	"Birdfoot's Grampa"
Sonnet	a fourteen-line lyric poem with a strict form and rhyme scheme	"On the Grasshopper and the Cricket"
Ode	a lyric poem on a serious subject, usually addressed to a person or thing	"Ode to Thanks"
Elegy	a lyric poem that laments the death of someone or the loss of something	"O Captain! My Captain!"

Identifying the form of poetry isn't very hard. If you want to see how form affects the tone or mood of the poem, try a strategy called **text reformulation.** With this strategy you rewrite any text in a different form. You could turn an ode into a sonnet or a ballad into an elegy. You could turn a ballad into a short story or a play. You could turn a news article into a ballad. You could turn a sonnet into a love song.

Your Turn Analyze Forms of Poetry

Find a news story in the newspaper. Reformulate the story as a ballad. You will have to find a gripping story, isolate a few key events, and find at least two characters. Think of a haunting or funny refrain.

A good way to find a story that has ballad potential is to scan the headlines. Look for a story that is tragic or heart-warming—though the old ballad singers preferred the tragic!

Reading Standard 2.5 Understand and explain the use of a complex mechanical device by following technical directions. **2.6** Use information from a variety of consumer, workplace, and public documents to explain a situation or decision and to solve a problem.

Strategy Lesson 7

How Do I Read for Information?

In one basic way, reading technical materials—like the booklet that comes with the thousand-piece starship you plan to build or the directions for assembling a bike—differs from reading stories. Can you figure out what that difference is? It's not that stories are usually fiction and technical matter is usually nonfiction. With both fiction and nonfiction you still have to

- process information
- think about what the text is saying
- compare and contrast
- predict what will happen next
- summarize what's already happened
- understand the sequence of events
- recognize the writer's point of view
- connect what you already know to what you are reading
- note the relationship of cause and effect
- make inferences
- draw conclusions

You use those skills whether you're reading fiction or nonfiction, so the truth or untruth of the selection isn't the difference. It's also not that some readers will say that nonfiction is boring and fiction is exciting or that fiction is boring and nonfiction is exciting. The boring-versus-exciting factor is more about the reader than the text. One reader may think that the article titled "Seventy-five Ways to Care for Your Boa Constrictor" is a wonderful article, while the next reader may think it squeezes the fun out of reading. The most basic difference comes from the fact that almost all fiction follows a narrative structure, and much of nonfiction follows an expository, or explanatory, structure. A narrative structure uses a narrator to tell you what happens, usually in time order. You generally don't have to wonder where you're going with narrative because a narrator helps you get there. There is no narrator talking to you in an expository text, however. This lack of a guide slows down some readers of expository texts.

Finding a Guide in Informative Texts

When you are reading an expository text, look for some guidelines, such as these:

1. If the text has numbered steps, think of the steps as a character telling you, "First, do this. Next, do that."

2. If the text has subtitles, think of the subtitles as characters telling you, "Look here! This is a new topic we're about to meet."

3. If the text has words or phrases in boldface or italic type, think of these graphic features as a character saying, "This is an important word or definition. Pay attention!"

4. If the text includes a graph or map or chart, think of these graphic features as another character, one who has decided to tell you in another way what the first character was saying. "Listen" carefully to this other character to pick up additional information or to see the information in graphic terms.

5. If the text uses phrases such as *on the other hand* or *by comparison* or *by contrast* or *still others believe,* think of them as a character telling you the other side of what's happened. Read carefully when you see these phrases, because you're about to get information that conflicts with what you've already read.

6. If the text uses phrases such as *as a result* or *consequently* or *this results in* or *therefore,* think of these words as coming from a guide who is explaining the effects of something that has happened.

Reading Standard 3.7 Analyze a work of literature, showing how it reflects the heritage, tradition, attitudes, and beliefs of its author. (Biographical approach)

Strategy Lesson 8

How Do I Ask Questions About the Writer?

It Says, I Say, And So

Read this conversation that I once had with a group of eighth-graders. See if you've ever had a reaction like Adam's:

> "So, what did you think about the story?" I asked.
> "I liked it," some said. Others just nodded. Some just sat.
> "Well, what can you tell me about the author from reading this story?" I asked.
> Silence for a while and finally Adam said, "I didn't read anything about the author, I just read the story."

Adam was right—he did just read the story—but he was also wrong. When reading a story, you can sometimes make inferences about its writer. Consider these situations:

- You read a story about a boy who goes hunting and shoots a deer and later feels remorse for having killed that animal. You might reach the conclusion that the author doesn't like hunting.

- You read a story about a character who goes through a number of tough experiences, but in the end she is rewarded for all her bravery and feels great happiness. You can guess that this story was written by a writer who believes that the world is fair and rewards good people.

- You read a story about a character who is very religious and finds comfort in his faith. You might determine that the writer holds some religious belief.

However, you can't always presume that writers have had all the experiences they write about. Consider these examples:

- You can't presume that E. B. White knows what a spider thinks, even though he wrote *Charlotte's Web*. (Remember that Charlotte, the main character, is a spider.)

- You can't presume that J.R.R. Tolkien is a hobbit, even though he wrote *The Hobbit*, a book about an imaginary creature called a hobbit who lives in a made-up setting called Middle Earth.

- You can't presume that Sandra Cisneros is an eleven-year-old girl, even though she wrote the short story titled "Eleven," which is told by an eleven-year-old girl.

You *can* conclude that E. B. White believed that helping people is important and that J.R.R. Tolkien knew a lot about mythology. You *can* conclude that Sandra Cisneros understands what it is *like* to be an eleven-year-old girl—and that she knows that being embarrassed hurts. You can make these assumptions because of the settings the writers have created, the situations their characters face, the ways their characters act and talk.

Your Writing Assignment: "Explain How This Work Might Reflect the Writer's Background"

If you are assigned the above topic to write about or discuss, here is a strategy that can help you dig into the text to find your answer: **It Says, I Say, And So.**

Your Turn Analyze a Work of Literature

Write "It Says," "I Say," and "And So," in three columns. In the "It Says" column, write down what the story says in a particular passage. Under the "I Say" column, write what you think the passage might reflect about the writer. Under the "And So" column, write your final inference about what the passage reveals. Here's an example from "A Retrieved Reformation" (page 831). Note the assumptions this student makes about O. Henry's background:

It Says	I Say	And So
Jimmy Valentine is released from prison as the story starts.	I know that O. Henry was in prison and began his writing career there.	I think Jimmy's character is based on someone O. Henry met in prison. He seems very real.
[Add your own notes.]	[Add your own notes.]	[Add your own notes.]

Handbook of Literary Terms

For more information about a topic, turn to the page(s) in this book indicated on a separate line at the end of the entries. To learn more about *Allusion* for example, turn to page 483. On another line there are cross-references to entries in the handbook that provide closely related information. For instance, at the end of *Autobiography* are cross-references to *Biography* and *Nonfiction*.

ALLITERATION **The repetition of consonant sounds in words that are close together.** Alliteration occurs mostly in poetry, though prose writers use it from time to time. Although alliteration usually occurs at the beginning of words, it can also occur within or at the end of words. In the following stanza, notice the repeated *s*, *m*, and *b* sounds:

> The sun was shining on the sea,
>   Shining with all his might:
> He did his very best to make
>   The billows smooth and bright—
> And this was odd, because it was
>   The middle of the night.
>
> —from "The Walrus and the
>   Carpenter" by Lewis Carroll

The repetition of vowel sounds in words that are close together is called **assonance.**

See also *Poetry*.

ALLUSION **A reference to a statement, a person, a place, or an event from literature, the arts, history, religion, mythology, politics, sports, or science.** Allusions enrich the reading experience. Writers expect readers to recognize allusions and to think about the literary work and the allusions contained in it almost at the same time. For example, "I Have a Dream" (page 773) alludes to the song "My Country, 'Tis of Thee." A reader who is not familiar with that song will miss some of the speech's intended meaning.

See page 483.
See also *Literary Devices*.

ANALOGY **A comparison made between two things to show how they are alike.** Writers often make analogies to show how something unfamiliar is like something well known or widely experienced. In "Raymond's Run" (page 485), the main character, Squeaky, uses an analogy that compares her feelings before a race to a dream of flying.

See also *Literary Devices, Metaphor, Simile*.

ANECDOTE **A brief story told to illustrate a point.** Anecdotes are frequently found in memoirs, biographies, autobiographies, and personal essays.

See also *Proposition and Support* in the Handbook of Reading and Informational Terms.

ANTAGONIST See *Protagonist*.

ASSONANCE See *Alliteration*.

ATMOSPHERE See *Mood*.

AUTHOR **The writer of a literary work or document.** Toni Cade Bambara is the author of "Raymond's Run" (page 485); Abraham Lincoln is the author of the "Gettysburg Address" (page 771).

AUTOBIOGRAPHY **A person's account of his or her own life or of part of it.** "Camp Harmony" (page 387) is an example of autobiographical writing.

See pages 258, 267.
See also *Biography, Nonfiction*.

BALLAD **A song or songlike poem that tells a story.** Ballads usually tell stories of tragedy, love, or adventure, using simple language and a great deal of repetition. They generally have regular rhythm and rhyme patterns that make them easy to memorize. "The Cremation of Sam McGee" (page 603) and are "The Dying Cowboy" (page 608) both ballads.

See page 601.
See also *Narrative Poem, Poetry.*

BIOGRAPHICAL APPROACH **A biographical approach to literary criticism takes into account details about the writer's life when evaluating his or her work.** Readers who use the biographical approach look for evidence of the writer's heritage, background, or beliefs in fictional texts.

See pages 796, 798, 805, 813, 829.

BIOGRAPHY **An account of a person's life or of part of it, written or told by another person.** The excerpt from *Harriet Tubman* (page 199) is part of a longer biography.

See page 197.
See also *Autobiography, Nonfiction.*

CHARACTER **A person or an animal in a story, a play, or another literary work.** Characters can be classified according to the changes they undergo. A **static character** does not change much in the course of a work. Abuelo in "An Hour with Abuelo" (page 128) is a static character. In contrast, a **dynamic character** changes as a result of a story's events. Squeaky in "Raymond's Run" (page 485) is a dynamic character.

A character's **motivation** is any force (such as love or fear or jealousy) that drives the character to behave in a particular way.

See pages 178, 180, 189, 197, 213.
See also *Characterization, Motivation, Protagonist.*

CHARACTERIZATION **The way a writer reveals the personality of a character.** A writer may simply tell readers that a character is amusing or evil or dull or brave. This method is called **direct characterization.** Most often, though, writers use **indirect characterization,** revealing personality in one or more of the following ways:

1. through the words of the character
2. through description of the character's looks and clothing
3. through description of the character's thoughts and feelings
4. through comments made about the character by other characters in the story
5. through the character's behavior

When a writer uses indirect characterization, we must use our own judgment and the evidence the writer gives to infer the character's **traits.**

See page 189.
See also *Character.*

CHRONOLOGICAL ORDER **The arrangement of events in the order in which they occurred.** Most stories are told in chronological order. Sometimes, however, a writer interrupts the chronological order to flash back to a past event or to flash forward to a future event. *The Diary of Anne Frank* (page 301), for example, begins in 1945, when Mr. Frank arrives at the hiding place. The main story, however, takes place from 1942 to 1944.

See pages 9, 411.
See also *Flashback.*

CLIMAX **The point in a story that creates the greatest suspense or interest.** At the climax something happens that reveals how the conflict will turn out.

See page 4.
See also *Drama, Plot, Short Story.*

RESOURCE CENTER **Handbook of Literary Terms**

Handbook of Literary Terms **879**

COMEDY **In general, a story that ends happily for its main characters.** The hero or heroine usually overcomes a series of obstacles to get what he or she wants. (In contrast, the main character in a **tragedy** comes to an unhappy end.) The word *comedy* is not always a synonym for *humor*. Some comedies are humorous; others are not.

See also *Tragedy*.

CONFLICT **A struggle between opposing characters or opposing forces.** In an **external conflict** a character struggles with an outside force, which may be another character, society as a whole, or a natural force. In contrast, an **internal conflict** takes place within a character's own mind. It is a struggle between opposing needs, desires, or emotions. Greg in "The Treasure of Lemon Brown" (page 17) has an external conflict with neighborhood thugs and an internal conflict over his relationship with his father.

See pages 15, 178, 379.
See also *Plot*.

CONNOTATION **A meaning, association, or emotion suggested by a word, in addition to its dictionary definition, or denotation.** Words that have similar denotations may have different connotations. For example, suppose you wanted to describe someone who rarely changes plans in the face of opposition. You could use either *determined* or *pigheaded* to describe the person. The two words have similar denotations, but *determined* has positive connotations and *pigheaded* has negative connotations.

See pages 583, 589.
See also *Diction, Style, Tone*.

COUPLET **Two consecutive lines of poetry that rhyme.** Couplets are often used in humorous poems because they pack a quick punch. "The Cremation of Sam McGee" (page 603) and "Casey at the Bat" (page 616) are both written in four-line stanzas consisting of two couplets in each stanza. Shakespeare uses couplets in many of his plays, often for a more serious purpose, to give closure to a speech or an act.

See also *Poetry, Rhyme, Stanza*.

DENOTATION See *Connotation*.

DESCRIPTION **Writing intended to re-create a person, a place, a thing, an event, or an experience.** Description uses images that appeal to the sense of sight, smell, taste, hearing, or touch. It is often used to create a mood or emotion. Writers use description in all forms of fiction, nonfiction, and poetry. This description of the effect of extreme cold on a dog and its owner may make you feel cold, too:

> The frozen moisture of its breathing had settled on its fur in a fine powder of frost, and expecially were its jowls, muzzle, and eyelashes whitened by its crystaled breath. The man's red beard and moustache were likewise frosted, but more solidly, the deposit taking the form of ice and increasing with every warm, moist breath he exhaled. Also, the man was chewing tobacco, and the muzzle of ice held his lips so rigidly that he was unable to clear his chin when he expelled the juice. The result was that a crystal beard of the color and solidity of amber was increasing its length on his chin. If he fell down, it would shatter itself, like glass, into brittle fragments.
>
> —from "To Build a Fire"
> by Jack London

See also *Imagery*.

DIALECT **A way of speaking that is characteristic of a certain geographical area or a certain group of people.** A dialect may have a distinct vocabulary, pronunciation system, and grammar. In a sense, we all speak a dialect. One dialect usually becomes dominant in a country or culture, however, and is accepted as the standard way of speaking and writing. In the United States, for example, the formal language is known as **standard English.** (It's the kind of English taught in schools, used in national newspapers and magazines, and spoken by newscasters on television.)

Writers often reproduce regional dialects or speech to bring a character to life and to give a story color. For example, the dialect Squeaky speaks in "Raymond's Run" (page 485) helps us see and hear her as a real person.

See pages 483, 496.
See also *Literary Devices.*

DIALOGUE **Conversation between two or more characters.** Most stage dramas consist entirely of dialogue together with stage directions. The dialogue in a drama must move the plot along and reveal character. Dialogue is also an important element in most stories and novels, as well as in some poems and nonfiction. By using dialogue, a writer can show what a character is like.

In the written form of a play, dialogue appears without quotation marks. In prose or poetry, however, dialogue is usually enclosed in quotation marks.

A **monologue** is a long speech by an actor to one or more other characters onstage. A **soliloquy** is a part of a drama in which one character who is alone onstage speaks aloud his or her thoughts and feelings. An **aside** is a comment spoken aloud by a character that is meant to be heard by the audience only; not by the other characters onstage.

See also *Drama.*

DICTION **A writer's or speaker's choice of words.** People use different types of words, depending on the audience they are addressing, the subject they are discussing, and the effect they are trying to produce. For example, slang words that would be suitable for a humorous piece like "Casey at the Bat" (page 616) would not be appropriate for a serious essay like "A Tragedy Revealed: A Heroine's Last Days" (page 412). Diction is an essential element of a writer's style and has a major effect on the tone of a piece of writing.

See pages 591, 600.
See also *Connotation, Style, Tone.*

DRAMA **A work of literature meant to be performed for an audience by actors.** (A drama, or **play,** can also be enjoyed in its written form.) The actors work from the **playwright's** script, which includes dialogue and stage directions. The script of a drama written for the screen is called a **screenplay** (if it's for TV, it's a **teleplay**), and it also includes camera directions.

The action of a drama is usually driven by a character who wants something and takes steps to get it. The main stages of a drama are often described as **exposition, complications, climax, and resolution.** Most dramas are divided into **acts** and **scenes.**

See also *Comedy, Tragedy.*

ELEGY **A poem of mourning, usually about someone who has died.** "O Captain! My Captain!" (page 634) is an elegy on the death of President Abraham Lincoln.

See page 632.
See also *Poetry.*

EPIC **A long narrative poem that is written in heightened language and tells stories of the deeds of a heroic character who embodies the values of a society.** One of the oldest surviving epics is *Gilgamesh,* which was put into writing around 2000 B.C. in ancient Mesopotamia. Homer's *Iliad* and *Odyssey,* dating from around 500 B.C. in Greece, are two of the best-known Western epics. *Beowulf* (page 613), from around A.D. 700, is the oldest surviving Anglo-Saxon epic. A **mock epic,** such as "Casey at the Bat" (page 616), imitates the epic style in a comical way in order to poke fun at its topic.

See page 611.
See also *Poetry.*

ESSAY **A short piece of nonfiction prose that examines a single subject.** Most essays can be categorized as either personal or formal.

The **personal essay** generally reveals a great deal about the writer's personality and tastes. Its tone is often conversational, sometimes even humorous, and there may be no attempt to be objective. In fact, in a personal essay the focus is the writer's feelings and response to an experience. Personal essays are also called **informal** or **familiar** essays. "Walking with Living Feet" (page 432) is a personal essay.

The **formal essay** is usually serious, objective, and impersonal in tone. Its purpose is to inform readers about a topic or to persuade them to accept the writer's views. The statements in a formal essay should be supported by facts and logic.

See also *Nonfiction, Objective Writing*.

EXAGGERATION **Overstating something, usually for the purpose of creating a comic effect.** *He's so thin that if he turned sideways, he'd disappear* is an example of exaggeration. Much of the humor in "The Cremation of Sam McGee" (page 603) comes from exaggeration. Exaggeration is also called **hyperbole.**

See page 601.
See also *Literary Devices, Understatement*.

EXPOSITION **The kind of writing that explains or gives information.** You'll find exposition in newspaper and magazine articles, encyclopedias and dictionaries, and textbooks and other nonfiction books. In fact, what you're reading right now is exposition.

In fiction and drama, **exposition** refers to the part of a plot that gives information about the characters and their problems or conflicts.

See also *Drama, Nonfiction, Plot, Short Story*.

FABLE **A brief story told in prose or poetry that contains a moral, a practical lesson about how to get along in life.** The characters of most fables are animals that speak and behave like people. Some of the most popular fables, such as "The Dog and The Wolf" (page 450), are attributed to Aesop, a storyteller of ancient Greece. Often a moral is stated at the end of a fable.

FICTION **A prose account that is made up rather than true.** The term *fiction* usually refers to **novels** and **short stories.** Fiction is often based on a writer's experiences or on historical events, but a writer may add or alter characters, events, and other details to create a desired effect. "The Inn of Lost Time" (page 81) is entirely made up. "The Circuit" (page 69), on the other hand, is based to some extent on the writer's experiences.

See also *Historical Fiction, Nonfiction*.

FIGURE OF SPEECH **A word or phrase that describes one thing in terms of another and is not meant to be understood as literally true.** Figures of speech always involve some sort of imaginative comparison between seemingly unlike things.

The most common figures of speech are the **simile** (*The sun was shining like a new penny*), the **metaphor** (*The sun was a huge, unblinking eye*), and **personification** (*The sun smiled down on the bathers*).

See pages 480, 496, 509.
See also *Literary Devices, Metaphor, Personification, Simile*.

FLASHBACK **Interruption in the present action of a plot to show events that happened at an earlier time.** A flashback breaks the normal forward movement of a narrative. Although flashbacks often appear in the middle of a work, they can also be placed at the beginning. They usually give background information the audience needs in order to understand the present action. The first scene of *The Diary of Anne Frank* (page 301) takes place about one year after the main action of the play. Almost the entire play, then, is a flashback to an earlier time. Flashbacks are common in stories, novels, and movies and sometimes appear in stage plays and poems as well.

See also *Plot*.

FOLK TALE **A story that has no known author and was originally passed on from one generation to another by word of mouth.** Unlike myths, which are about gods and heroes, folk tales are usually about ordinary people—or animals that act like people. Folk tales tend to travel, and you'll often find the same **motifs**—elements such as characters, images, or story lines—in the tales of different cultures. Cinderella, for example, appears as Aschenputtel in Germany, Yeh-Shen in China, Tam in Vietnam, and Little Burned Face among the Algonquin people of North America. "The People Could Fly" (page 288) is a folk tale.

See also *Fable, Legend, Myth, Tall Tale*.

FORESHADOWING **The use of clues or hints to suggest events that will occur later in the plot.** Foreshadowing is used to build suspense or anxiety in the reader or viewer. A gun found in a bureau drawer in Act One of a drama may foreshadow violence later in the play. In the early part of "Flowers for Algernon" (page 33), details hint at changes that will occur in the life of main character, Charlie.

See also *Suspense*.

FREE VERSE **Poetry without a regular meter or rhyme scheme.** Poets writing in free verse try to capture the natural rhythms of ordinary conversation—or, as in this free-verse poem, a very unusual conversation:

Love in the Middle of the Air

CATCH ME!
    I love you, I trust you,
    I love you
CATCH ME!
    catch my left foot, my right
    foot, my hand!
    here I am hanging by my teeth
    300 feet up in the air and
CATCH ME!
    here I come, flying without wings,
    no parachute, doing a double triple
    super flip-flop somersault
    RIGHT UP HERE WITHOUT A
    SAFETY NET AND
CATCH ME!
    you caught me!
    I love you!

now it's *your* turn

—from "Circus"
by Lenore Kandel

Poets writing in free verse may use **internal rhyme, repetition, alliteration, onomatopoeia,** and other sound effects. They also frequently use precise imagery and striking metaphors and similes. "I Hear America Singing" by Walt Whitman (page 639) is a famous poem written in free verse.

See page 637.
See also *Meter, Poetry, Repetition, Rhyme, Rhythm*.

HISTORICAL FICTION **A novel, story, or play set during a real historical era.** Historical events (such as battles that really happened) and historically accurate details give us an idea of what life was like during a particular period and in a specific setting.

See also *Fiction*.

HUMOR **The quality that makes something seem funny or amusing.** Humor appears in all types of writing, including poetry, short stories, essays, and plays. In literature as in real life, humor consists of the unexpected. We might laugh with surprise when we see someone slip on a banana peel, for example, or get a pie thrown in his or her face. Besides comic actions like these, humor comes in many verbal forms, such as puns, verbal irony, and exaggeration.

See also *Comedy, Exaggeration, Irony, Pun.*

HYPERBOLE See *Exaggeration.*

IAMBIC PENTAMETER **A line of poetry that contains five beats consisting of an unstressed syllable followed by a stressed syllable.** The iambic pentameter line is the most common in English poetry. Shakespeare's plays are written in iambic pentameter, and so is "On the Grasshopper and the Cricket" (page 625), as can be seen in the first line:

∪ / ∪ / ∪ / ∪ / ∪ /
The poetry of earth is never dead

See also *Meter, Poetry, Sonnet.*

IDIOM **An expression peculiar to a particular language that means something different from the literal meaning of the words.** *Hold your tongue* (Don't speak) and *Bury your head in the sand* (Ignore a difficult situation) are idioms of American English, as is the title "A Smart Cookie" (page 466).

See pages 112, 621.

IMAGERY **Language that appeals to the senses.** Most images are visual—that is, they create pictures in the reader's mind by appealing to the sense of sight. In "Mrs. Flowers" (page 229), Maya Angelou uses words to paint a picture of a smile: "A slow widening of her thin black lips to show even, small white teeth, then the slow effortless closing."

Images can also appeal to the senses of hearing, touch, taste, and smell, or even to several senses at once.

See also *Description.*

INVERSION **The reversal of the normal word order of a sentence.** For example, a writer might change *Her hair was long* to *Long was her hair,* inverting the sentence to emphasize the word *long* or to fit a poem's rhyme scheme (*Long was her hair—she had plenty to spare*). In "On the Grasshopper and the Cricket" (page 625), John Keats uses inversion in the line "The poetry of earth is ceasing never."

IRONY **A contrast between expectation and reality.** Irony can create powerful effects, ranging from humor to strong emotion. The following terms refer to three common types of irony:

1. **Verbal irony** involves a contrast between what is said or written and what is really meant. If you were to call a baseball player who has just struck out "slugger," you would be using verbal irony.
2. **Situational irony** occurs when what happens is very different from what we expected would happen. When Casey strikes out after we've been led to believe he will save the day in "Casey at the Bat" (page 616), the poet is using situational irony.
3. **Dramatic irony** occurs when the audience or the reader knows something a character does not know. *The Diary of Anne Frank* (page 301) is filled with dramatic irony. We know about the tragic fate of the people in the Secret Annex, but they do not. Note the irony in the following words spoken by Mr. Frank to Mr. Van Daan. "Didn't you hear what Miep said? The invasion has come! We're going to be liberated! This is a time to celebrate!" (Act Two, Scene 3)

See also *Style.*

LEGEND **A story of extraordinary deeds that is handed down from one generation to the next.** Legends are based to some extent on fact. For example, George Washington did exist, but he did not chop down his father's cherry tree when he was a boy.

See also *Fable, Folk Tale, Myth, Tall Tale.*

LIMERICK **A very short humorous or nonsensical poem.** A limerick has five lines, a definite rhythm, and an *aabba* **rhyme scheme.** It tells a brief story. President Woodrow Wilson is said to have written this limerick:

> I sat next to the Duchess at tea;
> It was just as I feared it would be;
>   Her rumblings abdominal
>   Were truly phenomenal,
> And everyone thought it was me!

See also *Poetry, Rhyme.*

LITERARY DEVICES **The devices a writer uses to develop style and convey meaning.** Common literary devices include allusion, analogy, dialect, exaggeration, figures of speech, imagery, irony, repetition, symbolism, and understatement. Literary devices that are used mostly in poetry include alliteration, assonance, meter, onomatopoeia, rhyme, and rhythm.

See page 483.
See also *Dialect, Diction, Figure of Speech, Irony, Style, Symbol.*

LITERARY PERSPECTIVE **The viewpoint from which a reader may analyze literature.** When you analyze a work of literature, you might consider its credibility, biographical context, or historical context, for example. You might also analyze the archetypes represented, the author's techniques, or even your own responses. Such perspectives are frequently used as a basis for literary criticism.

See pages 33, 199, 303, 473, 609.

LYRIC POEM **A poem that expresses the feelings or thoughts of a speaker rather than telling a story.** Lyric poems can express a wide range of feelings or thoughts. Both "A word is dead" and "The Word" (page 511) explore the speaker's feelings about words. Lyric poems are usually short and imply, rather than directly state, a single strong emotion or idea.

See page 583.
See also *Poetry.*

METAMORPHOSIS **A miraculous change from one shape or form to another one.** In myths and other stories, the change is usually from human or god to animal, from animal to human, or from human to plant. Greek and Roman myths contain many examples of metamorphosis. The myth of Narcissus, for example, tells how the vain youth Narcissus pines away for love of his own reflection and is finally changed into a flower.

METAPHOR **An imaginative comparison between two unlike things in which one thing is said to be another thing.** The metaphor is a figure of speech used in all forms of writing. Metaphors are also common in ordinary speech. When you say someone has a heart of stone, you do not mean that the person's heart is made of rock. You mean that the person is cold and uncaring.

Metaphors differ from **similes,** which use words such as *like, as, than,* and *resembles* to make comparisons. William Wordsworth's famous comparison "I wandered lonely as a cloud" is a simile because it uses *as.* If Wordsworth had written "I was a lonely, wandering cloud," he would have been using a metaphor.

"I'm running a loose ship."

Sometimes a writer hints at a connection instead of stating it directly. T. S. Eliot uses an **implied metaphor** in one of his poems when he describes fog as rubbing its back on windows, making a sudden leap, and curling around a house to fall asleep. By using words that we associate with a cat's behavior, Eliot implies a comparison without stating "The fog is a cat."

An **extended metaphor** is a metaphor that is extended, or developed, over several lines of writing or even throughout an entire work. "O Captain! My Captain!" (page 634) contains an extended metaphor in which the United States is compared to a ship and President Abraham Lincoln is compared to the captain of the ship.

See pages 507, 621, 632, 805, 811.
See also *Figure of Speech, Simile.*

METER A pattern of stressed and unstressed syllables in poetry. It is common practice to show this pattern in writing by using two symbols. The symbol ⁄ indicates a stressed syllable. The symbol ◡ indicates an unstressed syllable. Indicating the metrical pattern of a poem in this way is called **scanning** the poem. The following lines by William Shakespeare have been scanned in part. (The lines make up the epilogue, or speech at the end of the play, of the mischief-maker Puck, or Robin Good-fellow, in *A Midsummer Night's Dream*. *Reprehend* means "criticize"; *serpent's tongue* means "hissing"; *Give me your hands* means "Clap.")

If we shadows have offended,
Think but this, and all is mended,
That you have but slumbered here
While these visions did appear,
And this weak and idle theme,
No more yielding but a dream,
Gentles, do not reprehend.
If you pardon, we will mend.
And, as I am an honest Puck,
If we have unearned luck
Now to scape the serpent's tongue,
We will make amends ere long,
Else the Puck a liar call.
So, good night unto you all.
Give me your hands, if we be friends,
And Robin shall restore amends.

—from *A Midsummer Night's Dream* by William Shakespeare

See also *Poetry, Rhythm.*

MOOD The overall feeling or atmosphere of a work of literature. A work's mood can often be described in one or two adjectives, such as *scary, happy, sad,* or *nostalgic*. A writer produces a mood by creating images and using sounds that convey a particular feeling. "The Tell-Tale Heart" (page 473) is noted for its eerie atmosphere. The setting of a story can also contribute to its mood. For example, the hot sun beating down on the farmworkers in "The Circuit" (page 69) contributes to a mood of oppression.

See page 79.
See also *Tone.*

MOTIF See *Folk Tale.*

MOTIVATION The reasons a character behaves in a certain way. Among the many reasons for a person's behavior are feelings, experiences, and commands by others. In "Passage to Freedom: The Sugihara Story" (page 215), Mr. Sugihara risks his career to issue visas to fleeing refugees despite his government's refusal. His motivation is his concern for their safety.

See pages 180, 213, 227.
See also *Character.*

MYTH A story that explains something about the world and typically involves gods or other supernatural forces. Myths reflect the traditions and beliefs of the culture that produced them. Almost every culture has **creation myths,** stories that explain how the world came to exist or how human beings were created. Other myths explain different aspects of life and the natural world. One of the ancient Greek myths, for instance, tells how Prometheus gave humans the gift of fire. Most myths are very old and were handed down orally before being put in written form. The exact origin of most myths is not known.

See also *Fable, Folk Tale, Legend, Tall Tale.*

NARRATION The kind of writing that tells a story. Narration is the main tool of writers of fiction. It is also used in any piece of nonfiction that relates a series of events in the order in which they happened (for example, in historical writing and science articles).

See also *Exposition, Fiction, Nonfiction.*

NARRATIVE POEM A poem that tells a story. "Paul Revere's Ride" (page 593) and "Casey at the Bat" (page 616) are narrative poems.

See page 591.
See also *Poetry.*

NONFICTION Prose writing that deals with real people, things, events, and places. Popular forms of nonfiction are autobiography, biography, essay, and speech. "Mrs. Flowers" (page 229) is an excerpt from Maya Angelou's autobiography. Other examples of nonfiction are newspaper stories, magazine articles, historical writing, science reports, and even diaries and letters.

The purpose of nonfiction writing may be to provide information, express personal feelings, entertain, or persuade. Some elements of nonfiction texts include **main idea,** or the writer's most important message, and repetition. Nonfiction texts have logic, unity, consistency, coherence, and structural patterns. Structural patterns include chronological order, order of importance, and logical order.

See also *Autobiography, Biography, Essay, Fiction, Speech.*

NOVEL A long fictional story, usually longer than one hundred book pages. A novel uses all the elements of storytelling—plot, character, setting, theme, and point of view. It usually has more characters, settings, and themes and a more complex plot than a short story. A **novella** is a fictional story that is shorter than a novel and longer than a short story.

See also *Plot, Short Story.*

OBJECTIVE WRITING Writing that presents facts without revealing the writer's feelings and opinions. Most news reports in newspapers are objective writing.

See also *Essay, Subjective Writing.*

ODE A lyric poem, rhymed or unrhymed, written in praise of a subject. Odes are usually addressed to one person or thing. In "Ode to Thanks" (page 629), Pablo Neruda praises the word *thanks.*

See page 627
See also *Poetry.*

ONOMATOPOEIA **The use of words whose sounds imitate or suggest their meaning.** *Buzz, rustle, boom, ticktock, tweet,* and *bark* are all onomatopoeic words. In the following lines the poet suggests the sound of sleigh bells in the cold night air by using onomatopoeia:

> Hear the sledges with the bells—
> Silver bells!
> What a world of merriment their melody
> foretells!
> How they tinkle, tinkle, tinkle,
> In the icy air of night!
> While the stars that oversprinkle
> All the Heavens, seem to twinkle
> With a crystalline delight.
>
> —from "The Bells"
> by Edgar Allan Poe,

See page 601.

PARALLEL EPISODES **Repeated elements of the plot.** Three times the Big Bad Wolf goes to a little pig's house and says, "I'll huff and I'll puff and I'll blow your house in." Each time this happens, we have a parallel episode. Each of Melinda Alice's wishes in "Those Three Wishes" (page 10) is a parallel episode.

See page 31.
See also *Plot.*

PERSONIFICATION **A figure of speech in which an object or animal is spoken of as if it had human feelings, thoughts, or attitudes.** This poet writes about the moon as if it were a woman wearing silver shoes ("shoon"):

> Slowly, silently, now the moon
> Walks the night in her silver shoon;
> This way, and that, she peers, and sees
> Silver fruit upon silver trees.
>
> —from "Silver"
> by Walter de la Mare

See pages 513, 589.
See also *Figure of Speech.*

PERSUASION **A kind of writing intended to convince a reader to think or act in a certain way.** Examples of persuasive writing are found in newspaper editorials, in speeches, and in many essays and articles. The techniques of persuasion are widely used in advertising. Persuasion can use language that appeals to the emotions, or it can use logic to appeal to reason. When persuasive writing appeals to reason and not to the emotions, it is called **argument.** The "Gettysburg Address" (page 771) and "I Have a Dream" (page 773) are examples of persuasive writing.

See pages 438, 447, 448.
See also *Proposition and Support* in the Handbook of Reading and Informational Terms.

PLAYWRIGHT **The author of a play, or drama.** Playwrights Frances Goodrich and Albert Hackett wrote *The Diary of Anne Frank* (page 301), which they based on Anne Frank's diary and life story.

See also *Author, Drama.*

PLOT **The series of related events that make up a story.** Plot is what happens in a short story, novel, play, or narrative poem. Most plots are built from these basic elements: An **introduction,** or **exposition,** tells us who the characters are and usually what their conflict is. **Complications** arise when the characters take steps to resolve the conflict. Eventually the plot reaches a **climax,** the most exciting moment in the story, when the outcome is decided one way or another. The final part of the story is the **resolution,** in which the conflict is resolved and the story is brought to a close.

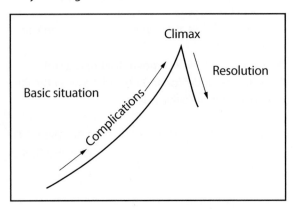

Not all works of fiction or drama have a traditional plot structure. Modern writers often experiment with plot. At times they eliminate some or almost all of the parts of a traditional plot in order to focus on other elements, such as character, point of view, or mood. In "Those Three Wishes" (page 10), the story ends with the climax. The reader infers the resolution.

See pages 4, 8, 13, 75, 115.
See also *Climax, Drama, Exposition, Parallel Episodes, Subplot.*

POETRY **A kind of rhythmic, compressed language that uses figures of speech and imagery designed to appeal to our emotions and imagination.** Poetry is usually arranged in lines. It often has a regular pattern of rhythm and may have a regular rhyme scheme. **Free verse** is poetry that has no regular pattern of rhythm or rhyme, though it is generally arranged in lines. Major forms of poetry include the **lyric,** the **narrative,** the **epic,** and the **ballad.**

See pages 572, 576, 581, 583, 591, 601, 611, 621, 623, 627.
See also *Ballad, Elegy, Epic, Figure of Speech, Free Verse, Imagery, Lyric Poem, Meter, Narrative Poem, Ode, Prose, Refrain, Rhyme, Rhythm, Sonnet, Speaker.*

POINT OF VIEW **The vantage point from which a story is told.** The most common points of view are the omniscient, the third-person limited, and the first person.

1. In the **omniscient** (all-knowing) **point of view,** the narrator knows everything about the characters and their problems. This all-knowing narrator can tell us about the past, the present, and the future of the characters. The narrator can also tell us what the characters are thinking and what is happening in several places at the same time. But the narrator does not take part in the story's action. Rather, the narrator stands above the action like a god. The omniscient is a familiar point of view; we have heard it in fairy tales since we were very young.

2. In the **third-person-limited point of view,** the narrator focuses on the thoughts and feelings of only one character. From this point of view, we observe the action through the eyes of only one of the characters in the story. "The Treasure of Lemon Brown" (page 17) is told from the third-person-limited point of view.

3. In the **first-person point of view,** one of the characters, using the personal pronoun *I,* tells the story. We become familiar with the narrator, but we can know only what this person knows and observe only what this person observes. All of our information about the story comes from this narrator, who may be unreliable. "The Circuit" (page 69) is told from the first-person point of view.

PROSE **Any writing that is not poetry.** Essays, short stories, novels, newspaper articles, and letters are all written in prose. Unlike poetry, prose is usually composed in paragraphs.

See also *Fiction, Nonfiction, Poetry.*

PROTAGONIST **The main character in a work of literature.** The protagonist is involved in the work's central conflict. If there is another character opposing the protagonist, that character is called the **antagonist.** In "Flowers for Algernon" (page 33), Charlie is the protagonist. In a subplot of the story, Joe Carp and Frank Reilly are his antagonists.

See also *Character.*

PUN **A play on the multiple meanings of a word or on two words that sound alike but have different meanings.** Most often puns are used for humor; they turn up in jokes all the time. *Where does an elephant put suitcases?* Answer: *In its trunk.* This pun is called a **homographic pun;** it is a play on a word (*trunk*) that has two meanings ("proboscis of an elephant" and "compartment in an automobile"). *Is Swiss cheese good for you?* Answer: *Yes, it is holesome.* This pun is called a **homophonic pun;** it is a play on words that sound alike but are spelled differently and have different meanings (*hole* and *whole*).

REFRAIN A repeated sound, word, phrase, line, or group of lines. Refrains are usually associated with songs and poems but are also used in speeches and other forms of literature. Refrains are most often used to build rhythm, but they may also provide emphasis or commentary, create suspense, or help hold a work together. Refrains may be repeated with small variations in a work to fit a particular context or to create a special effect. "Fallen cold and dead" is a refrain in the poem "O Captain! My Captain!" (page 634).

See page 769.

REPETITION The property of repeated words, sounds, syllables, and other elements that appear in a literary work. Repetition occurs in most poetry and some prose. The repetition might be of words or phrases (as in a refrain), of sounds (as in alliteration, assonance, and rhyme), of grammatical structures, or of events (as in parallel episodes). Speeches such as "I Have a Dream" (page 773), and free-verse poems, such as "I Hear America Singing" (page 639), especially, use repetition to emphasize their points and to create rhythm.

See also *Nonfiction, Poetry.*

RESOLUTION See *Plot.*

RHYME The repetition of accented vowel sounds and all sounds following them in words that are close together in a poem. *Mean* and *screen* are rhymes, as are *crumble* and *tumble*. The many purposes of rhyme in poetry include building rhythm, emphasizing ideas, organizing poems (for instance, into stanzas or couplets), providing humor or pleasure for the reader, and aiding memory.

End rhymes are rhymes at the ends of lines. In the following poem, *ought* and *thought* form end rhymes, as do *afternoon* and *soon*:

> **Condition**
> I have to speak—I must—I should
>   —I ought . . .
> I'd tell you how I love you if I thought
> The world would end tomorrow afternoon.
> But short of that . . . well, it might be
>   too soon.
>
> —Vikram Seth

Internal rhymes are rhymes within lines. The following line has an internal rhyme (*turning/burning*):

> Back into the chamber turning, all my soul
>   within me burning
>
> —from "The Raven"
> by Edgar Allan Poe

Rhyming sounds need not be spelled the same way: *Gear/here*, for instance, is a rhyme. Rhymes can involve more than one syllable or more than one word; *poet/know it* is an example. Rhymes involving sounds that are similar but not exactly the same are called **approximate rhymes** (or **near rhymes** or **slant rhymes**). *Leave/live* is an example of an approximate rhyme. Poets writing in English often use this kind of rhyme because they believe it sounds less artificial and more like real speech than exact rhymes do. Also, it is difficult to come up with fresh, original exact rhymes. Poets interested in how a poem looks on the printed page sometimes use **eye rhymes,** or **visual rhymes**—"rhymes" involving words that are spelled similarly but pronounced differently. *Tough/cough* is an eye rhyme. (*Tough/rough* is a "real" rhyme.)

The pattern of end rhymes in a poem is called a **rhyme scheme.** To indicate the rhyme scheme of a poem, use a separate letter of the alphabet for each end rhyme. For example, the rhyme scheme of the opening stanza of "Paul Revere's Ride" (page 593) is *aabba*.

See also *Free Verse, Poetry.*

RHYTHM A musical quality produced by the repetition of stressed and unstressed syllables or by the repetition of certain other sound patterns. Rhythm occurs in all forms of language, both written and spoken, but is particularly important in poetry.

The most obvious kind of rhythm is the regular repetition of stressed and unstressed syllables found in some poetry. In the following lines, which describe a cavalry charge, the rhythm echoes the galloping of the attackers' horses:

> The Assyrian came down like the wolf on the
>   fold,
> And his cohorts were gleaming in purple and
>   gold;
> And the sheen of their spears was like stars
>   on the sea,
> When the blue wave rolls nightly on deep
>   Galilee.
>
> —from "The Destruction of
>   Sennacherib" by George
>   Gordon, Lord Byron

Writers also create rhythm by repeating words and phrases or even by repeating whole lines and sentences. The following passage by Walt Whitman is written in free verse and does not have a regular pattern of rhythm or rhyme. Yet the lines are rhythmical because of Whitman's use of repetition.

> I hear the sound I love, the sound of the
>   human voice,
> I hear all sounds running together,
>   combined, fused, or following,
> Sounds of the city and sounds out of the city,
>   sounds of the day and night,
> Talkative young ones to those that like them,
>   the loud laugh of work-people at their
>   meals . . .
>
> —from "Song of Myself"
>   by Walt Whitman

See page 591.
See also *Meter*.

RISING ACTION See *Plot*.

SATIRE **Writing that ridicules something, often in order to bring about change.** Satire may poke fun at a person, a group of people, an attitude, a social institution, even all of humanity. Writers use satire to convince us of a point of view or to persuade us to follow a course of action.

SETTING **The time and place of a story, play, or narrative poem.** Most often the setting is described early in the story. For example, "The Treasure of Lemon Brown" (page 17) begins, "The dark sky, filled with angry, swirling clouds, reflected Greg Ridley's mood as he sat on the stoop of his building." Setting often contributes to a work's emotional effect. It may also play an important role in the plot, especially in stories involving a conflict between a character and nature such as in "The Cremation of Sam McGee" (page 603).

See pages 6, 8, 13, 67, 75, 79,
97, 101, 111, 115.
See also *Mood, Plot*.

SHORT STORY **A short fictional prose narrative.** A short story's plot usually consists of these basic elements: the **introduction (basic situation or exposition), complications, climax,** and **resolution.** Short stories are more limited than novels. They usually have only one or two major characters and one important setting.

See pages 154, 163.
See also *Fiction, Novel, Plot*.

SIMILE **A comparison between two unlike things, using a word such as *like, as, than*, or *resembles*.** *Her face was as round as a pumpkin* and *This steak is tougher than an old shoe* are similes.

See pages 513, 589.
See also *Figure of Speech, Metaphor*.

SONNET **A fourteen-line poem, usually written in iambic pentameter.** There are two kinds of sonnets: The **English,** or **Shakespearean, sonnet** has three four-line units and ends with a couplet. The **Italian,** or **Petrarchan, sonnet** (named after the fourteenth-century Italian poet Petrarch) poses a question or makes a point in the first eight lines. The last six lines respond to that question or point. "On the Grasshopper and the Cricket" (page 625) is in the form of an Italian sonnet.

See page 623.
See also *Iambic Pentameter, Poetry*.

SPEAKER **The voice talking to us in a poem.** The speaker is sometimes, but not always, the poet. It is best to think of the voice in the poem as belonging to a character the poet has created. The character may be a child, a woman, a man, an animal, or even an object.

See also *Poetry*.

SPEECH **A work delivered orally to an audience.** Its purpose is to unite an audience, inform them of something, or persuade them to do something. Speeches often include allusions that the audience will recognize and repetition. We can also read speeches, such as Lincoln's "Gettysburg Address" (page 771) and King's "I Have a Dream" (page 773).

See also *Allusion, Nonfiction, Repetition*.

STANZA **A group of consecutive lines in a poem that form a single unit.** A stanza in a poem is something like a paragraph in prose: It often expresses a unit of thought. A stanza may consist of any number of lines; it may even consist of a single line. The word *stanza* is an Italian word for "stopping place" or "place to rest." In some poems, such as "Casey at the Bat" (page 616), each stanza has the same rhyme scheme.

STEREOTYPE **A fixed idea about the members of a particular group of people that does not allow for any individuality.** Stereotypes are often based on misconceptions about racial, social, religious, gender, or ethnic groups. Some common stereotypes are the ideas that all football players are stupid, that all New Yorkers are rude, and that all politicians are dishonest.

STYLE **The way a writer uses language.** Style results from **diction** (word choice), sentence structure, tone, and the use of **literary devices.** One writer may use many figures of speech, for example; another writer may prefer straightforward language with few figures of speech.

See pages 462, 464, 469, 480, 483, 496, 507, 513, 515.
See also *Diction, Literary Devices, Tone*.

SUBJECTIVE WRITING **Writing in which the feelings and opinions of the writer are revealed.** Editorials, personal essays, and autobiographies are examples of subjective writing, as are many poems.

See also *Objective Writing*.

SUBPLOT **A minor plot that relates in some way to the main story.** In "Flowers for Algernon" (page 33), Charlie's relationship with Miss Kinnian and his problems at his job are subplots of the main plot, involving the surgery to make Charlie more intelligent.

See page 31.
See also *Plot*.

SUSPENSE **The uncertainty or anxiety that a reader feels about what will happen next in a story, novel, or drama.** In "The Tell-Tale Heart" (page 473), the suspense builds as the insane narrator describes his long vigil at his victim's door.

See also *Plot*.

SYMBOL **A person, a place, a thing, or an event that has meaning in itself and stands for something beyond itself as well.** Some symbols are so well known that we sometimes forget they are symbols. The bald eagle, for example, is a symbol of the United States; the Star of David is a symbol of Judaism; and the cross is a symbol of Christianity. In literature, symbols are often personal and surprising. In "Suéter / Sweater" (page 505), for example, a sweater symbolizes the grandmother's love and caring.

See also *Literary Devices*.

TALL TALE **An exaggerated, far-fetched story that is obviously untrue but is told as though it should be believed.** Almost all tall tales are humorous. "The Cremation of Sam McGee" (page 603) is a tall tale told in the form of a poem.

See also *Exaggeration, Folk Tale*.

THEME **The general idea or insight about life that a work of literature reveals.** A theme is not the same as a subject. The subject of a work can usually be expressed in a word or two: *love, childhood, death.* A theme is an idea or message that the writer wishes to convey *about* that subject. For example, one theme of "Camp Harmony" (page 387) might be stated as *Innocent people often suffer in times of conflict.* The same themes, such as *Good will triumph over evil,* that appear in works from different cultures and times, are called **recurring themes** or **universal themes.**

"If you were to boil your book down to a few words, what would be its message?

© The New Yorker Collection 1986 Edward Koren from cartoonbank.com. All Rights Reserved.

A work's themes (there may be more than one) are usually not stated directly. Most often the reader has to think about all the elements of the work and use them to make an **inference,** or educated guess, about what the themes are.

See pages 284, 286, 293, 295, 375, 385, 395, 399.

TONE **The attitude a writer takes toward his or her subject, characters, and audience.** For example, a writer's tone might be humorous, as in "Those Three Wishes" (page 10), or passionate and sincere, as in "I Have a Dream" (page 773). When people speak, their tone of voice gives added meaning to what they say. Writers use written language to create effects similar to those that people create with their voices.

See page 67.
See also *Connotation, Diction, Style.*

TRAGEDY **A play, novel, or other narrative in which the main character comes to an unhappy end.** A tragedy depicts serious and important events. Its hero achieves wisdom or self-knowledge but suffers a great deal—perhaps even dies. A tragic hero is usually dignified and courageous and often high ranking. The hero's downfall may be caused by a **tragic flaw** (a serious character weakness) or by external forces beyond his or her control. *The Diary of Anne Frank* (page 301) and Shakespeare's *Romeo and Juliet* are tragedies.

See also *Comedy, Drama.*

UNDERSTATEMENT **A statement that says less than what is meant.** Understatement is the opposite of exaggeration. It is usually used for comic effect. If you were to say that the Grand Canyon is a nice little hole in the ground, you would be using understatement.

See also *Exaggeration, Literary Devices.*

WORD CHOICE See *Diction.*

WORD PLAY See *Humor.*

Handbook of Reading and Informational Terms

For more information about a topic, turn to the page(s) in this book indicated on a separate line at the end of the entries. To learn about *Coherence*, for example, turn to page 745. On another line there are cross-references to entries in this Handbook that provide closely related information. For instance, *Chronological Order* contains a cross-reference to *Structural Patterns*.

ANALOGY   An **analogy** (uh NAL uh jee) compares one thing with another thing to show, point by point, how they are alike. Writers often use analogies to show how something unfamiliar is like something well-known. Writers of scientific and technical texts often use analogies to explain difficult concepts.

Another kind of analogy is a **word analogy.** This kind of analogy is sometimes used in tests. It asks you to compare two words and figure out how they are related to each other. To complete a word analogy,

1. figure out the relationship between the two words; then,
2. identify another pair of words that are related to each other in the same way.

In a word analogy, the symbol : means "is to." The symbol : : means "as." Once you get the hang of it, completing analogies is fun. Here's an example:

> Select the pair of words that best completes the analogy.
>   STANZA : POEM : : _____
>   **A**   metaphor : simile
>   **B**   chapter : book
>   **C**   fiction : nonfiction
>   **D**   words : music

The correct answer is B. The completed analogy should read: Stanza is to poem as chapter is to book. The relationship between stanza and poem is one of *part* to *whole*. Just as a stanza is part of a poem, a chapter is part of a book.

In another kind of word analogy, the words might be opposites:

> DRY : WET : : cold : hot
> Dry is to wet as cold is to hot.

ANECDOTE   See *Proposition and Support.*

CAUSE AND EFFECT   The **cause-effect pattern** is a structural pattern that writers use to explain how or why one thing leads to another. The **cause** is the reason that an action or reaction takes place. The **effect** is the result or consequence of the cause. A cause can have more than one effect, and an effect may have several causes. Writers may explain causes only or effects only. Sometimes a text is organized in a cause-and-effect chain. One cause leads to an effect, which causes another effect, and so on. Notice the cause-and-effect chain in the following paragraph from an interview with John Lewis in *The Power of Nonviolence:*

> In April, unknown people bombed the house of our attorney. It shook the whole area, and it shook us. How could we respond to the bombing and do something that would channel the frustration of the students in a nonviolent manner? We decided to have a march, and we sent the mayor a telegram letting him know that by noon we would march on city hall. And the next day, more than five thousand of us marched in twos in an orderly line to the city hall.

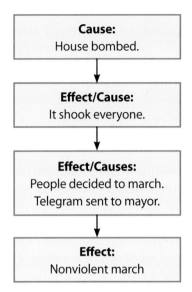

| Cause: |
| House bombed. |

↓

| Effect/Cause: |
| It shook everyone. |

↓

| Effect/Causes: |
| People decided to march. |
| Telegram sent to mayor. |

↓

| Effect: |
| Nonviolent march |

Writers use the cause-effect pattern in both narrative and informational texts. In many stories, events in the plot are connected in a cause-and-effect chain. Some words and phrases that are clues to the cause-effect pattern are *because, depended on, inspired, produced, resulting in, led to,* and *outcome.* Never assume, either in your reading or in real life, that one event causes another just because it happens before it.

See also *Coherence, Organizational Patterns, Structural Patterns.*

CHRONOLOGICAL ORDER Writers use **chronological order,** or time order, when they put events in the sequence in which they happened, one after the other. Chronological order is a common structural pattern in narratives, both fictional and non-fictional. Chronological order is frequently found in history texts and in science texts. You will also find chronological order in directions, from directions for a simple process, such as making hot chocolate, to technical directions for using a complex mechanical device, such as an electric generator. Some words and phrases that signal the chronological-order structural pattern are *first, after, finally, in the meantime, as soon as,* and *at this point.*

See pages 411, 737.
See also *Coherence, Organizational Patterns, Structural Patterns.*

CLASSIFICATION **Classification** is a structural pattern that organizes information into a group. Items in the group maybe related by size, location, importance, or any other order that will make sense to the reader.

See also *Structural Patterns.*

COHERENCE The Latin word *cohere* means "stick together." A text has **coherence** (koh HIHR uhns) when ideas stick together because they're arranged in an order that makes sense to the reader. To aid in coherence, writers often help you follow a text by using **transitions,** words and phrases that show how ideas are connected.

See page 745.
See also *Cause and Effect, Chronological Order, Comparison and Contrast, Order of Importance, Spatial Order.*

COMPARISON AND CONTRAST When you **compare,** you look at how two or more things are similar, that is, alike. When you **contrast,** you look at how things are different. Comparison and contrast is a structural pattern that discusses similarities and differences. There are two basic ways to organize a comparison-and-contrast text.

1. **Block method.** Discuss all the features (sometimes called **points of comparison**) of Subject 1 first; then, all the features of Subject 2. For each subject, discuss the same features in the same order. A block comparison and contrast of the two subjects Earth and Mars could be organized by subject.

Subject	Features
Earth	• planet surface • weather • length of day and year
Mars	• planet surface • weather • length of day and year

2. **Point-by-point method.** Discuss one feature at a time. First, talk about a feature in Subject 1; then, discuss the same feature in Subject 2.

Features	Subject
planet surface	• Earth • Mars
weather	• Earth • Mars
length of day and year	• Earth • Mars

Expect to see transitions that help you follow the ideas in both block structure and point-by-point structure. The transitions *both* and *neither* help you find similarities. Transitions such as *but* and *however* help you pinpoint differences.

A graphic organizer such as a Venn diagram, which uses overlapping circles to show relationships, can help you keep track of similarities and differences.

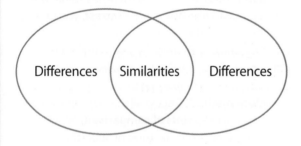

See pages 115, 411.
See also *Coherence, Organizational Patterns, Structural Patterns.*

CONCLUSION A **conclusion** is a final idea or judgment that you draw, or come to, after you've considered all the evidence. In his memoir *Woodsong,* Gary Paulsen tells how he observed his dog Columbia playing a joke on another dog. That observation leads him to a chain of reasoning based on what he knows about other animals. After he considers the evidence, he draws a conclusion.

> If Columbia could do that, I thought, if a dog could do that, then a wolf could do that. If a wolf could do that, then a deer could do that. If a deer could do that, then a beaver, and a squirrel, and a bird, and, and, and . . .
> And I quit trapping then.
> It was wrong for me to kill.

As you read, you draw conclusions based on information in the text combined with what you already know. You may or may not agree with Paulsen's reasoning and the conclusion it leads him to. Your own experiences with animals may tell you that a dog and a wolf may have a sense of humor— but that other animals might not. In that case, you might conclude that Paulsen's conclusion is valid (true and logical) for him, but not for you.

See page 515.

CONNECTIONS As you read you **make connections** between the text and what you already know from your own experience. Making connections helps you understand and evaluate what you read.

See pages 189, 813.

CONSISTENCY A text is **consistent** when its details focus on the main idea and are in agreement with it. Writers strive to maintain consistency because details that have little or nothing to do with the main idea of the text distract and confuse the reader. Why is the second sentence in the following passage inconsistent with the point of the passage?

> In the winter of 1866–1867 blizzards gripped the Sierra Nevada. Spring came early, and the weather was unusually warm on the East Coast. Dwellings were buried in blowing, shifting, drifting, driving snow.

A sentence about weather on the East Coast is inconsistent with a passage on conditions in the mountains of California.

See page 737.

CONSUMER DOCUMENTS See *Informational Texts.*

CONTEXT CLUE If you don't know the meaning of a word, **context clues,** the words and sentences surrounding it, can sometimes help you guess its meaning. The following chart gives you four types of context clues. In the examples the unfamiliar word appears in boldface (dark type). The context clue is underlined.

Definition: Look for words that define the unfamiliar word, often by giving a **synonym** for it.

> She peeled onions and grated potatoes for the **latkes,** the potato pancakes.

Restatement: Find words that restate the unfamiliar word's meaning.

> Ballet dancers perform on the **pointe** of their toeshoes—a platform about the size of a silver dollar.

Example: Look for examples that reveal the meaning of the unfamiliar word.

> Street vendors offered their **wares:** goods of all kinds were piled in their stalls.

Contrast: Find words that contrast the unfamiliar word with a word or phrase you already know.

> The land was **arid,** in contrast to the rich, fertile land we had left behind.

See page 437.

DETAIL It is important to **analyze details** in a text to help you understand elements of literature such a plot, setting, characters, theme, and style. For instance, the details in "The Inn of Lost Time" (page 81) reveal that the story takes place in a sixteenth-century Japanese farmhouse.

Useful details that help you follow both fiction and informational text are **transitional words.**

Common Transitional Words and Phrases	
Comparing Ideas also, and, moreover, too, similarly, another	**Contrasting Ideas** although, still, yet, but, on the other hand
Showing Cause-Effect for, since, as a result, therefore, so that	**Showing Importance** first, last, to begin with, mainly, more important
Showing Location above, across, over, there, inside, behind	**Showing Time** before, at last, when, eventually, at once

The details that are most important in a text are called **critical details.** If you e-mail a faraway friend about a film you've seen, you have to make decisions about which details to include and which to leave out. A critical detail is one that you must include for the text to make sense. Being able to separate critical details from minor ones is especially important in writing a summary.

See pages 67, 101.
See also *Proposition and Support, Summarizing.*

DOCUMENTS See *Informational Texts.*

FACT A **fact** is something that can be verified, or proved. It can be proved by direct observation or by checking a reliable reference source. The following statement is a fact:

> In 1860, Abraham Lincoln was elected president despite winning only 40 percent of the popular vote.

You can verify this fact by looking it up in a history book or in an encyclopedia. In fields where discoveries are still being made, you need to check facts in a recently published source. A Web site on the Internet may be current, but it may not be reliable. Remember that anybody can post a statement on the Internet. If you suspect that a statement given as a fact is not true, try to find the same fact in several sources.

See also *Opinion*.

FALLACIOUS REASONING Statements that seem reasonable at first may, if examined closely, prove to be based on **fallacious** (fuh LAY shuhs) **reasoning,** faulty reasoning, or mistakes in logic. (The word *fallacious* comes from a Latin word meaning "deceptive" or "tricky." The word *false* comes from the same root, as does the word *fallacy*.) Fallacious reasoning leads to false or incorrect conclusions. Here are some types of fallacious reasoning:

1. **Begging the question,** also called **circular reasoning,** assumes the truth of a statement before it has been proved. You appear to be giving a reason to support your opinion, but all you're doing is restating the same thing in different words.

> Everyone should be required to attend school sports events because mandatory attendance at such events is important.
>
> We can't control worldwide air pollution because every country in the world is guilty of polluting the air.

2. **Name-calling** uses labels to attack the person on the other side of the argument, instead of giving reasons or evidence to support the opposing point of view. This fallacy includes attacking the person's character, situation, or background.

> You're not seriously considering Latisha's childish ideas for the school dance, are you?
>
> Of course, Allen's not going to say that doctors make too much money. His mother's a doctor.

3. **Stereotyping** gives all members of a group the same (usually undesirable) characteristics. It assumes that everyone (or everything) in that group is alike. (The word *stereotype* comes from the word for a metal plate that was used to print the same image over and over.) Stereotypes are often based on misconceptions about racial, social, religious, gender, or ethnic groups.

> Smart kids are poor athletes.
> Actors are conceited.
> Big cities are dirty and dangerous.

4. **Hasty generalization** is a broad, general statement or conclusion that is made without sufficient evidence to back it up. A hasty generalization is often made on the basis of one or two experiences or observations.

> My brother is left-handed, and he's an artist. My aunt is left-handed, and she writes songs. I'm right-handed, and I have no artistic or musical talent at all.
> **Hasty generalization:** Left-handed people are more creative than right-handed people.

If any exceptions to the conclusion can be found, the generalization is not true.

5. **Either/or fallacy** assumes that there is only one correct choice or one solution, even though there may be many.

> Either we have free trade, or we return to the cold war.
> If you don't get good grades this year, you're not college material.

6. **False cause and effect** occurs when one event is said to be the cause of another event just because the two events happened in sequence. You cannot assume that an event caused whatever happened afterward.

> We got new uniforms, and our team won four straight games. The uniforms helped us win.
> Our mayor should be reelected. During her first term the crime rate in our city fell almost 10 percent.

GENERALIZATION A **generalization** is a broad statement that applies to many individuals, experiences, situations, or observations. A generalization is a type of conclusion that is drawn after considering as many of the facts as possible. A valid generalization is based on evidence, specific data, or facts. Here are some specific facts and a generalization based on them. Notice that each fact is one piece of evidence. The generalization then states what the

evidence adds up to, drawing a conclusion that applies to all members of the group.

> **Specific Facts:** My dog wags her tail when she's happy. Kathy's dog, Soot, wags his tail when he is happy.
> **Generalization:** All dogs I've seen wag their tails when they're happy.

A generalization jumps from your own specific experiences and observations to a larger, general understanding. To be **valid,** or true, a generalization must apply to every specific individual or instance within the group—including the millions in the group that are not mentioned or listed in arriving at the generalization.

See page 385.

GRAPHICS Many types of texts especially informational texts, can be enhanced by graphics. **Graphics** include graphs, tables, charts, maps, cartoons, and illustrations.

See page 707.
See also *Informational Texts.*

IDIOM An **idiom** (IHD ee uhm) is an expression peculiar to a particular language that means something different from the literal (dictionary) meaning of the words. If your brother tells you he's fallen for Angela, you know that he means he likes her a lot. Despite what the words say, you know he hasn't fallen down. Every language has its own idioms. When you grow up speaking a language, you understand its idioms without even thinking about them. When you're learning a new language, it's hard to figure out what its idioms mean, and it's even harder to use them correctly.

See pages 112, 621.

INFERENCE An **inference** is a guess based on clues. When you read, you make inferences based on clues that the writer provides. For example, you guess what will happen next in a story based on what the writer has already told you. You change your inferences as the writer gives you more information. Sometimes a writer will deliberately drop a clue that leads you, for a short time, to an incorrect inference about what is going to happen next. That's part of the fun of reading. Until you get to the end of a suspenseful story, you can never be sure about what will happen next.

When you're writing about a story or an informational text, you must be sure your inferences are supported by details in the text.

Supported inferences are based directly on evidence in the writer's text that you can point to and on reasonable prior knowledge. Some interpretation of the evidence is possible, but you cannot ignore or contradict facts in the text that the writer has given you.

Unsupported inferences are conclusions that are not logical. They ignore the facts in the text, or misinterpret them. Whenever you're asked to write an essay about a text, it's a good idea to re-read the text before and after you write your essay. Check each inference you make against the text to make sure you can find evidence for it. For example, if you write an analysis of a character in a story and you say that the character is self-centered, you should cite details from the text to support your inference.

See page 189.

INFORMATIONAL TEXTS When you're reading for your own enjoyment, a mystery story, for instance, you can read at your own pace. You can speed up to see what happens next. If you get bored, you can move on to another story. When you're **reading for information,** you need to read carefully, looking for main ideas and important details. Slow and careful reading is especially important when you're trying to get meaning from consumer, workplace, and public documents. These documents are often not written by professional writers, so they may be difficult to read.

Consumer documents are texts like warranties, contracts, product information, and instructional manuals. Here are some points to keep in mind when you read consumer documents:

1. Try to read the consumer document before you buy the product. Then you can ask the clerk to explain anything you don't understand.
2. Read all of the pages in whatever language comes most easily to you. (Many documents are printed in two or three languages.) You will often find important information where you least expect it, such as at the very end of the document.
3. Read the fine print; *fine*, here, means "tiny and barely readable." Some fine-print statements in documents are required by law. They are designed to protect you, the consumer, not the company that makes the product, so the company may not be interested in emphasizing these points.
4. Don't expect the document to be interesting or easy to read. If you don't understand a statement and you can't ask someone at the store that sold you the product, send an e-mail to the company that made it. It's okay to complain to the company if you find their consumer document confusing.
5. Before you sign anything, read everything on the page and be sure you understand what you're agreeing to. Ask to take the document home, and have your parent or guardian read it. If you are not of legal age in your state, an adult may be responsible for whatever you've signed. Make a copy of any document that you've put your signature to—and keep it in a place where you can find it.

Workplace documents include items like job applications, memos, instructional manuals, and employee handbooks. In addition to the points about reading consumer documents, you might want to keep these points in mind:

1. Take all the time you need to read and understand the document. Don't let anyone rush you or tell you that a document is not important, that it's just a formality.

2. Read directions carefully, even if they're just posted on the side of a device you're supposed to operate. Read all of the directions before you start. Ask questions if you're not sure how to proceed. Don't try anything out before you know what will happen next.

3. An employee handbook contains the "rules of the game" at a particular business. It tells you about holidays, work hours, break times, and vacations, as well as other important company policies. Read an employee handbook from cover to cover. Pay special attention to information about health benefits, probationary periods, and policies on sexual harassment.

Public documents are texts put out by public agencies and not-for-profit groups such as community-action organizations and church groups. They might inform readers about matters like health concerns, schedules, and records. As you get older, this type of document will become increasingly important to you. Practice reading public documents now, and talk about your understanding of them with your family.

Technical directions are instructions for assembling, installing, or operating mechanical or electronic devices or machines. As with workplace instructions, read technical directions very carefully before you try to carry out the task described.

Question Sheet for Informational Texts

1. What is the topic? _____
2. Do I understand what I'm reading? _____
3. What parts should I re-read? _____

4. What are the main ideas and details?
   Main idea: _____ Main idea: _____
   Details: _____ Details: _____
   Main idea: _____ Main idea: _____
   Details: _____ Details: _____
5. Summary of what I learned:
   _____
   _____

See pages 666, 668, 677, 693, 707, 736, 738.

JUDGMENT When you make **judgments,** you form opinions. As you read a text or watch TV, you're constantly making judgments about what you read and see. When you express your opinions in writing, it's important to support your judgments with evidence. If you're writing about a story's plot or characters, you should support your judgments with references to the text, to other works, or to your own experiences. Before you make judgments about a TV show or a movie, here are some points to keep in mind:

1. Identify the purpose of the program or film. You need to know the writer's goal before you say to what extent the goal was reached. If the writer's purpose was humor, you should judge it for its humor, not for the credibility of its characters and plot.

2. Think about the beliefs and assumptions that the work represents. For example, is violence considered funny? tragic? ordinary? Does the program attack or ignore stereotypes?

3. Evaluate the information presented, especially in a nonfiction TV program. What are the program's sources? How reliable are they? What biases or prejudices do you notice? Be sure to distinguish between provable facts and someone's opinions.

4. Make your own judgment. After you've observed the work critically, draw your own conclusions and support them with references to the work itself, to other works of the same type and purpose, and to your personal knowledge.

See also *Fallacious Reasoning, Opinion, Purposes of Texts.*

KWL CHART Before you start reading a text, it's a good idea to review what you already know about the subject. As you think about the subject, you'll come up with questions that the text may answer. Making a **KWL chart** can help you focus on a text. The following chart is based on the text from *Harriet Tubman: Conductor on the Underground Railroad* (page 199):

- In the **K** column, jot down what you already know about Harriet Tubman.
- In the **W** column, write any questions you have that the text might answer. Glancing through the text, looking at the pictures, if any, and reading subtitles and captions will help you come up with questions.
- As you read, note in the **L** column what you learn that supplements, answers, or contradicts what you wrote in the other two columns.

K	W	L
What I Know	What I Want to Know	What I Learned
She was African American.	What is an underground railroad?	

LOGIC is correct reasoning. A **logical text** supports statements with reasons and evidence. A text is illogical when it does not provide reasons backed by evidence (facts and examples). Notice how each sentence in the following text supports the sentence before:

Organizers of the Discovery Expedition took pains to be authentic but made concessions to time. Lewis, for instance, traversed the Ohio River with a keelboat using oars, poles, sails, or ropes for cordelling (pulling a boat along a waterway from the shore). In the reenactment, "Lewis" had a motor powering his craft.

See page 745.
See also *Logical Order*.

LOGICAL ORDER is a method of organization used in informational texts. In **logical order,** details are classified into related groups. Writers who use this order may use the **comparison-and-contrast** pattern to show similarities and differences among various groups. For an example of logical order, see "Apologies for Past Actions Are Still Appropriate Today" (page 765), an editorial about requesting forgiveness for slavery.

See page 745.
See also *Comparison and Contrast, Structural Patterns*.

MAGAZINE A **magazine** is a publication, usually in paperback, that comes out at regular intervals, such as weekly, monthly, or even annually. There are all kinds of magazines that appeal to general or special interests—from groups that love dogs (the magazine *Bark*) to people who enjoy reading about celebrities (the magazine *People*). A growing number of magazines are written especially for teenagers. Magazines may seek to entertain, to inform, or to persuade readers. Most have certain structural features in common:

- An attractive cover gives you the title, price, date of the magazine and usually some idea of what's inside. A brightly colored illustration is usually included on the cover to grab your attention.

- The table of contents page appears close to the beginning of the magazine. You may also find a list of contributors and letters to the editor in the opening pages.
- Most magazines contain photographs and other kinds of illustrations. Many include cartoons. Graphic features such as color and headings and subheadings in different sizes and fonts (printing styles), along with charts and maps, organize the text visually and often highlight information. You'll often find stories and articles printed in columns, but each page is designed for maximum appeal to the reader. Sidebars, short articles set off within the article, develop a topic related in some way to the main story.
- Many magazines are supported financially not by the price of the publication but by advertising revenues. Advertisers choose to sell their products in magazines that appeal to the kind of buyer they are looking for. Some readers think the splashy ads in some magazines are almost as entertaining as the magazine's features; whereas, others find that the ads interfere with the magazine's contents.

See also *Purposes of Texts.*

MAIN IDEA The **main idea** of a nonfiction text is the writer's most important point, opinion, or message. The main idea may be stated directly, or it may be only suggested or implied. If the idea is not stated directly, it's up to you to look at the details and decide on the idea they all seem to support. Try to restate the writer's main idea in your own words.

See also *Note Taking, Outlining, Proposition and Support, Summarizing.*

MAPS Maps show the natural landscape of an area. Shading may be used to show physical features, such as mountains and valleys. Colors are often used to show elevation (height above or below sea level). **Political maps** show political units, such as states and nations. The map of Europe in 1942 on page 298 is a political map. **Special-purpose maps** present information that is related to geography, such as the route that refugees escaping the Nazis took from Lithuania to Japan (page 217).

How to Read a Map
1. **Identify the map's focus.** The map's title and labels tell you its focus—its subject and the geographical area it covers.
2. **Study the legend.** The **legend,** or key, explains the symbols, lines, colors, and shading used in the map.
3. **Check directions and distances.** Maps often include a **compass rose,** a diagram that shows north, south, east, and west. If you're looking at a map that doesn't have one, assume that north is at the top, west is to the left, and so on. Many maps also include a **scale** to help you relate distances on the map to actual distances. One inch on a map may equal one, ten, or fifty miles or more.
4. **Look at the larger context.** The **absolute location** of any place on earth is given by its **latitude** (the number of degrees north or south of the equator) and **longitude** (the number of degrees east or west of the **prime meridian,** or zero degrees longitude). Some maps also include **locator maps,** which show the area depicted in relation to a larger area. Notice the locator map in the upper right corner of the map shown here:

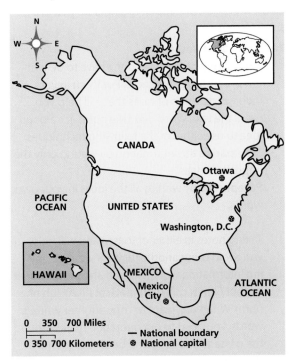

MEANING The most important idea or message of an informational text is called its **underlying meaning.** When you're reading or summarizing a text, to find the underlying meaning, you need to ask yourself the following questions:

- What is the writer's point? What is his or her reason for writing this text?
- What idea do all the critical details add up to?
- What connection can I make between the meaning of this text and the meaning of other texts I have read?
- What connection can I make between this text and my own life? What special meaning does this text have for me? How do I feel about what the writer is saying? Do I agree or disagree? What reasons can I give for my opinion?

See also *Summarizing.*

NOTE TAKING Taking notes is a good way to remember a writer's major ideas and interesting details. Notes are especially useful when you read an informational text such as a history or science assignment. You can jot down notes in a notebook such as the kind you might use for a reading log. Many students like to use three-by-five-inch note cards, which can be clipped together or filed in a small file box.

Tips for Taking Notes

1. **Your own words.** Notes don't have to be written in complete sentences. Put them in your own words, using phrases that will help you recall the text. When you take notes, it's a good idea to use either of the following techniques:
- **Summarize** the information by writing only the important ideas.
- **Paraphrase** by writing all the ideas in your own words.

Taking notes in either of these ways will help you avoid using another writer's words. Copying information word for word and presenting it as your own is called **plagiarism** (PLAY juh rihz uhm). When you want to copy another writer's words, you need to put quotation marks around the passage you copy and be sure to identify the writer.

2. **Main ideas.** Record each main idea at the top of its own page or note card. As you keep reading, add details that relate to that idea's page or to the note card.
3. **Write clearly.** Even though no one but you may ever see your notes (unless you become famous), try to write clearly for your own sake. You'll want to read your notes later, and decoding your own mysterious handwriting can take a lot of time. When you finish taking notes for the day, review them to make sure they make sense to you.

See pages 805.
See also *Detail, Main Idea.*

OPINION An **opinion** is a belief or an attitude. An opinion cannot be proved to be true or false. The following statement is an opinion:

> Lincoln was the best president the United States has ever had.

People have different opinions about who was the best president.

A **valid opinion** is an opinion that is supported by facts. The following opinion is valid. It is supported by two verifiable facts.

> Lincoln was a great president because he freed the slaves and led our country through the Civil War.

When you read a persuasive text, remember that statements of opinion can't be proved, but they can and should be supported by facts.

See also *Fact.*

ORDER OF IMPORTANCE is a structural pattern often used in informational texts. Writers of persuasive texts have to decide whether to give the strongest reason first or to present the weakest reason first and end with the strongest point. News articles always begin with the most important details because they want to grab the readers' attention immediately. The structure of a news article looks like an upside-down triangle, with the least important details at the bottom.

See also *Detail, Structural Patterns.*

ORGANIZATIONAL PATTERNS Writers of informational texts use a pattern of organization that will make their meaning clear. There are several ways writers can organize information. Don't expect a writer to use the same pattern throughout an entire text. Many writers switch from one pattern to another and may even combine patterns. Recognizing how a writer has organized a text— and noticing where and why the pattern changes—will help you understand what you read. Here are some of the organizational patterns you will find:

- **classification**—presenting information in groups, such as size, location, or any other sensible order
- **chronology,** time order, or sequence—putting events or steps in the order in which they occur
- **comparison-contrast**—pointing out and explaining similarities and differences
- **cause and effect**—showing how events happen as a result of other events
- **problem-solution**—explaining how a problem may be solved
- **question-answer**—asking questions, then giving the answers
- **spatial order**—showing how things relate to each other in space

See pages 137, 145, 149, 431.
See also *Cause and Effect, Chronological Order, Comparison and Contrast, Scope, Structural Patterns, Treatment.*

OUTLINING If you've taken notes on a text, you may want to organize your notes into an outline. Outlining puts main ideas and details in a form that you can review quickly. An **informal outline,** sometimes called a working outline, should have at least three main ideas. You put supporting details under each main idea, like this:

Informal Outline

First main idea
Detail supporting first main idea
Another detail supporting first main idea
Third detail supporting first main idea

Second main idea
[etc.]

A **formal outline** is especially useful if you're writing a research paper. You might start with a working outline and then revise it into a formal one. Your teacher may ask you to submit a formal outline with your completed research paper, so you have to be sure that it has the correct form. When you create a formal outline, you revise it, making changes as you revise your paper.

Formal outlines use Roman numerals (I, II, III), capital letters (A, B, C), and Arabic numerals (1, 2, 3) to show order, relationship, and relative importance of ideas. The headings in a formal outline should have the same grammatical structure, and you must be consistent in your use of either phrases or sentences (you can't move back and forth between them). There are always at least two divisions under each heading or none at all.

Here is the beginning of a formal outline of "The Scientific Method" (page 150):

Formal Outline

I. Basic Steps
 A. State the Problem
  1. Make an observation
  2. Come up with a research question
 B. Gather Information
  1. Search in books and journals

See also *Main Idea.*

PARAPHRASING Paraphrasing is usually used to restate a poem. In a **paraphrase,** you restate every line in your own words. A paraphrase is longer than a summary. In some cases, it may even be longer than the original text. A paraphrase can help you understand a complex text. Here is a paraphrase of the poem "A word is dead" by Emily Dickinson (page 511):

> In the first three-line stanza, the speaker says that some people claim that a word is "dead," that is, it no longer has meaning or importance, after it is spoken. In the second three-line stanza the speaker states an opposing opinion, that a word only begins to "live" after it is spoken. This means that a word, especially a loving or hateful word, is like a living thing—it can hurt or bring hope or happiness to people.

See pages 471, 591, 627, 632.

PREDICTIONS As you read a story, you may keep guessing about what will happen next. That means you're already using a reading strategy called **making predictions.** To make predictions, look for clues that the writer gives you. Try to connect those clues with other stories you've read and with experiences in your own life. As you continue to read and more information comes in from the writer, you'll change, or adjust, your guesses. Making predictions as you read helps you become involved with the story and its characters and their conflicts.

PREVIEWING When you **preview** a text, you look over the material to see what lies ahead. **Scan** (look specifically for) chapter titles, headings, subheadings, and terms printed in boldface or italics. Glance at the illustrations and graphics (such as charts, maps, and time lines), and **skim** (read quickly) a paragraph or two to check the vocabulary level and writing style.

PRIOR KNOWLEDGE The knowledge you already have about a topic before you read a text is called your **prior knowledge.** (*Prior* means "before.")

PROPOSITION AND SUPPORT In a **persuasive text,** the writer's most important idea or opinion, is called a **proposition.** A proposition should be supported by details and evidence. Example of evidence include **facts**, **statistics**, **examples**, **anecdotes** (especially those that tell about personal experiences), and statements or direct **quotations by experts** on the subject.

See pages 249, 759.

PUBLIC DOCUMENTS See *Informational Texts.*

PURPOSES OF TEXTS Texts are written for various purposes. The writer may want to
- inform
- persuade you to think or act a certain way
- express personal feelings
- entertain you

Readers also have different purposes: You read to get information, to enjoy a good story, to share an experience. Being aware of why you are reading helps you to **establish a purpose for reading,** which helps you to decide how you will read the text. If you are reading a science fiction novel just for fun, you might read quickly and eagerly to find out what happens next. If you decide to read that same novel for a book report, however, you would read more slowly and carefully.

You might even re-read some parts of the book to decide how you will evaluate it. Sometimes you read to find an answer to a particular question, such as "Where do penguins live?" To find the answer, you may need to use an index or table of contents first and then skim a text (read quickly) to locate the information you want.

See also *Magazine.*

QUESTIONS One way to monitor your understanding is to ask **questions** as you read. Get in the habit of carrying on a dialogue (in your head or in a reading notebook) with the writer. Make comments, ask questions, and note what puzzles you. Record facts that you might want to verify. Experiment with ways of noting questions, such as using sticky notes that you place by paragraphs. If you find yourself confused by a passage, try one of the following strategies:

- Re-read the passage more slowly.
- Read the passage aloud.
- Put the ideas into your own words.
- Look for context clues that might help you figure out the meaning of an unfamiliar word.
- Use a graphic organizer to jot down the text's ideas.

See also *Detail, Fallacious Reasoning.*

RETELLING A reading strategy called **retelling** helps you understand and recall what you read. As you're reading a text, stop often to retell the important events that have happened up to that point. You might want to tell a partner what has happened, or you can record notes in a reading notebook or journal. Retelling can be used in reading fiction and in reading historical and scientific texts.

See pages 15, 601, 611.
See also *Detail.*

SCANNING When you want to find particular information in a text, you quickly **scan** through it, searching for boldface key words and phrases and any other details that relate to your topic.

See also *Skimming.*

SCOPE The amount of information presented on a given topic is called **scope.** A treatment that covers many aspects of a topic is said to have a **broad** scope. A treatment that narrows the coverage of a topic is said to have a **limited** scope.

See pages 137, 145, 149, 431.
See also *Organizational Patterns, Treatment.*

SKIMMING When you want to quickly get the general idea of what a text is about, you **skim** through it, looking at the titles, heads, subheads, and the first lines of paragraphs.

See page 693.
See also *Scanning.*

SOMEBODY WANTED BUT SO Stories are built on conflict. A good way to summarize a story's plot is to reduce it to the following formula:

Somebody (name the main character):
_____

Wanted (tell what the main character wants):
_____

But (tell what complications develop that get between the main character and what he or she wants):
_____

So (tell how it all comes out in the end):
_____
_____

SPATIAL ORDER Spatial (SPAY shuhl) order is one of the patterns writers use to organize their texts. **Spatial order** shows where things are located. (The word *spatial* is related to the word *space*. Spatial order shows where things are located in space.) Spatial order is often used in descriptive writing. Here is an example from "Camp Harmony" (page 387):

> Our home was one room, about eighteen by twenty feet, the size of a living room. There was one small window in the wall opposite the one door. It was bare except for a small, tinny wood-burning stove crouching in the center.

See also *Organizational Patterns*.

STATISTICS See *Proposition and Support*.

STORY MAP A graphic organizer like the following one can help you map the plot structure of a story:

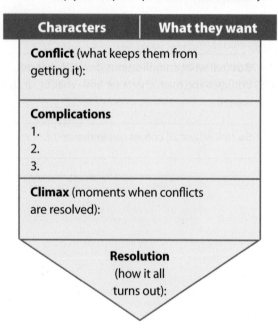

Characters	What they want
Conflict (what keeps them from getting it):	
Complications 1. 2. 3.	
Climax (moments when conflicts are resolved):	

Resolution
(how it all
turns out):

STRUCTURAL PATTERNS All texts have a structure. Without structure a piece of writing would fall apart—just as a house would fall down if its basic structure was faulty. The structure that holds a story together is called its **plot.** The structures that support the details in informative texts can be **chronology, order of importance, comparison and contrast,** or **cause and effect.**

Structural features, such as headings, graphics, captions, and boldface type, may be common to many types of texts. Other features may apply only to specific types of text. For example, only newspaper articles such as "Hawaiian Teen Named Top Young Scientist" (page 146) include datelines.

See pages 751, 759, 769.
See also *Cause and Effect, Chronological Order, Comparison and Contrast, Order of Importance, Organizational Patterns*.

SUMMARIZING When you **summarize**, you mention and explain only the most important ideas of a work. Because a summary is much shorter than the original text, you have to decide which ideas to include and which ones to leave out. To summarize an informational text, start by naming the title, the author, and the subject. Then, go on to state the main ideas and the **key details**, those that support the main idea or underlying meaning. Follow the same order that the writer used. If you quote any of the writer's words, be sure to put quotation marks around them.

See also *Main Idea*.

SUPPORT See *Proposition and Support.*

TECHNICAL DIRECTIONS See *Informational Texts.*

TIME LINE Use a **time line** to find out when events occurred.

A time line may show a vast span of time, such as thousands or millions of years.

Events on a time line are arranged in chronological order, with long-ago events at one end and more recent events at the other. The approximate date (year or century) of each event appears above, below, or beside the line.

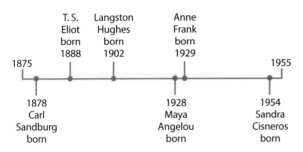

TRANSITIONAL WORDS See *Detail.*

TREATMENT The way of dealing with or discussing a topic or idea is called **treatment.** A section on slavery during the Civil War in a history textbook, for example, would present a thorough, **objective** explanation that would stick to the facts and avoid opinions. An editorial on the ramifications of slavery today might include the writer's **subjective,** or personal, comments and opinions.

See page 736.
See also *Organizational Patterns, Scope.*

UNITY When a text has unity, all its details support the texts main idea or topic. In a unified passage, each sentence relates to a single subject or topic.

See page 736.
See also *Coherence, Nonfiction.*

VISUALIZING When you visualize a text, you picture it in your own mind. You may visualize a character's appearance, the setting, the action, or any other details described in the text.

WORKPLACE DOCUMENTS See *Informational Texts.*

Glossary

The glossary that follows is an alphabetical list of words defined in the selections in this book. Use this glossary just as you would use a dictionary—to find the meaning of unfamiliar words. (Some technical, foreign, and more obscure words in this book are not listed here but instead are defined for you in the footnotes that accompany many of the selections.)

Many words in the English language have more than one meaning. This glossary gives the meanings that apply to the words as they are used in the selections in this book.

The following abbreviations are used:

adj.	adjective
adv.	adverb
n.	noun
v.	verb

Each word's pronunciation is given in parentheses. For more information about the words in this glossary or for information about words not listed here, consult a dictionary

A

abide (uh BYD) (with *by*) *v.* accept and follow.

abnormal (ab NAWR muhl) *adj.* not normal; unusual.

acquisition (ak wuh ZIHSH uhn) *n.* something purchased or gained.

aghast (uh GAST) *adj.* shocked; horrified.

amend (uh MEHND) *v.* make better.

amiably (AY mee uh blee) *adv.* good-naturedly.

ample (AM puhl) *adj.* as much as is needed; enough.

anguish (ANG gwihsh) *n.* emotional pain.

annihilation (uh ny uh LAY shuhn) *n.* complete destruction.

antiquated (AN tuh kway tihd) *adj.* old-fashioned.

appeal (uh PEEL) *n.* request for help or sympathy.

archaic (ahr KAY ihk) *adj.* out of date; old-fashioned.

arrogant (AR uh guhnt) *adj.* overly proud.

audacity (aw DAS uh tee) *n.* boldness.

authentic (aw THEHN tihk) *adj.* genuine.

authorization (aw thuhr uh ZAY shuhn) *n.* official permission.

B

barracks (BAR ehks) *n.* large buildings or groups of buildings in which many people live.

benign (bih NYN) *adj.* kindly; harmless.

boundaries (BOWN duh reez) *n.* where one thing ends and another begins.

breach (breech) *n.* opening caused by a break, such as in a wall or in a line of defense.

C

chaotic (kay AHT ihk) *adj.* confused.

cherished (CHEHR ihsht) *v.* used as *adj.* valued; well-loved.

circuit (SUR kiht) *n.* regular route of a job.

clemency (KLEHM uhn see) *n.* mercy; tolerance.

commemorate (kuh MEHM uh rayt) *v.* honor the memory of.

commotion (kuh MOH shuhn) *n.* noisy confusion; disturbance.

competition (kahm puh TIHSH uhn) *n.* contest.

compressed (kuhm PREHST) *adj.* pressed together.

compressed (kuhm PREHST) *v.* constricted; stifled, as if squeezed.

comrade (KAHM rad) *n.* companion; friend; associate.

conceded (kuhn SEED ihd) *v.* admitted; acknowledged.

confines (KAHN fynz) *n.* borders; boundaries.

conspicuous (kuhn SPIHK yoo uhs) *adj.* noticeable.

contradictory (kahn truh DIHK tuhr ee) *adj.* in disagreement; opposing.

corps (kawr) *n.* group of people with special training; a military unit.

correlate (KAWR uh layt) *v.* show the connection between things.

corresponding (kawr uh SPAHN dihng) *adj.* matching; equivalent.

credulity (kruh DYOO luh tee) *n.* quality of believing too readily.

creed (kreed) *n.* statement of belief or principles.

D

defiance (dih FY uhns) *n.* willingness to fight; rebellious feelings.

denounce (dih NOWNS) *v.* speak against.

derision (dih RIHZH uhn) *n.* contempt; ridicule.

descendants (dih SEHN duhnts) *n.* all the generations who come from one person.

desolate (DEHS uh liht) *adj.* lonely; miserable.

despicable (DEHS pih kuh buhl) *adj.* hateful; detested.

detect (dih TEHKT) *v.* discover; notice.

deterioration (dih tihr ee uh RAY shuhn) *n.* used as *adj.* worsening; declining.

detract (dih TRAKT) *v.* take away from; make less important.

diplomat (DIHP luh mat) *n.* person who handles issues with other countries.

disconnected (dihs kuh NEHK tihd) *v.* used as *adj.* not connected; cut off; separated.

discontinued (dihs kuhn TIHN yood) *v.* used as *adj.* not continued; stopped; ended.

dispel (dihs PEHL) *v.* get rid of by driving away.

displeasure (dihs PLEHZH uhr) *n.* annoyance; dissatisfaction.

dissuade (dih SWAYD) *v.* change someone's mind against; convince not to do.

domination (dahm ih NAY shuhn) *n.* act of controlling; power.

drifting (DRIHF tihng) *v.* being carried along as if by a current of air or water.

drone (drohn) *n.* continuous buzzing sound.

E

eloquence (EHL uh kwehns) *n.* ability to write or speak gracefully and convincingly.

elusive (ih LOO sihv) *adj.* hard to catch.

emaciated (ih MAY shee ay tihd) *v.* used as *adj.* extremely thin, as from starvation.

empowered (ehm POW uhrd) *adj.* given the power to do something.

excessive (ehk SEHS ihv) *adj.* too much; too great.

F

fate (fayt) *n.* what becomes of someone or something.

fatigue (fuh TEEG) *n.* exhaustion; tiredness.

ferocious (fuh ROH shuhs) *adj.* brutal; cruel.

fixated (FIHK sayt uhd) *adj.* focused with full attention.

forlorn (fawr LAWRN) *adj.* abandoned and lonely.

formulated (FAWR myuh lay tihd) *v.* stated clearly and logically.

foster (FAWS tuhr) *adj.* given shelter and care by people other than one's parents.

foundered (FOWN duhrd) *v.* broke down; failed.

frail (frayl) *adj.* weak; fragile.

frayed (frayd) *adj.* worn away; unraveled.

fugitives (FYOO juh tihvz) *n.* people fleeing from danger or oppression.

functions (FUHNGK shuhnz) *n.* uses; purposes.

G

gesticulations (jehs TIHK yuh LAY shuhnz) *n.* energetic movements or gestures.

gnarled (nahrld) *adj.* covered with knots; twisted.

grueling (GROO uhl ihng) *adj.* very tiring; demanding.

H

hazards (HAZ uhrdz) *n.* dangers; things that can cause danger.

hospitality (hahs puh TAL uh tee) *n.* friendly or generous treatment of guests.

host (hohst) *n.* army; large number.

hypocrisy (hih PAHK ruh see) *n.* false show of virtue or goodness.

hypothesis (hy PAHTH uh sihs) *n.* possible explanation or answer.

hysterically (hihs TEHR uh klee) *adv.* in an uncontrolled or wild manner.

I

ignorant (IHG nuhr uhnt) *adj.* without knowledge; uninformed.

immortality (ihm awr TAL uh tee) *n.* endless life.

impeccably (ihm PEHK uh blee) *adv.* flawlessly.

impetuous (ihm PEHCH yoo uhs) *adj.* impulsive; eager.

impromptu (ihm PRAHMP too) *adj.* unplanned.

incentive (ihn SEHN tihv) *n.* reason to do something; motivation.

incomprehensible (ihn kahm prih HEHN suh buhl) *adj.* impossible to understand.

indignantly (ihn DIHG nuhnt lee) *adv.* with anger caused by something felt to be unjust.

inert (ihn URT) *adj.* not moving; still.

inexplicable (ihn ihk SPLIHK uh buhl) *adj.* unable to be explained.

innumerable (ih NOO muhr uh buhl) *adj.* very many.

inquiring (ihn KWYR ihng) *v.* looking for answers; asking.

instinctively (ihn STIHNGK tihv lee) *adv.* automatically.

insulated (IHN suh layt ihd) *v.* shielded; protected.

intensified (ihn TEHN suh fyd) *v.* increased; strengthened.

intently (ihn TEHNT lee) *adv.* with close attention.

intolerant (ihn TAHL uhr uhnt) *adj.* unwilling to accept something.

introspective (ihn truh SPEHK tihv) *adj.* looking inward.

invasion (ihn VAY zhuhn) *n.* act of entering by force.

L

legitimate (luh JIHT uh miht) *adj.* allowed by law.

liable (LY uh buhl) *adj.* legally responsible.

liberation (lihb uh RAY shuhn) *n.* release from imprisonment or enemy occupation.

loathed (lohthd) *v.* hated.

M

majority (muh JAWR uh tee) *n.* larger part of something.

mass (mas) *n.* large group, in this case, of people.

mastered (MAS tuhrd) *v.* made oneself the master of; became skillful at.

merit (MEHR iht) *n.* worth.

mesmerized (MEHS muh ryzd) *v.* used as *adv.* hypnotized.

mimicking (MIHM ihk ihng) *v.* imitating; copying.

mind (mynd) *v.* take care of.

minority (muh NAWR uh tee) *n.* smaller part of something.

misled (mihs LEHD) *v.* fooled; led to believe something wrong.

monopoly (muh NAHP uh lee) *n.* total control over a particular business.

mournful (MAWRN fuhl) *adj.* full of deep sadness.

N

necessarily (nehs uh SAIR uh lee) *adv.* unavoidably; in every case.

negotiated (nih GOH shee ayt ihd) *v.* came to an agreement through discussion; talked.

negotiation (nih goh shee AY shuhn) *n.* process of reaching an agreement.

nobly (NOH blee) *adv.* in a manner that is excellent or heroic.

O

oasis (oh AY sihs) *n.* place or thing offering relief.

obscure (uhb SKYOOR) *v.* hide.

observation (ahb suhr VAY shuhn) *n.* act of noticing.

ominous (AHM uh nuhs) *adj.* threatening.

ostentatiously (ahs tehn TAY shuhs lee) *adv.* in a showy way.

P

patriots (PAY tree uhts) *n.* people who love and support their country.

perpetuate (puhr PEHCH yoo ayt) *v.* cause to continue.

petrified (PEHT ruh fyd) *adj.* paralyzed with fear.

poignant (POYN yuhnt) *adj.* causing sadness or pain; touching.

populated (PAHP yuh layt ihd) *v.* used as *adj.* lived in.

potentially (poh TEHN shuh lee) *adv.* possibly.

premonition (prehm uh NIHSH uhn) *n.* feeling that something will happen.

presumptuous (prih ZUHMP choo uhs) *adj.* overly bold or confident; expecting too much.

probing (PROHB ihng) *v.* used as *adj.* searching or investigating.

procession (proh SEHSH uhn) *n.* parade.

prodigy (PROD uh jee) *n.* child with exceptional talent.

proposal (pruh POHZ uhl) *n.* suggestion.

prototype (PROH tuh typ) *n.* first or original model of something.

proximity (prahk SIHM uh tee) *n.* state of being close by; nearness.

purge (purj) *v.* get rid of something harmful.

R

raucous (RAW kuhs) *adj.* loud and rough.

recite (rih SYT) *v.* present a memorized text orally, often in a formal manner.

recreation (rehk ree AY shuhn) *n.* used as *adj.* relaxation; amusement.

refugees (rehf yoo JEEZ) *n.* people who seek refuge, or safety, especially in another country.

regression (rih GREHSH uhn) *n.* return to an earlier or less advanced condition.

rehabilitate (ree huh BIHL uh tayt) *v.* restore to good standing.

reigns (raynz) *v.* dominates; exists.

re-invented (ree in VEHNT ihd) *v.* created again, or made new.

reputation (rehp yuh TAY shuhn) *n.* way others see a person.

resembles (rih ZEHM buhlz) *v.* looks like.

riveted (RIHV iht ihd) *v.* used as *adj.* intensely focused on.

rueful (ROO fuhl) *adj.* regretful.

ruefully (ROO fuhl lee) *adv.* with regret and embarrassment.

ruin (ROO uhn) *n.* great damage; devastation.

S

scholarship (SKAHL uhr shihp) *n.* money given to help a student continue to study.

scorn (skawrn) *n.* obvious disrespect or dislike for someone or something.

secure (sih KYUR) *v.* fix firmly in place.

serene (suh REEN) *adj.* calm; undisturbed.

shunning (SHUHN ihng) *v.* avoiding; having little to do with.

solace (SAHL ihs) *n.* comfort.

somber (SAHM buhr) *adj.* dark, melancholy.

spent (spehnt) *adj.* worn-out.

spirit (SPIHR iht) *n.* courage; liveliness.

staff (staf) *n.* pole.

stirred (sturd) *v.* moved; roused.

stoically (STOH uh kuhl lee) *adv.* here, stubbornly.

subject (SUHB jehkt) *adj.* likely to have; having a tendency.

suffrage (SUHF rihj) *n.* right to vote.

summoned (SUHM uhnd) *v.* called; requested to come.

superiors (suh PIHR ee uhrz) *n.* people of higher rank.

T

taut (tawt) *adj.* pulled tight.

tax (taks) *v.* here, burden; strain.

tedious (TEE dee uhs) *adj.* long and boring.

teeming (TEEM ihng) *adj.* full (in this case, of people); crowded.

tentatively (TEHN tuh tihv lee) *adv.* in an uncertain or hesitant way.

tersely (TURS lee) *adv.* briefly and clearly; without unnecessary words.

tranquility (trang KWIHL uh tee) *n.* calm; peace.

traumatic (traw MAT ihk) *adj.* emotionally painful; causing shock.

tread (trehd) *n.* footstep.

tremor (TREHM uhr) *n.* shaking movement; vibration.

tyranny (TIHR uh nee) *n.* cruel and unjust use of power.

V

vaguely (VAYG lee) *adv.* unclearly.

vehemently (VEE uh muhnt lee) *adv.* forcefully; passionately.

verify (VEHR uh fy) *v.* show to be true; confirm.

versatility (vur suh TIHL uh tee) *n.* ability to do many things well.

vexed (vehkst) *v.* disturbed; annoyed.

vigil (VIHJ uhl) *n.* keeping guard; act of staying awake to keep watch.

vile (vyl) *adj.* very unpleasant.

vital (VY tuhl) *adj.* of great importance or need.

W

weathered (WEHTH uhrd) *v.* survived; came through safely.

wholesome (HOHL suhm) *adj.* good for the mind and spirit.

writhed (rythd) *v.* twisted and turned.

Y

yearning (YURN ihng) *v.* used as *adj.* longing for; wanting badly.

Spanish Glossary

A

aborrecer *v.* odiar.

abundante *adj.* suficiente; tanto como se necesite.

acogido *adj.* que otras personas distintas de sus padres lo llevaron a su hogar y lo cuidaron.

acongojado *adj.* que tiene una tristeza profunda.

admitir *v.* reconocer; aceptar.

adquisición *sust.* algo que se compra o se obtiene.

afablemente *adv.* con amabilidad.

aislar *v.* apartar, proteger.

alivio *sust.* consuelo.

angustia *sust.* sensación de dolor o sufrimiento emocional.

anhelo *sust.* ansia; deseo grande.

aniquilación *sust.* destrucción completa.

anormal *adj.* que no es normal; inusual.

anticuado *adj.* pasado de moda.

apesadumbradamente *adv.* con arrepentimiento y vergüenza.

apreciado *adj.* valorado, querido.

arcaico *adj.* muy viejo o anticuado.

arrogante *adj.* excesivamente orgulloso.

asegurar *v.* fijar con firmeza en el lugar.

asemejarse *v.* ser parecido a.

atender *v.* ocuparse de.

atenerse *v.* aceptar algo y actuar acorde a ello.

atentamente *adv.* prestando mucha atención.

aterrorizado *adj.* alarmado; horrorizado.

audacia *sust.* atrevimiento; osadía.

autorización *sust.* permiso oficial.

autorizado *adj.* que tiene el poder de hacer algo.

B

barraca *sust.* edificio grande o grupo de edificios en los que viven muchas personas.

bastón *sust.* palo; poste.

beca *sust.* dinero que se da a un estudiante para que continúe sus estudios.

benigno *adj.* amable; inofensivo.

brecha *sust.* abertura, en general se refiere a una ruptura en una pared o en una línea de defensa.

C

camarada *sust.* compañero; amigo; socio.

caótico *adj.* confuso.

chillón *adj.* ruidoso y brusco.

circuito *sust.* recorrido habitual.

clemencia *sust.* compasión; tolerancia.

competición *sust.* competencia; partido.

comprimido *adj.* apretado.

comprimir *v.* apretar; contener; reducir.

confines *sust.* fronteras; límites.

conmemorar *v.* honrar la memoria de alguien.

conmoción *sust.* gran confusión; perturbación.

conmovedor *adj.* que causa tristeza o dolor; tierno.

conmover *v.* emocionar profundamente.

contorsionarse *v.* retorcerse.

contradictorio *adj.* que está en desacuerdo; que se opone.

convocar *v.* llamar; pedir que alguien asista a un lugar.

correlacionar *v.* establecer una relación entre dos o más cosas.

correspondiente *adj.* que coincide con algo; equivalente.

credo *sust.* proclamación de las creencias o principios.

credulidad *sust.* tendencia a creer algo con mucha facilidad.

cuerpo *sust.* grupo de personas con entrenamiento especial; unidad militar.

D

demacrar *v.* provocar extrema delgadez, por ejemplo, a causa del hambre.

denunciar *v.* expresarse en contra de algo.

deriva (ir a la) loc. *adv.* moverse empujado por una corriente de aire o agua.

desamparado *adj.* solo y abandonado.

descendientes *sust.* todas las generaciones que vienen de una persona.

desconectado *adj.* que no está conectado; aislado; separado.

desdén *sust.* falta de respeto o antipatía evidente por alguien o algo.

desmerecer *v.* quitar importancia; restar mérito.

desolado *adj.* desierto; triste.

despreciable *adj.* odioso; detestable.

destino *sust.* lo que le sucederá a alguien en el futuro.

detectar *v.* descubrir; darse cuenta de algo.

deteriorado *adj.* estropeado; dañado.

diplomático *sust.* persona que se encarga de las relaciones con otros países.

disgusto *sust.* desagrado; insatisfacción.

disipar *v.* hacer que algo desaparezca.

disuadir *v.* aconsejar a alguien que no haga algo; convencerlo para que no lo haga.

diversión *sust.* regocijo; pasatiempo.

dominación *sust.* acción de controlar; poder.

dominar *v.* sobresalir en algo; adquirir la habilidad de hacer algo.

dudosamente *adv.* de manera incierta o dubitativa.

E

elocuencia *sust.* habilidad para hablar o escribir con gracia y de manera convincente.

embaucar *v.* engañar; hacer creer a alguien algo que no es cierto.

emular *v.* imitar; copiar.

endeble *adj.* débil; frágil.

enmendar *v.* corregir, mejorar.

escarnio *sust.* desdén; burla.

escurridizo *adj.* difícil de atrapar.

espíritu *sust.* vigor; vivacidad.

estoicamente *adv.* aquí, testarudamente.

examinar *v.* investigar, explorar.

excesivo *adj.* que es demasiado; exagerado; desmesurado.

extenuante *adj.* que cansa; agotador.

F

fascinar *v.* hipnotizar.

fatiga *sust.* agotamiento; cansancio.

feroz *adj.* brutal; cruel.

formular *v.* explicar de manera clara y lógica.

fugitivo *sust.* persona que escapa del peligro o la opresión.

función *sust.* uso; objetivo.

G

genuino *adj.* auténtico.

gesticulación *sust.* movimientos enérgicos.

gravar *v.* aquí, cargar, pesar sobre alguien o algo.

H

hipocresía *sust.* acto de fingir virtudes o bondad.

hipótesis *sust.* explicación o repuesta posible.

histéricamente *adv.* de manera salvaje e incontrolada.

hospitalidad *sust.* trato generoso y amigable hacia los invitados.

hueste *sust.* ejército.

I

ignorante adj. alguien sin conocimientos; mal informado.

impecablemente *adv.* sin errores.

impetuoso *adj.* impulsivo; precipitado.

improvisado *adj.* que no estaba planeado.

incentivo *sust.* razón para hacer algo; motivación.

incomprensible *adj.* imposible de entender.

indagar *v.* buscar respuestas, preguntar.

indignadamente *adv.* con enojo causado por algo que se siente como una injusticia.

inerte *adj.* que no se mueve; quieto.

inexplicable *adj.* que no se puede explicar.

inmortalidad *sust.* vida sin fin.

innumerable *adj.* numeroso; incalculable.

inquietante *adj.* amenazante.

instintivamente *adv.* automáticamente.

intensificar *v.* aumentar, reforzar.

interrumpir *v.* hacer que algo se detenga, que no continúe.

intolerante *adj.* que no está dispuesto a aceptar algo.

introspectivo *adj.* que mira hacia el interior de sí mismo.

invasión *adj.* acto de entrar por la fuerza.

irritar *sust.* molestar; enojar.

L

lacónicamente *adv.* de manera breve y concisa; sin palabras innecesarias.

legítimo *adj.* permitido por la ley.

liberación *sust.* acto de dejar salir de prisión o liberar de la ocupación enemiga.

límites *sust.* línea que separa el fin de una cosa del principio de otra.

llamativo *adj.* que atrae la atención.

M

masa *sust.* grupo grande de personas.

mayoría *sust.* la mayor cantidad; la mayor parte de algo.

mérito *sust.* valor.

minoría *sust.* la menor cantidad; la menor parte de algo.

monopolio *sust.* control total sobre un negocio específico.

N

necesariamente *adv.* que no se puede evitar; en todos los casos.

negociación *sust.* proceso para llegar a un acuerdo.

negociar *v.* llegar a un acuerdo mediante el debate; hablar.

noblemente *adv.* de manera excepcional o heroica.

nudoso *adj.* lleno de nudos; retorcido.

O

oasis *sust.* lugar o cosa que ofrece alivio.

observación *sust.* acto de notar algo o darse cuenta de algo.

obsesionado *adj.* que centra toda su atención en algo.

ocultar *v.* esconder.

ostentosamente *adv.* de manera pomposa.

P

paso *sust.* pisada. **patriota** *sust.* persona que ama y apoya a su país.

perpetuar *v.* hacer que algo continúe.

pesaroso *adj.* arrepentido.

petrificado *adj.* paralizado por el miedo.

poblar *v.* vivir en.

potencialmente *adv.* posiblemente.

premonición *sust.* sentimiento de que algo malo va a suceder.

presuntuoso *adj.* que tiene demasiada seguridad en sí mismo; que pretende demasiado.

procesión *sust.* desfile.

prodigio *sust.* niño que tiene un talento excepcional.

propuesta *sust.* sugerencia.

prototipo *sust.* primer modelo o modelo original de algo.

proximidad *sust.* cercanía.

purgar *v.* deshacerse de algo que hace daño.

Q

quebrar *v.* hundirse; irse a pique.

R

raído *adj.* gastado en los bordes.

rebeldía *sust.* acto de oponerse a algo o a alguien con seguridad y determinación.

recitar *v.* repetir en voz alta, a menudo de manera formal.

refugiado *sust.* persona que busca refugio o seguridad, especialmente en otro país.

regresión *sust.* vuelta a una etapa anterior o menos avanzada.

rehabilitar *v.* hacer volver a un buen estado o posición.

rehuir *v.* evitar; rechazar.

reinar *v.* dominar, existir.

reinventar *v.* volver a crear algo nuevo.

repleto *adj.* lleno (en este caso, de personas); atestado.

reputación *sust.* opinión que tienen otras personas de uno.

responsable *adj.* que tiene que responder por algo.

riesgos *sust.* peligros; cosas que pueden ocasionar peligros.

ruina *sust.* daño grande; devastación.

S

saludable *adj.* bueno para el cuerpo y el alma.

sereno *adj.* en calma; tranquilo.

sombrío *adj.* oscuro; melancólico.

sortear *v.* sobrellevar; sobrevivir a algo y quedar a salvo.

sufragio *sust.* el derecho al voto.

sujeto *adj.* propenso; que tiene tendencia a.

sumirse *v.* concentrarse mucho en algo.

superior *sust.* persona que tiene un cargo o rango más alto.

súplica *sust.* petición de ayuda o compasión.

T

tedioso *adj.* extenso y aburrido.

temblor *sust.* sacudida; vibración.

tenso *adj.* tirante.

tiranía *sust.* ejercicio del poder de una manera cruel e injusta.

tranquilidad *sust.* calma; paz.

traumático *adj.* doloroso emocionalmente; que causa una impresión fuerte.

U

usado *adj.* gastado.

V

vagamente *adv.* sin claridad.

vehementemente *adv.* con fuerza; apasionadamente.

verificar *v.* probar que algo es cierto; confirmar.

versatilidad *sust.* habilidad para hacer bien muchas cosas.

vigilia *sust.* vigilancia; acción de estar despierto para hacer guardia.

vil *adj.* muy desagradable.

vital *adj.* de gran importancia o necesidad.

Z

zumbido *sust.* ruido continuo y bronco.

Academic Vocabulary Glossary

English/Spanish

The Academic Vocabulary Glossary in this section is an alphabetical list of the Academic Vocabulary words defined in this textbook. Use this glossary just as you would use a dictionary—to find out the meanings of words used in your literature class to talk about and write about literary and informational texts and to talk about and write about concepts and topics in your other academic classes.

For each word, the glossary includes the pronunciation, part of speech, and meaning. A Spanish version of the glossary immediately follows the English version. For more information about the words in the Academic Vocabulary Glossary, please consult a dictionary.

English

A

analyze (AN uh lyz) *v.* examine in detail.

approach (uh PROHCH) *n.* method or style of doing something.

articulate (ahr TIHK yuh layt) *v.* clearly express in words.

aspect (AS pehkt) *n.* one part of a situation, plan, or subject.

associations (uh soh see AY shuhnz) *n.* connections in the mind between different things.

attitude (AT uh tood) *n.* way of thinking about or viewing something.

C

characteristics (kar ihk tuh RIHS tihks) *n.* qualities or features of something.

coherence (koh HIHR uhns) *n.* clarity; logical connection.

complex (kuhm PLEHKS) *adj.* complicated; difficult to understand.

consistency (kuhn SIHS tuhn see) *n.* uniformity; regularity.

contemporary (kuhn TEHM puh rehr ee) *adj.* in the style of present time; modern.

critical (KRIHT uh kuhl) *adj.* vital, very important.

criticism (KRIHT uh sihz uhm) *n.* analysis and judgment of a work's strengths and weaknesses.

critique (krih TEEK) *v.* judge the quality of.

D

device (dih VYS) *n.* method used to produce a specific effect.

distinctive (dihs TIHNGK tihv) *adj.* special; different from others.

E

elements (EHL uh muhnts) *n.:* parts of which things are made up.

evaluate (ih VAL yoo ayt) *v.* judge.

evident (EHV uh duhnt) *adj.* plain; clear; obvious.

expository (ehk SPAHZ uh tawr ee) *adj.* containing an explanation.

F

factor (FAK tuhr) *n.* something that has an influence on something else.

I

insight (IHN syt) *n.* act of understanding how things work or how people think or act.

intent (ihn TEHNT) *n.* purpose; plan; aim.

interact (ihn tuhr AKT) *v.* behave toward one another.

interpret (ihn TUR priht) *v.* decide the intended meaning of something.

M

motivation (moh tuh VAY shuhn) *n.* reasons behind a person's action or actions.

R

reaction (ree AK shuhn) *n.* action in response to an influence or force.

relevance (REHL uh vuhns) *n.* quality of being important or meaningful.

response (rih SPAHNS) *n.* reply or reaction.

S

significant (sihg NIHF uh kuhnt) *adj.* meaningful; important.

specify (SPEHS uh fy) *v.* mention or describe in detail; give as a condition.

structural (STRUHK chuhr uhl) *adj.* associated with the arrangement of parts.

T

tradition (truh DIHSH uhn) *n.* a custom, belief, or way of doing things that is handed down, as in families.

traditional (truh DIHSH uh nuhl) *adj.* handed down, usually by word of mouth.

Spanish

A

actitud *sust.* manera de pensar o de ver las cosas.

analizar *v.* examinar en profundidad.

asociación *sust.* relación que se hace mentalmente entre cosas distintas.

aspecto *sust.* parte de una situación, plan o tema.

C

características *sust.* cualidades o rasgos de algo.

coherencia *sust.* conexión lógica; claridad.

complejo *adj.* complicado; difícil de entender.

constante *adj.* uniforme; que no varía.

contemporáneo *adj.* perteneciente al tiempo o época en el que se vive; moderno.

contribuir *v.* participar; colaborar.

crítica sust. análisis y opinión sobre los puntos fuertes y débiles de algo.

crìtico *adj.* vital; muy importante.

D

definir *v.* aclarar el significado de algo; explicar.

distintivo *adj.* característico; que lo hace diferente de otros.

E

elocuencia *sust.* expresar claramente mediante palabras.

enfatizar *v.* dar importancia; prestar especial atención a algo.

enfoque *sust.* método o estilo para hacer algo.

especificar *v.* explicar o describir en detalle; fijar una condición.

establecer *v.* instaurar; crear.

estratagema *sust.* método utilizado para conseguir una cosa.

estructural *adj.* manera en la que se disponen partes de una cosa. evaluar *v.* juzgar.

evaluar v. juzgar.

evidente *adj.* patente; claro; obvio.

explicativo *adj.* que contiene una explicación.

expresar *v.* demostrar; poner en palabras.

F

factor *sust.* algo que influye en otra cosa.

I

intención *sust.* objetivo; plan; propósito.

interactuar *v.* actuar conjuntamente.

interpretar *v.* decidir el verdadero significado de alguna cosa.

M

motivación *sust.* razones tras los actos de una persona.

P

perspicacia *sust.* capacidad para entender cómo funcionan las cosas o cómo piensan las personas.

R

reacción *sust.* respuesta.

relevancia *sust.* significativo; importante.

réplica *sust.* respuesta o reacción.

representar *v.* comunicar, expresar.

resultado *sust.* efecto; conclusión.

revelar *v.* dar a conocer.

S

significativo *adj.* importante.

suscitar *v.* provocar.

T

tradición *sust.* costrumbres, valores o ideas que se pasan de una generación a otra.

tradicional *adj.* que pasa de una generación a otra, por lo general verbalmente.

ACKNOWLEDGMENTS

For permission to reproduce copyrighted material, grateful acknowledgment is made to the following sources:

"Hawaiian Teen Named Top Young Scientist." Copyright © 2006 by **The Associated Press** and MetroSource. Reproduced by permission of the publisher.

"My Mother Pieced Quilts" by **Teresa Palomo Acosta** from *Festival de Flor y Canto: An Anthology of Chicano Literature,* edited by Alurista et al. Copyright © 1976 by El Centro Chicano, University of Southern California. Reproduced by permission of the author.

From "Oda a las gracias" from *Navegaciones y Regresos* by Pablo Neruda. Copyright © 1959, 2007 by Fundación Pablo Neruda. Reproduced by permission of **Agencia Literaria Carmen Balcells on behalf of Fundación Pablo Neruda.**

"The Treasure of Lemon Brown" by Walter Dean Myers from *Boys' Life Magazine,* March 1983. Copyright © 1983 by Walter Dean Myers. Reproduced by permission of **Miriam Altshuler Literary Agency, on behalf of Walter Dean Myers.**

Quote by James Baldwin from *Nobody Knows My Name: More Notes of a Native Son.* Copyright © 1954, 1956, 1958, 1959, 1960, 1961 by James Baldwin. Published by Vintage Books. Reproduced by permission of the **James Baldwin Estate.**

From "A Smart Cookie" from *The House on Mango Street* by Sandra Cisneros. Copyright © 1984 by Sandra Cisneros. Published by Vintage Books, a division of Random House, Inc., and in hardcover by Alfred A. Knopf in 1994. All rights reserved. Reproduced by permission of **Susan Bergholz Literary Services, New York, NY and Lamy, NM.**

"Gil's Furniture Bought and Sold" from *The House on Mango Street* by Sandra Cisneros. Copyright © 1984 by Sandra Cisneros. Published by Vintage Books, a division of Random House, Inc., and in hardcover by Alfred A. Knopf in 1994. All rights reserved. Reproduced by permission of **Susan Bergholz Literary Services, New York.**

"Redwing Sonnets" from *Homecoming: New and Collected Poems* by Julia Alvarez. Copyright © 1984, 1996 by Julia Alvarez. Published by Plume, an imprint of The Penguin Group (USA); originally published by Grove Press. All rights reserved. Reproduced by permission of **Susan Bergholz Literary Services, New York and Lamy, NM.**

"Valentine for Ernest Mann" from *Red Suitcase: Poems* by Naomi Shihab Nye. Copyright © 1994 by Naomi Shihab Nye. Reproduced by permission of **BOA Editions, Ltd.**

From *The Glass Menagerie* by Tennessee Williams. Copyright © 1945 by Tennessee Williams and Edwina D. Williams; copyright renewed © 1973 by Tennessee Williams. Reproduced by permission of **Georges Borchardt, Inc.**

From *Adrift: Seventy-Six Days Lost at Sea* by **Steven Callahan.** Copyright © 1986 by Steven Callahan. All rights reserved. "The Word" by Manuel Ulacia, translated by Jennifer Clement. Translation copyright © 1995 by **Jennifer Clement.** Reproduced by permission of the translator.

"An Air of Duty and Discipline" by Barbara Krasner-Khait from *Calliope* ©, vol. 12, no.9, May 2002. Copyright © 2002 by **Cobblestone Publishing Company,** 30 Grove Street, Suite C, Peterborough, NH 03458. All rights reserved. Reproduced by permission of the publisher.

"The Cook Legacy" by Robson from *Calliope* ©, vol. 12, no. 9, May 2002. Copyright © 2002 by **Cobblestone Publishing Company,** 30 Grove Street, Suite C, Peterborough, NH 03458. All rights reserved. Reproduced by permission of the publisher.

"The Inn of Lost Time" by Lensey Namioka from **Short Stories by Outstanding Writers for Young Adults,** edited by Donald R. Gallo. Copyright © 1989 by Lensey Namioka. All rights reserved. Reproduced by permission of **Ruth Cohen, for Lensey Namioka.**

"The Flying Machine" from *Golden Apples of the Sun* by Ray Bradbury. Copyright © 1953 and renewed © 1986 by Ray Bradbury. Reproduced by permission of **Don Congdon Associates, Inc.**

"The Fog Horn" by Ray Bradbury from *The Saturday Evening Post,* June 23, 1951. Copyright © 1951 by the Curtis Publishing Company; copyright renewed © 1979 by Ray Bradbury. Reproduced by permission of **Don Congdon Associates, Inc**

The Dragon (Graphic Version) by Ray Bradbury with art by Vicente Segrelles. Copyright © 1955 and renewed © 1983 by Ray Bradbury. Reproduced by permission of *Don Congdon Associates, Inc.*

Introduction to *The Dragon* (Graphic Version) by Ray Bradbury with art by Vicente Segrelles. Copyright © 1955 and renewed © 1983 by Ray Bradbury. Reproduced by permission of **Don Congdon Associates, Inc.**

From "A Shot at It" from *When I Was Puerto Rican* by Esmeralda Santiago. Copyright © 1993 by Esmeralda Santiago. Reproduced by permission of **Da Capo Press, a member of Perseus Books, L.L.C.**

From *The Cay* by Theodore Taylor. Copyright © 1969 by Theodore Taylor. Reproduced by permission of **Doubleday, a division of Random House, Inc.** and electronic format by permission of **Watkins/Loomis Agency, Inc.**

From *The Diary of a Young Girl: The Definitive Edition* by Anne Frank, edited by Otto H. Frank and Mirjam Pressler, translated by Susan Massoty. Copyright © 1995 by Doubleday, a division of Random House, Inc. Reproduced by permission of **Doubleday, a division of Random House, Inc., www.randomhouse.com.**

"The Puppy" from *Stories and Prose Poems* by Alexander Solzhenitsyn, translated by Michael Glenny. Translation copyright © 1971 by Michael Glenny. Reproduced by permission of **Farrar, Straus and Giroux, LLC.**

"Dancer" from *Simple Songs* by Vickie Sears. Copyright © 1990 by Vickie Sears. Reproduced by permission of **Firebrand Books.**

Sources Cited:

Quotations by Sandra Cisneros from *Interviews with Writers of the Post-Colonial World,* conducted and edited by Feroza Jussawalla and Reed Way Dasenbrock. Published by University Press of Mississippi, Jackson, MI, 1992.

Quotations by Francisco Jimenez from *Santa Clara Magazine,* vol. 38, no. 2, Spring 1999. Published by Santa Clara University, Santa Clara, CA.

PICTURE CREDITS

American Art Museum, Washington, D.C./Art Resource, NY; **198** (l), ©Richard Meek/Time & Life Pictures/Getty Images; (r), ©Scott Lituchy/Star Ledger/CORBIS; **200-208** (border), amygdala imagery/ShutterStock; **200** (b), ©CORBIS; **201** (b), ©CORBIS; **203,** ©Bettmann/CORBIS; **205** (b), ©Mary Evans Picture Library/ Alamy; **206,** (detail) Collection of The New-York Historical Society, Album file, PR-002-347.20; Digital id #aa02038; negative #37629; **212** (t), United States Holocaust Memorial Museum, Courtesy of Markus & Mary Nowogrodzki; (b), ©AP Images/ Kevin Frayer; **214** (l), Photo courtesy of Ken Mochizuki and Lee & Low Books; (r), ©Wolfgang KaehlerAlamy; **215** (l, r), United States Holocaust Memorial Museum, Courtesy of Markus & Mary Nowogrodzki; **218-219** (bkgd), United States Holocaust Memorial Museum, courtesy of Markus & Mary Nowogrodzki; **218** (l), United States Holocaust Memorial Museum, Courtesy of Hiroki Sugihara; (r), Photo by Setsuko Kikuchi, United States Holocaust Memorial Museum, Courtesy of Hiroki Sugihara; **219** (r), Courtesy Visas for Life Foundation; **228** (t), ©Dave Allocca/ DMI/Time & Life Pictures/Getty Images; (b), ©Frank Cantor; **230,** Gift of the Harmon Foundation. Smithsonian American Art Museum, Washington, DC, U.S.A./Art Resource, NY; **231,** Smithsonian American Art Museum, Washington, DC, U.S.A./Art Resource, NY; **235** (bkgd), Uladzimir Bakunovich/iStockphoto; **237** (t), Courtesy Babcock Galleries; **238** (bkgd), Uladzimir Bakunovich/iStockphoto; **240** (bkgd), Uladzimir Bakunovich/ iStockphoto; (b), ©Michael Newman/PhotoEdit, Inc.; **243** (bkgd), Uladzimir Bakunovich/iStockphoto; (t), ©Peter Hvizdak/The Image Works; **248,** ©AP Images/Mary Ataffer; **255** (tr), Robyn Beck/AFP/Getty Images; (bl), ©Rachel Epstein/The Image Works; **256** (b), Photo by Justin Sullivan/Getty Images; **262,** (bl) Victoria Smith/HRW; **280** (tl), Cover image from *The Clay Marble* by Minfong Ho. Copyright ©1991 by Holt, Rinehart and Winston. Reproduced by permission of the publisher; (tr), Cover image from *North by Night* by Katherine Ayres. Copyright ©1998 by Dell Publishing, a division of Random House, Inc. Reproduced by permission of the publisher; (bl), Cover image from *Call Me Maria* by Judith Ortiz Cofer. Cover illustration copyright ©2004 by Scholastic Inc. Reproduced by permission of Orchard Books, an imprint of Scholastic Inc.; (br), Cover image from *The Call of the Wild* by Jack London. Copyright ©1998 by Holt, Rinehart and Winston. Reproduced by permission of the publisher; **281** (tl), Cover image from *The Story of My Life* by Helen Keller. Copyright ©1990 by Bantam Books, a division of Random House, Inc. Reproduced by permission of the publisher; (tr), Cover image from *Freedom's Children* by Ellen Levine. Copyright ©1993 by Puffin Books, a division of Penguin Group (USA) Inc. Reproduced by permission of the publisher; (bl), Cover image from *Rescue: The Story of How Gentiles Saved Jews in the Holocaust* by Milton Metzer. Copyright ©1988 by HarperCollins Children's Books, a division of HarperCollins Publishers, Inc. Reproduced by permission of the publisher; (br), Cover image from *Lives of the Musicians* by Kathleen Krull. Copyright ©1993 by Harcourt, Inc. Reproduced by permission of the publisher; **283** (r), ©Herbert Spichtinger/zefa/CORBIS; **288** (shadow behind type), ©Getty Images; **289** (bl), from *The People Could Fly* by Virginia Hamilton, illustrated by Leo and Diane Dillon. Illustrations copyright ©1985 by Leo and Diane Dillon. Used by permission of Alfred A.

Knopf, an imprint of Random House Children's Books, a division of Random House, Inc.; **291** (t), From *The People Could Fly* by Virginia Hamilton, illustrated by Leo and Diane Dillon. Illustrations copyright ©1985 by Leo and Diane Dillon. Used by permission of Alfred A. Knopf, an imprint of Random House Children's Books, a division of Random House, Inc.; **292** (l), ©Getty Images; (bl), ©Arnold Adoff, used by permission; (br), ©Layne Kennedy/CORBIS; **294** (bkgd), ©Anne Frank House/ Hulton Archive/Getty Images; (foreground), ©Anne Frank House/Hulton Archive/Getty Images; **296,** ©Bettmann/CORBIS; **297,** ©Anne Frank House/Hulton Archive/Getty Images; **298** (l), ©Hulton-Deutsch Collection/CORBIS; **299** (bkgd), Maxim Pushkarev/iStockphoto; (tr), Library of Congress; (cl), ©Anne Frank House/Hulton Archive/Getty Images; **300** (bkgd), Maxim Pushkarev/iStockphoto; (r), ©Bettmann/CORBIS; **301** (bkgd), Maxim Pushkarev/iStockphoto; (bkgd), ©PEDRO UGARTE/AFP/ Getty Images; **304,** ©Anne Frank House/Hulton Archive/Getty Images; **309** (b), ©Anne Frank House/Hulton Archive/Getty Images; **311** (bkgd), Maxim Pushkarev/iStockphoto; **312** (b), ©Anne Frank House/Hulton Archive/Getty Images; **319** (bkgd), Maxim Pushkarev/iStockphoto; **320** (l, r), Netherlands Institute for War Documentation; **323** (b), ©Anne Frank House/Hulton Archive/Getty Images; **324** (bkgd), Maxim Pushkarev/ iStockphoto; **327,** Dutch Resistance Museum, Amsterdam; **329,** **333** (r), ©Anne Frank House/Hulton Archive/Getty Images; **340-341** (t), ©AP Images/Charles Rex Arbogast; **341,** ©Purestock/ Getty Images; **347** (bkgd), Maxim Pushkarev/iStockphoto; **349** (b), ©Anne Frank House/Hulton Archive/Getty Images; **351** (bkgd), Maxim Pushkarev/iStockphoto; **353,** ©James P. Blair/ CORBIS; **354,** ©Anne Frank House/Hulton Archive/Getty Images; **359** (bkgd), Maxim Pushkarev/iStockphoto; **361** (b), ©Anne Frank House/Hulton Archive/Getty Images; **362** (tr), Cameramann International; **363** (br), Cover image from *Immigrant Kids* by Russell Freedman. Copyright ©1980 by Puffin Books, a division of Random House, Inc. Reproduced by permission of the publisher; **367** (bkgd), Maxim Pushkarev/ iStockphoto; **369** (l, r), ©Anne Frank House/Hulton Archive/ Getty Images; **370** (t), ©Anne Frank House/Hulton Archive/Getty Images; (b), Maria Austria/Maria Austria Institute; **380** (bkgd), ©Anne Frank House/Hulton Archive/Getty Images; **381** (bkgd, r), ©Anne Frank House/Hulton Archive/Getty Images; **382** (bkgd), ©Anne Frank House/Hulton Archive/Getty Images; **386** (t), Photo Courtesy of Monica Sone; (c), courtesy of Dwight Okita; **388, 390,** Fair Street Pictures; **392,** Department of Special Collections, Young Research Library, University of California, Los Angeles. Box 719. Estelle Ishigo Papers (Collection 2010); **394,** ©Cynthia Hart, Designer/CORBIS; **398,** Kevin Dietsch/UPI/ Landov; **400** (t), ©Picture History; (b), ©CORBIS; **401,** ©David Buffington/Photodisc/Getty Images; **403,** ©Jeff Greenberg/The Image Works; **405** (border), ©M. Timothy O'Keefe/Alamy; **406** (bkgd), ©M. Timothy O'Keefe/Alamy; (t), ©Peter Turnley/CORBIS; **410,** ©David Sutherland/CORBIS; **412,** ©Michael St. Maur Sheil/ CORBIS; **415** (bkgd), ©Bettmann/CORBIS; (r), ©Michael Jenner/ Robert Harding World Imagery/Getty Images; **417,** ©Anne Frank House/Hulton Archive/Getty Images; **420** (t), ©epa/CORBIS; (b), ©Hulton Archive/Getty Images; **423,** United States Holocaust Memorial Museum; **425,** ©Sean Gallup/Getty Images; **426, 428,**

Tribune; **590,** Regional Gallery of Art, Astrakhan, Russia, Scala/ Art Resource, NY; **593** (bkgd), ©Charles O'Rear/CORBIS; (b), ©Randy Wells/Photographer's Choice/Getty Images; **594** (border), ©Charles O'Rear/CORBIS; (tl), Cover image from *The Glory Field* by Walter Dean Myers. Copyright ©1994 by Holt, Rinehart and Winston. Reproduced by permission of the publisher; (tr), Cover image from *Little Women* by Louisa May Alcott. Copyright ©1994 by Tom Doherty Associates, LLC. Reproduced by permission of the publisher; **595** (border), ©Charles O'Rear/CORBIS; (t), ©Kevin Fleming/CORBIS; (tl), Cover image from *The Boys' War* by Jim Murphy. Copyright ©1990 by Houghton Mifflin Company. Reproduced by permission of the publisher; (bl), Cover image from *Behind Rebel Lines* by Seymour Riet. Copyright ©1988 by Harcourt, Inc. Reproduced by permission of the publisher; (br), Cover image from *To Be a Slave* by Julius Lester. Copyright ©1968 by Penguin Putnam Books for Young Readers, a division of Penguin Group (USA) Inc. Reproduced by permission of the publisher; **596-597,** Stefano Paltera/North American Solar Challenge; **596** (border), ©Charles O'Rear/CORBIS; **597** (r), Stefano Paltera/North American Solar Challenge; ©Bettmann/CORBIS; **598** (bkgd), ©Charles O'Rear/ CORBIS; (b), Simple Stock Shots/IPN Stock Independent Photo Network; **601,** Alvin Ailey/Andrew Eccles/JBGPhoto; **602,** ©AP Images; **603** (t), Daryl Pederson/AlaskaStock Images; (b), Jeff Schultz/AlaskaStock Images; **604-605** (b), Jeff Schultz/ AlaskaStock Images; **604,** Courtesy of Media Relation Division, Space and Missile Systems Center, Los Angeles Air Force Base; **605** (t), ©Carol Kohen/The Image Bank/Getty Images; **606-607** (b), Jeff Schultz/AlaskaStock Images; **607** (r), ©Ashley Cooper/ CORBIS; **608** (r), ©Smithsonian Institution/CORBIS; **608-609** (bkgd), ©Jon Arnold Images/Alamy; **610,** ©Ursula Klawitter/ zefa/CORBIS; **612** (tr), British Library/The Art Archive; **612** (bl), Courtesy of the Harvard University Archives; (br), ©Steve Dunwell/Index Stock Imagery, Inc.; **613,** ©David Young-Wolff/ PhotoEdit, Inc.; (bkgd), ©Ted Spiegel/CORBIS; (b), National Museum, Copenhagen, Denmark, Erich Lessing/Art Resource, NY˜; **614-615** (bkgd), ©Ted Spiegel/CORBIS; **614,** Pacifica Skatepark, Department of Parks, Beaches and Recreation, City Hall, Pacifica, California; **615,** ©Ryan McVay/Photodisc/Getty Images; **616,** Mary Evans Picture Library; **617** (l, r), Mary Evans Picture Library; **618** (l, r), Mary Evans Picture Library; ©Jeff Greenberg/PhotoEdit, Inc.; **619,** Mark Raycroft/Minden Pictures; (l, r), Mary Evans Picture Library; **621** (t), Mike Randolph/ Masterfile; (b), ©Geraint Lewis/Alamy; **622** (t), Darrell Lecorre/ Masterfile; (b), ©Ron Chapple Stock/CORBIS; Private Collection, U.S.A., Erich Lessing/Art Resource, NY; **624** (l), National Portrait Gallery, London; (r), ©Massimo Listri/CORBIS; ©Mike Kemp/ Rubberball Productions/Gettty Images; **625,** Private Collection/ The Bridgeman Art Library; **626** (bkgd), ©Peter Dazeley/ Photodisc/Getty Images; (l), ©Stockbyte/Getty Images; (r), Alex Gumerov/iStockphoto; **628** (l), ©AP Images/Michel Lipchitz; (r), Jo Ann Snover/iStockphoto; **629,** ©altrendo nature/Altrendo/ Getty Images; **630** (bkgd), ©altrendo nature/Altrendo/Getty Images; **630** (b), ©Dirk V. Mallinckrodt/Alamy; Grafissimo/ iStockphoto; **632,** ©Jack Hollingsworth/Photodisc/Getty Images; **633** (bkgd), doodlemachine/iStockphoto; (l), Fair Street Pictures; (r), ©Corey Hochachka/Design Pics/CORBIS; **634-635** (bkgd), Peter Christopher/Masterfile; **634** (bkgd), doodlemachine/iStockphoto; (l), Prints & Photographs Division, Library of Congress, LC-USZ62-112729; **635, 636** (bkgd), ©Chad Baker/Photodisc/Getty Images; **638** (c), ©CORBIS; ©Ken

Kaminesky/Take 2 Productions/CORBIS; **639,** ©Todd Davidson/ Stock Illustration Source/Getty Images; **640,** ©Gilbert Mayers/ SuperStock; **650,** ©Myrleen Ferguson Cate/PhotoEdit, Inc.; **652,** Kinzie-Riehm, Inc./HRW; **662** (tl), Cover image from *In The Eyes of the Cat* by Demi. Copyright ©1992 by Henry Holt and Company, LLC. Reproduced by permission of the publisher; (tr), Cover image from *You Come Too: Favorite Poems for Young Readers* by Robert Frost. Copyright ©1959 by Henry Holt and Company, LLC. Reproduced by permission of the publisher; (bl), Cover image from *Canto Familiar* by Gary Soto. Copyright ©1995 by Harcourt, Inc. Reproduced by permission of the publisher; (br), Cover image from *This Same Sky,* selected by Naomi Shihab Nye. Copyright ©1992 by Simon & Schuster Books for Young Readers, an imprint of Simon & Schuster Children's Publishing Division. Reproduced by permission of the publisher; **663** (tl), Cover image for *Island of Hope* by Martin W. Sandler. Copyright ©2004 by Martin W. Sandler. Reproduced by permission of Scholastic, Inc.; (tr), Cover image from *Lincoln: A Photobiography* by Russell Freedman. Copyright ©1987 by Houghton Mifflin Company. Reproduced by permission of the publisher; (bl), Cover image from *A Great and Glorious Game* by A. Bartlett Giamatti. Copyright ©1998 by Algonquin Books of Chapel Hill, a division of Workman Publishing. Reproduced by permission of the publisher; (br), Cover image from *The Harlem Renaissance* by Veronica Chambers. Copyright ©1997 by Chelsea House Publishers, a subsidiary of a subsidiary of Haights Cross Communications. Reproduced by permission of the publisher; **664** (tl), Cover image from *Cobblestone Magazine,* February 1981, vol. 2, no. 2. Copyright ©1981 by Cobblestone Publishing Company, 30 Grove Street, Suite C, Peterborough, NH 03458. All rights reserved. Reproduced by permission of Carus Publishing Company; (tr), Cover image from *National Geographic Kids*, March 2007. Copyright ©2007 by National Geographic Kids. Reproduced by permission of National Geographic Society; (bl), Cover image from *Cricket Magazine,* June 1998, vol. 25, no. 10. Copyright ©1998 by Cobblestone Publishing Company, 30 Grove Street, Suite C, Peterborough, NH 03458. All rights reserved. Reproduced by permission of Carus Publishing Company; (br), Cover image from *Muse Magazine,* May/June 2003. Copyright ©2003 by Cobblestone Publishing Company, 30 Grove Street, Suite C, Peterborough, NH 03458. All rights reserved. Reproduced by permission of Carus Publishing Company; **665** (tr, bl), ©Image Source/CORBIS; (tl, br), ©Suza Scalora/Photodisc/Getty Images; **666** (bkgd), ©Jagdish Agarwal/ CORBIS; (l), Photo courtesy of Aimee Nezhukumatahil; (c), Cover image from *Miracle Fruit* by Aimee Nezhukumatahil. Copyright ©2003 by Tupelo Press. Reproduced by permission of the publisher; (r), Cover image from *At the Drive-In Volcano* by Aimee Nezhukumatathil. Copyright ©2003 by Tupelo Press. Reproduced by permission of the publisher; **684,** ©Bob Daemmrich/The Image Works; **700,** ©Jack Hollingsworth/ Photodisc/Getty Images; **736-737,** ©Images.com/CORBIS; **742,** Stocktrek Images/Getty Images; **743** (l), ©Royal Observatory, Edinburgh/Photo Researchers, Inc.; (r), ©Peter Arnold, Inc./ Alamy; **748** (r), ©Topham/The Image Works; **749,** National Oceanic and Atmospheric Administration/Department of Commerce; **751** (t), ©Smithsonian Institution/CORBIS; (b), North Wind Picture Archives; **754** (t), Map Division. Astor, Lenox and Tilden Foundations, The New York Public Library/Art Resource, NY; (b), ©AP Images/James Woodcock/Billings Gazette; **757** (b), ©AP Images/Robin Loznak/Great Falls Tribune; **760** (t), ©Richard

Picture Credits

RESOURCE CENTER

INDEX OF SKILLS

The boldface page numbers indicate an extensive treatment of the topic.

Reading: Word Analysis, Fluency, and Systematic Vocabulary Development

Reading Skills and Strategies

Writing Strategies and Applications

Standards Review

Written and Oral English-Language Conventions

Listening and Speaking Strategies and Applications/ Media Analysis

Read On: For Independent Reading

INDEX OF AUTHORS AND TITLES